ORGANIZATION & GOVERNANCE
IN HIGHER EDUCATION

Fifth Edition

ASHE Reader Series

Edited by M. Christopher Brown II

James L. Ratcliffe, ASHE Reader Series Editor

Pearson
Custom
Publishing

Cover Art: "Color Shapes," by Paul Klee.
Courtesy of the Barnes Foundation, Merion, PA/SuperStock, Inc.

Printed in the United States of America

10 9 8 7 6 5 4 3 2 1

Please visit our website at www.pearsoncustom.com

ISBN 0–536–60749–4

BA 992027

PEARSON CUSTOM PUBLISHING
75 Arlington Street, Boston, MA 02116
A Pearson Education Company

Contents

ACKNOWLEDGMENTS vii

EDITORIAL ADVISORY BOARD viii

A NOTE ON THE FIFTH EDITION x

FOREWORD BY ROBERT BIRNBAUM xi

INTRODUCTION xiii

PART I. CLASSIC ORGANIZATIONAL THEORY 1

    Chapter 1. Evolution of University Organization. 3
      —E. D. Duryea

    Chapter 2. Leadership in an Organized Anarchy. 16
      —Michael D. Cohen and James G. March

    Chapter 3. Educational Organizations as Loosely Coupled Systems 36
      —Karl E. Weick

    Chapter 4. The Professional Bureaucracy 50
      —Henry Mintzberg

    Chapter 5. Emerging Developments in Postsecondary Organization
           Theory and Research. 71
      —Marvin W. Peterson

PART II. TRADITIONAL ADMINISTRATIVE AND GOVERNANCE MODELS 83

    Chapter 6. Statement on Government of Colleges and Universities. 85
      —American Association of University Professors, American Council on
        Education, and Association of Governing Boards of Universities and
        Colleges

    Chapter 7. The Nature of Administrative Behavior in Higher Education . . 92
      —David D. Dill

    Chapter 8. Administrative and Professional Authority 111
      —Amitai Etzioni

    Chapter 9. Faculty Organization and Authority. 119
      —Burton R. Clark

Chapter 10. Alternative Models of Governance in Higher Education 128
    —J. Victor Baldridge, David V. Curtis,
    George P. Ecker, and Gary L. Riley

PART III. CAMPUS CLIMATE AND CULTURE 143

    Chapter 11. Organizational Culture in the Study of Higher Education. . . . 145
        —Andrew T. Masland

    Chapter 12. The Organizational Saga in Higher Education 153
        —Burton R. Clark

    Chapter 13. Culture in American Colleges and Universities 160
        —George D. Kuh and Elizabeth J. Whitt

    Chapter 14. Understanding Academic Culture and Climate 170
        —Marvin W. Peterson and Melinda G. Spencer

    Chapter 15. The Campus Racial Climate: Contexts of Conflict 182
        —Sylvia Hurtado

PART IV. LEADERSHIP ANALYSIS 203

    Chapter 16. The Ambiguity of Leadership 205
        —Jeffrey Pfeffer

    Chapter 17. Higher Education and Leadership Theory. 214
        —Estela M. Bensimon, Anna Neumann, and Robert Birnbaum

    Chapter 18. Symbolism and Presidential Perceptions of Leadership 223
        —William G. Tierney

    Chapter 19. The Latent Organizational Functions
                of the Academic Senate. 232
        —Robert Birnbaum

    Chapter 20. What Teams Can Do 244
        —Estela M. Bensimon and Anna Neumann

PART V. MANAGEMENT PRINCIPLES 259

    Chapter 21. The Management of Academic Culture 261
        —David D. Dill

    Chapter 22. Organizational Adaptation and Higher Education 273
        —Kim S. Cameron

    Chapter 23. Building Learning Organizations 287
        —Peter M. Senge

    Chapter 24. Balancing Corporation, Collegium, and Community 305
        —James Downey

    Chapter 25. Understanding Radical Organizational Change. 313
        —Royston Greenwood and C. R. Hinings

PART VI. INSTITUTIONAL CHANGE AND ASSESSMENT 337

    Chapter 26. Assessment with Open Eyes .339
        —Patrick T. Terenzini

Chapter 27. Sensemaking During Strategic Change in Academia 352
—*Dennis A. Gioia and James B. Thomas*

Chapter 28. The Applicability of Corporate Strategic
Principles to Diversified University Campuses. 379
—*David M. Brock and William B. Harvey*

Chapter 29. The Social Construction of Resource Stress 389
—*Anna Neumann*

Chapter 30. Creating a New Kind of Leadership
for Campus Diversity. 406
—*Blandina Cardenas Ramirez*

PART VII. PERSPECTIVES ON RACE AND GENDER 415

Chapter 31. Race in Organizations. 417
—*Stella M. Nkomo*

Chapter 32. An Organizational Analysis of Racism
in Higher Education. 436
—*Mark A. Chesler and James Crowfoot*

Chapter 33. Harnessing a Diversity of Views to
Understand Multiculturalism 470
—*Patricia L. Nemetz and Sandra L. Christensen*

Chapter 34. Re-writing Gender into Organizational Theorizing. 490
—*Marta B. Calás and Linda Smircich*

Chapter 35. Academic Structure, Culture and the Case
of Feminist Scholarship 508
—*Patricia J. Gumport*

PART VIII. CRITICAL APPROACHES TO ORGANIZATIONAL GOVERNANCE 521

Chapter 36. Organization Theory in the Postmodern Era. 523
—*Kenneth J. Gergen*

Chapter 37. Critical Leadership and Decision Making
in a Postmodern World 537
—*William G. Tierney*

Chapter 38. Organizational Change as Paradigm Shift 550
—*Hasan Simsek and Karen Seashore Louis*

Chapter 39. Postmodernism and Higher Education. 566
—*Harland G. Bloland*

Chapter 40. The Power of Symbolic Constructs in Reading Change
in Higher Education. 589
—*Hasan Simsek*

ADDITIONAL READINGS (WITH THE ASSISTANCE OF EBONI M. ZAMANI) 605

ABOUT THE EDITOR 609

Acknowledgments

The challenge of preparing the Fifth Edition of the *ASHE Reader on Organization and Governance in Higher Education* was daunting. I recall vividly my early conversations with four senior colleagues about this undertaking. Their ominous descriptions of the painstaking work involved were most accurate ("You told me so"). Despite the gargantuan task of reading, reviewing, and ranking hundreds of articles, book chapters, and microfiche versions of research on organizational theory and postsecondary governance, I received enormous assistance and support from many colleagues throughout the field. It is important to single out a few whose recommendations were central to the selection of readings for the revised reader: Ana Martinez Aleman (Boston College), Estela Bensimon (University of Southern California), Sue Estler (University of Maine), Lester Goodchild (University of Denver), Esther Gottlieb (West Virginia University), Steve Graham (University of Missouri), Linda Serra Hagedorn (University of Southern California), Karen Kellogg (ERIC Clearinghouse on Higher Education), John Levin (University of Arizona), Jeffrey Milem (University of Maryland), Jack Schuster (Claremont Graduate University), Meg Sidle (Central State University), Daryl Smith (Claremont Graduate University), and Marta Soto (University of Southern California).

I would also like to offer thanks to the two persons who edited the first four editions of the Reader, and also assisted with the development of the Fifth Edition—Marvin Peterson (University of Michigan) and Robert Birnbaum (University of Maryland). Marvin Peterson provided critical suggestions on classical selections, assisting in my effort to blend traditional and contemporary readings. Robert Birnbaum was excited and supportive of the revision from the very beginning. He offered his keen insight regarding ideal readings and authored the foreword for this edition.

Special thanks are warranted for two graduate students—Kimberly Clark and Eboni Zamani. Kimberly Clark located and photocopied all of the readings necessary for the review process. Many of the readings were not on file in the library and required initiative and persistence to be located. Eboni Zamani provided critical assistance in compiling and arranging all of the readings reviewed, as well as those selected for the bibliography. Finally, this Reader would not be possible without the guidance, encouragement, and active participation of the editorial advisory board. While the preparation of the Reader was collaborative in nature, all errors, mistakes, and omissions rest with the editor.

Editorial Advisory Board

A Note on the Fifth Edition

The *ASHE Reader on Organization and Governance in Higher Education* remains one of the primary teaching and research references in the study and practice of postsecondary education. The main purpose of the Fifth Edition of the Reader is to update the selections from the previous volume. In the nine years since the last edition of the Reader, research in higher education has provided new insights and recommendations for the management of postsecondary institutions. While the Fifth Edition seeks to maintain the strength and integrity of prior readers in covering classical theories and traditional models, it also intends to broaden the scope of readings to include current perspectives on campus governance and institutional change. To the extent that the Fifth Edition seamlessly blends classic and contemporary readings, it fulfills its primary aim.

The Fifth Edition was assembled utilizing a multi-phase synthesis process. First, a survey was issued to the ASHE membership via email. Respondents were asked to recommend up to six readings in each of the eight subject parts of the Reader. Simultaneously, an extensive bibliographic search was conducted. All of the membership responses were then rank ordered, read, and evaluated in conjunction with the bibliographic references. A proposed Reader table of contents was then forwarded to the editorial advisory board for their suggestions and modifications. The current compendium is the result of those changes, extensions, and replacements.

A Sixth Edition of the Reader is anticipated in five years. The editorial advisory board and I would welcome your comments on the current reader, as well as your suggestions for improvement. We would be particularly interested in information regarding new scholarship on organization theory, leadership models, and management principles in higher education. Please direct your comments and suggestions regarding the Fifth Edition of the *ASHE Reader on Organization and Governance in Higher Education* to the following address:

M. Christopher Brown II
Department of Educational Organization and Leadership
College of Education
University of Illinois
1310 South Sixth Street
Champaign, IL 61820

Foreword

As I write this foreword to the Fifth Edition of the *ASHE Reader in Organization and Governance in Higher Education* in January 2000, I have in front of me a copy of the First Edition, which I edited in 1983. It was created out of the kind of faculty desperation that often leads to academic invention. I wanted my students to read important journal articles. But even though in those benighted days we considered the making of photocopies for student use to be exempt from copyright laws, copying supplementary course materials was slower and more expensive than it is today. Putting together a packet of readings for a course was a hassle, and telling part-time commuting students instead to go to the library was functionally equivalent to identifying the readings as optional. What to do?

With the approval of the ASHE Board of Directors, and then-president Bob Clark, I set about the task of simplifying my life by putting readings from disparate journals into a single volume. I sent a proposed table of contents to about 30 ASHE members who specialized in administration and governance, made some revisions based on the responses, and sent off a batch of less-than-pristine photocopies to let Ginn Press worry about the details. The resultant ragged First Edition was the beginning of the *ASHE Reader* series which today offers volumes of foundational readings in over a dozen different specialized areas in the field of higher education.

If you were to see the 1983 edition today from a distance, you would immediately recognize it as an *ASHE Reader*. But up close, some major changes would be obvious. The first would be the difference in sheer size. The 1983 edition had 409 pages while the 2000 edition has 610 pages. In part this may reflect a burgeoning of the scholarship of higher education during the 1980s and 1990s. But it also reflects my concern in 1983 that if the price was too high no one would buy the Reader. Even though the number of pages was intentionally limited to control costs and encourage adoption, to break even the First Edition had to be sold for a (then) breathtaking $24.95—a price so much higher than the going rate for texts that there was fear that graduate students would not be able to afford it.

There are other obvious changes as well. For example, a quick flip through the First Edition would reveal a hodge-podge of photocopies from original sources; the Fifth Edition, in contrast, is set in a single type face. But the most significant differences are not in the appearance, but in the content. There were 26 "chapters" in the first edition, compared to 40 in the fifth edition. Surprisingly, only six of the chapters appear in both. Of these six, only half were authored by scholars whose primary area of scholarship has emphasized higher education. If higher education as a field has a canon, it appears to be a limited one.

One of the understandable reasons for the limited overlap is that the first edition included a number of articles focusing on current issues of the day that may no longer be seen as relevant or of general scholarly interest. Among these were chapters dealing with such matters as state coordination, collective bargaining, and institutional decline, crises that have in the fullness of time been replaced by more current crises. A somewhat less understandable difference is that the First Edition included articles dealing with the governance roles of trustees, presidents, and (would you believe it) even students. The Fifth Edition takes little notice of these institutional roles.

Another reason for the limited overlap is that it may take time for the significance of an article to be recognized. The Fifth Edition includes 11 articles that were originally published prior to 1983 and thus could have been included in the First Edition—but only six of them were. It is embarrassing to look back and note that the five missing included the AAUP/ACE/AGB Joint Statement on Governance, Mintzberg on the professional bureaucracy, Clark on the organizational saga, Pfeffer on the ambiguity of leadership, and Dill on the management of academic culture. Generous readers may accept the "it takes time" argument for the lapses. Others may with some justification attribute it to early editorial incompetence. Mea culpa.

But perhaps the most important reason for the limited overlap is the development of new ways of thinking about higher education in 2000 that were only dimly perceived in 1983. Both volumes have a sampling of literature dealing with administration, governance, and leadership. But the Fifth Edition also has an entire section on campus climate and culture, issues relatively unexplored in 1983, as well as a section on institutional change and assessment. These once peripheral topics have moved to the center of attention over the past 17 years.

Even more profound as an indicator of changes in our field, as well as in society at large, is the presence in the Fifth Edition of two new sections that, for lack of well-developed literatures, and the vocabulary and conceptual bases that such literatures provide, could not have been prepared in 1983. One of these sections provides perspectives on race and gender, issues of scholarly interest to an increasing number of ASHE members. The other takes a postmodern look at governance through the lens of critical theory. Both sections require us to reconsider traditional social and institutional practices from new perspectives, as well as to attend to longstanding questions of social justice. It is noteworthy, within this context, that of the 39 identified authors in 1983, only three (8 percent) were women; in the 2000 edition, 14 of 54 identified authors (35 percent) are women.

Of course, the differences between the First and Fifth editions didn't happen suddenly. The 2000 version is the culmination of efforts by a number of scholars who edited or participated in the development of intervening editions, each one of which added something to the evolutionary process. What will future editions of the *ASHE Reader* look like? The only safe predictions are that a small number of articles not now appreciated will join the canon, a large number of works now seen as essential will be dismissed as quaint, and some esoteric topic currently of interest to only a handful of scholars will move from marginal to central attention. The number of sections themselves—three in 1983 and eight in 2000—is likely to expand as our field of study further diversifies and becomes more complex. Alternatively, topics now combined in this single volume may split into separate volumes as the eternal battle between specialization and integration continues.

The largest single audience for this book consists of graduate students studying in programs of higher education. Some of you will have the thrill of seeing one or more of your own articles included in future editions of this Reader. Others will likely also be among the editors of these future Readers. You will find it challenging to select from among the best of what has been written, disheartening to reflect on how many articles of equal merit could not be included for lack of space, and gratifying to know that you are performing an important professional and scholarly service for your colleagues and their students.

—Robert Birnbaum
University of Maryland-College Park

Introduction

Organization and governance are the cornerstones of higher education as a field of study. The specifics of how colleges are governed vary from institution to institution. There are some campuses with presidents and some with chancellors. There are colleges with provost systems and others with deans. While no two institutional flow charts are identical, there are congruencies regarding the context, function, and performance of higher education administration.

This volume provides a collection of readings that aid in understanding the multiple nuances of how colleges are organized, governed, and administered. Colleges and universities are complex organizations of great diversity and scope. Consequently, they are among the most difficult of all institutions to administer or study. Because of the complex nature of the postsecondary institution, this ASHE Reader creates eight subject area lenses. Each lens allows the reader to engage the specific paradigms and phenomena related to that aspect of higher education. The areas are arranged in the following order: classic organization theory, traditional administrative and governance models, campus climate and culture, leadership analysis, management principles, institutional change and assessment, perspectives on race and gender, and critical approaches to organizational governance.

In the section on classic organization theory, readings are presented which describe the nature of the university as an organization. Treatment is given to the historical development of the college and its nexus with faculties, boards of trustees, and central administration. The chaotic context of higher education administration is also reviewed, particularly the theories on organized anarchy, loosely coupled systems, and professional bureaucracies. The section closes with an early look at the developments and dilemmas of organizational theory.

The next collection of readings is more specific about the functioning of the university. Focusing on traditional administrative behavior models, the readings provide a cogent presentation of how many institutions are organized. The confluence of power, authority, and influence is explored by several authors. The dual questions of who runs the college and who should run the college are also addressed.

Section three details the invisible organization structure of the university. The presentation of research on organizational culture, saga, and climate reveals the multiple threads woven into a given institution's "tapestry." Attention is paid to campus holidays, rituals, celebrations, and traditions in this unique body of scholarship. While it may be easy to identify the hierarchical arrangement of a given institution, it is more difficult to ascertain the unwritten histories which condition how the organization evolves. As an external observer it is possible to misread the administrative network. Hence, information regarding informal governance systems are presented and aid in detailing how myriad institutional factors conjoin.

Likewise, leadership is central to higher education management. Unlike studies of leadership in corporate or business systems, postsecondary education runs on a system of "primus inter pares"—first among equals—arrangements. The relationships between the leadership and the constituent groups are not necessarily hierarchical or hegemonic. Consequently, the higher education leadership models presented in this section explain the perennially unclear issues of power and chain-of-command inherent in postsecondary governance.

Section five of this collection explores management principles. The first readings offer guidance on managing academic units based on traditional higher education research. These chapters utilize academic culture as the context to discuss administrative leadership. However, the remaining chapters are more unconventional. Borrowing from both international higher education and the organizational behavior research community, the readings provide critical new insights into how radical change can be made in an organization. Notwithstanding, each chapter in this section treats change as a delicate merger between the competing interests of diverse institutional stakeholders.

Continuing the theme of change, the next unit covers institutional transformation and assessment. Reform, reorganization, and reinvention have become the "sound-bytes" of academic leadership. The readings investigate the above three "R's," as well as research on sensemaking, interpretation, and assessment. Each reading calls on higher education *writ-large* to establish "a new kind of leadership." Citing the growing calls to reinvent higher education, several of the authors address the need for change in postsecondary settings.

The seventh section offers research perspectives on race and gender in higher education governance. Several of the chapters focus on helping higher education researchers and practitioners identify the race and gender dynamics at work in organizational structures. Each reading provides an exemplar on how to engage the diverse constituencies within the academic structure. This section also includes a chapter on multiculturalism. This chapter is included because of the way it combines both the diversity and organizational theory literature into one coherent statement.

The book concludes by addressing the new frameworks for approaching higher education governance. Each author prognosticates an era of organizational change in higher education. Each author also suggests that a change in paradigm will be necessary if higher education research and practice in the organization and governance arenas will be poised to address the "postmodern" shifts. Finally, each of the chapters presented conclude with a challenge to the reader and to the field to exercise due caution and sound judgment in responding to the changing contexts within and surrounding institutions of higher education.

Organization and governance will continue to be central to the study and practice of higher education. The challenges of constituency, climate, and change are timeless concerns for scholars and administrators. Arguably, these issues will remain with the field of higher education for many years. Almost one century ago, Charles W. Eliot, the esteemed forty-year president of Harvard University, wrote about the unique attributes of postsecondary governance in his book—*University Administration* (1908). President Eliot pens the following words in the final paragraph of his book:

> Any one who makes himself familiar with all the branches of university administration in its numerous departments of teaching, in its financial and maintenance departments, its museums, laboratories, and libraries, in its extensive grounds and numerous buildings for very various purposes, and in its social organization, will realize that the institution is properly named the university.

PART I

CLASSIC ORGANIZATIONAL THEORY

CHAPTER 1

EVOLUTION OF UNIVERSITY ORGANIZATION

E. D. DURYEA

It has become customary in histories of American higher education to begin with a description of medieval origins. In general, there is good basis for looking back to those distant and turbulent days. The idea of a university itself as a formal, organized institution is a medieval innovation, which contrasts to the Greek schools and to the rudimentary organizational precedents in ancient Alexandria and in the Byzantine and Arabian cultures. The medieval universities instituted the use of many contemporary titles such as *dean, provost, rector,* and *proctor*. They initiated the idea of formal courses and of the curriculum leading to the baccalaureate and the master's and doctor's degrees. Our commencements are graced annually by the color and distinction of medieval garb. Fascinating anecdotes confirm that student violence has early precedents.

The point is, of course, that complex institutions such as universities do not appear full-blown at a particular point in time. They evolve through that complicated process by which men and cultures mingle over a history fraught with traditions and happenstance. Contemporary Western culture itself originated in the centuries that followed the "dark ages," and the university has served as one of the major institutions by which this culture has been transmitted over the years.

Within this context, certain aspects of the university's organization do have some important medieval precedents. Other aspects of its organization reflect the more direct influence of the English colleges of the sixteenth and seventeenth centuries. A history of American colleges and universities must be written also with due recognition of that educational revolution which took place in this country during the four decades following the Civil War. As Laurence R. Veysey (1965, p. 2) comments in his detailed interpretation of that era, "The American university of 1900 was all but unrecognizable in comparison to the colleges of 1860." The contemporary system of higher education dominated by the large, multifunctional university stands as a heritage of those years. Organizationally as well as educationally, its form and function were set by the time of the First World War. Its history during this century is primarily a chronicle of expansion and consolidation.

Reflecting these major historical influences, the following analysis examines the evolution of university organization from three major perspectives. The first deals with (1) the origins and use of the corporate form by which authority was granted to lay governing boards and (2) how their legal control has been modified by alumni and faculty influences that go back well into the nineteenth century. The second views the origins and expansion of the organizational structure of universities, an evolution epitomized by the comment that the old-time college president has all but disappeared behind a bureaucracy of academic and administrative offices and councils. In this sense the transition from the small, struggling colleges of the past to the large multiversity with its complex administration is first of all the history of the presidency. The third views the twentieth-century period of organizational expansion and consolidation. A concluding section identifies very briefly the evidences of dysfunction that have emerged in recent years.

Corporate Origins

By the twelfth century in Europe the church not only reigned supreme as a ruler of man's conscience but also exercised great temporal power over his mundane affairs. Rare were the individuals who would, when threatened with excommunication, choose to face an uncertain future in the hereafter. As the arbitrator of an ultimate destiny which included the possibility so vividly described in Dante's *Inferno* and as the only effective organization for all Europe, the church entered into the total life of the culture. But early in the thirteenth century, the more astute popes began to feel the rumblings of a shift of temporal power to political states and kings. The remote threat of hell began to give way to the more tangible thrust of the sword. As a result, the church hierarchy moved to bring its scattered organizations—religious orders, cathedral chapters, and universities—under more effective papal control. To this end, canon lawyers looked back to Roman law and its concept of corporations as fictitious legal entities. Their learned investigations led to a number of papal statements in the first decades of the thirteenth century and in 1243 to the famous bull or proclamation of Pope Innocent IV. The central idea in the Innocentean doctrine was that each cathedral chapter, collegiate church, religious fraternity, and university constituted a *Universitas*, i.e., a free corporation. Its corporate personality, however, was not something natural in the sense of a social reality but rather "an artificial notion invented by the sovereign for convenience of legal reasoning," existent only in the contemplation of law. This was a theoretical conception but nonetheless a very real one, since the corporation thereby derived its right to exist from an external authority and not from the intrinsic fact of its being (Brody, 1935, pp. 3–4).

The efforts of the papacy, the need of universities for protection against the immediate threats to their freedom from local bishops and townspeople, and the fact that the kings also intruded on their sovereignty—all these supported the corporate idea. The theory of corporate existence meant ultimately the end of the guild system and, for universities, of the idea of an independent association of scholars. The history of this development is complex and detailed, certainly beyond the scope of this particular analysis. It is sufficient to note that Emperor Frederick II rivaled Pope Gregory IX during the later years of the thirteenth century in the issuance of grants of authorization to universities, which in turn did not hesitate to strengthen their own hand by playing off pope against king (Rashdall, 1936, vol. 1, pp. 8–9). As national states gained dominance, however, universities ultimately had to look solely to kings for their charters and what the king gave the king could take away.

The concept of corporations which served as precedent for the early colleges in this country matured in England during the fifteenth and sixteenth centuries. It provided an effective legal means by which the king and later parliament would delegate in an orderly way authority for designated activities, not only to universities but to municipalities, trading companies, charitable establishments, and various other institutions. Charters provided for perpetual succession and the freedom for corporate bodies to set up and maintain the rules and regulations which in effect constituted internal or private governments. They also carried the right of supervision and visitation by representatives of the state. They established, in addition, legal protections associated with the rights of individuals in the sense that the corporation existed as an artificial or juristic individual. This conception of governmental grant of authority served also as the basis for the charters and statutes of the colleges of the English universities, which in general included provisions for external visitors or overseers, a head elected by the teaching staff or fellows, and a formal body constituted of these fellows which "exercised the legislative powers" (Davis, 1961, pp. 303–305).

The influence of this English college model was evident in the founding of the first two colonial colleges, Harvard (1636) and William and Mary (1693). For example, the language of the 1650 charter for Harvard is very similar to that of the royal charters for the colleges of Oxford and Cambridge (Morison, 1935, p. 10). Both these institutions were formed with governing councils composed of internal members (the presidents and teaching fellows) in tandem with external supervising boards that held final approval powers and the right of visitation.[1]

Another medieval precedent, however, came to the colonies with the early settlers and caused a significant modification of the English practice. In place of immediate control of the colleges by the teachers or professors, the practice evolved of granting complete corporate power to governing boards composed of external members. The origins of the use of external control lie in the medieval universities of northern Italy. Initially guilds of students who hired their professors, universities proved good for local business. The Italian towns competed for their presence in part by subsidizing salaries of outstanding teachers. The inexorable result was a blunting of student economic power and the establishment of municipal committees, in effect the first lay governing boards, to guard their financial interests (Rashdall, 1936, vol. 2, p. 59). Again, the detailing of the history of this tradition goes beyond the scope of this chapter. The lay board of control proved an appropriate mechanism for the direction of advanced education under the Calvinists at Geneva in the early sixteenth century, at the Dutch University of Leyden a few years later, at the Scottish universities of that same era, and finally at the Protestant Trinity College in Dublin. It was in part from these Dutch, Scottish, and Irish sources that the concept of lay boards came to the colonies (Cowley, 1964; 1971).

The English pattern of internal control by academics which was followed by Harvard and William and Mary did not set the precedent for university government in this country. That distinction fell to Yale College, established in 1701. Whether because of direct influences from the European Calvinistic practices noted above or simply because of parallel sectarian desires to maintain religious orthodoxy, the founders of Yale petitioned for a single nonacademic board of control. As a consequence, the colonial legislature of Connecticut granted authority to a board of "Trustees, Partners, or Undertakers" to "erect a collegiate school." Renamed in the revised 1745 charters as the "President and Fellows of Yale College," it continued as an external board with the right of self-perpetuation and with final control of the affairs of the institution (*The Yale Corporation*, 1952; see also Brody, 1935, Ch. 1).

Meanwhile, yet another deviation from English precedents also had begun to emerge. The right of the king and parliament to grant a charter carried with it an equal right to withdraw this charter. In fact, during the times of religious conflict in England this did occur, as first a Protestant and then a Catholic sovereign reconstituted the organization of the English universities in terms of religious biases. In the eighteenth century a new philosophy, that formalized by John Locke, gained acceptance, especially in the American colonies so strongly committed to a separation of church and state. This view stressed the nature of government as a compact among individuals, with sovereignty held by the people. In these terms of reference, having legal status as a person in law, although a fictitious or juridical person, corporations gained protection from legislative intrusions associated with the rights of individuals. Early in the nineteenth century court decisions began to interpret charters as contracts equally as binding upon the state as upon their recipients. The first intimation of this position regarding corporate autonomy appeared in the 1763 statement of President Clap of Yale to the colonial legislature. He was protesting a threatened legislative visitation of the college on the grounds that such action would be contrary to the nature of the charter and the private legal nature of the institution.[2] Clap's position was novel in his day, but after the turn of the eighteenth century support of a judicial theory which interpreted charters to private corporations as contracts or compacts between the state and the founders began to appear. This point of view received its legal judicial confirmation in the famous Dartmouth College case decision of the Supreme Court under Chief Justice Marshall. In that decision, the Court viewed the college as a private institution and interpreted its charter as a contract binding upon the state of New Hampshire as well as the trustees, "a contract, the obligation of which cannot be impaired without violating the constitution of the United States" (Wright, 1938, p. 45).

The Dartmouth College decision led to a reexamination of the state-college relationship. Faced with a loss of control, legislators understandably questioned the award of public funds to private corporations. As a result there emerged in subsequent decades a number of public or state colleges, but not as agencies of state government under ministers of education in the continental tradition. Rather, the early public colleges took the form of public corporations parallel in their general organization to the private colleges. In the nineteenth century, it became common practice for legislatures to delegate governing power over state institutions to boards of control established as public corporations.[3] These boards received authority to control property, contracts, finances, forms of internal governance, and relationships with internal personnel—students, faculty members, and administrative employees (Brody, 1935, Ch. 6).[4]

Modification of Board Control: Faculty and Alumni Participation

Whatever the legal authority inherent in lay governing boards, continuing modification of their actual power is documented by a history of university organization. Early in the nineteenth century, accounts of the administration of Jeremiah Day at Yale College attest to the influence of faculty members with whom Day conferred regularly on policy decisions. Students, while rarely a direct component of government until recent years, have traditionally participated as alumni.

Earlier precedents than Yale exist. Professor W. H. Cowley (1964, Ch. 7) has uncovered a number of such instances. Overall, it is clear from his analysis and from histories of the leading universities that faculties greatly expanded their influence over academic affairs during the nineteenth century. The period from 1869 to 1900 illustrates the gradual but decisive involvement of professors in academic policies (Morison, 1930, p. xxxiv). The trustees at Cornell in 1889, for example, established a University Senate of the president and full professors (Kingsbury, 1962, pp. 263–264). Similar arrangements existed at Michigan, Illinois, Wisconsin, and other Midwestern institutions. At Johns Hopkins and Chicago, professors were accepted as the guiding force for all matters concerned with education and research. Faculty influence reached the point that, by the 1890s, President Jacob G. Schurman of Cornell

saw his influence in educational affairs limited to final approval of appointments and his role as "the only man in the University who is a member of all boards, councils and organizations" (Kingsbury, 1962, p. 323).

By the turn of the century the trend to faculty participation was definite in the larger universities and major colleges. The decades that followed have chronicled the extension of faculty control over academic affairs, a development influenced by the policies and pressures of the American Association of University Professors subsequent to its founding in 1915.[5]

During the nineteenth century, alumni also entered actively into the government of colleges and universities. In doing this, they had well-established precedents in both England and Scotland, though little evidence exists to support a causal relationship. It is probably more accurate to explain alumni participation as the result of a unique commitment epitomized by the spirit of alma mater and reinforced by recollections of campus camaraderie. The college class has constituted a primary social as well as academic unit which, early in the history of the colleges, led to campus reunions and thus served regularly to reinforce the loyalty of graduates. In turn, it was natural for the members of governing boards and leaders of state governments to look to graduates of colleges for service on these boards when openings occurred. "From the very beginnings," Professor Cowley (1964, Ch. 10, p. 10) has written, "alumni have contributed to the support of private colleges and universities; and as legislators, lobbyists, and moulders of public opinion they have strategically influenced the subsidizing of civil institutions." Formal representation by means of elected members to governing boards first appeared at Harvard in 1865, a pattern that was followed by many other institutions in the subsequent decades.[6]

In summary, university government had coalesced into the pattern we know today by shortly after the turn of the century. It reflected a continuation of medieval and English precedents whereby institutional autonomy received a high degree of protection, modified perhaps in American higher education by a more overt sense of commitment to societal needs. Private colleges and universities had the protection afforded them by their status as corporations under law.[7] In practice, public institutions obtained much of this same autonomy through their status as public corporations under the control of boards established by state constitution or legislative law. But even before the end of the nineteenth century, evidences of growing restrictions upon the actual power of governing boards had begun to emerge.

Over and above any incipient faculty militance, the practical result of growing size and complexity necessitated the delegation of some policy-making and managerial responsibilities to presidents and faculties. Finally, the unique role and influence of presidents during this era require recognition. In contrast to earlier periods when presidents served more as principals responsible for campus conduct and morality—of professor and student alike—and trustees sat importantly at commencements to examine graduating seniors, by 1900 presidents had become a positive force. Every university to rise to major status did so under the almost dominating influence of such presidential leaders as Charles W. Eliot at Harvard, Andrew D. White at Cornell, Daniel Coit Gilman at Johns Hopkins, Charles R. Van Hise at Wisconsin, William Rainey Harper at Chicago, David S. Jordan at Stanford, and Benjamin Ide Wheeler at California. The office of president emerged as the central force that has given United States higher education a distinctive character among systems of higher education in the world. Whether one viewed the president as the alter ego of boards or as a discrete unit in institutional government had little bearing on practice. Whatever faculty voices may have been raised to the contrary, university government by the twentieth century centered upon the office of the president.

Administrative Structure

In his history of Williams College, *Mark Hopkins and the Log* (1956), Frederick Rudolph vividly portrays a typical college from 1836 to 1872. President Hopkins presides as the paternal head of a small and personal college family, responsible for the character of its children, the students. The curriculum was fixed and limited. In any event, what the students studied was secondary to the quality of personal moral life. In contrast, the "new education" of the last half of the nineteenth century reflected the new morality of the times, a turning away from Christian theology as the basis for life's judgments and toward values oriented far more to the marketplace and material success. In the words of Veysey (1965, Ch. 2), "discipline and piety" gave way to "utility" as the hallmark of a college education. Specialized knowledge replaced the "disciplining of the mind and character" as the raison d'être for higher education. Adherents of reform rallied to elective ideas which supported, to a degree at least, the rights of students to choose their subjects and thus to open the universities to the new studies of science and technology and of specialization in the humanities, all of which stressed the advancement of knowledge and a utilitarian commitment. By 1900 graduate studies, professional schools, and professors whose careers rested upon their published research rather than upon their role as teachers were moving to positions of the highest status in the academic hierarchy. Harvard University offered good evidence of the impact of this influence upon the curriculum. The 1850 catalog described the entire four years of undergraduate study on four pages; in 1920, 30 times that number of pages were required to list the courses offered at the university.

Two shifts in organizational structure inevitably followed. On the one hand, by the turn of the century departments and professional schools had become the basic units for academic affairs. The academic structure of the university coincided with the structure of knowledge. On the other hand, the impact of this "new education" fitted the times. In contrast to the declining enrollment of the 1840s and 1850s, the latter half of the nineteenth century marked the beginning of what has become a constantly increasing rate of college attendance. More students meant more professors, more buildings, more facilities and equipment, and, above all, more money from private and public sources. As chief executive, the president inherited the responsibility both for securing this support and for coordinating and managing the inevitable internal complexities that resulted. Initially, a vice-president and a few professors who served as part-time registrars, bursars, and librarians assisted him. By 1900, however, such staffs proved insufficient; the managerial burden of the president had begun to necessitate what has become a burgeoning administrative bureaucracy.

Academic Organization

Some imitations of the specialized departments and professional schools which have become the basic organizational units of universities do appear in the early colleges. The University of Virginia, for example, opened in 1825 with eight schools, each headed by a professor and each offering a program of studies. In that same year, the statutes reorganizing Harvard College established nine "departments" for instruction, each of which (in the pattern already set for medicine, law, and divinity) would be "governed by a board of its full professors" (Cowley, 1964, Ch. 7, p. 4). The use of departments appeared also in 1826 at the University of Vermont, a decade later at Wisconsin, and at Michigan in 1841. But these departments served only as progenitors of the disciplinary and professional units that fashioned the academic organization of universities later in the century.

The appearance of departments as organizational entities accompanied the expansion of knowledge—particularly scientific and technological—and the elective system, by means of which the adherents of specialized study forced their point of view into institutions with traditions of a fixed, classical curriculum. But the reason for the association of departments of scholars in this country (in contrast to the chair held by one professor in foreign universities) has not been documented historically. That they had become the established structural units by 1900 is evident nonetheless in the histories of all major universities.[8]

A similar development occurred in the various professional studies, which appeared with few exceptions first as departments and later as schools, which in turn procreated their own departments. Certainly by 1900 professional specializations in more than a dozen areas were well established, ranging from the traditional trinity of medicine, law, and theology to such new areas as business administration, veterinary medicine, journalism, librarianship, and architecture.

The departmental structure that followed in the wake of specialized knowledge was accompanied by other evidence of disciplinary and professional segmentation, such as journals and national societies. Professors, as the authorities for their respective specializations, assumed more and more control over academic affairs. This revolutionary change from the earlier colleges had evolved by 1910 to the extent that a study of physics departments complains about their having "too much autonomy." The report describes the department as "usually practically self-governing" in control of its own affairs—that is, its students, staff, and curriculum (Cooke, 1910).

Administrative Organization

Responding to the pressures of office work, travel, supervising new construction, employing new faculty, and initiating educational programs, in 1878 President Andrew Dickson White of the new Cornell University appointed a professor of modern languages and history, William C. Russel, as vice-president. Russel functioned as a kind of executive associate—hiring and dismissing junior faculty members, answering correspondence, and carrying out routine responsibilities as well as acting as institutional head in White's absence. The same year, a presidential colleague at Harvard, Charles W. Eliot, appointed Professor Ephriam W. Gurney as dean of the college faculty. In contrast to Russel's initial tasks, Dean Gurney's primary responsibility was to relieve the president of the burden of contacts with students.

These appointments at two major universities signaled the beginning of a trend. For the college growing into a large and complex university, the office of the president quickly ceased to be a one-man job. Those part-time assistants, usually professors, who served as librarian, bursar, or registrar had by 1900 turned into full-time administrative officers, and by the 1930s they were supervising large staffs. A 1936 study by Earl J. McGrath documents the trend. The author charts the growth from a median of three or four administrative officers in the 1880s to a median of nearly sixty for the larger universities by 1930. As noted previously in this chapter, the decades from 1890 to 1910 proved to be the turning point. The lines on McGrath's chart after 1890 turn upward abruptly, showing a doubling of these officers from an average of about 12 in that year to 30 in 1910.

What brought about this transformation of American universities into complex administrative systems, especially in contrast to the much simpler organization of European universities? Many determinants exerted influence, of course. In large part, administrative expansion responded to the need to coordinate and, to a degree, control the expansion of the academic structure. In part, it grew out of a relationship with the general society, unique to this country, which imposed on the university the task of securing financial support from both public and private sources and concurrently of attending to public relations. In part, the enlarged administration implemented an intricate credit system for student admissions and educational accounting.

Fundamentally, however, the administrative organization of universities resulted from the managerial role of the American college president, the coincidental result of the fact that early founders looked to the colleges of the English universities for their patterns. In doing this they carried over the concept of a permanent headship, designated in the English colleges as *warden, master, provost, president,* or *rector* (Cowley, 1971, Ch. 11, p. 10; Davis, 1961, p. 304).[9] In contrast to the English custom of election by the fellows of the college, the presidents in this country from the very beginning have been appointed by governing boards. Thus, the presidents of the early colleges had responsibilities as executives for boards. For the first two centuries this constituted a relatively simple and personal, almost paternal, relationship with student and teachers. When, after the Civil War, colleges ceased to be small and universities appeared with expanded enrollments, academic fragmentation, and diversified relationships with the external society, presidents found their responsibility elaborated and their need for staff assistance imperative.

By 1900 it could be said that the general administration had developed something like its full measure of force in American higher education. In 1902, President Nicholas Murray Butler assumed the presidency of Columbia complete with clerical staff, abetted by well-established offices for the registrar and bursar (Veysey, 1965, p. 307). Probably typical of its times, the University of North Carolina administration included a registrar, bursar, librarian, and part-time secretary for the university. The office of alumni secretary was not unknown by 1900 (McGrath, 1936). Although largely a product of this century, business officers commonly served as bursars or collectors of fees. By the turn of the century, librarians had established themselves on a full-time basis and had begun to employ assistants—in contrast with the rudimentary condition of these services 40 years previously. The first press bureau appeared at the University of Wisconsin in 1904 (Seller, 1963, p. 3). The office of registrar was nearly universal. The office of vice-president, usually assigned to handle specific functions such as university relations, academic affairs, medical affairs, or similar constellations of administrative services, had appeared in some numbers by the First World War.

Concurrently, presidents turned to the title of *dean* to further delegate their academic responsibilities. By 1900 this title was used for the heads of professional schools, especially medicine and law, and of schools or divisions of arts and sciences. The office of dean served in smaller colleges to designate the "second in command." In an 1896 reorganization at Cornell, for example, President Schurman appointed deans of academic affairs and of graduate studies. All the universities and two-thirds of the colleges included in the McGrath study had academic deans by 1900. The designation of the title of dean for student affairs also has precedent in the late nineteenth century. At Harvard, Eliot's appointment of Dean Gurney, as noted above, was a response to the pressures of his responsibilities for students. Similar appointments were made at Swarthmore, Oberlin, and Chicago in the 1890s. The same forces that had fragmented the unitary curriculum of the early colleges in support of specialized knowledge made the orientation of faculty members more intellectual and pushed into secondary or tertiary importance their concern with students. Into this void came the forerunners of contemporary student personnel services. Deans of women began to meet annually in 1903; directors of student unions appeared in 1914; the National Association of Deans of Men was organized in 1917.

In summary, then, the organizational structure of American universities was etched clearly enough by the first decade of this century. Its two mainstreams flowed to and from the offices of presidents: one an academic route to deans and thence to departmental chairmen; the other a managerial hierarchy. Whatever the organizational charts designated, as early as 1910 it had become apparent that initiative on the academic side had begun to rest heavily at the departmental level.

Twentieth-Century Expansion

If the late nineteenth century constitutes the formative years of American higher education, the present century has been an era of growth and consolidation. During the decades following the Civil War, colleges began their search for a personality appropriate to the times and to their position in society. As the years of maturity approached, each found its particular role in what has become a spectrum from small, unitary schools to large, complex universities which set the pace and pattern for the whole system. Diversity became the pervasive quality of the new era—diversity among institutions and within the major universities.

Expansion in this century has led to colleges and universities that number faculty members in the hundreds and thousands and students in the thousands and tens of thousands. Society's commitment to send youth to college as a major preparation for adult roles is evident in the steady increase from 52,000 students in 1869 to 2,650,000 in 1949 to more than double this by the 1970s. The less than 2 percent of the age group who attended college at the close of the Civil War has grown to more than 40 percent and approaches 50 percent. This expansion in numbers has carried with it a similar expansion in functions. By the early 1960s Clark Kerr, then president of the University of California, could comment that his university employed more people "than IBM . . . in over a hundred locations, counting campuses, experiment stations, agricultural and urban extension centers, and projects abroad involving more than fifty countries." He pointed to "nearly 10,000 courses in its catalogues; some form of contact with nearly every industry, nearly every level of government, nearly every person in its region" (Kerr, 1966, pp. 7–8). The "multiversity" has proved to be the ultimate outcome for the "new university" of 70 years ago.

Since 1900 no radical departures have altered the form of university organization or changed in any substantial way its function. In the retrospect of the last 60 years, the major thrusts that have characterized this era are the following: first, the expansion in numbers of both personnel and of units of the administrative structure, both academic and managerial; second, the consolidation of departmental control over academic matters; and, third, the diffusion of participation in government with a concurrent lessening of the influence of boards and presidents.

Administrative Expansion

Aside from the study by McGrath (1936) and a recent article by David R. Witmer (1966), little documentation exists to delineate the specifics of administrative expansion in this century. But the outward manifestations are obvious. What university of any size today lacks that imposing administration building located near the center of the campus? Within its walls dozens and even hundreds of clerks, typists, secretaries, bookkeepers, accountants, staff assistants, and a variety of administrative officers labor diligently over correspondence and reports, accounts and records, and a variety of managerial services—frequently in a high degree of efficient isolation from the classroom, laboratory, and library across the campus. In addition, one finds a plethora of service positions ranging from dietitians and delivery men to personnel for institutional research.

Paralleling the managerial services, the academic organization has had its own expansion of new functions and offices appended to departments and professional schools. It takes only a quick glance at the telephone directory of a major university to spot such activities as the animal facilities, athletic publicity and promotion, black studies program, carbon research, program in comparative literature, council for international studies, continuing education division, cooperative urban extension center, and creative art center at the top of the alphabet through to technical research services, theater program, upward bound project, urology studies, and urban studies council at the bottom. Each of these activities has its director or head who reports to a chairman, a dean, or a vice-president. Each has a professional staff of one to a dozen individuals aided by secretaries and research assistants. The totality presents a bewildering complex of functions requiring administrative coordination and control.

As one looks over charts for the period, what stands out clearly is the steady, inexorable increase in administrative personnel and services paralleling the increase in numbers of students and faculty members.

Departmental Influence

Specialization of knowledge has its counterpart in specialization of departments. But more than this it has led to what amounts to a monopoly of the expert. This specialization has left the university-wide administrators, and at times deans as well, unable to do more than respond to initiative on matters of personnel facilities, teaching, curriculum, and research. Authors Paul L. Dressel and Donald J. Reichard (1970, p. 387)[10] observed in their historical overview that the department "has become a potent force, both in determining the stature of the university and in hampering the attempts of the university to improve its effectiveness and adapt to changing social and economic requirements." As early as 1929 a study of departments in small colleges demonstrated that they exercised a major influence in matters related to teaching, curriculum, schedule, and promotion (Reeves & Russell, 1929). More recent studies confirm the trend toward departmental autonomy and control over its own affairs (Caplow & McGee, 1958), evidenced by what David Riesman (1958) has called an academic procession in which the less prestigious institutions have followed the leadership of the major, prestigious universities.

This departmental autonomy has come as a logical outgrowth of size and specialization and of the pressing necessity to delegate and decentralize if major administrators were not to find themselves overwhelmed. A new kind of professor, the specialist and expert and man of consequence in society, has replaced the teacher and has augmented his (the specialist's) influence with a national system of professional and disciplinary societies. Together they have set the standards and the values, both oriented to productive scholarship, that dominate the universities.

Diffusion of Government

Following hard on the downward shift of academic power, governing boards have withdrawn extensively from active involvement in university affairs. This condition was incipient in 1905, as noted by James B. Munroe, industrialist and trustee at Massachusetts Institute of Technology. The trustees, he observed then, "find less and less opportunity for usefulness in a machine so elaborate that any incursion into it by those unfamiliar may do infinite harm—(Munroe, 1913). Fifty years later, in the same vein, the 1957 report on The Role of Trustees of Columbia University, (Columbia University, 1957) stated flatly that, while governing boards may hold final legal authority, their actual role in government leaves them removed from the ongoing affairs of their institutions. And as Trustee Ora L. Wildermuth, secretary of the Association of Governing Boards of State Universities, commented in 1949: "If a governing board contents itself with the selection of the best president available and with him develops and determines the broad general principles ... and then leaves the administration and academic processes to the administrative officers and the Faculty, it will have done its work well." It serves best to select a president, hold title to property, and act as a court of last appeal, he summarized (Wildermuth, 1949, p. 238).

Pressing up from a departmental base, faculty members have moved into governmental affairs via the formalization of a structure of senates, councils, and associated committees. Evidence supports the contention that by 1910 professors were not hesitant to refer to their "rightfully sovereign power" (Veysey, 1965, p. 392). President Harper of Chicago formally stated in his decennial report that it was a "firmly established policy of the Trustees that the responsibility for the settlement of educational questions rests with the Faculties" (Bogert, 1945, p. 81). During the first half of this century the precedent of the major universities slowly carried over to other institutions. In 1941 a survey of 228 colleges and universities by the AAUP (American Association of University Professors) Committee T on College and University Government led to the comment that "in the typical institution the board of trustees appointed the president, the president appointed deans, and the deans in turn designated executives. . . . Consultation concerning personnel and budget . . . took place between administrative and teacher personnel through departmental executives—("The Role of Faculties . . ." 1948). A decade later, however, the same committee reported an increase in faculty communication with trustees, participation in personnel decisions, influence on personnel policies, consultation about budgetary matters, and control of academic programs ("The Place and Function . . ." 1953). By the late 1960s the basic position of the AAUP had the strength of general tradition; in the eyes of a new breed of faculty radicals it had become a conservative force. In essence, the AAUP's position was based upon five principles: (1) that faculties have primary responsibility over educational policies; (2) that they concur through established committees and procedures in academic personnel matters; (3) that they participate actively in the selection of presidents, deans, and chairmen; (4) that they are consulted on budgetary decisions; and (5) that appropriate agencies for this participation have official standing.

Precedents for student involvement in university and college government (distinct from extracurricular campus activities) have gained a new force, although their roots lie deep in the history of higher education. Professor Cowley (1964, Ch. 11, p. 16) has described the abortive two-year "House of Students" at Amherst in 1828 as a legislative body concerned with security on campus, study hours, and similar matters. In this century, something of the same spirit has appeared sporadically. At Barnard during the academic year 1921–22, students carried out a sophisticated analysis of the curriculum. At Dartmouth in 1924, a committee of 12 seniors submitted a critical review of the education program. At Harvard in 1946, following the publication of the faculty report General Education in a Free Society (Harvard Committee, 1946), students published an equally formidable document. Overall, as Cowley (1964, Ch. 11, p. 47) observes, "American students have continuously and sometimes potently affected the thinking and actions of professors, presidents, and trustees." Historically their influence has been an informal one. Their drive for direct participation on the governing councils and boards of colleges and universities generated real

potency only during the late 1960s.[11] Its effectiveness remains conjectural, although the evidence suggests that the student drive for participation will tend to dissipate further the influence of boards and presidents.

Alumni have maintained their traditional voice in government, although one can perceive an undermining of the spirit of alma mater and the significance of financial contributions so long associated with their institutional commitments. This participation was substantiated by a 1966 survey of 82 public and private universities and colleges which reported that 31 of the institutions have elected alumni trustees and an additional 24 have trustees nominated by alumni. Nearly all had alumni on their boards, however.[12] Cornell University's situation is typical of private institutions. In a 1966 letter the president of the Alumni Association noted that "a trustee is not required to be an alumnus of the University unless he is elected by the alumni. At present, however, of the 40 members, 35 are alumni." In retrospect, then, higher education is moving into the final decades of the twentieth century with a pattern of organization similar in its major dimensions to that with which it entered the century. The question readily comes to mind whether this form will continue to prove effective.

Conclusion

That the American university, the hallmark of the American system of higher education, has flourished as an institution uniquely fitted to its times stands without question. Its commitment to the expansion of knowledge and its application are emulated throughout the world. Similarly, its organizational arrangements have grown out of and suited well its particular kind of educational enterprise. Inevitably governing boards and presidents had to delegate as institutions expanded. That they did so in a manner that enhanced the effectiveness of the academic endeavor has proved to be no minor achievement. Departments, in turn, have served well by translating the essence of specialized knowledge into workable organizational forms. Student personnel administrators, in their turn, have filled that void between individual and organization left by the impersonalism inherent in a faculty pre-eminently concerned with the extension of knowledge. A faculty governing structure has given an organizational channel to the exercise of professorial influence, in turn an academically essential counterbalance to the authority of governing boards and external constituencies. In sum, universities have proved an effective organizational means by which scholarship and learning could flourish within the confines of large, complex organizations.

Yet, as the decade of the 1970s unfolds, a sense of uncertainty about just how well universities do perform has begun to settle over the campuses of the nation. Students in large universities, and even to a degree in smaller institutions, find themselves caught in a complex of increasingly impersonal relationships and an educational endeavor which enhances advanced study and research more than student learning. Both influences tend to dull any sense of intellectual awakening or of personal meaning for life on the part of students. Most faculty cling hard to the traditional fields of knowledge and to specialization despite a societal need for synthesis and application of what is known. As, historically, cultures and nations in their greatest flowering have begun to show their inherent weaknesses, so the university in the last few decades has provided evidence of its limitations. The changing nature of the social order, as it too reaches a pinnacle of scientific-technological achievement, amplifies these weaknesses.

A historical survey such as this would be inadequate indeed if it did not at least suggest some clues to the future. In conclusion, therefore, we note three pervasive organizational inadequacies. One can be attributed to size and complexity, a second to specialization and departmentalization, and the third to the shifting pattern of institutional government. All were incipient but generally underway as higher education emerged from the First World War.

The size and complexity of United States universities seem to dictate that they have become large bureaucracies. Actually, however, one finds two bureaucracies. On the one hand, over the past 50 years faculties have created a hierarchy of departments, schools, and senates or executive councils well larded with a variety of permanent and temporary committees. This bureaucracy claims rights of control over the totality of the academic function. On the other

hand, administrators have formed a separate hierarchy to grapple with the immense tasks of management of essential yet supportive services which maintain the university, not the least of which are budget and finance. The lines of relationship between the two bureaucracies have become tenuous. The different attitudes and values associated with each have driven a psychological wedge between faculty members and administrators. Faculty remain committed to a traditional ideal of the university as an integrated community, at the same time giving constant evidence that they fail to grasp its real operational nature and managerial complications. Administrators find their managerial tasks so consuming that they become forgetful of the nature of the academic enterprise.

The second evidence of dysfunction stems from the nature of the department as the organizational unit for disciplinary and professional specialization. The commitment to specialization energizes centrifugal forces that tend to push faculty loyalties out from the universities. Thus the university is often merely a base, temporary or permanent, from which the scholar pursues his primary concern with research activities. Specialization has produced a similar tendency toward fragmentation of the academic organization. While exercising a dominant influence on instruction, curriculum, research, and other academic matters, schools and departments show a low regard for university values and a high concern for disciplinary and professional values. Despite many evidences to the contrary during the student disruptions of the last few years, this condition is reinforced by academic condescension toward administrators, who are viewed as servants rather than leaders of the professorate. It reflects what one might call a faculty schizophrenia which categorizes administrators as minions while condemning them for failure to stand firmly as defenders of the academic faith in times of crisis.

At times this divergency threatens an atrophy in leadership for large universities in an era when leadership is of utmost importance. The remedy, however, inevitably must lie beyond the bounds of organizational factors. Forms of government serve only as well as they are supported in the general values and commitments of those affected by them. Any rectification of this condition, therefore, must stem from deep within the higher education enterprise. In particular, there must be some resolution of the conflict between the clear and direct rewards that accompany achievement in scholarship and research and the nominal recognition, despite societal expectation, accorded to the education of students. From this base line one moves into explorations of reward systems that conform to stated purposes. One also has to reflect upon organizational systems that prove responsive to changing conditions as against those that support existing arrangements.

The third problem—the shifting power in institutional government—was anticipated in 1903 by President Schurman of Cornell when he characterized his role as that of a mediator. Sixty years later Clark Kerr made the same observation with greater force. Presidential deference to faculty expertise in academic affairs is only one facet of the situation, however. The history of university organization in the twentieth century has been an account of the disintegration of the traditional form of government conceived in terms of formal authority granted to governing boards, which have exercised it through the president as executive officer.

The diffusion of government by means of dissipation of boards and presidential influence and dispersion of operating control to departments, administrative offices, and faculty governing bodies has been accompanied by the intrusion of external forces. Professional and disciplinary associations, accrediting agencies, agencies of the federal government for all institutions and state executive offices for public ones—all have tended to bypass presidents and boards. It appears that higher education has experienced one of those historic circles. Governing boards today serve much the way the original visitors or overseers did. What is lacking is a new corporation in the sense of a controlling or managerial council to fill the vacuum. As one English observer phrased it, organizationally American universities have tended to become "confederations of largely autonomous departments." It adds up to what he has characterized as "the hole in the centre" (Shils, 1970).

As universities enter the decade of the 1970s, the pressures on the established organization are evidenced in student dissent and the public reaction to it. The movement toward decentralization of control over educational and administrative functions has begun to come up against external demands for more forceful central authority to the end not only of "law and order" but of a "more efficient use of resources." Mass higher education and the possibility of almost universal higher education exacerbate the problems. More fundamentally, one finds growing evidences of academic inadequacies in the face of the need for new kinds of education and scholarship. These must relate to the role of the university in a society pressed by ecological and social dislocation stemming from scientific and technological achievement. One readily suspects that the organizational forms effective in 1900 may serve but poorly for the year 2000.

Notes

1. These arrangements for the College of William and Mary were stated in a manner that led to conflicts between the two boards during its early years, although essentially they remained in effect until it became a state institution shortly after 1900. At Harvard, however, practice nullified the apparent intent of the 1650 charter, so that by the eighteenth century the immediate governing council (the Corporation) had passed into the hands of external members. The practice was disputed from time to time by tutors until an 1825 vote of the Overseers finally and formally stated that "the resident instructors of Harvard University" did not have any exclusive right to be chosen members of the Corporation (Quincy, 1860, vol. 2, 324).

2. Yale historians apparently have tended to credit Clap with a successful defense. Recent investigation of this incident by Professor W. H. Cowley, however, discloses that a visitation was made the following year, about which one of the visitors later observed that "we touch'd them so gently, that till after ye Assembly, they never saw they were taken in, that we had made ourselves Visitors, & subjected them to an Annual Visitation" (a point made in correspondence with this author).

3. This precedent has undergone modification in more recent decades as state budget bureaus, civil service commissions, and coordinating boards have intruded directly into the internal affairs of public institutions.

4. Exceptions to these rights do exist, particularly in connection with the control of property and the borrowing of monies. Frequently special corporations are set up within the control of state universities to handle private

funds. Actual practice varies among the states, some of which limited the powers of boards in the founding legislation.

5. In recent decades the growth in academic status and influence of the disciplines and professional departments and schools has further strengthened faculty power within institutions. The status associated with productive scholarship and research has given faculty members a greatly improved position vis-á-vis administration in internal affairs, a condition documented by Theodore Caplow and Reece J. McGee in their classic study, *The Academic Marketplace,* 1958.

6. Amherst in 1874, Dartmouth in 1875, Rutgers in 1881, Princeton in 1900, Columbia in 1908, Brown in 1914. (In the 1865 modification of its charter, Harvard adopted a plan whereby alumni gained the right to elect all new members to the Board of Overseers, the body with ultimate responsibility for that institution.)

7. Little attention is given, unfortunately, to the uniquely significant role of the governing board in this country as the agency that both has protected internal autonomy and intellectual freedom and has served as a force to keep institutions relevant to the general society. This history badly needs doing. Despite occasional intrusions into internal affairs and matters related to academic freedom, the governing board has served as a point of balance for that essential dualism between institutional and academic autonomy and public accountability which has characterized American higher education. Current forces pressing for greater internal participation on

the one hand and increased public control on the other need tempering by the experience of the past in this connection.

8. For example, Harvard established 12 divisions, each including one or more departments, in 1891; Chicago had 26 departments in three faculties in 1893; Cornell, Yale, Princeton, Johns Hopkins, and Syracuse, among others, all reveal the trend toward departmentalization during the decade of the 1890s (Forsberg & Pearce, 1966).

9. Actually, the first head of Harvard had the title of master and that of Yale, rector. The Harvard custom lasted two years, that at Yale about forty. Both colleges shifted to the title of president.

10. This report anticipated a more complete study by Dressel, Marcus, and Johnson entitled The *Confidence Crisis,* Jossey-Bass, Inc., San Francisco, 1970.

11. In his 1970 book, *Should Students Share the Power?* Earl J. McGrath reports a survey of existing practice, noting that more than 80 percent of 875 institutions admit some students to membership in at least one policy-making body. In the same year the University of Tennessee admitted students to its trustee committees. A House bill submitted in 1969 in the Massachusetts legislature proposed an elected student member of each of the governing boards of public universities.

12. Conducted by Howard University with the sponsorship of the American Alumni Council. The questionnaire was mailed to 112 institutions, from which 82 usable responses were received.

CHAPTER 2

LEADERSHIP IN AN ORGANIZED ANARCHY

MICHAEL D. COHEN AND JAMES G. MARCH

The Ambiguities of Anarchy

The college president faces four fundamental ambiguities. The first is the ambiguity of *purpose*. In what terms can action be justified? What are the goals of the organization? The second is the ambiguity of *power*. How powerful is the president? What can he accomplish? The third is the ambiguity of *experience*. What is to be learned from the events of the presidency? How does the president make inferences about his experience? The fourth is the ambiguity of *success*. When is a president successful? How does he assess his pleasures?

These ambiguities are fundamental to college presidents because they strike at the heart of the usual interpretations of leadership. When purpose is ambiguous, ordinary theories of decision making and intelligence become problematic. When power is ambiguous, ordinary theories of social order and control become problematic. When experience is ambiguous, ordinary theories of learning and adaptation become problematic. When success is ambiguous, ordinary theories of motivation and personal pleasure become problematic.

The Ambiguity of Purpose

Almost any educated person can deliver a lecture entitled "The Goals of the University." Almost no one will listen to the lecture voluntarily. For the most part, such lectures and their companion essays are well-intentioned exercises in social rhetoric, with little operational content.

Efforts to generate normative statements of the goals of a university tend to produce goals that are either meaningless or dubious. They fail one or more of the following reasonable tests. First, is the goal clear? Can one define some specific procedure for measuring the degree of goal achievement? Second, is it problematic? Is there some possibility that the organization will accomplish the goal? Is there some chance that it will fail? Third, is it accepted? Do most significant groups in the university agree on the goal statement? For the most part, the level of generality that facilitates acceptance destroys the problematic nature or clarity of the goal. The level of specificity that permits measurement destroys acceptance.

Recent discussions of educational audits, of cost-benefit analysis in education, and of accountability and evaluation in higher education have not been spectacularly successful in resolving this normative ambiguity, even in those cases where such techniques have been accepted as relatively fruitful. In our judgment, the major contributions (and they are important ones) of operational analysis in higher education to date have been to expose the inconsistencies of current policies and to make marginal improvements in those domains in which clear objectives are widely shared.

Similarly, efforts to infer the "real" objectives of a university by observing university behavior tend to be unsuccessful. They fail one or more of the following reasonable tests. First, is the goal uniquely consistent with behavior? Does the imputed goal produce the observed behavior and is it the only goal that does? Second, is it stable? Does the goal imputed from past behavior reliably predict future behavior? Although it is often possible to devise a statement of the goals of a university by some form of revealed preference test of past actions, such goal statements have poor predictive power.

The difficulties in imputing goals from behavior are not unique to universities. Experience with the complications is shared by revealed preference theorists in economics and psychology, radical critics of society, and functionalist students of social institutions. The search for a consistent explanation of human social behavior through a model of rational intent and an imputation of intent from action has had some successes. But there is no sign that the university is one of the successes, or very likely to become one.

Efforts to specify a set of consciously shared, consistent objectives within a university or to infer such a set of objectives from the activities or actions of the university have regularly revealed signs of inconsistency. To expose inconsistencies is not to resolve them, however. There are only modest signs that universities or other organized anarchies respond to a revelation of ambiguity of purpose by reducing the ambiguity. These are organizational systems without clear objectives, and the processes by which their objectives are established and legitimized are not extraordinarily sensitive to inconsistency. In fact, for many purposes the ambiguity of purpose is produced by our insistence on treating purpose as a necessary property of a good university. The strains arise from trying to impose a model of action as flowing from intent on organizations that act in another way.

College presidents live within a normative context that presumes purpose and within an organizational context that denies it. They serve on commissions to define and redefine the objectives of higher education. They organize convocations to examine the goals of the college. They write introductory statements to the college catalog. They accept the presumption that intelligent leadership presupposes the rational pursuit of goals. Simultaneously, they are aware that the process of choice in the college depends little on statements of shared direction. They recognize the flow of actions as an ecology of games (Long, 1958), each with its own rules. They accept the observation that the world is not like the model.

The Ambiguity of Power

Power is a simple idea, pervasive in its appeal to observers of social events. Like *intelligence* or *motivation* or *utility*, however, it tends to be misleadingly simple and prone to tautology. A person has power if he gets things done, if he has power, he can get things done.

As students of social power have long observed, such a view of power has limited usefulness.[1] Two of the things the simple view produces are an endless and largely fruitless search for the person who has "the real power" in the university, and an equally futile pursuit of the organizational locale "where the decision is *really* made." So profound is the acceptance of the power model that students of organizations who suggest the model is wrong are sometimes viewed as part of the plot to conceal "the real power" and "the true locus of decision." In that particular logic the reality of the simple power model is demonstrated by its inadequacy.

As a shorthand casual expression for variations in the potential of different positions in the organization, *power* has some utility. The college president has more potential for moving the college than most people, probably more potential than any one other person. Nevertheless, presidents discover that they have less power than is believed, that their power to accomplish things depends heavily on what they want to accomplish, that the use of formal authority is limited by other formal authority, that the acceptance of authority is not automatic, that the necessary details of organizational life confuse power, (which is somewhat different from diffusing it), and that their colleagues seem to delight in complaining simultaneously about presidential weakness and presidential willfulness.

The ambiguity of power, like the ambiguity of purpose, is focused on the president. Presidents share in and contribute to the confusion. They enjoy the perquisites and prestige of the office. They enjoy its excitement, at least when things go well. They announce important events. They appear at important symbolic functions. They report to the people. They accept and thrive on their own importance. It would be remarkable if they did not. Presidents even occasionally recite that "the buck stops here" with a finality that suggests the cliché is an observation about power and authority rather than a proclamation of administrative style and ideology.

At the same time, presidents solicit an understanding of the limits to their control. They regret the tendency of students, legislators, and community leaders to assume that a president has the power to do whatever he chooses simply because he is president. They plead the countervailing power of other groups in the college or the notable complexities of causality in large organizations.

The combination is likely to lead to popular impressions of strong presidents during good times and weak presidents during bad times. Persons who are primarily exposed to the symbolic presidency (e.g., outsiders) will tend to exaggerate the power of the president. Those people who have tried to accomplish something in the institution with presidential support (e.g., educational reformers) will tend to underestimate presidential power or presidential will.

The confusion disturbs the president, but it also serves him. Ambiguity of power leads to a parallel ambiguity of responsibility. The allocation of credit and blame for the events of organizational life becomes—as it often does in political and social systems—a matter for argument. The "facts" of responsibility are badly confounded by the confusions of anarchy; and the conventional myth of hierarchical executive responsibility is undermined by the countermyth of the nonhierarchical nature of colleges and universities. Presidents negotiate with their audiences on the interpretations of their power. As a result, during the recent years of campus troubles, many college presidents sought to emphasize the limitations of presidential control. During the more glorious days

of conspicuous success, they solicited a recognition of their responsibility for events.

The process does not involve presidents alone, of course. The social validation of responsibility involves all the participants: faculty, trustees, students, parents, community leaders, government. Presidents seek to write their histories in the use of power as part of a chorus of history writers, each with his own reasons for preferring a somewhat different interpretation of "Who has the Power?"

The Ambiguity of Experience

College presidents attempt to learn from their experience. They observe the consequences of actions and infer the structure of the world from those observations. They use the resulting inferences in attempts to improve their future actions.

Consider the following very simple learning paradigm:

1. At a certain point in time a president is presented with a set of well-defined, discrete action alternatives.

2. At any point in time he has a certain probability of choosing any particular alternative (and a certainty of choosing one of them).

3. The president observes the outcome that apparently follows his choice and assesses the outcome in terms of his goals.

4. If the outcome is consistent with his goals, the president increases his probability of choosing that alternative in the future; if not, he decreases the probability.

Although actual presidential learning certainly involves more complicated inferences, such a paradigm captures much of the ordinary adaptation of an intelligent man to the information gained from experience.

The process produces considerable learning. The subjective experience is one of adapting from experience and improving behavior on the basis of feedback. If the world with which the president is dealing is relatively simple and relatively stable, and if his experience is relatively frequent, he can expect to improve over time (assuming he has some appropriate criterion for testing the consistency of outcomes with goals). As we have suggested earlier, however, the world in which the president lives has two conspicuous properties that make experience ambiguous even where goals are clear. First, the world is relatively complex. Outcomes depend heavily on factors other than the president's action. These factors are uncontrolled and, in large part, unobserved. Second, relative to the rate at which the president gathers experimental data, the world changes rapidly. These properties produce considerable potential for false learning.

We can illustrate the phenomenon by taking a familiar instance of learning in the realm of personnel policies. Suppose that a manager reviews his subordinates annually and considers what to do with those who are doing poorly. He has two choices: he can replace an employee whose performance is low, or he can keep him in the job and try to work with him to obtain improvement. He chooses which employees to replace and which to keep in the job on the basis of his judgment about their capacities to respond to different treatments. Now suppose that, in fact, there are no differences among the employees. Observed variations in performance are due entirely to random fluctuations. What would the manager "learn" in such a situation?

He would learn how smart he was. He would discover that his judgments about whom to keep and whom to replace were quite good. Replacements will generally perform better than the men they replaced; those men who are kept in the job will generally improve in their performance. If for some reason he starts out being relatively "humane" and refuses to replace anyone, he will discover that the best managerial strategy is to work to improve existing employees. If he starts out with a heavy hand and replaces everyone, he will learn that being tough is a good idea. If he replaces some and works with others, he will learn that the essence of personnel management is judgment about the worker.

Although we know that in this hypothetical situation it makes no difference what a manager does, he will experience some subjective learning that is direct and compelling. He will come to believe that he understands the situation and has mastered it. If we were to suggest to the manager that he might be a victim of superstitious learning, he would find it difficult to believe. Everything in his environment tells him that he understands the world, even though his understanding is spurious.

It is not necessary to assume that the world is strictly random to produce substantially the same effect. Whenever the rate of experience is modest relative to the complexity of the phenomena and the rate of change in the phenomena, the interpretation made of experience will tend to be more persuasive subjectively than it should be. In such a world, experience is not a good teacher. Although the outcomes stemming from the various learned strategies in the personnel management example will be no worse because of a belief in the reality of the learning, the degree of confidence a manager comes to have in his theory of the world is erroneously high.

College presidents probably have greater confidence in their interpretations of college life, college administration, and their general environment than is warranted. The inferences they have made from experience are likely to be wrong. Their confidence in their learning is likely to have been reinforced by the social support they receive from the people around them and by social expectations about the presidential role. As a result, they tend to be unaware of the extent to which the ambiguities they feel with respect to purpose and power are matched by similar ambiguities with respect to the meaning of the ordinary events of presidential life.

The Ambiguity of Success

Administrative success is generally recognized in one of two ways. First, by promotion: An administrator knows that he has been successful by virtue of a promotion to a better job. He assesses his success on the current job by the opportunities he has or expects to have to leave it. Second, by widely accepted, operational measures of organizational output: a business executive values his own performance in terms of a profit-and-loss statement of his operations.

Problems with these indicators of success are generic to high-level administrative positions. Offers of promotion become less likely as the job improves and the administrator's age advances. The criteria by which success is judged become less precise in measurement, less stable over time, and less widely shared. The administrator discovers that a wide assortment of factors outside his control are capable of overwhelming the impact of any actions he may take.

In the case of the college president all three problems are accentuated. As we have seen earlier, few college presidents are promoted out of the presidency. There are job offers, and most presidents ultimately accept one; but the best opportunity the typical president can expect is an invitation to accept a decent version of administrative semiretirement. The criteria of success in academic administration are sometimes moderately clear (e.g., growth, quiet on campus, improvement in the quality of students and faculty), but the relatively precise measures of college health tend neither to be stable over time nor to be critically sensitive to presidential action. For example, during the post-World War II years in American colleges, it was conventional to value growth and to attribute growth to the creative activities of administrative leaders. In the retrospective skepticism about the uncritical acceptance of a growth ethic, we have begun to reinterpret a simple history that attributed college growth to the conscious prior decision of a wise (or stupid) president or board. The rapid expansion of higher education, the postwar complex of student and faculty relations and attitudes, and the massive extension of governmental subsidies to the research activities of colleges and universities were not the simple consequences of decisions by Clark Kerr or John Hanna. Nor, retrospectively, does it seem plausible to attribute major control over those events to college administrators.

An argument can be made, of course, that the college president should be accustomed to the ambiguity of success. His new position is not, in this respect, so strikingly, different from the positions he has held previously. His probable perspective is different, however. Success has not previously been subjectively ambiguous to him. He has been a success. He has been promoted relatively rapidly. He and his associates are inclined to attribute his past successes to a combination of administrative savoir-faire, interpersonal style, and political sagacity. He has experienced those successes as the lawful consequence of his actions. Honest modesty on the part of a president does not conceal a certain awareness of his own ability. A president comes to his office having learned that he is successful and that he enjoys success.

The momentum of promotion will not sustain him in the presidency. Although, as we have seen, a fair number of presidents anticipate moving from their present job to another, better presidency, the prospects are not nearly as good as the hopes. The ambiguities of purpose, power, and experience conspire to render success and failure equally obscure. The validation of success is unreliable. Not only can a president not assure himself that he will be able to lead the college in the directions in which others might believe, he also has no assurance that the same criteria will be applied tomorrow. What happens today will tend to be rationalized tomorrow as what was desired. What happens today will have some relation to what was desired yesterday. Outcomes do flow in part from goals. But goals flow from outcomes as well, and both goals and outcomes also move independently.

The result is that the president is a bit like the driver of a skidding automobile. The marginal judgments he makes, his skill, and his luck may possibly make some difference to the survival prospects for his riders. As a result, his responsibilities are heavy. But whether he is convicted of manslaughter or receives a medal for heroism is largely outside his control.

One basic response to the ambiguities of success is to find pleasure in the process of presidential life. A reasonable man will seek reminders of his relevance and success. Where those reminders are hard to find in terms of socially validated outcomes unambiguously due to one's actions, they may be sought in the interactions of organizational life. George Reedy (1970) made a similar observation about a different presidency: "Those who seek to lighten the burdens of the presidency by easing the workload do no occupant of that office a favor. The workload—especially the ceremonial work load—are the only events of a president's day which make life endurable."

Leader Response to Anarchy

The ambiguities that college presidents face describe the life of any formal leader of any organized anarchy. The metaphors of leadership and our traditions of personalizing history (even the minor histories of collegiate institutions) confuse the issues of leadership by ignoring the basic ambiguity of leadership life. We require a plausible basic perspective for the leader of a loosely coupled, ambiguous organization.

Such a perspective begins with humility. It is probably a mistake for a college president to imagine that what he does in office affects significantly either the long-run position of the institution or his reputation as a president. So long as he does not violate some rather obvious restrictions on his behavior, his reputation and his term of office are more likely to be affected by broad social events or by the unpredictable vicissitudes of official responsibility than by his actions. Although the college library or administration building will doubtless record his presidency by appropriate portraiture or plaque, few presidents achieve even a modest claim to attention 20 years after their departure from the presidency; and those who are remembered best are probably most distinguished by their good fortune in coming to office during a period of collegiate good times and growth, or their bad fortune in being there when the floods came.

In this respect the president's life does not differ markedly from that of most of us. A leadership role, however, is distinguished by the numerous temptations to self-importance that it provides. Presidents easily come to believe that they can continue in office forever if they are only clever or perceptive or responsive enough. They easily come to exaggerate the significance of their daily actions for the college as well as for themselves. They easily come to see each day as an opportunity to build support in their constituencies for the next "election."

It is an old story. Human action is frequently corrupted by an exaggeration of its consequences. Parents are intimidated by an exaggerated belief in their importance to the process of child-rearing. Teachers are intimidated by an exaggerated belief in their importance to the process of learning. Lovers are intimidated by an exaggerated belief in their importance to the process of loving. Counselors are intimidated by an exaggerated belief in their importance to the process of self-discovery.

The major consequence of a heroic conception of the consequences of action is a distrust of judgment. When college presidents imagine that their actions have great consequences for the world, they are inclined to fear an error. When they fear an error, they are inclined to seek social support for their judgment, to confuse voting with virtue and bureaucratic rules with equity. Such a conception of the importance of their every choice makes presidents vulnerable to the same deficiencies of performance that afflict the parents of first children and inexperienced teachers, lovers, or counselors.

A lesser, but important, result of a heroic conception of the consequences of action is the abandonment of pleasure. By acceding to his own importance, the college president is driven to sobriety of manner. For reasons we have detailed earlier, he has difficulty in establishing the correctness of his actions by exhibiting their consequences. He is left with the necessity of communicating moral intent through facial intensity. At the same time, he experiences the substantial gap between his aspirations and his possibilities. Both by the requirements of their public face and by their own intolerant expectations, college presidents often find the public enjoyment of their job denied to them.

The ambiguities of leadership in an organized anarchy require a leadership posture that is somewhat different from that implicit in most discussions of the college presidency. In particular, we believe that a college president is, on the whole, better advised to think of himself as trying to do good than as trying to satisfy a political or bureaucratic audience; better advised to define his role in terms of the modest part he can play in making the college slightly better in the long run than in terms of satisfying current residents or solving current problems. He requires an enthusiasm for a Tolstoyan view of history and for the freedom of individual action that such a view entails. Since the world is absurd, the president's primary responsibility is to virtue.

Presidents occupy a minor part in the lives of a small number of people. They have some power, but little magic. They can act with a fair degree of confidence that if they make a mistake, it will not matter much. They can be allowed the heresy of believing that pleasure is consistent with virtue.

The Elementary Tactics of Administrative Action

The tactics of administrative action in an organized anarchy are somewhat different from the tactics of action in a situation characterized by clearer goals, better specified technology, and more persistent participation. Nevertheless, we can examine how a leader with a purpose can operate within an organization that is without one.

Necessarily, any presentation of practical strategies suggests a minor Machiavellianism with attendant complications and concerns. There is an argument that strategies based upon knowledge contribute to administrative manipulation. There is a fear that practical strategies may be misused for evil ends. There is a feeling that the effectiveness of the strategies may be undermined by their public recitation.

We are aware of these concerns, but not persuaded by them. First, we do not believe that any major new cleverness that would conspicuously alter the prevailing limits on our ability to change the course of history will be discovered. The idea that there are some spectacularly effective strategies waiting to be discovered by some modern Machiavelli seems implausible. Second, we believe that the problem of evil is little eased by know-nothingness. The concern about malevolent manipulation is a real one (as well as a cliché), but it often becomes a simple defense of the status quo. We hope that good people interested in accomplishing things will find a list of tactics marginally helpful. Third, we can see nothing in the recitation of strategic recommendations that changes systematically the relative positions of members of the organization. If the strategies are effective, it is because the analysis of organization is correct. The features of the organization that are involved are not likely to change quickly. As a result, we would not anticipate that public discussion of the strategies would change their effectiveness much or distinctly change the relative positions of those (e.g., students, presidents) who presumably stand to profit from the advice if it is useful.

As we will indicate later in this chapter, a conception of leadership that merely assumes that the college president should act to accomplish what he wants to accomplish is too narrow. A major part of his responsibility is to lead the organization to a changing and more complex view of itself by treating goals as only partly knowable. Nevertheless, the problems of inducing a college to do what one wants it to do are clearly worthy of attention. If presidents and others are to function effectively within the college, they need to recognize the ways in which the character of the college as a system for exercising problems, making decisions, and certifying status conditions their attempts to influence the outcome of any decision.

We can identify five major properties of decision making in organized anarchies that are of substantial importance to the tactics of accomplishing things in colleges and universities:

1. Most issues most of the time have *low salience* for most people. The decisions to be made within the organization secure only partial and erratic attention from participants in the organization. A major share of the attention devoted to a particular issue is tied less to the content of the issue than to its symbolic significance for individual and group esteem.

2. The total system has *high inertia*. Anything that requires a coordinated effort of the organization in order to start is unlikely to be started. Anything that requires a coordinated effort of the organization in order to be stopped is unlikely to be stopped.

3. Any decision can become a *garbage can* for almost any problem. The issues discussed in the context of any particular decision depend less on the decision or problems involved than on the timing of their joint arrivals and the existence of alternative arenas for exercising problems.

4. The processes of choice are easily subject to *overload*. When the load on the system builds up relative to its capabilities for exercising and resolving problems, the decision outcomes in the organization tend to become increasingly separated from the formal process of decision.

5. The organization has a *weak information base*. Information about past events or

past decisions is often not retained. When retained, it is often difficult to retrieve. Information about current activities is scant.

These properties are conspicuous and ubiquitous. They represent some important ways in which all organizations sometimes, and an organization like a university often, present opportunities for tactical action that in a modest way strengthen the hand of the participant who attends to them. We suggest eight basic tactical rules for use by those who seek to influence the course of decisions in universities or colleges.

Rule 1: Spend Time

The kinds of decision-making situations and organizations we have described suffer from a shortage of decision-making energy. Energy is a scarce resource. If one is in a position to devote time to the decision-making activities within the organization, he has a considerable claim on the system. Most organizations develop ways of absorbing the decision-making energy provided by sharply deviant participants; but within moderate boundaries, a person who is willing to spend time finds himself in a strong position for at least three significant reasons:

- By providing a scarce resource (energy), he lays the basis for a claim. If he is willing to spend time, he can expect more tolerant consideration of the problems he considers important. One of the most common organizational responses to a proposal from a participant is the request that he head a committee to do something about it. This behavior is an acknowledgment both of the energy-poor situation and of the price the organization pays for participation. That price is often that the organization must allow the participant some significant control over the definition of problems to be considered relevant.[2]

- By spending time on the homework for a decision, he becomes a major information source in an information-poor world. At the limit, the information provided need have no particular evidential validity. Consider, for example, the common assertions in college decision-making processes about what some constituency (e.g., board of trustees, legislature, student body, ethnic group) is "thinking." The assertions are rarely based on defensible evidence, but they tend to become organizational facts by virtue of the shortage of serious information. More generally, reality for a decision is specified by those willing to spend the time required to collect the small amounts of information available, to review the factual assertions of others, and to disseminate their findings.

- By investing more of his time in organizational concerns, he increases his chance of being present when something important to him is considered. A participant who wishes to pursue other matters (e.g., study, research, family, the problems of the outside world) reduces the number of occasions for decision making to which he can afford to attend. A participant who can spend time can be involved in more arenas. Since it is often difficult to anticipate when and where a particular issue will be involved (and thus to limit one's attention to key times and domains), the simple frequency of availability is relatively important.

Rule 2: Persist

It is a mistake to assume that if a particular proposal has been rejected by an organization today, it will be rejected tomorrow. Different sets of people and concerns will be reflected each time a problem is considered or a proposal discussed. We noted earlier the ways in which the flow of participants leads to a flow of organizational concerns.[3] The specific combination of sentiments and people that is associated with a specific choice opportunity is partly fortuitous, and Fortune may be more considerate another day.

For the same reason, it is a mistake to assume that today's victory will be implemented automatically tomorrow. The distinction between decision making and decision implementation is usually a false one. Decisions are not "made" once and for all. Rather they happen as a result of a series of episodes involving different people in different settings, and they may be unmade or modified by subsequent episodes. The participant who spends much time celebrating his victory ordinarily can expect to find the victory short-lived. The loser who spends his time weeping rather than reintroducing his ideas will persistently have something to weep about. The loser who persists in a variety of contexts is frequently rewarded.

Rule 3: Exchange Status for Substance

As we have indicated, the specific substantive issues in a college, or similar organization, typically have low salience for participants. A quite typical situation is one in which significant numbers of participants and groups of participants care less about the specific substantive outcome than they do about the implications of that outcome for their own sense of self-esteem and the social recognition of their importance. Such an ordering of things is neither surprising nor normatively unattractive. It would be a strange world indeed if the mostly minor issues of university governance, for example, became more important to most people than personal and group esteem.

A college president, too, is likely to become substantially concerned with the formal acknowledgment of office. Since it is awkward for him to establish definitively that he is substantively important, the president tends to join other participants in seeking symbolic confirmation of his significance.

The esteem trap is understandable but unfortunate. College presidents who can forgo at least some of the pleasures of self-importance in order to trade status for substance are in a strong position. Since leaders receive credit for many things over which they have little control and to which they contribute little, they should find it possible to accomplish some of the things they want by allowing others to savor the victories, enjoy the pleasures of involvement, and receive the profits of public importance.

Rule 4: Facilitate Opposition Participation

The high inertia of organizations and the heavy dependence of organizational events on processes outside of the control of the organization make organizational power ambiguous. Presi-

dents sense their lack of control despite their position of authority, status, and concern. Most people who participate in university decision making sense a disappointment with the limited control their position provides.

Persons outside the formal ranks of authority tend to see authority as providing more control. Their aspirations for change tend to be substantially greater than the aspirations for change held by persons with formal authority. One obvious solution is to facilitate participation in decision making. Genuine authoritative participation will reduce the aspirations of oppositional leaders. In an organization characterized by high inertia and low salience it is unwise to allow beliefs about the feasibility of planned action to outrun reality. From this point of view, public accountability, participant observation, and other techniques for extending the range of legitimate participation in the decision-making processes of the organization are essential means of keeping the aspirations of occasional actors within bounds. Since most people most of the time do not participate much, their aspirations for what can be done have a tendency to drift away from reality. On the whole, the direct involvement of dissident groups in the decision-making process is a more effective depressant of exaggerated aspirations than is a lecture by the president.

Rule 5: Overload the System

As we have suggested, the style of decision making changes when the load exceeds the capabilities of the system. Since we are talking about energy-poor organizations, accomplishing overload is not hard. In practical terms, this means having a large repertoire of projects for organizational action; it means making substantial claims on resources for the analysis of problems, discussion of issues, and political negotiation.

Within an organized anarchy it is a mistake to become absolutely committed to any one project. There are innumerable ways in which the processes we have described will confound the cleverest behavior with respect to any single proposal, however imaginative or subjectively important. What such processes cannot do is cope with large numbers of projects. Someone with the habit of producing many proposals, without absolute commitment to any one, may lose any one of them (and it is hard to predict a priori which one), but cannot be stopped on everything.

The tactic is not unlike the recommendation in some treatments of bargaining that one should introduce new dimensions of bargains in order to facilitate more favorable trades.[4] It is grounded in the observation that the press of proposals so loads the organization that a large number of actions are taken without attending to problems. Where decisions are made through oversight or flight, considerable control over the course of decision making lies in the hands of two groups: the initiators of the proposals, who get their way in oversight, and the full-time administrator, who is left to make the decision in cases of flight. The college president with a program is in the enviable position of being both a proposal initiator and a full-time administrator. Overload is almost certainly helpful to his program. Other groups within a college or university are probably also advantaged by overload if they have a positive program for action, but their advantage is less certain. In particular, groups in opposition to the administration that are unable to participate full time (either directly or through representatives) may wish to be selective in the use of overload as a tactic.

Rule 6: Provide Garbage Cans

One of the complications in accomplishing something in a garbage can decision-making process is the tendency for any particular project to become intertwined with a variety of other issues simply because those issues exist at the time the project is before the organization. A proposal for curricular reform becomes an arena for a concern for social justice. A proposal for construction of a building becomes an arena for concerns about environmental quality. A proposal for bicycle paths becomes an arena for discussion of sexual inequality.

It is pointless to try to react to such problems by attempting to enforce rules of relevance. Such rules are, in any event, highly arbitrary. Even if they were not, it would still be difficult to persuade a person that his problem (however important) could not be discussed because it is not relevant to the current agenda. The appropriate tactical response is to provide

garbage cans into which wide varieties of problems can be dumped. The more conspicuous the can, the more garbage it will attract away from other projects.

The prime procedure for making a garbage can attractive is to give it precedence and conspicuousness. On a grand scale, discussions of overall organizational objectives or overall organizational long-term plans are classic first-quality cans. They are general enough to accommodate anything. They are socially defined as being important. They attract enough different kinds of issues to reinforce their importance. An activist will push for discussions of grand plans (in part) in order to draw the garbage away from the concrete day-to-day arenas of his concrete objectives.

On a smaller scale, the first item on a meeting agenda is an obvious garbage can. It receives much of the status allocation concerns that are a part of meetings. It is possible that any item on an agenda will attract an assortment of things currently concerning individuals in the group, but the first item is more vulnerable than others. As a result, projects of serious substantive concern should normally be placed somewhat later, after the important matters of individual and group esteem have been settled, most of the individual performances have been completed, and most of the enthusiasm for abstract argument has waned.

The garbage can tactic has long-term effects that may be important. Although in the short run the major consequence is to remove problems from the arena of short-term concrete proposals, the separation of problem discussion from decision making means that general organizational attitudes develop outside the context of immediate decisions. The exercise of problems and the discussion of plans contribute to a building of the climate within which the organization will operate in the future. A president who uses the garbage can tactic should be aware of the ways in which currently irrelevant conversations produce future ideological constraints. The same tactic also provides a (partly misleading) device for the training and selection of future leaders of the organization. Those who perform well in garbage can debates are not necessarily good leaders, though they may frequently be identified as potential leaders. Finally, the tactic offers a practical buffer for the organization from the instabilities introduced by the entry and exit of problems that drift from one organization to another. In recent years universities have become an arena for an assortment of problems that might have found expression in other social institutions. Universities and colleges were available and accessible to people with the concerns. Although the resulting strain on university processes was considerable, the full impact was cushioned by the tendency of such problems to move to decision-irrelevant garbage cans, to be held there until they could move on to another arena in another institution.

Rule 7: Manage Unobtrusively

If you put a man in a boat and tell him to plot a course, he can take one of three views of his task. He can float with the currents and winds, letting them take him wherever they wish; he can select a destination and try to use full power to go directly to it regardless of the current or winds; or he can select a destination and use his rudder and sails to let the currents and wind eventually take him where he wants to go. On the whole, we think conscious university leadership is properly seen in third light.

A central tactic in high-inertia systems is to use high-leverage minor actions to produce major effects—to let the system go where it wants to go with only the minor interventions that make it go where it should. From a tactical point of view, the main objection to central direction and control is that it requires an impossible amount of attention and energy. The kinds of organizations with which we have been concerned are unable to be driven where we want them to go without making considerable use of the "natural" organizational processes. The appropriate tactics of management are unobstrusive and indirect.

Unobtrusive management uses interventions of greater impact than visibility. Such actions generally have two key attributes: (1) They affect many parts of the system slightly rather than a few parts in a major way. The effect on any one part of the system is small enough so that either no one really notices or no one finds it sensible to organize significantly against the intervention. (2) Once activated, they stay activated without further organizational attention. Their deactivation requires positive organizational action.

Given all the enthusiasm for elaborating a variety of models of organizations that bemoan bureaucracy and the conventional managerial tools associated with bureaucratic life, it is somewhat surprising to realize that the major instruments of unobstrusive management are bureaucratic. Consider the simple act of committing the organization by signing a piece of paper. By the formal statutes of many organizations, some people within the organization are conceded authority to sign pieces of paper. College presidents tend, in our judgment, to be timid about exercising such authority. By signing a piece of paper the president is able to reverse the burden of organizing the decision-making processes in the system. Many people have commented on the difficulty of organizing the various groups and offices in a college or university in order to do something. What has been less frequently noted is that the same problems of organization face anyone who wants to overturn an action. For example, the official charter of an institution usually has some kind of regulation that permits a desired action, as well as some kind of regulation that might be interpreted as prohibiting it. The president who solicits general organizational approval for action is more likely to obtain it if the burdens of overcoming organizational inertia are on his opposition. He reverses the burden of organization by taking the action.

Major bureaucratic interventions lie in the ordinary systems of accounting and managerial controls. Such devices are often condemned in academic circles as both dreary and inhibiting. Their beauty lies in the way in which they extend throughout the system and in the high degree of arbitrariness they exhibit. For example, students of business have observed that many important aspects of business life are driven by accounting rules. What are costs? What are profits? How are costs and profits allocated among activities and subunits? Answers to such questions are far from arbitrary. But they have enough elements of arbitrariness that no reasonable business manager would ignore the potential contribution of accounting rules to profitability. The flow of investments, the utilization of labor, and the structure of organization all respond to the organization of accounts.

The same thing is true in a college or university, although the process works in a somewhat different way because the convenient single index of business accounting, profit, is denied the university executive. Universities and colleges have official facts (accounting facts) with respect to student activities, faculty activities, and space utilization. In recent years such accounting facts have increased in importance as colleges and universities struggled first with the baby boom and now with fiscal adversity. These official facts enter into reports and filter into decisions made throughout the system. As a typical simple example, consider the impact of changing the accounting for faculty teaching load from number of courses to student credit hours taught. Or, consider the impact of separating in accounting reports the teaching of language (number of students, cost of faculty) from the teaching of literature in that language at a typical American university. Or, consider the impact of making each major subunit in a university purchase services (e.g., duplication services, computer services, library services) at prices somewhat different from the current largely arbitrary prices. Or, consider the consequences of allowing transfer of funds from one major budget line to another within a subunit at various possible discount rates depending on the lines and the point in the budget year. Or, consider the effect of having students pay as part of their fees an amount determined by the department offering the instruction, with the amount thus paid returning to the department.

Rule 8: Interpret History

In an organization in which most issues have low salience, and information about events in the system is poorly maintained, definitions of what is happening and what has happened become important tactical instruments. If people in the organization cared more about what happened (or is happening), the constraints on the tactic would be great. Histories would be challenged and carefully monitored. If people in the organization accepted more openly the idea that much of the decision-making process is a status-certifying rather than a choice-making system, there would be less dependence on historical interpretation. The actual situation, however, provides a tactically optimal situation. On the one hand, the genuine interest in keeping a good record of what happened (in

substantive rather than status terms) is minimal. On the other hand, the belief in the relevance of history, or the legitimacy of history as a basis for current action, is fairly strong.

Minutes should be written long enough after the event as to legitimize the reality of forgetfulness. They should be written in such a way as to lay the basis for subsequent independent action—in the name of the collective action. In general, participants in the organization should be assisted in their desire to have unambiguous actions taken today derived from the ambiguous decisions of yesterday with a minimum of pain to their images of organizational rationality and a minimum of claims on their time. The model of consistency is maintained by a creative resolution of uncertainty about the past.

Presidents and Tactics

As we observed at the outset, practical tactics, if they are genuine, will inevitably be viewed as somewhat cynical. We will, however, record our own sentiments that the cynicism lies in the eye of the beholder. Our sympathies and enthusiasm are mostly for the invisible members of an organized anarchy who make such tactics possible. We refer, of course, to the majority of participants in colleges and universities who have the good sense to see that what can be achieved through tactical manipulation of the university is only occasionally worth their time and effort. The validity of the tactics is a tribute to their reluctance to clutter the important elements of life with organizational matters. The tactics are available for anyone who wants to use them. Most of us most of the time have more interesting things to do.

But presidents, as full-time actors generally occupying the best job of their lives, are less likely to have more interesting things to do. In addition, these tactics, with their low visibility and their emphasis on the trading of credit and recognition for accomplishment, will not serve the interests of a president out to glorify himself or increase his chances to be one of the very few who move up to a second and "better" presidency. Instead, they provide an opportunity chiefly for those who have some conception of what might make their institution better, more interesting, more complex, or more educational, and are satisfied to end their tenures believing that they helped to steer their institutions slightly closer to those remote destinations.

The Technology of Foolishness

The tactics for moving an organization when objectives are clear represent important parts of the repertoire of an organizational leader.[5] Standard prescriptions properly honor intention, choice, and action; and college presidents often have things they want to accomplish. Nevertheless, a college president may sometimes want to confront the realities of ambiguity more directly and reconsider the standard dicta of leadership. He may want to examine particularly the place of purpose in intelligent behavior and the role of foolishness in leadership.

Choice and Rationality

The concept of choice as a focus for interpreting and guiding human behavior has rarely had an easy time in the realm of ideas. It is beset by theological disputations over free will, by the dilemmas of absurdism, by the doubts of psychological behaviorism, and by the claims of historical, economic, social, and demographic determinism. Nevertheless, the idea that humans make choices has proved robust enough to become a matter of faith in important segments of contemporary Western civilization. It is a faith that is professed by virtually all theories of social policy making.

The major tenents of this faith run something like this:

> Human beings make choices. Choices are properly made by evaluating alternatives in terms of goals and on the basis of information currently available. The alternative that is most attractive in terms of the goals is chosen. By using the technology of choice, we can improve the quality of the search for alternatives, the quality of information, and the quality of the analysis used to evaluate alternatives. Although actual choice may fall short of this ideal in various ways, it is an attractive model of how choices should be made by individuals, organizations, and social systems.

These articles of faith have been built upon and have stimulated some scripture. It is the scripture of the theories of decision making. The scripture is partly a codification of received doctrine and partly a source for that doctrine. As a result, our cultural ideas of intelligence and our theories of choice display a substantial resemblance. In particular, they share three conspicuous interrelated ideas:

The first idea is the *preexistence of purpose*. We find it natural to base an interpretation of human-choice behavior on a presumption of human purpose. We have, in fact, invented one of the most elaborate terminologies in the professional literature: "values," "needs," "wants," "goods," "tastes," "preferences," "utility," "objectives," "goals," "aspirations," "drives." All of these reflect a strong tendency to believe that a useful interpretation of human behavior involves defining a set of objectives that (1) are prior attributes of the system, and (2) make the observed behavior in some sense intelligent vis-à-vis those objectives.

Whether we are talking about individuals or about organizations, purpose is an obvious presumption of the discussion. An organization is often defined in terms of its purpose. It is seen by some as the largest collectivity directed by a purpose. Action within an organization is justified or criticized in terms of purpose. Individuals explain their own behavior, as well as the behavior of others, in terms of a set of value premises that are presumed to be antecedent to the behavior. Normative theories of choice begin with an assumption of a preexistent preference ordering defined over the possible outcomes of a choice.

The second idea is the *necessity of consistency*. We have come to recognize consistency both as an important property of human behavior and as a prerequisite for normative models of choice. Dissonance theory, balance theory, theories of congruency in attitudes, statuses, and performances have all served to remind us of the possibilities for interpreting human behavior in terms of the consistency requirements of a limited-capacity, information-processing system.

At the same time, consistency is a cultural and theoretical virtue. Action should be consistent with belief. Actions taken by different parts of an organization should be consistent with each other. Individual and organizational activities are seen as connected with each other in terms of their consequences for some consistent set of purposes. In an organization, the structural manifestation of consistency is the hierarchy with its obligations of coordination and control. In the individual, the structural manifestation is a set of values that generates a consistent preference ordering.

The third idea is the *primacy of rationality*. By rationality we mean a procedure for deciding what is correct behavior by relating consequences systematically to objectives. By placing primary emphasis on rational techniques, we have implicitly rejected—or seriously impaired—two other procedures for choice: (1) the processes of intuition, through which people do things without fully understanding why; and (2) the processes of tradition and faith, through which people do things because that is the way they are done.

Both within the theory and within the culture we insist on the ethic of rationality. We justify individual and organizational action in terms of an analysis of means and ends. Impulse, intuition, faith, and tradition are outside that system and viewed as antithetical to it. Faith may be seen as a possible source of values. Intuition may be seen as a possible source of ideas about alternatives. But the analysis and justification of action lie within the context of reason.

These ideas are obviously deeply embedded in the culture. Their roots extend into ideas that have conditioned much of modern Western history and interpretations of that history. Their general acceptance is probably highly correlated with the permeation of rationalism and individualism into the style of thinking within the culture. The ideas are even more obviously embedded in modern theories of choice. It is fundamental to those theories that thinking should precede action: that action should serve a purpose; that purpose should be defined in terms of a consistent set of preexistent goals; and that choice should be based on a consistent theory of the relation between action and its consequences.

Every tool of management decision making that is currently a part of management science, operations research, or decision-making theory, assumes the prior existence of a set of consistent goals. Almost the entire structure of microeconomic theory builds on the assumption that there exists a well-defined, stable, and consistent preference ordering. Most theories

of individual or organizational choice accept the idea that goals exist and that (in some sense) an individual or organization acts on those goals, choosing from among some alternatives on the basis of available information. Discussions of educational policy with their emphasis on goal setting, evaluation, and accountability, are in this tradition.

From the perspective of all of man's history, the ideas of purpose, consistency, and rationality are relatively new. Much of the technology currently available to implement them is extremely new. Over the past few centuries, and conspicuously over the past few decades, we have substantially improved man's capability for acting purposively, consistently, and rationally. We have substantially increased his propensity to think of himself as doing so. It is an impressive victory, won—where it has been won—by a happy combination of timing, performance, ideology, and persistence. It is a battle yet to be concluded, or even engaged, in many cultures of the world; but within most of the Western world individuals and organizations see themselves as making choices.

The Problem of Goals

The tools of intelligence as they are fashioned in modern theories of choice are necessary to any reasonable behavior in contemporary society. It is inconceivable that we would fail to continue their development, refinement, and extension. As might be expected, however, a theory and ideology of choice built on the ideas outlined above is deficient in some obvious, elementary ways, most conspicuously in the treatment of human goals.

Goals are thrust upon the intelligent man. We ask that he act in the name of goals. We ask that he keep his goals consistent. We ask that his actions be oriented to his goals. We ask that a social system amalgamate individual goals into a collective goal. But we do not concern ourselves with the origin of goals. Theories of individual, organizational, and social choice assume actors with preexistent values.

Since it is obvious that goals change over time and that the character of those changes affects both the richness of personal and social development and the outcome of choice behavior, a theory of choice must somehow justify ignoring the phenomena. Although it is unreasonable to ask a theory of choice to solve all the problems of man and his development, it is reasonable to ask how such conspicuous elements as the fluidity and ambiguity of objectives can plausibly be ignored in a theory that is offered as a guide to human choice behavior.

There are three classic justifications. The first is that goal development and choice are independent processes, conceptually and behaviorally. The second is that the model of choice is never satisfied in fact and that deviations from the model accommodate the problems of introducing change. The third is that the idea of changing goals is so intractable in a normative theory of choice that nothing can be said about it. Since we are unpersuaded of the first and second justifications, our optimism with respect to the third is somewhat greater than that of most of our fellows.

The argument that goal development and choice are independent behaviorally seems clearly false. It seems to us obvious that a description that assumes that goals come first and action comes later is frequently radically wrong. Human choice behavior is at least as much a process for discovering goals as for acting on them. Although it is true enough that goals and decisions are "conceptually" distinct, that is simply a statement of the theory, not a defense of it. They are conceptually distinct if we choose to make them so.

The argument that the model is incomplete is more persuasive. There do appear to be some critical "holes" in the system of intelligence as described by standard theories of choice. Incomplete information, incomplete goal consistency, and a variety of external processes facilitate goal development. What is somewhat disconcerting about the argument, however, is that it makes the efficacy of the concepts of intelligent choice dependent on their inadequacy. As we become more competent in the techniques of the model and more committed to it, the "holes" become smaller. As the model becomes more accepted, our obligation to modify it increases.

The final argument seems to us sensible as a general principle, but misleading here. Why are we more reluctant to ask how human beings might find "good" goals than we are to ask how they might make "good" decisions? The second question appears to be a more technical problem. The first seems more preten-

tious. It claims to say something about alternative virtues. The appearance of pretense, however, stems directly from the prevailing theory of choice and the ideology associated with it.

In fact, the conscious introduction of goal discovery for consideration in theories of human choice is not unknown to modern man. For example, we have two kinds of theories of choice behavior in human beings. One is a theory of children. The other is a theory of adults. In the theory of children, we emphasize choices as leading to experiences that develop the child's scope, his complexity, his awareness of the world. As parents, teachers, or psychologists, we try to lead the child to do things that are inconsistent with his present goals because we know (or believe) that he can develop into an interesting person only by coming to appreciate aspects of experience that he initially rejects.

In the theory of adults, we emphasize choices as a consequence of our intentions. As adults, educational decision makers, or economists, we try to take actions that (within the limits of scarce resources) come as close as possible to achieving our goals. We try to find improved ways of making decisions consistent with our perceptions of what is valuable in the world.

The asymmetry in these models is conspicuous. Adults have constructed a model world in which adults know what is good for themselves, but children do not. It is hard to react positively to the conceit. The asymmetry has, in fact, stimulated a large number of ideologies and reforms designed to allow children the same moral prerogative granted to adults—the right to imagine that they know what they want. The efforts have cut deeply into traditional childrearing, traditional educational policies, traditional politics, and traditional consumer economics.

In our judgment, the asymmetry between models of choice for adults and for children is awkward; but the solution we have adopted is precisely wrong-headed. Instead of trying to adapt the model of adults to children, we might better adapt the model of children to adults. For many purposes, our model of children is better. Of course, children know what they want. Everyone does. The critical question is whether they are encouraged to develop more interesting "wants." Values change. People become more interesting as those values and the interconnections made among them change.

One of the most obvious things in the world turns out to be hard for us to accommodate in our theory of choice: A child of two will almost always have a less interesting set of values (indeed, a worse set of values) than a child of 12. The same is true of adults. Values develop through experience. Although one of the main natural arenas for the modification of human values is the arena of choice, our theories of adult and organizational decision making ignore the phenomenon entirely.

Introducing ambiguity and fluidity to the interpretation of individual, organizational, and societal goals obviously has implications for behavioral theories of decision making. We have tried to identify and respond to some of those difficulties in the preceding chapters. The main point here, however, is not to consider how we might describe the behavior of systems that are discovering goals as they act. Rather it is to examine how we might improve the quality of that behavior, how we might aid the development of interesting goals.

We know how to advise a society, an organization, or an individual if we are first given a consistent set of preferences. Under some conditions, we can suggest how to make decisions if the preferences are consistent only up to the point of specifying a series of independent constraints on the choice. But what about a normative theory of goal-finding behavior? What do we say when our client tells us that he is not sure his present set of values is the set of values in terms of which he wants to act?

It is a question familiar to many aspects of ordinary life. It is a question that friends, associates, students, college presidents, business managers, voters, and children ask at least as frequently as they ask how they should act within a set of consistent and stable values.

Within the context of normative theory of choice as it exists, the answer we gave is: First determine the values, then act. The advice is frequently useful. Moreover, we have developed ways in which we can use conventional techniques for decision analysis to help discover value premises and to expose value inconsistencies. These techniques involve testing the decision implications of some successive approximations to a set of preferences. The

object is to find a consistent set of preferences with implications that are acceptable to the person or organization making the decisions. Variations on such techniques are used routinely in operations research, as well as in personal counseling and analysis.

The utility of such techniques, however, apparently depends on the assumption that a primary problem is the amalgamation or excavation of preexistent values. The metaphors—"finding oneself," "goal clarification," "self-discovery," "social welfare function," "revealed preference"—are metaphors of search. If our value premises are to be "constructed" rather than "discovered," our standard procedures may be useful: but we have no *a priori* reason for assuming they will.

Perhaps we should explore a somewhat different approach to the normative question of how we ought to behave when our value premises are not yet (and never will be) fully determined. Suppose we treat action as a way of creating interesting goals at the same time as we treat goals as a way of justifying action. It is an intuitively plausible and simple idea, but one that is not immediately within the domain of standard normative theories of intelligent choice.

Interesting people and interesting organizations construct complicated theories of themselves. To do this, they need to supplement the technology of reason with a technology of foolishness. Individuals and organizations sometimes need ways of doing things for which they have no good reason. They need to act before they think.

Sensible Foolishness

To use intelligent choice as a planned occasion for discovering new goals, we require some idea of sensible foolishness. Which of the many foolish things that we might do now will lead to attractive value consequences? The question is almost inconceivable. Not only does it ask us to predict the value consequences of action, it asks us to evaluate them. In what terms can we talk about "good" changes in goals?

In effect, we are asked either to specify a set of supergoals in terms of which alternative goals are evaluated, or to choose among alternatives *now* in terms of the unknown set of values we will have at some future time (or the distribution over time of that unknown set of future values). The former alternative moves us back to the original situation of a fixed set of values—now called "supergoals"—and hardly seems an important step in the direction of inventing procedures for discovering new goals. The latter alternative seems fundamental enough, but it violates severely our sense of temporal order. To say that we make decisions now in terms of goals that will be knowable only later is nonsensical—as long as we accept the basic framework of the theory of choice and its presumptions of preexistent goals.

As we challenge the dogma of preexistent goals, we will be forced to reexamine some of our most precious prejudices: the strictures against imitation, coercion, and rationalization. Each of those honorable prohibitions depends on the view of man and human choice imposed on us by conventional theories of choice.

Imitation is not necessarily a sign of moral weakness. It is a prediction. It is a prediction that if we duplicate the behavior or attitudes of someone else, not only will we fare well in terms of current goals but the chances of our discovering attractive new goals for ourselves are relatively high. If imitation is to be normatively attractive, we need a better theory of who should be imitated. Such a theory seems to be eminently feasible. For example, what are the conditions for effectiveness of a rule that one should imitate another person whose values are close to one's own? How do the chances of discovering interesting goals through imitation change as the number of people exhibiting the behavior to be imitated increases? In the case of the college president we might ask what the goal discovery consequences are of imitating the choices of those at institutions more prestigious than one's own, and whether there are other more desirable patterns of imitation.

Coercion is not necessarily an assault on individual autonomy. It can be a device for stimulating individuality. We recognize this when we talk about education or about parents and children. What has been difficult with coercion is the possibility for perversion, not its obvious capability for stimulating change. We need a theory of the circumstances under which entry into a coercive relationship produces behavior that leads to the discovery of interesting goals. We are all familiar with the

tactic. College presidents use it in imposing deadlines, entering contracts, making commitments. What are the conditions for its effective use? In particular, what are the conditions for goal-fostering coercion in social systems?

Rationalization is not necessarily a way of evading morality. It can be a test for the feasibility of a goal change. When deciding among alternative actions for which we have no good reason, it may be sensible to develop some definition of how "near" to intelligence alternative "unintelligent" actions lie. Effective rationalization permits this kind of incremental approach to changes in values. To use it effectively, however, we require a better idea of the metrics that might be possible in measuring value distances. At the same time, rationalization is the major procedure for integrating newly discovered goals into an existing structure of values. It provides the organization of complexity without which complexity itself becomes indistinguishable from randomness.

The dangers in imitation, coercion, and rationalization are too familiar to elaborate. We should, indeed, be able to develop better techniques. Whatever those techniques may be, however, they will almost certainly undermine the superstructure of biases erected on purpose, consistency, and rationality. They will involve some way of thinking about action now as occurring in terms of a set of future values different from those that the actor currently holds.

Play and Reason

A second requirement for a technology of foolishness is some strategy for suspending rational imperatives toward consistency. Even if we know which of several foolish things we want to do, we still need a mechanism for allowing us to do it. How do we escape the logic of our reason?

Here we are closer to understanding what we need. It is playfulness. Playfulness is the deliberate, temporary relaxation of rules in order to explore the possibilities of alternative rules. When we are playful, we challenge the necessity of consistency. In effect, we announce—in advance—our rejection of the usual objections to behavior that does not fit the standard model of intelligence.

Playfulness allows experimentation at the same time that it acknowledges reason. It accepts an obligation that at some point either the playful behavior will be stopped or it will be integrated into the structure of intelligence in some way that makes sense. The suspension of the rules is temporary.

The idea of play may suggest three things that are, in our minds, quite erroneous in the present context. First, play may be seen as a kind of "holiday" for reason, a release of the emotional tensions of virtue. Although it is possible that play performs some such function, that is not the function with which we are concerned. Second, play may be seen as part of some mystical balance of spiritual principles: fire and water, hot and cold, weak and strong. The intention here is much narrower than a general mystique of balance. Third, play may be seen as an antithesis of intelligence, so that the emphasis on the importance of play becomes a support for simple self-indulgence. Our present intent is to propose play as an instrument of intelligence, not a substitute.

Playfulness is a natural outgrowth of our standard view of reason. A strict insistence on purpose, consistency, and rationality limits our ability to find new purposes. Play relaxes that insistence to allow us to act "unintelligently" or "irrationally" or "foolishly" to explore alternative ideas of purposes and alternative concepts of behavioral consistency. And it does this while maintaining our basic commitment to intelligence.

Although play and reason are in this way functional complements, they are often behavioral competitors. They are alternative styles and alternative orientations to the same situation. There is no guarantee that the styles will be equally well developed, that all individuals, organizations, or societies will be equally adept in both styles; or that all cultures will be sufficiently encouraging to both.

Our design problem is either to specify the best mix of styles or, failing that, to assure that most people and most organizations most of the time use an alternation of strategies rather than persevering in either one. It is a difficult problem. The optimization problem looks extremely complex on the face of it, and the learning situations that will produce alternation in behavior appear to be somewhat less common than those that produce perseverance.

Consider, for example, the difficulty of sustaining playfulness as a style within contemporary American society. Individuals who are good at consistent rationality are rewarded early and heavily. We define consistent rationality as intelligence, and the educational rewards of society are associated strongly with it. Social norms press in the same direction, particularly for men. "Changing one's mind" is viewed as feminine and undesirable. Politicians and other leaders will go to enormous lengths to avoid admitting an inconsistency. Many demands of modern organizational life reinforce the same rational abilities and preferences for a style of unchanging purposes.

The result is that many of the most influential and best-educated citizens have experienced a powerful overlearning with respect to rationality. They are exceptionally good at maintaining consistent pictures of themselves, of relating action to purposes. They are exceptionally poor at a playful attitude toward their own beliefs, toward the logic of consistency, or toward the way they see things as being connected in the world. The dictates of manliness, forcefulness, independence, and intelligence are intolerant of playful urges if they arise. The playful urges that arise are weak ones, scarcely discernible in the behavior of most businessmen, mayors, or college presidents.

The picture is probably overdrawn, but we believe that the implications are not. Reason and intelligence have had the unnecessary consequence of inhibiting the development of purpose into more complicated forms of consistency. To move away from that position, we need to find some ways of helping individuals and organizations to experiment with doing things for which they have no good reason, to be playful with their conceptions of themselves. We suggest five things as a small beginning:

First, we can treat *goals as hypotheses*. Conventional theories of decision making allow us to entertain doubts about almost everything except the thing about which we frequently have the greatest doubt—our objectives. Suppose we define the decision-making process as a time for the sequential testing of hypotheses about goals. If we can experiment with alternative goals, we stand some chance of discovering complicated and interesting combinations of good values that none of us previously imagined.

Second, we can treat *intuition as real.* We do not know what intuition is or even if it is any one thing. Perhaps it is simply an excuse for doing something we cannot justify in terms of present values or for refusing to follow the logic of our own beliefs. Perhaps it is an inexplicable way of consulting that part of our intelligence and knowledge of the world that is not organized in a way anticipated by standard theories of choice. In either case, intuition permits us to see some possible actions that are outside our present scheme for justifying behavior.

Third, we can treat *hypocrisy as a transition.* Hypocrisy is an inconsistency between expressed values and behavior. Negative attitudes about hypocrisy stem mainly from a general onus against inconsistency and from a sentiment against combining the pleasures of vice with the appearance of virtue. It seems to us that a bad man with good intentions may be a man experimenting with the possibility of becoming good. Somehow it seems more sensible to encourage the experimentation than to insult it.

Fourth, we can treat *memory as an enemy.* The rules of consistency and rationality require a technology of memory. For most purposes, good memories make good choices. But the ability to forget or overlook is also useful. If you do not know what you did yesterday or what other people in the organization are doing today, you can act within the system of reason and still do things that are foolish.

Fifth, we can treat *experience as a theory.* Learning can be viewed as a series of conclusions based on concepts of action and consequences that we have invented. Experience can be changed retrospectively. By changing our interpretive concepts now, we modify what we learned earlier. Thus we expose the possibility of experimenting with alternative histories. The usual strictures against "self-deception" in experience need occasionally to be tempered with an awareness of the extent to which all experience is an interpretation subject to conscious revision. Personal histories and national histories need to be rewritten continuously as a base for the retrospective learning of new self-conceptions.

If we knew more about the normative theory of acting before thinking, we could say

more intelligent things about the functions of management and leadership when organizations or societies do not know what they are doing. Consider, for example, the following general implications.

First, we need to reexamine the functions of management decision making. One of the primary ways in which the goals of an organization are developed is by interpreting the decisions it makes, and one feature of good managerial decisions is that they lead to the development of more interesting value premises for the organization. As a result, decisions should not be seen as flowing directly or strictly from a preexistent set of objectives. College presidents who make decisions might well view that function somewhat less as a process of deduction or a process of political negotiation, and somewhat more as a process of gently upsetting preconceptions of what the organization is doing.

Second, we need a modified view of planning. Planning can often be more effective as an interpretation of past decisions than as a program for future ones. It can be used as a part of the efforts of the organization to develop a new consistent theory of itself that incorporates the mix of recent actions into a moderately comprehensive structure of goals. Procedures for interpreting the meaning of most past events are familiar to the memoirs of retired generals, prime ministers, business leaders, and movie stars. They suffer from the company they keep. In an organization that wants to continue to develop new objectives, a manager needs to be tolerant of the idea that he will discover the meaning of yesterday's action in the experiences and interpretations of today.

Third, we need to reconsider evaluation. As nearly as we can determine, there is nothing in a formal theory of evaluation that requires that criteria be specified in advance. In particular, the evaluation of social experiments need not be in terms of the degree to which they have fulfilled our prior expectations. Rather we can examine what they did in terms of what we now believe to be important. The prior specification of criteria and the prior specification of evaluational procedures that depend on such criteria are common presumptions in contemporary social policy making. They are presumptions that inhibit the serendipitous discovery of new criteria. Experience should be used explicitly as an occasion for evaluating our values as well as our actions.

Fourth, we need a reconsideration of social accountability. Individual preferences and social action need to be consistent in some way. But the process of pursuing consistency is one in which both the preferences and the actions change over time. Imagination in social policy formation involves systematically adapting to and influencing preference. It would be unfortunate if our theories of social action encouraged leaders to ignore their responsibilities for anticipating public preferences through action and for providing social experiences that modify individual expectations.

Fifth, we need to accept playfulness in social organizations. The design of organizations should attend to the problems of maintaining both playfulness and reason as aspects of intelligent choice. Since much of the literature on social design is concerned with strengthening the rationality of decision making managers are likely to overlook the importance of play. This is partly a matter of making the individuals within an organization more playful by encouraging the attitudes and skills of inconsistency. It is also a matter of making organizational structure and organizational procedures more playful. Organizations can be playful even when the participants in them are not. The managerial devices for maintaining consistency can be varied. We encourage organizational play by insisting on some temporary relief from control, coordination, and communication.

Presidents and Foolishness

Contemporary theories of decision making and the technology of reason have considerably strengthened our capabilities for effective social action. The conversion of the simple ideas of choice into an extensive technology is a major achievement. It is, however, an achievement that has reinforced some biases in the underlying models of choice in individuals and groups. In particular, it has reinforced the uncritical acceptance of a static interpretation of human goals.

There is little magic in the world, and foolishness in people and organizations is one of the many things that fail to produce miracles. Under certain conditions, it is one of several ways in which some of the problems of our current theories of intelligence can be overcome. It may be a good way, for it preserves the virtues of consistency while stimulating change. If we had a good technology of foolishness, it might (in combination with the technology of reason) help in a small way to develop the unusual combinations of attitudes and behaviors that describe the interesting people, interesting organizations, and interesting societies of the world. The contribution of a college president may often be measured by his capability for sustaining that creative interaction of foolishness and rationality.

Notes

1. For anyone who wishes to enter the literature, see by way of introduction Raymond Wolfinger (1971a, 1971b), and Frederick W. Frey (1971).
2. For a discussion of this point in the context of public school decision making, see Stephen Weiner (1972).
3. For a discussion of the same phenomenon in a business setting, see R. M. Cyert and J. G. March (1963).
4. See, for example, Iklé (1964) and Walton and McKersie (1965).
5. These ideas have been the basis for extended conversation with a number of friends. We want to acknowledge particularly the help of Lance Bennett, Patricia Nelson Bennett, Michael Butler, Soren Christensen, Michel Crozier, Claude Faucheux, James R. Glenn, Jr., Gudmund Hernes, Heiga Hernes, Jean Carter Lave, Harold J. Leavitt, Henry M. Levin, Leslie Lincoln, André Massart, John Miller, Johan Olsen, Richard C. Snyder, Alexander Szalai, Eugene J. Webb, and Gail Whitacre.

CHAPTER 3

EDUCATIONAL ORGANIZATIONS AS LOOSELY COUPLED SYSTEMS

KARL E. WEICK

In contrast to the prevailing image that elements in organizations are coupled through dense, tight linkages, it is proposed that elements are often tied together frequently and loosely. Using educational organizations as a case in point, it is argued that the concept of loose coupling incorporates a surprising number of disparate observations about organizations, suggests novel functions, creates stubborn problems for methodologists, and generates intriguing questions for scholars. Sample studies of loose coupling are suggested and research priorities are posed to foster cumulative work with this concept.

Imagine that you're either the referee, coach, player or spectator at an unconventional soccer match: the field for the game is round; there are several goals scattered haphazardly around the circular field; people can enter and leave the game whenever they want to, they can throw balls in whenever they want; they can say "that's my goal" whenever they want to, as many times as they want to, and for as many goals as they want to; the entire game takes place on a sloped field; and the game is played as if it makes sense (March, personal communication).

If you now substitute in that example principals for referees, teachers for coaches, students for players, parents for spectators and schooling for soccer, you have an equally unconventional depiction of school organizations. The beauty of this depiction is that it captures a different set of realities within educational organizations than are caught when these same organizations are viewed through the tenets of bureaucratic theory.

Consider the contrast in images. For some time people who manage organizations and people who study this managing have asked, "How does an organization go about doing what it does and with what consequences for its people, processes, products, and persistence?" And for some time they've heard the same answers. In paraphrase the answers say essentially that all organization does what it does because of plans, intentional selection of means that get the organization to agree upon goals, and all of this is accomplished by such rationalized procedures as cost-benefit analyses, division of labor, specified areas of discretion, authority invested in the office, job descriptions, and a consistent evaluation and reward system. The only problem with that portrait is that it is rare in nature. People in organizations, including educational organizations, find themselves hard pressed either to find actual instances of those rational practices or to find rationalized practices whose outcomes have been as beneficent as predicted, or to feel that those rational occasions explain much of what goes on within the organization. Parts of some organizations are heavily rationalized but many parts also prove intractable to analysis through rational assumptions.

"Educational Organizations as Loosely Coupled Systems," by Karl E. Weick, reprinted with permission from *Administrative Science Quarterly*, Vol. 26, No. 1, March 1976.

It is this substantial unexplained remainder that is the focus of this paper. Several people in education have expressed dissatisfaction with the prevailing ideas about organizations supplied by organizational theorists. Fortunately, they have also made some provocative suggestions about newer, more unconventional ideas about organizations that should be given serious thought. A good example of this is the following observation by John M. Stephens (1967: 9–11):

> (There is a) remarkable constancy of educational results in the face of widely differing deliberate approaches. Every so often we adopt new approaches or new methodologies and place our reliance on new panaceas. At the very least we seem to chorus new slogans. Yet the academic growth within the classroom continues at about the same rate, stubbornly refusing to cooperate with the bright new dicta emanating from the conference room . . . [These observations suggest that] we would be making a great mistake in regarding the management of schools as similar to the process of constructing a building or operating a factory. In these later processes deliberate decisions play a crucial part, and the enterprise advances or stands still in proportion to the amount of deliberate effort exerted. If we must use a metaphor or model in seeking to understand the process of schooling, we should look to agriculture rather than to the factory. In agriculture we do not start from scratch, and we do not direct our efforts to inert and passive materials. We start, on the contrary, with a complex and ancient process, and we organize our efforts around what seeds, plants, and insects are likely to do anyway. . . . The crop, once planted, may undergo some development even while the farmer sleeps or loafs. No matter what he does, *some* aspects of the outcome will remain constant. When teachers and pupils foregather, some education may proceed even while the Superintendent disports himself in Atlantic City.

It is crucial to highlight what is important in the examples of soccer and schooling viewed as agriculture. To view these examples negatively and dismiss them by observing that "the referee should tighten up those rules," "superintendents don't do that," "schools are more sensible than that," or "these are terribly sloppy organizations" is to miss the point. The point is although researchers don't know what these kinds of structures are like but researchers do know they exist and that each of the negative judgments expressed above makes sense only if the observer assumes that organizations are constructed and managed according to rational assumptions and therefore are scrutable only when rational analyses are applied to them. This paper attempts to expand and enrich the set of ideas available to people when they try to make sense out of their organizational life. From this standpoint, it is unproductive to observe that fluid participation in schools and soccer is absurd. But it can be more interesting and productive to ask, how can it be that even though the activities in both situations are only modestly connected, the situations are still recognizable and nameable? The goals, player movements, and trajectory of the ball are still recognizable and can be labeled "soccer." And despite variations in class size, format, locations, and architecture, the results are still recognized and can be labeled "schools." How can such loose assemblages retain sufficient similarity and permanence across time that they can be recognized, labeled, and dealt with? The prevailing ideas in organization theory do not shed much light on how such "soft" structures develop, persist, and impose crude orderliness among their elements.

The basic premise here is that concepts such as loose coupling serve as sensitizing devices. They sensitize the observer to notice and question things that had previously been taken for granted. It is the intent of the program described here to develop a language for use in analyzing complex organizations, a language that may highlight features that have previously gone unnoticed. The guiding principle is a reversal of the common assertion, "I'll believe it when I see it" and presumes an epistemology that asserts, "I'll see it when I believe it." Organizations as loosely coupled systems may not have been seen before because nobody believed in them or could afford to believe in them. It is conceivable that preoccupation with rationalized, tidy, efficient, coordinated structures has blinded many practitioners as well as researchers to some of the attractive and unexpected properties of less rationalized and less tightly related clusters of events. This paper intends to eliminate such blindspots.

The Concept of Coupling

The phrase "loose coupling" has appeared in the literature (Glassman, 1973; March and Olsen, 1975) and it is important to highlight the connotation that is captured by this phrase and by no other. It might seem that the word coupling is synonymous with words like connection, link, or interdependence, yet each of these latter terms misses a crucial nuance.

By loose coupling, the author intends to convey the image that coupled events are responsive, *but* that each event also preserves its own identity and some evidence of its physical or logical separateness. Thus, in the case of an educational organization, it may be the case that the counselor's office is loosely coupled to the principal's office. The image is that the principal and the counselor are somehow attached, but that each retains some identity and separateness and that their attachment may be circumscribed, infrequent, weak in its mutual affects, unimportant, and/or slow to respond. Each of those connotations would be conveyed if the qualifier loosely were attached to the word coupled. Loose coupling also carries connotations of impermanence, dissolvability, and tacitness all of which are potentially crucial properties of the "glue" that holds organizations together.

Glassman (1973) categorizes the degree of coupling between two systems on the basis of the activity of the variables which the two systems share. To the extent that two systems either have few variables in common or share weak variables, they are independent of each other. Applied to the educational situation, if the principal-vice-principal-superintendent is regarded as one system and the teacher-classroom-pupil-parent-curriculum as another system, then by Glassman's argument if we did not find many variables in the teacher's world to be shared in the world of a principal and/or if the variables held in common were unimportant relative to the other variables, then the principal can be regarded as being loosely coupled with the teacher.

A final advantage of coupling imagery is that it suggests the idea of building blocks that can be grafted onto an organization or severed with relatively little disturbance to either the blocks or the organization. Simon (1969) has argued for the attractiveness of this feature in that most complex systems can be decomposed into stable subassemblies and that these are the crucial elements in any organization or system. Thus, the coupling imagery gives researchers access to one of the more powerful ways of talking about complexity now available.

But if the concept of loose coupling highlights novel images heretofore unseen in organizational theory, what is it about these images that is worth seeing?

Coupled Elements

There is no shortage of potential coupling elements, but neither is the population infinite.

At the outset the two most commonly discussed coupling mechanisms are the technical core of the organization and the authority of office. The relevance of those two mechanisms for the issue of identifying elements is that in the case of technical couplings, each element is some kind of technology, task, subtask, role, territory and person, and the couplings are task-induced. In the case of authority as the coupling mechanism, the elements include positions, offices, responsibilities, opportunities, rewards, and sanctions and it is the couplings among these elements that presumably hold the organization together. A compelling argument can be made that *neither* of these coupling mechanisms is prominent in educational organizations found in the United States. This leaves one with the question what *does* hold an educational organization together?

A short list of potential elements in educational organizations will provide background for subsequent propositions. March and Olsen (1975) utilize the elements of intention and action. There is a developing position in psychology which argues that intentions are a poor guide for action, intentions often follow rather than precede action, and that intentions and action are loosely coupled. Unfortunately, organizations continue to think that planning is a good thing, they spend much time on planning, and actions are assessed in terms of their fit with plans. Given a potential loose coupling between the intentions and actions of organizational members, it should come as no surprise that administrators are baffled and angered when things never happen the way they were supposed to.

Additional elements may consist of events like yesterday and tomorrow (what happened yesterday may be tightly or loosely coupled with what happens tomorrow) or hierarchical positions, like, top and bottom, line and staff, or administrators and teachers. An interesting set of elements that lends itself to the loose coupling imagery is means and ends. Frequently, several different means lead to the same outcome. When this happens, it can be argued that any one means is loosely coupled to the end in the sense that there are alternative pathways to achieve that same end. Other elements that might be found in loosely coupled educational systems are teachers-materials, voters-school-board, administrators-classroom, process-outcome, teacher-teacher, parent-teacher, and teacher-pupil.

While all of these elements are obvious, it is not a trivial matter to specify which elements are coupled. As the concept of coupling is crucial because of its ability to highlight the identity and separateness of elements that are momentarily attached, that conceptual asset puts pressure on the investigator to specify clearly the identity, separateness, and boundaries of the elements coupled. While there is some danger of reification when that kind of pressure is exerted, there is the even greater danger of portraying organizations in inappropriate terms which suggest an excess of unity, integration, coordination, and consensus. If one is nonspecific about boundaries in defining elements then it is easy—and careless—to assemble these ill-defined elements and talk about integrated organizations. It is not a trivial issue explaining how elements persevere over time. Weick, for example, has argued (1974: 363–364) that elements may appear or disappear and may merge or become separated in response to need-deprivations within the individual, group, and/or organization. This means that specification of elements is not a one-shot activity. Given the context of most organizations, elements both appear and disappear over time. For this reason a theory of how elements become loosely or tightly coupled may also have to take account of the fact that the nature and intensity of the coupling may itself serve to create or dissolve elements.

The question of what is available for coupling and decoupling within an organization is an eminently practical question for anyone wishing to have some leverage on a system.

Strength of Coupling

Obviously there is no shortage of meanings for the phrase loose coupling. Researchers need to be clear in their own thinking about whether the phenomenon they are studying is described by two words or three. A researcher can study "loose coupling" in educational organizations or "loosely coupled systems." The shorter phrase, "loose coupling," simply connotes things, "anythings," that may be tied together either weakly or infrequently or slowly or with minimal interdependence. Whether those things that are loosely coupled exist in a system is of minor importance. Most discussions in this paper concern loosely coupled systems rather than loose coupling since it wishes to clarify the concepts involved in the perseverance of sets of elements across time.

The idea of loose coupling is evoked when people have a variety of situations in mind. For example, when people describe loosely coupled systems they are often referring to (1) slack times—times when there is an excessive amount of resources relative to demands; (2) occasions when any one of several means will produce the same end; (3) richly connected networks in which influence is slow to spread and/or is weak while spreading; (4) a relative lack of coordination, slow coordination or coordination that is dampened as it moves through a system; (5) a relative absence of regulations; (6) planned unresponsiveness; (7) actual causal independence; (8) poor observational capabilities on the part of a viewer; (9) infrequent inspection of activities within the system; (10) decentralization; (11) delegation of discretion; (12) the absence of linkages that should be present based on some theory—for example, in educational organizations the expected feedback linkage from outcome back to inputs is often nonexistent; (13) the observation that an organization's structure is not coterminus with its activity; (14) those occasions when no matter what you do things always come out the same—for instance, despite all kinds of changes in curriculum, materials, groupings, and so forth the outcomes in an educational situation remain the same; and (15) curricula or courses in educational organizations for which there are few prerequisites—the longer the string of prerequisites, the tighter the coupling.

Potential Functions and Dysfunctions of Loose Coupling

It is important to note that the concept of loose coupling need not be used normatively. People who are steeped in the conventional literature of organizations may regard loose coupling as a sin or something to be apologized for. This paper takes a neutral, if not mildly affectionate, stance toward the concept. Apart from whatever affect one might feel toward the idea of loose coupling, it does appear a priori that certain functions can be served by having a system in which the elements are loosely coupled. Below are listed seven potential functions that could be associated with loose coupling plus additional reasons why each advantage might also be a liability. The dialectic generated by each of these oppositions begins to suggest dependent variables that should be sensitive to variations in the tightness of coupling.

The basic argument of Glassman (1973) is that loose coupling allows some portions of an organization to persist. Loose coupling lowers the probability that the organization will have to—or be able to—respond to each little change in the environment that occurs. The mechanism of voting, for example, allows elected officials to remain in office for a full term even though their constituency at any moment may disapprove of particular actions. Some identity and separateness of the element "elected official" is preserved relative to a second element, "constituency," by the fact of loosely coupled accountability which is measured in two, four, or six year terms. While loose coupling may foster perseverance, it is not selective in what is perpetuated. Thus archaic traditions as well as innovative improvisations may be perpetuated.

A second advantage of loose coupling is that it may provide a sensitive sensing mechanism. This possibility is suggested by Fritz Heider's perceptual theory of things and medium. Heider (1959) argues that perception is most accurate when a medium senses a thing and the medium contains many independent ele-

ments that can be externally constrained. When elements in a medium become either fewer in number and/or more internally constrained and/or more interdependent, their ability to represent some remote thing is decreased. Thus sand is a better medium to display wind currents than are rocks, the reason being that sand has more elements, more independence among the elements, and the elements are subject to a greater amount of external constraint than is the case for rocks. Using Heider's formulation metaphorically, it could be argued that loosely coupled systems preserve many independent sensing elements and therefore "know" their environments better than is true for more tightly coupled systems which have fewer externally constrained, independent elements. Balanced against this improvement in sensing is the possibility that the system would become increasingly vulnerable to producing faddish responses and interpretations. If the environment is known better, then this could induce more frequent changes in activities done in response to this "superior intelligence."

A third function is that a loosely coupled system may be a good system for localized adaptation. If all of the elements in a large system are loosely coupled to one another, then any one element can adjust to and modify a local unique contingency without affecting the whole system. These local adaptations can be swift, relatively economical, and substantial. By definition, the antithesis of localized adaptation is standardization and to the extent that standardization can be shown to be desirable, a loosely coupled system might exhibit fewer of these presumed benefits. For example, the localized adaptation characteristic of loosely coupled systems may result in a lessening of educational democracy.

Fourth, in loosely coupled systems where the identity, uniqueness, and separateness of elements is preserved, the system potentially can retain a greater number of mutations and novel solutions than would be the case with a tightly coupled system. A loosely coupled system could preserve more "cultural insurance" to be drawn upon in times of radical change than in the case for more tightly coupled systems. Loosely coupled systems may be elegant solutions to the problem that adaptation can preclude adaptability. When a specific system fits into an ecological niche and does so with great success, this adaptation can be costly. It can be costly because resources which are useless in a current environment might deteriorate or disappear even though they could be crucial in a modified environment. It is conceivable that loosely coupled systems preserve more diversity in responding than do tightly coupled systems, and therefore can adapt to a considerably wider range of changes in the environment than would be true for tightly coupled systems. To appreciate the possible problems associated with this abundance of mutations, reconsider the dynamic outlined in the preceding discussion of localized adaptation. If a local set of elements can adapt to local idiosyncrasies without involving the whole system, then this same loose coupling could also forestall the spread of advantageous mutations that exist somewhere in the system. While the system may contain novel solutions for new problems of adaptation, the very structure that allows these mutations to flourish may prevent their diffusion.

Fifth, if there is a breakdown in one portion of a loosely coupled system then this breakdown is sealed off and does not affect other portions of the organization. Previously we had noted that loosely coupled systems are an exquisite mechanism to adapt swiftly to local novelties and unique problems. Now we are carrying the analysis one step further, and arguing that when any element misfires or decays or deteriorates, the spread of this deterioration is checked in a loosely coupled system. While this point is reminiscent of earlier functions, the emphasis here is on the localization of trouble rather than the localization of adaptation. But even this potential benefit may be problematic. A loosely coupled system can isolate its trouble spots and prevent the trouble from spreading, but it should be difficult for the loosely coupled system to repair the defective element. If weak influences pass from the defective portions to the functioning portions, then the influence back from these functioning portions will also be weak and probably too little, too late.

Sixth, since some of the most important elements in educational organizations are teachers, classrooms, principals, and so forth, it may be consequential that in a loosely coupled system there is more room available for self-determination by the actors. If it is argued that a sense of efficacy is crucial for human beings, then a sense of efficacy might be greater in a loosely coupled system with autonomous units than it would be in a tightly coupled system where discretion is limited. A further comment can be made about self-determination to provide an example of the kind of imagery that is invoked by the concept of loose coupling.

It is possible that much of the teacher's sense of—and actual—control comes from the fact that diverse interested parties expect the teacher to link their intentions with teaching actions. Such linking of diverse intentions with actual work probably involves considerable negotiation. A parent complains about a teacher's action and the teacher merely points out to the parent how the actions are really correspondent with the parent's desires for the education of his or her children. Since most actions have ambiguous consequences, it should always be possible to justify the action as fitting the intentions of those who complain. Salancik (1975) goes even farther and suggests the intriguing possibility that when the consequences of an action are ambiguous, the stated *intentions* of the action serve as surrogates for the consequences. Since it is not known whether reading a certain book is good or bad for a child, the fact that it is intended to be good for the child itself becomes justification for having the child read it. The potential trade-off implicit in this function of loose coupling is fascinating. There is an increase in autonomy in the sense that resistance is heightened, but this heightened resistance occurs at the price of shortening the chain of consequences that will flow from each autonomous actor's efforts. Each teacher will have to negotiate separately with the same complaining parent.

Seventh, a loosely coupled system should be relatively inexpensive to run because it takes time and money to coordinate people. As much of what happens and should happen inside educational organizations seems to be defined and validated outside the organization, schools are in the business of building and maintaining categories, a business that requires coordination only on a few specific issues—for instance, assignment of teachers. This reduction in the necessity for coordination results in fewer conflicts, fewer inconsistencies among activities, fewer discrepancies between categories and activity. Thus, loosely coupled systems seem to hold the costs of coordination to a minimum. Despite this being an inexpensive system, loose coupling is also a nonrational system of fund allocation and therefore, unspecifiable, unmodifiable, and incapable of being used as means of change.

When these several sets of functions and dysfunctions are examined, they begin to throw several research issues into relief. For example, oppositions proposed in each of the preceding seven points suggest the importance of contextual theories. A predicted outcome or its opposite should emerge depending on how and in what the loosely coupled system is embedded. The preceding oppositions also suggest a fairly self-contained research program. Suppose a researcher starts with the first point made, as loose coupling increases the system should contain a greater number of anachronistic practices. Loosely coupled systems should be conspicuous for their cultural lags. Initially, one would like to know whether that is plausible or not. But then one would want to examine in more fine-grained detail whether those anachronistic practices that are retained hinder the system or impose structure and absorb uncertainty thereby producing certain economies in responding. Similar embellishment and elaboration is possible for each function with the result that rich networks of propositions become visible. What is especially attractive about these networks is that there is little precedent for them in the organizational literature. Despite this, these propositions contain a great deal of face validity when they are used as filters to look at educational organizations. When compared, for example, with the bureaucratic template mentioned in the introduction, the template associated with loosely coupled systems seems to take the observer into more interesting territory and prods him or her to ask more interesting questions.

Methodology and Loose Coupling

An initial warning to researchers: the empirical observation of unpredictability is insufficient evidence for concluding that the elements in a system are loosely coupled. Buried in that caveat are a host of methodological intricacies. While there is ample reason to believe that loosely coupled systems can be seen and examined, it is also possible that the appearance of loose coupling will be nothing more than a testimonial to bad methodology. In psychology, for example, it has been argued that the chronic failure to predict behavior from attitudes is due to measurement error and not to the unrelatedness of these two events. Attitudes are said to be loosely coupled with behavior but it may be that this conclusion is an artifact produced because attitudes assessed by time-independent and context-independent measures are being used to predict behaviors that are time and context dependent. If both attitudes and behaviors were assessed with equivalent measures, then tight coupling might be the rule.

Any research agenda must be concerned with fleshing out the imagery of loose coupling—a task requiring a considerable amount of conceptual work to solve a few specific and rather tricky methodological problems before one can investigate loose coupling.

By definition, if one goes into an organization and watches which parts affect which other parts, he or she will see the tightly coupled parts and the parts that vary the most. Those parts which vary slightly, infrequently, and periodically will be less visible. Notice, for example, that interaction data—who speaks to whom about what—are unlikely to reveal loose couplings. These are the most visible and obvious couplings and by the arguments developed in this paper perhaps some of the least crucial to understand what is going on in the organization.

An implied theme in this paper is that people tend to overrationalize their activities and to attribute greater meaning, predictability, and coupling among them than in fact they have. If members tend to overrationalize their activity, then their descriptions will not suggest which portions of that activity are loosely and tightly coupled. One might, in fact, even use the presence of apparent over-rationalization as a potential clue that myth making, uncertainty, and loose coupling have been spotted.

J.G. March has argued that loose coupling can be spotted and examined only if one uses methodology that highlights and preserves rich detail about context. The necessity for a contextual methodology seems to arise, interestingly enough, from inside organization theory. The implied model involves cognitive limits on rationality and man as a single channel information processor. The basic methodological point is that if one wishes to observe loose coupling, then he has to see both what is and is not being done. The general idea is that time spent on one activity is time spent away from a second activity. A contextually sensitive methodology would record both the fact that some people are in one place generating events and the fact that these same people are thereby absent from some other place. The rule of thumb would be that a tight coupling in one part of the system can occur only if there is loose coupling in another part of the system. The problem that finite attention creates for a researcher is that if some outcome is observed for the organization, then it will not be obvious whether the outcome is due to activity in the tightly coupled sector or to inactivity in the loosely coupled sector. That is a provocative problem of interpretation. But the researcher should be forewarned that there are probably a finite number of tight couplings that can occur at any moment, that tight couplings in one place imply loose couplings elsewhere, and that it may be the *pattern* of couplings that produces the observed outcomes. Untangling such intricate issues may well require that new tools be developed for contextual understanding and that investigators be willing to substitute nonteleological thinking for teleological thinking (Steinbeck, 1941: chapter 14).

Another contextually sensitive method is the use of comparative studies. It is the presumption of this methodology that taken-for-granted understandings—one possible "invisible" source of coupling in an otherwise loosely coupled system—are embedded in and contribute to a context. Thus, to see the effects of variations in these understandings one compares contexts that differ in conspicuous and meaningful ways.

Another methodological trap may await the person who tries to study loose coupling. Suppose one provides evidence that a particular goal is loosely coupled to a particular action. He or she says in effect, the person wanted to do this but in fact actually did that, thus, the action and the intention are loosely coupled. Now the problem for the researcher is that he or she may simply have focused on the wrong goal. There may be other goals which fit that particular action better. Perhaps if the researcher were aware of them, then the action and intention would appear to be tightly coupled. Any kind of intention-action, plan-behavior, or means-end depiction of loose coupling may be vulnerable to this sort of problem and an exhaustive listing of goals rather than parsimony should be the rule.

Two other methodological points should be noted. First, there are no good descriptions of the kinds of couplings that can occur among the several elements in educational organizations. Thus, a major initial research question is simply, what does a map of the couplings and elements within an educational organization look like? Second, there appear to be some fairly rich probes that might be used to uncover the nature of coupling within educational organizations. Conceivably, crucial couplings within schools involve the handling of disciplinary issues and social control, the question of how a teacher gets a book for the classroom, and the question of what kinds of innovations need to get clearance by whom. These relatively innocuous questions may be powerful means to learn which portions of a system are tightly and loosely coupled. Obviously these probes would be sampled if there was a full description of possible elements that can be coupled and possible kinds and strengths of couplings. These specific probes suggest, however, in addition that what holds an educational organization together may be a small number of tight couplings in out-of-the-way places.

Illustrative Questions for a Research Agenda

Patterns of Loose and Tight Coupling: Certification versus Inspection

Suppose one assumes that education is an intrinsically uninspected and unevaluated activity. If education is intrinsically uninspected and unevaluated then how can one establish that it is occurring? One answer is to define clearly who can and who cannot do it and to whom. In an educational organization this is the activity of certification. It is around the issues of certification and of specifying who the pupils are that tight coupling would be predicted to occur when technology and outcome are unclear.

If one argues that "certification" is the question "who does the work" and "inspection" is the question "how well is the work done," then there can be either loose or tight control over either certification or inspection. Notice that setting the problem up this way suggests the importance of discovering the distribution of tight and loosely coupled systems within any organization. Up to now the phrase loosely coupled systems has been used to capture the fact that events in an organization seem to be temporally related rather than logically related (Cohen and March, 1974). Now that view is being enriched by arguing that any organization must deal with issues of certification (who does the work) and inspection (how well is the work done). It is further being suggested that in the case of educational organizations there is loose control on the work—the work is intrinsically uninspected and unevaluated or if it is evaluated it is done so infrequently and in a perfunctory manner—but that under these conditions it becomes crucial for the organization to have tight control over who does the work and on whom. This immediately suggests the importance of comparative research in which the other three combinations are examined, the question being, how do these alternative forms grow, adapt, manage their rhetoric and handle their clientele. Thus it would be important to find organizations in which the controls over certification and inspection are both loose, organizations where there is loose control over certification but tight control over inspection, and organizations in which there is tight control both over inspection and over certification. Such comparative research might be conducted among different kinds of educational organizations within a single country (military, private, religious schooling in the United States), between educational and noneducational organizations within the same country (for example, schools versus hospitals versus military versus business organizations) or between countries looking at solutions to the problem of education given different degrees of centralization. As suggested earlier, it may not be the existence or nonexistence of loose coupling that is a crucial determinant of organizational functioning over time but rather the patterning of loose and tight couplings. Comparative studies should answer the question of distribution.

If, as noted earlier, members within an organization (and researchers) will see and talk clearly about only those regions that are tightly coupled, then this suggests that members of educational organizations should be most explicit and certain when they are discussing issues related to certification for definition and regulation of teachers, pupils, topics, space, and resources. These are presumed to be the crucial issues that are tightly controlled. Increasing vagueness of description should occur when issues of substantive instruction—inspection—are discussed. Thus, those people who primarily manage the instructional business will be most vague in describing what they do, those people who primarily manage the certification rituals will be most explicit. This pattern is predicted *not* on the basis of the activities themselves—certification is easier to describe than inspection—but rather on the basis of the expectation that tightly coupled subsystems are more crucial to the survival of the system and therefore have received more linguistic work in the past and more agreement than is true for loosely coupled elements.

Core Technology and Organizational Form

A common tactic to understand complex organizations is to explore the possibility that the nature of the task being performed determines the shape of the organizational structure. This straightforward tactic raises some interesting puzzles about educational organizations. There are suggestions in the literature that education is a diffuse task, the technology is uncertain.

This first question suggests two alternatives: if the task is diffuse then would not any organizational form whatsoever be equally appropriate *or* should this directly compel a diffuse form of organizational structure? These two alternatives are not identical. The first suggests that if the task is diffuse then any one of a variety of quite specific organizational forms could be imposed on the organization and no differences would be observed. The thrust of the second argument is that there is one and only one organizational form that would fit well when there is a diffuse task, namely, a diffuse organizational form (for instance, an organized anarchy).

The second question asks if the task in an educational organization is diffuse then why do all educational organizations look the way they do, and why do they all look the same? If there is no clear task around which the shape of the organization can be formed then why is it that most educational organizations do have a form and why is it that most of these forms look identical? One possible answer is that the tasks of educational organizations does not constrain the form of the organization but rather this constraint is imposed by the ritual of certification and/or the agreements that are made in and by the environment. If any of these nontask possibilities are genuine alternative explanations, then the general literature on organizations has been insensitive to them.

One is therefore forced to ask the question, is it the case within educational organizations that the technology is unclear? So far it has been argued that loose coupling in educational organizations is partly the result of uncertain technology. If uncertain technology does not generate loose coupling then researchers must look elsewhere for the origin of these bonds.

Making Sense in/of Loosely Coupled Worlds

What kinds of information do loosely coupled systems provide members around which they can organize meanings, that is, what can one use in order to make sense of such fleeting structures? (By definition loosely coupled events are modestly predictable at best.) There is a rather barren structure that can be observed, reported on, and retrospected in order to make any sense. Given the ambiguity of loosely coupled structures, this suggests that there may be increased pressure on members to construct or negotiate some kind of social reality they can live with. Therefore, under conditions of loose coupling one should see considerable effort devoted to constructing social reality, a great amount of face work and linguistic work, numerous myths (Mitroff and Kilmann, 1975) and in general one should find a considerable amount of effort being devoted to punctuating this loosely coupled world and connecting it in some way in which it can be made sensible. Loosely coupled worlds do not look as if they would provide an individual many resources for sense making—with such little

assistance in this task, a predominant activity should involve constructing social realities. Tightly coupled portions of a system should not exhibit nearly this preoccupation with linguistic work and the social construction of reality.

Coupling as a Dependent Variable

As a general rule, any research agenda on loose coupling should devote equal attention to loose coupling as a dependent and independent variable. Most suggestions have treated loose coupling as an independent variable. Less attention has been directed toward loose coupling as a dependent variable with the one exception of the earlier argument that one can afford loose coupling in either certification or inspection but not in both and, therefore, if one can locate a tight coupling for one of these two activities then he can predict as a dependent variable loose coupling for the other one.

Some investigators, however, should view loose coupling consistently as a dependent variable. The prototypic question would be, given prior conditions such as competition for scarce resources, logic built into a task, team teaching, conflict, striving for professionalism, presence of a central ministry of education, tenure, and so forth, what kind of coupling (loose or tight) among what kinds of elements occurs? If an organization faces a scarcity of resources its pattern of couplings should differ from when it faces an expansion of resources (for instance, scarcity leads to stockpiling leads to decoupling). Part of the question here is, what kinds of changes in the environment are the variables of tight and loose coupling sensitive to? In response to what kinds of activities or what kinds of contexts is coupling seen to change and what kinds of environments or situations, when they change, seem to have no effect whatsoever on couplings within an organization? Answers to these questions, which are of vital importance in predicting the outcomes of any intervention, are most likely to occur if coupling is treated as a dependent variable and the question is, under what conditions will the couplings that emerge be tight or loose?

Assembling Loosely Connected Events

Suppose one assumes that there is nothing in the world except loosely coupled events. This assumption is close to Simon's stable sub-assemblies and empty world hypothesis and to the idea of cognitive limits on rationality. The imagery is that of numerous clusters of events that are tightly coupled within and loosely coupled between. These larger loosely coupled units would be what researchers usually call organizations. Notice that organizations formed this way are rather unusual kinds of organizations because they are neither tightly connected, nor explicitly bounded, but they are stable. The research question then becomes, how does it happen that loosely coupled events which remain loosely coupled are institutionally held together in one organization which retains few controls over central activities? Stated differently, how does it happen that someone can take a series of loosely coupled events, assemble them into an organization of loosely coupled systems, and the events remain both loosely coupled but the organization itself survives? It is common to observe that large organizations have loosely connected sectors. The questions are, what makes this possible, how does it happen? What the structure in school systems seems to consist of is categories (for example, teacher, pupil, reading) which are linked by understanding and legitimated exogenously (that is, by the world outside the organization). As John Meyer (1975) puts it, "the system works because everyone knows everyone else knows roughly what is to go on. . . . Educational organizations are holding companies containing shares of stock in uninspected activities and subunits which are largely given their meaning, reality, and value in the wider social market." Note the potential fragility of this fabric of legitimacy.

It remains to be seen under what conditions loosely coupled systems are fragile structures because they are shored up by consensual anticipations, retrospections, and understanding that can dissolve and under what conditions they are resilient structures because they contain mutations, localized adaptation, and fewer costs of coordination.

Separate Intending and Acting Components

Intention and action are often loosely coupled within a single individual. Salancik (1975) has suggested some conditions under which dispo-

sitions within a single individual may be loosely coupled. These include such suggestions as follows. (1) If intentions are not clear and unambiguous, then the use of them to select actions which will fulfill the intentions will be imperfect. (2) If the consequences of action are not known, then the use of intention to select action will be imperfect. (3) If the means by which an intention is transformed into an action are not known or in conflict, then the coupling of action to intention will be imperfect. (4) If intentions are not known to a person at the time of selecting an action, then the relationships between action and intention will be imperfect. This may be more common than expected because this possibility is not allowed by so-called rational models of man. People often have to recall their intentions after they act or reconstruct these intentions, or invent them. (5) If there exists a set of multiple intentions which can determine a set of similar multiple actions, then the ability to detect a relationship between any one intention and any one action is likely to be imperfect. To illustrate, if there is an intention A which implies selecting actions X and Y, and there is also an intention B which implies selecting actions X and Y, then it is possible that under both presence and absence of intention A, action X will be selected. Given these circumstances, an observer will falsely conclude that this relationship is indeterminate.

The preceding list has the potential limitation for organizational inquiry in that it consists of events within a single person. This limitation is not serious *if* the ideas are used as metaphors or if each event is lodged in a different person. For example, one could lodge intention with one person and action with some other person. With this separation, then all of the above conditions may produce loose coupling between these actors but additional conditions also come into play given this geographical separation of intention from action. For example, the simple additional requirement that the intentions must be communicated to the second actor and in such a way that they control his actions, will increase the potential for error and loose coupling. Thus any discussion of separate locations for intention and action within an organization virtually requires that the investigator specify the additional conditions under which the intending component can control the acting component. Aside from the problems of communication and control when intention and action are separated there are at least two additional conditions that could produce loose coupling.

1. If there are several diverse intending components all of whom are dependent on the same actor for implementing action, then the relationship between any one intention and any one action will be imperfect. The teacher in the classroom may well be the prototype of this condition.

2. The process outlined in the proceeding item can become even more complicated, and the linkages between intention and action even looser, if the single acting component has intentions of its own.

Intention and action are often split within organizations. This paper suggests that if one were to map the pattern of intention and action components within the organization these would coincide with loosely coupled systems identified by other means. Furthermore, the preceding propositions begin to suggest conditions under which the same components might be at one moment tightly coupled and at the next moment loosely coupled.

Conclusion: A Statement of Priorities

More time should be spent examining the possibility that educational organizations are most usefully viewed as loosely coupled systems. The concept of organizations as loosely coupled systems can have a substantial effect on existing perspectives about organizations. To probe further into the plausibility of that assertion, it is suggested that the following research priorities constitute a reasonable approach to the examination of loosely coupled systems.

1. Develop Conceptual Tools Capable of Preserving Loosely Coupled Systems

It is clear that more conceptual work has to be done before other lines of inquiry on this topic are launched. Much of the blandness in organizational theory these days can be traced to investigators applying impoverished images to organizational settings. If researchers immediately start stalking the elusive loosely coupled system with imperfect language and concepts, they will perpetuate the blandness of organizational theory. To see the importance of and necessity for this conceptual activity the reader should reexamine the 15 different connotations of the phrase "loose coupling" that are uncovered in this paper. They provide 15 alternative explanations for any researcher who claims that some outcome is due to loose coupling.

2. Explicate What Elements Are Available in Educational Organizations for Coupling

This activity has high priority because it is essential to know the practical domain within which the coupling phenomena occur. Since there is the further complication that elements may appear or disappear as a function of context and time, this type of inventory is essential at an early stage of inquiry. An indirect benefit of making this a high priority activity is that it will stem the counterproductive suspicion that "the number of elements in educational organizations is infinite." The reasonable reply to that comment is that if one is precise in defining and drawing boundaries around elements, then the number of elements will be less than imagined. Furthermore, the researcher can reduce the number of relevant elements if he has some theoretical ideas in mind. These theoretical ideas should be one of the outcomes of initial activity devoted to language and concept development (Priority 1).

3. Develop Contextual Methodology

Given favorable outcomes from the preceding two steps, researchers should then be eager to look at complex issues such as patterns of tight and loose coupling keeping in mind that loose coupling creates major problems for the researcher because he is trained and equipped to decipher predictable, tightly coupled worlds. To "see" loosely coupled worlds unconventional methodologies need to be developed and conventional methodologies that are underexploited need to be given more attention. Among the existing tools that should be refined to study loose coupling are comparative studies and longitudinal studies. Among the new tools that should be "invented" because of their potential relevance to loosely coupled systems are nonteleological thinking (Steinbeck, 1941), concurrence methodology (Bateson, 1972: 180–201), and Hegelian, Kantian, and Singerian inquiring systems (Mitroff, 1974). While these latter methodologies are unconventional within social science, so too is it unconventional to urge that we treat unpredictability (loose coupling) as our topic of interest rather than a nuisance.

4. Promote the Collection of Thorough, Concrete Descriptions of the Coupling Patterns in Actual Educational Organizations

No descriptive studies have been available to show what couplings in what patterns and with what strengths existed in current educational organizations. This oversight should be remedied as soon as possible.

Adequate descriptions should be of great interest to the practitioner who wants to know how his influence attempts will spread and with what intensity. Adequate description should also show practitioners how their organizations may be more sensible and adaptive than they suspect. Thorough descriptions of coupling should show checks and balances, localized controls, stabilizing mechanisms, and subtle feedback loops that keep the organization stable and that would promote its decay if they were tampered with.

The benefits for the researcher of full descriptions are that they would suggest which locations and which questions about loose coupling are most likely to explain sizeable portions of the variance in organizational outcomes. For example, on the basis of good descriptive work, it might be found that both tightly and loosely coupled systems "know" their environments with equal accuracy in which case, the earlier line of theorizing about "thing and medium" would be given a lower priority.

5. Specify the Nature of Core Technology in Educational Organizations

A surprisingly large number of the ideas presented in this paper assume that the typical coupling mechanisms of authority of office and logic of the task do not operate in educational organizations. Inquiry into loosely coupled systems was triggered partly by efforts to discover what *does* accomplish the coupling in school systems. Before the investigation of loose coupling goes too far, it should be established that authority and task are not prominent coupling mechanisms in schools. The assertions that they are not prominent seem to issue from a combination of informal observation, implausibility, wishful thinking, looking at the wrong things, and rather vague definitions of core technology and reward structures within education. If these two coupling mechanisms were defined clearly, studied carefully, and found to be weak and/or nonexistent in schools, *then* there would be a powerful justification for proceeding vigorously to study loosely coupled systems. Given the absence of work that definitively discounts these coupling mechanisms in education and given the fact that these two mechanisms have accounted for much of the observed couplings in other kinds of organizations, it seems crucial to look for them in educational organizations in the interest of parsimony.

It should be emphasized that if it *is* found that substantial coupling within educational organizations is due to authority of office and logic of the task, this does not negate the agenda that is sketched out in this paper. Instead, such discoveries would (1) make it even more crucial to look for patterns of coupling to explain outcomes, (2) focus attention on tight and loose couplings within task and authority induced couplings, (3) alert researchers to keep close watch for any coupling mechanisms other than these two, and (4) would direct comparative research toward settings in which these two coupling mechanisms vary in strength and form.

6. Probe Empirically the Ratio of Functions to Dysfunctions Associated with Loose Coupling

Although the word "function" has had a checkered history, it is used here without apology—and without the surplus meanings and ideology that have become attached to it. Earlier several potential benefits of loose coupling were described and these descriptions were balanced by additional suggestions of potential liabilities. If one adopts an evolutionary episte-mology, then over time one expects that entities develop a more exquisite fit with their ecologi-cal niches. Given that assumption, one then argues that if loosely coupled systems exist and if they have existed for some time, then they bestow some net advantage to their inhabitants and/or their constituencies. It is not obvious, however, what these advantages are. A set of studies showing how schools benefit and suffer given their structure as loosely coupled sys-tems should do much to improve the quality of thinking devoted to organizational analysis.

7. Discover How Inhabitants Make Sense Out of Loosely Coupled Worlds

Scientists are going to have some big problems when their topic of inquiry becomes low proba-bility couplings, but just as scientists have spe-cial problems comprehending loosely coupled worlds so too must the inhabitants of these worlds. It would seem that quite early in a research program on loose coupling, examina-tion of this question should be started since it has direct relevance to those practitioners who must thread their way through such "invisible" worlds and must concern their sense-making and stories in such a way that they don't bump into each other while doing so.

Karl E. Weick is a professor of psychology and organizational behavior at Cornell University.

This paper is the result of a conference held at La Jolla California, February 2–4, 1975 with sup-port from the National Institute of Education (NIE). Participants in the conference were in addi-tion to the author, W.W. Charters, Center for Edu-cation Policy and Management, University of Ore-gon; Craig Lundberg, School of Business, Oregon State University; John Meyer, Dept. of Sociology, Stanford University; Miles Meyers, Dept. of English. Oakland (Calif.) High School; Karlene Roberts, School of Business, University of Califor-nia, Berkeley; Gerald Salancik, Dept. of Business Administration, University of Illinois and Robert Wentz, Superintendent of Schools, Pomona (Calif.)

Unified School District. James G. March, School of Education, Stanford University, a member of the National Council on Educational Research, and members of the NIE staff were present as observers. This conference was one of several on organizational processes in education which will lead to a report that will be available from the National Institute of Education, Washington, D.C. 20208. The opinions expressed in the paper do not necessarily reflect the position or policy of the National Institute of Educa-tion or the Department of Health, Education, and Welfare.

References

Bateson, Mary Catherine. *Our Own Metaphor,* New York: Knopf, 1972.

Cohen, Michael D., and James G. March. *Leadership and Ambiguity.* New York: McGraw-Hill, 1974.

Glassman, R. B. "Persistence and Loose Coupling in Living Systems." *Behavioral Science,* 1973,18; 83-98.

Heider, Fritz. "Thing and medium." *Psychological Is-sues,* 1959, 1 (3); 1–34.

March, J. G., and J. P. Olsen, *Choice Situations in Loose-ly Coupled Worlds.* Unpublished manuscript, Stanford University, 1975.

Meyer, John W., *Notes on the Structure of Educational Organizations.* Unpublished manuscript, Stanford University, 1975.

Mitroff, Ian I., *The Subjective Side of Science.* New York: Elsevier, 1974.

Mitroff, Ian I., and Ralph H. Kilmann, *On Organiza-tional Stories: An Approach to the Design and Anal-ysis of Organizations Through Myths and Stories.* Unpublished manuscript. University of Pitts-burgh, 1975.

Salancik, Gerald R., *Notes on Loose Coupling: Linking Intentions to Actions.* Unpublished manuscript. University of Illinois, Urbana-Champaign, 1975.

Simon, H. A., "The architecture of complexity." *Pro-ceedings of the American Philosophical Society,* 106, 1969; 467–482

Steinbeck, John, *The Log from the Sea of Cortez.* New York: Viking, 1941.

Stephens, John M., *The Process of Schooling.* New York: Holt, Rinehart, and Winston, 1967.

Weick, Karl E., "Middle range theories of social sys-tems." *Behavioral Science,* 1974, 19; 357–367

CHAPTER 4

THE PROFESSIONAL BUREAUCRACY

HENRY MINTZBERG

Prime Coordinating Mechanism:	Standardization of skills
Key Part of Organization:	Operating core
Main Design Parameters:	Training, horizontal job specialization, vertical and horizontal decentralization
Contingency Factors:	Complex, stable environment, nonregulating, non-sophisticated technical system, fashionable

We have seen evidence at various points in this book that organizations can be bureaucratic without being centralized. Their operating work is stable, leading to "predetermined or predictable, in effect, standardized" behavior, but it is also complex, and so must be controlled directly by the operators who do it. Hence, the organization turns to the one coordinating mechanism that allows for standardization and decentralization at the same time, namely the standardization of skills. This gives rise to a structural configuration sometimes called *Professional Bureaucracy*, common in universities, general hospitals, school systems, public accounting firms, social work agencies, and craft production firms. All rely on the skills and knowledge of their operating professionals to function; all produce standard products or services.

The Basic Structure

The Work of the Operating Core

Here again we have a tightly knit configuration of the design parameters. Most important, *the Professional Bureaucracy relies for coordination on the standardization of skills and its associated design parameter, training and indoctrination. It hires duly trained and indoctrinated specialists—professionals—for the operating core, and then gives them considerable control over their own work. In effect, the work is highly specialized in the horizontal dimension, but enlarged in the vertical one.*

Control over his own work means that the professional works relatively independently of his colleagues, but closely with the clients he serves. For example, "Teacher autonomy is reflected in the structure of school systems, resulting in what may be called their structural looseness. The teacher works alone

"The Professional Bureaucracy," by Henry Mintzberg, reprinted from *The Structuring of Organizations—A Synthesis of the Research*, 1979, Prentice-Hall, Inc.

within the classroom, relatively hidden from colleagues and superiors, so that he has a broad discretionary jurisdiction within the boundaries of the classroom" (Bidwell, 1965, pp. 975–976). Likewise, many doctors treat their own patients, and accountants maintain personal contact with the companies whose books they audit.

Most of the necessary coordination between the operating professionals is then handled by the standardization of skills and knowledge, in effect, by what they have learned to expect from their colleagues. ". . . the system works because everyone knows everyone else knows roughly what is going on" (Meyer quoted in Weick, 1976, p. 14). During an operation as long and as complex as open-heart surgery, "very little needs to be said [between the anesthesiologist and the surgeon] preceding chest opening and during the procedure on the heart itself: lines, beats and lights on equipment are indicative of what everyone is expected to do and does—operations are performed in absolute silence, particularly following the chest-opening phase" (Gosselin, 1978). The point is perhaps best made in reverse, by the cartoon that shows six surgeons standing around a patient on the operating table with one saying, "Who opens?" Similarly, the policy and marketing courses of the management school may be integrated without the two professors involved ever having even met. As long as the courses are standard, each knows more or less what the other teaches.

Just how standardized complex professional work can be is illustrated in a paper read by Spencer (1976) before a meeting of the International Cardiovascular Society. Spencer notes that "Becoming a skillful clinical surgeon requires a long period of training, probably five or more years" (p. 1178). An important feature of that training is "repetitive practice" to evoke an "automatic reflex" (p. 1179). So automatic, in fact, that Spencer keeps a series of surgical "cookbooks" in which he lists, even for "complex" operations, the essential steps as chains of thirty to forty symbols on a single sheet, to "be reviewed mentally in sixty to 120 seconds at some time during the day preceding the operation" (p. 1182).

But no matter how standardized the knowledge and skills, their complexity ensures that considerable discretion remains in their application. No two professionals—no two surgeons or teachers or social workers—ever apply them in exactly the same way. Many judgments are required, as Perrow (1970) notes of policemen and others:

> There exist numerous plans: when to suspend assistance, when to remove a gun from its holster, when to block off an area, when to call the FBI, and when remove a child from the home. The existence of such plans does not provide a criterion for choosing the most effective plan . . . Instead of computation the decision depends upon human judgment. The police patrolman must decide whether to try to disperse the street corner gang or call for reinforcements. The welfare worker must likewise decide if new furniture is an allowable expense, and the high school counselor must decide whether to recommend a college preparatory or vocational program. Categories channel and shape these human judgments but they do not replace them (p. 216).

Training and indoctrination is a complicated affair in the Professional Bureaucracy. The initial training typically takes place over a period of years in a university or special institution. Here the skills and knowledge of the profession are formally programmed into the would-be professional. But in many cases that is only the first step, even if the most important one. There typically follows a long period of on-the-job training, such as internship in medicine and articling in accounting. Here the formal knowledge is applied and the practice of the skills perfected, under the close supervision of members of the profession. On-the-job training also completes the process of indoctrination, which began during the formal teaching. Once this process is completed, the professional association typically examines the trainee to determine whether he has the requisite knowledge, skills, and norms to enter the profession. That is not to say, however, that the individual is examined for the last time in his life, and is pronounced completely full, such that "After this, no new ideas can be imparted to him," as humorist and academic Stephen Leacock once commented about the Ph.D., the test to enter the profession of university teaching. The entrance examination only tests the basic requirements at one point in time; the process of training continues. As new knowledge is generated and new skills develop, the professional upgrades his expertise. He reads the journals, attends the conferences, and perhaps also returns periodically for formal retraining.

The Bureaucratic Nature of the Structure

All of this training is geared to one goal—the internalization of standards that serve the client and coordinate the professional work. In other words, *the structure of these organizations is essentially bureaucratic, its coordination—like that of the Machine Bureaucracy—achieved by design, by standards that predetermine what is to be done.* How bureaucratic is illustrated by Perrow's (1970) description of one well-known hospital department:

> . . . obstetrics and gynecology is a relatively routine department, which even has something resembling an assembly (or deassembly?) line wherein the mother moves from room to room and nurse to nurse during the predictable course of her labor. It is also one of the hospital units most often accused of impersonality and depersonalization. For the mother, the birth is unique, but not for the doctor and the rest of the staff who go through this many times a day (p. 74).

But the two kinds of bureaucracies differ markedly in the source of their standardization. *Whereas the Machine Bureaucracy generates its own standards—its technostructure designing the work standards for its operators and its line managers enforcing them—the standards of the Professional Bureaucracy originate largely outside its own structure, in the self-governing associations its operators join with their colleagues from other Professional Bureaucracies.* These associations set universal standards which they make sure are taught by the universities and used by all the bureaucracies of the profession. *So whereas the Machine Bureaucracy relies on authority of a hierarchical nature—the power of office—the Professional Bureaucracy emphasizes authority of a professional nature—the power of expertise* (Blau, 1967–68). Thus, although Montagna (1968) found internal as well as external rules in the large public accounting firms he studied, the latter proved more important. These were

imposed by the American Institute of Certified Public Accountants and included an elaborate and much revised code of ethics, a newly codified volume of principles of accounting, and revised auditing standards and procedures.

> These rules serve as a foundation for the firms' more specific internal rules, a few of which are more stringent, others of which merely expand on the external rules. Nearly to a man, the total sample [of accountants questioned] agreed that compared with internal rules, the external rules were the more important rules for their firms and for the profession as a whole (p. 143).

Montagna's findings suggest that the other forms of standardization are difficult to rely on in the Professional Bureaucracy. The work processes themselves are too complex to be standardized directly by analysts. One need only try to imagine a work study analyst following a cardiologist on his rounds or observing a teacher in a classroom in order to program their work. Similarly, the outputs of professional work cannot easily be measured, and so do not lend themselves to standardization. Imagine a planner trying to define a cure in psychiatry, the amount of learning that takes place in the classroom, or the quality of an accountant's audit. Thus, Professional Bureaucracies cannot rely extensively on the formalization of professional work or on systems to plan and control it.

Much the same conclusion can be drawn for the two remaining coordinating mechanisms. Both direct supervision and mutual adjustment impede the professional's close relationships with his clients. That relationship is predicated on a high degree of professional autonomy—freedom from having not only to respond to managerial orders but also to consult extensively with peers. In any event, the use of the other four coordinating mechanisms is precluded by the capacity of the standardization of skills to achieve a good deal of the coordination necessary in the operating core.

The Pigeonholing Process

To understand how the Professional Bureaucracy functions in its operating core, it is helpful to think of it as a repertoire of standard programs—in effect, the set of skills the professionals stand ready to use—which are applied to predetermined situations, called contingencies, also standardized. As Weick (1976) notes of one case in point, "schools are in the business of building and maintaining categories" (p. 8). The process is sometimes known as *pigeonholing*. In this regard, *the professional has two basic tasks: (1) to categorize the client's need in terms of a contingency, which indicates which standard program to use, a task known as diagnosis, and (2) to apply, or execute, that program.* Pigeonholing simplifies matters enormously. "People are categorized and placed into pigeonholes because it would take enormous resources to treat every case as unique and requiring thorough analysis. Like stereotypes, categories allow us to move through the world without making continuous decisions at every moment" (Perrow, 1970, p. 58). Thus, a psychiatrist examines the patient, declares him to be manic-depressive, and initiates psychotherapy. Similarly, a professor finds 100 students registered in his course and executes his lecture program; faced with 20 instead, he runs the class as a seminar. And the management consultant carries his own bag of standard acronymical tricks—MBO, MIS, LRP, PERT, OD. The client with project work gets PERT, the one with managerial conflicts, OD. Simon (1977) captures the spirit of pigeonholing with his comment that "The pleasure that the good professional experiences in his work is not simply a pleasure in handling difficult matters; it is a pleasure in using skillfully a well-stocked kit of well-designed tools to handle problems that are comprehensible in their deep structure but unfamiliar in their detail" (p. 98).

It is the pigeonholing process that enables the Professional Bureaucracy to decouple its various operating tasks and assign them to individual, relatively autonomous professionals. Each can, instead of giving a great deal of attention to coordinating his work with his peers, focus on perfecting his skills. As Spencer (1976) notes in the case of vascular surgery, "with precise diagnosis and expert operative technique excellent results could almost always be obtained" (p. 1177).

The pigeonholing process does not deny the existence of uncertainty in servicing a client. Rather, it seeks to contain it in the jobs of single professionals. As Bidwell (1965) notes, "The problem of dealing with variability in student abilities and accomplishments during a school year ... is vested in the classroom teacher, and one important component of his professional skill is ability to handle day-to-day fluctuations in the response to instruction by individual students and collectively by the classroom group" (p. 975). The containment of this uncertainty—what Simon characterizes as unfamiliarity in detail in the job of the single professional—is one of the reasons why the professional requires considerable discretion in his work.

In the pigeonholing process, we see fundamental differences among the Machine Bureaucracy, the Professional Bureaucracy, and the Adhocracy. The Machine Bureaucracy is a single-purpose structure: presented with a stimulus, it executes its one standard sequence of programs, just as we kick when tapped on the knee. No diagnosis is involved. In the Professional Bureaucracy, diagnosis is a fundamental task, but it is circumscribed. The organization seeks to match a predetermined contingency to a standard program. Fully open-ended diagnosis—that which seeks a creative solution to a unique problem—requires a third structural configuration, which we call Adhocracy. No standard contingencies or programs exist in that structure.

Segal (1974) refers to these three as "chain-structured," "mediatively-structured," and "adaptively-structured" organizations. The chain-structured organization relates to only a small part of the environment and accepts inputs only at one end; once ingested, these are processed through a fixed sequence of operations. The mediatively-structured organization—our Professional Bureaucracy—is designed "to channel external dissimilarity into uniform organizational categories" (p. 215). Segal cites the example of the welfare department:

> A glance at the telephone numbers individuals must call to initiate contact with the welfare department indicates that the potential client cannot simply need help, he must need help as defined by the organization—aging, adoption, children in trouble, landlord-tenant complaints, etc. (p. 215).

In other words, the welfare department leaves part of the diagnosis to the client. The adaptively-structured organization, or Adhocracy, "is not structured to screen out heterogeneity and uncertainty" (p. 217). It adapts to its client's individual problem rather than trying to fit it into one of its own categories. Segal provides an example of each of these three types of organizations from the field of mental health:

1. The chain-structured custodial unit responds to the pressure in the environment to keep mental patients out of the public eye and in physical captivity. The chain-structured custodial unit is thus designed to achieve the singular purpose of custodial behavior.

2. The individual treatment structure responds to other pressure in the environment by arranging its units and care to help each patient to fit into a *category* of behavior defined by society. This facility is thus categorically responsive as staff attempts to change patients' behavior so that it fits their own standards of "normality."

3. The adaptively-structured milieu treatment ward responds to a more relativistic environmental pressure. In this instance, units and roles are arranged so that the very definition of normality is a product of interaction between staff and patients (p. 218).[1]

It is an interesting characteristic of the Professional Bureaucracy that its pigeonholing process creates an equivalence in its structure between the functional and market bases for grouping. *Because clients are categorized—or, as in the case of the welfare recipients above, categorize themselves—in terms of the functional specialists who serve them, the structure of the Professional Bureaucracy becomes at the same time both a functional and a market-based one.* Two illustrations help explain the point. A hospital gynecology department and a university chemistry department can be called functional because they group specialists according to the knowledge, skills, and work processes they use, or market-based because each unit deals with its own unique types of clients—women in the first case, chemistry students in the second. Thus, the distinction between functional and market bases for grouping breaks down in the special case of the Professional Bureaucracy.

Focus on the Operating Core

All the design parameters that we have discussed so far—the emphasis on the training of operators, their vertically enlarged jobs, the little use made of behavior formalization or planning and control systems—suggest that *the operating core is the key part of the Professional Bureaucracy. The only other part that is fully elaborated is the support staff, but that is focused very much on serving the operating core.* Given the high cost of the professionals, it makes sense to back them up with as much support as possible, to aid them and have others do whatever routine work can be formalized. For example, universities have printing facilities, faculty clubs, alma mater funds, building and grounds departments, publishing houses, archives, bookstores, information offices, museums, athletics departments, libraries, computer facilities, and many, many other support units.

The technostructure and middle line of management are not highly elaborated in the Professional Bureaucracy. In other configurations (except Adhocracy), they coordinate the work of the operating core. But in the Professional Bureaucracy, they can do little to coordinate the operating work. The need for planning or the formalizing of the work of the professionals is very limited, so there is little call for a technostructure (except, as we shall see, in the case of the nonprofessional support staff). In McGill University, for example, an institution with 17,000 students and 1200 professors, the only units that could be identified by the author as technocratic were two small departments concerned with finance and budgeting, a small planning office, and a center to develop the professors' skills in pedagogy (the latter two fighting a continual uphill battle for acceptance).

Likewise, the middle line in the Professional Bureaucracy is thin. With little need for direct supervision of the operators, or mutual adjustment between them, the operating units can be very large, with few managers at the level of first-line supervisor, or, for that matter, above them. The McGill Faculty of Management at the time of this writing has fifty professors and a single manager, its dean.

Thus, Figure 4-1 shows the Professional Bureaucracy, in terms of our logo, as a flat structure with a thin middle line, a tiny technostructure, and a fully elaborated support staff. All these features are reflected in the organigram of McGill University, shown in Figure 4-2.

Decentralization in the Professional Bureaucracy

Everything we have seen so far tells us that *the Professional Bureaucracy is a highly decentralized structure, in both the vertical and horizontal dimensions.* A great deal of the power over the operating work rests at the bottom of the structure, with the professionals of the operating core. Often each works with his own clients, subject only to the collective control of his colleagues, who trained and indoctrinated him in the first place and thereafter reserve the right to censure him for malpractice.

The professional's power derives from the fact that not only is his work too complex to be supervised by managers or standardized by analysts, but also that his services are typically in great demand. This gives the professional mobility, which enables him to insist on considerable autonomy in his work. The professional tends to identify more with his profession than with the organization where he practices it. Thus, Perrow (1965, p. 959) talks of the "stronger grip" of the medical profession on its members than the specific hospital, while Beyer and Lodahl (1976) note in academia that "Many faculty members receive an important part of their rewards—recognition—from their scientific communities, and this reward is only secondarily reinforced by their universities" (p. 124). In these organizations, even "promotion is not related to the climbing of an administrative ladder but to professional progress, or the ability to handle more and more complex professional problems" (SIAR, 1975, p. 62). Thus, when the professional does not get the autonomy he feels he requires, he is tempted to pick up his kit bag of skills and move on.

One is inclined to ask why professionals bother to join organizations in the first place.

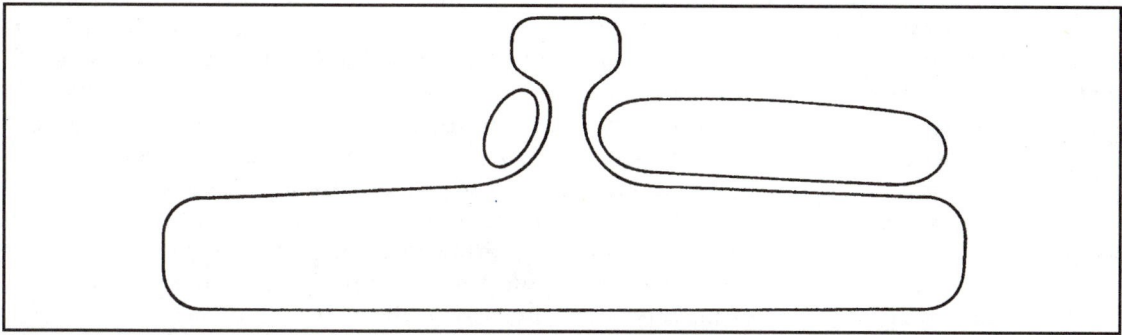

Figure 4-1 The Professional Bureaucracy

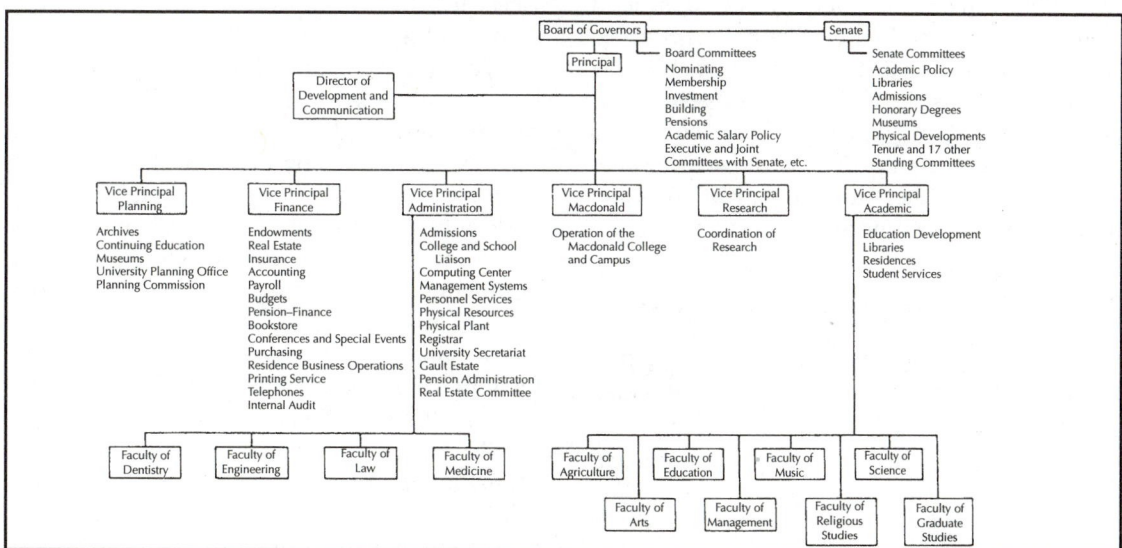

Figure 4-2 Organigram of McGill University (circa 1978, used by permission)

There are, in fact, a number of good reasons. For one thing, professionals can share resources, including support services, in a common organization. One surgeon cannot afford his own operating theater, so he shares it with others, just as professors share laboratories, lecture halls, libraries, and printing facilities. Organizations also bring professionals together to learn from each other, and to train new recruits.

Some professionals must join the organization to get clients. The clients present themselves to an organization that houses many different kinds of professionals, depending on it to diagnose their problem and direct them to the individual professional who can best serve them. Thus, while some physicians, have their private patients, others receive them from the hospital emergency department or from in-patient referrals. In universities, students select the department where they wish to study—in effect, diagnosing their own general needs—but that department, in turn, helps direct them into specific courses given by individual professors.

Another reason professionals band together to form organizations is that the clients often need the services of more than one at the same time. An operation requires at least a surgeon, an anesthesiologist, and a nurse; an MBA program cannot be run with less than about a dozen different specialists. Finally, the bringing together of different types of professionals allows clients to be transferred between them when the initial diagnosis proves incorrect or the needs of the client change during execution. When the kidney patient develops heart trouble, that is no time to change hospitals in search of a cardiologist. Similarly, when a law student finds his client needs a course in moral ethics, or an accountant finds his client needs tax advice, it is comforting to know that other departments in the same organization stand ready to provide the necessary service.

The Administrative Structure

What we have seen so far suggests that the Professional Bureaucracy is a highly democratic structure, at least for the professionals of the operating core. In fact, *not only do the professionals control their own work, but they also seek collective control of the administrative decisions that affect them*, decisions, for example, to hire colleagues, to promote them, and to distribute resources. Controlling these decisions requires control of the middle line of the organization, which professionals do by ensuring that it is staffed with "their own." Some of the administrative work the operating professionals do themselves. Every university professor, for example, carries out some administrative duties and serves on committees of one kind or another to ensure that he retains some control over the decisions that affect his work. Moreover, full-time administrators who wish to have any power at all in these structures must be certified members of the profession, and preferably be elected by the professional operators or at least appointed with their blessing. What emerges, therefore, is a rather democratic administrative structure. The university department chairmen, many of them elected, together with the deans, vice-presidents, and president—all of them necessarily academics—must work alongside a parallel hierarchy of committees of professors, many of them elected, ranging from the departmental curriculum committee to the powerful university senate (shown with its own subcommittees in Figure 4-2). This can be seen clearly in Figure 4-3, the organigram of a typical university hospital. The plethora of committees is shown on the right side, reporting up from the medical departments through the Council of Physicians and Dentists directly to the Board of Trustees, bypassing the managerial hierarchy entirely. (Notice also the large number of support services in the organization and the relative absence of technocratic units.)

The nature of the administrative structure which itself relies on mutual adjustment for coordination—indicates that the liaison devices, while uncommon in the operating core, are important design parameters in the middle line. Standing committees and ad hoc task forces abound, as was seen in Figure 4-3; a number of positions are designated to integrate the administrative efforts, as in the case of the ward manager in the hospital; and some Professional Bureaucracies even use matrix structure in administration.

Because of the power of their operators, Professional Bureaucracies are sometimes called "collegial" organizations. In fact, some professionals like to describe them as inverse

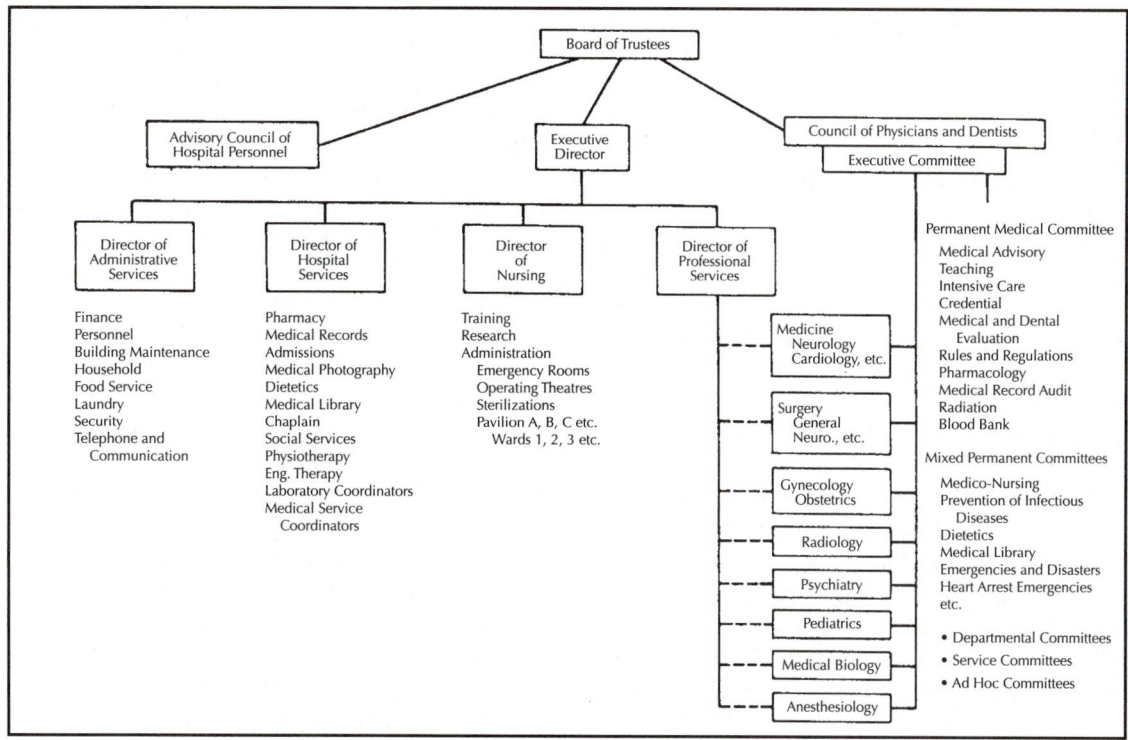

Figure 4-3 Organigram of a University Hospital Board of Trustees

pyramids, with the professional operators at the top and the administrators down below to serve them—to ensure that the surgical facilities are kept clean and the classrooms well supplied with chalk. Thus comments Amitai Etzioni (1959), the well-known sociologist:

> . . . in professional organizations the staff-expert line-manager correlation, insofar as such a correlation exists at all, is reversed. . . . Managers in professional organizations are in charge of secondary activities; they administer *means* to the major activity carried out by experts. In other words, if there is a staff-line relationship at all, experts constitute the line (major authority) structure and managers the staff. . . . The final internal decision is, functionally speaking, in the hands of various professionals and their decision-making bodies. The professor decides what research he is going to undertake and to a large degree what he is going to teach; the physician determines what treatment should be given to the patient (p. 52).

Etzioni's description may underestimate the power of the *professional* administrator—an issue we shall return to shortly—but it seems to be an accurate description of the nonprofes-

sional one, namely the administrator who manages the support units. For the support staff—often much larger than the professional one, but charged largely with doing nonprofessional work-there is no democracy in the Professional Bureaucracy, only the oligarchy of the professionals. Support units, such as housekeeping or kitchen in the hospital, printing in the university, are as likely as not to be managed tightly from the top. They exist, in effect, as machine bureaucratic constellations within the Professional Bureaucracy.

What frequently emerge in the Professional Bureaucracy are parallel administrative hierarchies, one democratic and bottom up for the professionals, and a second machine bureaucratic and top down for the support staff. As Bidwell (1965) notes: "The segregation of professional and nonprofessional hierarchies in school systems presumably permit this differentiation of modes of control" (p. 1016; see also Blau, 1967–68).

In the professional hierarchy, power resides in expertise; one has influence by virtue of one's knowledge and skills. In other words, a good deal of power remains at the bottom of the hierarchy, with the professional operators themselves. That does not, of course, preclude a pecking order among them. But it does require the pecking order to mirror the professionals' experience and expertise. As they gain experience and reputation academics move through the ranks of lecturer, and then assistant, associate, and full professor; and physicians enter the hospital as interns and move up to residents before they become members of the staff.

In the nonprofession hierarchy, power and status reside in administrative office; one salutes the stripes, not the man. The situation is that Weber originally described: "each lower office is under the control and supervision of a higher one" (cited in Blau, 1967–68, p. 455). Unlike the professional structure, here one must practice administration, not a specialized function of the organization, to attain status.

But "research indicates that a professional orientation toward service and a bureaucratic orientation toward disciplined compliance with procedures are opposite approaches toward work and often create conflict in organizations" (Blau, 1967–68, p. 456). Hence, these two parallel hierarchies are kept quite independent of each other. The two may come together at some intermediate level, as when a university dean oversees both the professional and secretarial staff. But often, as shown in Figure 4-4, they remain separate right up to the strategic apex. The hospital medical staff, as shown in Figure 4-3, does not even report to the executive director—the chief executive officer—but directly to the board of trustees. (Indeed, Charns, [1976] reports that 41 percent of physicians he surveyed in academic medical centers claimed they were responsible to no one!)

The Roles of the Professional Administrator

Where does all this leave the administrators of the professional hierarchy, the executive directors and chiefs of the hospitals and the presidents and deans of the universities? Are they as powerless as Etzioni suggests? Compared with their peers in the Simple Structure and the Machine Bureaucracy, they certainly lack a good deal of power. But that is far from the whole story. While the professional administrator may not be able to control the professionals directly, he does perform a series of roles that gives him considerable indirect power in the structure.

First, *the professional administrator spends much time handling disturbances in the structure.* The pigeonholing process is an imperfect one at best, leading to all kinds of jurisdictional disputes between the professionals. Who should teach the statistics course in the MBA program, the mathematics department or the business school? Who should perform mastectomies in hospitals, surgeons who specialize in operations or gynecologists who specialize in women? Seldom, however, can a senior administrator impose a solution on the professionals or units involved in a dispute. Rather the unit managers—chiefs, deans, or whoever—must sit down together and negotiate a solution on behalf of their constituencies. Coordination problems also arise frequently between the two parallel hierarchies, and it often falls to the professional administrator to resolve them.

Second, *the professional administrators—especially those at higher levels—serve key roles at the boundary of the organization, between the professionals inside and interested parties—governments, client associations, and so on—on the outside.* On one hand, the administrators are expected to protect the professionals' autonomy, to "buffer" them from external pressures. "The principal is expected to 'back the teacher up'—support her authority in all cases of parental 'interference' "(Melcher, 1976, p. 334). So, too, the executive director of the hospital is supposed to keep the government or the trustees from interfering in the work of the physicians. On the other hand, the administrators are expected to woo these outsiders to support the organization, both morally and financially. "...teachers consider it a prime responsibility of the administrator to secure for them the greatest possible amount of resources" (Hills, quoted in Melcher, 1976, p. 333), as do professors in universities and physicians in hospitals. Thus, the external roles of the manager—maintaining liaison contacts, acting as figurehead and spokesman in a public relations capacity, negotiating with outside agencies—emerge as primary ones in the job of the professional administrator.

Some view the roles professional administrators are called upon to perform as signs of weakness. Like Etzioni, they see these people as the errand boys of the professionals, or else as pawns caught in various tugs of war—between one professional and another, between support staffer and professional, between outsider and

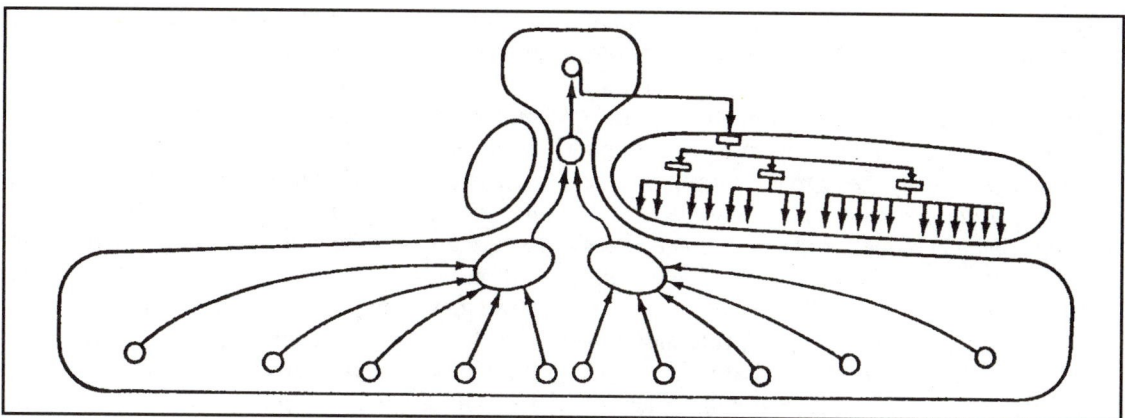

Figure 4-4 Parallel Hierarchies in the Professional Bureaucracy

professional. In fact, however, these roles are the very sources of administrator power. Power is, after all, gained at the locus of uncertainty. And that is exactly where the professional administrators sit. The administrator who succeeds in raising extra funds for his organization gains a say in how these are distributed. Similarly, the one who can reconcile conflicts in favor of his unit or who can effectively buffer the professionals from external influence becomes a valued—and therefore powerful—member of the organization. The professionals well know that "Without the 'superb politician,' metropolitan school systems, urban governments, universities, mental hospitals, social work systems, and similar complex organizations would be immobilized" (Thompson, 1967, p. 143).

Ironically, *the professional becomes dependent on the effective administrator.* The professional faces a fundamental dilemma. Frequently, he abhors administration, desiring only to be left alone to practice his profession. But that freedom is gained only at the price of administrative effort—raising funds, resolving conflicts, buffering the demands of outsiders. That leaves the professional two choices: to do the administrative work himself, in which case he has less time to practice his profession, or to leave it to administrators, in which case he must surrender some of his power over decision making. And that power must be surrendered, it should further be noted, to administrators who, by virtue of the fact that they no longer wish to practice the profession, probably favor a different set of goals. Damned if he does and damned if he doesn't. Take the case of the university professors oriented to research.

To ensure the fullest support for research in his department, he should involve himself in committees where questions of the commitment to teaching versus research are decided. But that takes time, specifically time away from research. What is the use of spending time protecting what one has no time left to do. So the professor is tempted to leave administration to full-time administrators, those who have expressed a disinterest in research by virtue of seeking fulltime administrative office.

We can conclude that *power in these structures does flow to those professionals who care to devote the effort to doing administrative instead of professional work*—a considerable amount of power, in fact, to those who do it well, especially in complex professional organizations, such as the modern hospital (Perrow, 1967). *But that, it should be stressed, is not laissez-faire power: the professional administrator keeps his power only as long as the professionals perceive him to be serving their interests effectively.* The managers of the Professional Bureaucracy may be the weakest among those of the five structural configurations, but they are far from impotent. *Individually,* they are usually more powerful than individual professionals—the chief executive remaining the single most powerful member of the Professional Bureaucracy—even if that power can easily be overwhelmed by the *collective* power of the professionals.

Strategy Formulation in the Professional Bureaucracy

A description of the strategy formulation process in the Professional Bureaucracy perhaps best illustrates the two sides of the professional administrator's power. At the outset it should be noted that strategy takes on a very different form in these kinds of organizations. Since their outputs are difficult to measure, their goals cannot easily be agreed upon. So *the notion of a strategy—a single, integrated pattern of decisions common to the entire organization—loses a good deal of its meaning in the Professional Bureaucracy.*

Given the autonomy of each professional—his close working relationships with his clients, and his loose ones with his colleagues—it becomes sensible to think in terms of a personal strategy for each professional. In many cases, each selects his own clients and his own methods of dealing with them—in effect, he chooses his own product-market strategy. But professionals do not select their clients and methods at random. They are significantly constrained by the professional standards and skills they have learned. That is, the professional associations and training institutions outside the organization play a major role in determining the strategies that the professionals pursue. Thus, to an important extent all organizations in a given profession exhibit similar strategies, imposed on them from the outside. These strategies—concerning what clients to serve and how—are inculcated in the professionals during their formal training and are modified as new needs emerge and the new methods developed to cope with them gain acceptance by the professional associations. In medicine, for example, researchers develop new forms of treatment and test them experimentally. They publish their results in the medical journals, these publications leading to more experimentation and elaboration until the methods are considered sufficiently safe to pass into standard practice—that is, to become part of the repertoire of programs of all hospitals. And this whole process is overseen by the professional associations, which pass judgments on acceptable and unacceptable practices, and through whose journals, newsletters, conferences, and training programs information on new practices is disseminated. This control of strategy can sometimes be very direct: in one of the McGill studies, a hospital that refused to adopt a new method of treatment was, in effect, censured when one of the associations of medical specialists passed a resolution declaring failure to use it tantamount to malpractice.

We can conclude, therefore, that *the strategies of the Professional Bureaucracy are largely ones of the individual professionals within the organization as well as of the professional associations on the outside.* Largely, but not completely. There are still degrees of freedom that allow each organization within the profession to adapt the basic strategies to its own needs and interests. There are, for example, mental hospitals, women's hospitals, and veterans' hospitals; all conform to standard medical practice, but each applies it to a different market which it has selected.

How do these organizational strategies get made? It would appear that *the Professional Bureaucracy's own strategies represent the cumulative effect over time of the projects, or strategic "initiatives," that its members are able to convince it to undertake*—to buy a new piece of equipment in a hospital, to establish a new degree program in a university, to develop a new specialty department in an accounting firm. Most of these initiatives are proposed by members of the operating core—by "professional entrepreneurs" willing to expend the efforts needed to negotiate the acceptance of new projects through the complex administrative structure (and if the method is new and controversial, through outside professional associations as well, and also through outside funding agencies if the project is an expensive one). A proposal for a new Ph.D. program in management at McGill University was worked out by an ad hoc committee and then approved within the Faculty of Management by its Graduate Program Committee, Academic Committee, and Faculty Council; from there it went to the Executive Committee and the Council of the Faculty of Graduate Studies; then it moved on to the Academic Policy Committee of the Senate of the University and then to the full Senate itself; from there it went to the University Programs Committee of the Quebec government Ministry of Education and then into the Ministry itself, and then back and forth between these bodies and the university administration a few more times until it was finally approved (as a joint program of four universities).

What is the role of the professional administrator in all this? Certainly far from passive. As noted earlier, administration is neither the forte nor the interest of the operating professional (for good reason, as should be clear from the example above!). So he depends on the full-time administrator to help him negotiate his project through the system. For one thing, the administrator has time to worry about such matters—after all, administration is his job; he no longer practices the profession. For another, the administrator has a full knowledge of the administrative committee system as well as many personal contacts within it, both of which are necessary to see a project through it. The administrator deals with the system every day; the professional entrepreneur may promote only one new project in his entire career. Finally, the administrator is more likely to have the requisite managerial skills, for example, those of negotiation and persuasion.

But the power of the effective administrator to influence strategy goes beyond helping the professionals. Every good manager seeks to change his organization in his own way, to alter its strategies to make it more effective. In the Professional Bureaucracy, this translates into a set of strategic initiatives that the administrator himself wishes to take. But in these structures—in principle bottom up—the administrator cannot impose his will on the professionals of the operating core. Instead, he must rely on his informal power, and apply it subtly. Knowing that the professionals want nothing more than to be left alone, the administrator moves carefully—in incremental steps, each one hardly discernible. In this way, he may achieve over time changes that the professionals would have rejected out of hand had they been proposed all at once.

To conclude, we have seen again that while the weak administrator of the Professional Bureaucracy may be no more than the errand boy of the professionals, the strong one—a professional himself, politically adept and fully aware of the power system of his organization—can play a major role in changing its strategies.

Conditions of the Professional Bureaucracy

This third structural configuration appears wherever the operating core of an organization is dominated by skilled workers—professionals—who use procedures that are difficult to learn yet are well defined. This means an environment that is both complex and stable—complex enough to require the use of difficult procedures that can be learned only in extensive formal training programs, yet stable enough to enable these skills to become well defined, in effect, standardized. Thus, the environment is the chief contingency factor in the use of the Professional Bureaucracy.

In contrast, the factors of age and size are of less significance. Larger professional organizations tend to be somewhat more formalized (Holdaway et al., 1975; Bidwell, 1965, p. 1017)[2] and to have more fully developed staff support structures (Bidwell, 1965, p. 977). But that does not preclude the existence of small Professional Bureaucracies, or, for that matter, of young ones as well. The Machine Bureaucracy has a start-up time because the standards need to be worked out within the organization. Thus, it passes through a period of Simple Structure before its procedures become routinized. In the Professional Bureaucracy, in contrast, the skilled employees bring the standards into the organization with them when they join. So there is little start-up time. Put a group of doctors in a new hospital or a group of lawyers in a new law office and in no time they are functioning as if they had been there for years. Size would seem to be a relatively minor contingency factor for the same reason, and also because the professionals to a large extent work independently. One accountant working on his own adheres to the same professional standards as 2000 working in a giant firm. Thus, Professional Bureaucracies hardly pass through the stage of Simple Structure in their formative years.

Technical system is an important contingency factor, at least for what it is not in the Professional Bureaucracy—neither highly regulating, sophisticated, nor automated. The professional operators of this structural configuration require considerable discretion in their work. It is they who serve the clients, usually directly and personally. So the technical system cannot be highly regulating, certainly not highly automated. As Heydebrand and Noell (1973) point out, the professional resists the rationalization of his skills—their division into simply executed steps—because that makes them programmable by the technostructure, destroys his basis of autonomy, and drives the structure to the machine bureaucratic form.

Nor can the technical system be sophisticated. That would pull the professional into a closer working relationship with his colleagues and push him to a more distant one with his clients, driving the organization toward another structural configuration—the adhocratic form. The surgeon uses a scalpel, the accountant a pencil. Both must be sharp, but are otherwise simple and commonplace instruments; yet both allow their users to perform independently what can be exceedingly complex functions. More sophisticated instruments—such as the computer in the accounting firm or the coronary care unit in the hospital—reduce the professional's autonomy by forcing him to work in multidisciplinary teams, as he does in the Adhocracy. These teams are concerned in large part with the design, modification, and maintenance of the equipment; its operation, because that tends to be regulating, and often automated, impersonalizes the relationship between the professional and his clients. Thus, *in the pure form of the Professional Bureaucracy, the technology of the organization— its knowledge base—is sophisticated but its technical system—the set of instruments it uses to apply that knowledge base—is not.*

Thus, the prime example of the Professional Bureaucracy is the *personal service organization,* at least the one with complex, stable work. Schools and universities, consulting firms, law and accounting offices, social work agencies all rely on this structural configuration as long as they concentrate not on innovating in the solution of new problems, but on applying standard programs to well-defined ones. The same is true of hospitals, at least to the extent that their technical systems are simple. (In those areas that call for more sophisticated equipment—apparently a growing number, especially in teaching institutions—the hospital is driven toward a hybrid structure, with characteristics of the Adhocracy. The research function would also seem to drive it, and the university as well, toward the same hybrid, research being oriented more than clinical practice and teaching to innovation.[3] The same effect results from dynamic environmental conditions—again increasingly common in teaching hospitals. But all these forces are strongly mitigated by the hospital's overriding concern with safety. Only the tried and true can be used on regular patients. Institutions entrusted with the lives of their clients have a natural aversion to the looser, organic structures such as Adhocracy.)

A good deal of the service sector of contemporary society in fact applies standard programs to well-defined problems. Hence, the Professional Bureaucracy structure tends to predominate there. And with the enormous growth of this sector in the last few decades, we find that the Professional Bureaucracy has emerged as a major structural configuration.

So far, all of our examples have come from the service sector. But Professional Bureaucracies are found in manufacturing too, notably where the environment demands work that is complex yet stable, and the technical system is neither regulating nor sophisticated. This is the case of the *craft enterprise,* an important variant of the Professional Bureaucracy. Here the organization relies on skilled craftsmen who use relatively simple instruments to produce standard outputs. The very term "craftsman" implies a kind of professional who learns traditional skills through long apprentice training and then is allowed to practice them free of direct supervision. Craft enterprises seem typically to have tiny administrations—no technostructures and few managers, many of whom, in any event, work alongside the craftsmen.

Many craftsmen were eliminated by the Industrial Revolution. Their jobs—for example, the making of shoes—were rationalized, and so control over them passed from the workers who did them to the analysts who designed them. Small craft enterprises metamorphosed into large Machine Bureaucracies. But some craft industries remain, for example, fine glasswork and handmade pottery, portrait photography, and gastronomic cuisine.[4] In fact, as these examples indicate, the term "craft" has today come to be associated with functional art, handmade items that perform a function but are purchased for their aesthetic value.

There is at least one major industry that has remained largely in the craft stage, and that is construction. In a paper entitled "Bureaucratic and Craft Administration of Production: A Comparative Study," Stinchcombe (1959–60) contrasts mass production and construction firms, describing the latter much as we have described Professional Bureaucracy. He notes that professionalization of the labor force in the construction industry serves the same functions as bureaucratic administration in mass production industries" (p. 169). In construction, "work processes [are] governed by the worker in accordance with the empirical lore that makes up craft principles" (p. 170). As a result, few clerks are needed (20 percent of the administrative personnel, versus 53 percent in mass production, where they are used, Stinchcombe explains, to effect machine bureaucratic control), the communication system is less formalized, and less emphasis is placed on the hierarchy of authority. Stinchcombe also cites another study of the construction industry that noted "the low development of distinctly bureaucratic production control mechanisms, such as cost accounting, detailed scheduling, regularized reporting of work process, and standardized inspection of specific operations" (p. 182).[5]

The markets of the Professional Bureaucracy are often diversified. As noted earlier, these organizations often bring together groups of professionals from different specialties who serve different types of clients. The hospital includes gynecologists to serve women, pediatricians to serve children, and so on, while the university has its philosophy professors to teach those interested in general knowledge and its management professors for those in search of specific career skills. Hypothesis 11 would lead us to the conclusion that such market diversity encourages the use of the market basis for grouping the professionals. In fact, we have already seen this to be the case (although we also saw that the market basis for grouping turns out to be equivalent to the functional one in Professional Bureaucracies, as a result of the way in which professional services are selected).

Sometimes the markets of Professional Bureaucracies are diversified geographically, leading to a variant we call the *dispersed professional bureaucracy*. Here the problem of maintaining loyalty to the organization becomes magnified, since the professionals do their autonomous work in remote locations, far from the administrative structure. The Royal Canadian Mounted Police, for example, were dispersed across the Canadian west and north late last century to bring order to what were then lawless districts of the country. Once sent out, each Mountie was on his own. The same situation exists today in intelligence (spy) agencies, forest ranger services, and international con-

sulting firms. As a result, these organizations must rely extensively on training and indoctrination, especially the latter. The employees are selected carefully, trained extensively, and indoctrinated heavily—often by the organization itself—before they are sent out to the remote areas to perform their work. Thus, even on their own, the Mounties carried the norms and skills of the R.C.M.P. with them and so served it resolutely. Moreover, the employees of the dispersed professional bureaucracy are frequently brought back to the central headquarters for a fresh dose of indoctrination, and they are often rotated in their jobs to ensure that their loyalty remains with the organization and does not shift to the geographical area they serve. The U.S. Forest Rangers, for example, are recruited largely from the forestry schools—having already demonstrated a commitment to forests and a love of the outdoors—and are then further trained and indoctrinated, and, once on the job, are rotated from post to post. Both the rotation and indoctrination "facilitate communication between headquarters and the field by keeping loyalties and career interests centrally directed" as well as keeping "the foresters independent of private interests in the regions or communities in which they serve . . ." (Wilensky, 1967, pp. 59–60; see also Kaufman, 1960).

This chapter has stressed the role of training in the Professional Bureaucracy more than indoctrination. Indoctrination only emerged as important in this last variant. But there is another variant, the *missionary organization*—common in religious orders, charitable foundations (Sills, 1957), and the like, and sometimes found also in business firms (Perrow, 1970, pp. 166-170)–where indoctrination replaces training as the key design parameter. Because this organization has an attractive mission, and perhaps a distinguished history as well, its members also share a strong ideology—a set of norms about the goals and strategies the organization pursues. The members may come by this naturally, or they may have been indoctrinated into the ideology when they first joined. In any event, because every member of the organization can be trusted to pursue its main goals and strategies, there can be an extensive decentralization to the level of the single individual, resulting in a structure that in some ways resembles the Professional Bureaucracy.

The Professional Bureaucracy is also occasionally found as a hybrid structure. In our discussion of hospitals earlier, we alluded to a possible combination with characteristics of the Adhocracy which we can call the *professional bureaucracy/adhocracy.* Another hybrid—the *simple professional bureaucracy*—occurs when highly trained professionals practicing standard skills nevertheless take their lead from a strong, sometimes even autocratic, leader, as in the Simple Structure. Consider, for example, the following description of a symphony orchestra, an organization staffed with highly skilled musicians who play standard repertoires:

> An orchestra is not a democracy but a dictatorship. The interpretation and presentation of this complex repertoire cannot be pieced together as a kind of consensus among the musicians.
>
> Such a system has been tried out, notably in Russia in the 1920's, but the famous conductorless orchestra, Persimfans, lasted only a few years. There were countless long rehearsals while the musicians argued about the treatment of every passage, and any one of the members was given the democratic right, in turn, to lay down his instrument and listen to the effect from the hall.
>
> It was finally decided that it would be much more efficient, and less costly, to allow one man of recognized ability to impose his ideas upon the rest of the orchestra, a conclusion the rest of the European orchestras had reached more than a century earlier . . .
>
> I think it was one of Szell's musicians who was quoted as saying: "He's a sonovabitch, but he makes us play beyond ourselves."[6]

Finally, we might note briefly the effects of the contingency factors of power, notably fashion and the influence of the operators. Professionalism is a popular word among all kinds of identifiable specialists today; as a result, *Professional Bureaucracy is a highly fashionable structure*—and for good reason, since it is a very democratic one. Thus, it is to the advantage of every operator to make his job more professional—to enhance the skills it requires, to keep the analysts of the technostructure from rationalizing those skills, and to establish associations that set industry-wide standards to protect those skills. In these ways, the operator can achieve what always escapes him in the Machine Bureaucracy—control of his work and the decisions that affect it.

Some Issues Associated with Professional Bureaucracy

The Professional Bureaucracy is unique among the five structural configurations in answering two of the paramount needs of contemporary men and women. It is democratic, disseminating its power directly to its workers (at least those who are professional). And it provides them with extensive autonomy, freeing them even of the need to coordinate closely with their peers, and all of the pressures and politics that entails. Thus, the professional has the best of both worlds: he is attached to an organization, yet is free to serve his clients in his own way, constrained only by the established standards of his profession.

As a result, professionals tend to emerge as responsible and highly motivated individuals, dedicated to their work and the clients they serve. Unlike the Machine Bureaucracy that places barriers between the operator and the client, this structure removes them, allowing a personal relationship to develop. Here the technical and social systems can function in complete harmony.

Moreover, *autonomy allows the professionals to perfect their skills, free of interference.* They repeat the same complex programs time after time, forever reducing the uncertainty until they get them just about perfect, like the Provençal potter who has spent his career perfecting the glazes he applies to identical pots. The professional's thought processes are "convergent"—vascular surgeon Spencer (1976) refers to them as deductive reasoning. Spencer quotes approvingly the bridge aficionado who stood behind champion Charles Goren during a three-day tournament and concluded: "He didn't do anything I couldn't do, except he didn't make any mistakes" (p. 1181). That captures nicely the secure feelings of professionals and their clients in Professional Bureaucracies. The Provençal potter expects few surprises when he opens his kiln; so, too, do Dr. Spencer's patients when they climb on to his operating table. They know the program has been executed so many times—by this surgeon as well as by the many whose experiences he has read about in the journals—that the possibility of mistakes has been minimized. Hospitals do not even get to execute new programs on regular patients until they have been thoroughly tested and approved by the profession. So the client of the Professional Bureaucracy can take satisfaction in the knowledge that the professional about to serve him will draw on vast quantities of experience and skill, will apply them in a perfected, not an experimental procedure, and will likely be highly motivated in performing that procedure.

But in these same characteristics of democracy and autonomy lie all the major problems of the Professional Bureaucracy. *For there is virtually no control of the work outside the profession, no way to correct deficiencies that the professionals themselves choose to overlook.* What they tend to overlook are the major problems of coordination, of discretion, and of innovation that arise in these structures.

Problems of Coordination

The Professional Bureaucracy can coordinate effectively only by the standardization of skills. Direct supervision and mutual adjustment are resisted as direct infringements on the professional's autonomy, in one case by administrators, in the other by peers. And standardization of work processes and of outputs are ineffective for this complex work with its ill-defined outputs. But *the standardization of skills is a loose coordinating mechanism at best, failing to cope with many of the needs that arise in the Professional Bureaucracy.*

There is, first of all, the need for coordination between the professional and the support staff. To the professional, that is simply resolved: he gives the orders. But that only catches the support staffer between two systems of power pulling in different ways, the vertical power of line authority above him, and the horizontal power of professional expertise to his side.

Perhaps more severe are the coordination problems between the professionals themselves. Unlike Machine Bureaucracies, Professional Bureaucracies are not integrated entities. They are collections of individuals who join to draw on the common resources and support services but otherwise want to be left alone. As long as the pigeonholing process works effec-

tively, they can be. But that process can never be so good that contingencies do not fall in the cracks between the standard programs. The world is a continuous intertwined system. Slicing it up, although necessary to comprehend it, inevitably distorts it. Needs that fall at the margin or that overlap two categories tend to get forced—artificially—into one category or another. In contemporary medicine, for instance, the human body is treated not so much as one integrated system with interdependent parts, as a collection of loosely coupled organs that correspond to the different specialties. For the patient whose malady slots nicely into one of the specialties, problems of coordination do not arise. For others—for example, the patient who falls between psychiatry and internal medicine—it means repeated transfers in search of the right department, a time-consuming process when time is critical. In universities the pigeonholing process can be equally artificial, as in the case of the professor interested in the structure of production systems who fell between the operations and organizational behavior departments of his business school and so was denied tenure.

The pigeonholing process, in fact, emerges as the source of a great deal of the conflict of the Professional Bureaucracy. Much political blood is spilled in the continual reassessment of contingencies, imperfectly conceived, in terms of programs, artificially distinguished.

Problems of Discretion

The assumption underlying the design of the Professional Bureaucracy is that the pigeonholing process contains all of the uncertainty in single professional jobs. As we saw above, that assumption often proves false to the detriment of the organization's performance. But even where it works, problems arise. For it focuses all the discretion in the hands of single professionals, whose complex skills, no matter how standardized, require the exercise of considerable judgment. That is, perhaps, appropriate for professionals who are competent and conscientious. Unfortunately not all of them are; and *the professional bureaucratic structure cannot easily deal with professionals who are either incompetent or unconscientious.*

No two professionals are equally skilled. So the client who is forced to choose among them—to choose in ignorance, since he seeks professional help precisely because he lacks the specialized knowledge to help himself—is exposed to a kind of Russian Roulette, almost literally so in the case of medicine, where single decisions can mean life or death. But that is inevitable: little can be done aside from using the very best screening procedures for applicants to the training schools.

Of greater concern is the unconscientious professional—the one who refuses to update his skills after graduation, who cares more for his income than his clients, or who becomes so enamored with his skills that he forgets about the real needs of his clients. This last case represents a means-ends inversion common in Professional Bureaucracies, different from that found in Machine Bureaucracies but equally serious. In this case, the professional confuses the needs of his clients with the skills he has to offer them. He simply concentrates on the program that he favors—perhaps because he does it best or simply enjoys doing it most—to the exclusion of all the others. This presents no problem as long as only those clients in need of that favorite program are directed his way. But should other clients slip in, trouble ensues. Thus, we have the psychiatrists who think that all patients (indeed, all people) need psychoanalysis, the consulting firms prepared to design the same planning system for all their clients, no matter how dynamic their environments, the professors who use the lecture method for classes of 500 students or 5, the social workers who feel the compulsion to bring power to the people even when the people do not want it.

Dealing with this means-ends inversion is impeded by the difficulty of measuring the outputs of professional work. When psychiatrists cannot even define the words "cure" or "healthy," how are they to prove that psychoanalysis is better for manic-depressives than chemical therapy would be? When no one has been able to measure the learning that takes place in the classroom, how can it be demonstrated with reliability that lectures are better or worse than seminars or, for that matter, than staying home and reading. That is one reason why the obvious solution to the problems of discretion—censure by the professional association—is seldom used. Another is that professionals are notoriously reluctant to act against

their own, to wash their dirty linen in public, so to speak. In extreme cases, they will so act—certain behavior is too callous to ignore. But these instances are relatively rare. They do no more than expose the tip of the iceberg of misguided discretion.

Discretion not only enables some professionals to ignore the needs of their clients; it also encourages many of them to ignore the needs of the organization. Professionals in these structures do not generally consider themselves part of a team. To many, the organization is almost incidental, a convenient place to practice their skills. They are loyal to their profession, not to the place where they happen to practice it. But the organization has need for loyalty, too—to support its own strategies, to staff its administrative committees, to see it through conflicts with the professional association. Cooperation, as we saw earlier, is crucial to the functioning of the administrative structure. Yet, as we also saw earlier, professionals resist it furiously. Professors hate to show up for curriculum meetings; they simply do not wish to be dependent on each other. One can say that they know each other only too well!

Problems of Innovation

In these structures, major innovation also depends on cooperation. Existing programs can be perfected by individual specialists. But new ones necessarily cut across existing specialties—in essence, they require a rearrangement of the pigeonholes—and so call for interdisciplinary efforts. As a result, the reluctance of the professionals to work cooperatively with each other translates itself into problems of innovation.

Like the Machine Bureaucracy, the Professional Bureaucracy is an inflexible structure, well suited to producing its standard outputs but ill-suited to adapting to the production of new ones. All bureaucracies are geared to stable environments; they are performance structures designed to perfect programs for contingencies that can be predicted, not problem solving ones designed to create new programs for needs that have never before been encountered.

The problems of innovation in the Professional Bureaucracy find their roots in convergent thinking, in the deductive reasoning of the professional who sees the specific situation in terms of the general concept. In the Professional Bureaucracy this means that new problems are forced into old pigeonholes. The doctoral student in search of an interdisciplinary degree—for, after all, isn't the highest university degree meant to encourage the generation of new knowledge—inevitably finds himself forced back into the old departmental mode. "It must be a D.B.A. or a D.Ed.; we don't offer educational administration here." Nowhere are the effects of this deductive reasoning better illustrated than in Spencer's (1976) comments that "All patients developing significant complications or death among our three hospitals . . . are reported to a central office with a narrative description of the sequence of events, with reports varying in length from a third to an entire page," and that six to eight of these cases are discussed in the one-hour weekly "mortality-morbidity" conferences, including presentation of it by the surgeon and "questions and comments" by the audience (p. 1181). An "entire" page and ten minutes of discussion for cases with "significant complications"! Maybe enough to list the symptoms and slot them into pigeonholes; hardly enough even to begin to think about creative solutions. As Lucy once told Charlie Brown, great art cannot be done in half an hour; it takes at least forty-five minutes!

The fact is that great art and innovative problem solving require *inductive* reasoning, that is, the induction of new general concepts or programs from particular experiences. That kind of thinking is *divergent*—it breaks away from old routines or standards rather than perfecting existing ones. And that flies in the face of everything the Professional Bureaucracy is designed to do.

So it should come as no surprise that Professional Bureaucracies and the professional associations that control their procedures tend to be conservative bodies, hesitant to change their well-established ways. Whenever an entrepreneurial member takes up the torch of innovation, great political clashes inevitably ensue. Even in the Machine Bureaucracy, once the managers of the strategic apex finally recognize the need for change, they are able to force it down the hierarchy. In the Professional Bureaucracy, with operator autonomy and bottom-up decision making, and in the professional

association with its own democratic procedures, power for strategic change is diffuse. Everybody must agree on the change, not just a few managers or professional representatives. So change comes slowly and painfully, after much political intrigue and shrewd maneuvering by the professional and administrative entrepreneurs.

As long as the environment remains stable, the Professional Bureaucracy encounters no problem. It continues to perfect its skills and the given system of pigeonholes that slots them. But dynamic conditions call for change—new skills, new ways to slot them, and creative, cooperative efforts on the part of multidisciplinary teams of professionals.

Dysfunctional Responses

What responses do the problems of coordination, discretion, and innovation evoke? Most commonly, those outside the profession—clients, nonprofessional administrators, members of the society at large and their representatives in government—see the problems as resulting from a lack of external control of the professional, and his profession. So they do the obvious: try to control the work with one of the other coordinating mechanisms. Specifically, they try to use direct supervision, standardization of work processes, or standardization of outputs.

Direct supervision typically means imposing an intermediate level of supervision, preferably with a narrow "span of control"—in keeping with the tenets of the classical concepts of authority—to watch over the professionals. That may work in cases of gross negligence. The sloppy surgeon or the professor who misses too many classes can be "spoken to" or ultimately perhaps fired. But specific professional activities—complex in execution and vague in results—are difficult to control by anyone other than the professionals themselves. So the administrator detached from the work and bent on direct supervision is left nothing to do except engage in bothersome exercises. As in the case of certain district supervisors who sit between one Montreal school board and its schools and, according to the reports of a number of principals, spend time telephoning them at 4:59 on Friday afternoons to ensure they have not left early for the weekend. The imposition of such intermediate levels of supervision stems from the assumption that professional work can be controlled, like any other, in a top-down manner, an assumption that has proven false again and again.

Likewise, the other forms of standardization, instead of achieving control of the professional work, often serve merely to impede and discourage the professionals. And for the same reasons—the complexity of the work and the vagueness of its outputs. Complex work processes cannot be formalized by rules and regulations, and vague outputs cannot be standardized by planning and control systems. Except in misguided ways, which program the wrong behaviors and measure the wrong outputs, forcing the professionals to play the machine bureaucratic game—satisfying the standards instead of serving the clients. Back to the old means-ends inversion. Like the policeman in Chicago who described to Studs Terkel (1972) the effects of various such standards on his work:

> My supervisor would say, "We need two policy arrests, so we can be equal with the other areas." So we go out and hunt for a policy operator. . . .
>
> A vice officer spends quite a bit of time in court. You learn the judges, the things they look for. You become proficient in testifying. You change your testimony, you change the facts. You switch things around 'cause you're trying to get convictions. . . .
>
> Certain units in the task force have developed a science around stopping your automobile. These men know it's impossible to drive three blocks without committing a traffic violation. We've got so many rules on the books. These police officers use these things to get points and also hustle for money. The traffic law is a fat book. He knows if you don't have two lights on your license plate, that's a violation. If you have a crack in your windshield, that's a violation. If your muffler's dragging, that's a violation. He knows all these little things.
>
> So many points for a robbery, so many points for a man having a gun. When they go to the scene and the man with the gun has gone, they'll lock up somebody anyway, knowing he's not the one. The record says, "Locked up two people for UUW"—unlawful use of weapons. The report will say, "When we got there, we saw these guys and they looked suspicious." They'll get a point even if the case is thrown out of court. The arrest is all that counts (pp. 137–140).

Graphic illustrations of the futility of trying to control work that is essentially professional in nature. Similar things happen when accountants try to control the management consulting arms of their firms—"obedience is stressed as an end in itself because the CPA as administrator is not able to judge the nonaccountant expert on the basis of that expert's knowledge" (Montagna, 1968:144). And in school systems when the government technostructure believes it can program the work of the teacher, as in that of East Germany described proudly to this author by a government planner, where each day every child in the country ostensibly opens the same book to the same page. The individual needs of the students—slow learners and fast, rural and urban—as well as the individual styles of the teachers have to be subordinated to the neatness of the system.

The fact is that complex work cannot be effectively performed unless it comes under the control of the operator who does it. Society may have to control the overall expenditures of its Professional Bureaucracies—to keep the lid on them—and to legislate against the most callous kinds of professional behavior. But too much external control of the professional work itself leads, according to Hypothesis 14, to centralization and formalization of the structure, in effect driving the Professional Bureaucracy to Machine Bureaucracy. The decision-making power flows from the operators to the managers, and on to the analysts of the technostructure. The effect of this is to throw the baby out with the bathwater. Technocratic controls do not improve professional-type work, nor can they distinguish between responsible and irresponsible behavior—they constrain both equally. That may, of course, be appropriate for organizations in which responsible behavior is rare. But where it is not—presumably the majority of cases—*technocratic controls only serve to dampen professional conscientiousness.* As Sorensen and Sorensen (1974) found, the more machine bureaucratic the large public accounting firms, the more they experienced conflict and job dissatisfaction.

Controls also upset the delicate relationship between the professional and his client, a relationship predicated on unimpeded personal contact between the two. Thus, Cizanckas, a police chief, notes that the police officer at the bottom of the pecking order in the "paramilitary structure is more than willing, in turn, to vent his frustration on the lawbreaker" (paraphrased by Hatvany, 1976, p. 73). The controls remove the responsibility for service from the professional and place it in the administrative structure, where it is of no use to the client. It is not the government that teaches the student, not even the school system or the school itself; it is not the hospital that delivers the baby, not the police force that apprehends the criminal, not the welfare department that helps the distraught family. These things are done by the individual professional. If that professional is incompetent, no plan or rule fashioned in the technostructure, no order from an administrator can ever make him competent. But such plans, rules, and orders can impede the competent professional from providing his service effectively. At least rationalization in the Machine Bureaucracy leaves the client with inexpensive outputs. In the case of professional work, it leaves him with impersonal, ineffective service.

Furthermore, the incentive to perfect, even to innovate—the latter weak in the best of times in professional bureaucracy—can be reduced by external controls. In losing control over their own work, the professionals become passive, like the operators of the Machine Bureaucracy. Even the job of professional administrator—never easy—becomes extremely difficult with a push for external control. In school systems, for example, the government looks top-down to the senior managers to implement its standards, while the professionals look bottom-up to them to resist the standards. The strategic apex gets caught between a government technostructure hungry for control and an operating core hanging on to its autonomy for dear life. No one gains in the process.

Are there then no solutions to a society concerned about its Professional Bureaucracies? Financial control of Professional Bureaucracies and legislation against irresponsible professional behavior are obviously necessary. But beyond that, must the professional be left with a blank check, free of public accountability? Solutions are available, but they grow from a recognition of professional work for what it is. *Change in the Professional Bureaucracy does not sweep in from new administrators taking office to announce major reforms, nor from government technostructures intent on bringing the professionals under control. Rather, change seeps in, by the slow process of changing the professionals—changing who can enter the profession, what they learn in its professional schools (ideals as well as skills and knowledge), and thereafter how willing they are to upgrade their skills.* Where such changes are resisted, society may be best off to call on the professionals' sense of responsibility to serve the public, or, failing that, to bring pressures on the professional associations rather than on the Professional Bureaucracies.

Notes

1. For an excellent related example—a comparison of the prison as a Machine Bureaucracy (custodial-oriented) and as a Professional Bureaucracy (treatment-oriented)—see Cressey (1958; or 1965, pp. 1044–1048). Van de Ven and Delbecq (1974) also discuss this trichotomy in terms of "systematized" programs, which specify both means and ends in detail, "discretionary" programs, which specify ends and a repertoire of means but require the operator to select the means in terms of the ends, and "developmental" programs, for highly variable tasks, which may specify general ends but not the means to achieve them.

2. Boland (1973) finds them also to be more democratic, which seems to stem from their being more formalized: "The faculty in the larger institutions are much more likely to develop a strong faculty government. Those in the smaller institutions, on the other hand, are more often subject to the decrees of administrative officials" (p. 636). This seems akin to the situation Crozier described, where the operators of large bureaucratic organizations force in rules to protect their interests. But that seems to work more to the operators' advantage in Professional rather than in Machine Bureaucracies, in the former case the rules setting up the means for true self-government, in the latter, serving only to protect the workers from the arbitrary whims of their bosses.

3. However, Kuhn's (1970) description of the practice of scientific research gives the distinct impression that most of the time—namely during periods of what he calls "normal" science, when the researchers are essentially elaborating and perfecting a given "paradigm"—the professional bureaucratic structure might be equally appropriate. Only

during scientific "revolutions" should the adhocratic one clearly be more relevant.

4. Restaurants can be viewed as falling into the manufacturing or service sectors, depending on whether one focuses on the preparation of the food or on the serving of it.

5. Stinchcombe also ascribes some of these structural characteristics to the dynamic nature of the construction industry's environment, which pushes the firms to adopt the organic features of Simple Structure or Adhocracy.

6. From "MSD Crisis Plus ça change" by E. McLean, Canada Wide Feature Service in the Montreal Star, December 4,1976. Used with permission.

CHAPTER 5

EMERGING DEVELOPMENTS IN POSTSECONDARY ORGANIZATION THEORY AND RESEARCH: FRAGMENTATION OR INTEGRATION

MARVIN W. PETERSON

ABSTRACT: Developments in theory and research on postsecondary institutions as organizations are proceeding in many different directions, threatening to fragment this critical area of research. This article examines the major developments and identifies dilemmas in theory development research methods, organizational behavior context, relating theory to practice, and identifying professional colleagues. These areas need to be understood and addressed to assure the continued, integrated development of postsecondary organization theory and research.

Reflecting on the emerging developments in organization theory and research in postsecondary education over the past decade suggests a major concern: There is a substantial tension between the current tendency to fragment and proliferate knowledge about organizational behavior in postsecondary education and the need to integrate it. Opening this topic brings to mind a few past warnings by some astute observers of colleges and universities.

In commenting on universities, Alfred North Whitehead (1928) said, "the heart of the matter is beyond all regulation" (p. 638).

Frederick Rudolph (1962) concludes his history of the *American College and University* with the observation that change in higher education is best typified as "drift, reluctant accommodation, and belated recognition that, while no one was looking, change had in fact taken place" (p. 491).

In a more current practical observation, Kingman Brewster (1965) suggests "the real trouble with attempting to devise a strategy, let alone a plan, for a university is that basically we (faculty) are all anarchists—significant thought, art, and action must have creativity. Creativity by definition defies predictions plan" (p. 45).

For those of us who think our work in postsecondary organizational behavior can make a difference, these observations should give reason to pause. Yet it is precisely these complexities and the variety of students, learning and research styles, faculty and administrative behavior, academic and administrative structures, external demands and pressures, and institutional roles, missions, structures, processes, and characteristics that challenge us to understand the patterns of organizational behavior in these institutions with their strong fragmenting tendencies. The organizing challenge is to preserve the positive aspects of that variety and richness while assuring that we accomplish our mutual educational and academic purposes and to make each college or university more effective. The dilemma is not whether to organize, but how to organize, to what degree, and for what purpose. The challenge of postsecondary organizational theory and research is to try to understand what holds together these fascinating institutions as organizations and what makes them more effective.

An Image of Adolescence

Before examining some of the recent developments and the dilemmas they raise, it is useful to recall that this is still an emerging scholarly arena. For example, the larger field of organizational behavior is almost entirely a post World War II phenomenon. It has grown rapidly as an interdisciplinary arena of study and has spawned graduate degree programs, departments, schools, and professional associations of scholars and practitioners. It has also produced an extensive literature and some highly sophisticated journals on organizational theory, research, and application. Indeed, Pfeffer (1982) describes it as a "thicket."

Although not yet of thicket proportions, the literature on organizational theory and research in postsecondary education is also growing rapidly. Using a human "developmental" rather than a "thicket" image, one might mark 1963 as the beginning of "infancy" of our interest in postsecondary organizational theory and research. In separate articles, McConnell (1963) of Berkeley and Henderson (1963) of Michigan decried the paucity of literature and research about the organization and administration of higher education. In the decade following, numerous practical and conceptual writings and some serious research efforts emerged.

By 1974, one might describe the area as past "early childhood" and entering "preadolescence." In that year, a comprehensive review of the research literature on "Organization and Administration in Higher Education" for Volume II of *Review of Research in Education* highlighted some of the theoretical and conceptual bases of the research, assessed the sophistication of the research, and attempted to identify major gaps (Peterson, 1974). An initial list of 500 publications was quickly reduced to less than 200, which were research based. That review noted that the quantity of research had increased substantially after 1970, that it was attracting researchers from several social science fields who were doing some excellent work, and that most major issues of the late 1960s and early 1970s were receiving attention. However, major concerns were noted and recommendations focused on the following:

1. The limited development or use of theoretical models or concepts from related disciplines and the need for greater emphasis in this area.

2. Studies were too often exploratory case studies or descriptive surveys. Longitudinal, before and after, field experiments, and comparative studies were almost nonexistent. Studies used exploratory as a rationale for avoiding conceptualization and/or quantification. Even quantitative surveys seldom used bivariate statistical analyses and ignored multivariate or causal path approaches, even when data might have allowed. There was a need for greater sophistication in research strategy, design, and methodology.

3. Replication studies and use of reliably constructed instruments on different populations to extend generalizability of any findings had seldom occurred and was needed.

4. Since the most sophisticated theoretical formulations and sophisticated designs came from scholars with disciplinary backgrounds, a professional network for involving them was needed.

The most recent decade has been one of substantial progress. Research that examines the organizational behavior of colleges and universities at the individual, group or process, organization, and interorganization of organization environment level has expanded both in quantity and sophistication. A formal review such as the one 10 years ago would be extensive. This paper only examines the high points and scans the major theoretical, methodological, and application developments and dilemmas that face us today. The current stage seems to be one of "advanced adolescence"—maturing rapidly, capable of extremes of sophistication and foolishness, and alternately confident and uncertain. The current high level of productivity is generating a wide array of theoretical, methodological, and application activities that create a tension that can either lead to proliferation and fragmentation or a new synthesis and integration.

As an "adolescent," the research area is struggling with problems of identity and commitment—what is the field? Where are developments in postsecondary organizational theory and research methods going and do we want to go there? It is struggling with the issue of relevance—are we dealing with important issues and relating theory to practice (or viceversa) in constructive ways? Also, it is struggling with the issue of legitimacy—what professional peer group provides intellectual criticism and guidance to direct these efforts? An overview of developments in five areas—theory, research, content, relation to practice, and peers—poses some interesting images and dilemmas to stimulate discussion about where we should go.

Because organizational behavior has few bounds, these comments focus primarily on organizational level phenomenon, that is, where the entire college or university or major segment of it is dealt with as an organization. Also, because the literature is growing rapidly, the attempt is not to summarize what we have learned but rather to ask: How is the area developing?

On Theory Development

Since the 1974 review that found limited use of theoretical concepts and models in higher education, the area has exploded. At that time there were three basic models of organization (six, if one includes their derivatives): bureaucracy or formal-rational and goal models; collegial and professional community models; and political and public bureaucracy models. These were basically internally oriented and used to analyze the pervading governance issues. In the intervening decade, conceptual discussions and research in postsecondary education now includes open systems, environmental contingency, organizational life cycle, and strategic models that reflect the increased concern for external developments and forces. Task-technology and information or resource models reflect our growing concern with the impact those changes have on us. The list now includes a variety of emergent social system

models. Temporary adaptive, loosely coupled, organized anarchy, and social network models reflect primarily internal models that attempt to account for some of the postsecondary education special characteristics. The cultural model, which Peters and Waterman (1982) have popularized, has also reemerged in higher education. Clark's (1970) *Distinctive Colleges* and Riesman, Gusfeld, and Gamson's (1970) study of *Academic Values and Mass Education* introduced us to the concern for culture 15 years ago. More recently, Dill (1982) has examined our changing institutional value systems at professional meetings, and researchers like Bess have been challenging us at professional meetings to examine the larger values that postsecondary institutions and educators should address. Closely related to the study of organizational cultures and values are proponents of the natural study of organizational phenomenon—an antimodel perspective. Finally, there are interorganizational models: Systems of organizations, organizational networks, organizational ecology, and industry models are being used to examine broader patterns of relationships among postsecondary organizations. (See Table 5-1.)

The list is not comprehensive and includes only organizational level models. The intent is not to examine each model; rather, the character of the list itself prompts some observations and raises issues about where we are going in the expansion of models and frameworks.

First, and perhaps most important, the pre-1974 models are what Pfeffer (1982) classified as "internal, purposive" models; they focus on a managed set of activities that impact on the organizations' performance—they see organizations as self directed. The recent models give more credence to technology, the environment, or the emergent social structure as the major determinants of action. (The distinction between "internal, purposive" and "emergent and social structure" will be discussed later.)

Second, as it did a decade ago, the list consists primarily of "borrowed" models. Admittedly, many have been distorted or modified to fit our postsecondary context, but only two—Cohen and March's (1974) model of organized anarchy and Weick's (1976) loosely coupled notion—were generated primarily to reflect the postsecondary context. Even those, however, have roots in other settings because neither are

Table 5-1	
Some Organizational Models in Postsecondary Education	
Internal purposive:	Formal-rational/goal Collegial/professional community Political/public bureaucracy
Environmental:	Open systems Contingency Strategic Life cycle
Technology:	Task/techno-structure Information system/resource models
Emergent social systems:	Temporary adaptive Organized anarchy Loosely coupled Social networks Organizational culture/values Organizational learning Natural/anti-models
Interorganizational:	Systems of organizations Organizational networks Ecology models Industry model

new concepts. It is ironic that in postsecondary education, which many argue is unique, so little attention is given to theory generation and so much reliance is placed on borrowing models from institutional settings. Clearly, theory generation deserves greater attention.

A third observation on the list of models has to do with the fragmented nature of the models themselves and with how one deductively builds theory.[1] Borrowing models has led to a multitude of models that focus on different phenomena. The models also vary in normative, analytic, or predictive purpose and often have different assumptions about explanatory forces (e.g., internal or external, guided or emergent). The concern is that little attention has been given either to *mapping* the organizational territory covered by these borrowed theories or to *examining* comparatively the nature of each model. The need to relate our theoretical models to organizational phenomena (the territory) to identify gaps is noted by Bess (1983) in his edited volume of *Review of Higher Education*.

The direct comparison of models dealing with a similar phenomenon is also useful to highlight their differing perspectives and content. Baldridge's (1971) comparison of bureau-

cratic, collegial, and political models over a decade ago covered the organizational and governance models in vogue at the time. More recently, we have many limited comparisons of models (or submodels) or concepts that focus on only one level or type of organizational phenomenon—for example, Cameron's (1984) comparison of four models of organizational adaption (population ecology, life cycles, strategic choice, and symbolic action) in the *Journal of Higher Education*. But many questions remain. For example, how does the loose-coupling model compare with a social network model? Is a coupling element the same as or different from a linkage element? Mapping our theories in relation to organizational phenomena and analytic comparison of models offers useful ways of reducing fragmentation and/or discovering overlaps; however, a comprehensive scheme for comparing all our models still needs considerable conceptual thought and effort.

The final observation is our failure to examine the "appropriateness" or "adequacy" of each of our borrowed models or constructs, evidently because they appear to be intuitively logical or seem to make sense. In much of the conceptual literature and research, writers have a tendency to become advocates of the model they are discussing. They seldom ask critical analytic questions. Is the model an analytic framework, a normative theory, or an explanatory or predictive theory? Does the model satisfy simple criteria for a good theory? Five come to mind (Pfeffer, 1982, p. 38). First, is there "clarity" in the phenomenon being examined and definition of key concepts and variables? Are conceptual and operational definitions of variables clear? For example, one still sees influence defined and measured in different ways, yet discussed without recognizing the differences. Second, is the model "parsimonious" in the number of variables it contains (or loaded with inexplicable contingencies)? Third, does the theory have a "logical coherence"? For example, Weick (1976) proposed "loose-coupling" as an idea and an analytic perspective that was yet to be defined, evaluated, and developed. However, several researchers have discussed it as if it were already an explanatory theory rather than challenging it (Lutz, 1982). Fourth, do we ask if the model exhibited "consistency" with real data and whether the conditions or "contingencies" are present? For example, organizational anarchy is a popular way of explaining some of our less predictable behavior but others have questioned its usefulness when "organizational slack," one of its key assumptions, is declining or not present. In a recent analysis of the review and reorganization of the biological sciences at Berkeley, Trow (1984) suggests it is not as useful as a more rational paradigm.

A fifth criterion for theory is "refutability." Do we attempt to refute or disconfirm our models? It prompts comments at two levels. First, as research has accumulated using some of these models or their key concepts, there has not been an inductive, balanced, and systematic examination of the convergent or divergent evidence for or against a particular model. Because so much organizational research in higher education is problem oriented, the research reviews have focused on categorizing the research around issues addressed, patterns of descriptive findings, types of institutions studied, methods used, and so forth—not on evidence converging with or diverging with a model or its prediction. There are few scholarly outlets for reviews of this nature, and it also appears that critical, comparative analysis of research findings is not a high priority that postsec-

ondary organizational researchers have emphasized. Many review articles and even entire books report only findings and insights supporting their argument for their model and do not systematically weigh the counter evidence. An exemplary exception is the research on attrition in which several careful research scholars have examined quantitative studies in a systematic and balanced fashion around theoretical frameworks (Pascarella & Terenzini, 1979; Tinto, 1982). But even this group has not used meta-analysis to statistically test the convergence of predictions and theory across studies.

The second concern about refuting or disconfirming the research models is that although organizational research is now more likely to be theoretically or conceptually oriented and to develop a hypothesis, it is often based on one model. The studies are designed either to support or not support the theory. Seldom do we use what Platt (1964) referred to in *Science* as "strong inference"—testing different models or competing hypotheses in the same study. Although she did not use statistical tests, Chaffee's (1984) recent study comparing adaptive vs. interpretive strategies in institutions that had suffered decline is one example of this approach.

This abbreviated overview of the organizational theories and models portrays it as a *muddled* arena and highlights one of our developmental dilemmas. Should postsecondary organizational research focus on theory *generation* that can more adequately reflect the uniqueness of higher education? Should it focus on *systematic synthesis* of the many theoretical models and extensive research to establish if there is more convergence or less fragmentation than appears? Should it focus on systematic model *testing*, which is the most convincing way to establish results but which is time consuming, expensive, and of limited practical interest? I shall return to the dilemmas later.

On Research Developments

In 1974, postsecondary organizational research was characterized as primarily descriptive surveys or exploratory case studies. Although these are still present, research strategies, methods, and techniques have also expanded and become more sophisticated. Before noting some of the changes, it is useful to note what has not changed. There is still little or no use of experimental research strategies and primary emphasis remains on field research. Few longitudinal, prepost, or quasi-experimental designs are noted. Some simulation strategies have been tried, but mostly in quantitative computer simulations. Cohen, March, and Olsen's (1972) test of their organized anarchy model and the many resource flow and forecasting simulations developed in the mid-1970s are most notable. Interestingly, behavioral simulations that have been used to model organizational behavior in other professional settings have received little use. The changes, on the other hand, are most instructive and are a product of our changing models, the conditions affecting higher education, and our increasing research sophistication.

First, comparative case studies that combine both structured qualitative and quantitative methods appear to be used more often. This enhances the opportunity to validate variables and causal patterns, enhances generalizability, and in some instances allows sophisticated statistical comparisons and even multivariate analysis. Mortimer's (1979) studies of resource decline processes emphasize content analysis of documents and interviews from several institutions, whereas Baldridge's (1979) study of the impact of management systems in several liberal arts colleges uses both qualitative and quantitative approaches for making comparisons.

Second, more large survey studies now incorporate institutional characteristics along with individual survey results and have led to enriched analysis examining the effects of individual and organizational variables. Baldridge's (1978) extensive study of governance in the mid to late 1970s, which produced numerous studies of different governance issues, is an example. Both the comparative case studies and large-scale surveys have on occasion used complex index building and even causal path modeling.

Third, there has been some increase in the use of standardized data bases of institutional characteristics for secondary analysis in large-scale studies. Birnbaum's (1983) study of changing patterns of institutional diversity and Zammuto's (1984) study of shifting patterns of liberal arts colleges and their enrollment are examples that draw on the HEGIS data base for an ecological analysis of our institutions.

Fourth, out of the renewed emphasis on organizational culture and the models reflecting less formal, more emergent phenomena (loose-coupling, organized anarchy, natural models, etc.) has come a substantial interest in less structured qualitative methods. Strategies such as content analysis of documents and interviews, use of unobtrusive measures, and ethnographic and phenomenological approaches appear to be used more frequently.

Large-scale studies that combine a thorough synthesis of research, carefully develop models and variables, employ institutional surveys with comparative case studies, and use both quantitative and qualitative methods are still rare. Cameron's (1983) current series of studies of effectiveness, Chaffee's (1984) studies of strategic management, and Peterson's (1978) study of the impact of black students on predominantly white colleges are examples. Such studies are expensive, time consuming, and require long-term commitments. Unfortunately, funding for such large-scale research has declined and is seldom available.

These observations on research strategies and methods highlight the fact that organizational research in higher education is becoming a complex "methodological maze" that is increasingly sophisticated and raises the second dilemma: Do we emphasize larger scale *quantitative* studies that yield greater generalizability and potential for statistical modeling but are expensive and uncertain, or *intensive qualitative* studies that may be more helpful in generating new theory and new ideas?

Organizational Behavior: The Contextual Debate

The previous theoretical and methodological dilemmas are a reflection of a debate that has been raging in the larger realm of organizational behavior for the past 5 years. Since the advances in postsecondary education have both been borrowed from and lag the developments in organizational behavior, it can be useful to examine that debate briefly. In an exaggerated form, it can be posed as a dialectic between two extreme positions or paradigms, as an argument about basic philosophical and metaphysical assumptions: What constitutes reality in organizations (the ontological issue)? How do we gain knowledge about them (the epistemological issue)? What are our assumptions about causation (the teleological dimension)? (See Table 5-2.)

Stated simply: The first is variously called the "Traditional," "Conservative," or "Social Fact" paradigm (Cummings, 1981; March, 1982; Meryl, 1981). It views organizational elements as objective, accepts them as positive facts, and is concerned with predicting events. The major focus is on structures, observable behaviors and organizational elements, and respondents' attitudes and self reports. Theories are posed in terms of how one set of variables varies with others, and the concern is to test them. The methodologies are primarily reductionist and quantitative in nature.

The second, the "Cultural," "Radical," or "Social Definition" paradigm views organizational elements as those that are subjective and must be interpreted, primarily by the organizational actors themselves. It is more concerned with diagnosis or final causes. The major focus is on emergent processes and dynamics. Theories are process theories, and the concern is mostly with development of theory. However, some supporters of this view reject the notion of any theoretical models and recommend describing or auditing the phenomenon under study. The methodologies tend to be more wholistic, viewing the entire context of organizational behavior and making more extensive use of qualitative research methods.

Setting aside the externally oriented and technological organizational models noted earlier, the distinction, although not as clear or sharp, has emerged in our postsecondary models. For example, prior to 1974 the formal-rational, political, and collegial models more closely fit the traditional paradigm. They all suggest that objective phenomena can be used to explain events and that institutions can be managed or intentionally directed if one understands the formal, political, or collegial patterns. All have been the basis of research using primarily statistical or other forms of objective analysis based on survey data of attitude and perceptions, on measures of individual and institutional characteristics, and on content of documents and structured interviews.

On the other hand, the more recent models such as social networks, loose-coupling, organizational learning, and examining institutions as cultures reject the more intentional and rational assumptions of the traditional models, and they often criticize their failure to account for much of what happens in higher education. These models choose to focus on understanding how people in higher education interpret events, how they are influenced by the setting and the content of events, and how they ascribe meaning to them. The focus is on the examina-

Table 5-2

Two Cultures of Organizational Theory and Research

Paradigm:	Traditional, Conservative or Social Fact	Cultural, Radical, or Social Definition
Elements of Reality:	Objective	Subjective
View of Knowledge:	Positivism	Interpretive
Causation:	Predictive	Diagnostic, Final Cause
Content Focus:	Structures, Patterns	Emergent Processes, Dynamics
Use of Theory:	Variance Testing	Process or Developmental
Research Design:	Planned	Audit
Methodology:	Reductionist	Wholistic
Measurement:	Quantitative	Qualitative

tion and diagnosis of behavior and how processes emerge or are shaped. Their methodologies tend to rely more on ethnography (intensive, anthropological case studies), in-depth interviews and participant observations, and phenomenological investigation.

Naturally, these two positions are extremes, and many of the discussions of theory, research, and methodology in postsecondary education either incorporate or acknowledge both perspectives. Nonetheless, the intensity of the debate that mirrors the two previous dilemmas does suggest a potential third one for the development of organizational theory and research in postsecondary education: Will these *dialectical views* continue as two potentially *divisive paradigms* or will there be an *accommodation?*

Theory to Practice

The second topic on our developmental agenda is the "relevance" issue, the relationship of theory and research to practice. Because organizational research on postsecondary education has often been heavily practice oriented, the topic is important. However, several changes appear to be reshaping this interface.

First, the tendency to be responsive to current practical issues continues and often leads to extremely descriptive research. Fortunately, the recent research on retrenchment or decline and on effectiveness (e.g., Cameron, 1983; Mortimer, 1979) have resisted this criticism by examining issues that are not ephemeral and by placing the problem in a sound conceptual framework. Given postsecondary education's current pressures, researchers need to weigh the temptation for visible, descriptive studies and give equal attention to research on important longer-term issues.

Second, there is an increasing administrative research capacity and sophistication in higher educational institutions. This can reduce the pressure on scholars for immediate useful studies. It can also provide faculty members interested in postsecondary organizational and administrative issues with greater opportunity to synthesize research and to translate it to knowledgeable administrators. This is a potentially useful development and is reflected in the increasing array of monograph series such as the *ASHE/ERIC Research Reports*, the

New Directions series from Jossey-Bass, and other association publications that provide opportunities for synthesis around current and practical issues.

Third, the increased emphasis on conceptual models and more complicated array of research strategies and methods previously noted may tend to make postsecondary organizational research either less useful or more difficult for administrators to comprehend. This makes the translation and dissemination of research results to practitioners more critical than it has been in the past. It is my observation that the issue of research utilization is getting less emphasis by postsecondary organizational researchers than in the past just when the need may be increasing. This issue, which has become a central concern to institutional researchers, is the topic of a recent *New Directions for Institutional Research* volume (Lindquist, 1981).

Fourth, closely related to the previous points is the tendency of current organizational research efforts to adopt an approach in which the researcher is viewed as neutral or noninvolved. In courses and literature on higher and postsecondary research design that I have reviewed, applied research techniques related to the practice of institutional research, policy analysis, and evaluation are approached largely from the perspective of a neutral researcher. Little attention is given to strategies of action research or organizational development where the researcher participates with the actors. Almost no attention is given to advocacy research. Yet many graduate students in postsecondary education enter administrative careers requiring such skills. However, scholars have recently made such contributions. For example, Gamson's (1984) *Varieties of Liberal Education* was based on her experience as a FIPSE project coordinator in which she assisted project institutions in designing and carrying out evaluations. Victor Baldridge has recently directed a project to design, implement, and evaluate attrition reduction programs in several schools in which he adopted a more active research role. Clifton Conrad, Robert Blackburn, and Robert Berdahl among others have participated in advocacy research roles for U.S. Department of Justice Investigations of desegregation in Louisiana. The point is that strategies of research involvement as well as dissemination may be called for in this theory to practice interface.

These observations suggest the fourth dilemma: Are researchers to become more isolated or more involved? The key issue is not so much, the interest in theoretical versus practical problems, but whether the postsecondary organizational researcher should emphasize roles as neutral or uninvolved experts who conceptualize and design, as intermediaries who translate and disseminate, or as involved research-practitioners or advocates.

Professional Peers

The final developmental topic is concerned with defining the legitimate professional colleagues and mentors in postsecondary organizational theory and research to whom one looks for criticism and guidance. Individuals who have done the conceptual writing and research are identifiable. However, there are still few programmatic efforts or organizations concentrating primarily on postsecondary organizational studies. Associations like AERA and ASHE do not have a formal special interest group devoted to this area alone. There is not a single postsecondary journal or monograph series with this focus, although all give it attention in special sections or special publications. In light of the fragmenting tendencies of the theory and research and absence of professional foci, a few brief comments on professional peers are appropriate.

First, the previous theory to practice discussion suggests a dilemma in the identification of peers. Are they other scholars or administrators? Clearly, other scholars should be a source of critical scholarly interchange. But what of administrators? Are we allies or increasingly aliens as our previous theory-practice dilemma hints? Off campus, a few postsecondary organizational researchers have found colleagues and rewards in institutional membership associations (e.g., AGB, ACE, etc.) and the other administrative associations (e.g., AIR, AAUA, etc.). On campus, administrators can be a source of stimulation in problem identification and provide access to applied projects, data, local resources, opportunities for dissemination, and even influence. One increasingly finds senior administrators with some organizational

theory or research expertise. Many institutions have an expanded institutional research and planning staff who have applied research assignments. Unfortunately budget pressures often make administrators reluctant to have their own faculty probing sensitive and often conflicting events and issues.

Second, among scholarly colleagues one also has some peer choices. In the field of education, the network of postsecondary researchers as noted is still embryonic or loosely coupled. On campus, other education school faculty are accessible, but the numbers interested in organizational concepts and research issues are limited and often have a heavy practitioner orientation. Educational statistics and research faculty often focus on or emphasize individual and small group level phenomena rather than organizations as the unit of analysis.

Outside of education, more faculty are involved in organization behavior, both on and off campus, they are but not as interested in Postsecondary education. As in any interdisciplinary field, one has the choice of an association-based disciplinary group (e.g., ASA's Organization Section), another professional school unit (e.g., a department of organization behavior in a business school), or a less clearly defined interdisciplinary network. As an example of the network, an "organizational behavior seminar" at the University of Michigan involves about 25 faculty from Law, Business, Education, Social Work, Engineering, Public Policy, Sociology, Psychology, Public Health, Political Science, and so on, and meets occasionally to share someone's research or to interact with an invited outside scholar. Interestingly, while many of the members have known each other for years, it did not become organized until a visiting scholar who had met us individually invited us all to lunch.

The point is that the sources of professional peers are numerous, but they are still ill defined as a resource for the criticism, guidance, and collaboration that are so useful in furthering this area of study. Stimulating such a network is probably a valuable activity, but involves basic choices about orientation and membership: practitioners or scholars; education lists, professionals, or disciplinarians. Resolving this dilemma may influence the direction on many of the previous dilemmas.

Dilemmas Revisited

This overview suggests there is a great deal of potential fragmentation in the rapidly developing area of postsecondary organizational theory and research highlighted by these five dilemmas. Further development may involve answering all five of them with a resounding, "Yes."

There is a *muddled array of models*. Yet we need to emphasize further theory "development" to find better ways to understand postsecondary education's uniqueness. The newer emergent models offer useful examples. But there is also a need to encourage theory and research "synthesis" to clarify the theories and constructs, to examine more critically the applicability of the borrowed models, and to see what has been learned conceptually as well as about practice. And there is a need to pursue more rigorous "testing" of individual models and the comparative testing of competing explanations to confirm or refute them, rather than continuing to advocate them.

The *methodological maze* that is necessary to understand the complexity of organizational behavior in any setting will continue to be many faceted. There is a need to continue the emphasis on large-scale comparative and survey research strategies and to utilize "quantitative" techniques and multivariate or causal analysis to enhance the generalizablity of our findings and to test our competing theories. But there is also a need to expand efforts in using the more intensive, "qualitative" strategies and methods to give construct validity to the quantitative variables, to examine the causal assumptions in the theories, and to generate new insights or models for more extensive examination.

It is useful not only to emphasize both paradigms but also to seek an integration to avoid becoming embroiled in an extended and exaggerated *philosophical dialectic*. The different models and theories and different research strategies and methods each need to be examined in relation to criteria for sound theory and methodology and to be used as appropriate to the purpose, problem, and setting of the research project. Sensitive manipulation and open-minded interpretation of quantitative approaches and causal models can lead to the refutation of existing models and the suggestion of questions for intensive qualitative explo-

ration. Examples that merge the two paradigms are the combined use of survey and comparative case studies employing both qualitative and quantitative approaches in large studies such as the NCHEMS research on effectiveness and decline and the use of grounded theory in more focused studies such as Richardson, Fisk, and Okun's (1983) study of literacy.

Clearly, the theory-practice or relevance dilemma is a product of the conflict between our expanded efforts in research and theory development and the urgent demands of postsecondary education today. There is a need for good "conceptualizers and designers" to place the practical findings in a broader context and to guide the development of explanatory frameworks. We need "translators" who can effectively disseminate the extensive array of theoretical and research literature. We also need "practitioner researchers" who can involve subjects in the research process and not just do research on practical problems. More importantly, we need more balanced attention to the range of methods from theory development and critique, to strategies of dissemination and utilization of research, and to research approaches that stress research involvement.

Rogers and Gamson (1982) have a recent article on "Evaluation as a Developmental Process." In a chapter of *Black Students on White Campuses* (Blackburn, Gamson, & Peterson, 1978), the authors discuss the use of an interracial team in the study of a sensitive social issue. There is a need to analyze and share our insights into how to do organizational research in postsecondary education. In these examples and in the theory to practice and professional roles discussion, the thesis is that, in the establishment of a "peer" group of colleagues and mentors, form follows function—it may be timely to bring colleagues together around some of the developmental issues in postsecondary organization theory and research.

Such efforts may determine whether postsecondary organizational theory and research survives its adolescent dilemmas and grows to wholesome, integrated maturity or becomes more fragmented and stifles its development.

Notes

1. For an excellent discussion of theory development in organizations, see Larry Mohr's

Explaining Organizational Behavior (Jossey-Bass, 1982) and Jeffrey Pfeffer's *Organizations and Organization Theory* (Pitman, 1982).

2. Two useful sources on nonquantitative research methods are *Administrative Science Quarterly*, Vol. 27, 1982, which is devoted to articles on qualitative methods, and a recent NDIR monograph by Kuhns and Martorana on *Qualitative Methods in Institutional Research* (1984).

3. Clifton Conrad's article discussing grounded theory in the *Review of Higher Education* (1982).

References

Baldridge, J. V. *Power and Conflict in the University*. San Francisco: Jossey-Bass, 1971.

_____. *Policy Making and Effective Leadership*. San Francisco: Jossey-Bass, 1978.

Baldridge, J. V. & Tierney, M. *New Approaches to Management*. San Francisco: Jossey-Bass, 1979.

Bess, J. "Maps and Gaps in the Study of College and University Organization." *Review of Higher Education*, 1983, 6; 239–251.

Birnbaum, R. *Maintaining Diversity in American Higher Education*. San Francisco: Jossey–Bass, 1983.

Blackburn, R., Gamson, Z., & Peterson, M. "Chronology of the Study and First Steps." In M. Peterson, et al. (Eds.), *Black Students on White Campuses*. Ann Arbor: Institute for Social Research, University of Michigan, 1978.

Brewster, K., Jr. "Future Strategy of the Private University." *Princeton Alumni Weekly*, 1965; 45–46.

Cameron, K. *A Study of Organizational Effectiveness and its Predictors*. Unpublished manuscript, 1983.

_____. "Organizational Adaptation and Higher Education." *Journal of Higher Education*, 1984, 55, (2); 122–144.

Chaffee, E. "Successful Strategic Management in Small Private Colleges." *Journal of Higher Education*, 1984, 55, (2); 212–241.

Clark, B. *The Distinctive Colleges*. Chicago: Aldine, 1970.

Cohen, M., & March, J. *Leadership and Ambiguity*. New York: McGraw-Hill, 1974.

Cohen, M., March, J., & Olsen, J. "A Garbage Can Model of Organizational Choice." *Administrative Science Quarterly*, 1972, 17, 1–25.

Conrad, C. "Grounded Theory: An Alternative Approach to Research in Higher Education." *Review Of Higher Education*, 1982, 5 (4); 239–249.

Cummings, L. L. "Organizational Behavior in the 1980's." *Decision Sciences*, 1981,12; 265–377.

Dill, D. "The Structure of the Academic Profession: Toward a Definition of Ethical Issues." *Journal of Higher Education*, 1982, 3; 255–267.

Gamson, Z. *Varieties of Liberal Educational*. San Francisco: Jossey-Bass, 1984.

Henderson, A. "Improving Decision-Making Through Research." In G. Smith (Ed.), *Current Issues in Higher Education*. Washington, DC: AAHE, 1963.

Kuhns, E., & Martorana, S.V. (Eds.). "Qualitative Methods in Institutional Research." In *New Directions for Institutional Research*. San Francisco: Jossey-Bass, 1982.

Lindquist, J. (Ed.). "Increasing the Use of Institutional Research." In *New Directions for Institutional Research*. San Francisco: Jossey-Bass, 1981.

Lutz, F. "Tightening up Loose Coupling in Organizations of Higher Education." *Administration Science Quarterly*, 1982, 27; 653–669.

March, J. *Handbook of Organizations*. Chicago: Rand McNally, 1965.

_____. "Emerging Developments in the Study of Organizations." *Review of Higher Education*, 1982, 6; 1–18.

McConnell, T. R. "Needed: Research in College and University Organization and Administration." In T. Lunsford (Ed.), *Study of Academic Organizations*. Boulder, CO: Western Institute Commission on Higher Education, 1963.

Meryl, L. "A Cultural Perspective on Organizations: The Need for and Consequences of Viewing Organizations as Culture-Bearing Milieux." *Human Systems Management*, 1981, 2; 246–258.

Mohr, L. *Exploring Organizational Behavior*. San Francisco: Jossey-Bass, 1982.

Mortimer, K. *The Three R's of the Eighties: Reduction, Reallocation, and Retrenchment*, (ERIC/AAHE Research Reports, No. 4). Washington, DC: AAHE, 1979.

Pascarella, E. T., & Terenzini, P. "Interaction Effects in Spady's and Tinto's Conceptual Models of College Dropout." *Sociology of Education*, 1979, 52; 197–210.

Peters, T., & Waterman, R. In *Search of Excellence*. New York, Harper and Row, 1982.

Peterson, M., et al. *Black Students on White Campuses*. Ann Arbor: Institute for Social Research, University of Michigan, 1978.

_____. "Organization and Administration in Higher Education: Sociological and Social-Psychological Perspectives." In F. Kerlinger (Ed.), *Review of Research in Education*, Vol. II. Itasca, IL: Peacock, 1974.

Pfeffer, J. *Organizations and organization theory*. Marshfield, MA: Pitman, 1982.

Platt, J. R. Strong inference. *Science*, 1964, 146, (3642); 347–353.

Richardson, R., Fisk, E., & Okun, M. *Literacy in the Open Access College*. San Francisco: Jossey-Bass, 1983.

Riesman, D., Gusfeld, J., & Gamson, Z. *Academic Values and Mass Education*. Garden City, NY: Doubleday, 1970.

Rogers, T., & Gamson, Z. "Evaluation as a Developmental Process." *Review of Higher Education*, 1982, 5, 225–238.

Rudolph, F. *The American College and University: A History.* New York: Knopf, 1962.

Tinto, V. "Limits of Theory and Practice in Student Attrition." *Journal of Higher Education*, 1982, 6; 687–700.

Trow M. "Reorganizing the Biological Sciences at Berkeley." *Change*, 1984, 28; 44–53.

Weick, K. "Educational Organizations as Loosely Coupled Systems." *Administrative Science Quarterly*, 1976, 21 (1); 1–19.

Whitehead, A. M. "Universities and Their Functions." *Atlantic Monthly*, 1928,141 (5); 638–644.

Zammuto, R. "Are the Liberal Arts an Endangered Species?" *Journal of Higher Education*, 1984, 55, (2); 184–211.

PART II

TRADITIONAL ADMINISTRATIVE AND GOVERNANCE MODELS

CHAPTER 6

STATEMENT ON GOVERNMENT OF COLLEGES AND UNIVERSITIES

AMERICAN ASSOCIATION OF UNIVERSITY PROFESSORS, AMERICAN COUNCIL ON EDUCATION, ASSOCIATION OF GOVERNING BOARDS OF UNIVERSITIES AND COLLEGES

Editorial Note. The Statement which follows is directed to governing board members, administrators, faculty members, students and other persons in the belief that the colleges and universities of the United States have reached a stage calling for appropriately shared responsibility and cooperative action among the components of the academic institution. The Statement is intended to foster constructive joint thought and action, both within the institutional structure and in protection of its integrity against improper intrusions.

It is not intended that the Statement serve as a blueprint for government on a specific campus or as a manual for the regulation of controversy among the components of an academic institution, although it is to be hoped that the principles asserted will lead to the correction of existing weaknesses and assist in the establishment of sound structure and procedures. The Statement does not attempt to cover relations with those outside agencies which increasingly are controlling the resources and influencing the patterns of education in other institutions of higher learning, e.g., the United States Government, the state legislatures, state commissions, interstate associations or compacts and other interinstitutional arrangements. However it is hoped that the Statement will be helpful to these agencies in their consideration of educational matters.

Students are referred to in this Statement as an institutional component coordinate in importance with trustees, administrators and faculty. There is, however, no main section on students. The omission has two causes: (1) the changes now occurring in the status of American students have plainly outdistanced the analysis by the educational community, and an attempt to define the situation without thorough study might prove unfair to student interests,[1] and (2) students do not in fact presently have a significant voice in the government of colleges and universities; it would be unseemly to obscure, by superficial equality of length of statement, what may be a serious lag entitled to separate and full confrontation. The concern for student status felt by the organizations issuing this Statement is embodied in a note "On Student Status" intended to stimulate the educational community to turn its attention to an important need.

This Statement, in preparation since 1964, is jointly formulated by the American Association of University Professors, the American Council on Education, and the Association of Governing Boards of Universities and Colleges. On October 12, 1966, the Board of Directors of the ACE took action by which the Council "recognizes the Statement as a significant step forward in the clarification of the respective roles of governing boards, faculties, and administrations," and "commends it to the institutions which are members of the Council." On

---

"Statement on Government of Colleges and Universities," by AAUP/ACE/AGB, reprinted with permission from *Academe*, Vol. 52, No. 4, December 1966.

October 29, 1966, the Council of the AAUP approved the Statement, recommended approval by the Fifty-Third Annual Meeting in April, 1967, and recognized that "continuing joint effort is desirable, in view of the areas left open in the jointly formulated Statement, and the dynamic changes occurring in higher education." On November 18, 1966, the Executive Committee of the AGB took action by which that organization also "recognizes the Statement as a significant step forward in the clarification of the respective roles of governing boards, faculties and administrations," and "commends it to the governing boards which are members of the Association."

I. Introduction

This Statement is a call to mutual understanding regarding the government of colleges and universities. Understanding, based on community of interest, and producing joint effort, is essential for at least three reasons. First, the academic institution, public or private, often has become less autonomous; buildings, research, and student tuition are supported by funds over which the college or university exercises a diminishing control. Legislative and executive governmental authority, at all levels, plays a part in the making of important decisions in academic policy. If these voices and forces are to be successfully heard and integrated, the academic institution must be in a position to meet them with its own generally unified view. Second, regard for the welfare of the institution remains important despite the mobility and interchange of scholars. Third, a college or university in which all the components are aware of their interdependence, of the usefulness of communication among themselves, and of the force of joint action will enjoy increased capacity to solve educational problems.

II. The Academic Institution: Joint Effort

A. Preliminary Considerations

The variety and complexity of the tasks performed by institutions of higher education produce an inescapable interdependence among governing board, administration, faculty, students and others. The relationship calls for ade-

quate communication among these components, and full opportunity for appropriate joint planning and effort.

Joint effort in an academic institution will take a variety of forms appropriate to the kinds of situations encountered. In some instances, an initial exploration or recommendation will be made by the president with consideration by the faculty at a later stage; in other instances, a first and essentially definitive recommendation will be made by the faculty, subject to the endorsement of the president and the governing board. In still others, a substantive contribution can be made when student leaders are responsibly involved in the process. Although the variety of such approaches may be wide, at least two general conclusions regarding joint effort seem clearly warranted: (1) important areas of action involve at one time or another the initiating capacity and decision-making participation of all the institutional components, and (2) differences in the weight of each voice, from one point to the next, should be determined by reference to the responsibility of each component for the particular matter at hand, as developed hereinafter.

B. Determination of General Educational Policy

The general educational policy, i.e., the objectives of an institution and the nature, range, and pace of its efforts, is shaped by the institutional charter or by law, by tradition and historical development, by the present needs of the community of the institution, and by the professional aspirations and standards of those directly involved in its work. Every board will wish to go beyond its formal trustee obligation to conserve the accomplishment of the past and to engage seriously with the future; every faculty will seek to conduct an operation worthy of scholarly standards of learning; every administrative officer will strive to meet his charge and to attain the goals of the institution. The interests of all are coordinate and related, and unilateral effort can lead to confusion or conflict. Essential to a solution is a reasonably explicit statement on general educational policy. Operating responsibility and authority, and procedures for continuing review, should be clearly defined in regulations.

When an educational goal has been established, it becomes the responsibility primarily of the faculty to determine appropriate curriculum and procedures of student instruction.

Special considerations may require particular accommodations: (1) a publicly supported institution may be regulated by statutory provisions, and (2) a church-controlled institution may be limited by its charter or bylaws. When such external requirements influence course content and manner of instruction or research, they impair the educational effectiveness of the institution.

Such matters as major changes in the size or composition of the student body and the relative emphasis to be given to the various elements of the educational and research program should involve participation of governing board, administration and faculty prior to final decision.

C. Internal Operations of the Institution

The framing and execution of long-range plans, one of the most important aspects of institutional responsibility, should be a central and continuing concern in the academic community.

Effective planning demands that the broadest possible exchange of information and opinion should be the rule for communication among the components of a college or university. The channels of communication should be established and maintained by joint endeavor. Distinction should be observed between the institutional system of communication and the system of responsibility for the making of decisions.

A second area calling for joint effort in internal operations is that of decisions regarding existing or prospective physical resources. The board, president and faculty should all seek agreement on basic decisions regarding buildings and other facilities to be used in the educational work of the institution.

A third area is budgeting. The allocation of resources among competing demands is central in the formal responsibility of the governing board, in the administrative authority of the president, and in the educational function of the faculty. Each component should therefore have a voice in the determination of short and long-range priorities, and each should receive appropriate analyses of past budgetary experience, reports on current budgets and expenditures, and short and long-range budgetary projections. The function of each component in budgetary matters should be understood by all; the allocation of authority will determine the flow of information and the scope of participation in decisions.

Joint effort of a most critical kind must be taken when an institution chooses a new president. The selection of a chief administrative officer should follow upon cooperative search by the governing board and the faculty, taking into consideration the opinions of others who are appropriately interested. The president should be equally qualified to serve both as the executive officer of the governing board and as the chief academic officer of the institution and the faculty. His dual role requires that he be able to interpret to board and faculty the educational views and concepts of institutional government of the other. He should have the confidence of the board and the faculty.

The selection of academic deans and other chief academic officers should be the responsibility of the president with the advice of and in consultation with the appropriate faculty.

Determinations of faculty status, normally based on the recommendations of the faculty groups involved, are discussed in Part V of this Statement; but it should here be noted that the building of a strong faculty requires careful joint effort in such actions as staff selection and promotion and the granting of tenure. Joint action should also govern dismissals; the applicable principles and procedures in these matters are well established.[2]

D. External Relations of the Institution

Anyone—a member of the governing board, the president or other member of the administration, a member of the faculty, or a member of the student body or the alumni—affects the institution when he speaks of it in public. An individual who speaks unofficially should so indicate. An official spokesman for the institution, the board, the administration, the faculty, or the student body should be guided by established policy.

It should be noted that only the board speaks legally for the whole institution, although it may delegate responsibility to an agent.

The right of a board member, an administrative officer, a faculty member, or a student to speak on general educational questions or about the administration and operations of his own institution is a part of his right as a citizen and should not be abridged by the institution.[3] There exist, of course, legal bounds relating to defamation of character, and there are questions of propriety.

III. The Academic Institution: The Governing Board

The governing board has a special obligation to assure that the history of the college or university shall serve as a prelude and inspiration to the future. The board helps relate the institution to its chief community: e.g., the community college to serve the educational needs of a defined population area or group, the church-controlled college to be cognizant of the announced position of its denomination, and the comprehensive university to discharge the many duties and to accept the appropriate new challenges which are its concern at the several levels of higher education.

The governing board of an institution of higher education in the United States operates, with few exceptions, as the final institutional authority. Private institutions are established by charters; public institutions are established by constitutional or statutory provisions. In private institutions the board is frequently self-perpetuating; in public colleges and universities the present membership of a board may be asked to suggest candidates for appointment. As a whole and individually when the governing board confronts the problem of succession, serious attention should be given to obtaining properly qualified persons. Where public law calls for election of governing board members, means should be found to insure the nomination of fully suited persons, and the electorate should be informed of the relevant criteria for board membership.

Since the membership of the board may embrace both individual and collective competence of recognized weight, its advice or help may be sought through established channels by other components of the academic community. The governing board of an institution of higher education, while maintaining a general overview, entrusts the conduct of administration to the administrative officers, the president and the deans, and the conduct of teaching and research to the faculty. The board should undertake appropriate self-limitation.

One of the governing board's important tasks is to ensure the publication of codified statements that define the over-all policies and procedures of the institution under its jurisdiction.

The board plays a central role in relating the likely needs of the future to predictable resources; it has the responsibility for husbanding the endowment; it is responsible for obtaining needed capital and operating funds; and in the broadest sense of the term it should pay attention to personnel policy. In order to fulfill these duties, the board should be aided by, and may insist upon, the development of long-range planning by the administration and faculty.

When ignorance or ill-will threatens the institution or any part of it, the governing board must be available for support. In grave crises it will be expected to serve as a champion. Although the action to be taken by it will usually be on behalf of the president, the faculty, or the student body, the board should make clear that the protection it offers to an individual or a group is, in fact, a fundamental defense of the vested interests of society in the educational institution.

IV. The Academic Institution: The President

The president, as the chief executive officer of an institution of higher education, is measured largely by his capacity for institutional leadership. He shares responsibility for the definition and attainment of goals, for administrative action, and for operating the communications system which links the components of the academic community. He represents his institution to its many publics. His leadership role is supported by delegated authority from the board and faculty.

As the chief planning officer of an institution, the president has a special obligation to innovate and initiate. The degree to which a president can envision new horizons for his institution, and can persuade others to see them and to work toward them, will often constitute the chief measure of his administration.

The president must at times, with or without support, infuse new life into a department; relatedly, he may at times be required, working within the concept of tenure, to solve problems of obsolescence. The president will necessarily utilize the judgments of the faculty, but in the interest of academic standards he may also seek outside evaluations by scholars of acknowledged competence.

It is the duty of the president to see to it that the standards and procedures in operational use within the college or university conform to the policy established by the governing board and to the standards of sound academic practice. It is also incumbent on the president to insure that faculty views, including dissenting views, are presented to the board in those areas and on those issues where responsibilities are shared. Similarly the faculty should be informed of the views of the board and the administration on like issues.

The president is largely responsible for the maintenance of existing institutional resources and the creation of new resources: he has intimate managerial responsibility for a large area of nonacademic activities, he is responsible for public understanding, and by the nature of his office is the chief spokesman of his institution. In these and other areas his work is to plan, to organize, to direct, and to represent. The presidential function should receive the general support of board and faculty.

V. The Academic Institution: The Faculty

The faculty has primary responsibility for such fundamental areas as curriculum, subject matter and methods of instruction, research, faculty status, and those aspects of student life which relate to the educational process. On these matters the power of review or final decision lodged in the governing board or delegated by it to the president should be exercised adversely only in exceptional circumstances, and for reasons communicated to the faculty. It is desirable that the faculty should, following such communication, have opportunity for further consideration and further transmittal of its

views to the president or board. Budgets, manpower limitations, the time element and the policies of other groups, bodies and agencies having jurisdiction over the institution may set limits to realization of faculty advice.

The faculty sets the requirements for the degrees offered in course, determines when the requirements have been met, and authorizes the president and board to grant the degrees thus achieved.

Faculty status and related matters are primarily a faculty responsibility; this area includes appointments, reappointments, decisions not to reappoint, promotions, the granting of tenure, and dismissal. The primary responsibility of the faculty for such matters is based upon the fact that its judgment is central to general educational policy. Furthermore, scholars in a particular field or activity have the chief competence for judging the work of their colleagues; in such competence it is implicit that responsibility exists for both adverse and favorable judgments. Likewise there is the more general competence of experienced faculty personnel committees having broader charge. Determinations in these matters should first be by faculty action through established procedures, reviewed by the chief academic officers with the concurrence of the board. The governing board and president should, on questions of faculty status, as in other matters where the faculty has primary responsibility, concur with the faculty judgment except in rare instances and for compelling reasons which should be stated in detail.

The faculty should actively participate in the determination of policies and procedures governing salary increases.

The chairman or head of a department, who serves as the chief representative of his department within an institution, should be selected either by departmental election or by appointment following consultation with members of the department and of related departments: appointments should normally be in conformity with department members' judgment. The chairman or department head should not have tenure in his office; his tenure as a faculty member is a matter of separate right. He should serve for a stated term but without prejudice to re-election or to reappointment by procedures which involve appropriate faculty consultation. Board, administration, and faculty should all bear in mind that the department chairman has a special obligation to build a department strong in scholarship and teaching capacity.

Agencies for faculty participation in the government of the college or university should be established at each level where faculty responsibility is present. An agency should exist for the presentation of the views of the whole faculty. The structure and procedures for faculty participation should be designed, approved and established by joint action of the components of the institution. Faculty representatives should be selected by the faculty according to procedures determined by the faculty.

The agencies may consist of meetings of all faculty members of a department, school, college, division or university system, or may take the form of faculty-elected executive committees in departments and schools and a faculty-elected senate or council for larger divisions or the institution as a whole.

Among the means of communication among the faculty, administration, and governing board now in use are: (1) circulation of memoranda and reports by board committees, the administration, and faculty committees, (2) joint *ad hoc* committees, (3) standing liaison committees, (4) membership of faculty members on administrative bodies, and (5) membership of faculty members on governing boards. Whatever the channels of communication, they should be clearly understood and observed.

On Student Status

When students in American colleges and universities desire to participate responsibly in the government of the institution they attend, their wish should be recognized as a claim to opportunity both for educational experience and for involvement in the affairs of their college or university. Ways should be found to permit significant student participation within the limits of attainable effectiveness. The obstacles to such participation are large and should not be minimized: inexperience, untested capacity, a transitory status which means that present action does not carry with it subsequent responsibility, and the inescapable fact that the other components of the institution are in a position of judgment over the students. It is important to recognize that student needs are strongly related to educational experience, both formal and informal. Students expect, and have a right to expect, that the educational process will be structured, that they will be stimulated by it to become independent adults, and that they will have effectively transmitted to them the cultural heritage of the larger society. If institutional support is to have its fullest possible meaning it should incorporate the strength, freshness of view and idealism of the student body.

The respect of students for their college or university can be enhanced if they are given at least these opportunities: (1) to be listened to in the classroom without fear of institutional reprisal for the substance of their views, (2) freedom to discuss questions of institutional policy and operation, (3) the right to academic due process when charged with serious violations of institutional regulations, and (4) the same right to hear speakers of their own choice as is enjoyed by other components of the institution.

Notes

1. Note: 1950, the formulation of the Student Bill of Rights by the United States National Student Association: 1956, the first appearance of *Academic Freedom and Civil Liberties of Students*, published by the American Civil Liberties Union: 1961, the decision in Dixon v. Alabama State Board of Education currently the leading case on due process for students: 1965, the publication of a tentative Statement on the Academic Freedom of Students, by the American Association of University Professors.

2. See the 1940 *Statement of Principles on Academic Freedom and Tenure* and the *1958 Statement on Procedural Standards in Faculty Dismissal Proceedings*. These statements have been jointly approved or adopted by the Association of American Colleges and the American Association of University Professors; the 1940 Statement has been endorsed by numerous learned and scientific societies and educational associations.

3. With respect to faculty members, the 1940 *Statement of Principles on Academic Freedom and Tenure* reads: "The college or university teacher is a citizen, a member of a learned profession, and an officer of an educational institution. When he speaks or writes as a citizen, he should be free from institutional censorship or discipline, but his special position in the community imposes special obligations. As a man of learning and an educational officer, he should remember that the public may

judge his profession and his institution by his utterances. Hence he should at all times be accurate, should exercise appropriate restraint, should show respect for the opinion of others, and should make every effort to indicate that he is not an institutional spokesman."

CHAPTER 7

THE NATURE OF ADMINISTRATIVE BEHAVIOR IN HIGHER EDUCATION[1]

DAVID D. DILL

The rapid growth of American higher education after World War II produced several outputs in large measure. In addition to the largest number of faculty members and students in the world, a significant volume of research and a vast and growing literature on the enterprise itself resulted. A sizable portion of the literature on higher education has addressed a still amorphous area usually referred to as higher education administration. The intent of this review is to focus on a particular slice of that literature: the research on administrative behavior.

The focus of the review was prompted by three important publications that appeared over a two-year period. In 1974, Peterson published the only extant review of the research literature on the organization and administration of higher education.[2] As his review made clear, the large volume of research as of 1974 addressed colleges and universities as organizations—their goals and purposes, organizational climate, institutional decision making, governance structures, patterns of influence, and processes of conflict, innovation, participation, and change. Peterson also identified and reviewed a growing literature on planning and management techniques in higher education. In contrast, empirical studies on administrative behavior or on what administrators in these settings actually did were rare, and Peterson identified this as a particular weakness of the literature at the time.

In the same year, March presented a classic but generally unknown address on educational administration.[3] In it, March argued that the training of higher education administrators should be based on knowledge of the context of education. This knowledge should ideally include the nature of educational organizations as well as what educational managers actually do. As March pointed out, a persistent difficulty with attempts to improve administrative effectiveness has been that efforts in that direction are often unrelated to the ordinary organization and conduct of administrative life. Unless one begins with some appreciation of what administrators do and why they organize their lives the way they do, such efforts are unlikely to improve administrative performance.

In the prior year, Mintzberg's landmark book, *The Nature of Managerial Work*, was published.[4] Mintzberg's original investigations as well as his codification of existing research revealed consistent patterns in managerial work. These patterns were at variance with existing models of administrative behavior that tended to emphasize the rational processes of planning, organizing, and controlling. Subsequent research by Kurke and Aldrich,[5] Kotter,[6] and Lau and his associates[7] has generally supported Mintzberg's findings. Taken as a whole, this research raised the question of whether or not the successful implementation of technologies and processes advocated for contemporary managers was seriously compromised by a failure to understand the nature of managerial work itself.

Following the lead of these three publications, this review will focus on the state of knowledge on administrative behavior in institutions of higher education.

Method

A review of research represents a fundamental activity in the behavioral sciences, but the methods, techniques, and procedures for conducting such reviews are sometimes ambiguous or unstated.[8] As a result, it is quite likely that two people conducting a similar review may arrive at substantially different conclusions. This variation may be due to the questions asked, the methods of selecting material, the form the analysis takes, and/or to unstated biases that shape each of the above. In sum, reviews of research are subject to the same sources of error as traditional research studies.

The review that follows is an integrative review, that is, a review "inferring generalizations about substantive issues from a set of studies directly bearing on those issues."[9] To increase the potential value of the review, several strategies were employed. First, the basic organization of the review was derived from a framework that is reliably grounded in the nature of managerial work. Second, some care was taken in selecting the material for the review. A computerized search was conducted of both the *Social Sciences Citation Index* and *ERIC*. The key words utilized were: "administrative behavior," "management," "leadership," "higher education," "college," and "university." Citations were collected for the period of 1974 (i.e., the date of the last such review by Peterson) through September 1983. This yielded 345 references. In addition, a separate review was made of the best known research journals in the field. These journals were: the *Educational Administration Quarterly, Higher Education, Journal of Higher Education, Research in Higher Education,* and *The Review of Higher Education.* This resulted in an additional 50 references. Each of these was reviewed to determine those articles that presented the results of empirical research, and 30 more references were identified. To these were added a number of articles and book chapters reporting research that was known to be relevant by the author but that had not been uncovered in the keyword search.

It is at this point that substantial bias can enter into a review. Therefore, one important control is for the author to state his or her own bias(es). The writer's own views of management and academic organizations have been heavily influenced by the writings of Clark,[10] March,[11] and Mintzberg.[12] As a result, personal knowledge of references in the field was likely to over-represent literature on subjects such as "ambiguity," "culture," "influence," and "political models," as well as research pertinent to the categories of Mintzberg's framework. In contrast, literature addressing "rational" analyses and techniques were apt to be underrepresented. Furthermore, although the techniques of decision analysis, cost-benefit analysis, and MBO may, if implemented, lead to improvements in academic management, the empirical research supporting the utility of such models for managerial work is scant in the writer's judgment. Finally, the author's knowledge of material relating to research universities is greater than for other types of institutions. Having stated these biases, it is incumbent on the writer to attend to contradictory research evidence in the articles reviewed.

An additional control employed in this review was the means of presenting and analyzing the results of the primary materials.[13] Because the variety of research methodologies and approaches employed in the field of higher education administration and management compromise the additive results of different studies, the present review will attend principally to general trends in research results as well as to issues related to methodology.

Finally, this discussion of method must conclude with an important *caveat.* The plan for selecting material for the review has limitations which may affect the results. In addition to the title keyword search, subject key words or key words reflecting the organizing or analytical framework employed in the review could have been pursued. Furthermore, dissertations and books could have been included along with journal articles. The decision to restrict the search and material considered was mandated by limitations of time and funds. One implication of the procedure used is that the review over-represents research published in traditional research journals. As such, the research results may under-represent new directions in inquiry not yet evident in published sources. However, it can be assumed that the review is representative of the accrued knowledge in the field to date.

Analytical Framework

The concept of "administrative behavior" refers to the behavior of those within the boundaries of organizations who occupy administrative positions.[14] Traditionally the research in this area has focused on leadership traits and patterns of individual or group decision making. The literature has also included normative prescriptions for the managerial activities of planning, coordinating, and controlling that have been based on little if any research. Because classical perspectives on administrative behavior have been supplanted by more recent observational approaches, the general managerial skill framework of Katz[15] will be linked with the empirically derived categories of Mintzberg[16] as a means of organizing and presenting the research analyzed in this review. Katz has argued that successful managers exhibit three categories of skills: human relations skills, conceptual skills, and technical skills. Anderson[17] has suggested that linking these categories with the behavior exhibited by the executives observed by Mintzberg provides greater insight to the understanding of managerial behavior (see Figure 7-1).

By human relations skills, Katz means those interpersonal skills that are applied when a manager relates to superiors, peers, and subordinates. They are thereby relevant to every managerial level. In terms of Mintzberg's research, human relations skills include: (1) peer-related behavior such as developing contacts in the organization, maintaining information networks, and negotiating and communicating with peers; (2) leadership behavior that relates to dealing effectively with subordinates; and (3) conflict resolution behavior.

Conceptual skills relate to the manager's ability to think through the coordination and integration of the organization's diverse activities, what in contemporary terms is thought of as "strategic thinking." Mintzberg discovered five types of behavior that may be categorized as conceptual skills: (1) information processing behavior or the monitoring of one's networks for obtaining information, extracting and assimilating information, and communicating the "pictures" the manager develops; (2) decision making in unstructured and ambiguous situations; (3) resource allocation behavior or the allocation of the organization's critical assets (i.e., time, money, and skill) among competing demands; (4) entrepreneurial behavior that relates to discovering problems and opportunities for which "improvement projects" will be initiated; and (5) introspective behavior that relates to the manager's understanding of the job, sensitivity to his or her personal impact, and learning from these insights.

By technical skill Katz means two things: first, the technique or expertise of "management" (e.g., knowledge of budgeting and

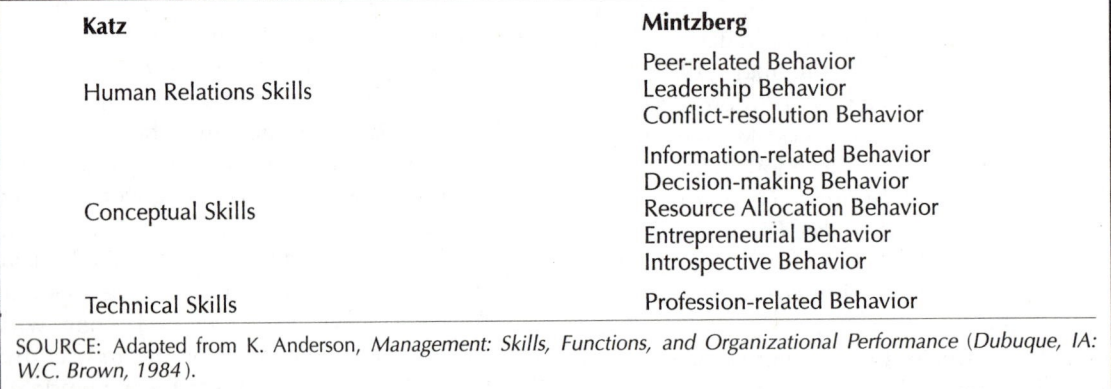

Katz	Mintzberg
Human Relations Skills	Peer-related Behavior Leadership Behavior Conflict-resolution Behavior
Conceptual Skills	Information-related Behavior Decision-making Behavior Resource Allocation Behavior Entrepreneurial Behavior Introspective Behavior
Technical Skills	Profession-related Behavior

SOURCE: Adapted from K. Anderson, *Management: Skills, Functions, and Organizational Performance* (Dubuque, IA: W.C. Brown, 1984).

Figure 7-1 Framework for Administrative Behavior Based Upon Katz and Mintzberg (1973, 1974)

accounting), and second, the professional expertise or skill that the individual practiced prior to becoming a manager. In the case of the academic manager, professional expertise is equivalent to academic expertise, that is, knowledge of a disciplinary field as well as acknowledged capabilities in teaching and research. Because several of Mintzberg's categories of observed management behavior (e.g., conflict resolution behavior, decision-making behavior, and resource allocation behavior) are relevant to Katz's first meaning of technical skill, technical skill in this review will be limited to a discussion of the relevance of the aspect of this skill area referred to as professional expertise. Both Katz and Mintzberg argue that professional expertise becomes less relevant as one moves up the managerial hierarchy and assumes responsibility for a broader range of activities. However, a distinctive aspect of academic management is the attempts of faculty members to sustain their professional expertise by teaching and conducting research while occupying administrative positions. Thus, the relationship of technical academic skills to managerial behavior is of special interest in higher education administration.

There is no assumption here that the research on administrative behavior in higher education will be evenly distributed among these various categories or that the results within each category will be unequivocal. Some categories will probably contain no research at all, and further, some material may well logically be placed in more than one of the classification categories. Nevertheless, by organizing the review in this fashion, the state of knowledge regarding what administrators in higher education do can be codified and implications for practice and research can be more effectively drawn.

Knowledge concerning the allocation of administrative time and patterns of communication is an important contribution of the research of Mintzberg and others who study managerial work. This review will begin with the related research on academic administrators as an introduction. In the sections of the review that follow, the published research will be reviewed in terms of the above categorization of administrative behavior. Put another way, what little is known about how administrators in higher education distribute their time will be discussed first. Then the skills and behavior associated with the categories of human relations skills, conceptual skills, and professional technical skills will be explored in turn.

Managerial Time in Academia

Mintzberg's study of five managers of large organizations concluded that the managers performed a great deal of work at an unrelenting pace; that managerial work was characterized by variety, fragmentation, and brevity; and that managerial work was conducted essentially in a verbal medium. Related analyses of the time allocations of college presidents and deans or department heads have reached similar conclusions about academic managerial work.

Cohen and March in a national survey of college presidents discovered that these executives worked an average of 60 hours a week.[18] This compared with 55 hours of weekly work for the average dean or department head in Lewis and Dahl's small sample study done at the University of Minnesota.[19] As Cohen and March have pointed out, such an average work week is consistent with reported work schedules of academics generally, and it is at the high end of the scales in terms of studies of managers in other fields.

Cohen and March's data on university presidents were comparable in other ways to those on general managers. For example, the presidents spent proportionately similar amounts of time around their office (approximately 30%), in the vicinity of the university (approximately 60%), and out of town (approximately 22%) as did the executives in Mintzberg's study. University presidents were also similar to the executives in terms of their distribution of contact time with other parties. Approximately one-third of their contact time was with those outside the organization, less than 10% was with trustees, and over 50% was with subordinates (i.e., students, faculty, and administrators). Although the university presidents came in contact with a wide variety of people, more time was spent by them with fellow administrators than with any other single group.

University presidents, department heads or deans, and managers from other fields are also alike in that they spend approximately 25% of their time alone, but over 40% of their time in meetings, usually with two or more people. Similarly, management in all settings is a reactive job. Further, the majority of meetings that all these managers attend is initiated by others.

The studies of academic managers reveal some interesting variations and similarities in role both by institution and administrative level. For example, presidents of large universities are more likely to be alone, in town, and spending time with "academic" administrators and dealing with people in groups. In contrast, deans and department heads reported only 45% of their time in administrative work. (The sample in the Lewis and Dahl study contained more department heads than deans.) Approximately 9% of their time was reported in the area of research, 16% in teaching, and over 20% in university service. Lewis and Dahl also reported that the administrators indicated greatest stress came from their administrative duties and that the greatest stress reducer would be increasing the number of hours each week voluntarily devoted to management. This is consistent with the survey results of Weisbord, Lawrence, and Chains of academics in a large medical complex who perceived the functions of research, teaching, patient care, and departmental administration as essentially conflicting functions.[20]

In summary, academic administrators lead a busy, reactive life in which they heavily utilize their verbal skills, particularly in meetings. Observed variations exist as a result of differences in role between full-time administrators (e.g., presidents) and part-time administrators (e.g., department heads). How academic managers apportion their time and contacts is of interest, but what do they actually do? That is, what are their characteristic administrative behaviors? In the following sections, the available research will be discussed according to the framework established for this review.

Human Relations Skill

There is high level of agreement in the literature on administrative behavior that human relations or interpersonal skills are critical to the role of manager, particularly as one moves up the hierarchy of an organization. Mintzberg clarified those skills by focusing on peer-

related behavior that deals with the manager's behavior in entering into and effectively maintaining peer or horizontal relationships. Leadership behavior, on the other hand, was conceived by Mintzberg (and many others as well) as the vertical relationships between managers and their subordinates. In this sense, leadership addresses the interpersonal processes of motivation, training, helping, and dealing with issues of authority and dependence. Conflict resolution behavior was described as attempting to mediate between conflicting individuals and decisions or handling disturbances.

Peer-Related Behavior

Cohen and March reported that the amount of time spent by university presidents on peer-related behavior was substantial. Over a third of their time was spent with outsiders and nearly 30% was spent with constituents (trustees, students, and faculty members) who were not direct subordinates. (Cohen and March also quoted very comparable data from a study conducted in New York State that included community college presidents.)

The large amount of external contact suggests that high level administrators become more distinct and isolated. Lunsford has argued: "The growth in size and importance of universities, together with increasing specialization, has sharpened the separation of administrators from the rest of university life. Their authority is consequently mixed and precarious."[21] In his ethnographic study at the University of California at Berkeley, Lunsford observed that certain core values or beliefs reinforced this isolation and made it a more significant problem for academic managers than for their industrial counterparts. These core values were beliefs in the esoteric quality of specialized research, in academic freedom, in "collegial" decision making, and in the separation of powers between academic and nonacademic decisions. Whitson and Hubert in a national study of department chairmen in large public universities confirmed that decision-making authority was perceived to reflect a separation of powers.[22] Department heads reported primary influence or greater influence than all other groups or individuals in personnel decisions, faculty selection and evaluation, salary decisions, dismissal and nonreappointment of faculty, and administration of the budget. Faculty were reported as having had primary influence in student admissions' policy, departmental academic standards, and the selection and recruitment of graduate students. Department heads and faculty had equal influence in tenure and promotion issues. Lunsford further suggested that academic beliefs in conjunction with the impacts of institutional growth and increased administrative accountability have led to the isolation of high-level administrators. The specialization of administrative tasks, the nature of associations (less with faculty and students, and more with trustees, alumni, and legislators), the visibility and prestige of executive status, and the unwelcome burden of conveying bad news have led in Lunsford's analysis to a separate administrative culture, one distinct and alien.

As a consequence of this separation, Lunsford observes that managers must spend time building channels of communication and support. This involves seeking opportunities for frequent, informal communication with internal constituents such as faculty and students (for example, through teaching a class as a means of staying in touch or using task forces composed of faculty members to address administratively defined problems). Another such possible means is through the use of special assistants drawn from the faculty at large. Stringer, in a study within a large public university, found these "colleague" special assistants to be the most influential of all "assistant-to" types.[23] The relationships of these assistants to executives was what Stringer termed, "collegial": that is, they participated in all major policy discussions and had frequent informal contacts with the executives. As Stringer pointed out, this type of staff role is unique to higher education.

The earlier analysis of administrator time devoted to peer contacts and this modest research suggests that peer-related behavior is both a significant part of an academic manager's job and, given the potential for isolation, a potentially critical component of behavior. However, little work has been done on the means managers use to develop and maintain their networks of contacts. Also lacking is knowledge about how academic managers negotiate with peers for needed resources or

how they consult effectively with the many colleagues and experts that they must utilize.

Leadership Behavior

Cohen and March reported that contact with direct subordinates, such as members of the president's staff as well as academic and nonacademic administrators, occupied the largest single block of the university president's time. There is also some evidence that this time is perceived as important to administrative success and satisfaction. Peterson asked four-year college presidents in public midwestern colleges to identify incidents critical to their success.[24] Staffing problems and subordinate ineffectiveness (i.e., subordinate incompetence in decision making or handling a problem that still necessitated presidential intervention) were mentioned by both new and experienced presidents as the major constraint on their productivity. Solmon and Tierney in a national study of administrative job satisfaction in higher education discovered that a great emphasis on authority relationships between leaders and subordinates was negatively correlated with satisfaction.[25] In contrast, when interpersonal behaviors were emphasized, satisfaction increased. Given the apparent importance of leadership behavior, how do higher education managers act in these kinds of situations?

A number of studies have been conducted with department chairpersons. Hoyt and Spangler, using a sample drawn from four diverse universities, studied the relationship between department chairperson management emphases and rated performance of the chair by the faculty.[26] Personnel management—faculty recruitment; allocating faculty responsibilities; stimulating research scholarship and teaching; maintaining faculty morale; and fostering faculty development—represented six of the nine positive relationships in this regard. Coltrin and Glueck,[27] and Glueck and Thorp[28] reported analyses of data collected from research-oriented departments at the University of Missouri. These studies revealed that a leadership style emphasizing ethical behavior, helpfulness in research projects, accurate and complete communication, frequency of communication, and a willingness to represent the interests of the staff was positively associated with faculty satisfaction with the department head in all departments. There was also some evidence that keeping track of research activities in progress through discussion rather than formal report was also positively related to faculty satisfaction. In contrast, attempts to restrict the selection of projects by researchers was negatively associated with faculty satisfaction. When given a choice of leader roles, faculty members consistently preferred the leader as a "resource person/coordinator." That is, they ideally saw the administrator as a "facilitator" or one who smoothed out problems and sought to provide the resources necessary for the research activities of faculty members. Researchers' perceptions of department heads' attempts to reward them were also positively associated with both satisfaction and effort (i.e., reported hours worked). However, there was no observed direct relationship between leader style and faculty publications, although a later reanalysis led Coltrin and Glueck to question whether an "ideal style" was or was not department independent.

This issue has also been raised in a number of related studies. Neumann and Boris found support that highly ranked paradigmatic departments (e.g., physics and chemistry) were characterized by task-oriented leaders, while lesser ranked paradigmatic departments and highly ranked preparadigmatic departments (e.g., sociology and political science) were both characterized by task and people-oriented department heads.[29] Similarly, Groner used the Group Atmosphere Scale of Fiedler to measure the quality of leader-member relations.[30] He found that the quality of department head-faculty member relations was positively associated with feelings of control over the destiny of the department. But, in both the community college and the university settings, leader-member relations also correlated positively with the amount of task clarity in the department (i.e., extent to which the department was paradigmatic). More specifically, in the university setting there was a strong negative relationship between the heterogeneity of faculty research interests and department head-faculty member relationships.

One traditional argument about the role of department chair is that it is a marginal position in which the chairperson is presented with conflicting demands from above to be a manager and from below to be an academic colleague. Carroll[31] applied the Kahn et al. model for studying role conflict with a sample of department heads from Florida universities.[32] He reported that intersender conflict, a situation in which the focal person perceives incompatible expectations from individuals having influence on his or her position, was most commonly reported and was negatively associated with chairperson satisfaction. As Carroll noted, intersender conflict appears to stem primarily from hierarchical relationships of superiors and subordinates.

Two studies, one within a single university and the other a survey of physical education departments, utilized the Leadership Behavior Description Questionnaire to study department heads. Madron, Craig, and Mendel found that high consideration by the department head was related to departmental morale.[33] They also found a negative relationship between morale and department size suggesting that departmental size may serve as a constraint on leadership style. Milner, King, and Pizzini discovered no significant difference between male and female department heads in their perceptions of ideal leadership qualities or in their rating of their actual qualities.[34] In contrast, faculty members in the departments reacted differently to the department head depending on their sex. Faculty members of both sexes tended to perceive heads of the same sex as more considerate.

When viewed from the perspective of research on leadership generally, the studies reported above offer at best modest insights. However, within this review, leadership behavior has been defined consistent with Mintzberg's emphasis as relational behavior between leaders and subordinates. Viewed from this perspective, the studies indicate the potential contribution that the quality of leader-subordinate relationships has for the morale and satisfaction of *both* parties. As well, the research gives some indication that the nature of leader-subordinate relations may vary by department size, type of department, and the sex match of leaders and followers. Nonetheless, it is unclear whether the findings about the leadership behavior of department chairpersons is generalizable to other levels of the academic hierarchy. What is clear from such studies, given their limitations, is that there is a need to investigate leadership behavior in the higher education context and to study the leadership of administrators at all levels of the organizational hierarchy. Uniquenesses and potentially substantial complexities argue for the need for carefully conducted studies that account for a variety of variables and control for known sources of variation. Conversely, the tendency to continue to rely on correlational research methods in leadership studies can be questioned in terms of the insights they will yield into the practice of leadership.

Conflict Resolution Behavior

Only two studies were found that directly addressed managerial mediation and disturbance-handling behavior. Hobbs focused on the management of academic disputes utilizing a critical incident methodology.[35] The disputes studied included those involving academic administrators, faculty, nonfaculty professionals, and ancillary personnel as well as community versus institutional personnel. In all categories, disputes were held sub rosa; they were avoided or muted whenever possible. The nature of disputes varied, however, among the constituencies. Non-professional personnel tended to have conflicts of interest, and faculty and administrators more often engaged in value conflicts. Administrative disputes were generally settled through compromise or resignation after due consideration of the tactical or sometimes strategic value of compromise. Compromising behavior was less characteristic of conflict resolution involving the other groups. Hobbs inferred that compromise was more endemic to the role of administrators—it was seen as more familiar and legitimate. Administrators also often assumed the third party role in disturbances involving other parties. They seldom served in the role of the mediator but, rather, as the intervenor—intruding into events after crises, adjudicating issues in question, and establishing parameters for future interactions. Intervention was most typical in disputes among ancillary personnel. In these cases, administrators imposed new arrangements in order to terminate controversy. With non-faculty professionals, administrators attempted to optimize the needs of both parties while observing institutional priorities. From the sides of the disputants, however, such interventions were usually perceived as one

more aspect of the conflict. The specific tactics of administrative intervention employed depended on astute timing and the use of the substance of the administrator's own participation. "I learned from watching (another third party administrator) when to act and when not to. At times he'd listen, at times he'd cajole and at times he'd question. But sometimes he'd say, 'stop; that's it; go no further.' And things would stop."[36] In contrast to this prevalent use of a personal style of intervention, Hobbs found little evidence of the use of quasi-legal practices such as grievance committees.

Some support for Hobbs' research comes from Weisbord, Lawrence, and Chains' study of conflict management practices in academic medical centers.[37] They found that bargaining or splitting differences in an attempt to maximize one's own interest was the preferred mode for resolving conflicts between departments as well as between faculty and administrators. Smoothing or letting people discuss issues in which differences existed without dealing with substantive issues was the second most preferred method of resolving conflict. Weisbord, Lawrence, and Chains suggested that these results contrasted dramatically with the industrial setting where confronting and forcing or where using power plays were identified as the major means of conflict management.

The research on conflict-resolution behavior is quite modest. Available research on peer-related behavior, leadership behavior, and conflict-resolution behavior in higher education partially confirms Mintzberg's research. Such behaviors are part of the managerial repertoire, and they are important components of overall managerial skill. The nature of behavior in this skill area is partially obscured by the researchers' tendencies to ignore it and by the tendency of some to fragment it through methodological reductionism. This problem was graphically revealed in the contrast of the rich insights on disturbance-handling behavior in Hobbs' research with the more limited observations on administrative behavior provided in other reported studies.

Conceptual Skills

Conceptual skills include the manager's capacity to collect and use different types of information for decision making in ambiguous situations. These decisions often entail allocating resources (e.g., money, space, and the manager's time). Mintzberg has provided additional insight into this area by his discovery that conceptual skills also involve the manager's capacity for identifying opportunities for change and gaining insight into the managerial role itself. Essentially these are the cognitive and creative behaviors of managers.

Information-Related Behavior

Fenker developed a questionnaire for evaluating administrators that he distributed among the faculty and staff of a single university[38] A factor analysis of the responses yielded four factors, one of which was an information/communication factor. Components of this factor included the accumulation of pertinent information before acting and communicating important information. Although information is important, Lunsford observed that it often comes from unconventional sources.[39] The hierarchical separation of academic administrators means they have restricted associations. Therefore, they place a premium on "political" information and informal knowledge of constituent attitudes as well as their academic knowledge based on past faculty experience. In contrast, the everyday knowledge of operating information for administrators is variable. Astin and Christian studied the variance between administrators' everyday knowledge of basic institutional information and the "actual" data.[40] The study, which was conducted in liberal arts colleges, resulted in the finding that there was an average error of between 6 and 8% among all administrators on data about student enrollment, faculty size, and finances or budgets. Directors of development had the greatest error and academic administrators the least. Presidents were most accurate on student-related data, least accurate on faculty data, and consistently overestimated revenues—what Astin and Christian characterized as "wishful thinking." Administrators use their political information and experience, Lunsford has argued, to explain and define the institution with "socially integrating myths."[41] These broad abstractions help to hold a loosely coordinated institution together and provide

members a sense of mission. Patrick and Caruthers in a national survey of college and university presidents provided some support for Lunsford's ethnographic insights.[42] The presidents perceived communicating institutional strengths to internal constituencies, trustees, and the public as a major current focus. There was almost universal agreement among the presidents, however, that data and analytical reports were of low priority. Adams, Kellogg, and Schroeder discovered that when administrators provided information to guide operational decision making, it was often limited.[43] That is, at most it included a due date, guidelines for a report format, and individual or group responsibilities. Rarely were administrators precise about the types of final output needed or about assumptions, constraints, or implementation issues. In sum, while information is deemed critical to administrators, the sources and uses of information appear somewhat unconventional when viewed in the light of the recommendations of traditional management texts.

Administrative behavior in relationship to management, especially computer-based, information systems, has received particular attention in the research literature. Wyatt and Zeckhauser conducted in-depth interviews at six different sized institutions including both public and private universities.[44] The attitudes of administrators toward quantitative data and management reports appeared to be a function of individual background, discipline, and prior experience. Size of institution[45] also seemed positively related to the use of such data. Some individuals with a non-quantitative background tended to hold a "technological mystique" and were unrealistic about the kind of improvements that were possible with improved management information. Management information systems that were in use were often manual, idiosyncratic, and ad hoc—the information was in an individual's head and the procedures were unwritten. Centralized information systems were criticized for being too late, being too hard to decipher, or lacking critical data. Baldridge in a comparable study of liberal arts colleges observed that reports contained too much "junk" (or unfocused data).[46] If administrators had to stop and translate raw data, it was perceived as slowing down the decision-making process. Baldridge also discovered that, to the extent data were used, their major value was in facilitating "hot spot" analyses—the data highlighted or made more obvious those issues previously neglected. Wyatt and Zeckhauser concluded that the difficulties with using existing information systems led to three typical administrative responses.[47] The first was to use data that were available on the spur of the moment, the second was to use interpreters who understood and could translate existing information, and the third was to create parochial or local level information systems.

Research on particular types of quantitative information has resulted in similar conclusions.[48] Large amounts of data are often available, but they are used principally for operating purposes and for outside reporting. The management applications of the information (e.g., for establishing recruitment costs per student admitted) are minimal, and relevant management analytical techniques (e.g., long-term cash budgeting) are rarely utilized. In concluding, Adams, Kellogg, and Schroeder argued that these results were due overwhelmingly to utilization rather than to availability factors.[49]

Feldman and March have provided insight into the information-related behavior of academic managers.[50] Consistent with the research just reviewed they observed that academic administrators appear to value information that has no great decision relevance—they gather information and do not use it, they ask for reports and do not read them, and they act first and ask for information later. Feldman and March suggested that this behavior can be understood as a function of belief, that is, a general academic commitment to reason and rational discourse as well as to a decision theory perspective on the nature of life. As a result, displaying the use of information symbolizes a commitment to rational choice and signals personal and organizational competence. This dichotomy between the symbolic and the real may be attributed to the background and training of academic managers as well as to the organizational characteristics of academic institutions. It can also be attributed, as Mintzberg discovered in business organizations, to a general ignorance about the true nature of managerial work among those who design and develop information systems.

Decision-Making Behavior

Research on decision-making behavior falls into three general arenas: the locus or location of decision making, the sources of influence on decision making, and actual decision-making behavior.

In a survey of Canadian community colleges, Heron and Friesen discovered a parallel between structuring and decentralization of decision making.[51] That is, as institutions grew and aged, the size of the administrative component and the use of formal documents in administration increased. But decentralization of decision making also increased in these institutions. This was particularly true when institutional growth was accompanied (as it usually was) by increasing academic specialization. Similarly, Ross, using a national data set found that organizational complexity and certain aspects of administrative apparatus, such as administrative use of the computer and presence of an institutional research office, were positively associated with decentralized decision making.[52] Ross concluded that culture—local traditions, beliefs, and values as influenced by an institution's history—may be a better predictor of the locus of decision making than are structural variables. Studies such as these are helpful in indicating the pitfalls of simplistic or dichotomous thinking about the location of decision making. Put another way, a large administrative structure or a high degree of structuring activity is not necessarily incompatible with decentralization of authority.

In studies of influences on managerial decision making, the type of decision influenced appears to vary with administrative positions.[53] Faculties, department heads, deans, and central level administrators in public universities were perceived as having primary influence on different clusters of decisions although they partially influence one another on many decisions. Demographic factors such as the region of the country, type of field, size, and existence of collective bargaining also affected the pattern of influence within an institution. McLaughlin, Montgomery, and Sullins suggested that the pattern of influence was associated with the decisions made by the chairmen.[54] When faculty were most influential, the chairman's goals were faculty oriented. In contrast, chair-dominated departments were characterized by goals less orientated to faculty development. There has also been limited research on the influence of individual differences on decision making. In a survey of public university administrators in California, Walker and Lawler discovered an association between political orientation, expectations regarding the impact of collective bargaining, and support for implementation of collective bargaining.[55] Strong opposition to collective bargaining was, therefore, partially explained by unfavorable perceptions and political attitudes. Two studies that investigated sex differences, however, suggested that the decision-making behavior of male and female academic administrators was more similar than dissimilar.[56] In sum, level in the hierarchy, distribution of influence, and personal perceptions and attitudes have all been found to relate to decision-making behavior.

In a study of administrators in community colleges, four-year colleges, and one university, Taylor provided one of the few direct studies of decision-making behavior.[57] Utilizing the well known Vroom-Yetton model of decision styles, in the study administrators chose a style of encouraging faculty participation over two-thirds of the time. They also preferred decision styles which protected the "quality" of a decision rather than those that ensured decision acceptance or implementation. Nonetheless, a closer analysis by Taylor revealed little relationship between the nature of the problem and the preferred style of decision making. For example, in those situations where more information was required, where commitment to the decision was critical to success, where non-acceptance could generate high conflict, or where fairness was at issue, the administrators often selected autocratic styles. Taylor's evidence also indicated support for faculty participation was an ideological response among department heads as opposed to an explicitly considered decision-making style. As Lunsford argued, administrators seemed to assume that universities are united by strongly shared and well understood values that provide guidelines for tough decisions.[58] The administrator, therefore, can make decisions as a benevolent representative of the institution. The interests of the institution, like the public interest, are assumed to be equivalent to the interests of all participants and thereby become a basis for choice. As a consequence, academic administrators rely

strongly on the myth of consultation as a legitimizing force for their decisions. Taylor's research, when combined with Lunsford's analysis, suggests a potential dichotomy between what is espoused and what is practiced in academic decision making. The gap is likely to vary by institution depending both on institutional history and on the prior socialization of faculty.

Several studies examined decision-making behavior related to substantive areas such as budgeting and program evaluation. Moyer and Kretlow in a national study of vice-presidents of finance in colleges and universities found little use of commonly employed business techniques in program evaluation decisions or in capital investment decisions.[59] Instead of capital evaluation techniques, current demand—usually expressed as demonstrated academic need—was not only the primary, but usually also the exclusive criterion. Adams, Kellogg, and Schroeder in an in-depth study of decision making and information systems at small colleges came to similar conclusions.[60] In faculty position allocations, institutional goal setting, and budgeting, decision making was responsive rather than anticipatory and was characterized by reacting to requests for expansion and setting goals only when demand was great. Again, the technical apparatus which might have been appropriate or supportive of these decision processes was not in evidence. At least well through the 1970s, therefore, decision making continued to be present oriented and subject to both influence and negotiation.

The research on decision-making behavior is not inconsistent with, and to some extent supports, the well known "garbage can" model of decision making developed by Cohen, March, and Olsen.[61] In this model, university decision making frequently does not resolve problems. Choices are more likely to be made in these settings by flight or oversight, and the decisions made are apt to be among those of intermediate importance rather than of most or least importance. The matching of problems, choices, and decision makers is partly determined by problem content, problem relevance, and the competence of the decision maker. However, decision choices are sensitive to timing, the current catalog of problems, and the overall load on the system. For example, Cohen and March suggested that decision-making style was apt to vary by institutional size and wealth as well as by changes in organizational slack or the relative availability of financial resources.[62] The research on decision making just reviewed, provides detailed insight into the dynamics of the garbage can model. The possible effects of demographic factors, influence, personality, beliefs, and technology are suggested, and the tendency toward decision making by flight and oversight is quite apparent.

Resource-Allocation Behavior

Mintzberg characterized resource allocation behavior as involving the allocation of all resources—the manager's time, the delegation of responsibility, and the allocation of financial resources. As discussed previously in the section on time-related behavior, academic administrators are similar to managers generally in the amount of their time that they allocate to different constituencies, activities, and media. That is, academic administrators allocate their largest block of work time to other administrators (peers and subordinates), to meetings and committee work, and to the verbal medium, particularly telephone conversations and informal discussions. Contact with faculty and students, and solitary work (and, by inference, reading and analytical activity) receive less time. Of particular importance is the fact that academic managers are largely responsive to the demands of others in allocating their time. The most distinctive characteristic of time allocation, particularly at the departmental level, is the high allocation of time to academic work (averaging between 45–50%) as contrasted to managerial or administrative work. Although this behavior undoubtedly diminishes as one moves up the administrative hierarchy, the continued allocation of time to academic work helps to explain much of the dissatisfaction and stress in academic administration as well as the frequent observation that academic institutions are undermanaged.[63] It also seems to influence the behavior of subordinates. Glueck and Thorp reported a negative relationship between perceived amount of time department heads spend on their own research and faculty satisfaction with the administrator.[64]

There was no direct research evidence on delegation behavior, although the previously discussed research on the decentralization of decision making and the use or non-use of participative decision making by department heads could be viewed from this perspective. There has, however, been substantial research on the allocation of financial resources. In a national sample of college presidents, Patrick and Caruthers discovered that fiscal resource allocation and reallocation were among the two highest current priorities for change.[65] Moyer and Kretlow reported that facilities allocations were usually based on presidential "wish lists." Although institutional standards for space needs had been developed, no institution in their study had assigned facilities costs to programs or used discounting methods of cost/revenue matching techniques.[66] Similarly, Adams, Kellogg, and Schroeder found little use of class size and teaching load standards or unit costs in the allocation of faculty positions and discretionary budgets.[67]

A series of related studies have suggested that administrators base their resource allocations on perceptions of influence and power. The results of the studies, all conducted in major research universities, reveal that universalistic criteria such as workload or numbers of students are less powerful predictors of the allocation of faculty slots and discretionary funds than are various measures of subunit power.[68] In the most recent test of this model, it was discovered that the state of paradigm development of a unit increases its power since high paradigm units are more likely to receive outside funds.[69] High paradigm departments also possess greater consensus and, therefore, act as a stronger coalition in fights for internal resources.[70] Power, operationalized as the ability to attract grants and contracts as well as student enrollments, was thus inferred to be a de facto administrative criterion for the allocation of scarce resources. Finally, power was a more important criterion during periods of resource scarcity, suggesting that attempts to develop more universalistic criteria for allocation decisions during retrenchment may run counter to normal managerial behavior.[71]

Of particular interest in the research on resource allocation behavior is the tendency toward present-oriented responsiveness to other's demands, the relative lack of independent criteria or values on which to base resource allocation decisions, and the avoidance by administrators of management technology or expertise as inputs to resource allocation decision processes.

Entrepreneurial Behavior

Mintzberg's concept of entrepreneurial behavior is metaphorically similar to the process of project management. Managers search their organizations for problems or opportunities for change and then initiate improvement projects to address them. Some of these projects are supervised personally, such as a study of the age distribution of faculty, and others are delegated by the manager to staff members while retaining responsibility for review and quality control. Implicit in Mintzberg's analysis are two critical assumptions: (1) that the manager is constantly involved in developing and implementing improvement projects and is juggling a number of such projects at any one time; and (2) that, like R and D projects, many improvement projects fail or lead to no implementable result. These insights derived from the observation of managers at work have a face validity for those who have been involved in academic management. Patrick and Caruthers in their national survey reported that college presidents identified with certain managerial change priorities and placed greater importance on developing procedures for managerial change than on reports and data analysis of results.[72] However, the research analyzed for this review does not directly address entrepreneurial behavior. In part, this may be due to a methodological or conceptual bias in which organizational change has been interpreted as a response to changes in the external environment.[73] For example, Manns and March discovered a measurable relationship between changes in resource availability and departmental curricula change at Stanford University, but because of the methods and variables selected, no insight was provided about how this process was managed at the departmental level.[74] Similarly, Salancik, Staw, and Pondy studied the relationship between external change and department chair turnover, and they concluded that the largest amount of turnover was explained by factors associated with organization and context, and was not directly affected by the individual capacities or characteristics of administrators (although these characteristics and capacities

were not measured and, therefore, could not be controlled in the study).[75] Mintzberg's interpretation of the manager as a change agent also conflicts with the prevailing model of organizational development which advocates an external change agent.[76] A possible result of such methodological and theoretical biases, therefore, is a relative lack of knowledge about the means by which academic managers act in an entrepreneurial manner to bring about change in their organizations. The implications of this will be explored below.

Introspective Behavior

Mintzberg suggested that managers need the capacity to thoroughly understand their jobs, that they should be sensitive to their own impact on their organizations, and that they should have the ability to learn by introspection. Argyris developed a model of organizational learning, based in part on research with academic administrators, that takes a similar position to that taken by Mintzberg.[77] Argyris advocates that academic professionals need the capacity to take technical actions and, simultaneously, to reflect on their practice. This in effect double-loop learning will become even more critical in the future, Argyris believes, because the management dilemmas that will be encountered will require examination of both current values and underlying policies. Argyris therefore advocates double loop learning as a theoretical basis for professional and executive education.

Academic managers, of course, are not by and large professionally trained in management. Further, research continually suggests that professionals learn little from seminars and continuing professional education opportunities; instead, they are most influenced by learning that takes place in conjunction with the job itself. What would be of most value for the higher education setting would be research on effective patterns of learning and introspective behavior of academic managers in the context of their work. Regrettably, such research does not appear to have been conducted. Lewis and Dahl's research suggested that academic administrators at the department head and dean levels either deny, resist, or do not fully comprehend the obligations of their administrative duties.[78] The greatest amount of stress was induced for these administrators because they appeared to resist allocating sufficient time to administrative demands. This suggests that accurate knowledge of the job, of the current demands of the job, and of their own preferences was inadequate. McLaughlin, Montgomery, and Sullins discovered a relationship between a chairperson's perception of who has influence and his or her own professional goals.[79] If these administrators perceived themselves in control or as making the major decisions, they characteristically spent more time in guiding the growth and development of the department as well as its personnel and programs, and had a greater desire to continue in administration. In contrast, if they perceived control to be above them, they typically spent more time in working with students, in doing liaison work, and in activities with expected return to the faculty. Similarly, Solmon and Tierney found that institutional reward systems that were perceived to foster acceptance of authority created less job satisfaction for administrators because they created a sense that the job was not challenging, that the administrator had little autonomy in decision making, and that the job had little variety.[80] Although this research can be related to the issue of introspective behavior, it is insufficiently illuminating because it does not provide any insight into the nature of the behavior itself.

Technical Skills: Profession-Related Behavior

Mintzberg suggested that managerial behavior can be separated from profession-related behavior in that the manager makes the transition from technical activity such as teaching and research to managerial activity. However, in the academic environment, this transition is rarely completed. Most academic administrators, in fact, continue to engage in academic responsibilities. The allocation of time between profession-related and administrative activities and its relationship to administrative stress and satisfaction has already been addressed. A more fundamental question involves the relationship between academic skill or background and interpersonal behavior, conceptual behavior, and overall management success. For example, research in a related setting—R and D organizations—suggests that scientific expertise is an important predictor of managerial

effectiveness.[81] The results from anecdotal evidence in recent publications on computer modelling provide an indication that the disciplinary background of senior academic administrators can be of primary importance in influencing the successful implementation of contemporary planning and management techniques.[82] It is worth noting that, although a number of the research studies reported here identify discipline or field as a variable with implications for faculty behavior, departmental leadership style, and centralized allocation behavior, no study directly examined the relationship between the technical and professional skills of administrators and administrative behavior.[83] This seems odd, because there is well validated research on substantive differences in behavior among faculty members from different disciplines.[84] Such studies suggest that the relationship between technical skill or background and administrative behavior could be a fruitful and particularly important component of research in higher education administration and would have practical implications for management selection, training, and development.

Discussion

In the sections above, the available research over the last ten years on administrative behavior in higher education has been analyzed utilizing the combined conceptual frameworks of Katz and Mintzberg. In this section some broader issues will be explored including the author's possible bias, methodological issues of research in this area, and implications for future research.

The available research on higher education suggests that the use and allocation of time among academic administrators is not untypical of managers generally. Academic managers: (1) perform a great quantity of work at a continual pace; (2) carry out activities characterized by variety, fragmentation, and brevity; (3) prefer issues that are current, specific, and ad hoc; (4) demonstrate a preference for verbal media (telephone calls, meetings, and brief discussions); and (5) develop informal information systems. Unlike their management counterparts in other organizations, academic managers are apt to sustain substantial academic technical activity while in their managerial roles. They are also, particularly department heads and deans, less likely to be comfortable with full-time administrative responsibilities. Both interpersonal skill and what Katz terms conceptual skill play an important part in academic managerial work. Research on interpersonal skills has been addressed somewhat in terms of leadership skills. Given the organizational structure and belief systems of academic organizations, the development of horizontal peer networks for information and influence could, however, be more important to academic administrators than to other managers. Unfortunately, there has been little definitive research on this topic. Similarly, conflict negotiation and dispute settlement deserve more attention, and Hobbs has suggested some fruitful leads in this regard.[85] In the category of conceptual behavior, substantial attention has been given to information-processing, decision-making, and resource allocation behavior, but relatively little is known about the entrepreneurial and introspective behavior of academic managers. Since the management of change is routinely advocated as the role of the administrator, the apparent paucity of research on how academic administrators *actually manage* change is somewhat surprising.

The writer began this review effort with a certain bias—that is, that academic management is an ambiguous process highly dependent on flows of influence and power, and subject to the beliefs and values of the academic culture. If anything, this bias has been strengthened by the analysis of available research. First, it is apparent that informal influence, negotiations, and networks of contacts are important aspects of academic administration as it is currently practiced. Second, the results of research on information-related behavior, decision making, and resource allocation provide some indication that academic management is still highly intuitive, tends to avoid the use of quantitative data or available management technology, and is subject to the political influence of various powerful groups and interests. Third, the traditions, beliefs, and values of individuals, disciplines, and institutions appear to play a more substantial role than is generally acknowledged in the extant prescriptive literature on management. In short, the garbage can

model of decision making and the institutional context of organized anarchy as articulated by March and his colleagues receives much support from the available research on administrative behavior.

Nevertheless, it is wise to be cautious about these generalizations. Although the models of ambiguity and influence may better fit the available data than do the highly rational models, current understandings are based on historical evidence. Furthermore, the contextual environment which obviously influences the development of current patterns of administrative behavior is currently changing, perhaps dramatically. Those studies that have sampled administrative behavior over time provide evidence of differing patterns of managerial behavior under various environmental circumstances. For example, Cohen, March, and Olsen's simulation of the garbage can model predicted modification of administrative decision-making behavior (i.e., organizational learning) over time and as organizational slack was reduced.[86] In other words, it is important to maintain a constant willingness to test models and biases against current empirical data.

In sum, available research, not surprisingly, prompts the notion that a better understanding of administrative behavior is critical to improved management: (1) for example, sophisticated information systems that are planned without sufficient attention to the needs and working habits of academic administrators appear to make little (immediate) impact; (2) further, since human beings need and seek meaning, an important part of academic administration involves the creation and maintenance of academic beliefs;[87] and finally, (3) interpersonal relationships and skills are an important part of management in organizations that depend for their effectiveness on the talent of autonomous, creative, and often "spikey" individuals. It is reasonable to assume that managerial behavior in academic organizations may change in response to new conditions. However, the understanding of that process is most apt to occur through research on the relationships between administrative behavior, technology, and structure.

The methodologies of studies reviewed deserve special attention. In the first place, sampling strategies vary substantially. Some studies are focused on single institutions and the elite, research institutions are over-represented in this respect. Other studies have surveyed particular clusters of institutions such as private liberal arts colleges, public universities, or community colleges. Overall, research seems to be heavily focused on larger research universities and published studies of administrative behavior in small or community colleges are far less common. While available information on the focus and source of data for each study was included in the analysis above, specificity in this regard was often difficult to ascertain. One of the consistently reliable findings of research in this area is that institutions of higher education vary in organization and management by type and level of institution.[88] The research reviewed here confirms that institutional type, level, region, size, and culture can all contribute to variance in administrative behavior. It is reasonable, of course, to argue that the study of a single case can provide a model suitable for testing in later studies. March and Pfeffer, and their colleagues, have demonstrated the value of this approach. However, among the research studies reviewed for this article, more than half seem to be unaware of the obvious weaknesses in terms of their focus and sampling procedures, or of the relevant research on institutional types. Future research on administrative behavior in higher education needs to give significantly greater attention to measuring and controlling for variance between types of institutions.

A second major issue relates to the conceptual frameworks employed in some of the studies. Studies tend to employ a psychological model that reduces behavior to the study of relationships between variables relevant to the psychological models used, or they employ a sociological unit of analysis which tends to bypass individual behavior altogether. There are, of course, fundamentally important reasons for such selectivity. The psychological approach places emphasis on precision of measurement and the potential for prediction, often with some penalty in overall understanding. The sociological logic has been well expressed by March.[89] Throughout his work, March has evolved a Tolstoyan perspective on academic administrators that argues that great leadership is unlikely, particularly in organizations of this type. Academic administration, in

this view, is an art of small adjustments in which larger and, by inference, slow-moving forces determine the evolution of events. But each of these two perspectives, the psychological and the sociological, limits the understanding of administrative behavior. The framework and precision of the psychological view causes researchers to overlook key interpersonal processes. For example, the means by which administrators build and maintain networks for information and influence were ignored by traditional management researchers until they were emphasized in the observational work of Mintzberg and his followers. Even today, there has been little informative research that suggests the relationships of importance in this domain. Although the sociological point of view provides an appropriate sense of humility toward administrative accomplishment, its results are similarly impoverished in terms of advancing knowledge. If the contribution of management is at the margin through small adjustments and improvements, then how is this accomplished? As the results of research on managers continually indicate, it is a profession of action. Therefore, illuminating the nature of administrative action and its consequences in different settings is apt to be of substantial value to theory and to practice. With the exception of a few of the studies reviewed, there is little insight into administrative behavior in action. This criticism is not a plea for a particular type of methodology but, rather, for a more creative application and interchange between the disciplines and methodologies available to inquirers.

Conclusion

The research on administrative behavior in higher education over the last ten years has helped to fill an important gap that Peterson observed in his 1974 review of the field. While the research is modest in amount and limited in approach, it provides some insight into the nature of managerial work in higher education as well as suggestions for promising directions in both research and practice.

The nature of academic organizations and of administration in these settings highlights the centrality of human behavior, beliefs, and values. Although organizational structure and management technology are very important, studies of those mechanisms and processes in the absence of an understanding of administrative behavior at best make a limited contribution to theory or to practice. Ironically, while the best known research on academic organizations provides a rich understanding of the role of human behavior, culture, and meaning in the development of these institutions (see, for example, the many writings of Burton Clark, James March, David Riesman, and Lawrence Veysey), it is currently the students of business organizations who argue most strongly for an emphasis on entrepreneurship, organizational culture, the development of human assets, and the importance of interpersonal skills.[90]

The intent of this review was to provide an integrative understanding of the current knowledge concerning administrative behavior in higher education. Taking stock at certain periods is a necessary and important part of the ongoing attempts to advance both practice and research. To paraphrase A. N. Whitehead, the scientist does not inquire in order to know, the scientist knows in order to inquire.

David D. Dill is Associate Professor of Education and Assistant to the Chancellor at the University of North Carolina at Chapel Hill.

References

1. The writer would like to acknowledge the help of Peter Cistone, Ralph Kimbrough, James Lemons, Sandra Reed, Jay Smout, John Walker, and two anonymous reviewers in the preparation of this article.
2. M. W. Peterson, "Organization and Administration in Higher Education: Sociological and Socio-Psychological Perspectives," in *Review of Research in Education*, Volume 2, F. N. Kerlinger and J. B. Carroll, eds. (Itasca, Ill.: F. E. Peacock, 1974).
3. J. G. March, "Analytical Skills and University Training of Educational Administrators," *Education and Urban Society* (6,4 (August 1974): 382–427.
4. H. Mintzberg, *The Nature of Managerial Work* (New York: Harper and Row, 1973).
5. L. B. Kurke and H. E. Aldrich, "Mintzberg Was Right!: A Replication and Extension of *The Nature of Managerial Work*" (Paper presented at the Annual Meeting of The Academy of Management, Atlanta, Ga., 1979).
6. J. P. Kotter, *The General Managers* (Glenco, Ill.: The Free Press, 1982).
7. C. M. Pavett and A. W. Lau, "Managerial Roles, Skills, And Effective Performance," *Pro-ceedings of the Forty-Second Annual Meeting of The Academy of Management* (New York: The Academy, 1982).
8. G. B. Jackson, "Methods for Integrative Reviews," *Review of Educational Research* 50, 3 (Fall 1980):438–460.
9. Ibid., p. 438.
10. Burton Clark's collective work on academic organizations has had a substantial impact on the field. For a useful synthesis of his findings, see B. R. Clark, *The Higher Education System* (Berkeley, Calif.: University of California Press, 1983).
11. M. D. Cohen and J. G. March, *Leadership and Ambiguity: The American College President* (New York: McGraw-Hill, 1973); M. O. Cohen, J. G. March, and J. P. Olsen, "A Garbage Can Model of Organizational Choice," *Administrative Science Quarterly* 17 (March 1972): 1–25; M. S. Feldman and J. G. March, "Information in Organizations as Signal and Symbol," *Administrative Science Quarterly* 26 (1981): 171–186; C. L. Manns and J. C. March, "Financial Adversity, Internal Competition and Curriculum Change in a University," *Administrative Science Quarterly* 23, 4 (1978): 541-552; and J. G. March, "How We Talk and How We Act: Administrative Theory and Administrative Life" (Seventh David D. Henry Lecture in Higher Education, University of Illinois, September, 1980).
12. Mintzberg, *Nature of Managerial Work*.
13. Jackson, "Methods for Integrative Reviews."
14. H. R. Bobbitt and O. C. Behling, "Organizational Behavior: A Review of the Literature," *Journal of Higher Education* 52, 1 (January/February 1981): 29–44.
15. R. L. Katz, "Skills of an Effective Administrator," *Harvard Business Review* (September/October 1974): 90–102.
16. Mintzberg, Nature of Managerial Work.
17. K. Anderson, *Management: Skills, Functions, and Organizational Performance* (Dubuque, Iowa: W. C. Brown Company, 1984).
18. Cohen and March, *Leadership and Ambiguity*.
19. D. R. Lewis and T. Dahl, "Time Management in Higher Education Administration: A Case Study," *Higher Education* 5 (1976): 49–66.
20. M. R. Weisbord, P. R. Lawrence, and M. P. Chains, "Three Dilemmas of Academic Medical Centers," *Journal of Applied Behavioral Sciences* 14, 3 (1978): 284–304.
21. T. F. Lunsford, "Authority and Ideology in the Administered University," in *The State of the University: Authority and Change*, C. E. Kruytbosch and S. L. Messinger, eds. (Beverly Hills, Calif.: Sage Publications, 1970).
22. L. J. Whitson and F. W. R. Hubert, "Interest Groups and The Department Chairperson: The Exertion of Influence in the Large Public University," *Journal of Higher Education* 53, 2 (1982): 163–176.

23. J. Stringer, "The Role of the 'Assistant To' in Higher Education," *Journal of Higher Education* 48, 2 (March/April): 193–201.

24. W. O. Peterson, "Critical Incidents for New and Experienced College and University Presidents," *Research in Higher Education* 3 (1975): 45–50.

25. L. C. Solmon and M. L. Tierney, "Determinants of Job Satisfaction among College Administrators," *Journal of Higher Education* 48,4 (July/August 1977): 412–431.

26. D. P. Hoyt and R. K. Spangler, "The Measurement of Administrative Effectiveness of the Academic Department Head," *Research in Higher Education* 10, 4 (1979): 291–303.

27. S. Coltrin and W. Glueck, "Effect of Leadership Roles on Satisfaction and Productivity of University-Research Professors," *Academy of Management Journal* 20, 1 (1977): 101-116.

28. W. F. Glueck and C. D. Thorp, "The Role of the Academic Administrator in Research Professors' Satisfaction and Productivity," *Educational Administration Quarterly* 10, 1 (Winter 1974): 72–90.

29. Y. Neumann and S. B. Boris, "Paradigm Development and Leadership Style of University Department Chairmen," *Research in Higher Education* 9 (1978): 291–302.

30. N. E. Groner, "Leadership Situations in Academic Departments: Relations among Measures of Situational Favorableness and Control," *Research in Higher Education* 8 (1978): 125–143.

31. A. B. Carroll, "Role Conflict in Academic Organizations: An Exploratory Examination of the Department Chairman's Experience," *Educational Administration Quarterly* 10, 2 (Spring 1974): 51–64.

32. R. L.Kahn, D. M. Wolfe, R. P. Quinn, J. O. Snoek, and R. A. Rosenthal, *Organizational Stress: Studies in Role Conflict and Ambiguity* (New York: John Wiley, 1964).

33. T. M. Madron, J. R. Craig, and R. M. Mendel, "Departmental Morale as a Function of the Perceived Performance of Department Heads," *Research in Higher Education* 5 (1976): 83–94.

34. E. K. Miner, H. A. King, and E. L. Pizzini, "Relationship Between Sex and Leadership Behavior of Department Heads in Physical Education," *Research in Higher Education* 10, 2 (1979): 113–121.

35. W. C. Hobbs, "The 'Defective Pressure-Cooker' Syndrome," *Journal of Higher Education* 45, 8 (1974): 569–581.

36. Ibid, p. 578.

37. Weisbord, Lawrence and Charns, "Three Dilemmas."

38. R. M. Fenker, "The Evaluation of University Faculty and Administrators: A Case Study," *Journal of Higher Education* 56, 6 (November/December 1975): 665–686.

39. Lunsford, "Authority and Ideology."

40. A. W. Astin and C. E. Christian, "What do Administrators Know about Their Institutions?" *Journal of Higher Education* 49, 4 (July/August 1977): 389–400.

41. Lunsford, "Authority and Ideology."

42. C. Patrick and J. K. Caruthers, "Management Priorities of College Presidents," *Research in Higher Education* 12, 3 (1980): 195–214.

43. C. R. Adams, T. E. Kellogg, and R. C. Schroeder, "Decision-Making and Information Systems in Colleges," *Journal of Higher Education* 47, 1 (January/February 1976): 33–49.

44. J. B. Wyatt and S. Zeckhauser, "University Executives and Management Information: A Tenuous Relationship," *Educational Record* 56, 3 (Summer 1975): 175–189.

45. R. C. Moyer and W. J. Kretlow, "The Resource Allocation Decision in U.S. Colleges and Universities: Practice, Problems and Recommendations," *Higher Education* 7 (1978): 35–46.

46. J. V. Baldridge, "Impact on College Administration: Management Information Systems and Management by Objectives Systems," *Research in Higher Education* 10, 3 (1979): 263–282.

47. Wyatt and Zeckhauser, "University Executives and Management Information."

48. Adams, Kellogg, and Schroeder, "Decision-Making and Information Systems"; and Moyer and Kretlow, "The Resource Allocation Decision."

49. Adams, Kellogg, and Schroeder, "Decision-Making and Information Systems."

50. Feldman and March, "Information Organizations."

51. R. P. Heron and D. Friesen, "Growth and Development of College Administrative Structures," *Research in Higher Education*, Vol. 1 (1973): 333–346.

52. R. D. Ross, "Decentralization of Authority in Colleges and Universities," *Research in Higher Education* 6, 2 (1977): 97–123.

53. G. W. McLaughlin, J. R. Montgomery, and W. R. Sullins, "Roles and Characteristics of Department Chairmen in State Universities as Related to Level of Decision Making," *Research in Higher Education* 6 (1977): 327–341; Whitson and Hubert, "Interest Groups and the Department Chairperson."

54. McLaughlin, Montgomery, and Sullins, "Roles and Characteristics."

55. J. M. Walker and J. D. Lawler, "University Administrators and Faculty Bargaining," *Research in Higher Education* 16, 4 (1982): 353–372.

56. O. Andruskin and N. J. Howes, "Dispelling a Myth: That Stereotypic Attitudes Influence Evaluations of Women as Administrators in Higher Education," *Journal of Higher Education* 51, 5 (1980): 475–496; and Mimer, King, and Pizzini, "Relationship between Sex and Leadership Behavior."

57. A. L. Taylor, "Decision-Process Behaviors of Academic Managers," *Research in Higher Education* 16, 2 (1982): 155–173.

58. Lunsford, "Authority and Ideology."
59. Moyer and Kretlow, "The Resource Allocation Decision."
60. Adams, Kellogg, and Schroeder, "Decision-Making and Information Systems."
61. Cohen, March, and Olsen, "A Garbage Can Model."
62. Cohen and March, *Leadership and Ambiguity*.
63. Adams, Kellogg, and Schroeder, "Decision-Making and Information Systems"; Lewis and Dahl, "Time Management"; and C. W. McLaughlin, J. R. Montgomery, and L. F. Malpass, "Selected Characteristics, Roles, Goals, and Satisfactions of Department Chairmen in State and Land-Grant Institutions," *Research in Higher Education* 3 (1975): 243–259.
64. Glueck and Thorp, "The Role of the Academic Administrator."
65. Patrick and Caruthers, "Management Priorities."
66. Moyer and Kretlow, "The Resource Allocation Decision."
67. Adams, Kellogg, and Schroeder, "Decision-Making and Information Systems."
68. F. S. Hills and T. A. Mahoney, "University Budgets and Organizational Decision Making," *Administrative Science Quarterly* 23, 3 (1978): 454–465; J. Pfeffer and G. R. Salancik, "Organizational Decision Making as a Political Process: The Case of a University Budget," *Administrative Science Quarterly* 19, 2 (1974): 135–151; G. R. Salancik and Jeffrey Pfeffer, "The Bases and Use of Power in Organizational Decision Making: The Case of a University," *Administrative Science Quarterly* 19, 4 (1974): 453–473; and Manns and March, "Financial Adversity."
69. J. Pfeffer and W. L. Moore, "Power in University Budgeting: A Replication and Extension," *Administrative Science Quarterly* 25, 4 (1994): 637–653.
70. Groner, "Leadership Situations"; and Pfeffer and Moore, "Power in University Budgeting."
71. Hills and Mahoney, "University Budgets"; and Pfeffer and Moore, "Power in University Budgeting."
72. Patrick and Caruthers, "Management Priorities."
73. D. Katz and R. L. Kahn, *Social Psychology of Organizations*, 2nd Edition (New York: John Wiley, 1978).
74. Manns and March, "Financial Adversity."
75. G. Salancik, B. Staw, and L. Pondy, "Administrative Turnover as a Response to Unman-

aged Organizational Interdependence." *Academy of Management Journal* 23, 3 (1980): 422–437.
76. Bobbitt and Behling, "Organizational Behavior."
77. C. Argyris, "Educating Administrators and Professionals," in *Leadership in the '80s*, C. Argyris and R. M. Cyert (Cambridge, Mass.: Institute for Educational Management/Harvard University, 1980).
78. Lewis and Dahl, "Time Management."
79. McLaughlin, Montgomery, and Sullins, "Roles and Characteristics."
80. Solmon and Tierney, "Determinants of Job Satisfaction."
81. N. Rosen, R. Billings, J. Turney, "The Emergence and Allocation of Leadership Resources Over Time in a Technical Organization," *Academy of Management Journal* 20 (1976): 165–183.
82. D. S. P. Hopkins and W. F. Massey, *Planning Models for Colleges and Universities* (Stanford, Calif.: Stanford University Press, 1981).
83. Coltrin and Glueck, "Effect of Leadership Roles"; Groner, "Leadership Situations"; Neumann and Boris, "Paradigm Development"; Pfeffer and Moore, "Power in University Budgeting"; Salancik, Straw, and Pondy, "Administrative Turnover."
84. J. M. Beyer and T. M. Lodahl, "A Comparative Study of Patterns of Influence," *Administrative Science Quarterly* 21 (1976): 104–129; and A. Biglan, "Relationships Between Subject Matter Characteristics and the Structure and Output of University Departments," *Journal of Applied Psychology* 57, 3 (1973): 204–213.
85. Hobbs, "The Syndrome."
86. Cohen, March, and Olsen, "A Garbage Can Model."
87. D. Dill, "The Management of Academic Culture," *Higher Education* 11, 3 (1982): 303–320.
88. J. V. Baldridge, D. V. Curtis, G. Ecker, and G. L. Riley, *Policy Making and Effective Leadership* (San Francisco: Jossey-Bass, 1978).
89. March, "How We Talk."
90. See, for example, T. E. Deal and A. A. Kennedy, *Corporate Cultures* (Reading, Mass.: Addison-Wesley, 1982); W. G. Ouchi, *Theory Z* (Reading, Mass.: Addison-Wesley, 1981); and T. J. Peters and R. H. Waterman, Jr., *In Search of Excellence* (New York: Harper and Row, 1982).

CHAPTER 8

ADMINISTRATIVE AND PROFESSIONAL AUTHORITY

AMITAI ETZIONI

The ultimate source of the organizational dilemmas reviewed up to this point is the incomplete matching of the personalities of the participants with their organizational roles. If personalities could be shaped to fit specific organizational roles, or organizational roles to fit specific personalities, many of the pressures to displace goals, much of the need to control performance, and a good part of the alienation would disappear. Such matching is, of course, as likely as an economy without scarcity and hence without prices. But even if all the dilemmas which result from the incomplete articulation of personality and organization were resolved, there still would remain those which are consequences of conflicting tendencies built into the organizational structure.

Probably the most important structural dilemma is the inevitable strain imposed on the organization by the use of knowledge. All social units use knowledge, but organizations use more knowledge more systematically than do other social units. Moreover, most knowledge is created in organizations and passed from generation to generation—i.e., preserved—by organizations. It is here that Weber overlooked one necessary distinction: He viewed bureaucratic or administrative authority as based on technical knowledge or training; the subordinates, he thought, accept rules and orders as legitimate because they consider being rational being right, and regard their superiors as more rational.[1] One is not "stretching" Weber much to suggest that he thought that the higher the rank of an official the better equipped he tends to be either in terms of formal education e.g., academic degrees or in terms of merit and experience. Examinations and promotion according to merit, Weber pointed out, help to establish such association between rank and knowledge. To a degree, this conception is valid. There is considerable evidence that persons who have only a high-school education will be more frequently found in lower ranks, and college-educated persons in the higher ones. There is probably some correlation between IQ and rank, in the sense that on the average the IQ of the top third of an organization is likely to be higher than that of the lowest third. One could argue that when the superiority-of-knowledge requirement is not fulfilled, when the higher in rank knows less or has a lower IQ than the lower in rank, his orders might still be followed because of his power to enforce them; but Weber would counter that such orders would not be considered legitimate and hence the official would have power but not authority.

Still the reader is correct in his intuition that there is something fundamentally wrong with the notion of viewing the bureaucracy as a hierarchy in which the more rational rule the less rational. There are two reasons. First, by far most of the trained members of the organization are found not in the highest but in the middle ranks, and not in the regular line or command positions but around them. Depending on the type of organization, they are referred to as experts, staff, professionals, specialists, or by the names of their respective professions. Second, the most basic principle

"Administrative and Professional Authority," by Amitai Etzioni, reprinted from *Modern Organizations*, 1964, Prentice-Hall, Inc.

of administrative authority and the most basic principle of authority based on knowledge—or professional authority—not only are not identical but are quite incompatible.

Administrative vs. Professional Authority

Administration assumes a power hierarchy. Without a clear ordering of higher and lower in rank, in which the higher in rank have more power than the lower ones and hence can control and coordinate the latter's activities, the basic principle of administration is violated; the organization ceases to be a coordinated tool. However, knowledge is largely an individual property; unlike other organization means, it cannot be transferred from one person to another by decree. Creativity is basically individual and can only to a very limited degree be ordered and coordinated by the superior in rank. Even the application of knowledge is basically an individual act, at least in the sense that the individual professional has the ultimate responsibility for his professional decision. The surgeon has to decide whether or not to operate. Students of the professions have pointed out that the autonomy granted to professionals who are basically responsible to their consciences (though they may be censured by their peers' and in extreme cases by the courts) is necessary for effective professional work. Only if immune from ordinary social pressures and free to innovate, to experiment, to take risks without the usual social repercussions of failure, can a professional carry out his work effectively. It is this highly individualized principle which is diametrically opposed to the very essence of the organizational principle of control and coordination by superiors—i.e., the principle of administrative authority. In other words, the ultimate justification for a professional act is that it is, to the best of the professional's knowledge, the right act. He might consult his colleagues before he acts, but the decision is his. If he errs, he still will be defended by his peers. The ultimate justification of an administrative act, however, is that it is in line with the organization's rules and regulations, and that it has been approved—directly or by implication—by a superior rank.

The Organization of Knowledge

The question is how to create and use knowledge without undermining the organization. Some knowledge is formulated and applied in strictly private situations. In the traditional professions, medicine and law, much work is carried out in non-organizational contexts—in face-to-face interaction with clients. But as the need for costly resources and auxiliary staff has grown, even the traditional professions face mounting pressures to transfer their work to organizational structures such as the hospital and the law firm. Similarly, while most artistic work is still conducted in private contexts, often in specially segregated sectors of society in which an individual's autonomy is particularly high, much of the cognitive creativity, particularly in scientific research, has become embedded in organizational structures for reasons similar to those in medicine and law.

In addition there are several professions in which the amount of knowledge (as measured in years of training) and the degree of personal responsibility (as measured in the degree to which privileged communications—which the recipient is bound not to divulge—or questions of life and death are involved) are lower than in the older or highly creative, cognitive professions. Engineering and nursing are cases in point. These professions can be more easily integrated into organizational structures than can medicine or law, for example. Most professional work at this level is carried out within organizations rather than in private practice, and it is more given to supervision by persons higher in rank (who have more administrative authority but no more, or even less, professional competence) than the work of the professions discussed above.

To some degree, organizations circumvent the problem of knowledge by "buying" it from the outside, as when a corporation contracts for a market study from a research organization; i.e., it specifies the type of knowledge it needs and it agrees with the research group on price, but then it largely withdraws from control over the professional work. There are, however, sharp limitations on the extent to which knowledge can be recruited in this way, particularly since organizations consume such large amounts of knowledge and they tend to need more reliable control on its nature and flow. There are three basic ways in which knowledge is handled within organizations:

1. Knowledge is produced, applied, preserved, or communicated in organizations especially established for these purposes. These are *professional organizations,* which are characterized not only by the goals they pursue but also by the high proportion of professionals on their staff (at least 50 per cent) and by the authority relations between professionals and non-professionals which are so structured that professionals have superior authority over the major goal activities of the organization, a point which is explored below. Professional organizations include universities, colleges, most schools, research organizations, therapeutic mental hospitals, the larger general hospitals, and social-work agencies. For certain purposes it is useful to distinguish between those organizations employing professionals whose professional training is long (5 years or more), and those employing professionals whose training is shorter (less than 5 years). The former we call *full-fledged professional* organizations; the latter, *semiprofessional* organizations. Generally associated with differences in training of the professionals in these two types of organizations are differences in goals, in privileges, and in concern with matters of life and death. "Pure" professional organizations are primarily devoted to the creation and application of knowledge; their professionals are usually protected in their work by the guarantee of privileged communication, and they are often concerned with matters of life and death. Semi-professional organizations are more concerned with the communication and, to a lesser extent, the application of knowledge, their professionals are less likely to be guaranteed the right of privileged communications, and they are rarely directly concerned with matters of life and death.

2. There are *service organizations* in which professionals are provided with the instruments, facilities, and auxiliary staff required for their work. The professionals however are not employed by the organization nor subordinated to its administrators.

3. Professionals may be employed by organizations whose goals are *non-professional*, such as industrial and military establishments. Here professionals are often assigned to special divisions or positions, which to one degree or another take into account their special needs.

We shall first discuss the relation between the two authority principles—that of knowledge and that of administration—in non-professional organizations, then in "full-fledged" professional organizations, in semiprofessional organizations, and finally in service organizations.

Professional Authority in Non-professional Organizations

Superiority of Administrative Authority

By far the largest and most common non-professional organizations are the production organizations which are privately owned and managed. The organizational goal of private business is to make profits. The major means are production and exchange. While professionals deal with various aspects of the production and exchange process—that is, with means such as engineering, quality control, and marketing—the manager (the corporation's equivalent of the administrator) is expected to coordinate the various activities in such a way that the major organizational goal—profit-making—will be maximized. This seems to be one of the reasons why modern corporations prefer to have as top executives people with administrative experience rather than professionals. (In a study of the occupational backgrounds of the chief executives of American industry in 1950, administration was found to have been the principal occupation of 43.1 per cent; 11.8 per cent were defined as entrepreneurs; finance had been the field of 12.4 per cent; and only 12.6 per cent had been engineers.[2] People with scientific backgrounds such as research workers are even less likely to become heads of private business. Only about 4 per cent of the presidents of American corporations had such a background.[3])

In general, the goals of private business are consistent with administrative orientations. The economic orientation of the organization and the bureaucratic orientation of the administrative role share an orientation toward rational combination of means and development of rational procedures to maximize goals which are considered as given. The social and cultural conditions that support modern economic activities also support modern administration (see below, Ch. 10). Professional and economic orientations are less compatible.

When people with strong professional orientations take over managerial roles, a conflict between the organizational goals and the professional orientation usually occurs. Homans reports an interesting case in which the influence of professionally oriented participants was greater than in most corporations.[4] He discusses an electrical equipment company which was owned, managed, and staffed by engineers. Management, which was in the hands of administration-oriented engineers, suffered from pressure to pursue uneconomic goals by the professionally oriented design engineers. The design engineers were charged with being indifferent to the "general welfare of the company"—that is, to profit-making—as "shown by their lack of concern with finance, sales, and the practical needs of the consumer and by their habit of spending months on an aspect of design that had only theoretical importance." This caused considerable tension between the managerial and professionally oriented groups, tension to which this company was especially sensitive because of its high dependence on professional work and the special structure of ownership. A power struggle resulted which ended with a clearer subordination of the design engineers (staff) to the managerial engineers (line). This was mandatory "if the company was to survive and increase its sales," as Homans put it. The treasurer (a nonprofessional in this context) became the most influential member of the new management. In short, in a corporation where the professionals exerted a strong influence, the existence of the organization was threatened, considerable internal tension was generated, and finally the

organizational power structure was changed toward a more usual structure, with the professionally minded more clearly subordinated. In other words, the organizational authority structure was made more compatible with the goals of the organization. The orientations of the managers and the goals of private business seem to match. When a professional orientation dominates, this tends to "displace" the profit goal of privately owned economic organizations.

Staff and Line

The way the two kinds of authority are combined in corporations and other non-professional organizations is often referred to as "staff and line." The managers, whose authority is administrative, direct the major goal activities; the professionals deal with knowledge as a means, and with the knowledge aspect of other means. They are in a subordinate position to the managers. Thus, in cases of conflict between the two criteria for decision-making, the organizational power structure is slanted in favor of the administrative authority. However, professional subordinates are treated differently from regular subordinates; they are not treated as are lower ranks in a line structure, but as "staff," a term which designates positions outside the regular chain of command or "line" and implies a certain amount of autonomy.

There are two interpretations of the relationship between staff and line. According to one approach, the staff has no administrative authority whatsoever. It advises the administrators (line authority) on what action to take. The staff does not issue orders to those lower in rank; if it desires any action or correction, this must be achieved through those in the line rank. According to the second approach, the staff, while advising the line on various issues, also takes responsibility for limited areas of activity.[5] That is, on some matters the staff directly issues orders to the lower participants.

Both combinations of the two authority principles generate considerable strain. In the first, where the line alone issues orders, the line tends to be overloaded by demands for decisions, and tends to repel at least some of the professional advice and requests for action of the staff. Line personnel have a large number of other functional requirements they must look after. They rarely comprehend fully the bases of actions requested by the staff, and they tend to neglect or at least to under-represent the staff demands. In the second approach the lower line is subordinated to two authorities at a time. There is a functional division of control between the two authorities, in the sense that professional matters are assigned to staff control and all the others to line control. In practice, while there are some matters that fall clearly into one category or the other, many issues can be viewed as either professional or administrative matters or both. This leads to the issuance of conflicting orders and gives the lower in rank the opportunity to play one authority against the other.

Dalton called attention to the tendencies of the higher- and lower-ranking line personnel to form a coalition against the staff personnel. He found the reason in the sociological differences that unite the line against the staff. The staff is generally younger and much more likely to be college-educated than the line, although the latter have greater organizational experience and hence resent advice and suggestions from the relatively inexperienced staff. Furthermore, the two groups are divided by differences in patterns of speech and dress, recreational preferences, etc.[6] In these areas, the higher-ranking line is often closer to the lower-ranking line than to the staff. Thus the tensions between staff and line derive not only from the organizational conflicts resulting from overloading or lack of clear division of authority, but also from differences in sociological background. (These differences might decline as more and more higher line officials gain college education, or a new division might emerge between the A.B. and B.S. on the one hand, and the Ph.D.'s on the other.)

In spite of important differences between the two approaches, staff authority in both is subordinate to line authority and the line is identified with administrative authority and the staff with professional authority. While it is obvious that there are some staff functions which are not carried out by professionals, and that there are some professionals among the line personnel, there is a high correlation between staff and professionals, and between line and non-professionals.

In organizations whose goal is non-professional (e.g., profit-making), it is considered desirable for administrators to have the major (line) authority because they direct the major goal activity. Professionals deal only with means, with secondary activities. Therefore it is functional for the organization that they have no, or only limited (staff), authority, and they be ultimately subordinated to administrators. This generally is the case in corporations and armies.

Professionals in Professional Organizations

In full-fledged professional organizations the staff-professional line-administrator correlation, insofar as such distinctions apply at all, is reversed. Although administrative authority is suitable for the major goal activities in private business, in professional organizations administrators are in charge of secondary activities; they administer *means* to the major activity carried out by professionals. In other words, to the extent that there is a staff-line relationship at all, professionals should hold the major authority and administrators the secondary staff authority. Administrators offer advice about the economic and organizational implications of various activities planned by the professionals. The final decision is, functionally speaking, in the hands of the various professionals and their decision-making bodies, such as committees and boards. The professor decides what research he is going to undertake and to a large degree what he is going to teach; the physician determines the treatment to be given to the patient.

Administrators may raise objections. They may point out that a certain drug is too expensive or that a certain teaching policy will decrease the number of students in a way that endangers the financing of a university. But functionally the professional is the one to decide on his discretion to what degree these administrative considerations should be taken into account. It is interesting to note that some of the complaints usually made against professionals in nonprofessional organizations are made against administrators in professional organizations: They are said to lose sight of the major goal of the organization in pursuit of their specific limited responsibilities. Professionals in private business are sometimes criticized as being too committed to science, craftsmanship, and abstract ideas; administrators in professional organizations are deprecated because they are too committed to their specialties—"efficiency" and economy.

Many of the sociological differences between professionals and managers in private business are reversed in professional organizations. Professionals enter professional organizations younger and at lower positions (i.e., as students, research assistants, or interns) than managers do. The range of mobility of administrators is usually relatively limited, and a professional is more likely to reach the top position of institutional head.

In private business, overinfluence by professionals threatens the realization of organizational goals and sometimes even the organization's existence. In professional organizations overinfluence by the administration, which takes the form of ritualization of means, undermines the goals for which the organization has been established and endangers the conditions under which knowledge can be created and institutionalized (as, for instance, academic freedom).

Who Is Superior?

Heading a professional organization constitutes a special dilemma. It is a typical case of institutionalized role conflict.[7] On the one hand, the role should be in the hands of a professional in order to ensure that the commitments of the head will match organizational goals. A professional at the head of the authority structure will mean that professional activity is recognized as the major goal activity, and that the needs of professionals will be more likely to receive understanding attention. On the other hand, organizations have needs that are unrelated to their specific goal activity. Organizations have to obtain funds to finance their activities, recruit personnel to staff the various functions, and allocate the funds and personnel which have been recruited. Organizational heads must know how to keep the system integrated by giving the right amount of attention and funds to the various organizational needs, including secondary needs. A professional may endanger the integration of the professional organization by over-emphasizing the major goal activity and neglecting

secondary functions. He may lack skill in human relations. In short, the role of head of professional organizations requires two incompatible sets of orientations, personal characteristics, and aptitudes. If the role is performed by either a lay administrator or a typical professional, one set of considerations is likely to be emphasized to the neglect of the other.

The severity of the dilemma is increased because of the motivational pattern of typical professionals. Most successful professionals are not motivated to become administrators. Some would refuse any administrative role, including the top one of university president or hospital chief, because of their commitment to professional values and ties to professional groups, and because they feel that they would not be capable of performing the administrative role successfully. Even those professionals who would not reject the distinguished and powerful role of organizational head avoid the administrative roles that are training grounds for and channels of mobility to these top positions. Thus many academicians refuse to become deans, not to mention associate or assistant deans, and try to avoid if possible the role of department chairman. Those who are willing to accept administrative roles are often less committed to professional values than their colleagues,[8] or view it as a transitional status, not a career. The same can be said about administrative appointments in hospitals. For instance, in the mental hospital studied by Stanton and Schwartz, the role of administrative psychiatrist is fulfilled at the beginning of the training period.[9] It is considered an undesirable chore that must be endured before turning to the real job. Psychiatrists who complete their training tend to withdraw to private practice. From other studies, especially those of state mental hospitals, it appears that those who stay are often less competent and less committed to professional values than those who leave.

The Professionally Oriented Administrator

There are various solutions to this dilemma. By far the most widespread one is the rule of the professionally oriented administrator. Such an administrator is one who combines a professional education with a managerial personality and practice. Goal as well as means activities seem to be handled best when such a person is the institutional head. Because of his training, he is more likely to understand the special needs of a professional organization and its staff than a lay administrator, and, because of his personal characteristics, he is more likely to be skilled in handling the needs and requests of his professional colleagues as well as those of the administrative staff.

There are two major sources of professionally oriented administrators. One is the professionals themselves. Some feel that they have little chance of becoming outstanding professionals in their field. Often the same people find that they are relatively more skilled in administrative activities. Thus they gravitate toward administrative jobs by serving on committees and by assuming minor administrative roles; some eventually become top administrators. Contrary to the popular belief, most university presidents are former professors. Wilson found that out of the 30 universities he studied, 28 had presidents who had been professors, albeit none a very eminent scholar.[10] It seems that academicians who are inclined to take administrative jobs, or who are organization-oriented, not only publish less in quantity and quality after they have entered administrative positions but also tended to publish less before they accepted such jobs.

Of the heads of mental hospitals studied, 74.2 per cent are physicians.[11] Although there is no study on their professional eminence as compared to that of private practitioners, it seems that the heads of mental hospitals do not include the most successful psychiatrists. Only about 22 per cent of the heads of general hospitals are physicians. Where these are full-time jobs, the statement made about the heads of mental hospitals seems to apply here also.

The second source of professionally-oriented administrators is special training. In recent years there has been a movement toward developing training programs for specialized administration, such as hospital administration and research administration. A considerable number of teachers, for example, return to universities to take courses in administrative education before they become school principals.

The advantages of specialized administrators over lay administrators are obvious. They are trained for their particular role and have considerable understanding of the organization in which they are about to function before they enter it. They are sensitized to the special tensions of working with professionals, and they share some of their professional values. On the other hand, they are less prepared for their role than the professionally oriented administrators from the first source who have a deeper commitment to professional values, command more professional respect, and have a greater number of social ties with professionals.

Although most professional organizations are controlled by professional or professionally oriented administrators, some are controlled by lay administrators. By lay administrators we mean, administrators who have no training in serving the major goal activities of the organization. This holds for 2 out of the 30 universities studied by Wilson, for fewer than 10 per cent of the schools, for 20.5 per cent of the mental hospitals, and for about 38 per cent of the general hospitals. (Wilson's study is small, the other data is based on large populations).

The strain created by lay administrators in professional organizations leads to goal displacement. When the hierarchy of authority is in inverse relation to the hierarchy of goals and means, there is considerable danger that the goals will be subverted. Of course there are many other factors which may have such a distorting influence; but lay administrators are more likely to cause displacement than are other administrators.

References

1. Max Weber (Talcott Parsons, ed.; A. M. Henderson and Talcott Parsons, trans.), *The Theory of Social and Economic Organization* (New York: Oxford University Press, 1947), p. 339.
2. M. Newcomer, *The Big Business Executive* (New York: Columbia University Press, 1955), p. 92.
3. See G. H. Copeman, *Leaders of British Industry* (London: Gee and Co., 1955).
4. George C. Homans, *The Human Group* (New York: Harcourt, Brace, 1950), pp. 369–414.
5. On the two approaches, see H. A. Simon, D. W. Smithburg, and V. A. Thompson, *Public Administration* (New York: Knopf, 1956), pp. 280–295; and A. W. Gouldner, *Patterns of Industrial Bureaucracy* (Glencoe, Ill.: The Free Press, 1954), PP. 224–228.
6. Melville Dalton, "Conflicts Between Staff and Line Managerial Officers," *American Sociological Review* 15: (1950): 342–351.

7. By role we mean the behavior expected from a person in the particular position. Seeman, "Role Conflict and Ambivalent Leadership," *American Sociological Review* 18 (1953), 373–380.

8. A. W. Gouldner, "Cosmopolitans and Locals: Toward an Analysis of Latent Social Roles," *Administrative Science Quarterly* (1957), 2:281–306. For a more recent study, see Barney C. Glaser, "Attraction, Autonomy, and Reciprocity in the Scientist-Supervisor Relations," *Administrative Science Quarterly* (1963), 8–379–398.

9. A. H. Stanton and M. S. Schwartz, *The Mental Hospital* (New York: Basic Books, 1954).

10. L. Wilson, *The Academic Man* (New York: Oxford University Press, 1942), p. 85.

11. L. Block, "Ready Reference Of Hospital Facts," *Hospital Topics* (1956), 34:23.

CHAPTER 9

FACULTY ORGANIZATION AND AUTHORITY

BURTON R. CLARK

As we participate in or study various faculties in American higher education, we observe decisions being made through informal interaction among a group of peers and through collective action of the faculty as a whole. Formal hierarchy plays little part, and we have reason to characterize the faculty as a collegium.[1] At the same time we sense that what we now observe is not a counterpart of the collegiality of the days of old. The modern faculty in the United States is not a body to be likened to the guilds of the medieval European university,[2] or to the self-government of a dozen dons in a residential college at Oxford or Cambridge,[3] or to the meagre self-rule that was allowed the faculty in the small liberal arts college that dominated American higher education until the end of the last century.[4] The old-time collegium has modern reflections, as in the Fellowships of the colleges at Yale, but for the most part it is no longer winningly with us, and the kind of collegiality we now find needs different conceptualization. We also observe on the modern campus that information is communicated through formal channels, responsibility is fixed in formally-designated positions, interaction is arranged in relations between superiors and subordinates, and decisions are based on written rules. Thus we have reason to characterize the campus as a bureaucracy. But, at the same time, we sense that this characterization overlooks so much that it becomes misleading. Though the elements of bureaucracy are strong, they do not dominate the campus; and though they grow, their growth does not mean future dominance if other forms of organization and authority are expanding more rapidly.

The major form of organization and authority found in the faculties of the larger American colleges and universities, and toward which many small campuses are now moving, is now neither predominantly collegial nor bureaucratic. Difficult to characterize, it may be seen as largely "professional," but professional in a way that is critically different from the authority of professional men in other organizations such as the business corporation, the government agency, and the hospital. To approach this unusual pattern, we will first discuss trends in the organization and culture of the campus as a whole and then turn to the related trends in the organization and authority of the faculty.

We begin with broad changes in the nature of the campus because they condition the structure of authority. Authority is conditioned, for example, by the nature of work, the technology of an organization. The mass assembly of automobiles does not allow much personal discretion on the part of the worker; surgery in the hospital operating room requires on-the-spot judgment and autonomous decision by the surgeon and one or two colleagues. To understand faculty authority, we need some comprehension of what academic work has in common with work in other settings and how it differs from work elsewhere. Authority is also conditioned by patterns of status. Status comes in part from formal assignment, hence men called deans usually have much of it, but status

Excerpt from *Faculty Organization and Authority*, by Burton R. Clark, October 1963. Reprinted with permission of Western Interstate Commission for Higher Education.

is also derived in academia from one's standing in a discipline, and this important source of status is independent of the official scheme.[5] Authority is also conditioned by traditional sentiments. Legends and ideologies have a force of their own. Conceptions of what should be are formed by what has been or by ideals handed down through the generations. The stirring ideologies of community of scholars and academic freedom are forces to be reckoned with when one is dealing with faculties and in understanding their organization. Thus, the work itself, the status system, the traditional sentiments, all affect authority.

Trends in the Social Organization of the Campus

Four trends in the campus, closely related, are as follows: unitary to composite or federal structure; single to multiple value systems; non-professional to professional work; consensus to bureaucratic coordination.

Unitary to Federal Structure

The history of American higher education is a history of movement from unitary liberal arts colleges to multi-structured colleges and universities. The American college of 1840 contained a half dozen professors and fifty to a hundred students;[6] in 1870, average size was still less than 10 faculty and 100 students (Table 9-1). All students in a college took the same

curriculum, a "program of classical-mathematical studies inherited from Renaissance education."[7] There was no need for sub-units such as division and department; this truly was a unitary structure. In comparison, the modern university and college is multi-structured. The University of California at Berkeley in 1962–63, with over 23,000 students and 1,600 "officers of instruction," was divided into some 15 colleges or schools (e.g., College of Engineering, School of Public Health); over 50 institutes, centers and laboratories; and some 75 departments (including Poultry Husbandry, Romance Philology, Food Technology and Naval Architecture). In three departments and three schools, the sub-unit itself contained over 50 faculty members. Such complexity is not only characteristic of the university: a large California state college contains 40 or so disciplines, grouped in a number of divisions; and even a small liberal arts college today may have 20 departments and three or four divisions.

The multiplication of sub-units stems in part from increasing size. The large college cannot remain as unitary as the small one, since authority must be extensively delegated and subsidiary units formed around the many centers of authority. The sub-units also stem from plurality of purpose; we have moved from single- to multi-purpose colleges. Goals are not only more numerous but also broadly defined and ambiguous. Those who would define the goals of the modern university speak in such terms as "preserving truth, creating new

Table 9-1

Size of Colleges, 1870–1956

Year	Colleges	Faculty		Students	
		Total Number	*Average Size*	*Total Number*	*Average Size*
1870	563	5,553	10	52,000	92
1880	811	11,552	14	116,000	143
1890	998	15,809	16	157,000	157
1900	977	23,868	24	238,000	244
1910	951	36,480	38	355,000	373
1920	1,041	48,615	47	598,000	574
1930	1,409	82,386	58	1,101,000	781
1940	1,708	146,929	86	1,494,000	875
1950	1,851	246,722	134	2,659,000	1,436
1956	1,850	298,910	162	2,637,000	1,425

Source: U.S. Bureau of the Census, *Historical Statistics of the United States, Colonial Times to 1957*, Washington, D.C.: Government Printing Office, 1960, pp. 210–211.

knowledge, and serving the needs of man through truth and knowledge."[8] The service goal has a serviceable ambiguity that covers anything from home economics for marriage to research and development for space. A tightly integrated structure could not be established around these goals. Organizational structure accommodates to the multiplicity of goals by dividing into segments with different primary functions, such as liberal arts and professional training, scientific research and humanistic education. The structure accommodates to ambiguity of goals with its own ambiguity, overlap, and discontinuity. We find some liberal arts disciplines scattered all over the campus (e.g., statistics, psychology), residing as components of professional schools and of "other" departments as well as in the appropriately-named department. No neat consistent structure is possible; the multiple units form and reform around functions in a catch-as-catch-can fashion. Needless to say, with a multiplicity of ambiguous goals and a variety of sub-units, authority is extensively decentralized. The structure is federal rather than unitary, and even takes on some likeness to a loosely-joined federation.

Single to Multiple Value Systems

Most colleges before the turn of the century and perhaps as late as the 1920s possessed a unified culture that extended across the campus,[9] and this condition still obtains in some small colleges of today. But the number of colleges so characterized continues to decline and the long-run trend is clear: the campus-wide culture splits into subcultures located in a variety of social groups and organizational units. As we opened the doors of American higher education, we admitted more orientations to college—college as fun, college as marriage, college as preparation for graduate school, college as certificate to go to work tomorrow, college as place to rebel against the Establishment, and even college as a place to think. These orientations have diverse social locations on campus, from fraternity house to *cafe espresso* shop to Mrs. Murphy's desegregated rooming house. The value systems of the students are numerous.

The faculty is equally if not more prone to diversity in orientation, as men cleave to their specialized lines of work and their different perspectives and vocabularies. Faculty orientations differ between those who commit themselves primarily to the local campus and those who commit themselves primarily to their farflung discipline or profession; between those who are scientists and those who are humanists; between those who think of themselves as pure researchers or pure scholars and those who engage in a professional practice and train recruits. The value systems of the faculty particularly cluster around the individual disciplines and hence at one level of analysis there are as many value systems as there are departments.

Non-Professional to Professional Work

Intense specialization characterizes the modern campus; academic man has moved from general to specific knowledge. The old-time teacher—Mr. Chips—was a generalist. He covered a wide range of subject-matter, with less intensity in any one area than would be true today, and he was engaged in pure transmission of knowledge. In the American college of a century ago, the college teacher had only a bachelor's degree (in the fixed classical curriculum) plus "a modest amount of more advanced training, perhaps in theology . . ."[10] There was no system of graduate education, no reward for distinction in scholarship, and the professor settled down into the groove of classroom recitation and the monitoring of student conduct. We have moved from this kind of professor, the teacher generalist, to the teacher of physics, of engineering, of microbiology, of abnormal psychology, and to the professor as researcher, as consultant, as professional-school demonstrator. We have moved from transmission of knowledge to innovation in knowledge, which has meant specialization in research. Taking the long view, perhaps *the* great change in the role of academic man is the ascendance of research and scholarship—the rise of the commitment to create knowledge. This change in the academic role interacts with rapid social change: research causes change, as in the case of change in technology and industrial processes; and such changes, in turn, encourage the research attitude, as in the case of competition between industrial firms, competition between nations, competition between universities. In short, the research component of the academic role is intimately related to major modern social trends.

In his specialism, modern academic man is a case of professional man. We define "profession" to mean a specialized competence with a high degree of intellectual content, a specialty heavily based on or involved with knowledge. Specialized competence based on involvement in knowledge is the hallmark of the modern professor. He is preeminently an expert. Having special knowledge at his command, the professional worker needs and seeks a large degree of autonomy from lay control and normal organizational control. Who is the best judge of surgical procedure—laymen, hospital administrators, or surgeons? Who is the best judge of theories in chemistry—laymen, university administrators, or professors of chemistry? As work becomes professionalized—specialized around esoteric knowledge and technique—the organization of work must create room for expert judgment, and autonomy of decision-making and practice becomes a hallmark of the advanced profession.

Not all professional groups need the same degree of autonomy, however. Professionals who largely give advice or follow the guidelines of a received body of knowledge require extensive but not great autonomy for the individual and the group. They need sufficient leeway to give an honest expert opinion or to apply the canons of judgment of their field. Those requiring great autonomy are those who wish to crawl along the frontiers of knowledge, with flashlight or floodlight in hand, searching for the new—the new scientific finding, the new reinterpretation of history, the new criticism in literature or art. Academic man is a special kind of professional man, a type characterized by a particularly high need for autonomy. To be innovative, to be critical of established ways, these are the commitments of the academy and the impulses of scientific and scholarly roles that press for unusual autonomy.

Consensual to Bureaucratic Coordination

As the campus has moved from unitary to composite structure, from single to multiple systems of values, from general to specialized work, it has moved away from the characteristics of community, away from "community of scholars." A faculty member does not interact with most other members of the faculty. In the larger places, he may know less than a fifth, less than a tenth. Paths do not cross. The faculty lounge is no more, but is replaced by coffee pots in dozens of locations. The professor retains a few interests in common with all others, such as higher salaries, but he has an increasing number of interests that diverge. Even salary is a matter on which interests may diverge, as men bargain for themselves, as departments compete for funds, as scientists are paid more, through various devices, than the men of the humanities.

In short, looking at the total faculty, interaction is down, commonality of interest is down, commonality of sentiments is down. With this, coordination of work and policy within the faculty is not so much now as in the past achieved by easy interaction of community members, by the informal give-and-take that characterizes the true community—the community of the small town where everyone knows nearly every one else, or the community of the old small college where the professors saw much of everyone else in the group. The modern campus can no longer be coordinated across its length and breadth by informal interaction and by the coming together of the whole. Informal consulting back and forth is still important; the administration and the faculty still use the lunch table for important business. But campus-wide coordination increasingly moves toward the means normal to the large-scale organization, to bureaucratic means. We appoint specialists to various areas of administration, give them authority, and they write rules to apply across the system. They communicate by correspondence, they attempt to make decisions fairly and impartially by judging the case before them against the criteria of the rulebook. Thus we move toward bureaucratic coordination, as the admissions officer decides on admissions, the registrar decides on the recording of grades, the business officer decides proper purchasing procedures, and various faculty committees decide on a wide range of matters, from tenure to travel funds to the rules of order for meetings of an academic senate.

In sum: the campus tends toward composite structure, toward a multiplicity of subcultures, toward intense professionalism, and toward some bureaucratic coordination.

Change in Faculty Organization and Authority

The organization and authority of the faculty accommodate to these trends in at least three ways: by segmentation, by a federated professionalism, and by the growth of individual power centers.

Segmentation

As campuses increase in size, complexity, and internal specialization, there is less chance that the faculty will be able to operate effectively as a total faculty in college affairs, less as the governmental body we have in mind when we speak of a community of scholars. The decision-making power and influence of the faculty is now more segmented—segmented by sub-college, by division, and particularly by department. Since the interests of the faculty cluster around the departments, faculty participation in government tends to move out to these centers of commitment. Who selects personnel, decides on courses, and judges students? The faculty as a whole cannot, any more than the administration. Indeed, as departments and professional schools grow in size and complexity, even they often do not; it is a wing of the department or a part of the professional school that has most influence. A liberal arts department that numbers 40 to 80 faculty members may contain six or eight or a dozen specialties. The day has arrived when a department chairman may not even know the name, let alone the face and the person, of the new instructors in "his" department.

What happens to the governmental organs designed for the faculty as a whole? They move in form from Town Hall to representative government, with men elected from the various "states" coming together in a federal center to legislate general rules, which are then executed by the administration or the faculty committees that constitute an administrative component of the faculty. With the move to representative government, there is greater differentiation in participation: a few Actives participate a great deal; a considerably larger group constitutes an alert and informed public and participates a modest amount; the largest group consists of those who are not very interested or informed and who participate very little. The structure of participation parallels that found in the larger democratic society, and apparently is normal to a representative mass democracy. The situation is, of course, vexing to those who care about faculty government.

Professionalization

The authority of the faculty which flows out toward the departments and other units of the campus becomes located in the hands of highly specialized experts; and, as suggested earlier, takes on some characteristics of professional authority. Almost everywhere in modern large-scale organizations, we find a tug-of-war going on between administrative and professional orientations. In the hospital, the basic conflict in authority lies between the control of the non-medical hospital administrator and the authority of the doctors. In industry, a fascinating clash is occurring between management and the scientist in the research and development laboratory.[11] The fantastic expansion of research and development has brought over 400,000 scientists and engineers into industry, there to be committed to innovation and to the development of new inventions to the point of practical utility. Many of these technologists have a high degree of expertise, a strong interest in research—often "pure" research—and they press for a large degree of freedom. Their fondest wish is to be left alone; they make the point that in scientific work it seems rational to do just that, that basic discoveries stem not from managerial direction but from the scientist following up his own initial hunches and the leads he develops as he proceeds. Management has found such men difficult to deal with; their morale suffers easily from traditional forms of management, and they present unusual demands on management to change and accommodate. In this situation, professional authority and bureaucratic authority are both necessary, for each performs an essential function: professional authority protects the exercise of the special expertise of the technologist, allowing his judgment to be preeminent in many matters. Bureaucratic authority functions to provide coordination of the work of the technologists with the other major elements of the firm. Bureaucratic direction is not capable of providing certain expert judgments; professional direction is not capable of providing the overall coordination. The problem presented by the scientist in industry is how to serve simultaneously the requirements of autonomy and the requirements of coordination, and how to accommodate the authority of the professional man and his group of peers to the authority of management and vice versa.[12]

The professional-in-the-organization presents everywhere this special kind of problem. He gains authority, compared to most employees, by virtue of his special knowledge and skills; he loses authority, compared to a man working on his own, by virtue of the fact that organizations locate much authority in administrative positions. The problem of allocation of authority between professionals and bureaucrats does, however, vary in intensity and form in different kinds of organizations. As mentioned earlier, advisers and practitioners need a modest degree of authority, while scientists and academics have perhaps the highest requirements for autonomy to engage in research, in unfettered teaching, and in scholarship that follows the rules of consistency and proof that develop within a discipline.

The segmentation of the faculty into clusters of experts gives professional authority a special form in academic organizations. In other situations, there usually are one or two major professional groups within the organization who, if they are influential, substitute professional control for administrative control. This occurs in the case of medical personnel in the hospital who often dominate decision-making. The internal controls of the medical profession are strong and are substituted for those of the organization. But in the college or university this situation does not obtain; there are 12, 25, or 50 clusters of experts. The experts are prone to identify with their own disciplines, and the "academic profession" overall comes off a poor second. We have wheels within wheels, many professions within a profession. No one of the disciplines on a campus is likely to dominate the others; at a minimum, it usually takes an alliance of disciplines, such as "the natural sciences" or "the humanities," to put together a bloc that might dominate others. The point is that with a variety of experts—chemists, educationists, linguists, professors of marketing—the collective control of the professionals over one another will not be strong. The campus is not a closely-knit group of professionals who see the world from one perspective. As a collection of professionals, it is decentralized, loose and flabby.

The principle is this: where professional influence is high and there is one dominant professional group, the organization will be integrated by the imposition of professional standards. Where professional influence is high and there are a number of professional groups, the organization will be split by professionalism. The university and the large college are fractured by expertness, not unified by it. The sheer variety of the experts supports the tendency for authority to diffuse toward quasi-autonomous clusters. Thus, faculty authority has in common with professional authority in other places the protection of individual and group autonomy. It is different from professional authority in other places in the extremity of the need for autonomy and in the fragmentation of authority around the interests of a large variety of groups of roughly equal status and power. The campus is a holding company for professional groups rather than a single association of professionals.

Individualization

When we speak of professional authority we often lump together the authority that resides with the individual expert and the authority that resides with a collegial group of experts. Both the individual and the group gain influence at the expense of laymen and the general administrator. But what is the division of authority between the individual and the group? Sometimes group controls can be very tight and quite hierarchical, informally if not formally, as young doctors learn in many hospitals, and as assistant professors learn in many departments. The personal authority of the expert varies widely with the kind of establishment, and often with rank and seniority. The campus is a place where strong forces cause the growth of some individuals into centers of power. We will review several of these sources of personal authority.

First, we have noted the expertise of the modern academy. The intense specialization alone makes many a man into king of a sector in which few others are able to exercise much judgment. Thus, *within* a department, men increasingly feel unable to judge the merits of men in specialties they know nothing about. The technical nature of the specialized lines of work of most academic men, then, is a source of personal authority. If we want to provide a course on Thomas Hardy, we are likely to defer on its content to the judgment of the man in the English Department who has been knee-deep in Hardy for a decade. The idea of such a course would really have been his in the first place; Hardy falls within his domain within the English Department, and his judgment on the need for the course will weigh more than the judgment of others.

Second, some professorial experts now have their personal authority greatly enhanced by money. Despite his location within an organization, the professor in our time is becoming an entrepreneur. It used to be that the college president was the only one on campus, other than an enterprising and dedicated member of the board of trustees, who was capable of being an entrepreneur. Many of the great presidents were great because they were great at coming home with the loot—adventurers who conquered the hearts and pocketbooks of captains of industry and then with money in hand raided wholesale the faculties of other institutions. Presidents who can raise money and steal faculty are still with us, but they have been joined by professors. Kerr has suggested that the power of the individual faculty member is going up while the power of the collective faculty is going down because the individual as researcher, as scholar, and as consultant relates increasingly to the grant-giving agencies of the Federal government and to the foundations.[13] He has direct ties to these major sources of funds and influence; indeed, he participates in their awarding of grants and even has problems of conflict of interest. A professor-entrepreneur, by correspondence and telephone and airplane trips, lines up money for projects. He sometimes arranges for the financing of an entire laboratory; occasionally he even brings back a new building. Even when the professor does little of the arranging, it is *his* presence that attracts these resources. He represents competence, and the grant-givers pursue competence.

The entrepreneurial activity and resources-gaining influence of professors, which extends down to assistant professors in the social as well as the natural sciences, has had remarkable growth since World War II, and the personal autonomy and power thus achieved in relation to others in the university is considerable. A professor does not have to beg postage stamps from a departmental secretary nor a two hundred dollar raise from the department chairman nor travel money to go to a meeting from a dean or a committee if he has monies assigned to him to the tune of $37,000, or $175,000, or $400,000. His funds from outside sources may be called "soft" funds, in the jargon of finance, but they are hard enough to hire additional faculty members and assistants, to cover summer salaries, and to provide for travel to distant, delightful places.

The following principle obtains: a *direct* relation of faculty members to external sources of support affects the distribution of influence within the campus, redistributing influence from those who do not have such contacts to those who do, and moving power from the faculty as a whole and as smaller collectivities to individual professors. In the university of old, members of the faculty achieved a high degree of influence by occupying the few professorial positions available in a structure that narrowed at the top. Their source of influence was structural and internal. The source of great influence in the modern American university is less internal and less tied to particular positions; it is more external and more tied to national and international prestige in a discipline, and to contact with the sources of support for research and scholarship that are multiplying and growing so rapidly.

This individualization in faculty organization and authority excites impulses in the faculty and the administration to establish some collective control, for much is at stake in the balance of the curriculum, the equality of rewards in the faculty, and even the character of the institution. But the efforts at control do not have easy going. Collective bodies of the faculty and the administration are hardly in a position, or inclined, to tell the faculty member he can have this contract but not that one, since the faculty member will define the projects as part of his pursuit of his own scholarly interests. When the faculty member feels that this sensitive right is infringed, he will run up the banners of academic freedom and inquiry, or he will fret and become a festering sore in the body politic of the campus, or he will retreat to apathy and his country house, or he will make it known in other and greener pastures that he will listen to the siren call of a good offer.

Third, personal authority of the professorial expert is increased in our time by the competitiveness of the job market. The expansion of higher education means a high demand for professors, and the job market runs very much in the professor's favor in bargaining with the administration. His favorable position *in* the market enhances his position on campus. He can demand more and get it, he can even become courageous. In the world of work, having another job to go to is perhaps the most important source of courage.

To recapitulate: faculty organization and authority tends in modern times to become more segmented, more professional in character, and somewhat more individualized. We are witnessing a strong trend toward a federated structure in colleges and especially in universities with the campus more like an United Nations and less like a small town and this trend affects faculty authority by weakening the faculty as a whole and strengthening the faculty in its many parts. Faculty authority becomes less of a case of self-government by a total collegium, and more of a case of authority exercised department by department, sub-college by sub-college. The *role* of faculty authority is shifting from protecting the rights of the entire guild, the rights of the collective faculty, to protecting the autonomy of the separate disciplines and the autonomy of the individual faculty member.

Faculty authority in our time tends to become professional authority in a federated form. We have a loose alliance of professional men. The combination of professional authority and loosely joined structure has the imposing function of protecting the autonomy of the work of experts amidst extensive divergence of interests and commitments. The qualities of federation are important here. The federation is a structure that gives reign to the quasi-autonomous, simultaneous development of the interests of a variety of groups. Within an academic federation, a number of departments, divisions, colleges, professional schools, insti-

tutes, and the like can co-exist, each pushing its own interests and going its own way to a rather considerable extent. Professional authority structured as a federation is a form of authority particularly adaptive to a need for a high degree of autonomous judgment by individuals and sub-groups.

This trend toward a federation of professionals is only part of the story. To hold the separate components of the campus together, we have a superimposed coordination by the administration, and, as Kerr has suggested, this coordination increasingly takes on the attributes of mediation.[14] The administration attempts to keep the peace and to inch the entire enterprise another foot ahead. The faculty, too, in its own organization, also counters this divisive tread with a machinery of coordination. The very fact of a diffusion of authority makes the faculty politician more necessary than ever, for the skills of politics and diplomacy are needed. There must be faculty mediators; men who serve on central committees, men with cast iron stomachs for lunch table discussions and cocktail parties, men who know how to get things done that must be done for the faculty as a whole or for part of the faculty. There must be machinery for setting rules and carrying them out impartially across the faculty. The modern campus is, or is becoming, too large and complicated for collegial or professional arrangements to provide the over-all coordination, and coordination is performed largely by bureaucratic arrangements—e.g., the rulebook, and definite administrative domains.

Federated professionalism within an organization, like many other trends, thus promotes counter-trends. Specialization and individualization seriously weaken the integration of the whole. The weakness of collegiality or professionalism in the large organization, as suggested earlier in the case of industry, is that it cannot handle the problem of order, it cannot provide sufficient integration. Thus the above trends in faculty organization and authority open the door to bureaucracy—more bureaucracy in the administration, more within the faculty itself. The modern large faculty, therefore, combines professionalism, federated structure, and bureaucracy perhaps in a mixture never before evidenced in human history.

This combination of what seem contradictory forms of organization perplexes observers of academia. Is the faculty collegial? Yes, somewhat. Is it split into fragments? Yes, somewhat. It is professional? Yes, somewhat. Is it unitary? Yes, somewhat. Is it bureaucratic? Yes, somewhat. Different features of the faculty strike us according to the occurrences of the week or the events we chance to observe. The ever-mounting paperwork firmly convinces us that the campus is doomed to bureaucratic stagnation. The fact that the president often gets what the president wants convinces us that he really has all the authority. The inability of a campus to change a department that is twenty years behind in its field convinces us that departmental autonomy has run amok and the campus is lacking in leadership and in capacity to keep up with the times. One observer will see the campus as a tight ship, the next will speak of the same campus as a lawless place where power lies around loose. No wonder we are confused and no wonder that outsiders are so often even more confused or more irrelevant in giving advice.

But in the combination of forms of organization and forms of authority that we find today within the campus and within the faculty itself, there are certain trends that are stronger than others and certain features that tend toward dominance. The society at large is tending to become a society of experts, and the campus has already arrived at this state. Expertise is a dominant characteristic of the campus, and organization and authority cluster around it. Because of its expertness, together with its ever-growing size, the faculty moves away from community, moves away from collegiality of the whole. The faculty moves toward decentralized or federated structure, and authority moves toward clusters of experts and the individual expert. Thus professional authority tends to become the dominant form of authority, and collegial and bureaucratic features fall into a subsidiary place. In short, when we say

college, we say expert. When we say expert, we say professional authority.

Burton R. Clark, Associate Research Sociologist, Center for the Study of Higher Education, University of California, Berkeley

References

1. A major type of collegiality is that involving collegial decision: "In such cases an administrative act is only legitimate when it has been produced by the cooperation of a plurality of people according to the principle of unanimity or of majority." Max Weber, *The Theory of Social and Economic Organization*, translated by A. M. Henderson and Talcott Parsons, New York: Oxford University Press, 1947, p. 400.
2. Hastings Rashdall, *The Universities in Europe in the Middle Ages*, edited by T. M. Powicke and A. B. Emden, Oxford: At the Clarendon Press, 1936, three volumes.
3. C. P. Snow, *The Masters*, New York: The Macmillan Co., 1951.
4. Richard Hofstadter and Walter P. Metzger, *The Development of Academic Freedom in the United States*, New York: Columbia University Press, 1955; George P. Schmidt, *The Liberal Arts College*, New Brunswick, New Jersey: Rutgers University Press, 1957.
5. Logan Wilson, *The Academic Man*, New York: Oxford University Press, 1942; Theodore Caplow and Reece J. McGee, *The Academic Marketplace*, New York: Basic Books, Inc., 1958.
6. Hofstadter and Metzger, op. cit., pp. 222–223.
7. Ibid., p. 226.
8. Clark Kerr, *The Uses of the University*, The Godkin Lectures, Harvard University, 1963.
9. Hofstadter and Metzger, *op. cit.,*: Schmidt, *op. cit.*
10. Hofstadter and Metzger, *op. cit.*, p. 230.
11. See William Kornhauser, *Scientists in Industry: Conflict and Accommodation*, Berkeley: University of California Press, 1962; and Simon Marcson, *The Scientist in American Industry*, New York: Harpers and Brothers, 1960.
12. Kornhauser, *op. cit.*
13. Kerr, *op. cit.*
14. *Ibid.*

CHAPTER 10

ALTERNATIVE MODELS OF GOVERNANCE IN HIGHER EDUCATION

J. VICTOR BALDRIDGE, DAVID V. CURTIS,
GEORGE P. ECKER, AND GARY L. RILEY

Organizations vary in a number of important ways: they have different types of clients, they work with different technologies, they employ workers with different skills, they develop different structures and coordinating styles, and they have different relationships to their external environments. Of course, there are elements common to the operation of colleges and universities, hospitals, prisons, business firms, government bureaus, and so on, but no two organizations are the same. Any adequate model of decision making and governance in an organization must take its distinctive characteristics into account.

This chapter deals with the organizational characteristics and decision processes of colleges and universities. Colleges and universities are unique organizations, differing in major respects from industrial organizations, government bureaus, and business firms.

Distinguishing Characteristics of Academic Organizations

Colleges and universities are complex organizations. Like other organizations they have goals, hierarchical systems and structures, officials who carry out specified duties, decision-making processes that set institutional policy, and a bureaucratic administration that handles routine business. But they also exhibit some critical distinguishing characteristics that affect their decision processes.

Goal Ambiguity

Most organizations are goal-oriented, and as a consequence they can build decision structures to reach their objectives. Business firms want to make a profit, government bureaus have tasks specified by law, hospitals are trying to cure sick people, prisons are in the business of "rehabilitation."

By contrast, colleges and universities have vague, ambiguous goals and they must build decision processes to grapple with a higher degree of uncertainty and conflict. What is the goal of a university? This is a difficult question, for the list of possible answers is long: teaching, research, service to the local community, administration of scientific installations, support of the arts, solutions to social problems. In their book *Leadership and Ambiguity,* Cohen and March comment:

> Almost any educated person could deliver a lecture entitled "The Goals of the University." Almost no one will listen to the lecture voluntarily. For the most part, such lectures and their companion essays are well-intentioned exercises in social rhetoric, with little operational content. Efforts to generate normative statements of the goals of the university tend to produce goals that are either meaningless or dubious [Cohen and March, 1974, page 195].

Goal ambiguity, then, is one of the chief characteristics of academic organizations. They rarely have a single mission. On the contrary, they often try to be all things to all people. Because their existing goals are unclear, they also find it hard to reject new goals. Edward Gross (1968) analyzed the goals of faculty and administrators in a large number of American universities and obtained some remarkable results. To be sure, some goals were ranked higher than others, with academic freedom consistently near the top. But both administrators and faculty marked as important almost every one of forty-seven goals listed by Gross!

Not only are academic goals unclear, they are also highly contested. As long as goals are left ambiguous and abstract, they are readily agreed on. As soon as they are concretely specified and put into operation, conflict erupts. The link between clarity and conflict may help explain the prevalence of meaningless rhetoric in academic policy statements and speeches. It is tempting to resort to rhetoric when serious content produces conflict.

Client Service

Like schools, hospitals, and welfare agencies, academic organizations are "people-processing" institutions. Clients with specific needs are fed into the institution from the environment, the institution acts upon them, and the clients are returned to the larger society. This is an extremely important characteristic, for the clients demand and often obtain significant input into institutional decision-making processes. Even powerless clients such as schoolchildren usually have protectors, such as parents, who demand a voice in the operation of the organization. In higher education, of course, the clients are quite capable of speaking for themselves—and they often do.

Problematic Technology

Because they serve clients with disparate, complicated needs, client-serving organizations frequently have problematic technologies. A manufacturing organization develops a specific technology that can be segmented and routinized. Unskilled, semiskilled, and white collar workers can be productively used without relying heavily on professional expertise. But it is hard to construct a simple technology for an organization dealing with people. Serving clients is difficult to accomplish, and the results are difficult to evaluate, especially on a short-term basis. The entire person must be considered; people cannot be separated easily into small, routine, and technical segments. If at times colleges and universities do not know clearly *what* they are trying to do, they often do not know *how* to do it either.

Professionalism

How does an organization work when its goals are unclear, its service is directed to clients, and its technology is problematic? Most organizations attempt to deal with these problems by hiring expertly trained professionals. Hospitals require doctors and nurses, social welfare agencies hire social workers, public schools hire teachers, and colleges and universities hire faculty members. These professionals use a broad repertoire of skills to deal with the complex and often unpredictable problems of clients. Instead of subdividing a complicated task into a routine set of procedures, professional work requires that a broad range of tasks be performed by a single employee.

Sociologists have made a number of important general observations about professional employees, wherever they may work:

1. Professionals demand *autonomy* in their work. Having acquired considerable skill and expertise in their field, they demand freedom from supervision in applying them.

2. Professionals have *divided loyalties.* They have "cosmopolitan" tendencies and loyalty to their peers at the national

level may sometimes interfere with loyalty to their local organization.

3. There are strong tensions between *professional values* and *bureaucratic expectations* in an organization. This can intensify conflict between professional employees and organizational managers.

4. Professionals demand *peer evaluation* of their work. They believe that only their colleagues can judge their performance, and they reject the evaluations of others, even those who are technically their superiors in the organizational hierarchy.

All of these characteristics undercut the traditional norms of a bureaucracy, rejecting its hierarchy, control structure, and management procedures. As a consequence, we can expect a distinct management style in a professional organization.

Finally, colleges and universities tend to have *fragmented* professional staffs. In some organizations there is one dominant professional group. For example, doctors are the dominant group in hospitals. In other organizations the professional staff is fragmented into subgroups, none of which predominates. The faculty in a university provides a clear example. Burton R. Clark comments on the fragmented professionalism in academic organizations:

> The internal controls of the medical profession are strong and are substituted for those of the organization. But in the college or university this situation does not obtain; there are twelve, twenty-five, or fifty clusters of experts. The experts are prone to identify with their own disciplines, and the "academic profession" overall comes off a poor second. We have wheels within wheels, many professions within a profession. No one of the disciplines on a campus is likely to dominate the others . . . The campus is not a closely knit group of professionals who see the world from one perspective. As a collection of professionals, it is decentralized, loose, and flabby.
>
> The principle is this: where professional influence is high and there is one dominant professional group, the organization will be integrated by the imposition of professional standards. Where professional influence is high and there are a number of professional groups, the organization will be split by professionalism. The university

and the large college are fractured by expertness, not unified by it. The sheer variety supports the tendency for authority to diffuse toward quasi-autonomous clusters [Clark, 1963, pages 37, 51].

Environmental Vulnerability

Another characteristic that sets colleges and universities apart from many other complex organizations is environmental vulnerability. Almost all organizations interact with their social environment to some extent. But though no organization is completely autonomous, some have considerably greater freedom of action than others. The degree of autonomy an organization has vis-à-vis its environment is one of the critical determinants of how it will be managed.

For example, in a free market economy, business firms and industries have a substantial degree of autonomy. Although they are regulated by countless government agencies and constrained by their customers, essentially they are free agents responsive to market demands rather than to government control. At the other extreme, a number of organizations are virtually "captured" by their environments. Public school districts, for example, are constantly scrutinized and pressured by the communities they serve.

Colleges and universities are somewhere in the middle on a continuum from "independent" to "captured." In many respects they are insulated from their environment. Recently, however, powerful external forces have been applied to academic institutions. Interest groups holding conflicting values have made their wishes, demands, and threats well known to the administrations and faculties of academic organizations in the 1970s.

What impact does environmental pressure have on the governance of colleges and universities? When professional organizations are well insulated from the pressures of the outside environment, then professional values, norms, and work definitions play a dominant role in shaping the character of the organization. On the other hand, when strong external pressure is applied to colleges and universities, the operating autonomy of the academic professionals is seriously reduced. The faculty and administrators lose some control over the curriculum, the goals, and the daily operation of the institution. Under these circumstances, the academic professionals are frequently reduced to the role of hired employees doing the bidding of bureaucratic managers.

Although colleges and universities are not entirely captured by their environments, they are steadily losing ground. As their vulnerability increases, their governance patterns change significantly.

"Organized Anarchy"

To summarize, academic organizations have several unique organizational characteristics. They have ambiguous goals that are often strongly contested. They serve clients who demand a voice in the decision-making process. They have a problematic technology, for in order to serve clients their technology must be holistic and adaptable to individual needs. They are professionalized organizations in which employees demand a large measure of control over institutional decision processes. Finally, they are becoming more and more vulnerable to their environments.

The character of such a complex organizational system is not satisfactorily conveyed by the standard term "bureaucracy." Bureaucracy carries the connotation of stability or even rigidity; academic organizations seem more fluid. Bureaucracy implies distinct lines of authority and strict hierarchical command; academic organizations have blurred lines of authority and professional employees who demand autonomy in their work. Bureaucracy suggests a cohesive organization with clear goals; academic organizations are characteristically fragmented with ambiguous and contested goals. Bureaucracy does adequately describe certain aspects of colleges and universities, such as business administration, plant management, capital outlay, and auxiliary services. But the processes at the heart of an academic organization—academic policy making, professional teaching, and research—do not resemble the processes one finds in a bureaucracy. Table 10-1 summarizes the differences between the two types of organizations.

Perhaps a better term for academic organizations has been suggested by Cohen and March. They describe the academic organization as an "organized anarchy"—a system with little central coordination or control:

> In a university anarchy each individual in the university is seen as making autonomous decisions. Teachers decide if, when, and what to teach. Students decide if, when, and what to learn. Legislators and donors decide if, when, and what to support. Neither coordination . . . nor control [is] practiced. Resources are allocated by whatever process emerges but without explicit accommodation and without explicit reference to some superordinate goal. The "decisions" of the system are a consequence produced by the system but intended by no one and decisively controlled by no one [Cohen and March, 1974, pages 33–34].

The organized anarchy differs radically from the well-organized bureaucracy or the consensus-bound collegium. It is an organization in which generous resources allow people to go in different directions without coordination by a central authority. Leaders are relatively weak and decisions are made by individual action. Since the organization's goals are ambiguous, decisions are often by-products of unintended and unplanned activity. In such fluid circumstances, presidents and other institutional leaders serve primarily as catalysts or facilitators of an ongoing process. They do not so much lead the institution as channel its activities in subtle ways. They do not command, but negotiate. They do not plan comprehensively, but try to apply preexisting solutions to problems.

Decisions are not so much "made" as they "happen." Problems, choices, and decision makers happen to come together in temporary solutions. Cohen and March have described decision processes in an organized anarchy as

> sets of procedures through which organizational participants arrive at an interpretation of what they are doing and what they have done while they are doing it. From this point of view an organization is a collection of choices looking for problems, issues and feelings looking for decision situations in which they might be aired, solutions looking for issues for which they might be the answer, and decision makers looking for work [Cohen and March, 1974, page 81].

TABLE 10-1

Organizational Characteristics of Academic Organizations and More Traditional Bureaucracies

	Academic organizations (colleges and universities)	*Traditional bureaucracies (government agency, industry)*
Goals	Ambiguous, contested, inconsistent	Clearer goals, less disagreement
Client service	Client-serving	Material-processing, commercial
Technology	Unclear, nonroutine, holistic	Clearer, routinized, segmented
Staffing	Predominantly professional	Predominantly nonprofessional
Environmental relations	Very vulnerable	Less vulnerable
Summary image	"Organized anarchy"	"Bureaucracy"

The imagery of organized anarchy helps capture the spirit of the confused organizational dynamics in academic institutions: unclear goals, unclear technologies, and environmental vulnerability.

Some may regard "organized anarchy" as an exaggerated term, suggesting more confusion and conflict than really exist in academic organizations. This is probably a legitimate criticism. The term may also carry negative connotations to those unaware that it applies to specific organizational characteristics rather than to the entire campus community. Nevertheless, "organized anarchy" has some strong points in its favor. It breaks through the traditional formality that often surrounds discussions of decision making, challenges our existing conceptions, and suggests a looser, more fluid kind of organization. For these reasons we will join Cohen and March in using "organized anarchy" to summarize some of the unique organizational characteristics of colleges and universities: (1) unclear goals, (2) client service, (3) unclear technology, (4) professionalism, and (5) environmental vulnerability.[1]

Models of Academic Governance

Administrators and organization theorists concerned with academic governance have often developed images to summarize the complex decision process: collegial system, bureaucratic network, political activity, or participatory democracy. Such models organize the way we perceive the process, determine how we analyze it, and help determine our actions. For example, if we regard a system as political, then we form coalitions to pressure decision makers. If we regard it as collegial, then we seek to persuade people by appealing to reason. If we regard it as bureaucratic, then we use legalistic maneuvers to gain our ends.

In the past few years, as research on higher education has increased, models for academic governance have also proliferated. Three models have received widespread attention, more or less dominating the thinking of people who study academic governance. We will examine briefly each of these models in turn: (1) the bureaucracy, (2) the collegium, and (3) the political system. Each of these models has certain points in its favor. They can be used jointly to examine different aspects of the governance process.

The Academic Bureaucracy

One of the most influential descriptions of complex organizations is Max Weber's (1947) monumental work on bureaucracies. Weber discussed the characteristics of bureaucracies that distinguish them from less formal work organizations. In skeleton form he suggested that bureaucracies are networks of social groups dedicated to limited goals and organized for maximum efficiency. Moreover, the regulation of a bureaucratic system is based on the principle of "legal rationality," as contrasted with informal regulation based on friendship, loyalty to family, or personal allegiance to a charismatic leader. The hierarchical structure is held together by formal chains of command and systems of communication. The bureaucracy as Weber described it includes such elements as tenure, appointment to office, salaries as a rational form of payment, and competency as the basis of promotion.

Bureaucratic characteristics of colleges and universities

Several authors have suggested that university governance may be more fully understood by applying the bureaucratic model. For example, Herbert Stroup (1966) has pointed out some characteristics of colleges and universities that fit Weber's original description of a bureaucracy. They include the following:

1. Competence is the criterion used for appointment.

2. Officials are appointed, not elected.

3. Salaries are fixed and paid directly by the organization, rather than determined in "free-fee" style.

4. Rank is recognized and respected.

5. The career is exclusive; no other work is done.

6. The style of life of the organization's members centers on the organization.

7. Security is present in a tenure system.

8. Personal and organizational property are separated.

Stroup is undoubtedly correct in believing that Weber's paradigm can be applied to universities, and most observers are well aware of the bureaucratic factors involved in university administration. Among the more prominent are the following.

1. The university is a complex organization under *state charter*, like most other bureaucracies. This seemingly innocent fact, has major consequences, especially as states increasingly seek to exercise control.

2. The university has a *formal hierarchy*, with offices and a set of bylaws that specify the relations between those offices. Professors, instructors, and research assistants may be considered bureaucratic officers in the same sense as deans, chancellors, and presidents.

3. There are *formal channels of communication* that must be respected.

4. There are definite *bureaucratic authority relations*, with certain officials exercising authority over others. In a university the authority relations are often vague and shifting, but no one would deny that they exist.

5. There are *formal policies and rules* that govern much of the institution's work, such as library regulations, budgetary guidelines, and procedures of the university senate.

6. The bureaucratic elements of the university are most vividly apparent in its *"people-processing" aspects*: record keeping, registration, graduation requirements, and a multitude of other routine, day-to-day activities designed to help the modem university handle its masses of students.

7. *Bureaucratic decision-making processes* are used, most often by officials assigned the responsibility for making routine decisions by the formal administrative structure. Examples are admissions procedures, handled by the dean of admissions; procedures for graduation, routinely administered by designated officials; research policies, supervised by specified officials; and financial matters, usually handled in a bureaucratic manner by the finance office.

Weaknesses in the bureaucratic model

In many ways the bureaucratic model falls short of encompassing university governance, especially if one is primarily concerned with decision-making processes. First, the bureaucratic model tells us much about authority—that is, legitimate, formalized power—but not much about informal types of power and influence, which may take the form of mass movements or appeals to emotion and sentiment. Second, it explains much about the organization's formal *structure* but little about the dynamic *processes* that characterize the organization in action. Third, it describes the formal structure at one particular time, but it does not explain changes over time. Fourth, it explains how policies may be carried out most efficiently, but it says little about the critical process by which policy is established in the first place. Finally, it also ignores political issues, such as the struggles of various interest groups within the university.

The University Collegium

Many writers have rejected the bureaucratic model of the university. They seek to replace it with the model of the "collegium" or "community of scholars." When this literature is closely examined, there seem to be at least three different threads running through it.

A description of collegial decision making

This approach argues that academic decision making should not be like the hierarchical process in a bureaucracy. Instead there should be full participation of the academic community, especially the faculty. Under this concept the community of scholars would administer its own affairs, and bureaucratic officials would have little influence (see Goodman, 1962). John Millett, one of the foremost proponents of this model, has succinctly stated his view:

> I do not believe that the concept of hierarchy is a realistic representation of the interpersonal relationships which exist within a college or university. Nor do I believe that a structure of hierarchy is a desirable prescription for the organization of a college or university . . .
>
> I would argue that there is another concept of organization just as valuable as a tool of analysis and even more useful as a generalized observation of group and interpersonal behavior. This is the concept of community . . .
>
> The concept of community presupposes an organization in which functions are differentiated and in which specialization must be brought together, or coordination, if you will, is achieved not through a structure of superordination and subordination of persons and groups but through a *dynamic of consensus* [Millett, 1962, pages 234–235].

A discussion of the faculty's professional authority

Talcott Parsons (1947) was one of the first to call attention to the difference between "official competence," derived from one's office in a bureaucracy, and "technical competence," derived from one's ability to perform a given task. Parsons concentrated on the technical competence of the physician, but others have extended this logic to other professionals whose authority is based on what they *know* and can *do*, rather than on their official position. Some examples are the scientist in industry, the military adviser, the expert in government, the physician in the hospital, and the professor in the university.

The literature on professionalism strongly supports the argument for collegial organization. It emphasizes the professional's ability to make his own decisions and his need for freedom from organizational restraints. Consequently, the collegium is seen as the most reasonable method of organizing the university. Parsons, for example, notes (page 60) that when professionals are organized in a bureaucracy, "there are strong tendencies for them to develop a different sort of structure from that characteristic of the administrative hierarchy . . . of bureaucracy. Instead of a rigid hierarchy of status and authority there tends to be what is roughly, in formal status, a company of equals."

A utopian prescription for operating the educational system

There is a third strand in the collegial image. In recent years there has been a growing discontent with our impersonal contemporary society. The multiversity, with its thousands of students and its huge bureaucracy, is a case in point. The student revolts of the 1960s and perhaps even the widespread apathy of the 1970s are symptoms of deeply felt alienation between students and massive educational establishments. The discontent and anxiety this alienation has produced are aptly expressed in the now-famous sign worn by a Berkeley student: "I am a human being—do not fold, spindle, or mutilate."

As an alternative to this impersonal, bureaucratized educational system, many critics are calling for a return to the "academic community." In their conception such a community would offer personal attention, humane education, and "relevant confrontation with life." Paul Goodman's *The Community of Scholars* (1962) still appeals to many who seek to reform the university. Goodman cites the need for more personal interaction between faculty and students, for more relevant courses, and for educational innovations to bring the student into existential dialogue with the subject matter of his discipline. The number of articles on this subject, in both the mass media and the professional journals, is astonishingly large. Indeed, this concept of the collegial academic community is now widely proposed as one answer to the impersonality and meaninglessness of today's large multiversity. Thus conceived, the collegial model functions more as a revolutionary ideology and a utopian projection than a description of actual governance processes at any university.

Weaknesses in the collegial model

Three themes are incorporated in the collegial model: (1) decision making by consensus, (2) the professional authority of faculty members, and (3) the call for more humane education. These are all legitimate and appealing. Few would deny that our universities would be better centers of learning if we could somehow implement these objectives. There is a misleading simplicity about the collegial model, however, that glosses over many realities.

For one thing, the *descriptive* and *normative* visions are often confused. In the literature dealing with the collegial model it is often difficult to tell whether a writer is saying that the university is a collegium or that it ought to be a collegium. Discussions of the collegium are frequently more a lament for paradise lost than a description of reality. Indeed, the collegial image of round-table decision making is not an accurate description of the processes in most institutions.

Although at the department level there are many examples of collegial decision making, at higher levels it usually exists only in some aspects of the committee system. Of course, the proponents may be advocating a collegial model as a desirable goal or reform strategy. This is helpful, but it does not allow us to understand the actual workings of universities.

In addition, the collegial model fails to deal adequately with the problem of *conflict*. When Millett emphasizes the "dynamic of consensus," he neglects the prolonged battles that precede consensus, as well as decisions that actually represent the victory of one group over another. Proponents of the collegial model are correct in declaring that simple bureaucratic rule making is not the essence of decision making. But in making this point they take the equally indefensible position that major decisions are reached primarily by consensus. Neither extreme is correct, for decisions are rarely made by either bureaucratic fiat or simple consensus.

The University as a Political System

In *Power and Conflict in the University* (1971), Baldridge proposed a "political" model of university governance. Although the other major models of governance—the collegial and the bureaucratic—have valuable insights to offer, we believe that further insights can be gained from this model. It grapples with the power plays, conflicts, and rough-and-tumble politics to be found in many academic institutions.

Basic assumptions of a political model

The political model assumes that complex organizations can be studied as miniature political systems. There are interest group dynamics and conflicts similar to those in cities, states, or other political entities. The political model focuses on policy-forming processes, because major policies commit an organization to definite goals and set the strategies for reaching those goals. Policy decisions are critical decisions. They have a major impact on an organization's future. Of course, in any practical situation it may be difficult to separate the routine from the critical, for issues that seem minor at one point may later be decisive, or vice versa. In general, however, policy decisions bind an organization to important courses of action.

Since policies are so important, people throughout an organization try to influence them to reflect their own interests and values. Policy making becomes a vital target of interest group activity that permeates the organization. Owing to its central importance, then, the organization theorist may select policy formation as the key for studying organizational conflict and change, just as the political scientist often selects legislative acts as the focal point for his analysis of a state's political processes. With policy formation as its key issue, the political model operates on a series of assumptions about the political process.

1. To say that policy making is a political process is not to say that everyone is involved. On the contrary, *inactivity* prevails. Most people most of the time find the policy-making process an uninteresting, unrewarding activity. Policy making is therefore left to the administrators. This is characteristic not only of policy making in universities but of political processes in society at large. Voters do not vote; citizens do not attend city council meetings; parents often permit school boards to do what they please. By and large, decisions that may have a profound effect on our society are made by small groups of elites.

2. Even people who are active engage in *fluid participation*. They move in and out of the decision-making process. Rarely do people spend much time on any given issue. Decisions, therefore, are usually made by those who persist. This normally means that small groups of political elites govern most major decisions, for they invest the necessary time in the process.

3. Colleges and universities, like most other social organizations, are characterized by fragmentation into *interest groups* with different goals and values. When resources are plentiful and the organization is prospering, these interest groups engage in only minimal conflict. But they are likely to mobilize and try to influence decisions when resources are tight, outside pressure groups attack, or internal groups try to assume command.

4. In a fragmented, dynamic social system *conflict* is natural. It is not necessarily a symptom of breakdown in the academic community. In fact, conflict is a significant factor in promoting healthy organizational change.

5. The pressure that groups can exert places severe *limitations on formal authority* in the bureaucratic sense. Decisions are not simply bureaucratic orders but are often negotiated compromises between competing groups. Officials are not free simply to issue a decision. Instead they must attempt to find a viable course acceptable to several powerful blocs.

6. *External interest groups* exert a strong influence over the policy-making process. External pressures and formal control by outside agencies—especially in public institutions—are powerful shapers of internal governance processes.

The political decision model versus the rational decision model

The bureaucratic model of organizational structure is accompanied by a rational model of decision making. It is usually assumed that in a bureaucracy the structure is hierarchical and well organized, and that decisions are made through clear-cut, predetermined steps. Moreover, a definite, rational approach is expected to lead to the optimal decision. Graham T. Allison has summarized the rational decision-making process as follows:

1. *Goals and objectives.* The goals and objectives of the agent are translated into a "payoff" or "utility" or "preference" function, which represents the "value" or "utility" of alternative sets of consequences. At the outset of the decision problem the agent has a payoff function which ranks all possible sets of consequences in terms of his values and objectives. Each bundle of consequences will contain a number of side effects. Nevertheless, at a minimum, the agent must be able to rank in order of preference each possible set of consequences that might result from a particular action.

2. *Alternatives.* The rational agent must choose among a set of alternatives displayed before him in a particular situation. In decision theory these alternatives are represented as a decision tree. The alternative courses of action may include more than a simple act, but the specification of a course of action must be sufficiently precise to differentiate it from other alternatives.

3. *Consequences*. To each alternative is attached a set of consequences or outcomes of choice that will ensue if that particular alternative is chosen. Variations are generated at this point by making different assumptions about the accuracy of the decision maker's knowledge of the consequences that follow from the choice of each alternative.

4. *Choice*. Rational choice consists simply of selecting that alternative whose consequences rank highest in the decision maker's payoff function [Allison, 1971, pages 29–30].

The rational model appeals to those who regard their actions as essentially goal-directed and rational. Realistically, however, we should realize that the rational model is more an ideal than an actual description of how people act. In fact, in the confused organizational setting of the university, political constraints often undermine the force of rationality. A political model of decision making requires us to answer some new questions about the decision process:

The first new question posed by the political model is *why* a given decision is made at all. The formalists have already indicated that "recognition of the problem" is one element in the process, but too little attention has been paid to the activities that bring a particular issue to the forefront. Why is *this* decision being considered at *this* particular time? The political model insists that interest groups, powerful individuals, and bureaucratic processes are critical in drawing attention to some decisions rather than to others. A study of "attention cues" by which issues are called to the community's attention is a vital part of any analysis.

Second, a question must be raised about the right of any person or group to make the decisions. Previously the *who* question was seldom raised, chiefly because the decision literature was developed for hierarchical organizations in which the focus of authority could be easily defined. In a more loosely coordinated system however, we must ask a prior question: Why was the legitimacy to make the decision vested in a particular person or group? Why is Dean Smith making the decision instead of Dean Jones or why is the University Senate dealing with the problem instead of the central administration? Establishing the right of authority over a decision is a political question, subject to conflict, power manipulation, and struggles between interest groups. Thus the political model always asks tough questions: Who has the right to make the decision? What are the conflict-ridden processes by which the decision was located at this point rather than at another? The crucial point is that often the issue of *who* makes the decision has already limited, structured, and pre-formed *how* it will be made.

The third new issue raised by a political interpretation concerns the development of complex decision networks. As a result of the fragmentation of the university, decision making is rarely located in one official; instead it is dependent on the advice and authority of numerous people. Again the importance of the committee system is evident. It is necessary to understand that the committee network is the legitimate reflection of the need for professional influence to intermingle with bureaucratic influence. The decision process, then, is taken out of the hands of individuals (although there are still many who are powerful) and placed into a network that allows a *cumulative buildup* of expertise and advice. When the very life of the organization clusters around expertise, *decision making is likely to be diffused, segmentalized, and decentralized*. A complex network of committees, councils, and advisory bodies grows to handle the task of assembling the expertise necessary for reasonable decisions. Decision making by the individual bureaucrat is replaced with decision making by committee, council, and cabinet. Centralized decision making is replaced with diffuse decision making. The process becomes a far-flung network for gathering expertise from every corner of the organization and translating it into policy [Baldridge, 1971, page 190].

The fourth new question raised by the political model concerns alternative solutions to the problem at hand. The rational decision model suggests that all possible options are open and within easy reach of the decision maker. A realistic appraisal of decision dynamics in most organizations, however, suggests that by no means are all options open. The political dynamics of interest groups, the force of external power blocs, and the opposition of powerful professional constituencies may leave only a handful of viable options. The range of alternatives is often sharply limited by political considerations. Just as important, there is often little time and energy available for seeking new solutions. Although all possible solutions should be identified under the rational model, in the real world administrators have little time to grope for solutions before their deadlines.

In *Power and Conflict in the University*, Baldridge summed up the political model of decision making as follows:

First, powerful political forces—interest groups, bureaucratic officials, influential individuals, organizational subunits—cause a given issue to emerge from the limbo of on-going problems and certain "attention cues" force the political community to consider the problem. Second, there is a struggle over locating the decision with a particular person or group, for the location of the right to make the decision often determines the outcome. Third, decisions are usually "preformed" to a great extent by the time one person or group is given the legitimacy to make the decision; not all options are open and the choices have been severely limited by the previous conflicts. Fourth, such political struggles are more likely to occur in reference to "critical" decisions than to "routine" decisions. Fifth, a complex decision network is developed to gather the necessary information and supply the critical expertise. Sixth, during the process of making the decision political controversy is likely to continue and compromises, deals, and plain head cracking are often necessary to get any decision made. Finally, the controversy is not likely to end easily. In fact, it is difficult even to know when a decision is made, for the political processes have a habit of unmaking, confusing, and muddling whatever agreements are hammered out.

This may be a better way of grappling with the complexity that surrounds decision processes within a loosely coordinated, fragmented political system. The formal decision models seem to have been asking very limited questions about the decision process and more insight can be gained by asking a new set of political questions. Thus the decision model that emerges from the university's political dynamics is more open, more dependent on conflict and political action. It is not so systematic or formalistic as most decision

theory, but it is probably closer to the truth. Decision making, then, is not an isolated technique but another critical process that must be integrated into a larger political image [Baldridge, 1971, pages 191–192].

It is clear that a political analysis emphasizes certain factors over others. First, it is concerned primarily with problems of goal setting and conflicts over values, rather than with efficiency in achieving goals. Second, analysis of the organization's change processes and adaptation to its environment is critically important. The political dynamics of a university are constantly changing, pressuring the university in many directions, and forcing change throughout the academic system. Third, the analysis of conflict is an essential component. Fourth, there is the role of interest groups in pressuring decision makers to formulate policy. Finally, much attention is given to the legislative and decision-making phases—the processes by which pressures and power are transformed into policy. Taken together these points constitute the bare outline for a political analysis of academic governance.

The revised political model: an environmental and structuralist approach. Since the political model of academic governance originally appeared in *Power and Conflict in the University*, we have become aware that it has several shortcomings. For this reason we offer a few observations about some changes in emphasis, a few corrections in focus.

First, the original political model probably underestimated the impact of routine bureaucratic processes. Many, perhaps most, decisions are made not in the heat of political controversy but according to standard operating procedures. The political description in *Power and Conflict in the University* was based on a study of New York University. The research occurred at a time of extremely high conflict when the university was confronted with two crises, a student revolution and a financial disaster. The political model developed from that study probably overstresses the role of conflict and negotiation as elements in standard decision making, since those were the processes apparent at the time. Now we would stress that it is important to consider routine procedures of the governance process.

Second, the original political model, based on a single case study, did not do justice to the broad range of political activity that occurs in different kinds of institutions. For example, NYU is quite different from Oberlin College, and both are distinctive institutions compared to local community colleges. Many of the intense political dynamics observed in the NYU study may have been exaggerated in a troubled institution such as NYU, particularly during the heated conflicts of the late 1960s.

Third, we want to stress even more strongly the central role of environmental factors. The NYU analysis showed that conflict and political processes within the university were linked to environmental factors. But even more stress on the environmental context is needed.

Finally, as developed in *Power and Conflict in the University,* the political model suffered from an "episodic" character. That is, the model did not give enough emphasis to long-term decision-making patterns, and it failed to consider the way institutional structure may shape and channel political efforts. Centralization of power, the development of decision councils, long-term patterns of professional autonomy, the dynamics of departmental

power, and the growth of unionization were all slighted by the original model. There are other important questions concerning long-term patterns: What groups tend to dominate decision making over long periods of time? Do some groups seem to be systematically excluded from the decision-making process? Do different kinds of institutions have different political patterns? Do institutional characteristics affect the morale of participants in such a way that they engage in particular decision-influencing activities? Do different kinds of institutions have systematic patterns of faculty participation in decision making? Are decision processes highly centralized in certain kinds of institutions?

Finally, we are not substituting the political model for the bureaucratic or collegial model of academic decision making. In a sense, they each address a separate set of problems and, taken together, they often yield complementary interpretations. We believe, however, that the political model has many strengths, and we offer it as a useful tool for understanding academic governance. See Table 10-2 for a comparison of the three decision-making models.

Table 10-2			
Three Models of Decision Making and Governance			
	Bureaucratic	*Collegial*	*Political*
Assumptions about structure	Hierarchical bureaucracy	Community of peers	Fragmented, complex professional federation
Social	Unitary: integrated by formal system	Unitary: integrated bypeer consensus	Pluralistic: encompasses different interest groups with divergent values
Basic theoretical foundations	Weberian bureaucracy, classic studies of formal systems	Professionalism literature, human-relations approach to organization	Conflict analysis, interest group theory, community power literature
View of decision-making process	"Rational" decision making; standard operating procedures	Shared collegial decision: consensus, community participation	Negotiation, bargaining, political brokerage, external influence
Cycle of decision making	Problem definition; search for alternatives; evaluation of alternatives; calculus; choice; implementation	As in bureaucratic model, but in addition stresses the involvement of professional peers in the process	Emergency of issue out of social context; interest articulation; conflict; legislative process; implementation of policy; feedback

Images of Leadership and Management Strategies

Thus far we have made two basic arguments: (1) colleges and universities are unique in many of their organizational characteristics and, as a consequence, it is necessary to create new models to help explain organizational structure, governance, and decision making; and (2) a political model of academic governance offers useful insights in addition to those offered by the bureaucratic and collegial models. In this section we will suggest that some alternative images of leadership and management style are needed to accommodate the unique characteristics of academic organizations.

Leadership Under the Bureaucratic Model

Under the bureaucratic model the leader is seen as a hero who stands at the top of a complex pyramid of power. The hero's job is to assess problems, propose alternatives, and make rational choices. Much of the organization's power is held by the hero. Great expectations are raised because people trust the hero to solve their problems and to fend off threats from the environment. The image of the authoritarian hero is deeply ingrained in most societies and in the philosophy of most organization theorists.

We expect leaders to possess a unique set of skills with emphasis on problem-solving ability and technical knowledge about the organization. The principles of "scientific management," such as Planning, Programming, Budgeting Systems (PPBS) and Management by Objectives, are often proposed as the methods for rational problem solving. Generally, schools of management, business, and educational administration teach such courses to develop the technical skills that the hero-planner will need in leading the organization.

The hero image is deeply imbedded in our cultural beliefs about leadership. But in organizations such as colleges and universities it is out of place. Power is more diffuse in those organizations; it is lodged with professional experts and fragmented into many departments and subdivisions. Under these circumstances, high expectations about leadership performance often cannot be met. The leader has neither the power nor the information necessary to consistently make heroic decisions. Moreover, the scientific management procedures prescribed for organizational leaders quickly break down under conditions of goal ambiguity, professional dominance, and environmental vulnerability—precisely the organizational characteristics of colleges and universities. Scientific management theories make several basic assumptions: (1) the organization's goals are clear; (2) the organization is a closed system insulated from environmental penetration; and (3) the planners have the power to execute their decisions. These assumptions seem unrealistic in the confused and fluid world of the organized anarchy.

Table 10-3			
Images of Leadership and Management Under Three Models of Governance			
	Bureaucratic	*Collegial*	*Political*
Basic leadership image Leadership skills	Hero Technical problem-solving skills	"First among equals" Interpersonal dynamics	Statesman Political strategy, interpersonal dynamics, coalition management
Management Expectation	"Scientific management" Very high: people believe that hero-leader can solve problems and he tries to play the role	Management by consensus Modest: leader is developer of consensus among professionals	Strategic decision making Modest: leader marshalls political action, but is constrained by the counter efforts of other groups

Leadership Under the Collegial Model

The collegial leader presents a stark contrast to the heroic bureaucratic leader. The collegial leader is above all the "first among equals" in an organization run by professional experts. Essentially, the collegial model proposes what John Millett calls the "dynamic of consensus in a community of scholars." The basic role of the collegial leader is not so much to command as to listen, not so much to lead as to gather expert judgments, not so much to manage as to facilitate, not so much to order but to persuade and negotiate.

Obviously, the skills of a collegial leader differ from those required by the scientific management principles employed by the heroic bureaucrat. Instead of technical problem-solving skills, the collegial leader needs professional expertise to ensure that he is held in high esteem by his colleagues. Talent in interpersonal dynamics is also needed to achieve consensus in organizational decision making. The collegial leader's role is more modest and more realistic. He does not stand alone since other professionals share the burden of decision making with him. Negotiation and compromise are the bywords of the collegial leader; authoritarian strategies are clearly inappropriate.

Leadership Under the Political Model

Under the political model the leader is a mediator or negotiator between power blocs. Unlike the autocratic academic president of the past, who ruled with an iron hand, the contemporary president must play a political role by pulling coalitions together to fight for desired changes. The academic monarch of yesteryear has almost vanished. In his place is not the academic hero but the academic statesman. Robert Dahl has painted an amusing picture of the political maneuvers of Mayor Richard Lee of New Haven, and the same description applies to academic political leaders:

> The mayor was not at the peak of a pyramid but rather at the center of intersecting circles. He rarely commanded. He negoti-

ated, cajoled, exhorted, beguiled, charmed, pressed, appealed, reasoned, promised, insisted, demanded, even threatened, but he most needed support and acquiescence from other leaders who simply could not be commanded. Because the mayor could not command, he had to bargain [Dahl, 1961, page 204].

The political interpretation of leadership can be pressed even further, for the governance of the university more and more comes to look like a "cabinet" form of administration. The key figure today is not the president, the solitary giant, but the political leader surrounded by his staff, the prime minister who gathers the information and expertise to construct policy. It is the "staff," the network of key administrators, that makes most of the critical decisions. The university has become much too complicated for any one man, regardless of his stature. Cadres of vice-presidents, research men, budget officials, public relations men, and experts of various stripes surround the president, sit on the cabinet, and help reach collective decisions. Expertise becomes more critical than ever and leadership becomes even more the ability to assemble, lead, and facilitate the activities of knowledgeable experts.

Therefore, the president must be seen as a "statesman" as well as a "hero-bureaucrat." The bureaucratic image might be appropriate for the man who assembles data to churn out routine decisions with a computer's help. In fact, this image is fitting for many middle-echelon officials in the university. The statesman's image is much more accurate for the top administrators, for here the influx of data and information gives real power and possibilities for creative action. The statesman is the innovative actor who uses information, expertise, and the combined wisdom of the cabinet to plan the institution's future; the bureaucrat may only be a number manipulator, a user of routine information for routine ends. The use of the cabinet, the assembly of expertise, and the exercise of political judgment in the service of institutional goals—all this is part of the new image of the statesman leader which must complement both the hero leader and the collegial leader.

Table 10-3 presents a summary and comparison of the three basic images of leadership and management we have just described.

Summary

Colleges and universities are different from most other kinds of complex organizations. Their goals are more ambiguous and contested, they serve clients instead of seeking to make a profit, their technologies are unclear and problematic, and professionals dominate the work force and decision-making process. Thus colleges and universities are not standard bureaucracies, but can best be described as "organized anarchies" (see Cohen and March, 1947).

What decision and governance processes are to be found in an organized anarchy? Does the decision process resemble a bureaucratic system, with rational problem solving and standard operating procedures? Does it resemble a collegial system in which the professional faculty participate as members of a "community of scholars"? Or does it appear to be a political process with various interest groups struggling for influence over organizational policy? Each image is valid in some sense; each image helps complete the picture. Finally, we question the standard image of leadership and management. Classic leadership theory, based on a bureaucratic model, suggests the image of the organizational leader as a hero who uses principles of scientific management as the basis for his decisions. We have suggested that the leader's image should be that of the academic statesman, and that management should be considered a process of strategic decision making.

The research reported in this paper was supported by the Stanford Center for Research and Development in Teaching, by funds from the National Institute of Education (contract no. NE-C-00-3-0062.

Note

1. Our list of characteristics of an organized anarchy extends Cohen and March's, which contains (1) and (3), plus a characteristic called "fluid participation."

References

Allison, Graham T. *Essence of Decision.* Boston: Little, Brown, 1971.

Baldridge, J. Victor. *Power and Conflict in the University.* New York: John Wiley, 1971.

Clark, Burton R. "Faculty Organization and Authority." *The Study of Academic Administration,* edited by Terry Lunsford. Boulder, Colo.: Western Interstate Commission for Higher Education, 1963. Reprinted as chapter 4 in this volume.

Cohen, Michael D., and March, James G. *Leadership and Ambiguity: The American College President.* New York: McGraw-Hill, 1974.

Dahl, Robert. *Who Governs?* New Haven, Conn.: Yale University Press, 1961.

Goodman, Paul. *The Community of Scholars.* New York: Random House, 1962.

Gross, Edward, and Grambsch, Paul V. *Changes in University Organization, 1964–1971.* New York: McGraw-Hill, 1974.

Gross, Edward. *University Goals and Academic Power.* Washington, D.C.: Office of Education, 1968.

Millett, John. *The Academic Community.* New York: McGraw-Hill, 1962.

Parsons, Talcott. "Introduction." *The Theory of Social and Economic Organization,* by Max Weber. New York: Free Press, 1947.

Stroup, Herbert. *Bureaucracy in Higher Education.* New York: Free Press, 1966.

Weber, Max. *The Theory of Social and Economic Organization.* New York: Free Press, 1947.

PART III

CAMPUS CLIMATE AND CULTURE

CHAPTER 11

ORGANIZATIONAL CULTURE IN THE STUDY OF HIGHER EDUCATION

ANDREW T. MASLAND

The pervasive influence of organizational culture has recently recaptured the attention of those who study organizations. Ouchi's *Theory Z* (1981), Pascale and Athos' *The Art of Japanese Management* (1981), and Deal and Kennedy's *Corporate Cultures* (1982) describe how organizational culture profoundly influences managerial behavior. This paper first defines organizational culture and briefly examines how the concept has been applied to colleges and universities. It then describes possible approaches and techniques for uncovering the influence of organizational culture. Finally, the paper explores why the study of organizational culture is relevant to researchers and practitioners. Thus, the paper defines and illustrates the application of a useful perspective on higher education.

The literature has previously recognized that there is more to organizations than formal structure. The classic elements of organizational design such as hierarchical structure, formalization, rationality, and specialization are important (Tosi, 1975), but they do not fully explain organizational behavior. Leadership, for example, can transform an organization with a formal structure of rules and objectives into an institution that is a responsive, adaptive organism (Selznick, 1957, p. 5).

Pettigrew (1979) expands upon Selznick's study of organizations. Pettigrew views leadership and values as one part of a concept he calls organizational culture. He defines organizational culture "as the amalgam of beliefs, ideology, language, ritual, and myth" (1979, p. 572). Pettigrew argues that an organization is a continuing social system and the elements of culture exert a powerful control over the behavior of those within it. Organizational culture induces purpose, commitment, and order; provides meaning and social cohesion; and clarifies and explains behavioral expectations. Culture influences an organization through the people within it.

The recent popular literature on Japanese management techniques highlights the influence of organizational culture. Pascale and Athos (1981) describe organizational culture as the glue that holds an organization together. It is a "bass clef" that conveys at a deep level what management really cares about. Theory Z (Ouchi, 1981) is a specific configuration of cultural beliefs and values. Ouchi asserts that this particular combination of cultural elements is largely responsible for the success of Japanese businesses. In contrast to Ouchi, Deal and Kennedy (1982) propose that a variety of corporate cultures can increase organizational effectiveness. A strongly articulated culture tells employees what is expected of them and how to behave under a given set of circumstances. The coherence of thought and action a strong culture produces thus enhances organizational success. Corporations with weak cultures do not have the sense of purpose and direction that is found in those with strong cultures, and are often less successful (Deal & Kennedy, 1982).

It is somewhat ironic that widespread interest in the interaction of culture and management grew out of studies of Japanese firms. As Chait (1982), Dill (1982), and Wyer (1982) note, traditional administrative practices common in American colleges and universities are similar to Japanese management styles. Shared governance and collegiality are participatory management. Academic departments, in discussions of future direction, quality control, and problem resolution, function like quality circles. Tenure traditionally provides the economic and psychological benefits of lifetime employment. Although colleges and universities have long benefited from these managerial practices, they have not been identified as "organizational culture."

The concept of organizational culture is not new to higher education, however. Clark (1980) notes that the lofty doctrines associated with colleges and universities elicit almost religious emotions. He defines four cultural spheres that affect academic life in this way. They are (a) the cultures of specific academic disciplines, (b) the culture of the academic profession, (c) institutional cultures, and (d) the cultures of national systems of higher education. These four elements reflect academic structures. This paper focuses on the third category, the cultures of specific institutions.

The strength of institutional culture depends on several factors (Clark, 1980). Primary among them is the scale of the organization. Small organizations tend to have stronger cultures than do large organizations. Second is the tightness of the organization. Colleges with highly interdependent parts have stronger cultures than those with autonomous parts. Third is the age of the organization. As discussed below, culture develops over time and an institution with a long history simply has a larger foundation upon which to build its culture. Finally, the institution's founding influences the strength of its culture. A traumatic birth or transformation, like a long history, provides a stronger base upon which to build cultural values and beliefs. In colleges with stronger cultures there is greater coherence among beliefs, language, ritual, and myth. Weak cultures lack this coherence.

Clark's description of organizational saga is a classic embodiment of academic culture. Saga is a "collective understanding of unique accomplishment in a formally established group" (Clark, 1972, p. 179). It is a set of beliefs and values tied together in a story about the institution's past. A saga strengthens the bond between the organization and students, alumni, faculty, and staff. A saga shapes social reality on the campus and thus helps control behavior. According to Clark saga intensifies organizational commitment and feelings of membership in a special community. The trust and loyalty a saga produces are valuable resources in preserving organizational strength.

At the institutional level culture affects many aspects of campus life. There is a long history of interest in student culture and its effects (see, for example, Feldman & Newcomb, 1969, Becker, Geer, Hughes, & Strauss, 1961). Similar to the study of student culture is research on organizational climate—the atmosphere or style of life on a campus (Pace, 1968). A wide variety of instruments measure climate, but they classify institutions by standard typologies and are heavily influenced by psychological constructs. Organizational culture, on the other hand, focuses on the shared values, beliefs, and ideologies which are unique to a campus. Thus measures of climate do not illuminate culture.

Organizational culture also affects curriculum and administration. Masland (1982), for example, demonstrates that organizational culture influences how academic computing fits into an institution's curriculum. As might be expected, a college that values a traditional liberal arts education is less apt to introduce a technical computing major. On the other hand, a college that primarily teaches business and management will want to introduce its students to the practical applications of computing that support business decisions. Along somewhat similar lines, an organization's culture affects the management of computer resources. A belief that students should have free access to computer resources in the same way that they have unlimited library resources is part of some campus cultures. But when computer resources are scarce, allocating them among competing users is a difficult task. This problem would not arise if institutional values did not stress unlimited access to educational resources.

Thus, the literature on higher education has begun to apply the concept of organizational culture—the implicit values, beliefs, and ideologies of those within an organization. In particular, research demonstrates that in higher education culture can affect student life, administration, and curriculum.

While organizational culture is becoming more widely used and accepted, it is still difficult to find clear and succinct methods of uncovering an institution's culture. Typical of the means given for discovering organizational culture is this description.

> All one has to do to get a feel for how the different cultures of competing businesses manifest themselves is to spend a day visiting each. . . . There are characteristic ways of making decisions, relating to bosses, and choosing people to fill key jobs (Schwartz & Davis, 1981, p. 30).

Although this may be true, the advice is rather vague for the researcher who wants to study organizational culture. The difficulty in studying culture arises because culture is implicit, and we are all embedded in our own cultures. In order to observe organizational culture, the researcher must find its visible and explicit manifestations (Schein, 1981).

Windows on Organizational Culture

Fortunately, there are methods available which uncover manifestations of organizational culture. Each involves looking for a specific influence of culture at work and from that evidence deducing something about the culture itself. Examination of organizational history, for example, often illuminates culture and its influences because culture develops over time through the actions and words of organizational leaders. Cultural manifestations can also be seen in current actions. The methods used to make decisions, agendas of meetings, and personnel policy are common arenas for cultural influences. To understand an organization's culture one must pay close attention to the details of daily life. There are a number of windows on organizational culture that make it easier to see both past and present cultural influences. This article focuses on four in particular: saga, heroes, symbols, and rituals. While there are a variety of ways to "see" culture, these four are particularly helpful, in part

because they are easy to understand and apply. These four windows are closely related and may seem redundant, yet there are subtle differences among them.

Saga Like Heroes: Symbols and Rituals

Saga (Clark, 1972) is the first window on organizational culture in higher education. A saga usually has its roots in an organization's history, and it describes a unique accomplishment of the organization. An institution's saga codifies what sets a college apart from others. Key faculty members, students, and alumni usually support an institution's saga, as do unique academic program elements and images about the institution. Clark uses Antioch, Swarthmore, and Reed as examples of three colleges with strong sagas. He demonstrates how the sagas at these schools profoundly influence institutional life. At Reed College, for example, the saga dates from the school's founding in 1910 by William T. Foster. The first president established a college known for "hard-won excellence and nonconformity" (Clark, 1972, p. 180). Antioch's saga arose from the influence of reformer Arthur E. Morgan who completely restructured Antioch and launched a saga based on combining work, study, and community participation.

Heroes

Organizational heroes or Saints (Deal & Kennedy, 1982; Dill, 1982) are a second window on organizational culture. Heroes are people who are important to an organization and often represent ideals and values in human form. They may play a central role in an institution's saga because heroes are people who have made crucial decisions or who exemplify behavior suitable to the college. They are role models, set standards, and preserve what makes the organization unique. People in an organization tell stories about heroes and the examples they set. The stories about heroes are another way to see organizational culture. They are passed down to newcomers in an organization as examples of successful behavior in the past.

Often, a college's founder is an organizational hero. The examples of Reed and Antioch cited above illustrate such heroes. Another example is a small college that has always combined liberal arts with career-oriented programs for women. Its founder stated that he wanted to provide women with an education that would make them self-sufficient. The college does this, and it did so long before the current trend towards career education began. The school's founder set an example personnel at the college endeavor to follow. A hero at a business college provides a final illustration. He was a long-time faculty member and administrator who fought for accreditation from an important agency. His long battle demonstrated and validated the value college personnel place on excellence.

Symbols

Symbols are a third window on organizational culture. A symbol can represent implicit cultural values and beliefs, thus, making them tangible. Personnel can point to a symbol as a concrete example much the same way that a hero personifies cultural values. Symbols also can serve an important external function. While heroes and stories may only be known to those within an organization, the public may recognize organizational symbols.

The business college mentioned above provides an excellent example of how a symbol gives insight into culture. The college has fairly extensive computer resources. It uses them to introduce students to the techniques and knowledge they will need in tomorrow's business environment. The desire to do this stems in part from the value the college places on leadership and excellence in business education. The computer facilities are a symbol of this value.

Metaphor is another type of symbol that is helpful in understanding organizational culture. The language people use when they talk about an organization reveals its culture. As with other symbols, metaphors make explicit normally implicit cultural values and beliefs (Beaudoin, 1981). Because metaphors help express that which usually is difficult to verbalize, they are an excellent key for unlocking culture. Masland (1982) examined a college that described its computer facilities as "supermarket computing." This is a vivid metaphor that invokes an image of practicality and value in the institution's approach to computing.

Rituals

Rituals are another means of identifying cultural values, beliefs, and ideologies. Rituals are a useful tool for uncovering culture because they translate culture into action. They provide tangible evidence of culture. An outstanding teaching award ceremony, for example, can demonstrate to an academic community the strength of the institution's values. Is such a ceremony taken seriously and the recipient seen as receiving a great honor, or is it dismissed as meaningless? If the institution values excellence in teaching, the former is more likely than the latter. Rituals provide continuity with the past. They demonstrate that old values and beliefs still play a role in campus life. Rituals also provide meaning. In an organization with ambiguous goals and uncertain outcomes, the annual convocation ceremony may provide a sense of meaning and direction for personnel. This kind of ritual reinforces the institution's culture. Moreover, daily rituals of interaction between faculty and administrators illustrate the relative importance of each group and the ideologies surrounding their roles.

Collecting Cultural Data

Saga, heroes, rituals, and symbols are means of exploring an organization's culture. In a strong culture they work in unison and illustrate the culture. But the researcher still needs specific methodologies to learn about each window. The common techniques described below are useful ways of examining the four cultural windows and thus culture itself.

Interviews, observation, and document analysis are three basic techniques. Of the three, interviews may be the most important. According to Gorden (1975), interviews are the most effective means of gathering data on beliefs, attitudes, and values. But because culture is implicit interview questions cannot ask about culture directly. Instead the researcher should probe the four cultural windows discussed above. Asking respondents what makes their college distinct or unique, or what makes it stand apart from similar schools a prospective applicant might consider, uncovers organizational saga. Similar questions focus on the school's educational philosophy and what is unique about its academic mission. Respondents draw upon their understanding of the institution's saga when answering such questions. They disclose what the college means to them. They also refer to the symbols and rituals that represent this meaning in a more tangible form. Thus listening carefully to responses in an interview is an excellent means of uncovering manifestations of organizational culture.

Interviewees may also respond positively to questions about organizational heroes, although referring to them as heroes may be counterproductive. It can be helpful to ask respondents to describe who the organization remembers and why they are remembered. Questions about organizational heroes are closely connected to questions about institutional history. Because cultural values and beliefs become institutionalized slowly over a period of time, their influence on past events is often apparent. Interviews are an excellent means of gathering such data.

Members of various campus constituencies such as faculty, students, administrators, and staff should be included in the interview sample. Snowball sampling (Murphy, 1980), in which one respondent suggests others who might also have valuable information, is one useful sampling method. With such a sampling plan the investigator can locate those individuals who have the greatest knowledge of the college.

Observation, a second useful technique, can be used concurrently with interviews. It is not simply classical observation of decision makers at work, committee meetings, or faculty members' teaching. Rather, it is also observing from many sources what is important in daily life on the campus. Through observation one can learn which issues receive careful attention and close scrutiny. Such issues are often central to the organization's culture.

Observation is a valuable means of learning more about cultural symbols, rituals, and heroes. As an outsider, an observer often sees symbols to which community members have become habituated. Thus, the observer may recognize the implicit meaning and importance of symbols that an insider takes at face value. As with symbols, an outsider may see rituals that insiders do not notice. These are the small, daily rituals that illustrate the relative value placed on different people or positions in the organization. Moreover, the memories of

heroes are often immortalized in paintings, statues, or buildings.

A third technique is analysis of written documents. Document analysis is a useful means of filling in the gaps interviews and observation leave. It is also a valuable addition because documents are not subject to problems of selective recall and reinterpretation in light of the contemporary situation (Murphy, 1980).

Document analysis is an efficient method of gathering background information on the college. It is well suited for collecting data on institutional history. Historical accounts provide past examples of cultural influences while also illuminating the development of values, beliefs, and ideologies. Presidential annual reports often reference particularly important or traumatic events and decisions. Similarly, reports of blue ribbon committees may contain information about organizational culture. Campus newspapers may refer to key events and decisions. Those that create controversy often come closest to important cultural values and beliefs. Document analysis is also a means of learning more about the college's curriculum and its relationship to the campus culture. Worth noting are the unique features of a curriculum and why they exist. Finally, documents often highlight important and continuing rituals such as convocations or award ceremonies.

Several types of documents lend themselves to cultural analysis. These can include, but are not limited to, official college publications, correspondence, minutes of meetings, campus newspapers, and college histories. Institutional mission statements, planning documents, and self-studies for accreditation may also be useful. While such documents may seem trite (Chait, 1979), they are part of an organization's culture. Particularly in an organization with a strong culture, a mission statement reflects the institution's culture.

In summary, the use of interviews, observation, and document analysis encourages triangulation (Denzin, 1970). Each technique can confirm, disconfirm, or modify data obtained using the other two. Differences among the data must be investigated and the reasons for inconsistencies uncovered. In organizations with a strong culture, data from each source should confirm the other two because written statements, actions, and oral descriptions all form a coherent whole. Discrepancies among the data sources may indicate a weak or fractured culture.

Analysis of Cultural Data

Qualitative data collected while investigating organizational culture are usually complex and voluminous. Analysis begins and is concurrent with data collection. While gathering information, researchers may begin to see themes and trends in what people say about the organization and what they observe. These preliminary findings are then tested and further explored as the data collection process continues.

A basic technique for analyzing cultural data is thematic analysis—finding the recurrent cultural themes in the data (Schatzman & Strauss, 1973). Using this approach, the analyst structures and codes the data in order to distill important aspects of the organizational culture. Once researchers discover the underlying themes, they must determine how the themes fit together. Gradually, the analyst refines the principal ideas that recur throughout and begins to develop the central "story line" on the institution's culture. On a campus with a strong culture the analytic process is relatively straightforward because the data are consistent. If the culture is weak, the themes will not be as strong and the data may show discrepancies.

Consistency in cultural images takes several forms. Each respondent often refers to the same organizational heroes. Trends or problems which reappear over the history of the organization point to important cultural elements. Rituals and symbols support the culture. The clarity of values and the ways in which people act on them will be apparent. Another key to analysis is to look for the repeated use of symbols and rituals. Those repeated in many different contexts point to fundamental cultural features (Ortner, 1973). Important parts of the organization's culture are often associated with several different symbols or rituals.

Why Study Organizational Culture?

Over the past decade the perspectives on academic governance have expanded from the bureaucratic model to include political concepts and those of organized anarchies (Baldridge, 1971; Cohen & March, 1974). The concept of organizational culture may also provide valuable insight into colleges and universities. On a theoretical level, cultural analysis is another tool for researchers. Understanding the culture of a particular institution may further explain campus management because culture appears to influence managerial style and decision practices. Analysis of culture may expose conflicting cultural elements which could lead to ineffective behavior and plans. It might also help explain variations in curriculum and resistance to curricular change. Additional empirical research is needed to explore this area.

There is another argument that makes the study of organizational culture appear even more central to higher education. Organizational culture is what Leifer (1979) calls an unobtrusive organizational control. Unobtrusive controls operate in conjunction with two other levels of control mechanisms. Explicit controls (such as formal regulations and direct comments) and implicit controls (such as specialization and hierarchy) also influence organizational life. But when explicit and implicit controls are weak, the unobtrusive forces such as organizational culture become more important. A college or university campus is the classic example of an organization with weak explicit and implicit control mechanisms (Cohen & March, 1974; March & Olsen, 1976). Thus, it seems all the more appropriate to study organizational culture in higher education in greater depth.

Organizational culture is also useful on a practical level. Exploration of organizational culture may help explain how an organization arrived at its current state. Culture may explicate past influences on decisions and actions. It may provide an underlying rationale for institutional development. This understanding can then provide a better foundation for administrators' decision making (Smith & Steadman, 1981).

Finally, as colleges and universities confront the challenges of the eighties, a better comprehension of organizational culture may be vital at a broader level. As institutions and systems of higher education expand, academic culture fragments (Clark, 1980; Dill, 1982). Larger institutions, increased autonomy of institutional units, and specialization within disciplines contribute to what Clark calls the move from an "integrated academic culture" to "the many cultures of the conglomeration" (1980, p. 25). If, as this paper suggests, culture is a critical element of institutional life and management, it deserves careful attention. In fact, Dill (1982) argues that administrators must "manage" academic cultures during these times of decline because an institution derives strength from its culture. Institutional culture relieves some of the pressures and strains that decline puts on the social fabric of an organization. It does this because culture is a force that provides stability and a sense of continuity to an ongoing social system such as a college or university. Managing a force such as culture is a difficult task at best. The first step is acknowledging culture's existence and trying to understand the cultures of individual campuses. The techniques outlined above are useful in this respect.

In conclusion, exploring organizational culture is another means of learning more about colleges and universities. Traditional approaches to studying governance and decision making provide useful insights into why and how higher education works the way it does. But the perspective of cultural influences supplements the traditional approaches. It may further explain the variations found among colleges and universities. Although organizational culture is difficult to identify and study, it is worth the effort. Further investigation of organizational culture is needed to uncover its specific influence on the college and university campus. Before this is possible, however, culture needs to become part of the common parlance of researchers in higher education.

References

Baldridge, J. V. *Power and Conflict in the University.* New York: John Wiley, 1971.

Beaudoin, D. B. *Presidents' Metaphors and Educational Leadership.* Unpublished manuscript. Harvard University, Harvard Graduate School of Education, Cambridge, 1981.

Becker, H. S., Geer, B., Hughes, E. C., & Strauss, A. L. *Boys in White.* Chicago: University of Chicago Press, 1961.

Chait, R. P. Mission madness strikes our colleges. *The Chronicle of Higher Education,* 16 July 1979; p. 36.

Chait, R. P. Look who invented Japanese management! *AGB Reports,* 1982, March/April; pp. 3–7.

Clark, B. R. The organizational saga in higher education. *Administrative Science Quarterly,* 1972, 17; 179–194.

Clark, B. R. *Academic Culture.* Working Paper. IHERG-42, Yale University, Higher Education Research Group, March 1980.

Cohen, M. D., & March. J. G. *Leadership and ambiguity.* New York: McGraw-Hill, 1974.

Deal, T. E., & Kennedy, A. A. *Corporate Cultures.* Reading, MA: Addison-Wesley. 1982.

Denzin, N. K. *The Research Act: A Theoretical Introduction to Sociological Methods.* Chicago: Aldine Publishing, 1970.

Dill, D. D. The management of academic culture: Notes on the management of meaning and social integration. *Higher Education,* 1982, 11; 303–320.

Feldman, K. A., & Newcomb, T. M. *The Impact of College on Students.* San Francisco: Jossey-Bass, 1969.

Gorden, R. L. *Interviewing: Strategy, Techniques, and Tactics.* Homewood, IL: Dorsey Press, 1975.

Leifer, R. *The Social Construction of Reality and the Evolution of Mythology as a Means for Understanding Organizational Control Processes.* Paper presented at the international meeting of the Institute of Management Science, Honolulu, Hawaii, June 1979.

March, J. G., & Olsen, J. P. *Ambiguity and Choice in Organizations.* Bergen, Norway: Universitetsforlaget, 1976.

Masland, A. T. *Organizational Influences on Computer Use in Higher Education.* Unpublished doctoral dissertation, Harvard University. Cambridge, 1982.

Murphy, J. T. *Getting the Facts: A Field Guide for Evaluation and Policy Analysis.* Santa Monica, CA: Goodyear Publishing, 1980.

Ortner, S. B. On key symbols. *American Anthropologist,* 1973, 75; 1338–1346.

Ouchi, W. *Theory Z: How American Business Can Meet the Japanese Challenge.* Reading, MA: Addison-Wesley, 1981.

Pace, C. R. The measurement of college environments. In R. Tagiuri & G. H. Litwin (Eds.), *Organizational Climate.* Boston: Harvard University, Division of Business Research, 1968; 127–147.

Pascale, R. T., & Athos, A. G. *The Art of Japanese Management.* New York: Simon & Schuster, 1981.

Pettigrew, A. M. "On Studying Organizational Cultures." *Administrative Science Quarterly,* 1979, 24; 570–581.

Schatzman, L., & Strauss, A. L. *Field Research: Strategies for a Natural Sociology.* Englewood Cliffs, NJ: Prentice Hall, 1973.

Schein, E. H. "Does Japanese Management Have a Message For American Managers." *Sloan Management Review,* 1981, 23(1); 55–68.

Schwartz, H., & Davis, S. M. "Matching Corporate Culture and Business Strategy." *Organizational Dynamics,* 1981, 10; 30–48.

Selznick, P. *Leadership in Administration.* New York: Harper & Row, 1957.

Smith, G. D., & Steadman, L. E. Present value of corporate history. *Harvard Business Review,* 1981, 59(6); 164–173.

Tosi, H. C. *Theories of Organization.* Chicago: St. Clair Press, 1975.

Wyer, J. C. "Theory Z—The Collegial Model Revisited: An Essay Review." *The Review of Higher Education,* 1982, 5(2); 111–117.

CHAPTER 12

THE ORGANIZATIONAL SAGA IN HIGHER EDUCATION

BURTON R. CLARK

An organizational saga is a collective understanding of a unique accomplishment based on historical exploits of a formal organization, offering strong normative bonds within and outside the organization. Believers give loyalty to the organization and take pride and identity from it. A saga begins as strong purpose, introduced by a man (or small group) with a mission, and is fulfilled as it is embodied in organizational practices and the values of dominant organizational cadres, usually taking decades to develop. Examples of the initiation and fulfillment of sagas in academic organizations are presented from research on Antioch, Reed, and Swarthmore.[1]

Saga, originally referring to a medieval Icelandic or Norse account of achievements and events in the history of a person or group, has come to mean a narrative of heroic exploits, a unique development that has deeply stirred the emotions of participants and descendants. Thus a saga is not simply a story but a story that at some time has had a particular base of believers. The term often refers also to the actual history itself, thereby including a stream of events, the participants, and the written or spoken interpretation. The element of belief is crucial, for without the credible story, the events and persons become history; with the development of belief, a particular bit of history becomes a definition full of pride and identity for the group.

Introduction

An *organizational saga* is a collective understanding of unique accomplishment in a formally established group. The group's definition of the accomplishment, intrinsically historical but embellished through retelling and rewriting, links stages of organizational development. The participants have added affect, an emotional loading, which places their conception between the coolness of rational purpose and the warmth of sentiment found in religion and magic. An organizational saga presents some rational explanation of how certain means led to certain ends, but it also includes affect that turns a formal place into a beloved institution, to which participants may be passionately devoted. Encountering such devotion, the observer may become unsure of his own analytical detachment as he tests the overtones of the institutional spirit or spirit of place.

The study of organizational sagas highlights nonstructural and nonrational dimensions of organizational life and achievement. Macroorganizational theory has concentrated on the role of structure and technology in organizational effectiveness (Gross, 1964; Litterer, 1965; March, 1965; Thompson, 1967; Price, 1968; Perrow, 1970). A needed corrective is more research on the cultural

"The Organizational Saga in Higher Education," by Burton R. Clark, reprinted with permission from *Administrative Science Quarterly*, Vol. 17, No. 2, June 1972.

and expressive aspects of organizations, particularly on the role of belief and sentiment at broad levels of organization. The human-relations approach in organizational analysis, centered largely on group interaction, showed some awareness of the role of organization symbols (Whyte, 1948: ch. 23), but this conceptual lead has not been taken as a serious basis for research. Also, in the literature on organizations and purposive communities, "ideology" refers to unified and shared belief (Selznick, 1949; Bendix, 1956; Price, 1968: 104–110; Carden, 1969); but the concept of ideology has lost denotative power, having been stretched by varying uses. For the phenomenon discussed in this paper, "saga" seems to provide the appropriate denotation. With a general emphasis on normative bonds, organizational saga refers to a unified set of publicly expressed beliefs about the formal group that (a) is rooted in history, (b) claims unique accomplishment, and (c) is held with sentiment by the group.

To develop the concept in this paper, extreme cases and exaggerations of the ideal type are used; but the concept will be close to reality and widely applicable when the phenomenon is examined in weak as well as strong expression. In many organizations, even some highly utilitarian ones, some segment of their personnel probably develop in time at least a weak saga. Those who have persisted for some years in one place will have had at minimum, a thin stream of shared experience, which they elaborate into a plausible account of group uniqueness. Whether developed primarily by management or by employees, the story helps rationalize for the individual his commitment of time and energy for years, perhaps for a lifetime, to a particular enterprise. Even when weak, the belief can compensate in part for the loss of meaning in modern work, giving some drama and some cultural identity to one's otherwise entirely instrumental efforts. At the other end of the continuum, a saga engages one so intensely as to make his immediate place overwhelmingly valuable. It can even produce a striking distortion, with the organization becoming the only reality, the outside world becoming illusion. Generally the almost complete capture of affect and perception is associated with only a few utopian communities, fanatical political factions, and religious sects. But some formal rationalized organizations, as

for example business and education, can also become utopian, fanatical, or sectarian.

Organizational sagas vary in durability. They can arise quickly in relatively unstructured social settings, as in professional sports organizations that operate in the volatile context of contact with large spectator audiences through the mass media. A professional baseball or football team may create a rags-to-riches legend in a few months' time that excites millions of people. But such a saga is also very fragile as an ongoing definition of the organization. The story can be removed quickly from the collective understanding of the present and future, for successful performance is often unstable, and the events that set the direction of belief can be readily reversed, with the great winners quickly becoming habitual losers. In such cases, there seems to be an unstable structural connection between the organization and the base of believers. The base of belief is not anchored within the organization nor in personal ties between insiders and outsiders, but is mediated by mass media. Such sagas continue only as the organization keeps repeating its earlier success and also keeps the detached followers from straying to other sources of excitement and identification.

In contrast, organizational sagas show high durability when built slowly in structured social contexts; for example, the educational system, specifically for the purposes of this paper, three liberal arts colleges in the United States. In the many small private colleges, the story of special performance emerges not in a few months but over a decade or two. When the saga is firmly developed, it is embodied in many components of the organization, affecting the definition and performance of the organization and finding protection in the webbing of the institutional parts. It is not volatile and can be relegated to the past only by years of attenuation or organizational decline.

Since the concept of organizational saga was developed from research on Reed, Antioch, and Swarthmore, three distinctive and highly regarded colleges (Clark, 1970), material and categories from their developmental histories are used to illustrate the development of a saga, and its positive effects on organizational participation and effectiveness are then considered.[2]

Development of Saga

Two stages can be distinguished in the development of an organizational saga, initiation and fulfillment. Initiation takes place under varying conditions and occurs within a relatively short period of time: fulfillment is related to features of the organization that are enduring and more predictable.

Initiation

Strong sagas do not develop in passive organizations tuned to adaptive servicing of demand or to the fulfilling of roles dictated by higher authorities (Clark, 1956, 1960). The saga is initially a strong purpose, conceived and enunciated by a single man or a small cadre (Selznick, 1957) whose first task is to find a setting that is open, or can be opened, to a special effort. The, most obvious setting is the autonomous new organization, where there is no established structure, no rigid custom, especially if a deliberate effort has been made to establish initial autonomy and bordering outsiders are preoccupied. There a leader may also have the advantage of building from the top down, appointing lieutenants and picking up recruits in accord with his ideas.

Reed College is strongly characterized by a saga, and its story of hard-won excellence and nonconformity began as strong purpose in a new organization. Its first president, William T. Foster, a thirty-year-old, high-minded reformer, from the sophisticated East of Harvard and Bowdoin went to the untutored Northwest, to an unbuilt campus in suburban Portland in 1910, precisely because he did not want to be limited by established institutions, all of which were, to his mind, corrupt in practice. The projected college in Oregon was clear ground, intellectually as well as physically, and he could there assemble the people and devise the practices that would finally give the United States an academically pure college, a Balliol for America.

The second setting for initiation is the established organization in a crisis of decay. Those in charge, after years of attempting incremental adjustments (Lindblom, 1959), realize finally that they must either give up established ways or have the organization fail. Preferring that it survive, they may relinquish the leadership to one proposing a plan that promises revival and later strength, or they may even accept a man of utopian intent. Deep crisis in the established organization thus creates some of the conditions of a new organization. It suspends past practice, forces some bordering groups to stand back or even to turn their backs on failure of the organization, and it tends to catch the attention of the reformer looking for an opportunity.

Antioch College is a dramatic example of such a setting. Started in the 1860s, its first sixty years were characterized by little money, weak staff, few students, and obscurity. Conditions worsened in the 1910s under the inflation and other strains of World War I. In 1919 a charismatic utopian reformer, Arthur E. Morgan, decided it was more advantageous to take over an old college with buildings and a charter than to start a new one. First as trustee and then as president, he began in the early 1920s an institutional renovation that overturned everything: as president he found it easy to push aside old, weak organizational structures and usages. He elaborated a plan of general education involving an unusual combination of work, study, and community participation; and he set about to devise the implementing tool. Crisis and charisma made possible a radical transformation out of which came a second Antioch, a college soon characterized by a sense of exciting history, unique practice, and exceptional performance.

The third context for initiation is the established organization that is not in crisis, not collapsing from long decline, yet ready for evolutionary change. This is the most difficult situation to predict, having to do with degree of rigidity. In both ideology and structure, institutionalized colleges vary in openness to change. In those under church control, for example, the colleges of the more liberal Protestant denominations have been more hospitable than Catholic colleges, at least until recently, to educational experimentation. A college with a tradition of presidential power is more open to change than one where the trustees and the professors exert control over the president. Particularly promising is the college with a self-defined need for educational leadership. This is the opening for which some reformers watch, the sound place that has some ambition to increase its academic stature, as for example, Swarthmore College.

Swarthmore began in the 1860s, and had become by 1920 a secure and stable college, prudently managed by Quaker trustees and administrators and solidly based on traditional support from nearby Quaker families in Pennsylvania, New Jersey, and Maryland. Such an organization would not usually be thought promising for reform, but Frank Aydelotte, who became its president in 1920, judged it ready for change. Magnetic in personality, highly placed within the élite circle of former Rhodes scholars, personally liked by important foundation officials, and recommended as a scholarly leader, he was offered other college presidencies, but he chose Swarthmore as a place open to change through a combination of financial health, liberal Quaker ethos, and some institutional ambition. His judgment proved correct, although the tolerance for his changes in the 1920s and 1930s was narrow at times. He began the gradual introduction of a modified Oxford honors program and related changes, which resulted in noteworthy achievements that supporters were to identify later as "the Swarthmore saga" (Swarthmore College Faculty, 1941).

Fulfillment

Although the conditions of initiation of a saga vary, the means of fulfillment are more predictable. There are many ways in which a unified sense of a special history is expressed; for example, even a patch of sidewalk or a coffee room may evoke emotion among the believers; but one can delimit the components at the center of the development of a saga. These may center, in colleges, on the personnel, the program, the external social base, the student subculture, and the imagery of the saga.

Personnel

In a college, the key group of believers is the senior faculty. When they are hostile to a new idea, its attenuation is likely; when they are passive, its success is weak; and when they are devoted to it, a saga is probable. A single leader, a college president, can initiate the change, but the organizational idea will not be expanded over the years and expressed in performance unless ranking and powerful members of the faculty become committed to it and remain committed even after the initiator is gone. In committing themselves deeply, taking some credit for the change and seeking to ensure its perpetuation, they routinize the charisma of the leader in collegial authority. The faculty cadre of believers helps to effect the legend, then to protect it against later leaders and other new participants who, less pure in belief, might turn the organization in some other direction.

Such faculty cadres were well developed at Reed by 1925, after the time of its first two presidents; at Antioch, by the early 1930s, after Morgan, disappointed with his followers, left for the board of directors of the new TVA; and at Swarthmore, by the 1930s, and particularly, by 1940, after Aydelotte's twenty years of persistent effort. In all three colleges, after the departure of the change agent(s), the senior faculty with the succeeding president, a man appropriate for consolidation, undertook the full working out of the experiment. The faculty believers also replaced themselves through socialization and selective recruitment and retention in the 1940s and 1950s. Meanwhile, new potential innovators had sometimes to be stopped. In such instances, the faculty was able to exert influence to shield the distinctive effort from erosion or deflection. At Reed, for example, major clashes between president and faculty in the late 1930s and the early 1950s were precipitated by a new change-oriented president, coming in from the outside, disagreeing with a faculty proud of what had been done, attached deeply to what the college had become, and determined to maintain what was for them the distinctive Reed style. From the standpoint of constructing a regional and national model of purity and severity in undergraduate education, the Reed faculty did on those occasions act to create while acting to conserve.

Programs

For a college to transform purpose into a credible story of unique accomplishment, there must be visible practices with which claims of distinctiveness can be supported; that is, unusual courses, noteworthy requirements, or special methods of teaching. On the basis of seemingly unique practices, the program becomes a set of communal symbols and rituals, invested with meaning. Not reporting grades to the students becomes a symbol, as at Reed, that the college cares about learning for learning's sake; thus mere technique becomes part of a saga.

In all the three colleges, the program was seen as distinctive by both insiders and outsiders. At Swarthmore it was the special seminars and other practices of the honors program, capped by written and oral examination by teams of visiting outsiders in the last days of the senior year. At Antioch it was the work-study cycle, the special set of general education requirements, community government, and community involvement. At Reed it was the required freshman lecture-and-seminar courses, the junior qualifying examination, and the thesis in the senior year. Such practices became central to a belief that things had been done so differently, and so much against the mainstream, and often against imposing odds, that the group had generated a saga.

Social Base

The saga also becomes fixed in the minds of outside believers devoted to the organization, usually the alumni. The alumni are the best located to hold beliefs enduringly pure, since they can be as strongly identified with a special organizational history as the older faculty and administrators and yet do not have to face directly the new problems generated by a changing environment or students. Their thoughts can remain centered on the past, rooted in the days when, as students, they participated intimately in the unique ways and accomplishments of the campus.

Liberal alumni as those of Reed, Antioch, and Swarthmore here, seek to conserve what they believe to be a unique liberal institution and to protect it from the conservative forces of society that might change it—that is, to make it like other colleges. At Reed, for example, dropouts as well as graduates were struck by the intellectual excellence of their small college, convinced that college life there had been unlike college life anywhere else, and they were ready to conserve the practices that seemed to sustain that excellence. Here too, conserving acts can be seen for a time as contributing to an innovation, protecting the full working out of a distinctive effort.

Student Subculture

The student body is the third group of believers, not overwhelmingly important but still a necessary support for the saga. To become and remain a saga, a change must be supported by the student subculture over decades, and the ideology of the subculture must integrate with the central ideas of the believing administrators and faculty. When the students define themselves as personally responsible for upholding the image of the college, then a design or plan has become an organizational saga.

At Antioch, Reed, and Swarthmore, the student subcultures were powerful mechanisms for carrying a developing saga from one generation to another. Reed students, almost from the beginning and extending at least to the early 1960s, were great believers in the uniqueness of their college, constantly on the alert for any action that would alter it, ever fearful that administration or faculty might succumb to pressures that would make Reed just like other colleges. Students at Antioch and Swarthmore also offered unstinting support for the ideology of their institution. All three student bodies steadily and dependably transferred the ideology from one generation to another. Often socializing deeply, they helped produce the graduate who never quite rid himself of the wish to go back to the campus.

Imagery of Saga

Upheld by faculty, alumni, and students, expressed in teaching practices, the saga is even more widely expressed as a generalized tradition in statues and ceremonies, written histories and current catalogues, even in an "air about the place" felt by participants and some outsiders. The more unique the history and the more forceful the claim to a place in history, the more intensely cultivated the ways of sharing memory and symbolizing the institution. The saga is a strong self-fulfilling belief; working through institutional self-image and public image, it is indeed a switchman (Weber, 1946), helping to determine the tracks along which action is pushed by men's self-defined interests. The early belief of one stage brings about the actions that warrant a stronger version of the same belief in a later period. As the account develops, believers come to sense its many constituent symbols as inextricably bound together, and the part takes its meaning from the whole. For example, at Antioch a deep attachment developed in the 1930s and 1940s to Morgan's philosophy of the whole man and to its expression in a unique combination of work, study, community participation, and many practices thought to embody freedom and nonconformity. Some of the faculty of those years who remained in the 1940s and 1950s had many memories and impressions that seemed to form a symbolic whole: personnel counselors, folk dancing in Red Square, Morgan's towering physique, the battles of community government, the pacifism of the late 1930s, the frequent dash of students to offcampus jobs, the dedicated deans who personified central values. Public image also grew strong and sharp, directing liberals and radicals to the college and conservatives to other places. The symbolic expressions themselves were a strong perpetuating force.

Conclusion

An organizational saga is a powerful means of unity in the formal place. It makes links across internal divisions and organizational boundaries as internal and external groups share their common belief. With deep emotional commitment, believers define themselves by their organizational affiliation, and in their bond to other believers they share an intense sense of the unique. In an organization defined by a strong saga, there is a feeling that there is the small world of the lucky few and the large routine one of the rest of the world. Such an emotional bond turns the membership into a community, even a cult.

An organizational saga is thus a valuable resource, created over a number of years out of the social components of the formal enterprise. As participants become ideologues, their common definition becomes a foundation for trust and for extreme loyalty. Such bonds give the organization a competitive edge in recruiting and maintaining personnel and helps it to avoid the vicious circle in which some actual or anticipated erosion of organizational strength leads to the loss of some personnel, which leads to further decline and loss. Loyalty causes individuals to stay with a system, to save and improve it rather than to leave to serve their

self-interest elsewhere (Hirschman, 1970). The genesis and persistence of loyalty is a key organizational and analytical problem. Enduring loyalty follows from a collective belief of participants that their organization is distinctive. Such a belief comes from a credible story of uncommon effort, achievement, and form.

Pride in the organized group and pride in one's identity as taken from the group are personal returns that are uncommon in modern social involvement. The development of sagas is one way in which men in organizations increase such returns, reducing their sense of isolation and increasing their personal pride and pleasure in organizational life. Studying the evocative narratives and devotional ties of formal systems leads to a better understanding of the fundamental capacities of organizations to enhance or diminish the lives of participants. The organization possessing a saga is a place in which participants for a time at least happily accept their bond.

Burton R. Clark is a professor of sociology at Yale University.

Notes

1. Revised version of paper presented at the 65th Annual Meeting of the American Sociological Association, September, 1970, Washington, D.C. I wish to thank Wendell Bell, Maren L. Carden, Kai Erikson, and Stanley Udy for discussion and comment. Parts of an early draft of this paper have been used to connect organizational belief to problems of governance in colleges and universities (Clark, 1971).
2. For some discussion of the risks and tensions associated with organizational sagas, particularly that of success in one period leading to later rigidity and stagnation, see Clark (1970: 258–261). Hale (1970) gives an illuminating discussion of various effects of a persistent saga in a theological seminary.

References

Bendix, R., *Work and Authority in Industry*. New York: John Wiley, 1956.

Carden, M. L., *Oneida: Utopian Community to Modern Corporation*. Baltimore: The Johns Hopkins Press, 1960.

Clark, B. R., *Adult Education in Transition: A Study of Institutional Insecurity*. Berkeley: University of California Press, 1956.

———. *The Open Door College. A Case Study*. New York: McGraw-Hill, 1960.

_____. *The Distinctive College: Antioch, Reed, and Swarthmore.* Chicago: Aldine, 1970.

_____. "Belief and loyalty in college organization," *Journal of Higher Education*, 1971, XLII, 6: 499–515.

Gross, B. M., *The Managing of Organizations.* (2 vols.) New York: Free Press, 1964.

Hale, J. R. *The Making and Testing of an Organizational Saga: A Case-Study of the Lutheran Theological Seminary at Gettysburg, Pennsylvania, with Special Reference to the Problem of Merger, 1959–1960.* Unpublished Ed.D. dissertation, Columbia University, 1970.

Hirschman, A. O., *Exit, Voice, and Loyalty.* Cambridge, Mass.: Harvard University Press, 1970.

Lindblom, C. E. "The science of 'muddling through.'" *Public Administration Review,* 1950 19:79–88.

Litterer, J. A. *The Analysis of Organizations.* New York: John Wiley, 1965.

March, J. G. (ed.), *Handbook of Organizations:* Chicago: Rand McNally, 1965.

Perrow, C. *Organizational Analysis.* Belmont, California: Wadsworth, 1970.

Price, J. L. Organizational Effectiveness: An Inventory of Propositions. Homewood, Illinois: Richard D. Irwin, 1968.

Selznick, P. *TVA and the Grass Roots.* Berkeley: University of California Press, 1949.

_____. Leadership in Administration. New York: Harper & Row, 1957.

Swarthmore College Faculty. *An Adventure in Education: Swarthmore College Under Frank Aydelotte.* New York: Macmillan, 1941.

Thompson, J. D. Organizations in Action. New York: McGraw-Hill, 1967.

Weber, M. *From Max Weber: Essays in Sociology.* Translated and edited by H. H. Gerth and C. Wright Mills. New York: Oxford, 1946.

Whyte, W. F. *Human Relations in the Restaurant Industry.* New York: McGraw-Hill, 1948.

CHAPTER 13

CULTURE IN AMERICAN COLLEGES AND UNIVERSITIES

GEORGE D. KUH AND ELIZABETH J. WHITT

Culture Defined and Described

If there were any word to serve the purpose as well, I would unhesitatingly use it in preference to one that seems at times downright slippery and at other times impossibly vague and all-embracing. But although "culture" has uncomfortably many denotations, it is the only term that seems satisfactorily to combine the notions . . . of a shared way of thinking and a collective way of behaving (Becher 1984, p. 166).

Certain ideas burst upon the intellectual landscape with such a force that they seem to have the potential to resolve all fundamental problems and clarify all obscure issues facing a field (Langer, cited in Geertz 1973). Cultural perspectives have been widely used in a general, all-encompassing manner to subsume almost every concept, event, or activity that might occur in an organized setting (Deal and Kennedy 1982; Schwartz and Davis 1981). Some (see, for example, Morgan 1986) have suggested that culture is a metaphor for organizations. Because culture lacks conceptual clarity, however, its utility as a metaphor for colleges and universities seems limited, perhaps even confusing. Indeed, unless more precision is achieved, cultural perspectives may obscure more than they reveal. That is, if cultural elements are not more clearly explicated, the insights into college and university life promised by cultural views will be blurred, thus reducing their power and utility (Trice and Beyer 1984).

Risks are inherent, however, in attempting to flesh out or specify the elements of culture. For example, thinking about cultural properties as distinct institutional attributes (e.g., beliefs, stories, norms, and so on) that can be separated and independently analyzed is compatible with conventional assumptions undergirding organizational rationality. The perception that culture can be intentionally controlled does violence to some important properties of culture, such as its complex, holistic character (Geertz 1973), an entity greater than the sum of its parts (Morgan 1986). Nevertheless, when talking about and studying culture, we do separate properties, such as language, from rituals, stories, belief systems, and values. In doing so, however, we must acknowledge the contradiction inherent between analysis and holistic perception and the distortion that results whenever a single element is isolated in the complex web of history, traditions, and patterns of behaviors that have developed in a college or university (Taylor 1984).

The Invisible Tapestry: Culture in American Colleges and Universities by George D. Kuh and Elizabeth J. Whitt, ASHE-ERIC Higher Education Report No. 1, Washington, D.C.: Association for the Study of Higher Education, 1988.

Toward a Definition of Culture

[We] have been entrusted with the difficult task of speaking about culture. But there is nothing in the world more elusive. One cannot analyze it, for its components are infinite. One cannot describe it, for it is Protean in shape. An attempt to encompass its meaning in words is like trying to seize the air in the hand when one finds that it is everywhere except within one's grasp (Lowell, cited in Kroeber and Kluckhohn 1952, p. 7).

Asked to define the institution's culture, an MIT student, "without batting an eye, ... responded by saying: 'It's everything we aren't tested on in the classroom'" (Van Maanen 1987, p. 5). Although most social scientists would not be satisfied with this level of precision, her response is consistent with the myriad meanings and connotations of culture reported in the literature. Indeed, culture cannot be succinctly defined because it is an inferential concept (Cusick 1987), "something that is perceived, something felt" (Handy 1976, p. 185).

Culture is described as a social or normative glue (Smircich 1983)—based on shared values and beliefs (see Pascale and Athos 1981)—that holds organizations together and serves four general purposes: (1) it conveys a sense of identity; (2) it facilitates commitment to an entity, such as the college or peer group, other than self; (3) it enhances the stability of a group's social system; and (4) it is a sense-making device that guides and shapes behavior. In addition, the culture of a college or university defines, identifies, and legitimates authority in educational settings (Gage 1978; Goodlad 1984). Therefore, studies of institutional culture have implications for policy and strategies for institutional change (Elmore 1987).

Most definitions of culture convey one or more of the following properties (Schein 1985): (1) observed behavioral regularities (Goffman 1959, 1961; Van Maanen 1979), such as the hours faculty spend in the office; (2) norms (Homans 1950) or specific guides to conduct, some of which (e.g., mores) are more salient than others (Broom and Selznick 1973); (3) dominant values espoused by the organization (Deal and Kennedy 1982), such as the importance of inquiry in research universities and the commitment to undergraduate teaching in lib-

eral arts colleges; (4) the philosophy that guides an organization's attitudes and actions toward employees or clients (Ouchi 1981; Pascale and Athos 1981); (5) rules for getting along in the organization (Schein 1968; Van Maanen 1979); and (6) the feeling or organizational climate and the manner in which members of the culture interact with those outside the culture (Tagiuri and Litwin 1968).

Behavioral regularities should not be overemphasized as a manifestation of culture (Schein 1985). Who talks with whom may be more a function of environmental contingencies, such as physical proximity, rather than a behavioral manifestation of deeper assumptions and beliefs at the "core" of culture. For example, inferring cultural groupings based on the location of faculty offices may or may not be appropriate. Faculty with adjoining offices could share cultural bonds—or the arrangement might merely reflect a confluence of factors, such as random space assignment following renovation of the physical plant or historical accident.

The "small homogenous society" analogue used in anthropological studies of culture (discussed later) is sorely strained when applied to many contemporary institutions of higher education. Large public, multipurpose universities are comprised of many different groups whose members may or may not share or abide by all of the institution's norms, values, practices, beliefs, and meanings. Instead of viewing colleges and universities as monolithic entities (Martin and Siehl 1983), it is more realistic to analyze them as multicultural contexts (March and Simon 1958; Van Maanen and Barley 1984) that are host to numerous subgroups with different priorities, traditions, and values (Gregory 1983).

Culture is potentially divisive. If routine patterns of behavior within one group are considered normal, different activities performed by another subgroup may be judged abnormal (Morgan 1986, p. 120). Such ethnocentric behavior may be a form of cultural nearsightedness (Broom and Selznick 1973) or socialized differences that increase the possibility that misunderstandings and conflicts will occur (Gregory 1983).

Faculty in the humanities are socialized into "a structure of values, attitudes, and ways of thinking and feeling" (Clark and Corcoran 1986, p. 30) quite different from the structure to which physicists and chemists are socialized.

Career path patterns of faculty in "pure" disciplines (e.g., biology, history) and "applied" fields (e.g., engineering, education) are different. Faculty in the former group learn how to behave by working side by side with senior professors in the laboratory as postdoctoral research associates. Faculty in the latter group are more likely to learn about the academic profession "on the job" during the first years of a professorial appointment after postdoctoral experience as a practicing professional in private industry, government, medicine, law, or education (Becher 1984). These and other differences (epistemological and ideological views, for example) encourage the formation of separate academic clans or subcultures, a topic examined in more depth later.

So how, then, does one define culture? Three and one-half decades ago, Kroeber and Kluckhohn (1952) reported 164 different definitions of culture. Given the myriad qualities contained in the concept of culture, it is not surprising that a common definition remains elusive (Smircich 1983), but it has been defined, for example, as:

> The core set of assumptions, understandings, and implicit rules that govern day-to-day behavior in the workplace (Deal and Kennedy 1983, p. 498);
>
> The shared philosophies, ideologies, values, assumptions, beliefs, expectations, attitudes, and norms that knit a community together (Kilmann et al. 1985, p. 5);
>
> The traditional and social heritage of a people; their customs and practices; their transmitted knowledge, beliefs, law, and morals, their linguistic and symbolic forms of communication, and the meanings they share (Becher 1984, p. 167);
>
> An interpretive paradigm ... both a product and process, the shaper of human interaction and the outcome of it, continually created and recreated by people's ongoing interactions (Jelinek, Smircich, and Hirsch 1983, p. 331).

Based on a review of the literature, another definition of culture is "the shared values, assumptions, beliefs, or ideologies that participants have about their organization (colleges and universities)" (Peterson et al. 1986, p. 81). While this definition is parsimonious, it does not explicitly acknowledge the influence culture has on the behavior of faculty and students, the holistic, evolutionary qualities of culture, and the influence of the external environment on institutional culture.

For the purposes of this report, then, culture in higher education is defined as *the collective, mutually shaping patterns of norms, values, practices, beliefs, and assumptions that guide the behavior of individuals and groups in an institute of higher education and provide a frame of reference within which to interpret the meaning of events and actions on and off campus*. This definition emphasizes normative influences on behavior as well as the underlying system of assumptions and beliefs shared by culture bearers.

Properties of Culture

This section describes many of the subtle aspects of experience subsumed under the concept of culture as a complex whole, paying particular attention to artifactual manifestations of culture as they can be observed and providing clues to hidden properties (e.g., values and assumptions).

Culture and meaning are inextricably intertwined (Hall 1976).

> The more we have learned about colleges, the more we have been struck by their uniqueness. True, colleges run to "types," and types ultimately converge on a national academic model. One might therefore lump together the Universities of Massachusetts and Connecticut, or Harvard and Yale, or Boston College and Fordham, or San Francisco State and San Diego. But on closer inspection these colleges appear to draw on quite different publics and to have quite different flavors (Riesman and Jencks 1962, p. 132).

Because culture is bound to a context, every institution's culture is different. Therefore, the meaning of behavior can be interpreted only through a real-life situation within a specific college's cultural milieu (Hall 1976). To attempt to divorce an interpretation of behavior "from what happens—at this time or in that place, what specific people say, what they do, what is done to them, from the whole vast business of the world—is to divorce it from its applications and render it vacant" (Geertz 1973, p. 18). Thus, descriptions and interpretations of events and actions from one institution are not generalizable to other institutions. "The essential task [is] not to generalize across cases but to generalize within them" (Geertz 1973, p. 20).

The manner in which culture is transmitted and through which individuals derive meaning from their experiences within the cultural milieu are essentially tacit (Geertz 1973; Hall 1976; Schein 1985). In this sense, culture is an "unconscious infrastructure" (Smircich 1983), a paradigm for understanding nuances of behavior shaped by shared understandings, assumptions, and beliefs. The cultural paradigm serves as an organizing framework within which to determine rewards and punishments, what is valued and what is not, and moral imperatives (see, for example, Gardner 1986; Schein 1985) that bond individuals and groups and order behavior. Culture provides contextual clues (Hall 1976) necessary to interpret behaviors, words, and acts and gives these actions and events meaning within the culture bearers' frame of reference (Corbett, Firestone, and Rossman 1987). Culture also enhances stability in a college or university through the socialization of new members (Van Maanen and Barley 1984). Because culture exists largely below the level of conscious thought and because culture bearers may themselves disagree on the meaning of artifacts and other properties of culture, describing the culture of a college or university in a way that all faculty and students find satisfactory may not be possible (Allaire and Firsirotu 1984).

> [Culture is] a process of reality construction that allows people to see and understand particular events, actions, objects, utterances, or situations in distinctive ways. These patterns of understanding also provide a basis for making one's own behavior sensible and meaningful . . . [Culture is] an active living phenomenon through which people create and recreate the worlds in which they live (Morgan 1986, pp. 128, 131).

Thus, although culture is fairly stable, it is always evolving, continually created and recreated by ongoing patterns of interactions between individuals, groups, and an institution's internal and external environments. Although these patterns of interaction may change over time to reflect changing assumptions, values, and preferences, they are stable enough to define and shape what is acknowledged to be appropriate behavior in a particular setting. Thus, the dominant constellation of assumptions, values, and preferences introduces and socializes new members into the accepted patterns of behavior, thereby perpetuating—for all practical purposes—many of the dominant assumptions and beliefs of the culture. In this sense, culture provides stability for a college during turbulent periods and also contributes to the general effectiveness of the institution (Smircich 1983) by reminding students and faculty of what the institution values and by punishing undesirable behavior.

The press toward behaving in culturally acceptable ways, which is invariably an outcome of a strong culture (Deal and Kennedy 1982; Gregory 1983), may constrain innovation or attempts to do things differently. A dominant culture presents difficulties to newcomers or members of underrepresented groups when trying to understand and appreciate the nuances of behavior. At worst, culture can be an alienating, ethnocentric force that goads members of a group, sometimes out of fear and sometimes out of ignorance, to reinforce their own beliefs while rejecting those of other groups (Gregory 1983).

The relative strength of a culture or subculture is impossible to determine (Van Maanen and Barley 1984). While this question begs for an empirical answer, the weight of the argument seems to be on the side of those who claim that cultures do vary in the degree to which they influence members' behavior and guide institutional responses in times of crisis (Deal and Kennedy 1982; Peters and Waterman 1982).

Some writers have developed typologies or inventories of organizational characteristics based on their observations of what seem to be "healthy" cultures (see, for example, Peters and Waterman 1982; Peterson et al. 1986). Given the context-bound, perspectival qualities of culture, however, attempts to determine whether one institutional culture is better than another seem wrongheaded. Some institutional cultures clearly support research activity over undergraduate instruction and vice versa (Riesman and Jencks 1962). University trustees, state legislators, and students will continue to be wary of prevailing norms that encourage faculty to cloister themselves in library carrels or in the research laboratory rather than increase the number of office hours to meet with students. Standards for academic productivity, such as papers published or number of courses and students taught, are different in a church-related liberal arts college, a state-supported university whose mission is teacher education, and a research-oriented university (Austin and Gamson 1983; Baldridge et al. 1977).

Any culture has two basic components: (1) "substance, or the networks of meanings contained in its ideologies, norms, and values; and (2) forms, or the practices whereby these meanings are expressed, affirmed, and communicated to members" (Trice and Beyer 1984, p. 654). In this sense, culture is both a product and a process.

Culture has been discussed as both an independent and a dependent variable (Ouchi and Wilkins 1985; Peterson et al. 1986). Culture, when viewed as an independent variable, is a complex, continually evolving web of assumptions, beliefs, symbols, and interactions carried by faculty, students, and other culture bearers (Smircich 1983) that cannot be directly purposefully controlled by any person or group. Culture as a dependent variable is the constellation of shared values and beliefs manifested through patterns of behavior like rituals, ideologies, and patterns of interactions. An administrator may attempt to change seemingly dysfunctional aspects of a culture by encouraging different behaviors on the part of faculty and students, and suggestions have been offered about how one might attempt to manipulate organizational culture (Kilmann et al. 1985; Ouchi 1981; Peters and Waterman 1982). The culture of a college or university—as substance and form, as process and product, and as independent and dependent variables—shapes human interactions and reflects the outcomes of mutually shaping interactions (Louis 1980; Siehl and Martin 1982; Smircich 1983).

Levels of Culture

Some find the essence of culture to be the tacit assumptions and beliefs that influence the way a group of people think and behave (Schein 1985). These guiding assumptions and beliefs, which are below the surface of conscious thought, are manifested in observable forms or artifacts. In an effort to increase analytical precision and avoid unnecessary confusion, Schein (1985) divided culture into a conceptual hierarchy comprised of three levels: artifacts, values, and basic assumptions and beliefs.

Artifacts

"Meanings are 'stored' in symbols" (Geertz 1973, p. 127). Because artifacts are largely symbols of culture, they represent a multitude of meanings and emotions. Evidence of an institution's culture may be found in norms, mores, formal and informal rules, routine procedures, behaviors that are rewarded or punished, customs, folkways, myths, daily and periodic rituals, ceremonies, interaction patterns, signs, and a language system common to the culture bearers (Broom and Selznick 1973; Morgan 1986; Schein 1985; Tierney 1985, 1987; Van Maanen and Barley 1984). A rite combines discrete cultural forms into an integrated, unified public performance. A ceremonial is the linking of several rites into a single occasion or event (Chapple and Coon 1942). For example, most commencement ceremonies are made up of discrete rites: the formation of candidates for degrees into one or more lines, the procession of faculty and students, the commencement address, the conferral of honorary degrees, the conferral of various degrees (baccalaureate, master's, professional school, Ph.D.), the hooding of doctoral degree recipients, the alumni association's welcome to those receiving degrees, the tossing of mortarboards into the air at the conclusion of the formal event, and the recession from the site of commencement.

Table 13-1 defines other frequently mentioned cultural forms (see also Boje, Fedor, and Rowland 1982). To underscore the connectedness and cumulative contributions of what appear to be discrete artifacts to the "whole" of culture, ritual, language, stories, and myths are discussed in some detail.

Rituals communicate meaning within a college community by calling attention to and transmitting important values, welcoming and initiating new members (Gardner 1986), and celebrating members' accomplishments. Essentially a social construction, rituals—such as convocations, graduations, presidential inaugurations, activities of secret societies, and dedications (Bushnell 1962)—help to create, maintain, and invent "patterns of collective action and social structure" (Burns 1978, p. 265; see also Turner and Turner 1985). "Above all, rituals are dramas of persuasion. They are didactic, enacted pronouncements concerning the meaning of an occasion and the nature and worth of

Table 13-1

Definitions of Frequently Studied Cultural Forms

Rite	Relatively elaborate, dramatic, planned sets of activities that consolidate various forms of cultural expressions into one event (e.g., dissertation defense meeting); carried out through social interactions, usually for the benefit of an audience.
Ceremonial	A system of several rites connected with a single occasion or event (e.g., commencement, orientation).
Ritual	A standardized, detailed set of techniques and behaviors that manage anxieties but seldom produce intended technical consequences of practical importance (e.g., freshman induction convocation, required chapel).
Myth	A dramatic narrative of imagined events, usually used to explain origins or transformations of something; also, an unquestioned belief about the practical benefits of certain techniques and behaviors that is not supported by demonstrated facts.
Saga	A historical narrative describing the unique accomplishments of a group and its leaders, usually in heroic terms (see Clark 1972).
Legend	A handed-down narrative of some wonderful event that is based in history but has been embellished with fictional details.
Story	A narrative based on true events, often a combination of truth and fiction.
Folktale	A completely fictional narrative.
Symbol	Any object, act, event, quality, or relation that serves as a vehicle for conveying meaning, usually by representing another thing (e.g., school mascot, campus statues, or other objects, such as the axe that symbolizes rivalry between the University of California at Berkeley and Stanford—Basu 1984).
Language	A particular form or manner in which mem bers of a group use vocal sounds and written signs to convey meanings to each other (e.g., an institution's fight song or Alma Mater).
Gesture	Movements of parts of the body used to express meanings.
Physical setting	Those things that surround people physically and provide them with immediate sensory stimuli as they carry out culturally expressive activities.
Artifact	Material objects manufactured by people to facilitate culturally expressive activities.

Source: Adapted from Trice (1984) and Trice and Beyer (1984).

the people involved in the occasion" (Myerhoff 1977, p. 22). Thus, rituals make statements about the quality of life within the community and set standards against which people are asked to compare and modify behavior, values, activities, and relationships (Manning 1987).

Rituals are staged, public, and stylized versions of how things should be and beliefs about how things are that eloquently describe and shape cultural patterns (Goody 1977). Although the possibilities for expression are endless, similar patterns are repeated over time and become part of, as well as reflect, a group's history. These patterns teach cooperation, the importance of tradition, social relations and solidarity, tasks and goals of the group, and the place of authority (Burns and Laughlin 1979; Moore and Myerhoff 1977).

Rituals have certain properties:

1. A collective dimension in which the social meaning inherent in the community is expressed

2. Repetition in content, form, and occasion

3. Self-conscious or deliberate action by the participants as part of the special behavior or stylized performance

4. Orderly action achieved through exaggerated precision and

5. Evocative style of presentation and staging to engage and focus the attention of the audience (Manning 1987; Myerhoff 1977).

Rituals depend on a system of *language* to communicate important ideas and feelings

(Gordon 1969). Language is more than an inventory of words and expressions to describe objects and behaviors; it is a guide to social reality that typifies, stabilizes, and integrates experience into a meaningful whole (Pettigrew 1979). All cultures have a language that links "the collective, cultural, and cognitive domains" of everyday living (Forgas 1985, p. 252). Language systems are based on symbols and metaphors and serve as analogues of life that convey thoughts, perceptions, and feelings associated with experiences in a particular social context (Bredeson 1987; Langer 1953). "Language is not (as commonly thought) a system for transferring thoughts or meaning . . . but a system for organizing information and releasing thoughts and responses in other organisms" (Hall 1976, p. 49). Thus, symbols and metaphors do not so much reflect reality as translate it in a form that can be shared and understood by others (Morgan, Frost, and Pondy 1983). Because colleges and universities are rich in symbolism and ceremony, an awareness of the systems of symbols that mediate meaning between individuals and their cultures is important to understanding events and actions (Kuh, Whitt, and Shedd 1987; Masland 1985).

Symbols, such as organizational signs, communicate the value placed on time, space, and communication, different modes by which institutional agents express their feelings about others, and the activities of a college.

> Signs exist as fluid examples of how people define and give meaning to organizational culture. Thus, signs change over time and acquire and lose power due to the constantly shifting nature of the organization and its participants (Tierney 1987, pp. 20-21).

The significance of analyzing how leaders spend their time, where they spend it, and how they communicate (writing, speaking from written notes) leads to different understandings about how people within a college may influence organizational leadership and decision making. For example, how faculty members or administrators spend time can be effective at one university and inefficient elsewhere because of the cultural meaning given to time in their institutional context (Tierney 1985). Organizational time has three different dimensions: formal/informal, historical, and seasonal/ceremonial (Tierney 1985). The formal

and informal use of time refers to how individuals structure their own time, such as appointments and meetings, versus dropping in for a visit (Deal and Kennedy 1982; Peters and Waterman 1982).

Historical time refers to the manner in which individuals and organizations use the experience of the past in responding to current challenges (Gadamer 1979), while seasonal or ceremonial time refers to the institutional events with which people attempt to synchronize their own activities. Seasonal festivals, the beginning and ending of academic years, the informal coffee hour, the preregistration period, the change in athletic seasons, the movement from outdoors to indoors in the winter and vice versa in the spring all impart organizational meaning and have an influence on how faculty and students perceive and act in a college or university. Problems can arise when administrators rely on a functional interpretation of time that violates the institution's conception of ceremonial time.

> At one institution, . . . Honors Day and Founders Day traditionally were in the fall. A new president and a new academic vice president decided to delay the ceremonies until springtime. They had proposed a massive overhaul of the academic and fiscal sides of the institution, and they did not believe they had time to spend on Honors Day or Founders Day. . . .
>
> The community decried the move. One observer noted, "It's kind of chintzy if you ask me. It used to be really special and everything." Another person said, "Those days stand for what we're about. Everybody got involved, and in one fell swoop they just decided to get rid of them, tell us that we've got to stick to our desks" (Tierney 1985, p. 17).

How time is used influences sense making. What is appropriate use of time in one institutional culture may be inappropriate at another (Tierney 1985).

Stories are narratives—complete with plots, protagonists, antagonists, and action—that shape other aspects of the institutional culture, such as behavioral norms. Stories serve at least five functions: (1) providing information about rules in the institution or subculture; (2) reflecting the beliefs that faculty, students, and alumni have about how past events occurred, thereby keeping the institutional memory sharp (Wilkins 1983); (3) increasing commitment and loyalty to the institution; (4) undergirding and reinforcing other artifacts of culture; and (5) connecting current faculty and students with the institution's past and present (Brown, cited in Kelly 1985). Although stories provide distinctive information about a college, certain characteristics of stories are similar at many institutions (Martin et al. 1983). For example, written histories of colleges often describe the founders of the institution as heroes and depict, in sagalike language, the trials and travails endured in establishing the college (Clark 1970, 1972).

As stories are passed from one student generation to another (Trippet 1982), the stories sometimes take on legendary proportions and become tightly woven into the fabric of the institutional culture. Stories are told at Wabash College in Indiana about the founders of the college kneeling in the snow watching the burning of South Hall, the marching off to war of the "entire" student body in the 1860s, and the bloody class fights on Washington's birthday. Such stories, perpetuated by faculty members and administrators alike, sometimes have more influence on decisions and institutional commitments than policies or data from management information systems (Martin and Powers 1983).

Myths are substantially fictional narratives of events, usually expressed in symbolic terms and often endowed with an almost sacred quality (Allaire and Firsirotu 1984; Cohen 1969). Myths develop over time "to mediate and otherwise 'manage' basic organizational dilemmas," such as ambiguity and uncertainty (Boje, Fedor, and Rowland 1982, p. 27). Myths perform five functions: (1) legitimizing and rationalizing intended or completed actions and consequences; (2) mediating between political interests and competing values; (3) explaining or creating causal relationships; (4) dealing with turbulence in the external environment through rationalization; and (5) enriching the life of the institution or group (Boje, Fedor, and Rowland 1982). An innovative campus, the University of California–Santa Cruz attracted students with liberal social attitudes and developed the reputation for being "flaky" and "touchy-feely." A mythical tale about the origins of the school circulated among students during the 1960s:

Like other conspiracy theories of the sixties, the myth was laced with paranoia and hysteria. The central administration of the University of California, the story went, had planned the Santa Cruz campus as a home for radical students. Like some enormous Venus's fly trap, innovation would attract the unorthodox. But the rural setting, decentralized structure, and close student-faculty contact envisioned for Santa Cruz would effectively disarm radical criticism of the university, turning potentially angry humanists into compliant and hard-working students (Adams 1984, pp. 21-22).

As with many myths, a kernel of truth was imbedded in this example. In the 1950s, predating student activism by about a decade, Clark Kerr, then president of the University of California system, and Dean McHenry, Kerr's assistant for academic planning (who later became chancellor of the Santa Cruz campus), envisioned the need for a campus that would be committed to innovative undergraduate education (Grant and Riesman 1978). Kerr and McHenry had no interest in isolating radicals; they were, however, committed to minimizing the bureaucracy of the research-oriented university in an effort to personalize the experience at Santa Cruz (Adams 1984).

Sometimes additional insights into culture can be gleaned from an analysis of organizational structure (Clark and Trow 1966) and substantive products like policy statements and standard operating procedures. Structure, as represented by an organizational chart, provides a point of reference for the way people think about and make sense of the contexts in which they work (Deal and Kennedy 1982). Written statements of institutional philosophy, mission, and purpose may communicate important messages to faculty, students, and others about what is valued in the institution. Artifacts also may take the form of technologies, such as ways of organizing work, how decisions are made, and course reservation and registration procedures for students (Kuh, Whitt, and Shedd 1987).

Identifying artifacts is relatively easy. It is much more difficult to determine how the nested patterns of assumptions and beliefs represented by artifacts influence the behavior of individuals and groups across time (Schein 1985). Slogans, symbols, language patterns, stories, myths, ceremonials, and rituals provide clues to a deeper, pervasive system of meaning. To understand the culture of a college or university is "to understand how this system, in its mundane as well as its more dramatic aspects, is created and sustained" (Morgan 1986, p. 133). Such understanding can be acquired by linking or contrasting artifacts with the values used in decision making (Schein 1985).

Values

The second level of culture (Schein 1985) is made up of values—widely held beliefs or sentiments about the importance of certain goals, activities, relationships, and feelings. Four values influence the academic enterprise: justice, competence, liberty, and loyalty (Clark 1984). Some institutional values are conscious and explicitly articulated; they serve a normative or moral function by guiding members' responses to situations. Most institutional values, however, are unconsciously expressed as themes (e.g., academic freedom, tradition of collegial governance) or are symbolic interpretations of reality that give meaning to social actions and establish standards for social behavior (Clark and Trow 1966). They often take the form of context-bound values that are related directly to a college's vitality and well-being (Clark 1970; Riesman and Jencks 1962; Sanford 1967).

In *The Small Room* (Sarton 1961), the faculty of a selective Eastern liberal arts college face a dilemma: The institution's literary journal published a promising student's paper that contained plagiarized material. The appropriate institutional response is problematic because the faculty feel they may have placed an undue amount of pressure on the student to perform brilliantly. The discussion among several faculty directly involved in the matter reveals the tension between the values of academic integrity, honesty, intellectual achievement, and the student's social-emotional well-being:

> "Well," Lucy swallowed and paused, then began in a rather stiff cold voice, "I think I am clear that Jane was put under more stress than she could stand. It looks to me as if she broke down not after the affair exploded, but that the real breakdown was clear in the act itself of stealing the Weil essay, and that she did it as a way out of unbearable pressure" . . .
>
> "You suggest that Professor Cope asked too much out of Jane?" . . .

> "Do you feel that there is an overemphasis on intellectual achievement in the college as a whole? Is that the essence?"
>
> ". . . If Lucy is right . . . then a serious attack is being made on the values of this college. We are going to have to do some hard thinking" . . .
>
> ". . . With your permission, I am going to call the faculty [together] and present Jane's case in light of all we have been saying. I shall try to move away from the passions all this has aroused to the big questions that confront us . . . (pp. 179-81).

Cultural values are likely to be tightly linked to, or at least congruent with, basic beliefs and assumptions (the deepest level of culture, to be discussed next) and are embodied in the institution's philosophy or ideology, a "relatively coherent set of beliefs that bind some people together and that explain their worlds [to them] in terms of cause-and-effect relations" (Beyer 1981, p. 166). In this sense, values provide the basis for a system of beliefs (Allaire and Firsirotu 1984).

An illustration of using institutional values to work through dilemmas is provided in a description of Ryke College (a pseudonym), an urban, midwestern Protestant liberal arts college (1,635 full-time equivalent students) founded in 1874 that—like many institutions in the 1970s—was confronted with financial troubles precipitated by declining enrollments (Chaffee 1983). Three major traditions characterized Ryke's history: (1) a mutually supportive relationship with and commitment to its urban setting, (2) an openness to international perspectives, and (3) involvement in social causes. Although Ryke's faculty were receptive to new curricular ideas, any changes were cautiously integrated into the existing classical liberal arts curriculum. The strategy Ryke College followed was to hold fast to the image of "a small, fine liberal arts college" (Chaffee 1983, p. 182).

Ryke's values served as a bridge between artifacts and basic assumptions and beliefs. Ryke's new president attempted to make the college visible again within the urban community. The faculty renewed their commitment to a core liberal arts curriculum consistent with the institution's original mission. The college also made certain its mission statement and recruitment and socialization practices for faculty and students were consistent with the guiding values of the institution. Apparently, the key to the survival of this institution was "being true to its historical liberal arts mission . . ." (Chaffee 1983, p. 183).

Values sometimes surface as exhortations about what is right or wrong, what is encouraged or discouraged—what "ought" to be. For example, statements by the chief academic officer about the importance of teaching or by the chief student life officer about the debilitating consequences of the inappropriate use of alcohol can, under certain circumstances (e.g., when the statements are repeated often and are accompanied by behavior suggesting the authenticity of the statements), communicate the institution's values. Of course, some values are merely espoused (Argyris and Schon 1978) and predict what people will say in certain situations but may not represent what they do. Espoused values are more like aspirations or rationalizations (Schein 1985). Examples of espoused values abound in many colleges and universities: commitment to increasing minority representation in the student body and faculty, assertions about the importance of undergraduate instruction in research universities, and mission statements underscoring an institution's commitment to students' holistic development.

Basic assumptions and beliefs

The third level, believed to be the core of culture, consists of basic but often unstated assumptions that undergird artifacts and values (Schein 1985). These assumptions and beliefs are learned responses to threats to institutional survival and exert a powerful influence over what people think about, what they perceive to be important, how they feel about things, and what they do (Schein 1985). Indeed, assumptions and beliefs determine the way reality is perceived and (albeit unconsciously) guide behavior. These conceptions are so deeply ingrained that they are by definition taken for granted, "not confrontable or debatable" (Schein 1985, p. 18); thus, such assumptions are difficult to identify.

The difficulty in identifying assumptions and beliefs is acknowledged in the advocacy of the use of a culture audit to systematically review aspects of an organization that reflect culture (Wilkins 1983). Tacit assumptions and beliefs are not possible to articulate. Assumptions may be implied, however, through concrete examples. ("I can't explain it in so many words, but I can give you a lot of examples"— Wilkins 1983, p. 27). Thus, to discover distinctive patterns of beliefs and assumptions, one must sift through numerous, diverse artifacts and talk with students and faculty at great length.

The existence of subcultures also adds to the challenge of mapping core assumptions. Clashes of subcultures may point to conflicting core assumptions (Wilkins 1983), such as students' expectation that the institution should prepare them for a vocation, while faculty assume the institution should provide adequate resources for them to pursue scholarly interests. Faculty expect that collegial governance structures can and should be used to guide the direction of the institution, while administrators, under pressure to make decisions and allocate resources, behave in what may appear to faculty to be a unilateral, rigidly bureaucratic manner.

Summary

Culture is a complex set of context-bound, continually evolving properties that potentially includes anything influencing events and actions in a college or university (Tierney 1988). As a result, precise definitions of culture remain elusive. Rituals, stories, language, and other artifacts are observable manifestations of culture that reflect deeper values and help faculty, students, staff, alumni, and others understand what is appropriate and important under certain situations. The core of culture is comprised of assumptions and beliefs shared—to some degree—by members of the institution that guide decision making and shape major events and activities.

Colleges and universities are not monolithic entities. Subgroups have their own artifacts and values, which may differ from the host's institutional culture. The next section reviews the disciplinary perspectives that have been used to study cultural phenomena.

CHAPTER 14

UNDERSTANDING ACADEMIC CULTURE AND CLIMATE

MARVIN W. PETERSON AND MELINDA G. SPENCER

The current interest in organizational culture and climate makes these two complex and confusing concepts an important arena for institutional researchers to understand and to add to their research arsenal.

The optimist looked at the institutional research report on a rather mediocre, entering freshman class and commented, "What an interesting group of students. It will be an exciting challenge to see how much we can help their learning development," The pessimist retorted, "Another mediocre group of students. It's going to be difficult to teach them anything." Clearly these comments reflect two typical but different value sets regarding the central teaching-learning function of their institution and the purpose or meaning of that work. Those comments, heard and interpreted by others, no doubt set the tone for student and faculty attitudes and behavior toward each other and toward the teaching-learning process. The underlying values, beliefs, and meaning in the comments in part constitute the institution's *culture.* The resultant attitudes and behavior in part establish the *climate.* Implicitly we understand both concepts, but they are still among the most complex and confusing in the array of tools we use to research the dynamics of institutional behavior and to foster or manage improvement.

This volume may reflect the well-documented tension in organizational theory and research between rational, empirical, explicit approaches to understanding organizational behavior and the less rational, qualitative, intuitive approaches (Peterson, 1985). This paradigm shift reflects a longer-term debate in many disciplines (Lincoln, 1989) and is emerging in institutional research via topics such as qualitative methods, quality-improvement approaches, and the importance of context. Examination of the topic of culture and climate in institutional research reflects a conceptual and methodological shift toward the less rational, more intuitive side of the paradigm, adding a significant new set of concepts and tools to the analytic artillery. This chapter attempts to (1) clarify the concepts of organizational culture and climate and distinguish between them, (2) identify some of the conceptual approaches to culture and climate that raise some general research issues, and (3) identify some of the organizational research issues and institutional research implications of explicitly examining culture and climate.

"Understanding Academic Culture and Climate," by Marvin W. Peterson and Melinda G. Spencer, reprinted with permission from *Assessing Academic Climates and Cultures*, edited by W. G. Tierney. *New Directions for Institutional Research*, No. 68, Winter 1990.

An Emergent Phenomenon

Despite conceptual confusion and the "soft" nature of the constructs, organizational climate and culture have emerged as one of the most active arenas of scholarly and practical research conducted by individuals from a variety of disciplines. This interest is more than just an academic curiosity about paradigm shifts and a desire to create new models or research approaches. Rather, the concepts of culture and climate are proving useful as a way of understanding the complexities of organizational operations.

The concepts of organizational culture and climate, as they have evolved, perform several important functions. The highly visible and popular research on effective organizations has identified culture as a major factor in effectiveness (Tichy, 1983). Organizational climate has long been seen as an important concept related to individual performance (Blackburn and Pitney, 1988). Culture and climate provide members with and reflect their understanding of the purpose or meaning of their organization and their work. They provide a mechanism for attracting, selecting, and socializing new members. Often culture and climate provide a sense of organizational identity for members by providing them with a sense of what is unique or distinctive about their organization or how it differs from similar places. This organizational identity is not completely static and may mature or change over time. When communicated externally, this cultural identity can function to create an image and establish legitimacy with various outside constituencies. Finally, organizational culture and climate provide a reasonable framework for making sense of the nonrational and informal aspects of an organization that are not captured in formal documents and procedures, objective characteristics of its members, quantitative measures of resources and performance, or organizational charts.

Although the major interest and research activity related to culture and climate has occurred outside of higher education institutions, interest within is also expanding. Growing constituent demands for more accountability and for proof of educational improvement and the inadequacy of specific quantitative measures to reflect performance have increased faculty, administrator, and policymaker interest in developing alternative frameworks for evaluating organizational performance. The concept of culture represents a paradigm for providing a holistic perspective on organizational functioning. In an era of growing institutional competition for students and funding, an institutional image reflecting a positive culture and climate on a few key dimensions is often sought.

While research on culture in higher education is not new, its complex and elusive nature has limited attempts to study it comparatively. Major classic studies are mostly case studies of single institutions, for example, Lunsford (1963), Foote, Mayer, and Associates (1968), Clark (1970), and Riesman, Gusfield, and Gamson (1970). The distinctive nature and unique character of higher education institutions have long been recognized and accepted both within and outside higher education (Veysey, 1965; Martin, 1985). A few comprehensive studies of institutions conducted by Chaffee and Tierney (1988), Tierney (1988), and Peterson, Cameron, Jones, Mets, and Ettington (1986) suggest that the culture of an institution is pivotal in determining the success of organizational improvement efforts. (Two recent syntheses of organizational culture research in higher education are by Peterson, Cameron, Jones, Mets, and Ettington, 1986; and Kuh and Whitt, 1988. More-focused reviews are Cameron and Ettington, 1988; Chaffee and Tierney, 1988; and Tierney, 1988). There are numerous studies of subcultures and subclimates within institutions, such as the work by C. P. Snow (1959) and Burton Clark (1987).

Research on organizational climate, which was quite popular in the 1960s and 1970s, is far more extensive. Much of it has involved the design and development of instruments to measure student, faculty, and administrative views of a wide variety of organizational phenomena. Among those elements studied are organizational missions and goals (Clark, 1970; Davies, 1986), academic workplaces (Austin and Gamson, 1983), organizational functioning (Blau, 1973), academic images and reputations (Webster, 1985; Heverson, 1987), and student, faculty, and administrator environments (Feldman and Newcomb, 1969; Locke, Fitzpatrick, and White, 1983; Blackburn, Horowitz, Edington, and Klos, 1986). Much of this literature is descriptive or compares various institutions, rather than relating the culture and climate measures to other organizational variables (Peterson, Cameron,

Table 14-1		
Primary Distinctions of Culture and Climate		
Organizational Concept	Culture	Climate
Basis of concept	Deeply shared values, assumptions, beliefs, or ideologies of members	Common member perception of attitudes toward and feelings about organizational life
Primary conceptual sources	Anthropology, sociology, linguistics, and organizational behavior	Cognitive and social psychology and organizational behavior
Organizational perspective	Holistic primary emergent patterns	Pervasive, various organizational patterns, often focused on specific arenas
Major purposes of concept	Instrumental (Is): social interpretation, behavior control, and adaptation Interpretive (Has): metaphor or meaning	Extrinsic: member control Intrinsic: member motivation
Primary elements or emphasis	Superordinate meaning	Common view of participants
Primary values or use	Identifies uniqueness in relation to other organizations	Comparison among organizations or over time
Major characteristics	Embedded or enduring	Current patterns or atmosphere
Nature of change	Cataclysmic or long-term and intensive efforts	More malleable, various direct or indirect means

Jones, Mets, and Ettington, 1986). Even so, one is able to get a sense of the interrelatedness and interdependency of the various elements within the institutional environment.

Thus, although the higher education research on organizational culture and climate is not as extensive as in the larger field of organizational behavior, a significant groundwork has been laid. It is apparent from the findings outside of higher education that these concepts are linked to other important organizational variables (Deal and Kennedy, 1982; Peters and Waterman, 1982; Deming, 1986). Within higher education preliminary results suggest the same. More important, some of the current organizational processes and problems may benefit from research on these concepts.

Definitions, Dimensions, and Distinctions

Culture and climate are terms that have been used to describe somewhat abstract phenomena and that emanate from disciplines as diverse in interests as anthropology, sociology, psychology, linguistics, and organizational behavior (Ott, 1989). The two terms have been used to describe quite different levels of behavior (societies, nations, tribes, professions, social groups, organizations, subcultures/subclimates), often in different time frames (current context or historical evolution) and for both single-context and comparative purposes. Consequently, there are numerous subtleties and distinctions in the definitions, and often little common ground. Within higher education the terms environment, culture, and climate are often used interchangeably to describe a wide array of different organizational phenomena.

Definitions

From the perspective of institutional researchers, our primary concern is to focus on organizational behavior, especially that of major subgroups. For the purposes of this discussion, the term *environment* is the broadest concept, potentially including all internal and external, organizationally related phenomena. *Culture* and *climate* are seen as concepts describing a subset of the internal environment of an institution. While definitions of culture and climate vary, it is useful to define them in ways that capture their central essence and that circumscribe a set of phenomena important to understanding higher education institutions (see Table 14-1).

Culture, as a construct or concept, emanates primarily from anthropology, sociology, linguistics, and, more recently, studies of organizational behavior and psychology. It focuses on the deeply embedded patterns of organizational behavior and the shared values, assumptions, beliefs, or ideologies that members have about their organization or its work. Organizational culture is a holistic perspective. It may serve purposes that are (1) *instrumental:* social interpretation of what the organization *is* or *does,* a form of member control, or a mode of organizational adaptation to problems and challenges and (2) *interpretive:* a sense of what the organization *has,* a sense of meaning for members about the organization or their work (Peterson, Cameron, Jones, Mets, and Ettington, 1986). The major features of culture are that it (1) serves to emphasize an organization's unique or distinctive character, which provides a subordinate meaning to members, (2) is deeply embedded and enduring, and (3) is not malleable, changed primarily by cataclysmic events or through slower, intensive, and long-term efforts. As a holistic interpretation of the institution, culture is often captured in sagas about the organization (Clark, 1970), its heroic and revered figures (Deal and Kennedy, 1982), its often ritualistic or symbolic patterns and events (Zucker, 1988), and strongly held images, beliefs, or myths about the place

(Koproski, 1983). For anyone familiar with colleges or universities, culture has face validity. It is the dominant behavioral or belief pattern that reflects or holds the institution together—a kind of "organizational glue."

Climate, as a construct or concept, emanates primarily from cognitive and social psychology and studies of organizational behavior. Although the terms climate and culture are often used interchangeably, the two can be usefully distinguished. Climate can be defined as the current common patterns of important dimensions of organizational life or its members' perceptions of and attitudes toward those dimensions. Thus, climate, compared to culture, is more concerned with current perceptions and attitudes rather than deeply held meanings, beliefs, and values (Hellrigel and Slocum, 1974).

The purposes served by organizational climate reflect its psychological base and individual-level focus as opposed to culture's more holistic approach. Climate is usually viewed as serving extrinsic purposes (member control) and intrinsic purposes (member motivation). The major features of climate are (1) its primary emphasis on common participant views of a wide array of organizational phenomena that allow for comparison among groups or over time, (2) its focus on current patterns of beliefs and behaviors, and (3) its often ephemeral or malleable character. Climate is pervasive, potentially inclusive of a broad array of organizational phenomena, yet easily focused to fit the researcher's or the administrator's interest. Again, the concept of organizational climate has face validity for anyone familiar with higher education. If culture is the "organizational value," climate is the "atmosphere," or "style." One interesting analogy suggests that culture is the meteorological zone in which one lives (tropical, temperate, or arctic) and climate is the daily weather patterns.

Dimensions

Several dimensions or variables are useful in examining both culture and climate. *Distinctiveness, content,* and *continuity* are three dimensions that contrast culture and climate. A focus on distinctiveness or uniqueness is key to understanding culture. Since culture is seen as an emergent pattern that reflects what the organization is or has, the focus is on those elements, such as behavioral patterns, values, beliefs, or ideologies, that make the institution unique (Schein, 1985). Comparison or contrast of institutions is thus based on and limited to content differences. Climate, on the other hand, focuses on common participant views of various organizational phenomena (Allaire and Firsirotu, 1984). This makes it possible to specify the phenomena and easier to compare changes in a specific arena of climate in a single institution over time or across various institutions or subgroups.

Since culture emphasizes an institution's uniqueness, it is difficult also to prescribe the content of culture a priori. Since colleges and universities are educational organizations, both the research literature and common sense suggest some broad categories of possible cultural elements, such as the governance pattern, philosophy of education, perspectives on teaching/learning, the nature of an educational or academic community, and the commitment to clientele. However, identification of the specific content of culture is critical to understanding its unique meaning, to being able to contrast it with other institutions or subgroups, and to assessing its content change over time.

Climate, on the other hand, deals with more clearly focused elements. Thus, it is possible to prescribe the organizational phenomena one wishes to examine. Common categories are institutional goals and functioning, governance and decision patterns, teaching and learning processes, participant behaviors, effort, and interaction patterns, and work patterns or workplace dynamics. Unlike culture, the content of which cannot be easily specified, the options with climate are extensive, so it is important to identify the content of the climate one is examining.

Finally, on the dimension of continuity, culture, by definition, focuses on enduring patterns of embedded values, beliefs, and the like and is difficult to change. Climate, on the other hand, may be enduring but focuses on less embedded attitudes and behaviors. Consequently, climate is more likely to change than culture, and to change more rapidly.

Culture and climate also share four dimensions that are useful in clarifying the existence of the elements of culture or climate being examined. *Strength*, the degree to which culture or climate variables are valued and shape or control members' behavior, is important to understanding the effect of each variable and the ease with which it might be changed. Three dimensions that undergird strength are also useful in establishing the reliability and validity of its existence as a variable. Those are the *congruence* among the subelements of culture (related values, beliefs and so on) and climate (related perceptions or attitudes), the *clarity* or explicit nature of the content of the culture or climate variable, and the *consensus* among institutional members about the strength or importance of the variable.

Continuum, Complementary, or Contrast

Obviously, the confusion about culture and climate are the results of their multiple disciplinary sources; the different purposes and perspectives involved; their different emphases, uses, and characteristics; and some contrasting key dimensions, Yet, the dilemma remains: Are climate and culture merely a continuum ranging from a broad spectrum of attitudes and perceptions of organizational life (climate) to a cluster of those that are deeply embedded and valued (culture)? Are they two separate concepts focusing on similar phenomena that provide complementary views of an organization? Or, are culture and climate focusing on different phenomena and providing contrasting views of organizational life? This chapter cannot definitively answer these questions. In part, the answer depends on the content of the culture and climate on which one chooses to focus. More important, from the perspective of the institutional researcher, these definitions and dimensions suggest that both culture and climate can be distinguished and used to enhance our understanding of college and university environments.

Models of Culture and Climate

Use of the concepts of culture and climate to study colleges and universities has some interesting implications for research approaches and methodology. While there are many diverse and often nitpicking definitions and distinctions for both culture and climate and models of how to conceptualize each, it is possible to identify some of the more popular descriptive frameworks that may be useful to institutional researchers.

Cultural Models: Focusing Content

The numerous approaches and typologies for understanding and studying organizational culture can generally be grouped under the following four broad categories: geospatial; traditions, myths, artifacts, and symbolism; behavioral patterns and processes; and espoused versus embedded values and beliefs (see Figure 14-1). These define the organizational phenomena examined and affect research methodology.

Geospatial approaches focus on tangible and visible physical elements that have shared meaning within the culture. An example is the considerable attention in recent years given to the campus physical plant and architecture. Campus structures, styles, and patterns have often served as visible manifestations of deeper institutional beliefs or as signals of future institutional directions. The somewhat facetious "edifice complex" or preoccupation of many presidents and alumni with initiating major building projects is a well-known phenomenon within higher education (Thelin and Yankovich,

1985). However, the nature, location, condition, and design of campus structures, statues, sculptures, traffic patterns, and other construction can convey a wealth of information about the shared values and beliefs of the culture. Since these elements are relatively permanent, the role that they play within the campus culture, the shared meanings they convey, and the sense of the historical context and present status can make them critical elements in shaping or perpetuating cultural meaning. Descriptive studies of these elements are straightforward, but what they mean is a matter of interpretation, judgment, or opinion.

A second set of approaches focuses on the traditions, myths, and artifacts found within the organizations. As symbols these elements convey more than simple actions. A graduation ceremony, for example, symbolizes more than a simple graduation (Ott, 1989). The celebrations and major campus events, the heroes and villains of the institution, the major sagas of the institution's successes or failures, and the language and jargon used to describe them are all forms of institutional culture that can provide great insight into the past and current ideologies and assumptions that members hold important and that guide their actions. Studies of these phenomena can provide a broad range of information about the shared assumptions, values, and beliefs members hold about their

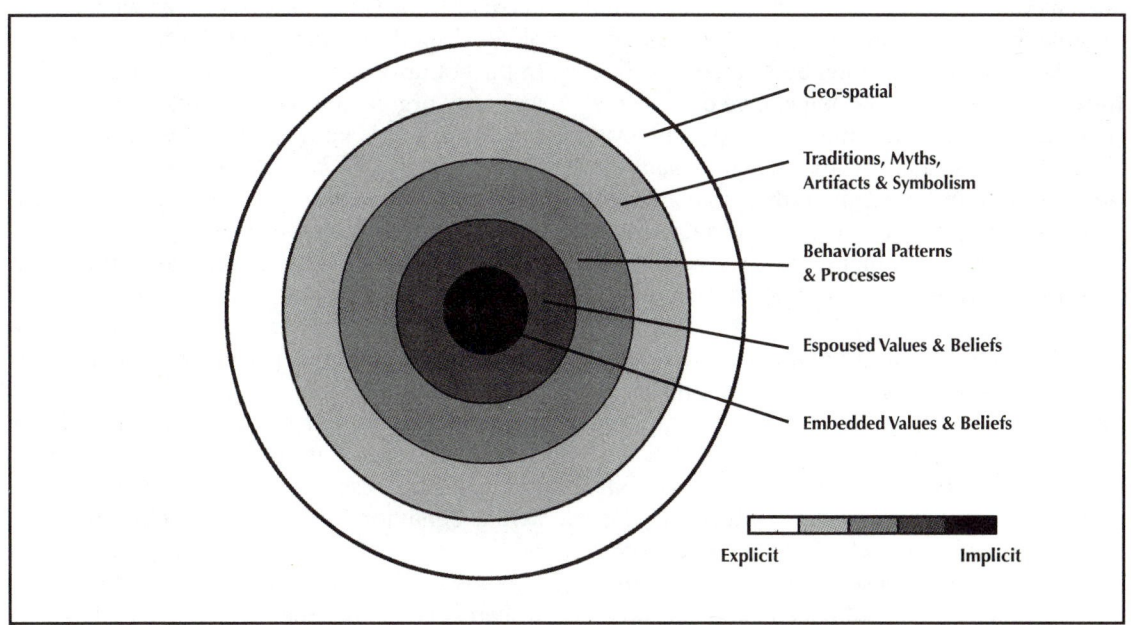

Figure 14-1 Conceptual Model of Organizational Culture

Note: Adapted from Schein, 1985; Ott, 1989.

organization, but they can also be time consuming to conduct. Often, these elements illustrate the idealized view of the institution, highlighting values and beliefs that are avowed but not necessarily practiced.

Behavioral patterns and processes comprise a third set of approaches for studying organizational culture. This category includes the manifest patterns of behavior that are present in the organization's operations, and that have been referred to as the "social architecture" of the organization (Jaccaci, 1989). These patterns and processes can be distinguished from other artifacts in that they involve behavioral activities with relatively standard content and form, sustained and repeated over time. They may be either formally defined by the organization or informally developed and supported by members within the organization. Because patterns and processes are manifested behaviors, studies of these elements can be relatively simple to execute (Sherkenback, 1988). However, determining the cultural impact of these elements requires careful consideration of the manifested processes, the subsequent reactions to them, and their meanings within the organization.

A final set of approaches to considering organizational culture focuses on the values and beliefs that the members share about their organization. These may be explicitly stated, such as those found in mission statements and organizational charters, or implicitly held and revealed only through members' actions. While the espoused values and beliefs are often those that are widely communicated and that form the institutional identity, they often present the organization in its ideal, rather than actual, form. The implicit, or embedded, values and beliefs are those that members carry with them and that provide a real sense of the meaning of their organizational reality (Schein, 1985). It is this latter level of values and beliefs that actually guides members' daily actions. Studies of values and beliefs, while critical in determining the shared meanings that guide member and organizational behavior, are also the most difficult and time-consuming to conduct. The fact that these cultural values and beliefs often function in the unconscious of the individual, where they go unchallenged and unrecognized, makes them difficult to discern (Wilkins, 1983). Often, the researcher is forced to consider other elements within the culture and make an interpretive "leap of faith" regarding the values and beliefs that guide members' behavior.

Researching Culture

While each of these approaches reveals important information and provides insight into the institution, the picture that emerges is essentially incomplete. The culture of an organization is holistic and cannot be completely understood by limiting study to only one of these approaches to culture or one aspect of organizational functioning. Further, the meaning attached to the various elements within the culture is not always readily apparent nor can it be externally derived. Rather, the significance of these "culture bearing" elements can only be determined with qualitative methods within the context of the organization (Ouchi and Wilkins, 1988).

Climate Models: Focusing Content

The conceptual foundations for climate studies are also extensive. They include psychological concerns for attitude formation processes, expectancy theory, and cognitive process models of attitudes and perceptions, as well as sociological models addressing the formation and impact of norms, role modeling, group dynamics, and organizational socialization. For the purposes of this volume and most institutional researchers, three broad categories of climate help to delineate the conceptual content of climate research (Peterson, 1988).

Objective climate focuses on patterns of behavior or formal activity in an institution that can be observed directly and objectively. Certain practices and procedures, characteristics, and quantifiable patterns of behavior of academic management are examples. These fixed, prescribed patterns are relatively easy to identify and research. However, focusing on actual behavior requires observation and can be time consuming. In addition, patterns may not always be obvious. A major concern for researchers is whether objective patterns of behavior and those formally prescribed or required are similar or different, and whether these differences are critical and have dysfunctional consequences. While this research on objective climate is useful, it fails to get at the attitudes toward and perceptions and motivational consequences of organizational climate.

Perceived climate focuses on the cognitive images that participants have of how organizational life actually does function and how it should function. These perceptions may be accurate or inaccurate, but they represent reality from the perspective of participants. They shape norms that guide behavior and expectations and that may underscore motivation. Generally, research on perceived climate focuses on how participants view various institutional patterns and behaviors. Perceptions of institutional goals and functioning, governance and decision making, effort and participation, and workplace dynamics are commonly examined in higher education. Within this rubric, interview approaches, fixed-response instruments, and survey techniques are well-understood and commonly used methodologies. While useful, the critical issue in conducting perceived climate studies is to select from among the many aspects of organizational life that could be addressed and then to determine what to do with data that often present mixed results. The comparison of actual and ideal views reflecting the differences between perceived reality and expectations is often the most informative contrast.

Psychological or felt climate is the motivational, rather than perceptual, dimension that focuses on how participants feel about their organization and their work. These measures are the least used, yet potentially most constructive, climate dimensions. Unlike the objective and perceptual measures of climate, many motivational climate dimensions have been linked to individual and organizational performance measures. Examples include measures of members' loyalty and commitment, their morale and satisfaction, their beliefs about their quality of effort or involvement, and their sense of belonging. These dimensions are included in numerous studies of administrators, faculty, and students in higher education. While interviews, fixed-response instruments, and survey techniques are well understood, there are few well-designed psychological climate or motivational instruments that have been calibrated to fit faculty and administra-

tors in higher education. Development of such instruments involves sophisticated research skills, can be expensive and time consuming, and is usually not a high priority for institutional research offices.

Some Organizational Research Issues

While these definitions, dimensions, distinctions, and models of culture and climate are helpful in bringing pertinent concepts into focus, and such research can provide insights that are useful to an institution of higher education, the resulting picture is still unclear. Research on culture and climate raises a set of broad organizational research issues that also need to be understood and addressed.

Holistic Versus Focused (Comprehensive or Specific)

In studying climate, the array of phenomena that can be addressed is unlimited. Within this framework, it is understood that the choice of a broad focus or specific focus needs to be addressed. However, the advantage of a cultural approach is its emphasis on a holistic view of the organization or unit under study. For a cultural approach to be most useful, it is not possible to focus on only one aspect of organizational functioning or on one type of content. Each aspect needs to be understood within a total context (Schein, 1985). A decision to conduct a cultural audit or study is an extensive and long-term endeavor, cutting across many organizational functions and levels of content suggested by the cultural model. Climate studies, however, can be either comprehensive or focused on specific organizational dimensions, depending on the purpose of the research.

Instrumental Versus Interpretive (Is or Has)

Studying culture places one in the center of a complex (and sometimes esoteric) argument that asks whether culture is something an organization is or has. The former perspective likens culture to an individual's personality interpretable only from the standpoint of its meaning to the participant. This perspective suggests that predefined research protocols, methods, and analytic approaches that attempt to analyze culture are not useful. Rather, research must be phenomenologically oriented, interpreting organizational culture through ethnographically thick descriptions of its context and meaning to its participants (Geertz, 1973). This type of research, while often insightful and fascinating, is not likely to prove fruitful to the overloaded institutional researcher seeking to improve some aspect of his or her institution. However, a more interpretive approach, which assumes culture is what an organization has, allows the researcher to apply his or her own interpretation to the pattern of functioning that is being described. In complex organizations, adopting a holistic perspective and examining multiple layers of cultural evidence can be a fruitless or confusing effort, as the results are open to very different interpretations.

Intrinsic Versus Extrinsic (Individual or Organization)

A slightly different issue in research on climate involves the question of whether climate is an intrinsic measure of participants' motivation or an extrinsic measure of organizational patterns that control member behavior. While the distinction of perceived (extrinsic) and psychological (intrinsic) climate is clear in principle, in practice it can be quite opaque. The administrative implications, however, are clear. Changing external controls to influence perceptions is much easier than changing individuals' motivation and involves very different change strategies.

Quantitative Versus Qualitative Methods (Distinctiveness and Insight Versus Reliability and Comparison)

Research on organizational climate can be approached systematically using either qualitative methods (interviews, observations, focus groups, document content analyses, and so on) or quantitative approaches (fixed-response instruments, survey sampling, and statistical analysis). The former offers significant insight on new emergent issues and organizational phenomena. The latter provides information that can be statistically

compared and contrasted. However, when studying organizational culture, the primary methods are qualitative, involving ethnographically thick descriptions drawn from participant observation by the researcher, examination of institutional records and documents, and open-ended interviews. Even more structured attempts at case studies, triangulation of data, or use of grounded theory are primarily qualitative.

Some researchers have attempted to build institutional typologies for quantitatively measuring institutional culture. However, this approach requires the use of a prescribed set of dimensions and renders the identification of distinctive features of the culture less likely. For example, Cameron has attempted to classify institutions on an internal-external orientation and a member-control dimension of flexibility-rigidity that yields a fourfold classification of the organizational culture as market, clan, adhocracy, or hierarchy (Cameron and Ettington, 1988). As yet, the efficacy of such cultural typologies measured by quantitative instruments has not been proven in higher education. Thus, the researcher is left with the choice of either a qualitative approach that allows the institution's distinctive features to be identified but renders comparison to other institutions problematic or a quantitative approach that may be statistically reliable and allow cross-institution comparison but fails to capture the critical cultural or climate features.

Independent, Intervening, or Dependent (or All Three)

Another issue for studies of culture and climate is the question of whether these variables are (1) *independent*, affecting individual behavior and institutional functioning, (2) *intervening* between administrative action or strategy and performance, or (3) *dependent*. To even suggest such a distinction in culture studies assumes culture is instrumental, rather than interpretive, in nature. In most higher education research, culture has been studied for its own sake, and climate similarly or for institutional comparisons. Conceptually, climate and culture can be seen as all three types of variables. Consequently, it is important for researchers to consider carefully the research model and research questions they are attempting to answer.

Loose Coupling (Rationalizing Muddled Results)

While the notion of colleges and universities as loosely coupled organizations has been discussed, it is important to keep this notion in mind when addressing research on culture and climate. Both are "soft" variables. Climate is, by definition, a variable that is subject to change for many reasons. Culture, by definition, is enduring and not easily changed. Researchers and administrators focusing on culture and climate should not expect to see close relationships between their decisions or actions and changes in these variables. Rather, the two variables need to be examined over longer time frames and in light of other simultaneous changes that may affect them.

Paradox (A Researcher's Paradise)

One of the advantages of a cultural perspective is that it can force administrators to recognize that paradoxes existing within their institution are not always detrimental. A paradox is the simultaneous existence of two seemingly contradictory values or purposes ("We want to be an inner-city institution" and "We want to focus on excellence or quality"). The existence of seemingly contradictory views, if carefully documented, can be a focus for creative discussions and problem solving. But, if left unrecognized or unattended, those contradictions can lead to internal conflicts.

Subcultures/Climates (And How Many)

Most participants in higher education know their institutions are seldom monolithic and that important subunits or groups are quite different. Those differences are often critical in mitigating conflict, guiding broad participation, or stimulating productive competition or cooperation. Nowhere is this insight more important than in the study of organizational culture and climate. The literature on differing perceptions of administrators, faculty, and students and on the differences among disciplines and professions is extensive. Sensitivity to the potential existence of subcultures and subclimates is important for anyone doing research in this arena (and for tactful presentation of findings).

The Role of Institutional Research: Some Implications

Although the study of institutional culture and, to a lesser degree, climate have been of greater academic than practical interest, it is apparent that institutional researchers will be drawn into or influenced by research in this arena. While the research issues are clear, there are several roles or stances that institutional researchers can assume as the interest in and usefulness of these concepts continues to evolve and expand.

Awareness

Attempt to develop, unobtrusively, an understanding of important cultural and climate dimensions in our institutions of higher education. This can be done by reviewing past studies, doing some purposive exploration, or engaging key participants in focused discussions.

Establish Cultural Context

Try to define important dimensions of institutional culture and climate as context for other research studies to help convey what the dimensions mean and to aid in their interpretation.

Build Benchmarks

Since long-term research is needed and causal links are difficult to establish in culture and climate research, conduct a series of one-time investigations on important cultural or climate conditions to serve as benchmarks at a future date.

Active Program of Culture/Climate Studies

Although time consuming and often not of immediate concern, launching a series of studies geared toward important goals such as clarifying institutional image and improving the climate for undergraduate education can be a good way to make such studies useful and to learn about and improve the methodology. It may also be a way to involve a different group of faculty in institutional research.

Culture/Climate Change Expert

Managing or changing an institution's climate or culture usually involves administrative strategies not often practiced in colleges and universities. The institutional research office could be a repository of some of this expertise.

To summarize, each institution has its own culture and climate for the practice of institutional research—the value placed on systematic research on institutional dynamics, problems, and pressures. Perhaps the primary focus of the institutional research office could or should be to build a supportive culture and climate for conducting this research and systematically using it to improve the institution over time—for the sake of institutional research and the institution.

MARVIN W. PETERSON is director of the Center for the Study of Higher and Postsecondary Education and chair of the Program in Higher and Adult Continuing Education at the University of Michigan, Ann Arbor.

MELINDA G. SPENCER is a doctoral student in higher education at the University of Michigan, Ann Arbor.

References

Allaire, Y, and Firsirotu, M. E. "Theories of Organizational Culture." *Organizational Studies*, 1984, 5, 193–226.

Austin, A. E., and Gamson, Z. F. *Academic Workplace: New Demands, Heightened Tensions.* ASHE-ERIC Higher Education Report No. 10. Washington, D.C.: Association for the Study of Higher Education, 1983.

Blackburn, R. T., Horowitz, S. M., Edington, D. W, and Klos, D. M. "University Faculty and Administrator Response to Stresses: Correlations with Health and Job/Life Satisfactions." *Research in Higher Education*, 1986, 25 (1), 31–41.

Blackburn, R. T., and Pitney, J. A. *Performance Appraisal for Faculty: Implications for Higher Education.* Ann Arbor: National Association for Research to Improve Postsecondary Teaching and Learning, University of Michigan, 1988.

Blau, P. M. *The Organization of Academic Work.* New York: Wiley, 1973.

Cameron, K. S., and Ettington, D. R. "The Conceptual Foundations of Organizational Culture." In J. C. Smart (ed.), *Higher Education: Handbook of Theory and Research.* Vol. 4. New York: Agathon, 1988.

Chaffee, E. E., and Tierney, W G. *Collegiate Culture and Leadership Strategies.* New York: American Council on Education and Macmillan, 1988.

Clark, B. R. *The Distinctive College: Antioch, Reed, and Swarthmore.* Chicago: Aldine, 1970.

Clark, B. R. *The Academic Life: Small Worlds, Different Worlds.* Princeton, N.J.: Princeton University Press, 1987.

Davies, G. K. "The Importance of Being General: Philosophy, Politics, and Institutional Missions Statements." In J. C. Smart (ed.), *Higher Education: Handbook of Theory and Research.* Vol. 2. New York: Agathon, 1986.

Deal, T. E., and Kennedy, A. A. *Corporate Cultures: The Rites and Rituals of Corporate Life.* Reading, Mass.: Addison-Wesley, 1982.

Deming, W. E. *Out of the Crisis.* Cambridge, Mass.: Center for Advanced Engineering Study, Massachusetts Institute of Technology, 1986.

Feldman, K. A., and Newcomb, T. M. *The Impact of College on Students.* San Francisco: Jossey-Bass, 1969.

Foote, C., Mayer, H., and Associates. *The Culture of the University: Governance and Education.* San Francisco: Jossey-Bass, 1968.

Geertz, C. *The Interpretation of Cultures.* New York: Basic Books, 1973.

Hellriegel, D., and Slocum, J. W. Jr. "Organizational Climate: Measures, Research, and Contingencies." *Academy of Management Journal*, 1974, 17, 255–279.

Heverson, E. D. "Boosting Academic Reputations: A Study of University Departments." *Review of Higher Education*, 1967, 11, 177–197.

Jaccaci, A. T. "The Social Architecture of a Learning Culture." *Training & Development Journal*, 1989, 43 (11), 49–51.

Koproski, E. J. "Cultural Myths: Clues to Effective Management." *Organizational Dynamics*, 1983, 12 (2), 39–51.

Kuh, G. D., and Whitt, E. J. *The Invisible Tapestry: Culture in American Colleges and Universities.* ASHE-ERIC Higher Education Report No. 1. Washington, D.C.: Association for the Study of Higher Education, 1988.

Lincoln, Y. S. "Trouble in the Land: The Paradigm Revolution in the Academic Disciplines." In J. C. Smart (ed.), *Higher Education: Handbook of Theory and Research.* Vol. 5. New York: Agathon, 1989.

Locke, E. A., Fitzpatrick, W., and White, F. M. "Job Satisfaction and Role Clarity Among University and College Faculty." *Review of Higher Education*, 1983, 6, 343–365.

Lunsford, I. F. (ed.). *The Study of Campus Cultures.* Boulder, Colo.: Western Interstate Commission on Higher Education, 1963.

Martin, J. "Can Organizational Culture Be Managed?" In P. J. Frost, L. F. Moore, M. R. Louis, C. C. Lundberg, and J. Martin (eds.), *Organizational Culture.* Newbury Park, Calif.: Sage, 1985.

Ott, J. S. *The Organizational Culture Perspective.* Chicago: Dorsey, 1989.

Ouchi, W. G., and Wilkins, A. L. "Organizational Culture." In A. Westoby (ed.), *Culture and Power in Educational Organizations.* Philadelphia: Open University Press, 1988.

Peters, T. J., and Waterman, R. H. *In Search of Excellence: Lessons from America's Best-Run Companies.* New York: Harper & Row, 1982.

Peterson, M. W. "Emerging Developments in Postsecondary Organization Theory and Research: Fragmentation or Integration." *Education Researcher,* 1985, 14 (3), 5–12.

Peterson, M. W. "The Organizational Environment for Student Learning." In J. S. Stark and L. A. Mets (eds.), *Improving Teaching and Learning Through Research.* New Directions for Institutional Research, no. 57. San Francisco: Jossey-Bass, 1988.

Peterson, M. W., Cameron, K. S., Jones, P., Mets, L. A., and Ettington, D. *The Organizational Context for Teaching and Learning: A Review of the Research Literature.* Ann Arbor: National Center for Research to Improve Postsecondary Teaching and Learning, University of Michigan, 1986.

Reisman, D., Gusfield, J., and Gamson, Z. F. *Academic Values and Mass Education: The Early Years of Oakland and Monteith.* New York: Doubleday, 1970.

Schein, E. H. *Organizational Culture and Leadership: A Dynamic View.* San Francisco: Jossey-Bass, 1985.

Sherkenback, W. W. *The Deming Route to Quality and Productivity: Road Maps and Roadblocks.* Washington, D.C.: CEEP Books, 1988.

Snow, C. P. *The Two Cultures and the Scientific Revolution.* New York: Cambridge University Press, 1959.

Thelin, J. R., and Yankovich, J. "Bricks and Mortar: Architecture and the Study of Higher Education." In J. C. Smart (ed.), *Higher Education: Handbook of Theory and Research.* Vol. 1. New York: Agathon, 1985.

Tichy, N. M. *Managing Strategic Change: Technical, Political, and Cultural Dynamics.* New York: Wiley, 1983.

Tierney, W. G. "Organizational Culture in Higher Education." *Journal of Higher Education,* 1988, 59, 2–21.

Veysey, L. R. *The Emergence of the American University.* Chicago: University of Chicago Press, 1965.

Webster, D. S. "James McKeen Cattell and the Invention of Academic Quality Ratings, 1903–1910." *Review of Higher Education,* 1985, 8, 107–121.

Wilkins, A. L. "The Culture Audit: A Tool for Understanding Organizations." *Organizational Dynamics,* 1983, 12 (2), 24–38.

Zucker, L. G. "Where Do Institutional Patterns Come from? Organizations as Actors in Social Systems." In L. G. Zucker (ed.), *Institutional Patterns and Organizations: Cultures and Environment.* Cambridge, Mass.: Ballinger, 1988.

CHAPTER 15

THE CAMPUS RACIAL CLIMATE: CONTEXTS OF CONFLICT

SYLVIA HURTADO

Racial conflict was becoming commonplace on American college campuses throughout the 1980s, with more than one hundred college campuses reporting incidents of racial/ethnic harassment and violence in each of the last two years of the decade [40]. The most highly publicized racial incidents, ranging from verbal harassment to violent beatings, occurred at some of the most elite institutions in the country [25, 56]. In many cases students organized protests as a direct response to these problems, or to express solidarity with students facing similar problems at other institutions [60]. Although these events have provided the impetus for examining the quality of race relations on individual college campuses, researchers have not explored at any great length the nature of campus race relations across a variety of institutional contexts.

The research on minorities in higher education is extensive, yet a surprisingly small number of empirical studies have focused specifically on campus racial climates. Only a few studies include measures of campus race relations in their models of student persistence [54, 57, 58], academic achievement [2, 41, 42, 46], and social involvement [1]. Although this is an important step toward developing appropriate models that describe the college experiences of minority students, these studies have revealed a conflicting pattern of relations between hostile racial climates and student outcomes [29]. Part of the problem is that we need a better understanding of what constitutes a racially tense interpersonal environment before considering how these climates are related to student development.

Drawing upon previous work on race relations, inequality, and campus diversity, the goal of this study is to examine comparative institutional data that may help identify contexts for racial conflict. This study offers a unique opportunity to examine racial tension on campus because it focuses on the experiences of a student cohort that attended predominantly white colleges from 1985 to 1989, a period when racial incidents occurred on many campuses. A central premise of the study is that such incidents are part of a wide range of climate issues on college campuses that require our attention. Much of what we observe on campus is undoubtedly influenced by the general social context, yet we can learn a great deal about the nature of our campuses by examining black, Chicano, and white student perceptions in institutional contexts associated with campus racial tension.

The Social Context

The civil rights movement, the elimination of *de jure* segregation in the public sector (*Brown v. the Board of Education* [16]), litigation in areas related to the Civil Rights Law (Title VI), and a surge in minority enrollments up until the mid-1970s raised the level of public consciousness regarding inequalities in the education of minority groups. These events represented tremendous strides in progress toward eliminating overt aspects of discrimination in educational institutions, making such practices illegal and unethical in the public mind. However, scholars concede that institutional compliance with legal injunctions for increased minority participation in higher education continues to be problematic [59, 61, 65], the system of higher education remains racially stratified [62], and vestiges of discrimination exist in everyday administrative practices [50]. Thus, important progress has yet to be made in removing some of the more intractable forms of racial inequality and discrimination at both the institutional and individual level.

The research literature suggests that instances of overt racial conflict can no longer be viewed as aberrations or isolated incidents, but rather are indicators of a more general problem of unresolved racial issues in college environments and in society at large. Researchers investigating racial climates in the mid-1970s found that though college campuses exerted considerable energy in initiating programs and services in response to the initial entrance of black students, institutions did not attend to minority-majority relations or the psychological climate [49]. Recent studies have shown that even on relatively calm campuses there are differences in students' racial attitudes and considerable social distance among students of different racial or ethnic backgrounds [37, 38]. Alienation from the mainstream of campus life is also reported to be particularly acute among minority students on predominantly white campuses [2, 46, 53]. The 1989 American Council on Education (ACE) survey of academic administrators revealed that only one in four felt their campus provided an "excellent" to "very good" climate for black students, and only 21 percent felt they provided a supportive climate for Hispanics [23]. If these issues have been left unattended since the influx of minorities into higher education in the 1960s, it is no wonder that campuses continue to deal with racial tensions.

External forces and the events of the past decade have helped to make these unresolved issues more salient. The resurgence of overt hostilities on campuses, reported as early as 1979 [54], accompanied events that signaled the questioning of affirmative action practices (for example, *Bakke*), declining federal commitment to issues that affect minorities, renewed Ku Klux Klan activity, and increasing racial discord in urban communities [25, 33, 59]. At the same time, college campuses reflected a political shift toward conservatism in the country during the 1980s. Students who identified with the far right and political conservatives became more vocal, while their classmates shied away from the liberal label and increasingly characterized their political views as middle-of-the road [22]. Moreover, significant policy trends that are connected with issues of inequality directly affected institutions of higher education. For example, reductions in federal aid programs during the Reagan years resulted in changes in financial aid packaging policy at the institutional level, which many contend have disproportionately affected blacks and Hispanics in their decisions to attend or remain in college [8, 19, 43, 44. 56]. Diminishing federal support for Pell grants and minority-targeted fellowships promises to complicate institutional efforts to stem the decline of college participation rates for low-income and minority groups [17, 18, 30, 45].

Institutional Contexts

Although the general social context influences all institutions, researchers have found considerable institutional variability in reports of racial conflict and responses to improve the racial climate. Early studies found that institutional selectivity and size were both positively associated with student unrest involving campus racial policies [5]. Researchers offered two alternative interpretations: (a) selective institutions and large campuses are environments that are more likely to attract protest-prone students, and (b) large institutions are characterized by an impersonal atmosphere and lack of concern for the individual student, thereby promoting student discontent. The first interpretation suggests that conflict on campus is largely due to the types of students an institution recruits. Studies support the notion that elite institutions tend to attract students with strong ideological commitments and foster political liberalism [7, 28]. The second interpretation states that institutional size may be a proxy for attention to students, suggesting that the extent to which institutions are supportive of students helps maintain a conflict-free environment. Recent research shows that higher rates of institutional spending (per student) in the areas of student services and student aid (non-repayable grants and fellowships) are correlated with student perceptions of relatively low racial tension on campuses [29]. Although there is research support for both interpretations, one focuses on the individual as the source of conflict, while the other suggests that institutional contexts are largely responsible for setting the stage for conflict. These interpretations were tested in the current study, along with others which suggest that both size and selectivity are proxies for other phenomena that include changes in minority enrollment and institutional priorities that help shape the climate.

One of the most comprehensive studies of the racial climate, initiated on the campuses of thirteen four-year institutions, systematically documented the historical and environmental forces that accompanied substantial increases in black student enrollment from 1968 to 1975 [49]. In addition to campus site visits, extensive surveys of administrators, faculty, and students at four of the large institutions explored three broad areas of institutional responsiveness to the entrance of black students: institutional commitment, program responses, and the attitudinal or perceptual climate. Although the large institutions had invested a fair amount of time and funds in minority programs and services, researchers found that these institutions differed substantially in ratings of relative priorities placed on the recruitment of black students, provision for nonacademic support, and commitment to affirmative action. They also observed that campuses paid little attention to the interpersonal aspects of race relations, which were characterized by "voluntary segregation or by indifference thinly covering interracial conflicts and feelings of mistrust" [49, p. 319]. They concluded that a failure to deal with any of the issues at the institutional, programmatic, or individual level was "likely to become a source of difficulty at some point in these institutions' relationships with minorities" [49, p. 316]. Although researchers antici-

pated problems with minority students, they did not foresee the extent to which an institution's relationship with majority students would become equally problematic in matters such as admissions (for example, *Bakke*), student organizations (fraternities), and student publications (for example, *Dartmouth Review*). Still, these early findings hold important implications for the examination of contemporary racial tension with regard to the role of institutional priorities and the impact of changing enrollments.

The 1989 ACE survey of academic administrators at 456 institutions revealed distinct differences by institution type in priorities for cultural diversity, programmatic activity, and the amount of racial tension reported on campus [23]. Administrators at doctoral institutions reported the most programmatic activity to improve minority participation at all levels of the university, including efforts to increase the number of minority faculty and increase the enrollment of minority students at the undergraduate level. Comprehensive universities were the next most active in this regard. At the same time, however, racial tensions were reported more often at comprehensive and doctoral institutions than at other types of institutions. In direct contrast, administrators from private baccalaureate institutions reported the least racial tension among the four-year institutions; but also gave their institutions the lowest ratings in their ability to attract black and Hispanic students. These ratings, from one of the top academic administrators at each campus, indicate distinct differences among four-year institutions that include both a public/private dichotomy and contradictions in campus racial climates.

Conducted some fourteen years apart, both studies suggest that despite visible programmatic activity, institutions continue to vary considerably in their commitment to diversity and in the amount of racial conflict on campus. These findings run counter to the commonly held assumption that the introduction of a few programs would essentially lead to better racial climates. Apparently, a shift in institutional priorities for diversity is more difficult to achieve and may involve resolving a more complex set of institutional priorities or problems. Richardson and Skinner's [51] model of institutional adaptation to diversity proposes that goals for quality and diversity may be seen as sources of conflict within institutions. Scholars have raised questions regarding this issue, stating that the assumptions underlying these concepts may inappropriately place the two goals in conflict [53]. Though there has been substantial attention to the debate regarding the relationship between the two priorities, there has been little concern about whether the quest for institutional quality or a shift in priorities of institutional commitment to diversity may be related to racial tension on campus.

The adaptation model has several underlying premises that are reexamined here in relation to the campus climate. The model equates quality with individual achievement, suggesting that the focus of selective institutions is high on achievement and low on diversity, whereas the reverse is true for open-access institutions. The problem with this logic is that all educational institutions have a concern for individual achievement; the difference between these types of institutions is that student achievement must be proven *prior* to admission with selective institutions, whereas open-access institutions are willing to allow students to prove achievement *during* college. Therefore, selective institutions may have less to do with improving individual achievement than with maintaining institutional status and reputation [6]. This forces us to reexamine the conflict in priorities: the source of conflict is not between diversity and achievement but originates from differences in institutional priorities that work to preserve inequalities. For example, although campus race relations is not an aspect of the adaptation model, researchers acknowledge that "our society has historically treated minority populations as inferior" [51] and report that the social environment of the large predominantly white universities has been problematic, even for minority students with strong academic preparation [52, p. 487]. Traditional notions of quality are often linked to both selectivity and an institutional preoccupation with resource accumulation and reputation enhancement [6]. It may be that minority students are generally undervalued (regardless of their achievement characteristics), whereas high achieving white students are viewed as resources. Therefore, priorities that guide an institution and its members may have underlying ideological assumptions that are linked with racial issues.

A theoretical tradition supports the view that our institutions, particularly our schools, have embedded ideologies that work to preserve inequality [14, 27]. Research on racial inequality and attitudes has adopted a similar notion of dominant ideological interests. Arce [4] introduced the concept of "academic colonialism" when referring to Chicano participation in academe. Academic colonialism refers to the imposition of dominant ideologies (for example, intellectual premises, concepts, practices) and/or the uncritical acceptance of these ideologies by subordinate groups. Similarly, others assert that dominant group interests are served in maintaining a status quo that justifies unequal social relations and achieves some level of consensus about such arrangements among subordinate groups [31, 32, 38]. Viewed from this perspective, the conflict between quality and diversity appears contrived and arguments for "quality" may be used as a way to uniformly exclude minorities (faculty and students) and their perspectives.

When "harmonious inequality" is challenged by subordinates, dominant groups are forced to defend their privilege [32]. This perspective suggests that mean-spirited acts of racial harassment on the part of white students may represent a reassertion of group dominance in an era when prevailing dominant group ideologies are in question. However, the defense of dominant group privilege is less often characterized by such acts of "traditional" racism on campus and more often takes on a sophisticated guise as an expressed concern for the individual that is consistent with prevailing democratic values—so long as one chooses to ignore *both* the historical and continuous disadvantages under which subordinate groups operate. As researchers point out, this concern for individual privilege is at the heart of the meritocratic ethic in higher education [38]. It is also at the center of contention with regard to virtually every institutional response to eliminate inequalities and discriminatory practices for various groups, including affirmative action, the development of disciplinary codes to prohibit harassment, and the practice of providing minority-targeted scholarships.[1] Although this view suggests dominant group opposition to institutional commitment to diversity, we have yet to obtain evidence which shows that diversity priorities are related to racial tension on predominantly white campuses.

Race relations theorists propose that racial conflict arises out of a sense of threat to group position, when the dominant group perceives the risk of losing power, resources, or other advantages [12, 63]. Work in the area of relative numbers of underrepresented groups suggests that the proportions of socially and culturally different people in a group are critical in shaping the dynamics of social interaction [35]. Blalock hypothesized that "as the minority percentage increases, we would expect to find increasing discriminatory behavior" [11, p. 148] because more members of the minority group will be in direct competition with someone from the dominant group. Recent research on racial attitudes shows decreases in white support for integration and increases in perceived threat from blacks as the relative size of the black population increased in communities [26]. Thus, differences in minority enrollment may account for variations in racial tension and contradictions observed in studies of institution type and the racial climate. Faced with impending changes in the ethnic composition of the college-age population [24], such effects may have important implications for college campuses.

Student Perceptions and Ethnic Group Differences

Researchers have found that student perceptions vary by race in college environments, yet only a handful of studies have compared perceptions of the racial climate among black, Chicano, and white college students [64]. A study at one predominantly white university showed that although a higher percentage of blacks than Chicanos reported that they have personally experienced discrimination, these reports were positively correlated with feelings of alienation only among Chicano students [46]. Loo and Rolison [37] also found that the majority of white students (68 percent) thought that the university was generally supportive of minority students, while only 28 percent of the black and Chicano students expressed the same opinion. In the same study, certain behaviors (for example, ethnic group clustering) were interpreted by white students as racial segregation, whereas minority students tended to view them as modes of cultural support within a larger unsupportive environment. In a comparative study of two institutions [48], researchers found black students were most likely to perceive a hostile racial climate on campus, but Hispanics were also more likely than white students to perceive such hostility. Perceptions of the racial climate also differed by institution, although it appears that dimensions of location and ethnic composition of the campus were confounded with group differences. These studies show that ethnic groups differ in their view of the racial climate, highlighting the need to conduct comparative group analyses across institutions to understand environments with considerable racial tension.

Method

Conceptual Framework

The structural properties of the environment are central to shaping social interaction and the individual's attitude and behavior within it [36]. These structural properties are often assessed with measures that social psychologists refer to as "contextual variables" [36] or distal characteristics [34]. In higher education research these measures are often institutional characteristics such as size, type, control, selectivity, and racial composition of the college. In Jessor's [34] view, there are a multiplicity of environments in which human interaction takes place. These multiple environments can be ordered along a continuum according to proximity to the individual. Demographic and structural attributes of environments are considered distal, whereas the perceived environment is considered the most proximal and is of immediate significance to the actor. Studies have begun to validate the notion that proximal measures are more important than distal characteristics in relation to student outcomes [47, 55]. Research in social psychology also suggests that proximal measures mediate the effect of these distal characteristics on other outcomes [34, 39]. In this particular study the distal environmental dimensions include size, selectivity, ethnic enrollments, and campus expenditures. The proximal environment is represented by student perceptions of institutional priorities that reflect institutional commitment to cultural diversity, a resource/reputation orientation, and a student-centered orientation. Within this framework, the proximal measures (student perceptions of the environment) are hypothesized to have a greater influence than the distal measures of the environment on student perceptions of racial tension.

Data Sources

This study draws upon several major data sources. The primary source of student data came from responses to a four-year longitudinal survey, the 1989 Follow-up Survey (FUS) to the 1985 Freshman Survey, a project of the Cooperative Institutional Research Program (CIRP) and the Higher Education Research Institute at UCLA. The 1985 Freshman Survey was administered during freshman orientation and the FUS was sent to the student's home address in the summer and fall of 1989, four years after college entry. The FUS was administered according to two different sampling techniques to address the need for national normative data and to facilitate separate group analyses. The first sample was drawn from the population of first-time, full-time freshmen (192,453) responding to the 1985 Survey. A stratified, random procedure was used to ensure representation of students based on sex within the different types of institutions in higher education. (Stratification involved 23 cells reflecting institutional selectivity, control, race, sex, and the type of institution). Based on patterns of response observed in earlier FUS studies, a random sample (20,317) was selected to yield a minimal number (175) of respondents in each stratification cell. This yielded data on 4,672 respondents (23 percent response rate), which were statistically adjusted for nonresponse and weighted to approximate the national population of students. (The statistical weighting methodology used in HERI Follow-up surveys can be found in all FUS reports [30]).

Although this sampling procedure is well suited for analyses of national normative data, the numbers of minority students drawn randomly across institutions remains extremely small for the purposes of separate group analyses. A second procedure was necessary to yield a sample more conducive to analyses on ethnic groups. Four-year institutions were selected to maximize variability according to student academic programs and minority enrollment in addition to institutional type, control, and selectivity. Full cohorts of students (34,323) were surveyed, yielding 10,640 respondents (31 percent response rate). A secondary data sampling procedure was employed to select only those students representing three ethnic groups (black, Chicano, and white students) from among respondents at 116 predominantly white institutions. Each institution was considered a separate stratum with stratified, random sampling conducted on a 3:1 white/minority ratio. The purpose of this procedure was to yield a sample of white students that was distributed across institutions in a manner similar to the distribution of minority students. Most institutions had both black and Chicano students but in some institutions, due to distinct patterns of college attendance among minorities, white students were matched with only one of these ethnic groups. This final selection criteria yielded a sample of 1,825 white students, 328 black, and 340 Chicano students. The major part of the study utilized the data from this selected sample for separate group analyses.

Institutional characteristics and undergraduate ethnic enrollments were obtained from the data files of the U.S. Department of Education's Integrated Postsecondary Data System (IPEDS, formerly HEGIS).[2] Black, Hispanic, and total enrollment data for 1982, 1986, and 1988 at each institution were obtained from this national source. These years were used to create enrollment change variables for the ethnic groups in each institution. Financial data on 1985 expenditures (per student) for student services and grants/fellowships were similarly obtained, and all institutional data were merged with student survey data for analyses.

Measures

A total of 21 independent variables were selected for the analyses. Variable definitions are shown on table 15-A1, along with coding schemes and scales. The dependent variable consisted of a factorially confirmed scale representing student perceptions of racial tension among students, faculty, and campus administrators [29]. Items constructing all scales are shown on table 15-A2. The rationale for including specific measures in analyses is described below.

Because the distribution of students across different college environments is never random, one of the basic features of any research design is to control for student characteristics at the point of initial exposure to the environment. For example, selective institutions tend to attract students who are more critical of their environments (for example, liberal and protest "prone"), come from families with higher incomes, and have higher academic ability [5, 7]. Parental income and student academic performance (high-school grade point average) served as control variables, along with a number of student self-rating and value measures on the 1985 Freshman Survey. Measures that controlled for predispositions in student perceptions included student self-ratings of political view, estimated chances of becoming involved in campus protest, and the importance attributed to the goal of helping to promote racial understanding. Aside from the need for statistical control, additional student background characteristics were included in analyses because they are established correlates of racial attitudes and perceptions. For example, females are generally more supportive of affirmative action and racial integration [13]; the well-educated tend to be more supportive of principles of racial integration (but not decidedly more willing to support specific equity policies) [31, 32]; and age is negatively associated with racial integration [26]. Previous research has also suggested that a sense of interpersonal accomplishment or social self-confidence may be an important precursor to social involvement among minorities [2] and perceptions of racial tension on campus among white students [29]. Therefore, additional student background variables included gender, mother's and father's level of education, age, and a social self-confidence scale.

Factor scales constructed from student perceptions of their environment included institutional priorities that reflect a commitment to diversity, a reputation/resource orientation, and a student-centered orientation. Parallel measures, obtained independent of student observation, for an institution's student-centered priorities included campus expenditures (per student) in the areas of student services and student aid (non-repayable grants and fellowships). High expenditures in these areas reflect student-centered priorities, particularly in an era of budget constraint and shrinking governmental resources. Measures reflecting the college composition, the proportion of black and Hispanic undergraduate enrollment in 1986 and ethnic enrollment changes over a six-year period (1982–88), served to test race relations theories based on relative numbers. They also controlled for institutional differences that were observed in previous studies of the racial climate [23], and as parallel measures of institutional commitment to diversity. The enrollment change measures were designed to capture changes in student diversity at each institution prior to and during the enrollment of the 1985–89 cohort. Two additional college composition variables, institutional size and selectivity, served to test alternative interpretations regarding campus conflict [5].

Five factors derived from previous climate studies [20, 29] were used in the regression analyses of campus racial tension on student and institutional characteristics. Because items were on similar scales (table 15-A2), new variables were created by summing responses on each item to construct a factor scale. Table 15-1 shows that all the scales have fairly high reliabilities that are similar across groups. The range on reliabilities across groups for a socioeconomic status factor was too wide to be considered a generalizable construct in analyses across groups, therefore, multiple indicators (parental income and the level of mother's and father's education) were entered in the equation with full recognition that this might underestimate the effects of each indicator. The effects of these variables and other complex relationships among the independent variables were carefully monitored prior to and after entry into the equation using a computer software program, *Betaview*, designed for this purpose [21].

Analyses

Student perceptions of racial climate issues at all types of four-year institutions were examined using bivariate analyses of national normative data. Ethnic group differences on all variables were assessed using two-tailed tests of significance on the selected sample of black, Chicano, and white students. Because ethnic groups differed significantly in their perceptions of the environment, separate group analyses were conducted using multiple regression techniques to assess the relationship between perceptions of campus racial tension and student and institutional characteristics. Variables

Table 15-1

Factor Scales: Estimates of Internal Consistencies (Alpha) by Student Sample

Factor Scale	Number of Items	Black	Chicano	White
Campus racial tension	3	0.66	0.66	0.64
Social self-confidence	3	0.76	0.75	0.73
Institutional commitment to diversity	4	0.88	0.86	0.80
Student-centered orientation	5	0.75	0.80	0.83
Resource/reputation orientation	5	0.77	0.79	0.76

NOTE: Confirmatory and exploratory procedures used to develop factors are reported in Hurtado [29] and Dey [20]. Items constituting each scale are reported in table A-2.

were entered in three stages to observe changes in regression coefficients. The first stage explored the extent to which perceptions of racial tension were a function of the cultural and psychological baggage that students bring with them to college, including demographic attributes and tendencies that might suggest a precollege bias in their views regarding the climate. Institutional priorities, hypothesized to be the primary explanatory variables that would diminish the impact of college composition variables (size and selectivity), were entered in the next stage. College composition variables were entered in the final stage to determine if these structural aspects of the environment remain central to shaping perceptions of the climate. Interaction terms representing (1) high resource/reputation priorities and institutional commitment to diversity and (2) high resource/reputation and student-centered priorities were forward entered in a second regression model for each group to determine if these combinations could account for a significant addition in the proportion of variance in the dependent variable.

Results

National normative data are presented in table 15-2 to provide an overview of student perceptions of the racial climate, highlighting differences among four-year colleges and universities. Student views on the existence of racial discrimination show the least variation across all institution types. Only about 12 percent of all students at four-year institutions agreed with the statement that "racial discrimination is no longer a problem in America," indicating

that most undergraduates feel that this form of discrimination is still an issue to contend with in our society. At the same time, items measuring student perceptions of campus race relations reflect a much wider range of responses between institution types. This suggests that though most students acknowledge the existence of racial discrimination, their perceptions of race relations on campus vary according to their experiences in different institutional contexts.

Data show that approximately one in four students at all four-year institutions perceive considerable racial conflict; however, this proportion is higher in university settings (approximately one in three students). It is also important to note that most students agree that "students of different ethnic origins communicate well with one another" on their campus, with the lowest proportion of students agreeing with this statement at private (59 percent) and public universities (61 percent). When compared with other institution types, students at both public and private universities were also more likely to report a lack of trust between minority student groups and administrators (36 and 39 percent, respectively). These results support accounts of racial incidents and related protests occurring primarily at public and private universities from 1985 to 1989 [25].

Private four-year colleges fared better than universities and public four-year colleges on most racial climate measures. Students at Catholic institutions are least likely to report racial conflict (12 percent) or mistrust between minority groups and administrators (16 percent); and are most likely to report good communication among ethnic groups (82 percent).

Table 15-2

Student Perceptions of Racial Issues at Four-Year Colleges and Universities, 1989 Follow-up Survey of Fall 1985 Freshmen

| | All Institutions | Universities | | Four-Year Colleges | | | | Institutional Range (high to low) |
		Public	Private	Public	Private Nonsectarian	Catholic	Protestant	
Agreement with the Statement:[1]								
Racial discrimination is no longer a problem in America	12	11	9	15	11	8	12	7
Statements about the Institution:[1]								
There is a lot of campus racial conflict here	25	34	34	21	17	12	16	22
Many courses include minority perspectives	47	46	41	49	50	43	47	9
Students of different ethnic origins communicate well with one another	68	61	59	69	77	82	76	23
There is little trust between minority student groups and administrators	31	36	3	34	21	16	19	23
Most faculty here are sensitive to the issues of minorities	67	61	65	65	76	70	81	20
Institutional Priorities:[2]								
Create a diverse multicultural environment on campus	42	43	40	42	42	45	37	8
Develop among faculty and students an appreciation for a multicultural society	31	36	40	42	46	45	45	10
Increase minority representation in the faculty and administration	29	30	25	32	27	23	22	10
Recruit more minority students	41	40	40	47	36	29	33	18

Source: National normative data, Higher Education Research Institute, UCLA. Responses are statistically adjusted to correct for non-response and weighted to) approximate the national population of 1985 first-time, full-time freshmen. (For weighting procedures see Higher Education Research Institute, 1991).
1. Percent who "agree strongly" or "agree somewhat."
2. Percent rating priority is "high" or "highest."

While over two-thirds of all students report that most faculty are sensitive to the issues of minorities, a higher proportion of students at Protestant (81 percent) and nonsectarian four-year colleges (76 percent) perceive this to be the case. In addition, a general measure of curriculum integration shows that the highest proportion of undergraduates (50 percent) report that many courses include minority perspectives at nonsectarian four-year colleges.

Two general observations are made regarding student perceptions of specific institutional priorities for cultural diversity. First, there is a somewhat smaller institutional range of student views on diversity priorities compared with views on campus race relations, indicating diversity priorities may be more consistent across institutions. Institutions differed most on priorities to diversify the student body, faculty, and the administration. Students at public four-year colleges (47 percent) and universities (40 percent) are more likely than students at private four-year colleges to report minority student recruitment was a "high" or the "highest priority" at their institution. Students at public institutions were also more likely than students at private institutions to report that increasing the representation of minorities in the faculty and administration was a high priority (30–32 percent).

Although these differences in priorities for diversity may be cause for concern, perhaps a more general concern is related to the second observation: less than a third of the students perceive specific goals to change the racial composition of the institution, and less than half perceive general goals for fostering cultural or racial diversity to be a high institutional priority. Given public statements regarding the importance of diversity and the general nature of items reflecting priorities to "create a diverse multicultural environment on campus" and "develop an appreciation for a multicultural society among faculty and students," one wonders why more students do not perceive these to be a high priority on campuses. To what extent are students' perception of racial tension on campus related to their view of institutional priorities for cultural diversity? What can explain the institutional contradictions between priorities and race relations observed here and in previous studies [49, 23]? While institutional type and control are helpful

in locating the problems within the higher education system, they are of limited practical significance to administrators in addressing problems within institutional settings. Subsequent analyses focused on the relationship between institutional priorities and campus racial tension, with appropriate controls for student and institutional characteristics, to provide insights into contexts for conflict and contradiction.

Table 15-3 shows means, standard deviations, and tests of significance on all measures used in analyses of the selected sample of black, Chicano, and white students. This table describes the sample and shows that significant group differences were detected on most freshmen characteristics and perceptions of the environment. The Chicano students came from families with significantly lower levels of educational attainment and lower incomes ($\overline{X} \approx$ \$27,850) than either their black or white classmates. Upon college entry in 1985, Chicanos were also less likely to characterize themselves as politically liberal. Black students entered college with significantly higher social self-confidence. They were more likely than other students in the sample to become involved in campus protest, characterize their views as politically liberal, and place a high value on helping to promote racial understanding. In contrast, white students had significantly higher GPAs, college-educated parents, higher family incomes ($\overline{X} \approx$ \$42,100), and were less likely to place a high value on promoting racial understanding than the minority students. These results suggest that these are important student background characteristics to take into account in assessing institutional contexts that inform perceptions of campus racial tension.

Given these freshmen differences in relative status and social views, we would expect their perceptions of the environment to vary considerably four years after college entry. Black students were more critical of their environments than the other student groups: they perceive relatively higher levels of racial tension and lower levels of institutional commitment to diversity at their institutions. Chicanos were least likely to perceive that their institution had student-centered priorities. However, there appeared to be consensus across all groups on institutional priorities for resource and reputation enhancement, as there were no significant differences among groups. Significant group

Table 15-3

Means, Standard Deviations, and Tests of Significance on Variables by Group

Variables	White (n = 1821) Mean	S. D.	Black (n = 325) Mean	S. D.	Chicano (n = 340) Mean	S. D.	Significant Differences		
1985 Student Characteristics									
Sex (female)	1.58	0.49	1.61	0.49	1.64	0.48		C*	
Age	3.12	0.47	3.03	0.48	3.19	0.53	A**	B**	C*
High-school GPA	6.36	1.39	5.59	1.60	5.95	1.41	A**	B**	C**
Mother's education	5.36	1.78	5.07	1.95	3.50	2.10	A**	B**	C**
Father's education	6.10	1.90	4.87	2.11	3.89	2.37	A**	B**	C**
Income	9.19	2.97	6.73	3.18	6.54	3.12	A**		C**
Social self-confidence	10.78	1.95	10.99	2.17	10.55	2.03		B**	
Expect to protest	2.35	0.83	2.44	0.83	2.24	0.87		B**	C**
Political view (liberal)	3.06	0.78	3.32	0. 64	3.02	0.71	A**	B**	
Promote racial understanding	2.27	0.83	3.14	0.79	2.55	0.83	A**	B**	C**
Institutional Characteristics									
Institutional Priorities									
Expenditures:									
Student services	865.32	701.54	899.54	618.67	842.93	764.22			
Non-repayable aid	1345.88	939.09	1576.17	1008.69	1124.31	730.68	A**	B**	C**
Student Perceptions:									
Student-oriented	12.45	2.98	12.39	2.66	11.78	3.11		B**	C**
Resource/reputation-oriented	14.33	3.23	14.35	3.30	14.61	3.47			
Commitment to diversity	9.51	2.73	8.94	3.38	9.57	3.08	A**	B**	
College composition:									
Selectivity (Average SAT)	105.38	14.27	108.16	15.72	98.42	13.64	A**	B**	C**
Enrollment:									
Size (total FTE)	6.28	2.16	5.72	1.95	6.39	2.38	A**	B**	
Black percent in 1986	4.68	3.10	5.53	3.35	4.21	2.45	A**	B**	C**
Hispanic percent in 1986	5.60	6.84	3.30	5.33	14.29	16.27	A**	B**	C**
Black increase (1982–89)	1.64	0.48	1.57	0.50	1.70	0.46	A*	B**	C*
Hispanic increase (1982–88)	2.55	0.83	2.48	0.87	2.69	0.73		B**	C**
Dependent Variable									
Campus Racial Tension	6.70	1.90	7.85	2.07	6.73	2.03	A**	B**	

NOTE: Variable scales are reported in table A-1. Significant group differences, *$p \le 0.05$. ** $p \le 0.01$ (two-tailed probability): A = white/black difference, B = black/Chicano difference, C = Chicano/white difference.

differences were also detected among college composition variables (size, selectivity, ethnic enrollment). This is due primarily to the distinct distribution of Chicano and black students among institution types: Chicanos were concentrated in larger, less selective institutions with a higher proportion of Hispanic enrollment.

Table 15-4 shows the regression results for the three ethnic groups. Beta coefficients are shown at two steps: β^1 is the value of each regression coefficient at the step where all student characteristics are controlled, and β^2 represents the value of the coefficient at the final step of the equation. The β^1 coefficient represents the effect of a variable, net of student characteristics and prior to competing with other environmental variables in the equation. These coefficients are shown to (1) consider alternative interpretations that can be derived from other models that may exclude some of the environmental measures and (2) evaluate the performance of some of the data obtained independent of student observation (expenditures and enrollments) in comparison to student perceptions. T-ratios represent the magnitude of the coefficient, taking into account its standard error of estimate; these values are presented in lieu of unstandardized coefficients to compare effects across groups at the final step of the equation. Overall, the regression models account for 36 percent of the variance in campus racial tension in the Chicano, 24 percent in the black, and 19 percent in the white student samples.

Student Characteristics

Results show that white students who entered college expecting to become involved in campus protest, white females, and black students who characterized their views as politically liberal are inclined to perceive racial tension on campus. It may be that these types of students are predisposed to view the climate critically and are sensitive to issues of racial and social inequality. In the wake of harassment incidents on campus, these students may have also found themselves in the forefront of protests to pressure institutions into formulating a response. Prior to the entry of institutional characteristics in the equations, the significant betas (β^1) of other student variables show that perceptions of racial tension are also prevalent among Chicanos who expected to become involved in

campus protest. Additional characteristics of white students who perceive racial tension include those with a higher level of social self-confidence, parental income, mother's education, and a higher GPA. These latter student characteristics do not maintain significant coefficients in the final steps of the regression equations due to their association with institutional characteristics that have relatively strong effects (for example, selectivity). Thus, perceptions of racial tension are not created solely in the minds of specific individuals, but rather are rooted in a shared institutional reality.

Institutional Characteristics

Across all groups, students perceive low racial tension at institutions with high student-centered priorities. This relationship remains significant after controlling for institution size, college composition variables, and other institutional priorities. Betas at the step where all student characteristics are controlled (β^1) also indicate that institutional spending priorities may play an indirect role in relation to campus racial tension. Campus expenditures for student aid (among Chicano and white students) and student services (among black and white students) are negatively associated with perceptions of racial tension. The changes in the coefficients for these expenditure measures were monitored throughout the equations, revealing that perceptions of student-centered priorities account for much of their effect on perceptions of racial tension. These institutional spending priorities are associated with perceptions of an overall environment of student support that, in turn, are associated with perceptions of lower racial tension. Results on these parallel measures of student support extend earlier findings that were derived from a model of campus racial tension that included only expenditure measures (distal measures) [29].

Data support the notion that an institutional commitment to diversity can substantially improve minority and, to some extent, white student perceptions of race relations on campus. Perceptions of institutional commitment to diversity maintained a strong negative association with perceptions of racial tension among black and Chicano students. Similarly, white students' perceptions of institutional commitment to diversity were associated with a

Table 15-4

Regression of Campus Racial Tension on Student and Institutional Characteristics by Group

Standardized Regression Coefficients and T Ratios for:

	White (n = 1821)			Black (n = 325)			Chicano (n = 340)		
	β¹	β²	t	β¹	β²	t	β¹	β²	t
1985 Student Characteristics									
Sex (female)	0.02	0.06	2.65	0.02	0.05	0.86	−0.05	0.03	0.64
Age	−0.03	−0.01	−0.56	−0.03	−0.01	0.23	−0.02	0.06	1.11
High-school GPA	0.10**	0.01	0.53	0.01	−0.06	−1.10	0.04	−0.04	−0.86
Mother's education	0.04*	0.04	1.64	−0.03	−0.02	−0.32	−0.02	−0.00	−0.04
Father's education	0.02	−0.01	−0.35	−0.01	−0.00	−0.05	−0.10	−0.13	−1.88
Income	0.05*	0.01	0.48	0.05	−0.03	−0.47	0.08	0.01	0.22
Social self-confidence	0.06*	0.03	1.55	0.01	0.05	1.00	0.03	−0.01	−0.21
Expect to protest in college	0.15**	0.12	5.20	0.06	0.04	0.70	0.18**	0.10	1.89
Political view (liberal)	0.02	0.02	0.85	0.23**	0.18	3.41	0.09	0.04	0.88
Goal: helping to promote racial understanding	0.00	0.02	0.68	0.02	0.04	0.70	0.06	0.09	1.70
Institutional Characteristics									
Institutional Priorities									
Expenditures (per student):									
Student services	−0.09**	0.01	0.48	−0.15**	−0.08	−1.17	−0.07	−0.04	−0.60
Non-repayable student aid	−0.09**	−0.00	−0.05	−0.11	−0.12	−1.32	−0.19**	0.01	0.14
Student Perceptions of Priorities:									
Student-centered	−0.28**	−0.20	−7.48	−0.29**	−0.22	−3.58	−0.38**	−0.18	−3.06
Resource/reputation	0.17**	0.06	2.64	0.20**	0.12	2.15	0.22**	0.08	1.57
Commitment to diversity	−0.05*	−0.03	−1.28	−0.28**	−0.18	−3.14	−0.23**	−0.20	−4.03
College composition:									
Selectivity (Average SAT)	0.16**	0.19	5.56	0.09	0.17	2.13	0.31**	0.29	3.17
Enrollment:									
Size (total FTE)	0.23**	0.14	3.48	0.14**	−0.12	−1.42	0.36**	0.10	0.97
Black percent in 1986	0.07**	0.11	5.09	−0.05	0.00	−0.01	−0.13*	0.05	0.68
Hispanic percent in 1986	−0.08**	−0.05	−2.15	−0.03	0.02	0.42	−0.31**	−0.07	−0.64
Black increase (1982–88)	0.13**	0.06	2.08	−0.06	0.01	0.14	0.28**	0.13	1.94
Hispanic increase (1982–88)	0.07**	−0.02	−0.66	−0.12*	−0.10	−1.65	0.12*	0.04	0.62
R²	0.19			0.24			0.36		

NOTE: β¹ is reported at the step where all student characteristics were controlled, (* $p = \leq 0.05$. ** $p = \leq 0.01$); β² is reported at final step of the evaluation. T ratios (reported at the final step) of approximately 1.96 or greater are significant at the 0.05 level, and 2.59 or greater are significant at the 0.01 level.

small negative effect on racial tension prior to controlling for other environmental characteristics (β^1). However, the effect for white students became non-significant when measures of student-centered priorities were controlled (β^2). This difference between white and minority groups will be discussed in the latter part of this article. It is important to note here, however, that perceptions of institutional commitment to diversity do not significantly contribute to white student perceptions of racial tension.

Although college selectivity and priorities for resource/reputation enhancement are often associated with traditional notions of quality, they maintain unique effects on racial tension in the black and white student samples and are more closely linked in the Chicano sample. Black and white students who perceive that their institutions have high resource and reputation priorities perceive high racial tension. In addition, institutional selectivity was a positive indicator of perceptions of racial tension across all ethnic groups. The unique effects of selectivity on perceptions of racial tension are maintained over and above student characteristics and campus priorities for resource and reputation enhancement. This suggests that selectivity is not merely a proxy for the type of student an institution recruits, nor can priorities for resource/reputation enhancement fully explain why we observe racial conflict in selective institutions.

Interaction terms that represent (1) high resource/reputation and institutional commitment to diversity and (2) high resource/reputation and student-centered orientation were introduced in subsequent models (not shown) to test whether these combinations of priorities were significantly related to racial tension. The interaction terms did not contribute significantly to the proportion of variance explained in the dependent measure. Therefore, these dimensions of institutional priorities appear to work independently and are not likely to have an additive effect on perceptions of racial tension.

Differences among the ethnic groups are evident in the relationship between enrollments and perceptions of racial tension. The effect of institutional size on perceptions of racial tension was diminished substantially by other institutional measures in all student groups, yet it maintains a positive association with perceptions of racial tension among white students. Similarly, the various effects of the ethnic enrollment measures on minority student perceptions of racial tension were diminished when other institutional characteristics were taken into account (β^2). In contrast, white students' perceptions of racial tension were significantly influenced by minority enrollments. The proportion of black students and increases in black enrollment are positively associated and Hispanic enrollment is negatively associated with white students' perception of racial tension on campus. There are at least two possible explanations for this difference between white and minority students and the contradictory effect of Hispanic enrollment: (1) as some race relations theories propose, white students may feel threatened by the presence of an increasing number of black students [11] or (2) ethnic enrollment differences in the institutional sample may indicate that the effects of the minority composition of a college on racial tension may be nonlinear.

To investigate nonlinear effects, the quadratic and cubic terms of the proportion of black students were added hierarchically to the regression models for each group. Although the cubic term was significant in the white student sample, when compared with the base model, there was no change in the direction of effects and the additional proportion of variance accounted for was too small to determine a nonlinear trend in the data. Still, the different distribution of black and Hispanic enrollments at the institutions in this sample may be indicative of nonlinear effects. None of the institutions had a black student population higher than 26 percent, and two institutions in the sample were Hispanic-serving institutions (HSIs)[3] with Hispanic enrollments approaching 30 and 50 percent respectively. Moreover, these institutions were located in cities with predominantly Hispanic populations. It may be that white students' perceptions of racial tension are lower in these institutional contexts not so much because of the ethnicity of the changing population, but because of the higher proportion of culturally diverse students and the general multicultural context of community in which they are located.

Summary and Discussion

National data show that approximately one in four students perceived considerable racial conflict at four-year institutions in the late 1980s. Considering the substantial media attention devoted to racial issues on campus in recent years, some may think this proportion is small. However, the proportion of students reporting racial conflict was higher in university settings (approximately one-third). This proportion is significant given that racial tension escalated to the point of creating serious disruptions at several campuses [25, 60]. At the same time that institutions were experiencing racial conflict, students were critical of institutional priorities to improve the racial climate. Less than a third of the students reported priorities to increase the representation of minorities through student and administrator/faculty recruitment, and less than half reported that general goals for fostering a multicultural environment were a high priority at their institution.

Although there are slight differences in reporting categories, results from the 1989 Follow-up of students replicate several general findings of the 1989 ACE survey of academic administrators [23]. Perceptions of campus race relations and various diversity priorities are not uniform across different institutional contexts. A higher proportion of universities and public four-year colleges have initiated efforts to diversify their environments, yet these institutions also have relatively higher racial tension than private four-year colleges. There also appears to be a public/private institutional dichotomy among four-year colleges in the quality of race relations and priorities for diversity: students at private four-year colleges perceive better overall campus race relations than public four-year institutions. At the same time, a smaller proportion of students perceive that the recruitment of minority students and administrators/faculty is a high priority at private four-year institutions. Ethnic group analyses revealed that these contradictory patterns may be due to differences in college composition and distinct institutional priorities that shape the general campus climate.

Institutions may foster racial tension when they support priorities that work against promoting a better climate. Specifically, traditional notions of quality based on selectivity and resource/reputation priorities are associated with perceptions of high racial tension. Selective institutions are unique environments, they are not simply contexts of individual achievement as proposed in the adaptation model for diversity [51]. They represent an extreme in American wealth and privilege, are staunch promoters of tradition, and are the rungs to powerful positions in society. Although resistance to change may be greatest at these institutions, they are also birthplaces for progressive thought. Racial tension may be highest in these contradictory environments because institutional commitment to diversity is often ambivalent, mitigated by other institutional actions that systematically exclude minorities and their perspectives.

In retrospect, the narrow focus on the enhancement of reputation and resources and moves to increase the selectivity of institutions may have more to do with maintaining inequalities than with actually improving the overall quality of college environments. Our definition of quality and its implementations are laden with assumptions that carry implicit messages to members of the campus community. Narrow conceptions of "quality" often favor elitism rather than egalitarianism, homogeneity rather than diversity, and the unequal distribution of resources. Institutions have opposed diversification of the curriculum, student body, and faculty; concentrated resources in a few individuals (for example, "faculty stars"); and often excluded minorities—all in the name of "quality." This justification is constructed to maintain" harmonious inequality" and may heighten racial tension when groups challenge these actions and their underlying assumptions. The apparent link between racial tension and traditional notions of quality should serve as the impetus for reframing our conceptions of quality to focus on improving the overall condition of life on campus. The quality of life on campus includes both the campus racial climate and the environment of support for students.

Along these lines, black and Chicano student perceptions of institutional commitment to diversity are associated with perceptions of relatively low racial tension. Among white students, this relationship is weaker and appears to be indirect: institutional commitment to diversity is tied to how an institution treats students (student-centered priorities), which in turn, affects perceptions of racial tension on campus. The difference between groups may be partially explained by results that show white students are less likely to perceive racial tension. Minorities are more aware of racial tension both for historical reasons and because they, unlike white students who are a numerical majority, must depend on constant interracial contact in social, learning, and work spheres on predominantly white campuses.

History reflects that substantial barriers delayed minority progress to attain full participation in American life, and removal of these barriers for racial integration and participation in education required both collective action and institutional change [15]. This progress is still in evolution in our society, as minorities continue to enter college from substantially different social backgrounds (income and parental education) compared to white classmates. Black and Chicano students may feel that institutional initiatives can improve the condition of a racial climate that affects daily interactions, whereas white students may feel the same way about more general climate issues. Thus, institutions that increase their commitment to diversity may significantly improve minority student perceptions of the racial climate. Results also indicate that institutional commitment to diversity does not fuel perceptions of racial tension among the majority of white students. A small proportion (12 percent) of students believe that racial discrimination is no longer a problem in our society, suggesting that only a small (sometimes vocal) group may oppose measures designed to improve the climate for diversity.

A central finding of this study is that racial tension may arise in environments where there is a lack of concern for individual students. Across all groups, perceptions of student-centered priorities were important predictors of perceptions of low racial tension. These results provide empirical support for the importance of "setting a 'tone' that is congenial to all students" [47, p. 645] on college campuses. It may be that racial tensions are higher in environments where students believe that particular groups have special privileges or receive more attention when, in fact, all groups are experiencing a decline in the quality of support for students. Expenditures in the areas of student services

and student grant/scholarship aid secure the environment of support for student development, resulting in a more favorable climate. Institutions should stand firm on issues that maintain support for students, particularly in light of declining federal commitment to issues that affect minority and low-income students. Campuses should seek opportunities to reconfigure resources and rewards to create student-centered priorities that will benefit all students. For example, institutions may devote more attention to student-centered approaches that involve faculty in both the personal and academic development of students. This approach may both reduce racial tension and improve social and academic outcomes for students.

Researchers have proposed that the effect of institutional size on campus conflict and racial policies was due to the impersonal environment of large campuses and their ability to attract more liberal or protest "prone" students [5]. Controls for student characteristics and student-centered priorities in the analyses show that these conclusions are only partially supported. While certain types of students may be more critical of the racial climate and an environment of student support was found to be essential, institutional size remains a significant predictor of perceptions of racial tension among white students. This suggests that there is more to large campus environments and their differential impact on racial/ethnic groups than we understand. Minority student perceptions of racial tension may be mediated by other institutional characteristics (for example, ethnic enrollments) and perhaps their ability to develop their own niche in large institutional settings [10]. Although all students may use this adaptive strategy, white students may view the prevalence of "niches" developed along mutual interests and ethnicity as increasing racial tension on large campuses. This area requires further research to understand how minority and white students make sense of large environments and whether their approaches may be conducive to relations across ethnic groups.

Results from assessing the effect of ethnic composition of a college, or the "compositional hypothesis" [26], are mixed. Increases in black enrollment over the last six years and the proportion of black enrollment are associated with white students' perception of high racial tension; however, the proportion of Hispanic enrollment had the opposite effect. It is difficult to determine whether different effects of relative size of the two ethnic groups may be due to substantially different relations with white students or may be explained by institutional sampling variability. Institutions with a broad range of ethnic enrollments should be added to the sample in the future to settle the question of whether there is a population "threshold" point that determines differences in relations among various ethnic groups on college campuses.

In any case, predominantly white campuses may be relatively unprepared for some of the problems accompanying change in their student bodies—particularly in the wake of impending demographic changes [24]. These findings indicate, and reports of racial incidents confirm [25], that black-white relations are generally in need of improvement on college campuses where enrollment shifts are occurring. Race relations theorists would conclude that, due to competition for resources, white students view black students as a threat to their group position [11]. The fact that student-centered priorities are associated with lower racial tension suggests that some campuses may have minimized feelings of competition among groups. The relative status differences among students of different racial/ethnic groups (social background and relative size of the groups) suggest structural conditions that may inform a sense of group position, however, it is not clear whether white students feel they are in competition with black students for limited institutional resources. The actual motivations for racial tension require further research to conclusively determine how different ethnic groups perceive one another in relation to their environments.

Conclusion

This study has shown that perhaps no single element of the environment may work to produce racial tension on college campuses. It is a configuration of external influences (historical and contemporary), structural characteristics of institutions and group relations, and institutionalized ideologies. Each of these areas requires our attention in efforts to promote civility and foster values in students that will

serve them in an increasingly multicultural society. These efforts should be guided by a willingness to question our assumptions, consideration of the experiences of different ethnic groups, and an overriding concern for a quality of life on campus that will be conducive to student development. Further research on the experiences of different ethnic groups may help determine elements of our environments that uniquely contribute to the development of each group.

Notes

1. In the case of minority-targeted scholarships, the defense of individual privilege ran counter to group norms. As the Bush Administration questioned the legality of minority-targeted scholarships, the 1990 General Social Survey showed that the majority of the American public (69 percent of the white and 95 percent of the black population) supported special college scholarships for black students who maintain good grades [13]. Shaky legal rationale was used to defend individual privilege [45], even while there was widespread public support for minority-targeted scholarships.

2. The U.S. Department of Education still collects and reports data on Chicanos under the umbrella category of "Hispanic" even though census data and educational data show dramatic differences among Latino groups [24]. Chicanos represent the majority of the Hispanic enrollment in this sample of institutions.

3. According to the Hispanic Association of Colleges and Universities (HACU), a Hispanic-serving institution is one that meets a Hispanic enrollment minimum of 25 percent.

References

1. Allen, W. R. "Black Student, White Campus: Structural, Interpersonal, and Psychological Correlates of Success." *Journal of Negro Education*, 54 (1985), 134–37.

2. _____. "Black Students in U.S. Higher Education: Toward Improved Access, Adjustment, and Achievement," *The Urban Review*, 20 (1988), 165–87.

3. American Council on Education. "Bush's Plan Would Reduce Pell Grants." *Higher Education and National Affairs*, 40 (11 March 1991).

4. Arce, C. H. "Chicano Participation in Academe: A Case of Academic Colonialism," *Grito del Sol: Chicano Quarterly*, 3 (1978), 75–104.

5. Astin, A. W. "New Evidence on Campus Unrest, 1969–70." *Educational Record,* (Winter 1971), 41–46.

6. _____. *Achieving Educational Excellence.* San Francisco: Jossey-Bass, 1985.

7. _____. *Four Critical Years.* San Francisco: Jossey-Bass. 1977.

8. _____. *The Black Undergraduate: Current Status and Trends in the Characteristics of Freshmen.* Los Angeles: Higher Education Research Institute, 1990.

9. Astin, A. W., and J. W. Henson. "New Measures of College Selectivity." *Research in Higher Education, 7* (1977), 1–9.

10. Attinasi, L. C., Jr. "Getting In: Mexican Americans' Perceptions of University Attendance and the Implications for Freshman Year Persistence." *Journal of Higher Education,* (May/June 1989), 247–77.

11. Blalock, J. M., Jr. *Toward a Theory of Minority-Group Relations.* New York: Wiley, 1967.

12. Blumer, H. "Race Prejudice as a Sense of Group Position." *Pacific Sociological Review, 1* (1958), 3–7.

13. Bobo, L., and J. R. Kluegel. "Opposition to Race-Targeting: Self-interest, Stratification Ideology, or Prejudice?" A paper delivered at the American Association of Public Opinion Research, Phoenix, Arizona, May 1991.

14. Bowles, S., and H. Gintis. *Schooling in Capitalist America.* London: Routledge and Kegan Paul, 1977.

15. Branch, T. *Parting the Waters: America in the King Years, 1954–63.* New York: Simon and Schuster. 1989.

16. Brown v. Board of Education, 347 US 483 (1954).

17. Carter, D. J., and R. Wilson. *Minorities in Higher Education: Eighth Annual Status Report.* Washington, D.C.: American Council on Education, 1990.

18. _____. *Minorities in Higher Education: Ninth Annual Status Report.* Washington, D.C.: American Council on Education, 1991.

19. Carter-Williams, M. "The Eroding Status of Blacks in Higher Education: An Issue of Financial Aid." In *Black Education: A Quest for Equity and Excellence,* edited by W. D. Smith and E. W. Chunn. New Brunswick, N.J.: Transaction Publishers, 1989.

20. Dey, E. L. *Perceptions of the College Environment: An Analysis of Organizational, Interpersonal, and Behavioral Influences.* Ph.D. dissertation, University of California, Los Angeles, 1991. Ann Arbor: University Microfilms International. No: 9119161.

21. _____. *Beta View.* [Computer program]. Los Angeles: Higher Education Research Institute, 1990.

22. Dey, E. L., A. W. Astin, and W. S. Korn. *The American Freshman: Twenty-Five Year Trends.* Los Angeles: Higher Education Research Institute, 1991.

23. El-Khawas, E. *Campus Trends, 1989.* Higher education panel reports, no. 78. Washington, D.C.: American Council on Education, 1989.

24. Estrada, L. F. "Anticipating the Demographic Future." *Change, 20* (1988), 14–19.

25. Farrell, W. C. Jr., and C. K. Jones. "Recent Racial Incidents in Higher Education: A Preliminary Perspective." *The Urban Review, 20* (1988). 211–33.

26. Fossett, M. A., and K. J. Kiecolt. "The Relative Size of Minority Populations and White Racial Attitudes." *Social Science Quarterly, 70* (1989), 820–35.

27. Giroux, H. A. "Theories of Reproduction and Resistance in the New Sociology of Education: A Critical Analysis." *Harvard Educational Review, 53* (1983). 257–93.

28. Gurin, P., and E. Epps. *Black Consciousness, Identity, and Achievement: A Study of Students in Historically Black Colleges.* New York: Wiley, 1975.

29. Hurtado, S. *Campus Racial Climates and Educational Outcomes.* Ph.D. dissertation, University of California. Los Angeles, 1990. Ann Arbor: University Microfilms International, No: 9111328.

30. Higher Education Research Institute. *The American College Student, 1989: National Norms for 1985 and 1987 College Freshmen.* Los Angeles: Higher Education Research Institute, 1991.

31. Jackman, M. R. "Prejudice, Tolerance, and Attitudes Toward Ethnic Groups." *Social Science Research, 6* (1977), 145–69.

32. Jackman, M. R., and M. J. Muha. "Education and Intergroup Attitudes: Moral Enlightenment. Superficial Democratic Commitment, or Ideological Refinement?" *American Sociological Review, 49* (1984), 751–69.

33. Jacob, J. E. "Black America 1987: An Overview." In *The State of Black America, 1988,* edited by J. Dewart. New York: National Urban League, 1988.

34. Jessor, R. "The Perceived Environment in Psychological Theory and Research." In *Toward a Psychology of Situations: An Interactional Perspective,* edited by D. Magnusson. Hillsdale, N.J.: Lawrence Erlbaum Associates, 1981, 297–317.

35. Kanter, R. M. "Some Effects of Proportions on Group Life: Skewed Sex Ratios and Responses to Token Women." *American Journal of Sociology, 82* (1977), 965–89.

36. Kiecolt, K. J. "Recent Developments in Attitudes and Social Structure." *Annual Review of Sociology, 14* (1988), 381–403.

37. Loo, C. M., and G. Rolison. "Alienation of Ethnic Minority Students at a Predominantly White University." *Journal of Higher Education, 57* (1986), 58–77.

38. McClelland, K. E., and C. J. Auster. "Public Platitudes and Hidden Tensions: Racial Climates at Predominantly White Liberal Arts

Colleges." *Journal of Higher Education,* 61 (November/December 1990), 607–42.

39. Moos, R. H. *Evaluating Educational Environments.* San Francisco: Jossey-Bass, 1979.

40. National Institute against Prejudice and Violence, "Conflict Continues on U.S. Campuses." *Forum,* 5 (November 1990), 1–2.

41. Nettles, M. T. "Black and White Students' Academic Performance in Majority White and Majority Black College Settings." In *Desegregating America's Colleges and Universities,* edited by J. B. Williams III. New York: Teachers College Press, 1988.

42. Nettles, M. T., A. R. Thoeny, and E. J. Gosman. "Comparative and Predictive Analyses of Black and White Students' College Achievement and Experiences." *Journal of Higher Education,* 57 (1986), 289–318.

43. Olivas, M. A. "Research and Theory on Hispanic Education: Students, Finance, and Governance." *Atzlan, International Journal of Chicano Studies Research,* 14 (1983), 111–46.

44. _____. "Research on Latino College Students: A Theoretical Framework for Inquiry." In *Latino College Students,* edited by M. A. Olivas. New York: Teachers College Press, 1986.

45. _____. "Federal Law and Scholarship Policy: An Essay on the Office for Civil Rights, Title VI, and Racial Restrictions." *Journal of College and University Law,* 18 (1991), 21–28.

46. Oliver, M. L., C. J. Rodriguez, and R. A. Mickelson. "Brown and Black in White: The Social Adjustment and Academic Performance of Chicano and Black Students in a Predominantly White University." *The Urban Review: Issues and Ideas in Public Education,* 17 (1985), 3–24.

47. Pascarella, E. T., and P. T. Terenzini. *How College Affects Students.* San Francisco: Jossey-Bass, 1991.

48. Patterson, A. M., W. E. Sedlacek, and F. W. Perry. "Perceptions of Blacks and Hispanics in Two Campus Environments." *Journal of College Student Personnel,* 25 (1984), 513–18.

49. Peterson, M. W., et al. *Black Students on White Campuses: The Impacts of Increased Black Enrollments.* Ann Arbor: Institute for Social Research, 1978.

50. Reyes, M. D., and J. J. Halcón. "Racism in Academia: The Old Wolf Revisited." *Harvard Educational Review,* 58 (1988), 299–314.

51. Richardson, R. C., Jr., and E. F. Skinner. "Adapting to Diversity: Organizational Influences on Student Achievement." *Journal of Higher Education,* 61 (September/October 1990), 485–511.

52. Skinner, E. F., and R. C. Richardson, Jr. "Making it in a Majority University." *Change,* 20 (May/June 1988), 34–42.

53. Smith, D. G. "The Challenge of Diversity: Involvement or Alienation in the Academy?" *ASHE-ERIC Higher Education Report* 5, 1989. Washington: George Washington University.

54. Smith, D. H. "Social and Academic Environments of Black Students on White Campuses." *Journal of Negro Education,* 50 (1981). 299–306.

55. Stoecker, J., E. T. Pascarella, and L. M. Wolfle. "Persistence in Higher Education: A 9-year Test of a Theoretical Model." *Journal of College Student Personnel,* 29 (1988), 196–209.

56. Sudarkasa, N. "Black Enrollment in Higher Education: The Unfulfilled Promise of Equality." In *The State of Black America,* edited by J. Dewart. New York: National Urban League, 1988.

57. Tracey, T. J., and W. E. Sedlacek. "A Comparison of White and Black Student Academic Success Using Noncognitive Variables: A LISREL Analysis." *Research in Higher Education,* 27 (1987), 333–48.

58. Tracey, T. J., and W. E. Sedlacek. "Noncognitive Variables in Predicting Academic Success by Race." *Measurement and Evaluation in Guidance,* 16 (1984), 171–78.

59. Trent, W. T. "Student Affirmative Action in Higher Education: Addressing Underrepresentation." In *The Racial Crisis in American Higher Education,* edited by P. G. Altbach and K. Lomotey. Albany: State University of New York Press, 1991.

60. Vellela, T. *New Voices: Student Activism in the '80s and '90s.* Boston: South End Press, 1988.

61. Vera, R. *Texas' Response to the Office of Civil Rights: Progress Made Under the Texas Equal Educational Opportunity Plan for Higher Education.* Claremont: Tomas Rivera Policy Center, 1989.

62. Verdugo, R. R. "Educational Stratification and Hispanics." In *Latino College Students,* edited by M. A. Olivas. New York: Teachers College Press, 1986.

63. Wellman, D. T. *Portraits of Whim Racism.* New York: Cambridge University Press, 1977.

64. White, T. J., and W. E. Sedlacek. "White Student Attitudes Toward Blacks and Hispanics: Programming Implications." *Journal of Multicultural Counseling and Development,* 15 (October 1987), 171–83.

65. Williams, J. B., III. "Title VI Regulation of Higher Education." In *Desegregating America's Colleges and Universities,* edited by J. B. Williams Ill. New York: Teachers College Press, 1988.

The Exxon Education Foundation provided generous support for the administration of surveys at selected institutions, thereby facilitating analyses by ethnic group. This funding was provided as part of a project on the outcomes of general education conducted at the Higher Education Research Institute, UCLA. Research was conducted in UCLA's Department of Sociology and the Graduate School of Education with the support of the University of California President's Postdoctoral Fellowship. The author extends her appreciation for Walter R. Allen's and Michael A. Olivas's helpful comments on an earlier draft of this article.

Table 15-A1

Variable Definition and Coding Scheme

Dependent Variable
Campus Racial Tension | Four-item factor scale, (see table 15-A2 for items).

1985 Student Characteristics

Sex | Dichotomous: 1 = "male"; 2 = "female."
Age | Ten-point scale: 1 = "16 or younger," to 10 = "55 or older."

High-school GPA (self-report) | Eight-point scale: 1 = "D," to 8 = "A or A+."
Mother's education | Eight-point scale: 1 = "grammar school or less," to 8 = "graduate degree."

Father's education | Eight-point scale: 1 = "grammar school or less," to 8 = "graduate degree."

Parental Income | Fourteen-point scale: 1 = "less than $6000," to 14 "$150,000 or more."

Social self-confidence (see Table 15-A2). | Three-item factor scale based on student self ratings

Expect to protest in college | Four-point scale: 1 = "very little chance," to 4 = "very good chance."

Political view (self-rating) | Five-point scale: 1 = "far right," to 5 = "far left."

Helping to promote racial understanding | Four-point scale: 1 = "not important," to 4 = "essential."

Institutional Characteristics

Institutional Priorities

Expenditures per student:

Student services | Expenditures for admissions and all activities designed to contribute to the emotional, physical, intellectual, cultural, and social development of students outside the formal educational program

Non-repayable aid | Monies given in the form of grants and scholarships to students enrolled in formal coursework. Excludes college work study and Pell grants.

Student Perceptions of Priorities:
Student-centered | Five-item factor scale. (see table 15-A2 for item scales).
Resource/reputation | Five-item factor scale. (see table 15-A2 for item scales).
Commitment to diversity | Four-item factor scale. (see table 15-A2 for item scales).

College composition:
Selectivity | Average SAT of entering freshmen divided by 10 (ACT converted to SAT equivalents using Astin & Henson. 1977).

Enrollment:
Size (total FTE)[1] | Total graduate and undergraduate FTE.

Black percent in 1986 | Black undergraduate FTE divided by total undergraduate FTE.

Hispanic percent in 1986 FTE. | Hispanic undergraduate FTE divided by total undergraduate.

Black increase (1982-88)[2] | Dichotomous: 1 = "decrease," 2 = "increase" (absolute numbers of undergraduate FTE).

Hispanic increase (1982- 88) | Three-point scale: 1 = "decrease," 2 = "no change." 3 = "increase" (absolute numbers of undergraduate FTE).

1. Three part-time students are equivalent to one FTE.
2. All institutions in the sample experienced change in black undergraduate enrollment over six years.

Table 15-A2

Items Constituting Factor Scales

Social Self-Confidence Factor
(Student self-rating compared to the average person his/her age)
    Leadership ability[1]
    Popularity[1]
    Self-Confidence (social)[1]

Campus Racial Tension Factor
(Statements about the freshman college)
    There is a lot of campus racial conflict here[2]
    Students of different racial/ethnic origins communicate well with one another[3]
    There is little trust between minority student groups and campus administrators[2]

Institutional Priority: Commitment to Diversity Factor
(Priorities of the freshman college)
    Increase the representation of minorities in the faculty and administration[4]
    Develop among students and faculty an appreciation for a multicultural society[4]
    Recruit more minority students[4]
    Create a diverse multicultural environment on campus[4]

Institutional Priority: Resource/Reputation Factor
(Priorities of the freshman college)
    Increase or maintain institutional prestige[4]
    Enhance the institution's national image[4]
    Hire faculty "stars"[4]
    Raise money for the institution[4]
    Conduct basic and applied research[4]

Institutional Priority: Student-centered Factor
(Statements about the freshman college)
    It is easy to see faculty outside of office hours[5]
    Most students are treated like "numbers in a book"[6]
    Faculty here are interested in students' personal problems[2]
    Faculty here are strongly interested in the academic problems of undergraduates[2]

NOTE: Full details of the exploratory and confirmatory procedures used to develop factors are reported in Hurtado (1990) and Dey (1991).
1. Five- point scale: 1 = "bottom 10%" to 5 = "highest 10%."
2. Four-point scale: 1 = "Disagree strongly" to 4 = "Agree strongly."
3. Four-point scale: 1 = "Agree strongly" to 4 = "Disagree strongly" (reversed for analyses).
4. Four-point scale: 1 = "Low Priority" to 4 = "Highest priority."
5. Three-point scale: 1 = "Not descriptive" to 3 "Very descriptive."
6. Three-point scale: 1 = "Very descriptive" to 3 "Not descriptive" (reversed for analyses).

PART IV

LEADERSHIP ANALYSIS

CHAPTER 16

THE AMBIGUITY OF LEADERSHIP[1]

JEFFREY PFEFFER

Problems with the concept of leadership are addressed: (a) the ambiguity of its definition and measurement, (b) the issue of whether leadership affects organizational performance, and (c) the process of selecting leaders, which frequently emphasizes organizationally-irrelevant criteria. Leadership is a process of attributing causation to individual social actors. Study of leaders as symbols and of the process of attributing leadership might be productive.

Leadership has for some time been a major topic in social and organizational psychology. Underlying much of this research has been the assumption that leadership is causally related to organizational performance. Through an analysis of leadership styles, behaviors, or characteristics (depending on the theoretical perspective chosen), the argument has been made that more effective leaders can be selected or trained or, alternatively, the situation can be configured to provide for enhanced leader and organizational effectiveness.

Three problems with emphasis on leadership as a concept can be posed: (a) ambiguity in definition and measurement of the concept itself; (b) the question of whether leadership has discernible effects on organizational outcomes; and (c) the selection process in succession to leadership positions, which frequently uses organizationally irrelevant criteria and which has implications for normative theories of leadership. The argument here is that leadership is of interest primarily as a phenomenological construct. Leaders serve as symbols for representing personal causation of social events. How and why are such attributions of personal effects made? Instead of focusing on leadership and its effects, how do people make inferences about and react to phenomena labelled as leadership (5)?

The Ambiguity of the Concept

While there have been many studies of leadership, the dimensions and definition of the concept remain unclear. To treat leadership as a separate concept, it must be distinguished from other social influence phenomena. Hollander and Julian (24) and Bavelas (2) did not draw distinctions between leadership and other processes of social influence. A major point of the Hollander and Julian review was that leadership research might develop more rapidly if more general theories of social influence were incorporated. Calder (5) also argued that there is no unique content to the construct of leadership that is not subsumed under other, more general models of behavior.

Kochan, Schmidt, and DeCotiis (33) attempted to distinguish leadership from related concepts of authority and social power. In leadership, influence rights are voluntarily conferred. Power does not require goal compatability—merely dependence—but leadership implies some congruence

"The Ambiguity of Leadership," by Jeffrey Pfeffer, reprinted with permission from *Academy of Management Review*, Vol. 12, No. 1, January 1977.

between the objectives of the leader and the led. These distinctions depend on the ability to distinguish voluntary from involuntary compliance and to assess goal compatibility. Goal statements may be retrospective inferences from action (46, 53) and problems of distinguishing voluntary from involuntary compliance also exist (32). Apparently there are few meaningful distinctions between leadership and other concepts of social influence. Thus, an understanding of the phenomena subsumed under the rubric of leadership may not require the construct of leadership (5).

While there is some agreement that leadership is related to social influence, more disagreement concerns the basic dimensions of leader behavior. Some have argued that there are two tasks to be accomplished in groups—maintenance of the group and performance of some task or activity—and thus leader behavior might be described along these two dimensions (1, 6, 8, 25). The dimensions emerging from the Ohio State leadership studies—consideration and initiating structure—may be seen as similar to the two components of group maintenance and task accomplishment (18).

Other dimensions of leadership behavior have also been proposed (4). Day and Hamblin (10) analyzed leadership in terms of the closeness and punitiveness of the supervision. Several authors have conceptualized leadership behavior in terms of the authority and discretion subordinates are permitted (23, 36, 51). Fiedler (14) analyzed leadership in terms of the least-preferred-co-worker scale (LPC), but the meaning and behavioral attributes of this dimension of leadership behavior remain controversial.

The proliferation of dimensions is partly a function of research strategies frequently employed. Factor analysis on a large number of items describing behavior has frequently been used. This procedure tends to produce as many factors as the analyst decides to find, and permits the development of a large number of possible factor structures. The resultant factors must be named and further imprecision is introduced. Deciding on a summative concept to represent a factor is inevitably a partly subjective process.

Literature assessing the effects of leadership tends to be equivocal. Sales (45) summarized leadership literature employing the authoritarian-democratic typology and concluded that effects on performance were small and inconsistent. Reviewing the literature on consideration and initiating structure dimensions, Korman (34) reported relatively small and inconsistent results, and Kerr and Schriesheim (30) reported more consistent effects of the two dimensions. Better results apparently emerge when moderating factors are taken into account, including subordinate personalities (50), and situational characteristics (23, 51). Kerr, et al. (31) list many moderating effects grouped under the headings of subordinate considerations, supervisor considerations, and task considerations. Even if each set of considerations consisted of only one factor (which it does not), an attempt to account for the effects of leader behavior would necessitate considering four-way interactions. While social reality is complex and contingent, it seems desirable to attempt to find more parsimonious explanations for the phenomena under study.

The Effects of Leaders

Hall asked a basic question about leadership: is there any evidence on the magnitude of the effects of leadership (17, p. 248)? Surprisingly, he could find little evidence. Given the resources that have been spent studying, selecting, and training leaders, one might expect that the question of whether or not leaders matter would have been addressed earlier (12).

There are at least three reasons why it might be argued that the observed effects of leaders on organizational outcomes would be small. First, those obtaining leadership positions are selected, and perhaps only certain, limited styles of behavior may be chosen. Second, once in the leadership position, the discretion and behavior of the leader are constrained. And third, leaders can typically affect only a few of the variables that may impact organizational performance.

Homogeneity of Leaders

Persons are selected to leadership positions. As a consequence of this selection process, the range of behaviors or characteristics exhibited by leaders is reduced, making it more problematic to empirically discover an effect of leadership. There are many types of constraints on the selection process. The attraction literature suggests that there is a tendency for persons to like those they perceive as similar (3). In critical decisions such as the selections of persons for leadership positions, compatible styles of behavior probably will be chosen.

Selection of persons is also constrained by the internal system of influence in the organization. As Zald (56) noted, succession is a critical decision, affected by political influence and by environmental contingencies faced by the organization. As Thompson (49) noted, leaders may be selected for their capacity to deal with various organizational contingencies. In a study of characteristics of hospital administrators, Salancik (42) found a relationship between the hospital's context and the characteristics and tenure of the administrators. To the extent that the contingencies and power distribution within the organization remain stable, the abilities and behaviors of those selected into leadership positions will also remain stable.

Finally, the selection of persons to leadership positions is affected by a self-selection process. Organizations and roles have images, providing information about their character. Persons are likely to select themselves into organizations and roles based upon their preferences for the dimensions of the organizational and role characteristics as perceived through these images. The self-selection of persons would tend to work along with organizational selection to limit the range of abilities and behaviors in a given organizational role.

Such selection processes would tend to increase homogeneity more within a single organization than across organizations. Yet many studies of leadership effect at the work group level have compared groups within a single organization. If there comes to be a widely shared, socially constructed definition of leadership behaviors or characteristics which guides the selection process, then leadership activity may come to be defined similarly in various organizations, leading to the selection of only those who match the constructed image of a leader.

Constraints on Leader Behavior

Analyses of leadership have frequently presumed that leadership style or leader behavior was an independent variable that could be selected or trained at will to conform to what research would find to be optimal. Even theorists who took a more contingent view of appropriate leadership behavior generally assumed that with proper training, appropriate behavior could be produced (51). Fiedler (13), noting how hard it was to change behavior, suggested changing the situational characteristics rather than the person, but this was an unusual suggestion in the context of prevailing literature which suggested that leadership style was something to be strategically selected according to the variables of the particular leadership theory.

But the leader is embedded in a social system, which constrains behavior. The leader has a role set (27), in which members have expectations for appropriate behavior and persons make efforts to modify the leader's behavior. Pressures to conform to the expectations of peers, subordinates, and superiors are all relevant in determining actual behavior.

Leaders, even in high-level positions, have unilateral control over fewer resources and fewer policies than might be expected. Investment decisions may require approval of others, while hiring and promotion decisions may be accomplished by committees. Leader behavior is constrained by both the demands of others in the role set and by organizationally prescribed limitations on the sphere of activity and influence.

External Factors

Many factors that may affect organizational performance are outside a leader's control, even if he or she were to have complete discretion over major areas of organizational decisions. For example, consider the executive in a construction firm. Costs are largely determined by operation of commodities and labor markets; and demand is largely affected by interest rates, availability of mortgage money, and economic conditions which are affected by governmental policies over which the executive has little control. School superintendents have little control over birth rates and community economic development, both of which profoundly affect school system budgets. While the leader may react to contingencies as they arise, or may be a better or worse forecaster, in accounting for variation in organizational

outcomes, he or she may account for relatively little compared to external factors.

Second, the leader's success or failure may be partly due to circumstances unique to the organization but still outside his or her control. Leader positions in organizations vary in terms of the strength and position of the organization. The choice of a new executive does not fundamentally alter a market and financial position that has developed over years and affects the leader's ability to make strategic changes and the likelihood that the organization will do well or poorly. Organizations have relatively enduring strengths and weaknesses. The choice of a particular leader for a particular position has limited impact on these capabilities.

Empirical Evidence

Two studies have assessed the effects of leadership changes in major positions in organizations. Lieberson and O'Connor (35) examined 167 business firms in 13 industries over a 20 year period, allocating variance in sales, profits, and profit margins to one of four sources: year (general economic conditions), industry, company effects, and effects of changes in the top executive position. They concluded that compared to other factors, administration had a limited effect on organizational outcomes.

Using a similar analytical procedure, Salancik and Pfeffer (44) examined the effects of mayors on city budgets for 30 U.S. cities. Data on expenditures by budget category were collected for 1951–1968. Variance in amount and proportion of expenditures was apportioned to the year, the city, or the mayor. The mayoral effect was relatively small, with the city accounting for most of the variance, although the mayor effect was larger for expenditure categories that were not as directly connected to important interest groups. Salancik and Pfeffer argued that the effects of the mayor were limited both by absence of power to control many of the expenditures and tax sources, and by construction of policies in response to demands from interests in the environment.

If leadership is defined as a strictly interpersonal phenomenon, the relevance of these two studies for the issue of leadership effects becomes problematic. But such a conceptualization seems unduly restrictive, and is certainly inconsistent with Selznick's (47) concep-

tualization of leadership as strategic management and decision making. If one cannot observe differences when leaders change, then what does it matter who occupies the positions or how they behave?

Pfeffer and Salancik (41) investigated the extent to which behaviors selected by first-line supervisors were constrained by expectations of others in their role set. Variance in task and social behaviors could be accounted for by role-set expectations, with adherence to various demands made by role-set participants a function of similarity and relative power. Lowin and Craig (37) experimentally demonstrated that leader behavior was determined by the subordinate's own behavior. Both studies illustrate that leader behaviors are responses to the demands of the social context.

The effect of leadership may vary depending upon level in the organizational hierarchy, while the appropriate activities and behaviors may also vary with organizational level (26, 40). For the most part, empirical studies of leadership have dealt with first line supervisors or leaders with relatively low organizational status (17). If leadership has any impact, it should be more evident at higher organizational levels or where there is more discretion in decisions and activities.

The Process of Selecting Leaders

Along with the suggestion that leadership may not account for much variance in organizational outcomes, it can be argued that merit or ability may not account for much variation in hiring and advancement of organizational personnel. These two ideas are related. If competence is hard to judge, or if leadership competence does not greatly affect organizational outcomes, then other, person-dependent criteria may be sufficient. Effective leadership styles may not predict career success when other variables such as social background are controlled.

Belief in the importance of leadership is frequently accompanied by belief that persons occupying leadership positions are selected and trained according to how well they can enhance the organization's performance. Belief in a leadership effect leads to development of a set of activities oriented toward enhancing leadership effectiveness. Simultaneously, persons managing their own careers are likely to place emphasis on activities and developing behaviors that will enhance their own leadership skills, assuming that such a strategy will facilitate advancement.

Research on the bases for hiring and promotion has been concentrated in examination of academic positions (e.g., 7, 19, 20). This is possibly the result of availability of relatively precise and unambiguous measures of performance, such as number of publications or citations. Evidence on criteria used in selecting and advancing personnel in industry is more indirect.

Studies have attempted to predict either the compensation or the attainment of general management positions of MBA students, using personality and other background information (21, 22, 54). There is some evidence that managerial success can be predicted by indicators of ability and motivation such as test scores and grades, but the amount of variance explained is typically quite small.

A second line of research has investigated characteristics and backgrounds of persons attaining leadership positions in major organizations in society. Domhoff (11), Mills (38), and Warner and Abbeglin (52) found a strong preponderance of persons with upper-class backgrounds occupying leadership positions. The implication of these findings is that studies of graduate success, including the success of MBA's, would explain more variance if the family background of the person were included.

A third line of inquiry uses a tracking model. The dynamic model developed is one in which access to elite universities is affected by social status (28) and, in turn, social status and attendance at elite universities affect later career outcomes (9, 43, 48, 55).

Unless one is willing to make the argument that attendance at elite universities or coming from an upper class background is perfectly correlated with merit, the evidence suggests that succession to leadership positions is not strictly based on meritocratic criteria. Such a conclusion is consistent with the inability of studies attempting to predict the success of MBA graduates to account for much variance, even when a variety of personality and ability factors are used.

Beliefs about the bases for social mobility are important for social stability. As long as persons believe that positions are allocated on meritocratic grounds, they are more likely to be satisfied with the social order and with their position in it. This satisfaction derives from the belief that occupational position results from application of fair and reasonable criteria, and that the opportunity exists for mobility if the person improves skills and performance.

If succession to leadership positions is determined by person-based criteria such as social origins or social connections (16), then efforts to enhance managerial effectiveness with the expectation that this will lead to career success divert attention from the processes of stratification actually operating within organizations. Leadership literature has been implicitly aimed at two audiences. Organizations were told how to become more effective, and persons were told what behaviors to acquire in order to become effective, and hence, advance in their careers. The possibility that neither organizational outcomes nor career success are related to leadership behaviors leaves leadership research facing issues of relevance and importance.

The Attribution of Leadership

Kelley conceptualized the layman as:

> an applied scientist, that is, as a person concerned about applying his knowledge of causal relationships in order to exercise control of his world (29, p. 2).

Reviewing a series of studies dealing with the attributional process, he concluded that persons were not only interested in understanding their world correctly, but also in controlling it.

> The view here proposed is that attribution processes are to be understood not only as a means of providing the individual with a veridical view of his world, but as a means of encouraging and maintaining his effective exercise of control in that world (29, p. 22).

Controllable factors will have high salience as candidates for causal explanation, while a bias toward the more important causes may shift the attributional emphasis toward causes that are not controllable (29, p. 23). The study of attribution is a study of naive psychology—an examination of how persons make sense out of the events taking place around them.

If Kelley is correct that individuals will tend to develop attributions that give them a feeling of control, then emphasis on leadership may derive partially from a desire to believe in the effectiveness and importance of individual action, since individual action is more controllable than contextual variables. Lieberson and O'Connor (35) made essentially the same point in introducing their paper on the effects of top management changes on organizational performance. Given the desire for control and a feeling of personal effectiveness, organizational outcomes are more likely to be attributed to individual actions, regardless of their actual causes.

Leadership is attributed by observers. Social action has meaning only through a phenomenological process (46). The identification of certain organizational roles as leadership positions guides the construction of meaning in the direction of attributing effects to the actions of those positions. While Bavelas (2) argued that the functions of leadership, such as task accomplishment and group maintenance, are shared throughout the group, this fact provides no simple and potentially controllable focus for attributing causality. Rather, the identification of leadership positions provides a simpler and more readily changeable model of reality. When causality is lodged in one or a few persons rather than being a function of a complex set of interactions among all group members, changes can be made by replacing or influencing the occupant of the leadership position. Causes of organizational actions are readily identified in this simple causal structure.

Even if, empirically, leadership has little effect, and even if succession to leadership positions is not predicated on ability or performance, the belief in leadership effects and meritocratic succession provides a simple causal framework and a justification for the structure of the social collectivity. More importantly, the beliefs interpret social actions in terms that indicate potential for effective individual intervention or control. The personification of social causality serves too many uses to be easily overcome. Whether or not leader behavior actually influences performance or effectiveness, it is important because people believe it does.

One consequence of the attribution of causality to leaders and leadership is that leaders come to be symbols. Mintzberg (39), in his discussion of the roles of managers, wrote of the symbolic role, but more in terms of attendance at formal events and formally representing the organization. The symbolic role of leadership is more important than implied in such a description. The leader as a symbol provides a target for action when difficulties occur, serving as a scapegoat when things go wrong. Gamson and Scotch (15) noted that in baseball, the firing of the manager served a scapegoating purpose. One cannot fire the whole team, yet when performance is poor, something must be done. The firing of the manager conveys to the world and to the actors involved that success is the result of personal actions, and that steps can and will be taken to enhance organizational performance.

The attribution of causality to leadership may be reinforced by organizational actions, such as the inauguration process, the choice process, and providing the leader with symbols and ceremony. If leaders are chosen by using a random number table, persons are less likely to believe in their effects than if there is an elaborate search or selection process followed by an elaborate ceremony signifying the changing of control, and if the leader then has a variety of perquisites and symbols that distinguish him or her from the rest of the organization. Construction of the importance of leadership in a given social context is the outcome of various social processes, which can be empirically examined.

Since belief in the leadership effect provides a feeling of personal control, one might argue that efforts to increase the attribution of causality to leaders would occur more when it is more necessary and more problematic to attribute causality to controllable factors. Such an argument would lead to the hypothesis that the more the *context* actually effects organizational outcomes, the more efforts will be made to ensure attribution to *leadership*. When leaders really do have effects, it is less necessary to engage in rituals indicating their effects. Such rituals are more likely when there is uncertainty and unpredictability associated with the organization's operations. This results both from the desire to feel control in uncertain situations and from the fact that in ambiguous contexts, it is easier to attribute consequences to leadership without facing possible disconfirmation.

The leader is, in part, an actor. Through statements and actions, the leader attempts to reinforce the operation of an attribution process which tends to vest causality in that position in the social structure. Successful leaders, as perceived by members of the social system, are those who can separate themselves from organizational failures and associate themselves with organizational successes. Since the meaning of action is socially constructed, this involves manipulation of symbols to reinforce the desired process of attribution. For instance, if a manager knows that business in his or her division is about to improve because of the economic cycle, the leader may, nevertheless, write recommendations and undertake actions and changes that are highly visible and that will tend to identify his or her behavior closely with the division. A manager who perceives impending failure will attempt to associate the division and its policies and decisions with others, particularly persons in higher organizational positions, and to disassociate himself or herself from the division's performance, occasionally even transferring or moving to another organization.

Conclusion

The theme of this article has been that analysis of leadership and leadership processes must be contingent on the intent of the researcher. If the interest is in understanding the causality of social phenomena as reliably and accurately as possible, then the concept of leadership may be a poor place to begin. The issue of the effects of leadership is open to question. But examination of situational variables that accompany more or less leadership effect is a worthwhile task.

The more phenomenological analysis of leadership directs attention to the process by which social causality is attributed, and focuses on the distinction between causality as perceived by group members and causality as assessed by an outside observer. Leadership is associated with a set of myths reinforcing a social construction of meaning which legitimates leadership role occupants, provides belief in potential mobility for those not in leadership roles, and attributes social causality to leadership roles, thereby providing a belief in the effectiveness of individual control. In analyzing leadership, this mythology and the process by which such mythology is created and supported should be separated from analysis of leadership as a social influence process, operating within constraints.

Jeffrey Pfeffer (Ph.D.—Stanford University) is Associate Professor in the School of Business Administration and Associate Research Sociologist in the Institute of Industrial Relations at the University of California, Berkeley.

Notes

1. An earlier version of this paper was presented at the conference, Leadership: Where Else Can We Go?, Center for Creative Leadership, Greensboro, North Carolina, June 30 July 1, 1975.

References

Bales, R. F. *Interaction Process Analysis: A Method for the Study of Small Groups*, Reading, Mass.: Addison-Wesley, 1950.

Bavelas, Alex. "Leadership: Man and Function," *Administrative Science Quarterly*, 1960, 4; 491–498.

Berscheid, Ellen, and Elaine Walster. *Interpersonal Attraction*, Reading, Mass.: Addison-Wesley, 1969.

Bowers, David G., and Stanley E. Seashore. "Predicting Organizational Effectiveness with a Four-Factor Theory of Leadership," *Administrative Science Quarterly*, 1966, 11; 238–263.

Calder, Bobby J. "An Attribution Theory of Leadership," in B. Slaw and G. Salancik (Eds.), *New Directions in Organizational Behavior*, Chicago: St. Clair Press, 1976, in press.

Cartwright, Dorwin C., and Alvin Zander. *Group Dynamics: Research and Theory*, 3rd ed., Evanston, Ill.: Row, Peterson, 1960.

Cole, Jonathan R., and Stephen Cole. *Social Stratification in Science*, Chicago: University of Chicago Press, 1973.

Collins, Barry E., and Harold Guetzkow. *A Social Psychology of Group Processes for Decision-Making*, New York: Wiley, 1964.

Collins, Randall. "Functional and Conflict Theories of Stratification," *American Sociological Review*, 1971, 36; 1002–1019.

Day, R. C., and R. L. Hamblin. "Some Effects of Close and Punitive Styles of Supervision," *American Journal of Sociology*, 1964, 69; 499–510.

Domhoff, G. William. *Who Rules America?* Englewood Cliffs, N.J.: Prentice-Hall, 1967.

Dubin, Robert. "Supervision and Productivity: Empirical Findings and Theoretical Considerations," in R. Dubin, G. C. Homans, F. C. Mann, and D. C.

Miller (Eds.), *Leadership and Productivity*, San Francisco: Chandler Publishing Co., 1965; 1–50.

Fiedler, Fred E. "Engineering the Job to Fit the Manager," *Harvard Business Review*, 1965, 43; 115–122.

Fiedler, Fred E. *A Theory of Leadership Effectiveness*, New York: McGraw-Hill, 1967.

Gamson, William A., and Norman A. Scotch. "Scapegoating in Baseball," *American Journal of Sociology*, 1964, 70; 69–72.

Granovetter, Mark. *Getting a Job*, Cambridge, Mass.: Harvard University Press, 1974.

Hall, Richard H. *Organizations: Structure and Process*, Englewood Cliffs, N.J.: Prentice-Hall, 1972.

Halpin, A. W., and J. Winer. "A Factorial Study of the Leader Behavior Description Questionnaire," in R. M. Stogdill and A. E. Coons (Eds.), *Leader Behavior: Its Description and Measurement*, Columbus, Ohio: Bureau of Business Research, Ohio State University, 1957; 39–51.

Hargens L. L. "Patterns of Mobility of New Ph.D.'s Among American Academic Institutions," *Sociology of Education*, 1969, 42; 18–37.

Hargens, L. L., and W. O. Hagstrom. "Sponsored and Contest Mobility of American Academic Scientists," *Sociology of Education*, 1967, 40; 24–38.

Harrell, Thomas W. "High Earning MBA's," *Personnel Psychology*, 1972, 25; 523–530.

Harrell, Thomas W., and Margaret S. Harrell. "Predictors of Management Success." *Stanford University Graduate School of Business, Technical Report No. 3 to the Office of Naval Research.*

Heller, Frank, and Yukl, Gary. "Participation, Managerial Decision-Making and Situational Variables," *Organizational Behavior and Human Performance*, 1969, 4; 227–241.

Hollander, Edwin P., and James W. Julian. "Contemporary Trends in the Analysis of Leadership Processes," *Psychological Bulletin*, 1969, 71; 387–397.

House, Robert J. "A Path Goal Theory of Leader Effectiveness," *Administrative Science Quarterly*, 1971, 16; 321–338.

Hunt, J. G. "Leadership-Style Effects at Two Managerial Levels in a Simulated Organization," *Administrative Science Quarterly*, 1971, 16; 476–485.

Kahn, R. L., D. M. Wolfe, R. P. Quinn, and J. D. Snoek. *Organizational Stress: Studies in Role Conflict and Ambiguity*, New York: Wiley, 1964.

Karabel, J., and A. W. Astin. "Social Class, Academic Ability, and College 'Quality'," *Social Forces*, 1975, 53; 381–398.

Kelley, Harold H. *Attribution in Social Interaction*, Morristown, N.J.: General Learning Press, 1971.

Kerr, Steven, and Chester Schriesheim. "Consideration, Initiating Structure and Organizational Criteria—An Update of Korman's 1966 Review," *Personnel Psychology*, 1974, 27; 555–568.

Kerr, S., C. Schriesheim, C. J. Murphy, and R. M. Stogdill, "Toward A Contingency Theory of Leadership Based Upon the Consideration and Initiating Structure Literature," *Organizational Behavior and Human Performance*, 1974, 12; 62–82.

Kiesler, C., and S. Kiesler. *Conformity*, Reading, Mass.: Addison-Wesley, 1969.

Kochan, T. A., S. M. Schmidt, and T. A. DeCotiis. "Superior-Subordinate Relations: Leadership and Headship," *Human Relations*, 1975, 28; 279–294.

Korman, A. K. "Consideration, Initiating Structure, and Organizational Criteria—A Review," *Personnel Psychology*, 1966, 19; 349–362.

Lieberson, Stanley, and James F. O'Connor. "Leadership and Organizational Performance: A Study of Large Corporations," *American Sociological Review*, 1972, 37; 117–130.

Lippitt, Ronald. "An Experimental Study of the Effect of Democratic and Authoritarian Group Atmospheres," *University of Iowa Studies in Child Welfare*, 1940, 16; 43–195.

Lowin, A., and J. R. Craig. "The Influence of Level of Performance on Managerial Style: An Experimental Object-Lesson in the Ambiguity of Correlational Data," *Organizational Behavior and Human Performance*, 1968, 3; 440–458.

Mills, C. Wright. "The American Business Elite: A Collective Portrait," in C. W. Mills, *Power, Politics, and People*, New York: Oxford University Press, 1963; 110–139.

Mintzberg, Henry. *The Nature of Managerial Work*. New York: Harper and Row, 1973.

Nealey, Stanley M., and Milton R. Blood. "Leadership Performance of Nursing Supervisors at Two Organizational Levels," *Journal of Applied Psychology*, 1968, 52; 414–442.

Pfeffer, Jeffrey, and Gerald R. Salancik. "Determinants of Supervisory Behavior: A Role Set Analysis, *Human Relations*, 1975, 28; 139–154.

Pfeffer, Jeffrey, and Gerald R. Salancik. "Organizational Context and the Characteristics and Tenure of Hospital Administrators," *Academy of Management Journal*, 1977, 20, in press.

Reed, R. H., and H. P. Miller. "Some Determinants of the Variation in Earnings for College Men," *Journal of Human Resources*, 1970, 5; 117–190.

Salancik, Gerald R., and Jeffrey Pfeffer. "Constraints on Administrator Discretion: The Limited Influence of Mayors on City Budgets," *Urban Affairs Quarterly*, in press.

Sales, Stephen M. "Supervisory Style and Productivity: Review and Theory," *Personnel Psychology*, 1966,19; 275–286.

Schutz, Alfred. *The Phenomenology of the Social World*, Evanston, Ill.: Northwestern University Press, 1967.

Selznick, P. *Leadership in Administration*, Evanston, Ill.: Row, Peterson, 1957.

Spaeth, J. L., and A. M. Greeley. *Recent Alumni and Higher Education*, New York: McGraw-Hill, 1970.

Thompson, James D. *Organizations in Action*, New York: McGraw-Hill, 1967.

Vroom, Victor H. "Some Personality Determinants of the Effects of Participation," *Journal of Abnormal and Social Psychology,* 1959, 59; 322–327.

Vroom, Victor H., and Phillip W. Yetton. *Leadership and Decision-Making,* Pittsburgh: University of Pittsburgh Press, 1973.

Warner, W. L., and J. C. Abbeglin. *Big Business Leaders in America,* New York: Harper and Brothers, 1955.

Weick, Karl E. *The Social Psychology of Organizing,* Reading, Mass.: Addison-Wesley, 1969.

Weinstein, Alan G., and V. Srinivasan. "Predicting Managerial Success of Master of Business Administration (MBA) Graduates," *Journal of Applied Psychology,* 1974, 59; 207–212.

Wolfle, Dael. *The Uses of Talent,* Princeton: Princeton University Press, 1971.

Zald, Mayer N. "Who Shall Rule? A Political Analysis of Succession in a Large Welfare Organization," *Pacific Sociological Review,* 1965, 1; 52–60.

CHAPTER 17

HIGHER EDUCATION AND LEADERSHIP THEORY

ESTELA M. BENSIMON, ANNA NEUMANN, AND ROBERT BIRNBAUM

This section examines works on leadership in the literature of higher education from the perspective of theories discussed in the previous section, suggesting implications of these studies for effective leadership in higher education.

Although studies of leadership in higher education have traditionally been atheoretical, a resurgence of theoretical research has occurred in recent years, and several works have attempted to integrate findings in the higher education literature with more general theories of leadership. A review of the strengths and weaknesses of several conceptual approaches to studying leadership in the context of academic organizations, for example, provides a clear and concise summary of the major theories of leadership along with a comprehensive annotated bibliography of works on leadership, corporate management, and higher education administration keyed to each theory (Dill and Fullagar 1987). Another essay emphasizes the role of leaders in organizational improvement and gives considerable attention to characteristics and behaviors of leaders as developed through the Ohio State leadership studies (Fincher 1987), not only recognizing the contingent nature of leadership but also including a critical analysis of several works on the presidency.

Trait Theories

Trait theory continues to be influential in images of effective leadership in higher education, even though it is no longer a major approach to research among organizational theorists. Works concerned primarily with describing successful presidents, with identifying the characteristics to look for in selecting individuals for positions of leadership, or with comparing the characteristics of effective and ineffective leaders are the most likely to reflect a trait approach. Even though trait theory may not necessarily be the authors' primary orientation, the tendency to associate leaders with specific traits is so common that many works on leadership refer to traits or individual qualities (see, e.g., Kerr 1984; Kerr and Gade 1986; Vaughan 1986; Walker 1979).

Successful academic leaders have been described in terms of personal attributes, interpersonal abilities, and technical management skills (Kaplowitz 1986). Personal attributes include humor, courage, judgment, integrity, intelligence, persistence, hard work, vision, and being opportunity conscious; interpersonal abilities include being open, building teams, and being compassionate. Technical management skills include producing results, resolving conflicts, analyzing and evaluating problems, being able to shape the work environment, and being goal oriented (Gilley, Fulmer, and Reithlingshoefer 1986; Vaughan 1986).

"Higher Education and Leadership Theory," by Estela Bensimon, Anna Neumann, and Robert L. Birnbaum, reprinted from *Making Sense of Administrative Leadership, ASHE-ERIC Research Report*, No. 1, 1989, Association for the Study of Higher Education.

A portrait of the effective president suggests the following personal traits:

> . . . a strong drive for responsibility, vigor, persistence, willingness to take chances, originality, ability to delegate, humor, initiative in social situations, fairness, self-confidence, decisiveness, sense of identity, personal style, capacity to organize, willingness to act or boldness . . . (Fisher 1984, p. 24).

A belief persists that in selecting candidates for positions of leadership, one should look for individuals who appear to have such characteristics. Most often cited are confidence, courage, fairness, respect for the opinions of others, and sensitivity. Undesirable characteristics include being soft-spoken, insecure, vain, concerned with administrative pomp, and graveness (Eble 1978). The trouble, of course, is that judgments on the presence or absence of these characteristics are highly subjective. No research has shown, for example, that a college president who speaks in an assertive and strong voice will be more effective than a soft-spoken president. One study of presidential effectiveness compares the traits and behaviors of 412 presidents identified as highly effective by their peers with a group of 412 "representative" presidents (Fisher, Tack, and Wheeler 1988). The prototypical effective president was self-described as a "strong risk-taking loner with a dream" who was less likely to form close collegial relationships than typical presidents, worked longer hours, made decisions easily, and confided less frequently in other presidents. Closer examination of the data reveals, however, that effective and representative presidents were probably more alike than different. In four of five leadership factors derived from a factor analysis of survey items (managing style, human relations, image, and social reference), no significant differences were found between the two groups of presidents. Significant differences were found only for the confidence factor, which consisted of items that assessed the extent to which presidents believed they can make a difference in their institutions.

While this study suggests that effective leaders are "loners" who maintain social distance, the findings of another study suggest that successful colleges are headed by presidents who are "people-oriented—caring, supportive, and nurturing" (Gilley, Fulmer, and Reithlingshoefer 1986, p. 115). Similarly, while the former study maintains that effective leaders are risk takers, the other says that successful presidents "work feverishly to minimize risk at every step of the way" (p. 65). These studies' conflicting findings suggest the problems of analyzing the effectiveness of leadership from a trait perspective. Few people exhibit consistent traits under all circumstances, so that both "distance" and "nurturing" may accurately represent effective leadership as manifested in different situations. If this in fact is the case, these studies provide a strong argument for the need to define the effectiveness of leadership in dynamic rather than static terms.

Power and Influence Theories

Power and influence theories fall into two types, those that consider leadership in terms of the influence or effects that leaders may have on their followers (social power theory and transformational leadership theory) and those that consider leadership in terms of mutual influence and reciprocal relationships between leaders and followers (social exchange theory and transactional leadership theory).

Social Power Theory

From this perspective, effective leaders are those who can use their power to influence the activities of others. Concepts of social power appeared to be an important influence in shaping presidents' implicit theories of leadership in one study (Birnbaum 1989a). When asked to explain what leadership meant to them, most of the presidents participating in an extensive study of institutional leadership provided definitions describing leadership as a one-way process, with the leader's function depicted as getting others to follow or accept their directives. For a small minority, the role of the leader was not to direct the group but to facilitate the emergence of leadership latent within it. Definitions that included elements of other conceptual orientations (trait theories, contingency theories, and symbolic theories) were mentioned infrequently.

The most likely sources of power for academic leaders are expert and referent power rather than legitimate, coercive, or reward powers (see the discussion of power and influence theories in the previous section): it has been proposed that college presidents can exert influence over their campuses through charismatic power, which has been questionably identified as analogous to referent power (Fisher 1984). This particular perspective maintains that academic leaders can cultivate charismatic power by remaining distant or remote from constituents, by attending to their personal appearance and style, and by exhibiting self-confidence. To establish distance and remoteness, presidents are counseled not to establish close relationships with faculty, not to be overly visible, and to emphasize the importance of the trappings of the office as symbols of its elevated state. Style consists of presidential comportment, attitude, speech, dress, mannerisms, appearance, and personal habits. Self-confidence relates to cultivating a style of speaking and walking that conveys a sense of self-assuredness. The concept of charismatic power that has been proposed here appears to be much different from referent power, which traditionally has been defined as the willingness of followers to accept influence by a leader they like and with whom they identify.

Practitioners and scholars tend to question the importance given to charismatic traits as well as whether leaders stand to gain by creating distance between themselves and their constituents. It has been suggested (Keohane 1985) that a leader who is concerned with creating an image of mystery and separateness cannot be effective at building coalitions, a critical part of leadership. High levels of campus discontent have been attributed to leaders who were considered to be too distant from their internal and external constituencies and who tended to take constituents' support for granted or to feel it was not needed (Whetten 1984). Reacting to the current preoccupation with charismatic leadership, a recent commentary published in *The Wall Street Journal* says "leadership is more doing than dash."

> It has little to do with "leadership qualities" and even less to do with "charisma . . . Charisma becomes the undoing of leaders. It makes them inflexible, convinced of their own infallibility, unable to change. This is what happened to Stalin, Hitler, and Mao, and it is a commonplace in the study of ancient history that only Alexander the

Great's early death saved him from becoming an ineffectual failure" (Drucker 1988).

Social Exchange Theory/Transactional Theory

College and university presidents can accumulate and exert power by controlling access to information, controlling the budgetary process, allocating resources to preferred projects, and assessing major faculty and administrative appointments (Corson 1960). On college campuses, however, the presence of other sources of power—the trustees' power to make policy and the faculty's professional authority—seriously limits the president's discretionary control of organizational activities. For this reason, social exchange theory is particularly useful for examining the principles of shared governance and consultation and the image of the president as first among equals, which undergirds much of the normative values of academic organizations.

Transactional theory can be particularly useful for understanding the interactions between leaders and followers. The idiosyncrasy credit (IC) model (Hollander 1987), a major transactional approach to leadership, is of particular relevance to the understanding of leaders' influence in academic organizations. This model suggests that followers will accept change and tolerate a leader's behavior that deviates from their expectations more readily if leaders first engage in actions that will demonstrate their expertise and conformity to the group's norms. The IC model, for example, explains why new presidents initially may find it beneficial to concentrate on getting to know their institutions' history, culture, and key players before proclaiming changes they plan to introduce. A study of new presidents suggests that first-time presidents, not wanting to appear indecisive, may overlook the potential benefits of "getting to know" and "becoming known" by the institution. In contrast, experienced presidents, in assuming office at a new institution, recognized the importance of spending time learning about the expectations of followers (Bensimon 1987, 1989a).

Two works relate presidential failure and success in accomplishing change to presidents' initial actions. These studies show the relevance of concepts underlying the IC model. For example, a member of a new university administration attributed the failure to implement radical changes and reforms to the inability of the new president and his academic administrators to build loyalty—and to gain credits—among respected members of the faculty.

> We succeeded in infusing new blood . . . but we failed to recirculate the old blood. We lost an opportunity to build loyalty among respected members of the veteran faculty. If veteran faculty members had been made to feel that they, too had a future in the transformed university, they might have embraced the academic reorganization plan with some enthusiasm. Instead the veteran faculty members were hurt, indignant, and—finally—angry (Bennis 1972, p. 116).

In contrast, another study illustrates that time spent accumulating credits (e.g., fulfilling the expectations of constituents) can lead to positive outcomes (Gilley, Fulmer, and Reithlingshoefer 1986). The authors observed that presidential success was related to gaining acceptance and respect from key constituents through low-key, pleasant, and noncontroversial actions early in the presidential term. In their judgment, change and departure from established patterns were tolerated because "of the safety zone of good will they ha[d] created" (p. 66).

The influence of social exchange theory can also be detected in works that downplay the charismatic and directive role of leaders. These studies portray leaders as coordinators of ongoing activities rather than as architects of bold initiatives. This view of leadership is related to the anarchical (Cohen and March 1974), democratic-political (Walker 1979), atomistic (Kerr and Gade 1986), and cybernetic (Birnbaum 1988) models of university leadership that will be discussed in the next section.

Transformational Theory

This perspective suggests that effective leaders create and promote desirable "visions" or images of the institution. Unlike goals, tasks, and agendas, which refer to concrete and instrumental ends to be achieved, vision refers to altered perceptions, attitudes, and commit-

ments. The transforming leader must encourage the college community to accept a vision created by his or her symbolic actions (Green 1988b; Hesburgh 1979).

Transformation implies a "metamorphosis or a substitution of one state or system for another, so that a qualitatively different condition is present" (Cameron and Ulrich 1986, p. 1). Fear that higher education is suffering a crisis in leadership has made calls for transformational leadership a recurrent theme in recent studies. Some suggest it is an "illusion, an omnipotent fantasy" (Bennis 1972, p. 115) for a change-oriented administrator to expect that academic organizations would be receptive to this kind of leadership. In higher education, transformational leadership more appropriately may refer to the inspirational role of the leader. For example, the description of leadership as the "poetic part of the presidency" that "sweeps listeners and participants up into the nobility of intellectual and artistic adventures and the urgency of thinking well and feeling deeply about the critical issues of our time" (Keller 1983, p. 25) is unmistakably transformational in tone, as is the following eloquent and inspiring call:

> . . . in the years ahead, higher education will be sorely tested. If we believe that our institutions have value, we must articulate that value and achieve adequate understanding and support. We must find leaders who are dedicated enough to the purpose of higher education that they will expend themselves, if necessary, for that purpose . . . The qualities of transforming leadership are those that restore in organizations or society a sense of meaning and purpose and release the powerful capacity humankind has for renewal (Kauffman 1980, pp. 114–15).

A modern example of the transformational leader may be found in Theodore Hesburgh, who has been described as "brilliant, forceful, and charismatic . . . a legend on campus, where stories of students scampering up the fire escape outside his office for a glimpse of the great man are a part of the Notre Dame lore, like winning one for the Gipper" (Ward 1988, pp. 32–33). Images like this one, along with the popular belief that transformational leaders are concerned with "doing the right things" while managers are concerned with "doing things right" (Bennis and Nanus 1985; Cameron and Ulrich 1986), make transformational leadership irresistible to leaders and nonleaders alike.

A five-step agenda derived from an analysis of the qualities possessed by great leaders like Ghandi, Martin Luther King, Jr., and Winston Churchill attempts to put transformational leadership into practical terms (Cameron and Ulrich 1986). The list includes the following steps: (1) create readiness for change by focusing attention on the unsatisfactory aspects of the organization; (2) overcome resistance by using non-threatening approaches to introduce change; (3) articulate a vision by combining rational reasoning and symbolic imagery; (4) generate commitment; and (5) institutionalize commitment. Suggested approaches on how to implement each step came mostly from examples drawn from industry and tested in case studies of two colleges in crisis whose presidents took actions that corresponded to the agenda prescribed for transformational leadership. Of course, while following these steps might result in changes that make the campus more adaptable to the demands of the environment, it might not result in changes in the perceptions, beliefs, and values of campus constituents that are at the core of transformational leadership as initially proposed (Burns 1978).

The nature of colleges and universities appears to make the exercise of transformational leadership extremely difficult except under certain conditions. Three such conditions have been suggested—institutional crisis, institutional size, and institutional quality (Birnbaum 1988). Institutional crisis is likely to encourage transformational leadership because campus members and the external community expect leaders to take strong action. Portrayals of presidents exercising transformational leadership can be found in case-study reports of institutions suffering adversity (see, e.g., Cameron and Ulrich 1986; Chaffee 1984; Clark 1970; Riesman and Fuller 1985). Transformational leadership is also more likely to emerge in small institutions where leaders can exert a great deal of personal influence through their daily interactions with the campus. Leaders in 10 small private liberal arts colleges identified as having high faculty morale displayed characteristics of the transformational orientation (Rice and Austin 1988). These leaders were seen by others as powerful influences in the life

of their colleges and were credited with single-handedly turning their institutions around. Institutions that need to be upgraded to achieve comparability with their peers also provide an opportunity for transformational leadership. Such presidents have been described as "pathbreaking leaders" (Kerr and Gade 1986).

Although with few exceptions (see Bass 1985) leaders tend to be considered as being either transactional or transformational, a recent study comparing the initial activities of new presidents in institutions in crisis suggests that leaders who use transactional means (e.g., conforming to organizational culture) may be more successful in attaining transformational effects (e.g., improving the organizational culture) than leaders whose behavior reflects the pure form (one-way approach) of transformational leadership (Bensimon 1989c). Even in institutions in distress, a leadership approach that conforms to the group's norms while also seeking to improve them may be of greater benefit than heroic attempts at redesigning an institution.

Behavioral Theories

Behavior of the Leader

These theories examine whether the leader is task (initiating structure) or people (consideration) oriented or both. Blake and Mouton (1964) adapted their managerial grid into an academic grid and applied it to higher education. Their model suggests five styles of academic administration (Blake, Mouton, and Williams 1981): caretaker, authority-obedience, comfortable-pleasant, constituency-centered, and team. The optimum style is identified as team administration, which is characteristic of leaders who scored high on both concern for institutional performance and concern for people on their grid.

Some limited empirical tests of this theory have been performed. A study of department chairs found that those judged as effective by the faculty scored high both in initiating structure (task) and consideration of people (Knight and Holen 1985). On the other hand, a case study of a single institution reports that departments with high faculty morale had chairs who scored high on measures of consideration of people and participative leadership style but not in initiating structure (Madron, Craig, and Mendel 1976). The academic grid appears to have found its greatest use as a tool for self assessment. For example, the grid was adapted into a questionnaire to assist department chairs in determining their personal styles of leadership (Tucker 1981).

Presidents' perceptions of the similarity of their role to other leadership roles were used to describe two types of presidents—mediative and authoritative, which are roughly comparable to emphasizing consideration of people and initiating structure (task), respectively (Cohen and March 1974). Mediative presidents tended to define their roles in terms of constituencies, while authoritative presidents appeared to be more directive. Additionally, mediative presidents were more likely to measure their success on the basis of faculty respect, while authoritative presidents were more likely to base it on the quality of educational programs.

Administrative styles based on the self-reported behaviors of presidents were found to be related to faculty and student outcomes in 49 small private liberal arts colleges (Astin and Scherrei 1980). These findings, however, may be influenced by the size of the institutions.

Managerial Roles

A comprehensive essay (Dill 1984) reviews the literature on administrative behavior in higher education, employing the behavioral framework developed by Mintzberg (1973). The findings (p. 91) suggest that like managers in other settings, senior administrators in higher education:

- Perform a great variety of work at a continuous pace;
- Carry out activities characterized by variety, fragmentation, and brevity;
- Prefer issues that are current, specific, and ad hoc;
- Demonstrate preference for verbal media (telephone calls, meetings, brief discussions); and
- Develop informal information systems.

Although academic leaders are likely to learn from their actions, almost no attention has been

given to what leaders learn on the job. A qualitative study based on interviews with 32 presidents reports that what presidents learn from their actions varies, depending on whether they feel the action they took was wrong (substantive error) or whether they feel the action was justified but the process used (process error) was inappropriate (Neumann 1988). New presidents who made substantive errors learned how to sense situational differences that called for diverse (and new) responses, they began to identify new behaviors that were more appropriate to their new settings, and they gave up the behaviors that worked in their old settings but appeared to be dysfunctional in their new ones. From process errors, presidents tended to learn the degree of influence organizational members have on what presidents can accomplish. Some presidents also made action errors, which consisted of taking action when none should have been taken. From these errors, presidents gained respect for personal and organizational limitations.

Contingency Theories

From this perspective, effective leadership requires adapting one's style of leadership to situational factors. Applying four contingency theories to higher education, Vroom (1983) found that if used to determine the kind of leader best suited to chair academic departments, each would prescribe a different type of leader. Situational variables in Fiedler's contingency model and in House's path-goal theory prescribe a task-oriented leader who would do whatever is necessary to drive the group to complete a job. In contrast, Hersey and Blanchard's life-cycle theory and the Vroom-Yetton decision process theory identify individuals with a delegating and participative style of leadership. The contradictory prescriptions may be the result of their development in organizational settings with clearly delineated superior and subordinate roles. Thus, they may have limited applicability to the study of leadership in higher education. The Vroom-Yetton model appears to be better suited to higher education organizations, because it uses multiple criteria to determine participative or autocratic decision making (Floyd 1985).

Although the observation that "a president may be egalitarian one day and authoritarian the next" (Gilley, Fulmer, and Reithlingshoefer 1986, p. 66) is commonplace, little systematic application of contingency theory has occurred to determine under what conditions alternative forms of leadership should be displayed. Generally, contingency theories have found their greatest applicability in the study of leadership in academic departments, probably because decision making at this level is less equivocal than at higher levels of the academic organization. An application of the Vroom-Yetton model to the study of decision making among department chairs concludes that they frequently chose autocratic styles of decision making in situations where a consultative style would have increased the likelihood of the faculty's acceptance of the decision (Taylor 1982). Hersey and Blanchard's theory was used to develop a questionnaire that would help department chairs determine departmental level of maturity and select a corresponding style of leadership (Tucker 1981). An analysis of studies on the behavior of leaders (Dill 1984) suggests that "when given a choice of leader roles, faculty members consistently preferred the leader as a . . . 'facilitator' or one who smoothed out problems and sought to provide the resources necessary for the research activities of faculty members" (p. 79).

Kerr and Jermier's theory of substitutes for hierarchical leadership may be highly relevant for academic organizations. Despite being one of the few contingency theories in which leadership is not seen as residing solely with the official leader, it has received little attention in the study of academic leadership. If leadership in higher education were to be viewed from this perspective, one could conclude that directive leadership may not be effective because characteristics of academic organizations (such as faculty autonomy and a reward structure that is academic discipline and peer-based) substitute for or neutralize the influence of leaders (Birnbaum 1989a). Similarly, a consideration of the influence of administrators on the faculty's motivation asks, "What are university administrators to do in the face of so many 'substitutes' for their leadership?" (Staw 1983, p. 312). Because alternatives such as stressing local (e.g., primary identification is with the institution) rather than professional orientation (e.g., primary identification is with the academic discipline) or reducing self-gov-

ernance and self-motivation are not in the best interests of the university, it may be more fruitful for administrators to assume the role of facilitator than controller.

Cultural and Symbolic Theories

Occasionally effective leaders give symbolic meaning to events that others may see as perplexing, senseless, or chaotic. They do so by focusing attention on aspects of college life that are both familiar and meaningful to the college community. Cultural and symbolic approaches to studying leadership appear in works on organizations as cultural systems (Chaffee and Tierney 1988; Kuh and Whitt 1988). Understanding colleges and universities as cultures was originally introduced in a now-classic case study of Reed, Swarthmore, and Antioch (Clark 1970, 1972). This study suggests that leaders may play an important role in creating and maintaining institutional sagas. The role of academic leaders in the preservation of academic culture may be even more critical today than in the past, because increased specification, professionalization, and complexity have weakened the values and beliefs that provided institutions with a common sense of purpose, commitment, and order (Dill 1982). Although leaders may not be able to change culture through management, their attention to social integration and symbolic events may enable them to sustain and strengthen the culture that already exists (Dill 1982).

Cultural and symbolic perspectives on leadership have figured prominently in a small handful of recent works that examine the actions of leaders and their effects on campus during times of financial decline. A recent study suggests that college presidents who are sensitive to the faculty's interpretation of financial stress are more likely to elicit the faculty's support for their own leadership (Neumann 1989a). One of the most important contributions to the understanding of leadership from a cultural perspective is the work on the role of substantive and symbolic actions in successful turn-around situations (Chaffee 1984, 1985a, 1985b). The examination of managerial techniques of presidents in institutions suffering financial decline discloses three alternative strategic approaches—linear, adaptive, and interpretive. Linear strategists were concerned with achieving goals. Adaptive strategists were concerned with aligning the organization with the environment, for example, by changing the organizational orientation to meet current demands and thus to ensure the continued flow of resources. Interpretive strategists reflected the cultural/symbolic perspective in that they were concerned with how people saw, understood, and felt about their lives. Interpretive leaders believed that effective action involves shaping the values, symbols, and emotions that influence the behaviors of individuals. The use of interpretive strategy in combination with adaptive strategy was considerably more effective in turning institutions around than the use of adaptive strategy alone (Chaffee 1984). Presidents who employed interpretive strategies were careful to protect the essential character of their institutions and to refrain from actions and environments that compromise or disrupt the institution's self-identity and sense of integrity by only introducing new programs that were outgrowths of the old ones. For example, they reaffirmed the existing institutional mission and did not attempt to pursue programmatic thrusts that were outside the expertise of the faculty.

Strategies of change that make sense to institutional members and that therefore are likely to elicit acceptance and support may depend upon leaders' understanding an organization from cultural perspectives. To do so, leaders may be required to act as anthropologists uncovering the organizational culture by seeking to identify metaphors embedded in the language of the college community (Corbally 1984; Deshler 1985; Peck 1983; Tierney 1988). Frameworks for organizational cultures suggest that leaders can begin to understand their institutional cultures by identifying internal contradictions or incongruities between values and structure, by developing a comparative awareness, by clarifying the identity of the institution, by communicating so as "to say the right things and to say things right," and by acting on multiple and changing fronts (Chaffee and Tierney 1988, pp. 185–91).

Leaders should pose organizational questions to help them identify characteristics of the organizational environment, the influence of institutional mission on decision making, pro-

cesses of socialization, the uses of information, the approaches used to make decisions, and constituents' expectations of leaders (Tierney 1988). Researchers also can gain insights into leadership by examining the symbols embedded in the language of leaders. A study of 32 presidents reveals that they used six categories of symbols—metaphorical, physical, communicative, structural, personification, and ideational—when they talked about their leadership role. Understanding the use of symbolism can help academic leaders to become more consistent by sensitizing them to contradictions between the symbols they use and the behaviors they exhibit on their campuses. Leaders may become more effective by using symbols that are consistent with the institution's culture (Tierney 1989).

The "techniques of managing meaning and social integration are the undiscussed skills of academic management" (Dill 1982, p. 304). For example, it has been suggested that leaders in community colleges have consistently failed to interpret and articulate their missions and to create positive images among their publics (Vaughan 1986). While it is clear that cultural and symbolic leadership skills are becoming increasingly important to presidents, scholars still have much to learn about the characteristics of these skills and effective ways of teaching them to present and aspiring leaders (Green 1988b). A recent examination of colleges and universities from a cultural perspective provides administrators with the following insights: Senior faculty or other core groups of institutional leaders provide continuity and maintain a cohesive institutional culture; institutional policies and practices are driven and bound by culture; culture-driven policies and practices may denigrate the integrity and worth of certain groups; institutional culture is difficult to modify intentionally; and organizational size and complexity work against distinctive patterns of values and assumptions (Kuh and Whitt 1988, p. vi).

Cognitive Theories

Cognitive theories have important implications for perceptions of leaders' effectiveness. In many situations, presidential leadership may not have measurable outcomes other than social attribution—or the tendency of campus constituents to assign to a president the credit or blame for unusual institutional outcomes. From this perspective, leaders are individuals believed by followers to have caused events (Birnbaum 1989b). Leaders themselves, in the absence of clear indicators, are subject to cognitive bias that can lead them to make predictable errors of judgment (Birnbaum 1987) and to over-estimate their effectiveness in campus improvements (Birnbaum 1986).

Summary

Trait theories and power and influence theories appear to be particularly influential in works on leadership in higher education. Several of the works reviewed tend to relate effectiveness of leaders to individual characteristics, although not necessarily the same ones. For example, while some consider "being distant" as a desirable characteristic, others propose that "being nurturing" is more important.

Even though exchange theories are more relevant to the understanding of leadership in academic organizations, works that consider leadership from the perspective of power and influence theories tend to emphasize one-way, leader-initiated and leader-directed approaches. Transformational theory, in particular, has received considerable attention, while transactional theory has for the most part been ignored.

Behavioral and contingency theories may have limited application in higher education because these theories focus their attention on the relationship between superior and subordinate roles. Within the category of behavioral theories, the most promising approach may be in the study of administrative behavior, particularly as a way of understanding how leaders learn from their actions and mistakes. Examining how leaders learn from a behavioral perspective may provide new directions and ideas for the design of training programs for academic leaders.

Within the category of contingency theories, Kerr and Jermier's theory of substitutes for hierarchical leadership may be of greatest use, even though it has been almost totally overlooked by scholars of academic leadership.

Although cultural and symbolic perspectives on leadership were first suggested in the early 1970s in Burton Clark's case study of Reed, Swarthmore, and Antioch, only recently has this view of leadership attracted serious attention. Cultural and symbolic perspectives have been shown to be especially useful for understanding the internal dynamics of institutions in financial crisis, particularly in differentiating the strategies leaders use to cope with financial stress and to communicate with constituents. Cognitive theories offer a promising new way of studying leadership, but their use in higher education to date has been limited.

CHAPTER 18

SYMBOLISM AND PRESIDENTIAL PERCEPTIONS OF LEADERSHIP

WILLIAM G. TIERNEY

In the last decade, organizational researchers have shown considerable interest in the interpretive aspects of organizational life. Rather than viewing an organization as rational and objective, theorists have used the perspective that organizations are socially constructed and subjective entities. Symbolism has emerged as a critical theme. For example, Birnbaum (in press) has investigated the symbolic aspects of the academic senate, Pfeffer (1981) has considered management as symbolic action; and Tierney has undertaken a semiotic analysis of a private, liberal arts college (1987).

Researchers have also noted the significance of a leader's use of symbols. "The only thing of real importance that leaders do is to create and manage culture," asserts Edgar Schein. "The unique talent of leaders is their ability to work with culture" (1985, 2). Birnbaum has commented, "To emphasize the importance of leadership as myth and symbol is not to denigrate the role of leaders, but rather to identify a particularly critical function that they play" (1988, 208). If a central task of leadership is managing the symbolic aspects of the organization, then obviously it is helpful to investigate what leaders perceive leadership to be and what activities leaders perceive they have used to realize those perceptions.

This paper seeks to shed light on the discussion of leadership in higher education from the perspective of its symbolic dimensions. By investigating presidential perceptions of leadership using the National Center of Postsecondary Governance and Finance's Institutional Leadership Project, I developed a schema of symbolic categories leaders use to accomplish their goals. First, I consider leadership and symbolism from an interpretive perspective. Second, I discuss the methodology and how I developed the symbolic categories; I then incorporate the data used from the Institutional Leadership Project to examine the symbolic aspects of presidential perceptions of leadership. I conclude by discussing the implications for administrators of understanding the symbolism of their leadership.

Leadership and Symbolism

First, how does one think about a symbol? Second, how does symbolism enhance and help define leadership? Third, what constraints does the organization impose on a leader's use of symbols?

The Nature of Symbols

Organizational theorists (Dandridge, Mitroff, and Joyce 1980; Peters and Waterman 1982; Pettigrew 1979; Trice and Beyer 1984) have tended to view symbols either as objects or as reified objects that serve as vehicles for conveying meaning. I assume, however, that symbols connote more than objectivized meaning, and they are not simply vehicles in which meaning resides—tabernacles which hold institutional beliefs.

Symbols exist within an organization whether or not the organization's participants are aware of these symbols. To speak of organizations is to speak of interpretation and symbols. An organization void of symbolism is an organization bereft of human activity. Given that symbols exist wherever human activity occurs, a central question for researchers is how to define and uncover symbols in organizations. Particularly germane for this paper is how to interpret symbols of leadership.

Symbols reside in a wide variety of discursive and nondiscursive message units: an act, event, language, dress, structural roles, ceremonies, or even spatial positions in an organization. Hence, we must understand the context in which symbols function and how leaders communicate symbols to create and interpret their organizational reality.

Symbols and Leadership

As with any act of communication, the audience that receives a message must necessarily interpret what the message means. A manager who walks around a building, casually talking with subordinates, for example, may be considered a symbol of management's respect for everyone in the organization. Conversely, organizational participants may feel that the leader is "checking up" on everyone and that such symbolic behavior is intrusive.

Similarly, leaders who remain in their offices, and never converse informally with subordinates may symbolize in their business-oriented approach the message that formalized tasks, rules, and procedures are what the organization values. The point is not that a leader must use this or that trait to be an effective leader. Rather, I suggest that "management by walking around," as well as any other management strategy, is a symbolic act, open to interpretation. Indeed, a manager's informal style can symbolize any number of messages to different constituencies—friendship, accessibility, intrusiveness, or harassment, to name but a few possible interpretations.

As conscious or unconscious forms for participant understanding of the organization, symbols change and evolve due to historical ruptures, responses to the exterior environment, and individual influence. Individuals attach significance to any number of phenomena, and it is in the context of the organization itself that symbols acquire shared meaning. Thus, the key to understanding organizational symbols lies in delineating the symbolic forms whereby the participants communicate, perpetuate, and develop their knowledge about and attitudes toward life (Geertz 1973).

Conversely, symbolism enhances and helps define leadership. Clifford Geertz observes that leaders

> ... justify their existence and order their actions in terms of a collection of stories, ceremonies, insignia, formalities, and appurtenances that they have either inherited ... or invented. It is these—crowns and coronations, limousines and conferences—that mark the center as center and give what goes on there its aura of being not merely important but in some odd fashion connected with the way the world is built (1983, 124).

Symbolism is intertwined with participants' expectation and understanding of leadership. The symbolic role of a college or university president allows an individual to try to communicate a vision of the institution that other individuals are incapable of communicating. We understand leadership through such symbols as the president's yearly speech at convocation or, as will be shown, by a host of activities that "mark the center as center."

Organizational Constraints

Yet leaders are not entirely free to define what is or is not symbolic. Organizations channel activity and interpretation, constraining a leader's use of symbols. Merely because a college president intends for an open door to signify open communication does not assure that the faculty will so interpret it. Almost all leaders in higher education inherit organizations with a history; thus, the parameters of the organization's culture and ideology help fix not only what is or is not symbolic but also what that symbol signifies.

Organizational participants need to feel that they comprehend what is going on in the organization. To do so, they interpret abstractions, often following suggestions made by their leaders. Bailey notes, "We focus on some things and ignore others; we impose a pattern on the flow of events, and thus 'falsify' them if only by simplifying the diversity and the complexity . . . and so make the real world comprehensible" (1983, 18).

College presidents highlight some activities and ignore others; they employ a wide variety of symbolic forms to communicate their messages to different constituencies. To adequately understand how leaders make sense of the organizational universe for their followers, it is important to deconstruct the underlying conceptual orientations that presidents bring to their leadership roles and contexts. It is these concepts and ideologies that shape presidents' perceptions of their organizations and presidential actions within those organizations. Symbolism both defines leadership and is defined by the organization in which the leader resides.

Methodology and Data

Research teams collected data through on-site, semi-structured interviews with the presidents of thirty-two colleges and universities participating in the Institutional Leadership Project (ILP), a five-year longitudinal study conducted by the National Center for Postsecondary Governance and Finance. (For the purposes of the ILP and its purposive stratified sampling procedure, see Birnbaum, Bensimon, and Neumann 1989.)

Data for this paper comes from the presidents' responses to three analytical questions.

1. What is the meaning of "good" presidential leadership?

2. What have you done as a presidential leader?

3. What are you like as a presidential leader?

I reviewed the transcripts of presidential responses, looking especially for comments that were symbolic in nature. Building on previous discussions of what defines a symbol (Deal and Kennedy 1982; Eco 1979; Trice and Beyer 1984), 1 then disaggregated the data into six categories: metaphorical, physical, communicative, structural, personification, and ideational. These categories are not always mutually exclusive; a symbol may fall within more than one category or reinforce another symbolic category. Nor do these six categories necessarily cover all organizational symbols. This is an "essay" in the root sense of the word—a trial of some ideas.

It is also important to point out that I built the categories from previous work on symbolism. The presidents did not devise them. Needless to say, when presidents act they do not generally think, "I am now using a structural symbol." Indeed, one intent of this paper is to provide a provisional framework which presidents might use in reflecting on their leadership acts and thinking about the use of symbols.

In reviewing the data I neither found differences due to institutional type in how presidents symbolically perceived leadership nor did I find substantial differences between presidents appointed within the last three years and "old" presidents. Instead, I found similarities across type and between new and old presidents, as well as differences within type and among the same presidential generation. However, as we will see, what is particularly important when we analyze symbols in an organization is the manner and intention with which presidents use symbols. That is, two presidents may use the same symbolic form with the same frequency, but their purposes will be quite different.

The limitations of this study have already been referred to in the Introduction to these articles. We have analyzed presidents' responses but not the context surrounding those responses. That is, the data of this paper comes from the mouths of presidents. Analyzing the data of faculty and other constituents about their perceptions of presidential symbols is yet to come. It also was not my purpose to count or gradate the frequency of symbolic categories. Prior to such a task we will first need a clearer understanding of symbolic categories. What follows is a discussion of each category that highlights how presidents act symbolically.

Metaphorical Symbols

Metaphors are figures of speech. Presidents provide figures of speech for themselves, their organization, environment, and activities as if something were that particular other. The metaphors an individual uses provide participants with a portrait of how the organization functions. One president noted:

> My philosophy of leadership is to have a team approach to managing the university. The executive committee is a group that shares certain values and expectations, and we push each other hard for the good of the college. What is essential is that we have an effective team, and that we portray that to the board and the community.

Another individual consistently mentioned how it was important "to provide the glue" so that the organization "sticks together." And still another president spoke of organizational participants as "troops" that needed to be rallied.

Presidents also use different metaphors to describe themselves. "I am militaristic . . . like a football coach," observed one. "I am their counselor," commented another. And a third individual was a maestro: "Being president is like an orchestra conductor."

Metaphors give participants a way of seeing and, hence, of acting in the organizational universe. The organization where the participants see themselves as a team presumably interacts differently than the organization led by a general who commands troops. Similarly, an organization that needs glue is different from an organization where it is unimportant to stick together but where a prime metaphorical value concerns "everyone pulling his or her own weight."

Presidents perceive themselves as leaders in a multitude of ways. By focusing on particular metaphors, a president simplifies the organizational universe by providing an image of leadership and the organization. However, the success or failure of a metaphor as a strategy may depend on how the metaphor fits with the organization's culture. That is, a faculty that sees itself as an academy of scholars may rebel at the idea that they are troops being led by a general.

Physical Symbols

Physical symbols refer to objects that are meant to mean something other than what they really are and are perhaps the most common symbols. Artifacts are tangible examples of a particular message. However, as with all symbols, physical symbols may not signify what the leader intends. For example, one president said that getting personal computers for each faculty member made "a statement about the distinctiveness of the learning experience here. The purpose of this action was not to give PC's to the faculty but to set forth a philosophy, to make a statement that we are changing teaching here."

As the president notes, the intention was to make a statement with physical symbols. Clearly, on some campuses, alternative interpretations may exist. A humanities faculty might interpret the uninvited appearance of computers in their offices as the sciences' encroachment on their turf. A science faculty who already owned personal computers but worked in a building that needed renovation could interpret computers as a sign that the president was pandering to the liberal arts. The point is not that one interpretation is right and the other wrong, but rather that physical objects need to be seen within the context of the organization and its constituencies.

New libraries, attention to the grounds, a faculty club, school ties and scarves, and a host of other physical artifacts are designed as symbolic representations to various constituencies by presidents. Another president observed that the university had remained open when students took over the administration building. The president noted how the campus "carried on." By the president's symbolic use of space the president intended for the community to understand that the college was more than buildings and that, even under duress, the institution would continue.

Communicative Symbols

Communication entails not only symbolic acts of oral discourse but also written communicative acts and nonverbal activities that convey particular meanings from a president to a constituency. "I try to rub elbows with students and faculty on a regular basis," related one president. "I spend evenings in the student center. I try to make faculty council meetings, and I talk to faculty on campus." Another individual reported, "I call each of the faculty by their first name. During the year, all of them will be entertained in my home. I send birthday cards to all full-time faculty," noted a third leader. And a fourth commented:

> During a normal workday I will walk over to some other person's office maybe seven or eight times. It is really time consuming to be doing that, and I could save time by just picking up the phone. But I get mileage out of doing that, however, that is immeasurable . . . I am visible.

Given the popularity of such texts as *In Search of Excellence* and *Corporate Cultures,* it is commonplace to hear leaders refer to their style as "management by walking around." And, indeed, many leaders do "walk around." As American organizations struggle to emulate what they perceive to be Japanese models of effectiveness and efficiency, communicative symbols serve as functional vehicles for organizational success.

Talking with students "on their turf," entertaining faculty, strolling around campus, or walking into offices are all presidential perceptions of symbolic communication. Most often, the symbol is meant to communicate presidential concern; presidents think of themselves as caring individuals when they talk with students about student concerns. To use yet another symbolic metaphor, presidents perceive themselves as understanding their constituencies when they know everyone's first name or send someone a birthday card.

Structural Symbols

Symbolic structures refer to institutional structures and processes that signify more than who reports to whom. Of the six symbolic forms mentioned in this paper, the structural form most often differentiates new presidents from old. New presidents, those in office three years or less, often feel the need to alter the organizational structure to signify change. Birnbaum has noted, "New presidents . . . may talk off the

record to colleagues . . . and complain (but with a certain degree of pride), 'You wouldn't believe the mess I found when I got here, but I've finally begun to get it turned around'" (1986, 392). Although I have not uncovered any aggregated differences between new and old presidents' symbolic perceptions—including the structural form—within the structural form, I have found Birnbaum's comment correct. That is, the intent of new presidents differs from that of old presidents when they use the structural form.

New presidents tend to embrace decision-making structures as symbols of change more than individuals who have served in their positions longer. Although older presidents use structures as symbols, structures do not necessarily connote change. Instead they may imply any number of significations. Commented one new president: "I did not create the faculty council. It was here when I arrived. But under my predecessor, people on that council were selected by the president and it was an at large position. I have changed that so that there is one faculty representative per division and they are elected by the faculty."

Another new president set up a task force primarily composed of senior faculty who helped the president create fundamental changes in the university. An older president said, "When I came in, I developed the traditional vice presidential offices. The first thing I did was to create a traditional administrative structure, an administrative team."

One new college president spoke indirectly about the symbolic implications of structural changes:

> I created two vice president positions—one for academic affairs and the other for public relations; I upgraded the dean of research to vice president. More reorganization took place at the deans' level too. I had to change the football coach and the athletic director. This situation enabled me to establish the fact that the president would be running the university, not the athletic director.

None of these examples, indeed, no examples of symbols in general, serve a singular purpose. When a president takes office, it is certainly conceivable that an administrative structure may be unsuitable to the president's style or needs. Changing such a structure may achieve particular goals. At the same time, by changing a structure the president also signals to the college community that life as it previously existed will change. From this perspective, the president's action accounts not only for structural change but also for the perception of change.

Borrowing from Merton (1957), Birnbaum (in press) has termed symbols such as those noted here as functionally "latent." Although structural change may produce needed outcomes, Birnbaum contends that some latent functions "are meeting less obvious, but still important, organizational needs." The findings from the data tend to suggest that new presidents use structural change in large part because of its latent function; they draw heavily on structural symbols to place their imprimatur on the institution.

Task forces may provide someone with good ideas and a different electoral system may be an improvement upon a previous system; but in essence, the president uses these devices to symbolize change. An older president commented, "During my time, we have elaborated the administrative style of the university. [My predecessor] was more of a one-person operator." Again, the administrative structure had come into play as a presidential perception of structural change or evolution.

Personification Symbols

Symbolic personification refers to a leader's intent to represent a message with an individual or group. For example, on a national level, we often find political appointees who symbolize an elected leader's commitment to a particular constituency. President Reagan's appointing a woman to the Supreme Court was intended to symbolize his concern for women.

College presidents also perceive that particular groups or individuals symbolize particular messages to different communities. One president noted, "When we changed the governance structure, we put the president of the student government on [it]; and he or she is involved in everything we discuss. The individual is a full member of the administrative structure." Thus, the president perceived not only that the administrative structure symbolized a message but also that who sat on the governing body symbolized, in this case, concern for student ideas.

Another president commented about the rising quality of the student body and noted, "We have finally started getting the recognition we deserve to have." This recognition was that the Big Eight accounting firms had been recruiting on campus. The presence of major marketing companies symbolized a rise in the institution's quality.

One college president felt the need to emphasize "excellent teaching." A potent symbol was appointing "three campus deans and a VP who have all had teaching experience and have had department chair experience. And I told the deans that they were required to teach also." Thus, this president's perception of leadership was to use personal symbols as a means of reorienting the culture of the organization.

Presidents also see themselves as symbols of the institution. One president spoke for many: "I had to get out in the community because no one had been out there before. I wanted people to think of the college as entering a new era." The presidents' willingness to meet the public was perhaps the most tangible example of symbolic personification. Presidents are the university; or, at least, they perceive themselves to be.

Ideational Symbols

Ideas as symbols refer to images leaders convey about the mission and purpose of the institution. Presidents generate ideas that serve as symbolic ideologies about their institutions. Clark's (1980) concept of an institutional saga is a cogent example of an ideational symbol by which leaders attempt to seize a unique role for their institution. A president perceives that leadership is often inextricably bound up with the symbolic generation of an institutional mission or ideology.

Ideational symbols are often the most difficult symbols for constituents to interpret if the symbol is divorced from tangible contexts. That is, particular ideas that presidents perceive as important may appear to be no more than presidential rhetoric to a constituency if the symbol cannot be palpably interpreted to them.

"I wanted a new image, a comprehensive quality," commented one leader. A second downgraded the importance of football at the institution:

> The first statement I would make as president would be about athletics, and I knew that it would be heard throughout all the towns and cities. I wanted it to be a statement not about athletics but about what the institution would be and do in the future. I want us to be known for great education and not great athletics. I wanted it to be a statement about the kind of students we want.

The images that presidents struggle to convey to their constituencies are symbolic representations of institutional values. What a president perceives to be the value of the institution is oftentimes what the institution will struggle to achieve. By definition, an institution with a unique identity cannot be all things to all people. The symbolic idea serves as the unifying principle for the organization. Many colleges and universities are committed to distinctive ideas. College presidents who emphasize one idea over another impart to constituents what they believe to be the primary goal of the institution.

Discussion

I offer organizational leaders three suggestions about the symbolic aspects of leadership. Rather than formulaic prescriptions of how to function in the organizational universe, I tender three proposals for understanding one's own perceptions and the culture in which one operates. The suggestions are components of a diagnostic frame of reference, a way of interpreting one's organization. I propose ways for leaders to identify what they must do to comprehend the symbolic dimensions of their leadership.

1. Symbols Demand Corroboration

As noted, the research team queried the presidents about how they defined good leadership and what they had done as leaders. The interviews revealed several contradictions between what the individuals used as a symbol and how they acted. That is, on occasion discrepancies existed between what leaders perceive as good leadership and how they actually act.

One president who believes in visibility, for example, meets formally with the faculty only once a year. Another president's ideational symbol was "excellence" and to be known as a top-rate institution yet later in the interview spoke of institutional survival as the top priority. A third president cited the faculty council as a structural-personal symbol to communicate the critical importance of the faculty, yet no formal vehicles existed whereby the president actually met with them. Still another president tried to communicate symbolically that open, frank discussion was extremely important yet simultaneously demanded "extraordinary loyalty" to the president.

The point is not that individuals seek to deceive their constituencies. Instead, leaders should be aware of how symbolic forms may contradict one another. Walking around a campus or stressing "teamwork" does not necessarily confirm that collegiality exists. Leaders need to contextualize their perceptions and search for contradictions. We all have discrepancies between what we say and what we do. For an organizational leader, greater consistency between words and deeds allows followers a clearer understanding of a leader's intention.

2. Use Symbols Consistent with the Organization's Culture

The culture of an organization is a social construction, dependent not only on the perceptions of a leader but also on the unique history of the organization, the individual orientations and perceptions of followers, and larger environmental influences. The cultural paradigm assumes that an organization does not consist of rational, "real" entities (Tierney 1988).

Everyday existence is a constant matter of interpretation among organizational participants. Rather than assume a functional view of symbols and a passive view of individuals, we need to reconceptualize culture as an interpretive dynamic whereby a leader's symbols may or may not be interpreted the way he or she intended. Thus, dissonance will occur even when a president's symbols corroborate each other if he or she has used symbols that are inconsistent with the organization's culture.

A new president, for example, may want to symbolize care and concern for the faculty and structurally reorganize the decision-making process, adding councils and committees to make it more participative. The president's perception and symbolic intent is to highlight a structural symbol. The strategy may fail, however, if the culture has relied for a generation on presidential informality and one-on-one conversations with faculty.

The challenge for the president is not only to search for contradictions in symbolic forms but also to understand how those symbolic forms exist within the organization's culture. If symbols are neither reified nor functional, then we must necessarily investigate their contextual surroundings to understand them.

3. Use All Symbolic Forms

Leaders, not unlike most individuals, are intuitively aware that particular objects or activities are highly imbued with symbolism. This essay has reported on the use of new buildings or new computers to convey a message. Similarly, the well-read manager today believes that management tips about communication hold symbolic value.

Yet as we have seen, leaders may employ a wide array of symbolic forms. Within each category exist a potential multitude of symbols. Further, an abundance of activities, acts, and the like also exist within a symbolic form. Rather than rely on the symbolic content of a single convocation speech every year, a president might benefit from employing a wide array of consistent symbolic forms. We tend to compartmentalize activities to simplify them, yet that is not how organizational participants experience reality.

All acts within an organization are open to interpretation. Virtually everything a leader does or says (or does not do or say) is capable of symbolic intent or interpretation. To acknowledge the pervasiveness of symbols in an organization does not imply that a leader is in charge of an anarchic organization that interprets messages any way it wants. Instead, a central challenge for the leader is to interpret the culture of the organization and to draw upon all of the symbolic forms effectively so that organizational participants can make sense of organizational activities.

Conclusion

A symbolic view of leadership and organizations needs to move beyond functionalist definitions of organizational symbolism. We need to pay attention to the processes whereby organizational members interpret the symbolic activities of leaders, rather than assume that all individuals march to the same organizational beat. We need to investigate why a particular symbol may be potent in one organization at one particular time and relatively useless in another organization.

The assumption at work in this paper has been that, although both the structure and expressions of colleges and universities change, the inner necessities that drive them do not. "Thrones may be out of fashion," states Geertz, "and pageantry too; but authority still requires a cultural frame in which to define itself and advance its claims" (1983, 143). If symbolism helps define authority, then we should continue the quest to understand the symbolic manifestations of organizational life and leadership.

William G. Tierney is assistant professor and research associate, Center for the Study of Higher Education, Pennsylvania State University.

This document was prepared with financial support from the Office of Educational Research and Improvement/Department of Education (OERI/ED). However, the opinions expressed herein do not necessarily reflect the position, policy, or official endorsement of the OERI/ED.

References

Bailey, Frederick George. *The Tactical Uses of Passion.* Ithaca, NY: Cornell University Press, 1983.

Birnbaum, Robert. *How Colleges Work: The Cybernetics of Academic Organization and Leadership.* San Francisco: Jossey-Bass Publishers, 1988.

———. "Leadership and Learning." *Review of Higher Education* 9, no. 4 (1986): 381–95.

———. "The Latent Organizational Functions of the Academic Senate." *Journal of Higher Education* in press.

Birnbaum, Robert, Estela M. Bensimon, and Anna Neumann. "Leadership in Higher Education: A Multidimensional Approach to Research." *Review of Higher Education* 12, no. 2 (Winter 1989): 101–105.

Clark, Burton R. "The Making of an Organizational Saga." In *Readings in Managerial Psychology,* edited by Harold J. Leavitt and Louis R. Pondy. Chicago: University of Chicago Press, 1980.

Dandridge, Thomas C., Ian Mitroff, and William F. Joyce. "Organizational Symbolism: A Topic to Expand Organizational Analysis." *Academy of Management Review* 5, no. 1 (1980): 77–82.

Deal, Terrence, and Allan A. Kennedy. *Corporate Cultures: The Rites and Rituals of Corporate Life.* Reading, Mass.: Addison-Wesley, 1982.

Eco, Umberto. *A Theory of Semiotics.* Bloomington: Indiana University Press, 1979.

Geertz, Clifford. *The Interpretation of Cultures.* New York City: Basic Books, 1973.

_____. "Reflections on the Symbolics of Power." In *Local Knowledge,* edited by Clifford Geertz. New York City: Basic Books, 1983.

Merton, Robert K. *Social Theory of Social Structure.* Glencoe, Ill.: Free Press, 1957.

Peters, Thomas J., and Robert H. Waterman, Jr. *In Search of Excellence.* New York: Harper and Row, 1982.

Pettigrew, Andrew M. "On Studying Organizational Cultures." *Administrative Science Quarterly* 24 (1979): 570–81.

Pfeffer, Jeffrey. "Management as Symbolic Action." In *Research in Organizational Behavior,* edited by Larry L. Cummings & Barry Staw. Greenwich, Conn.: JAI Press, 1981.

Schein, Edgar H. *Organizational Culture and Leadership.* San Francisco: Jossey-Bass Publishers, 1985.

Tierney, William G. "The Semiotic Aspects of Leadership: An Ethnographic Perspective." *The American Journal of Semiotics* 5, no. 1 (1987): 223–50. In press-a.

_____. "Organizational Culture in Higher Education: Defining the Essentials." *Journal of Higher Education* 59, no. 1 (1988): 2–21. In press-b.

Trice, Harrison M., and Janice M. Beyer. "Studying Organizational Cultures through Rites and Ceremonials." *Academy of Management Review* 9 (1984): 653–69.

CHAPTER 19

THE LATENT ORGANIZATIONAL FUNCTIONS
OF THE ACADEMIC SENATE

ROBERT BIRNBAUM

Academic senates[1] are generally considered to be the normative organizational structure through which faculty exercise their role in college and university governance at the institutional level [1]. Although no complete census is available, analysis of data in past studies [23, 25] suggest that senates may exist in one or another form on between 60 to 80 percent of all campuses.

With the advent of faculty collective bargaining in the late 1960s, concern was expressed that senates, unable to compete with the more adversarial and aggressive union, might disappear on many campuses [351. Not only has this prediction proven to be false [5, 6], but there is evidence that the proportion of institutions with senates has increased over the past decades [3].

This growth is somewhat perplexing in view of the stream of criticisms that increasingly has been directed against the senate structure. It has been called weak, ineffective, an empty forum, vestigial, unrepresentative, and inept [2, 12, 24, 33, 35, 38]. Its detractors have referred to it as "slowly collapsing and becoming dormant" [24, p. 61] and "purely ceremonial" [7]. In a 1969 national study, 60 percent of faculty respondents rated the performance of their campus senate or faculty council as only "fair" or "poor" [11]. A more recent consideration of faculty governance has stated that "traditional structures do not appear to be working very well. Faculty participation has declined, and we discovered a curious mismatch between the agenda of faculty councils and the crisis now confronted by many institutions" [12, p. 12.].

These negative evaluations of faculty governance structures are not new. A trenchant observer in 1918 [47, p. 186] noted the administrative use of faculty "committees-for-the-sifting-of-the-saw-dust" to give the appearance, but not the reality, of participation, and called them "a nice problem in self-deception, chiefly notable for an endless proliferation" (p. 206).

There is not complete agreement that the senate has no real instrumental value. Blau's [9] finding of a negative correlation between senate participation and educational centralization at over one hundred colleges and universities, for example, led him to state that "an institutionalized faculty government is not mere window dressing but an effective mechanism for restricting centralized control over educational programs, in accordance with the professional demands of the faculty. Formal institutionalization of faculty authority fortifies it" (p. 164). Another supporter of the senate [21], after reviewing the literature, reported that the senate continued to be "a useful mechanism for campus-wide faculty participation" (p. 26) at certain types of research universities and elite liberal arts colleges in some governance areas, although it was less useful in others. But despite the support of a small number of observers, the clear weight of evidence and authoritative opinion suggests that, except perhaps in a small number of institutions with particular characteristics, the academic senate does not work. Indeed, it has been suggested that it has never worked [2]. Yet it survives and, in many respects, thrives.

After citing a litany of major criticisms of the senate and proposing reasons for its deficiencies, Lieberman [30, p. 65] added, "what is needed is not so much a critique of their inherent weaknesses, but an explanation of their persistence in spite thereof." Similarly, Hobbs [22], in looking at the functions of university committees, suggested that rather than focusing attention on recommending ways in which these committees might be made more effective, greater attention should be given to examining their roles in university organization. This article will conduct such an examination by considering the roles that senates are presumed to play—and the roles they actually play—within four alternative organizational models that consider the senate as part of bureaucratic, collegial, political, or symbolic organizational systems.

Manifest and Latent Functions

The manifest functions of an organizational structure, policy, or practice can be thought of as those for which behavior leads to some specified and related achievement. Institutional processes that usually lead to expected and desired outcomes should be expected to persist. Often, however, organizations engage in behavior that persists over time even though the manifest function is clearly not achieved. Indeed, such behavior may persist even when there is significant evidence that the ostensible function *cannot* be achieved. There is a tendency to label such organizational behavior as irrational or superstitious and to identify an institution's inability to alter such apparently ineffectual behavior as due to "inertia" or "lack of leadership."

Merton's [36] concept of functional analysis suggests an alternative explanation. Some practices that do not appear to be fulfilling their formally intended functions may persist because they are fulfilling unintended and unrecognized latent functions that are impor-

tant to the organization. As Merton describes it, functional analysis examines social practices to determine both the planned and intended (manifest) outcomes and the unplanned and unintended (latent) outcomes. This is particularly useful for the study of otherwise puzzling organizational behavior because it "clarifies the analysis of seemingly irrational social patterns . . ., directs attention to theoretically fruitful fields of inquiry . . ., and precludes the substitution of naive moral judgments for sociological analysis" (p. 64–66, 70). In particular, it points towards the close examination of persistent yet apparently ineffective institutional processes or structures to explore the possibility that they are meeting less obvious, but still important, organizational needs. "We should ordinarily (not invariably) expect persistent social patterns and social structures to perform positive functions which are at the time not adequately fulfilled by other existing patterns and structures" [36, p. 72]. The senate may do more than many of its critics believe, and "only when we attend to all the functions and their social contexts can we fully appreciate what it is that the senate does" [42, p. 174].

This article shall examine two major questions. First, and briefly, what are the manifest functions of the academic senate that its critics claim appear not to be fulfilled, and what organizational models do they imply? Second, and at greater depth, what may be the latent functions of the academic senate that may explain its growth and persistence despite its failure to meet its avowed purposes, and how do these functions relate to organizational models?

The Manifest Functions of the Academic Senate

In general, those who criticize the senate have not clearly articulated the criteria they have employed, and their analyses tend to be narrative and anecdotal with no explicit conceptual orientation. Their comments and conclusions, however, suggest that they evaluate the senate implicitly using the three traditional models of the university as a bureaucracy, as a collegium, and as a political system.

Probably the most prevalent implicit model is that of the university as bureaucracy. In his study of the effectiveness of senates (which is one of the few studies to specify desired outcomes) Millett established eight criteria that "would provide some reasonable conclusions about the contributions and the effectiveness of campus-wide governance to the process of institutional decision making" [38, p. xiv]. These included the extent to which senates clarified institutional purpose, specified program objectives, reallocated income resources, and developed new income sources, as well as the extent to which they were involved in issues such as the management of operations, degree requirements, academic behavior, and program evaluation. The identification of the senate's role in decision making and the emphasis upon goal-setting, resource allocation, and evaluation suggest an implicit view of the senate as an integral part of a hierarchical, rational organization. This bureaucratic orientation is also seen in one of the two "modal" university committee types identified by Hobbs [22]. This type, among other characteristics, meets often, has a decision-making function, records minutes, prepares written reports for administrative officers, and has a clear sense of task. Other analysts have also used language that either explicitly or metaphorically identifies the senate in bureaucratic terms. Senates are needed to deal with "the full range of academic and administrative matters" [12, p. 13], their purpose "approximates that of the college's management" [24, p. 126], and they assist "the discovery and employment of techniques to deal with deficit spending, with increasing enrollments, with healing the wounds resulting from student dissent, with curriculum expansion, with faculty salary increases in a tight budget, with parking, and so forth" [41, p. 40].

A second model implicitly views the senate as part of a political system. In this model the senate is seen as a forum for the articulation of interests and as the setting in which decisions on institutional policies and goals are reached through compromise, negotiation, and the forming of coalitions. Senates serve as a place for campus politicians to exercise their trade, which in its worst sense may identify them as "poorly attended oratorical bodies" [24, p. 127] and in the best sense means that they can "provide a forum for the resolution of a wide range of issues involving the mission and operation of the institution" [1, p. 57]. Given the significant differences that typify the interest groups

that make up its constituencies, the senate enables participants to deal with inevitable conflict as they "engage one another civilly in dispute" [22, p. 242].

The model of the university as collegium is less explicitly identified in analyses of the senate than the other two models, but it appears to be recognized through constant references in the literature to the concept of collegiality. The senate in this view would be a forum for achieving Millett's [37] goal of a dynamic of consensus.

Depending upon the organizational assumptions used, an observer might consider the senate to be effective in governance either (a) to the extent that it efficiently considered institutional problems and, through rational processes, developed rules, regulations, and procedures that resolved them, or (b) to the extent that, perceived as fully representative of its constituencies, it formulated and clarified goals and policies, or (c) to the extent that, through interaction in the senate forum, it developed shared values leading to consensus. But senates often appear to do none of these things well. From the bureaucratic perspective they are slow and inefficient, from a political position they are oligarchical and not representative, and from a collegial viewpoint faculty interactions may be as likely to expose latent conflict as to increase feelings of community [39].

These alternative organizational models suggest a range of activities, processes, and outcomes as the manifest functions of the senate. Because these functions do not appear to be performed adequately, the senate has been judged to be ineffective. In many ways the senate appears to be a solution looking for problems. Millett, for example, provides a list of eight specific problems and questions raised by student activism in the 1960s (such as the role of higher education in defense research, or the role of higher education in providing community service to the disadvantaged) to which appropriately comprised senates were presumably an answer. He found that there was "very little evidence that organs of campus-wide governance, after they were established, were particularly effective in resolving these issues" [38, p. 200]. Because its manifest functions are not being fulfilled, the persistence of the senate suggests that it is filling important latent functions. What might some of these be?

The Latent Functions of the Academic Senate

The Senate as Symbol

In addition to whatever effects they may have upon outcomes, organizational structures and processes also often have symbolic importance to participants [20]. Academic senates may fill a number of important symbolic purposes. We will consider three: the senate may symbolize institutional membership in the higher education system, collective and individual faculty commitment to professional values, and joint faculty-administration acceptance of existing authority relationships.

Faculty participation in governance is generally accepted as an essential characteristic of "mainstream" colleges and universities. Since 1950 there has been a significant increase in the types and kinds of institutions that many consider only marginally identified with higher education. These include, for example, community colleges with strong administrative hierarchies, unselective state colleges with traditions rooted in teacher education and the paternalistic practices of school systems, and small and unselective independent institutions with authoritarian presidents. By establishing an academic senate structure that was more typical of the system to which they aspired than it was of the one from which they developed, an institution could suggest the existence of faculty authority even when it did not exist. This structural symbol of a faculty voice could support a claim to being a "real" college.

The development of a senate can also symbolize a general faculty commitment to substantive values. The most visible and public matters of faculty concern at some institutions have been related to faculty collective bargaining, which has tended to focus upon employee issues that in many ways were similar to those of other workers. Particularly in the public sector, but sometimes in the private sector as well, faculty emphasis upon salary, working conditions and other mundane matters has eroded in the minds of the public their claim to professional status. Creating a senate may be a response to that erosion, symbolizing a commitment to professional values and faculty concern for more purely academic matters. This helps to legitimate the institution's desire to be treated differently than other organizations and the faculty's claim to be treated differently than other groups of workers. Through a senate, the faculty can symbolically endorse such desirable attributes or outcomes as increased quality, standards, and integrity even though (or perhaps because) they cannot define either the problems or their solutions in operational terms. The senate may thus serve as a forum through which, individually and collectively, faculty may symbolically embrace values in lieu of actual behavior. Within the senate, academics who have never had controversial new ideas can publicly defend academic freedom, and those without scholarly interests can argue for reduced teaching loads to encourage research. In this way even faculty who cannot do so through the publication of scholarship or research, can publicly display their academic *bona fides*.

Senates may also serve as symbols of campus authority relationships. A major criticism directed against the senate is that it exists at the pleasure of the administration and board of trustees [3, 30]. Because of this, its authority has been described as "tenuous" [39, p. 26]. However, the fact is that although trustees have rejected senate recommendations, they have not abolished senates (except in rare circumstances involving the introduction of faculty collective bargaining). Indeed, administrations support senates and believe them to be even more "effective" than do faculty members [23]. Why should both the faculty and the administration continue to support the senate structure? It is obvious that faculty would wish to maintain senates because they are a symbol of administrative acceptance of the idea of faculty participation in governance. Administrators may support senates because voluntary faculty participation in such bodies is a tacit acknowledgement by the faculty that they recognize and accept the ultimate legal authority of the administration and board. The senate is thus a symbol of cooperation between faculty and administration. As in other organizational settings, parties may cooperate in perpetuating an already established structure even when the objective utility of the structure is agreed by the parties to be of little value [17]. The continued existence of the senate therefore is not only a visible manifestation of the ability of the parties to cooperate but also reflects an intent to further increase cooperative activities.

The symbolic value of the senate is so strong that even those like Millett [38] who after study have concluded that the senate is ineffective when evaluated against specific criteria, continue to support it. Even if it doesn't work in terms of its ostensible aims, it may be preferable that an institution have a nonfunctioning senate than that it have no senate at all.

The Senate as Status Provider

Cohen and March [13] have suggested that "most people in a college are most of the time less concerned with the content of a decision than they are with eliciting an acknowledgment of their importance within the community. . . . Faculty members are more insistent on their right to participate in faculty deliberations than they are on exercising that right" (pp. 201–2). In an analogous vein, the existence of a senate certifies the status of faculty members by acknowledging their right to participate in governance, while at the same time not obligating them to do so. The vigorous support of faculty for a strong and active voice in campus governance, coupled with their reluctance to give the time that such participation would require [16, 18], should therefore not be surprising.

The senate also offers a route of social mobility for older and less prestigious faculty locals whose concern for status based on traditional norms is frustrated by a lack of scholarly achievement [27]. Participation in committee affairs and opportunities it brings to work with higher status administrators provides a local means for enhancing their own importance.

In addition to certifying the status of participants in general, providing an opportunity for individuals to serve as senator is a means of conferring status that protects the institution from two quite different, but potentially disruptive, elements: informal leaders and organizational deviants.

Universities are normative organizations that rely upon the manipulation of symbols to control the behavior of their members [19]. Unlike organizations characterized by control through coercive or utilitarian power, normative organizations tend to have more "formal leaders" (those who influence others both through their personal power and through the organizational positions they hold) and fewer informal leaders (personal power only) or officials (positional power only). Formal leadership provides a relatively effective means of exercising power in a decentralized and loosely coupled system. By the same token, the development of informal leaders can be dysfunctional by facilitating the development of semi-autonomous subgroups that can diminish the formal leader's influence.

Formal leaders cannot prevent the development of informal leaders, but in normative organizations "to the degree that informal leaders arise . . ., the tendency is to recruit them and gain their loyalty and cooperation by giving them part-time organizational positions. . . . The tendency is for the informal leaders to lose this status within the given organization and for control to remain largely in the hands of the formal leaders" [19, p. 64]. Membership in a prestigious body such as a senate with presumed quasi-administrative responsibilities can be used towards the same end "of providing alternative channels of social mobility for those otherwise excluded from the more conventional avenues for 'social advancement'" [36, p. 76]. Senate membership provides legitimate organizational roles in which informal leaders can participate and have their status confirmed while at the same time preventing them from disrupting ongoing organizational structures and processes.

There is a second group of campus participants whose activities, if not channelled through a legitimate structure such as a senate, might prove disruptive to the organization. They are the institutional deviants, often highly vocal persons with a single-minded devotion to one or another cause. Senates offer these deviant faculty a legitimized opportunity to vent their grievances and solicit potential support. Election of such persons may sometimes lead administrators to discount the senate as "nonrepresentative" and may be seen by them as yet another example of senate weakness. On the other hand, the need for even deviants to allocate attention means that time spent acting in the relatively stable environment of the senate is time they do not have available for participating in relatively more vulnerable settings, such as the department. The senate may thus serve as a system for absorbing the energies of potentially disruptive faculty members. Because the senate, like the administration, is subject to overload, it can attend to only a small number of items at any one time. The difficulty of convincing senate colleagues of the justice of their position is more likely to reduce aspirations of deviants than would be constant rebuffs by administrators or departmental colleagues; if a faculty member cannot convince his or her colleagues, how can the administration possibly be convinced?

The Senate as Garbage Can and Deep Freeze

Sometimes a college or university can use rational processes to make choices and solve problems when it is called upon to make a decision. However, this becomes difficult when unexpectedly other people become involved in the decision process, new problems are introduced, and new solutions are proposed. These independent streams of participants, problems, and solutions may somehow become attached to each other, often by chance, just as if they were all dumped into a large container, leading to what has been referred to as "garbage can decision making" [15]. Choices become more difficult as they become increasingly connected with "garbage" (that is, with problems, potential solutions, or new participants who, at least to the decision maker, appear irrelevant). Choices become easier if they can be made either before these irrelevant matters become attached to them (decision making by oversight), or after these irrelevant matters can be made to leave the choice (decision making by flight). Because of the essential ambiguity of the college and university processes, any choice point can become a garbage can. One of the latent functions of the senate may be to function as a structural garbage can, and the inability of the senate to make speedy decisions may increase its effectiveness in this role by putting some problems into an organizational "deep freeze."

An administrator who wishes to make a decision but finds it difficult to do so because irrelevant problems have become associated with it, can refer those irrelevant problems to the senate. The decision can then be made by flight while the attention of participants is directed elsewhere.

The deliberate speed of the senate makes it possible for many problems that are referred to it to resolve themselves over time with no need for any specific action. This kind of outcome is shown by the disparaging statement of one faculty member: "The committees [of the senate] report, but usually it has taken so long to 'study the issue' that the matter is long since past" [3, p. 80].

Other issues, particularly those that deal with goals and values and thus might be divisive if an attempt were made to resolve them, may be referred to the senate with the justifiable expectation that they will absorb a significant amount of energy and then will not be heard of again. Still, the senate debate has an important outcome even if it does not lead to taking action. Through the presentation of alternative positions and arguments, participants come to realize that an issue whose resolution initially appeared to be self-evident and therefore enjoying wide support is in fact complex and contentious. As the attractiveness of simplistic solutions is reduced, aspirations are modified and potential conflict is therefore managed.

The Senate as Attention Cue

The number of problems available in a university searching for decision opportunities and forums in which they can be resolved, although perhaps finite in number, is at any specific time far greater than can be acted upon. Administrative attention is in comparatively short supply, and as administrators "look for work" they must decide to which of many different potential attention cues they should pay attention. This is a nontrivial issue, because the ability of problems, solutions, decision makers, and choice opportunities to become coupled through temporal rather than through logical relationships makes it exceptionally difficult for an administrator to know on an *a priori* basis what is most important. In the absence of a calculus or an algorithm that permits administrators to predict how important any specific problem may prove to be, they must rely on heuristics (such as "oil the squeaky wheel") to indicate when an item may have reached a level of concern sufficient to require administrative attention. There are many sources of such cues: a telephone call from a state legislator or an editorial in the local paper or student press are examples. So too is discussion and action (potential or actual) by the senate. As Mason [33] and others have commented, senate agendas "tend to be exceedingly crowded . . . [and] even if a senator has succeeded in placing a policy-question in the agenda 'it will not be reached until the meeting has gone on so long that the member's one overwhelming desire is to go home'" [p. 75]. As a result, not every item that is proposed for the senate agenda actually gets on it, and not every item that gets on it is attended to. The presence of a specific item on an agenda that becomes the subject of extended discussion and possible action therefore signifies that it is of unusual importance and worth an investment of administrative time. By the same token, a matter proposed to the senate but not considered by it can be used as a justification for administrative indifference. The senate thus operates in the university in a manner similar to that of a public agency before a budget subcommittee. When there are no more than the usual level of complaints, no action need be taken. But when "an agency shouts more loudly than usual, subcommittee members have a pretty good idea that something is wrong" [46, p. 154].

Because most items which someone wants discussed by the senate are never acted upon, the use of the senate as an attention cue is an efficient way of allocating attention. It relieves the administration of responsibility for dealing with every problem, establishes a rationale for a system of priorities, provides a justification for inattention to some items, and maintains the symbolic relationship of administration responsiveness to faculty concerns.

The Senate as Personnel Screening Device

Universities constantly have to fill administrative positions, and it is often less disruptive institutionally as well as desirable financially to do so with faculty members. However, not every faculty member is acceptable, and at least two characteristics not often found in combination are desirable: a person should have the confidence of faculty colleagues and should also be sympathetic to the administrative point of view. The senate provides a forum in which such persons can be more easily identified and evaluated.

Election to the senate itself provides strong (although not absolutely reliable) evidence of acceptability to faculty colleagues, and working with administrators in preparing reports or other committee assignments allows senators to demonstrate through the equivalent of on-the-job participation their commitment to administrative values.

Anecdotal evidence indicates that administrators are often selected from among faculty "committeemen," [27, p. 83], and case study material [34] has shown how the intimate involvement of faculty committee members with administrative officers in policy formulation has meant that "many senate committee members have moved easily and naturally into regular administrative positions" [34, p. 103]. Of course, persons selected for administrative positions because they perform well in the kinds of ideological and noninstrumental debates of the senate may turn out not to be the most effective institutional leaders [13].

The Senate as Organizational Conservator

More attention has traditionally been given to the presumed negative consequences of the university's acknowledged resistance to change than to the potentially positive aspects of maintaining the ongoing system. From a functional perspective, ongoing organizational processes and structures exist in an equilibrium that is a response to and a resultant of a number of forces operating upon and within the institution. As with any open system, the university is homeostatic in nature and tends to react to the instability caused by change by responding in a manner that returns it to its former state. The senate, by inhibiting the propensity to change that increasingly characterizes the administration, serves as a major element in this homeostatic process of organizational conservation.

Administrators in general, and presidents in particular, usually do not wish to change the university in dramatic ways, and the processes through which they are selected and socialized tend to make their roles conservative [13]. Yet they occupy boundary positions in the organization and find themselves exposed, as faculty members are not, to the demands of the external environment as well as those of the organization. In that external environment there are a number of factors that implicitly or explicitly pressure university administrators to become more intrusive in organizational life [see, for example, 24]. Administrators may attempt to introduce new institutional policies in response to regulations enacted or proposed by state agencies, calls for accountability by external study groups, or potential fiscal emergencies based on worse-case scenarios. These policies almost always seek to increase administrative authority. Faculty are less likely to be directly influenced by such pressures and therefore less likely to be persuaded that dramatic action is required. By opposing such administrative initiatives, senates act not only as "an effective mechanism for restricting centralized control over academic programs" [9, p. 164], but also serve as a constraint upon an ambitious administration [18].

In addition to external pressures, there are powerful, if less obvious, reasons for increased administrative activism, and these reasons are related to the increased availability of institutional information. The movement toward the "management" of higher education has, among other things, led to complex systems for the collection and analysis by administrators of previously inaccessible institutional data. These data illuminate anomalies, inequities, and nonstandard practices that must then be justified or abolished and therefore provoke administrative intervention. But as Trow [43] has pointed out, it is precisely the obscurity caused by bad data collection that may permit the diversity and innovation upon which institutional quality is based. The senate's ability to resist administrative initiatives can therefore be seen, at least in some cases, as protecting the institution from making changes based upon measurable but ultimately unimportant factors and thus preserving those enduring organizational and institutional qualities that are beyond routine measurement.

In addition to the increased quantity of data, there are also changes in the processes through which data reach administrators in executive positions, as well as in the speed with which they move through the organization. In the past, data might eventually have come to administrative attention after having first been passed through and manipulated by a series of committees and long after corrective administrative measures could be applied. Today these same data may be transmitted directly to the president from a state coordinating board, often with a time lag measured in

weeks rather than years. The effect on a university can be similar to that in other social systems characterized by "symptoms of communication failures based on a superabundance of information, inadequately assimilated, rather than its scarcity" [Douglas Cater, cited in 31, p. 1]. Today administrators may face an endless and often real-time stream of data calling for corrective action before there is time to plan, consult, or fully consider.

The existence of a senate reduces administrative aspirations for change and increases the caution with which the administration acts. This not only protects much of value within the organization but also prevents the unwitting disruption of ongoing but latent systems through which the university keeps the behavior of organizational participants within acceptable bounds. The senate thus is the structure through which, in Clark Kerr's [26] terms, the faculty serve as the institution's balance wheel, "resisting some things that should be resisted, insisting on more thorough discussion of some things that should be more thoroughly discussed, delaying some developments where delay gives time to adjust more gracefully to the inevitable. All this yields a greater sense of order and stability" (p. 100).

The Senate as Ritual and as Pastime

Senates usually meet on a regular schedule, follow a standard agenda format, involve the same core of participants, and engage in their activities under stipulated rules of order. In an organization typified by ambiguity, it is often comforting to engage in scheduled and structured activities in which the behaviors of others can be generally predicted. The senate thus serves as a ritual, a "formality of procedure or action that either is not directed towards a pragmatic end, or if so directed, will fail to achieve the intended aim" [10, cited in 32, p. 164]. The identification of the senate as "theatrical and debate-oriented" [24, p. 127] underscores its ritualistic qualities.

The rituals of senates serve a number of important organizational functions. Among other things, it helps stabilize and order the organization, it provides assurances that mutually expected interactions will occur, and it reduces anxiety [32]. Senates also provide organizational participants with opportunities for engaging in acceptable behavior when faced with ambiguous or uncertain stimuli. When one doesn't know what else to do, participating in senate debate can appear to be a contribution towards solutions and can enable faculty members to "pretend that they are doing something significant" [3, p. 80].

Ritual provides participants with a sense of membership and integration into an organization and into a profession. For others, however, the senate may be enjoyed purely as a pastime. It is a place where one can meet friends, engage in political intrigues, gossip about the administration, and complain about parking—all common forms of faculty recreation. It is also a place where speeches can be made, power can be displayed, nits can be picked, and the intricacies of Robert's Rules of Order can be explored at infinite depth. Those faculty who do enjoy such things have a vested interest in perpetuating the senate, for without it a forum for their involvement would be lost.

The Senate as Scapegoat

The best-laid plans of institutions often go awry. To some extent, this may be due to cognitive limits to rationality that suggest that only a small proportion of potentially important variables may be attended to at any given time. Equally as important may be the organizational characteristics of colleges and universities as decentralized and loosely coupled systems [44]. In such systems it is often difficult to predict events, and intentions, actions, and outcomes may be only modestly related. Even the power of the president, usually considered the single most influential person in the institution, is severely circumscribed.

When plans are not enacted or goals not achieved, organizational constituents search for reasons. In order to meet psychological needs, these reasons must of course blame others and not oneself; and in order to meet political needs, these reasons must be specific rather than conceptual. A president is unlikely to blame an institutional failure on weak presidential performance, and a board of trustees is not likely to accept a president's argument that a certain task cannot be performed because it is beyond the capabilities of a loosely coupled system. On the other hand, Boards can understand a president's assertion that a specific act was made difficult or impossible because of opposition by the senate and may even entertain a claim that it would be impossible to implement a program because of the likelihood of future senate opposition. In the same way, faculty members at the department or school level can argue against considering a new policy on the grounds that the senate would not approve it and can blame the senate when a program supported by the senate breaks down when implemented at lower organizational levels.

Cause and effect relationships are extremely difficult to assess in the equivocal environment of the college or university. The actions (or lack thereof) of a structure such as the senate, which has high visibility and an ambiguous charge, can plausibly be blamed for deficiencies of all kinds in institutional operation. An academic department can use the senate as a scapegoat for its own unwillingness to make the difficult choices necessary to strengthen its departmental curriculum as easily as a politically incompetent president can accuse it of scuttling a major policy initiative. In these and in similar cases, the senate helps the participants "make sense" of an exceptionally complex system while at the same time preserving their self-images of acumen and professional competence.

Academic Senates in Symbolic Organizational Systems

This article began by discussing the perceived shortcomings of senates when traditional organizational models of the bureaucracy, collegium, and political system are used to assess their effectiveness. It then suggested a number of important latent functions that senates may play. Let us now consider these latent functions in the context of newer models that view organizations as symbolic or cultural systems.

Our world is too complex, equivocal, and confusing to be understood completely, and people must find ways of simplifying and interpreting it if they are to function effectively. There are many ways in which the world can be interpreted, and organizations can be seen as groups of people who interact regularly in an attempt to construct and understand reality, to make sense of ambiguous events, and to share meanings in distinctive ways. Through their regular interactions they develop a culture, which may be defined as "the values or social ideals and the beliefs that organizational members come to share. These values or beliefs are manifested by symbolic devices such as myths, rituals, stories, legends, and specialized language" [40, p. 344].

Within the context of these cultural inventions, people decide what is important, take indeterminate relationships and develop them into coherent beliefs about cause and effect, and retrospectively make sense of events that were too equivocal to be understood as they occurred. A major organizational model built upon these ideas is that of the "organized anarchy," an institution characterized by problematic goals, unclear technology and fluid participation. "The American college or university is a prototypical organized anarchy. It does not know what it is doing. Its goals are either vague or in dispute. Its technology is familiar but not understood. Its major participants wander in and out of the organization. These factors do not make the university a bad organization, or a disorganized one; but they do make it a problem to describe, understand, and lead" [13, p. 3].

An organized anarchy is a loosely coupled system in which individuals and subunits within the organization make essentially autonomous decisions. Institutional outcomes are a resultant of these only modestly interdependent activities and are often neither planned nor predictable. It is difficult in such an environment to make inferences about cause and effect, to determine how successful one is, or even to be certain in advance whether certain environmental changes or evolving issues will turn out to be important or trivial. In this situation of great ambiguity, people spend more time in sense making than in decision making [45] and in engaging in activities that verify their status. The decoupling of choices and outcomes makes symbolic behavior particularly important, and particular choices, problems, solutions, and participants often become associated with one another because of their temporal, rather than their logical relationships.

Organized anarchies need structures and processes that symbolically reinforce their espoused values, that provide opportunities for individuals to assert and confirm their status, and that allow people to understand to which of many competing claims on their attention they should respond. They require a

means through which irrelevant problems and participants can be encouraged to seek alternative ways of expressing themselves so that decision makers can do their jobs. They should also be able to "keep people busy, occasionally entertain them, give them a variety of experiences, keep them off the streets, provide pretexts for storytelling, and allow socializing" [45, p. 264].

Given these requirements, the issue of the "success" of the academic senate can be seen from a completely different perspective. Questions concerning its rationality, efficiency, ability to resolve important issues, representatives, and community-building effectiveness, which may be important under other models, are of less consequence here. If one uses notions of symbolic or cultural systems to consider a college or university as an organized anarchy, academic senates may be effective indeed. This may be the reason they have survived and prospered even though they have not fulfilled the manifest purposes that their charters claim. If senates did not exist, we would have to invent them.

It's time to say something nice about senates. The concept of organized anarchy appears to capture a significant aspect of the role of the senate on many campuses but certainly not of all senates on all campuses at all times. There are many examples of senates that have taken responsibility for resolving a specific problem and have done so in a timely and efficient manner. There are senates in which important institutional policy has been determined and through whose processes of interaction faculty have developed shared values and increased feelings of community. Given the comments of observers of the senate, however, these appear to be exceptional rather than common occurrences.

Those who observe the workings of senates and find them deficient should be particularly careful in making recommendations for change, because these changes might affect not only performance of manifest functions but their important latent functions as well. This is particularly true when making recommendations based upon normative and ultimately moral concepts such as "shared authority" or "representativeness." Merton [36, p. 71] warned that "since moral evaluations in a society tend to be largely in terms of the manifest consequences of a practice or code, we should be prepared to find that analysis in terms of latent functions at times runs counter to prevailing moral evaluations. For it does not follow that the latent functions will operate in the same fashion as the manifest consequences which are ordinarily the basis of these judgments."

Anyone who recommends that senates change or be eliminated in favor of some other organizational structure should carefully consider their latent functions. As a general principle, "any attempt to eliminate an existing social structure without providing adequate alternative structures for fulfilling the functions previously fulfilled by the abolished organization is doomed to failure [and] is to indulge in social ritual rather than social engineering" [36, p. 81]. Functional analysis also enables us to evaluate more clearly warnings such as that senates are "ineffective because faculty [are] not active participants. If faculty do not become involved in . . . senate . . . affairs, the ominous predictions about the demise of faculty governance may come true" [4, p. 345–46]. To the extent that the organized anarchy model is an appropriate one, the future of the senate in governance is unlikely to be related to increased faculty involvement.

Presented at the Annual Meeting of the Association for the Study of Higher Education, San Diego, California, 14–17 February 1987.

The project presented or reported herein was prepared pursuant to a grant from the Office of Educational Research and Improvement/Department of Education (OERI/ED). However, the opinions expressed herein do not necessarily reflect the position or policy of the OERI/ED, and no official endorsement by the OERI/ED should be inferred.

Robert Birnbaum was professor of higher education at Teachers College, Columbia University, when this article was written. He is currently professor of higher education at the University of Maryland, College Park, and project director at the National Center for Postsecondary Governance and Finance.

Notes

1. The term "academic senate" is used in this article to identify a formal, representative governance structure at the institutional level that may include only faculty (a "pure" senate), or one that, in addition to a faculty majority, may also include representatives of other campus constituencies, such as administrators, aca-

demic staff members, and/or students (a "mixed" senate), as defined by the Report of the AAHE Task Force on Faculty Representation and Academic Negotiations [1, p. 34].

References

American Association for Higher Education. *Faculty Participation in Academic Governance.* Washington, D.C.: American Association for Higher Education, 1967.

Baldridge, J. V. "Shared Governance: a Fable about the Lost Magic Kingdom." *Academe,* 1982, 68; 12–15.

Baldridge, J. V., D. V. Curtis, G. Ecker, and G. L. Riley. *Policy Making and Effective Leadership.* San Francisco: Jossey-Bass, 1978.

Baldridge, J. V., and F. R. Kemerer. "Academic Senates and Faculty Collective Bargaining." *Journal of Higher Education,* July/August 1976, 47; 391–411.

Baldridge, J. V., F. R. Kemerer, and Associates. *Assessing The Impact of Faculty Collective Bargaining.* Washington, D.C.: American Association for Higher Education, 1981.

Begin, J. P. "Faculty Collective Bargaining and Faculty Reward Systems." In *Academic Rewards in Higher Education,* edited by L. Becker. Cambridge: Ballinger, 1979.

Ben-David, J. *American Higher Education: Directions Old and New.* New York: McGraw-Hill, 1972.

Berry, M. F. "Faculty Governance." In *Leadership for Higher Education,* edited by R. W. Heyns. Washington, D.C.: American Council on Education, 1977.

Blau, P. M. *The Organization of Academic Work.* New York: John Wiley and Sons, 1973.

Burnett, J. H. "Ceremony, Rites, and Economy in the Student System of an American High School." *Human Organization,* 1969, 28; 1–10.

Carnegie Commission on Higher Education. *Governance of Higher Education: Six Priority Problems.* New York: McGraw-Hill, 1973.

Carnegie Foundation for the Advancement of Teaching. "A Governance Framework for Higher Education." *Educational Record,* 1983, 64; 12–18.

Cohen, M. D. and J. G. March. *Leadership and Ambiguity: The American College President.* New York: McGraw-Hill, 1974.

_____. "Decisions, Presidents, and Status." In J. G. March and J. P. Olsen, *Ambiguity and Choice in Organizations,* 2d ed., Bergen: Universitetsforlaget, 1979.

Cohen, M. D., J. G. March, and J. P. Olsen. "A Garbage Can Model of Organizational Choice." *Administrative Science Quarterly,* 1972, 17; 1–25.

Corson, J. J. *Governance of Colleges and Universities.* New York: McGraw-Hill, 1960.

Deutsch, M. *The Resolution of Conflict: Constructive and Destructive Forces.* New Haven: Yale University Press, 1973.

Dykes, A. R. *Faculty Participation in Academic Decision Making.* Washington, D.C.: American Council on Education, 1968.

Etzioni, A. *Modern Organizations.* Englewood Cliffs, N.J.: Prentice-Hall, 1964.

Feldman M. S. and J. G. March. "Information in Organizations as Signal and Symbol." *Administrative Science Quarterly,* 1981, 26; 171–86.

Floyd, C. E. *Faculty Participation in Decision Making: Necessity or Luxury?* Washington, D.C.: Association for the Study of Higher Education, 1985.

Hobbs, W. C. "Organizational Roles of University Committees." *Research in Higher Education,* 1975, 3; 233–42.

Hodgkinson, H. L. *The Campus Senate: Experiment in Democracy.* Berkeley: Center for Research and Development in Higher Education, 1974.

Keller, G. *Academic Strategy: The Management Revolution in American Higher Education.* Baltimore: The Johns Hopkins University Press, 1983.

Kemerer, F. R., and J. V. Baldridge. *Unions on Campus.* San Francisco: Jossey-Bass, 1975.

Kerr, C. *The Uses of the University.* Cambridge, Mass.: Harvard University Press, 1964.

Ladd, E. C., Jr., and S. M. Lipset. *Professors, Unions, and American Higher Education.* Washington, D.C.: American Enterprise Institute for Public Policy Research, 1973.

Lee, B. A. *Collective Bargaining in Four-Year Colleges.* Washington, D.C.: American Association for Higher Education, 1978.

_____. "Contractually Protected Governance Systems at Unionized Colleges." *Review of Higher Education,* 1982,5; 69–85.

Liberman, M. "Representational Systems in Higher Education." In *Employment Relations in Higher Education,* edited by S. Elam and M. H. Moskow. Washington, D.C.: Phi Delta Kappa, 1969.

Magarrell, J. "The Social Repercussions of an 'Information Society'." *Chronicle of Higher Education,* 1980, 20; 1, 10.

Masland, A. T. "Simulators, Myth, and Ritual in Higher Education." *Research in Higher Education,* 1983, 18; 161–77.

Mason, H. L. *College and University Government: A Handbook of Principle and Practice.* New Orleans: Tulane University, 1972.

McConnell, T. R. "Faculty Government." In *Power and Authority,* edited by H. L. Hodgkinson and L. R. Meeth. San Francisco: Jossey-Bass, 1971.

McConnell, T. R., and K. P. Mortimer. *The Faculty in University Governance.* Berkeley: Center for Research and Development in Higher Education, 1971.

Merton, R. K. *Social Theory and Social Structure,* rev. ed. Glencoe, Ill.: The Free Press, 1957.

Millett, J. D. *The Academic Community.* New York: McGraw-Hill, 1962.

_____. *New Structures of Campus Power.* San Francisco: Jossey-Bass, 1978.

Mortimer, K. P., and T. R. McConnell. *Sharing Authority Effectively: Participation, Interaction and Discretion.* San Francisco: Jossey-Bass, 1978.

Smircich, L. "Concepts of Cultural and Organizational Analysis." *Administrative Science Quarterly,* 1983, 28; 339–58.

Stone, J. N., Jr. "Achieving Broad-Based Leadership." In *Leadership for Higher Education,* edited by R. W. Heyns. Washington, D.C.: American Council on Education, 1977.

Tierney, W. G. "Governance by Conversation: An Essay on the Structure, Function, and Communicative Codes of a Faculty Senate." *Human Organization,* 1983, 42; 172–77.

Trow, M. "The Public and Private Lives of Higher Education." *Daedalus,* 1975, 104; 113–27.

Weick, K. E. "Educational Organizations as Loosely Coupled Systems." *Administrative Science Quarterly,* 1976, 21; 1–19.

_____. *The Social Psychology of Organizing,* 2nd ed. Reading, Mass.: Addison-Wesley, 1979.

Wildavsky, A. *The Politics of the Budgetary Process,* 2nd ed. Boston: Little, Brown, 1974.

Veblen, T. *The Higher Learning in America.* New York: Sagamore Press, 1957. (Originally published in 1918.)

CHAPTER 20

WHAT TEAMS CAN DO: HOW LEADERS USE— AND NEGLECT TO USE—THEIR TEAMS

ESTELA M. BENSIMON AND ANNA NEUMANN

In this chapter, we describe how the fifteen college and university presidents participating in our study made use of their teams. We compare presidents who involved their teams broadly in institutional affairs, giving team members a huge share of responsibility and authority in the thinking, feeling, and doing of leadership, with the presidents who saw leadership as a more restricted dynamic, making individual team members responsible for "segments" of institutional leadership rather than making them aware of larger wholes. We saw the former set of presidents as adhering to the view of the team as a cultural whole and the latter set as adhering to the more conventional view of a team as composed of segments that are merely summed together.

It has been suggested that college presidents have an all but impossible job (Birnbaum 1989), in part because their control of organizational resources is often illusory (Cohen & March 1974). Top-level leadership teams, particularly the president's cabinet or inner circle of administrative colleagues, may represent one of the few resources over which presidents in fact have some influence. On the basis of our study, we believe that a college's top-level leadership team can be an important resource for its president. Our discussions with a variety of people in administrative positions other than the presidency lead us to believe that teams can also be an important resource for vice presidents, college deans, department chairs, and other institutional leaders. However, we also believe that presidents and other leaders need to understand the nature of that resource—for example, how teams work, what they can do, and what they cannot do.

Our research suggests that while many presidents acknowledge the usefulness of their teams in a general way, often because intuitively they believe that teams are important, they frequently have trouble explaining exactly how or why they are useful. Some presidents, in fact, take their institution's top leadership group (i.e., their administrative circle) for granted without giving much thought as to how well it is working. Some presidents are oblivious to serious team dysfunctions that some of their vice presidents, and even many faculty, see clearly. We believe that because most presidents, and most people in leadership positions generally, lack a conceptual map of the functions that teams can fulfill, they may tend *not* to utilize their teams as fully as they might. In the next section we present a three-part framework for thinking about the functions of leadership teams.

To reiterate the point we made in chapter 2, we, do not see these functions as restricted to or focused on particular individuals on the team but as encompassing the team as a total unit. At the same time, it is important to consider the fact that the individuals on the team are likely to shape its nature depending on whether they take a cultural or a conventional approach to thinking about it. Given the president's often prominent role as a team builder, we turn now to the question of how presidents conceive of their teams' functions.

Three Functions of Presidential Teams

One of the major findings of this study is that presidents who are effective team builders think in complicated ways about their team's work. In an analysis of how the fifteen presidents in this study view their teams, Estela Mara Bensimon (1991b) discovered that they construe the work of their teams in terms of three functions: utilitarian, expressive, and cognitive.* She pattern-coded (Miles & Huberman 1984) presidents' descriptions of their teams, utilizing the following question as a guiding frame: "In what ways does President X find his/her team useful?" The analysis yielded the three functions that we present, with specific examples, in this chapter. Table 20-1 also summarizes the findings of Bensimon's study.

The Team's Utilitarian Function

From a utilitarian perspective, presidents view their teams as formal structures for achieving "rational organization" and for maintaining control over institutional functioning. Viewed as a utilitarian tool, the presidential team keeps the institution running and gets necessary jobs done. Moreover, it is purposive and task-oriented, engaging in instrumental activities such as: (a) providing information, (b) coordinating and planning, and (c) making decisions. While we define these three activities below, we also highlight the fact that each activity may manifest itself in more than one way.

Providing Information

Depending on a president's orientation, the act of providing information can be an educative activity (information sharing), or it can serve as a perfunctory recital of facts that the "president needs to know" to avoid being surprised (information delivery).

In our study, the presidents who viewed this informational activity as *educative* were typically concerned with how "news" would affect the team as a whole, rather than just the president. As one president put it, "The team plays an important role in getting each other up to speed," and he described the team's information-sharing ritual of "going around the table and giving progress reports." Another president added that this kind of information sharing is important not only for instrumental reasons but because it is "important [that] we all hear certain things together." The presidents who spoke from the educative standpoint usually saw new information as an opportunity to establish a common ground for decision making.

In contrast, presidents who saw the provision of information more as an act of "delivery"—as a means for keeping *themselves* aware of institutional events—tended not to worry as much about the team's understanding of collegiate issues. These presidents portrayed themselves as individuals who were uncomfortable with the "unexpected," and they saw information delivery as a means of assuring that they (as individuals) would always have a ready response to whatever institutional difficulty confronted them. They were less concerned with a team response, including what that would look like in the public eye, than with their own personal response and what *they* would look like.

These presidents usually construed information as a resource over which they needed to establish control. They were apt to let their teams know (as one of our presidents did) that "being kept informed is a sacred matter" to them. One of the presidents we interviewed told the members of his team, "I have a right to the information in your brain; . . . to withhold information, . . . not to be candid with me is a cardinal sin."

The presidents oriented toward information delivery described themselves as possessing a team, but unlike the presidents who were concerned with the educative aspects of information provision, they typically did not see the team as a leadership group. Rather, they saw it as a "doing" group, and one of the things that

---

*The following discussion elaborates on a research report by Estela Mara Bensimon titled, "How College Presidents Use Their Administrative Groups: Real and Illusory Teams," *Journal for Higher Education Management* 7 (1991): 35–51.

Table 20-1 Three Functions of Presidential Teams

Team Function	Image	Purpose	Behavior	Activities
Utilitarian	Formal	Help president achieve a sense of rationality and maintain control over institutional functioning	Task related	Deliver information, coordinate and plan, make decisions
Expressive	Social	Help reinforce a sense of groupness or connectedness among individuals involved in a joint venture	Integrative, associative	Provide mutual support, provide counsel to the president
Cognitive	Sense making	Enlarge span of intelligence of individual team members, enable the group to behave as a creative system and also as a corrective system	Intellective, dialogical	View problems from multiple perspectives; question, challenge, argue; act as monitor and feedback system

they saw their group "doing" was connecting the president to the campus. In fact, these presidents often saw the team as their *only* connection to the campus. In their determination to stay connected—to know and see it all—these presidents would often assume a highly authoritarian tone as they demanded information from their vice presidents.

Teams that work this way—whose dominant function is the delivery of information to the president for the president's own benefit—cannot be regarded as real teams because they just provide information, without talk or input. Information provision is always a critical team activity. The challenge for presidents who are concerned with building truly effective teams is not to allow informational activity to become the sole reason for regular meetings of their administrative group.

In our study, presidents who limited the team's role to information delivery were a source of unhappiness for many of their administrative officers. A vice president on one of these teams put his concerns this way:

> I guess the most important thing is hearing what goes on at meetings at the state sys-

tem level, but this is not necessarily what should be going on. Ideally I would like to see it [the team meeting] as a place [where] institution-wide issues could be discussed with a certain amount of candor. A team needs to know the major issues. While I do not have responsibility for academic programs I should be able to contribute my ideas. There should be open debate. The institution benefits from different perspectives. We also need to examine, jointly, where our energies are going. But rarely are those issues introduced. We are just informed when something is brought to the table. If you venture too far out of your territory you are told so.

In sum, this vice president saw information delivery as a constraining activity that impinged on open and creative team thinking and team learning.

To summarize, we agree with yet another interviewee who quietly told us, "If the purpose of team meetings is to keep the president on top of what is happening, there are probably a lot [of] better ways of doing that than through a weekly cabinet meeting."

Coordination and Planning

Teams that were active in goal setting and strategic planning for the purpose of institutional coordination, a utilitarian aim, generally did not limit members to their official areas of responsibility and expertise (e.g., academic affairs or student affairs). Rather, they sought to involve team members, regardless of their divisional responsibilities, in the "crafting of an institutional agenda that [was] representative of all constituent parts."

As one president pointed out, "The key thing about the annual goals statement [is that it is the outcome of extensive] consultation with the group." Another president asserted his belief that the team's involvement in institutional goal setting was important in that it avoided "disparity" among the vice presidents with regard to where they saw "the institution going." In the words of the president, "Everyone knows what is the most important driving force," He added that, as a result of their participation in the making of the "institutional agenda," team members felt more committed to it.

The majority of presidents in our study were quick to recognize their team's usefulness for coordination and planning in the abstract sense, but when we asked them to elaborate with examples or explanation, many were unclear as to how the coordination and planning actually occurred. Additionally, not all presidents were aware of the practical and symbolic advantages of team involvement in broad-based campus matters (e.g., via strategic planning). One president said that his team was "least useful" in terms of "long-range issues, such as where the institution should be five or ten years from now." For this president, the team was more useful for specific, short-range issues such as determining "how an action in one area may influence other areas" and then adjusting accordingly. But this president saw the team's contribution to other matters—particularly if they were out of the ordinary—as wasteful and uncomfortable, mainly because he feared that the diversity of the individuals involved would lead to a "loss of coherence." He pointed out to us that the campus's best long-range planners were himself and the executive vice president, and he excluded all other team members from all but the most basic of administrative functions.

Decision Making

Another important activity related to the team's utilitarian function is decision making. In this study this was particularly true among presidents who had adopted consensus procedures within the team whereby each member had a significant voice and sometimes a vote. A consensus approach to decision making was particularly useful in assessing policy issues affecting the whole institution or in the allocation of financial resources. According to one president, "When decisions involve money, we hash it out in the group. Together we decide whether hiring a new counselor is more important than adding a new faculty member."

Decision making frequently involved giving members a formal say in the final decision, but this was not always the case. We found several utilitarian teams in which team members contributed to decision making in a more distanced advisory sense. For example, they provided the president with ideas, suggestions, and alternatives for consideration, but it was clear that the final decision would be made by the president. As one president told us, "We do not vote. After I have heard all I need to on an issue, I will come to a decision and I will set the assignments."

Although decision making would appear to be a critical administrative activity for a presidential team, surprisingly few presidents in our study considered their teams useful in terms of either voting or giving advice, in this activity. We believe the presidents undervalued the teams' decisionmaking usefulness because they viewed group decision making negatively. For example, some admitted to not "having the patience" required for decision making by consensus. Others viewed consensus as "a way in which individuals can avoid responsibility." Still others shied away from this kind of decision making because they felt that it made them appear indecisive or overly dependent on others. As one president put it, "You should be able to tie your own shoes."

We disagree. Our belief is that decision making can be enhanced when it is approached as a collaborative effort. We recognize, however, that the president's team is not the institution's supreme decision-making body. Other decision-making groups, most prominently the board of trustees, play important roles. We also recognize that the consensus model, as we commonly think of it, may be flawed. We pursue these points further in chapter 6.

The Team's Expressive Function

To develop the team's expressive function, presidents need to view their team as a social structure aimed at meeting team members' needs for collegial relations and affiliation as well as the president's needs for counsel and commitment. Through the expressive function, a team reinforces its sense of "groupness" or internal connectedness. We believe that "groupness" is important because it comprises the setting or ground on which the substantive work of collaboration may occur.

Our study identified two key activities that fall within the expressive domain of team functioning: (*a*) providing mutual support, and (*b*) providing counsel to the president.

Providing Mutual Support

The capacity of the presidential team to provide mutual support was the expressive activity mentioned most often by the presidents in our study. Presidents said that it is important for the institution's top leadership group to "have a coherent chemistry" so that its members can be "supportive of one another in achieving the goals of the university." When administrative officers "have problems in their own areas," it is reassuring to them—and to their president—to know they are able "to get help from others on the team." Because top-level administrators have "lonely jobs," said one president, they need to act as "a support group for each other."

Some interviewees described the team as a place to go when campus life became particularly hard to take: "Faculty and students cannot appreciate some of the torment we go through. You are always confronted with the lack of resources, silly rules, . . . so if you do not have a group of people with whom you can laugh you can get burned out in administration." Others described the team as simultaneously creative and supportive: "The meetings have an agenda. We follow a certain form. But we also share our dreams, clear the air, compliment each other. That is the free-flowing creative aspect—it helps us all. I can rely on each of them to support me and not to become an adversary."

Our sample also contained several presidents who were uncomfortable with the expressive function, including the provision of mutual support. These presidents were very open in telling us that they did not want to "personalize relationships" on the team and preferred "to emphasize the responsibilities of the office." Our view, however, is that presidents who think this way are, in effect, forcing an artificial split between the personal and the professional and that, in doing so, they contribute to the suppression of connectedness. We do not believe that collaborative work, particularly collaborative thinking, can occur in thin air. We believe, instead, that such work requires a solid base of patterned interdependencies—a team that becomes the *setting* within which collaborative teamwork may occur.

We conclude from this that teams need to strive for relationships that consist of more than politically expedient alliances among individuals with different values and desires. For a group to exist there needs to be groupness.

Providing Counsel to the President

While one would think that presidents would view their administrative groups as playing an important counseling role, our study suggests that few actually do. Among the presidents in our study who saw the team as their primary advisory group, one said, "I use the group as a sounding board. . . . If I don't have background on an issue, I lean on them for counsel." A second added, "They are there to guide and advise me."

Apart from offering substantive, instrumental advice to their president, the team can act as a mirror: team colleagues can provide presidents with feedback that lets them see themselves as others do. Presidents (especially new presidents) often want to know how they are doing, that is, how others see them, and their teams are a key source of this sort of information. One president said, "They [the presidential team] are expected to be candid and frank with me with regard to my leadership." Teams can also prevent presidents from taking action that would damage their leadership image. One president said, "I express my dependency on staff quite openly. I count on them not to let me go off on a crazy tangent. It is helpful to have people tell the emperor he has no clothes. I'd rather be foolish in a small group than in a large group."

Obviously, the extent to which top-level leadership teams can fulfill the role of counselor to the president depends heavily on whether the president-team relationship is based more on intimacy and collegiality than on purely official ties. The team's ability to fulfill a counseling role also requires a president who is able to rely strongly and openly on the team, to recognize that doing it all alone is impossible. Such presidents must also be willing to open themselves to scrutiny. Not all presidents can accept such terms. In fact, many of the presidents in this study preferred to establish relationships based on loyalty rather than on interdependence.

Although a relationship based on loyalty need not preclude a counseling role for the institution's top leadership team, the concept of "loyalty to the president" communicates stiffness, and it connotes a rigid president-team relationship. When presidents talk of loyalty, they mean that the group has "to identify with the president" or "protect the president" or "be ready to sacrifice themselves" for the president's needs. The biggest difference between "counseling the president" and "showing loyalty to the president" is that the former suggests a relationship between peers and colleagues, while the latter is a demonstration of commitment by subordinates to a superior.

It is also important to distinguish between loyalty to an individual and loyalty to an institution. The former refers to team members' loyalty to the president alone, while the latter refers to their loyalty to the group. Loyalty to an institution may involve showing support for decisions that the group has made, or it may involve taking responsibility, both for wise choices and for choices made in error. Finally, the concept of loyalty suggests that each team member works "for the good of something." In the case of loyalty to an institution, this may require one or more team members to bring bad news to the group (for example, bring up something the team would prefer not to hear or deal with) or to be constructively critical of an idea within the group despite the group's attachment to the idea.

We conclude this section with a warning: highly associative teams risk insularity. They may inadvertently distance themselves from the rest of the campus. Thus, while a team may feel that it is engaged in collaborative decision making, the rest of the campus can feel left out.

It sometimes takes a newcomer to the team to recognize that this is happening: "The few people on the cabinet were in agreement," said a new president, "but they failed to produce a consensus on campus." An interviewee on another campus described what he saw as his team's predicament:

> We are not great in communicating to the rest of the campus, . . . telling them what is going on and what the direction is. The president does try to do this by writing memos and through faculty meetings. I think that there is a tremendous consensus among us [the team] on the institutional purpose and the philosophy. We have a shared sense of purpose. We understand that what each of us does affects the others. But communicating that outside, . . . we are very bad at doing that.

The Team's Cognitive Function

Presidents are likely to find the cognitive function to be the most challenging, if not the most problematic, to develop within the team. Yet of the three functions, this is without doubt the most critical. Our studies suggest that in order to bring the cognitive function into being, a president must view the institution as a complex system in which the team is the sense maker—that is, its members are collectively involved in perceiving, analyzing, learning, and thinking. Simply put, in its cognitive function the team is a brainlike social structure that enlarges the intelligence span of individual team members. Intellectual expansion allows the group to behave as a creative system when unusual events occur, and as a warning and corrective system in the case of dysfunction.

The team's cognitive function comprises mostly intellective and analytical activity, including: (a) viewing problems from multiple perspectives, (b) questioning, challenging, and arguing, and (c) acting as a monitor and feedback system.

Unless presidents make clear that they expect and welcome substantive and analytical questions and issues within the context of the team, the cognitive function may be compromised. For example, a highly influential member of one of our sample teams informed us that even though he brings many issues to the group, he never "brings anything without checking with the president first." Undoubtedly, this preliminary tête-à-tête between the president and the vice president risks undermining the team's cognitive usefulness. We would hope that presidents would actively discourage this "checking it out first with the president" form of behavior.

Viewing Problems from Multiple Perspectives

According to the presidents who defined the usefulness of their teams in cognitive terms, the most widely valued cognitive activity is generating multiple, diverse perspectives on problems at hand. Even though presidents consider it important for their teams to have a "common sense of the institution's values, its vision, its purposes, its goals and its priorities," they also expect their teams to produce "varying ideas on how to accomplish those things." As one president put it, "I would hope that [team members] would not all be clones of myself or anyone else—that they [would] be individuals in their own right."

Effective presidential teams act in ways that allow problems or issues to be examined from multiple points of view and along more than one value dimension. By bringing "individual [members'] perspectives" to bear on an issue, and by "suggesting alternative courses of action," these teams can be very useful in expanding the ways in which presidents come to view their institutions' special circumstances or problems. As one of the study presidents explained, "The team brings more ideas to me than I bring to them." Another president described how he looks to the team to be sure that all possible perspectives on an issue have been tried out and that all problem-solving options have been explored: "Usually only two or three alternatives may be considered, when in reality there is a fourth and a fifth. . . . I find that once these other alternatives are raised, an issue is more complicated than I realized, and strategies that I had not envisioned suddenly become evident."

Reconsidering a problem through multiple lenses might make the problem look more complex and might make a person feel that the problem is becoming less and less manageable. However, as a problem unfolds in its largeness, looking frighteningly more complicated all the time, its previously hidden facets may suggest solutions not seen when it was defined in simpler terms. Not to be overlooked is the well-known administrative fact that multiple solutions to a complex problem can make the problem less daunting and easier to handle.

Questioning, Challenging, and Arguing

Presidents who nurture the team's cognitive function purposefully strive to avoid oversimplifying problems that come before the team. They also try to avoid bringing premature closure to questions that need substantial thought and exploration. They urge their teams to raise sensitive questions, to challenge the status quo, and to argue points of inconsistency or contradiction.

One of the presidents participating in this study—a person who deliberately sought to strengthen his team's cognitive function—told us that he expects his group to "push me." Another said that he openly invites debates within the team in considering why "a chosen course of action may not be a prudent one." A third president told us that he sees a need to have group members "stand up to me and question my biases."

In teams where questions, challenges, and arguments such as these were possible, we learned from team members that, in their eyes, it was the president's style that made it all possible. In one such team, a member told us that the president "encourages interchange and disagreement and candor, . . . so much so that it would feel odd if we were not having arguments with him." Elaborating further, this member said: "I think most faculty would be surprised at how often the president is challenged in the cabinet. We take him on all the time. I think a president needs this kind of thing. The trust we have with him gives us the freedom to do this. When he is challenged, it forces him to reflect, and that has an impact."

Questioning, challenging and arguing occur more often when the president's relationship with the group is collegial. One president said, "I love it when people argue because I learn," but he was also sufficiently perceptive to realize that a norm of questioning and argument is not easy to come by, that it takes time to nurture as a way of team life. This president added, "Now that people are more familiar . . .

they seem less afraid of me. . . . They will argue more, they are more inclined to question." At the beginning of a presidential term, people may not be fully attuned to such expectations. To challenge authority is, after all, antithetical to convention. One president's method of countering members' expectations was to choreograph "heated debates with team members until they came to realize that I wanted to see a problem from all angles" and "that it was all right to argue with the president."

Monitoring and Feedback

A presidential team can act as a monitoring and feedback mechanism in two ways: First, it may search for and attend to signs indicating that the institution is deviating from its desired course. One of the presidents participating in this study explained this process as "continually assessing" how well the "critical path we established for the college" is being followed. She also said that team members typically "keep their ear to the ground" in order to take "readings" of the state of the institution. Then periodically, she and others on the team "pause to reflect on these readings [to] gauge whether we are all functioning well [and to assess if we are getting bogged down" in issues or details that might "make us lose sight of where the institution is headed."

Another way in which a presidential team can act as a monitoring and feedback system is by guarding the institution against pursuing outdated or no longer viable courses of action. For example, after commenting on how hard it can be to keep ideas going, a president explained that by challenging one another and by constantly stimulating the organization, the institution's top leadership group kept the college from becoming "entrenched, overly satisfied, and routinized."

For the team to be effective there has to be some tolerance for disorder on the part of the president as well as other team members. Teams that are truly effective (that think out loud, that challenge each other, and that argue among themselves) frequently consider new, unfamiliar, or unclear courses of action. They deviate often from what is comfortable and known to them. Presidents should bear in mind that creative problem solving is more likely to

emerge from unstructured talks, which appear chaotic and wasteful to those who are impatient to get to the point, than from carefully ordered, formal agendas. The dialogues most conducive to successful monitoring and course adjustment are more likely to take place in informal settings that "allow the conversation to take the group" in unexpected directions and toward new or different understandings.

We should note, however, that in some institutions, unstructured discussion seldom takes place unless the president actively encourages group members to think and talk about "what [they] are hearing and seeing" rather than simply to deliver information in a utilitarian fashion. When the president demands information only, the group is likely to act only as a messenger. When the president asks the group to ponder what lies beneath the information that comes to the table, the group assumes the more complex role of information processor, sense maker, and information user and creator.

"Real" and "Illusory" Teams: How Presidents Use Their Teams

The three functions that teams may serve—utilitarian, expressive, and cognitive—are important in that together they respond to the diverse needs and expectations associated with collegiate operations. A president or other team builder who can conceive of all three functions, rather than being limited to just one, is in a position to mold a real team, one capable of meeting important administrative, human relations, and intellective issues. Real teams are complex because through their multiple functions they are able to address a diverse range of institutional issues.

Presidents with Real Teams

In our study, presidents with real teams tended to fit a consistent profile: First, when they described the nature of their teamwork, they presented their team as performing at least one useful activity in each of the three functional domains—the utilitarian, the expressive, and the cognitive. Second, virtually all the presidents with real teams cast their team's utilitarian function in terms of decision making and planning. Only one of the presidents with real teams was concerned about the team's information-delivery capacities. In sum, presidents with real teams thought of them in complex ways.

Presidents with Illusory Teams

Unlike the presidents with real teams, presidents with illusory teams utilized their groups only partially in that they focused on team functions in only one or two of the three domains presented in this chapter. For the most part, the illusory teams missed both the cognitive and expressive domains; they functioned at the most basic, utilitarian level of "doing," giving little attention to their processes of thinking and simply being together.

As we will note later, some of the presidents who openly stated a preference for what we call the illusory team, worried about the cacophony, confusion, and disorder that might ensue when multiple ideas move into motion, as they often do in the more complex, real teams. They seemed to distance themselves purposely from the idea of teamwork in its real form as we have presented it thus far. However, as we launched into interviews with these people, none of them stopped us with something like, "Your questions are irrelevant to me because I do not have a team." Rather, all but one of the eight presidents whose teams we deemed illusory told us that, in fact, they had teams. For these presidents, a cabinet composed of vice presidents was tantamount to a team, regardless of how limited that team's, functions might be. Our observation was that these presidents' framework for thinking about teamwork was much narrower than the three-part framework that we discovered among the presidents engaged in real teamwork.

Presidents with illusory teams often told us that they felt more comfortable working with their administrative officers one to one—a sharp contrast to the group-oriented presidents with real teams. One president explained that he met only with "groups of two or three [because] when you get the five or six of us together it is not coherent." Another illusory team lacked the routines and symbols often associated with real teamwork, including regularly scheduled meetings.

In sum, presidents with illusory teams made use of their top administrative groups in limited, narrowly defined ways. The domains they bypassed most often were the expressive and the cognitive. They tended to describe their team's usefulness in terms of the utilitarian domain, particularly the team's ability to deliver information, rather than to think, question, challenge, or argue. Presidents with illusory teams were also concerned with exacting the loyalty of their administrators. They were not concerned with building a sense of closeness among team members. One president summed it up this way: "It is not that important to have scotch together on Friday afternoon. 'Living together' is not the issue." In contrast to this president's view, research suggests that effective groups typically balance solidarity, on the one hand, with task accomplishment on the other. Thus the time team members spend together over a drink on Fridays may be as important to the team's functioning as time spent getting things done (Goleman 1988) in a more utilitarian fashion. What stands out distinctively about the presidents with illusory teams is that they do not identify cognition as a useful team function.

A Once "Real" Team That Became "Illusory": The Case of Southern Plains College

The difference between real and illusory teamwork is stark when we watch a team change from one form to the other. A change such as this lets us see not only that people behave differently in the two models but also that their thinking and feeling differ. To illustrate just such a change, and to sharpen the contrast between real and illusory teamwork, we offer here the story of Southern Plains College (previously published in Bensimon 1990a).

Soon after taking office, the new president of Southern Plains let the "inherited" chief administrative officers know of his intention to discontinue the team approach to decision making to which they had become accustomed. Under the previous president the team had functioned like a "real" team. The chief administrators had been together for a long time and shared a strong sense of "groupness." The prevailing belief among all members of the group was that by acting as a cohesive body they had greater access to information and were more effective problem solvers than when they acted individually. For example, one said, "We used to look forward to cabinet meetings to find out about little things that can bite you if you are unaware of them." The cabinet meetings also provided a forum of interaction for busy administrators. One described it this way: "I don't have time to find my colleagues to chitchat on a daily basis, so the meetings were good for that. We shared things, we passed information to one another, we questioned each other about small incidents." Essentially, these administrators were united in their faith that their manner of organizing and working "expanded their intelligence."

However, the group ceased to function as a real team. The processes that had contributed to making them a real team—a meeting held always on the same day and hour of every week, informal brainstorming as a problem-solving approach, sharing of information (including gossip and rumors) in an open manner, and consensual decision making—were suddenly replaced by a considerably more structured and formal process. The new president had learned and preferred to work with administrators individually and not as a group. The idea of a single conference table, with all the chief administrative officers getting involved in each other's domains, was quite outside his immediate experience. Before the new president took over, the administrative group's meetings had been organized around a loose and impromptu agenda, which allowed issues to be raised spontaneously. But to the new president, this approach seemed disorderly; it prompted conversations that were unfocused, making it appear that time was being wasted on seemingly irrelevant matters. These "problems" were addressed by the president's introduction of new processes: the agenda for the meeting was drawn up several days in advance, and each item was classified according to a predetermined category (information items, decision items, and so on).

The new structuring of the agenda elicited a new mode of interaction. Instead of engaging in prolonged debates and arguments as they had in the past, now each administrator gave a formal report on the status of her or his items. One administrator described the procedure as follows: "Now you are essentially making a presentation to the president, and your peers are your audience. Now you are looking for an okay from the president, where before we would all get involved in the discussion and in making the decision. But now, after you present the agenda item, you say, 'Mr. President, on the basis of what I have summed up, I'd like to recommend . . .,' without the others chiming in." Another administrator summed up the effect of these changes by observing that suddenly "it felt like we were moving from family cooking to restaurant cooking."

While the newly imposed structure made it possible to deal more efficiently with single and unified problems, it could not accommodate issues that did not neatly fit into one of the prescribed agenda categories. To conform to the president's penchant for an orderly agenda, the chief administrators stopped bringing problems that were so abstract, complex, and value laden as to preclude quick and clean resolution. Unbeknownst to the president, who looked at the situation purely from his standpoint, efficiency was gained at the cost of the team's cognitive role, and what could have been a critical source of information and analysis for the newly installed president was shut off.

What is obvious about the change at Southern Plains College is that the team, as initially configured, featured a prominent expressive function. The team felt good together; members were comfortable with each other; they were completely open with each other. In this initial setting, the cognitive function also flourished. Members brainstormed together, offered insights, and tendered constructive criticism. This was a real team.

Under the new president, however, the more planned and organized agenda, rather than providing guidance and form, served to restrict conversation to all but the most utilitarian of activities (information giving, decision making). Moreover, the team's new internal process, which was highly formal and rational, served to constrain the type of personal and thinking-out-loud "chitchat" that characterized the team in its former existence, when thinking together and being together were more important than doing together.

What Gets in the Way? Conditions That Deter the Building of Real Teams

While in later chapters we discuss aspects of leadership and institutional life that are likely to facilitate the building of real teams, we consider here some of the barriers to real teamwork. What are the impediments to the building of teams that serve more than the utilitarian function, that provide emotional support, and that contribute cognitive effort? What stands in the way of the real team? As the case of Southern Plains College shows, the orientation of the team builder—in this case, the president—is a key factor in determining the real versus illusory character of the team.

The Team Builder's Leadership Orientation

The team builder may stand as a barrier to the full functioning of the team. The team builder's approach to teamwork may reflect, for example, the characteristics (including the limitations) of that person's approach to leadership generally. For example, some presidents (i.e., those designated as having illusory teams) may not use their teams for expressive or cognitive purposes because demanding loyalty and limiting access to information is consistent with their view of managerial success. They see the manager as the "guardian of the organization's knowledge base to heighten the importance of exclusivity" (Zuboff 1988, p. 238). Or, like the president of Southern Plains College, a team builder may be so concerned with orderliness and control as to openly impede expressive and cognitive activity among team members, at least during team meetings or at other official gatherings. At Southern Plains College the team conformed to the new, official team structure. However, the team members' informal exchanges and networking practices continued outside the rigid structure of the cabinet meetings and without the president's participation.

The converse is also true: Presidents and other administrators who use a democratic/political approach for institutional problem solving and goal-setting generally are likely to be effective in developing real teamwork (see Walker 1979). Leaders, and especially presidents, who tend toward a democratic/political style are likely to adhere to principles of administration based on open communication and free access to information, and they are likely to favor the use of negotiation, compromise, and persuasion in resolving problems; their approach to managing the larger organization is likely to parallel their approach to managing the work of their administrative teams. Moreover, leaders who use a democratic/political leadership style are particularly adept at developing real teams because they recognize that no one person is strong in all areas, because they are able to share and give credit to others, and because they recognize that conflict is a natural condition of human organization. We will discuss such aspects of team building again in chapter 6.

Institutional Context

Another factor that may affect real teamwork, particularly at the executive level, is institutional context. Our study shows that presidents in small institutions are more apt to have real teams. The opposite is true for presidents of large institutions, where we are likely to find very few real teams (Bensimon 1991b).

Contrary to what one might expect, our study suggests that as institutional size and complexity increase, real teams are likely to become more difficult to achieve. One explanation may be that characteristics of large and complex institutions, such as task specialization and loose coupling (Weick 1979), make them incompatible with real (and more tightly coupled) teamwork. Illusory teamwork may more closely match the organizational worlds of the large institutions. On the other hand, because smaller institutions are more tightly coupled, they may be more conducive settings for the tightly coupled real teams.

Specifically, we found that real teams are more likely to exist in small, private, four-year colleges than in large, public universities. This is consistent with the collegial governance model (Baldridge et al. 1978, Millett 1962, Rice & Austin 1988) typically attributed to small, private institutions. The absence of real teams in universities may be related to the strongly political nature of these institutions (Baldridge 1971), to their anarchic qualities (Cohen & March 1974), and to their tendencies to act like "adhocracies" (Weick 1983). Leadership in such institutions is likely to rely on power tactics, negotiation, coalitional dynamics, and persistence more than on collaboration. Again, what is true of the institution as a whole may be true also of the team.

This is not to say that real teams cannot exist in large universities. But it must be recognized that just as small colleges reflect characteristics that are conducive to real teamwork, universities possess characteristics (e.g., a high degree of differentiation among structural units, loose coupling) that are antithetical to real and complex teamwork. Consequently, university presidents who desire the benefits of teamwork that blends all three functions—cognitive, expressive, and utilitarian—must exert substantial effort to create a climate that supports it.

Our previous research (Neumann & Bensimon 1990) shows that university presidents are more likely to be externally focused than internally connected, for example, as they turn their attention to fundraising or to network building in the state and the nation. The typical university president has little time for the internal and rather contained activity of team building. Although teamwork was less evident at the executive level in universities, our research revealed that university presidents rely very heavily on their executive officers, using them, as one said, to "execute things because the president cannot do it all" and because they feel that they need to "resist getting dragged down to a level of inappropriate detail." University presidents described themselves as "aggressive at developing a formal reporting system" and as creating structures to alert them to problems "before they become full blown."

While university presidents appear to be particularly adept at using their teams for relatively utilitarian purposes (e.g., to "execute things because the president cannot do it all"), they may yet need to learn how to use their teams for reflective dialogue. A team may represent a time and place—an opportunity—to examine the meaning of issues and problems in light of the institution's mission, values, and aspirations. It may represent a setting within which meaning generally can be constructed. This, however, requires the team's ability to think together (the cognitive function) and also

to support each other in their joint thinking (the expressive function).

Regardless of the president's position with regard to teams, the fact that teams do not typically exist at the upper reaches of university administration should not nullify the likelihood of their existence at middle or lower institutional levels. Because of the monumental complexity of university life, and because of the deep political rifts that often mark top-level university deliberations, these institutions may be able to support real teams and teamwork only at the level of the college or academic department. At this level, the turf battles (against opposing departments or colleges) characteristic of politically alive, loosely coupled systems, may actually inspire tight coupling within the academic unit—namely, the formation of teamlike structures. While we speculate that in the university teams are *not* absent but rather that they are situated differently than in small colleges, this is a question in need of further research.

Other Conditions That Affect Real Teamwork

A number of other conditions may affect the ability of a team to engage in real teamwork:

1. Whether or not the president feels at ease in sharing organizational leadership and decision making with the cabinet and whether or not the president wants to create a workplace that operates according to an egalitarian ethic are likely to affect the emergence or suppression of real teamwork (Lewis 1975 cited in Dyer 1987). Because the cognitive function requires exploration of areas beyond those that are known or seen as legitimate, it requires the ability to explore conceptions that range beyond the ordinary. This is likely to involve listening to voices that have not traditionally been at the center of the decision process rather than favoring conventional (and dominant) views.

2. Whether or not trust exists between the team builder and other team members and how comfortable all members feel in disclosing their vulnerabilities are also likely to affect the quality of team-

work. The expressive function is based on openness toward and trust in others. The cognitive function requires people to speak their thoughts openly—to risk being wrong and awkward—as the team searches for new ways to think about issues and problems. Without the openness and without the risk, a team is likely to withdraw into utilitarian behavior.

3. Whether or not there is a sense of respect for team members is also likely to affect the quality of teamwork. In the ideal team, meetings are taken seriously and are not canceled and rescheduled to fit the lead administrator's (or chairperson's) calendar. In one of our study institutions, we heard this complaint: "We schedule to meet weekly, but that is often canceled because of the president's schedule. That is had because it does not show respect for our time. The exceptions are too numerous." Complaints such as this were common on teams that we defined as primarily utilitarian and, therefore, illusory. They were not typically characteristic of real teams. In addition to the symbolic message of disrespect that this kind of schedule changing sends out to team members, there is also the more basic problem of substance. As a member of an illusory team noted, when the team fails to meet, it also "fail[s] to look at longer range issues, and [it] fail[s] to notice early warnings before a crisis hits." A brief qualification follows, however: some administrators may convene their teams too frequently, making members feel that they are at the beck and call of the lead administrator and that they must limit work outside the domain of the team. This kind of "over-meeting," with the schedule in the hands of the lead administrator, is as harmful as not meeting at all.

Summary

We have shown that presidential teams can function in diverse ways. They are likely to differ not only in terms of their utilitarian, expressive, and cognitive emphases but also in the amount of power they wield in their potential effect on institutional life. Some teams, for example, may play strong and active leadership roles in their institutions. Others may play the roles of subordinate staff. Teams enjoy different degrees of influence. For example, teams with strong cognitive functions may exert significant leadership because they are actively involved in interpreting meaning. Cognitively oriented teams are in a position to shape, alter, and otherwise fashion the team builder's and other team members' understandings of a given situation, as well as the team's potential responses to that situation. This perspective differs radically from the conventional belief that the team builder (in many cases, the lead administrator) should shape the views of those who work with her or him.

We have also differentiated teams that are real—those that fulfill utilitarian, expressive, and cognitive functions—from those that are illusory—those focusing predominantly on the utilitarian function. In this study, the presidents who had real teams espoused a collectivist orientation to teamwork. They encouraged team members to think about global institutional issues rather than limiting them to specific domains of activity. They also described the team as an opportunity "to philosophize" jointly about institutional direction, and they frequently referred to their group's "ongoing conversations" and "shared sense of the institution."

In contrast, the presidents with illusory teams approached teamwork from an individualistic standpoint. They related to their administrators through formal (as opposed to personal) means. They were careful to maintain clear hierarchical distinctions between people in superior and subordinate roles. They used authoritarian language to emphasize the status difference between the president and the rest of the team. They restricted team members to specific institutional segments (e.g., academic affairs, budgetary matters) rather than acquainting them with the institution as a totality. Comments such as the following were quite common among this set of presidents:

I expect [the team] to carry out my orders.

They [team members] are more comfortable knowing the boundaries and who is God.

They carry forth to the campus my vision and goals.

They understand what I want to know and what I don't want to know.

Another difference between presidents with real teams and those with illusory teams is that the former tended to rely on the first-person plural ("we" and "us") in describing team actions, a verbal gesture that reinforced these presidents' collectivist orientation. In contrast, the presidents with illusory teams made more frequent use of the first-person singular pronoun ("I"), a gesture that defined them as separate, even remote, from the team. Presidents with illusory teams also tended toward paternalism more than did presidents with real teams. Their interviews were spiced with statements such as, "I make them [the team] believe I need them," or "I set an example for them, . . . I work hard so they will work hard." While some team builders may see the team as merely a utilitarian appendage to their own superordinate leadership, others see the very essence of leadership in the team rather than within themselves. Presidents in the team-building role who take the latter view—emphasizing the team rather than the self as leader—typically present themselves as their teams' care givers rather than as their heads.

Finally, in setting out the three functions of leadership teams we have tried to point out that there is more than just one way to be a team. Some teams fulfill only one basic function (utilitarian). Others, of a more complex variety, fulfill the basic function alongside other more sophisticated ones (cognitive and expressive). We turn now to what we deem the team's central task—thinking together. This is what separates an elemental, utilitarian team from a complex team engaged in sense making. It is also what separates the illusory from the real team.

PART V

MANAGEMENT PRINCIPLES

CHAPTER 21

THE MANAGEMENT OF ACADEMIC CULTURE: NOTES ON THE MANAGEMENT OF MEANING AND SOCIAL INTEGRATION

DAVID D. DILL

Abstract: This article is concerned with the management of the symbolic life of academic organizations, an area strangely neglected in discussions of academic management. The adoption by higher education of the techniques of market-based businesses comes at a time when these businesses are being criticized for lack of attention to organizational culture. Academic institutions may best be understood as value-rational organizations grounded in strong cultures described as ideologies and belief systems. Some thoughts on the management of academic culture, on the management of meaning and social integration, are developed.

No community, no organization, no institution . . . can exist for long without a belief or set of beliefs so deeply and widely held that it is more or less exempt from ordinary demands that its goodness or rightness be demonstrable at any given moment . . . [But] dogma and faith unsupported by the bonds of structure are, as comparative religion teaches us, notoriously fragile. Robert Nisbet (pp. 23, 40)

Introduction

We are members of academic communities, but we manage academic organizations. When we seek to give meaning to the term "academic community" we speak of symbolic context: the distinctive history and traditions of our particular university, past sacrifices by notable faculty members on the behalf of academic freedom. When we seek to give meaning to the term "academic management" we speak of rational processes: goal setting, evaluation, cost analysis. A necessary condition for the management of academic organizations is the assumption that they are academic communities; the faculty are committed to a common set of beliefs. Yet academic managers do not discuss the actions by which a common set of beliefs can be maintained. We assume a common academic culture; we do not manage it.

The strength of academic culture is particularly important when academic institutions face declining resources. During these periods the social fabric of the community is under great strain. If the common academic culture has not been carefully nurtured during periods of prosperity, the

"The Management of Academic Culture: Notes on the Management of Meaning and Social Integration," by David D. Dill, reprinted from *Higher Education*, Vol. 11, 1982, Kluwer Academic Publishers, Netherland.

result can be destructive conflicts between faculties, loss of professional morale, and personal alienation.

The basic argument to be presented is that academic institutions possess distinctive cultures which are developed and sustained by identifiable actions of the community members. These actions include the presentation of symbolic events, such as honoring a distinguished researcher, which emphasize the core values of the institution; this process will be termed "the management of meaning." These actions also include designing structural bonds, such as the joint appointment of faculty members, which help transmit the core values of the institution; this process will be termed the management of social integration. The techniques of managing meaning and social integration are the undiscussed skills of academic management.

To understand the relevance of these skills we must first explore three interrelated phenomena: first, the part culture plays in models of management; second, the traits which distinguish universities from other organizations and make the management of culture of particular importance; third, the reasons for the decline of the existing academic culture. From this discussion we can begin to develop the threads of a distinctive process critical to maintaining academic institutions—the management of academic culture.

The Trends in Management: Academic

Many academic institutions in the United States are confronting the issue of survival. To the issues of financial stress which dominated the 1970s—soaring fuel costs, rapid inflation, inadequate budgeting and investment strategies, decreased federal support for research—has been added the decline in available numbers of traditional age students. Recent policy decisions to cut federal support for student loan funds can further decrease, dramatically, student enrollments, thereby intensifying the competition between institutions.

The response to this on the part of academic institutions has been conventional. If academic institutions are engaged in a competitive market—competing for scarce financial resources from multiple and shifting supporters, competing for able students and faculty, competing for social prestige—then it is argued they should adopt the managerial techniques of market-based businesses: strategic planning, marketing, and management control. Strategic planning refers to the organization defining its distinctive competence in such a way that it occupies a special niche in the market and is thereby assured of resources necessary for survival. Marketing refers both to discerning the needs of the market place and advertising the institution's distinctive competence to potential customers and supporters. Management control refers to accounting mechanisms such as cost and workload analyses which assure that critical resources are used to attain the strategic plans.

There is ample evidence in the United States that this is indeed the trend of events. The survival of academic institutions will depend upon the application of the skills of American management once extolled by Servan-Schreiber in *The American Challenge* (1968). The Institute for Educational Management at Harvard University, which provides continuing education for provosts, chancellors, and deans of distinguished institutions, emphasizes these skills. Contemporary books on academic management argue that only through this type of managerial attention may academic institutions survive (Anthony and Herzlinger, 1980; Balderston, 1975; Mayhew, 1979). Continuing education, pamphlets, and consulting enterprises in these areas abound. The trend in the management of academic organizations is clearly towards the adoption of the tools of management originally developed in the business sector.

The Trends in Management: Business

The trends in business management tend to be flowing in the other direction. Many American business corporations are also confronting the issue of survival. A mounting criticism of these corporations is that they have focused so heavily on a management orthodoxy of market driven behavior and strict management controls that they are managing American corporations to economic decline (Hayes and Abernathy, 1980). As the competitive advantage that American business enjoyed since World War II has eroded, numerous observers are arguing the superiority of European and particularly Japanese management methods. Now Servan-Schreiber has written *The World Challenge* (1981), which addresses the managerial advantage of other countries with emphasis on Japan. Recent American publications such as *Japan as Number One* (Vogel, 1979), *Theory Z* (Ouchi, 1981), and *The Art of Japanese Management* (Pascale and Athos, 1981) dissect Japanese management techniques and urge their adoption in the United States.

While Japanese organizations employ similar techniques of strategic planning, marketing and management control as those used by American businesses and currently advocated for adoption by universities, they also emphasize several "soft" techniques of management traditionally under-represented in the American management literature (Pascale and Athos, 1981). These soft techniques address the management of human resources with particular attention to:

1. procedures for recruiting, socializing and training personnel;

2. the cultural style of organization visible in various traditions and ceremonies;

3. the values or meanings in which the work of the organization is grounded.

In this sense, Japanese organizations "make meaning" for their workers, and design the organization to enhance interdependence and personal development. Consequently, it is argued, Japanese organizations are highly productive and command uncommon loyalty and commitment from their workers.

Similarly, Ouchi (1981) argues that the high commitment and effectiveness of Japanese workers derives from certain distinctive structural characteristics of the organizations. Lifetime employment, for example, is more common in Japanese business. The promotion of personnel is less frequent and status distinctions between employees are not as pronounced. The evaluation of personnel is more informal, decision making is consensual and collective, and personnel are regularly rotated. Explicit use is made of symbols such as key promotions and public meetings to express the critical values of the organization.

Each of these writers suggest that while these management techniques are consistent with Eastern cultural traditions, they are not solely dependent upon Japanese or oriental culture for their success. IBM is consistently cited as one American company which has created uncommon commitment to the firm by emphasizing the management of human resources, the culture of the organization, and techniques which enhance the contact and communication between personnel (Pascale and Athos, 1981). IBM makes substantial use of a system of basic beliefs—respect for the individual, customer service, and excellence—and a set of supporting fundamental principles. These core values are maintained by stressing an attitude of ascetic conformity (e.g., required white shirts), a common symbol system (e.g., the THINK signs), and a stress on an interdependent social life (e.g., a rich program of recreation for employees and families). Partially as a result of these managerial techniques, which are remarkably similar to those employed in Japanese organizations such as Matsushita Corporation, IBM is regarded as possessing a distinctive identity, high employee loyalty, and as one of the most effective of Western organizations.

In summary, there are three critical points to this brief review of management trends. First, the long-term effectiveness of the tools advocated for adoption by academic organizations—strategic planning, marketing and management control—is being seriously questioned within the business community. (This is particularly true in the case of market-driven planning and financial controls.) Second, increased attention is being given to the management of Japanese organizations. Ironically the organizations in Western society which most approximate the essential characteristics of Japanese firms are academic institutions. That is, they are also characterized by life-time employment, collective decision making, individual responsibility, infrequent promotion, and implicit, informal evaluation (Ouchi, 1981). Third, the Japanese management techniques place particular emphasis on the development of human resources and the maintenance of an organizational culture.

Organizational Culture

The most striking aspect of this recent work on Japanese organizations is its stress on the symbolic features of organizational life. The writers direct attention to social activities within Japanese organizations which eventually generate purpose, commitment, and order for organizational members. This phenomenon has been termed organizational culture, the system of "publicly and collectively accepted meanings operating for a given group at a given time" (Pettigrew, 1979, p. 574). For individuals to function in any organized setting, they must have some continuing sense of the reality in which they work. It is the expressive social fabric surrounding them that gives meaning to the individual tasks and objectives they pursue.

Organizational culture, then, is the shared beliefs, ideologies, or dogma of a group which impel individuals to action and give their actions meaning. Because of the distinctive nature of academic institutions, organizational culture plays a significant role in their functioning.

The Nature of Universities

The philosopher William James once said that any difference that is a difference should make a difference. What is the difference, if any, about universities as organizations which should be taken into account in their management? Satow (1975) has argued that organizations dominated by professionals must be viewed as "value-rational" organizations, in which members have absolute belief in the values of the organization for their own sake, independent of the values' prospects for success. The very authority of the enterprise therefore rests on obedience to a set of values or ideological norms. For example, the legitimacy of rules and regulations within academic institutions is determined by their consistency with the goals of academic ideology. When professional commitment to these norms (e.g., the pursuit of truth), comes into conflict with bureaucratic rules (e.g., government requirements that researchers obtain the consent of their subjects) priority is given to ideology (e.g., many researchers ignore the regulations in conducting their research). The notion that even academic organizations are grounded in an ideology, or dogma, has been neatly described by Madden (in Nisbet, 1971, p. viii–ix):

Every institutionalization of human activity is grounded on an unquestioned (not unquestionable!) faith which must be maintained in order to sustain the institution itself and the human function it embodies. If dogma seems the opposite of scholarship, which should be based upon the principle of open inquiry, then consider the case of science, an institution unquestionably devoted to inquiry. Every scientific inquiry is an act of faith in the worth of inquiry itself, every testing of an hypothesis is an act of faith in the idea that not only positive but even negative findings produce knowledge. Every inquiry must stabilize its premises in order even to locate its problems. These are parts of the dogma of science, and in fact of scholarship in general, including the humanities.

Satow further suggests that value-rational organizations are not only identified by their ideologies, but bound together by them. For example: selection of staff is based in part on their ideological commitment, for instance, schools of thought in economics; performance evaluation of faculty members is not dependent upon a set of standards to which behavior can be compared as in bureaucratic organizations, but upon flexible professional judgments based on shared tradition; policy is not determined hierarchically, but collegially, and premised upon common values and beliefs. Thus the nature of the enterprise, both its pattern of authority and its basic techniques of social organization, vary from market-based businesses.

Clark (1981) has suggested that the ideology or culture of academic organizations is much more complex than that of other organizations. Ideologies, or systems of belief, permeate academic institutions at at least three different levels: the culture of the enterprise, the culture of the academic profession at large, and the culture of academic discipline.

In Western society the culture of the academic enterprise has been powerful in terms of tradition and symbolic life. Through the language of titles and degrees, the specified curriculum and examinations which form the *rites de passage* of student life, and the characteristic organization of facilities, colleges, deans and chancellors, western universities can trace a direct lineal relationship to medieval universities, thereby providing the powerful symbol of ageless continuity to academic work (Haskins, 1957). Because the foundings of many European and American universities were supported by various religious groups, the search for truth and the transmission of knowledge have been historically associated with the sacred, and the reverence still awarded these centers of learning cannot fully be explained by their contemporary secular importance.

Certain institutions—in the United States, often smaller private colleges—have developed a particularly intense and localized form of enterprise culture, which Clark has termed a saga: "a collective understanding of current institutional character that refers to an historical struggle and is embellished emotionally and loaded with meaning to the point where the organization becomes very much an end-in-itself" (Clark, 1981, pp. 12–13). In this sense the common institutional tradition and shared symbols provide meaning and reward to organizational members, engendering commitment, loyalty, and uncommon effort.

The second level of culture is that of the collected academic profession. In Europe, the academic profession or guild has a substantial history, although its contemporary basis for meaning and identity has been eroded by the autonomy of faculties and chairs and the absence of any national system of professional identification. In the United States the development of the American Association of University Professors (AAUP) in the second decade of this century came in response to the strong and suppressive administrative groups at various institutions which were antagonistic to the emerging scholarly and scientific ideology in support of free inquiry. The AAUP therefore attempted to foster the shared identity of an academic profession grounded in a common dogma and articulated in the symbol of academic freedom and the ritual of tenure. The AAUP employed the symbolic activities of traditional religious organizations: the identification and celebration of martyrs (dismissed faculty), excommunication (the AAUP "blacklist" of offending institutions), the liturgical study group (AAUP chapter meetings), and the codification of gallant effort (the written history of the AAUP). The conduct of the AAUP was informed by scientific and scholarly values; the guidelines for an AAUP institutional investigation read like the methodological imputations

of the field researcher. The result of these efforts was an influential group of believers who were successful in altering the bylaws and contracts of many institutions to a form consistent with that of a value-rational organization.

Finally, we can also speak of the cultures or distinctive ideologies of the academic disciplines (Becher, 1981). These systems of shared belief clearly evoke the greatest meaning, commitment, and loyalty from contemporary academics. It is a culture with its own symbols of status and authority in the forms of professional awards, research grants, and publications, its ritualistic behavior at professional meetings, and its distinguishing articles of faith. For example, Becher (1981, p. 115) describes physicists as possessing a strong common identity and a "shared, 'almost religious,' belief in the unity of nature." Because this faith is developed during the intense socialization of graduate work, and because it is so central to the belief systems of adherents, it is rarely recognized as such until a paradigmatic shift occurs in a theoretical perspective, or methodological given. A shift, for example, from a qualitative-comparative method to a highly quantitative approach. At these times the intensity of the clash in belief systems within the discipline itself dramatizes the value systems at work beneath the surface of the field. These clashes would do justice to any conflict between religious sects over basic faith.

The difference that makes a difference, then, about academic institutions is that they are value-rational organizations whose members are committed to, and find meaning in, specified ideologies. These ideologies are manifest in a symbolic life or culture at the level of the enterprise, the profession, and discipline. Given the contemporary attention to the means by which Japanese managers create and maintain the culture of their organizations, one would expect that academic administrators would have a comparable skill in presenting and nurturing the ideologies or belief systems of their organizations. In fact, discussion and attention to the management of meaning, and the mechanisms of social structure necessary to maintain a common culture are as absent in American academic organizations as in American business corporations.[1] This is because both the overall strength of academic culture and the skills for managing it have declined.

The Decline of Academic Culture

Viewed from the perspective of value-rational organizations, the decline of academic institutions in the West cannot be attributed only to inattention to modern skills of management such as strategic planning, marketing and management control. Some portion of the decline must be attributed to the loss of a unifying system of belief, of a center of personal and collective identity, or of what Robert Nisbet has termed the "Degradation of the Academic Dogma" (Nisbet, 1971). Ideology or culture is not self-preserving. It requires the exercise of symbolic management and certain forms of social organization to keep it alive. In reviewing Clark's (1981) analysis of academic belief systems, it becomes obvious that the cultures which once commanded loyalty and gave meaning to the enterprise and the profession at large have been dissipated.

This decline or degradation can be attributed to the steady erosion of an enterprise culture originally based upon sectarian religious beliefs and to two other interrelated phenomena:

1. the rapid growth of systems of higher education;

2. an orientation toward the individual, discipline-based, career.

These latter two phenomena have produced faculty members who are socially and psychologically independent of the enterprise and the profession. One example of this change is evident in language. Faculty members who a generation ago would define themselves in terms of their institution—"I am a member of the Harvard faculty"—now identify themselves in terms of their field—"I am a sociologist, currently at Harvard."

In the United States the loss of meaning of enterprise culture has been relatively rapid. In only a hundred years we have moved from colleges and universities with the symbols and traditions of required chapel, a liberal education heavily based upon religious and moral precepts, and baccalaureate services at graduation, to secular institutions which retain many of these symbols and rituals but have discarded the underlying religious faith which gave these symbols meaning. In its place, we have adopted a faith in disciplinary ideology. But at the enterprise level we have failed to develop a corresponding culture rich enough in symbol and ritual to provide a unifying sense of belief. While even public universities possessed some religious rituals, the secular commitment to the separation of church and state inevitably led to their demise as significant symbols. The rapid growth of individual institutions, notably public institutions, further attenuated the bonds of enterprise culture. Commitment and loyalty to institution, a sense of shared belief, tended to remain strong only at those private colleges which retained a religious identity, substituted a secular version of distinctive purpose in the form of a saga or were capable, as were Harvard, Yale and a few other private research universities, of creating an institution-wide belief system dedicated to the academic dogma.

Similar to the decline of enterprise culture has been the decline of the academic profession as a unifying belief system. The rapid growth of American higher education was not constrained as in other countries by centralized traditions as to what constituted an appropriate discipline or field, or as to what institutions were eligible to offer advanced degrees. As a result, fields, disciplines, and Ph.D. recipients proliferated so rapidly after World War II as to eliminate the shared traditions, the identification to a common calling, the sense of a single profession which the AAUP attempted to establish at the turn of the century. At that time it was feasible to develop a professional identity through the mechanism of a collective association. The professoriate was small in size and the number of doctoral-granting universities limited in number. The disciplinary associations were in their early stages of development. Finally, the actions by some administrators to dismiss outspoken faculty members presented a sufficient threat against survival of the profession to galvanize faculty into developing a common culture of meaning and importance. Today the AAUP is a collective bargaining agent, one of several in the United States, and its moral force for the academic profession has withered. Similarly, the shared identity and meaning of an academic profession among faculty members in the United States has also disappeared.

Nisbet (1971) suggests that the principal reason for this decline in enterprise culture, and the culture of the profession at large, is the identification of the faculty members with the culture of the discipline. But a more useful conception is the identification of individual faculty members with their *professional careers* (Blankenship, 1977). Specific organizational conditions of the last several decades have provided status and prestige directly to the individual faculty member and have thereby compromised the authority of the faculties at all levels—discipline, enterprise, profession—to maintain the norms of academic culture by conferring conventional status. These organizational conditions were byproducts of the rapid growth of higher education and high social investment in scholarly and scientific work: easy promotion brought about by an insufficient supply of able faculty members; frequent movement between institutions; relatively plentiful funds to promote individual involvement in professional associations; ready access to grants, leaves, and research funds; and sharp gains in salary. In a time of academic decline, these conditions which fostered identification with an individual career are changing to conditions which will make the individual career rewards less attractive. Under these circumstances we can anticipate substantial numbers of faculty members choosing early retirement should that option be made available.

An additional problem is that of isolation. The focus on an individual career draws the faculty member toward increasing specializa-tion, particularly in research. This specialization results in declining involvement in institutional requirements for teaching, counselling and administration, and a lessening of social ties with disciplinary and institutional colleagues. Recent research on professionals suggests that a decline in satisfaction from interpersonal contacts in professional life may produce professional non-involvement and a search for satisfaction in areas unrelated to the core activities of the professional craft (Korman et al., 1981). Thus contemporary reports of "burn out," of loss of professional commitment and satisfaction, of declining motivation for professional work, may be related to the erosion of academic culture at all levels.

Before turning to a discussion of the management of academic culture, let us review the argument to this point. Under pressure to survive, academic institutions, particularly in the United States, are adopting the management techniques of market-based businesses. At the same time, these techniques are being criticized within the business community as insufficient, and attention has been drawn to the emphasis of Japanese organizations on organizational culture. Not only do academic organizations possess several key traits of Japanese organizations, e.g., lifetime employment, but they are organizations in which organizational culture plays a dominant role. Furthermore, critical segments of the academic culture—the culture of the profession and the culture of the enterprise—have fallen into decline, while the culture of the discipline has strengthened. The

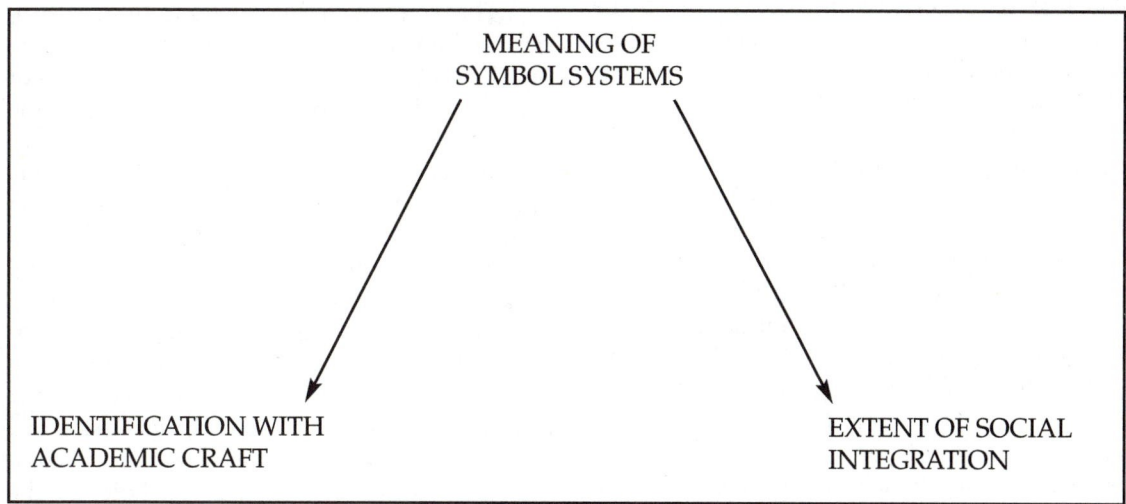

Figure 21-1 Meaning of Symbol Systems

primary meaning for academics has thus become not profession, not institution, but their professional career, and external conditions may decrease the meaningfulness of that orientation as well. Academic managers therefore face the real potential of alienation at the level of the profession, the enterprise and the discipline.

The techniques of increasing commitment and providing meaning in academic life are the same at the level of the discipline, the enterprise and the academic profession. These techniques, the mechanisms of coordination and control in professional organizations, are the meaning of symbol systems and the extent of social integration (Blankenship, 1977).

As Figure 21-1 suggests, the meaning of symbol systems and the extent of social integration are mutually related. Each directly affects identification with the academic discipline/enterprise/profession. To increase commitment and involvement in academic life, we might explore the means of increasing the meaning of symbol systems and increasing social integration. We might explore the management of academic culture.

The Management of Academic Culture: Meaning

To begin to talk about the management of meaning, we must become more specific about the concept of organizational culture. The nurturance of the symbolic life of academic organizations requires attending to the symbolism of concrete social events and occasions, to the constructions which faculty members place upon publicly expressed academic life (Geertz, 1973). To do this we need to view culture as composed of the more specific components: myth, symbol, and ritual (Pettigrew, 1979).

Myth is to be defined, not as false belief, but as the distinctive history of an institution or group embodied in written documents, reminiscences, legends and the physical properties of a place. Myths help to anchor the present in the past, and provide meaning which legitimates the social practices of academic life. Symbols are those "objects, acts, relationships or linguistic formations that stand ambiguously for a multiplicity of meanings, evoke emotions, and impel men to action" (quoted in Pettigrew, 1979, p. 574). The term ritual has come to mean ceremonies devoid of meaning. As used here, however, a ritual is a patterned sequence of social activity which expresses and articulates meaning. While the management of myth, symbol, and ritual can occur at any level of the academic belief system—enterprise, profession at large, or discipline—the following discussion will focus on enterprise culture.

Many academic administrators have an exquisite sense of myth and are skilled in its presentation and maintenance. This requires insuring that the history of an institution or group is not forgotten, that it is rewritten, read and known, that individuals who embody that history in their lives are visible and active in the community, and that traditional ceremonies of the community are scrupulously maintained. The management of myth would require that additions to the physical home of the community are tied to and reinvest the myth, and that any public activity is an opportunity to proclaim and celebrate the myth.

Academic institutions abound with symbols. An example is liberal education. Liberal education is symbolic in that it cannot be tangibly grasped, defined or specified. It is an ideology which serves the purpose of providing a unifying belief among individuals whose primary belief systems are anchored in their disciplines. The symbol of liberal education is thereby a critical component of enterprise academic culture: the belief in liberal education suggests that members of the academic community have a meaningful purpose in working together, that they are in fact a community.

The symbol of liberal education is supported by ritual, the formal attempts to define it. These attempts invariably occur after major shocks to the social fabric of society and to the worth of the academic dogma. Thus the general education program emerged at Columbia after World War I and the Harvard Report on general education after World War II. Most recent attempts to strengthen and define liberal education occurred after the campus disruptions of the Vietnamese War and the racial crisis. In this sense, the outcome of the ritual—the curriculum defined—is relatively meaningless. It is the ritual of discipline-wide discussion of a symbolic idea which creates meaning and commitment to the institution as a whole. By the same token, the emerging sense of cynicism about this ritual, the perception of departmental politicking to sustain enrollments necessary for their budget base, also suggests the loss of meaning, the decline in the power of this symbol to create a common system of belief.

If a chancellor, dean, or department head were to think seriously about the creation of meaning, or more responsibly, the nurturing of existing academic culture, what myths or symbols should be emphasized? This is the critical issue, and one for which corporate and industrial examples offer little insight. It is this selection and heightening of critical values which is at the heart of the creative dimension of leadership. It can only be said, that the values chosen for emphasis must be necessary conditions to the core technologies of academic life: research, scholarship and teaching. In this sense it is obvious that the major symbols and supporting rituals of American universities—athletic valor and team play—important as they may be for creating meaning among alumni and financial supporters, do little to strengthen academic culture. The celebration of academic values such as honesty, sustained curiosity, the communication of knowledge, and continued intellectual growth should be necessary conditions for any vital academic culture.[2] Vital in the sense that the myths, symbols and rituals comprising the culture would preserve the distinctive identity of the academic craft, specify the behaviors necessary to the sustenance of the craft, and provide meaning to these behaviors. While many academic institutions possess rituals such as founding day, or graduation, what myths, symbols and rituals exist which draw institution-wide attention to critical academic values, which celebrate and help sustain them? What proportion of the expressive lives of academic administrators is spent in symbolic activity of this type?

One difficulty with academic symbols and their supporting rituals is that they are often abstract.[3] They do not immediately communicate with the everyday behaviors of academic life. One means of animating symbols, which helps to communicate their meaning to academic life as it is lived, is the canonization of exemplars. Saints are individuals who in harsh or extreme circumstances have personified values necessary for the community to function, thereby earning our respect, our adoration and emulation. Who might be saints to serve as vital symbols for the contemporary academic community? Individuals who have made substantial contributions to knowledge with little or no research support, individuals whose dedication to teaching and scholarship has been marked by self-sacrifice and disinterest in worldly goods, individuals who have resisted the suppression of knowledge, individuals who have made dramatic and significant shifts in fields in the latter stages of their careers, and so on. The selection, canonization and celebration of faculty exemplars in the life of an academic institution becomes a powerful symbol in time of stress and hardship as to the values of the enterprise essential to survival. People as symbols provide meaning in work, because identification with the symbol offers courage to the organizational members to live through difficult periods.

A final means of managing symbolic life is through the ritual of the guild. A guild is a sworn brotherhood of persons following a common craft and seeking to preserve the distinctive identity of that craft. In this sense the AAUP, the faculty of a given institution, and particularly the faculty of a specific discipline, can be viewed as guilds. The decline of the AAUP and the faculty of an institution as guilds can then be understood as the loss of a common identity. If we wish to strengthen the culture of the enterprise, to nurture a system of belief of potential meaning, we might consider the formation of guilds. Guilds provide a powerful means of socialization, communication and camaraderie. The meetings and activities of a guild satisfy needs for affiliation and provide the sense of involvement in an activity of long-term importance.

How might the structure of the guild be employed to manage meaning? One example is teaching. Teaching is a distinctive characteristic of the academic craft in which all members engage. But which members of the community act to superintend or preserve teaching, act to maintain faith in the importance of teaching, act to define the necessary values in teaching which distinguish the "sacred" from the "profane"? Where is the academic guild of teachers? Occasionally the university acts to honor great teachers by identifying them, offering an award, and celebrating their gifts. Often, too, universities debase their basic values by conferring this status in the form of a cash award or salary increase, rather than in symbolically meaningful terms. Following their celebration, these great teachers are then ignored by the organization and play no special role in the life of the academic community. An alternative scenario might be to induct each individual into a formal guild of the elect; to assign to that guild the authority and responsibility of selecting future members; to provide the guild with distinctive facilities and perquisites; to involve the guild in means to improve teaching on a campus such as dispensing funds for innovation in teaching; to request that the guild oversee the orientation of new faculty members to the campus; and to encourage the guild to hold distinctive ceremonies and activities which maintain belief in the importance of teaching. A comparable guild could be developed for research and scholarship which might serve as an antidote to the current system which confers status in the form of faculty chairs with high salaries; a system which builds no community of scholars dedicated to the preservation of the craft, but superintends belief in financial remuneration as the ultimate reward for the pursuit of knowledge.

In summary, one aspect of the management of academic culture involves the management of meaning. Some important tools in the management of meaning, include the nurturance of myth, the identification of unifying symbols, the ritual observance of symbols, the canonization of exemplars, and the formation of guilds. These are critical managerial tools in value-rational organizations, because it is through shared beliefs and traditions that such organizations can be coordinated and controlled and professional loyalty, commitment, and identity can be maintained.

The Management of Academic Culture: Social Integration

The intensity of an academic culture is determined not only by the richness and relevance of its symbolism for the maintenance of the professional craft, but by the bonds of social organization. These bonds are created by the mechanism of collegial communication with feedback about professional activity (Hage,

1974). For this mechanism to operate the institution needs to take specific steps to socialize the individual to the belief system of the organization, and promote joint activities between colleagues from throughout the enterprise. The decline of academic culture is thus partially traceable to the rapid growth of academic communities, the isolation of specialities, and the inattention given to the process of social organization necessary to nurture academic culture. The management of academic culture therefore involves both the management of meaning and the management of social integration.

One example of this inattention to social integration can be seen in the development of new fields. During periods of rapid growth organizations frequently grow by adoption rather than extension. Adoption entails the appointment of a specialist in the new field who subsequently makes independent critical decisions about additional staff. If the new staff is socialized at all, it is within the department or field, rarely to institutional norms. Development of the curriculum, definition of degrees and the process of teaching and research, are carried out in isolation from other colleagues, responsive at best to broadly stated institutional policies or to distant mechanisms of review. The potential for conflict over time with basic institutional beliefs becomes obvious. This was frequently experienced during the 1970s in new professional programs, or new fields such as ethnic studies, where faculty members did not fully subscribe to the ideology of the parent institution and as a result issues of quality control and academic integrity became a continuing source of debate. By contrast, some more selective institutions grew by extension. For example, the recently developed School of Organization and Management at Yale University was begun around a core of professors from existing disciplines already on the campus. Selection of new faculty members frequently required joint appointment to an existing discipline thus assuring that traditional academic values of the institution were observed in the definition of new positions. While broad searches for new faculty members were conducted, new appointments were most typically made from a small core of selective graduate schools where students had been intensely socialized to academic values consistent with those of Yale University. Thus the techniques of extension: growth around a faculty core already committed to the academic culture, selection of new appointees by emphasizing harmony between their socialization and institutional belief systems, and appointment of new recruits who subscribe to existing disciplinary ideologies, all tend to insure the strength of the academic culture and the maintenance of academic norms.

The intensive socialization of new students to a college or department is a matter of course. Intensive socialization of faculty members to the traditions and values of the institution is much more rare. The assumption has been that prior socialization in graduate training has been appropriate and sufficient. Given the growth and fragmentation of academic systems, this traditional assumption may no longer be valid. If one instead wished to consider socialization to the values of the enterprise, there are several ways this might be accomplished: by particular rituals such as social occasions with older, prestigious faculty drawn from across the institution (e.g., the aforementioned guilds); the gift of a history of the institution to all new faculty members; programs nominally introducing new appointees to teaching and research support services provided by the institution, but which also include substantial inculcation to institutional values and tradition. The most powerful socialization device, one institutionalized by Japanese organizations, in the "Sempai-Kohai" (senior-junior) relationship, is that of mentoring (Pascale and Athos, 1981). The mentoring process in this sense focuses not on technical skill, but on norms and values which the mentor possesses and which the new appointee will learn. To be effective in an academic context, mentors might be assigned to new faculty from senior faculty in a related but separate discipline, thereby providing vertical (across ranks) and horizontal (across fields) integration, and avoiding conflict with peer evaluation.

In addition to the process of socialization are the organizational policies and procedures which promote interdepartmental communication or vertical and horizontal integration. In academic organizations these might include: extradepartmental faculty involvement in the definition of new positions; the requirement of extradepartmental faculty participation in faculty search committees, encouragement of joint appointments; systematic encouragement of joint research and teaching through targeted funding; and the requirement of outside department members on doctoral committees. There is nothing exceptional about these suggestions, although an analysis of the policies and practices of many academic institutions will reveal that such practices have steadily deteriorated, and that contemporary academic management is noticeably inattentive to the principles of vertical and horizontal social integration.

Ouchi (1981) has argued that Japanese organizations have promoted interdependence and organizational loyalty by minimizing specialized career paths. Frequent rotation is a specific means employed by Japanese industries to lessen the isolation of specialization. Recognizing that faculty members often broaden perspective over their careers, from highly specialized inquiry in their early years to issues of greater scope in later life, we might adapt the technique of rotation to one of "internal sabbaticals" in which faculty members are released from present duties and reappointed in different but related departments or fields at the same institution for a specified period of time.

The maintenance of academic culture depends to a substantial extent upon careful management of the technique of social organization critical for sustaining common belief systems. These techniques involve an emphasis on socialization and policies which promote organizationwide communication principally through joint activities featuring vertical and horizontal integration. These facets of social organization coupled with a strongly shared system of belief are the primary methods of coordination and control in value-rational organizations.

Conclusion

The major perspective of this article has been that while the techniques of market-based bureaucrats may aid the short-term survival of academic organizations, they may do little to increase the productivity, commitment and loyalty of the professional staff. Indeed, these techniques may clash substantially with the core ideologies of academic life. The revival of academic institutions in a time of diminishing resources must also address the management of academic culture: the nurturing of the expressive life of academic institutions and the strengthening of social integration.

The notion that academic culture can be managed may suggest an overweening confidence in the capacity of managers. Certainly self-conscious efforts at social engineering have a dubious track record. It is wise to be modest about what can be accomplished. The major thesis of this article, however, has not been to argue for the creation of new systems of value in academic life, but to maintain existing ones. The issue is not whether academic culture should be managed. The issue is whether those with the principal responsibility of superintending academic values have focused on the appropriate means of accomplishing the task.

Given the distinctive nature of academic organization the maintenance of the expressive aspects of academic community deserves much more attention than it has received in discussions of academic management. The nurturance of the symbolic life of academic organizations and the distinctive skills of social organization necessary for their coordination and control are unique skills of academic management which must be rediscovered and accentuated or they will be lost. To begin, we must first discuss the management of academic culture not as anthropologists, sociologists, educators, theologians, or journalists, but seriously.

This is a revised version of a paper originally presented at the Fifth International Conference on Higher Education, University of Lancaster, 2 September 1981. I am indebted to Philip Altbach, Tony Becher, Zelda Gamson, and the members of Study Group Six for their constructive criticisms of the original paper.

David D. Dill is at the School of Education, University of North Carolina, U.S.A.

Notes

1. James G. March, an astute observer of academic organizations has recently argued that the management of symbols is an underemphasized aspect of administration. See, James G. March, "How We Talk and How We Act," David D. Henry, Lecturer in Higher Education, University of Illinois, September, 1980.
2. For some thinking about values which may be necessary conditions for effective university teaching, see the special issue on "Ethics and the academic profession," *Journal of Higher Education* May/June, 1982.
3. I am indebted to the Reverend Robert W. Duncan for his creative thinking on these issues.

References

Anthony, R. N. and Herzlinger, R. E. *Management Control in Nonprofit Organizations.* Homewood, Ill: Irwin, 1980.

Balderston, F. E. *Managing Today's University.* San Francisco: Jossey-Bass, 1975.

Becher, T. "Towards a Definition of Disciplinary Cultures," *Studies in Higher Education*, 1981, 6; 109–122.

Blankenship, R. L. "Toward a Theory of Collegial Power and Control," in Ralph Blankenship, (ed.) *Colleagues in Organization.* New York: John Wiley, 1977.

Clark, B. R. "Belief," March (unpublished paper), 1981.

Geertz, C. *The Interpretation of Cultures.* New York: Basic Books, 1973.

Hage, H. *Communication and Organizational Control.* New York: John Wiley, 1974.

Hayes, R. H. and Abernathy, W. J. "Managing Our Way to Economic Decline," *Harvard Business Review*, 1980, 58; 67–77.

Haskins, C. H. *The Rise of Universities.* Ithaca, New York: Cornell University, 1957.

Korman, A. K., Wittig-Berman, U. and Lang, D. "Career Success and Personal Failure: Alienation in Professionals and Managers." *Academy of Management Journal*, 1981, 24; 242–260.

Mayhew, L. B. *Surviving the Eighties.* San Francisco: Jossey-Bass, 1979.

Nisbet, R. *The Degradation of the Academic Dogma.* New York: Basic Books, 1971.

Ouchi, W. G. *Theory Z.* Reading, Mass: Addison-Wesley, 1981.

Pascale, R. T. and Athos, A. G. *The Art of Japanese Management.* New York: Simon and Schuster, 1981.

Pettigrew, A. M. "On Studying Organizational Cultures," *Administrative Science Quarterly*, 1979, 24; 570–581.

Satow, R. L. "Value-Rational Authority and Professional Organizations: Weber's Missing Type," *Administrative Science Quarterly*, 1975, 20; 526–531.

Servan-Schreiber, J. *The American Challenge.* New York: Atheneum, 1968.

Servan-Schreiber, J. *World Challenge.* New York: Simon and Schuster, 1981.

Vogel, E. F. *Japan as Number One.* New York: Harper and Row, 1979.

CHAPTER 22

ORGANIZATIONAL ADAPTATION AND HIGHER EDUCATION

KIM S. CAMERON

The recent report of the National Commission on Excellence in Education [46] concluded that "the educational foundations of our society are presently being eroded by a rising tide of mediocrity that threatens our very future as a nation and a people. What was unimaginable a generation ago has begun to occur—others are matching and surpassing our educational attainments. The explicit objective of the commission's report was to generate reform of our educational system in fundamental ways and to renew the nation's commitment to schools and colleges of high quality throughout the length and breadth of our land."

A variety of recommendations were made in the report, which called for innovation and adaptation on the part of educational institutions. These recommendations focused both on elementary and secondary schools and on colleges and universities. However, before educational institutions can implement these recommendations, they must become both knowledgeable and adept at instituting organizational change. They will need to become effective at implementing innovation, reform, and adaptation. One purpose of this special issue of the *Journal of Higher Education* is to point out ways in which reforms, innovations, and adaptations can and have occurred successfully. Hopefully, these articles will contribute to the renewal of America's educational institutions in general and of liberal arts colleges in particular.

Our focus in this issue is mainly on liberal arts colleges, for reasons pointed out in the *Introduction*, and on the concept of adaptation, as opposed to innovation or reform, for reasons that will become clear later. This article reviews what is known about organizational adaptation and points out types of adaptation that will be needed in institutions of higher education in the future. The focus is a conceptual one, and specific adaptive actions taken by institutions are not reviewed. Rather, the purpose is to give the reader a framework within which to comprehend adaptation in educational organizations.

In the first section, major conceptual approaches to organizational adaptation are reviewed. The second section discusses the probable environment that institutions of higher education are likely to face in the future that will require adaptation. The third section discusses some adaptive strategies and institutional characteristics that will be needed by colleges and universities if they are to remain effective.

Section 1: Approaches to Organizational Adaptation

"Organizational adaptation" refers to modifications and alterations in the organization or its components in order to adjust to changes in the external environment. Its purpose is to restore equilibrium to an imbalanced condition. Adaptation generally refers to a process, not an event, whereby changes are instituted in organizations. Adaptation does not necessarily imply reactivity on the part of an organization (i.e., adaptation is not just waiting for the environment to change and then reacting to it) because proactive or anticipatory adaptation is possible as well. But the emphasis is definitely on responding to some discontinuity or lack of fit that arises between the organization and its environment.

This kind of organizational change is not the same as "planned change," or what is often called Organization Development (OD). Adaptation focuses on changes motivated by the external environment; OD focuses on changes motivated from within the organization. OD is generally oriented toward changes in individual attitudes and behaviors and in the organization's culture; adaptation is more concerned with organization-level change (see, e.g., [12]). Goodman and Kurke [23] differentiated adaptation and planned change in the following ways:

> Planned organizational change deals with the basis of change; adaptation deals with the conditions or sources of change. Planned organizational change focuses primarily on change within the organization, but the adaptation literature focuses primarily on populations of organizations, and on organization-environment interfaces, and on changes within an organization that are environmentally dictated. The planned organization literature emphasizes the process of actually creating change rather than writing about the processes of change (adaptation literature). The planned organizational change literature is devoted to methods and techniques, but the adaptation literature is devoted to theorizing about the change processes or outcomes. [23, p. 4]

This article, and this issue in general, focuses on the process of adaptation because of the pervasive influence of the external environment on liberal arts colleges. Several articles in this issue (e.g., Zammuto, Pfnister, Martin) point out the threats that face liberal arts colleges because of changing environments. Most observers agree that environmental turbulence and complexity have greatly accelerated in recent years (see [58, 59, 41, 52]) and that the ability of organizations to cope with those changes is being stretched. As Toffler noted:

> I gradually came to be appalled by how little is actually known about adaptivity, either by those who call for and create vast changes in our society, or by those who supposedly prepare us to cope with those changes. Earnest intellectuals talk bravely about "educating for change," or "preparing people for the future." But we know virtually nothing about how to do it. In the most rapidly changing environment to which man has ever been exposed, we remain pitifully ignorant of how the human animal copes. [58, p. 2]

Toffler's observation, that little is known about adaptation, is beginning to be rectified somewhat on the organization level. The body of literature on organizational adaptation is relatively new (most of it has appeared since 1970), but it has nevertheless become quite extensive. In fact, it is so extensive that a summary of it must, of necessity, be selective and abridged. Therefore, in this first section, general themes are discussed and examples are used, but a comprehensive survey is not attempted.

One way to organize the conceptual approaches to organizational adaptation is to use a continuum anchored on one end by the assumption that managers have *no* power to influence the adaptability and long-term survival of their organizations. On the other end of the continuum is the assumption that managers have *complete power* to create adaptability and to ensure long-term survival. Figure 22-1 summarizes the major approaches to organizational adaptation on the basis of this continuum. These approaches to adaptation are briefly explained below.

Approaches Assuming Little or No Managerial Influences

Aldrich [2], Aldrich and Pfeffer [3], Hannan and Freeman [24], Birnbaum [8], McKelvey [39], and others have proposed and elaborated a "population ecology" or "natural selection" view of organizational adaptation. The population ecology approach to adaptation focuses on changes in environmental "niches" (i.e., subunits of the environment that support organizations). Two types of "niche" change can occur that lead to organizational adaptation. One is a change in the size of the niche, or the amount of resources available to organizations. The other is a change in the shape of the niche, or the type of organizational activities supported. Zammuto and Cameron [68] pointed out what adaptations are required of populations of organizations when faced with these different types of changes in environmental niches. For example, when a population of organizations encounters a change in niche shape (e.g., certain organizational activities are no longer supported), generalist organizations—those involved in a wide range of activities—are most adaptative. Successful adaptation requires becoming more diversified. On the other hand, when populations of organizations encounter changes in niche size (e.g., fewer resources are available), specialist organizations—those that are especially good at a narrow range of activities—are most adaptive. Successful adaptation requires organizations to specialize.

The population ecology approach suggests that adaptation is meaningful only if viewed from the population level of analysis (i.e., single organization changes are largely irrelevant). According to advocates, this level of analysis is important because of the many constraints and inertias inhibiting managerial action in organizations (i.e., formal structure, past history, norms, policies, and so on). The only meaningful change occurs as major shifts among entire populations of organizations, not as minor adjustments in existing organizational forms. The environment is viewed as such a powerful and pervasive force that it selects those organizational forms (or adaptations) that are to persist and other organizational forms die out. (For example, Hannan and Freeman [24]) suggest that unstable environments select generalist organizations and stable environments select specialist organizations.)

The process is considered to be much like biological selection theories. The fittest species—those that evolve characteristics that are compatible with the environment—survive while other species become extinct. Most organizations adapt, therefore, not because of intelligent or creative managerial action but by the random or evolutionary development of characteristics that are compatible with the environment. Managerial discretion and influence is neither present nor relevant.

Another approach to adaptation that emphasizes evolutionary change and the powerful role of the environment but that allows for more managerial discretion is the "life cycles" approach to adaptation (see [13, 14, 51] for reviews). Single organizations are the preferred units of analysis, and they are assumed to progress through at least four sequential stages of development. At each stage, unique organizational features develop in order to overcome certain general problems encountered by all organizations. Without direct managerial intervention to alter this natural evolution, organizational adaptations tend to follow

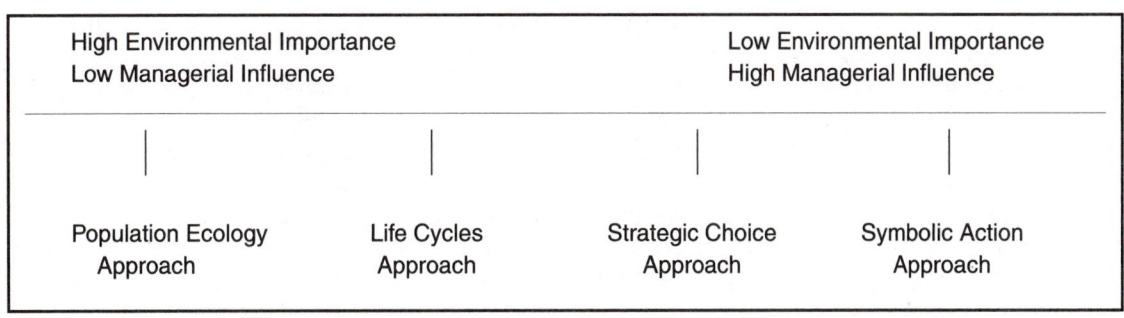

Figure 22-1 Categories of Approaches to Organizational Adaptation

a predictable sequence. Cameron and Whetten summarized the sequence as follows:

> Organizations begin in a stage, labelled "creativity and entrepreneurship," in which marshalling resources, creating an ideology, and forming an ecological niche are emphasized. [The problem faced by the organization in this stage is to build legitimacy and acquire the resources needed to survive.] The second stage, the "collectivity" stage, includes high commitment and cohesion among members, face-to-face communication and informal structures, long hours of dedicated service to the organization, and an emerging sense of collectivity and mission. The organizational emphasis is on internal processes and practices, rather than on external contingencies. [The problem faced by the organization is mobilizing the work force and building interdependence.] In the third stage, "formalization and control," where procedures and policies become institutionalized, goals are formalized, conservatism predominates, and flexibility is reduced. The emphasis is on efficiency of production. [The organizational problem in this stage is coordinating and stabilizing the work force and improving efficiency.] The fourth stage emphasizes "elaboration of structure" where decentralization, domain expansion, and renewed adaptability occur, and new multipurpose subsystems are established. (The organizational problem is overcoming rigidity and conservatism and expanding to meet new constituency demands.) [13, p. 527]

In each new stage of development, certain problems are encountered that are overcome by progressing on to the next life-cycle stage. That is, organizations encounter similar issues as they develop over time, and adaptation occurs by acquiring characteristics of the next life-cycle stage. This new stage solves the issues encountered in the previous stage but also generates issues that motivate further life-cycle development. Therefore, this approach to adaptation assumes that there is a natural tendency in organizations to follow a life-cycle pattern of development.

Two assumptions modify this approach and make it less deterministic than the population ecology view. The first assumption is that managers can speed up, slow down, or even abort this sequential development by their actions. That is, they can cause an organization to stay in an early stage for a long time, to move through the sequence very rapidly, or to go out of business before ever reaching subsequent stages. Second, these stages are most typical of the early history of organizations. After the fourth stage is reached, organizations may recycle through the sequence again as a result of unusual environmental events, leadership turnover, organizational membership changes, and so on. Managerial action can help determine which stage is returned to after stage 4 (see [14]).

Approaches Assuming Substantial Managerial Influence

On the other end of the continuum are approaches to adaptation that consider the decisions and actions of managers, not the external environment, to be the most important causes of organizational adaptation. They emphasize that managers can choose which environment the organization operates in, they can control and manipulate the environment, they can scan and thereby predict in advance environmental events, and so on. In short, organizations are not assumed to be at the mercy of an immutable environment; rather, they can act and influence their environment. The diverse literature on adaptation resulting from managerial action is organized into two major categories for the purpose of review. Several different models of adaptation are subsumed under each category.

One major category of adaptation models is the "strategic choice" approach [17, 3, 5]. A sampling of the different models summarized by this approach includes the "resource dependence" model [49], the "political economy" model [61], the "strategy-structure" model [16], and models by Miles and Snow [40], Miles and Cameron [42], March [35], and Miller and Friesen [43]. Whereas these authors recognize the importance of external environmental influences and the need for a fit between environment and an organization's structure and process [31], a variety of strategies are available to managers that can modify the environment and determine the success or failure of adaptation. As Chamberlain stated:

Organizations are obviously not pushed and pulled and hauled by market forces which overwhelm them; rather, they demonstrably choose to follow a certain course of action which differs from other courses which they might have chosen and which, indeed, some of their number do elect to follow. Discretion is present. How important it is in the end result is still a moot point, but at least there is no basis for pretending that it has no effect. [15, p. 47]

The strategic choice approach is illustrated by Miles and Cameron [42], who found that organizations adapted very successfully to an extremely turbulent and hostile environment by implementing three types of strategies in sequence: "domain defense" strategies (designed to enhance the legitimacy of the organization and buffer it from environmental encroachment), "domain offense" strategies (designed to expand in current areas of expertise and exploit weaknesses in the environment), and "domain creation" strategies (designed to minimize risk by diversifying into safer or less turbulent areas of the environment). (See Cameron [11]) for a discussion of these strategies in higher education organizations.)

Miles and Snow [40] suggested that organizations develop a particular orientation—a "strategic competence"—that leads them to implement these various types of strategies at different times and in different ways. For example, "prospector" organizations are inclined to be "first in," to implement strategies early and innovatively. "Analyzer" organizations are inclined to wait for evidence that the strategy will be successful before implementing new adaptations. "Defenders" seek for stability and are slow to adapt. "Reactors" implement strategies sporadically and are often unable to follow through with a consistent adaptive response. Miles and Snow [40] and Snow and Hrebiniak [57] have found empirical evidence linking these strategic orientations to effective adaptation under varying environmental conditions.

Miller and Friesen [43] studied thirty-six organizations and 135 different organizational adaptations in order to identify how organizations adapted over time. They used historical case studies so a longitudinal time-frame could be observed. Evidence for the strategic choice approach was found as they identified several

major "archetypes of organizational transition." The most prominent archetypes among successful organizations were entrepreneurial revitalization, scanning and troubleshooting, consolidation, centralization and boldness, and decentralization and professionalization. These authors concluded that "there do not appear to be a very great number of common transition types" [43, p. 288]. That is, only a few major adaptation strategies implemented by managers are typical of a large variety of organizations.

One major issue that permeates the strategic choice approach is whether adaptations are implemented incrementally (i.e., small, piecemeal changes are put into place by managers) or in a revolutionary way (i.e., major shifts occur affecting many organizational elements). On the one hand, some writers suggest that organizations adapt by "muddling through" or by implementing "a succession of incremental changes" [32]. Change occurs without requiring major aberrations from the routine. As March put it:

Managers and leaders propose changes, including foolish ones; they try to cope with the environment and to control it; they respond to other members of the organization; they issue orders and manipulate incentives. Since they play conventional roles, organizational leaders are not likely to behave in strikingly unusual ways. And if a leader tries to march toward strange destinations, an organization is likely to deflect the effort. Simply to describe leadership as conventional and constrained by organizational realities, however, is to risk misunderstanding its importance. Neither success nor change requires dramatic action. The conventional, routine activities that produce most organizational change require ordinary people to do ordinary things in a competent way. [35, p. 575]

On the other hand, Miller and Friesen [44] represent those who argue that adaptation occurs in a revolutionary way. They point out that organizations possess a great deal of momentum, or inertia, that serves to inhibit alterations or reforms. Past strategies, structures, goals, political coalitions, myths and ideologies, and so on contribute to that momentum, so that major adjustments in a substantial part of the organization have to be made in order for adaptation to occur.

Organizational adaptation is likely to be characterized by periods of dramatic revolution in which there are reversals in the direction of change across a significantly large number of variables of strategy and structure. Revolutions that display reversals for a high proportion of variables occur with very significantly high frequency. These major reorientations seem to take place because many excesses or deficiencies have developed during periods of pervasive momentum or because a new strategy requires realignments among many variables. Thus there follows a myriad of structural and strategic reversals. [44, pp. 593, 612]

The second category of adaptation models on this end of the continuum is called the "symbolic action" approach [48, 47, 18, 7]. It differs from the strategic choice approach by focusing on change in symbols, interpretations, and stories as opposed to change in structure and technology. The logic of this approach is that organizations are glued together mainly by the presence of common interpretations of events, common symbols, common stories or legends, and so on or by a "social construction of reality" [7]. Social construction of reality means that the interpretation of reality in an organization is a product of social definition. Shared meanings are much more important than are events themselves. Part of the socialization process in organizations is giving members access to these common meanings. The role of the manager, in turn, is to create, manipulate, or perpetuate these meanings so that they are accepted in the organization and thereby influence organizational behavior. Pfeffer summarized this perspective in the following way:

> The activity of management is viewed as making what is going on in the organization meaningful and sensible to the organizational participants, and furthermore developing a social consensus and social definition around the activities being undertaken. Management involves more than labeling or sense making—it involves the development of a social consensus around those labels and the definition of activity. [48, p. 21]

Organizational adaptation comes about through the use of a variety of strategies involving language, ritual, and symbolic behavior designed to modify organization members' shared meanings. Weick [65] referred to this as "enacting" the external environment. Several of the more prominent methods of adaptation in this approach are as follows:

1. *Interpreting history and current events.* "The effectiveness of a leader lies in his ability to make activity meaningful for those in his role set—not to change behavior but to give others a sense of understanding what they are doing and especially to articulate it so they can communicate about the meaning of their behavior. . . . If in addition the leader can put it into words, then the meaning of what the group is doing becomes a social fact. . . . This dual capacity . . . to make sense of things and to put them into language meaningful to large numbers of people gives the person who has it enormous leverage" [50, pp. 94–95].

2. *Using rituals or ceremonies.* Gameson and Scotch [22] noted the ritualistic function of firing managers and coaches of professional sports teams whose win-loss records were bad. The firings did not so much represent a substantive change as they did a symbolic one designed to give the impression that things would get better. Inaugurations, ceremonies, and commencements are symbolic functions used frequently to manage meanings and interpretations in order to influence organizational adaptation.

3. *Using time and measurement.* Time spent is one measure of the importance of organizational activities (47). Therefore, spending more time at one activity than another helps managers convey messages of priority to other organization members. Similarly, what is measured almost always receives more attention in organizations than what is not measured. Adaptation is facilitated by managers, therefore, through their use of time and quantitative measurement.

4. *Redesigning physical space.* Providing a new physical setting often conveys the message that something new is going on

or that a different direction is being pursued. Similarly, attributes of physical settings often are interpreted as manifestations of power in offices and buildings (e.g., larger space, higher space, more central space, and so on). Pfeffer noted that "skilled managers understand well the importance of physical settings for their symbolic value. The size, location, and configuration of physical space provide the backdrop against which other managerial activity takes place, and thereby influence the interpretation and meaning of that other activity" [48, p. 41].

5. *Introducing doubt.* "The introduction of doubt into a loosely coupled system is a much more severe change intervention than most people realize. Core beliefs, such as the presumption of logic and the logic of confidence, are crucial underpinnings that hold loose events together. If these beliefs are questioned, action stops, uncertainty is substantial, and receptiveness to change is high" [66, p. 392].

Each of these strategies of adaptation under the symbolic action approach assumes substantial power on the part of managers to change the definition of the external environment and to change organizational behavior in response to those definitions. The environment is not assumed to be immutable (as with the population ecology approach); on the contrary, it is assumed to be almost entirely a product of social definition. Adaptation occurs by changing definitions.

Review

By way of review, approaches to organizational adaptation can be organized into at least four categories based on the importance of the roles played by the external environment and by management in influencing organizational survival. The population ecology approach assumes a prominent role for the environment and virtually no role for management action. The life cycles approach assumes a prominent role for the environment and evolutionary forces, but some discretion is assumed for management in altering those naturalistic forces.

The strategic choice approach assumes a prominent role for both environment and management, but the balance is shifted toward management. The strategies implemented by managers can change the external environment as well as the organization. The symbolic action approach assumes a prominent role for management, through the ability to manipulate symbols and social definitions, and a less prominent role for the external environment.

Having reviewed the major approaches to adaptation, the question remains: What does this mean for institutions of higher education? Is one approach to adaptation better than another? What should managers and administrators in institutions do to make their organizations more adaptable?

To answer these questions, it is necessary to review the environmental conditions that are likely to face institutions of higher education in the future. That is, to understand how colleges should adapt, it is first necessary to understand what conditions will be characteristic of the external environment that perpetuate imbalances and require adaptation. The next section speculates on what future environments will be like for educational organizations.

Section 2. The Nature of Postindustrial Environments

It is generally acknowledged that factors in the external environment are increasing in their influence on organizations. Organizations are more frequently being required to be good at adaptation in order to survive. Roeber noted, for example:

> The characteristic mode of change in Western industrialized countries has been integrative, and the key characteristic is loss of slack. Partial equilibrium solutions are becoming less satisfactory, particularly where interaction between organizations and their social environment is involved. Consequently, the environment is becoming more of a factor inside organizations and requires more explicit attention. [52, p. 154]

Roeber's point, that the environment is becoming more dominant at the same time that organizations are faced with less slack, suggests that adaptive strategies should constitute a critical concern of future managers.

Several authors have discussed the changes that are occurring in the external environment that make attention to it more crucial than ever before. These changes are leading to what some call postindustrial society [56, 6], the technetronic era [9], the information society [38], the telematic society [37], and the third wave [59]. These authors all point out that environments in the future will be radically different for institutions than are the current environments of industrialized society. In a recent provocative article, for example, Huber [28] pointed out several ways in which postindustrial environments will be different from present or past environments. He stated that "postindustrial society will be characterized by more and increasing knowledge, more and increasing complexity, and more and increasing turbulence. These, in combination, will pose an organizational environment qualitatively more demanding than those in our experience" [28, p. 4].

Taking "increasing knowledge" as an example, environments of the future will contain a great deal more knowledge than is currently available. Because knowledge feeds on itself, the current knowledge explosion is likely to continue at exponential rates. The availability of computers that are more "friendly" (i.e., little, if any, training needed), more "intelligent" (i.e., able to coach the user), and more up-to-date (i.e., have access to more cutting-edge data) will contribute to both the availability of existing knowledge to institutions and the generation of new knowledge. Because knowledge will be able to be distributed rapidly, managers and administrators in institutions will have more information upon which to base decisions and less need to interact in face-to-face meetings to obtain it. Knowledge will become more continuous in its availability, more wide-ranging in the subjects it covers, and more direct in its sources.

This increase in knowledge and its availability through computer technology is also likely to produce increased complexity in the environment. Complexity is generally defined by three dimensions: numerosity, specialization or diversity, and interdependence. Miller explained the relationship between these three factors: "As a system's components become more numerous, they become specialized, with resulting increased interdependence" [45, p. 5]. That is, managers and administrators in institutions in a postindustrial environment will be exposed to a greater number of environmental elements (i.e., time and distance buffers will be greatly reduced by communication and transportation technologies, and more elements in the environment will become directly relevant). This abundance of environmental elements will force a greater degree of specialization of managers and administrators since overload could quickly occur otherwise. Increased specialization will, in turn, lead to the requirement of even greater interdependence among managers and institutions. Although institutions will have to be more loosely coupled in structure to cope with this environmental complexity [31], they will also need to become more tightly coupled in their information exchange.

The knowledge explosion and the increased complexity of the environment also contribute to a greater degree of turbulence. That is, increased access to information will require more rapid decision making and action implementation. Events in this kind of an environment will, as a result, occur more rapidly, and the timeliness required of managers will produce a tendency toward short timeframe strategies. More decisions in less time, along with a tendency toward shorter and more numerous events, will lead to a major increase in the turbulence of organizational environments (see [28] for an elaboration).

Increases in knowledge, complexity, and turbulence in postindustrial environments will place enormous strains on managers of educational organizations. In particular, although the necessity of designing and implementing adaptive strategies will dramatically increase, the "bounded rationality" [36] of managers will act as a constraint on their ability to do so. That is, the cognitive capacity of managers can be exceeded easily by the necessity to consider all the information and events present in a postindustrial environment. It is simply impossible for managers to initiate adaptive strategies in the same ways in postindustrial environments as they do now. The institutions themselves will have to be designed so as to enhance their ability to adapt, aside from the manager's specific strategies. Simon explained this requirement in the following way:

Organizational decision making in the organizations of the postindustrial world shows every sign of becoming a great deal more complex than the decision making of the past. As a consequence of this fact, the decision-making process, rather than the processes contributing immediately and directly to the production of the organization's final output, will bulk larger and larger as the central activity in which the organization is engaged in the postindustrial society, the central problem is not how to organize to produce efficiently (although this will always remain an important consideration), but how to organize to make decisions—that is, to process information. [56, pp. 269–70]

In view of these turbulent conditions, it becomes clear that all four approaches to organizational adaptation will be required as managers and administrators encounter the postindustrial environment. Institutional forms will have to emerge that are compatible with a diversity of environmental elements (the population ecology approach). Transitions to new stages of development will have to be closely monitored and planned for since they will occur more rapidly and sporadically in a postindustrial environment (the life cycles approach). Strategic choices by managers will be required that enhance the adaptability of the institution by expanding information search capacities while constraining information-processing requirements in order to make the choices more reasonable (the strategic choice approach). Interpreting the environment for the institution will become an even more critical task for managers due to its complexity and turbulence (the symbolic action approach).

Although none of these activities (i.e., designing diversity into institutions, managing rapid organizational transitions, implementing strategic choices, and interpreting the environment) are unknown to managers and administrators, the nature of the postindustrial environment and the phenomenon of bounded rationality will require that they be implemented in the kinds of institutions that have not been common in the past. That is, the nature of the institutions themselves will need to be different if they are to be adaptive to this new environment. The third section of this article proposes some characteristics that will be required by institutions of higher education

and by managers in order to remain adaptable in future environments.

Section 3. Adaptability and the Janusian Institution

In discussing the challenges of managing organizations during turbulent times, Drucker observed some characteristics that managers must assure if organizations are to survive. "The one certainty about the times ahead, the times in which managers will have to work and to perform, is that they will be turbulent times. And in turbulent times, the first task of management is to make sure of the institution's capacity for survival, to make sure of its structural strength and soundness, of its capacity to survive a blow, to adapt to sudden change, and to avail itself of new opportunities" [19, p. 1]. For managers and administrators in higher education to assure capacity for survival, strength and soundness, adaptability to sudden change, and the ability to take advantage of new opportunities in a postindustrial environment with turbulence, information overload, rapid-fire events, and complexity all increasing at exponential rates, they will need to become Janusian thinkers and develop Janusian institutions.

Janusian Thinking

Rothenburg [53] introduced the concept of "Janusian thinking" while investigating the creative achievements of individuals such as Einstein, Mozart, Picasso, and O'Neill, as well as fifty-four highly creative artists and scientists in the United States and Great Britain. Janusian thinking is named after the Roman god Janus, who was pictured as having at least two faces looking in different directions at the same time. Janusian thinking occurs when two contradictory thoughts are held to be true simultaneously. The explanation or resolution of the apparent contradiction is what leads to major breakthroughs in insight.

> In Janusian thinking, two or more opposites or antitheses are conceived simultaneously, either as existing side by side, or as equally operative, valid, or true. In an apparent defiance of logic or of physical possibility, the creative person consciously

formulates the simultaneous operation of antithetical elements and develops those into integrated entities and creations. It is a leap that transcends ordinary logic. What emerges is no mere combination or blending of elements: the conception does not only contain different entities, it contains opposing and antagonistic elements, which are understood as coexistent. As a self-contradictory structure, the Janusian formulation is surprising when seriously posited in naked form. [54, p. 55]

The surprising nature of Janusian formulations results from the pre-conception that two opposites cannot both be valid at the same time. However, holding such thoughts engenders the flexibility of thought that is a prerequisite for individual creativity. Such flexibility is also the key to effective problem solving. As pointed out by Interaction Associates:

Flexibility in thinking is critical to good problem solving. A problem solver should be able to conceptually dance around the problem like a good boxer, jabbing and poking, without getting caught in one place or "fixated." At any given moment, a good problem solver should be able to apply a large number of strategies. Moreover, a good problem solver is a person who has developed, through his understanding of strategies and experiences in problem solving, a sense of appropriateness of what is likely to be the most useful strategy at any particular time. [30, p. 15]

Similarly, perpetuating Janusian characteristics in institutions also has the effect of producing flexibility and adaptability, and it enables organizations to cope better with unpredictable environmental events. A large variety of sometimes contradictory characteristics must be present in order to make adaptation effective on the institution level. For example, Weick pointed out some of these contradictory characteristics by asserting:

The problem of organizational effectiveness has traditionally been punctuated into conclusions such as those that the effective organization is flexible and productive, satisfies its members, is profitable, acquires resources, minimizes strain, controls the environment, develops, is efficient, retains employees, grows, is integrated, communicates openly, and survives. I would like to propose a different set of punctuations.

Specifically, I would suggest that the effective organization is (1) garrulous, (2) clumsy, (3) superstitious, (4) hypocritical, (5) monstrous, (6) octopoid, (7) wandering, and (8) grouchy. [64, p. 193]

Several Janusian characteristics are discussed below that are proposed as necessary in effective higher education institutions in postindustrial environments.

Janusian Institutions

In addition to being aware of and implementing all four of the approaches to adaptation discussed previously, managers and administrators will need to perpetuate the following characteristics in their postindustrial institutions. Both loose coupling and tight coupling will be required. A loosely coupled system is one where connections among elements are weak, indirect, occasional, negligible, or discontinuous (see [62, 66]). Diffusion from one part of the organization to another occurs unevenly, sporadically, and unpredictably, if it occurs at all. Loose coupling refers to process looseness, not necessarily structural looseness. Tightly coupled systems, on the other hand, are controlled and coordinated so as to achieve specified goals. Centralization and hierarchy are prevalent so that all organizational action is directed toward similar purposes. Structure and process are interdependent (see [55]).

Lutz [33, 34] recently pointed out that the main responsibility of managers in higher education is to reinforce and perpetuate the tightly coupled elements in their institutions. Weick's statement is used as support for this point of view: "The chief responsibility of the administrator in a loosely coupled system is to reaffirm and solidify those ties that do exist" [67, p. 276]. Lutz responded: "That is exactly the point I was trying to make in my article, hence its title. To reaffirm and strengthen organizational ties or couplings is the administrator's chief responsibility. As university administrators fail in that responsibility, higher education is going to be in trouble" [34, p. 297].

The point of view advocated in this article is contrary to that of Lutz. In order for institutions to be adaptive in postindustrial environments, both tight and loose couplings will need to be reinforced and reaffirmed by administrators.

Neither can predominate permanently over the other. One reason for this is that initiating innovations requires loose coupling, but implementing innovation requires tight coupling. "During the initiation (discovery) stage, the organization needs to be as flexible and as open as possible to new sources of information and alternative courses of action.... During the implementation stage, however.... a singleness of purpose is required ... in order to bring the innovation into practice" [20, p. 175].

Postindustrial institutions of higher education will be required to remain loose enough to develop multiple, innovative adaptations. At the same time, they must be tight enough to implement them quickly and to change major components of the organization as needed. The self-design characteristics called for by Hedberg, Nystrom, and Starbuck [26], Weick [63], and Galbraith [21]—where high levels of experimentation and temporariness exist—will need to be matched with the ability to communicate and act quickly and efficiently through tight coupling. To do this, new arrangements such as ad hoc structures, collateral or parallel processes, or matrix arrangements may have to become much more common.

Actions designed both to achieve stability and to achieve flexibility will be required. Adaptation, in a technical sense, is designed to re-establish equilibrium between the organization and its environment. As mentioned earlier, adaptation is motivated by an imbalance or discontinuity between the requirements of the environment and the organization. Adapting to meet these requirements, therefore, makes the organization more stable but also less flexible. Adaptation establishes a certain organizational history that provides continuity, but it makes less likely radical departures from current functioning.

Adaptability, on the other hand, generally refers to the ability to cope with novel changes in the environment by maintaining a repertoire of unique, unconnected responses. It is synonymous with flexibility. Maintaining adaptability requires that organizational histories be at least partially forgotten so that improvisations can occur as required. Too much flexibility inhibits a sense of continuity and identity, and too much stability inhibits the ability to respond to completely new environmental features [66].

In postindustrial environments, institutions will need to be both stable (i.e., maintain a strong identity and a common interpretation of the environment) and at the same time be flexible (i.e., have a high degree of experimentation, trial-and-error learning, detours, randomness, and improvisation) as they encounter environmental elements that they have never before experienced. Because pressures will be present to fragment institutions, a strong identity and sense of institutional history is needed, but that identity and history must be systematically ignored in some circumstances. Mechanisms designed to erase organizational memory and to kill previous frameworks will be as important as mechanisms designed to operationalize current frameworks and reinforce the institution's culture. Short-term stability and long-term adaptability will both be prerequisites of effectiveness.

A wider search for information as well as mechanisms to inhibit information overload will be required. Postindustrial environments will require that institutions increase their sensing and receptor capabilities because of the tremendous amount of knowledge that will be available. Not being aware of critical elements in the environment could lead to an institution's demise. With increasing turbulence and complexity coupled with an exponential growth in the amount of knowledge available, managers and administrators will have to increase markedly their abilities to acquire that knowledge (see [25]).

On the other hand, these same environmental characteristics can quickly lead to information overload. There will simply be too many fragmented elements to consider at one time. Because of the constraints of bounded rationality [36], mechanisms will have to be present to filter knowledge and reduce the amount that must be attended to [1].

To satisfy these two contradictory requirements, institutions may need to develop specialized scanning units, ad hoc probing and sensing groups, formalized interpretation systems, boundary spanning units, and so on [28]. The purpose of such units would be to both gather more information and to reduce, synthesize, or select out information required for adaptation decisions.

More consensus in decision making while also having more heterogeneity will be needed.

In institutions where a high level of consensus exists, change and adaptation can occur both rapidly and efficiently. Time is not required to consider multiple, conflicting points of view or coalitional interests. The institution can be mobilized much more quickly when faced with disruptive environmental events than when the multiple stake holders do not agree on a common action.

Ashby's [4] "law of requisite variety" indicates, however, that complexity in one element must always be matched by equal complexity in another element. Contingency theorists (e.g., [10, 31]) have found that this principle applies to the relationship between organizations and their environments. Complexity in the environment must be met with complexity (i.e., heterogeneity) in the organization for equilibrium to occur. There will be a requirement in postindustrial environments, therefore, for intraorganizational heterogeneity (i.e., multiple viewpoints, specialization, diversity) to exist in order for institutions to maintain adaptability. Too much homogeneity, on the one hand, can lead to "groupthink" phenomena [29] and to narrowness of strategic alternatives. Too much heterogeneity can lead to revolution and anarchy in adaptation. Both consensus and homogeneity as well as diversity and heterogeneity, therefore, are needed simultaneously as prerequisites of adaptability.

To achieve these two contradictory states simultaneously, institutions will need to rely on new kinds of computer decision support systems that allow preferences and interests to be instantaneously aggregated and compared [28], new varieties of consensus-building group decision processes [60], formalized diffusion mechanisms that gather preferences and build commitment among institutional members when adaptation is required, redundant structures and process mechanisms that function independently, and so on.

Other characteristics of Janusian institutions also will be important to cope with postindustrial environments, such as high specialization as well as high generality of roles, proactivity and reactivity in strategic decisions, continuity of leadership and the infusion of new leaders with new ideas, deviation amplifying and deviation reducing processes, and so on. These characteristics are not elaborated here because of the constraint of space. However, the important point to be made is that the adaptability needed by institutions in postindustrial environments will require that Janusian characteristics be present. The deliberate redesign and restructuring of institutions will be a necessary prerequisite for these new environments.

The presence of Janusian thinking in individuals and Janusian characteristics in organizations often appears to be frightening (because of unpredictability) or even silly (because of inconsistency). However, it is precisely because of this attribute that both individuals and organizations operate successfully in turbulent and unknown environments. Initiating both continuity and change in leadership, specialization and generalization, proactivity and reactivity, and other seemingly contradictory characteristics will produce the adaptability necessary for effective institutions of higher education in the future.

Summary

The first section of this article reviewed different approaches to organizational adaptation. These approaches were categorized according to the amount of discretion they assumed for managers and the importance of the external environment. It was argued in the second section that each of these approaches will be required to operate simultaneously in institutions of higher education in a postindustrial environment. That environment was described as being characterized by more and increasing knowledge, complexity, and turbulence.

In addition to relying on these four common approaches to adaptation, however, it was proposed that managers and administrators will also be required to help design and perpetuate characteristics and processes in their institutions that have been somewhat uncommon in the past. That is, self-contradictory attributes will need to be developed and reinforced both in individual administrators and in their institutions in order to maintain adaptability in a postindustrial environment. Educational institutions with these characteristics and processes were labelled "Janusian" institutions because of the presence of contradictory phenomena that operate simultaneously within them.

The intent of this article, then, has been not only to review and provide a framework for the organizational adaptation literature but to propose how adaptation might be best facilitated in institutions of higher education. Liberal arts colleges, like other types of colleges and universities, will survive and prosper as they become adept at implementing adaptive strategies in the required ways and as they develop characteristics that match with the demands of the postindustrial environment.

Reprinted by permission from The Journal of Higher Education, *Vol. 55, April/May 1984, pp. 122–144. Copyright © 1984 by the Ohio State University Press. All rights reserved.*

Kim S. Cameron is director, Organizational Studies Program, National Center for Higher Education Management Systems.

References

Ackoff. R. L. "Management Misinformation Systems." *Management Science,* 1967, 14; 147–56.

Aldrich, H. *Organizations and Environments.* Englewood Cliffs, N.J.: Prentice-Hall, 1979.

Aldrich, H., and J. Pfeffer. "Environments of Organizations." *Annual Review of Sociology,* 1976, 2; 79–105.

Ashby, W. R. "Principles of the Self-Organizing Dynamics System." *Journal of General Psychology,* 1947, 37; 13–25.

Barnard, C. I. *The Functions of the Executive.* Cambridge, Mass.: Harvard University Press. 1938.

Bell, D. *The Coming of Postindustrial Society.* New York: Basic Books, 1973.

Berger, P., and T. Luckmann. *The Social Construction of Reality.* New York: Doubleday, 1967.

Birnbaum, R. *Maintaining Diversity in American Higher Education.* San Francisco: Jossey-Bass, 1983.

Brezezinski, Z. *Between Two Ages: America's Role in the Technetronic Era.* New York: Viking Press, 1970.

Burns, T., and G. M. Stalker. *The Management of Innovation.* London: Tavistock. 1961.

Cameron, K. S. "Strategic Responses to Conditions of Decline: Higher Education and the Private Sector." *Journal of Higher Education,* July/August 1983, 54; 359–90.

Cameron, K. S., and R. E. Quinn. "The Field of Organizational Development." In *Classics in Organization Development,* edited by R. E. Quinn and K. S. Cameron. Oak Park, Ill.: Moore Publishing, 1983.

Cameron, K. S., and D. A. Whetten. "Perceptions of Organizational Effectiveness Over Organizational Life Cycles." *Administrative Science Quarterly,* 1981, 26; 525–44.

_____. "Models of the Organization Life Cycle: Applications to Higher Education." *Review of Higher Education,* in press.

Chamberlain, N. W. *Enterprise and Environment: The Firm in Time and Place.* New York: McGraw-Hill, 1968.

Chandler, A. D. *Strategy and Structure: Chapters in the History of the American Enterprise.* Cambridge, Mass.: M.I.T. Press, 1962.

Child, J. "Organizational Structure, Environment, and Performance: The Role of Strategic Choice." *Sociology,* 1972, 6, 1–22.

Cohen, M. D., and J. G. March. *Leadership and Ambiguity: The American College President.* New York: McGraw-Hill, 1974.

Drucker, P. F. *Managing in Turbulent Times.* New York: Harper and Row, 1980.

Duncan, R. B. "The Ambidextrous Organization: Designing Dual Structures for Innovation." in *The Management of Organization Design: Strategies and Implementation,* edited by R. H. Kilmann, L. R. Pondy, and D. P. Slevin, New York: Elsevier North Holland, 1976; 167–88.

Galbraith, J. R. "Designing the Innovating Organization." *Organizational Dynamics,* 1982, 11; 5–25.

Cameson, W. A., and N. R. Scotch. "Scapegoating in Baseball." *American Journal of Sociology,* 1964, 70; 69–76.

Goodman, P. S. and L. B. Kurke. "Studies of Change in Organizations: A Status Report." in *Change in Organizations,* edited by P. S. Goodman, San Francisco: Jossey-Bass, 1982; 1–46.

Hannan, M. T., and J. Freeman. "The Population Ecology of Organizations." *American Journal of Sociology,* 1977, 82; 929–64.

Hedberg, B. L. T. "How Organizations Learn and Unlearn." In *Handbook of Organizational Design.* Vol. 1, edited by P. C. Nystrom and W. H. Starbuck. New York: Oxford University Press, 1981; 3–27.

Hedberg, B. L. T., P. C. Nystrom, and W. H. Starbuck. "Camping on Seesaws: Prescriptions for a Self-Designing Organization." *Administrative Science Quarterly,* 1976, 21; 41–65.

Huber, G. P. "Decision Support Systems: Their Present Nature and Future Applications." In *Decision Making: An Interdisciplinary Inquiry,* edited by G. R. Ungson and D. N. Braunstein. Boston: Kent, 1982.

_____. "The Nature and Design of Postindustrial Organizations." *Management Science,* in press.

Janis, I. *Victims of Groupthink.* Boston: Houghton-Mifflin. 1972.

Interaction Associates. *Tools for Change.* San Francisco: Interaction Associates, 1971.

Lawrence, P., and J. W. Lorsch, *Organization and Environment.* Homewood, Ill.: Irwin, 1967.

Lindblom. C. E. "The Science of Muddling Through." *Public Administration Review,* 1959, 20; 79–88.

Lutz, F. W. "Tightening Up Loose Couplings in Organizations of Higher Education." *Administrative Science Quarterly,* 27 (1982), 653–69.

_____. "Reply to More on Loose Coupling." *Administrative Science Quarterly*, 1983, 28; 296–98.

March, J. G. "Footnotes to Organizational Change." *Administrative Science Quarterly*, 1981, 26; 563–77.

March, J. G., and H. A. Simon. *Organizations*. New York: Wiley, 1958.

Martin J. *Telematic Society: The Challenge for Tomorrow*. Englewood Cliffs, N.J.: Prentice-Hall, 1981.

Masuda. Y. *The Information Society*. Bethesda, Md.: World Future Society, 1980.

McKelvey, W. *Organizational Systematics: Taxonomy, Evolution, and Classification*. Berkeley: University of California Press, 1982.

Miles, R. E. and C. C. Snow. *Organizational Strategy, Structure, and Process*. New York: McGraw-Hill, 1978.

Miles. R. H. *Macro Organizational Behavior*. Glenview, Ill.: Scott Foresman, 1980.

Miles, R. H., and K. S. Cameron. *Coffin Nails and Corporate Strategies*. Englewood Cliffs, N.J.: Prentice-Hall, 1982.

Miller, D., and P. H. Friesen. "Archetypes of Organizational Transition." *Administrative Science Quarterly*, 1980, 25; 268–99.

_____. "Momentum and Revolution in Organizational Adaptation." *Academy of Management Journal*, 1980, 23; 591–614.

Miller, J. G. "Living Systems: The Organization." *Behavioral Science*. 1972, 17; 1–182.

National Commission on Excellence in Education. *A Nation at Risk: The Imperative for Educational Reform*. Report to the Secretary of the U.S. Department of Education, Washington, D.C., 1983.

Peters, T. J. "Symbols, Patterns, and Settings: An Optimistic Case for Getting Things Done." *Organizational Dynamics*, 1978, 7; 3–23.

Pfeffer, J. "Management as Symbolic Action: The Creation and Maintenance of Organizational Paradigms." In *Research in Organizational Behavior*, Vol. 3, edited by I. I. Cummings and B. M. Staw, Greenwich, Conn.: JAI Press, 1981; 1–52.

Pfeffer, J., and G. R. Salancik. *The External Control of Organizations*. New York: Harper and Row. 1978.

Pondy, L. R. "Leadership Is a Language Game." In *Leadership: Where Else Can We Go?*, edited by M. W. McCall and M. M. Lombardo. pp. 87–99. Durham, N.C.: Duke University Press, 1978.

Quinn, R. E., and K. S. Cameron. "Organizational Life Cycles and Shifting Criteria of Effectiveness: Some Preliminary Evidence." *Management Science*, 1983, 29; 33–51.

Roeber, R. J. C. *The Organization in a Changing Environment*. Reading, Mass.: Addison-Wesley, 1973.

Rothenburg, A. *The Emerging Goddess*. Chicago: University of Chicago Press, 1979.

_____. "Creative Contradictions." *Psychology Today*, June 1979; 55–62.

Scott, W. R. *Organizations: Rational, Natural, and Open Systems*. Englewood Cliffs, N.J.: Prentice-Hall, 1981.

Simon, H. A. "Applying Information Technology to Organization Design," *Public Administration Review*, 1973, 34; 268–78.

Snow, C. C., and L. G. Hrebiniak. "Strategy, Distinctive Competence, and Organizational Performance." *Administrative Science Quarterly*, 1980, 25; 317–35.

Toffler, A. *Future Shock*. New York: Random House, 1970.

_____. *The Third Wave*. New York: Morrow, 1980.

Van Gundy, A. B. *Techniques of Structured Problem Solving*. New York: Van Nostrand Reinhold, 1981.

Wamsley, G., and M. N. Zald. *The Political Economy of Public Organizations*, Lexington, Mass.: D. C. Heath, 1973.

Weick, K. E. "Educational Organizations as Loosely Coupled Systems." *Administrative Science Quarterly*, 1976, 21; 1–19.

_____. "Organizational Design: Organizations as Self-Designing Systems." *Organizational Dynamics*, 1977, 6; 30–46.

_____. "Repunctuating the Problem." In *New Perspectives on Organizational Effectiveness*, edited by P. S. Goodman and J. M. Pennings, San Francisco: Jossey-Bass, 1977; 146–84.

_____. *The Social Psychology of Organizing*. Reading, Mass.: Addison-Wesley. 1979.

_____. "Managing Change Among Loosely Coupled Elements." In *Change in Organizations*, edited by P. S. Goodman, pp. 375–408. San Francisco: Jossey-Bass, 1982.

_____. "Administering Education in Loosely Coupled Schools." *Phi Delta Kappan*, 1982, 63; 673–76.

Zammuto, R. F., and K. S. Cameron. "Environmental Decline and Organizational Response." Discussion paper. National Center for Higher Education Management Systems, Boulder, Colorado, 1983.

CHAPTER 23

BUILDING LEARNING ORGANIZATIONS

PETER M. SENGE

The Leader's New Work:
Building Learning Organizations

Over the past two years, business academics and senior managers have begun talking about the notion of the learning organization. Ray Stata of Analog Devices put the idea succinctly in these pages last spring: "The rate at which organizations learn may become the only sustainable source of competitive advantage." And in late May of this year, at an MIT-sponsored conference entitled "Transforming Organizations," two questions arose again and again: How can we build organizations in which continuous learning occurs? and, What kind of person can best lead the learning organization? This article, based on Senge's recently published book, The Fifth Discipline: The Art and Practice of the Learning Organization, begins to chart this new territory, describing new roles, skills, and tools for leaders who wish to develop learning organizations.

Human beings are designed for learning. No one has to teach an infant to walk, or talk, or master the spatial relationships needed to stack eight building blocks that don't topple. Children come fully equipped with an insatiable drive to explore and experiment. Unfortunately, the primary institutions of our society are oriented predominantly toward controlling rather than learning, rewarding individuals for performing for others rather than for cultivating their natural curiosity and impulse to learn. The young child entering school discovers quickly that the name of the game is getting the right answer and avoiding mistakes—a mandate no less compelling to the aspiring manager.

"Our prevailing system of management has destroyed our people," writes W. Edwards Deming, leader in the quality movement.[1] "'People are born with intrinsic motivation, self-esteem, dignity, curiosity to learn, joy in learning. The forces of destruction begin with toddlers—a prize for the best Halloween costume, grades in school, gold stars, and on up through the university. On the job, people, teams, divisions are ranked—reward for the one at the top, punishment at the bottom. MBO, quotas, incentive pay, business plans, put together separately, division by division, cause further loss, unknown and unknowable."

Ironically, by focusing on performing for someone else's approval, corporations create the very conditions that predestine them to mediocre performance. Over the long run, superior performance depends on superior learning. A Shell study showed that, according to former planning director Arie de Geus, "a full one-third of the Fortune '500' industrials listed in 1970 had vanished by 1983."[2] Today, the average lifetime of the largest industrial enterprises is probably less than *half* the average lifetime of a person in an industrial society. On the other hand, de Geus and his colleagues at Shell also found a small number of companies that survived for seventy-five years or

"The Leader's New Work: Building Learning Organizations," by Peter M. Senge, reprinted from *Sloan Management Review,* Fall 1990, MIT Sloan School of Management, Cambridge, MA.

longer. Interestingly, the key to their survival was the ability to run "experiments in the margin," to continually explore new business and organizational opportunities that create potential new sources of growth.

If anything, the need for understanding how organizations learn and accelerating that learning is greater today than ever before. The old days when a Henry Ford, Alfred Sloan, or Tom Watson learned for the organization are gone. In an increasingly dynamic, interdependent, and unpredictable world, it is simply no longer possible for anyone to "figure it all out at the top." The old model, "the top thinks and the local acts," must now give way to integrating thinking and acting at all levels. While the challenge is great, so is the potential payoff. "The person who figures out how to harness the collective genius of the people in his or her organization," according to former Citibank CEO Walter Wriston, is going to blow the competition away.

Adaptive Learning and Generative Learning

The prevailing view of learning organizations emphasizes increased adaptability. Given the accelerating pace of change, or so the standard view goes, "the most successful corporation of the 1990s," according to Fortune magazine, "will be something called a learning organization, a consummately adaptive enterprise."[3] As the Shell study shows, examples of traditional authoritarian bureaucracies that responded too slowly to survive in changing business environments are legion.

But increasing adaptiveness is only the first stage in moving toward learning organizations. The impulse to learn in children goes deeper than desires to respond and adapt more effectively to environmental change. The impulse to learn, at its heart, is an impulse to be generative, to expand our capability. This is why leading corporations are focusing on generative learning, which is about creating, as well as adaptive learning, which is about coping.[4]

The total quality movement in Japan illustrates the evolution from adaptive to generative learning. With its emphasis on continuous experimentation and feedback, the total quality movement has been the first wave in budding learning organizations. But Japanese firms'

view of serving the customer has evolved. In the early years of total quality, the focus was on "fitness to standard," making a product reliably so that it would do what its designers intended it to do and what the firm told its customers it would do. Then came a focus on "fitness to need," understanding better what the customer wanted and then providing products that reliably met those needs. Today, leading edge firms seek to understand and meet the "latent need" of the customer—what customers might truly value but have never experienced or would never think to ask for. As one Detroit executive commented recently, "You could never produce the Mazda Miata solely from market research. It required a leap of imagination to see what the customer might want."[5]

Generative learning, unlike adaptive learning, requires new ways of looking at the world, whether in understanding customers or in understanding how to better manage a business. For years, U.S. manufacturers sought competitive advantage in aggressive controls on inventories, incentives against overproduction, and rigid adherence to production forecasts. Despite these incentives, their performance was eventually eclipsed by Japanese firms who saw the challenges of manufacturing differently. They realized that eliminating delays in the production process was the key to reducing instability and improving cost, productivity, and service. They worked to build networks of relationships with trusted suppliers and to redesign physical production processes so as to reduce delays in materials procurement, production set up, and in-process inventory—a much higher-leverage approach to improving both cost and customer loyalty.

As Boston Consulting Group's George Stalk has observed, the Japanese saw the significance of delays because they saw the process of order entry, production scheduling, materials procurement, production, and distribution as an integrated system. "What distorts the system so badly is time," observed Stalk—the multiple delays between events and responses. "These distortions reverberate throughout the system, producing disruptions, waste, and inefficiency."[6] Generative learning requires seeing the systems that control events. When we fail to grasp the systemic source of problems, we are left to "push on" symptoms rather than eliminate underlying causes. The best we can ever do is adaptive learning.

The Leader's New Work

"I talk with people all over the country about learning organizations, and the response is always very positive," says William O'Brien, CEO of the Hanover Insurance companies. "If this type of organization is so widely preferred, why don't people create such organizations? I think the answer is leadership. People have no real comprehension of the type of commitment it requires to build such an organization."[7]

Our traditional view of leaders—as special people who set the direction, make the key decisions, and energize the troops—is deeply rooted in an individualistic and nonsystemic worldview. Especially in the West, leaders are heroes—great men (and occasionally women) who rise to the fore in times of crisis. So long as such myths prevail, they reinforce a focus on short-term events and charismatic heroes rather than on systemic forces and collective learning.

Leadership in learning organizations centers on subtler and ultimately more important work. In a learning organization, leaders' roles differ dramatically from that of the charismatic decision maker. Leaders are designers, teachers, and stewards. These roles require new skills: the ability to build shared vision, to bring to the surface and challenge prevailing mental models, and to foster more systemic patterns of thinking. In short, leaders in learning organizations are responsible for building organizations where people are continually expanding their capabilities to shape their future—that is, leaders are responsible for learning.

Creative Tension: The Integrating Principle

Leadership in a learning organization starts with the principle of creative tension.[8] Creative tension comes from seeing clearly where we want to be, our "vision," and telling the truth about where we are, our "current reality," The gap between the two generates a natural tension (see Figure 23-1).

Creative tension can be resolved in two basic ways: by raising current reality toward the vision, or by lowering the vision toward

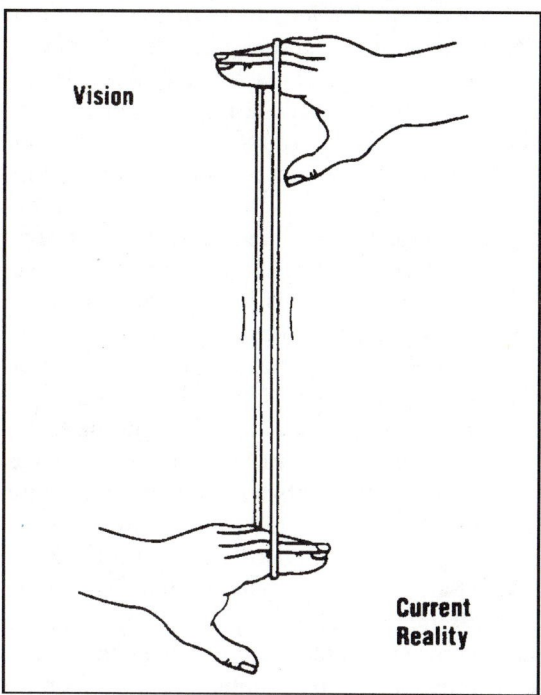

Figure 23-1 The Principle of Creative Tension

current reality. Individuals, groups, and organizations who learn how to work with creative tension learn how to use the energy it generates to move reality more reliably toward their visions.

The principle of creative tension has long been recognized by leaders. Martin Luther King, Jr., once said, "Just as Socrates felt that it was necessary to create a tension in the mind, so that individuals could rise from the bondage of myths and half truths . . . so must we . . . create the kind of tension in society that will help men rise from the dark depths of prejudice and racism."[9]

Without vision there is no creative tension. Creative tension cannot be generated from current reality alone. All the analysis in the world will never generate a vision. Many who are otherwise qualified to lead fail to do so because they try to substitute analysis for vision. They believe that, if only people understood current reality, they would surely feel the motivation to change. They are then disappointed to discover that people "resist" the personal and organizational changes that must be made to alter reality. What they never grasp is that the natural energy for changing reality comes from holding a picture of what might be that is more important to people than what is.

But creative tension cannot be generated from vision alone; it demands an accurate picture of current reality as well. Just as King had a dream, so too did he continually strive to "dramatize the shameful conditions" of racism and prejudice so that they could no longer be ignored. Vision without an understanding of current reality will more likely foster cynicism than creativity. The principle of creative tension teaches that an accurate picture of current reality is just as important as a compelling picture of a desired future.

Leading through creative tension is different than solving problems. In problem solving, the energy for change comes from attempting to get away from an aspect of current reality that is undesirable. With creative tension, the energy for change comes from the vision, from what we want to create, juxtaposed with current reality. While the distinction may seem small, the consequences are not. Many people and organizations find themselves motivated to change only when their problems are bad enough to cause them to change. This works for a while, but the change process runs out of steam as soon as the problems driving the change become less pressing. With problem solving, the motivation for change is extrinsic. With creative tension, the motivation is intrinsic. This distinction mirrors the distinction between adaptive and generative learning.

New Roles

The traditional authoritarian image of the leader as "the boss calling the shots" has been recognized as oversimplified and inadequate for some time. According to Edgar Schein, "Leadership is intertwined with culture formation." Building an organization's culture and shaping its evolution is the "unique and essential function" of leadership.[10] In a learning organization, the critical roles of leadership—designer, teacher, and steward—have antecedents in the ways leaders have contributed to budding organizations in the past. But each role takes on new meaning in the learning organization and, as will be seen in the following sections, demands new skills and tools.

Leader as Designer

Imagine that your organization is an ocean liner and that you are "the leader." What is your role?

I have asked this question of groups of managers many times. The most common answer, not surprisingly, is "the captain." Others say, "The navigator, setting the direction." Still others say, "The helmsman, actually controlling the direction," or, "The engineer down there stoking the fire, providing energy," or, "The social director, making sure everybody's enrolled, involved, and communicating." While these are legitimate leadership roles, there is another which, in many ways, eclipses them all in importance. Yet rarely does anyone mention it.

The neglected leadership role is the designer of the ship. No one has a more sweeping influence than the designer. What good does it do for the captain to say, "Turn starboard 30 degrees," when the designer has built a rudder that will only turn to port, or which takes six hours to turn to starboard? It's fruitless to be the leader in an organization that is poorly designed.

The functions of design, or what some have called "social architecture," are rarely visible; they take place behind the scenes. The consequences that appear today are the result of work done long in the past, and work today will show its benefits far in the future. Those who aspire to lead out of a desire to control, or gain fame, or simply to be at the center of the action, will find little to attract them to the quiet design work of leadership.

But what, specifically, is involved in organizational design? "Organization design is widely misconstrued as moving around boxes and lines," says Hanover's O'Brien. "The first task of organization design concerns designing the governing ideas of purpose, vision, and core values by which people will live." Few acts of leadership have a more enduring impact on an organization than building a foundation of purpose and core values.

In 1982, Johnson & Johnson found itself facing a corporate nightmare when bottles of its bestselling Tylenol were tampered with, resulting in several deaths. The corporation's immediate response was to pull all Tylenol off the shelves of retail outlets. Thirty-one million capsules were destroyed, even though they were tested and found safe. Although the immediate cost was significant, no other action was possible given the firm's credo. Authored almost forty years earlier by president Robert Wood Johnson, Johnson & Johnson's credo states that permanent success is possible only when modern industry realizes that:

- service to its customers comes first;
- service to its employees and management comes second;
- service to the community comes third; and
- service to its stockholders, last.

Such statements might seem like motherhood and apple pie to those who have not seen the way a clear sense of purpose and values can affect key business decisions. Johnson & Johnson's crisis management in this case was based on that credo. It was simple, it was right, and it worked.

If governing ideas constitute the first design task of leadership, the second design task involves the policies, strategies, and structures that translate guiding ideas into business decisions. Leadership theorist Philip Selznick calls policy and structure the "institutional embodiment of purpose."[11] "Policy making (the rules that guide decisions) ought to be separated from decision making," says Jay Forrester.[12] "Otherwise, short-term pressures will usurp time from policy creation."

Traditionally, writers like Selznick and Forrester have tended to see policy making and implementation as the work of a small number of senior managers. But that view is changing. Both the dynamic business environment and the mandate of the learning organization to engage people at all levels now make it clear that this second design task is more subtle. Henry Mintzberg has argued that strategy is less a rational plan arrived at in the abstract and implemented throughout the organization than an "emergent phenomenon." Successful organizations "craft strategy" according to Mintzberg, as they continually learn about shifting business conditions and balance what is desired and what is possible.[13] The key is not getting the right strategy but fostering strategic thinking. "The choice of individual action is only part of . . . the policymaker's need," according to Mason and Mitroff.[14] "More important is the need to achieve insight into the nature of the complexity and to formulate concepts and world views for coping with it."

Behind appropriate policies, strategies, and structures are effective learning processes; their creation is the third key design responsibility in learning organizations. This does not absolve senior managers of their strategic responsibilities. Actually, it deepens and extends those responsibilities. Now, they are not only responsible for ensuring that an organization have well-developed strategies and policies, but also for ensuring that processes exist whereby these are continually improved.

In the early 1970s, Shell was the weakest of the big seven of companies. Today, Shell and Exxon are arguably the strongest, both in size and financial health. Shell's ascendance began with frustration. Around 1971 members of Shell's "Group Planning" in London began to foresee dramatic change and unpredictability in world oil markets. However, it proved impossible to persuade managers that the stable world of steady growth in oil demand and supply they had known for twenty years was about to change. Despite brilliant analysis and artful presentation, Shell's planners realized, in the words of Pierre Wack, that they "had failed to change behavior in much of the Shell organization."[15] Progress would probably have ended there, had the frustration not given way to a radically new view of corporate planning.

As they pondered this failure, the planners' view of their basic task shifted: "We no longer saw our task as producing a documented view of the future business environment five or ten years ahead. Our real target was the microcosm (the 'mental model') of our decision makers." Only when the planners reconceptualized their basic task as fostering learning rather than devising plans did their insights begin to have an impact. The initial tool used was "scenario analysis," through which planners encouraged operating managers to think through how they would manage in the future under different possible scenarios. It mattered not that the managers believed the planners' scenarios absolutely, only that they became engaged in ferreting out the implications. In this way, Shell's planners conditioned managers to be mentally prepared for a shift from low prices to high prices and from stability to instability. The results were significant. When OPEC became a reality, Shell quickly responded by increasing local operating company control (to enhance maneuverability in the new political environment), building buffer stocks, and accelerating development of non-OPEC sources—actions that its competitors took much more slowly or not at all.

Somewhat inadvertently, Shell planners had discovered the leverage of designing institutional learning processes, whereby, in the words of former planning director de Geus, "Management teams change their shared mental models of their company, their markets, and their competitors."16 Since then, "planning as learning" has become a byword at Shell, and Group Planning has continually sought out new learning tools that can be integrated into the planning process. Some of these are described below.

Leader as Teacher

"The first responsibility of a leader," writes retired Herman Miller CEO Max de Pree, "is to define reality."[17] Much of the leverage leaders can actually exert lies in helping people achieve more accurate, more insightful, and more empowering views of reality.

Leader as teacher does not mean leader as authoritarian expert whose job it is to teach people the "correct" view of reality. Rather, it is about helping everyone in the organization, oneself included, to gain more insightful views of current reality. This is in line with a popular emerging view of leaders as coaches, guides, or facilitators.[18] In learning organizations, this teaching role is developed further by virtue of explicit attention to people's mental models and by the influence of the systems perspective.

The role of leader as teacher starts with bringing to the surface people's mental models of important issues. No one carries an organization, a market, or a state of technology in his or her head. What we carry in our heads are assumptions. These mental pictures of how the world works have a significant influence on how we perceive problems and opportunities, identify courses of action, and make choices.

One reason that mental models are so deeply entrenched is that they are largely tacit. Ian Mitroff, in his study of General Motors, argues that an assumption that prevailed for years was that, in the United States, "Cars are status symbols. Styling is therefore more important than quality."[19] The Detroit automakers didn't say, "We have a mental model that all people care about is styling." Few actual managers would even say publicly that all people care about is styling. So long as the view remained unexpressed, there was little possibility of challenging its validity or forming more accurate assumptions.

But working with mental models goes beyond revealing hidden assumptions. "Reality," as perceived by most people in most organizations, means pressures that must be borne, crises that must be reacted to, and limitations that must be accepted. Leaders as teachers help people *restructure their views of reality* to see beyond the superficial conditions and events into the underlying causes of problems—and therefore to see new possibilities for shaping the future.

Specifically, leaders can influence people to view reality at three distinct levels: events, patterns of behavior, and systemic structure.

Systemic Structure
(Generative)
↓
Patterns of Behavior
(Responsive)
↓
Events
(Reactive)

The key question becomes *where do leaders predominantly focus their own and their organization's attention?*

Contemporary society focuses predominantly on events. The media reinforces this perspective, with almost exclusive attention to short-term, dramatic events. This focus leads naturally to explaining what happens in terms of those events: "The Dow Jones average went up sixteen points because high fourth-quarter profits were announced yesterday."

Pattern-of-behavior explanations are rarer, in contemporary culture, than event explanations, but they do occur. "Trend analysis" is an example of seeing patterns of behavior. A good editorial that interprets a set of current events in the context of long-term historical changes is another example. Systemic, structural explanations go even further by addressing the question, "What causes the patterns of behavior?"

In some sense, all three levels of explanation are equally true. But their usefulness is quite different. Event explanations—who did what to whom—doom their holders to a reactive stance toward change. Pattern-of-behavior explanations focus on identifying long-term trends and assessing their implications. They at least suggest how, over time, we can respond to shifting conditions. Structural explanations are the most powerful. Only they address the underlying causes of behavior at a level such that patterns of behavior can be changed.

By and large, leaders of our current institutions focus their attention on events and patterns of behavior, and, under their influence, their organizations do likewise. That is why contemporary organizations are predominantly reactive, or at best responsive—rarely generative. On the other hand, leaders in learning organizations pay attention to all three levels, but focus especially on systemic structure; largely by example, they teach people throughout the organization to do likewise.

Leader as Steward

This is the subtlest role of leadership. Unlike the roles of designer and teacher, it is almost solely a matter of attitude. It is an attitude critical to learning organizations.

While stewardship has long been recognized as an aspect of leadership, its source is still not widely understood. I believe Robert Greenleaf came closest to explaining real stewardship, in his seminal book Servant Leadership.[20] There, Greenleaf argues that "The servant leader *is* servant first. . . . It begins with the natural feeling that one wants to serve, to serve *first*. This conscious choice brings one to aspire to lead. That person is sharply different from one who is leader first, perhaps because of the need to assuage an unusual power drive or to acquire material possessions."

Leaders' sense of stewardship operates on two levels: stewardship for the people they lead and stewardship for the larger purpose or mission that underlies the enterprise. The first type arises from a keen appreciation of the impact one's leadership can have on others. People can suffer economically, emotionally, and spiritually under inept leadership. If anything, people in a learning organization are more vulnerable because of their commitment and sense of shared ownership. Appreciating this naturally instills a sense of responsibility in leaders. The second type of stewardship arises from a leader's sense of personal purpose and commitment to the organization's larger mission. People's natural impulse to learn is unleashed when they are engaged in an endeavor they consider worthy of their fullest commitment. Or, as Lawrence Miller puts it, "Achieving return on equity does not, as a goal, mobilize the most noble forces of our soul."[21]

Leaders engaged in building learning organizations naturally feel part of a larger purpose that goes beyond their organization. They are part of changing the way businesses operate, not from a vague philanthropic urge, but from a conviction that their efforts will produce more productive organizations, capable of achieving higher levels of organizational success and personal satisfaction than more traditional organizations. Their sense of stewardship was succinctly captured by George Bernard Shaw when he said,

> This is the true joy in life, the being used for a purpose you consider a mighty one, the being a force of nature rather than a feverish, selfish clod of ailments and grievances complaining that the world will not devote itself to making you happy.

New Skills

New leadership roles require new leadership skills. These skills can only be developed, in my judgment, through a lifelong commitment. It is not enough for one or two individuals to develop these skills. They must be distributed widely throughout the organization. This is one reason that understanding the disciplines of a learning organization is so important. These disciplines embody the principles and practices that can widely foster leadership development.

Three critical areas of skills (disciplines) are building shared vision, surfacing and challenging mental models, and engaging in systems thinking.[22]

Building Shared Vision

How do individual visions come together to create shared visions? A useful metaphor is the hologram, the three-dimensional image created by interacting light sources.

If you cut a photograph in half, each half shows only part of the whole image. But if you divide a hologram, each part, no matter how small, shows the whole image intact. Likewise, when a group of people come to share a vision for an organization, each person sees an individual picture of the organization at its best. Each shares responsibility for the whole, not just for one piece. But the component pieces of the hologram are not identical. Each represents the whole image from a different point of view. It's something like poking holes in a window shade; each hole offers a unique angle for viewing the whole image. So, too, is each individual's vision unique.

When you add up the pieces of a hologram, something interesting happens. The image becomes more intense, more lifelike. When more people come to share a vision, the vision becomes more real in the sense of a mental reality that people can truly imagine achieving. They now have partners, co-creators; the vision no longer rests on their shoulders alone. Early on, when they are nurturing an individual vision, people may say it is "my vision." But, as the shared vision develops, it becomes both "my vision" and "our vision."

The skills involved in builing shared vision include the following:

- **Encouraging Personal Vision.** Shared visions emerge from personal visions. It is not that people only care about their own self-interest—in fact, people's values usually include dimensions that concern family, organization, community, and even the world. Rather, it is that people's capacity for caring is personal.

- **Communicating and Asking for Support.** Leaders must be willing to continually share their own vision, rather than being the official representative of the corporate vision. They also must be prepared to ask, "Is this vision worthy of your commitment?" This can be difficult for a person used to setting goals and presuming compliance.

- **Visioning as an Ongoing Process.** Builing shared vision is a never-ending process. At any one point there will be a particular image of the future that is predominant, but that image will evolve. Today, too many managers want to dispense with the "vision business" by going off and writing the Official Vision Statement. Such statements almost always lack the vitality, freshness, and excitement of a genuine vision that comes from people asking, "What do we really want to achieve?"

- **Blending Extrinsic and Intrinsic Visions.** Many energizing visions are extrinsic—that is, they focus on achieving something relative to an outsider, such as a competitor. But a goal that is limited to defeating an opponent can, once the vision is achieved, easily become a defensive posture. In contrast, intrinsic goals like creating a new type of product, taking an established product to a new level, or setting a new standard for customer satisfaction can call forth a new level of creativity and innovation. Intrinsic and extrinsic visions need to coexist; a vision solely predicated on defeating an adversary will eventually weaken an organization.

- **Distinguishing Positive from Negative Visions.** Many organizations only truly pull together when their survival is threatened. Similarly, most social movements aim at eliminating what people don't want: for example, anti-drugs, anti-smoking, or anti-nuclear arms movements. Negative visions carry a subtle message of powerlessness: people will only pull together when there is sufficient threat. Negative visions also tend to be short term. Two fundamental sources of energy can motivate organizations: fear and aspiration. Fear, the energy source behind negative visions, can produce extraordinary changes in short periods, but aspiration endures as a continuing source of learning and growth.

Surfacing and Testing Mental Models

Many of the best ideas in organizations never get put into practice. One reason is that new insights and initiatives often conflict with established mental models. The leadership task of challenging assumptions without invoking defensiveness requires reflection and inquiry skills possessed by few leaders in traditional controlling organizations.[23]

- **Seeing Leaps of Abstraction.** Our minds literally move at lightning speed. Ironically, this often slows our learning, because we leap to generalizations so quickly that we never think to test them. We then confuse our generalizations with the observable data upon which they are based, treating the generalizations as if they were data. The frustrated sales rep reports to the home office that "customers don't really care about quality, price is what matters," when what actually happened was that three consecutive large customers refused to place an order unless a larger discount was offered. The sales rep treats her generalization, "customers care only about price," as if it were absolute fact rather than an assumption (very likely an assumption reflecting her own views of customers and the market). This thwarts future learning because she starts to focus on how to offer attractive discounts rather than probing behind the customers' statements. For example, the customers may have been so disgruntled with the firm's delivery or customer service that they are unwilling to purchase again without larger discounts.

- **Balancing Inquiry and Advocacy.** Most managers are skilled at articulating their views and presenting them persuasively. While important, advocacy skills can become counterproductive as managers rise in responsibility and confront increasingly complex issues that require collaborative learning among different, equally knowledgeable people. Leaders in learning organizations need to have both inquiry and advocacy skills.[24]

Specifically, when advocating a view, they need to be able to:
—explain the reasoning and data that led to their view;
—encourage others to test their view (e.g., Do you see gaps in my reasoning? Do you disagree with the data upon which my view is based?); and
—encourage others to provide different views (e.g., Do you have either different data, different conclusions, or both?).

When inquiring into another's views, they need to:
—actively seek to understand the other's view, rather than simply restating their own view and how it differs from the other's view; and
—make their attributions about the other and the other's view explicit (e.g., Based on your statement that . . .; I am assuming that you believe . . .; Am I representing your views fairly?).

If they reach an impasse (others no longer appear open to inquiry), they need to:
—ask what data or logic might unfreeze the impasse, or if an experiment (or some other inquiry) might be designed to provide new information.

- **Distinguishing Espoused Theory from Theory in Use.** We all like to think that we hold certain views, but often our actions reveal deeper views. For example, I may proclaim that people are trustworthy, but never lend friends money and jealously guard my possessions. Obviously, my deeper mental model (my theory in use), differs from my espoused theory. Recognizing gaps between espoused views and theories in use (which often requires the help of others) can be pivotal to deeper learning.

- **Recognizing and Defusing Defensive Routines.** As one CEO in our research program puts it, "Nobody ever talks about an issue at the 8:00 business meeting exactly the same way they talk about it at home that evening or over drinks at the end of the day." The reason is what Chris Argyris calls "defensive routines," entrenched habits used to protect ourselves from the embarrassment and threat that come with exposing our thinking. For most of us, such defenses began to build early in life in response to pressures to have the right answers in school or at home. Organizations add new levels of performance anxiety and thereby amplify and exacerbate this defensiveness. Ironically, this makes it even more difficult to expose hidden mental models, and thereby lessens learning.

The first challenge is to recognize defensive routines, then to inquire into their operation. Those who are best at revealing and defusing defensive routines operate with a high degree of self-disclosure regarding their own defensiveness (e.g., I notice that I am feeling uneasy about how this conversation is going. Perhaps I don't understand it or it is threatening to me in ways I don't yet see. Can you help me see this better?)

Systems Thinking

We all know that leaders should help people see the big picture. But the actual skills whereby leaders are supposed to achieve this are not well understood. In my experience, successful leaders often *are* "systems thinkers" to a considerable extent. They focus less on day-to-day events and more on underlying trends and forces of change. But they do this almost completely intuitively. The consequence is that they are often unable to explain their intuitions to others and feel frustrated that others cannot see the world the way they do.

One of the most significant developments in management science today is the gradual coalescence of managerial systems thinking as a field of study and practice. This field suggests some key skills for future leaders:

- **Seeing Interrelationships, Not Things, and Processes, Not Snapshots.** Most of us have been conditioned throughout our lives to focus on things and to see the world in static images. This leads us to linear explanations of systemic phenomena. For instance, in an arms race each party is convinced that the other is the cause of problems. They react to each new move as an isolated event, not as part of a process. So long as they fail to see the interrelationships of these actions, they are trapped.

- **Moving beyond Blame.** We tend to blame each other or outside circumstances for our problems. But it is poorly designed systems, not incompetent or unmotivated individuals, that cause most organizational problems. Systems thinking shows us that there is no outside—that you and the cause of your problems are part of a single system.

- **Distinguishing Detail Complexity from Dynamic Complexity.** Some types of complexity are more important strategically than others. Detail complexity arises when there are many variables. Dynamic complexity arises when cause and effect are distant in time and space, and when the consequences over time of interventions are subtle and not obvious to many participants in the system. The leverage in most management situations lies in understanding dynamic complexity, not detail complexity.

- **Focusing on Areas of High Leverage.** Some have called systems thinking the "new dismal science" because it teaches that most obvious solutions don't work—at best, they improve matters in the short run, only to make things worse in the long run. But there is another side to the story. Systems thinking also shows that small, well-focused actions can produce significant, enduring improvements, if they are in the right place. Systems thinkers refer to this idea as the principle of "leverage." Tackling a difficult problem is often a matter of seeing where the high leverage lies, where a change—with a minimum of effort—would lead to lasting, significant improvement.

- **Avoiding Symptomatic Solutions.** The pressures to intervene in management systems that are going awry can be overwhelming. Unfortunately, given the linear thinking that predominates in most organizations, interventions usually focus on symptomatic fixes, not underlying causes. This results in only temporary relief, and it tends to create still more pressures later on for further, low-leverage intervention. If leaders acquiesce to these pressures, they can be sucked into an endless spiral of increasing intervention. Sometimes the most difficult leadership acts are to refrain from intervening through popular quick fixes and to keep the pressure on everyone to identify more enduring solutions.

While leaders who can articulate systemic explanations are rare, those who can will leave their stamp on an organization. One person who had this gift was Bill Gore, the founder and long-time CEO of W.L. Gore and Associates (makers of GoreTex and other synthetic fiber products). Bill Gore was adept at telling stories that showed how the organization's core values of freedom and individual responsibility required particular operating policies. He was proud of his egalitarian organization, in which there were (and still are) no "employees," only "associates," all of whom own shares in the company and participate in its management. At one talk, he explained the company's policy of controlled growth: "Our limitation is not financial resources. Our limitation is the rate at which we can bring in new associates. Our experience has been that if we try to bring in more than a 25 percent per year increase, we begin to bog down. Twenty-five percent per year growth is a real limitation; you can do much better than that with an authoritarian organization." As Gore tells the story, one of the associates, Esther Baum, went home after this talk and reported the limitation to her husband. As it happened, he was an astronomer and mathematician at Lowell Observatory. He said, "That's a very interesting figure." He took out a pencil and paper and calculated and said, "Do you realize that in only fifty-seven and a half years, everyone in the world will be working for Gore?"

Through this story, Gore explains the systemic rationale behind a key policy, limited growth rate—a policy that undoubtedly caused a lot of stress in the organization. He suggests that, at larger rates of growth, the adverse effects of attempting to integrate too many new people too rapidly would begin to dominate. (This is the "limits to growth" systems archetype explained below.) The story also reaffirms the organization's commitment to creating a unique environment for its associates and illustrates the types of sacrifices that the firm is prepared to make in order to remain true to its vision. The last part of the story shows that, despite the self-imposed limit, the company is still very much a growth company.

The consequences of leaders who lack systems thinking skills can be devastating. Many charismatic leaders manage almost exclusively at the level of events. They deal in visions and in crises, and little in between. Under their leadership, an organization hurtles from crisis to crisis. Eventually, the worldview of people in the organization becomes dominated by events and reactiveness. Many, especially those who are deeply committed, become burned out. Eventually, cynicism comes to pervade the organization. People have no control over their time, let alone their destiny.

Similar problems arise with the "visionary strategist," the leader with vision who sees both patterns of change and events. This leader is better prepared to manage change. He or she can explain strategies in terms of emerging trends, and thereby foster a climate that is less reactive. But such leaders still impart a responsive orientation rather than a generative one.

Many talented leaders have rich, highly systemic intuitions but cannot explain those intuitions to others. Ironically, they often end up being authoritarian leaders, even if they don't want to, because only they see the decisions that need to be made. They are unable to conceptualize their strategic insights so that these can become public knowledge, open to challenge and further improvement.

New Tools

Developing the skills described above requires new tools—tools that will enhance leaders' conceptual abilities and foster communication and collaborative inquiry. What follows is a sampling of tools starting to find use in learning organizations.

Systems Archetypes

One of the insights of the budding, managerial systems-thinking field is that certain types of systemic structures recur again and again. Countless systems grow for a period, then encounter problems and cease to grow (or even collapse) well before they have reached intrinsic limits to growth. Many other systems get locked in runaway vicious spirals where every actor has to run faster and faster to stay in the same place. Still others lure individual actors into doing what seems right locally, yet which eventually causes suffering for all.[25]

Some of the system archetypes that have the broadest relevance include:

- **Balancing Process with Delay.** In this archetype, decision makers fail to appreciate the time delays involved as they move toward a goal. As a result, they overshoot the goal and may even produce recurring cycles. Classic example: Real estate developers who keep starting new projects until the market has gone soft, by which time an eventual glut is guaranteed by the properties still under construction.

- **Limits to Growth.** A reinforcing cycle of growth grinds to a halt, and may even reverse itself, as limits are approached. The limits can be resource constraints, or external or internal responses to growth. Classic examples: Product life cycles that peak prematurely due to poor quality or service, the growth and decline of communication in a management team, and the spread of a new movement.

- **Shifting the Burden.** A short-term "solution" is used to correct a problem, with seemingly happy immediate results. As this correction is used more and more, fundamental long-term corrective measures are used less. Over time, the mechanisms of the fundamental solution may atrophy or become disabled, leading to even greater reliance on the symptomatic solution. Classic example: Using corporate human resource staff to solve local personnel problems, thereby keeping managers from developing their own interpersonal skills.

- **Eroding Goals.** When all else fails, lower your standards. This is like "shifting the burden," except that the short-term solution involves letting a fundamental goal, such as quality standards or employee morale standards, atrophy. Classic example: A company that responds to delivery problems by continually upping its quoted delivery times.

- **Escalation.** Two people or two organizations, who each see their welfare as depending on a relative advantage over the other, continually react to the other's advances. Whenever one side gets ahead, the other is threatened, leading it to act more aggressively to reestablish its advantage, which threatens the first, and so on. Classic examples: Arms race, gang warfare, price wars.

- **Tragedy of the Commons.**[26] Individuals keep intensifying their use of a commonly available but limited resource until all individuals start to experience severely diminishing returns. Classic examples: Shepherders who keep increasing their flocks until they overgraze the common pasture; divisions in a firm that share a common salesforce and compete for the use of sales reps by upping their sales targets, until the salesforce burns out from overextension.

- **Growth and Underinvestment.** Rapid growth approaches a limit that could be eliminated or pushed into the future, but only by aggressive investment in physical and human capacity. Eroding goals or standards cause investment that is too weak, or too slow, and customers get increasingly unhappy, slowing demand growth and thereby making the needed investment (apparently) unnecessary or impossible. Classic example: Countless once-successful growth firms that allowed product or service quality to erode, and were unable to generate enough revenues to invest in remedies.

The Archetype template is a specific tool that is helping managers identify archetypes operating in their own strategic areas (see Figure 23-2).[27] The template shows the basic structural form of the archetype but lets managers fill in the variables of their own situation. For example, the shifting the burden template involves two balancing processes ("B") that compete for control of a problem symptom. The upper, symptomatic solution provides a short-term fix that will make the problem symptom go away for a while. The lower, fundamental solution provides a more enduring solution. The side effect feedback ("R") around the outside of the diagram identifies unintended exacerbating effects of the symptomatic solution, which, over time, make it more and more difficult to invoke the fundamental solution.

In the "shifting the burden" template, two balancing processes (B) compete for control of a problem symptom. Both solutions affect the symptom, but only the fundamental solution treats the cause. The symptomatic "solution" creates the additional side effect (R) of defer-

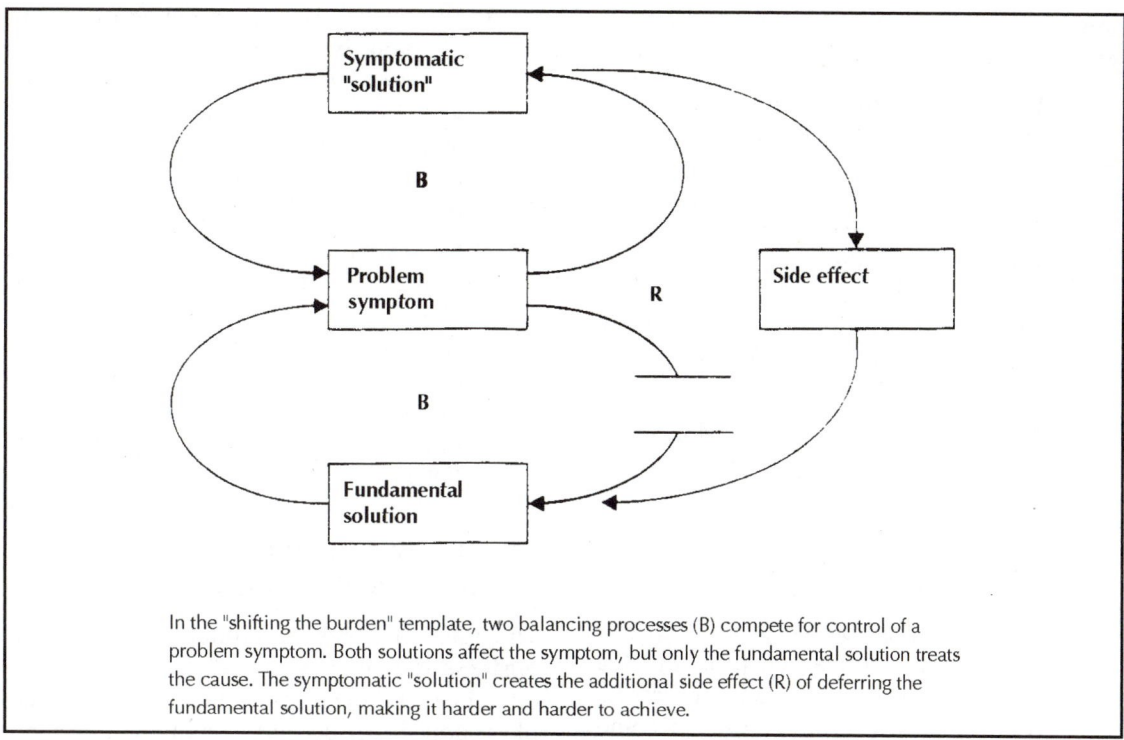

In the "shifting the burden" template, two balancing processes (B) compete for control of a problem symptom. Both solutions affect the symptom, but only the fundamental solution treats the cause. The symptomatic "solution" creates the additional side effect (R) of deferring the fundamental solution, making it harder and harder to achieve.

Figure 23-2 "Shifting the Burden" Archetype Template

ring the fundamental solution, making it harder to achieve.

Several years ago, a team of managers from a leading consumer goods producer used the shifting the burden archetype in a revealing way. The problem they focused on was financial stress, which could be dealt with in two different ways: by running marketing promotions (the symptomatic solution) or by product innovation (the fundamental solution). Marketing promotions were fast. The company was expert in their design and implementation. The results were highly predictable. Product innovation was slow and much less predictable, and the company had a history over the past ten years of product-innovation mismanagement. Yet only through innovation could they retain a leadership position in their industry, which had slid over the past ten to twenty years. What the managers saw clearly was that the more skillful they became at promotions, the more they shifted the burden away from product innovation. But what really struck home was when one member identified the unintended side effect: the last three CEOs had all come from advertising function, which had become the politically dominant function in the corporation, thereby institutionalizing the symptomatic solution. Unless the political values shifted back toward product and process innovation, the managers realized, the firm's decline would accelerate—which is just the shift that has happened over the past several years.

Charting Strategic Dilemmas

Management teams typically come unglued when confronted with core dilemmas. A classic example was the way U.S. manufacturers faced the low cost-high quality choice. For years, most assumed that it was necessary to choose between the two. Not surprisingly, given the short-term pressures perceived by most managements, the prevailing choice was low cost. Firms that chose high quality usually perceived themselves as aiming exclusively for a high quality, high price market niche. The consequences of this perceived either-or choice have been disastrous, even fatal, as U.S. manufacturers have encountered increasing international competition from firms that have chosen to consistently improve quality and cost.

In a recent book, Charles Hampden-Turner presented a variety of tools for helping management teams confront strategic dilemmas creatively.[28] He summarizes the process in seven steps:

- **Eliciting the Dilemmas.** Identifying the opposed values that form the "horns" of the dilemma, for example, cost as opposed to quality, or local initiative as opposed to central coordination and control. Hampden-Turner suggests that humor can be a distinct asset in this process since "the admission that dilemmas even exist tends to be difficult for some companies."

- **Mapping.** Locating the opposing values as two axes and helping managers identify where they see themselves, or their organization, along the axes.

- **Processing.** Getting rid of nouns to describe the axes of the dilemma. Present participles formed by adding "ing" convert rigid nouns into processes that imply movement. For example, central control versus local control becomes "strengthening national office" and "growing local initiatives." This loosens the bond of implied opposition between the two values. For example, it becomes possible to think of "strengthening national services from which local branches can benefit."

- **Framing/Contextualizing.** Further softening the adversarial structure among different values by letting "each side in turn be the frame or context for the other." This shifting of the "figure-ground" relationship undermines any implicit attempts to hold one value as intrinsically superior to the other, and thereby to become mentally closed to creative strategies for continuous improvement of both.

- **Sequencing.** Breaking the hold of static thinking. Very often, values like low cost and high quality appear to be in opposition because we think in terms of a point in time, not in terms of an ongoing process. For example, a strategy of investing in new process technology and developing a new production-floor culture of worker responsibility may take time and money in the near term, yet reap significant long-term financial rewards.

- **Waving/Cycling.** Sometimes the strategic path toward improving both values involves cycles where both values will get "worse" for a time. Yet, at a deeper level, learning is occurring that will cause the next cycle to be at a higher plateau for both values.

- **Synergizing.** Achieving synergy where significant improvement is occurring along all axes of all relevant dilemmas. (This is the ultimate goal, of course.) Synergy, as Hampden-Turner points out, is a uniquely systemic notion, coming from the Greek syn-ergo or "work together."

"The Left-Hand Column": Surfacing Mental Models

The idea that mental models can dominate business decisions and that these models are often tacit and even contradictory to what people espouse can be very threatening to managers who pride themselves on rationality and judicious decision making. It is important to have tools to help managers discover for themselves how their mental models operate to undermine their own intentions.

One tool that has worked consistently to help managers see their own mental models in action is the "left-hand column" exercise developed by Chris Argyris and his colleagues. This tool is especially helpful in showing how we leap from data to generalization without testing the validity of our generalizations.

When working with managers, I start this exercise by selecting a specific situation in which I am interacting with other people in a way that is not working, that is not producing the learning that is needed. I write out a sample of the exchange, with the script on the right-hand side of the page. On the left-hand side, I write what I am thinking but not saying at each stage in the exchange (see sidebar).

The left-hand column exercise not only brings hidden assumptions to the surface, it shows how they influence behavior. In the example, I make two key assumptions about Bill: he lacks confidence and he lacks initiative. Neither may be literally true, but both are evident in my internal dialogue, and both influence the way I handle the situation. Believing that he lacks confidence, I skirt the fact that I've heard the presentation was a bomb. I'm afraid that if I say it directly, he will lose what little confidence he has, or he will see me as unsupportive. So I bring up the subject of the presentation obliquely. When I ask Bill what we should do next, he gives no specific course of action. Believing he lacks initiative, I take this as evidence of his laziness; he is content to do nothing when action is definitely required. I conclude that I will have to manufacture some form of pressure to motivate him, or else I will simply have to take matters into my own hands.

The exercise reveals the elaborate webs of assumptions we weave, within which we become our own victims. Rather than dealing directly with my assumptions about Bill and the situation, we talk around the subject. The reasons for my avoidance are self-evident: I assume that if I raised my doubts, I would provoke a defensive reaction that would only make matters worse. But the price of avoiding the issue is high. Instead of determining how to move forward to resolve our problems, we end our exchange with no clear course of action. My assumptions about Bill's limitations have been reinforced. I resort to a manipulative strategy to move things forward.

The Left-Hand Column: An Exercise

Imagine my exchange with a colleague, Bill, after he made a big presentation to our boss on a project we are doing together. I had to miss the presentation, but I've heard that it was poorly received.

Me: How did the presentation go?

Bill: Well, I don't know. It's really too early to say. Besides, we're breaking new ground here.

Me: Well, what do you think we should do? I believe that the issues you were raising are important.

Bill: I'm not so sure. Let's just wait and see what happens.

Me: You may be right, but I think we may need to do more than just wait.

Now, here is what the exchange looks like with my "left-hand column":

What I'm Thinking

Everyone says the presentation was a bomb.

Does he really not know how bad it was? Or is he not willing to face up to it?

He really is afraid to see the truth. If he only had more confidence, he could probably learn from a situation like this.

I can't believe he doesn't realize how disastrous that presentation was to our moving ahead.

I've got to find some way to light a fire under the guy.

What Is Said

Me: How did the presentation go?

Bill: Well, I don't know. It's too early to say. Besides, we're breaking new ground here.

Me: Well, what do you think we should do? I believe that the issues you were raising are important.

Bill: I'm not so sure. Let's just wait and see what happens.

Me: You may be right, but I think we may need to do more than just wait.

Learning at Hanover Insurance

Hanover Insurance has gone from the bottom of the property and liability industry to a position among the top 25 percent of U.S. insurance companies over the past twenty years, largely through the efforts of CEO William O'Brien and his predecessor, Jack Adam. The following comments are excerpted from a series of interviews Senge conducted with O'Brien as background for his book.

Senge: Why do you think there is so much change occurring in management and organizations today? Is it primarily because of increased competitive pressures?

O'Brien: That's a factor, but not the most significant factor. The ferment in management will continue until we find models that are more congruent with human nature.

One of the great insights of modern psychology is the hierarchy of human needs. As Maslow expressed this idea, the most basic needs are food and shelter. Then comes belonging. Once these three basic needs are satisfied, people begin to aspire toward self-respect and esteem, and toward self-actualization—the fourth- and fifth-order needs.

Our traditional hierarchical organizations are designed to provide for the first three levels, but not the fourth and fifth. These first three levels are now widely available to members of industrial society, but our organizations do not offer people sufficient opportunities for growth.

Senge: How would you assess Hanover's progress to date?

O'Brien: We have been on a long journey away from a traditional hierarchical culture. The journey began with everyone understanding some guiding ideas about purpose, vision, and values as a basis for participative management. This is a better way to begin building a participative culture than by simply "letting people in on decision making." Before there can be meaningful participation, people must share certain values and pictures about where we are trying to go. We discovered that people have a real need to feel that they're part of an enobling mission. But developing shared visions and values is not the end, only the beginning.

Next we had to get beyond mechanical, linear thinking. The essence of our jobs as managers is to deal with "divergent" problems—problems that have no simple answer. "Convergent" problems—problems that have a "right" answer—should be solved locally. Yet we are deeply conditioned to see the world in terms of convergent problems. Most managers try to force-fit simplistic solutions and undermine the potential for learning when divergent problems arise. Since everyone handles the linear issues fairly well, companies that learn how to handle divergent issues will have a great advantage.

The next basic stage in our progression was coming to understand inquiry and advocacy. We learned that real openness is rooted in people's ability to continually inquire into their own thinking. This requires exposing yourself to being wrong—not something that most managers are rewarded for. But learning is very difficult if you cannot look for errors or incompleteness in your own ideas.

What all this builds to is the capability throughout an organization to manage mental models. In a locally controlled organization, you have the fundamental challenge of learning how to help people make good decisions without coercing them into making *particular* decisions. By managing mental models, we create "self-concluding" decisions—decisions that people come to themselves—which will result in deeper conviction, better implementation, and the ability to make better adjustments when the situation changes.

Senge: What concrete steps can top managers take to begin moving toward learning organizations?

O'Brien: Look at the signals you send through the organization. For example, one critical signal is how you spend your time. It's hard to build a learning organization if people are unable to take the time to think through important matters. I rarely set up an appointment for less than one hour. If the subject is not worth an hour, it shouldn't be on my calendar.

Senge: Why is this so hard for so many managers?

O'Brien: It comes back to what you believe about the nature of your work. The authoritarian manager has a "chain gang" mental model; "The speed of the boss is the speed of the gang. I've got to keep things moving fast, because I've got to keep people working." In a learning organization, the manager shoulders an almost sacred responsibility: to create conditions that enable people to have happy and productive lives. If you understand the effects the ideas we are discussing can have on the lives of people in your organization, you will take the time.

The exercise not only reveals the need for skills in surfacing assumptions, but that we are the ones most in need of help. There is no one right way to handle difficult situations like my exchange with Bill, but any productive strategy revolves around a high level of self-disclosure and willingness to have my views challenged. I need to recognize my own leaps of abstraction regarding Bill, share the events and reasoning that are leading to my concern over the project, and be open to Bill's views on both. The skills to carry on such conversations without invoking defensiveness take time to develop. But if both parties in a learning impasse start by doing their own left-hand column exercise and sharing them with each other, it is remarkable how quickly everyone recognizes their contribution to the impasse and progress starts to be made.

Learning Laboratories: Practice Fields for Management Teams

One of the most promising new tools is the learning laboratory or "microworld": constructed microcosms of real-life settings in which management teams can learn how to learn together.

The rationale behind learning laboratories can best be explained by analogy. Although most management teams have great difficulty learning (enhancing their collective intelligence and capacity to create), in other domains team learning is the norm rather than the exception—team sports and the performing arts, for example. Great basketball teams do not start off great. They learn. But the process by which these teams learn is, by and large, absent from modern organizations. The process is a continual movement between practice and performance.

The vision guiding current research in management learning laboratories is to design and construct effective practice fields for management teams. Much remains to be done, but the broad outlines are emerging.

First, since team learning in organizations is an individual-to-individual and individual-to-system phenomenon, learning laboratories must combine meaningful business issues with meaningful interpersonal dynamics. Either alone is incomplete.

Second, the factors that thwart learning about complex business issues must be eliminated in the learning lab. Chief among these is the inability to experience the long-term, systemic consequences of key strategic decisions. We all learn best from experience, but we are unable to experience the consequences of many important organizational decisions. Learning laboratories remove this constraint through system dynamics simulation games that compress time and space.

Third, new learning skills must be developed. One constraint on learning is the inability of managers to reflect insightfully on their assumptions, and to inquire effectively into each other's assumptions. Both skills can be enhanced in a learning laboratory, where people can practice surfacing assumptions in a low-risk setting. A note of caution: It is far easier to design an entertaining learning laboratory than it is to have an impact on real management practices and firm traditions outside the learning lab. Research on management simulations has shown that they often have greater entertainment value than educational value. One of the reasons appears to be that many simulations do not offer deep insights into systemic structures causing business problems. Another reason is that they do not foster new learning skills. Also, there is no connection between experiments in the learning lab and real life experiments. These are significant problems that research on learning laboratory design is now addressing.

Developing Leaders and Learning Organizations

In a recently published retrospective on organization development in the 1980s, Marshall Sashkin and N. Warner Burke observe the return of an emphasis on developing leaders who can develop organizations.[29] They also note Schein's critique that most top executives are not qualified for the task of developing culture.[30] Learning organizations represent a potentially significant evolution of organizational culture. So it should come as no surprise that such organizations will remain a distant vision until the leadership capabilities they demand are developed. "The 1990s may be the period," suggest Sashkin and Burke, "during which organization development and (a new sort of) management development are reconnected."

I believe that this new sort of management development will focus on the roles, skills, and tools for leadership in learning organizations. Undoubtedly, the ideas offered above are only a rough approximation of this new territory. The sooner we begin seriously exploring the territory, the sooner the initial map can be improved—and the sooner we will realize an age-old vision of leadership:

> The wicked leader is he who the people despise.
> The good leader is he who the people revere.
> The great leader is he who the people say, "We did it ourselves."
> —Lao Tsu

References

1. P. Senge, *The Fifth Discipline: The Art and Practice of the Learning Organization* (New York: Doubleday/Currency, 1990).

2. A. P. de Geus, "Planning as Learning," *Harvard Business Review*, March–April 1988, pp. 70–74.

3. B. Domain, *Fortune*, 3 July 1989, pp. 48–62.

4. The distinction between adaptive and generative learning has its roots in the distinction between what Argyris and Schon have called their "single-loop" learning, in which individuals or groups adjust their behavior relative to fixed goals, norms, and assumptions, and "double-loop" learning, in which goals, norms, and assumptions, as well as behavior, are open to change (e.g., see C. Argyris and D. Schon, *Organizational Learning: A Theory-in-Action Perspective* (Reading, Massachusetts: Addison-Wesley, 1978)).

5. All unattributed quotes are from personal communications with the author.

6. G. Stalk, Jr., "Time: The Next Source of Competitive Advantage," *Harvard Business Review*, July–August 1988, pp. 41–51.

7. Senge (1990).

8. The principle of creative tension comes from Robert Fritz' work on creativity. See R. Fritz, *The Path of Least Resistance* (New York: Ballantine, 1989) and Creating (New York: Ballantine, 1990).

9. M. L. King, Jr., "Letter from Birmingham Jail." *American Visions*, January–February 1986, pp. 52–59.

10. E. Schein, *Organizational Culture and Leadership* (San Francisco: Jossey-Bass, 1985). Similar views have been expressed by many leadership theorists. For example, see: P. Selmick, *Leadership in Administration* (New York: Harper & Row, 1957); W. Bennis and B. Nanus, *Leaders* (New York: Harper & Row, 1985); and N. M. Tichy and M. A. Devanna, *The Transformational Leader* (New York: John Wiley & Sons. 1986).

11. Selznick (1957).

12. J. W. Forrester, "A New Corporate Design," *Sloan Management Review* (formerly *Industrial Management Review*), Fall 1965, pp. 5–17.

13. See, for example, H. Mintzberg, "Crafting Strategy," *Harvard Business Review*, July–August 1987, pp. 66–75.

14. R. Mason and I. Mitroff. *Challenging Strategic Planning Assumptions* (New York: John Wiley & Sons, 1981), p. 16.

15. P. Wack, "Scenarios: Uncharted Waters Ahead," *Harvard Business Review*, September–October 1985, pp. 73–89.

16. de Geus (1988).

17. M. de Pree, *Leadership Is an Art* (New York: Doubleday, 1989) p. 9.

18. For example, see T. Peters and N. Austin, *A Passion for Excellence* (New York: Random House, 1985) and I. M. Kouzes and B. Z. Posner, *The Leadership Challenge* (San Francisco: Jossey-Bass, 1987).

19. I. Mitroff, *Break-Away Thinking* (New York: John Wiley & Sons, 1988), pp. 66–67.

20. R. K. Greenleaf, *Servant Leadership: A Journey into the Nature of Legitimate Power and Greatness* (New York: Paulist Press, 1977).

21. L. Miller, *American Spirit: Visions of a New Corporate Culture* (New York: William Morrow, 1984), p. 15.

22. These points are condensed from the practices of the five disciplines examined in Senge (1990).

23. The ideas below are based to a considerable extent on the work of Chris Argyris, Donald Schon, and their Action Science colleagues: C. Argyris and D. Schon, *Organizational Learning: A Theory-in-Action Perspective* (Reading, Massachusetts: Addison-Wesley, 1978); C. Argyris, R. Putnam, and D. Smith, *Action Science* (San Francisco: Jossey-Bass, 1985); C. Argyris, *Strategy, Change, and Defensive Routines* (Boston: Pitman, 1985); and C. Argyris, *Overcoming Organizational Defenses* (Englewood Cliffs, New Jersey: Prentice-Hall, 1990).

24. I am indebted to Diana Smith for the summary points below.

25. The system archetypes are one of several systems diagramming and communication tools. See D. H. Kim, "Toward Learning Organizations: Integrating Total Quality Control and Systems Thinking" (Cambridge, Massachusetts: MIT Sloan School of Management, Working Paper No. 3037-89-BPS, June 1989).

26. This archetype is closely associated with the work of ecologist Garrett Hardin, who coined its label: G. Hardin, "The Tragedy of the Commons," Science, 13 December 1968.

27. These templates were originally developed by Jennifer Kemeny, Charles Kiefer, and Michael Goodman of Innovation Associates, Inc., Framingham, Massachusetts.

28. C. Hampden-Turner, *Charting the Corporate Mind* (New York: The Free Press, 1990).

29. M. Sashkin and W. W. Burke, "Organization Development in the 1980s" and "An End-of-the-Eighties Retrospective," in *Advances in Organization Development*, ed. F. Masarik (Norwood, New Jersey: Ablex, 1990).

30. E. Schein (1985).

CHAPTER 24

BALANCING CORPORATION, COLLEGIUM, AND COMMUNITY

JAMES DOWNEY

It has been customary, at least since John Henry Newman (1852), to speak of "the idea of the university." Many books have been written bearing that title or alluding to it. Of no other social institution do we converse in quite the same way. We do not speak so naturally of "the idea of the hospital," or "the idea of the school," or "the idea of the corporation," or "the idea of the trade union," or even "the idea of the church." This is because no other social institution is so dedicated to the life of the mind, to thinking, reasoning, and imagining—in other words, to ideas—as the university.

Another reason why we speak of the *idea* of the university is, I think, because the idealized character of the university, which is to say its essence, always seems to elude definitional capture. Dictionary definitions describe the coil but not the current. Consider, for example, this definition from the *American Heritage Dictionary:*

> *University.* 1. An institution of higher learning with teaching and research facilities that awards undergraduate and postgraduate degrees. 2. The buildings and grounds of a university. 3. The students, teaching staff, and governing body of a university, regarded collectively.

That's the enterprise all right; what is missing is the purpose, which is the raison d'être, which is the essence. What is missing is the *idea* of the university.

Still, in an important sense, as Karl Jaspers says in his own book on *The Idea of the University* (1959), "the university exists only to the extent that it is institutionalized" (p. 83). Jaspers continues:

> The idea becomes concrete in the institution. The extent to which it does this determines the quality of the university. Stripped of its ideal the university loses all value. Yet "institution" necessarily implies compromises. The idea is never perfectly realized. Because of this a permanent state of tension exists [in] the university between the idea and the shortcomings of the institutional and corporate reality. (p. 83)

In its institutional form, however, a university is not a unity but a trinity; three simultaneous incarnations in one. It is corporation, collegium, and community. Each contains elements which are essential to the realization of the idea of the university, but each also contains elements and tendencies which are not readily harmonized.

"The University as Trinity: Balancing Corporation, Collegium, and Community," by James Downey, reprinted from *Innovative Higher Education*, Winter 1996, Human Sciences Press. Reprinted by permission.

The easiest of the three to describe, and for the lay person to understand, is the university as corporation. Corporations have existed in various forms for many centuries. They have been found so useful and durable that they have survived countless political and economic upheavals. They may be privately owned and managed; they may be publicly owned and managed; they may be a combination of both, as is the case with Canadian crown corporations. They may exist for profit or not for profit; either way they are creations of the state and answerable to it.

For the most part universities in Canada are legal corporate entities of the provincial governments and, like other corporations, have the right to appoint officers, own property, make contracts, sue in the courts, and have perpetual possession. Their administrative powers are held by delegation from the civil authority and are contained usually in an act of parliament which, like other statutes, may from time to time be amended. They are also generally bound by the same laws that apply to all corporations in the conduct of business. Whatever "institutional autonomy" and "academic freedom" may mean, these concepts cannot be used to argue that the corporation, its officers, or employees may operate outside the law.

Corporations have long been a principal legal and economic instrument of democracies, but they are not in their operations particularly democratic. They have a hierarchical structure, with authority vested in a corporate board and delegated to designated officers. Because legal compliance across a range of accountabilities is required of it, the university as corporation cannot afford to operate as a consensual community; it needs the administrative levers to act, and its structure provides them. The corporation doesn't have colleagues: it has officers, employees, and clients, and for its own integrity it must deal with them as such.

In exchange for its compliance in the ways indicated, the state confers on the university as corporation, and through the mechanism of a lay board of directors, a considerable measure of institutional autonomy in the conduct of its affairs. The body corporate therefore is a shield as well as a shell.

It is also a vehicle. It provides an orderly environment in which the business of the academy may be transacted. Through the cor-poration the state, clients, and donors provide the material resources without which scholarly endeavour is impossible. The corporation's systems of financial accounting, personnel management, plant operation, and resource allocation are essential preconditions for the research, teaching, and service that constitute the principal activities of the modern university. If the academic corporation is not well structured, financed, governed, and managed, the cause of scholarship will be, depending on the degree of deficiency, impeded or imperiled. No one would claim that the corporation is itself the essence of the university. To the extent, however, that it makes possible the institutional autonomy, the material resources, and the administrative order essential for the conduct of the work of the university, it is an indispensable vehicle for that essence.

More people would be prepared to claim, especially among the professoriate, that the second modality of my trinity, the collegium, is indeed the essence of the university. I would argue that while it is essential to, it is not the essence of, the academy. The collegium is the complex network of assumptions, traditions, protocols, relations, and structures within the university which permit the professoriate to control and conduct the academic affairs of the institution, determining, among other things, who shall be admitted, who shall teach and research, what shall be taught and researched, and what standards shall be set for which rewards. The collegium is thus the practical realization of academic freedom.

It may be worth emphasizing what academic freedom is and is not, so important is it to an understanding and the functioning of the collegium. Academic freedom and constitutional free speech are sometimes conflated. They should not be; they may be sisters, but they are not identical twins. Academic freedom does not entitle professors to rights as citizens over those enjoyed by other citizens. To quote Jaspers again: "Academic freedom . . . does not mean the right to say what one pleases. Truth is much too difficult and great a task that it should be mistaken for the passionate exchange of half-truths spoken in the heat of the. moment. It exists only where scholarly ends and commitment to truth are involved. Practical objectives, educational bias, or political propaganda have no right to invoke academic freedom" (p. 142).

Academic freedom therefore has both an individual and collective connotation. For the individual faculty member it means the greatest reasonable measure of autonomy in the performance of his or her academic duties. Only through the possession of such a right, it is argued, can the pursuit of truth be guaranteed. For the collectivity it means the right of faculty members conferring together through departmental, faculty, and university councils, to determine the academic content and character of their institution.

If the corporation rests on the principle of hierarchical authority, the collegium rests on the principle of hieratic authority, on the notion that the professoriate constitutes a priesthood when it comes to matters of academic policy and principle. Students and staff and alumni may be invited to offer views, but it is the ordained members of the community who make decisions. While the collegium as part of the community is anything but democratic, within the collegium there is ample scope for the practice of democracy. Any faculty member may speak his or her mind with impunity, any objection may be raised, any argument made, any decision challenged.

It is through this time-intensive process that the consensus is formed which is so essential to concerted action. At the same time, it is also the process which often seems to those outside the university, not to say many within, to inhibit unreasonably institutional responsiveness to social change. When under pressure to respond with dispatch, most universities of course find ways of doing so, especially when institutional self-interest is involved. The recent incident, however, of Yale University's having to return a multi-million dollar gift to a donor after a couple of years' inability to decide whether the donation could be used as intended, illustrates how the interests of corporation and collegium may sometimes collide.

Then there is the university as community. If the vertical axis of this complex organizational graph represents the corporation and the horizontal axis represents the collegium, the community is all of the interstitial space around and between. Among our manifold social institutions none so approximates a complete community as a university. No other institution has such an impressive range of communal attributes. There is first the physical infrastructure of land, buildings, roads, sewers, communication and transportation systems, and cultural and athletic facilities. There is as well the infrastructure of a different sort; this is the impressive range of services provided to citizens—personal, professional, social, recreational, and of course educational. There is finally the professional and demographic diversity of the citizenry, representing the broadest possible range of interest, competence, and ethnicity. It is the least structured, most malleable of the three components of the university. It is also the most encompassing. Everyone belongs to and has equity in the university as community.

Unlike the corporation, there is nothing neat and orderly about the community, nothing straightforward, nothing unambiguous, not much clearly defined. We cannot speak of the community, as we can of the corporation, as a structure. It is a culture in which things grow. It accommodates itself, if it is a good culture, to the gray and grainy nature of our lives as we live them: it makes way for the eccentric, it tolerates the absurd, it protects the vulnerable, it subsumes differences into common cause, it grounds in democratic perspective the elitisms inherent in the corporation and the collegium. Without such a community, neither the corporation nor the collegium will prosper.

All three dimensions of the university are being tested at present in Canada, as I believe they are in the United States, and it might be instructive to reflect for a moment on how and why. For the corporation there are the contractions and adjustments necessitated by declining government support. Ours in Canada is almost exclusively a state-supported system of higher education. For the past generation government has supplied more than 75% of the revenues of universities, with student fees accounting for about 15%. In the 90s, as governments have attempted to do combat with Canada's monstrous public debt, fiscal transfers to universities on a per-student basis have decreased significantly. Now, at least in Ontario, which represents approximately 40% of the higher-education system in Canada, a precipitous drop in government support will occur this year.

With this dramatic reduction in government support will likely come a partial deregulation of tuition fees. These two actions together will place great stress upon the corporation in meeting its obligations to the state, on the one hand, and to students, faculty, and staff, on the other. It now seems clear that in the short run major reductions will have to be made to the numbers of employees, to wages and benefits, and, conceivably, to the range and perhaps quality of courses and programs. For all the short-term dislocation, however, the prospects for the corporation look reasonably good. There seems little doubt that as reliance on bloc grants from government decreases and market-place competition for students increases, boards of governors and university officers will have more scope for strategic management, which is to say, more scope for both fiscal success and failure, than is true at present. In becoming more directly accountable to the client, whether the student who will pay much higher fees or the agency which commissions research or consulting service, the corporate aspect of the university will unavoidably be accentuated.

Will this accentuation of the corporate come at the expense of the collegium? Our tradition is that of a bicameral system, under which an institution has both a board of governors, generally lay persons, and an academic senate. Will the strengthening of corporate governance weaken further the bicameral system of university governance which has been under siege for some time? It is by no means foreordained that bicameralism will wane as corporatism waxes; it will depend in large part on what imaginative power the concept of the collegium still holds for academics. There is, I believe, general agreement that the bicameral system has been considerably weakened over the past quarter-century. There is also agreement about the factors which have contributed to this malaise.

The widespread unionization of faculty in the 1970s has been perhaps the most significant constraint on the powers of both boards of governors and academic senates. For ill-prepared boards, as Professor David Cameron explains so well in his book, *More than an Academic Question* (1991), the nature of the contracts negotiated with well-orchestrated faculty unions left them with very weak management

rights. Since boards have been little more than proxies for government in the negotiation of salaries and benefits, and while government was prepared to provide more or less adequate funding on a generally unrestricted basis, this system worked well enough. In the present state of fiscal crisis, however, and contemplating a future where neither adequacy of funds nor equity of their distribution is assured, boards will have to accept greater responsibility for the health and perhaps the very survival of the institutions they govern. I believe that boards will do this; either they will recover through negotiations the tools they need for effective governance in the new environment or they will be given them by government intervention. My own decided preference is for the former; the latter way could be at the expense of the institutional autonomy which boards exist in part to protect.

As for academic senates, the heart of the collegium, I am less sanguine about their prospects. At the same time that faculty unionization limited the discretionary powers of boards of governors, it removed from academic senates several important jurisdictions over the terms and conditions of employment of faculty, promotion and tenure criteria and procedures being only the most obvious example. There is little in the situation evolving in Canada to suggest that faculty are prepared to transfer any jurisdiction from their collective agreements or memoranda of agreement back to their senates. In fact, the current crisis in funding might well have the opposite effect, strengthening the syndical aspects of faculty life and weakening the collegial. In the end, faculty unions tend to strengthen the corporation at the expense of the collegium.

The second powerful factor which has helped to circumscribe the scope and effectiveness of bicameralism is the pronounced tendency of Canadian governments in the past to prefer regulation rather than competition as a means of ensuring accountability. As our most respected cultural critic, Robert Fulford, said recently,

> Canadians love regulation. What rice is to the Japanese, what wine is to the French, regulation is to the Canadians. When any new phenomenon appears on the horizon, whether it is *in vitro* fertilization or super-conductivity, our first response is always

the same: how do we regulate this sucker? An Ottawa bureaucrat's highest word of praise for an industry is "orderly," meaning well regulated. The BNA Act promises "peace, order, and good government," but the only one we absolutely insist on is order." (Toronto *Globe & Mail*, 22 December, 1993)

The tendency of governments to limit through regulation the sphere of decision-making has had a debilitating effect upon boards of governors, making their most important function one of ensuring that their institutions are in compliance with increasingly more intrusive and detailed legislation.

Affecting the bicameral system too, and weakening collegial self-determination, has been the growing litigiousness of Canadian society, which has resulted in many more complaints being referred for resolution outside the university, to adjudicators, tribunals, human-rights commissions, and the courts. No one is prepared, it seems, to take no for an answer, or even a "yes, but," until it comes from the highest authority to which it can be appealed. Unlike Americans, Canadians have had a written charter of rights and freedoms for only little more than a decade, and we are still somewhat in its thrall. Such thralldom sits ill with the more informal, less definitive methods of dispute resolution characteristic of the traditional collegium.

Finally, as the knowledge intensity of the modern university has grown, and with it the technology intensity of modem scientific knowledge, universities have assumed an importance in strategic economic development never before known in Canada. The perishable nature of much scientific and technological knowledge has meant that the slow, consensual decision-making processes of the collegium have been inadequate. Both the corporation and the individual faculty members with marketable intellectual property have had to find faster ways to respond to transfer opportunities. University-owned technology-transfer offices and, in some cases, corporations have been established to facilitate the corporation's responsiveness. Many professors, their academic freedom ensuring their ownership of the intellectual property they have created, incorporate to market their inventions. In themselves these developments are not only not bad

but may be essential to the competitiveness of the provincial and national economies. They are, however, a further short-circuiting of the collegial system, and they leave many gifted professors with no time to assume collegial governance responsibilities and little time even for teaching.

The forces just described have also affected the university as community. I spoke earlier of the physical, social, and cultural infrastructures which provide the basis for the university as community. But these are not its essence. There is another meaning of community. It is the spirit of concern and caring, of regard and respect, of cooperation and sharing which is the communal bonding agent. This is the essence which harmonizes divergent interests and creates cohesion. It is this spirit which is being severely tested in our universities at the moment, as it is in our society at large.

As the fiscal belt tightens, the several groups that make up the university become more concerned about their own interests—administration, faculty, staff, students, and occasionally alumni. In a new book, *Troubled Times for American Higher Education* (1994), that wise man Clark Kerr writes: "Additionally, the campus, as also the external society, is becoming more a series of enclaves divided by race/ethnic group, by gender, by political orientation, by 'old guard' citizens versus 'guest workers' whose basic allegiances lie elsewhere" (p. 13). I do not believe that things are that bad at most Canadian universities, just as they are not that bad at many American universities, but the dangerous tendencies of which Kerr speaks are all there to be observed.

Where then does all this leave us in thinking about the modern university and assessing its prospects? What if anything can be done to balance the legitimate claims of corporation, collegium, and community, and to ensure that the university of the 21st century, as it has been for most of the 20th, is an institution characterized by "a fruitful interaction in a dynamic state of tension" (Jaspers, 1959, p. 20)?

In the first place it is important to understand that none of these three modalities of the university is its essence. It is almost as important to understand that each carries within it elements of that essence, elements without which the university is in some respect deficient. There never has been a time perhaps when all of these elements have been fully present and perfectly balanced, but present dangers of imbalance are greater than they have been in a long time. The spirit of the times is corporate, not communal, and certainly not collegial. Corporate is about the production of wealth and the exercise of power; communal and collegial are about the sharing of wealth and power. There is a strong sense in both Canada and the United States that we have for too long been too concerned about the bottom rung and not enough about the bottom line. The governments we have of late elected with unambiguous mandates have assured us they will correct this imbalance. We in the universities are not immune to the political temper of the times, any more than we are to the fiscal and social policies that our governments enact. It seems clear by now that, in Canada at least, universities will participate in a process of corporate restructuring similar to that which has characterized business and, more recently, government. This may be neither fair nor reasonable, given how effectively universities have adapted over the past generation to changing social needs, but the forces at work are powerful and undiscriminating. Corporate restructuring will occur, and as it does it will confer salience on the economic utility and responsiveness of the university.

This is not in itself a bad thing, as long as we recognize and seek to redress its potentially distorting tendencies on the other two cultures of the university. There are, after all, many inside as well as outside the academy who have argued of late that the exercise of faculty control through the collegium has led to abuses, in the neglect of teaching, the pursuit of irrelevant research and scholarship, using tenure to protect the incompetent, and a general failure to make honest and rigorous judgments about each other's work. Whatever the validity of these criticisms, we would be ill-advised to ignore them and well-advised to seize the opportunity presented by the fiscal changes that will be forced on us to ask ourselves the most basic of questions, which is, what is the *idea* of the university on the cusp of a new millennium?

Three ingredients are, I believe, essential. One is responsiveness to the economic and social stresses and challenges facing society and the people, organizations, and institutions that comprise it. It is not enough merely to be good at what we do; we must also be focused and relevant. For universities like Georgia and Waterloo this will not come as anything other than commonplace thinking. But Canada has no land grant tradition to point the way to a more practical and applied approach to higher education, and in much of Canada there has been too sharp a distinction drawn between the role of universities and the role of colleges of applied arts and technology. Universities, even among many who support them, have an image of aloofness and indifference to society's urgent needs, a readiness to criticize but not to help.

Lest the point I am making here be assumed to constitute my entire philosophy of education, let me hasten to affirm that the primary mission of the university, as I embrace it, is not just to train, though training is essential to all learning, but to educate, not just to prepare students for work, but to make them wiser and more civilized people. And this is true for all students, even those learning the technical and mental skills of a profession.

I believe that, while there will always be some tension between the university's role as critic of society and its role as society's servant, there is ultimately no contradiction between the two. We not only can, but we must, prepare our students to live fuller and more capacious lives as individuals and citizens even as we equip them with the skills and knowledge and attitudes necessary for earning a living. We not only can, but we must, continue to pursue fundamental knowledge through research and scholarship even as we look for outreach opportunities for the products of that work. Indeed, I have long since been persuaded that the better we do the one the better we shall do the other.

The second element that will need to be present in our universities is a deeper sense of community, which is to say, a stronger sense of academic citizenship and a greater willingness to participate in and contribute to the *vita communitatis*. For their part, and it is a vital part, professors find their loyalties divided between the institution that employs them and the disciplines they pursue. Not infrequently, the colleagues with whom they most closely confer are in the same disciplines at other universities. Modern means of communication and transportation make those collaborations easier, while pressures to perform research and to publish often leave too little time, energy, or interest for citizenship duties within the university.

In the 22 September 1995 issue of *Science*, William H. Danforth, former president of Washington University in St. Louis and now chairman of the board, writes as follows:

> If it was ever true that faculty members' pursuit of individual interests automatically created a great university, it is certainly not so now. Rather, the loosening of institutional ties has become a major risk, for today's successful university requires effective internal operations aimed at agreed-upon goals. Because faculty do the essential work of teaching and research, their participation and leadership are key. Also, faculty must embody and serve as guardians of the values that should permeate the institutional culture, including, at a minimum, freedom of exploration and expression, commitment to excellence in scholarship and teaching, and tolerance for differences. Promotion of such values requires time, effort, and devotion.

I am glad Danforth put it in terms of values and personal commitment on the part of faculty because that is what it comes down to. For the most part students, staff, and alumni are, I have observed, only too willing to make the commitments of which Danforth speaks. What is often missing is the essential leadership that only a significant cadre of the best faculty can provide. We need it in our departmental and faculty councils, we need it in our senates and on our committees, we need it at the numerous and nuanced interfaces where the several estates of the university—the students, the staff, the alumni, the faculty, and friends—come together to plan, to transact, or merely to enjoy.

Finally, we need in our institutions a fresh infusion of idealism, a renewed affirmation of faith in the central, civilizing purpose of the university. We need to remind ourselves in fresh and uninhibited language of the great ennobling tradition we have inherited. I'm not talking about the survival of the university. An institution that has weathered the vagaries, vagrancies, and vicissitudes of the past eight hundred years has obviously acquired an impressive capacity for adaptation to changing circumstances. And there is no good reason to think that we in our time will lack the wit or the resolve to lead our institutions into a new

century. There is, I believe, no cause for despair. What I lament is that there seems too little disposition for celebration.

In his book, *A Free and Ordered Space*, Bart Giamatti (1988) reminds us in many places and many ways of what is too often missing in our collegial life, distracted and preoccupied as we are with the ceaseless ebb and flow of debate about curriculum and course loads and political correctness. Here is one such reminder:

> Intellectual and civic in nature, pluralistic in purpose and composition, hierarchical in structure, the University exists for that play of restrain and release in each of its individual members. Through that creative play of opposites in teaching, learning, and research, the university nourishes at its core the humanizing and spacious acts of the individual imagination. Those acts are found in every area of study, whether lasers, literature, or law, and are proof of the human capacity to make and impose a design. Those designs made by the imagination are the signs of our ability to shape instinct and flux, to find or reveal patterns in the seemingly unplanned. The University is the guardian of the imagination that both defines and asserts our humanity. (pp. 48 - 49)

Ah, to be able to catch a glimpse of that from time to time, to feel that *this* is the enterprise of which we are a part, to sense our pulses quickened and our spirits lifted by the realization that all around us new fields of understanding are being explored and minds illumined and lives liberated by the knowledge and skills we impart and cultivate.

More than we need strategic planning or new facilities or organizational re-engineering or revised curricula or more resources, we need a reawakening of our sense of the wonder and grandeur of it all. And if that sounds too much like Cardinal Newman, I do not apologize. Though I share neither his religious faith nor his academic philosophy, his reverence for the idea of the university is the kindly light we still need to lead us amid the encircling gloom.

References

Cameron, D. M. *More than an academic question: Universities, government, and public policy in Canada.* Halifax, NS: Institute for Research on Public Policy.

Danforth, W. H.. Universities are our responsibility. *Science*, 269 (5231), 1651, 1995.

Giamatti, A. B. *A free and ordered space: The real world of the University*. New York: W. W. Norton, 1988, pp. 48–49.

Jaspers, K. *The idea of the university*. Karl. W. Deutsch (Ed.). Boston: Beacon Press. 1959.

Kerr, C., Gade, M. & Kawaoka, M. *Troubled times for American higher education: The 1990s and beyond*. Albany: State University of New York Press, 1994.

Newman, J. H. *The idea of a university defined and illustrated*. I. In nine discourses delivered to the Catholics of Dublin (1852). II. In Occasional lectures and essays addressed to the members of the Catholic University (1858). I. T. Kerr (Ed.). Oxford: Clarendon, 1976.

Toronto *Globe and Mail* (22. December, 1993).

CHAPTER 25

UNDERSTANDING RADICAL ORGANIZATIONAL CHANGE

ROYSTON GREENWOOD AND C. R. HININGS

The complexity of political, regulatory, and technological changes confronting most organizations has made radical organizational change and adaptation a central research issue. This article sets out a framework for understanding organizational changes from the perspective of neo-institutional theory. The principal theoretical issue addressed in the article is the interaction of organizational context and organizational action. The article examines the processes by which individual organizations retain, adopt, and discard templates for organizing, given the institutionalized nature of organizational fields.

The complexity of political, regulatory, and technological changes confronting most organizations has made organizational change and adaptation a central research issue of the 1990s. The ability to cope with often dramatically altering contextual forces has become a key determinant of competitive advantage and organizational survival (D'Aveni, 1994). The purpose of this article is to set out a framework for understanding organizational change from the perspective of neo-institutional theory (Powell & DiMaggio, 1991). Institutional theory is used as a starting point because it represents one of the more robust sociological perspectives within organizational theory (Perrow, 1979), and it makes sense, as Dougherty pointed out, to "integrate some theoretical threads regarding the specific issue of transformation by building on already developed theories" (1994: 110). We use the term *neo-institutional* to capture the developments that have taken over the past decade (Powell & DiMaggio, 1991).

In their review of the state of institutional theory, DiMaggio and Powell (1991: 13) distinguished between the old and the new institutionalism (cf. Table 25-1). In the old institutionalism, issues of influence, coalitions, and competing values were central, along with power and informal structures (Clark, 1960, 1972; Selznick, 1949, 1957). This focus contrasts with the new institutionalism with its emphasis on legitimacy, the embeddedness of organizational fields, and the centrality of classification, routines, scripts, and schema (DiMaggio & Powell, 1983; Meyer & Rowan, 1977). Scott (1987) suggested that institutional theory was at the stage of adolescence. Later, he saw considerable progress, namely: "I see convergent developments among the approaches of many analysts as they recognize the importance of meaning systems, symbolic elements, regulatory processes, and governance systems" (Scott, 1994: 78). It is this convergence around multiple themes, the coming together of the old and the new institutionalism that we label *neo-institutionalism*. The convergence that Scott (1994) wrote about involves all of the elements of the old and new institutional theory.

Institutional theory is not usually regarded as a theory of organizational change, but as usually an explanation of the similarity ("isomorphism") and stability of organizational arrangements in a given population or field of organizations. Ledford, Mohrman, Mohrman, and Lawler (1989: 8), for example, concluded that institutional theory offers not "much guidance regarding change." Buckho (1994: 90) observed that institutional pressures are a "powerful force" *against* transformational change. Here we present the opposite view, agreeing with Dougherty that the theory contains "an excellent basis" (1994: 108) for an account of change, first, by providing a convincing definition of radical (as opposed to convergent) change, and, second, by signaling the contextual dynamics that precipitate the need for organizational adaptation (Leblebici, Salancik, Copay, & King, 1993; Oliver, 1991). As formulated, however, neo-institutional theory is weak in analyzing the *internal* dynamics of organizational change. As a consequence, the theory is silent on why some organizations adopt radical change whereas others do not, despite experiencing the same institutional pressures. Nevertheless, neo-institutional theory contains insights and suggestions that, when elaborated, provide a model of change that links organizational context and intraorganizational dynamics.

In this article, then, the central purpose is to provide an explanation of both the incidence of radical change and of the extent to which such change is achieved through evolutionary or revolutionary pacing. The explanation has three themes. First, we establish that a major source of organizational resistance to change derives from the normative embeddedness of an organization within its institutional context. This statement is a central message of institutional theory. Second, we suggest that the incidence of radical change, and the pace by which such change occurs, will vary across institutional sectors because of differences in the structures of institutional sectors, in particular in the extents to which sectors are tightly coupled and insulated from ideas practiced in other sectors. Third, we propose that both the incidence of radical change and the pace by which such change occurs will vary *within* sectors because organizations vary in their internal organizational dynamics. In order to understand differences in organizational responses, organizations are conceptualized as heterogeneous entities composed of functionally differentiated groups pursuing goals and promoting interests. How organizations "respond" to institutional prescriptions, in particular, whether they undergo radical change, and, if they do, how quickly, is a function of these internal dynamics.

By addressing the interplay of organizational context and organizational action, this article is consistent with recent developments in organization theory. The initial polarization of perspectives offered, on the one hand, by population ecologists, with their essential denial of radical organizational change and emphasis upon peremptory environmental determinism (e.g., Hannan & Freeman, 1989) and, on the other hand, by strategic choice theorists, with their emphasis upon the pivotal role of executive action (e.g., Child, 1972; Tichy, 1983; Tichy & Devanna, 1986) has given way to attention to the interaction of choice and context. Hrebiniak and Joyce (1985), Van de Ven and Poole (1988), Astley and Van de Ven (1983), Pettigrew (1987), and Wilson (1994) have lodged pleas for theoretical understanding of how contextual pressures are interpreted and acted upon by organizational actors. To date, however, existing accounts have "not been successful" (Van de Ven & Poole, 1988: 327). Ledford and colleagues (1989: 4) dismissively described them as "of limited help." Here we seek to provide a more complete account for understanding organizational interpretations of, and responses to, contextual pressures, by stressing the political dynamics of intraorganizational behavior and the normative embeddedness of organizations within their contexts.

It is beyond the scope of this article to summarize the extensive literature on organizational change, but it is important to establish two aspects of change of particular concern here: first, the difference between convergent and radical change and, second, the difference between revolutionary and evolutionary change. A distinction is frequently drawn between convergent and radical change (Greenwood & Hinings, 1988; Miller & Friessen, 1984; Mohrman, Mohrman, Ledford, Cummings, & Lawler, 1989: Nadler & Tushman, 1989; Nadler, Shaw, Walton & Associates, 1995: Tushman & Romanelli, 1985). Radical organizational change, or "frame bending" as it is sometimes evocatively known, involves the busting loose from an existing "orientation" (Johnson, 1987; Miller, 1982, 1990) and the transformation of the organization. Convergent change is fine tuning the existing orientation. It is radical, not convergent change in which we are interested.

Revolutionary and evolutionary change are defined by the scale and pace of upheaval and adjustment. Whereas evolutionary change occurs slowly and gradually, revolutionary change happens swiftly and affects virtually all parts of the organization simultaneously. Tushman and Romanelli's (1985) punctuated-equilibrium model describes revolutionary change. Pettigrew's (1985; 1987) model of continuity and change reflects the process of evolutionary change.

The remainder of the article is divided into two sections. We begin the following section by outlining the current contribution of institutional theory to understanding change. We then develop a more complete account of intraorganizational dynamics and their interaction with contextual dynamics. In the final section, we draw attention to a number of key issues and discuss possible directions for research.

Institutional Theory and Change

Scott (1987: 493), in a seminal review of institutional theory, advised that "the beginning of wisdom in approaching institutional theory is to recognize that there is not one but several variants." At the outset, however, we begin by briefly reviewing three salient characteristics of what has become known as neo-institutional theory. The theory of change that can be derived from those characteristics is then elaborated.

The Impact of the Institutional Context

Institutional theorists declare that regularized organizational behaviors are the product of ideas, values, and beliefs that originate in the institutional context (Meyer & Rowan, 1977; Meyer, Scott, & Deal, 1983; Zucker, 1983). To survive, organizations must accommodate institutional expectations, even though these expectations may have little to do with technical notions of performance accomplishment

(D'Aunno, Sutton, & Price, 1991; DiMaggio & Powell, 1991; Scott, 1987). For example, an accounting firm may be organized as a professional partnership, not because that form of governance has been analyzed and found to facilitate efficient and effective task performance, but because that form is defined as the appropriate way of organizing the conduct of accounting work. Institutional theory, in other words, shows how organizational behaviors are responses not solely to market pressures, but also to institutional pressures (e.g., pressures from regulatory agencies, such as the state and the professions, and pressures from general social expectations and the actions of leading organizations).

Templates of Organizing, Isomorphism, and Convergence

Institutional pressures lead organizations to adopt the same organizational form. That is, the institutional context provides "templates for organizing" (DiMaggio & Powell, 1991: 27). The idea of templates connects to the growing interest in "configurational" research (for a review, see Meyer, Tsui, & Hinings, 1993). Configurational researchers conceptualize organizations holistically, seeking to recognize archetypal patterns in the display of structures and systems (Drazin & Van de Ven, 1985; Mintzberg, 1983; Miller & Friesen, 1984). Greenwood and Hinings (1993), consistent with the neo-institutionalist emphasis upon values, suggested that the configuration or pattern of an organization's structures and systems is provided by underpinning ideas and values, that is, an interpretive scheme (Barley, 1986; Bartunek, 1983; Ranson, Hinings, & Greenwood, 1980).

Thinking of organizational arrangements in terms of templates or archetypes (Greenwood & Hinings, 1993) provides a robust definition of radical and convergent change. Convergent change occurs within the parameters of an existing archetypal template. Radical change, in contrast, occurs when an organization moves from one template-in-use to another. That is, an accounting firm operating as a professional partnership may institute representative democracy in place of more broadly based democratic involvement in order to accommodate the exigencies of growth and large size. Such a change would be consistent with prevailing core ideas and values of the importance of clan rather than bureaucratic bases of authority (Ouchi, 1980), and it is convergent change. If, in contrast, a firm were to move from one template to another, the change would be radical, because it represents the breaking of the mold defined by an interpretive scheme. For example, if members of a professional partnership hired a nonaccountant as chief executive officer charged with formal responsibility for monitoring and evaluating senior professionals, there would be a discordant structure within the professional partnership and an indication of possible movement toward a new template (e.g., the "corporate" model). The new structures and responsibilities would not fit the clan orientation and would be more consistent with bureaucratic values.

Stressing ideas, beliefs, and values as the basis for identifying templates of structures and systems is not unique to institutional theory. The same idea is found in Miller's (1991: 8) "stable central themes," Blau and McKinley's (1979: 200) "work motifs," and Pettigrew's (1987: 658)dominating beliefs or ideologies." It is also present in much of the culture literature. Institutional theorists are different because they stress ideational templates as originating outside of the organization and being relevant to a population of organizations within an organizational field. As a consequence, institutional theory draws attention to institutionally derived and created templates of organizing to which organizations converge, rather than to the uniqueness of individual organizational cultures. Organizational convergence, not uniqueness, is implied.

DiMaggio and Powell (1983, 1991b: 63) stressed the convergence of organizations by bluntly framing *the* question as "Why [is there] such startling homogeneity, not variation?" The same authors discussed the primary processes (coercive, mimetic, and normative) by which convergence might occur as organizations seek to become isomorphic with their contexts. Underlying DiMaggio and Powell's (1991a) analysis is that organizations conform to contextual expectations of appropriate organizational forms to gain legitimacy and increase their probability of survival.

The focus of neo-institutional theory is thus not upon the individual organization but

upon a category or network of organizations. Even though much of the early empirical work (e.g., Meyer & Rowan, 1977) was based upon individual organizations, or case studies, neo-institutional theorists treat organizations as a population within an organizational field. These theorists stress that the institutional context is made up of vertically and horizontally interlocking organizations[1] and that the pressures and prescriptions within these contexts apply to all of the relevant classes of organizations.

Resistance to Change

According to early contributions to institutional theory, the organizational field and the templates of organizing within it become infused with a taken-for-granted quality, in which actors unwittingly accept the prevailing template as appropriate, right, and the proper way of doing things. DiMaggio and Powell (1983) and Fligstein (1985) noted that a template rationale for an individual organization may not be rational for large numbers of organizations. There is, in short, a normative tone to institutional discussions (Meyer & Rowan, 1977; Oliver, 1991; Zucker, 1977). For this reason, institutional theorists stress the stability of organizational arrangements and the characteristic of inertia rather than change (Tolbert, 1985; Tolbert & Zucker, 1983). Stressing inertia may be slightly misleading in that organizations constantly experience unfolding change. To the institutional school, however, the prevailing nature of change is one of constant reproduction and reinforcement of existing modes of thought and organization (i.e., change is convergent change).

By emphasizing archetypes/templates that originate in the institutional context and around which networks of organizations converge, institutional theorists actually show a likely dynamic of inertia, which can be illustrated from the accounting industry. The accounting profession mimicked the law (and the clergy) and adopted the partnership organizational form, which has endured and become almost synonymous with the very meaning of "professional," with its emphasis on independence, autonomy, and responsible conduct. Development of the profession during the 19th century and structuration of the accounting industry field followed much the same path as DiMaggio (1991) described for the museum profession. Thus, the values of the professional partnership became reinforced by professional associations that worked closely with universities and state agencies to promulgate and protect the self-regulating independence and autonomy of accounting firms. As a result, strong reciprocal exchanges have developed between the accounting field and any one accounting firm, such that the firm both accommodates the expectation of the field by observing appropriate behaviors and practices, and in doing so, acts as a role model within the field to other accounting firms. Thus, there are strong mimetic, normative, and coercive processes at work.

These mimetic, normative, and coercive processes are part of the institutional context. Such contexts differ in the strength of these kinds of pressures (i.e., the degree of embeddedness and in the extent to which change may occur because of deinstitutionalization (Oliver, 1992). Radical change is thus problematic not solely because of weak organizational learning (as emphasized by strategic choice theorists such as Kanter, 1983, and Johnson, 1987) or the constraints of strategy "commitments" (Ghemawat, 1991) or the difficulty of mobilizing internal support (as emphasized by Tichy, 1983, and Fombrun, 1992)—although these forces for inertia may and often do occur—but because of the normative embeddedness of an organization within its institutional context (Baum & Oliver, 1991). Also, the greater the embeddedness, the more problematic is the attainment of radical change. Indeed, Powell and DiMaggio (1991a) noted that the greater the extent to which organizations are tightly coupled to a prevailing archetypal template within a highly structured field, the greater the degree of instability in the face of external shocks. That is, the rigidity of tight coupling and high structuredness produces resistance to change; however, should institutional prescriptions change dramatically, the resultant organizational response would be revolutionary, not evolutionary (in terms of the scale and pace of upheaval and adjustment).

The above starting points may be summarized as follows:

Hypothesis 1: Organizations are structured in terms of archetypes (templates of organizing), which are institutionally derived.

Hypothesis 2: Radical change (movement from one archetype to another) is problematic because of the normative embeddedness of an organization within its institutional context. Convergent change is the more normal occurrence.

Hypothesis 3: The greater the normative embeddedness of an organization within the institutional context, the more likely that when change occurs it will be revolutionary rather than evolutionary (i.e.. the pace of upheaval will be fast, not gradual, and the scale large, not modest).

The Possibility for Change

Institutional theory, in summary, emphasizes convergence around institutionally prescribed templates. Indeed, Powell (1991a: 183) was particularly critical of such theory for its "static, constrainted, and over-socialised views of organizations." DiMaggio and Powell (1991a: 29) asked the question, "If institutions exert such a powerful influence over the ways in which people can formulate their desires and work to attain them, then how does institutional change occur?" Three streams of work within institutional theory give insights into the possible processes and likelihood of radical change, and it is these streams that lead us to a neo-institutional perspective. Early contributions (e.g.. Tolbert & Zucker, 1983) proposed a two-stage dissemination model of change. In the early (youthful) development of an organizational field, technical performance requirements are more important than in later (mature) stages of the field, at which point institutional pressures become more salient (Tolbert & Zucker, 1983; Baron, Dobbin, & Jennings, 1986). Subsequent authors have examined the "mechanisms of imitation" (Haunschild, 1993: 564), paying particular attention to the role of interlocking directorates (e.g., Davis, 1991; Davis & Powell, 1992; Haveman, 1993; Palmer, Jennings, & Thou, 1993) or the object of imitation (e.g., Burns & Wholey, 1993; Galaskiewicz & Wasserman, 1989; Haveman, 1993; O'Reilly, Main, & Crystal, 1988).

A second line of development within institutional theory, which has implications for understanding change, considers the structure of the institutional context (i.e., the *extent of tight coupling* and the *extent of sectoral permeability*). Regarding tight coupling, sectors usually have been perceived as having clearly legitimated organizational templates and highly articulated mechanisms (the state, professional associations, regulatory agencies, and leading organizations) for transmitting those templates to organizations within the sector (Fligstein, 1991; Haveman, 1993; Hinings & Greenwood, 1988a; Kikulis, Slack, & Hinings, 1995; Tolbert, 1985; Wholey & Burns, 1993). Furthermore, much of this work has assumed ideological consensus within an institutional field. Tight coupling, in other words, refers to the existence of mechanisms for dissemination and the monitoring of compliance combined with a focused and consistent set of expectations.

In practice. there can be variation across institutional sectors in the degree of tight coupling. Carroll, Goodstein, and Gyenes (1988), for example, questioned the probability of ideological consensus. Fligstein (1991: 316) noted that the possibility of "innovative behavior" is higher in "ill-formed" organizational fields. Barnett and Carroll (1987) documented how during the founding years of the telephone industry, high political differentiation in the markets enabled several organizational forms to flourish (i.e., high political differentiation was associated with low institutional consensus over templates). DiMaggio and Powell (1991a), Scott (1991), Powell (1991), Oliver (1991). and D'Aunno and colleagues (1991) accepted that institutional fields may have multiple pressures providing inconsistent cues or signals, opening the possibility for idiosyncratic interpretation and either deliberate or unwitting variation in practices.

Mechanisms for dissemination also can vary across institutional fields. In mature sectors, such as accounting and law, there are very clear mechanisms, and thus normative, coercive, and mimetic pressures (for conformity) are high. In governmental sectors, too, regulatory pressures are usually clear and reinforced (Hinings & Greenwood, 1988b; Kikulis, Slack, & Hinings. 1995). In less well-developed sectors such as biotechnology, the existence of leading organizations is less clear and there is no developed network of regulatory agencies comparable to accounting bodies (Powell, 1993). As a consequence, there is no stipulated template for organizing, and thus pressures for conformity are much less pronounced. Thus,

Hypothesis 4: Radical change in tightly coupled institutional fields will be unusual, but when it occurs, it will be revolutionary.

Hypothesis 5: Radical change in loosely coupled fields will be more common (than in tightly coupled fields), and when it occurs it will be evolutionary.

Institutional fields vary in their insulation from other fields. Same fields lack permeability (i.e., they are relatively closed to or not exposed to ideas from other institutional arenas). Other fields are more open and thus more likely to permit variation and change. Child and Smith (1987), for example, described the transfer of ideas that happen as contractors service firms in different industries. Similarly, members of accounting firms inevitably work in several fields (by consulting or by conducting audits) and become exposed to and potentially influenced by the ideas prevailing in those fields. Because of the tight coupling within the accounting industry, however, the influence of other fields traditionally has been limited (consistent with Hypothesis 4). Because of looming performance crises, however, members of accounting firms are beginning to consider other fields for possible solutions (e.g., the partnership form of governance is under review, *European Accounting Focus*, 1995). That is, permeable boundaries enable radical change because of the availability of new archetypal solutions. Thus,

Hypothesis 6: Institutional fields that are impermeable will be associated with low rates of radical change.

Hypothesis 7: Radical change that occurs in impermeable institutional fields will be revolutionary in pace.

Hypothesis 8: Institutional fields that are permeable will be associated with a higher incidence of radical change than will occur in impermeable institutional fields.

Hypothesis 9: Institutional fields that are permeable will be associated with evolutionary change.

These elaborations are significant because through them we admit to the possibility and even the likelihood of *alternative* templates within an institutional context.[2] In tightly structured contexts, the occurrence of such alternatives may be infrequent, and it may be dependent partly on a serious decline in performance (as in the law industry described by Cooper, Hinings, Greenwood, and Brown, in press, and in the municipal sector of the United Kingdom as described by Hinings and Greenwood, 1988a) and partly on the permeability of the sector. In less tightly coupled contexts, the occurrence of alternative templates may be more frequent but less coherently formulated. The central point is that organizations are recipients of prescribed ideas about appropriate templates of organizing whose relative salience and clarity *may change over time*. Particular organizations do not respond to a template of organizing, but they do respond over time to evolving and competing prescriptions. This conclusion leads to two issues: how do individual organizations respond *and why do they differ in their responses*.[3]

Intraorganizational Dynamics

In the old institutionalism (e.g., Selznick. 1949). issues of influence, coalitions, and competing values were central, and the emphasis was placed on the ways in which the formal, rational mission of an organization is diverted by the operation of group interests. Thus, the key forms of cognition are values, norms, and attitudes; conflicts of interest and vested interests are central; and the individual organization is the locus of institutionalization and the primary unit of analysis. Selznick (1957: 17) wrote of institutionalized organizations being "infused with value," becoming ends in themselves, and thus operating within essentially moral frames of reference.

Similarly. Clark (1960) emphasized that actual organizational practices diverge from expressed organizational goals. In further work, Clark (1972) showed how values may be "precarious." That is, newly appointed administrators attempted to signal shifts in values and expectations through changes in structures. However, the organizational implications of the new values and meanings were imperfectly understood, and it took a long time for the new values to be embodied in practice.

Brint and Karabel (1991: 344) related with the "old institutionalism" of Selznick (1949) and Clark (1960, 1972), building primarily "on the insights of the 'conflict' tradition in sociology, rather than on the insights of the Durkheimian tradition which have proven so fruitful for the new institutionalism." They also drew on the insights that Michels (1962) generated about the role of interests in organizations, which allow diversions to occur from original goals. As Brint and Karabel (1991: 352) observed, old institutionalism "emphasizes the details of an organization's interactions with its environment over time" and pays attention to the beliefs and actions of those who have the power to define directions and interests.

New institutionalism emphasizes the regulative, the normative, and the cognitive. In this case, rather than values and moral frames, it is cognition that is important. As Meyer and Rowan (1977: 341) put it, "normative obligations ... enter into social life primarily as facts." The key units of analysis are organizations-in-sectors and their relation to societal institutions.

From the point of view of understanding change, the old institutionalism suggests that change is one of the dynamics of organizations as they struggle with differences of values and interests. The new institutionalism emphasizes persistence. Combining the two into neo-institutionalism gives the possibility of dealing with the question asked by DiMaggio and Powell (1991: 29): If institutions exert such a powerful influence over the ways in which people can formulate their desires and work to attain them, then how does institutional change occur?"

Oliver (1992), building upon the work of Zucker (1987), began to provide a way of bringing these two perspectives together in her examination of the antecedents of deinstitutionalization. Oliver suggested (1992: 584) that "the persistence and longevity of institutionalized values and activities may be less common than the emphasis of institutional theory on cultural persistence and the diffusion of enduring change implies." Oliver (1992) introduced the notion of *dissipation,* a gradual deterioration in the acceptance and use of a particular institutionalized practice, which provided an overall conceptual framework for understanding that process. Her framework involves both environmental and organizational features that can produce deinstitutionalization. Among the organizational features are, inter alia, changing values, conflicting internal interests, and increasing social fragmentation.

Our aim is to bridge the old and the new institutionalisms by explaining the response of the individual organization to pressure in the institutional field as a function of the organization's internal dynamics. Oliver (1992) did this partly, but only in outline, and there is no expansion of how the characteristics of the organizational field *interact* with the internal characteristics of an organization. Also, Oliver emphasized how institutionalized practices break down and are replaced by new ones. Our aim is to understand both persistence and change. We do so by focusing upon four aspects of an organization's internal dynamics—interests, values, power dependencies, and capacity for action.

Given the institutionalized nature of organizational sectors, what are the processes by which individual organizations adopt legitimated templates and change them? DiMaggio and Powell (1991a: 27) suspected that "something has been lost in the shift from the old to the new institutionalism" and "the goal must be a sounder multidimensional theory, rather than a one-sidedly cognitive one." They go on to suggest that "power and interests have been slighted topics in institutional analysis" (1991a: 30). This line of thought leads to the conclusion that the role of intraorganizational dynamics in accepting or rejecting institutionalized practices is critical.

The framework for understanding organizational change that we wish to advance is summarized in Figure 25-1. The Figure encompasses exogenous (market context, institutional context) and endogenous dynamics (interests, values, power dependencies, and capacity for action).

One difficulty with representing a model of change dynamics in a diagram is that the representation itself is essentially cross-sectional and linear. In fact, radical organizational change, which is shown as the outcome of the model in Figure 25-1, would become the input to market

and institutional contexts. For example, an organization that adopted a new organizational form and achieved competitive success in the marketplace would produce pressures on other organizations to adopt the same organizational form. Organizations, as Fligstein (1991: 316) noted, "extensively monitor one another," and successful practices are mimicked and institutionalized.

Exogenous variables have been discussed previously. In order to elaborate the model, first, we summarize the endogeneous components of the framework that act as precipitating dynamics and, second, we summarize those that are enabling dynamics.

Precipitating Dynamics

From our perspective, it is necessary to take seriously the internal complexity of organizations (i.e., every organization is a mosaic of groups structured by functional tasks and employment status). Thus, in accounting firms there are separate functional groups for audit work, tax activities, small business practices, insolvency, and management consultancy. Within each of these groups are "students," "managers," and "partners." Blau's (1974) analysis of organizational structuring demonstrated that complex organizations handle growth and/or contextual complexity by differentiation into groups, each of which is focused on specialized tasks. The process of specialization leads to significant differences between groups in terms of structural arrangements (e.g., Lawrence & Lorsch, 1967) and orientation (e.g., Payne & Mansfield, 1973; Payne & Pugh, 1976; Pheysey, Payne, & Pugh, 1971).

However, central to our perspective is the role of "interests" and "value commitments." Functionally differentiated groups are not neutral and indifferent to other groups. Much of the work on differentiation and conflict in organizations (Lawrence & Lorsch, 1967) shows how technical boundaries between departments and sections are reinforced and buttressed by cognitive boundaries. Thus, in any organization are the seeds of alternative ways of viewing the purposes of that organization, the ways in which it might be appropriately organized, and the ways in which actions might be evaluated. This view is very much reflected in the old institutionalism of Selznick (1949).

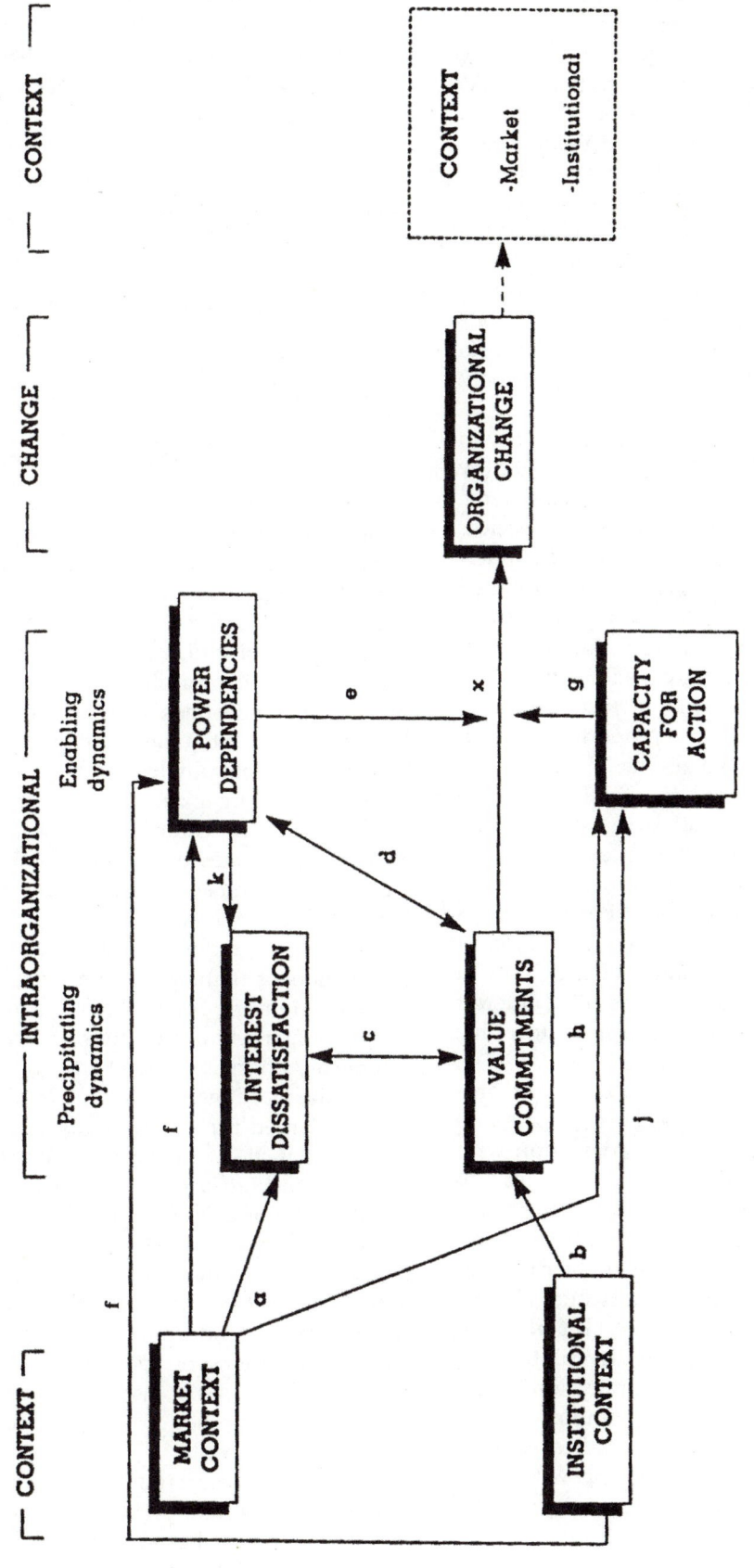

Figure 25-1 Model for Understanding Organizational Change

One outcome of such organizational differentiation is that groups seek to translate their interests into favorable allocations of scarce and valued organizational resources. As Palmer, Jennings, and Zhou (1993: 103) put it: "Organizations are. . . . arenas in which coalitions with different interests and capacities for influence vie for dominance." A potential pressure for change and/or inertia, therefore, is the extent to which groups are dissatisfied with how their interests are accommodated within an organization. A high measure of dissatisfaction becomes a pressure for change (Covaleski & Dirsmith, 1988; Walsh, Hinings, Greenwood, & Ranson, 1981).

We would expect organizations to vary in the extent to which they are characterized by interest dissatisfaction, for two reasons. First, organizations develop portfolios of services that vary in scope and balance. Arthur Andersen, for example, has aggressively promoted management consulting (especially in information technology), and the result has been that consulting income constitutes 45% of the firm's income (*Public Accounting Report*, 1995). In other accounting firms, the proportion is much lower. Arthur Andersen also has a smaller proportion of partners to total members employed, and the result is that income per partner is higher than the industry average. These differences in operating practices influence the relative sizes of different groups within the organization and their position of advantage and disadvantage. Hence, even in the same market context, the extent of interest dissatisfaction can vary from firm to firm (line a in Figure 25-1).

Dissatisfaction, however, does not provide direction for change. Intense pressure for change arising from dissatisfaction with accommodation of interests will not lead to *radical* change, unless dissatisfied groups recognize the connection between the prevailing template (which shapes the distribution of privilege and disadvantage) and their position of disadvantage.[4] It is the possibility of an alternative template that allows recognition of that connection. Thus, what becomes critically important in explaining the possibility of radical change is the *pattern of value commitments* within the organization, of which four generic patterns can be identified:

1. *Status quo commitment*, in which all groups are committed to the prevailing institutionalized template-in-use.

2. *Indifferent commitment*, in which groups are neither committed nor opposed to the template-in-use. This situation is frequently one of unwitting acquiescence.[5]

3. *Competitive commitment*, in which some groups support the template-in-use, whereas others prefer an articulated alternative. (The articulated alternative would have its origins in the institutional context.)

4. *Reformative commitment*, in which all groups are opposed to the template-in-use and prefer an articulated alternative.

Organizations will vary in their patterns of value commitments partly because of their different locations within the institutional sector (line b in Figure 25-1). As Leblebici and colleagues (1991) showed, organizations that are more peripheral and thus less embedded are less committed to prevailing practices and readier to develop new ones. They lack the intensity of commitment to the status quo found in firms that are more centrally located within the institutional field. Organizations also vary in their patterns of value commitments because they have different rates of success in the marketplace and respond accordingly. Thus, the growing maturity in the audit market coupled with the decline in perceived client loyalty (Greenwood, Cooper, Hinings, & Brown. 1993) has caused accounting firms to develop more professional marketing functions. Similarly, the complexity of organizational arrangements following the mega mergers of the 1980s led some of the enlarged firms to strengthen the human resource function. By hiring nonaccountants from *other institutional sectors*, new sets of expectations and thus commitments to ways of doing things are built into the organization (line b in Figure 25-1). Put more formally, organizations with *high structural differentiation* (Lawrence. & Lorsch, 1967) tend to have greater conflict among the groups of specialists. Each group may adhere to a set of institutional norms that is different from other groups, producing competitive commitment.

Thus far, interests and values have been described as discrete precipitators of pressure for change. In fact, they are linked (line c in Figure 25-1). One of the crucial attributes of values is that they become taken for granted and can serve to mute or temper expressions of dissatisfaction. That is, dissatisfied groups may not recognize that the prevailing template is a cause of that disadvantage. The role of value commitments is thus critical. because there is no direct link from interests to radical change, only from interests to convergent change. Radical change will occur only if interests become associated with a competitive or reformative pattern of value commitment (line x in Figure 25-1).

For example, management consultants within the accounting industry became cuckoos in the nest, increasingly producing greater shares of revenues and growth and yet being denied full reward (in terms of remuneration and status) for doing so. As a consequence, management consultants in several accounting firms became dissatisfied with their interests and began to question the organizational assumptions of how things were done (i.e., their commitment to the template-in-use, which favored the accounting profession, began to erode). The pattern of value commitments in these firms thus moved from a status quo pattern to a competitive pattern, *even though institutional pressures were unchanged*. In most accounting firms, an uneasy tension arose between accountants and consultants, as each profession became committed to different archetypes (*Business Week*, 1988; Stevens, 1991).

Competitive commitments, we have noted, can occur even in tightly coupled institutional fields, but if the degree of structuring is relatively modest, ideas and possibilities become more easily expressed and articulated. In situations of inconsistent cues and the absence of reinforcing institutional mechanisms, alternative templates develop and can be promoted by dissatisfied groups (line c in Figure 25-1). In this way, market and institutional contexts interact with interests and value commitments to create pressures for change. Pressures from the market and institutional contexts, in other words, precipitate the desire for change and, as we have stressed, the intensity of the pressure will likely vary from one organization to the next. The *direction* of change or of inertia is a function of the pattern of value commitments. Thus,

Hypothesis 10: Radical change will occur if the pattern of value commitments is competitive or reformative, irrespective of market and institutional pressures.

Hypothesis 11: Interest dissatisfaction will lead to radical change only if it is associated with a competitive or reformative pattern of value commitments. Otherwise, interest dissatisfaction will precipitate convergent change.

Hypothesis 12: A reformative or competitive pattern of value commitments is more likely to occur (a) in peripheral rather than core organizations, (b) in organizations with a complex portfolio of product/services, and (c) in institutional contexts that are loosely structured.

In terms of the speed of change, it seems reasonable to suggest that a reformative commitment will be associated with revolutionary change because of the absence of resistance. A competitive change, in contrast, is more likely to be evolutionary in pacing as resistance occurs. Thus,

Hypothesis 13: A reformative commitment will be associated with revolutionary change.
Hypothesis 14: A competitive commitment will be associated with evolutionary change.

Enabling Dynamics

Internal pressures for change, in summary, derive from interest dissatisfaction and the pattern of value commitments. The intensity of those pressures is the outcome of their links with market and institutional contexts. Radical change, however, will occur only in conjunction with an appropriate "capacity for action" and supportive power dependencies. Capacity for action and power dependencies are the *enablers* of radical change.

A political model of organizational change that starts from groups with different beliefs and interests must incorporate power (Clegg, 1975). Groups use favorable power dependencies to promote their interests (line k in Figure 25-1): As Fligstein (1991: 313) noted, "Change . . . can only occur when either a new set of actors gains power or it is in the interest of those in power to alter the organization's goals." An interesting twist in recent studies has been recognition that radical change cannot be nakedly prescribed, but it is better accomplished by appeals to normative "visions" (Collins & Porras, 1991).

Organizationally defined groups vary in their ability to influence organizational change because they have differential power. Some groups and individuals are listened to more keenly than others. Some have more potential or less potential for enabling or resisting change. The relations of power and domination that enable some organizational members to constitute and recreate organizational structures according to their preferences thus becomes a critical point of focus (Pettigrew, 1985: Ranson et al., 1980). The operation of values and interests can be conceptualized and understood only in relation to the differential power of groups.

There is a reciprocal relationship between power dependencies and value commitments (line d in Figure 25-1). Any normative scheme implies differential access to and control over key decision processes within organizations. In this sense, the prevailing archetypal template in an organization "gives" power to some groups and not to others. To the extent that groups recognize this link, it will be to their advantage to promote the norms of that template. Positions of power also can be used to buttress the prevailing archetype (Covaleski & Dirsmith, 1988). Hence, in a situation of a competitive pattern of commitment, radical change would not be the likely outcome, *unless* those in positions of privilege and power were in favor of the proposed change. Power dependencies either enable or suppress radical organizational change (line e in Figure 25-1).

It is when one explores the role of power that the interaction of market and institutional contexts becomes apparent. The resource dependence model (Pfeffer & Salancik, 1978) expresses one logic of change by tracking the effects that changes in market pressures have on power dependencies within the organization, which then enables change. That is, the precipitator of change (for the resource dependence model) is the market context, which, when the salience of some issues is raised relative to others (e.g.. the need for aggressive marketing of accounting services), alters the relative power of groups (line t in Figure 25-1) within the organization (e.g., marketing specialists. vis-à-vis audit practitioners) and leads to the executive succession link. The new executive

then introduces radical organizational change. That is, the resource dependence model posits a direct link among market changes, power dependencies, and radical change. (This line of reasoning is consistent with Fligstein's, 1991, account of the evolution of the M-Form organization in the United States. Fligstein showed how changes in the market context led to changes in the relative power of functional groups within the American corporation—specifically, from manufacturing, to sales and marketing, to finance—which led to shifts in strategy and organization from the vertically integrated undiversified form, through the related diversification model, to the unrelated diversified corporation.)

We suggest that the resource dependence thesis complements the institutionalist perspective, because market pressures may well reconfigure power relationships within an organization. However, the institutional context also acts to configure the power and status of groups within an organization (line i in Figure 25-1) and not necessarily in a manner consistent with market exigencies. For example, accounting firms universally have accorded high status and power to professional accountants, compared to both consultants and professional managers (e.g., marketing and human resource) despite the growing importance of these latter professions in generating revenue. In other words, the institutional context might *nullify* pressures from the market context. Alternatively, institutional pressures, even without market pressures, might shift power dependencies in favor of groups that prefer an alternative template to the existing one.

Most important, shifts in power dependencies, whether brought about by market and/or institutional pressures, will produce radical change *only* if the dominant coalition recognizes the weaknesses of existing template arrangements *and* is aware of potential alternatives. That is, users of the resource dependence model *assume* that there exists a competitive value commitment within an organization (which may not be correct) and also assume that as changes in power occur, alternative templates will be introduced. In our model, we propose that there are *several* possible patterns of commitment, which means that changes in power dependencies within an organization may or may *not* lead to radical change.

Enabling power dependencies will lead to radical change *only* if alternatives to the prevailing archetypal template are *known*. This is similar to Fligstein's note that "shocks or instability still require that actors develop a set of solutions based on their interpretation of the shock, which will generally reflect their position in the organization and the interests of that position" (1991: 316). Change occurs where power dependencies *combine* with either a competitive or reformative pattern of value commitments. Thus,

> *Hypothesis 15: Radical change will not occur without an enabling pattern of power dependencies combined with either a reformative or competitive pattern of value commitments.*

The second enabling dynamic—capacity for action—is the ability to *manage* the transition process from one template to another, which has three aspects.[6] Radical change cannot occur without the organization's having sufficient *understanding* of the new conceptual destination, its *having* the skills and competencies required to function in that new destination, *and* its having the ability to manage how to get to that destination. The importance of capacity for action has been alluded to by other authors (Carnall, 1990; Clarke, 1994; Fombrun, 1992; Nadler & Tushman, 1989; Tichy, 1983). Nadler and Tushman (1990), in their discussion of leadership and change, distinguished among three sets of leadership activities: charismatic (envisioning, energizing, and enabling), instrumental (structuring, controlling, and rewarding), and institutional (ensuring changes stick). These activities have to be performed by multiple actors. In our terms, capacity for action embraces both the *availability* of these skills and resources within an organization *and* their *mobilization*. Mobilization, in this sense, is the act of leadership. Capacity for action is also consistent with Amburgey and colleagues' work (1993), which showed that organizations with recent experience of change are more likely to attempt further change. In our terms, experience increases capacity for action. Capacity for action is an enabling dynamic because without it radical organizational change will not occur (line g in Figure 25-1). By itself, however, capacity for action would not be expected to precipitate change—there has to be a motivation for change driven by the precipitating dynamics. Thus,

> *Hypothesis 16: Radical change will not occur without a sufficient enabling capacity for action combined with either a reformative or competitive pattern of value commitments.*

Capacity for action may influence the speed by which radical change is accomplished. A clear understanding of the new destination and of how to get to that destination may give an organization the confidence to push ahead rapidly with change. On the other hand, lack of clarity and lack of expertise may promote lack of sureness and slower, almost experimental steps. Thus,

> *Hypothesis 17: High capacity for action will be associated with revolutionary change.*

Figure 25-1 shows capacity for action linked to the market context (line h). The recruitment of marketing and human resource management specialists into accounting firms illustrates how the market context is connected to capacity for action. Recruited ostensibly to introduce new marketing and human resource management practices, these employees often brought to the organization the experience of governing and organizing in fundamentally different ways. Their previous employment in corporate organizations (e.g., Proctor and Gamble) introduced within the accounting firm an awareness of alternatives to the professional partnership form of organization and a knowledge of how to operate such alternatives. Similarly, the experience of mega mergers undertaken in response to perceived market pressures (Greenwood, Hinings, & Brown, 1994) provided accounting firms with significant experience of managing change. In other words; developments in the market context can have an impact on the level of capacity for action in the organization, increasing the *possibility* for radical change.

The capacity for action might also be shaped or constricted by the institutional context (line j in Figure 25-1). Deeply embedded firms may be prevented by the institutional context from developing an action capability. That is, organizations that are centrally located within an institutional context may be less likely to develop the specialties and competencies of an alternative archetype. Peripheral organizations, in contrast, may develop these competencies because they are less fully socialized by the context. In this sense, the institutional context can act to limit the development of capacities for action in some but not all organizations. However, the context itself might fundamentally shift and articulate a new template, as occurred in Hinings and Greenwood's (1988a) study of municipal governments in the United Kingdom. In this scenario, the institutional context serves to articulate the need for new competencies and promotes the development of capacities for action.

Power dependencies and capacity for action are necessary but not sufficient conditions for radical organizational change. By themselves they will not lead to radical change, but they can and do enable or constrain it.

Conclusions

In the introduction to a collection of articles that summarized the current position of institutional theory, DiMaggio and Powell (1991a: 27) stated that "one of the principal goals of this volume is to address head on the issues of change, power, and efficiency." They saw these three issues as neglected in the historical development of institutional theory. Our emphasis has been to develop the contribution of institutional theory in order to understand radical organizational change. In particular, we have focused on the interplay of contextual forces and intraorganizational dynamics.

In making this attempt we also see ourselves dealing with two other points made by DiMaggio and Powell (1991a). The first point relates to the relationship between the "old" and "new" institutionalism (DiMaggio & Powell, 1991a: 11–5, especially Table 1.1). New institutionalism, these authors suggest, is primarily related to organizations-in-sectors, whereas the old institutionalism centers on the individual organization. We have attempted to build something of a bridge over this gap, both posing and trying to answer the question: What are the processes by which individual organizations adopt and discard templates for organizing, given the institutionalized nature of organizational fields (neo-institutionalism)? We have tried to show how the external processes of deinstitutionalization have to be

understood (organizations-in-sectors) *together with* the internal dynamics of interpretation, adoption, and rejection by the individual organization.

We have also suggested that the understanding of radical change requires more than an analysis of the institutional arena or sector. There must be a concern with patterns of value commitments, power dependencies, interests, and capacity for action within the organization. Typically, institutional theorists have informed our thinking about the nature of institutional pressures toward conformity and uniformity. They have emphasized the exogenous nature of change, which emanates from the realm of ideas and legitimacy. But understanding change is about understanding variations in response to the same pressures, which can only be done by analyzing the features of organizations that produce adoption and diffusion rather than resistance and inertia. The model of radical change developed here is about such understanding.

Future Directions

A central message of this article is that to understand the incidence and pacing of radical organizational change, in particular the differences between organizations as they respond to apparently similar contextual pressures, it is necessary to understand the play of intraorganizational dynamics. These dynamics have been defined as the pattern of value commitments, dissatisfaction with interests, power dependencies, and capacities for action. These dynamics are largely the product of ongoing studies into the accounting and law industries (Hinings, Brown, & Greenwood, 1991) and earlier work into the municipal sector in the United Kingdom (Hinings & Greenwood, 1988a; Greenwood & Hinings, 1993). An obvious requirement is examination of the applicability of the ideas to other sectors, especially less mature and less homogeneous sectors. Our suggestions at this point, however, concern the role of the dynamics in explaining why organizations respond differently to the same contextual pressures, which implies comparisons between organizations in the same sector. Two questions seem particularly important:

1. What are the determinants of a reformative or competitive commitment (i.e., of normative fragmentation)?

2. How do precipitating and enabling dynamics interact to respond to increasing pressures for change?

What are the determinants of normative fragmentation? Central to the framework is that radical organizational change will occur only if the pattern of value commitments is either reformative or competitive (*and* associated with favorable power dependencies and capacity for action). A key research endeavor, therefore, would be to identify what increases the likelihood of a competitive or reformative pattern of value commitments. In which situations is the researcher likely to find erosion of commitment to a prevailing archetype-in-use and development of either a competitive or reformative commitment? What are the precursors of "deinstitutionalization" (Oliver, 1992) *within* the organization?

Numerous factors might cause such an erosion of commitment, and several are noted in the change literature. In particular, performance problems and crises act to trigger political dissensus over existing arrangements and permit groups less committed to prevailing practices to more legitimately raise and promote alternative perspectives (e.g., Child & Smith, 1987; Oliver, 1992; Pettigrew, 1985; Tushman & Romanelli, 1985). This occurred in the local government sector of the United Kingdom, as groups such as corporate planning units and administrative departments espoused the logic of corporate planning as preferable to traditional professional practices as a means of handling social and urban problems (Hinings & Greenwood, 1988a). The pressure for change was contextual but amplified by groups within the organization. The push of management consultants within accounting firms for a new approach to management, in contrast, was the product of the dissatisfaction with their share of organizational resources (compensation *and* influence) rather than poor organizational performance. Precipitators of change, as we have shown previously, can be contextually or internally driven.

Hinings and Greenwood (1988b) pointed out that it may be quite unusual for the market and institutional contexts to produce strong, consistent signals about the need to change to a new archetype. There may well be conflictive institutional signals. This conflict currently can be seen in the law sector, where there are not only pressures from the market for organizations to become more corporate but also pressures from regulators for organizations to remain groups of autonomous professionals. The result may well be high levels of competitive commitment and the existence of sedimentation of values, structures, and systems (Cooper et al., In press) and unresolved excursions (Hinings & Greenwood, 1988a).

A second possible cause of erosion of commitment to a prevailing archetype would be increasing representation of ideas and views within the workforce, which cause "normative fragmentation" (Oliver, 1992: 575). An increasing representation of ideas and views would follow changes in the composition of the workforce (e.g., increasing diversity, turnover of personnel), changes in the portfolio of activities (e.g., the development of new "products," such as management consultancy within accounting firms), and changes in specializations within the organization (e.g., the growth of forensic accountants). The common theme of these developments is that organizational differentiation, both in the way that Lawrence and Lorsch (1967) and Blau and Schoenherr (1971) used those terms, increases the possibility of normative disagreement.

Even a superficial reflection on the forces that might lead to normative fragmentation indicates that some contemporary organizations are likely to experience fragmentation. Most studies of the future workplace stress increasing workforce diversity (e.g., Boyett & Conn, 1991; Krahn & Lowe, 1993). Similarly, the trend of contemporary society has been toward increased specialization of knowledge and thus of occupational differentiation. (For example, the accounting profession has for some years operated through four major divisions: audit and accountancy, insolvency/corporate recovery, tax, and small/independent business.) Recently, however, new specializations have developed—forensic accounting, environmental accounting. and so forth (Lawrence, 1993). These trends suggest that more organizations will experience normative fragmentation and dissensus than may have been the case previously.

This line of research would explore the extent to which increasing workforce diversity and structural differentiation is associated with normative fragmentation and thus competitive value commitments. Sites where this might occur would include companies growing through mergers and/or acquisitions or organizations that have recently experienced severe market/funding challenges. In these situations, it would be informative to trace how the changes either "produce" or "do not produce" competitive commitments.

Hinings and Greenwood (1988a), from their studies of municipalities, found that change occurs more quickly where organizational size is small, where there is low structural and task complexity, and where mergers and amalgamations sharpen the search for a relevant organizational form to cope with the new situation.

How do precipitating and enabling dynamics interact in response to pressure for change? Understanding the causes or conditions of normative fragmentation is a preface to the key task of uncovering how precipitating and enabling dynamics interact in response to pressures for change. At present. we know relatively little of these interactions. Probably, both detailed case comparisons and broader examinations are required.

Kikulis and colleagues (1995) and Fligstein (1991) gave indications of how broad surveys might provide insights into the play of intraorganizational dynamics. Kikulis and colleagues examined the adoption by sports organizations in Canada of a more professional approach to management. They showed how some organizations were much earlier movers than others and how some retained more traditional practices. By comparing these three groups (early movers, late movers, and nonmovers) it would be possible to ascertain whether the timing or absence of movement was a function of differences in precipitating and/or enabling dynamics. Given a large enough sample, researchers could gain insights into whether early movers tend to be those with reformative commitments (i.e., no resistance) and that have a high capacity for action, or whether there is a range of configurations conducive to early movement (e.g., competitive commitment plus favorable power dependencies plus capacity for action). Similarly, it would be interesting and not too difficult to observe whether late movers begin either with unfavorable precipitating dynamics

(e.g., status quo commitment) or with unfavorable enabling dynamics (inappropriate power dependencies and/or low capacity for action). Furthermore, late movers would provide some understanding of what it is that changes in order that change can occur (is it a shift from reformative to competitive commitments, or reconstitution of power dependencies, or acquisition of capacity for action?).

Fligstein's (1991) study of the adoption of strategies of diversification and associated organizational structures, by the *Fortune* 100, from 1919 to 1979, provides another example of how some of the basic parameters of the intraorganizational dynamics might work. He showed that organizational change followed appointment of a CEO from a different functional background, who provided a "new view of the firm's strategy" (Fligstein, 1991: 334). Appointment of a CEO with a new functional background reflected a redistribution of power dependencies. From our perspective, it is the analysis of historical data of large numbers of organizations and the comparison of early and late movers that enables some insights to be gleaned into the workings of intraorganizational dynamics.

Comparative studies that have the scope of those conducted by Fligstein (1991) and by Kikulis and colleagues (1995) can only go so far in uncovering the role of intraorganizational dynamics. Equally necessary are more detailed studies that permit the careful assessment of nonlinear processes. Previously we suggested that the study of sports organizations could have identified first movers and late movers and traced differences between them. But to fully understand (a) *how* new archetypal templates are uncovered, (b) *which* organizational actors uncover them (e.g., by monitoring other organizations), and (c) how they are *used* within the organization requires the case study method. Is it usually disadvantaged groups (i.e., those with high interest dissatisfaction) that are sensitive to new archetypal possibilities, or is it those with greater exposure to contextual change? For example, are members who cross the organizational boundary and come into contact with new ideas and possibilities more likely to question existing archetypal arrangements, or is it those who are dissatisfied with their share of scarce and valued organizational resources?

There is also the need to understand how new ideas become legitimated within the organization. In situations of a competitive commitment, power dependencies determine which view prevails. However, how do groups that do not have power but prefer change obtain sufficient power to effect change? Do these groups convince others that changes are desirable? From an institutional perspective, changes brought about by the latter method are more likely to be sustainable. But under what circumstances and for what reasons do privileged groups accept radical change and diminished privilege?

Our previous work on the adoption of new archetypes in a highly institutionalized sector, British local government, provides some insight into how these dynamics might play out (Hinings & Greenwood, 1988a). The development of movement away from an archetype depends on the existence of an articulated alternative organizational form and a leadership and power structure that allows alternatives to be expressed in arenas that matter. For an organization to move toward an institutionally novel archetype, a high degree of organizational capacity is needed. That initial movement toward a new archetype is consolidated through a spreading of commitment to change and a gradual tightening of the power structure. However, in an organization, a high value propensity to change and a low resistance to change are sufficient conditions to produce structural change, regardless of context, interests, and power.

In contrast, change can be blocked through a concentrated power structure (elite domination) and/or an active, transformational leadership that continuously reaffirms the importance. efficiency, and effectiveness of the current archetype. Sufficient conditions for no change become a high resistance to change by a dominant coalition with a concentrated power structure, regardless of the values held by the non-elite.

Both of the (big) questions we have raised as future directions generate questions of relationship with two other areas of theorizing, organizational cognition and organizational learning. Scott (1991) suggested that the new institutionalism places more emphasis on cognitive factors than did the old institutionalism, and DiMaggio and Powell (1991a: 29) charac-

terized our previous work as institutional theory with "a cognitive spin." Walsh (1995: 311) reviewed the field of managerial and organizational cognition, examining the "representation, use, and development of the content and structure of knowledge structures." Clearly, in dealing with value commitments and capacity for action, we are dealing with knowledge structures and hypothesizing that radical change involves changes in them. A link can be made to the questions that Walsh (1995: 307) raised, such as "the rate, magnitude, and locus of knowledge structure change" that is involved in radical organizational change and the extent to which institutional redefinition involves changes in knowledge structures. Certainly, the possible overlap of conceptual categories should be examined.

Similarly, organizational change requires organizational learning. Not only is there a link between change and learning but there is also a link between learning and cognition. Change from one archetype to another involves designing new organizational structures and systems, learning new behaviors, and interpreting phenomena in new ways. How do group members acquire and learn these new behaviors and interpretations? How are the values contained in new archetypes diffused to different groups in the organization?

Methodological Assumptions

The previous discussion has touched on a number of methodological themes that require amplification. The first is that archetypes exist and can be observed empirically: indeed, they have to be because they are the basis of the definition of radical change. The means of uncovering and measuring archetypes has been provided in other studies (Greenwood & Hinings, 1993). It involves immersion within an institutional sector such that a detailed understanding is obtained of that sector. In particular, the different interpretive schemes have to be unearthed, and the implications they have for organizational design must be worked through.

Using archetypes as the basis for understanding the dynamics of organizational change means that research has to be based on populations of organizations that are subject to similar institutional pressures. Most likely this will be situated in an industry sector, something which is quite usual in institutional theory. However, it could be based on organizational sets from different sectors, in which there are similar pressures for organizational change, for example, the work exemplified in Fligstein's (1991) study of the *Fortune* 100. Large-scale comparative studies such as those of Tolbert and Zucker (1991), Fligstein (1991), Baum and Oliver (1991), Palmer et al. (1993), and Kikulis et al. (1995) are necessary to establish (a) the changes in structures and systems that have taken place in a population and (b) the ways in which these changes coincide with institutional templates. However, these studies are limited in what they can show regarding the processes and dynamics through which individual organizations either do or do not adopt new institutional prescriptions.

As a result, detailed comparative case studies are required, and, if possible, in real time. There are a number of reasons for case studies. First, the conceptual framework that we have outlined in Figure 25-1 contains a number of concepts that are difficult to measure (e.g., power, interests, and leadership). These concepts tend to be highly sensitive to context in their operation. Second, radical organizational change takes place over lengthy periods of time. A number of researchers (cf. Nadler & Tushman, 1989; Miller, 1990; Huber & Van de Ven, 1995) suggested that not less than three years is required to gain some indication of how such changes are proceeding. To establish the interactions of precipitating and enabling dynamics in the light of institutional pressures over such time periods requires careful case study research (cf. Barley, 1986).

The third and very important point is that it is likely that radical organizational change is the product of processes that are oscillatory and iterative. Much organization theory operates, at least implicitly, with a linear perspective. That is, outcomes (in the present instance, radical organizational change) are treated as the product of sequential interactions between a given set of variables. In one sense, Figure 25-1 is laid out in this fashion. However, radical organizational change occurs in ways that are iterative, and close attention to such iterations is required to truly understand the dynamics. It is improbable that a single, simple line of causation will explain the occurrence of radical change. Instead, different combinations

of interactions between precipitating and enabling dynamics are possible.

Concluding Remarks

It would be possible to elaborate further possible research directions, each based on some combination of the elements of the intraorganizational dynamics. However, our concluding and key points are somewhat more general. The first is that institutional theory does, in fact, have a contribution to make to understanding organizational change, which goes beyond the ideas of inertia and persistence. But this can only happen when the old and the new institutionalism are combined in a neo-institutionalist framework. As so often happens in the evolution of theoretical areas, there is a period of movement away from starting points, a process of rediscovery of those starting points, and the "reincorporation" of these points into existing theory. We have attempted to start this task.

A second key point is that it is when theorists research the *interaction* of organizational actors with institutionalized contexts that they will find new directions. It is in the intersection of two forces that explanations of change and stability can be found. On the one hand, institutions are shapers of organizational arrangements (Jepperson, 1991; Jepperson & Meyer, 1991). On the other hand, key actors in organizations articulate views of strategy and have the power to implement that view (Fligstein, 1991). As Brint and Karabel (1991: 343) put it, "we wish to make a distinction, then, between the sociology of institutional forms and the sociology of institutional change." This distinction raises questions of why particular archetypal templates are chosen over possible alternatives and why those templates change in particular directions over time.

This observation leads directly to our final key point. The action of values, interests, power, and capacity within an organization must be brought into play. *However*, this action has to be located in the groups that make up any particular organization. Action is not disembodied; it comes from organizational actors who have positions, skills, commitments, and histories that are primarily found in the groups of which those actors are members. Change and stability are understood through the ways in which organizational group members react to old and new institutionally derived ideas through their already existing commitments and interests and their ability to implement or enforce them by way of their existing power and capability.

References

Amburgey, T. L., Kelly, D., & Barnett, W. P. 1993. Resetting the clock: The dynamics of organizational change and failure. *Administrative Science Quarterly*, 38: 51–73.

Astley, W. G., & Van de Ven, A. 1983. Central perspectives and debates in organization theory. *Administrative Science Quarterly*, 28: 245–273.

Barley, S. R. 1986. Technology as an occasion for structuring: Evidence from observations of CT scanners and the social order of radiology departments. *Administrative Science Quarterly*, 31: 78–108.

Barnett, W. P. & Carroll, G. R. 1987. Competition and mutualism among early telephone companies. *Administrative Science Quarterly*, 32: 400–421.

Baron, J. P., Dobbin, F., & Jennings, P. D. 1986. War and peace: The evolution of modern personnel administration in the U.S. industry. *American Journal of Sociology*, 92: 250–283.

Bartunek, J. M. 1984. Changing interpretive schemes and organizational restructuring: The example of a religious order. *Administrative Science Quarterly*, 29: 355–372.

Baum, J., A. & Oliver, C. 1991. Institutional linkages and organizational mortality. *Administrative Science Quarterly*, 36: 187–218.

Blau, P. M. 1974. *On the nature of organizations.* New York: Wiley.

Blau, P. M., & McKinley, W. 1979. Ideas, complexity and innovation. *Administrative Science Quarterly*, 24: 200–219.

Blau, P. M. & Schoenherr, R. A. 1971. *The structure of organizations.* New York: Basic Books.

Boyett, J. H. & Conn, H. P. 1991. *Workplace 2000: The revolution reshaping American business.* New York: Dutton.

Brint, S. & Karabel, J. 1991. Institutional origins and transformations: The case of American community colleges. In W. W. Powell & P.J. DiMaggio (Eds.), *The new institutionalism in organizational analysis,* 337–360. Chicago: University of Chicago Press.

Buchko, A. A. 1994. Barriers to strategic transformation. In P. Shrivastava, A. Huff, & J. Dutton (Eds.), *Advances in strategic management,* vol. 10: 81–106. Greenwich, CT: JAI Press.

Burns, L R. & Wholey, D. R. 1993. Adoption and abandonment of matrix management programs: Effects of organizational characteristics and interorganizational networks. *Acedemy of Management Journal*, 36: 106–138.

Business Week. 1988. An identity crisis at Arthur Andersen. October 24: 34.

Carnall, C. A. 1990. *Managing change in organizations.* New York: Prentice Hall.

Carroll, G. R, Goodstein, J., & Gyenes, A. 1988. Organizations and the state: Effects of the institutional environment on agricultural cooperatives in Hungary. *Administrative Science Quarterly*, 33: 233–256.

Child, J., 1972. Organization structure, environment and performance: The role of strategic choice. *Sociology.* 6:1–22.

Child, J., & Smith, C. 1987. The context and process of organizational transformation. *Journal of Management Studies.* 24: 585–593.

Clark. B. R. 1960. *The open-door colleges: A case study.* New York: McGraw-Hill.

Clark, B. R. 1972. The organizational saga in higher education. *Administrative Science Quarterly.* 17: 178–184.

Clarke, L. 1994. *The essence of change.* New York: Prentice Hall.

Clegg, S. 1975. *Power, rule and domination.* London: Routledge & Kegan Paul.

Collins, J. C., & Porras, J. I. 1991. Organizational vision and visionary organizations. *California Management Review.* 34(1): 30–52.

Cooper, D. J., Hinings, C. R., Greenwood, R., & Brown, J. L. In press. Sedimentation and transformation in professional service firms. *Organization Studies.*

Covaleski, M. A.. & Dirsmith, M. W. 1988. An institutional perspective on the rise, social transformation, and fall of a university budget category. *Administrative Science Quarterly.* 33: 562–587.

D'Aunno, T., Sutton, R. I., & Price, R. H. 1991. Isomorphism and external support in conflicting institutional environments: A study at drug abuse treatment units. *Academy of Management Journal.* 34: 636–681.

D'Aveni, R. A. 1994. *Hyper-competition.* New York: Free Press.

Davis, G. F. 1991. Agents without principles? The spread of the poison pill through the intercorporate network. *Administrative Science Quarterly.* 36: 583–613.

Davis, G. F., & Powell, W. W. 1992. Organization-environment relations. In M. D. Dunette & L. M. Hough (Eds.), *Handbook of industrial and organizational psychology:* 315–376. Palo Alto, CA: Consulting Psychologists Press.

DiMaggio, P. J. 1991. Constructing an organizational field as a professional project: U.S. art museums, 1920–1940. In W. W. Powell & P. J. DiMaggio (Eds.), *The new institutionalism in organizational analysis:* 287–292. Chicago: University of Chicago Press.

DiMaggio, P. J., & Powell, W. W. 1983. The iron cage revisited: Institutional isomorphism and collective rationality in organizational fields. *American Sociological Review*. 48:147–160.

DiMaggio, P. J. & Powell. W. W. 1991a. Introduction. In W. W. Powell & P. J. DiMaggio (Ed.), *The new institutionalism in organizational analysis*: 1–38. Chicago: University of Chicago Press.

DiMaggio. P. J.. & Powell. W. W. 1991b. The iron cage revisited: Institutional isomorphism and collective rationality in organizational fields. In W. W. Powell & P. J. DiMaggio (Ed.), *The new institution in organizational analysis*: 63–82. Chicago: University of Chicago Press.

Dougherty, D. 1994. Commentary. In P. Shrivastava, A. Huff & J. Dutton (Eds.), *Advances in strategic management*. vol. 10: 107–112. Greenwich. CT: JAI Press.

Drazin, R. & Van de Ven, A. H. 1985. Alternative forms of fit in contingency theory. *Administrative Science Quarterly*. 30: 514–539.

European Accounting Focus. 1994. KPMG Incorporation. October: 1.

Fligstein, N. 1985. The spread of the multidivisional form among large firms, 1919–1979. *American Sociological Review,* 50: 377–391.

Fligstein. N. 1991. The structural transformation of American industry: An institutional account of the causes of diversification in the largest firms, 1919–1979. In W. W. Powell & P. J. DiMaggio (Eds.), *The new institutionalism in organizational analysis*: 311–336. Chicago: University of Chicago Press.

Fombrun, C. 1992. *Turning points: Creating strategic change in corporations*. New York: McGraw-Hill.

Galaskiewicz, J., & Wasserman, S. 1989. Mimetic and normative processes within an interorganizational field: An empirical test. *Administrative Science Quarterly*. 34: 454–479.

Ghemawat, P. 1991. *Commitment: The dynamic of strategy*. New York: Free Press.

Gilson, R. J., & Mnookin, R. H. 1988. Coming of age in a corporate law firm: The economics of associate career patterns. *Stanford Law Review*, 41: 567–595.

Greenwood, R., Cooper, D. J., Hinings, C. R., & Brown, J. L. 1993. Biggest is best? Strategic assumptions and actions in the Canadian audit industry. *Canadian Journal of Administrative Sciences*, 10: 308–321.

Greenwood, R., & Hinings, C. R. 1988. Design archetypes, tracks and the dynamics of strategic change. *Organization Studies*, 9: 293–316.

Greenwood, R., & Hinings, C. R. 1993. Understanding strategic change: The contribution of archetypes. *Academy of Management Journal*. 36: 1052–1081.

Greenwood, R., Hinings, C. R., & Brown,. 1990. The P2-form of strategic management: Corporate practices in the professional partnership. *Academy of Management JournaL* 33:725–755.

Greenwood, R., Hinings, C. R., & Brown, J. L. 1994. Merging professional service firms. *Organization Science*. 5: 239–257.

Hannan, M. T., & Freeman, J. H. 1989. *Organizational ecology*. Cambridge, MA.:Harvard University Press.

Haunschild. P. R. 1993. Interorganizational imitation: The impact of interlocks on corporate acquisition activity. *Administrative Science Quarterly*. 38: 564–592.

Haveman, H. A. 1993. Follow the leader Mimetic isomorphism and entry into new markets. *Administrative Science Quarterly*. 38: 564–592.

Hinings, C. R., Brown, J. L., & Greenwood, R. 1991. Change in an autonomous professional organization. *Journal of Management Studies*. 28: 375–393.

Hinings, C. R., & Greenwood, R. 1988a. *The dynamics of strategic change*. Oxford. England: Basil Blackwell.

Hinings, C. R. & Greenwood. R. 1988b. The normative prescription of organizations. In L. Zucker (Ed.), *Institutional patterns and organizations*: 53–70. Cambridge, MA: Ballinger.

Hinings, C. R., Greenwood, R., Brown, J. L., & Cooper, D. In press. Organizational change: The role of archetypes, environmental dynamics and institutional ideas. *Scandinavian Journal of Management*.

Hrebiniak, L G., & Joyce, W. F. 1985. Organizational adaptation: Strategic choice and environmental determinism. *Administrative Science Quarterly*, 30: 336–349.

Huber, G. P. & Van de Ven, A. H. (Eds.). 1995. *Longitudinal field research methods*. Thousand Oaks, CA: Sage.

Jepperson, R. L. 1991. Institutions, institutional effects, and institutionalism. In W. W. Powell & P. J. DiMaggio (Ed.). *The new institutionalism in organizational analysis*: 143–163. Chicago: University of Chicago Press.

Jepperson, R. L., & Meyer, J. W. 1991. The public order and the construction of formal organizations. In W. W. Powell & P.J. DiMaggio (Eds.), *The new institutionalism in organizational analysis*: 204–231. Chicago: University of Chicago Press.

Johnson, G. 1987. *Strategic change and the management process*. Oxford, England: Basil Blackwell.

Kanter, R. M. 1983. *The change masters*. New York: Simon & Schuster.

Kikulis, L. M., Slack, T., & Hinings, C. R. 1995. Sector-specific patterns of organizational design change. *Journal of Management Studies,* 32: 87–100.

Krahn, H. J., & Lowe, G. S. 1993. *Work, industry and Canadian society* (2nd ed.). Scarboro: Nelson.

Lawrence, P. R., & Lorsch, J. W. 1967. *Organization and environment*. Boston: Harvard Business School Press.

Lawrence, T. 1993. *Institutional entrepreneurs in emerging industries*. Unpublished doctoral dissertation, University of Alberta.

Leblebici, H., Salancik, G. R., Copay, A., & King, T. 1991. Institutional change and the transformation of interorganizational fields: An organizational history of the U.S. radio broadcasting industry. *Administrative Science Quarterly*, 36: 333–363.

Ledlord, G. E., Mohrman, A. M., & Lawler, E. E. 1989. The phenomenon of large-scale organizational change. In A. M. Mohrman, S. A. Mohrman, G. E. Ledford, T. G. Cummings, E. E. Lawler, & Associates (Eds.), *Large-scale organization change*: 1–31. San Francisco: Jossey.Bass.

Meyer, A. 0., Tsui, A. S., & Hinings, C. R. 1993. Guest co-editors' introduction: Configurational approaches to organizational analysis. *Academy of Management Journal*, 36: 1175–1195.

Meyer, J. W., & Rowan, B. 1977. Institutionalized organizations: Formal structure as myth and ceremony. *American Journal of Sociology*, 83: 340–363.

Meyer, J. W., Scott, W. R., & Deal, T. 1983. Institutional and technical sources of organizational structure. In H. D. Stein (Ed.), *Organization and the human services*: 151–178. Philadelphia: Temple University Press.

Michels, R. 1962. *Political parties*. New York: Collier Press.

Miller, D. 1981. Towards a new contingency approach: The search for organizational gestalts. *Journal of Management Studies*, 18: 1–26.

Miller, D. 1982. Evolution and revolution: A quantum view of structural change in organizations. *Journal of Management Studies*. 19: 131–151.

Miller, D. 1987. Strategy making and structure: Analysis and implications for performance. *Academy of Management Journal*. 30: 7–32.

Miller, D. 1990. *The Icarus paradox*. New York: Harper Collins.

Miller, D., & Friesen, P. H. 1984. *Organizations: A quantum view*. Englewood Cliffs, NJ: Prentice Hall.

Mintzberg, H. 1983. *Structure in fives: Designing effective organizations*. Englewood Cliffs, NJ: Prentice Hall.

Mohrman, A. M., Mohrman, S. A., Ledford, G. E., Cummings, T. G., & Lawler, E. E., III. 1989. *Large-scale organizational change*. San Francisco: Jossey-Bass.

Nadler, D. A., Shaw, R. B., Walton, A. E., & Associates, 1995. *Discontinuous change*. San Francisco: Jossey-Bass.

Nadler, A. D., & Tushman, M. L. 1989. Organizational frame bending: Principles for managing reorientation. *Academy of Management Executive*. 3(3): 194–203.

Nadler, D. A. & Tushman, M. L. 1990. Beyond the charismatic leader: Leadership and organizational change. *California Management Review*. 32: 77–79.

Oliver, C. 1991. Strategic responses to institutional processes. *Academy of Management Review*. 16: 145–179.

Oliver, C. 1992. The antecedents of deinstitutionalization. *Organization Studies*. 13: 563–588.

O'Reilly, C. A., Main, B. G., & Crystal, G. S. 1988. CEO compensation as tournament and social comparison: A tale of two theories. *Administrative Science Quarterly*, 33: 257–274.

Ouchi, W. G. 1980. Markets, bureaucracies, and clans. *Administrative Science Quarterly*. 25: 129–141.

Palmer, D. A., Jennings, P. D. & Zhou, X. 1993. Late adoption of the multidivisional form by large U.S. corporations: Institutional, political, and economic accounts. *Administrative Science Quarterly*. 38: 100–131.

Payne, R. L. & Mansfield, R. 1973. Relationship of perceptions of organizational climate to organizational structure, context and hierarchical position. *Administrative Science Quarterly*. 8: 515–526.

Payne, R. L. & Pugh. D. S. 1976. Organizational structure and climate. In M. D. Dunnette (Ed.), *Handbook of industrial and organizational psychology*: 1125–1173. Chicago: Rand McNally.

Perrow, C. l985b. Overboard with myth and symbols. *American Journal of Sociology*. 91:151–155.

Perrow, C. 1979. *Complex organizations: A critical essay* (2nd ed.). New York: Random House.

Pettigrew, A. 1985. *The awakening giant*. Oxford, England: Basil Blackwell.

Pettigrew, A. 1987. Context and action in the transformation of the firm. *Journal of Management Studies*. 24: 649–670.

Pfeffer, J. 1981. *Power in organizations*. Boston: Pitman.

Pfeffer, J. 1992. *Managing with power*. Boston: Harvard Business School Press.

Pfeffer, J., & Salancik, C. H. 1978. *The external control of organizations: A resource dependence perspective*. New York: Harper & Row.

Pheysey, D. C., Payne, R. L., & Pugh, D. S. 1971. Influence of structure at organizational and group levels. *Administrative Science Quarterly*. 19: 61–73.

Powell, W. W. 1991. Expanding the scope of institutional analysis. In W. W. Powell, & P. J. DiMaggio (Eds.), *The new institutionalism in organizational analysis*: 183–203. Chicago: University of Chicago Press.

Powell, W. W. 1993. *The social construction of an organizational field: The case of biotechnology*. Paper presented at the Warwick-Venice Workshop on perspectives on strategic change. University of Warwick.

Powell, W. W., & DiMaggio, P. J. (Eds.). 1991. *The new institutionalism in organizational analysis*. Chicago: University of Chicago Press.

Public Accounting Report. 1995. Annual survey of national accounting firms. May 31:1.

Ranson, S., Hinings, C. R., & Greenwood, R. 1980. The structuring of organizational structures. *Administrative Science Quarterly*, 25: 1–7.

Scott, W. R. 1987. The adolescence of institutional theory. *Administrative Science Quarterly*, 32: 493–511.

Scott, W. R. 1991. Unpacking institutional arguments. In W. W. Powell, & P. J. DiMaggio (Eds.). *The new institutionalism in organizational analysis:* 164–182. Chicago: University of Chicago Press.

Scott, W. R. 1994. Institutions and organizations: Toward a theoretical synthesis. In W. R. Scott & J. W. Meyer (Eds.), *Institutional environments and organizations:* 55–80. Thousand Oaks, CA: Sage.

Scott, W. R., & Meyer, J. W. 1983. The organization of societal sectors. In J. W. Meyer & W. R. Scott (Eds.), *Organizational environments, Ritual and rationality:* 129–153.

Scott, W. R., & Meyer, J. W. 1991. The organization of societal sectors: Propositions and early evidence. In W. W. Powell & P. J. DiMaggio (Eds.), *The new institutionalism in organizational analysis:* 108–140. Chicago: University of Chicago Press.

Scott, W. R., & Meyer, J. W. (Eds.). 1994. *Institutional environments and organizations.* Thousand Oaks, CA: Sage.

Selznick, P. 1949. *TVA and the grass roots.* Berkeley: University of California Press.

Selznick, P. 1957. *Leadership in administration.* Evanston, IL: Row, Peterson.

Slack, T. 1994. Institutional pressures and isomorphic change: An empirical test. *Organization Studies.* 15: 803–827.

Stevens, M. 1991. *The big six.* New York: Simon & Schuster.

Tichy, N. M. 1983. *Managing strategic change.* New York: Wiley.

Tichy, N. M., & Devanna, M. A. 1986. *The transformational leader.* New York: Wiley.

Tolbert, P. S. 1985. Resource dependence and institutional environments: Sources of administrative structure in institutions of higher education. *Administrative Science Quarterly.* 30: 1–13.

Tolbert, P. S. & Zucker, L. G. 1983. Institutional sources of change in the femoral structure of organizations: The diffusion of civil service reform. 1880–1935. *Administrative Science Quarterly*, 28: 22–39.

Tushman, M. L., Newman, W., & Romanelli, E. 1986. Convergence and upheaval: Managing the unsteady pace of organization evolution. *California Management Review.* 29: 29–44.

Tushman, M. L. & Romanelli, E. 1985. Organizational evolution: A metamorphosis model of convergence and reorientation. In L. L. Cummings & B. M. Staw (Eds.). *Research in organizational behavior.* vol. 7: 171–222. Greenwich, CT: JAI Press.

Van de Ven, A. H., & Poole, M. S. 1988. Paradoxical requirements for a theory of organizational change. In R. E. Quinn & K. S. Cameron (Eds.), *Paradox and transformation:* 330–341. Cambridge, MA: Ballinger.

Virany, B., Tushman, M. L., & Romanelli, E. 1992. Executive succession and organization outcomes in turbulent environments: An organization learning approach. *Organization Science.* 3: 72–91.

Walsh, J. P. 1995. Managerial and organizational cognition: Notes from a trip down memory lane. *Organization Science.* 6: 280–321.

Walsh, K., Hinings, C. R., Greenwood, R. & Ranson, S. 1981. Power and advantage in organizations. *Organization Studies*, 2:131–152.

Wholey, D., & Burns, L. R. 1993. Organizational transitions: Form changes by health maintenance organizations. In S. Bacharach (Ed.), *Research in the sociology of organizations:* 257–293. Greenwich, CT: JAI Press.

Wilson, D. C. 1994. *A strategy of change.* New York: Routledge.

Zucker, L. G. 1977. The role of institutionalization in cultural persistence. *American Sociological Review*, 42: 726–743.

Zucker, L. G. 1983. Organizations as institutions. In S. B. Bacharach (Ed.), *Research in the sociology of organizations:* 1–42. Greenwich, CT: JAI Press.

Zucker, L. G. 1987. Institutional theories of organizations. *Annual Review of Sociology*, 13: 443–464.

Zucker, L. G. (Ed.). 1988. *Institutional patterns and organizations: Culture and environment.* Cambridge, MA: Ballinger.

Royston Greenwood is the AGT Professor in the Department of Organizational Analysis, Faculty of Business, at the University of Alberta. He received his Ph.D. degree from the University of Birmingham, England. His research interests include the management of professional service organizations, strategic organizational change, and the institutional specificity of design archetypes.

C. R. Hinings is the Thornton A. Graham Professor of Business in the Department of Organizational Analysis, University of Alberta. His research interests include the management and dynamics of strategic organizational change, with particular reference to professional service firms.

Notes

1. Scott and Meyer (1991: 108) referred to the institutional context as the *societal sector*, defined "to include all organizations within a society supplying a given type of product or service together with their associated organizational sectors: suppliers, financiers, regulators, and so forth."

2. In our model, we assume that "archetypes" exist within institutional sector. As such the model presented is of archetype diffusion, not archetype creation.

3. Our model and hypotheses are based on the existence of archetypes, so they are about the adoption of those archetypes by individual organizations, which for those organizations is radical, second-order change. Here we do not deal with the creation of archetype with-

in sectors. For a preliminary approach to this latter issue, see Hinings, Greenwood, Brown, and Cooper (In press).

4. We believe that groups often do *not* recognize how the existing organizational design is disadvantageous to their interests. Indeed, the most effective way by which advantaged groups maintain their privileged positions is through an organizational archetype that is regarded by disadvantaged groups as legitimate (Walsh et al., 1981).

5. We deliberately use what may seem like a conceptual oxymoron (indifferent commitment) to represent the situation of group members being neither for nor against particular changes. It also represents the midpoint that occurs on all scales used to measure values.

6. Some institutional studies have shown how organizations may make significant changes to their structures, in order to meet institutional expectations, but without fundamentally affecting the technical processes at the core of the organization (e.g., Meyer & Rowan, 1977). Such changes would not require a capacity for action because the new structures are not intended to accomplish anything (other than legitimacy). In our model, radical changes are intended to be substantive, not a matter of appearance, hence the need for "capacity for action."

PART VI

INSTITUTIONAL CHANGE AND ASSESSMENT

CHAPTER 26

ASSESSMENT WITH OPEN EYES

PATRICK T. TERENZINI

Pitfalls in Studying Student Outcomes

There can be little doubt that "assessment" is here to stay. At least seven national reports have appeared in the last five years, all critical of higher education in America and all giving a central role to "assessment"—the measurement of the educational impact of an institution on its students. At least eleven states have adopted formal assessment requirements [10], as many more are moving in that direction, and regional accrediting associations are writing student outcomes assessment activities into their reaccreditation requirements.

The fact that the origins of the push toward assessment are external to most campuses is significant. Surveys indicate that while "over 50 percent of college administrators support assessing general education. . . . only 15 percent report doing anything about it. In the more complex area of 'value-added' assessment, some 65 percent support the concept but less than 10 percent are fielding value-added programs" [10, p. 25]. The clear implication of these findings is that for many colleges and universities, assessment is a relatively new undertaking: they are either just beginning to explore and implement assessment programs, or they have not yet even begun.

In fact, through such activities as course examinations, senior comprehensive examinations, periodic program evaluations, or some types of student, alumni and employer surveys, many campuses have been engaged in "assessment," by one definition or another, for some time. These efforts, however, are typically undertaken by individuals or by individual offices or committees and are not coordinated in any way. Nor are they part of any comprehensive, institutional plan for ongoing, systematic self-study and improvement. Much of the discussion which follows will be useful to such discrete, individual assessment activities (for example, a department's evaluation of its courses or programs), but because the major thrust of state boards or agencies and regional accrediting bodies is for systematic, campus-wide assessment activities, this article focuses on potential problems in the development of institution-wide assessment programs.

Moreover, as Astin [1] has pointed out, we have for years tended to think of undergraduate program "quality" as synonymous with "resources invested." The "best" colleges and universities are frequently thought to be those with high-ability and high-achieving students, more books in their library, more faculty with terminal degrees, lower student-faculty ratios, larger endowments and so on. Although a reasonable argument can be made that undergraduate program quality and resources invested are not independent, the increased emphasis on assessment has radically altered the nature of discussions of undergraduate program quality. Increasingly, claims to quality must be based not on resources or processes, but on outcomes. The benefits to institutions and students of this reformulation of the issues are substantial. Because they are detailed elsewhere, however [for example, 9, 23], the major ones will be only suggested here.

Perhaps most importantly, assessment requires a redirection of institutional attention from resources to education. Now that the costs of a college education are identifiable and measurable, important people (for example, legislators, parents, students) now want to know what the return is on their investments. What *does* one get out of a college education? The question forces a fundamental introspection on the part of both individual faculty members and institutions. Assessment requires reconsideration of the essential purposes and expected academic and nonacademic outcomes of a college education. It also requires a clarity of institutional and programmatic purpose as well as a specificity of practice often absent on many campuses or hidden in the generalities of recruiting materials. What *should* students get out of attending college? What should they get out of attending *this* college? In addition, assessment requires that we try to understand whether the things we do and believe to be educational in fact produce the intended outcomes.

These are all substantial benefits. Many campuses, however, fail to recognize them, instead viewing assessment as merely one more external reporting obligation, as something to be done as quickly and as painlessly as possible. When assessment is seen in this light, significant opportunities to enhance educational programs are likely to be lost.

But though advice on how assessment programs should be designed and implemented is easy to come by, the pitfalls of assessment are more obscure, typically treated only cursorily (if at all) in the literature. This article calls attention to some of those pitfalls and suggests, however briefly, how at least some of them might be avoided. The article is not intended to discourage institutions from developing assessment programs. On the contrary. Its purpose is twofold: first, to identify some of the serious conceptual, measurement, organizational, and political problems likely to be encountered in the process of designing

and implementing an assessment program; and second, by identifying some of the pitfalls, to help people who are involved in assessment to "do" it well. To accomplish these purposes, the article focuses on three major areas: (1) definitional issues, (2) organizational and implementational issues, and (3) methodological issues.

Definitional Issues

One of the most significant and imposing obstacles to the advancement of the assessment agenda at the national level is the absence of any consensus on precisely what "assessment" means. Some have used the term to mean testing individual student achievement levels in various academic areas. To others it means a review of the general education program and an evaluation of whether students are receiving a "liberal education." To still others it means a series of surveys of current students, alumni, or even employers, undertaken for program evaluation and planning purposes. And to still others, it means nothing less than institution-wide self-study, applicable to teaching, research, service, and administrative and management functions. Lack of clarity about exactly what this term means on a campus constitutes a significant threat to the success of any assessment effort.

In thinking about what "assessment" can mean, it is useful to keep three questions in mind, for the answers will have a powerful influence on the kind of assessment in which a campus becomes involved, as well as on the issues and problems it will face. The first question is: "What is the *purpose* of the assessment?" *Why* is the assessment program being designed? Although something of an oversimplification, the answers to this question generally fall into one (or both) of two categories: assessment for the enhancement of teaching and learning or assessment for purposes of accountability to some organizationally higher authority, whether internal or external to an institution. The answers to this question parallel the purposes of formative and summative evaluations: the first is intended to guide program modification and improvement, while the second is undertaken to inform some final judgment about worth or value.

The second question is: "What is to be the *level* of assessment?" *Who* is to be assessed? Will the assessment focus on individual students, where the information gathered on each student is inherently interesting? Or will it focus on groups, where individual information is aggregated to summarize some characteristic of the group (for example, average performance on some measure)? In this instance, "group" refers to any of a wide variety of student aggregations, such as at the course, program, department, college/school, campus, or system level; or to students grouped by sex, race/ethnicity, class year, major, place of residence, or whatever.

The third question is: "*What* is to be assessed?" On which of a variety of possible educational outcomes will assessment efforts be focused? Several "outcomes" taxonomies are available [for example, 5, 6, 16, 17]. A simple yet useful general typology has been given by Ewell [9, 11], who suggests four basic dimensions of outcomes: (1) knowledge (both breadth and depth) outcomes; (2) skills outcomes (including basic, higher-order, and career-related skills); (3) attitudes and values out-

comes (frequently overlooked); and (4) behavioral outcomes (what students do, both during and after college). If these three questions are juxtaposed in a three-dimensional matrix such as figure 26-1, one can begin to see how varying approaches to assessment can be categorized.

Some would assert that assessment in its purest form has the improvement of learning and teaching as its primary purpose and that it focuses on individual students. In this approach, most notably practiced at Alverno College, but also at King's College in Pennsylvania and Clayton State College in Georgia, analysis of individual student performance is an integral part of the teaching and learning process. Students receive regular feedback on their knowledge and skill development, and teachers use the same information to shape their teaching strategies, activities and styles, as well as to guide individual student learning.

Some other standard assessment practices also fall in this category. For example, placement examinations and other diagnostic measures are clearly teaching- and learning-focused at the individual level. They are intended to determine a student's learning readiness and to

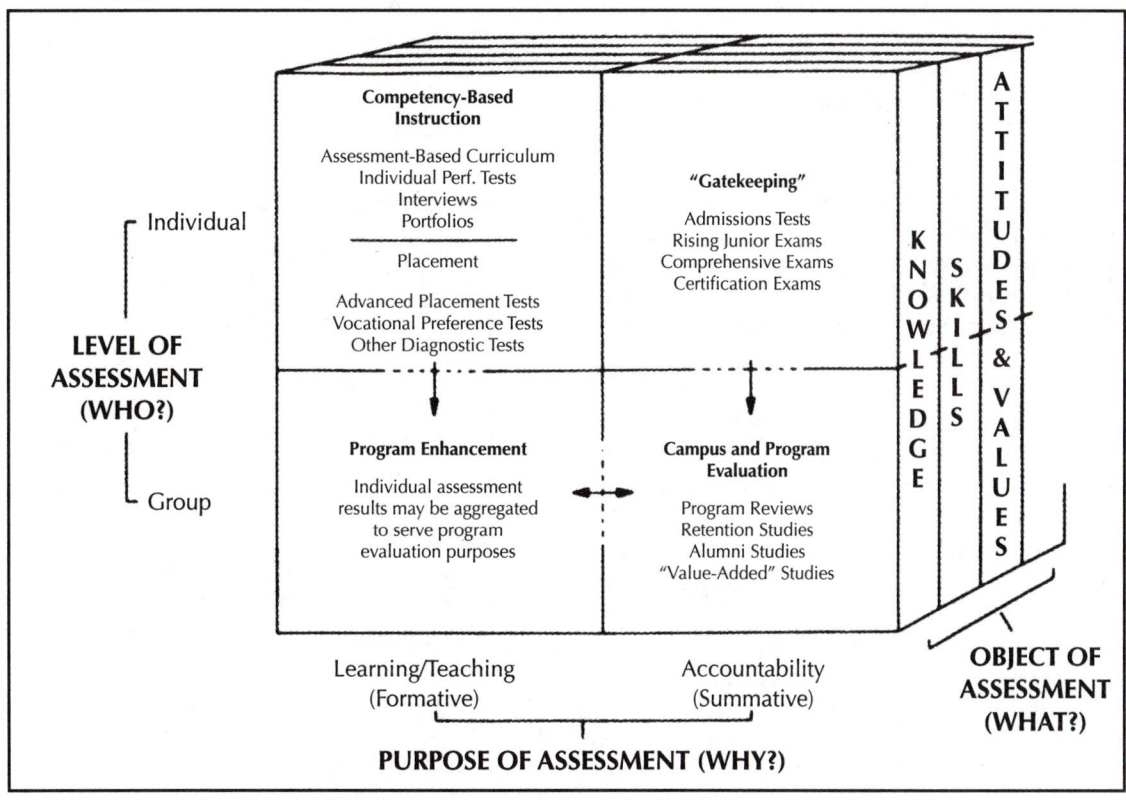

Figure 26-1 A Taxonomy of Approaches to Assessment

permit assignment of the student to the most beneficial learning sequence (for example, developmental studies or honors programs).

Individual assessment results may, of course, be aggregated to evaluate program effectiveness where the evaluation is intended to be formative, facilitating program modifications and increased effectiveness. (The multiple, often overlapping uses of assessment data are indicated by the broken lines and arrows between the cells in figure 26-1.) For example, assessments of general education program outcomes might fall in this category, unless of course the major purpose of such an assessment is for accountability purposes (that is, summative).

Moving to the right-hand column of figure 26-1, one can note that assessment programs with a clear accountability orientation can be of two varieties. At the individual level, assessment serves a gatekeeping function, sifting and sorting the qualified from the unqualified. This category includes such practices as admissions testing (for example, ACT, SAT, and others) and "rising junior" examinations employed in Florida, Georgia, and elsewhere. Other varieties of the accountability-oriented conception of assessment include comprehensive examinations in the student's academic major field (a practice enjoying a revival) and certification examinations in professional fields (for example, nursing).

These latter sorts of examinations may, of course, also serve accountability assessment purposes at the group level. Assessment programs comprising this group-accountability cell focus on group mean scores rather than on individual scores. The principal interest is in program enhancement, in determining the level of effectiveness or quality at which a program, department, school or entire campus is functioning. Assessment activities in this cell include academic program reviews, analysis of student attrition rates and reasons, alumni follow-up studies, and various forms of "value-added" assessment. The focus or purpose is primarily evaluative and administrative, and the information so obtained may be used for accounting to external bodies, although it may also be highly useful for internal program improvement and planning and for enhancing teaching and learning.

Each institution must decide for itself, consistent with its mission, what the character of its assessment program is to be on each of these three dimensions (and for subsets within these major categories). The point, here, is the importance of being clear on a more-or-less campus-wide basis about why assessment is being undertaken, who is to be assessed, and what educational outcomes are to be assessed. Time spent in committee work and in other forms of public discussion of these three questions will be time extremely well spent. An inadequate conceptual foundation for an assessment program will produce confusion, anxiety, and more heat than light.

Organizational and Implementational Issues

Assuming some reasonable level of agreement is reached on the purposes and objects of assessment, it is important to keep always in mind that institutional change is embedded in any conception of assessment. Depending upon where the changes occur and how they are managed, they can produce higher levels of individual and organizational performance and pride in accomplishment, or they can produce internal insurrection. Several significant organizational and implementational hazards must be addressed at the outset.

Mobilizing Support

A vital and difficult task involves enlisting the support of concerned parties. The active and visible support of senior executive officers (particularly the president and chief academic officer) is absolutely necessary but, unfortunately, not sufficient. Faculty support is also needed, and without it prospects for a successful assessment program are dim. According to Ewell, faculty objections are likely to come from either or both of two sources: first, the fear of being negatively evaluated, and second, a philosophical opposition based on the belief that the outcomes of college are inherently unmeasurable and that the evidence from such studies is "misleading, oversimplifying, or inaccurate" [9, p. 73].

If sufficient attention has been given to public discussions and review of the program's purposes and objects, much will already have been done to allay the fears of faculty members and others. Assessment—even when required by an external body—should be, and be seen by all, as a developmental, not punitive, undertaking. It should be a vehicle for individual and institutional improvement, not as a search for documentation on which to evaluate individual faculty members, or to cut budgets or retrench programs. Indeed, in some institutions (for example, in Tennessee and at Northeast Missouri State University), it is used not as a basis for withdrawing departmental support but for increasing it, whether to reward good work or to help a unit improve. Some basic level of trust must be established, and good faith participation in assessment activities should not be discouraged.

Ewell [12] recommends being publicly clear about what an assessment program is not intended to do. This would include a clear and public specification of what data are to be collected, by whom, for what purposes, the conditions under which the data will be made available, and to whom they will be available. Northeast Missouri State University [19], one of the assessment pioneers, recommends against using assessment data to support negative decisions, and Rossmann and El-Khawas [23] caution against mixing assessment procedures with faculty evaluation procedures. These latter authors also recommend sensitivity to the timing of the initiation of assessment efforts. If a financial crisis, retrenchment, or major reorganization is imminent (or underway), individual and unit anxiety levels may already be high enough without introducing a potentially threatening program [23].

Yanikoski [29] has suggested thinking and speaking in terms of *"progress* assessment," rather than "outcomes assessment." The switch can be important symbolically as well as conceptually. "Assessing outcomes" implies a certain finality: that a summative evaluation and judgment are to be made, that the "bottom line" is about to be drawn. "Assessing progress," by contrast, implies an ongoing, formative process, which, in turn, suggests that time remains to make any necessary improvements. The whole tone of "progress assessment" is more positive, less threatening.

Faculty reservations about the measurability of outcomes must also be addressed, and

several approaches are possible. One powerful way to allay faculty concerns about evaluation and the measurability of student progress is to include faculty in the design and implementation of the process and especially in the interpretation of results and development of recommendations. Respected faculty opinion leaders should be involved, and faculty members with technical specialties in research design, measurement, and other important areas should be recruited as consultants. Faculty members on most campuses constitute a significant, but untapped, source of technical and political support for an assessment effort.

Another way to ease concerns about the measurability of student progress is to ensure that multiple measures are incorporated into one's assessment program. The concept of triangulation in astronomy, surveying and map reading, and of successive approximations in probability theory, are familiar to most faculty members. Multitrait, multi-method matrices can be highly useful, arraying in the rows those content and skill areas to be assessed and across the columns the assessment techniques and approaches that might be used to assess each trait. One can then judge the extent to which each assessment area will be covered by multiple measures. Adoption of multiple measures is likely to have a face validity that will appeal to faculty members as well as increase the confidence that can be placed in interpretations of the data. The psychometric importance of using multiple measures is discussed further below.

Whatever approach is taken, however, everyone involved must recognize that judgments of program and institutional quality are made all the time by many different people. The issue is not really whether "assessments" should be made, but rather what is to be the nature, sources, and quality of the evidence on which those judgments are based.

Finally, assessment programs that start small, perhaps on a pilot basis, are more likely to draw support than elaborate plans. Most successful programs began small and grew incrementally [12]. The assessment efforts at Alverno College and Northeast Missouri State University have been underway for a decade and a half. It should be clear to all concerned, however, that any "pilot" project is not a test of whether the campus will proceed with assessment, but of how to do so in the most efficient and effective manner.

An inventory of current data collection activities (including the use of standardized measures, program review results, surveys, and standard institutional research studies) can be a politically and practically useful beginning. All academic and administrative offices should be surveyed to identify the information already on hand about students and about the effectiveness of their unit's activities. Such an inventory is likely to reveal far greater involvement in "assessment" than might be first have been believed.

In sum, one cannot overstate the importance of laying a strong political foundation. Without it, the assessment structure cannot stand. Faculty members, department heads, and deans are keen observers of their administrative superiors and readily discern which attitudes and behaviors are rewarded and which are not. For any assessment program to succeed, there simply must be some payoff for faculty members, whether in the form of additional funding to correct identified program deficiencies, rewards for a job well-done (say, some extra travel money), or other incentives to engage in assessment and enhance the quality of teaching and learning in a department.

Coordination

Assessment requires the involvement of a wide variety of people and offices, crossing not only academic departmental lines, but vice-presidential areas as well. Alternative approaches to the campus-wide coordination problem include assignment of coordinating responsibility to a currently existing office already significantly engaged in assessment and controlling many of the necessary resources (for example, the office of institutional research), creation of a new office, or assignment to a committee with representatives from the major affected organizational areas [12]. Each of these approaches has its assets and liabilities, of course, and though space precludes a detailed discussion of each, the reporting line(s) for the office or group should be given careful attention. Whatever approach is adopted, what will be the likely effects on traditional areas of responsibility and lines of authority? On informal power

networks? On traditional distinctions between academic and student affairs? Ways will have to be found to coordinate activities in such a way that lines of authority and responsibility are clear, existing functions and activities are not duplicated, and support is received from each area [12]. As noted earlier, experience indicates that the support of the institutions' top executives, particularly the president and chief academic officer, must be active and visible, especially in the early stages of the program's development.

Costs

How much should an institution invest in its assessment program? The answer, of course, will depend upon the purposes and the extensiveness of the assessment program and its activities. Ewell and Jones have argued that the real question is one of marginal costs: "How much *more* money beyond that already committed to outcomes-related information gathering do we have to spend to put in place an assessment program that is appropriate to our needs?" [13, p. 34]. These costs are incurred in four areas: (1) instruments, (2) administration, (3) analysis, and (4) coordination [13]. Rossmann and El-Khawas [23] also note start-up costs, which can include consultant services, conference attendance and visits to other campuses, on-campus workshops, and faculty and staff time for organizing and perhaps instrument development.

According to Rossman and El-Khawas [23, p. 20], campuses with ongoing assessment programs spend $10–15 per enrolled student. Ewell and Jones [13], after making a series of assumptions about the nature of the assessment program likely to be mounted by institutions of varying types and sizes, estimate incremental costs ranging from $30,000 (for a small, private, liberal arts college) to $130,000 (for a major public research university). These latter estimates do not include personnel costs associated with faculty involvement in assessment.

Finally, opportunity costs must also be considered. Institutional resources (including time) invested in assessment are not available for investment elsewhere. Moreover, Governor Kean [15] of New Jersey has advised institutions not to ask for additional funds to cover assessment costs. According to Kean, legislators are unlikely to respond favorably to requests for money to determine whether past and current appropriations are being effectively utilized. If that is true, reallocation of currently appropriated funds will probably be necessary, although a variety of other sources are available, including grants from public agencies, private foundations, individuals, or even student fees to cover testing directly beneficial to students [23].

In considering the costs of assessment, however, the costs of not assessing educational outcomes must also be placed in the balance. Important opportunities may be missed, including, for example, the chance to clarify institutional goals, to review and revise (or reconfirm the value of) existing curricular purposes and structures, and to examine the successes and failures of current policies and practices. The costs of rejecting or deferring assessment may be substantial, if difficult to calculate.

Methodological Issues

The third major category of potential assessment pitfalls is methodological. Some of these problems are specific to particular approaches to assessment, whereas others are merely common and frequent violations of the canons of good research. Within this general area, potential problems fall into three subcategories: (1) design limitations, (2) measurement difficulties, and (3) statistical hazards.

Design Problems

From the outset it is important to keep in mind that research design is a series of compromises. Designs that increase the power of a study in one area come almost invariably at the expense of some other aspect of the study. Whenever something is gained, something else is given away. The key to useful and psychometrically sound inquiry is to know what is being gained and what is being given away [see 25].

The dominant theme in the chorus of demands for "accountability" through assessment is the need to demonstrate that college and university attendance makes a difference, that students leave colleges and universities with knowledge, skills, attitudes, and values they did not have when they arrived. An impressive number of studies [for example, 6, 20] demonstrate the fact that students change in a variety of ways between their freshman and senior years. The problem lies in specifying the *origins* of those changes. Students may change during the college years in response to many influences, including their own precollege characteristics and their noncollege experiences, not to mention normal maturation. Thus, collegiate impact is only one of the possible sources of freshman-to-senior year change. Collegiate experiences may be a significant source of change, but knowing with any degree of certainty whether and to what extent college has an effect is a very complicated matter.

A common approach to the assessment of change in students is the use of a successive cross-sections design, typically involving cross-sectional samples of current freshmen and senior students. The freshmen (the control group) are compared with the seniors (the treatment group) on some measure of the variable(s) on which change is being studied. Observed differences are then taken as an indication of the effects of the college on students. Such designs have a number of limitations, however, including the need to assume that current seniors, at the time they matriculated, were similar in important respects to current freshmen—a questionable proposition. Such designs also leave selective dropout during the college years uncontrolled. Not all students who begin college will finish it, and students who complete a college program, compared with those who do not, are likely to have higher aptitude and achievement records and greater commitment to college. Given such self-selection during the college years, freshman and senior group score means would probably be different even if the two classes had been identical at the time they entered college. Any changes over the period in admissions standards or recruiting strategies might also have produced initially nonequivalent groups in the two classes.

Pascarella [21] suggests several ways to reduce the nonequivalent-groups problem inherent in this design. One possibility is to control for age and entering academic aptitude through statistics, matching, or both. Use of samples of freshman and senior students of the same age is another option. Both are preferable, if imperfect, alternatives to the typical, unadjusted, successive cross-sections design.

Longitudinal designs are a frequently recommended alternative. One might measure the characteristics of an entering freshman class in a variety of areas and then, after a period of time (for example, two or four years) study the group again and compare students with themselves at the time they entered college, controlling for entering characteristics. At least some of the same people are being studied at the two different times, but the tendency of subjects to drop out of a study over time can be a significant problem with longitudinal research, particularly research that covers an extended period of time (for example, four years). As the response rates drop, study generalizability is threatened.

Ideally, one would follow over the same period of time a control group of high-school graduates who do not attend college (but who are presumably personally and academically equivalent to one's freshmen) and who could be compared after some period of time with the freshman group who have presumably benefited from college attendance. Although the equivalency of groups might be questioned even under this sampling plan, the design has obvious advantages over a successive cross-sections design. Obtaining a sample of students who do not attend college may be difficult, however, it may be reasonable for institutions serving a largely local or regional population (for example, community and commuting colleges). Institutions that draw students from a national base will probably find this alternative impractical.

The price paid for adopting a longitudinal design comes in several forms. Because of the unavoidable subject mortality problem, longitudinal designs also require larger samples. Increased sample sizes mean higher direct and indirect costs for personnel and materials as well as more complex data management requirements. Finally, longitudinal studies take longer to complete, and all too often the need for information is (or is thought to be) immediate.

Another group assessment pitfall arises in developing a sampling plan. Have clearly in mind the kinds of subgroup analyses that are planned, for as the number of groups grows, or if one or more subgroups come from a small population (for example, minority students), simple random sampling may be inappropriate. Experience indicates, for example, that successful assessment programs provide unit-specific information. It is easy for deans or department heads to disregard assessment information when it comes from students or alumni of other schools or departments. The implication of this advice, however, often overlooked until it is too late, is that a census, not a sample, of students must be taken. Otherwise, group sizes may be too small to have face validity, political believability, or statistical stability. Costs and workload will, of course, go up accordingly.

Measurement Problems

However one defines "assessment," it will involve some form of measurement, and sooner or later one must deal with the problems and hazards of instrument selection. The common dilemma is whether to "buy, build, or borrow." Should one adopt a commercially available measure (for example ACT's COMP or Collegiate Assessment of Academic Proficiency [CAAP], or ETS's Academic Profile)? Or should one devise an instrument locally, or perhaps use a measure developed for similar purposes on some other campus? As noted previously, research is a series of compromises. Nationally available measures have several advantages, the first of which is that they have been developed by experts. Second, they have been field-tested, and their psychometric properties are known. Third, national scores or norms are usually available so one can compare one's students with those of other campuses of similar size, type, and purpose. Finally, use of commercial instruments can save substantial amounts of time and expense that would be required for local instrument development.

Such advantages come at a cost, however. In order to be usable in a variety of settings and for a variety of purposes, commercial measures are necessarily general and lack the specificity needed to focus in any detail on local conditions. Standardized achievement measures also focus unavoidably on a limited number of learning objectives. Do the substantive knowledge and skills measured by those instruments coincide with those that faculty want students to learn? Centra calls attention to the "faulty assumption . . . that commercial, standardized tests will adequately measure the student learning objectives of a typical general education program. But in fact it is unlikely that any of the tests measures more than half of what most faculty members believe should be part of general education" [7, p. 2]

Moreover, the format of any given measure constrains the range of what it can assess. For example, many standardized tests employ a multiple-choice structure that, no matter how clearly items may be written, limits the range of aspects of an educational outcome that can be examined [2]. One must remember that standardized, machine-scored tests were developed (and are popular) because they are comparatively easy to use, not because they are the best way to measure something. Centra [7] recommends, if commercial instruments are adopted, that they be supplemented with local measures.

On the other hand, though locally developed measures may be more carefully tailored to local purposes and educational objectives, they are also likely to be untested (at least in the short run) and, consequently, of unknown reliability and validity. Moreover, instrument construction is neither inexpensive nor an activity for novices. Many faculty members will have neither the time, commitment, nor competence to develop local measures.

As suggested earlier, the validity of assessments can be increased through the use of multiple measures. The allegory of the blind men seeking to describe the elephant has an important lesson to offer. Psychometricians know that each type of measurement has its characteristic sources of error [24], and reliance on one measure (or type of measure) is likely to produce data systematically biased by that measure's characteristic source(s) of error. In adopting multiple measures, one samples their strengths and their weaknesses, and as the number of different measures increases, so does the likelihood that any given measure's weakness(es) will be counterbalanced by the strength(s) of another.

One source of error characteristic of many of the assessment measures currently in use (commercially or locally developed) is their reactivity. Respondents to tests and surveys know they are being studied and that knowledge may influence their responses in varying and unknown ways. Such intrusive methods influence and shape, as well as measure. Unobtrusive measures—ones that do not require a conscious response from the subject, can be highly useful as well as efficient. For example, if one wishes to know whether students are receiving a general education, one alternative to the intrusive testing of students is an analysis of their transcripts. How many credits does the typical undergraduate take in various disciplinary areas? When are those credits earned (for example lower- or upper-division years)? How do these course-taking patterns vary across major fields? Transcript analysis is a reasonable basis for inference about the breadth and depth of students' formal learning [27], and numerous other unobtrusive measures are available to creative researchers [26].

Even if one successfully avoids these measurement pitfalls, however, additional hazards lie ahead as one begins the analysis of the data those assessment devices produce. The certainty implied by statistical testing can mask problems that may lead to the serious misinterpretation of results.

Statistical Problems

As noted previously, assessment (particularly the accountability strain) has embedded in it the expectation that change will occur, that the institution's contribution to student learning can be made apparent and even measured with some precision. Unfortunately, we rely almost without exception on average changes (for example, a comparison of a group mean at Time 1 with the same group's mean at Time 2). Group change, however, often masks individual change. Any observed freshman-to-senior year group change is related to the number of students who change and to the amount of change each student experiences. It may be useful to give attention to the frequency, direction, and magnitude of individual changes [see 14, pp. 52–69].

Moreover, change is often construed as "value-added," a frequently-heard phrase that can be highly misleading and damaging if not understood. Warren [27] and Pascarella [21] offer thoughtful and detailed discussions of this concept, but certain aspects of it require attention here. "Value-added" is both a metaphor and a research design. As a metaphor, it is a vivid and useful term focusing our attention on institutional effects rather than resources. Unfortunately, it can sometimes be too vivid, leading people inside and outside the academy to expect more of our assessment programs than can possibly be delivered. The reason for this lies not only in the metaphor's implication that "change" occurs, but also that it is positive change or growth. Can "value" be "added" without positive change? Legislators and others are likely to say "No." And therein lies the perniciousness of the metaphor, for it is important to distinguish "change" from collegiate "impact." As Pascarella notes: "In some areas of development . . . the impact of college (or other educational experiences) may be to prevent or retard decline rather than to induce major positive changes. Consequently, approaches to value-added assessment which focus only on pre- to post-changes may be overlooking important college effects" [21, p. 78]. For example, Wolfle [28] found that mathematics performance among a national sample of high-school graduates declined over the seven years following graduation. The data suggest, however, that the effects of college attendance may be to maintain precollege mathematics performance levels, whereas math achievement declines among those who do not go to college.

Similarly, it will be well to remember that one variable (for example, some aspect of the college experience) can influence another variable (for example, some outcome measure) in both direct and indirect ways. For example, evidence indicates that whereas participation in a pre-matriculation orientation program has no direct influence on freshman persistence into the sophomore year, attendance at an orientation session does positively influence students' level of social integration, which, in turn, is positively related to sophomore year enrollment [22]. Thus, any "value-added" approach that fails to take into account the indirect, as well as the direct, effects of college is likely to underestimate the full range of the collegiate influence [20].

One must also remember that college effects may not manifest themselves right away. For example, it is probably unreasonable to expect significant student progress over a one- or two-year period in acquiring the intellectual and personal knowledge, skills, attitudes, and values presumed to characterize a liberal education. Faculty, administrators, students, parents, and legislators must not expect (nor be led to expect) more of assessment programs than can reasonably be delivered. The benefits college is supposed to impart are not acquired overnight, and the programs intended to assess these benefits take time to design, implement, and fine-tune.

The "value-added" metaphor also promotes an analytical design that is correspondingly simple but potentially more dangerous. Common sense suggests that if one wishes to know whether something changes over time, one should measure it at Time 1 and again at Time 2. The difference between the pre- and post-test scores, the "change" score, presumably reflects the effects of some process. To many, this change score reflects the institutional "value-added." In this instance, however, common sense may harm more than help. Indeed, change scores have some positively alarming characteristics.

For example, simple difference scores are highly unreliable, and they can be shown to be negatively correlated with pretest scores [4, 18]. Second, it can also be shown that the higher the correlation between pre- and post-test measures, the lower the reliability of the gain score [18]. Such unreliability makes detection of reliable associations with other variables (for example, aspects of the institutional experience thought to produce a portion of the change) more difficult.

Third, simple difference scores are also subject to ceiling effects: students with high pre-test scores have little room for improvement and thus are likely to show smaller gains than students with lower initial scores. Similarly, gain scores are subject to regression effects, the tendency—due strictly to measurement error—for initially high (or low) scores to move ("regress") toward the group mean upon subsequent retesting.

One or more of the reasons probably lies behind the results reported by Banta, Lambert, Pike, Schmidhammer, and Schneider [3]. Many institutions are unable or unwilling to wait the usual two-to-four years needed for a longitudinal study following a cohort of entering freshmen through to the completion of a degree program. For that reason, and using the correlation between students' senior year "College Outcomes Measures Project" (COMP) scores and their freshman year ACT Assessment Composite scores, the American College Testing Program (ACT) has constructed concordance tables which permit institutions to estimate the COMP score gain, or value-added, that might have been recorded if the students had taken the COMP test in both freshman and senior years. [3].

In a series of tests on these estimated gain scores, Banta et al. [3] made a number of striking (if not to say bizarre) findings. They found, for example, that the estimated gains for University of Tennessee-Knoxville students were underestimated by as much as 60 percent. Moreover, a large number of seniors had no ACT Assessment Composite score from which to estimate a gain score, and the students without assessment scores tended to be older, black, and from lower socioeconomic families, raising serious questions about the generalizability of any study based on estimated gain scores. Finally, the correlations between estimated gain scores and certain demographic and institutional variables were the opposite of what was expected. For example, the greatest gain scores tended to be those of students who had high school averages lower than 3.0, did not receive a scholarship, whose fathers did not graduate from college, who did not participate in honors mathematics sections, and who did not take more than two mathematics courses [3, p. 15]. In all likelihood, these startling findings are due to the unreliability of gain scores, as well as to ceiling and regression effects.

Such results raise serious questions about the reliability and validity of any estimated gain score, not just those produced using the ACT's COMP and assessment instructions. Indeed, Banta and her colleagues are quick to praise COMP as a "valuable tool for stimulating faculty discussion about the general education curriculum, and modes of instructions. . . . What is called into question is the usefulness, the validity, of employing *estimated* student score gain on the COMP for the purpose of making precise judgments about program quality that can serve as the basis for decisions about the allocation of resources in higher education" [3, p. 19]. And though one might infer from this that the use of actual gain scores may be a way of circumventing the problems Banta and her colleagues identified, the same problems afflict actual gain scores as well.

Thus, in considering the use of the "value-added" metaphor in a specific measurement setting, one would be well advised to follow the suggestion of Cronbach and Furby, who advised "investigators who ask questions regarding gain scores . . . [to] . . . frame their questions in other ways" [8, p. 80]. Centra recommends "a criterion-referenced approach in which the level and content of student learning is compared to standards and objectives established by the faculty and staff of a college" [7, p. 8]. A variant on that approach is to examine the trend over time in the proportion of students who score above a faculty-determined threshold of "acceptable" performance on any given measure. Linn and Slinde [18] and Pascarella [21] suggest a number of other alternatives, although space precludes their review here. The point is that there are conceptually understandable and methodologically preferable alternatives to the use of simple difference scores.

Finally, whether one is dealing with design, measurement, or analytical issues, it will be well to remember that campus-based assessment programs are intended to gather information for instructional, programmatic and institutional improvement, not for journal publication. Methodological standards for research publishable in scholarly and professional journals can probably be relaxed in the interests of institutional utility and advancement. The most appropriate test of the suitability of a design, measure, or analytical procedure is probably that of reasonableness [21]: Was the study conducted with reasonable fidelity to the canons of sound research? Given the constraints on the research methods used and the data produced, is it reasonable to infer that college has had an effect on student change? Although the methodological issues reviewed here cannot and should not be ignored, neither should one's concern about them stifle action.

Conclusion

The assessment of student outcomes has much to offer colleges and universities. In linking stated institutional and programmatic goals to the measurement of progress toward their achievement, assessment represents a significant refocusing of institutional efforts on the purposes and effectiveness of undergraduate education. Assessment requires consideration of three questions: (1) What should a student get out of college?, (2) What should a student get out of attending this college?, and (3) What does a student get from attending this college? Addressing these questions in a systematic, periodic assessment program is likely to foster increased clarity about the purposes of an undergraduate program (one can also engage in assessment at the graduate level), increased consensus on those goals, and a better understanding of the consequences of educational policies and programs. In many respects, assessment is really only something higher education should have been doing all along.

The assessment of student outcomes, however, is not something that can be done quickly or casually. Several conceptual, administrative, political, and methodological issues may prove troublesome in developing a successful and beneficial assessment program. At the same time, and with a little preparation and care, those pitfalls can be rather easily avoided. This article has sought to help in those preparations by increasing the likelihood that when a campus starts down the path to assessment, it will do so with open eyes.

An earlier version of this article was presented at the Fifth Annual Conference on Research in Post-secondary Education at the University of Georgia, Institute of Higher Education, Athens, Georgia, December 1987.

Patrick T. Terenzini is professor of Higher Education at the Institute of Higher Education, University of Georgia.

References

1. Astin, A. W. *Achieving Educational Excellence.* San Francisco: Jossey-Bass, 1985
2. Baird, L. L. "Diverse and Subtle Arts: Assessing the Generic Academic Outcomes of Higher Education." Paper presented to the Association for the Study of Higher Education, Baltimore, MD, 1987.
3. Banta, T. W., et al. "Estimated Student Score Gain on the ACT COMP Exam: Valid Tool for Institutional Assessment?" *Research in Higher Education*, 27 (1987), 195–217.
4. Bereiter, C. "Some Persisting Dilemmas in the Measurement of Change." In *Problems in Measuring Change*, edited by C. W. Harris, pp. 3–20. Madison: University of Wisconsin Press, 1963.
5. Bloom, B. S., et al. *Taxonomy of Educational Objectives: Handbook 1, Cognitive Domain.* New York: McKay, 1956.
6. Bowen, H. R. *Investment in Learning: The Individual and Social Value of American Higher Education.* San Francisco: Jossey-Bass, 1977.
7. Centra, J. A. "Assessing the Content Areas of General Education." Paper presented to the Association for the Study of Higher Education, Baltimore, MD, 1987.
8. Cronbach, L. J., and L. Furby, "How We Should Measure 'Change'—or Should We?" *Psychological Bulletin.* 74 (1970), 68–80.
9. Ewell, P. T. *The Self-Regarding Institution: Information for Excellence.* Boulder, Colo.: National Center for Higher Education Management Systems, 1984.
10. _____ "Assessment: Where Are We?" *Change,* 19 (January/February 1987).
11. _____ "Establishing a Campus-based Assessment Program." In *Student Outcomes Assessment: What Institutions Stand to Gain*, edited by D. F. Halpern, pp. 9–24. *New Directions for Higher Education*, No. 59. San Francisco: Jossey-Bass, 1987, 23–28.
12. _____ "Implementing Assessment: Some Organizational Issues." In *Implementing Outcomes Assessment: Promise and Perils*, edited by T. W. Banta and H. S. Fisher. *New Directions for Institutional Research*, No. 59. San Francisco: Jossey-Bass, 1988.
13. Ewell, P. T. and D. Jones, "The Costs of Assessment." In *Assessment in American Higher Education: Issues and Contexts*, edited by C. Adelman, pp. 33–46. Washington, D.C.: U.S. Office of Education, Office of Educational Research and Improvement, 1986. (U.S. Government Printing Office, Document No. OR 86–301).
14. Feldman, K. A., and T. M. Newcomb. *The Impact of College on Students.* San Francisco: Jossey-Bass, 1969.
15. Kean, T. H. "Time to Deliver Before We Forget the Promises We Made," *Change,* 19 (September/October 1987). 10–11.
16. Krathwohl, D. R., B. S. Bloom, and B. B. Masia. *Taxonomy of Educational Objectives: The Classification of Educational Goals, Handbook II: Affective Domain.* New York: McKay, 1964.
17. Lenning, O. T. *The Outcomes Structure: An Overview and Procedure for Applying It in Postsecondary Education Institutions.* Boulder, Colo.: National Center for Higher Education Management Systems, 1979.
18. Linn, R. L., and J. A. Slinde. "The Determination of the Significance of Change Between Pre- and Post-testing Periods." *Review of Educational Research,* 47 (Winter 1977), 121–50.
19. Northeast Missouri State University. *In Pursuit of Degrees with Integrity: A Value-Added Approach to Undergraduate Assessment.*

Washington, D.C.: American Association of State College and Universities, 1984.

20. Pace, C. R. *Measuring the Outcomes of College: Fifty Years of Findings and Recommendations for the Future.* San Francisco: Jossey-Bass, 1979.

21. Pascarella, E. T. "Are Value-Added Analyses Valuable?" In *Assessing the Outcomes of Higher Education*, pp. 71–91. Proceedings of the 1986 ETS Invitational Conference, Princeton, N.J.: Educational Testing Service, 1987.

22. Pascarella, E. T., P. T. Terenzini, and L. M. Wolfle. "Orientation to College and Freshman Year Persistence/Withdrawal Decisions." *Journal of Higher Education,* 57 (March/April 1986). 155–75.

23. Rossmann, J. E., and E. El-Khawas. *Thinking About Assessment: Perspectives for Presidents and Chief Academic Officers.* Washington, D.C.: American Council on Education, 1987.

24. Sechrest, L., and M. Phillips. "Unobtrusive Measures: An Overview." In *Unobtrusive Measurement Today,* edited by L. Sechrest, pp. 1–17.

New Directions for Methodology of Behavioral Science, No. 1. San Francisco: Jossey-Bass, 1969.

25. Terenzini, P. L. "An Evaluation of Three Basic Designs for Studying Attrition." *Journal of College Student Personnel*, 21 (May 1980), 257–63.

26. _____. "The Case for Unobtrusive Measures." In *Assessing the Outcomes of Higher Education*, pp. 47–61. Proceedings of the 1986 ETS Invitational Conference, Princeton, N.J.: *Educational Testing Service*, 1987.

27. Warren, J. "The Blind Alley of Value Added." *AAHE Bulletin*, 37 (September 1984), 10–13.

28. Wolfle, L. M. "Effects of Higher Education on Ability for Blacks and Whites." *Research in Higher Education,* 19 (1983), 3–10.

29. Yanikoski, R. A . Comments made as part of a panel discussion on "Measuring the Value of College" at the annual meeting of the Illinois Association for Institutional Research, Champaign, IL, November 1987.

CHAPTER 27

SENSEMAKING DURING STRATEGIC CHANGE IN ACADEMIA

DENNIS A. GIOIA AND JAMES B. THOMAS

This study investigates how top management teams in higher education institutions make sense of important issues that affect strategic change in modern academia. We used a two-phase research approach that progressed from a grounded model anchored in a case study to a quantitative, generalizable study of the issue interpretation process, using 611 executives from 372 colleges and universities in the United States. The findings suggest that under conditions of change, top management team members' perceptions of identity and image, especially desired future image, are key to the sensemaking process and serve as important links between the organization's internal context and the team members' issue interpretations. Rather than using the more common business issue categories of "threats" and "opportunities," team members distinguished their interpretations mainly according to "strategic" or "political" categorizations.

Higher education is an industry that has experienced significant shifts in recent years. Less than a generation ago academic institutions thrived in an environment of predictable funding and student enrollment with little overt competition among institutions (cf. Cohen and March, 1974; Keller, 1983). Recent economic, demographic, and political changes, however, have cast colleges and universities into an ambiguous arena that looks more and more like a competitive marketplace. Such a dynamic environment calls for institutions to change to meet these new conditions—behavior that is virtually taken for granted in business but is still relatively unfamiliar in academe. There is a growing insistence not only that change occur but that it be accomplished quickly in institutions that historically have been comfortable only with slower, self-paced, incremental change. Given the market character of the environment, with its attendant emphasis on competition, many academic institutions are trying to adopt a more business-like orientation to accomplish intended changes (Milliken, 1990). Administrators are reexamining longstanding notions of egalitarianism in an effort to prioritize departments, colleges, and programs according to new strategic goals. Thus "strategic change" in academia is a phrase that introduces its own ambiguity into institutions not accustomed to thinking and acting strategically.

Parallels with business approaches to strategic change are not exact, however. Most notably, there are few bottom-line measures like profit or return on investment that apply to the generation and dissemination of knowledge. Therefore, assessing an institution's standing and establishing its competitive advantage depends on more subjective factors. For this reason, perceptions of an institution's prestige or ranking come to the fore, often taking precedence over measurable substance (Alvesson, 1990) in an institution's attempt to achieve prominence (Fombrun and Shanley, 1990). Under such conditions, the management of image becomes a critical strategic issue. As Dutton and Dukerich (1991) noted, image (i.e., perceptions of how others perceive the institution) is often tied to identity (i.e., how members perceive their organization). Therefore, it is unlikely that a change in image can be sustained without an associated change in identity. The assumption that image and identity can be altered within the compressed time frame demanded by modern academic environments implies that these concepts must be more fluid than the organizational literature has suggested. Identity, in particular, is typically taken to be that which is central, distinctive, and enduring about an organization (Albert and Whetten, 1985). A key question thus becomes: Can identity be enduring if strategic change is to occur?

Managing change requires a consideration of the effects of change on the interpretive schemes of organization members (Ranson, Hinings, and Greenwood, 1980; Bartunek, 1984). Unfamiliar expressions and actions that are consistent with a new vision for an institution and clearly inconsistent with the taken-for-granted way of seeing tend to destablize existing identity and image (Gioia et al., 1994). Under conditions of strategic change, then, it is not existing identity or image but, rather, envisioned identity and image—those to be achieved—that imply the standards for interpreting important issues. Our concern with shifting identity and image and their role in issue interpretation derives from a case study that investigated the research question "How do top management teams make sense of issues when managing strategic change in an academic institution?" Because we initially used a grounded approach and then consulted relevant literature to investigate this question, the theoretical framework underlying the paper emerged in large part from the study itself. Our ultimate purpose, however, was to refine the emergent model with a more generalizable, quantitative investigation of a broad range of academic institutions. The overall project thus combines a qualitative case study with a quantitative survey of colleges and universities in the U.S.

A Grounded Theoretical Overview of Strategic Sensemaking

We first foreshadow the elements of the grounded theoretical framework as a means of structuring the findings that emerged. In general we found: (1) that the strategy the top management team was currently pursuing and the information-processing structure they were using most influenced their sensemaking activities; (2) that the top management team's perceptions of institutional identity and image (both present and desired in the future) constituted the major "lenses" through which the team interpreted organization-level issues; and (3) that these issues were not conceived in the usual "threat/opportunity" categories seen in business organizations, but in terms of more general categories of "strategic" and "political" issues.

The "Internal" Context for Sensemaking

Although changes in the external environment obviously influence the interpretation process, "internal" contextual features also exert considerable influence. Of these, the strategies in use (Daft and Weick, 1984) and the organizational structures in place, especially information-processing structures (Thomas, Shankster, and Mathieu, 1994), play important roles in guiding interpretation. The organization's strategy amounts to a statement of intention that influences top management's perceptions of key issues (Thomas and McDaniel, 1990). The strategy in use thus constitutes a key element in the institution's enacted environment (Weick, 1979) and tightens top management's interpretive focus (Draft and Weick, 1984). Similarly, patterns of informational interaction among team members influence interpretations; characteristics such as frequency of interaction and degree of participation by members in decision making affect the identification and interpretation of issues (Thomas and McDaniel, 1990). Both the strategy and the information-processing structure, then, shape interpretive predispositions that focus attention on some information or issues and exclude others (Dutton and Duncan, 1987).

Identity and Image as Perceptual Lenses

Central to the top management team's perceptions of the organization are the notions of identity and image. Both concepts have been explored at various levels of analysis using a number of different perspectives. For example, personal (self) identity and social (collective) identity have long been recognized as critical constructs in the organizational behavior literature (Ashforth and Mael, 1989). At the organizational level, corporate or organizational identity concerns those features of the organization that members perceive as ostensibly central, enduring, and distinctive in character that contribute to how they define the organization and their identification with it (Albert and Whetten, 1985; Sutton and Callahan, 1987; Dutton and Dukerich, 1991). Our focus here is on the organizational identity held by the top management team, i.e., the team members' perceptions of the qualities of the organization that answers the question: "What kind of organization is this?" (Albert and Whetten, 1985).

Image generally has been defined in the organizational literature as how members believe others view their organization (Dutton, Dukerich, and Harquail, 1994). This descriptive view, labeled as "construed external image," complements a more projective view of the concept in the work of Whetten, Lewis, and Mischel (1992). Whetten, Lewis, and Mischel refer to image as characteristics organizational elites want stakeholders to ascribe to the firm (which can be termed a desired or communicated image). The thread that runs through these definitions is that organizational image is tied to perceptions of how external constituencies view the organization, regardless of whether these views are normative or manipulated. In this study, we focus on the top management team members' perceptions of their organization's image in the context of strategic change. Both identity and image act as perceptual screens or mirrors that affect team members' information processing and, ultimately, their interpretation of key issues.

Although most writers have assumed conditions of relative stability, under conditions of proactive change it is necessary to reconsider the assumed durability and distinctiveness of identity and image. In general, strategic change implies a revision in the interpretive schemes not only of the top management team but of the organization's members and constituencies as well. Any major change, perhaps especially a strategic change, must be accompanied by a significant alteration in the overall perception of the organization (Fiol, 1991). Therefore, taking substantive change seriously demands reconsidering existing identity and image. Our focus, therefore, is not only on identity and

image per se but also on the management of changing identity and image. What does "enduring" mean when changing environments demand that even not-for-profit institutions behave strategically, thus encouraging the malleability of identity and image? What does "distinctive" mean when institutional processes emphasize mimetic behavior (Scott, 1987) as a path to achieving a desired identity and image? This line of argument suggests that under conditions of change, it is not only existing identity or image that affects interpretation but also those yet to be achieved.

Issue Interpretation Labels

Research on interpretation in business organizations usually presumes that the labeling of issues influences decisions and actions (Dutton and Jackson, 1987; Thomas, Clark, and Gioia, 1993). This research has identified two issue categories that have come to dominate the literature: whether managers see issues as "opportunities" or as "threats" (Jackson and Dutton, 1988). Given that the study of strategic change in not-for-profit domains is in an early stage, it might be premature to presume that these interpretation categories translate directly to the academic arena. A categorization scheme that distinguishes issues in more general terms might be more useful. Rather than threats and opportunities, for instance, top management team members might initially categorize issues as either "strategic" or non strategic, but nonetheless "important." Similarly, academic traditions encourage participatory, consensus-based decision making, which might foster sensitivity to issues that affect the delicate balancing of factional preferences. The dominance of existing issue categorization schemes might be obscuring such issue categorizations, perhaps inadvertently resulting in a lack of empirical attention, although such categories might be quite germane to this context.

Qualitative Case Study

We conducted the initial stage of the project at a large, public research university that was in the midst of managing a strategic change effort that had been launched earlier. The stated goal of the change effort was to match internal capabilities with external conditions so that the university would be better positioned to deal with the "realities of the '90s." The administration had pointedly noted that "strategic" thinking and planning would be a hallmark of the change effort, to emphasize that the university now needed to see itself as "competing," not only with other universities but also with other organizations vying for public and private funding. The guiding symbolic vision for the change was that of making the institution a "Top 10" public university, which emerged early in the change process. The three members of the top management team, consisting of the president, the executive vice president/ provost, and the vice provost, were the architects of the change effort.

The orientation toward change had already produced several significant alterations in the administrative and academic structure and actions of the university, including the creation of a new school, the elimination of several programs, the combining of two colleges into a new unit, the establishment of a research park, and the pursuit of several large-scale, potentially profit-making projects. In addition, the university had recently become affiliated with a new athletic conference, and lucrative commercial tie-ins with corporations were in place. These changes were all relatively fresh and were still somewhat unsettling to various factions within a university that had historically seen itself as traditional, or normative (Albert and Whetten, 1985), in character. These factions remained politically active in trying to influence change actions toward their preferred agendas. Nonetheless, the top management team viewed the university as "having a momentum for change" and was actively engaged in setting the future direction of the university.

Method

The initial phase of the research was qualitative and fundamentally interpretive in its approach, so as to tap into the interpretation and meaning system of the top management team. Because meaning is essentially a socially constructed phenomenon, we treated the interpretation system as an intersubjectively negotiated framework of understanding. Therefore, we paid particular attention to the ways that the members themselves understood their context and experience and how they communicated that understanding among themselves and to others.

Informants and research procedures. All three members of the top management team agreed to participate in the study. We conducted multiple, in-depth interviews with each member over a six-month period, during which the team was actively engaged in the strategic change process. These were ethnographic-style interviews (Spradley, 1979): They were semistructured and allowed open-ended probes, but they also encouraged the informants to use their own terminology and to steer the interview toward issues and concepts that they felt best represented their own experiences. The interviews allowed the informants to engage in a stream of consciousness and to provide "thick," descriptive data.

Both authors took part in each interview, one having primary responsibility for questioning and the other taking notes, seeking clarification, and asking supplementary questions. During data gathering, we observed several rules of interviewing and qualitative data handling (Spradley, 1979; Yin, 1984; Bourgeois and Eisenhardt, 1988). First, we audiotaped all interviews and transcribed them verbatim. Second, we discussed the interviews and notes and did preliminary analyses in accordance with a "24-hour rule" to capitalize on the immediacy of the data. Third, we interviewed each informant multiple times so that we could affirm or revise interpretations, seek clarifications and explanations, and ask follow-up questions. Ultimately, the interview transcripts and notes served as the primary data base for the qualitative study.

We also interviewed other members of the upper echelons of the university, former officers (to gain a historical perspective), and members of the top management teams of other universities. In all, there were 25 interviews; for our focal data base we selected 11 of the interviews with the top management team members that focused on key aspects of their interpretation processes. We also used internal documents, including memos and limited-circulation reports, as well as speeches and all publicly available documentation, including newspaper accounts, to build our understanding of the change process.

We analyzed the transcripts according to two related but different analytical systems, one a categorization and theme analysis derived from Miles and Huberman's (1984) qualitative data analysis techniques and the other a domain analysis derived from Spradley's (1979) ethnographic interview techniques. We performed these different analyses as a form of triangulation (Jick, 1979) to provide confidence in the findings. Because both systems generated highly corroborative findings we report only the details of the categorical analysis.

Categorical analysis. Figure 27-1 shows the progression of the categorical analysis. During the initial readings of the transcriptions, we identified numerous first-order (informant) terms and concepts (Van Maanen, 1979). An example is the often-used "top 10 public university" phrase. We devoted subsequent readings to assembling these concepts into categories that defined similar ideas, issues, or relationships that had relevance for the informants (see column 1 of Figure 27-1). Next, we used a form of constant comparison (Glaser and Strauss, 1967) to triangulate comparative data from different informants and times to discern the shared concepts and/or processes used in managing the change effort. We developed comprehensive cross-reference lists to keep track of category commonality (e.g., politics and influence), relationships among major concepts (e.g., "top ten" and image), and the emerging themes (e.g., concern with the university's prestige or image).

We next used two different analysts to further explore the data via theoretical sampling (Strauss, 1987); they focused on convergent concepts, quotes, decisions, actions, etc., and their relation to the evolving categories and themes that emerged from the first stage of the analysis. On the basis of this analysis, we merged some overlapping categories. Then we assigned second-order, theoretical labels to the emergent themes (column 2 of Figure 27-1). We used these second-order themes (Van Maanen, 1979) to capture the informant categories at a higher level of abstraction. We derived these labels either by developing a more general label that subsumed the first-order categories or by reference to the existing literature that described the emergent themes well (e.g., "image" and "identity"). We then conducted a final iteration of constant comparison to decide whether enough evidence existed to support an identified theme as a reportable "finding." Finally, we assembled the second-order themes into aggregate analytical dimensions that provided a superordinate organizing framework for organizing the emerging findings (column 3 of Figure 27-1).

Gestalt analyses. In addition to these qualitatively rigorous analyses, both authors and a different research assistant conducted an impressionistic analysis (Van Maanen, 1988) to try to gain a general sense of patterns in the data. Overall, then, we assessed convergence across the multiple analytical techniques to establish confidence in our findings. We have structured the findings below according to the dominant emergent themes: we present them mainly in second-order terms, because these representations most clearly show the underlying concepts in operation. We have, however, included quotes from informants to demonstrate the character of the emergent themes. The grounded approach used in the case study in some ways is the inverse of the most common mode of interpretation research: Rather than using prior theory to drive the data gathering, the theoretical perspective is grounded in and emerges from the data (Glaser and Strauss, 1967; Gioia and Chittipeddi, 1991).

Findings

Because the initial focus of the study was on issue interpretation, we first present these findings and work back toward a description of their relationship to the other major informant dimensions (i.e., top management team perceptions and the sensemaking context). After describing the character of the interpretations and perceptions, we formulate several relational propositions between these dimensions and begin to construct the grounded model. Finally, after presenting the findings on the sensemaking context, we formulate propositions relating this dimension to the interpretation and perception dimensions, thus completing the tentative model. This presentational strategy also shows the basis for operationalizing concepts that permit a nomothetic investigation of the model in the second, quantitative study.

Issue interpretations. Early in the research it became clear that the top management team distinguished issues as either "strategic" or "political." Although both types of issues were important, the informants saw strategic issues as "most important" because they affected the long-term well-being of the university. As the vice provost described it: "I carry around in my

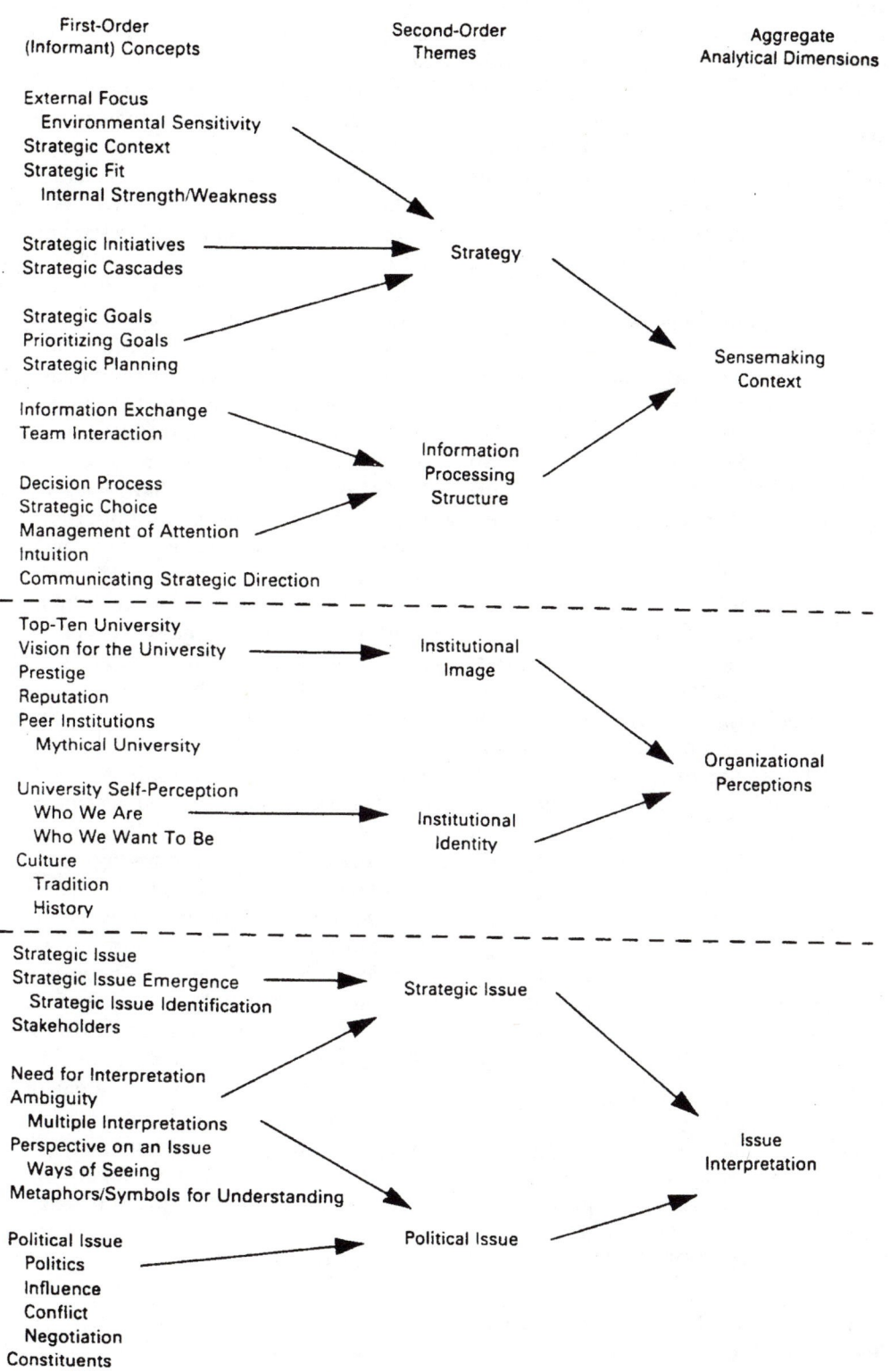

First-Order
(Informant) Concepts

Second-Order
Themes

Aggregate
Analytical Dimensions

External Focus
  Environmental Sensitivity
Strategic Context
Strategic Fit
  Internal Strength/Weakness

Strategic Initiatives
Strategic Cascades

Strategic Goals
Prioritizing Goals
Strategic Planning

Strategy

Information Exchange
Team Interaction

Decision Process
Strategic Choice
Management of Attention
Intuition
Communicating Strategic Direction

Information
Processing
Structure

Sensemaking
Context

Top-Ten University
Vision for the University
Prestige
Reputation
Peer Institutions
  Mythical University

Institutional
Image

University Self-Perception
  Who We Are
  Who We Want To Be
Culture
  Tradition
  History

Institutional
Identity

Organizational
Perceptions

Strategic Issue
Strategic Issue Emergence
  Strategic Issue Identification
Stakeholders

Strategic Issue

Need for Interpretation
Ambiguity
  Multiple Interpretations
Perspective on an Issue
  Ways of Seeing
Metaphors/Symbols for Understanding

Political Issue
  Politics
  Influence
  Conflict
  Negotiation
Constituents

Political Issue

Issue
Interpretation

* Indented labels indicate subcategories we merged during analysis as a result of constant comparison and cross-reference procedures.

Figure 27-1 Progression of the categorical analysis.*

head distinctions between content and process, in terms of what is a strategic issue and what is a political issue. I spend a lot of time smoothing feathers, but I concentrate on what will get the job done."

Strategic issues. The interpretation of an issue as strategic had to do with identifying or pursuing initiatives that would create or convey the image of a top-10 academic institution. As the president said, "When you are looking at strategic issues, you ask yourself: What would a top-10 place look like? That's how you consider issues that you are going to deal with." He defined them as "issues that relate to how the university serves the state economy and society more generally." The vice president was even more pointed: "What makes an issue strategic? It's whether it relates to [our] drive for prestige in becoming a top-10 place." Seen in these terms, enrollment, faculty recruiting, the creation of high-visibility schools and programs, and, perhaps especially, funding issues were defined as strategic because they "relate to the quality of the enterprise and the image of the institution" (executive vice president). Defining an issue as strategic implied "hard-nosed prioritizing" in a culture that was not receptive to such blatantly business-like processes. Nonetheless, the team emphatically dismissed the idea that all colleges, departments, and programs should somehow be treated "equally," although they were keenly aware that those units not favored would argue that such a "slash and burn approach" was not in the traditions of academia. The president put it in stark terms:

> You can't treat all these departments and programs equally. You begin to make some judgments about those areas that are strong and ought to continue to be strong, those areas that are weak and need to be strengthened, those areas that are weak and should be left with benign neglect, and those areas that are actually going to disappear.

Within the team, the frequently invoked metaphor of a "three-legged stool" captured the idea of being strategic. The legs of the metaphorical stool were (1) increased state funding, (2) increased private funding, and (3) strategic planning. Trying to identify strategic issues and prioritize according to a nebulous top-10 vision, however, was not a clear-cut process, especially in a university in which consensus and egalitarianism were historically valued. Therefore, another prominent type of issue also captured interpretive attention: political issues.

Political issues. The informants defined political issues as those that involved the management of competing interests and preferences, especially if the issue could compromise the attempt to achieve top-10 status. Those issues labeled (and treated) as political included pressures for administrative structural changes and concerns with diversity, as well as student involvement in the governance of the university. As the president explained about student involvement, "Nobody is going to rise or fall based on that issue, unless you say you don't believe it's important." These issues obviously were important and delicate in trying to manage the change process, but they led to a different way of thinking about issue interpretation: "How do you make the judgment call on navigating this thicket? Information is seldom on the substance of the issue; it is on the personalities involved, people's attitudes, and the politics of getting from here to there" (executive vice president).

The idea of change itself became a political issue simply because it challenged many people's preference for *not* changing—and because it involved powerful parties: "We want to change the place, but it is a question of what you can get away with. Historically, we have a very conservative board. We have to pay serious attention to that. Prepare them for thinking of the place as top 10 and understanding what that means we have to do" (president). The notion of prioritization as a strategic planning process, as well as the intention to designate certain colleges and programs to receive extra funding to try to become a top-10 institution, plunged the team directly into dealing with political issues because some powerful factions demanded that their programs be treated as strategically important, even if they were not:

> You cannot ignore [that college] in this university, even if they have little to do with achieving top 10 status. . . . It is not insignificant that a number of our very influential trustees are graduates of that program and have a proprietary attitude about its health. That is a big political issue

and a political fact of life. Now the real issue is whether it will help us get strategic excellence nationally. It won't, so you can't make it a strategic priority. But you better pay attention to it. You will get kicked out of here very fast if you are not sensitive to them. (Vice president)

In general, political issues were almost exclusively internally focused, but an issue that appears prototypically political—dealing with the governor and state legislature—top management team members instead construed as a strategic issue. They wanted to garner more state funding (one of the legs of the three-legged stool), which would enable more strategic initiatives. To do so, they wanted to affect the governor's perceptions of the university; they wanted to co-opt him by having him see himself "as a stakeholder in this university, instead of as a member of the audience" (president), and interpret the top-10 vision as his own and see such status as a goal of the state. If successful, the university might avoid the draining, yearly budget battles that consistently resulted in lower appropriations than needed. Overall, the top management team recognized that the change effort would not be sustained unless both internal and external stakeholders and constituencies could be convinced to accept the top-10 vision and the top management team's issue interpretations. As the vice president explained, "We want to try to get people to think the way we would like them to think. We want to try to raise their aspirations." They chose language so that their issue interpretations would be influential.

In addition to these findings, there also was a corollary finding that we termed a "strategic cascade": As team members labeled certain issues as strategic, they then came to see other issues as strategic as a consequence. Designating one program as a strategic priority, for instance, sometimes meant that they then designated other programs as strategic, in turn. Similarly, they sometimes classified current "political" issues as having the likelihood of evolving or cascading into future strategic issues. Minority enrollment, for example, which they classified as a political issue, they also saw as a strategic-issue-in-waiting, simply because future demographic projections show dramatic escalations in minority enrollment, and enrollment was predictably a strategic

issue. Likewise, although they also interpreted diversity as a political issue, its future status was likely to be strategic, especially as it concerned faculty recruiting. Lastly, the president noted that it was also possible for sticky political issues to turn into strategic issues if they created such a furor that they prevented strategic action or subverted the processes or goodwill necessary to accomplish strategic action. All these types of cascades were important in revealing future issues to be dealt with, either because they identified untenable political states or because they suggested previously overlooked strategic possibilities.

Overall, our findings concerning issue interpretation showed that in this organization, which was inexperienced in the strategic change process, the informants dichotomized issues into "strategic" and "political" categories, rather than the threat and opportunity categories common in business organizations. Of some note, late in the research when we asked one of the informants if he conceived issues in terms of threats or opportunities, his response was, "If you ask me to think in those terms, I can, but that isn't the way I normally do it. Those terms don't necessarily relate to what I am doing in this job." What became clear to us is that the way team members interpreted issues related to the way they saw the organization's identity and image.

Top management team perceptions. The top-10 vision that served as the symbol for launching the strategic change effort some years earlier had become pervasive at the time of this study. The concept of "top 10" had an aura of apparent specificity, but the top management team and many other members of the university community acknowledge that it was a much more ill-defined notion than it first appeared: "The top-10 vision is inspirational and is plausible. It doesn't have to be realistic, but it is plausible" (executive vice president). This vision communicated not only aspirations for the future but also the message that the university was not yet in the elite circle, although by implication it could be and would be if the change effort were successful: "Top-10 status is a way of articulating our intent to be, and be seen, as a major player" (executive vice president). It was clear, too, that the team wanted to maintain the ambiguity of the top-10 idea to allow a variety of interpretations, while minimizing the likelihood of in-fighting over exact standards of assessment: "The top-10 idea? Kind of a vague concept, eh? Yeah. It has to be. It needs to allow room to mean different things to different people and different factions" (president). In fact, the informants slyly noted that by various accounts the top-10 probably contained 15 or 20 universities. Many in the university were aware of the varied make-up of top-10 lists but conveniently overlooked the discrepancies because it permitted them to argue for status according to face-saving or self-serving choices of ratings lists used. The team viewed the inconsistency as useful, however, because it allowed political sensitivities to be managed.

The overriding concern with the top-10 vision led to a studied consideration of the prototypical characteristics of top universities as an approach to defining what a top-10 school looked like: "There is a profile in an experienced administrator's mind of what a great university looks like, and we are attempting to match that profile. We're not there yet" (vice president). The "we're not there yet" notion appeared in all informants' accounts and emphasized their desire for a different future "look" for the university. They originally cast this desired image in terms of a "mythical university," a phrase meant to convey idealism and high standards. In practice, the idea of a mythical university came to focus on the features of "peer institutions" perceived as already holding the elusive top-10 status. Those features included not only academic strength but also a utilitarian orientation with a demonstrated ability to raise funds and pursue enterprises that could "make a few bucks to support all the things we do." As the president phrased it:

> I look at the best places I can find that have certain traits that we don't have now, but are capable of having, and should have in the future. . . . I'm a great believer in peer comparisons. You look at the people who have the reputation and the clout for doing the best job and you say to yourself: "Why aren't we doing those things?"

Overall, in this process of comparing perceived top-10 universities with their own espoused top-10 vision, the team used two related but different consensual concepts to express their perceptions of the university: identity and image. At the first-order level of meaning, identity concerned "how you see yourself" as an institution; image focused implicitly on "how we think others see us [now]," but more overtly on "how we want others to see us in the future."

Identity. The adoption of the top-10 vision had led initially to a look inward at the team's sense of the institutional identity, as manifested in references to its history, traditions, symbols, practices, and "philosophy," as well as an assessment of the strength with which beliefs were held. Conclusions about identity and the strength of entrenched values and beliefs were not positive, especially given the desire for the university to change in some substantial ways. The president described the university as having had "a little hardening of the arteries," a description meant to suggest a recalcitrance toward change and a dysfunctional focus on political jockeying for resources. The team had therefore voiced a strong concern with changing the existing identity: "We just need to get [the university] to think better of itself. It's not easy; there is a lot of tradition around here that can get in the way of changing the way people think about themselves" (vice president). Such observations suggested that not only was the character of identity (e.g., emphasizing academic and/or economic values) an important consideration in anticipating critical issues, but that strength-of-identity perceptions also would affect current or emerging understandings of key issues. Talk among the top management team focused on the need for instilling a change orientation in members' perception of the university: "Top-10 is shorthand for saying that we are moving, that we are changing. It gives us a notion of who we will be in the future" (executive vice president).

At the time of this study, it was clear that the top management team had left its prior conception of the institution's identity behind in favor of a conception transformed in terms of a "top-10 public research institution." It also was clear that members of the team saw identity as necessarily malleable, but perhaps not easily so. They also indicated that they probably could not accomplish an identity change by focusing mainly on identity, because they were aware that people do not easily alter such belief structures. Therefore, instead of appealing directly to identity issues, they concentrated overtly on the related notion of image: ". . . if we start with trying to change identity, we might not get anywhere. But, if we start by laying out an image that people want to achieve, that will make it easier to move them off the current way of seeing themselves. That's what top-10 is all about" (vice president).

Image. The image dimension took the foreground in our data, appearing in a number of forms in the language of the informants, who often interchangeably used such terms as "prestige," "status," "impression," "stature," "visibility," and, somewhat loosely, "reputation." Of these first-order terms, the notions of prestige ("prestige is the goal") and our chosen representative label, "image," occurred most often: "Image is important! If you have the image, then people say: 'Oh yeah, he's from a good place.' They start by saying he must be pretty good. Then they look at what he's actually done" (executive vice president).

It soon became apparent that the issues the team interpreted as "strategic" were those they associated with achieving the desired future image for the university; those designated as "political" they associated with the status quo. Also, they did not construe image as "hand-waving" at the expense of substance; rather, they assumed that acceptance of the future image would lead to subsequent substantive improvements. The working logic was that the desired image would motivate a change in identity that would produce a desire for quality improvements, thus facilitating changes and strategic adaptation to the changing environment:

> Image has to be backed up by reality. It can't be fraudulent or it won't work. But if you tell people that your vision is that in five, ten, or fifteen years down the road they will be seen as graduates of a great university, they will buy into it. As you go along from here, you deliver, and you deliver by images, by people's impressions of who they will have become. (Executive vice president)

This belief was captured in the recurring story of a now-famous, high-quality institution that ostensibly had "bought" an image by convincing alumni to make major financial contributions to their then-mediocre university, so that the current administration could use the money to acquire resources and highly reputed faculty. The administrators argued that after using the donations to improve the university, the contributors would later be seen as having graduated from an elite school, even though the one they actually graduated from was not. In this fashion, later revisionist history would help to alter identity. Thus, the team saw image and identity as interdependent processes affecting each other over time. Although identity was an important concern, the current concentration was on projecting a desired future image: "We are trying to create an opportunity to articulate a vision of what the place ought to look like when it grows up. . . . What I am trying to do is manage the meaning of stature. A lot of us in the education business are trying to increase the future stature of the university" (vice president).

Identity and image took on a qualitatively different form within the strategic-change context of this study. Image, in particular, had a pronounced future-oriented tense to its expression. The characterization of both notions also implied that each was essentially changeable, but members clearly saw the desired, top-10 future image as the "key to change." Although they cast both perceptions against a backdrop of the existing tradition and culture of the university ("This was a stodgy institution . . ."), instead of the usual expression of "this is who we are and how we are seen," team members usually couched their expressions in terms of "this is who we want to be and how we want to be seen after the strategic change is accomplished." Overall, then, not only were image and identity important and vivid in the team members' perceptual processes, they also influenced the interpretation of issues. In particular, present and desired future image differed in their associations with strategic and political interpretations. These findings suggest several related propositions that capture key elements of an emerging model and provide grounds for further empirical investigation:

Proposition 1: Perceptions of identity and image will be differentially related to issue interpretation.

Proposition 1a: Present image will be related to political interpretation.

Proposition 1b: Desired future image will be related to strategic interpretation.

The remaining questions concern possible relationships between organizational perceptions and issue interpretations and the internal context within which sensemaking occurred.

Sensemaking context. We found two dominating contextual influences on how the top management team made sense of issues important to the change effort: strategy and information processing structure. Both are internal to the organization rather than external, as "the environment" is usually assumed to be. These internal "devices" (the informants' term) facilitated the understanding of the external environment.

Strategy. The strategy originally adopted under the aegis of this team several years earlier was based on the now-ubiquitous top-10 vision, and it guided administrative goals, plans, budgets, etc. Most notable, the mundane notion of "planning" had been recast as strategic planning and was framed as "a set of devices for making sense of things, motivating people, eliciting information, and justifying decisions" in pursuit of the top-10 vision:

> The vision is a clear, almost deceptively simple generalization. . . . The vision is decoupled from the strategic and is not easily monkeyed with. And maybe it has another important characteristic—it is not very easy to give up. Strategy is the operationalization of the vision. . . . It is the strategy that gets elaborated and explained and tinkered with and all that. Not the vision. Strategy is what makes it possible to achieve the vision. (Executive vice president)

The existing strategy constituted a means for identifying and focusing attention on issues relevant to managing the change process and in fact was influential in deciding which issues were actually strategic. As is evident in Figure 27-1, above, the strategy implied increased sensitivity to the external environment, assessments of the university's fit with environmental demands, an orientation toward strategic goals and planning, and an entrepreneurial stance. Proposed changes, impending changes, and actual changes (e.g., new schools, colleges, and programs that modeled top-10 universities) all provided symbolic evidence of the vision coming to realization. The team now pointedly interpreted all budgeting and funding issues in light of the strategy and selectively prioritized goals and initiatives accordingly—a change that engendered resistance

and political activity among powerful factions in the university (e.g., the deans).

Information processing structure. In keeping with the aims of the revised strategy, the top management team developed an information processing structure and supporting infrastructures that oriented information toward issues important to the whole institution, rather than the former concern with "provincial" decision making: "The administrative structure now facilitates the gathering and processing of information that we need to make strategic decisions. It never did before" (president). Meetings, information exchanges, and scanning activities assigned to specific roles or positions focused attention on important issues. In particular, interactions among the team members were frequent and typically open and informal; there were, however, several standing meetings designed to structure information and obtain input from outside sources, such as deans, other university officers, and ad hoc committees. Similarly, all team members participated in all major issue decisions: "We now have a much bigger sieve, and we have a much more matrix-like arrangement in terms of communication and decision making inside and a much more permeable membrane between the inside and the outside" (executive vice president).

The president had implemented this revised information processing structure because he felt that the "total organization" was not attuned to strategic issues but more to local, political issues that affected individual units: "The farther down you get, the harder you have to work to get issues recognized." The executive vice president noted differences by college: "Some deans didn't know what was going on and didn't have their own ears to the ground, except to protect their own territory, but we don't have many of them left." This suggested that the information processing structure also had a political use. Overall, the top management team set up an information processing structure characterized by interaction, informality, and participation so as to stay attuned to both strategic and political issues.

The internal sensemaking context thus had two main components: the strategy (put in place during the strategic change initiation process), which served as both an attention-directing device and a symbol of a university "on the move," and the top management team's information processing structure, which they used to deal with information on important issues. These findings, in juxtaposition with those concerning top management team perceptions and issue interpretations allow us to formulate a set of relational propositions that complete the emergent model and also lay the groundwork for testing and refining that model in the second phase of the study, a quantitative analysis of survey data.

> **Proposition 2:** Strategy and information processing structure will be related to issue interpretation.

> **Proposition 2a:** Strategy will be related to strategic issue interpretation.

> **Proposition 2b:** Information processing structure will be related to both strategic and political issue interpretation.

Similar evidence and reasoning lead to parallel propositions concerning the relationships among strategy, information processing structure, identity, and image:

> **Proposition 3:** Strategy and information processing structure will be related to organizational identity and image.

Because we do not have compelling empirical evidence suggesting specific differential relationships, we specify only the general relational proposition. Taken together, however, these findings and propositions suggest an emergent, grounded model, as shown in Figure 27-2.

The emergent model in this graphic form also allows the clearest specification of a final mediational proposition:

> **Proposition 4:** Perceptions of image and identity will partially mediate the relationship between the sensemaking context and issue interpretation.

We refined the emergent model from this qualitative, ideographic case study by investigating these propositions in a quantitative, nomothetic survey study. The main research question remained: How do top management teams make sense of issues when managing strategic change in academia? Two corollary questions also guided the quantitative study, however: (1) Does the emergent theoretical model apply to other academic institutions of different size, type, ownership, and location? If so, (2) What are the relationships between the key emergent concepts (strategy, information processing structure, identity, and image) and the interpretation of issues?

Quantitative Survey Study

Sample

We chose a stratified sample of 439 higher-education institutions representing two differ-

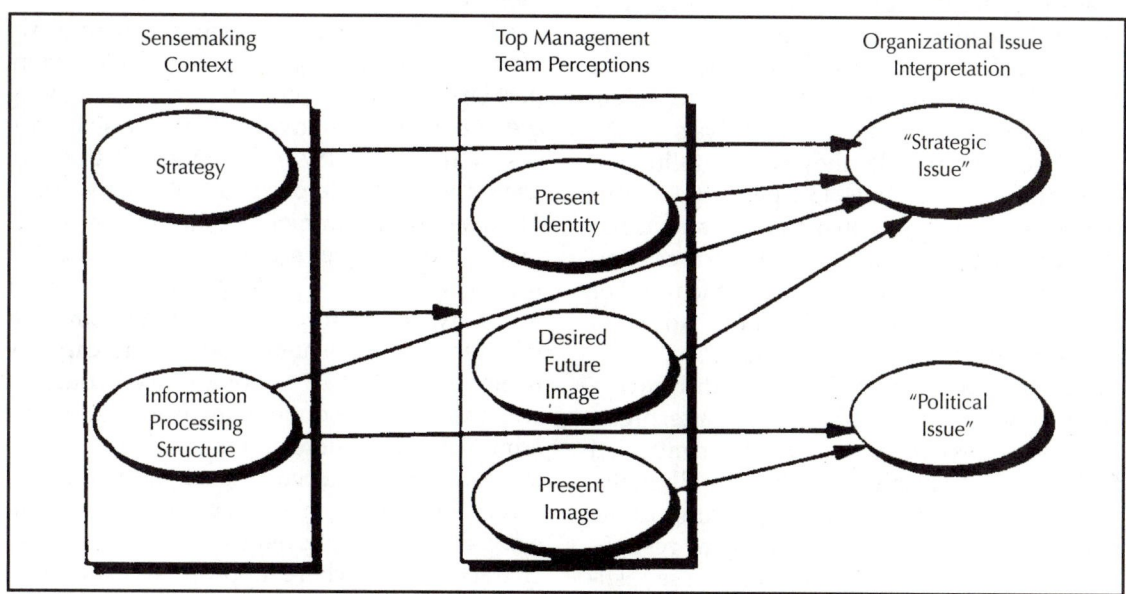

Figure 27-2 Emergent model of sensemaking in academic administration

ent ownership classifications (public and private) and three different degree-granting types (four-year baccalaureate, master's, and doctorate). There were approximately 75 institutions in each of the resulting six cells. We based our selection process on the regional distribution of the population of higher-education institutions to insure that all regions of the U.S. (Northeast, South, Midwest, West) were well represented. We selected no more than 33 percent of the institutions in each cell from any one region. We sent questionnaires to three top-level administrators at each of the 439 institutions. The positions including the following: the president or chancellor; executive vice president, provost, or vice president of academic affairs; and vice president or dean of admissions. If there was no vice president or dean of admissions, we sent a questionnaire to the chief financial officer or controller. We pretested the questionnaire via structured interviews lasting approximately one to two hours with five higher-education executives and professionals.

Of 1,317 questionnaires sent out, we received 611 usable questionnaires, representing 372 universities and colleges (individual response rate = 46 percent; institutional rate = 85 percent). Chi-square analysis revealed that in terms of size (number of full-time students), ownership, and type, there was no significant difference between the respondents and nonrespondents. There was a significant difference by region (χ^2 = 22.1, p < .0001), for which we controlled in subsequent analyses. The number of respondents from each institution ranged from one to three, with an average of 1.64. An analysis of the response rate by title showed the following distribution: presidents (33 percent), executive vice presidents (40 percent), and other top administrators (27 percent). Further analyses showed that neither title nor the number of respondents from an institution had a significant effect on the findings. Size, type, ownership, and region, however, did have a significant effect on some of the interpretation responses. Therefore, we also controlled for these demographic variables in all analyses. Of the 372 institutions responding to the questionnaire, 178 had more than one respondent. Interrater reliabilities across these institutions were greater than .80 for all percep-

tual variables, suggesting an acceptable level of agreement.

Variables

We conducted a literature search to help us operationalize the main concepts that emerged in the case study. We were especially interested in identifying research on higher education and in which the constructs of interest were operationalized. From the results of this search we constructed a questionnaire that included multi-item scales with 7-point Likert response formats for all variables. We averaged the items in each scale to calculate a score. The Appendix provides the complete scales for all variables. Cronbach alphas were greater than .70 for all scales.

Perceived contextual variables. The relevant variables associated with the sensemaking context were strategy and the information processing structure of the top management team. The eight items measuring the institution's strategy derived from Miles' (1982) conceptual framework and adaptation of specific items that Hambrick (1981) used to measure the strategies of higher-education institutions. Two main types of strategies anchored the primary scale: domain offensive (institutions engaging in new programs, curricula, and market developments) and domain defensive (institutions maintaining positions, engaging in little program development, concerned with efficiency). Items were coded so that higher scores meant more offensive-oriented behavior.

For information processing structure, we were interested in the degree of interaction, participation, and process formality among the top managers involved in decision processes (Duncan, 1973). To measure this, we used a 9-item scale derived from the work of Thomas and McDaniel (1990). We scaled the items so that higher scores represented higher interaction, higher participation, and lower formality, indicating an information processing structure with higher processing capacity (Galbraith, 1973). Although we collected responses for these variables from individual administrators, these scales referred to processes or actions occurring at the institution level. Thus, the survey instructions emphasized that items referred to institutional/team characteristics, where appropriate, and that top management team members were acting as informants on the team. We then calculated aggregate values for these variables from item averages across multiple respondents within each university.

Top management team perceptions. The main top management team perceptions of interest were identity and image. Identity refers to "how the institution sees itself" (Dutton and Dukerich, 1991). Following Albert and Whetten (1985), who drew heavily from university settings in their theory development, we assessed the type of organizational identity as perceived by the top management team respondents through items that measured whether they saw the institution as more "utilitarian" or more "normative." When members perceive the organization's character to be oriented mainly toward economic factors, identity is more utilitarian; when they perceive the organization's character to be oriented mainly toward ideological and value-based concerns, identity is more normative. We reverse-coded the 9-item scale so that low scores indicated a more utilitarian identity.

Because the data from the qualitative study suggested that top management team members were concerned not only with identity per se, but also with the extent to which members held the values and identity of the institution, we included a strength-of-identity measure in addition to the type-of-identity measure. This strength-of-identity variable refers to administrators' beliefs about various facets of the organization's cultural values (Martin et al., 1983; Milliken, 1990) irrespective of the type of identity (normative or utilitarian) they perceive. We adapted Milliken's six-item scale, which had been used in a higher-education research setting, for use in this research. Higher scores indicated a stronger sense of identity by top management team members.

Image refers to how members think others see the institution (Dutton and Dukerich, 1991) or how top management would like others to see the institution (Whetten, Lewis, and Mischel, 1992). Dutton, Dukerich, and Harquail (1994) also referred to this notion as "construed external image." We identified two variations of the image concept from the case study—present and desired future image—and measured both using 10-item Likert (1–7) scales. We assessed present image by asking respondents how they perceived other peer institutions

would currently rate their institution along ten dimensions (e.g., quality of students, academic climate; see Appendix for details). Because the findings from the case study indicated that the emulation of "peer" institutions with desired attributes was the basis for a desired future image, we assessed desired future image by first asking respondents what peer institutions (up to three) they would want their own institution to emulate. Next, we asked them to indicate (using the same ten items) the extent to which they desired to emulate the institutions they identified earlier (i.e., how respondents wanted their institution to be seen in the future).

Issue interpretation. Through our case study interviews and a subsequent literature search we identified 26 issues that top administrators typically face at modern institutions of higher education. We asked a panel of five experts (three higher-education professors and two high-level administrators) to rank the issues in terms of how important they felt higher-education administrators would perceive them to be. Five issues appeared in the top rankings of all five raters: faculty satisfaction, minority issues, external funding, student educational satisfaction, and changes in academic programs. For each of these issues, we used two, 4-item scales to assess the extent to which respondents felt each was a strategic and/or political issue. Issues are strategic if they can alter the institution's position in the market, can significantly affect the whole institution, and can have an effect on the institution's goals and missions (Ginsberg, 1988). Issues are political if they involve conflict, negotiation, or influence attempts by individuals or groups to gain their preferences (Pfeffer, 1981).

Data analysis. We tested propositions 1–3 using path analysis. We used two path models, each utilizing one of the image variables (present vs. future) to test the differential relationships of image to interpretation. The path analytical technique allowed us to identify the relative magnitudes of the direct and indirect effects of the sensemaking context and image/identity variables on the interpretation of key institutional issues. We tested proposition 4 by using the three-regression-equations procedure suggested by Baron and Kenny (1986). We used multivariate regression to test the overall relationships between sets of variables.

Table 27-1

Means, Standard Deviations, Alphas, Interrater Reliabilities and Zero-order Correlations

Variable	Mean	S.D.	Alpha*	IRR†	1	2	3	4	5	6	7	8	9	10	11
1. Size‡	3.65	.47	NA	NA											
2. Type	1.99	.78	NA	NA	.61••										
3. Ownership	1.47	.50	NA	NA	-.37••	-.06									
4. Region	2.87	.61	NA	NA	.06	.01	-.20••	-.04							
5. Identity type	3.85	.68	.71	.92	.13•	-.02	-.16••	-.03	-.20••						
6. Identity strength	5.60	.78	.82	.90	-.13•	-.07	.20••	-.06	-.19••	.53••					
7. Present image	5.07	.71	.88	.92	-.05	.07•	.25••	-.02	-.10	.16••	.22••				
8. Desired future image	5.27	.65	.86	.91	.02	-.03	.07	.06	-.35••	.05	.08•	.04			
9. Strategy	3.86	.92	.76	.86	.14••	.13•	-.01	.03	-.08	.39••	.26••	-.10•	-.07		
10. Information processing structure	4.81	.74	.88	.91	-.02	-.07	-.04								
11. Strategic interpretation	5.44	.61	.88	.91	.04	.07	.05	-.01	-.20••	-.19••	.15••	.15••	.10•	.18••	
12. Political interpretation	3.63	.89	.92	.81	.15••	.12••	-.14••	.09	-.01	-.24••	-.10•	.07	.08•	.19••	.22••

•$p < .05$; ••$p < .01$.
∗ Cronbach alphas calculated across all informants ($N = 611$).
† Interrater reliability for those institutions with more than one informant ($N = 178$).
‡ Raw size range was 188 to 66,909 students.

Control variables. We controlled for the effects of size, type, ownership, and region for each of the regression equations in the path analyses, as well as the test for mediation, after initial ANOVA analyses revealed links to the study's variables. Size was the number of full-time students enrolled, which we calculated by using the nine size groups used in the U.S. Department of Education's *Digest of Educational Statistics* (1 = less than 200 students; 9 = more than 30,000). Because the distribution was skewed (Kologorov-Smirnov Z-Test = 4.80, $p < .001$), we applied a logarithmic transformation. We coded type in terms of highest degree offered, with bachelor's degree equal to 1; master's degree, 2; and Ph.D. and beyond, 3. We coded ownership as either public (1) or private (2). We coded region as Northeast (1), Midwest (2), South (3), or West (4). We based this coding scheme and the states representing these regions on the *Digest* categories.

Results

Because neither extant theory nor the findings from the case study permitted issue-specific propositions or hypotheses, we averaged the scores for the five issues in terms of their perceived strategic and political content to form higher strata strategic interpretation and political interpretation measures, respectively. The overall Cronbach alpha for the strategic interpretation scale was .88; for the political interpretation scale it was .92 (reliability alphas for the individual issues were all above .72). Second-order factor analyses revealed that the issue loaded significantly on the single higher-order latent (strategic/political) variable (all parameter estimates > .50, $p < .01$). Table 27-1 provides the descriptive statistics and zero-order correlations for the combined interpretation scales and the other scales and variables.

Multivariate analysis indicated that, across all respondents, the set of independent variables (strategy, information processing structure, present/future image, identity type, and identity strength) was significantly related to the set of dependent variables (strategic and political interpretation). Multivariate results were Wilks' lambda = .69; $F_{18,720} = 12.56$, $p < .0001$.

Proposition testing. Results of testing the proposed differential relationship between the perceptual measures (i.e., image and identity)

and interpretation (proposition 1) indicated that identity type was related to the interpretation of organizational issues as strategic. This means that top management teams perceiving their institutions as more utilitarian tended to interpret issues as more strategic; those teams perceiving their institutions as more normative tended to interpret issues as less strategic. The strength-of-identity measure was positively related to the interpretation of issues as strategic and negatively related to the interpretation of issues as political. Further, although present image was significantly related to political interpretation, desired future image was not, supporting proposition 1a. Desired future image was related only to strategic interpretation and to political interpretation, as predicted by proposition 1b. Overall, the pattern of relationships among the variables indicated that identity type, identity strength, and desired future image were related to strategic interpretation, while only strength of identity and present image were related to political interpretation. Table 27-2 presents all the results from the path analyses.

In testing proposition 2 (that context would relate directly to issue interpretation), we found a direct link between information processing structure and the interpretation of issues as political, as well as the interpretation of issues as strategic. This negative relationship between information processing structure and political interpretation indicates that higher degrees of information processing structure are associated with top management teams perceiving organizational issues as less political. There was no significant direct relationship, however, between strategy and interpretation. Thus, the data support proposition 2b (that the information processing structure related to both strategic and political interpretation), but not proposition 2a (that strategy will be related to strategic issue interpretation).

We had formulated a general proposition that strategy and information processing structure would be related to identity and image, respectively (proposition 3). After controlling for size, type, ownership, and region, we found that strategy was a significant predictor of both identity measures, as shown in Table 27-2. The negative relationship between strategy and identity type means that offense-oriented strategies were associated with more utilitarian (less normative) identities. Although informa-

Table 27-2

Path Analysis and Regression Results[*]

Variable	B	t	R^2	F
Strategic Interpretation			.15	6.93[**]
Region	-.02	-.56		
Type	.00	.05		
Ownership	.04	.71		
Size	.12	1.77		
Information processing structure	.15	2.89[**]		
Strategy	.04	.76		
Image—present (future)	.05 (.11)	.03 (1.97[*])		
Identity (type)	-.20	-3.67[**]		
Identity (strength)	.12	1.96[*]		
Political Interpretation			.17	8.33[***]
Region	.07	1.46		
Type	.05	.77		
Ownership	-.10	-.18		
Size	.08	1.11		
Information processing structure	-.19	-3.63[***]		
Strategy	.08	1.55		
Image—present (future)	.11 (.08)	1.89[*] (1.01)		
Identity (type)	-.07	-1.23		
Identity (strength)	-.26	-4.24[***]		
Identity (Type)			.17	12.78[***]
Region	-.02	-.48		
Type	-.14	-2.29[*]		
Ownership	-.09	-1.73		
Size	.24	3.68[***]		
Information processing structure	-.05	-1.21		
Strategy	-.35	-7.27[***]		
Identity (Strength)			.22	17.23[***]
Region	-.01	-.31		
Type	.01	.04		
Ownership	.18	3.40[***]		
Size	-.08	-1.27		
Information processing structure	.40	8.67[***]		
Strategy	.08	2.19[*]		
Image (Present/Future)			.13	9.34[***]
Region	-.24	-.49		
Type	.14	2.28[*]		
Ownership	.21	3.76		
Size	-.07	-1.16		
Information processing structure	.26	5.35[***]		
Strategy	.03	.63		

[*]$p < .05$; [**]$p < .01$; [***]$p < .0001$.
[*]Standardized betas and t-values in parentheses are for future image when significance level changed as a result of substitution for present image.

tion processing structure was linked to strength of identity, present image, and desired future image, it was not significantly related to the type of identity. Thus, proposition 3 was broadly supported in that there was a general pattern of significant relationships between the sensemaking context and organizational perceptions. This can be seen clearly in Figure 27-3, which summarizes the findings graphically.

To test for mediation (proposition 4), we estimated the following three regression equations for each path in Figure 27-3: first, regressing the mediator (top management team perceptions) on the independent variable (sensemaking con-

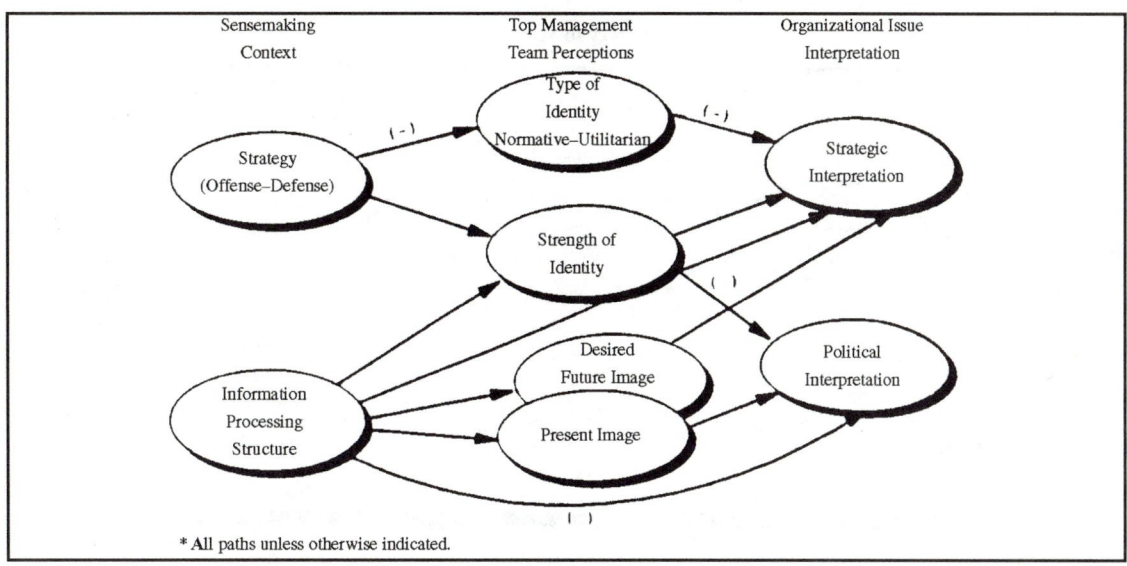

Figure 27-3 Revised model based on results of path analyses.*

text); second, regressing the dependent variable (issue interpretations) on the independent variable; and third, regressing the dependent variable on both the independent variable and the mediator. If the independent variable has no effect when controlling the mediator, there is full mediation; if the effect of the independent variable on the dependent variable is less in the third regression equation than in the second, then there is partial mediation (Baron and Kenny, 1986). This procedure revealed only one path (Strategy → Identity Type → Strategic Interpretation) that was fully mediational (i.e., the regression coefficient for strategy went from a .01 significance level to nonsignificance when controlling identity type). A second path (Information Processing Structure → Present Image → Political Interpretation) showed no mediation effects. All other paths were partially mediated by the top management team's perceptions of image and identity. Thus, these results provide only partial support for proposition 4.

When coupled with the case study findings, the path and mediation analyses indicate three primary paths, as shown in Figure 27-4. The first suggests that strategy's relationship to strategic interpretations is through the type and strength of the top management team's perceptions of organizational identity. Paths 2 and 3 of Figure 27-4 deal with the direct and indirect effects of information processing structure on interpretation. In path 2, we found that information processing structure affects the political interpretation of organizational issues both directly and indirectly through the strength of identity. There is no significant indirect path through the type of identity, present image, or desired future image. In path 3, the effect of information processing structure on strategic interpretation is also both direct and indirect. The partially mediated effect is through strength of identity and desired future image (but not present image). Again, there is no path through identity type.

Discussion

A Grounded View of Identity, Image, and Issue Interpretation in Academia

Of the findings from the case study, those concerning top management team perceptions (identity and image) and issue interpretations (strategic and political) have the greatest implications for theory. An underlying assumption of the informants was that their institution would not change markedly without somehow altering aspects of the central qualities of their institution—their identity. One of the most pronounced findings was the intense focus on the projection of a desired *future* image as a means of changing the currently held identity. There are several implications here. The first is that these team members assumed (or needed) identity to be somewhat fluid; actually, they viewed it as already in a state of flux as they

Path 1: Strategy to Strategic Interpretation

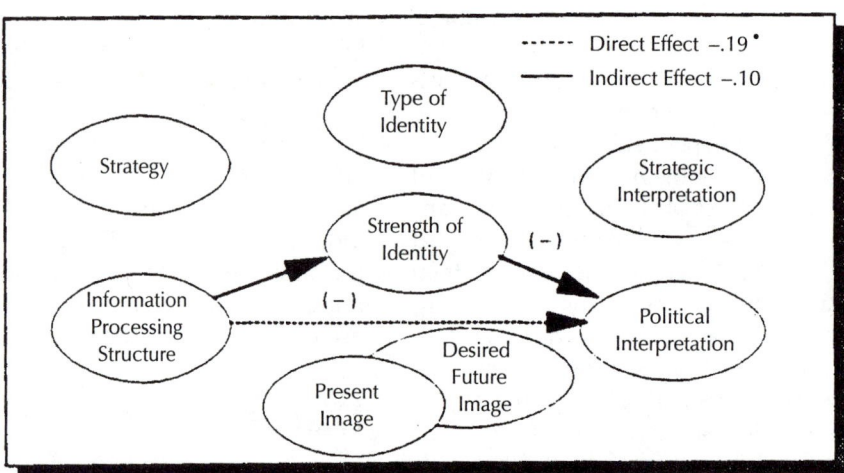

Path 2: Information Processing Structure to Political Interpretation

Path 3: Information Processing Structure to Strategic Interpretation

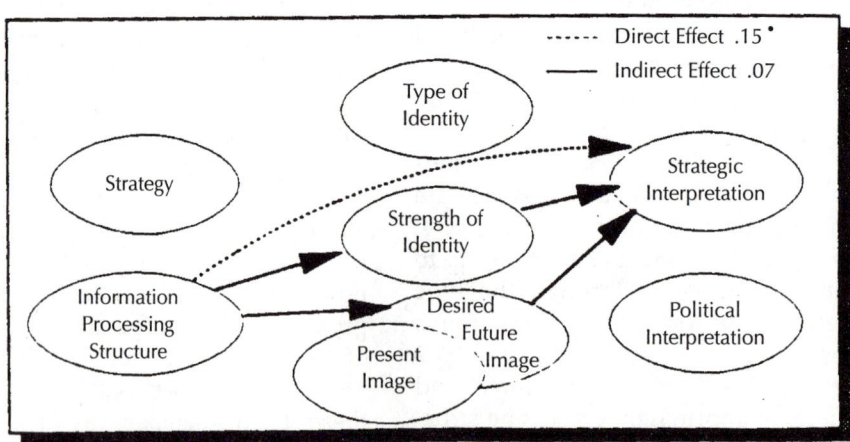

Figure 27-4 Primary mediated paths and direct effects compared.

tried to manage the strategic change effort that was currently underway. The top management teams' orientation is of some significance for theory, in that they construed organizational identity as changeable over relatively short periods of time, which is at odds with a key element of the currently accepted definition of identity as that which is central, distinctive, and *enduring* (Albert and Whetten, 1985; Dutton and Dukerich, 1991; Whetten, Lewis, and Mischel, 1992). The definition of identity as enduring obscures an important aspect of identity within the context of organizational change: for substantive change to occur, some basic features of identity also must change. What does "enduring" mean if organizational actors presume identity to be (and treat it as) malleable as a matter of practical necessity? In light of our findings, it seems appropriate to soften the stricture on the conception of identity as more or less fixed to include a dimension of fluidity.

Another theoretically important issue concerns the relationship of identity and image. Do changes in identity lead to changes in image or vice versa? And what implications might an answer to this question have for accomplishing organizational changes in identity and image? One line of thought would be that top management could first try to foster a change in identity that would produce a change in image (identity as the progenitor of image). Another line of thought would be that management could project a desired future image that would serve as a catalyst for changing identity (image as the shaper of identity). In the case study, the top management team believed that altering image was the path to altering identity, that the projection of a compelling future image would destabilize identity and "pull" it into alignment with the desired image. Presumably, the changing identity would further motivate progress toward the desired future image, which would further strengthen the new identity, etc.

A stream of theory and research that merges with this future-oriented sense of image as an impetus for change is the literature on organizational vision. Vision connotes the idea of a mythical organization that, as Nonaka and Takeuchi (1995) suggested, creates both chaos and order: chaos because it challenges members to think differently about the organi-

zation, and order because it offers direction. Collins and Porras (1991) argued that vision must be rooted in a guiding philosophy—the core beliefs and values of the organization—before it can be coupled with a tangible image of the future. It is in this articulation of a vision for change that past, present, and future come together. Against the backdrop of the organization's current and historical identity, top managers begin to mold new images of how they would like the organization to be perceived by external (and internal) stakeholders. As our informants suggested, new or redefined "sensible" identities that depart from past- and present-oriented views of the organization's self-concept then need to be generated to fit this desired future image. The range and level of abstraction of that departure are critical considerations during strategic change. In particular, members must determine which ostensibly enduring elements of the organization's identity should change and how much they should change to affect and ultimately reflect a desired future image of the organization. These proposed changes must at once capture members' imagination as well as their commitment (Hart, 1992). Thus, strategic change requires navigating between the maintenance of continuity and the management of disruption.

Dutton and Dukerich (1991) argued that deterioration of image is an important trigger for action. The findings of our case study suggested that the top management team was trying to think ahead, to do a kind of prospective sensemaking in constructing a desired image based on emulating other successful universities. The emphasis on emulation raised another caution about using a definition of identity as that which is "distinctive." Given our finding that the university administrators were seeking a new image by trying to mimic others already in the "top-10," they arguably were trying to achieve prominence by becoming *non*-distinctive from this elite referent group. Perhaps they intended to distinguish themselves along some fine-grained lines of difference within the elite group, but that point is not obvious from our data. With emulation as the chosen path to a desired future image, mimetic processes (Scott, 1987; DiMaggio and Powell, 1991) operated to diminish, not foster, distinctiveness as a component of some projective identity. Our findings also stand in contrast to Martin et al.'s

(1983) and Kinda's (1992) assertions that organizations often claim uniqueness when they are in fact not unique. The lack of uniqueness that emerged here was, for all practical purposes, intentional.

The most obvious difference between the findings of the case study and the existing literature was in the use of strategic/political categories, rather than the expected opportunity/threat categories. Our data, and our experiences in gathering it, lead us to believe that these categories pertain to a more general or coarse-grained level of categorization and labeling (Rosch, 1978) more appropriate to the context studied here. Cognitive categories emerge at a fairly general level and through experience develop finer gradations of distinction (Rosch and Mervis, 1975). Furthermore, such coarse-grained interpretations might be precursors to the development of more refined categories with commonly recognized issue labels like threats and opportunities (Dutton, Stumpf, and Wagner, 1990). We studied a context that featured an industry, an organization, and an executive team who were relatively unfamiliar with competition and with the strategic change stance that is so common in the business arena. For this domain, the team did not use the threat/opportunity labels. One might therefore see this finding as an artifact of the domain studied, and indeed it might be, but if so, it is an informative artifact because it suggests that taken-for-granted categories from the business literature do not necessarily translate well to other domains in which top managers are now engaging in strategic processes.

Discussion of the Quantitative Results

The broad-based survey results offer general support, clarification, and refinement of the grounded findings of the case study. These results demonstrate that image and identity have strong and systematic relationships with top management team interpretations of the key issues confronting higher-education institutions. Furthermore, image and identity not only directly affected issue interpretation, but they also served as influential linkages between the organizational sensemaking context and issue interpretation. The refined model also indicates firm support for the grounded model's focus on the existing strat-

egy in use and the information processing structure in place. Although changes in the external environment are clearly influential, strategy and information processing structure create an internal context for interpreting those changes. Thomas and McDaniel (1990), using an information processing perspective, found a linkage between these internal contextual features and interpretation, but they did not identify or explore the means by which this linkage occurred. This study locates the conceptual and empirical connection in the top management team's perceptions of the organization (i.e., identity and image).

With respect to the specific path relationships, we would like to highlight several key results evident in Figures 27-3 and 27-4. First, we found that strategy was linked only to the identity measures. When top management teams perceived their institutions as utilitarian and domain offensive, they tended to see the issues they faced as being strategic, whereas those who perceived their institutions as normative and domain-defensive saw the same issues as less strategic. Why might this pattern hold? On one hand, perhaps a declared domain-offensive strategy influences an orientation or reorientation toward a utilitarian identity. Such an identity implies that institutional decisions and actions are aimed at dealing with a competitive environment. On the other hand, domain defensive strategies are associated with more traditional, normative identities that de-emphasize an external, market orientation and thus do not facilitate perceptions of key issues from the environment in strategic terms.

There also was a positive relationship between strength of identity and the interpretation of issues as strategic. This result modifies the findings of Milliken (1990) by suggesting that strong, not weak, identities are linked to interpretations of issues as strategic. Rather than a strong identity providing confidence that the institution can weather, or even ignore, environmental changes, our findings suggest the possibility that a strong identity (especially when linked to a domain-offensive strategy) might instead provide the confidence to be proactive. This difference might be because of the number of issues examined (one in Milliken's study versus five in this study) or to the type(s) of higher-education institutions studied (four-year, privately owned versus all types and ownership). This suggests that defense-oriented strategies in modern academia, although usually linked to an identity that stresses the traditional norms of higher education, seem to be weak platforms for building strategic interpretations of critical issues. Rather, it appears that more offense-oriented strategies are associated with identities that promote strategic thinking. The quantitative results also indicate that the strength-of-identity measure is negatively related to interpretations of organizational issues as political. That is, when top management team members perceived their institutions as having stronger (i.e., more embedded and firmly understood) identities, they tended to interpret issues as less political. Stronger perceptions of institutional identity by the top management team perhaps foster the commitment and social control (Ouchi and Price, 1978) that minimizes the need for political speculation around the key issues facing the team.

We also found that richer information processing structures (i.e., those with more participation and interaction and less formality) were related to stronger identities and to the two image measures. Information processing structure clearly is an influential mechanism for institutionalizing the extent to which identity is held by organization members. Moreover, it affects both present and desired future image. If the emphasis is on "who we are," information processing structure provides the means for justifying and reinforcing the status quo; if the emphasis is on "who we want to be," information processing structure becomes a driver for legitimizing an altered image, whereas strategy might be the driver for altering or retaining identity.

As Figure 27-3 shows, present image relates only to political interpretations. This suggests that an emphasis on present image (especially in dynamic environments) leads to issue interpretations that are more focused on the status quo, thus steering the top management team away from interpretations that might facilitate strategic change. The conspicuously absent linkage between present image and strategic interpretation is counterintuitive, given the external focus of the concept of image. We found that desired future image, however, relates only to strategic interpretation, suggesting that future image fosters a

more strategic focus. The mythical organization that is embodied in desired future image appears to guide interpretation toward those aspects of an issue that, when acted upon, can help accomplish strategic reorientation in a changing environment. Desired future image thus contributes an interpretive template for strategic change.

Concluding Observations

Taken together, the findings and emergent model of the grounded qualitative case study and the results and broader scope of the quantitative survey study provide some revealing insights. Several notable outcomes suggest implications for our theoretical views of changing organizations, perhaps especially those in an industry like higher education, which is just becoming familiar with the elements of strategic change.

Perhaps because change in the external environment is now virtually a given, it is useful conceptually to observe that top management teams in academia construe the proximal context for sensemaking mainly in internal terms. This finding is consistent with Thomas and McDaniel (1990) and Thomas, Clark, Gioia (1993) and Weick's (1995) recent theorizing. Also, strategy is construed here more as an input to the sensemaking process than as an output or product of sensemaking, as it is usually treated. The combined qualitative findings and quantitative results, in conjunction with prior work, suggest that both strategy and information processing structure might better be viewed as recursive phenomena that over time are both medium and outcome of the sensemaking process.

The findings on identity and image as they relate to strategic change were among the most revealing. If the concern is to make intentional, substantive change, then some fundamental organizational attributes must change. This apparently simple observation implies that even that which we usually presume to be essentially immutable (i.e., identity) might instead be fluid and malleable. Although existing organizational theories have viewed identity as somewhat changeable, typically over a long term (Albert and Whetten, 1985) or as an incremental adaptation to deteriorating image over time (Dutton and Dukerich, 1991), the kind of change now demanded of academic institutions calls for altering aspects of identity and image within dramatically shorter time horizons. Consequently, the conceptualization of identity should include dimensions that account for the ability of organizations to learn and adapt quickly.

This study also suggests that changes to identity can be encouraged by design and, further, that an influential avenue to a changed identity is a changed image. Thus, a prime role for leaders of strategic change is to frame that change in aspirational terms. As Thayer (1988: 250, cited in Weick, 1995) noted, "a leader does not tell it 'as it is'; [she or] he tells it 'as it might be'...." A plausible, attractive, even idealistic future image would seem to help organization members envision and prepare for the dynamic environment implied by strategic change. When strategic change is articulated in desired states, we get a picture of people thinking and talking in the future tense. This picture not only portrays identity and image as fluid, it also portrays organizations as more capable of change than is typically assumed. Practically speaking, it suggests that formulating a compelling future image that people can associate with and commit to eases the launching and eventual institutionalizing of strategic change.

Given our findings about image, should we conclude that higher-education institutions that engage in strategic change are likely to move from a focus on substance to a focus on image (Alvesson, 1990), such that the image becomes an overriding goal in itself? Perhaps, but it is important to note that because many of their products and services are intangible, institutions of higher education must rely (and historically have relied) on image to some extent, albeit not as an impetus for strategic change. It also is apparent that there is a link between substance and image. Achieving an improved image fosters substantive improvement. The progression, therefore, might not be simply from substance to image but, rather, from substance to image to substance, as organization members seek congruence between the two. Of course, there are limits to the degree to which an organization can change its identity and image. Gagliardi (1986) even argued that the primary strategy of an organization is to maintain its identity and that organizations change so that they can preserve the essence of their identities. There is a resolution to this seeming paradox if one assumes that organizational change is natural, so that organizational identity is naturally presumed to evolve. Gagliardi's apparent paradox also assumes that organizational change and identity are independent. They are not. This study suggests that substantive strategic change implies a shift in the lenses used not only to reflect but also to guide the changing organization. Barring drastic contradictions or unmanageable discontinuities between present and projected identity, top managers can induce identity changes by working toward the desired future image.

The original premises and research questions for these integrated studies sought to explore how top management team members make sense of their shifting environments in modern academia. We found that under conditions of change, team members' perceptions of identity and image, and especially desired future image, were key to their interpretations of issues, which they categorized as either strategic or political in character. We believe that our grounded, emergent model in its refined form can serve as a basis for further research concerning some of the distinctive features of strategic change in academia. We also hope it will encourage research in other organizational settings in which strategic change is a less familiar process than in the business domain.

References

Albert, Stuart, and David A. Whetten,. 1985. "Organizational identity." In L. L. Cummings and B. M. Staw (eds.), *Research in Organizational Behavior*, 7: 263–295. Greenwich, CT: JAI Press.

Alvesson, Mats, 1990. "Organization: From substance to image?" *Organization Studies*, 11: 373–394.

Ashforth, Blake E., and Fred Mael, 1989. "Social identity theory and the organization." *Academy of Management Review*, 14: 20–39.

Baron, Reuben M., and David A. Kenny, 1986. "The moderator-mediator distinction in social psychological research: Conceptual strategic, and statistical consideration." *Journal of Personality and Social Psychology*, 51: 1173–1182.

Bartunek, Jean M., 1984. "Changing interpretive schemes and organizational restructuring: The example of a religious order," *Administrative Science Quarterly*, 29: 355–372.

Bourgeois, L. J., II, and Kathleen M. Eisenhardt, 1988. "Strategic decision process in high velocity environments: Four cases in the microcomputer industry." *Management Science*, 34: 816–835.

Cohen, Michael D., and James G. March, 1974. *Leadership and Ambiguity: The American College President*. New York: McGraw-Hill.

Collins, James C., and Jerry L. Porras, 1991. "Organizational vision and visionary organizations." *California Management Review*, 34(1): 31–52.

Daft, Richard L., and Karl Weick, 1984. "Toward a model of organizations as interpretive systems." *Academy of Management Review*, 9: 284–295.

DiMaggio, Paul J., and Walter W. Powell, 1991. "The iron cage revisited: Institutional isomorphism and collective rationality in organizational fields." In W. W. Powell and P. J. DiMaggio (eds.), *The New Institutionalism in Organizational Analysis: 63–82*. Chicago: University of Chicago Press.

Duncan, Robert B., 1973. "Multiple decision making structures in adapting to environmental uncertainty: The impact of organizational effectiveness." *Human Relations*, 26: 705–725.

Dutton, Jane E., and Janet M. Dukerich, 1991. "Keeping an eye on the mirror: The role of image and identity in organizational adaptation." *Academy of Management Journal*, 34: 517–554.

Dutton, Jane E., Janet M. Dukerich, and Celia V. Harquail, 1994. "Organizational images and member identification." *Administrative Science Quarterly*, 39: 239–263.

Dutton, Jane E., and Robert B. Duncan, 1987. "The creation of momentum for change through the process of strategic issue diagnosis." *Strategic Management Journal*, 8: 279–295.

Dutton, Jane E., and Susan E. Jackson, 1987. "Categorizing strategic issues: Links to organizational actions." *Academy of Management Review*, 1: 76–90.

Dutton, Jane E., Stephen A. Stumpf, and David Wagner, 1990. "Diagnosing strategic issues and managerial investment of resources." In P. Shrivestava and R. Lamb (eds.), *Advances in Strategic Management*, 6: 143–167. Greenwich, CT: JAI Press.

Fiol, Marlene, 1991. "Managing culture as a competitive resource: An identity-based view of sustainable competitive advantage." *Journal of Management*, 17: 191–211.

Fombrun, Charles, and Mark Shanley, 1990. "What's in a name? Reputation-building and corporate strategy." *Academy of Management Journal*, 33: 233–258.

Gagliardi, Pasquale, 1986. "The creation and change of organization cultures: A conceptual framework." *Organization Studies*, 7: 117–134.

Galbraith, Jay R., 1973. *Designing Complex Organizations*. Reading, MA: Addison-Wesley.

Ginsberg, Ari, 1988. "Measuring and modeling changes in strategy: Theoretical foundations and empirical directions." *Strategic Management Journal*, 9: 559–575.

Gioia, Dennis A., and Kumar Chittipeddi, 1991. "Sensemaking and sensegiving in strategic change initiation." *Strategic Management Journal*, 12: 443–448.

Gioia, Dennis A., James B. Thomas, Shawn M. Clark, and Kumar Chittipeddi, 1994. "Symbolism and strategic change in academia: The dynamics of sensemaking and influence." *Organization Science*, 5: 363–383.

Glaser, Barney G., and Anselm L. Strauss, 1967. *The Discovery of Grounded Theory*. Chicago: Aldine.

Hambrick, Donald C., 1981. "Environment, strategy, and power within top management teams." *Administrative Science Quarterly*, 26: 253–275.

Hart, Stuart, 1992. "An integrative framework for strategy-making processes." *Academy of Management Review*, 17: 327–351.

Jackson, Susan E., and Jane E. Dutton, 1988. "Discerning threats and opportunities." *Administrative Science Quarterly*, 33: 370–387.

Jick, Todd D., 1979. "Mixing qualitative and quantitative methods: Triangulation in action." *Administrative Science Quarterly*, 24: 602–611.

Keller, George, 1983. *Academic Strategy: The Management Revolution in American Higher Education*. Baltimore: Johns Hopkins University Press.

Kunda, Gideon, 1992. *Engineering Culture*. Philadelphia: Temple University Press.

Martin, Joanne, Martha S. Feldman, Mary Jo Hatch, and Sim B. Sitkin, 1983. "The uniqueness paradox in organizational stories." *Administrative Science Quarterly*, 28: 438–453.

Miles, Matthew B., and A. Michael Huberman, 1984. *Qualitative Data Analysis: A Source Book of New Methods*. Beverly Hills, CA: Sage.

Miles, Robert H., 1982. *Coffin Nails and Corporate Strategies*. Englewood Cliffs, NJ: Prentice-Hall.

Milliken, Frances J., 1990. "Perceiving and interpreting environmental change: An examination of college administrators' interpretation of changing demographics." *Academy of Management Journal*, 33: 42–63.

Nonaka, Ikujiro, and Hirotaka Takeuchi, 1995. *The Knowledge Creating Company*. New York: Oxford University Press.

Ouchi, William G., and Robert L. Price, 1978. "Hierarchies, clans, and theory Z: A new perspective on organizational development." *Organizational Dynamics*, 7: 25–44.

Pfeffer, Jeffrey, 1981. *Power in Organizations*. Marshfield, MA: Pitman.

Ranson, Stewart, Bob Hinings, and Royston Greenwood, 1980. "The structuring of organizational structures." *Administrative Science Quarterly*, 25: 1–17.

Rosch, Eleanor, 1978. "Principles of categorization." In E. Rosch and B. Lloyd (eds.), *Cognition and Categorization: 27–47*. Hillsdale, NJ: Erbaum.

Rosch, Eleanor, and C. Mervis, 1975. "Family resemblances: Studies in the internal structure of categories." *Cognitive Psychology*, 7: 573–605.

Scott, W. Richard, 1987. "The adolescence of institutional theory." *Administrative Science Quarterly*, 32: 493–511.

Spradley, James P., 1979. *The Ethnographic Interview.* New York: Holt Rinehart and Winston.

Strauss, Anselm L., 1987. *Qualitative Analysis for Social Scientists.* Cambridge: Cambridge University Press.

Sutton, Robert I., and Anita L. Callahan, 1987. "The stigma of bankruptcy: Spoiled organizational image and its management." *Academy of Management Journal*, 30: 405–436.

Thayer, L., 1988. "Leadership/communication: A critical review and a modest proposal." In G. M. Goldbar and G. A. Barnett (eds.), *Handbook of Organizational Communication*: 70–97. Norwood, NJ: Ablex.

Thomas, James B., Shawn M. Clark, and Dennis A. Gioia, 1993. "Strategic sensemaking and organizational performance: Linkages among scanning, interpretation, action, and outcomes." *Academy of Management Journal*, 36: 239–270.

Thomas, James B., and Reuben R. McDaniel, Jr., 1990. "Interpreting strategic issues: Effects of strategy and top management team information processing structure." *Academy of Management Journal*, 33: 286–306.

Thomas, James B., Laura Shankster, and John Mathieu, 1994. "Antecedents to organizational issue interpretation: The roles of single-level, cross-level, and content cues." *Academy of Management Journal*, 37: 1252–1284.

Van Maanen, John, 1979. "The fact of fiction in organizational ethnography." *Administrative Science Quarterly*, 24: 539–550.

_____. 1988. *Tales of the Field: On Writing Ethnography*, Chicago: University of Chicago Press.

Weick, Karl E., 1979. *The Social Psychology of Organizing.* Reading, MA: Addison-Wesley.

_____. 1995. *Sensemaking in Organizations.* Newbury Park, CA: Sage.

Whetten, David A., Debra Lewis, and Leann J. Mischel, 1992. "Towards an integrated model of organizational identity and member commitment." Paper presented at the Academy of Management Annual Meeting, Las Vegas.

Yin, Robert K., 1984. *Case Study Research: Design and Methods.* Beverly Hills, CA: Sage.

Appendix: Questionnaire

Questionnaire items were all measured on 7-point Likert scales.

Identity Type (U = Utilitarian, N = Normative)

To what extent . . .

a. do top administrators feel that your institution should *not* be "competing" for students as if they were clients or customers? (N)

b. are symbols and ceremonies important to the functioning of your institution? (N)

c. have budget cuts or increases usually been made across-the-board? (N)

d. are financial returns (e.g., from athletics, economic development, etc.) a measure of success for your institution? (U)

e. is your institution's mission focused on academic quality? (N)

f. is there a feeling that the university should be (or continue to be) actively engaged in marketing campaigns to attract students? (U)

g. are budget cuts or increases made selectively across departments or colleges at your institution? (U)

h. is cost-effectiveness the major criterion that guides programmatic or administrative change? (U)

i. is economic performance considered to be important to fulfilling your institution's missions or goals? (U)

Identity Strength

To what extent . . .

a. do the top management team members of your institution have a strong sense of the institution's history?

b. do your institution's administrators have a sense of pride in the institution's goals and missions?

c. do top administrators feel that your institution has carved out a significant place in the higher education community?

d. do the top management team members *not* have a well-defined set of goals or objectives for the institution?

e. does your institution have administrators who are knowledgeable about the institution's history and traditions?

f. does your institution have administrators, faculty, and students who identify strongly with the institution?

Present Image

In general, how do you think *peer institutions* would rate your institution in terms of:

a. the quality of program offerings?
b. the quality of faculty?
c. the quality of students?
d. the quality of the administrators?
e. overall academic climate?
f. academic innovativeness?
g. overall reputation and prestige?
h. financial/economic status?
i. your goals?
j. your administrative structure?

Future Image

After identifying up to three institutions that the respondent institution would like to emulate, respondents were asked: "To what extent is the reason for wanting to emulate these institutions based on..." The survey then presented the same characteristics provided for present image.

Strategy (O = Offense, D = Defense)

To what extent does your institution...

a. tend to ignore external changes that have little immediate, direct impact on current operations? (D)
b. try to be in the forefront of new programs or market developments in higher education? (O)
c. offer a more limited range of programs, but emphasize higher program quality, superior student services, etc? (D)
d. respond rapidly to early signals concerning areas of opportunity? (O)
e. maintain relatively stable curricula and programs? (D)
f. try to maintain superior strength in all of the areas it enters? (D)

g. operate within a broad program/curriculum domain that undergoes periodic reshaping? (O)
h. value being "first in" with new programs or market activities? (O)

Information Processing Structure of the Top Management Team

To what extent...

a. are views other than those of top administrators included in executive decision processes?
b. can planning concerning important issues be characterized as participative?
c. are written rules and procedures followed during executive decision processes?
d. are committees such as ad hoc task groups formed to deal with important issues?
e. can decision processes around important issues be characterized as interactive?
f. do one or two people dominate the handling of important issues?
g. is there a free and open exchange of ideas between those affected by a given issue?
h. do people affected by an issue typically feel that the definition of the issue and the manner in which it was resolved were imposed upon them?
i. can decision making be characterized as a formal process involving rules and policies?

Interpretation (S = Strategic, P = Political)

Informants were presented with five issues for which they were asked to respond to eight items. Four items measured the extent to which the informant saw the issue as strategic, four items the extent to which they perceived the issue as political.

Example

To what extent is *faculty satisfaction* considered by your institution to be . . .

a. a strategic issue? (S)

b. an issue that has consequences for the institution's position in the marketplace? (S)

c. an issue that involves attempts among individuals or groups in the institution to influence preferences? (P)

d. a political issue? (P)

e. something that affects the whole institution? (S)

f. an area in which there is conflict within the institution over control of the issue? (P)

g. an issue that could impact the institution's mission and goals? (S)

h. a topic that is associated with bargaining, compromise, and negotiation among top administrators? (P)

We would like to acknowledge helpful reviews on earlier drafts of this paper from Michael Dooris, Janet Dukench, Marlene Fiol, Kristian Kreiner, Ajay Mehra, and Majken Schultz. We also acknowledge the assistance of Shawn Clark, David Ketchen, Lee Ann Joyce, and Mark Youndt in the data analysis.

CHAPTER 28

THE APPLICABILITY OF CORPORATE STRATEGIC PRINCIPLES TO DIVERSIFIED UNIVERSITY CAMPUSES

DAVID M. BROCK AND WILLIAM B. HARVEY

The organizational strategy literature has made a definite distinction between *corporate* and *business* strategy. A corporation, for the purpose of this distinction, is comprised of one or more businesses, and is concerned with allocating resources among these businesses and placing the businesses in certain environments, with the overall long-term interests of the corporation in mind. A business is a singular entity, with its context and resources determined by its parent corporation. A business strategy has thus been summarized as *how to compete* in a given market (Hofer & Schendel, 1978), while corporate strategy involves establishing "What *set* of businesses should we be in—now and in the future?" (Thompson & Strickland, 1981).

The concept of strategy was initially borrowed by business from the military, and from there was adopted by many noncommercial fields, like education, politics and health care. In the higher education literature, the emphasis has been on adapting *business* strategic ideas to colleges and universities. Although there has been significant expansion in terms of publications of this kind (Chaffee, 1984 and 1985; Chaffee & Tierney, 1988; Kotler & Fox, 1985; Morrison, Renfro, and Boucher, 1984), there seems to be some difficulty in applying strategic management principles and techniques to academic settings. As a result, "higher education's use of strategy lags behind that of business both in scope and in sophistication" (Chaffee, 1985). This paper will build on the perceived difficulty of using *business* strategies in universities. Because the singularity of purpose that the business strategy literature reflects is seldom seen in these large, diversified, complex institutions of higher education, we suggest that the use of *corporate* strategic principles is more suitable for academe.

For the purposes of this paper, a "university" will be defined as an educational institution, composed of more than one college, that provides instruction in many branches of advanced learning, and awards degrees. This definition does not exclude institutions that are limited to undergraduate education, although in reality most universities have facilities for graduate and professional study, and support some level of research.

Using universities as a unit of analysis, we propose the use of corporate strategic principles in the management of institutions of higher education. We will argue that all universities, as they are defined in this paper, are diversified with respect to products, markets, technology, and other resources, and thus are more analogous to corporations than to businesses. [No presumption is made that corporations are the same as universities, but simply that there are significant similarities. A useful analogy may be to consider academics to be an industry, or a set of related industries, and universities of various sizes and forms to be some organizations that operate in those industries.]

This analysis will be presented in three parts. The first part explains some serious differences between businesses and universities, which limit the scope of a university to function like a business for strategic purposes. The second section points out the broad and practical similarities and differences between corporations and universities. The concluding section presents a selection of corporate strategic techniques and suggest how they might be adapted to higher education.

Why Universities Are Not Like Businesses

Many researchers in higher education have borrowed from the business strategy literature (Chaffee, 1985; Hearn, 1988). This has been possible because the strategy literature is based in turn on the organizational theory literature, which emphasizes the commonalities among all organizations, public or private, profit seeking or not. Due to space limitations in this paper, small social, casual, and philanthropic groups shall be excluded from the analysis. This approach allows a focus on larger, more permanent organizations that are essentially comparable, like businesses, institutions of higher education, and government agencies. On the face of it, there are many common principles underlying all these organizations. The most prevalent principle is that they all provide jobs, permanent and temporary, lucrative and poorly paid, to different classes of people. Because peoples' livelihoods depend on the organization, and these people often wield significant decision-making power, the organizations all tend to perpetuate themselves, seeking ways to survive and even grow, in good times as well as bad times. The organizations are often vitally dependent on external support, be it in the form of clientele, federal funding, or public support in fund raising. They all need people to want or need their products and services, and thus provide this external support. Support for this reasoning may be found among resource dependence theorists (Pfeffer & Salancik, 1978; Aldrich & Pfeffer, 1976) who stress how decisions within the organization

are affected by interdependence with environmental elements. Further, population ecologists have measured and noted how groups of similarly structured organizations seem to proliferate or dwindle, depending on changes in environmental resources (Aldrich, 1979; Zammuto & Cameron, 1985).

Lately, the forces of economic competition have been used to justify the similarities across types of organizations. The "privatization" (or deregulation) spirit in major Western democracies like the United States and Great Britain has insisted that organizations cannot easily be protected from market forces by claiming to be in the "public interest." As a result competition has occurred, and thus acceptance of similar procedures and resources, between commercial- and government-sponsored telephone companies, mail carriers, airlines, universities, clinics, security forces, media, weapons manufacturers, personnel agencies, kindergartens, and intelligence agencies. These competitive interactions have further led to expanding of the similarities and minimizing of the differences that previously were more apparent among nonprofit organizations and businesses that were not in competition with each other.

Apart from these broad similarities, there are many differences between universities and business organizations that seriously limit the usefulness of business strategy principles in universities. For one, higher educational organizations have multiple, often conflicting goals (Thuckman & Chang, 1988). These conflicts are less problematic when different parts of the organization differ, but more disturbing when colleagues in one department, with supposedly identical jobs, differ with respect to goals. While the former situation is not uncommon in corporations, the latter is often the case in universities. Business organizations may have feuding departments (Walton & Dutton, 1969). For instance, at the National Broadcasting Corporation (NBC), the news department strives for efficient gathering and transmission of the news, the sales (advertising) people want to attract viewership, while the creative division aims for quality of programming. The job of management at NBC is to coordinate these departments. Managers may tell the news people to compromise on their standards, save costs, or broaden viewership. It is unlikely, however, that irreconcilable differences in goals will be found among members of one department, as often happens in universities.

It is, however, common in colleges and universities where research is valued, to find professors who are ostensibly hired to teach but are rewarded primarily on the basis of research productivity. The professors' jobs may have originally been created by having sufficient students or classes that needed instructors, and the funds for the positions are thus justified in terms of demand by fee-paying students. However, some professors, knowing that promotion and salary increases depend largely on research, will often choose to spend only a small portion of their efforts on teaching. Simultaneously, other professors in the same department, may believe that the primary place of a professor is in the classroom, and so, they will emphasize teaching. Others will spend their time on departmental administration or school-level politics, trying to further their careers in this way. At evaluation time, the departmental head has the difficult job of balancing these conflicting directions of the professors with the needs of the department and distributing the available resources for rewarding the people.

Another feature that differentiates universities from business is that outcomes are largely intangible (Chaffee, 1985), making meaningful measurement of performance impossible in the short and medium terms. The inability to measure performance on a quarterly or annual basis takes an essential management tool away from university administrators, making management, at least in the traditional sense (Drucker, 1974), impossible.

Other "differences" that frustrate attempts to manage universities like businesses include commitment of many faculty members to professional, rather than institutional issues; decentralization of decision making; and tenure (Chaffee, 1985). These reasons reflect the fact that universities tend to be functionally fragmented, inherently factional, loosely coupled, and not analogous to business organizations. One cannot, for instance, easily visualize a "growing" or a "peoples'" university, in which the marine biology department, graduate school, dental school, revenue sports, library, agricultural extension service, traffic office, and computer services all share the same vision of "growth" or "service to the people."

For these reasons, the concept of business strategy is inappropriate for these large institutions. By the same token, NBC, Kidder-Peabody, RCA, General Electric Government Services, and General Electric Medical Services cannot all grow or adopt community service missions just because they are all part of the same corporation. Clearly, a management approach that recognizes differences among subunits, and aims to manage the whole organization in spite of these differences is necessary for universities. This paper proposes that corporate strategic theory provides such an approach.

The University as a Corporation

There are some immediate similarities in concept between corporations and universities. There are also some major differences. In this section we shall investigate some of these similarities and differences in an attempt to judge whether the two types of organizations share enough common features so that we may consider the application of corporate strategic theory to universities. Six major areas are reviewed and summarized in table 28-1.

First, we shall consider the *raison d'être*, mission, or major goals of corporations and universities. On the surface, there are major differences. Universities are meant to be institutions for the pursuit and transfer of knowledge and understanding. Corporations exist for the pecuniary gain of their owners or stockholders. In practice, however, there are other motives that underlie the major decisions made in both types of organizations. Some insight into the real, or *emergent* goals pursued by corporations and universities can be gained by examining the motives of the senior executives that steer both types of organization.

Recent business literature has shown how managers aim for goals that are consistent with their own interests, such as enhanced power bases and terms and continuity of employment, and not necessarily maximization of shareholder wealth (Amihud & Lev, 1981; Blackburn & Lang, 1989; Fruhan, 1984). The widespread usage of takeover defenses such as golden parachutes and poison pills also attests to managers' penchant for personal wealth and control (Nussbaum & Dobryznsky, 1987; Singh

	Table 28-1	
Similarities and Differences Between Corporations and Universities		
ISSUE	CORPORATIONS	UNIVERSITIES
Stated Raison d'être	maximize owner's wealth	knowledge, research, teaching
Emergent goals	self interest	self interest
Ownership	public, private, institutions, labor, managers	public (political), private
Appointment of top executives	stockholders	trustees

Form: Single business
    Related
    Unrelated
    Vertical Integration
	possible
	common
	common
	common
		[rare]
		common
		limited extent
		common

Decision making	de- or centralized	de- or centralized
Ability to acquire and divest	common	rare

& Harianto, 1989). Similarly, in higher education, researchers are finding that most of the major goals of administrators relate to personal enrichment (Cowley, 1980; Robinson, 1982; Thuckman & Chang, 1988). In fact, of the eight goals for administrators listed by Thuckman & Chang, only one, "to contribute to student and faculty learning" is not directly self-serving. The other goal that does not relate directly to personal enrichment is "to ensure the perpetuation and growth of the institution," which is similar to the corporate ethic.

The second major area of possible dissimilarity between corporations and universities is ownership. Corporations may be either owned by a single individual, a few individuals, labor, managers, another institution, many dispersed private stockholders, or any combination of these stakeholders. Corporate strategy formulation would differ among many of these forms of ownership. For instance, if owned by a financial institution, one would expect the corporation to be managed primarily with certain financial performance measures in mind. On the other hand, if managers or labor are powerful stockholders, the personal interests of these groups, such as stock-related benefit packages or lifetime employment benefits would emerge as primary goals. Universities may be owned by a political entity, like a state or city, or by private individuals and organiza-

tions. As with corporations, the nature of ownership will affect the strategic processes. However, there may be more similarities than differences in strategy formulation caused by ownership between some corporations and universities. For instance, in private universities and some corporations, a few powerful individuals may dominate. These individuals may derive their power through large stockholdings, donations, or simply charisma. A state university's governance in an election year may resemble that of a corporation with strong labor ownership, as both groups strive for short-term benefits for current employees. In other years the situation may be similar or different, depending on the political climate. These arguments lead to the conclusion that no defining practical differences arise between corporations and universities as a result of the ownership issue.

The third area of possible difference between corporations and universities is the appointment of top executives. The chairperson of the board of directors of a corporation (the corporate CEO) is elected by the majority of the shareholders, and can be replaced at the discretion of the same body. The chancellor or president (CEO) of a university is appointed by the board of trustees. In practice, though, a CEO is seldom appointed without substantial input from current administrators and faculty, and often from students and alumni (Birnbaum, 1988; Bolman, 1965).

The difference between these two organizational types may be important. Unpopular corporate CEOs, or those hired to implement unpopular policies, initially have the full sanction of the body that appoints them, which gives them strong legitimate power in the organization (French & Raven, 1959). Because faculty and others currently operating in the organization are so instrumental in selection of CEOs, it is far less likely to find an unpopular or tyrannical appointee. The implication of this relative lack of power of university CEOs as against their corporate counterparts for applicability of strategic principles may be significant in certain cases. The powerlessness will often diminish the viability of certain corporate strategic tactics in certain circumstances, as will be discussed in the following section.

The fourth area is organizational form or structuring. Just as universities take many forms, so do corporations (Rumelt, 1974). A corporation may have only one business, or it may have few but *related* businesses. An example of the latter form is a corporation that owns department stores, drug stores, and wholesale grocery merchants. Corporations also may be diversified in an unrelated fashion, like General Electric and Sears who each own businesses in very different industries. Another strategic dimension that a corporation may take is *vertical integration:* having businesses that are each others' customers and suppliers. Thus, an oil refinery could acquire an oilfield, a department store could merge with a clothing manufacturer, or a wholesaler and a shipping firm could unite.

Universities may similarly have various forms. [The variety is narrowed somewhat in this paper because single-college institutions have been excluded from the definition of universities, so the "single business" form, usually called "colleges" in North America, will not be considered.] A university's research emphasis may be primary or secondary, confined to certain departments or permeating every school. Professional schools such as business and law may be enclaves, set apart from the main campus. There may be a hospital, with all its ancillary services, containing medical, dental, and paramedical schools. Some universities have agricultural departments at farms in the locality.

Continuing education and extension services may be offered by some combination of regular faculty members and nonacademic employees, on campus, in special buildings, or at a client's premises. Although there are some common patterns, the extent to which facilities, services, and personnel may be shared often differs from campus to campus. Clearly both corporate and university forms are so flexible and broadly defined that no rules that apply to one are likely to be entirely inapplicable to the other.

Fifth, the degree of decentralization of decision making also differs among and within corporations, and among and within universities. Many business CEOs have almost complete autonomy, while others find corporate managers making many decisions for them. Although it is less common to find an autonomous dean, with outstanding leaders and in professional, financially independent schools, this sometimes is the case. As with the question of appointment of the CEO mentioned above, the decentralized CEOs will have a broader range of tactics at their disposal. However, because no systematic difference seems to exist in the decentralization of decision-making ability between university chancellors versus corporate CEOs, this point will not be considered as an impediment for the adoption of corporate principles in higher education.

The sixth and final major point of possible difference between corporations and universities is that it is common for a corporation to acquire and divest businesses, while universities seldom do so. It is possible for a business to be privately owned one day, to be acquired by a corporation the next, and to be the target of a leveraged buy-out a few months later. It is possible, but quite unusual for a school or college to change affiliations. The implications of this difference do not seem to differentiate seriously between the two kinds of institutions. One conclusion could be that a school would be more likely to display more loyalty and a closer identity with its university than a business would to its parent corporation. However, because higher education is typified by decentralization and independence, with multiple affiliations of professors to current and past schools as well as to professional associations, leads one to doubt whether there is a significant loyalty difference between corporations and universities due to the former's ability to acquire and divest.

The above points of similarity and difference between corporations and universities are summarized in table 28-1. These comparisons show more similarities than differences between these two types of organizations. This is not to say that universities are equivalent to corporations. There are many differences, many of which are obvious. The point here is that there are sufficient similarities between their goals, the way that they operate, their forms, and their internal processes to assume that some principles of strategic management that apply to one may well apply to the other.

The following section examines some aspects of corporate strategy with a view to useful applications thereof to universities.

Some Applications of Corporate Strategy to Universities

Having established some broad similarities between universities and corporations, we shall now look to the theory of corporate strategy for lessons that may be relevant to higher educational administration. In doing so some basic alternative corporate strategies are presented, and then the applicability of the portfolio approach to universities is investigated.

The Basic Alternatives of Corporate Strategy

The objectives of corporate strategies are somehow to create synergy, or add value to the parts of the corporation by their association, or to make the whole exceed the sum of its parts. The sources of this added value may be shared expertise, economies of scale (efficiency through size), access to new markets and resources, and reduction of risk through diversification (Hofer & Schendel, 1978). Thompson and Strickland (1981) list nine basic corporate strategic options as (1) concentration on a single business, (2) vertical integration, (3) concentric (or related) diversification, (4) conglomerate (or unrelated) diversification, (5) merger and acquisition, (6) joint ventures, (7) retrenchment, (8) divestiture, and (9) liquidation.

The process of strategy formulation will differ from corporation to corporation. It is true to say, however, that it is a process that is performed irregularly and seldom, and that the nature of this process will depend on the values and ideology of the decision makers, and the politics and coalitions at the strategic apex of the organization (Bower & Doz, 1979; Narajanan & Fahey, 1982). Once a corporation takes on one of the above nine strategic options, it is likely to pursue that strategy for many years. For instance, Exxon is vertically integrated, and General Electric is an unrelated conglomerate. Each may use retrenchment or divestiture on an occasional basis, but the overall corporate strategies change very little from year to year. A small university may decide in 1990 to pursue a strategy of related diversification, building on a strong undergraduate humanities curriculum by adding and expanding courses in the natural sciences, liberal arts, and education. Having made this decision, all other decisions and activities within the university and its components should be aimed to reinforce this strategy. Five years later the same institution may decide to adopt a strategy of vertical integration, using its current resources (plant, faculty, and top students) to build graduate curricula in modern languages, political science, history, and philosophy.

All these strategies are already used to some extent in universities. Some are fairly commonplace, such as the diversification that occurs when universities add new colleges or incorporate existing schools. Apart from sharing of human and other resources, universities improve their attractiveness to some professors by being diversified, offering them a choice of programs on which to teach, as well as diverse research and service opportunities.

Examples of vertical integration occur when the better-prepared graduates from a university's undergraduate programs may be recruited to continue with graduate or professional studies at the same institution. The same computer that is used as a data bank for university records and the payroll can be a resource when starting a research center. Importantly, the reputation and legitimacy gained through service to the community, or through an excellent basketball program, can often be used to get state funding for various faculty interests.

Joint ventures, such as research centers administered, staffed, and sponsored by neighbor institutions are now common: the Research Triangle of North Carolina began with such a joint venture between three universities.

In all these strategies, universities may be slower to act, and more limited by geographic and political constraints than some corporations; but because these impediments are common to the entire industry, the utility of these strategies to universities in the higher education industry should not be diminished by these constraints.

The rest of the basic corporate strategies, namely, merger and acquisition, retrenchment, divestiture, and liquidation, are more difficult to transplant in the field of higher education. Although we know that each can be and has been used in higher education, the relative lack of power of university CEOs noted above causes doubts as to whether these strategies can be counted among those that are ready options in higher education. A corporation can acquire or dispose of a business with one telephone call to an investment banker. Most chancellors of universities would have a major political campaign to accomplish the same result. The conclusion must be drawn, therefore, that some corporate strategies are not applicable to higher education in the same way as they are to the business world. This situation is in no way an indication of a lack of suitability for corporate, strategy as a whole for universities. It is simply a characteristic of academe, or the academic industry. Just as a CEO of an utility corporation or a railroad has less flexibility than the CEO of an acquisitive conglomerate, such as Donald Trump, so, too, do university CEOs have industry-specific constraints on their range of strategic options.

Higher education is an industry where structural change has traditionally taken place somewhat slowly (Carnegie Council on Policy Studies in Higher Education, 1980, p. 9), reducing the flexibility of strategists. However, there are indications that the rate of change is quickening. For instance, Zammuto (1981) noted that the organizational failure (or death) rate of universities was higher than for private businesses. This implies that the academic industry is now changing faster than ever. Not only do these changes increase the usefulness of corporate strategic techniques in the university set-

ting, but they also demand that administrators turn to more sophisticated management techniques, many of which are to be found within the area of corporate strategy.

The Portfolio Approach

The second and final application of corporate strategy to education that will be considered is the so-called portfolio approach (Newbould, 1980). This is an approach to evaluation of businesses within a corporation with a view to formulation of business strategies that relate to how each business is to be treated and managed.

For example, an institution may have formulated a strategy of unrelated diversification with some vertical integration. A set of questions will arise regularly about how to manage each business (division, school or college), to which to allocate more resources, perhaps allowing a program gradually to diminish.

Although many variations have been proposed, the basic idea is to plot business units on two-dimensional space, the dimensions being (1) some measure of industry attractiveness (or growth rate) and (2) competitive strength (or market share) of the business (Hedley, 1978; Thompson & Strickland, 1981). An example is shown in figure 28-1, with the size of the circles representing the value of the business to the corporation (for example, in revenue or assets).

The four quadrants of the matrix are often given names to describe their place in the corporate portfolio. The set of names popularized by the Boston Consulting Group (BCG) will be used in this paper. "Cash cows" in the low-attractiveness/ high-strength corner are businesses that generate significant amounts of cash for the corporation. Typical strategies are to appropriate these "milked" funds to business units where the cash is needed to survive or to fund growth. The usual beneficiaries are the "question marks" in weak positions in attractive industries. "Stars," while successful, merit reinvestment of generated cash in their own promising areas. Appropriate strategies for "dogs" are divestment, retrenchment, and liquidation. Thus portfolios help corporations in evaluating the position of their businesses in terms of two critical competitive dimensions, and thus assist in the strategy formulation process.

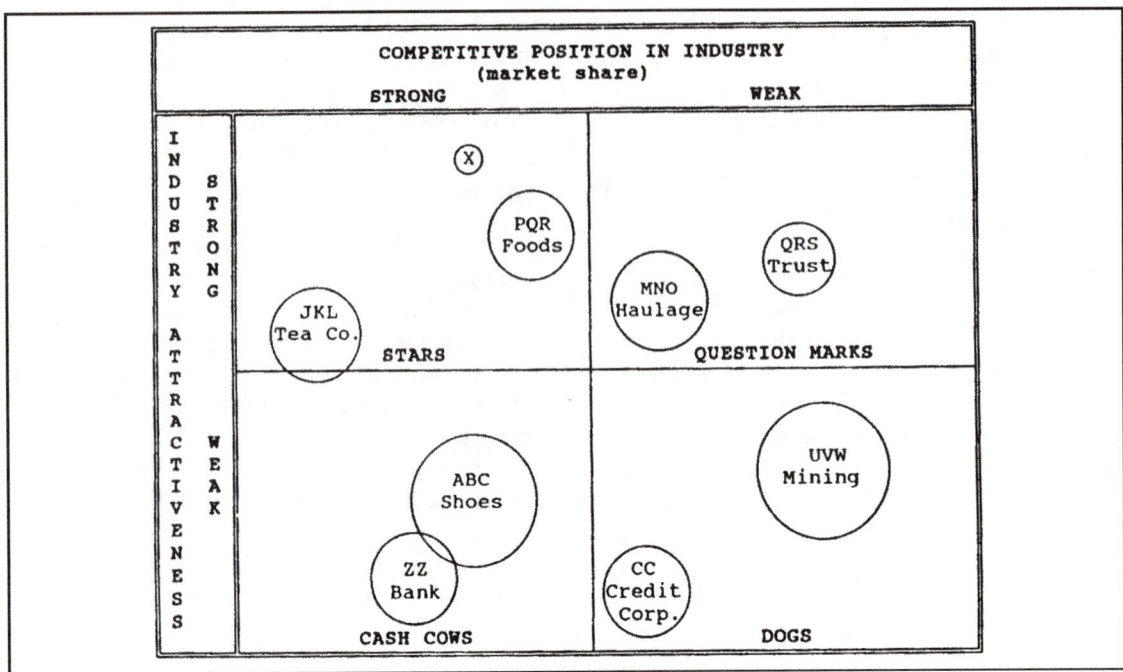

Figure 28-1 A Typical Portfolio for a Corporation

Another use to which corporations put portfolios is evaluating portfolio "balance." This concept refers to the need for corporations to have businesses of matching size, cash generation and needs, on the appropriate parts of the matrix. For example, a few "question marks" are desirable because those that succeed will be the future "stars" and "cash cows" of the corporate portfolio. However, "cash cows" of sufficient productivity are needed to fund these fledgling businesses.

Universities can readily use portfolios (Newbould, 1980). For example, ABC University may label its undergraduate program (it is a source of major endowment funds) and revenue sports as "cash cows." Engineering and Continuing Education may be "stars", the School of Veterinary Science and College of Education may be "question marks"; and the School of Design and nonrevenue sports could be called "dogs." This hypothetical situation is depicted in figure 28-2.

Many of the lessons of the portfolio approach have not been lost on university administrators. For instance, revenue sports have long been used to fund other sports and even fund academic and administrative functions. Budgetary surpluses from one school indirectly fund less lucrative areas. There are at

least two further lessons that universities can learn from these techniques. The first is to *classify* schools, colleges, and student activities in terms of a relevant portfolio. The benefit of this arrangement is to assist in determining the resources of the institution during the strategy formulation process. The second lesson is actively to seek a portfolio *balance* of established, lucrative, questionable, and growing units, to take advantage of the synergy of internal funding that may be possible.

There are also some limitations on the use of these techniques. As has been argued above, strategies that serve to diminish the power of existing stakeholders, like divestment and liquidation, are difficult to implement in higher education. In addition, the general complexity of the power structure, and consequent slowness of the decision-making processes necessitate procedural changes in the corporate strategic formulation model to suit it to universities. Just as in business, no department likes to be called a dog. Different nomenclature should be found to suit the needs of higher education.

Conclusions

This paper has pointed out some broad similarities between corporations and universities. Simi-

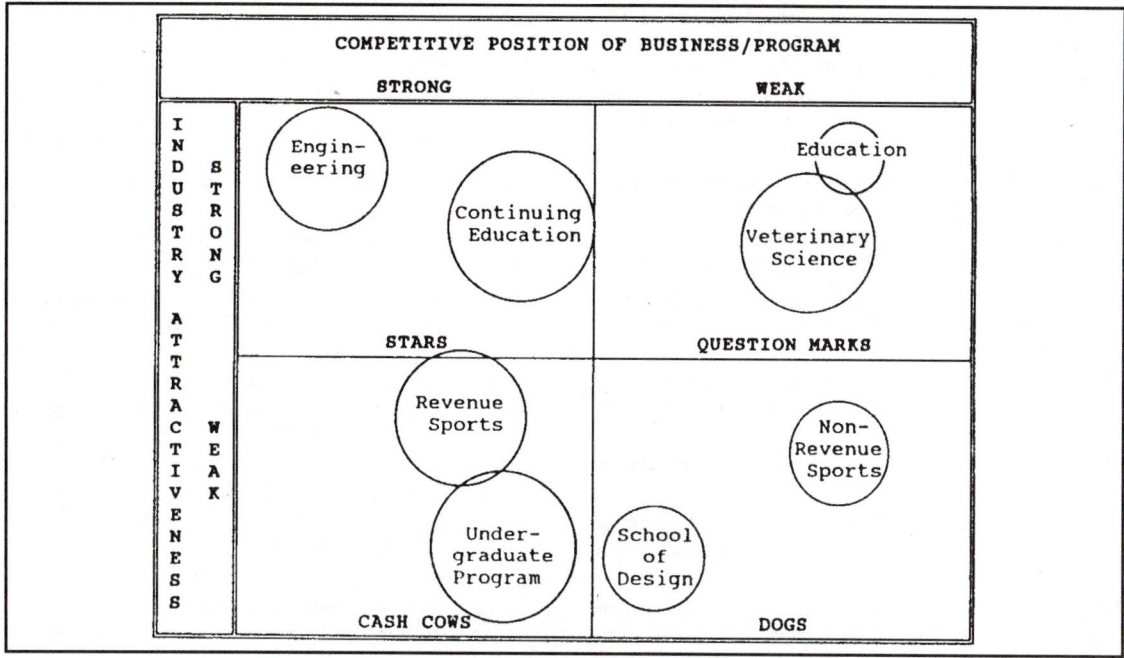

Figure 28-2 A Hypothetical Portfolio for a University

larities in mission, structure, and internal processes may be considered sufficiently comparable to consider the applicability of some corporate strategic techniques. Specific references were made to corporate strategic options available in the strategy formulation process, and to the portfolio analysis approach to evaluating and positioning the components of the institution.

These observations show how the broad techniques and goals of corporate strategy may be applied to universities. Further research is needed into specific applications of corporate theory to universities. In the area of mergers and acquisitions, for example, there may be substantial benefit to be gained by neighboring institutions if the necessary techniques could be developed to merge and divest colleges and schools. Another level of analysis, namely, the university system, may be an even more suitable area for application of corporate strategic theory.

References

Aldrich, H. (1979). *Organizations and environments*. Englewood Cliffs, NJ: Prentice-Hall.

Aldrich, H. & Pfeffer, J. (1976). Environments of organizations. In A. Inkeles, J. Colemen, & N. Smelser (Eds.), *Annual review of sociology, Vol. 2.* (pp. 79–105). Palo Alto, CA: Annual Reviews.

Amihud, Y. & Lev, B. (1981). Risk reduction as a managerial motive for conglomerate mergers. *Bell Journal of Economics*, 12, 605–617.

Birnbaum, R. (1988). Presidential searches and the discovery of organizational goals. *Journal of Higher Education*, 59, 489–509.

Blackburn, V. & Lang, J. (1989). Toward a market/ownership theory of merger behavior. *Journal of Management*, 15: 77–88.

Bolman, D. (1965). *How college presidents are chosen*. Washington, D.C.: American Council on Education.

Bower, J. & Doz, Y. (1979). Strategy formulation: A social and political process. In D. E. Schendel & C. W. Hofer (Eds.), *Strategic management: A new view of business policy and planning*. Boston: Little, Brown.

Carnegie Council on Policy Studies in Higher Education. (1980). *Three thousand futures: The next twenty years for higher education*. San Francisco: Jossey-Bass.

Chaffee, E. E. (1984). Successful strategic management in small private colleges. *Journal of Higher Education*, 55 (2), 212–241.

— (1985). The concept of strategy: From business to higher education. In J. C. Smart (Ed.), *Higher education handbook of theory and research: Vol. 1.* (pp. 133–172). New York: Agathon Press.

Chaffee, E. & Tierney, W. (1988). *Collegiate culture and leadership strategies*. New York: Macmillan.

Cowley, W. (1980). *Presidents, professors and trustees*. San Francisco: Jossey-Bass.

Drucker, P. (1974). *Management: Tasks, responsibilities, practices.* New York: Harper & Row.

French, J. & Raven, B. (1959). The bases of social power. In D. Cartwright (Ed.), *Studies in social power.* Ann Arbor: Institute for Social Research, University of Michigan.

Fruhan, W. (1984). How fast should your company grow? *Harvard Business Review, 62,* 84–93.

Hearn, J. (1988). Strategy and resources: Economic issues in strategic planning and management in higher education. In J. C. Smart (Ed.), *Handbook of theory and research in higher education.* New York: Agathon Press.

Hedley, B. (1978, December). A fundamental approach to strategy development. *Long-range planning,* 2–11.

Hofer, C. & Schendel, D. (1978). *Strategy formulation: Analytical concepts.* St. Paul: West.

Kotler, P. & Fox, K. (1985). *Strategic marketing for educational institutions.* Englewood Cliffs, N.J.: Prentice-Hall.

Morrison, J., Renfro, W. & Boucher, W. (1984). Futures research and the strategic planning process: Implications for higher education. *ASHE-ERIC higher education research report No. 9.*

Narajanan, V. & Fahey, L. (1982). The micro-politics of strategy formulation. *Academy of Management Review, 7,* 25–34.

Newbould, G. D. (1980). Product portfolio diagnosis for U.S. universities. *Akron Business and Economic Review.* Spring, 39–45.

Nussbaum, B. & Dobryznski, J. (1987, May 18). The battle for corporate control. *Business Week,* 102–109.

Pfeffer, J. & Salancik, G. (1978). *The external control of organizations: A resource dependence perspective.* New York: Harper & Row.

Robinson, D. (1982). Reflections of a trustee. *Academe, 68,* 6–8.

Rumelt, R. (1974). *Strategy, structure, and economic performance.* Boston, MA: Harvard University Press.

Singh, H. & Harianto, F. (1989). Management-board relationships, takeover risk, and the adoption of golden parachutes. *Academy of Management Journal, 32,* 7–24.

Thompson, A. & Strickland, A. (1981). *Strategy and policy: Concepts and cases.* Plano, TX: Business Publications, Inc.

Thuckman, H. & Chang, C. (1988). Conflict, congruence and generic university goals. *Journal of Higher Education, 59,* 611–633.

Walton, R. E. & Dutton, J. M. (1969, March). The management of interdepartmental conflict: A model and review. *Administrative Science Quarterly,* 73–84.

Zammuto, R. F. (1981). *Assessing organizational effectiveness: Systems change, adaptation, and strategy.* Albany: SUNY Press.

Zammuto, R. & Cameron K. (1985). Environmental decline and organizational response. *Research in Organizational Behavior, 7,* 223–262.

CHAPTER 29

THE SOCIAL CONSTRUCTION OF RESOURCE STRESS

ANNA NEUMANN

Financial troubles seem with us always, appearing in different forms (for example, declining revenues, soaring costs) and places, even among the most established institutions [11, 13, 14, 26, 37], and persisting over various lengths of time. Even during times of financial calm, institutional leaders worry about what the future will bring. For example, before the now all too common stories of real economic hardship in higher education [8, 9, 10, 17, 24, 25, 30], top administrators worried that they would soon be challenged more by finances than any other issue, including curriculum, diversity, and quality [1]. At the same time, analysts, pointing at imminent financial difficulty [16, 19, 20, 44], urged these leaders to prepare for inevitable change [12, 18, 27, 28, 31]. Looking back, we must wonder whether these premonitions and predictions of financial trouble foretold an inescapable future—or whether they helped create it.

Given leaders' enduring concerns about "tough times," in the present moment or in anticipation, it is not surprising that researchers are devoting substantial attention to the question of what leadership should look like in a changed economic environment [43]—in particular, what leaders should do to resolve or prevent money problems (see reviews by Zammuto [46] and Leslie [23]). Although this question, based in contingency theory [42], is important, given the hard times many institutions are currently experiencing, its focus on how leaders respond to conditions external to the leaders themselves obscures the possibility that leaders (or others) may, in fact, be creating those conditions.

Contingency theory, the prevailing lens for interpreting resource stress, assumes that leaders guide their organizations in responding to external change, whether by taking action in anticipation of such change or after the fact [21, 22, 38, 42]. Because contingency theory begins with the premise that organizations and their leaders respond to a world existing objectively outside of them, it cannot consider the extent to which leaders and other organizational members may contribute, knowingly or not, to the psychic construction of that world—that is, the world as leaders and others come to know it from within themselves. Contingency theory portrays the external world as given and as waiting to be discovered in its one true form by individuals looking outwardly, beyond themselves.

Alternatively, social constructivism views this world as a human creation: human beings construct it, personally and in interaction with each other. Moreover, "discovery," in the constructivist view, proceeds from individual and communal self-reflection—that is, looking within rather than outward. Whereas contingency theory begins by considering changes in a world that is presumed to exist objectively outside its human observers, constructivism begins by considering those observers' habits and changes of mind, including what they know and how they learn, individually and in communion [6, 29, 39, 41].

My purpose in this article is to turn from contingency theory to social constructivism as a vantage point for examining leadership and resource realities in higher education. Although what we see is different when we switch between one understanding and the other, what we ask is even more so. The following questions frame this constructivist study: To what extent might a leader, in this case a college president, contribute to the construction of a college's resource context— whether in creating "hard times" or "good times"—and by what means? For example, how might a college president (through words, actions, gestures, and stances enacted symbolically) contribute to the intensification of distress flowing from resource concerns or to the alleviation of such stress? How may others around the president, and particularly those not in positions of administrative leadership, understand and experience their president's words and actions, and how does such interaction between leader and others contribute to the construction of a college's financial condition?

To address these questions, rooted in social constructivism, I examined people's beliefs and feelings about their college's resource condition—including their recollections of how they formed those beliefs—at two colleges of differing financial status: Arcadia College, which is financially stable and strong with a growing resource base, and Industrial College,[1] caught in economic decline and facing steep and continuous hardship.[2] Though the colleges differ by Carnegie type and control (one is private, the other public), both are small (under 6000 FTE) and focused on undergraduate teaching. In addition, although the presidents of these two colleges are dissimilar in their tenure (one is very experienced, the other is new), they are remarkably alike in a social constructivist view of their leadership: Both are highly complex in how they construct the presidency [36]; they exhibit a prominent interpretive strategy [35], symbolic competence [5], and a well-defined learning orientation [34] and span multiple cognitive perspectives [4, 5]. Both also construct complex "thinking teams" which they orchestrate in complex ways [33] and toward complex ends [3].[3]

In this article I examine presidential leadership at Arcadia College and Industrial College in light of the quandary I posed at the beginning of this article, asking whether college leaders' efforts at financial "fortune telling" (central to contingency theory) mask an underlying process of "fortune creating" (the constructivist view). I present no final answers to this question, only some data to support a constructivist perspective, and thereby offer balance to well-entrenched contingency interpretations of resource stress.

Method

Arcadia College and Industrial College are part of a sample of eight colleges and universities, located throughout the United States, that participated in a study of higher education leadership and resource stress through the Institutional Leadership Project (ILP) of the National Center for Postsecondary Governance and Finance. During 1988–89 I visited the study sites for three days to interview persons engaged in or knowledgeable about campus leadership: the president, a trustee, members of the president's administrative team, between four and six faculty members, such as the head of the faculty senate and other influential or knowledgeable faculty leaders, and other campus observers. In addition, ILP interviewers had visited these sites during 1986–87, and the cases that comprise this article draw also on those data and documentary sources.

Although this article presents only two of the eight study institutions, it reflects what I learned comparatively and cumulatively from examining the other study sites as well [45]. This process resembles what Frederick Erickson [15] refers to as a search for "concrete universals arrived at by studying a specific case in great detail and then comparing it with other cases studied in equally great detail," as opposed to searching, in a positivist vein, for "abstract universals arrived at by statistical generalization from a sample to a population" [15, p. 130].

In the following pages I describe Arcadia College and Industrial College in my own voice, bringing out the patterns of meaning that I saw and heard on site and that, in retrospect, I continued to pursue. My first-person voice is a reminder to the reader that what follows is my interpretation and thereby my construction, worked and reworked, of various college members' interpretations of the campus worlds that they had jointly constructed at the time of the research visits.

Financially Sound and Solid: Arcadia College

As I enter the center of campus I see students rushing from building to building in a soft rain. Even on a gray morning, Arcadia College looks dignified, groomed, cared for. My first impressions bear out as I talk to faculty and administrators. These people radiate dignity, humble confidence, and security in their collective identity, and dedication to caring for even the smallest details of their life together.

Though Arcadia is not among the wealthiest colleges of its type in the country or in the study sample, it ranks among the most financially healthy, always balancing its budget and increasing its total resource flows at a rate markedly above that of most other American colleges and universities. While total resources increase yearly, the enrollment of Arcadia remains relatively steady, although occasional dips cause momentary anguish—among faculty more than administrators. The types of students who enroll at Arcadia are as predictable as the number. Joshua Anderson, Arcadia's president, defines the college's approach to student recruitment as focused on "who?" as opposed to "how many?" In his words, "We are not looking for numbers but for the right applicants."

Presidential Leadership and College Resources

I found that interviewees were clear and consistent in their image of Joshua Anderson and that, with some recent exceptions, Anderson's view of his own leadership coincided closely with theirs. In this section I sketch what I heard of that image.

Complexity in role: expanding the breadth of presidential attention. Anderson is as firm in attending to some things as to their opposites, even if, at times, this is uncomfortable for him. For example, though he prefers to look after the "day to day" details and routines of campus life, he "forces" himself to attend only to those that he sees as having "a major impact on the institution," and he restrains himself from attending to those that do not. Senior faculty leaders understand and appreciate his approach. "[Joshua] is interested in the nooks and crannies of the campus," said one interviewee, "(but] he does not get lost in minutiae." But in addition to attending to meaningful details, Anderson "forces" himself to focus on "high impact initiatives... big issues," although these are less appealing to him.

Anderson is particularly self-conscious about his natural tendency to be "an inside president"—doing "a good job in communicating what we have done internally" to the faculty and staff, but not giving enough attention "to translating this beyond the bounds of the campus... so people (outside the college) really understand." "It is beating the drum," Anderson explains. "I am not naturally inclined to this kind of thing. I tend more to soft sell. I don't really put pressure on people to give. I try to demonstrate that we do something worth supporting... We need to be a little more aggressive and hard-hitting."

Anderson's "forced" stretching and balancing of perspectives is not always so discomforting, and he handles many such tasks with ease and grace while campus members watch, usually approving. The trustees, for example, appreciate how carefully he attends to Arcadia's "economy and culture." And the faculty praise his attention to "people rather than buildings or pizzazz" while simultaneously applauding his "excellent management of the budget and its priorities." Even Anderson sees "the economy and culture' dynamic at play in his mind. On the one hand, he describes his "natural inclination toward finances" and says that he can "tell you any major figure on the institution's books"; at the same time he insists, "I don't see what I am doing with the administrators as the core—but rather what we are doing with the faculty."

Anderson presents himself as equally effective in balancing consultation and directiveness. Faculty members say that he "seeks input" and "has a good ear," but that he knows when to "make decisions" and that he is "careful as to communicating [the] reasons" for them.

Commitments in role: delimiting considerations. Though Joshua Anderson is known for his diverse and flexible perspective, he is known just as well for his firm, even unbending adherence to several commitments and beliefs.

First, Joshua Anderson views himself, and is viewed by others as financially cautious and conserving—as running "a pretty tight ship . . . not risk-taking . . . not spending money that we don't have." Faculty members say that he often reminds them that "our basic limitation is money," and he says that he will not commit the college to "doing more than resources would allow us to do well" and that "not balancing our budget is not an option."

Second, President Anderson is unequivocal about his need to remain engaged in campus life. Although he knows that some people criticize him for being "too concerned about what is happening day to day" and not concerned enough about "the external presidency . . . [and] fundraising," he asserts, "I cannot be an absentee president or a figurehead." He sees these external tasks as extensions of, rather than as substitutes for, his core internal role. "I don't do well when I am not hands on," he explains. "I have to have the pulse of the place—my fingers in the campus pie. I don't feel good off-campus talking if I am not speaking from concrete experience. If I can't talk about students and the curriculum, I can't be effective. . . . It is an inherent conflict."

Third, Anderson expresses more concern about how resources are used and about how people make sense of how resources are expended, than about how they are acquired in the first place: "I am sensitive to priorities and how we use our resources."

Fourth, he believes that in faculty members' minds financial value is often equated with assumptions about personal value, but that in reality these two forms of value can rarely align. He believes that leaders are responsible for managing this discrepancy and that they can do so by demonstrating competent institutional management and good-faith efforts to compensate or otherwise reward faculty fairly. In his words, "Our faculty always live with the tension of not having the income that they need and what they are worth. . . . [But] the faculty believe that we are doing the best that we can by them. Our resources are managed well. We are open about what we are doing. We understand the priorities. They can live with that."

Finally, while Anderson devotes substantial time and energy to financial and administrative matters, he looks at them through an educational lens: "I [have] fixed in my own frame of reference the commitment that what happens in the daily life of students is the most important consideration in what decisions we make. If we lose sight of that we lose the purpose of our being. An example of how Anderson uses this educational lens to address financial concerns is captured in a well-known campus story: When he first came to Arcadia, Joshua Anderson found "years of red ink," an inadequate operating budget that "we were not managing well," and several expensive academic programs that were not working. Rather than dealing with the financial problem in financial terms (for example, by economizing, fundraising, or marketing), he tackled it from the perspective of academic quality—pushing for cuts in ineffective programs, rethinking the curriculum and instructional format, hiring new faculty, and instituting "a rigorous system" of faculty and instructional evaluation.

Looking back, Anderson rationalizes these and related actions as "building quality" first, and then "pushing our price up" as people came to appreciate and value the product that resulted. "I think that people are always attracted to quality," he says. "Our building of quality experiences for students—that is the foundation of what we do. If we don't have that base, we won't get students or donors. Ours is not a 'big bang' approach to fundraising but building solidly and developing confidence over the long haul." Anderson believes that educational quality is a necessary precedent to (rather than an outcome of) financial development, and that it is this strategy that "put the institution on its financial feet." A top-level administrator comments, "It is hard to separate how [the president] has influenced the financial condition from how he has influenced the reputation and the total program . . . His question is: How do you put together a college that puts out a good product?" A senior faculty member adds, "Joshua Anderson came here and led a revolution—to a new era of growth and . . . leadership that respects faculty involvement. . . . He put a lot of money into people and [instructional] hardware [and in so doing, he] left a legacy of this."

This was the presidential image that I put together: The members of Arcadia College know Anderson as a person of diverse and complex abilities but clear commitments. Though this image remained constant over the two research visits, by 1988–89 there were shadows of change.

Self in role. During my visit in 1988–89 Anderson speaks at length about the importance of internal presidential leadership and educational priorities just as he did during 1986–87, but he adds something new: Over the past two years he has been using his time differently, immersing himself in major fundraising drives that have, in his words, "taken a lot of my psychological energy." A close administrative colleague explains, "The President is [now] very committed to expanding the financial base of the college, and he is giving nearly all his time to that. In his early years he tried to be an inside president. He still knows the people here but is not as involved in the day to day. He has a greater appreciation for fundraising." Although campus members approve of the president's search for new resources, several are concerned that he does not "know much about . . .tapping resources" and that now "he can't be as much of an in-house president any more." One person describes a change in the campus mood—that there is "discomfort internally" and "comments [like] 'Joshua is gone again. We have to wait 'til he gets back.'" And another adds, "[Joshua] is less visible on campus and that may have created problems. . . . Maybe he is more disassociated."

As I speak to Anderson during this second visit, I hear unexpected words. He tells me that the college "needs more resources" and that it needs a president who can raise them. "I would like to take time, . . ." he says, "to step back and re-evaluate; . . . maybe [Arcadia] needs someone other than Joshua Anderson, or maybe Joshua Anderson needs a different role." When I ask Anderson to tell me about the kind of leadership that Arcadia needs now, he refers to the college's needs and his own: "We need leadership that can generate resources, . . . we have millions of dollars in needs. . . . If someone can do better than me, then the institution needs to own up to this. My

wife and I are asking at what point we need to back off. I can see myself phasing out."

Resources and Stress

President Anderson describes the college's financial condition as positive but modest, explaining that resources have "not really changed, . . . if anything, they have strengthened; . . . we are strengthened materially." The vice presidents give "mixed" reviews. Although they see the college as "more stable than ever before," with continuously "balanced budgets" and "better facilities than we have ever had," they worry about the continued availability of revenues, believing that the college could face "a real tough situation." All administrators say that the cabinet faces "painful" decisions each year as they struggle with limits. In the words of one, "We are looking from one year to the next with a small margin. There are hard choices each year about what is important; . . . programs are always fighting for a minimal increase."

Most faculty interviewees simultaneously present two different views of Arcadia's financial condition: They echo administrators' positive assessments ("no deficit," "no red"), but they also see an Arcadia that is "right on the edge." One faculty member talks about the healthy "steady state" that has resulted from years of careful management, but she also refers to a "precarious balance, . . . feeling like the college is always one year away from disappearing." "We always seem to be balancing," she comments. "If we do this, what are we not going to do?" Another faculty member describes Arcadia as "running very hard to keep enrollment steady, . . . shuddering with each annual tuition increase will students continue to come here?" Others point to a variety of trouble spots—"staffing restrictions . . . library holdings [that] have not expanded well . . . [and needs for] more financial aid." When I ask a senior faculty member how these perceptions affect the faculty, he explains, "We are a community that thrives and anguishes together—we have a sense of emotional pain that faculty feel when things don't go well. We feel it if the college hurts and not just down in our pocketbooks. . . . We have had both good and bad [financial] news, . . . decreases and increases. The faculty follow this."

Although my analysis of Arcadia's finances, according to rough but standard measures, yielded a very positive picture (especially relative to other colleges and universities nationally), most faculty interviewees portrayed the college as financially stressed. Their stress was particularly prominent at four points: in descriptions of how people communicate about finances, in views of growth and stability, in comparisons of Arcadia to a peer group, and in speculations about the future.

Communicating about finances. When I ask faculty interviewees how they learn about the college's financial condition, they refer to "the grapevine," "word of mouth," and "gossip in the lunchroom." Some faculty also refer to meetings where the president "tells us about the state of financial affairs," including "the number of students, . . . the budget pie and how it is expended, future plans, shifts in distribution." But they also say that the president rarely has the last word on how faculty understand the budget because just as he finishes these presentations, "the grapevine" takes over "giving finesse" to his "statistics. As one faculty member explains, "His statistics, . . . what they mean, . . . how we are doing, . . . that gets fleshed out informally."

Administrators say that few faculty "have a complete [financial] picture or could have one" even though administrators "work at it all the time." "If there is a slight decrease," says one, "people get scared. We have to be careful how we explain downturns. . . . The faculty panic early. . . . We need to interpret it to the faculty carefully. . . . You have to help them see the possibilities and not just the costs. So much of it is how you say things in faculty meetings." Another adds that although Arcadia's financial status continues to change "for the better," that "this is not widely understood" by faculty, and that there is a need now for administrators "to meet with faculty. They don't have the context. We need to lay out for them past years of enrollment and [what) we have brought in, . . . [that] we have increased quality and raised more money."

Thinking about stability and growth. In 1986–87 President Anderson says that Arcadia needs "qualitative" growth—"challenging what we do and how we do it, . . . exploring new ways of achieving"—and that it should avoid the "major changes in mission" that physical growth can bring, even if this requires academic departments "restraining themselves." "We are an institution with about [number] students," says a close administrative colleague. "The facilities are geared that way, as are the faculty and the staff. . . . The question is: Will we continue to be an institution of [number], or will we become larger? That would be a major change, . . . would require a different institutional thrust. . . . We will have to hang on to where we are at. We can have no major new thrust."

By 1988–89 a small but voluble proportion of the faculty, several of them young and recently hired, had started to question this strategy and senior faculty members' trusting acceptance of it. In the words of one interviewee, "There is both an old and a young Arcadia faculty, . . . [facing] a philosophical and generational struggle. The older faculty are content to . . . let administrators administer. The younger faculty . . . are more snoopy and questioning." One of the younger faculty members describes the emerging point of view: "We need aggressive leadership in program and fundraising initiatives. You can't have a standard program. You have to go out to the community. It will make the college grow. If you have a laid-back leadership, the college won't grow. It will be death. . . . You can't hold back."

Comparing the college to its peers. In assessing their financial well-being, Arcadia's administrators usually compare themselves to three peer groups on a variety of performance indicators, such as enrollment, faculty salaries, academic program offerings, and revenues. Depending on the peer group to which they compare themselves and the indicator they select as the basis of their comparison, Arcadia can look moderately priced or expensive, financially solid or undersupported. In the words of a key administrator, Arcadia's financial position "varies depending on what you look at and what measure you use."

Whereas administrators view Arcadia's financial condition from several different vantage points, faculty usually rely on just one comparison group and on fewer performance indicators. For example, a cabinet-level administrator defines Arcadia's financial status relative to the three sets of peers—a small cluster of its "biggest competitors," a larger group of similar colleges "in this part of the country,"

Institutional Change and Assessment   395

and the total population of similar colleges in the United States, and he focuses equally on "revenue production" and "quality reputation" as markers of successful performance. In contrast, a key faculty leader compares Arcadia only to the "biggest competitor" group and then only in relation to revenues.

The resulting differences are not surprising. The administrators who look broadly see a broad range of outcomes, and they are able to consider how strengths may balance weaknesses. "From a marketing perspective . . . it is risky," an administrator speaks, "but we have more stable enrollment, . . . [and] we are well established in our position." The faculty, who typically take a narrower view, see a narrower band of outcomes—for example, that Arcadia is "on the low end" relative to its peers and "in continual risk of pricing [itself] out of the market."

Speculating about the future. At Arcadia people typically see the present as improved financially over the past, but they usually project a more difficult financial future. Thus administrators might refer to "an increase in our yield on applications" over past years, but at the same time they caution, "We all understand what the next five years will be like, . . . recruitment will be tougher." Even when the present day brings a real financial crunch, college members give less attention to how it is affecting the college in its immediacy than to how it might escalate or reemerge in the future. A faculty member describes how a recent dip in revenues caused a scare grounded less in what it was in the present than in people's speculations about what it might become in the future: "We have had a lean year (because of the) shortfall. The faculty would not notice much of a difference [this year]. There were no program cuts, no staff cuts. . . . Next year it may be the same. This could be serious if it became a pattern."

Retrospective

When I compare the Arcadia of 1986–87 and 1988–89, especially in terms of the president's growing concerns about revenues and his increased involvement in fundraising (and his concomitant distancing from campus life), I have to ask what happened in the interim. When I cast the question this way, my impulse is to indulge in contingency-based speculation, searching for an "environmental shift" that would require, from the president, a different response: Did support for the college drop, forcing the president to look for new sources of funds? Did key resource providers stop giving, or were they threatening to do so? Were students leaving? My answers, on all counts, was "no." Yet I knew that the level of felt stress on campus had increased over the two years between the research visits.

Approaching the pattern of events at Arcadia College from the perspective of social construction yields a different story: By 1988–89 President Anderson was clearly acting differently (he had become more of an "outside president") than he had been two years earlier and, according to campus sources, than he had been throughout his long term of office. Puzzled and frustrated by Anderson's changing relationship with the campus, key faculty members were reading their own meanings into his new stance. I viewed the faculty as disturbed by the president's departure from the daily routine of campus life and also as more concerned than they had been two years before about the college's uncertain future. By 1988–89 Arcadia's financial "story line" was muddled, at least as faculty saw it. Faculty members generated interpretations of the college's resource condition more volubly than the president did; in his absence this could happen. And faculty members' understandings of college financial indicators were, for the most part, inconsistent with and more negative than that of the president. Despite the discrepancy in the president's and the faculty's beliefs, administrators made few attempts to mediate the thinking of the faculty.

As the president distanced himself from the college—for example, by giving attention to external matters in ways he had not done previously—the faculty's concerns about him and the college's financial state seemed to escalate. These concerns were exacerbated by the entry of a new cadre of faculty who did not understand the relationship that had grown between the campus and the president over his many years in office. To these junior faculty, Anderson appeared not to be working hard or well enough at his external tasks. To the senior faculty, he appeared to be spending too much time outside the institution.

Although the research, as designed, kept me from examining how and why the president distanced himself from the campus, one pattern was clear: in his distancing, the president was losing "the pulse" of institutional life. What struck me particularly was that in losing the unique understanding and relationship that "having the pulse" represented—a habit he had long valued and which others, too, had long valued in him—he seemed to risk losing the institution's heart altogether. In his distancing, Joshua Anderson contradicted one of his core values (closeness to the campus) and one that the campus, probably through his example, had come to share. Moreover, the distancing made little sense to many faculty. In his distancing, Anderson created ambiguity.

By all objective measures this was a campus that, in 1988–89, should have reflected the same feelings of financial security and satisfaction that it had two years earlier. A social constructivist view suggests that the change may have been due, not to financial changes objectively defined (the contingency view), but to more subtle (and perhaps more powerful) subjective shifts within the mind of the president, within the minds of campus members, and within the relationship between the president and the campus.

Financially Strapped: Industrial College

Industrial College, located in downtown Thomasville, feels a world away from the mainstream urban center I have just left. Thomasville has a tattered, hard-work look about it. Unemployment is high, and residents say that they live in one of the poorest regions of the country. Although I am sure that the damp, cold weather colors my perceptions, I am struck, during both visits, by the run-down neighborhoods I pass—aging paint, loose shutters, homes in disrepair.

In contrast to Arcadia, Industrial College reflects one of the weakest financial records in the research sample. Its resources increase yearly at a rate substantially lower than the average for all American colleges and universities. Over recent years, Industrial has experienced several major resource reductions, and the possibility of more losses hangs in the air.

When I first visited Industrial College in 1986–87, 1 saw it as a financially troubled institution set in an equally troubled region. However, in revisiting two years later, I have the sense that life—or the feeling of life—in the college differs now from how life must feel in the outside community. A receptionist greets me cheerfully as I enter the main building, ready to provide college information or directions. I glance at what I remember as a blank gray wall now boasting a colorful bulletin board covered with newspaper cutouts—pictures and stories about faculty, students, administrators, individual and group accomplishments, collegiate events. People walk briskly down hallways and around me, talking to each other about students, reminding each other of tasks, rehashing recent meetings. There is the hum of a busy morning in the air. My feeling, gut-level, is that Industrial College is more ordered, more purposeful, more active—perhaps more alive—than I had found it before.

Presidential Leadership and College Resources

Rebecca Keeton, the president of Industrial College, strikes a sharp, consistent image in people's minds. What follows is an account of that picture as faculty members and administrators, including the president, presented it to me.

Complexity in role: expanding the breadth of presidential attention. When Rebecca Keeton thinks of Industrial College, its strengths and vulnerabilities, she considers its faculty, staff, and students ("The institution [is] only as good as [its] people." She also considers the quality of their work ("excellent teaching") and their dedication in accomplishing it ("We have some of the finest, most dedicated, student-oriented faculty that I have ever worked with"). However, like Joshua Anderson at Arcadia, Keeton also thinks of the college in more inanimate terms—as a structure of "resources," explaining that as president she has to "see the overall picture . . . the sources of funds and where the expenses go."

Given these two divergent understandings of college life—the human and the technical—Rebecca Keeton, like Joshua Anderson, simultaneously practices two very different brands of leadership. From the human perspective, she is "a cheerleader, . . . a coach, . . . a mentor, . . . providing encouragement and support." From the more technical and economic perspective, she tracks "external funding, . . . putting [money] where we most need it." The faculty see this dualism in her—that she is a "humanist" and "interested in people in the raw," but that she is also "an astute money manager."

Keeton's complex outlook shows itself in other ways, for example, in her pursuit of opportunities for change and especially in fundraising. She is known for her ability to "form alliances" with resource providers, "making them aware of what the college can provide" and winning their support. But at the same time, she insists on preserving what the college already is, and especially what it is already doing in the name of educational quality. In her fundraising drives, she is far more likely to concentrate on clarifying to outsiders what educational quality means at Industrial College, how the educational program works, and why it is deserving of support, rather than promising to adapt it to their differing expectations. In the words of faculty members, Keeton "works for the college" by "molding and affecting [the] opinions" of those who would support what it stands for.

I hear other examples of Keeton's complex outlook, several of which are reminiscent of Arcadia's president. For example, she is careful to "take her time . . . [to] give attention to the details" that are meaningful to campus life, but at the same time, she is assiduous in keeping "the big picture" before her, including the "economic . . . political . . . and social trends . . . [that may] impact on an institution." She is also careful to blend directiveness with consultation, especially when facing difficult decisions, much as Anderson is. An administrator describes her as "standing firm in her convictions . . . not wishy-washy," but as someone with whom you can argue and who "can be persuaded." And the faculty say that "she has very definite ideas, but is willing to be cooperative, to modify."

Commitments in role: delimiting considerations. Despite her flexible perspective, Keeton presents herself as committed—even immovable—on several fronts. First, unlike Anderson who is always careful to assure that there is money to spend before spending it, Keeton is committed to living with higher

degrees of financial risk, especially when the college's educational priorities are at stake. During the interview, she tells of how the college, virtually "in the hole," purchased some expensive instructional hardware. Even though she knew that "this is . . . money that we can't spend," she heeded the advice of academic leaders who urged, "We can't pretend that we are educating with quality if we don't have this. Although she knew the expenditure would weaken the college's operating base, she believed that, educationally, the college would "get a much better product." "If the faculty can teach well," she says, "that compensates some for salary problems, . . . if they have pride in what they are doing, if they are teaching the state of the art." A top-level administrator echoes her views, "we would have had more money in the bank if not for the president, . . . but we would not be accomplishing as much as we are."

Second, although Keeton realizes how important it is to engage in fundraising, like Anderson, she expresses primary commitment to the internal, educational core of the college. Her earliest actions in office resembled those of Anderson: assessing evaluation criteria, recognizing students who excel beyond expectations and teachers who encourage them, reshaping academic programs in the name of "quality" and "efficiency," and bringing in some new faculty and staff committed to the college's brand of educational quality. In sum, Keeton, like Anderson, started by building quality (locally defined) into the college's educational core, using it as a base for later resource development.

Third, Keeton also resembles Anderson in that she attends equally to resource acquisition and resource use. While asserting that a college president "can't spend enough time out there . . . looking for opportunities and building community relations," she personally attends to the internal allocation of hard-won dollars. Her strong involvement in the decision to buy instructional hardware is a case in point.

Fourth, Keeton, like Anderson, is sensitive to how faculty view the value of their efforts, especially as this is reflected in the college's reward system. Although Keeton can do little to affect the availability of monetary rewards, she creates substitutes, some coming directly from her. A faculty member explains, "Dr. Keeton tells us we are good teachers and we like to hear that . . . [she] gives us a lot of stroking. . . . She loses no opportunity just to say this, . . . gives us pep talks and makes us feel good, makes us feel we want to live up to the image she has of us." Keeton also provides rewards in more subtle and round-about but equally powerful ways, for example, by going out of her way to stay in touch with the faculty about their professional work. And she creates rewards for the academic community as a whole—in the form of public acknowledgment and appreciation—by reeducating the local citizenry about what college faculty are doing to "enhance the quality of life" in the region.

Self in role. Keeton's leadership image is distinctive in several ways. First, she is known for removing obstacles to faculty pursuits. Unlike many presidents who begin their terms by creating new bureaucratic processes and structures, she did just the opposite, dissolving large sections of a "gridlock" bureaucracy. An academic leader explains, "Before this president came we were running into brick walls. Now we can't climb all the stairs, but we are not losing step because we can't go where we want. I am tired, but it is a good tired. I am able to expect more of others." Keeton is also known for "setting an example" of hard work and accomplishment. People say that "her work ethic is unbelievable," that she has "vigor" and is "in tune," and that she is "aggressive, assertive"—in sum, that she is "most adept at doing what she is doing." Finally, she is recognized for cultivating the college's base of support, if not financially (due to unmanageable external constraints), then politically. She is known for recruiting key officials and citizens to be "very helpful in a public relations way . . . [and to] speak in support of the college."

Despite these accomplishments she emphasizes how hard it has been to lead during "financially chaotic" times. "I have dealt with some of the most difficult situations that you could ever imagine," she says. "Ambiguity, . . . coping with existential anxiety, the uncertainty about what does all of this mean, if anything?" As she describes the leadership that the college needs, she also expresses what she, as its presidential leader, needs: "[I have to] keep a sense of humor . . . [to] keep things in perspective, . . . being able to see the ridiculous side of our behavior. We take so seriously

things that aren't too significant. You have to be able to see the absurd side of our behavior. That is important for mental health and well-being. You can't be serious all the time. It helps in my leadership that I can laugh and hug someone . . . that I am a caring person and that I can demonstrate that through my behavior, that I am not cold and removed from the faculty's concerns."

Resources and Stress

During both visits the president and other top administrators report unequivocally that resources are in "continual erosion," and Keeton confesses, "I feel like I am walking right on the edge." The faculty repeat what administrators and faculty leaders tell them (that "the situation is worse," but they express less anxiety. "We almost laugh at it," says a faculty member, "the same old thing; . . . you have to laugh at things you have no control over. . . . [It] does not make us depressed, . . . nor do we act well on it all the time. It's always been some type of restraint as far as resources go." A key faculty leader adds, "I tend not to be interested in financial matters. . . . My feeling is that we keep crying wolf, . . . but I always get paid. . . . I have never missed a paycheck." In describing their work, nearly all faculty interviewees show hope and purpose ("feeling beleaguered but courageous"), and they see the college as "moving along, . . . moving forward, . . . not [staying at] the status quo." One faculty leader sums up the faculty's feelings as "fatalism blended with lifted spirits" and adds, "Things can't get worse so maybe they will get better. We have been down so long. The only way is up."

Whereas the stress I had felt among Arcadia's faculty led me to ask why it was there and what might be causing it, at Industrial College I had to ask why, on the whole, the faculty felt so good. In reviewing my visit, I am drawn to three factors: how the president communicates financial matters, how college members conceive of growth, and how faculty members center their attention on the immediate present.

Communicating about finances. President Keeton meets regularly with the faculty to "go through the whole budget picture, . . . develop a picture of the institution's finances—where the revenues come from, and where the expenses are going, . . . showing that over several years." Academic leaders say that the president's presentations help the faculty "see the implications of budgetary decisions" and "understand what is happening," and that this generates trust by bringing the president's priorities to light. In the words of one, "The faculty have seen that we have put more money into instruction than ever before, and they know where the money came from. . . . If in the upcoming year she has to reorganize, the faculty have the sense that she is not making things up or hiding money."

Faculty leaders report that they rely heavily on the president's definition of the college's finances, and this bears out when I hear them repeat phrases that she has also used in answering my interview questions. The faculty also comment on her presentational style. One faculty leader says, "We never get a bunch of numbers that mean nothing," and another adds, "She presents clearly, . . . does not leave people feeling bewildered." In addition to her formal budgetary meetings with the faculty, Rebecca Keeton is available informally to fill in gaps in people's knowledge, and in these sessions she is just as "open" and "clear" as in the more formal meetings.

Whereas Keeton confronts the "chaos" of financial events, the faculty confront an equally frightening but more orderly view: They get "the problem as it is defined in her mind." They also hear what she is doing about it, where she succeeds, and where she is limited. Thus they understand that in many ways, "her hands are tied" and that "given the situation, . . . there is little a president can do." An academic leader explains how this kind of understanding affects faculty morale: "Our resources have decreased even though the enthusiasm and morale remain high. The underlying financial factor is seen to be the external factor that we can't get control over—the problem we are having is not an internal factor. It is not us." Besides understanding the limitations, the faculty realize that the college administration "is doing all that it can to support what [the faculty] are all about." "(The president] has our interests at heart," says a faculty member. "Her heart, time, and efforts are devoted to this college; . . . we have the feeling that we count. . . . It is important for us to feel that our interests are being considered and cared for."

Rethinking growth. At Industrial College people are searching for a different vision of growth and change, and they say that they want their leadership to help them find it. According to one campus member, "WE need a president to encourage us to find new ways of doing what we are already doing while remaining within our current confines. . . . We need to try to encourage people to expand the college in more subtle ways." Interviewees see the president as meeting this need in two ways: by seeking external support for what the college is already doing well, and by "focusing on the management of what we do have."

Though no one defines this wished-for growth more specifically, there are clues in the interviews about what it might entail. Faculty, for example, refer to "how much we [do] with so little," and an academic administrator says that you have to focus on "how far you can stretch the buck" and "how well utilized [the equipment and buildings] are," and not just how you can maintain them or acquire more. A cabinet level administrator suggests the importance of "not expecting that you will get what you need just by asking for it," but rather, by being "creative" and patient ("an eternal optimist") . He also refers to an ethic of working and thinking closely with others and of arguing openly over points of view rather than resources. For example, he says that he calls other members of the president's administrative team several times a day to get alternate views on decisions and problems. And he comments on the absence of animosity over resource allocation: "[The cabinet officers] do argue but we share; . . . we have a dependence on each other; . . . we don't have the time to fight over money." There is little argument in this institution about how resources should be divided up among college divisions, or when and where the college might find more, as concerns about acquisition turn to concerns about best use.

Centering on the immediate present. At Industrial most faculty prefer to focus on everyday professional tasks—teaching classes, meeting students, developing courses—and the president, in promoting teaching and learning, strongly encourages this. Although Industrial's faculty worry about what the future will bring, few are concerned that President Keeton should be attending to other than what she is. This is very different from Arcadia, where the faculty are less accepting of Joshua Anderson's desire to attend to the routine of the present moment and where they are more direct than the faculty of Industrial in urging their president to think more about the future.

The view of time at Industrial differs from the view at Arcadia in another way. Given a time frame of past, present, and future, Arcadia's faculty see the present as the high point—as improved over the past and possibly as better than the uncertain future; at Arcadia the future holds the possibility of negative change. At Industrial, the faculty see continued financial decline: The past was difficult, the present is worse, the future will proceed on the same course; they expect little change in a world they know well.

Retrospective

If we begin an analysis of Industrial College by noting the change in faculty morale between 1986–87 and 1988–89, we might ask what happened in the college to induce that change. Just as at Arcadia, the financial condition at Industrial had not changed according to objective measures, though stasis at Industrial meant continued decline rather than continued security (as was the case at Arcadia). The faculty at Industrial College had become hopeful and optimistic—about their college, themselves, and their leadership—not because the college's financial fortunes had improved, but because through their new president, they seemed to find new (and renewed) meaning in their work together. The pattern was just the opposite at Arcadia, where the faculty's sense of comfort fell, not in relation to any objectively measured resource change, but because something had changed in the relationship between the president and the campus.

A social constructivist perspective that views people's communication and learning, rather than economic measures, as central to faculty morale sheds additional light on life within Industrial College: On entering office, Rebecca Keeton moved quickly to the heart of what she saw as mattering to the faculty (good teaching), she articulated this value clearly to the faculty and to citizens in the college's surrounding community, and she took action that was consistent with her words (for example, investing in instructional equipment even when she knew this might break the budget). Viewed purely from a contingency standpoint,

such actions might be questioned: During times of financial hardship, should a president not be more prudent about expenditures, and should she not put her mind to fundraising, delegating faculty leadership to academic administrators? Was the investment in expensive instructional equipment during particularly tough times truly wise?

Conversely, viewed from the standpoint of social constructivism, Keeton's actions were extraordinarily appropriate in that they communicated, to the faculty, consistency between their values and those of the president (Keeton responded to the faculty's teaching needs even while risking financial collapse). Moreover, Keeton made clear efforts to enhance her own understanding of what the faculty believed and how they felt about their financial condition—and she also tried to respond meaningfully to the faculty's questions and worries, voiced and unvoiced—at the same time that she addressed financial factors instrumentally, conventionally, and in the spirit of contingency thinking. In brief, she was just as concerned with how campus members understood and felt about the college's financial condition as their experienced reality—that is, its social construction—as she was with changing its more inanimate, objectivized, business-based features. Her attentiveness did not escape the faculty who praised her both for her business acumen and human caring.

Unlike Anderson at Arcadia, Rebecca Keeton moved closer to (as opposed to further away from) the faculty by building up her understanding of what faculty members were thinking, by communicating that she cared about what they thought and felt, and by mediating their interpretations of what she was doing to alleviate financial hardship, and why. While working amidst extraordinarily difficult financial conditions, Rebecca Keeton used a constructivist approach to alleviate distress among college members.

Reinterpreting the Leadership of Hard Times and Good Times from a Constructivist Stance

For both Arcadia and Industrial, a conventional contingency perspective would focus strongly on whether the president responded successfully to resource challenges, for example, by increasing revenues or decreasing loss, with the expectation that such accomplishments would boost faculty morale. However, the contingency perspective would overlook the possibility that how people understand their resource condition (be it bad or good), including the role of leadership in mediating their understanding, is more closely related to their morale than is the badness or goodness of their financial situation defined objectively. This study's surprising finding—that faculty at the rich and stable college (Arcadia) were dispirited and anxious while faculty at the impoverished college (Industrial) were optimistic, even buoyant—emerged from constructivist consideration. As such, it forces us to reconsider traditional assumptions about the centrality of money in academic organizations. Perhaps other factors emerging from constructivist thought—such as leaders' abilities to pick up and work with people's understandings, commitments, and anxieties, and their abilities also to interpret institutional events (including resource issues)—are just as central. In this section I present several summary propositions about the social construction of resource stress and leadership based on the cases of Arcadia College and Industrial College:

Proposition 1: Finances, like dramatic props, may contribute to the social construction of campus reality.

At Arcadia and Industrial, leaders often work with, through, or around finances, using them to rationalize what they do, what they do not do, or what they believe they (and others) should or should not be doing. In both cases, leaders use money as a medium for the construction of collegiate reality.

Proposition 2: Financial distress (including concerns about how leaders are managing finances) may result from deficits in what people know about their financial condition and how leaders are handling it. In neglecting her or his interpretive role, a president may foster such distress, knowingly or not.

Among the faculty, feelings of financial distress seem to result more from the absence of understanding (as at Arcadia College) than from the absence of money (as at Industrial

College). As we see at Arcadia, a president who neglects to develop the faculty's understanding of college resources—or to talk about her or his own approach to financial management—is likely to engender distress regardless of how good the college's financial condition might be.

Proposition 3: Feelings of financial distress may result from practices that make good sense from a contingency perspective, for example, the accumulation of money, the comparison of a college to its peers, and the president's engagement in external resource hunting.

Contingency theory views the organization as highly dependent for its existence on an erratic environment and requires that organizational members should, therefore, constantly monitor resource availability, compare themselves to competitors, and engage in resource hunting.

Viewed in a constructivist light, however, these practices may be more harmful than helpful. For example, the case of Arcadia College suggests that the possession of money may be a source of distress. The existence of a substantial budget gives the cabinet something to fight over, and it forces leaders to acknowledge that regardless how large the pot, they must deal with limitations. The situation at Industrial is diametrically opposite: because the college has little money to begin with, there is little to fight over, and limitations, defined on the basis of competitive resource allocation, are a non-issue for administrators and faculty alike.

At Arcadia distress also emerges as faculty compare their college's financial condition to that of selected peers. However, because Arcadia's president and other leaders neglect to participate in setting the faculty's comparative frame, the faculty construct multiple frames, some yielding negative and frightening views and differing substantially in their completeness and content from the president's and other administrators' usually more complex, studied interpretations.

Finally, the case of Arcadia suggests that resource hunting can do as much to distance a president from the faculty as to endear her or him to them. Joshua Anderson's new-found interest in fundraising represents his departure from the faculty's everyday lives, which they feel emotionally. At Industrial, Rebecca Keeton also engages in external fundraising, but she makes it a point to remain engaged with the faculty, something that Arcadia's Joshua Anderson does not do.

> **Proposition 4:** Just as presidents may foster distress by neglecting their interpretive tasks, so may they foster hope by attending, through conversation, to what people know, believe, and feel about their college's financial condition and about the meaning and value of their collective work.

Whereas the case of Arcadia shows that faculty members' confusion about their financial well-being may intensify their distress even in positive circumstances, the case of Industrial suggests that the inculcation of understanding may alleviate distress even during times of severe financial decline. Industrial's president, a good model of "leader as teacher," takes great pains to assemble an understandable financial lesson for the faculty. Because she can do little to resolve the college's real financial problem (declining revenues), she works at reducing the ambiguity that surrounds it, for example, by defining essential facts, clarifying constraints, and in general, providing an understandable picture of what is happening and why. Moreover, at Industrial, the president is firmly in the campus conversation, in fact, orchestrating it so that the most prominent comparison is the college to itself—its past to its present, its progress despite great odds ("how much we have done with so little"), the realization that things have gotten better incrementally despite the odds ("we've never had it so good"). The focus is on the management of "what we do have"—the present, the concern of the moment—and preserving its inherent "quality" rather than worrying about what tomorrow will bring. In contrast, at Arcadia the president withdraws from conversation, and as the campus's focus falls on the college's "biggest competitors" and on questions about the college's ability to survive a seemingly malevolent future, attention to the present gives way to anxiety about the future.

Finally, the lived reality of Industrial College centers, not on financial news (as it does at Arcadia), but on conversation about the faculty's teaching. Rebecca Keeton's ability to clarify and amplify the personal meaning of the faculty's chosen professional work, and her efforts

to extend support (in multiple forms) for their continued efforts, moderate financial hardship. Although Industrial's financial condition remains irritating (there are "grumblings," it fails to diminish the faculty's optimism.

> **Proposition 5:** A college president may contribute to the social construction of collegiate reality by balancing expansiveness of thought (cognitive complexity) with adherence to central values (enacted commitment).

A number of studies have suggested that leadership entails a good match between an organization's complexity and the leader's, or the core leadership team's, cognitive complexity [2, 7, 33]. Cognitive complexity might be defined as the ability to think in expansive and unconventional (even counterrational) terms about everyday organizational life—for example, viewing quality as a foundation for resource development rather than linearly as its outcome (as Keeton and Anderson did early in their terms), or assuming that when resources are tight, spending money may be more productive than putting it away (as Keeton did when she invested in expensive instructional equipment during tough times).

Though the concept of cognitive complexity is attractive in its reach beyond the conventional and rational, its neglect of limits raises questions: Where are the personal boundaries that separate the things that a person will consider enacting from those she would deem unacceptable? Where and when does the complex of possible considerations stop, and what causes this? Although the presidents of Arcadia and Industrial strive for cognitive expansiveness, there are some considerations that neither will tolerate, given their essential commitments (for example, concern for people over funding and administration). In both cases, the points where cognitive expansiveness ends and delimited commitment begins are marked by personal values. In both cases, complexity and commitment appear as integral to each other.

> **Proposition 6:** Leadership that leads to learning-related change is likely to be interactive and dialogic rather than unidirectional, and the learning it induces is as likely to touch the president as those with whom the president engages.

Communication between leaders and others around them (for example, faculty) may be unidirectional in the model of dissemination, or it may be interactive in the form of dialogue [32]. One example of interactive, dialogic communication is the president speaking (at least briefly), then listening for how faculty make sense of her words and for what they believe and want, then shaping (or reshaping) her leadership efforts based on what she has just learned about what is already in their minds. This approach views the president as initiating and encouraging an institutional conversation, though not directing it. Rather, the persons with whom she interacts (faculty) wield substantial power in shaping institutional discourse—for example, as they indicate their knowledge and expectations, as she reformulates her thinking in response to theirs, and as they, in turn, stretch to capture her meaning just as she has stretched to grasp theirs. Because communication of this sort is tailored closely to interactants' understandings, constructed reciprocally on the spot [41], it would also seem to lead more effectively (than the unidirectional model would allow) to learning-related change (although slowly and painstakingly) through incremental adjustment in the minds of both leader and other. Leadership that is based in interactive, dialogic communication and reciprocal learning requires the full presence and engagement of the interactants, something Keeton provided her college but which Anderson, over time, did not.

Conclusion

Whereas contingency theory focuses on how leaders respond to a contained, prespecified conception of the institutional context (including its financial status), social constructivism illuminates how people—leaders and others—create (and recreate) their conceptions of their institutional worlds, including their beliefs about how well their college is doing financially. Constructivism also illuminates people's personal experiences of these institutional worlds, often emphasizing how such experiences may differ from person to person, and why. As such, constructivism helps us understand the social life of colleges and universities, and the personal lives within them, in ways

that contingency theory does not. It also permits us to ask why collegiate realities are constructed as they are at any moment and to search for more humane and educationally liberating alternatives. Thus, social constructivism is helpful, not only in the framing of research on leadership, but in day-to-day leadership practice as well.

Although I have tried in this article to argue for constructivist interpretations of organizational life, I conclude with a caveat and a warning: Social constructivism, like most things, is only as good as its users. As researchers and as campus leaders, we can use constructivism to promote selected ends (good or bad) just as we may use contingency theory for selected purposes. Thus, we have the power to construct research designs and campus agendas, goals, and settings selfishly, heartlessly, or simply unthinkingly, just as we have the power to construct them humanistically, consciously, and critically. Moreover, though in this article I associate constructivist views with dialogic and empowering leadership, we can imagine, just as easily, a constructivism that controls, delimits, and disempowers—for example, as in the case of a leader who reserves dialogue for a select few, who tells only part of what she or he knows to favor a particular agenda, or who outrightly deceives. Constructivism may help us see and understand more as we research and as we lead, but it does not necessarily make us better people.

Despite this caveat, it is important to note that social constructivism helps us see, more clearly than we would otherwise, the values, intents, and experiences of those we study. In contrast, contingency theory keeps us from seeing the personal and subjective "insides" of college life. With a constructivist vision, we can at least begin to grapple with what we, and those we study, are doing, thinking, and feeling, and also, why. What we do with such knowledge—whether we use it to better our lives together, or to pursue selfish, even harmful aims—is an altogether different question, yet one we dare not leave unasked.

Notes

1. In order to abide by promises of research confidentiality, I have disguised numerous features of institutional and personal identity.

Arcadia College and Industrial College are pseudonyms, and although I refer to them as "colleges," I use the word in the most generic sense and without reference to a particular Carnegie (institutional) type. The gender that I ascribe to individuals does not necessarily reflect a person's true gender. All position titles (for example, president, head of faculty senate, and so on), names of official groups (for example, cabinet), and other identifying features of institutional life are given generically. I present institutional statistics (for example, enrollment) in terms of rough categories rather than specific numbers.

2. I initially examined patterns of change in FTE enrollment and total raw revenues for the time period 1985–86 through 1988–89 for eight institutions participating in a study of leadership and resource stress in higher education. Arcadia's rate of inflation-adjusted revenue increases was well above the average growth rate of all American colleges and universities, ranking the college among the top three of the eight study institutions. Industrial's rate of inflation- adjusted change was well below the national average, ranking the college among the lowest three in the study sample. Comparisons were based on the Higher Education Prices and Price Indexes, compiled by Research Associates of Washington [40].

3. Because contingency-based studies view institutional context as given and as determining the content and composition of leadership, their designs typically require study sites to be similar on features believed to define context (for example, institutional type). In a contingency study, context is the analytic point of departure. Constructivist studies, on the other hand, assume that leaders (and others) construct their contexts moment by moment; thus leadership and other human processes are the more appropriate points of departure. In a constructivist study, context is that which is determined. Thus, rather than choosing two sites identical in terms of institutional type or other contextual features associated with contingency thinking, I selected two presidents whose leadership was similar on key constructivist factors. This design helped me trace how the two presidents contributed to the enactment of their collegiate contexts.

References

1. American Council on Education (ACE) . "Administrators' Views of Challenges Facing Institutions in the Next Five Years." From table reprinted in *The Chronicle of Higher Education Almanac*, 5 September 1990, p. 28.

2. Ashby, W. R. *An Introduction to Cybernetics.* London: Chapman and Hall Ltd./University Paperbacks, 1956.

3. Bensimon, E. M. "How College Presidents Use Their Administrative Groups: 'Real' and 'Illusory' Teams." *Journal for Higher Education Management*, 7 (1991), 35–51.

4. _____. "Viewing the Presidency: Perceptual Congruence between Presidents and Leaders on Their Campuses." *The Leadership Quarterly*, 1 (1990), 71–90.

5. _____. "The Meaning of 'Good Presidential Leadership': A Frame Analysis." *Review of Higher Education*, 12 (Winter 1989), 107–23.

6. Berger, P. L., and T. Luckmann. *The Social Construction of Reality.* New York: Doubleday, 1967.

7. Birnbaum, R. *How Colleges Work: The Cybernetics of Academic Organization and Leadership.* San Francisco: Jossey-Bass, 1988.

8. Blumenstyk, G. "City Budget Cuts Take Another Toll on the Nation's Urban Institutions." *Chronicle of Higher Education*, 4 December 1991, p. A38.

9. Cage, M. C. "Mid-Year Budget Cuts Reported by Public Colleges in 22 States." *Chronicle of Higher Education*, 12 February 1992.

10. _____. "Public-College Employees Pay the Price for States' Political Disputes." *Chronicle of Higher Education*, 24 July 1991, pp. A17, A18.

11. Chira, S. "How Stanford, Wealthy and Wise, Is Cutting Costs to Stay that Way." *The New York Times*, 8 July 1990, pp. 1, 13.

12. Daniels, L. A. "Raising Money Tops Agenda of Many Colleges for 1990s." *The New York Times*, 17 December 1989, pp. 1, 46.

13. DePalma, A. "With Deficit, Can Yale Still Be Great?" *The New York Times*, 4 December 1991, p. B7.

14. _____. "As a Deficit Looms, 26 Threaten to Quit Key Columbia Posts." *The New York Times*, 27 November 1991, pp. Al, B6.

15. Erickson, F. "Qualitative Methods in Research on Teaching." In *Handbook of Research on Teaching*, 3rd ed., edited by M. C. Wittrock, pp. 119–61. New York: Macmillan, 1986.

16. Grassmuck, K. "Clouded Economy Prompts Colleges to Weigh Changes." *Chronicle of Higher Education*, 31 January 1990, pp. 1, 28, 30.

17. Hill, R. "Md. Professors Say Budget Cuts Will Hurt Quality of Education." *The Washington Post*, 24 November 1991, p. B3.

18. Jacobson, R. L. "Academic Leaders Predict Major Changes for Higher Education in Recession's Wake." *Chronicle of Higher Education*, 20 November 1991, pp. Al, A35, A36.

19. Jaschik, S. "State Funds for Higher Education Drop in Year; First Decline since Survey Began 33 Years Ago." *Chronicle of Higher Education*, 6 November 1991, pp. Al, A38, A39.

20. _____. "States Spending $40.8-Billion on Colleges This Year; Growth Rate at a 30-Year

Low." *Chronicle of Higher Education*, 24 October 1990, pp. A1, A26.

21. Kast, F. E., and J. E. Rosenzweig. *Organization and Management, A Systems and Contingency Approach*. 4th ed. New York: McGraw-Hill, 1985.

22. Katz, D., and R. L. Kahn. *The Social Psychology of Organizations*. 2nd ed. New York: John Wiley and Sons, 1978.

23. Leslie, L. L. "Financial Management and Resource Allocation." In *Key Resources on Higher Education Governance, Management, and Leadership*, edited by M. W. Peterson and L. A. Mets, pp. 194–217. San Francisco: Jossey-Bass, 1987.

24. Lively, K. "State Colleges Grapple with Tough Decisions on How to Downsize." *Chronicle of Higher Education*, 3 February 1993, pp. A23, A28.

25. _____. "Governors of Montana and Oregon Call on Colleges to Merge or Cut Programs." *Chronicle of Higher Education*, 13 January 1993, pp. A22, A23.

26. Magner, D. K. "New Princeton President Seeks to Allay Faculty's Fears Over Style and Budget." *Chronicle of Higher Education*, 29 September 1989, pp. 18, 20, 21.

27. McMillen, L. "College Endowments Gained Modest 7.2% in 1990–91 as Recession Cured Earnings for 2nd Year in Row." *Chronicle of Higher Education*, 12 February 1992, pp. A31, A32, A33.

28. _____. "Higher Education Is Said to Face Its Toughest PR Challenge Ever." *Chronicle of Higher Education*, 24 July 1991.

29. Mead, G. H. Mind, Self and Society, from the Standpoint of a Social Behaviorist. In *Works of George Herbert Mead*, vol. 1, edited by C. W. Morris. Chicago: University of Chicago Press, 1962.

30. Mooney, C. J. "Death of a Campus." *Chronicle of Higher Education*, 24 June 1992.

31. National Center for Postsecondary Governance and Finance (NCPGF). "Colleges Urged to Use Financial Savvy." *Centerpiece*, 4 (April 1989), 1, 7.

32. Neumann, A. "Double Vision: The Experience of Institutional Stability." *Review of Higher Education*, 15 (Summer 1992), 341–71.

33. _____. "The Thinking Team: Toward a Cognitive Model of Administrative Teamwork in Higher Education." Journal of Higher Education, 62 (September/October 1991), 485–513.

34. _____. "Making Mistakes: Error and Learning in the College Presidency." *Journal of Higher Education*. 61 (July/August 1990), 386–407:

35. _____. "Strategic Leadership: The Changing Orientations of College Presidents." *Review of Higher Education*, 12 (Winter 1989), 137–51.

36. Neumann, A., and E. M. Bensimon. "Constructing the Presidency: College Presidents' Images of Their Leadership Roles, A Comparative Study." *Journal of Higher Education*, 61 (November/December 1990), 678–701.

37. Nicklin, J. L. "Harvard U. Reports $42-Million Deficit, Its First since 1974." *Chronicle of Higher Education*, 26 February 1992, pp. A33, A34.

38. Pfeffer, J., and G. R. Salancik. *The External Control of Organizations: A Resource Dependence Perspective*. New York: Harper and Row, 1978.

39. Rabinow, P., and W. M. Sullivan (eds.). *Interpretive Social Science. A Reader*. Berkeley: University of California. 1979.

40. Research Associates of Washington. *Higher Education Prices and Price Indexes: 1988 Update*. Washington, D.C.: Research Associates of Washington, September 1988.

41. Schutz, A. *The Phenomenology of the Social World*, translated by G. Walsh and F. Lehnert. Chicago: Northwestern University Press, 1967.

42. Scott, W. R. *Organizations: Rational, Natural, and Open Systems*. 3rd ed. Englewood Cliffs, N.J.: Prentice Hall, 1992.

43. Whetten D. A. "Organizational Decline: A Neglected Topic in Organizational Science." *The Academy of Management Review*, 5 (October 1980), 577–88.

44. Wilson, R. "College Recruiting Gimmicks Get More Lavish as Competition for New Freshmen Heats Up." *Chronicle of Higher Education*, 7 March 1990, pp. 1, 34.

45. Yin, R. K. *Case Study Research: Design and Methods*. Beverly Hills: Sage, 1984.

46. Zammuto, R. F. "Managing Declining Enrollments and Revenues." In *Key Resources on Higher Education Governance, Management, and Leadership*, edited by M. W. Peterson and L. A. Mets, pp. 347–65. San Francisco: Jossey-Bass, 1987.

I am grateful to Estela M. Bensimon, Robert Birnbaum, Susan Florio-Ruane, Ken Kempner, Kathryn Moore, Aaron M. Pallas, Robert J. Silverman, and the *Journal of Higher Education* reviewers for helpful criticism and advice. An earlier version of this article was presented at the annual meeting of the Association for the Study of Higher Education, Portland, Oregon, November 1990.

This document was prepared pursuant to a grant from the office for Educational Research and Improvement/Department of Education (OERI/ED). However, the opinions expressed herein do not necessarily reflect the position or policy of OERI/ED, and no official endorsement should be inferred.

Anna Newmann is associate professor in higher, adult, and lifelong education at Michigan State University.

Chapter 30

Creating a New Kind of Leadership for Campus Diversity

Blandina Cardenas Ramirez

Over the course of the next several decades, American higher education institutions will be called on to serve an unprecedented configuration of race and culture, gender and age, and individuals with special needs. Moreover, colleges and universities will be required to prepare those they serve to function as professionals and scholars in what may be the most culturally and racially complex society since the creation of the modern nation state. Creating institutional capacity for the diversity represented by these changes will require authentic leadership with the integrity and the vision, indeed the creativity and staying power, to accomplish four distinct but interrelated tasks.

1. To eliminate the gap in the participation, persistence, and success of members of underrepresented groups as students, faculty, and leaders in higher education institutions

2. To prepare students for cross-cultural transactions born out of tolerance, respect, and appreciation for individuals and groups unlike themselves

3. To promote scholarship among faculty and students that will develop and apply a more complete and accurate body of knowledge necessary to the society's ability to solve problems rooted in the persistent effects of historical inequities, understand the opportunities inherent in diversity, and develop the full range of creative and productive capacities in a diverse population

4. To engage the institution's diverse constituencies, both internal and external, in the activities, rituals, and symbols that will develop the capacity of students to create community in the context of diversity, define a common stake, and envision a common future

Few individuals who currently make up the leadership pool in American higher education have had either the training or experiences necessary to provide leadership for the diversity that is beginning to characterize their institutions today and will constitute a central characteristic in the future. At best, the last several decades in American higher education have been characterized by additive responses to diversity or inequity—seldom by transformative ones. While institutions have generally turned away from the policies of de jure and de facto exclusion that characterized the period before 1950, and although most institutions embrace diversity as a goal, few understand the scope of the change required, and the challenge of developing a well-planned strategy to build institutional capacity for diversity remains unclear for many. The development of leaders and leadership strategies to guide institutions to and through these change processes is imperative. In

"Creating a New Kind of Leadership for Campus Diversity," by Blandina Cardenas Ramirez in *Educating a New Majority: Transforming America's Educational System for Diversity*. Jossey-Bass Publishers, San Francisco, 1996.

On Becoming a Leader, Bennis (1989) cites John W. Gardner's description of the power of leadership: "'Leaders have a significant role in creating the state of mind that is the society. They can serve as symbols of the moral unity of the society. They can express values that hold the society together. Most important they can conceive and articulate the goals that lift people out of their petty preoccupations, carry them above the conflicts that tear a society apart, and unite them in pursuit of objectives worthy of their best efforts'" (p. 13).

If we substitute the terms *institution, school, department, board of trustees, students, faculty,* and *staff* where Gardner has used *society*, we begin to understand the crucial need for leadership on diversity, not only at the top of institutional hierarchies but throughout the academic community.

Diversity presents formidable challenges in capacity building for institutions, but it is the historical separateness and inequality that have characterized American society that make the challenge of leadership for diversity exponentially more demanding. Since World War II, institutions of higher education have experienced formidable growth and success while operating with little if any consideration for issues of diversity or equity. Individual faculty careers, departments, research units, and schools have acquired resources, recognition, and prestige by concentrating on matters other than diversity. Issues of intergroup understanding and tolerance have been marginal, at best. Moreover, the reluctance of the academy to engage issues of differences and inequality has been strongly reinforced by a society that has great difficulty talking openly about race, culture, gender, sexual orientation, or conditions of disability. Leadership for diversity, then, must be prepared to deal with several layers of values, attitudes, and feelings in addition to the ones encountered in the pursuit of innovation and change in general.

Leadership Development for Diversity

If the complexity of diversity in our society is unprecedented and likely to increase and if the instrumentalities by which we develop leaders for our institutions have paid little attention to diversity until now, how then do we develop leadership for diversity and how can individuals currently in leadership positions become more authentic and effective as they confront the challenges in this arena?

Diversity, like leadership, does not lend itself to neat formulas, weekend workshops, or summer institutes where leadership skills for diversity may be modulized and acquired. Diversity calls up the most deeply felt passions about who we are, as individuals and as members of multiple groups, and about the kind of society we aspire to shape. The stakes associated with engaging diversity are high. One can begin to understand the complexities associated with diversity and acquire the strength to lead for diversity only if one recognizes and accepts the limited understandings of diversity acquired in contemporary life and contemporary education.

There are no all-knowing leaders in the struggle for equity and community in the face of diversity, but not knowing what to do to respond creatively to diversity in every instance is not an indication of either stupidity, apathy, racism, or sexism. It is a reflection of the failure of our society to value diversity sufficiently to incorporate it into the many processes by which we are educated. But accepting our limitations and therefore our fallibility is only half the equation; the potential leader for diversity must also be able to see possibilities. And the vision of those possibilities must serve as passionate motivation to embark on and persist in a journey in search of a deeper understanding of self as a cultural being in a diverse and often unequal society.

In this chapter, I will explore the development of leadership for diversity from two different perspectives. The first has to do with the individual journey on which anyone who pretends to lead in contemporary culturally and racially complex organizations must embark: *the journey of leadership and self-invention.* The second has to do with the *leader's role in shaping organizational culture in the face of diversity and inequality.*

Leadership and Self-Invention

In the early 1980s, when most of the nation was being led to retreat from efforts to reverse the persistent effects of discrimination, American higher education saw itself coming face to face with the demographic reshaping of the United States. The fact that students from groups that today we call minority would make up a rapidly increasing share of the market from which colleges would draw their students was accompanied by the realization that unless colleges and universities became far more proactive, too few minority students would be prepared to knock on the college door, much less walk in and stay in. Moreover, racial and gender tensions on college campuses were escalating as students who had lived largely segregated lives came in contact with students culturally, racially, and often socioeconomically different from themselves.

Given the political climate of the times, the response of the organized higher education community and of individual higher education leaders was heroic. It was grossly insufficient, however, in that the attempted solutions were often simplistic and almost always far too limited in scope. The result was that many college and university leaders found themselves in lose-lose situations. Confident in the rightness of their cause and their intentions and accustomed to solving problems with direct action, they prescribed responses to issues of underrepresentation and tensions associated with race, gender, and sexual preference that almost always put them at the center of backlashes from every direction. For some constituencies, nothing was ever enough; for others, anything was too much. And it was often the best of these leaders who suffered the greatest personal pain in the face of this turbulence.

Turbulence is inevitable in the face of the massive changes that U.S. higher education institutions will face in the next several decades. The polarization of the population on the basis of age, race, and ethnicity as well as socioeconomic groups will exacerbate the competition for resources and directly affect what happens on college campuses. The men and women who would effect leadership in those institutions—whether as faculty, staff, administrators, or members of a governance team—will have to draw on the resources of their *authentic* self to dare to shape answers to questions few have framed before.

Bennis identifies the basic ingredients of leadership as a guiding vision that clearly projects what the leader wants to do: an underly-

ing passion for the promise of life and a course of action; integrity that proceeds from self-knowledge, candor, and maturity; trust that is earned and not acquired; and curiosity and daring that result in risk taking, experimentation, and learning from adversity.

While Bennis (1989, p. 50) does not address diversity, he describes the essential task of becoming a leader in terms that precisely frame the challenge of diversity for individuals, groups, and the whole of society:

> I cannot stress too much the need for self-invention. To be authentic is literally to be your own author (the words derive from the same Greek root), to discover your own native energies and desires, and then to find your own way of acting on them. When you've done that, you are not existing simply in order to live up to an image posited by the culture or by some other authority or by a family tradition. When you write your own life, then no matter what happens, you have played the game that was natural for you to play.

To develop the authentic self on which to draw in exercising leadership on issues of diversity, however, it is necessary to risk learning in multiple modes. One must be willing to design a personal course of study and exploration that will enable one to learn not only facts but *truths, feelings, and interpretations.* Learning must be intellectual, but it must also be experiential, physical, and emotional. The journey to self-knowledge in the context of diversity can at times be undertaken with the aid of a teacher or in partnership with a peer and can be strengthened by group experiences, but ultimately it requires that one make time and space to make the journey in the company of one's self, with time for reflection, again and again and again.

The Journey to Self-Invention

On a recent visit to a community college in a small Texas city, I encountered a woman for whom the quest to understand diversity was providing the capacity to write her own life. A single white woman, born and raised in East Texas and the only daughter of only children, she retained the speech patterns that were the only clue to an upbringing marked by absolute separation of the races. It did not take long to see that she clearly loved teaching English to the African American and Hispanic students who made up a majority of the campus population. Her examination of gender issues in the curriculum had led her in turn to initiate a number of faculty development efforts to increase the faculty's understanding of multiculturalism, and she was clearly hungry for any insight that would strengthen her ability to understand and teach in the context of diversity. Our conversation flowed easily from the professional to the personal.

As she and my African American hostess drove me to several functions, I began to notice the absolute absence of subtle affectation or hidden strain in her manner or conversation. Somehow she was breaking all the bonds that maintain distance between African Americans, Hispanics, and non-Hispanic whites in Texas, particularly when race and culture are the topic. She was "discovering her own native energies and desires and finding her own way of acting on them."

In later conversation, my new friend revealed "her curiosity and daring which resulted in risk taking, experimentation, and learning from adversity." She told me about a summer-long immersion in Hispanic studies she had developed with colleagues and about a life-changing trip to Africa. "When I arrived in Africa, I felt as if I had arrived where I belonged. The people were warm and accepting and I was happier than I had ever been. When I came home, I found myself missing the people in Africa more than I had ever missed anyone with whom I had grown up." "I don't know exactly how," she said "but I know that I am going to find a way to make a difference."

Although she did not yet see herself as a formidable leader, my new friend was well on her way to becoming a strong leader for diversity. She had an underlying passion for the promise of life and for the broad outlines of a course of action and she was developing a guiding vision. Her self-invention radiated integrity and she was ready to take risks.

Indeed she was already, as a member of the faculty, exercising leadership among her peers and her students. In her enthusiastic search for understanding, she carried others along. In the discussion that followed my presentation on diversity, a young African American woman asserted the joy of her identity and two young

Hispanic women kept repeating that they had never experienced an event that had such an impact. As an experienced lecturer, I knew that the students and I had both been led that evening by a white, Anglo-Saxon Protestant woman born and raised in the separate and unequal world of East Texas who was in the process of inventing herself.

Of course few of us, regardless of gender, race, or culture believe ourselves to be as free to self-invent as my East Texas friend. Family, children, community, and professional standing and relationships root us deeply in the investments we have made in shaping the self to the contours of tradition and safety. As academicians we are trained to search for new knowledge primarily in close proximity to the boundaries of existing knowledge. Moreover, we hold ourselves to a high standard of "objective" and "rational" understanding in the application of new knowledge.

Who then is a candidate for self-invention on issues of diversity? The answer is almost anyone who aspires to influence their environment. The journey to self-invention in the face of diversity is by definition never complete. While people who are members of groups for whom the effects of historical discrimination persist may have added insight into the experience that enables them to more easily understand groups other than their own, they too must seek out facts, truths, feelings, and interpretations about a configuration of culture and gender that neither their education nor their experience has prepared them for. Chauvinism is not the exclusive domain of any group.

As a Hispanic woman raised in Deep South Texas, my world was largely defined by people we called *Anglos* and people like me who called themselves *mexicanos*. While there were a few African American families in our communities, we led separate lives until after 1954, when the state's response to the Supreme Court mandate for integration was to integrate the African American children with the Mexican children. African Americans became our close friends, but they were few in number and for the most part adapted to us, speaking Spanish and even our brand of "Spanglish." We convinced ourselves that "they" were just like "us" and that this made them worthy of being our friends, except "of course" when it came to interracial dating. I grew up knowing little about African Americans.

An early interest in the history of civil rights policy in this country made me a student of African American history, but it was my immersion in civil rights that led to the experiences and relationships that began to deepen my understanding and identification with the African American experience. The learning has taken many forms, but it must have been walking down Auburn Avenue in Atlanta from the Martin Luther King Center to the offices of the multigenerational African American newspaper that I finally felt the power of the African American struggle in this country. Just as sitting in the Longhouse on the Orandaga Reservation listening to Chief Lloyd Elm's stories of the teachings of his grandfather had connected me to the American Indian experience, it was being in the presence of three African American women laughing about their adventures and tribulations with demanding professors at Fisk University that gave me a glimpse into the power and the lessons of this country's historically black colleges and universities. You can neither "read" yourself nor "think" yourself into competence on issues of diversity; when it comes to diversity, self-invention requires a willingness to "experience."

But my journey to self-invention in the light of diversity is far from over. Indeed it has come full circle. One of the major cultural forces in Central Texas is Christian fundamentalism. For years I have known of its existence, but my understanding of what is clearly a culture has been minimal. It took less than a few weeks of teaching a graduate course in education for me to realize that as many as half my students were products of homes where Christian fundamentalism was a central focus in the development of cognition, language, problemsolving strategies, world views, and values. And if these professionals were at least onethird of my class, they would be at least onethird of the educational settings I was trying to affect. I would need to learn, to reinvent my biases, to allow the experience of Christian fundamentalists to reach deep into my understandings. I began by going to Christian bookstores. I sought out Christian fundamentalist ministers, trying to understand the origins of the questions posed by my students. I listened to the ministers on Sunday morning television.

I do not know that I will ever be able to identify with fundamentalists in the way I can with the African Americans, but I have found much to value in the lives of my students and my understanding is growing. Most important, I have examined myself in relation to this group of people and I will never again think about educational reform in Central Texas without considering the role of Christian fundamentalism in the culture of the area.

When we search for an understanding of the culture of others, we cannot help but begin to identify the power of culture in our own formation. It is as an aid to self-knowledge that cultural exploration holds the greatest promise for members of the dominant culture. Just as my well-to-do Mexican cousins do not need to assert their cultural identity and probably seldom think about it, many members of the dominant culture in the United States find it bothersome and even difficult to define their own cultural identity. But we are all a product of the strengths and frailties, enlightenment and ignorance, struggles, defeats, victories, and guiding values of the generations that have gone before us. When we can understand and appreciate the ways others have been formed by their own unique cultural tradition, we can begin to appreciate the power and the sanctity of the cultural traditions that have formed ourselves, and from self-knowledge can come self-invention.

Leadership, Diversity, and Organizational Culture

In the course of the last quarter of a century, this country has invested billions of dollars in developing, implementing, and evaluating educational strategies designed to reverse historical inequality in educational opportunity. Substantial scholarly and leadership resources have also been focused on the development of knowledge emerging from the history and contemporary experiences of populations largely ignored by traditional scholarship.

Whether at the elementary, secondary, or higher education level, these strategies and research recommendations have shown at least modest short-term benefit to the participants and many have proven highly successful. But in spite of their success, all but a few of these strategies and scholarly works that have explicitly built on experience and perspectives based on race, culture, and gender remain at the margin of institutional life. Attempts to weave these strategies and scholarly works into the core of institutional practices have usually met with great resistance, often generating hostility toward the leadership, faculty, staff, and students involved in the innovation. Building the capacity of the academic culture to recognize, learn from, and incorporate diversity at its core remains a daunting task.

Higher education leaders, whether president or department chairperson, know that their success in meeting any goal is dependent on realities that flow from the history, personalities, long-standing as well as emerging formal and informal power structures, and comprehensive and inclusive planning processes. These realities—the "politics" of the organization—can make or break any initiative. Even in the best of circumstances, initiatives that focus on the building of institutional capacity for diversity enjoy a fragile configuration of support from the status quo culture of the institution.

The leader who would increase capacity for diversity must develop a two-pronged strategy for the exercise of leadership. First, the leader must develop specific strategic objectives that are doable, measurable and time specific, and that have the potential for demonstrating that commitment can lead to results. Such strategies may proceed from comprehensive institutional planning, as recommended by the American Council on Education in its *Handbook on Diversity* (1989), or may proceed from an "innovation incubator" approach in which diversity initiatives receive adequate fiscal and administrative support as the critical mass of institutional capacity necessary for comprehensive planning is developed.

There is no lack of models for adapting institutional practices to the needs of an increasingly diverse student population. Some models are merely collections of projects, others are more systemic. In *Sources: Diversity Initiatives in Higher Education* (1993), the Office of Minorities in Higher Education of the American Council on Education has compiled an exhaustive collection of diversity initiatives in higher education. The Association of Governing Boards has collected best practices in prekindergarten through graduate education programs in *Power in the Pipeline* (1992), the American Council on Education and the Coun-

cil of Graduate Schools have examined the increased participation of diverse populations in graduate education, the National Association of Student Personnel Administrators has documented early outreach programs across the country, and the Education Commission of the States has done the same. The National Association of Independent Colleges and Universities, the American Association of Community Colleges, the American Association of State Colleges and Universities, and virtually every other higher education organization have published either collections of best practices by their member institutions or recommendations for action.

What is missing is not sufficient thinking on what needs to be done, but sufficient will and resources to do things on a scale broad enough to affect the numbers of students necessary to reduce the gap between groups. Higher education leaders must become advocates for private and public support of policies that will lead to the resources necessary to bring members of under-represented groups to a level of parity in higher education.

The second imperative for diversity focuses on the development of an institutional culture that can recognize, learn from, support, and incorporate diversity at its core. The leader's fundamental challenge is to understand the institutional culture and to marshal the resources necessary to shape it to a new vision.

Deal and Peterson (1990) see the term *institutional culture* as describing the "character of a school as it reflects deep patterns of values, beliefs, traditions that have been formed over the course of its history." The authors state: "Beneath the conscious awareness of everyday life in any organization there is a stream of thought, sentiment and activity. This invisible, taken for granted flow of beliefs and assumptions gives meaning to what people say and do. It shapes how they interpret hundreds of daily transactions. This deeper structure of life in organizations is reflected and transmitted through symbolic language and expressive action. Culture consists of the stable, underlying social meanings that shape beliefs and behavior over time" (pp. 9–10).

This "invisible, taken for granted flow of beliefs and assumptions" is also the greatest challenge for leaders who would address diversity. It is into this substratum of beliefs and assumptions that the status quo has dug its strongest roots, nurtured on a daily basis by the success experiences of those individuals, departments, research units, and formal and informal governance units for whom the status quo works well. Groups formerly excluded from both the set of beliefs and assumptions and the success experiences that nurture them tend to see the resistance to diversity aimed primarily at "keeping them out," when the aims are more likely to be "keeping us in" and "keeping things as they have worked for years." As one particularly candid corporate executive said to a feminist activist, "The purpose of the glass ceiling is not to keep you down, it is to keep me up."

But even when individual interests are not the only consideration, it is not easy to convince members of a culture that has worked well for them and for the institution, to change the culture by incorporating individuals and ideas that are genuinely different.

On matters of diversity, however, the essential leadership task is to penetrate the beliefs and assumptions maintaining that the mission of the institution can only be achieved when things remain as they have always been. The leader for diversity must bring to the institution her or his own vision of an institution, school, or department carrying out its mission in a changing world—one that demands a more complete and accurate picture of our history, contemporary condition, and future as that reflects the totality of the human experience, one that demands the intentional inclusion of a different configuration of individuals who can define problems and opportunities within a broader context. It is only when the leader can first envision and then communicate—through word, symbol, ritual, and action—the melding of the institution's mission with the social challenges posed by diversity and equity that balkanization can be avoided. It is in the formulation of this vision and its articulation that the leader must be able to call up both the courage and creativity that can only be earned through a process of self-knowledge and self-invention in the light of diversity.

Knowing the context in which change is to occur is an important tool for leadership in any situation, but it is an absolute prerequisite for leadership on diversity. The context must be understood on two levels. First, it is necessary to understand that the higher education experience with diversity is in many ways *generationally* determined. That is, higher education has been both influenced and defined by consecutive iterations of the nation's attempts to deal with exclusion and inequality. In a sense, much of the ethos relative to diversity in any institution is shaped by the particular level of intensity with which it has selectively engaged those iterations over time. If an institution's best memories of its engagement with exclusion and inequality are set in the 1960s, the people in the institution are likely to approach diversity first from a bipolar perspective (that is, black and white) and from a benevolent integrationist perspective (that is, "we will let you in so that you can become more like us because you are already enough like us to make you deserving of being let in"). The individuals who hold this ethos are not necessarily racist or sexist; they simply have not been able to progress in their thinking beyond that which was their noblest moment. Often individuals who were the most courageous in those prior periods of integration have the greatest difficulty in dealing with efforts to incorporate diversity into the institution at its core simply because they have invested much in their mid-1960s perspective on inclusion.

Subsequent generations of members of the academy have experienced the struggle for inclusion in diverse ways. The reaction to affirmative action, for example, will vary between and among members of diverse groups, depending on the historical period in which they engaged the practice as well as on the way practice has affected them or those close to them.

A second force affecting the leader's efforts to reshape organizational culture in the face of diversity is generated by a fundamental difference between members of the dominant culture and members of historically excluded groups in their approach to issues of *group identification* versus *individualism*.

Generally speaking, Americans of European origin have profited from an identity based on individualism. While every immigrant group initially experienced group-based discrimination and severe hardship, thinking of themselves as individuals allowed European Americans, usually within one to one and a half generations of immigration, to take full advantage of the promise of the country's expanding territory and economy. Indeed individualism was the epitome of the "American identity." Extolled in popular culture, it was the common person's greatest weapon against the bonds of centuries of feudalism and class-based societies. It also served as a psychological buffer for any conscious responsibility for the historical treatment of other Americans on the basis of group identity.

Cultural diversity, by definition, is antithetical to this construct of an American identity. The individuals who gave up their claim to a cultural and linguistic connectedness to the generations that preceded them—whether willingly or by force—have for the most part extinguished the memory of the loss and focused on its benefits and utility. The process is locked deep in the milieu of beliefs and values of most individuals in the dominant culture and the institutions they control. Indeed, individualism is so deeply held a belief that non-Hispanic whites often seem incapable of recognizing the many ways in which their behavior is group based.

In contrast, generally speaking, members of historically excluded groups continue to struggle with the competing values of an identity based on individualism and one based on group membership. The promise of individualism was never an option for members of groups historically excluded de jure from the rights and privileges of full citizenship. While individual resiliency was critical to survival and heroic individual effort was necessary for success, it was the collective experience and the group's struggle and adaptation to its condition that defined the values that shape identity.

Regardless of educational or economic status, members of historically excluded groups continue to experience at least occasional treatment based on group membership. It is inevitable; just when you think you have gotten through any experience, something or someone reminds you that you are not an individual, you are a member of a group. In most cases, this intermittent reinforcement of a group identity keeps most members of historically discriminated groups connected to the group experience and to the persistent effects of historical discrimination that define contemporary conditions for the group. Struggle for

the group, moreover, is a value deeply embedded in many families from groups that today we call minority. It is the stuff of which family myths and heroes are made, passed down in oral histories from generation to generation, and it is, for many, the source of most individual achievement.

Whereas successful Americans of European origin have essentially separated their individual realization from that of members of their group, successful Americans who are members of historically excluded groups may chafe at the diminution of their individual effort or achievement, but they are far more likely to invest themselves heavily in the advancement of the group as a whole and to continue to struggle against the exclusion or devaluing of the group. This latter identity is not ambiguous, it is simply complex.

Understanding organizational culture as it engages, for better or worse, the challenge of diversity is but the base of leadership. The leader must be able to marshal the resources for shaping the culture to meet new realities. These resources include: the leader's vision; the administrative, faculty, and staff resources as these are augmented, deployed, and developed over time; the rituals, traditions, and symbols that give meaning to the institution; and the internal and external constituencies that influence the institution.

Identifying, recruiting, and incorporating individuals who can understand and support the leader's vision for an institution that engages the challenges and promise of diversity is essential to the leader's chances of success. In this regard, it is critical that the goal of the leader should be well thought out and go beyond efforts to recruit, hire, and retain minorities and women in an affirmative action mode. Indeed, the whole of the human resource identification, hiring, training, and rewards and punishment system requires adaptation to the demands of creating institutional capacity for diversity. The leader must understand that it is in adding and redeploying individuals within the organization that he or she wishes to shape, that an organizational culture capable of dealing positively with diversity will be strengthened or weakened. The organization must have as a goal the creation of a leadership team that reflects the diversity of the populations that are of central concern, and such a team must have the capacity to focus on a common stake and a common vision for the institution.

Sustaining the focus of the institution on a vision that engages the challenge and promise of diversity is infinitely more difficult than formulating and communicating one. Not only is it essential for the leader to create the mechanisms, events, and decisions that continue to communicate the vision; the leader must also ensure that diversity is at the center of institutional goals as additional innovation and improvement initiatives demand institutional attention. Total Quality Management, Community Engagement, Initiatives to Improve Teaching, Assessment, and other initiatives must incorporate diversity efforts, not replace them.

Conclusion

Dealing with issues of diversity will be one of the central themes in American higher education for the foreseeable future. Institutions will be either enhanced by the process or debilitated by it; they cannot avoid it. How well institutions fare in the face of diversity depends on the quality of leadership not only at the top of the organizational hierarchy, but throughout the organization. Leadership for diversity by definition implies leadership that is inspired, shared, and cohesive. It is leadership that is focused not only on strategies, projects, and programs but that entails the development of a new organizational culture. The leader who would embrace diversity is playing out a journey to self-knowledge and self-invention with ever-expanding possibilities.

References

American Council on Education. *Sources: Diversity Initiatives in Higher Education*. Washington, D.C.: Office of Minorities in Higher Education, 1993.

American Council on Education, Office of Minorities in Higher Education. *Handbook on Diversity*. Washington, D.C.: American Council on Education, 1989.

Association of Governing Boards of Universities and Colleges. *Power in the Pipeline*. Washington, D.C.: Association of Governing Boards of Universities and Colleges, 1992.

Bennis, W. *On Becoming a Leader*. Reading, Mass.: Addison-Wesley, 1989.

Deal, T. E., and Peterson, K. D. *The Principal's Role in Shaping School Culture*. Office of Educational Research and Improvement, U.S. Department of Education, Washington, D.C.: U.S. Government Printing Office, 1990.

Part VII

Perspectives on Race and Gender

Chapter 31

RACE IN ORGANIZATIONS

STELLA M. NKOMO

This article analyzes how race has been studied in organization scholarship and demonstrates how our approaches to the study of race reflect and reify particular historical and social meanings of race. It is argued that the production of knowledge about race must be understood within a racial ideology embedded in a Euro-centric view of the world. Finally, a "re-vision" of the very concept of race and its historical and political meaning is suggested for rewriting "race" as a necessary and productive analytical category for theorizing about organizations.

"Now, is not that magnificent?" said both the worthy officials. "Will your Majesty deign to note the beauty of the patterns and the colors?" And they pointed to the bare loom for they supposed that all the rest could certainly see the stuff. "What's the meaning of this?" thought the Emperor. "I can't see a thing! This is terrible! Am I stupid? Am I not fit to be Emperor? That would be the most frightful thing that could befall me." "Oh, it's very pretty, it has my all highest-approval!" said he, nodding complacently and gazing on the empty loom: of course, he wouldn't say he could see nothing. The whole of the suite he had with him looked and looked, but got no more out of that than the rest. However, they said, as the Emperor said: "Oh, it's very pretty!" And they advised him to put on this splendid new stuff for the first time, on the occasion of a great procession which was to take place shortly . . .

So the Emperor walked in the procession under the beautiful canopy, and everybody in the streets and at the windows said: "Lord! How splendid the Emperor's new clothes are. What a lovely train he has to his coat! What a beautiful fit it is!" Nobody wanted to be detected seeing nothing: that would mean that he was no good at his job, or that he was very stupid.

"But he hasn't got anything on!" said a little child. . . . "Why he hasn't got anything on!" The whole crowd was shouting at last; and the Emperor's flesh crept, for it seemed to him they were right. "But all the same," he thought to himself, "I must go through with the procession." So he held himself more proudly than before, and the lords in waiting walked on bearing the train—the train that wasn't there at all. (Excerpt from "The Emperor's New Clothes," by Hans Christian Anderson, 1968: 104–107)

The children's fairy tale, "The Emperor's New Clothes," is an excellent allegory for the primary way in which organization scholars have chosen to address race in organizations. For the most part, research has tended to study organization populations as homogeneous entities in which distinctions of race and ethnicity are either "unstated" or considered irrelevant. A perusal of much of our research would lead one to believe that organizations are race neutral (Cox & Nkomo, 1990).

Although the emperor, his court suitors, and his tailors recognize that he is naked, no one will explicitly acknowledge that nakedness. Even as the innocent child proclaims his nakedness, the emperor and his suitors resolutely continue with the procession. Similarly, the silencing of the importance of race in organizations is mostly subterfuge because of the overwhelming role of race and ethnicity in every aspect of society.

Race in the United States has been a profound determinant of one's political rights, one's location in the labor market, one's access to medical care, and even one's sense of identity (Omi & Winant, 1986). Its immediacy is manifested in everyday life experiences and social interactions (Blauner, 1989; Essed, 1991; van Dijk, 1987). Most important, race is one of the major bases of domination in our society and a major means through which the division of labor occurs in organizations (Reich, 1981). As I will argue later, race has been present all along in organizations, even if silenced or suppressed.

One might ask, why use a European fairy tale to call attention to the exclusion of race in the study of organizations? I have purposefully used a Eurocentric parable to signify this problem through parody, in the African-American tradition of what Gates (1988: 82) has called "black signifyin(g)"—the figurative difference between the literal and the metaphorical, between surface and latent meaning. In this article, the emperor is not simply an emperor but the embodiment of the concept of Western knowledge as both universal and superior and white males as the defining group for studying organizations. The court suitors are the organizational scholars who continue the traditions of ignoring race and ethnicity in their research and excluding other voices. All have a vested interest in continuing the procession and not calling attention to the omissions.

Who then is most likely to call attention to these omissions? As has been the case in other disciplines, it is most likely to be the *other*, the excluded, who is assumed to be childlike and inferior. Even as these *other* voices point to the omissions and errors and the need for inclusiveness, the dominant group refuses to hear the message and continues with the procession. The real issue for the *others* is getting truly heard, rather than simply "added on." As noted by Minnich (1990), it is difficult to add new knowledge to anything that has been defined as the whole. The challenge must strike directly at the center of the kingdom and its attendant theoretical foundations.

The purpose of this article then is to analyze how race has been written into the study of organizations in incomplete and inadequate

ways. It demonstrates how our approaches to the study of race reflect particular historical and social meanings of race, specifically a racial ideology embedded in a Eurocentric view of the world. This view is evident first in the general exclusion of race when organizational theories are developed and, second, in the theoretical and methodological orientation of the limited body of research on race. Finally, suggestions are made for ways of making race a necessary and productive analytical category for theorizing about organizations. Perspectives are drawn from several disciplines including African-American studies and race and ethnic relations. The intent is not to provide a specific theory of race but to suggest ways of "re-visioning" the study of race in organizations.

On the Exclusion of Race in the Study of Organizations

Why do we as organizational scholars continue to conceptualize organizations as race neutral? Why has race been silenced in the study of organizations? One way of explaining this exclusion is to examine what Minnich (1990) has called intellectual errors in the production of knowledge. The root error might be labeled faulty generalization or noninclusive universalization. This error occurs when we take a dominant few (white males) as the inclusive group, the norm, and the ideal of humankind (Minnich, 1990). The defining group for specifying the science of organizations has been white males. Only recently have we begun to study the experiences of women in management, and even this body of literature focuses mainly on white women (Nkomo, 1988). We have amassed a great deal of knowledge about the experience of only one group, yet we generalize our theories and concepts to all groups. We do not acknowledge that these universal theories emanate from an inadequate sample and, therefore, there is the possibility that the range of a theory or construct is limited (Cox & Nkomo, 1990).

According to Minnich (1990), faulty generalization leads to a kind of hierarchically invidious monism. Not only are dominant group members the defining group, but they are taken to be the highest category—the best—and all other groups must be defined and judged solely with reference to that hegemonic category (Keto, 1989). Other racial and ethnic groups are relegated to subcategories; their experiences are seen as outside of the mainstream of developing knowledge of organizations.

This point can be illustrated by examining the use of prefixes in the description of research samples in our work. The prefix "white" is usually suppressed, and it is only other racial groups to which we attach prefixes (Minnich, 1990). "Race" becomes synonymous with *other* groups, and whites do not have "race." A study based on a sample of white male managers is unlikely to state that the results may be valid only for that group. More likely than not the term *manager* will be used. The problem is the usurpation of the category *manager* by the dominant group and the lack of awareness that white managers also have race.

Concomitantly, a study that has a minority group sample will rarely be accepted for developing and generalizing organization theory. The results of the study would be viewed as valid only for that group with minimal or little relevance for organization knowledge. Thus, instead of race being an analytical category critical to the fundamental understanding of organizations, it is marginalized. Unless the study is explicitly about race (e.g., affirmative action or bias in performance ratings) or has a minority-group sample, it is not included as an important variable, even when contextual factors may indicate otherwise.

The faulty generalization error stems mainly from bias in science. The practices of science reflect the values and concerns of dominant societal groups (Harding, 1986). The concepts and approaches used in Western academia help to maintain the political and intellectual superiority of Western cultures and people (Joseph, Reddy, & Searle-Chatterjee, 1990). Kuhn (1962) argued that problem selection and the search for explanations by scholars are influenced by the social and political conditions of the times. To the extent that white males have dominated the production of knowledge, their values and concerns are predominant. The study of race is an especially sensitive issue because scholars must not only be aware of how prevailing societal race relations influence their approach to the study of race but they must also understand the effects of their own racial identity and experiences on their work (Alderfer, 1982).

The tendency toward faulty generalization is further explained by the adherence to the assumption, embedded in Western philosophy from Socrates to the Enlightenment, that there is one ultimate objective truth and the scholar's mission is to search for that truth. This truth cannot come from *other* non-Western views of knowledge (Keto, 1989). Hence, there is a relationship between the desire for universal theories and the suppression of the experience of *others*. Researchers who ignore the influence of race in understanding organizations may reflect a veiled hope that, indeed, management theories and constructs are universal. Once there is acceptance of the idea that the major theories and concepts of the field of management do not address all groups, the holding of and search for universal theories is undermined.

It is illusory to think that other views are socially located while one's own are not. We cannot avoid the implicit influence of the scholar's perspective and values in the theories we develop (Morgan, 1983). The research questions that are asked and not asked and the chosen methodology of research on race in organizations parallel the dominant theoretical, political, and social meanings of race.

Theoretical and Ideological Foundations of Research on Race

Before race can be re-visioned as an analytical category in the formulation of organization theory, a first step is to understand the historical and theoretical foundations of research on race and its influence on the ways in which we have studied race in organizations.

According to Omi and Winant (1986), the meaning, transformation, and significance of racial theories are shaped by actual existing race relations in any given historical period. Blanton (1987) added that within any given historical period, a particular racial theory is dominant, despite the existence of competing paradigms. The dominant racial theory provides society with a framework for understanding race relations and serves as a guide for research with implications for the kinds of questions scholars address. The dominant racial paradigm in the field of race and ethnic studies for the last half century has been that of ethnicity (Blanton, 1987; Omi & Winant, 1986; Thompson, 1989).

The Ethnicity Paradigm

The basic premises and assumptions of this paradigm are reflected in much of the research and writing in the management literature. Ethnicity-based theory emerged in the 1920s as a challenge to biological and social Darwinian conceptions of race (Blanton, 1987). Sociological concepts primarily replaced biological ones, and racial and ethnic forms of identification and social organizations were viewed as "unnatural" (Thompson, 1989). Becoming predominant by World War II, the ethnic paradigm has shaped academic research about race and guided policy formation (Omi & Winant, 1986). Despite serious challenges from alternative paradigms during the 1970s and 1980s, the rise of neoconservatism in the United States has led to a resurgence of ethnicity theory in a new guise, which has been labeled the *new ethnicity* (Omi & Winant, 1986; Steinberg, 1981; Thompson, 1989).

Ethnicity theorists' main empirical reference point was the study of immigration and the social patterns and experiences of European immigrants (Omi & Winant, 1986). Dominated by two recurrent oppositional themes, assimilation versus cultural pluralism, ethnicity theory was focused on the incorporation and separation of ethnic minorities, the nature of ethnic identity, and the impact of ethnicity on life experiences (Omi & Winant, 1986). One of the earliest explications of assimilationalism appeared in Park's 1939 essay, "The Nature of Race Relations" (Park, 1950/1939). Park focused on the problem of European migration and what he called *culture contact*. Park's famous *race relations cycle* became the basis for further development of assimilation theory (e.g., Gordon, 1964). Park argued that this cycle "which takes the form of contacts, competition, accommodation and eventual assimilation is apparently progressive and irreversible" (Park, 1950/1939: 150). Despite Park's (1950/1939) acknowledgment that it was possible that a particular stage might be prolonged, assimilation was viewed as the most logical and natural antidote for racism and ethnocentricism. The widespread view of assimilation as a process of interpenetration and fusion in which persons and groups acquire the mentality, sentiments, and attitudes of dominant groups led to the well-known *melting pot* concept (Omi & Winant, 1986). For example, much of the early research on management was developed during a period of widespread European immigration to the United States. The new immigrants, urban white workers, particularly the Irish and people from Eastern Europe, were often degraded as "children" and "savage" and as being more interested in seeking lower rather than higher pleasures (Takai, 1979: 127). These early factory workers were scolded for their idleness and their lack of punctuality and industry (Gutman, 1977: 20). The theme of assimilation pervaded efforts by industrial capitalists to teach these workers the requisite attitudinal and work ethic skills needed to perform industrial jobs.

Other early proponents of assimilation theory included Myrdal (1944) and Gordon (1964). Gunnar Myrdal's classic work, *The American Dilemma*, called into question the contradiction between continued discrimination against African-Americans and the democratic ideals of equality and justice espoused in U.S. society. Both Myrdal's and Gordon's works attempted to extend ethnicity theory, which has been largely derived from the experience of European immigrants, to the situation of African-Americans (Thompson, 1989). It was assumed that the experience of racial minorities could be theorized in much the same way as the experience of ethnic immigrants. Thus, race in the United States was largely reduced to a question of integration and assimilation of racial minorities into the mainstream of a consensus-based society (van den Berghe, 1967). Within the assimilation framework, legal remedies like the Civil Rights Act of 1964 were viewed as necessary for removing barriers so that racial minorities would encounter the same conditions as white ethnics (Omi & Winant, 1986; Thompson, 1989). However, preferential treatment remedies like affirmative action were not supported (Glazer, 1987; Gordon, 1964). Blauner (1972: 2) pointed out that research on racial minorities (i.e., African-Americans, Latinos, Asian Americans, and Native Americans) from the ethnicity perspective was premised on several assumptions: (a) racial groups were not viewed as central or persistent elements of society; (b) racism and racial oppression were ultimately reducible to other causal determinants—usually economic or psychological; and (c) there were no essential long-term differences between the experience of racial minorities and the European ethnic groups that immigrated to the United States.

Research on race emanating from the ethnic-based paradigm centered on questions of why racial minorities were not becoming incorporated or assimilated into mainstream society. Or directly stated, "What obstructs assimilation?" Much of this research was devoted to problems of prejudice and discrimination and grew out of social psychological approaches to the study of intergroup relations (Oudenhoven & Willemsen, 1989). It was based on the belief that relations between dominant group members and racial minorities resulted from prejudiced attitudes of individuals. For example, Merton (1949) argued that discrimination might be practiced by unprejudiced people who were afraid not to conform to the prejudices of others. Adorno, Frenkel-Brunswick, Levinson, and Sanford (1950: 8) studied the relationship between prejudice and personality. He argued that prejudiced persons differed from tolerant persons in central personality traits—specifically, that they exhibited *authoritarian personalities*. Allport (1954) suggested that there was a direct link between prejudiced people and discriminatory acts. Unlike Adorno et al. (1950), Allport (1954) did not view prejudice as an aberrant cognitive distortion. Allport argued that prejudice was a natural extension of normal cognitive processes (Pettigrew, 1979). Thus, prejudice and discrimination were mainly reduced to either an individual aberration or faulty generalization (Henriques, 1984). Adorno's and Allport's emphasis on prejudice as an attitude also found widespread acceptance because of its amenability to quantification and statistical measurement (Henriques, 1984).

This traditional stress on the expressive function of prejudice by individuals is still manifested in much of contemporary social psychology research on race (Oudenhoven & Willemsen, 1989). For example, dominant contemporary social psychology theories for explaining prejudice include social identity or social categorization theory, social attribution theory, and the contact hypothesis (Dovidio & Gaertner, 1986).

The phenomenological approach of social identity or social categorization theory postulates that an individual's identity depends to a large extent on social group memberships where individuals seek positive social identity (Tajfel, 1969, 1970; Tajfel & Turner, 1979, 1986). The evaluation of one's own group is determined with reference to specific other groups through social comparisons in terms of value-laden attributes and characteristics. This mechanism is basic to the evaluation of one's social identity. These comparisons involve perceptual accentuation of similarities of people belonging to the same group and differences between people belonging to a different social group or category (Tajfel, 1981). Accordingly, if categorization is in terms of a racial or an ethnic criterion, then it is likely that this process is responsible in part for the prejudices found in the judgment of people belonging to different groups. Tajfel (1981) stressed the influence of the social factors of status, power, and material interdependence in the categorization process.

Social attribution theory or intergroup attribution theory refers to "how members of different social groups explain the behavior and social condition of members of their own group (ingroup) and other social groups (outgroups)" (Hewstone, 1989: 25). In this case, research emphasis is placed on explaining the behavior of individuals who act as members or representatives of social groups. An important explanatory concept in this theory is the fundamental attribution error—the phenomenon that one tends to explain the behavior of others by internal factors rather than situational factors (Oudenhoven & Willemsen, 1989). The extreme manifestation of social attribution is what Pettigrew has called the ultimate attribution error—"a systematic patterning of intergroup misattributions shaped in part by prejudice" (Pettigrew, 1979: 464). On the one hand, when blacks or other minority group members behave in a manner perceived to be negative, majority group members, especially those who are prejudiced, are likely to attribute this behavior to the personal character of the group (Pettigrew, 1979). On the other hand, prejudiced majority group members can explain away behavior that is seen as positive by attributing it to (a) the exceptional, special-case individual who is contrasted with his or her group; (b) luck or special advantage, which is viewed as unfair; (c) high motivation and effort, which is ultimately unsustainable; or (d) a manipulated situational context (Pettigrew, 1979: 469). Therefore, the ingroup (majority group) can still hold negative assessments of the outgroup (minority group), despite contrary evidence.

Finally, a third social psychology theory used to explain prejudice is the contact hypothesis. This is best understood as a solution to intergroup conflict which posits that positive contacts between ingroups and outgroups will reduce prejudice (Wilder, 1986). The success of contact is contingent upon the favorability of the interaction, especially the ingroup's perception of the interaction. Proponents of this theory underscore the important role of structuring the situation to promote cooperation rather than competition (Pettigrew & Martin, 1987). A major assumption underlying the contact hypothesis is that frequent positive contact between groups will minimize the information-processing errors (e.g., stereotyping) by ingroup members.

Although social psychologists like Tajfel argued that the major contribution of their work was its focus on the group rather than on individuals, making it more social and progressive, a close reading reveals it also ultimately relies on individual cognitive processing to explain prejudice and discrimination (Henriques, 1984). The results of Tajfel's minimal intergroup laboratory experiments led him to conclude that the mere perception of belonging to two distinct groups (i.e., social categorization per se) is sufficient to trigger intergroup discrimination favoring the ingroup. In other words, ingroup bias is a natural feature of intergroup relations. Therefore, if groups have no real bases for conflict, then discrimination lies in failures in the mechanism of individual cognition (Henriques, 1984).

Additionally, the primary solution offered by these social psychological approaches—the contact hypothesis—falls within the assimilation approach through the assumption that the reduction of the salience of group boundaries will improve intergroup interaction (Oudenhoven & Williemsen, 1989).

The New Ethnicity

During the mid-1970s, the ethnic-based paradigm was reformulated (Thompson, 1989). The upheavals during the Civil Rights movement of the 1960s and the urban riots of the 1970s underscored the fact that for African-Americans assimilation into dominant society was less than forthcoming. The major failure of assimilationists to explain the lack of African-American assimilation spawned a new paradigm, which has been called the *new ethnicity* (Steinberg, 1981; Thompson, 1989; Yinger, 1986). The *new* in *new ethnicity* is not so much a significant shift in theory as an attempt by assimilationists to explain the enduring nature of racial stratification (Thompson, 1989). According to Thompson (1989: 91), this paradigm is based on two interrelated positions: (a) that ethnic and racial criteria have become major forms of group-based sociopolitical behavior because of the changing nature of industrial society and (b) that ethnic and racial groups ought to maintain their separate boundaries and seek their separate interests provided such interests recognize and respect the multitude of other, different ethnic interests (i.e., the cultural pluralism creed). The popular origins of the new ethnicity lie in the revival of the ethnic consciousness of white ethnics in response to the perceived preferential treatment of racial minority groups (Steinberg, 1981).

The theoretical dilemma that existed within the new ethnicity paradigm was how to explain the persistence of racial and ethnic stratification. Two different explanations have been offered. One explanation is that the persistence of racial and ethnic stratification reflects biological tendencies and that people, by nature, have a basic, primordial need for group identification. This explanation is grounded in sociobiology and primordialism. In his more recent work, entitled *Human Nature, Class and Ethnicity*, Gordon (1978), one of the major early proponents of assimilation theory, emphasized the importance of understanding human nature (i.e., biological predisposition) and its interaction with the social and cultural environment. Gordon (1978: 74) wrote, "Some observers, including myself, . . . have begun to wonder whether there are not biological constants or propensities in human behavior which fall short of the instinct category but which predispose the actor to certain kinds of behavior." In a similar vein, van den Berghe (1981: 80) theorized that ethnic and racial sentiments are extensions of kinship sentiments and, as such, express the sociobiological principle of inclusive fitness. In his analysis, van den Berghe (1981) argued that genetic predisposition for kin selection causes people to behave in racist and ethnocentric ways. Accordingly, racism and discrimination in society and culture were viewed as the sum of individually motivated behaviors that were rooted in genetic predisposition. **According to this essentialist explanation, racial and ethnic stratification are viewed as an almost permanent and inevitable part of human society.**

The alternate explanation rejects biological criteria and relies upon social psychological theories that attribute the failure of minority group assimilation to improper attitudes of majority group members or the lack of self-reliance on the part of minorities (Thompson, 1989). The common denominator for all of these explanations is that they stress some essential property of individuals.

Problems with the Ethnic Paradigm

There are several problems with the ethnic-based paradigm and its so-called *new* form for producing knowledge for understanding race in organizations. In this paradigm, the dualistic oppositional categories of assimilation versus pleuralism are emphasized as the solution to questions of discrimination and racism (Glazer & Moynihan, 1970; Omi & Winant, 1986; Thompson, 1989).

Assimilationalism is basically individualistic in its ontology, and in this case, race is largely conceptualized as a problem of prejudiced attitudes or personal and cultural inadequacies of racial and ethnic groups (Thompson, 1989). The fact that certain groups have not been successfully assimilated is not due to the structure of U.S. society and institutions but to psychological or personality characteristics of both whites and minorities (Henriques, 1984; Thompson, 1989). Assimilation is conceptualized as a one-way process that requires non-European, non-English-speaking groups to change to fit the dominant culture (Feagin, 1987). Consequently, researchers have tended to focus on other groups as having race, and

questions of "why aren't they like us, or how can they become like us?" dominate. Herein lies one of the major deficiencies in the very premise of the assimilation approach. Inequality is accepted as a natural feature of U.S. society or any other complex social structure and, therefore, inequality itself is a "nonissue" and not part of the analysis (Thompson, 1989: 85).

Assimilation represents an inadequate model for understanding racial hierarchy in organizations. Its best answer to why racial and ethnic minorities are underrepresented in higher level positions in organizations would lie in social psychological explanations, which emphasize cognitive causes of prejudice and discrimination. Sole emphasis on microlevel or individualistic remedies are unlikely to affect existing social and power relations in organizations. Billig (1985) noted that the emphasis placed upon explaining cognitive biases by social categorization theory and other cognitive theories winds up confirming the status quo in the sense that changing the cognitions of individuals is often viewed as less amenable to intervention. Users of the individual-focused social psychology approaches are silent on the sociohistorical dynamics of the capitalist system in creating and maintaining inequality in organizations. Such explanations detract from issues of power and domination in racial dynamics and reflect a failure to analyze both the historically specific experience of racial minorities in U.S. society and the influence that this history has had on their status in organizations (Foner & Lewis, 1982; Takai, 1979).

Furthermore, assimilation within the ethnic paradigm often leads to a "blame-the-victim" explanation of why certain groups have not been assimilated as successfully as other groups (Omi & Winant, 1986). According to Thompson (1989), one of the less explicit assumptions of the ethnic paradigm is the acceptance of the neoclassical view of the very nature of a capitalist economy. In this view, individual opportunity is widely available, and the kind of job one has is a function of choice and skill level. People who fail are seen as making bad choices or not exhibiting the appropriate character traits (Sowell, 1975). Minority group members who do not succeed have abnormal cultural patterns or other deficiencies.

The essentialist element of this argument often results in tautological explanations of success whereby a minority group that has not been subjected to the social and historical conditions of another group is seen as a "good group," which has been successfully assimilated. For example, the contemporary view of Asian Americans as the model minority reinforces the notion that only "good groups," whose members do the right thing, become assimilated. Successful achievement and mobility reflect a group's willingness and ability to accept the norms and values of the majority group.

The theoretical alternative to assimilation, cultural pluralism, supposedly allows for the possibility that groups do not assimilate but remain distinct in terms of cultural identity. However, similar to users of assimilation theory, proponents of cultural pluralism still maintain the existence of an allegedly "normal" (understood to mean superior) majority culture, to which other groups are juxtaposed (Omi & Winant, 1986). Further, they suggest that separation of racial and ethnic groups is natural and immutable. Steinberg (1981) pointed out that cultural pluralism is not a viable option in a society where inequality exists because true cultural pluralism would be based on equality among different groups. In the words of Henriques (1984: 63), "It is a case of putting the ideal cart before the real horse."

Unfortunately, cultural pluralism has often been superficially interpreted as an opportunity to celebrate difference (Yinger, 1986). For example, the influence of this school of thought is reflected in the nascent "managing diversity" discourse appearing in management literature (Thomas, 1990). Yet underlying some work in this area are assumptions like. "Minority workers are less likely to have had satisfactory schooling and training. They may have language, attitude, and cultural problems that prevent them from taking advantage of the jobs that will exist" (Johnston & Packer, 1987: xxvi).

The Writing of Race in the Organization Literature

The influence of the ethnic paradigm and its assumptions are reflected in much of the extant research on race found in the organization literature. Thus, not surprisingly, when management researchers have studied race, much of

the research is narrowly focused, ahistorical, and decontextualized; in this research, race is mainly treated as a demographic variable. In their review of 20 journals during the period 1965–1989, Cox and Nkomo (1990) identified 201 articles focusing on race. They reported a notable decline in this type of research during the 1980s. For the most part, the topics and approaches in these articles reproduced the standard organization literature with emphasis on five content areas: affirmative action/equal employment opportunity; staffing, including test validation; job satisfaction; job attitudes and motivation; and performance evaluation.

Research designs were dominated by comparative studies of black and white workers to the neglect of other racial and ethnic groups (Cox & Nkomo, 1990). Within these studies, race was treated mainly as a demographic variable whereby blacks and whites were compared on a standard organizational theory or concept. Studies in the area of job satisfaction typically compared job satisfaction levels of black and white workers (e.g., Jones, James, Bruni, & Sell, 1977; Konar, 1981; Milutinovich & Tsaklanganos, 1978; Moch, 1980; Slocum & Strawser, 1972; Veechio, 1980; Weaver, 1978). Results in this area were largely inconsistent—some studies reported that white employees were more satisfied than black employees, and other studies reported the opposite effect. Although a few of these studies attempted to identify the factors that contributed to differences in levels of satisfaction (e.g., Konar, 1981), in general, the research provides little insight into the complexity of the psychological, organizational, and societal variables that may account for such findings. Often, the results appear to be tautological. For example, to explain their finding that whites were more satisfied with their jobs and that whites associated overall satisfaction more closely with promotion than nonwhites, O'Reilly and Roberts (1973) concluded that whites and nonwhites approach their jobs with different frames of reference.

One of the pervasive questions found within all topics was: "Does discrimination exist?" In this research, emphasis was placed on searching for objective and quantifiable evidence of racial discrimination. For example, a majority of the early articles in the area of affirmative action/equal employment opportunity were focused on whether or not discrimination existed in the occupational distribution of jobs (e.g., Franklin, 1968; Kovarshy, 1964; Northrop, 1969; Taylor, 1968). Representative questions included: To what extent are blacks overrepresented in lower socioeconomic jobs? (Franklin, 1968); Where are blacks employed within the aerospace industry? (Northrop, 1969); and Is there discrimination within the governmental apprentice training program? (Kovarshy, 1964). In the area of staffing, research was focused on discrimination and bias in recruitment and selection outcomes for blacks and whites in organizations (e.g., Brown & Ford, 1977; Newman, 1978; Newman & Krzytofiak, 1979; Stone & Stone, 1987; Terpstra & Larsen, 1980). Typically, explanations were centered on the stereotyping of minority groups.

Over the years, a number of studies have been used to examine bias in performance ratings and evaluation. The level of activity in this area is evidenced by the existence of three comprehensive literature reviews on the subject (Dipboye, 1985; Kraiger & Ford, 1985; Landy & Farr, 1980). According to some studies, ratees received significantly higher ratings from evaluators of their own race (e.g., Schmitt & Lappin, 1980), whereas other studies failed to support the existence of significant race effects on performance evaluation (Mobley, 1982). Still other studies reported results that indicated a complex interaction between the race of the ratee and his or her performance (Hamner, Kim, Baird, & Biogness, 1974). In their 1985 meta-analysis, Kraiger and Ford concluded that ratees tend to receive higher ratings from raters of the same race and that these effects were more pronounced in field studies than in laboratory ratings. Only a handful of researchers explored the processes underlying differences (Cox & Nkomo, 1986; Dipboye, 1985; Pettigrew & Martin, 1987). Most often the explanations were based on a social psychology perspective with an emphasis on rater bias, including stereotyping and perceptual error in information processing.

The other prototypical question underlying much of this literature was: Do racial and ethnic minorities have what it takes to succeed in organizations? or more concisely, Why aren't they like us? Illustrative of this theme are studies that were conducted regarding job attitudes, motivation, and affirmative action. A common question in the research on job attitudes was: Do blacks have different attitudes toward their jobs and work environment than whites? (Alper, 1975; Gavin & Ewen, 1974). Several studies were focused on race differences in motivation (e.g., Bhagat, 1979; Bankart, 1972; Brenner & Tomkiewicz, 1982; Greenhaus & Gavin, 1972; Miner, 1977; Watson & Barone, 1976). An unstated assumption in much of this research might be labeled the deficit hypothesis—whether or not minorities possessed the necessary motivational profile and values needed by organizations. Bhagat (1979) created a model to explain how black ethnic values coupled with negative job experiences have prevented a large majority of the black population from identifying strongly with the work ethic. The approach used in these studies included using a well-known theory of motivation and comparing scores of black employees to white employees. In the few studies that addressed the behavioral dimensions of affirmative action, authors emphasized the assimilation of minorities into organizations. Typical questions included: What changes are needed to assimilate the hard-core black into organizations? (Domm & Stafford, 1972) and Can the Afro-American be an effective executive? (Goode, 1970).

The final theme permeating much of this research was an emphasis on the legal, technical, and mechanical aspects of how organizations could comply with affirmative action and Title VII guidelines. Indeed, the highest concentration of research on race was conducted on the topic of affirmative action (e.g., Hitt & Keats, 1984; Marimont, Maize, Kennedy, & Harley, 1976; Marino, 1980). Some of the authors prescribed mathematical and computer simulation models for effectively implementing affirmative action programs (e.g., Hopkins, 1980; Ledvinka & Hildreth, 1984; Solomon & Messmer, 1980). Effectiveness in this area was most often defined by specifying the technical requirements of affirmative action and equal employment opportunity and fitting those requirements to existing organizational systems. Only a few studies were used to examine the behavioral and social ramifications of affirmative action and equal employment (e.g., Goodman, 1969; Lakin, 1966; Rubin, 1967). A similar emphasis on techniques and mechanics is found in the test validation literature where the issue of differential validity dominated personnel/human resource management research for a number of years (e.g., Bartlett & O'Leary, 1969; Bayroff, 1966; Boehm, 1977; Hunter, Schmidt, & Hunter, 1979; Schmidt, Pearlman, & Hunter, 1980). In this area there was very little discussion of theory about why researchers expected differential validity to occur among different racial and ethnic groups or why test score differentials persisted (Arvey & Faley, 1988). Little attention was given regarding the roles that educational opportunities and other societal factors play in explaining differences or that "universal knowledge" may not be value free.

Several observations can be drawn from the way race was considered in management studies. Much of the research lies along the prejudice-discrimination axis, with an emphasis on discovering objective evidence of racial discrimination and racial differences in behavior, primarily between blacks and whites. This is consistent with the premises underlying the ethnicity paradigm that race can largely be understood as a problem of prejudiced attitudes or personal and cultural inadequacies of racial minorities. A notable exception was the work of Alderfer, Alderfer, Tucker, and Tucker (1980). Using an intergroup framework that emphasized the interaction of power differences at the group, organizational, and societal levels, they examined the broad issue of *race relations* within an organizational setting.

What is most striking about the management literature is researchers' fixation on searching for differences. Although this fixation may reflect the positivist approach to research adopted by many management scholars, it raises important issues for how race has been conceptualized. When no significant differences were found, authors were likely to conclude that race had no effect. This might be interpreted as an affirmation of the universality of management concepts. Another interpretation, consistent with the theoretical premises of the ethnicity paradigm, is that there really are no differences between racial minority groups and the European immigrants who successfully achieved assimilation. In contrast, when significant behavioral differences were reported, explanations were often focused on inadequate socialization of racial minorities to the norms and requirements for successful accomplishment or prejudice or stereotyping

by majority group members. Conspicuously absent from these articles is any suggestion or recognition of the different sociohistorical experience of African-Americans or other racial minorities in the United States. There was little awareness that racial minorities may have something to contribute to organizations or that perhaps race can inform our understanding of organizations in other ways. For the most part, in this literature, race has been considered an issue or a problem. Or race enters the discussion of organizations only when minority employees are studied. Aside from Alderfer and his colleagues (1980), there were no researchers in the studies reviewed who examined the meaning of race for majority group members. This omission reflects an unconscious assumption by organizational researchers that majority group members do not have a racial identity and, consequently, it is a "nontopic" for research.

In summary, the questions that addressed race in the organizational literature echo the assumptions and themes of the ethnicity paradigm. Further, lest we think that the *managing diversity* discourse represents a *new* approach, we should be reminded that it may be only as *new* as the *new ethnicity*. Our conceptualization of race in organizations has been constrained by these theoretical orientations, and, consequently, a necessary step toward rewriting race is recognizing these influences.

Rewriting Race into the Study of Organizations

To rewrite race, we must not continue the emperor's procession by remaining silent about race or studying it within the narrowly defined ethnicity-based paradigm that has dominated much of our research. First, we must acknowledge that the emperor is indeed naked. Organizations are not race-neutral entities. Race is and has been present in organizations, even if this idea has not been explicitly recognized. Second, rewriting race is not a matter of simply clothing the emperor, but the emperor must be dethroned as the universal, the only reality. We need to revise our understanding of the very concept of race and its historical and political meaning. Only then can race be used as a productive analytical concept for understanding the nature of organizations.

Alternative Frameworks

A useful starting point is to examine alternative theoretical frameworks for understanding the complexity and nature of race. For example, power-conflict theories of race and ethnic relations offer ways to move beyond sole reliance on assimilation models.

Power-conflict approaches to race and ethnicity emphasize issues of economic power, inequalities in access to material resources and labor markets, and the historical development of racism (Bonacich, 1980; Cox, 1948; Reich, 1981). One of the earliest proponents of these approaches (Cox, 1948) argued that racial exploitation and race prejudice developed with the rise of capitalism and nationalism. In Cox's analysis, American colonies imported African slaves to fill a particular labor need and simultaneously incorporated the ideology of racism as a justification of slavery. He contended that the idea of racial inferiority didn't precede the use of minority groups as servile labor but that an ideology of racial inferiority developed to maintain Africans and other racial minorities in a servile status. According to Cox, the racial division of labor into white and black workers hindered any positive contact between the white and black masses. Thus, the persistence of racial stratification in society was not a function of atomistic individuals or cultural deficiencies of minorities but was rooted in the class positions of workers.

Reich's (1981) class-conflict theory of racial inequality attempts to explain the meaning of race within the context of an advanced capitalist system. Like Edwards (1979), Reich (1981) conceptualized the workplace as contested terrain wherein workers and capitalists engage in power struggles over income distribution and material resources. White workers do not benefit from racial inequality but capitalists do, and the very organization of jobs in the workplace is structured to exploit the existence of racial and other divisions among workers. Racial antagonism among workers inhibits the collective strength of workers and sustains the power of capitalists.

These and other power-conflict theories attempt to analyze race within the relations of capitalists' production without reducing it to an epiphenomenon (Thompson, 1989; Wilhelm, 1983).

Thus, if applied to organizational analysis, power-conflict theories would focus our attention on understanding how organizations have become racially constructed, the power relations that sustain racial divisions and racial domination, and the important role of capitalist modes of production in maintaining these divisions.

Omi and Winant's (1986) racial-formation theory represents another alternative formulation of race. They argued that race is preeminently a sociohistorical concept whose meanings and categories are given concrete expression by the specific social relations and historical context in which they are embedded. They noted, for example, that in the United States with the consolidation of racial slavery, a racially based understanding of society was set in motion, which resulted in the shaping of a specific racial identity for both slaves and European settlers. Africans with specific ethnic identities became simply "black," and European settlers previously identified as Christian or English and free became "white" (Omi & Winant, 1986: 64).

Race occupies a central position in our understanding of social relations, and in their theory, Omi and Winant (1986: 66) distinguish between two levels of social relations: micro and macro. At the microlevel, race is a matter of individuality, of the formation of identity. The ways we understand ourselves, our experiences, our interactions with others, and our day-to-day activities are all shaped by racial meanings and racial awareness. At the macrolevel, race is a matter of collectivity, of the formation of social structures. These authors conceived of social structures as a series of economic, political, and cultural/ideological sites, which represented a region of social life with a coherent set of constitutive social relations. For example, at the economic level, the very definition of labor and the allocation of jobs among workers have been dependent on race as an organizing principle. Consequently, in this case, the racial order is organized and enforced by the continuity and interaction between the microlevel and macrolevel of social relations. Racial discrimination within the economic structure has consequences for individual identity at the microlevel.

The term *racial formation* in Omi and Winant's (1986: 61) model refers to the process by which social, economic, and political forces determine the content and importance of racial categories and the subsequent process through which these categories are, in turn, shaped by racial meanings. Accordingly, the meaning of race is defined and contested throughout society, in both collective action and personal practice. In the process, racial categories themselves are formed, transformed, destroyed, and reformed. These authors caution not only against the tendency to view race as an essence (i.e., as something fixed or objective) but also against the tendency to view race as a mere illusion that will disappear with the correct social order.

Similarly, Essed (1991) argued that because *race* is an organizing principle of many social relations, the fundamental social relations of society are *racialized* relations. She conceptualized race as both an ideological and a social construction with structural expressions. Using cross-cultural empirical data, Essed (1991) developed a theory of everyday racism, which attempts to build upon both the micro and macro perspectives of race and ethnicity. Essed defined *everyday racism* as "a process in which (a) socialized racist notions are integrated into meanings that make practices immediately definable and manageable, (b) practices with racist implications become in themselves familiar and repetitive, and (c) underlying racial and ethnic relations are actualized and reinforced through these routine or familiar practices in everyday situations" (1991: 52). The three main practices are marginalization (a form of oppression), containment (a form of repression), and problematization (ideological constructions legitimizing exclusion through hierarchical organization of difference). The integration of racism into everyday situations through these practices activates and reproduces underlying power relations.

Omi and Winant's (1986) theory of racial formation and Essed's (1991) theory of everyday racism emphasize the instability of race as a natural category and the impossibility of maintaining the essentialist position about race that sustains the ethnicity paradigm. At the same time, these theories help in understanding the reproduction of race from its historical to contemporary site in particular forms that

occupy every part of society. They suggest that we have left out an important analytical concept for understanding organizations and that if race forms the core of individual, social, and institutional life in the United States, then we need explicit theories of race and ethnicity to overcome this omission.

Other theoretical approaches that have race at the center can be found in the literature and research in African-American and African studies, Asian studies, and Chicano/Latino studies. This literature can also provide a focus for developing theoretical content specifically about race and can help us to ask different questions than those that stem solely from the ethnicity paradigm.

For example, African-American and African studies, or Black studies, are ideologically and philosophically distinct from European social scientific theory because in them Africa is viewed as the genesis and foundation of knowledge and study of black people (Anderson, 1990). *Black studies* has been defined as "an analysis of the factors and conditions which have affected the economic, political, psychological, and legal status of African-Americans as well as the African in the Diaspora from the social reality of their own experience" (Gordon, 1978: 231). The early work of Black studies scholars called attention to the exclusion of the culture and experience of blacks from textbooks and curricula of educational institutions (Karenga, 1984). Despite this exclusion from mainstream academia, a great deal of scholarly work had been previously produced and generated about the experience of black people (e.g., Bennett, 1966; Diop, 1955; Du Bois, 1961; Fanon, 1963). Initial goals of Black studies were to add to the body of knowledge about blacks within the various disciplines. Taylor (1990) noted that most early attempts failed to move theory substantially beyond the extant paradigms of mainstream social science and research centered around relabeling familiar concepts and adapting existing research strategies.

A second strand of Black studies emerged that has been devoted to a critical assessment of traditional social science paradigms and the systematic articulation of a "black perspective," from which the development of new theories and alternative interpretation of the black community and its relation to the larger society could be advanced (e.g., Cheek, 1987; Gates, 1985; Kershaw, 1990). An effort was made to move away from the "pathological behavior" model of the black community. These strands have appeared as black psychology and black sociology, and they can be found in many other social science disciplines.

For example, within black psychology the attempt has been to build conceptual models to organize, explain, and understand the psychosocial behavior of African-Americans. These models are based on the primary dimensions of an African-American world view instead of the traditional psychology concerned mainly with categorization, mental measurement, and the establishment of norms (Azibo, 1990; Guthne, 1976; White, 1984). Cross (1978) and others (e.g., Parham, 1989) have developed a model of racial identity for African-Americans. The model describes a process of psychological Nigrescence that hypothesizes the kinds of changes that occur in the racial identity of African-Americans at various points in the life cycle. Research addressing specific applications of Nigrescence theories can be found in the areas of value orientations (Carter & Helms, 1987) and self-actualization (Parham & Helms, 1985). More recently, research has been focused on models of white racial identity (Helms, 1990). Another useful concept for understanding the experiences of racial and ethnic minorities that has been widely used is *biculturalism* (Bell, 1990), or what Du Bois (1961) called *double consciousness*. Users of this concept recognize that African-Americans have both Afrocentric and Eurocentric elements of culture and racial identity.

Within the discipline of history, scholars researching African-American experiences have sought to correct the theoretical and methodological errors that questioned the historical actuality of African societies (Davidson, 1991; Rodney, 1974) and the nature and effect of slavery upon African-Americans. By examining slave narratives, songs, and other historical documents, scholars in the field have offered re-visions that characterize slaves as more than empty vessels who were acted upon, shaped, and dominated by their European American enslavers (Blassingame, 1979; White, 1984). Slaves had cultural, psychological, and technical resources from their African heritage that not

only contributed to the development of the United States but also helped them to resist the devastation of slavery. Revisiting the early history of African-American and other minority workers and their exclusion from skilled industrial jobs in organizations also can inform our understanding of their present status (Foner & Lewis, 1982; Takai, 1979).

A third strand of research has developed, which calls attention to the need for theoretical development and construction of ideas toward building a new social science (Taylor, 1990). The aim of such research is to move beyond explanations of black institutional life and behavior toward theoretical formulations that build upon a more expansive lens. That is, how would social science concepts differ if we used race as a core analytical concept? What concepts and constructs have been omitted? Other areas of development include analyses that examine the intersection of race with gender and class (e.g., Hill-Collins, 1990; King, 1988; Wilson, 1984).

Implications of Alternative Frameworks

Although I have expanded upon African-American studies as a body of knowledge from which management studies can draw, analogous work can be found for other racial groups. My purpose is not to suggest the replacement of Eurocentric theories with Afrocentric or Asian-centered ones. Yes, these approaches do imply efforts toward accounting for the absence of or any reference to perspectives from other groups in understanding organizations; they also imply that we not view racial minorities solely as deviants or problems in the study of organizations. Yet, such changes do not simply mean *adding* on studies of these groups. The major point is that we re-vision the very way we "see" organizations. Clearly, the specific historical context of race should be considered in the development and use of concepts. A ready example can be found in Thomas's (1989) study of mentoring in organizations. He explicitly draws on the historical impact of social taboos from our legacy of slavery in order to understand the dynamics of present-day cross-race mentoring relationships. Finally, new approaches would suggest different questions about race in organizations. Table 31-1 contains a comparison of the questions that have emanated from the ethnicity paradigm and the kinds of questions supported from the alternative theoretical frameworks and bodies of literature discussed in this section.

Rewriting race also suggests recognizing the limitations of positivist research methods. Research strategies determine the kinds of knowledge produced, and a realistic view of the research process encourages us to use these strategies in different ways (Morgan, 1983). A majority of the organizational studies mentioned in this article relied upon comparative designs in which race was categorized as a two-level variable (i.e., black and white). There are two basic problems with this approach. First, comparative designs too often adopt a position of cultural monism that assumes equivalence of groups across race (Azibo, 1990). In such a case, meaningful and valid interpretations of any observed differences are hindered. An awareness of the appropriate use of emic (within culture) and etic (cross-culture) approaches is critical (Triandis, 1972). Azibo (1990) noted that researchers must seek a balance between the assumption that cultures can best be understood in their own terms and the desire to establish universal theories of human behavior. Research efforts in this direction can be found in the works of Marin and Triandis, 1985; Triandis, Marin, Lisanky, and Betancourt, 1984; and Cox, Lobel, and McLeod, 1991.

Table 31-1

Asked and Unasked Questions About Race

Research Questions From Ethnicity Paradigm

Does discrimination exist in recruitment, selection, etc?

Can the Afro-American be an effective executive?

Do blacks identify with the traditional American work ethic?

Do blacks' and whites' problem-solving styles differ?

How can blacks/minorities be assimilated into organizations?

How can organizations manage diversity?

How can organizations comply with equal employment opportunity/affirmative action requirements?

Do blacks and whites have the same job expectations?

Are there different levels of motivation between black and white employees?

Is there racial bias in performance ratings?

What is the role of stereotyping in job bias?

Does differential test validity exist?

Silenced Research Questions From Alternative Paradigms

How are societal race relations reproduced in the workplace?

How did white males come to dominate management positions?

To what extent is race built into the definition of a "manager"?

What are the implications of racial identity for organization theories based on individual identity?

How does racial identity affect organizational experiences?

How does the racial identity of white employees influence their status and interaction with other groups?

Why, despite national policies like affirmative action, does inequality still exist in the workplace?

Are assimilation and managing diversity the only two means of removing racial inequality in the workplace?

How do organizational processes contribute to the maintenance of racial domination and stratification?

Are white male-dominated organizations also built on underlying assumptions about gender and class?

What are the patterns of relationships among different racial minorities in organizations?

Second, categorization of subjects is an essentialist view of race as a discrete, demographic variable that can be objectively observed and measured. Reconceptualizing race not as a simple property of individuals but as an integral dynamic of organizations implies a move toward phenomenological and historical research methods that would contribute toward building theories and knowledge about both how race is produced and how it is a core feature of organizations.

Conclusion

I have argued that we should not continue our silence about race, and when we do study it, that we expand our approaches beyond the ethnicity-based paradigm that has implicitly dominated much of our research. This expansion would allow race to become a productive analytical category used in understanding organizations. What does it mean to use race as an analytical category? This use suggests a view of organizations as made up of *race relations* played out in power struggles, which includes the realization that "race" is not a stable category. Then, not only would we not conduct research on "race in organizations" the way we have done it in the past, but we would also need to rethink the very nature of organizations.

Finally, it is important to point out that race is just one part of a more complicated web of socially constructed elements of identity formation such as gender and class. Race, gender, and class can form interlocking bases of domination in social relations (Hill-Collins, 1990; Spelman, 1988). Although each part may be manifested in its own peculiar and distinct way, the common factor is domination based on notions of inferiority and superiority. To the extent that each system reinforces and reproduces the other, an analysis of organizations cannot exclude the importance of these significant elements of identity. Indeed, the challenge before us becomes much more complex than simply clothing the emperor!

An earlier version of this article was presented at the 1989 annual meeting of the Academy of Management.

Stella M. Nkomo received her Ph.D. at the University of Massachusetts, Amherst. She is an associate professor of management at the University of North Carolina at Charlotte. Her current research interests include race and gender effects on women's careers.

References

Adorno, T. W., Frenkel-Brunswick, E., Levinson, D. J., II, & Sanford, R. N. 1950. *The authoritarian personality.* New York: Harper & Row.

Alderfer, C. P. 1982. Problems of changing white males' behavior and beliefs concerning race relations. In P. S. Goodman & Associates (Eds.), *Change in organizations:* 122–165. San Francisco: Jossey-Bass.

Alderfer, C. P., Alderfer, C. J., Tucker, L., & Tucker, R. 1980. Diagnosing race relations in management: *Journal of Applied Behavioral Science,* 16: 135–165.

Allport, G. 1954. *The nature of prejudice.* New York: Doubleday.

Alper, S. W. 1975. Racial differences in job and work environment priorities among newly hired college graduates. *Journal of Applied Psychology,* 60: 120–134.

Anderson, H. C. 1958. *Forty-two stories* (M. P. James, Trans.). London: Faber & Faber.

Anderson, T. (Ed.). 1990. *Black studies: Theory, method, and cultural perspectives.* Pullman: Washington State University Press.

Arvey, R. D., & Faley, R. H. 1988. *Fairness in selecting employees.* Reading, MA: Addison-Wesley.

Azibo, D. A. Y. 1990. Personality, clinical, and social psychological research on blacks: Appropriate & inappropriate research frameworks. In T. Anderson (Ed.), *Black studies: Theory, method and cultural perspectives:* 25–41. Pullman: Washington State University Press.

Bankart, P. C. 1972. Attribution of motivation in same-race and different race stimulus persons. *Human Relations,* 215: 35–45.

Bartlett, C. J., & O'Leary, B. S. 1969. A differential prediction model to moderate the effects of heterogeneous groups in personnel selection and classification. *Personnel Psychology,* 22: 1–18.

Bayroff, A. 1966. Test technology and equal employment opportunity. *Personnel Psychology,* 19: 35–39.

Bell, E. L. 1990. The bicultural life experiences of career-oriented black women. *Journal of Organizational Behavior,* 11: 459–477.

Bennett, L. 1966. *Before the Mayflower: A history of the negro in America. 1619–1964.* Baltimore: Penguin Books.

Bhagat, R. 1979. Black-white ethnic differences in identification with the work ethic: Some implications for organizational integration. *Academy of Management Review,* 4: 381–391.

Billig, M. 1985. Prejudice, categorization and particularization: From a perceptual to a rhetorical approach. *European Journal of Social Psychology,* 15: 79–103.

Blanton, M. 1987. *Racial theories*. Cambridge: Cambridge University Press.

Blassingame, J. 1979. *The slave community: Plantation life in the antebellum south*. New York: Oxford University Press.

Blauner, R. 1972. *Racial oppression in America*. New York: Harper & Row.

Blauner, B. 1989. *Black lives, white lives: Three decades of race relations in America*. Berkeley: University of California Press.

Boehm, V. R. 1977. Differential prediction—A methodological criest. *Journal of Applied Psychology*, 52: 146–154.

Bonasich, E. 1980. Class approaches to ethnicity and race. *Insurgent Sociologist*, 10: 9–33.

Brenner, O. C., & Tomkiewicz, J. 1982. Job orientation of black and white college graduates in business. *Personnel Psychology*, 35: 89–103.

Brown, H. A., & Ford, D. L. Jr. 1977. An exploratory analysis of discrimination in the employment of black MBA graduates. *Journal of Applied Psychology*. 52: 50–56.

Carter, R. T., & Helms, J. E. 1987. Relationship of black value orientation to racial identity attitudes. *Measurement and Evaluation in Counseling and Development*. 19: 185–195.

Cheek, D. K. 1987. Social science: A vehicle for white supremacy? *International Journal for the Advancement of Counseling*, 10: 59–69.

Cox, O. C. 1948. *Caste, class, and race: A study in social dynamics*. New York: Doubleday.

Cox. T., Jr., & Nkomo, S. M. 1986. Differential appraisal criteria based on race of the ratee. *Group and Organization Studies,* 11: 101–119.

Cox. T., Jr., & Nkomo, S. M. 1990. Invisible men and women: A status report on race as a variable in organization behavior research. *Journal of Organizational Behavior*, 11: 419–431.

Cox. T., Jr., Lobel, S., & McLeod, P. 1991. Effects of ethnic group cultural differences on cooperative versus competitive behavior in a group task. *Academy of Management Journal*, 34: 827–847.

Cross, W. E. 1978. The Cross and Thomas models of psychological nigrescence. *Journal of Black Psychology*, 5: 13–19.

Davidson, B. 1991. *African civilization revisited*. Trenton, NJ: Africa World Press.

Diop, C. A. 1955. *The African origin of civilization: Myth or reality*. Paris: Presence Africaine.

Dipboye, R. L. 1985. Some neglected variables in research on discrimination in appraisals. *Academy of Management Review*. 10: 116–127.

Domm, D., & Stafford, J. 1972. Assimilating blacks into the organization. *California Management Review*. 15(1): 46–51.

Davidio, J. F., & Gaertner, S. L. (Eds.). 1986. *Prejudice, discrimination, and racism*. Orlando, FL: Academic Press.

Du Bois, W. E. 1961. *The souls of black folk*. Greenwich, CT: Fawcett.

Edwards, R. 1979. *Contested terrain*. New York: Basic Books.

Essed, P. 1991. *Everyday racism*. Newbury Park, CA: Sage.

Fanon, F. 1963. *The wretched of the earth*. New York: Grove Press.

Feagin, J. 1987. Changing black Americans to fit a racist system? *Journal of Social Issues*, 43(1): 85–89.

Foner, P. S., & Lewis, R. L. (Eds.). 1982. *The black worker: A documentary history from colonial times to the present*. Philadelphia: Temple University Press.

Franklin, R. 1968. A framework for the analysis of inter-urban negro-white economic differentials. *Industrial and Labor Relations Review*, 2: 209–223.

Gavin, J., & Ewen, R. 1974. Racial differences in job attitudes and performance—Some theoretical considerations and empirical findings. *Personnel Psychology*, 27: 455–464.

Gates, H. L. Jr. 1985. Editor's introduction: Writing "race" and the difference it makes. In H. L. Gates, Jr. (Ed.), *"Race," writing, and differences*: 1–20. Chicago: University of Chicago Press.

Gates, H. L., Jr. 1988. *The signifying monkey: A theory of Afro-American literary criticism*. New York: Oxford University Press.

Glazer, N. 1987. *Affirmative discrimination: Ethnic inequality and public policy*. Cambridge, MA: Harvard University Press.

Glazer, N., & Moynihan, D. P. 1970. *Beyond the melting pot: The Negroes, Puerto Ricans, Jews, Italians, and Irish of New York City*. Cambridge, MA: MIT Press.

Goode, K. 1970. Can the Afro-American be an effective executive? *California Management Review*, 13(1): 27–30.

Goodman, R. 1969. A hidden issue in minority employment: *California Management Review*, 11(1): 22–26.

Gorden, M. M. 1954. *Assimilation in American life: The role of race, religion, and national origin*. New York: Oxford University Press.

Gorden, M. M. 1978. *Human nature, class, and ethnicity*. New York: Oxford University Press.

Guthne, R. V. 1976. *Even the rat was white: A historical view of psychology*. New York: Harper & Row.

Guzman, H. G. 1977. *Work, culture, and society in industrializing America*. New York: Knopf.

Greenhaus, J., & Gavin, J. 1972. The relationship between experiences and job behavior for white and black employees. *Personnel Psychology*, 25: 449–455.

Hamner, W. C., Kim, J. S., Baird, L., & Biogness, W. J. 1974. Race and sex as determinants of ratings by potential employers in a simulated work-sampling task. *Journal of Applied Psychology*, 59: 705–711.

Harding, S. 1986. *The science question in feminism*. Ithaca, NY: Cornell University Press.

Helms, J. G. 1990. *Black and white racial identity: Theory, research, and practice*. Westport, CT: Greenwood Press.

Henriques, J. 1984. Social psychology and the politics of racism. In J. Henriques, W. Hollway, C. Urwin, C. Venn, & V. Walkerdine (Eds.), *Changing the subject: Psychology, social regulations and subjectivity:* 60–89. London: Methuen.

Hewstone, M. 1989. Intergroup attribution: Some implications for the study of ethnic prejudice. In J. P. Van Oudenhoven & T. M. Williemsen (Eds.), *Ethnic minorities: Social psychological perspectives*: 25–42. Amsterdam: Sivets & Zeitlinger.

Hill-Collins, P. 1990. *Black feminist thought: Knowledge consciousness, and the politics of empowerment*. Boston: Unwin Hyman.

Hitt, M., & Keats, B. 1984. Empirical identification of the criteria for effective affirmative action programs. *Journal of Applied Behavioral Science*, 20: 203–222.

Hopkins, D. 1980. Models for affirmative action planning and evaluation. *Management Science*, 26: 994–1006.

Hunter, J. E., Schmidt, F. L., & Hunter, R. 1979. Differential validity of employment tests by race: A comprehensive review and analysis. *Psychological Bulletin*. 85: 721–735.

Johnston, W., & Packer, A. 1987. *Workforce 2000: Work and workers for the 21st century*. Indianapolis, IN: Hudson Institute.

Jones, A. P., James, L. R., Bruni, J. R., & Sell, S. B. 1977. Black white differences in work environment perceptions and job satisfaction and its correlates. *Personnel Psychology*, 30: 5–16.

Joseph, G. G., Reddy, V., & Searle-Chatterjee, M. 1990. Eurocentrism in the social sciences. *Race & Class*, 31(4): 1–26.

Karenga, R. 1984. *Introduction to black studies*. Los Angeles: Kawaida Publications.

Kershaw, T. 1990. The emerging paradigm in black studies. In T. Anderson (Ed.), *Black studies: Theory, method, and cultural perspectives*: 17–24. Pullman: Washington State University Press.

King, D. K. 1988. Multiple jeopardy, multiple consciousness: The context of black feminist ideology. *Signs*, 14: 42–72.

Keto, C. T. 1989. *The Africa centered perspective of history*. Blackwood, NJ: KA Publications.

Konar, E. 1981. Explaining racial differences in job satisfaction: A reexamination of the data. *Journal of Applied Psychology*, 66: 522–524.

Kovarshy, I. 1964. Management, racial discrimination, and apprentice training programs. *Academy of Management Journal*, 7: 196–203.

Kraiger, K., & Ford, J. 1985. A meta-analysis of ratee race effects in performance ratings. *Journal of Applied Psychology*, 70: 56–65.

Kuhn, T. 1962. *The structure of scientific revolutions*. Chicago: University of Chicago Press.

Lakin, M. 1966. Human relations training and interracial social action: Problems in self and client definition. *Journal of Applied Behavioral Science*, 2(2): 139–149.

Landy, F. J., & Farr, S. L. 1980. Performance rating. *Psychological Bulletin*, 87: 72–107.

Ledvinka, J., & Hildreth, W. B. 1984. Integrating planned change intervention and computer simulation technology: The case of affirmative action. *Journal of Applied Behavioral Science*, 20(2): 125–140.

Lefkowitz, J. 1972. Differential validity: Ethnic groups as a moderator in predicting tenure. *Personnel Psychology*, 25: 223–240.

Marimont, R. B., Maize, B., Kennedy, P., & Harley, E. 1976. Using FAIR to set numerical EEO goals. *Public Personnel Management*, 5(3): 191–198.

Marin, G., & Triandis, H. C. 1985. Allocentrism as an important characteristic of the behavior of Latin Americans and Hispanics. In R. Diaz-Guerrero (Ed.), *Cross-cultural and national studies in social psychology*: 85–104. Amsterdam: Elsevier Science.

Marino, K. E. 1980. A preliminary investigation into the behavioral dimensions of affirmative action compliance. *Journal of Applied Psychology*, 65: 346–350.

Merton, R. K. 1949. Discrimination and the American creed. In R. MacIver (Ed.), *Discrimination and national welfare*: 99–126. New York: Harper & Row.

Milutinovich, J. S., & Tsaklanganos, A. 1976. The impact of perceived community prosperity on job satisfaction of black and white workers. *Academy of Management Journal*, 19: 49–65.

Miner, J. 1977. Motivational potential for upgrading among minority and female managers. *Journal of Applied Psychology*, 62: 691–697.

Minnich, E. K. 1990. *Transforming knowledge*. Philadelphia: Temple University Press.

Mobley, W. 1982. Supervisor and employee race and sex effects on performance appraisals: A field study of adverse impact and generalizability. *Academy of Management Journal*, 25: 598–606.

Moch, M. 1980. Racial differences in job satisfaction: Testing four common explanations. *Journal of Applied Psychology*, 65: 299–306.

Morgan, G. 1983. Toward a more reflective social science. In G. Morgan (Ed.), *Beyond method: Strategies for social research*: 368–376. Beverly Hills, CA: Sage.

Myrdal, G. 1944. *An American dilemma*. New York: Harper & Row.

Newman, J. M. 1978. Discrimination in recruitment: An empirical analysis. *Industrial and Labor Relations Review*, 32: 15–23.

Newman, J. M., & Krzytofiak, F. 1979. Self-reports versus unobtrusive measures: Balancing method variance and ethical concerns in employment discrimination research. *Journal of Applied Psychology*, 64: 2–85.

Nkomo, S. M. 1988. Race and sex: The forgotten case of the black female manager. In S. Rose & L. Larwood (Eds.). *Women's careers: Pathways and pitfalls:* 133–150. New York: Praeger.

Northrop, H. 1969. The negro in aerospace work. *California Management Review*, 11(4): 11–26.

Omi, M., & Winant, H. 1986. *Racial formation in the United States: From the 1960s to the 1980s.* New York: Routledge & Kegan Paul.

O'Reilly, C. A., & Roberts, K. M. 1973. Job satisfaction among whites and nonwhites: A cross-cultural approach. *Journal of Applied Psychology*, 57: 295–299.

Oudenhoven, J. P. V., & Williemsen, T. M. (Eds.). 1989. *Ethnic minorities: Social psychological perspectives.* Amsterdam: Sivets & Zeitlinger.

Parham, T. A. 1989. Cycles of psychological nigrescence. *Counseling Psychologist*, 17(2): 187–225.

Parham, T. A., & Helms, J. E. 1985. Relation of racial identity attitudes to self-actualization and affective statements of black students. *Journal of Counseling Psychology*, 32: 431–440.

Park, R. E. 1950. *Race and culture.* Glencoe, IL: Free Press. (Original work published in 1939)

Pettigrew, T. F. 1979. The ultimate attribution error. Extending Allport's cognitive analysis of prejudice. *Personality and Social Psychology* Bulletin, 5: 461–476.

Pettigrew, T. F., & Martin, J. 1987. Shaping the organizational context for black American inclusion. *Journal of Social Forces*, 43(1): 41–78.

Reich, M. 1981. *Racial inequality.* Princeton, NJ: Princeton University Press.

Rodney, W. 1974. *How Europe underdeveloped Africa.* Washington, DC: Howard University Press.

Rubin, I. 1967. The reduction of prejudice through laboratory training. *Journal of Applied Behavioral Science.* 3(1): 29–51.

Schmidt, F. L., Pearlman, K., & Hunter, J. 1980. The validity and fairness of employment and educational tests for Hispanic Americans: A review and analysis. *Personnel Psychology.* 33: 705–724.

Schmitt, N., & Lappin, M. 1980. Race and sex as determinants of the mean and variance of performance ratings. *Journal of Applied Psychology*, 65: 428–435.

Slocum, J., Jr., & Strawser, R. 1972. Racial differences in job attitudes. *Journal of Applied Psychology*, 56: 28–32.

Solomon, R. J., & Messmer, D. J. 1980. Implications of the Bakke decision in implementing affirmative action programs: A decision model. *Decision Sciences.* 11: 312–324.

Sowell, T. 1975. *Race and economics.* New York: David McKay.

Spelman, E. V. 1988. *Inessential woman: Problems of exclusion in feminist thought.* Boston: Beacon Press.

Steinberg, S. 1981. *The ethnic myth.* New York: Atheneum.

Stone, D. L., & Stone, E. F. 1987. Effects of missing application-blank information on personnel selection decisions: Do privacy protection strategies bias the outcome? *Journal of Applied Psychology*, 72: 452–456.

Tajfel, H. 1969. Cognitive aspects of prejudice. *Journal of Social Issues.* 25(4): 79–97.

Tajfel, H. 1970. Experiments in intergroup discrimination. *Scientific American*, 223(5): 96–102.

Tajfel, H., & Turner, J. C. 1979. *An integrative theory of intergroup conflict: The social psychology of intergroup relations.* Monterey, CA: Brooks/Cole.

Tajfel, H. 1981. *Human groups and social categories.* Cambridge: Cambridge University Press.

Tajfel, H., & Turner, J. C. 1986. The social identity of theory of intergroup behavior. In S. Worchel & W. G. Austin (Eds.), *Psychology of intergroup relations:* 7–24. Chicago: Nelson-Hall.

Takai, R. 1979. *Iron cages: Race and culture in nineteenth-century America.* New York: Knopf.

Taylor, D. 1968. Discrimination and occupational wage differences in the market for unskilled labor. *Industrial and Labor Relations Review*, 21: 373–390.

Taylor, Ronald L. 1990. The study of black people: A survey of empirical and theoretical models. In T. Anderson (Ed.), *Black studies: Theory, method and cultural perspectives:* 11–15. Pullman: Washington State University Press.

Terpstra, D., & Larsen, M. 1985. A note on job type and applicant race as determinants of hiring decisions. *Journal of Occupational Psychology*, 53(3): 117–119.

Thomas, D. A. 1989. Mentoring and irrationality: The role of racial taboos. *Human Resource Management*, 28: 279–290.

Thomas, D. A. 1990. From affirmative action to affirming diversity. *Harvard Business Review*, 68(2): 107–117.

Thompson, R. H. 1989. *Theories of ethnicity: A critical appraisal.* New York: Greenwood Press.

Triandis, H. C. 1972. *The analysis of subjective culture.* New York: Wiley.

Triandis, H. C., Marin, G., Lisansky, J., & Betancourt, H. 1984. Simpatia as a cultural script of hispanics. *Journal of Personality and Social Psychology*, 47: 1363–1375.

van den Berghe, P. 1967. *Race and racism.* New York: Wiley.

van den Berghe, P. 1981. *The ethnic phenomenon.* New York: Elsevier.

van Dijk, T. A. 1987. *Communicating racism: Ethnic prejudice in thought and talk.* Newbury Park, CA: Sage.

Veechio, R. 1980. Worker alienation as a moderator of the job quality—job satisfaction relationship: The case of racial differences. *Academy of Management Journal*, 23: 479–486.

Watson, J. G., & Barone, S. 1976. The self-concept, personal values, and motivational orientations of black and white managers. *Academy of Management Journal*, 19: 36–48.

Weaver, C. N. 1978. Black-white correlates of job satisfaction. *Journal of Applied Psychology*, 53: 255–258.

White, J. L. 1984. *The psychology of blacks: An African-American perspective*. Englewood Cliffs, NJ: Prentice-Hall.

Wilder, D. A. 1986. Cognitive factors affecting the success of intergroup contact. In S. Worchel & W. G.

Austin (Eds.), *Psychology of intergroup relations*: 49–66. Chicago: Nelson Hall.

Wilhelm, S. 1983. *Black in White America*. Cambridge, MA: Schenkman.

Wilson, W. J. 1984. *The declining significance of race*. Chicago: Chicago University Press.

Yinger, J. M. 1986. Intersecting strands in the theorization of race and ethnic relations. In J. Rex & D. Mason (Eds.), *Theories of race and ethnic relations*: 20–41. Cambridge: Cambridge University Press.

CHAPTER 32

AN ORGANIZATIONAL ANALYSIS OF RACISM IN HIGHER EDUCATION[1]

MARK A. CHESLER AND JAMES CROWFOOT

The Program in Conflict Management Alternatives: The Program in Conflict Management Alternatives was established in January, 1986, by a grant from the William and Flora Hewlett Foundation, and additional funds from the University of Michigan. These basic grants were renewed in July, 1988. The Program supports an agenda of research, application, and theory development. PCMA also establishes links among other University research and teaching efforts relevant to conflict management alternatives, and maintains liaison and collaboration with similar efforts in other Universities and Practitioner agencies. The Program staff's own work focuses explicitly on the relationship between social justice and social conflict, specifically: (a) the use of innovative settlement procedures and roles for disputants and third parties; (b) the institutionalization of innovative mechanisms and the adoption of organizational and community structures that permanently alter the way conflicts are managed; and (c) the fundamental differences and inequalities between parties that often create conflict and threaten its stable resolution.

We examine these issues primarily in United States' settings, in conflicts arising within and between families, organizations and communities, and between different racial, gender, and economic constituencies. These specific efforts are supported by a variety of research and action grants/contracts with governmental agencies, foundations, and private and public organizations/agencies.

I. Introduction

Complexity, contradiction and confusion are paramount in American race relations. Our national history is fraught with contradictory messages about "equal rights" and "slavery," about "equality of opportunity" and the "reproduction of poverty," about "affirmative action" and "reverse discrimination." Overriding this confusion, our history of racial injustice is maintained through contemporary policies and practices, and is reflected in the dramatic differentials in life expectancy, opportunity and other outcomes that still exist between people of color and white persons. In addition, in order to defend and sustain the moral imperative of democracy and equality, we have created ideologies that legitimate and justify these racial differentials as reflections of minority inadequacy or as aberrations from the otherwise fair workings of an open and meritorious political and economic system. As a result, even people who perceive obvious racial inequalities often find it difficult to recognize the injustice embedded in these inequalities. It is hard to act with fairness when we do not understand the basis upon which fairness applies, or what it even means when applied

"Racism in Higher Education: An Organizational Analysis," CRSO Center for Research on Social Organization, *The Working Paper Series*, by Mark A. Chesler and James Crowfoot, PCMA Working CRSO Work, Paper #21 Paper #412, November 1989

to people of color and to situations involving racial inequality.

If individuals' moral choices regarding racial relations and racial injustice are generally difficult, they are even more difficult when set within an organizational context. Here there are collective as well as individual choices to make, and actors must act amidst diffuse (and often impersonal) organizational criteria and competing claims. Moreover, the organizational imperative often requires individual claims (moral, economic and otherwise) to be subordinated to collective priorities. Sometimes organizational rules and cultures are so pervasive that there is an inability to perceive realities other than those posed or promulgated by the organization, or if choices are perceived people are unable to act on them. Nevertheless, organizational actors must make decisions, allocate resources and adjudicate competing claims. To the extent that organizations play powerful roles in providing their members and customers with access to vital life resources and opportunities, these decisions are profoundly moral and have crucial and lasting consequences.

Organizations propagate (implicitly or explicitly) frameworks within which individuals operating in the name or context of the organization make choices and engage in formal and informal behavior. Most organizations go further; they provide quite specific rewards and sanctions for behavior that is deemed to be appropriate or inappropriate (e.g., with regard to white collar crime, pursuit of prudent decisions in the interest of stockholders, sexual harassment on the job, stealing competitors' secrets, bribery that serves the organization's welfare, whistle blowing that surfaces malfeasance, etc.). Some organizations, moreover, have an explicitly moral agenda: school systems, particularly, have a goal of preparing the young to recognize moral issues and to make choices consistent with the values of prior generations. Colleges and universities are at the apex of educational systems, and as the secularization of society has progressed, they have increasingly replaced churches and synagogues as purveyors of core values and standards. The public often expects organizations of higher education to embody and articulate traditional moral values and to prepare students for exemplary lives.

When the complex realities of organizational life are joined with the confusing and often contradictory nature of race relations in American life, we enter very difficult territory. Clear understanding of relevant racial issues, let alone a capacity for wise and appropriate behavior, is difficult. The sheer invisibility of racism to white people makes it difficult to perceive (and correctly interpret) the reality of organizational life as it exists for people of color. Since this invisibility is historic as well as contemporary, white people also often are blind to their enmeshment in well established patterns of racial advantage and disadvantage, and to the privileges they and their ancestors have gained thereby. Without such clarity, or pressures to be clear, it is hard to own and take personal or organizational responsibility for injustice, or for the need to strive for justice. Thus, patterns of institutional racism often operate without white people being aware of them and without their conscious intent. Nevertheless, these patterns of racism reproduce themselves: they are aided by the ways in which people with power and advantage in the society, white people and people with wealth, cannot see racism clearly, deny responsibility for action to remove it, and thus passively if not actively contribute to the maintenance of the status quo.

One essential component of morally appropriate behavior is an ability to see the issues clearly: in the context of organizational racism that means clarity about the organization's impact on peoples' options, the existence and operation of racism in the organization, and the role and impact of racism in the lives of people of color and white people. As noted, what is hard to perceive at a personal level is even harder to see clearly at an organizational level, where individual capacities for clarity and responsibility often are obscured by organizational rules and norms. Without such clarity and responsibility, the potential for sound organizational decision making and implementation of decisions—including those necessary to achieve change—is virtually non-existent.

Our purpose in this paper is to contribute to an understanding of race relations and racism, and actions to combat racism, in institutions of higher education. We do so by conducting a conceptually based diagnosis and analysis of the operations of racism in typical colleges and universities. This analysis grows out of our work as white male faculty members and administrators at a major university. These background and role characteristics shape our perspectives in certain ways, and undoubtedly in ways that differ from those of people of a different race, status, gender, etc. Our hope in this paper is to move beyond a discussion of white peoples' individual attitudes and behaviors, or guilt and responsibility, or choice and non-choice; we focus on racism occurring at an organizational level—institutional racism. Moreover, we place organizational/institutional racism in the context of the specific activities and operations of colleges and universities, relatively unique kinds of organizations. The potential for organizational change to reduce racism also is described briefly.

II. From Individual Incidents To Institutional Racism

Numerous scholars and activists have drawn attention to the historic state of race relations and racial injustice in American higher education (Astin, 1982; Blauner, 1972; Clark and Plotkin, 1963; Fleming et al, 1978; Peterson et al, 1978; Thomas, 1981; Vetter et al, 1982). Many of these early efforts were spurred by the turbulence of the late 1960s and early 1970s. As relative "peace" returned to the campus, however, concern with these issues gradually receded. Fiscal crises, debates about appropriate public-sector private-sector relationships, potential declines in student applications and other issues became more important. Recent events have spurred new empirical and political analyses of institutional racism in our colleges and universities (Allen, 1986; Steele, 1989; Sudarkasa, 1988; Wilson and Carter, 1988).

Recent attention to racism on campus has been galvanized by a series of noteworthy public "incidents." Included among these incidents reported at 174 different colleges (Bayh, 1989) have been the following:

Citadel—A group of white students dressed in white sheets and hoods threatened a Black cadet with racial obscenities and a burnt cross.

Dartmouth—White students destroyed shanties erected in protest of corporate investment in South Africa.

Macalester College—The room of five Asian women was vandalized with the letters KKK written on the door.

Michigan State University—Threatening phone calls and written messages were received by students of color.

University of Massachusetts—Physical attacks were made on Black students by a mob of white students.

The University of Michigan—Black women were harassed in dormitories with flyers announcing an intention to "get them" and suggesting they go back to Africa.

University of Mississippi—Arson destroyed a Black fraternity house.

University of Wisconsin—A group of fraternity men held a mock auction of Black slaves with white pledges wearing blackface and Afro wigs.

Yale University—A swastika and racist comments were written on the Afro-American cultural center.

When first noted by administrators and faculty, many of these incidents were described as accidents, as departures from norms of civility and justice, or at least tolerance, prevailing on our campuses; indeed, they often were analyzed as not being "racial incidents" at all, but as instances of drunkenness, playfulness or political protest (e.g., Hurst, 1987). Moreover, they were seen as evidence of problems residing in the student community, reflecting ill on the state of mind of American college youth. And finally, they often were analyzed as individual actions, as the behaviors of one or a small group of individuals who were presumed to be ignorant, prejudiced, filled with hate or perhaps partially deranged.

It is of course true that growing up in America predisposes most white people to ignorance, indifference and fear or antipathy toward people of color. For some, this is learned through deliberate instruction at home and in school, instruction explicitly designed to maintain racial distance and to pass on accumulated social lessons regarding the inferiority of people of color. For others, this is incidental learning, messages gathered as a result of seeing how people of color are treated as systematically inferior and undeserving of the privileges and advantages of an affluent society.

For our society to maintain the illusion that it is democratic and just, the young must perceive the oppressed position of people of color as their own due, as the deserved result of their own inadequacies. In an uncertain world, these lessons have great psychic and social import, protecting us from our own insecurities as well as from the intrusion of others and discomforting ideas. Thus, the workings of institutional racism are deeply embedded in the psyches of white people, as well as in the structure of social, political, and economic relationships. They also impact on these psychic and social structures in ways that maintain and reproduce inequality over generations.

We suggest, however, that those analytic frames that focus primarily on prejudice, or that depend primarily on individual or incidental explanations of racism, are inadequate and thereby erroneous. More than that, they serve to distract attention from the true nature of racism on the university campus. What is real is neither incidental nor accidental; what is real is not located merely in the minds and actions of a few students; what is real is not solely individual ignorance or prejudice. What is real is institutional racism on campus, just as institutional racism is real throughout the warp and woof of the American society.

The path to a reanalysis of these phenomena, from explanations of individual incidents to explanations of institutional structure and process, often is provided in the extended nature of the incidents themselves, and in campus responses to them. For instance, in response to incidents occurring at the University of Michigan in early 1987, groups of students of color presented the University administration with the series of proposals/demands illustrated in Figure 32-1. Examination of the demands makes it obvious that these students have discerned some of the organizational roots of the incidents of individual racism practiced by white students. Indeed, the proposals focus on changes in the programs and structures of the University, and not solely on the behavior of students. In follow-up conversations and confrontations, these students have identified the behaviors (and non-behaviors) of faculty and administrators that encourage, permit or tolerate (even unconsciously) continued harassment and discrimination against students of color.

This list is in many ways quite similar to the list of demands presented to the University of Michigan administration by the original Black Action Movement, in 1970 (see Figure 32-2). The similarity of concerns, and therefore demands, is not surprising, since the character of racism at most colleges and universities has remained quite similar to the situation in 1970. Responses made at that time focused on new services, but not on changing the institutional basis of racism. The result has been a continuation of the conditions of disadvantage and discrimination that have led again to overt conflict and protest in the late 1980s.

For instance, when incidents of racial harassment surfaced at the University of Michigan, and when students of color voiced their concerns and grievances, most academic Deans and senior officials of the University expressed shock and surprise at the level and consistency of humiliation and discrimination these students reported. For so many well-meaning officials to be so poorly-informed about the experiences of this constituency is in itself revealing. It suggests, of course, that academic administrators (and often much of the faculty as well) are out of touch with and ignorant about student life in general, and of the conditions faced by students of color in particular. This lack of information is neither accidental nor individual. It is socially constructed ignorance, and is created by the separate cultures, life experiences and responsibilities of whites and of people of color—in the society, in the neighborhood and in the University. Moreover, it is ignorance that was permitted to exist because most individuals did not inquire proactively into the conditions of life of students of color: there was no payoff for such concern and no sanctions for such ignorance.

The situation at the University of Michigan is instructive, but not, we think, unique.[2] The institutional racism existing at the University of Michigan is quite probably no greater or lesser than that which exists at many other major institutions of higher education. What may be different at Michigan, however, is the University's tradition of student activism, and

---

UCAR Anti-Racist Proposals

1. Submit a specific plan to guarantee a substantial increase in black student enrollment.

2. Establish an Office of Minority Affairs with an autonomous supervisory commission elected by the minority campus community.

3. Create a Financial Aid Appeals Board to make sure no student is forced out of the University because of economic discrimination.

4. Establish a mandatory workshop on racism and diversity for all incoming students.

5. Set up a program of orientation for minority students to meet and talk with already enrolled minority students and faculty to minimize feelings of isolation.

6. Institute a program of tuition waivers for all under-represented and economically disadvantaged minority students until the goals for minority enrollment are realized.

7. Create a Minority Student Lounge and Office in the Michigan Union where minority students can meet in a comfortable and supportive atmosphere on a regular basis.

8. Establish a required course on diversity and bigotry to be taken by all matriculated students before graduation from the University, with input from the Center for Afroamerican and African studies.

9. Full observance of the Dr. Martin Luther King holiday including cancellation of classes and the closing of offices.

10. Honorary degree for S. African leader Nelson Mandela at May commencement.

11. Full, public and immediate investigation of all reported incidents of racial harassment, and a mechanism set up, to facilitate the on-going reporting and documentation of such incidents.

Figure 32-1: Selected Student Proposals/Demands to Counter Racism at the University of Michigan[3]

of student leadership in highlighting and protesting various campus and societal problems. Thus, these challenges to racism, and learning about it as well as changing it, are more publically and vigorously debated, advocated, and resisted.

In an analysis of the 1960–1970 state of race relations and race conflict on campus, Blauner drew attention to the differing analytic frames often used then by (even liberal) white academics and students of color (1972, p 276–278).

> . . . (For) the liberal professor . . . racism connotes conscious acts, where there is an intent to hurt or degrade or disadvantage others because of their color or ethnicity . . . He does not consider the all-white or predominantly white character of an occupation or an institution in itself to be racism. He does not understand the notion of covert racism, that white people maintain a system of racial oppression by acts of omission, indifference, and failure to change the status quo. The Third World definition of racism . . . focuses on the society as a whole

and on structured relations between people rather than on individual personalities and actions. From this standpoint, the university is racist because people of color are and have been systematically excluded from full and equal participation and power— as students, professors, administrators, and, particularly, in the historic definition of the character of the institution and its curriculum.

These different perspectives still exist. What is this concept of institutional racism?

Individual Racism and Institutional Racism

It is not new to argue, as have a number of scholars of race relations, that individual racial attitudes or behaviors must be analyzed in the context of organizational and societal parameters and frames of reference (Alvarez and Lutterman, 1979; Carmichael and Hamilton, 1976; Jones, 1970; Knowles and Prewitt, 1969; Schwartz and Disch, 1970; Omi and Winant,

1. Ten percent black enrollment by Fall, 1973;

2. Nine hundred new black students by Fall, 1971—450 freshmen, 250 transfers, 300 graduate students;

3. An adequate supportive services program including financial aid to finance black students' education;

4. Graduate and undergraduate recruiters (9) to recruit black students;

5. A referendum on the March Student Government Council ballot to have students vote on assessing themselves $3.00 for one year for the Martin Luther King Scholarship Fund;

6. Tuition waivers for minority group students who are also residents of the state of Michigan;

7. The establishment of a Community-located Black Student Center;

8. All work of a permanent nature on the Black Studies program is to be halted until an effective input is fully developed by a Community-University forum;

9. The creation of a University-wide appeal board to rule on the adequacy of financial aid grants to students;

10. A revamping of the Parent's Confidential Statement;

11. There should be one recruiter for Chicano students to assure 50 Chicano students by Fall, 1970;

12. Black students are to be referred to as Black and not as Negro or anything else

Figure 32-2 Summary of the Original BAM Demands (1970)[4]

1986; USCCR, 1981). Much like other forms of human behavior, racism would not persist as an individual attitude or behavior were there not organizational and societal norms teaching, supporting, and rewarding such activity.

The establishment and maintenance of racial difference, and the political, economic and cultural dominance of white people and groups, is part of the history of our nation. No serious student need be reminded by an examination of the history of colonization and its impact on Native Americans and Latinos, or by a re-reading of the Constitution and other founding documents of the Republic, of the ways in which support for white superiority and domination, slavery and a non-citizen class of people of color is part of our birthright as a nation. Nor do the facts of subsequent generations of white people's political and economic privilege and dominance, and the deprivation and oppression of people of color need retelling.

But it often is more difficult to see how this racially discriminatory history is sustained in the present, and how large-scale institutional structures currently operate to "pass on" and reinforce historic patterns of privilege and disadvantage and dominance. In Figure 32-3, Fea-

gin and Feagin emphasize the especially potent roles of Direct Institutionalized Discrimination and Indirect Institutionalized Discrimination in this process (1986, p. 28).

"Direct Institutionalized Discrimination refers to organizationally-prescribed or community-prescribed actions which have an intentionally differential and negative impact on members of subordinate groups . . . carried out . . . routinely by a large number of individuals guided by the rules of a large scale organization" (1986, p. 30). Examples include deliberate efforts to track (or counsel) minority students into certain colleges and universities and into certain career paths, or to exclude minority content from the curriculum or social life of an institution.

Of even greater subtlety, and therefore interest to those of us working within manifestly "liberal" and "non-discriminatory" organizations, is Indirect Institutionalized Discrimination. This category "refers to practices having a negative and differential impact on minorities and women even though the organizationally prescribed or community-prescribed norms or regulations guiding these actions were established, and are carried out, with no prejudice or no intent to harm laying immedi-

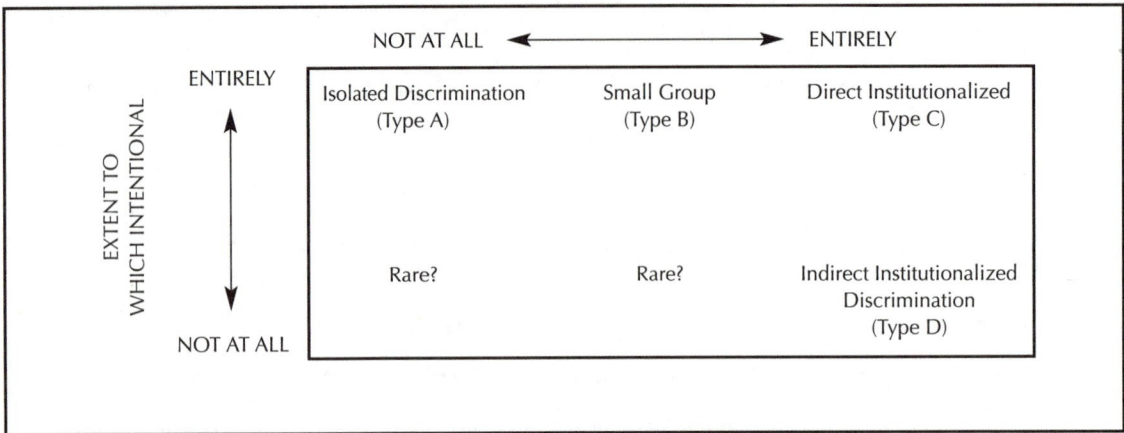

Figure 32-3. Types of Discriminatory Behavior
Extent of Imbeddedness in Larger Organizations

ately behind them. On their face and in their intent, the norms and resulting practices appear fair or at least neutral" (p. 31). It is important to emphasize the minimal role that conscious intent or personal prejudice plays in Indirect Institutionalized Discrimination, since many people (white people, especially, and certainly much of the white judiciary) continue to think of racism as involving conscious discriminatory purposes. The very point of institutional racism is that organizational procedures can have discriminatory impact even if individual actors are unaware of such impacts or are non-discriminatory in their personal beliefs, and even if their behavior appears to be a fair-minded application of "race-neutral" or "colorblind" rules and norms. Examples of such subtle racism in organizational operations include denying minority scholars access to faculty positions because of their lack of "appropriate" or traditional credentials (which credentials were denied them because of prior discrimination), or because they lack some attributes of white males that are assumed to be relevant for certain positions but which, on examination, may not be. It also would include acts of omission, such as the failure to vigorously recruit minority students/scholars, the failure to generate hiring criteria more appropriate to the pool of minority scholars, or the failure to confront racism when it occurs; such failures subtly reinforce the continuation of discrimination. Given our legacy of racial oppression and disadvantage, apparently fair and racially neutral or color-blind policies and practices continue to have discriminatory impact. In order to overcome racism, self-conscious anti-discriminatory actions are required; and they in turn will require changes in current organizational structures and processes.

III. Organizational Factors Promoting Institutional Racism In Universities

Understanding institutional racism in universities requires attention to the general nature of these organizations and their operations. Moreover, a thorough and coherent diagnosis should not only identify the institutional nature of racism in these organizations, but should also point the way for change. Drawing from a framework first generated by Terry (1981), we suggest that five elements of all organizations' operations influence universities' policies and practices, including those that affect members of different racial groups. These elements are: mission, culture (not identified as a separate element by Terry), power, structure and resources. This certainly is not the only model or typology of complex organizations that could direct diagnostic and change planning. Tichy reviews a series of useful examples on the way to creating his own emphasis on the technical, political and cultural sub-systems in complex organizations (1983, especially Chapter 2). Baldridge and Deal's analysis of change processes in higher educational institutions uses a taxonomy which has several points of overlap with

Terry's (1975, taken from Udy): it includes goals, environment, technology, formal structure and group-individual factors. Our preference for Terry's model (with modifications) is based on its heuristic value in noting specific elements which could be the basis of local college/university or unit diagnoses and change efforts. The model, and specific elements of the five-part taxonomy, is presented in Figure 32-4.

Mission refers to the official and unofficial vision and purposes of the organization, as these purposes or goals are reflected both in written policy statements and informal under-

standings and priorities. The emphasis on strategic planning, with regard to market concerns, program development and human resource management, generally flows from or creates clarification of an organization's mission, as it may be challenged by current circumstances and future options. Moreover, most organizations have several different submissions, and the complementarity or balance among them becomes quite critical, as in the ways in which different universities seek to satisfy the tri-partite commitment to research, teaching, and public service. Mission may

---

MISSION
Statement of goals and purposes
Vision of the future
Source of legitimacy for status quo or for change
Relates organizational goals to broader society's goals
Includes multiple or conflicting goals or subunits
Relatively not open to debate
Official (manifest) or unofficial (latent) purposes

CULTURE
Dominant belief systems reflected in values, rituals, technology, styles and customs
Norms for "proper" behavior and criteria for success
Degree of monoculturalism or pluralism of the approved culture
Standard for the allocation of rewards and sanctions
Includes alternative (complementary or conflicting) cultures based on age, gender, race, class, etc.
May include procedures for negotiating dominant and alternative cultures
"Rules of the game"
Belief system justifying basic organizational tasks and procedures

POWER
Formal decision-making hierarchies and procedures
Degree to which access to power hierarchy is closed or open
Degree to which power hierarchy is open to people of different race, gender, class, internal status, age, etc.
Constituencies that influence power-holders
Degree of grass roots participation in key decisions
Procedures for dealing with alternative power bases, formal (unions) and informal
Decentralized unit control

STRUCTURE
Division of labor among units and subunits, and related roles
Technology for achieving organizational goals (pedagogy)
Networks of social interaction and communication
Planned activities that help accomplish basic tasks
Boundary systems mediating organization's relationship with the external social and physical world
Procedures used to achieve goals

RESOURCES
Materials required to accomplish organization's goals
People
Money
Plant and facilities
Raw materials and markets
Information

Figure 32-4 Universal Organizational Elements

become a focus of conflict when vigorous debates center on the relative priorities of these three standards for excellence, or when public and private universities differentially commit themselves to research productivity, undergraduate education or public service as priorities. Gross (1968) indicates how faculty members and administrators in different institutions may differentially rank goals such as training young scholars and researchers, maintaining university prestige or doing applied research, depending on the public or private status of their college/university. In addition, internal conflict may occur when different university units (e.g., Engineering, Social Work and Liberal Arts) espoused different goals, or when various constituencies (e.g., students, faculty, administrators) rank goals very differently. Mission-centered conflict also can result from divergent public pressures, as when white and Black or Latino people (or other people of color) and their political representatives seek different racial compositions for the student body, faculty and administration of the university, or promote different instructional, service and research programs.

All organizations also develop a culture that permeates institutional functioning (Deal and Kennedy, 1982; Peters and Waterman, 1982; Van Maanen and Barley, 1984). The organizational culture consists of those core values which are reflected in the common understandings, assumptions or preferences regarding how people are expected to behave in the organization—from dress to deportment, whether competitively or cooperatively, whether caringly or sneeringly (Tichy, 1983). These preferences may, of course, differ at different status levels and for different task assignments within the organization. College and university cultures help define the unique styles of different educational institutions, as Clark points out in his research with small innovative, liberal arts colleges (Clark, 1970). Organizational cultures are deeply rooted in the history of each college or university, and serve to give special meaning to life at a particular institution (Dill, 1982; Masland, 1985). As many other organizations, a large university generally exists with several different sub-cultures simultaneously operative and potentially in conflict: at least a dominant culture and a counter-culture, in which the latter often serves as "a safe haven for the

development of innovative ideas (Martin and Siehl, 1983, p. 52)"; a faculty culture and a student culture; a scientific culture and a humanities culture; an academic culture and an athletic culture, etc.

The power element in an organization is manifest in its decision-making structures and processes. The typical hierarchial and centralized organization concentrates formal power at the top, in the hands of a relatively small number of persons—usually white men. Other actors in the system also exercise formal power, generally as the agents of senior stakeholders. Just how much latitude middle level managers and administrators have, as well as whether their power is formal or informal, is a clue to the level of participatory or decentralized decision-making in the system. Regardless of how tightly controlled the organizational power system is, lower level employees (front-line services providers) always have some discretionary power, and can implement or not implement higher level decisions, can engage in compliance or sabotage, etc. (March and Simon, 1958). In the modern university, administrative power typically is located in central offices ruled by a white patriarchy of Presidents and Vice-Presidents, but these decision-makers often are dependent upon Collegiate Deans or Department Heads for the implementation of new policies and procedures. Faculty members have minimal opportunity for decisional input in university policies, and only are able to exert formal institutional influence at the sub-unit level. Their decisional roles generally are limited to the curriculum and their own research programs. Especially in the classroom, however, they have unilateral and often exclusive power to decide what to teach, and how to do it. Students, the nominal clients of the institution, have little power to affect major decisions. So, too, are lower level staff members (some of whom have very significant impact on students) generally excluded from decisions.

Organizational structure refers to those procedures, technologies and activities that define the ways in which the organization acts to meet its goals. The definition of the functions and roles of specific units, through which decisions are implemented, constitute the core of organizational structures. The social network of units and subunits, and their lines of communication and social interaction, represent the threads by which various units and activities are integrated. Reflecting the power system, university structures often are highly decentralized, and multiple activities organize the life of faculty, students, and staff members. The dominant instructional pedagogy, an activity explicitly focused on realizing the organization's educational goals, typically involves high faculty autonomy and one-way transmission of knowledge to students in isolated classrooms.

Resources are those goods, people and funds (capital) that constitute the raw materials that organizations transform into finished products or services. The degree to which an organization is a material-processing or people-processing system helps determine just what resources are crucial to its activities (Katz & Kahn, 1978). For universities, people (students, faculty and staffs), and funds (private and public), are among the most crucial tangible resources, with the development and renewal of plant and equipment also occupying a lot of administrative energy.

Most organizational theorists and researchers would agree that these five elements are basic to all organizations, although many would use different labels and names (Baldridge and Deal, 1975; Katz and Kahn, 1978). Scholars disagree, however, on which of these elements is most likely to be dominant; i.e., which most influences the others. As a theologian and social ethicist, Terry himself emphasizes the primacy of mission and culture (1981); the structural-functional school of social thought emphasizes the role of structure and culture; and power elite theorists emphasize the vital driving force of power in organizations. In addition, some observers would argue that the university primarily reflects the organization of wealth and power in the society at large, and that an elite capitalist structure lies at the root of contemporary and historic patterns of institutional racism. While we are quite sympathetic to the latter point of view, and to the powerful role of external influences, in this paper we elect to focus attention on the internal organizational system of the university and/or college.

These five elements can be examined separately, but they are interdependent with and generally reinforce one another. In terms of our specific concerns, they fit together to create what Katz has called a "web" of organizational discrimination (1978, p. 75). Thus, for instance, the mission of a university influences its culture and vice versa. Moreover, if the resource base changes dramatically the mission might change (as in the search for a "smaller but better" university in the wake of fiscal crises of the early 1980s), and then the structure itself might follow suit. If the culture promotes inadequate respect for or unfair treatment of people of color, it is unlikely that the mission will articulate (explicitly) a concern for racial justice. If the mission and culture do not express a concern for reducing racial injustice or ignorance, it is unlikely that resources will be allocated to such an agenda on any other than a temporary and crash basis. Without specifically allocated resources, structures and power systems are not likely to operate in ways that pursue anti-racist goals and practices.

At the same time that this set of interdependent elements operates in an integrated fashion, there is also constant internal contradiction and conflict in diverse, complex organizations. Multiple missions and cultures exist, and subsidiary ones constantly struggle overtly or covertly with the dominant tradition. For instance, universities seek to pass on the history and traditions of their society as well as to prepare students to make new history and create or at least adapt a new social order. The culture of the young student and the culture of the middle-aged professional strive to co-exist. Although formal power structures represent and extend the prevailing culture, the organization is populated with myriad informal influence arrangements. Interest groups of all kinds curry favor and wheedle special deals that depart from and may even sabotage the decisions and policies of the formal system.

Such contradictions and conflicts in the organization's dominant patterns of operation are essential points of access and opportunity for people committed to change, for here is where the greatest potential for innovation and reform lies. Thus, as we discuss the pervasive and powerful character of institutional racism in universities, we constantly seek to identify the sources of contradiction and deviance from this dominant pattern. These inconsistencies, whether or not they are manifest in overt conflict, present us with the hope, the opportunity and perhaps the resources (including conflict) for change.

In Terry's own language, racism is evident when a group intentionally or unintentionally (1981, p. 124):

> perpetuates an unclear and/or dehumanizing mission (M)
> refuses to share power (P)
> denies appropriate support and challenge, and maintains inflexible and unresponsive structures(S)
> inequitably distributes resources to another racial/ethnic group for either group's supposed benefit (R)
> rationalizes (any of) the(se) process(es) by blaming or ignoring the other group.

To which we add:

> promulgates a monocultural or exclusionary set of values/styles (C)

With this overview in mind, we now discuss the operations of and evidence for institutional racism within each of these organizational elements of organization of colleges and universities. Figure 32-5 provides examples of institutional racism present within each element.

Mission

The mission statements of colleges and universities are expressions of the vision of why the organization exists and what it seeks to achieve. They are likely to be highly abstract and sometimes vague statements of generally agreed upon principles and goals. Most statements of mission advocate transmitting Western cultural traditions, advancing knowledge, providing an education to the young, and per-

---

MISSION
    Lack of explicit attention to justice and racial equity as a goal
    Lack of recognition of plural goals
    Commitment to the status quo . . . of the society and the institution
    Creators are limited to whites

CULTURE
    Monocultural norms for success are promulgated
    No explicit rewards for anti-racist behavior of the faculty, staff
    Diversity and excellence are seen as competitive/contradictory/played off
    Alternative cultures are not explicitly recognized or promoted
    Stance toward "racial incidents" is reactive
    Rituals and technology reflect white and Eurocentric dominance/exclusivity (graduation ceremonies, athletic mascots, pedagogy, etc.

POWER
    Power holders in senior positions are overwhelmingly white
    Informal access to the power hierarchy is limited to the "white male club"
    Constituencies of people of color have no formal access to power holders
    Protests by students of color are seen as trivial and disruptive and are dealt with via short term resolutions
    Sub units are not required to deal with racism proactively

STRUCTURE
    Opportunities do not exist for (re)training the white faculty to deal with students of color
    Social networks of the faculty generally exclude people of color
    Traditional pedagogies for classroom instruction are unaltered
    Social relations among students of different races are not seen as a university-wide concern. If they are so seen, they are seen as a curriculum concern
    Curriculum does not explicitly address issues of racism
    No coherent policy of response to racial harassment exists
    An Office of Minority Affairs exists but is not a central part of the university structure

RESOURCES
    Funds generally not available to support new anti-racist practices
    Community and physical settings usually include pervasive racism
    Active recruitment of students and faculty of color does not exist
    Post-recruitment support for students and faculty of color is minimal

Figure 32-5 Institutional Racism in Higher Education Organizations

forming public service. In general, they speak more to the conservation of tradition than to the creation of change.

The emphasis on preserving and passing on the traditions of Western (Eurocentric and Anglo-Christian) civilization reflects higher education's origins in service by and for privileged white males. Although recent history has extended college to more people of color and to women, little systematic attention in general education requirements is given to Asian, African and Southern American civilizations, although some concern for international and global problems may be expressed. Likewise, Hispanic, Black and Native American civilizations and traditions seldom are mentioned specifically as vital elements of the U.S.'s cultural tradition.

Mission statements rarely are debated or discussed vigorously, except in times of major change, major reallocations of external resource bases, dramatic alterations in relations with state or federal governments, or presidential transitions. Yet, daily matters of what and how knowledge and wisdom is sought (e.g., which cultural traditions and epistemologies), who is to be educated (which regional, racial, gender and socioeconomic groups), what public services are to be performed (e.g., for which interest groups or stakeholders) and what leadership should be committed to doing (e.g., what characteristics and commitments they should reflect), are precisely the cornerstone issues and conflictual choices that underlie a university's mission. For the most part these crucial issues are dealt with by default, typically via omission rather than specific commission, and thus the stage is set for the promotion and continuation of established traditions, including racism promulgated in the larger society of which the university is a part.

Jackson and Holvino (1988) emphasize the importance of establishing a clear mission or a concrete vision for the direction of change in institutions, especially when the changes involve matters as complex as anti-racism or multiculturalism. They also provide several competing images and definitions of organizations that are monocultural (committed to enhancing the dominance, privilege and access to those in power who are white and male, etc.), non-discriminating (committed to bringing people of different cultures together without changing the way things operate) and multicultural (committed to diverse and equitable distributions of power and influence that actively support the elimination of oppression).

Although some institutions of higher education include in their mission statements a deliberate and conscious policy to fight injustice, a commitment to go beyond non-discrimination to a multicultural, anti-discrimination or pro-social justice stance is rare in other than a few religious, private and small colleges. In large universities, this oversight may create conflict with subunits that do explicitly state an emphasis on service to traditionally oppressed or excluded constituencies (most notably Schools of Social Work, Education, Public Health or Community Service). The inclusion of a deliberate and articulate commitment to reduce institutional racism appears to be a high risk act for a contemporary public and secular university. It often appears to be a partisan agenda, anathema to the university's desire for a non-controversial stance and the maintenance of an illusion of value-free research and learning. It often appears as a change-oriented agenda, anathema to an institution devoted to conserving and transmitting the cultural and intellectual heritage of a nation. And it often appears to be an ideological agenda, anathema to an institution committed to transmitting information and factual knowledge in a "non-ideological" way (yet within the prevailing societal value system and organizational culture).

Culture

The culture of contemporary colleges and universities reflects, for the most part, the core values of the society/community with which they operate. Indeed, one basic mission of a university, at the apex of an extensive system of public and semi-public education, is to prepare the young for (at least partial) acceptance of and participation in the dominant culture—with individual freedom, democratic governance, etc. The socialization of the young into conformity with adult values does not occur without conflict, however, and the intergenerational tensions that mark the university reflect both the cultural distance between these age groups as well as their differential access to organizational power and autonomy.

Generally the ruling values and modes of operation in the university are those of white,

Western and Eurocentric civilization. They are not necessarily seen as such; people who are not aware of the existence and shape of white culture may see these as universal moral principles or behavioral norms. Nonetheless, as Katz points out (1988, p. 10):

> The white culture that exists is the synthesis of ideas, values and beliefs coalesced from descendents of white European ethnic groups in the United States. White culture is the dominant cultural norm in the United States and acts as the foundation of our institutions. The truth is that the white cultural system is one system and yet many people believe it is the only system.

A particular (positivist) version of the scientific method has also come to dominate university life and the scientific curriculum—physical, biological and social. In the search for the authority and expertise of universal principles grounded in empirically established facts, whole systems and their elements are subjected to positivist and reductionist methods, whereby phenomena are taken apart into their constituent elements and then reconstructed. Distance and detachment is maintained between the knower and the (to be) known. Emotion or intuition and preference (now seen as bias), rather than being seen as potentially rich and productive forces in human inquiry, generally are shunned and depreciated (Keller, 1985). They ultimately are seen as biases or vices to be controlled, perhaps only of central importance to the arts.

The social organization of science, based upon this rationalist and formal culture and its associated procedures, carries innumerable conflicts and tensions as well. Individual scientific knowledge-seekers compete with one another to test, confirm and/or disconfirm one another's theories. They typically work in isolation or in small cadres, with substantial conflict among competing departments, universities or schools of thought. Hierarchies of seniority and prestige, themselves often a focus of conflict, dominate the professions, the scientific disciplines and the university. As Ernst Benjamin, general secretary of the AAUP, argues (1989, p. 64):

> Our participation in institutional policies fostering individual entrepreneurship rather than collective responsibility has

contributed to lower median salaries as well as to the uncertainty inherent in academic careers. Our pursuit of institutional prestige has fostered a campus climate that subordinates teaching, mentoring, collegial responsibility and mutual tolerance to the disciplinary market and institutional status.

When such disciplinary prestige is taken as primary evidence of merit, scholars outside of one another's specialized tradition may no longer understand (or care) what others are doing, and no one may care for the life of the local institution or community.

As these modes of inquiry and social relations dominate the culture of the university, they accompany the instructor into the college classroom. Zorn argues that the culture of the university is passed on by faculty members as they act on and interact with students in the classroom (1986, p. 8):

> . . . most of what students learn about the faculty's values comes from observing the examples set by individual faculty functioning in the teacher/scholar role. The structure of courses and curricula, the use of language, the priorities on use of time and the mode of student-faculty interaction all convey faculty values in an implicit and sustained way that can be understood by every student.

The culture of the lone and specialized expert and the moral commitment to maintain adult control of the young, is transferred into the authority of the teacher as the font of wisdom in and out of class. This wisdom is transmitted to students, or "banked" into them in the language of Friere (1970). Seldom are students seen as reliable resources for co-instruction of their peers and the instructor, let alone as having expertise or wisdom based upon their own life experiences. The teacher as dispassionate expert, with specialized and empirically verified information, is center stage and the primary focus of attention and control in the classroom. Moreover, the organization's support for the cultural values of academic freedom and freedom of speech are generally interpreted as meaning that faculty members can do and say almost anything in the classroom. These same principles often are invoked to resist evaluation, or even comment upon, instructors' choices of classroom substance or procedure.

Students and faculty members of different races, with different cultural values and styles, often make new and different demands on this traditional system and culture. As Kochman (1981) points out, most Black people and members of white ethnic groups are embedded in different cultures than are most white-anglos. As such, these groups often have different ways of talking, relating, fighting, learning—and undoubtedly teaching and administering as well. Although anyone discussing such differences must be cautious about overgeneralizations and stereotypes, substantial additional evidence suggests that white people (students and faculty) and people of color perceive and experience university environments quite differently. For instance, in the Stanford University self-study, most of the white faculty agreed that the University administration was "genuinely committed (to) promoting multiracial understanding and cooperation," but only a minority of the Black and Asian and Hispanic faculty agreed with this statement (Stanford University Committee on Minority Issues, 1989, p. 24). There is a long history of social scientific studies, from many different public and institutional arenas, indicating that whites and people of color often disagree on whether people of different races are being treated equally, whether policy-makers or administrators are acting fairly with regard to racial issues, and whether the nation (or community or organization, etc.) is making progress on eliminating or reducing racism (see, for example, Alderfer et al., 1980; Campbell and Schuman, 1968; Schuman et al., 1985).

Since most contemporary universities are enmeshed in the white-anglo culture, the entrance of substantial numbers of people of color (or of lower class origins) inevitably escalates perceptual contrasts and cultural conflict, and creates extraordinary pressures on these newer populations. These added pressures and realities in the lives of people of color (such as racial and cultural differences and experiences of racism) typically are seen as extra-classroom or extra-professional issues, and typically go unrecognized and unchecked in the classroom. At best, they are seen as matters appropriately dealt with by "student services" units, and not germane to the disciplinary or classroom agenda. Whereas alternative pedagogies and epistemologies might allow room for the expression and satisfaction of different styles of learning and relating (to knowledge and to one another), the maintenance of traditional cultures and classroom procedures creates deviance out of non-normative preferences, inadequacy out of different adequacies, and continues to disadvantage students and colleagues with different cultural styles and preferences.

Several scholars have indicated how difficult it is for students of color to negotiate the alien and often hostile culture of predominantly white colleges and universities. Allen argues, for instance, that in addition to the individual background and talent characteristics of Black students, their collegiate outcomes are influenced strongly by the organizational environment, by (1988, p. 412):

> ... situational and interpersonal characteristics: the quality of life at the institution, the level of academic competition, university rules/procedures/resources, relationships with faculty, and friend support networks.

These aspects of the organizational culture also are reported as crucial to the success of Hispanic students. Fiske (1988) emphasizes the problems encountered by Hispanic students who have to find their way "in institutions built around an alien (Anglo) culture (p. 29)," and Richardson et al. (1987) note that successful programs for minority students "rely on the student culture to establish an environment conducive to involvement and achievement (p. 23)."

In some institutions Ethnic and Gender Studies' Departments have begun to challenge the dominant culture of the (white and male) scientific establishment, to suggest the need for alternative research espistemologies and methodologies, and alternative classroom pedagogies. To the extent such Programs or Departments accept the dominant culture, but serve special interest groups, they can be maintained on the fringe of the established system. But if and when they challenge the assumptions underlying the dominant tradition they potentially create change, and thereby encounter conflict. Then they typically are characterized as ideological rather than scholarly in character, and as social service centers for (marginal) faculty of color, rather than as meaningful loci for intellectual discourse. Debates about the intellectual viability and vitality of these Programs often reflect underlying assumptions of the superiority of white (and male) cultures and norms for scholarly pursuits. For instance, the argument that women/feminist and Black or Hispanic scholars might engage in a legitimately different kind of science by virtue of their gender and racial experiences, per se, and that these alternatives might contribute positively to the broader body of scientific methods and knowledge, is generally dismissed. Epps (1989) argues that the dominant culture of the university determines what the faculty will support as appropriate intellectual (research and teaching) priorities. As a result, "the minority scholar is constrained by the culture of the major research university to select research paradigms, research topics and publication outlets that conform to the traditionals of institutions that have historically excluded minorities (1989, p. 24)." Thus, he notes, "African-American, Hispanic and Native-American students and faculty encounter a culture that rejects them as legitimate participants in the life of the academy (p. 25)."

The dominance of a monocultural orientation in colleges and universities thus encourages unidimensional standards of evaluation. Students and faculty are sorted by these limited, and often quite skewed, expectations. Departments and programs, as well as students and faculty, are ranked, like baseball teams and their players. The "star system" seldom questions the definition of star qualities, and unidimensional criteria for academic excellence are raised to a level of abstraction that is seen as transcending considerations of race or gender. Thus, race and gender diversity can be ignored or discounted as having no relevance to defining or achieving excellence. They may be seen as necessary parts of a diverse environment, but not as necessary for the enrichment or modification of monocultural settings and standards. People who do not do well by the star metric are labelled as inferior— not as different or as valued—and generally they are perceived as being responsible for their own mediocre or otherwise flawed and deviant status and performance to boot.

The reward metric, focused predominantly on research, and research as it is determined and evaluated by a specific (usually white and male) peer group, seldom identifies combating racism as an essential area of performance for the faculty or administration in higher education. To the contrary, serious efforts to reduce racism require new forms of research and service in the university and in the community, in K-12 education, in student services, in campus and community housing and law enforcement, etc. If service as an arena of activity is little valued it is unlikely that anti-racist service activities that extend work beyond the boundary of the university will occur, even in publicly supported systems (Checkoway, 1989). Moreover, combating racism in the classroom requires substantial new designs for teaching and learning. If teaching and service are of minor importance compared to research activity, it is quite unlikely that this challenge can be met in the system "as is."

All too often, efforts to achieve racial diversity are seen as undermining the cultural commitment to academic excellence. At the University of Michigan, for instance, over the course of two years, various Presidents first articulated the need for "Excellence," then for "Achieving Diversity without Compromising Excellence," then for "Balancing Excellence with Diversity," then for "Diversity as part of Excellence," and finally for "Diversity as a Necessary Component of Excellence." At each step of the way, of course, there was conflict and pressure to maintain the status quo (in language and in practice).

In a recent welcoming address to students in Yale University's Graduate and Professional Schools, Dean Rosenberg suggested that the prevailing culture of many universities could be challenged by an increased public and private "commitment to decency and civility for minorities (1988, p. 47)." He illustrated this alternative cultural commitment with a code of conduct that students and faculty had prepared for Yale's School of Medicine (ibid.):

> Teaching, learning, research, and the delivery of medical care are best carried out in an atmosphere of civil relationships. Such relationships are possible only where there is mutual respect, decency, and sensitivity one to another—students, faculty, staff, and patients. Overt racism is not only morally wrong. It interferes with the quality of care received by patients, is debilitating to the victims, and compromises the integrity and stature of the offender. Less obvious forms

of racism such as disparaging comments, inappropriate labels, or subtle innuendoes which unfairly classify or criticize others on the basis of race are equally unacceptable. Wherever and whenever racist or insensitive remarks are heard or inappropriate actions witnessed, it should be the duty of every one of us to protest and to inform the offender about the reasons for our disapproval. Furthermore, it is our responsibility to help those who have been wronged to obtain satisfactory redress.

Such affirmations of positive and proactive anti-racist behaviors are rare, and more often applauded in rhetoric than followed in practice. They do, however, provide us with alternative visions of our options.

The culture of the university usually is not perceived or analyzed clearly, and it operates as part of the "givens" or general and unquestioned assumptions by which we go about our daily business. Only when open challenges are made, or when different cultures come into contact with one another, do we readily identify and critically evaluate the domains of the dominant culture. This is but one more reason it is so difficult to diagnose, as well as to alter, the monocultural basis of institutional racism in universities.

Power

The public trust of public and private universities generally is established and protected by appointed or elected boards of trustees made up of individuals from outside the academic organization. In practice, these trustees represent only a part of the general public, that part that is most white, most male and most upper middle class in origin and orientation (Ridgeway, 1968). Quite naturally, they establish policies and govern in ways that reflect the prevailing values and perspectives of these dominant constituencies. As in the political and economic spheres of the society in general, the dominant perspectives of these trustees, and the constituencies they represent, generally do not include the quest to increase racial justice as a high priority.

Where people in authority are predominantly white and male, and where authority is silent on the unfairness of this pattern and does not include explicit and concerted means

of changing it, racism and sexism are present and maintained. Established authorities in higher education claim to be operating in the interest of everyone in the college and university. Again and again, however, faculty, students and staff of color assert that their needs are not met and that they are not treated as favorably as are their white counterparts. Individual and institutional racism prevents authorities from fully perceiving and meeting the needs of people of color who are part of the organization.

Without representation in centers of institutional power and authority, and often having different needs and cultural styles, students of color often are alienated and regularly experience discrimination. In an extraordinarily honest self-study, MIT reports minority students' perspectives on the collegiate environment as follows (McBay, 1986, p. 5):

Feelings of isolation;
Insecurity about their admission because of the perception that others at the Institute believe lower standards are used when admitting minority students;
Belief that others consider all minority students as high risks;
Anxiety about their families' ability to provide the financial assistance expected by the Institute;
Perceived contempt from non-minority students, faculty, administrators, and staff;
Feelings of non-acceptance by faculty; and
The existence of a generally non-supportive environment in which minorities must constantly prove they are equal, both intellectually and socially.

The message of isolation and rejection is obvious.

Institutional racism also helps authorities rationalize why they are not meeting the needs students or faculty members of color. It typically is asserted that their special needs are inappropriate, their problems a result of their own inadequacies, their demands a call for unfair favoritism, etc. Without access to institutional power, people who are mistreated seldom can gain attention to their concerns, let alone redress. One stunning example of the kinds of demeaning and discriminatory treatment experienced by Black scholars is provided in reports of Harvard University Law Professor and constitutional scholar Derrick Bell's encounter with the Stanford Law School. While he was a visiting lecturer at Stanford in 1986, "white students and professors, dissatisfied with his performance as a teacher, surreptitiously created a series of lectures to supplement his course on constitutional law (Kennedy, 1989, p. 1767; Bell, 1986)." The Dean and faculty of the Stanford Law School have long since formally apologized to Bell, but that this should occur (both the level of expressed dissatisfaction and the collusion of white faculty and students in creating a covert substitute) to such a prominent Black scholar, only emphasizes the regularity with which other faculty of color must also encounter subtle and not so subtle forms of disdain and disregard.

From chief executives to faculty, students and staff members at all levels, the organizational power arrangements of universities are subject to hierarchical administrative control. As a result, Birnbaum (1988) argues, it is crucial for university presidents to go out of their way to demonstrate their commitment to a social justice and anti-racist agenda if it is to be acted on by administrative staff and faculty. Generally, he notes, presidents act vigorously only when things go wrong; it is important to counter this trend by engaging in proactive and preventive leadership. This same theme is echoed in a report from the University of California system (Justus et al., 1987). Regardless of the style (management or leadership) of the President and senior administrators (1987, p. 59):

> Available research on effective faculty affirmative action, however, does stress the importance of leadership at all levels within the university—from the chief executives to deans to department chairs... Significantly, at the most successful institutions we were told that CEOs, whether called Chancellors or Presidents, do make a difference; that the commitment of an institution can be measured by the relative weight the chief executive places on affirmative action success, and his/her ability to translate commitment into action.

Commitment, in this arena, includes the visible exercise of both formal authority and responsibility and informal power and influence.

The senior administration of a college or university, and its key deans, set the tone and context for dealing with racism and race relations on campus. Whether they do so actively or passively, overtly or covertly, by example of courageous acts or of acts of omission and ignorance, they set the stage. Administrative pronouncements and actions (especially actions, because policies are often not believed unless followed by explicit actions) can help create climates of fear or of hope, of concern or of disregard, of open discussion or of secretive conversation, of positive change or of negative retreat. They create the context and the conditions within which faculty, staff and students must deal with one another and, unfortunately, often play out their concerns and antagonisms upon one another.

The authority that Presidents and Vice-Presidents have can be exercised in a variety of forms, but it often is implemented most effectively and practically via a series of budgetary and financial policies, supplemented by centrally controlled personnel policies. Although these policies and practices can have major impact on subunit programs and priorities, they also have their limits—especially in our most elite research universities. Efforts to alter the prevailing power structure of the university, such as required in challenges to racism, can be resisted readily by the decentralized academic control of specialized units (Schools and Departments). Principles of unit autonomy and academic freedom permit each major unit of a university to retain decision making control over its own curricula, personnel and financial policies; thus they can resist innovations generated by the central administration on "a legitimate 'non-racist' basis (Exum, 1983, p. 390)." This delicate balance of centralized and decentralized power makes it very difficult for centrally mandated programs of change to be effective or for institution-wide changes to be implemented. At the same time, of course, it invests considerable room for innovation in local units, should they take the lead in generating programs to reduce racial injustice.

It is especially difficult to mobilize a broad consensus on reducing racism in predominantly white and monocultural systems of higher education where narrowly specialized areas of expertise and departmental loyalties are the basis of individual legitimacy and influence. Thus, we seldom see progressive initiatives developing from the white faculty at large or from faculty-led units of the system. When all the responsibility for initiating and implementing anti-racism programs remains with the central administration, the problems of unit and faculty resistance loom large.

In most large universities, the faculty as a group has little power to affect institutional priorities directly. Their role generally is limited to advice and debate on administrative decisions, and to passive (and covert) resistance to dicta with which they disagree individually or collectively. Traditions of collaborative decision-making, or multi-level involvement in participatory decision-making, are not readily represented in systems of higher education. This tradition constantly places the power of the faculty in an institutionally reactive mode. Just as the culture of the university supports the exercise of authoritative (and often authoritarian) power in the classroom, it reproduces that style in administrative-faculty relations at the departmental and central unit level.

Students, a subordinate group in the power structure of higher educational systems, typically are perceived by faculty and administrators as marginal and temporary members of the community. The experience of marginality, in turn, often gives students an impetus and opportunity (even a freedom) to organize and exert influence through extraordinary and even illegitimate channels. Students of color are doubly marginalized and disempowered, both on grounds of their racial as well as student status. As a result, their only path to the expression of their unique needs and desires for change may be through public protest, disruption and demonstration. The history of minority protest and challenge to racism throughout our society lends support and legitimacy to this tradition in the exercise of power in institutions of higher education (a large body of literature on student protest movements, and on oppressed social movements generally, supports this view).

Indeed, in the aftermath of the current spate of "racial incidents" occuring across campuses, it is the students of color who have taken the lead in demanding institutional change. More than faculties of color, more than white staff members or faculty or administrators, students of color have correctly noted that such incidents of harassment are not incidental or unique, that they represent the overt manifestations of deeply entrenched cultural and structural racism within our institutions. When their concerns and demands have gone unheeded and unmet, as so often has been the case when white faculty and administrators have been "caught by surprise" or have resisted change, these students have generated the initial thrust for change. The power of these students of color, stemming from their historic experience and contemporary need, has been the major energizer of change in racism in many universities.

In turn, many university faculty and administrations have been prone to see these expressions of student and minority power as illegitimate and ill-conceived, possibly dangerous to the welfare of the university as well as to their sense of students' more appropriate priority on classroom learning. Since the culture of the university promotes a view of itself as a non-partisan, objective and non-political system, it (administrators and faculty and students in the dominant cultural group) normally is shocked and outraged at a moral level by political protest of any sort, and especially from students—the most temporary and non-expert members of the system. When the students are people of color the emotional reaction often is even stronger.

Structure

The organizational structures of most colleges and universities create a large number of decentralized units defined by particular academic specializations. These specialized units, and the behavior of faculty members associated with them, are heavily influenced by external forces, especially their national scientific and/or professional societies. To the extent that prestige and merit are based upon evaluation standards rooted in these disciplinary and professional associations, faculty members are more likely to invest in these "cosmopolitan" reference groups than in "provincial" arenas within the local university. The trend for the most prestigious faculty to invest externally heightens the degree to which local units and departments become "feudal estates"; they often are seen as the concern only of those faculty who have been "left behind," and as such faculty influence is once more trivialized. This dynamic also reduces faculty commitment to their unit, particularly as it involves changes requiring greater time and energy for "local" or "provincial" pursuits.

However, these semi-autonomous local units, buttressed by concerns for faculty autonomy and academic freedom, remain the arena for most of the faculty's exercise of decisional authority. Some prestigious senior faculty always have private access to key decision-makers, and their "invisible influence" can be very effective. To alter racism in the curriculum, research programs and teaching pedagogies of local units generally requires challenges not only to the intellectual bases of the professions and disciplines, but also to the senior and influential faculty in these units.

To the extent that the structure and technology of instruction (pedagogy) relies on teacher dominance and student obedience, lone teacher and massed students, teacher expertise and student ignorance, it establishes a structure of social relations between the faculty and students that is pernicious and destructive of mutual respect and maximum learning opportunities. This sort of limited pedagogy is systematically insensitive to many students' needs: it falls especially hard on students of color. Authoritarian control of the classroom is most destructive to students with the least power to resist such dominance; cultural insensitivity in the classroom is most destructive to students whose cultures are most divergent from the mainstream; difficulty in gaining personal contact with the faculty is most disadvantageous to students with a minimal history of positive contact with white faculty; and so on. Any form of oppression and insensitivity falls hardest on the most vulnerable members of the system; thus the "normal" workings of the institutional structure of the classroom and the university organization most severely disadvantage students of color.

Crenshaw (1989) details several ways in which white faculty (Law School faculty, in her experience and examples, but we think the implications are nearly universal) may place students of color in a "difficult situation." She argues that problems of objectification, subjectification and alienation of minority students occur when white faculty fail to understand that what they consider to be "objective or neutral is often the embodiment of a white middle-class world view (p. 3)." Crenshaw labels this

unawareness (or disregard) of the race or class basis of one's approach to the world or to academic subject matter "perspectivelessness." Objectification occurs when discussions are framed as simple exercises in the application of general rules, and when students are required to keep their comments within that system of rules. Since most legal, social and academic rules predominately reflect white persons' consciousness and rule-making power, and often are unfair to people of color, such exercises often require a student to "abstract herself from her identity as African-American" (ibid, p. 5) and to deny or ignore much of her own experience in the world. Subjectification occurs when students of color "are unexpectedly dragged into the classroom by an instructor to illustrate a point or to provide a basis for a command performance of 'show and tell' (ibid, p. 6)." Such "testifying" not only focusses substantial (and often undesired) attention on the student, and implies that any student of color can be an expert on her culture, it also suggest limits to other areas of probable expertise attributable to that student. Alienation occurs when "discussions focus on problems, interests and values that either minorities do not share or that obscure or overlook issues that are particularly relevant to minorities (ibid, p. 9)." Certainly not every student will be "touched" by every topic in the collegiate curriculum, but when problems of taxation, savings, family life, natural resources depletion, psychotherapy, congressional decision-making, illness, etc., are discussed in apparently race-neutral or race-irrelevant ways, they subtly suggest that white and middle-class ways of experiencing and coping with these issues are the only experiences and perspectives that are relevant.

Partly as a result of prior discrimination in educational organizations, and partly as a result of the attitudes and behaviors of the white professoriat, students of color are generally expected to know less and perform less well than their white counterparts. People of color in a class of mostly whites often are less frequently called on to offer their ideas and questions in discussions, laboratories and studios. Not surprisingly, then, people of color generally volunteer less often to participate in classroom discussions than do their white counterparts. College and university faculty rarely receive preparatory training of any kind for teaching; they subsequently are not taught ways of creating more anti-racist or equitable approaches to classroom instruction. Only recently, for instance, have the following criteria for what constitutes equitable or multicultural or anti-racist science instruction appeared in sources like the *American Biology Teacher* (Gardner, Mason & Matyas, 1989, p. 73):

Criteria for Equitable Science Activities

- Teacher is enthusiastic and has equal expectations for all students.

- Written materials and verbal instructions use gender-free language.

- Relevance of activity to students' lives is stressed.

- "Hands-on" experience is required for all students.

- Small group work is used.

- Activity develops science process skills.

- Exercise does not demand one "right" answer.

- Activities do not utilize materials and/or resources exclusively familiar to white, male students.

- Career information relevant to the activity is presented.

- Examples of female and minority role models are included in the follow-up.

The MIT self-study highlights the cost of such inexperience, indicating that while most minority students positively evaluated the quality of their education at the institution, they felt that faculty members' behaviors often created and escalated problems (McBay, 1986, p. 11–12).

> The majority of the respondents (55%) communicated generally negative perceptions of the personal and academic support provided by MIT faculty members (of the remainder, 26% indicated positive perceptions, 12% were mixed, and 7% had minimal interactions); 31% voluntarily said that faculty members expected failure or a lack of ability in Blacks; many (32%) voluntarily said that they developed negative attitudes about going for help; and some (15%) voluntarily mentioned specific racial incidents involving MIT faculty members.

> Comments on low expectations and incidents:

> The main effect of being Black was the teachers' expectations—they think that you automatically won't make it in the class. I was very frustrated. You had to be in the absolute top to overcome that.

> One professor had a hang-up about Black people. I went to talk to him about a grade, and he said that "maybe you people should go somewhere and do things you people can do." This was not uncommon. Many of my friends had this happen. Some departments were worse than others.

> Blacks were discriminated against in some departments. I had a professor who talked about reverse discrimination and how unfair it was for Blacks to be given the opportunity when they did not deserve it. He said the Institute should not help Black students through various programs like interphase because things were not like that in the real world. He said we were given an unfair advantage. I went to him after I graduated and he apologized to me and said I was an exception.

> One classmate had a professor tell her that Blacks don't do well in math because they lack spatial sense and math sense. She was a straight "A" student and this blew her mind—and mine.

These experiences certainly are not unique to MIT.

In addition to the necessity of dealing with racism in the classroom, it is important to deal with racism (or anti-racism) as part of the formal curriculum. Teaching about racism has not been a required part of the curriculum in most institutions, nor has the topic of reducing institutional and individual racism been a popular concern (Takaki, 1989). Faculties in several major universities currently are debating whether or not to have a curriculum requirement focused on racism and ethnic studies. In the Spring of 1989 faculty at the University of Michigan voted against such a requirement, while faculty at the University of Wisconsin and the University of California (Berkeley) voted for it. In 1987, "Stanford University expanded its required Western Culture Program to include the study of minorities, women, other cultures and class issues (Maclay, 1988, p. 15)." Stanford's recent experience with incidents of racial harassment might have had an impact on this decision. For instance, the report of the Stanford University Committee on Minority Issues notes that (1989, p. 5):

Many students who participated in these incidents said they simply did not understand why their actions offended minority students or how their actions could be interpreted by others on campus as derogatory racial stereotyping.

Such "widespread ignorance about the history and culture of American racial minorities" (ibid, p. 5) may be shocking, but it is by no means rare. Nor is it limited to students. Widespread ignorance is a product of the culture and structure of invisibility which surrounds people of color in a white-dominated society or organization. While it may not constitute intentional or purposive discrimination it certainly is part of the passive racism and "indirect institutionalized discrimination" that pervades life in our colleges and universities.

Public ignorance of the culture and life-experience of people of color deprives and diminishes us all. People of color suffer because their culture is not represented in the institution of which they ostensibly are a part; dominant groups suffer because they fail to see or hear the full richness of the human experience. Racism mutes and sometimes obliterates the voices of people of color in two ways; directly, by denying them access to the institution or to institutional platforms for self expression; and, indirectly, by having white "experts" on people of color speak for them. To counter both problems it is important for the voices of people of color to be heard in direct and powerful ways, in the curriculum, in admissions/hiring, in discussions of public policies and issues, etc.

Many faculty members, themselves socialized in predominantly or exclusively white environs, educated in predominantly or exclusively white undergraduate and graduate schools, teaching in predominantly white universities, and living in predominantly white communities do not have the knowledge and skills required to live in, no less teach in, a multicultural environment. Thus, for much of the faculty, problems arise with regard to recognition and management of the following race-related issues:

How to recruit a multiracial student body into a class.

Whether and how to deal with racially self-segregated seating patterns in a class.

How to counsel students of color.

How to deal with culturally different learning styles.

How to facilitate students of different racial groups working together in learning teams.

How to respond to students of color who find traditional presentations of course material alienating or "offensive."

How to explain the lack of senior scholars of color in a given field.

How to deal with a "racial incident" that occurs in class.

Whether and how to respond in class to a "racial incident" that occurred elsewhere on campus.

How to counsel whites who feel threatened by students of color.

How to critically review course content and design in order to identify changes that could reduce racism and move toward multicultural understandings and relationships.

The day-to-day acts of teaching and research occur within individual classrooms, laboratories, studios, etc., where there are deeply entrenched traditions of faculty autonomy and freedom. This emphasis on the academic freedom and autonomy of the individual faculty makes it quite difficult to challenge and change customary ideas and procedures. In the case of racism, a poorly understood, self-interest based, deeply ingrained phenomenon, it is especially difficult. For instance, consider the dilemma of a faculty member who overhears (or is told about) a colleague making a prejudicial remark to or about a student of color (or engaging in sexual harassment of a student). General norms of civility and racially appropriate behavior suggest that such remarks or actions should be confronted: gently perhaps, in an educational frame perhaps, but confronted. But what if the colleague who has engaged in such behavior is senior, and holds informal or implicit review and reward power over the would-be-confrontor? How do we deal with a lack of consensus on the meaning of racist comments (or of sexual harassment)? How do we deal with the lack of a common culture that promotes dialogue, exchange and feedback of this sort among faculty members? Under these circumstances, it is the would-be-confrontor who violates the norms of civility, who potentially tears the fabric of academic freedom, who is seen as acting in a manner disloyal to his/her colleagues and the "club," who stands the risk of arrogantly alleging that she/he knows things that one's colleague does not. The structure and culture of the university mitigates strongly against individual faculty initiatives to challenge racism within the ranks of the faculty itself. When challenged on its own behavior, the faculty tends to adopt a "fortress mentality," to close ranks (and eyes and ears) against the threat from students or from deviants within its own ranks.

All these efforts to alter the infrastructure of the educational organization require new thinking about the place and manner of teaching in the university's system of priorities. Indeed, Richardson and de los Santos point out the need to go beyond the recruitment of faculty of color, but to influence "colleges and universities to value diversity among their faculties and to reward good teaching (including sensitivity to cultural differences, high expectations for all students, and caring and mentoring) through staff development, recruitment procedures, and criteria for tenure and promotion (1988, p. 326)." Unfortunately, deficiencies in the skills required for effective education in a multicultural or anti-racist environment seldom are dealt with via university programs attempting to (re)educate or influence the faculty; rather, the faculty that is already presumed to be fully competent and experienced in teaching students is assumed to be competent in teaching a diverse student body as well. Thus, by default such issues are ignored, and ignorance, denial and the continuation of racism are subtly (and perhaps unconsciously) reinforced.

In universities, like other organizations, social relationships are both formally and informally patterned, and these social patterns affect processes of racial interaction, communication and influence. Patterns of social relationships often exclude faculty of color from (white dominated) informal social networks, or treat them awkwardly when they are included. As social networks go, so go professional networks; thus, these practices of exclusion and awkwardness have major impact on people's professional lives and affect opportunities for promotion, advance and achievement, long after initial hiring decisions. In fact, Smelser and Content (1980) refer to a "succession of exclusions" that carry the "potential at every point for discrimination, both overt and insti-

tutionalized, conscious and unconscious (Exum, 1983, p. 394)." As a potential antidote, Blackwell (1989) emphasizes the necessity of expanded mentoring programs to aid the retention, development and achievement of faculty members of color. Perhaps proactive collegiality is a better model than mentoring, since most sustained exchanges of wisdom and caring are reciprocal rather than unidirectional. Such collegial relationships can explore the rules of the faculty game, journals most appropriate or rewarded as publication outlets, information about which colleagues can/should be avoided and which deferred to, the real balance of teaching and research and service in a department, avenues for research funding, assistance in teaching or in contacting teaching assistants, and in general the "politics of tenure" (Blackwell, 1989).

It also is quite common for graduate students of color to "miss out on" important but informally communicated information concerning opportunities for funding, time-tested ways of preparing dissertation proposals and contacts with influential people in their field of specialization. When faculty (or graduate students) of color are unable to participate effectively in or influence formal and informal networks, they may form their own social and professional groups. Frequently, however, there is resistance to racially homogeneous groups of people of color. Such "caucuses" are apparently offensive or threatening to whites, even though they may be important for personal and professional identity, safety and collegiality in a white dominated environment (Blakey, 1989).

The unique situation of faculty of color in white-dominated institutions results in a number of special burdens and responsibilities. The white faculty's ignorance of these "special tasks" presents serious dilemmas for the scholar of color. For instance, it is possible for most white scholars, regardless of their personal values, to do their work and live their lives without paying serious attention to racism and racial discrimination. It is improbable that faculty of color can do the same: one's personal experience, demands from students, community needs, and pressure to "serve the cause" create quite different responsibilities. Brooks reviews some of these special (often defined simply as service) burdens and responsibilities as follows (1986):

white students' difficult time dealing with minority professors

minority students' desire for problem-solving, advice and counselling

community organizations' search for assistance and role models

pressure to address issues of special interest to Black Americans

Several observers indicate that these and other special tasks create significant conflicts with traditional role definitions and with the multiple audiences who are served by and who evaluate faculty members' work (Elmore and Blackburn, 1983; Exum, 1983; Moore and Wagstaff, 1974). Blakey notes, however, that whites often see the demand/request to deal with such issues, in the definition or reward system for these service, teaching or research roles, as political, non-objective or self-serving, and as an excuse for not meeting traditional academic and organizational expectations (Blakey, 1989). Blackwell states the institutional duality of this situation well: "I don't think there is a campus in this country that will not dump every single thing minority on that particular person. Then we turn around . . . and say, well, you haven't published enough (1989, p. 13)."

A parallel danger, but one standing in sharp contrast to non-recognition or denial of the distinctive status/situation/interests of faculty of color, is the potential for stereotyping these colleagues only as faculty of color. Just as minority students sometimes are expected to be (or are limited to being) expert testifiers on their culture (see Crenshaw, 1989), minority faculty sometimes are expected only to conduct research or teaching on matters related to Black or Hispanic concerns, or only to be interested in alternative scholarly paradigms. Thus, faculty of color may be "tracked" into Ethnic Studies Centers, or hired with funds allocated specifically for these purposes, regardless of their scholarly predispositions or preferences. This sort of automatic coding represents another form of stereotyping. The university organization that seeks both to recognize the unique interests of faculty of color, and to deal sensitively with the unique interests and styles of every one of its faculty members as individuals, often will confront this dilemma. While this may be a very complex dilemma, avoiding it with either polar response (non-recognition of

differences or tracking on the basis of assumed differences) engages in sustained stereotyping.

The structure of social and professional relations that dominate the faculty, and the classroom, inevitably permeate the student culture itself. Since the administration and the faculty generally pay little attention to internal processes in the student culture or to the racial intricacies of the student peer system, students learn to ignore these issues as well. Students structure their lives in ways that sustain racially separated and insensitive domains; thus all are protected from discomfort . . . and from contact that might be enriching . . . and from contact that might reduce systematic stereotypes and ignorance. The inevitable outcome of these separated structures of learning and living are both isolated incidents and regular actions that discriminate against students of color. It is easy to see these incidents as isolated acts, as the behaviors of individually insensitive or hateful students. A more adequate analysis would see these incidents as a natural outgrowth of a culture, power structure and set of social and intellectual relations that teach people who are different from one another not to bother to understand or respect or work well with one another.

An interesting innovation in most university structures at this juncture in history is a special office or offices in charge of minority group affairs. Generally such an office is in charge of the "care and feeding" (recruiting, counselling, financing) of minority students; occasionally it has a broader organizational agenda of achieving affirmative action or of reducing institutional racism. Whatever its charge, its relative priority is indicated by its location in the academic structure, its access to resources, and related factors. If its creation is not reflected in the mission or goal statement of the university, we understand it as an "add-on" rather than a basic change in the organization's direction. If it is a staff office/position rather than a line office/position we understand that there is little authority or power connected to it. If it is located solely in the central administration, and not also represented in each subunit of the system, we know it is likely to be isolated from the places where critical decisions are implemented. If it is staffed by other than prestigious faculty members, we understand that it is not likely to have significant impact on the majority of the faculty. If it is charged with dealing with social relationships, and not with pedagogical and curricular change, we understand it strikes at the margin but not at the heart of the academic enterprise. If it cannot influence (through incentives) the institution's research program, and faculty review and promotion processes, we understand it will not carry significant intellectual power. And if students (especially students of color) are not involved in its formation, staffing, and ongoing functioning, we understand it will be unlikely to reflect their unique experiences of racism in the university and their visions of how things might be different.

Finally, an essential part of the organization's structure is its boundary system or interface with other, external, organizations (Brown, 1983). The influence of external social environments on colleges and universities and their interactions with other units across organizational boundaries also involves racism. Whatever their internal focus, higher educational organizations generally are expected to ignore racist practices in other institutions. For example, the recent actions of several law schools to deny the FBI the right to recruit because of court findings of discrimination in this agency was greeted with shock, surprise, and anger. So, too, would university efforts to advocate alteration of discriminatory municipal housing, hiring or policing practices. The university that is not sensitive to issues of racism often fails to attend to the community environment that diminishes and demeans the lives of many faculty and students of color. Societal racism often affects faculty and students of color, in housing opportunities, K-12 educational systems, relations with local police departments, and access to community services. People of color who must fend for themselves in dealing with these issues encounter an alienating community as well as a disinterested university. Similarly, as colleges and universities more aggressive recruit high school students of color, they are likely to become involved in programs of educational assistance or improvement that inevitably draw them into potential conflicts with community and school system practices that support racism. Consistent and effective anti-racist practices necessarily will involve universities in aiding the struggle for justice in community organizations: most are not prepared to undertake such action.

In a reciprocal fashion, federal and state anti-discrimination laws and policies may have substantial impact on the internal dynamics of higher educational organizations. Unfortunately, many colleges and universities have argued that such laws should not apply to them; despite federal judicial and executive decisions that these organizations are not exempt from anti-discriminatory laws, their implementation at the higher educational level still encounters resistance in the form of claims of institutional autonomy and the pursuit of excellence.

In summary, among the most alienating realities of these institutional structures and operations for faculty of color are:

- the failure to receive respect from white colleagues
- the inability of white colleagues to discuss issues of racism
- the unwillingness of colleagues to confront/challenge outrageously racist comments or memos made by other faculty or administrators
- the lack of reward for pro-actively anti-racist work
- the failure of white colleagues to appreciate different research priorities and a need for active engagement in racism
- the unwillingness of colleagues to confront racism in the community
- the perception that white faculty are not committed to students of color

In a restatement of the issues dealt with in this section, Payne argues that (1989, p. 21):

> If departments are to send the right "message" to current and prospective faculty, they must learn to ask the hard questions about the quality of interaction, social professional opportunities, cultural integrity, professional respect, common goals, social styles, aspirations, conflict, freedom and independence, entrepreneurial interest, quality of housing, and community support—all those aspects of higher education that make professional life on a campus attractive and self-fulfilling.

To ask these questions, and to discover the answers, would do much to advance the quality of life for faculty of color. The extent to which attention to such issues might improve the life of all faculty emphasizes the degree to which none of us will be free and fulfilled until all of us are.

Resources

The key resources utilized by colleges and universities are financial, physical and human. In the process of garnering these resources higher educational organizations encounter a variety of constraints and dilemmas. Sometimes perceived constraints or dilemmas lead to efforts to shape the organization's or unit's image and program to appeal to wealthy and powerful individuals, private corporations, or public agencies. An emphasis on social change, on altering structures of social privilege and oppression, on challenging racism, may not "sell well" to these constituencies. On the contrary, anti-racist mission statements and programs may be disquieting and alienating to people and organizations whose donations and other financial support might make a difference for key programs. They may see a university's efforts to create a plural culture or an anti-racist program as cavilling to special interests, as "selling out" western civilization, as bending core values under pressure, or as sacrificing excellence.

Indeed, when the University of Michigan's alumni magazine printed a story about campus racial incidents, and on a negotiated agreement reached between the President and leaders of student protest groups, several alumni responded with letters and commentary. Although some letters praised the magazine's "honest and courageous" approach, and even the University administration's commitment to dealing with racism, others adopted the critical perspective and language suggested above (*Michigan Alumnus*, 1987):

> . . . this "problem" does not warrant the attention it has been receiving.
>
> . . . The regents and the administration . . . succumbed to the pressure.
>
> I have never seen so much bull printed in a single copy . . . The University's reactions to racial incidents is that of nervous Nellies seeking refuge in phraseology and chasing their own tails.
>
> It is, in my mind, inconceivable that the administration and the regents could accede to the demands of a group of law-

breakers . . . shows a lack of moral fortitude.

> What we've witnessed on campus by UCAR, BAM III, Jesse Jackson and sadly, *Michigan Alumnus*, is nothing more than an amoral, political partisan purge . . . your publication perpetuate(s) ignorance and bias.

Rarely is there a concerted and committed effort to inform all alumni and potential funders about the university's commitments, policies, and programs designed to combat racism. Thus, the defensive and reactive posture of the university on these matters is "affirmed" by alumni donor patterns, and vice versa.

As universities and colleges appeal to wealthy and powerful people for resources, they often must deal with allegations by conservative media that they pursue politics favorable to left-wing radicals and unfairly penalize conservative scholars and students. A recent *Wall Street Journal* editorial (1989), "The Privileged Class," is a clear example of this biased picture of higher education. This editorial, among other claims, depicts higher education's efforts to combat racism as an example of the operation of a "privileged ideology," and alleges that "radical teachers . . . have insistently dominated discussion in recent years." Similar analyses by conservative media and political activists (see, for example, Finn, 1989) blame radical faculty for curricular changes that enhance student exposure to and knowledge of cultures other than the traditional white Western culture. They see efforts at an anti-racist or multi-cultural curriculum as evidence that colleges are overrun by left-wing "ideological indoctrination." This argument is made in the face of incontrovertible evidence of rapid globalization of the economy, communication systems and policy making, changes which require graduates to understand and deal with cultures other than one's own. Other informed observers and analysts continually have indicated that politically left-wing and actively anti-racist faculty are very much a minority in higher education and, while often outspoken, certainly do not dominate discussions or decisions on the curriculum or on campus policies in general. Nevertheless, such media perspectives and political presentations play on fears and stereotypes, and contribute to privileged groups' desires to resist higher education's efforts to control racism and to continue to develop multi-cultural learning opportunities. At the very least, they make it that much more difficult for colleges and universities to raise funds for these objectives.

Research grants and contracts are an increasingly important source of revenue for both private and public universities. Most such projects are funded by government or corporate interests to achieve goals related to economic prosperity, national defense or medical and educational improvements. Research in the areas of public health, environmental quality, social welfare and poverty occur, but at a much lower level of resources. Although support is available for studies of racial attitudes, rarely are there well-funded efforts to analyse institutional racism in different societal sectors, or policies and programs designed to ameliorate the structures of wealth and power that support racism over time.

The vast majority of research funds are decided upon and allocated by powerful social institutions, most of which suffer from the same enmeshment in systems of institutional racism as universities themselves, and most of which also benefit from the racism of the status quo. Despite this situation, universities can apply pressure to fund basic and applied research in the area of institutional racism. In all likelihood, however, such opportunities will not be successful without deliberate and concerted action and without the application of pressure by collectivities of concerned constituencies in universities and communities.

Student tuition is another important source of a university's financial resources. To a major extent, the ability to pay tuition is dependent upon a family's wealth, and since many students of color come from less wealthy families, they often are not able to pay as large a portion of their own tuition as are students from white families. They also are less likely to have extra resources available for entertainment and other collegiate expenses. Thus, they are more dependent upon the largess of the university in the allocation of funds to cover educational expenses.

Several scholars have pointed to the importance of an adequate financial support package to the collegiate success of students of color. Often, aid packages do not allow students of color to live comfortably and to partic-

ipate fully in the institutional culture dominated by people from wealthier backgrounds. Thus, racism once again is manifest—this time in definitions of financial need. Fields provides one example from inquiries conducted in the University of California system (1988, p. 25):

> Expanded financial aid, better information about it and simplified financial aid processing were among the more important things that students (at California State-Long Beach) said the campus might do to help them remain in college.

Note that it is not merely financial aid that is important, but notification and processing of applications in ways that are simple and that avoid additional stigma. When the university fails to explain the reasons for such need-based grants, and its commitment to their social necessity on the basis of concerns for justice and institutional excellence, white students' images of "reverse discrimination" and unfair advantages to students of color are heightened.

Public universities' appropriations from state legislatures are to a certain extent dependent upon the university's ability to satisfy the interests of concerned state officials. Because of the ways in which public policies generally favor the interests of white and upper middle class people, and their young who are college students, support for university efforts to combat racism and create a multicultural environment are, for the most part, not a priority. When state legislatures or their subcommittees do seek to analyze university race relations and their impacts, or pressure the university to reduce racism, their efforts often are seen as unwarranted intrusions on the academic freedom of the institution, or perhaps as an example of special interest group publicity-seeking. Rather than take advantage of these rare opportunities for legislative support or community collaboration in a broad change effort, the university leadership generally reacts negatively, both to deny its own problems and to resist external influence attempts.

Put simply, because the bulk of financial resources available to institutions of higher education do not come from people of color, or from the institutions they control, these resources are generally not allocated nor sought with an interest in combatting racism.

Colleges and universities are labor intensive organizations, and faculty/staff salaries constitute a major (and unyielding) portion of the overall budget. Most of their faculties are white and male. Most of their top administrative staffs are white and male as well. Their clerical, secretarial, and plant staffs may be more diverse; certainly Black and Hispanic employees are concentrated here. Moreover, most of the student body is likely to be white. Of course, there are exceptions to these patterns in historically Black or Hispanic colleges, and in some urban universities. If people are a crucial resource in the labor-intensive environment of higher education, the recruitment, employment, retention and development (growth and promotion) of people of color must be a crucial issue in the creation/deployment of anti-racist resources for the organization. However, it is common knowledge that despite rhetoric and policies of affirmative action, routing recruitment and hiring practices have generally failed to employ and sustain substantial numbers of people of color in faculty and senior staff roles. When employed, many people of color fail to be affirmed and sustained in a racist environment, and often leave or are pushed out of the organization (in spirit if not in body).

White faculty who are opposed to affirmative action programs, whether on principle, in particular cases, or because of a general resistance to racial change, often make faculty of color "feel uncertain about the reasons for their faculty appointments, consultantships and committee appointments . . . African-Americans are continuously confronted by the racist notion among colleagues that our successes are not achieved or merited, that affirmative action has allowed substandard scholars to rise to positions formerly held by meritorious whites (Blakey, 1989, pp. 18–17)." White faculty and administrators know such conversations occur: mostly in private but not always; mostly with white colleagues but sometimes with students. Faculty of color know it as well. Ironically, this stance does more than demean and humiliate faculty of color; it also ignores the history of preferential hiring of whites, which has itself led to problems in ethnocentrism, incompetence and inadequacy in some spheres of intellectual labor.

Wilson (1987, p. 3) argues that some additional reasons for the failure to make significant progress on the hiring of faculty of color rest in four widely-believed myths that often accompany faculty recruiting efforts:

- the myth that the problem is the "availability" of minorities with the terminal degree (no available data sustains this assumption).
- the myth that minority women are "prime hires" because they represent two "protected groups." (in fact minority women often are at the very bottom of the professional ladder).
- the myth that minority Ph.D.s in science and engineering are so rare that they can command top salaries and that many colleges cannot afford them (in fact they attain promotion and tenure at a lower rate than do whites).
- the myth that there is no necessary correlation between commitment to equity on the part of academic leaders and the number of minorities in those leaders' student bodies and faculties.

One of the reasons frequently cited for not recruiting more students or faculty of color is the lack of a suitable pool of candidates for these respective roles. Seldom is it acknowledged that the definition of the suitability of these students or faculty members affects the boundaries and make up of the candidate pool. The so-called pool is not a given, it is in itself a product of the mission and culture of the organization; and it can be redefined to enable more people of color to be included. Moreover, colleges and universities seldom take responsibility to remedy the social conditions that influence whether or not adequate numbers of people of color are included in a pool of candidates. (e.g., through work in local/regional elementary and secondary schools, job training or economic development programs). Higher educational organizations certainly have the capability (in research and service activities) to help alter those social conditions that lead to the exclusion of minorities from the pool they wish to use in selecting students and faculty members. To cite the absence of people of color in a pool of potential candidates for university positions, without taking some responsibility for the social conditions shaping the make-up of the pool, is obfuscatory at best and self-serving at worst.

It is important to expand the numbers of people of color, but not only from the standpoint of social justice or equity; it also is a matter of excellence. A diverse faculty and staff can exercise valuable modelling and leadership for others—if provided with the opportunity and support for such initiatives. Students and faculty who come from middle and upper middle-class white communities typically bring to their teaching and learning (and research and service) the racial attitudes and behaviors of their families of origin. They reflect the alienation and biases of the communities and class groupings of which they are a part. These "legacies" generally include little experience interacting as peers with people of color, and subtle notions of their inferiority. Whites may be curious about the living patterns of people of color, but they also are awkward with and ignorant of their life styles. Under these circumstances, living and working together is a challenging and difficult enterprise. So is creating a high quality and diverse educational environment. Although many universities seek to counter this awkwardness and ignorance through dormitory and extra-curricular programs, or even in rare circumstances through the curriculum, it cannot be accomplished without the substantial presence of people of color themselves.

Racial diversity also enhances academic excellence by broadening the intellectual content and methods that are part of a teaching and research program. Many people of color in colleges and universities bring with them constituency liaisons, topical interests, pedagogies and epistemologies that differ from many of their white colleagues. This occurs because of sub-cultural influences and because the values and interests of many people of color and many white people are affected by their socialization into different subordinate and superordinate statuses in the society. Intellectual diversity cannot be divorced from social diversity, and academic excellence cannot be achieved without maximum intellectual diversity. In pursuing intellectual diversity it is absolutely necessary to have a faculty and student body that has been socialized in different subcultures and in different socio-economic status groups—and that can and will communicate to and share their perspectives with one another.

Racial ignorance, awkwardness and isolation lead to a waste of key human potential and educational resources. They not only affect white students' views and relationships with students of color in the dormitories and residence halls, they affect their perceptions and expectations of these students' performance in class. They not only affect faculty behavior with students of color in the classroom, they affect faculty behavior with colleagues of color. They not only affect staff members' behavior as they counsel, advise or otherwise serve students of color, they affect their interactions with staff members of color as well. In general, the human capital of the university, the labor and educational resources themselves, are demeaned and limited by the institution's inability to create or take advantage of a diverse community or an anti-racist educational environment.

The physical plants of most colleges and universities are located in or near white neighborhoods and predominantly white communities. These settings carry a history of racial exclusion, and often are uncomfortable environs for people of color to enter and sustain themselves within. It is to be expected, moreover, that the art and architecture of these settings are generally more reflective of white and Western culture than of others. These settings further serve to make students of color feel they are in "strange territory." Even those universities located in the hearts, or on the margins, of communities of color, generally are so heavily invested in land ownership patterns that further the economic exploitation and alienation of poor and minority communities (Jacobs, 1963), that they fare no better on these dimensions.

Because the post-Korean era of growth in higher education is over, resource reallocation rather than resource growth has become the dominant theme in college and university budgeting. New goals have to be pursued by reallocating scarce funds from other programs and priorities. Such changes in financial patterns are notoriously controversial and ridden with conflict, and the conflict is likely to be escalated when reallocated resources appear to benefit people of color. All the ancient stereotypes and concerns about racial inferiority and unfair advantage are likely to surface. New efforts to recruit and admit minority students, to recruit and hire and promote minority faculty, to recruit and hire and promote minority staff leaders, to achieve changes in instructional and research programs so as to combat racism, and to move toward an anti-racist university will involve significant battles over the reallocation of financial resources.

Summary

Each of these major institutional elements operates in ways that pass on societal racism and that constrain the potential for change. At the same time, within each of these elements conflicts exist, as day-to-day realities are at odds with institutional ideals, as people of color and their allies seek improved opportunities, and as external pressures of internationalization, domestic demographics, improved human resource development systems, and renewed pursuit of social justice impact on institutions of higher education. Universities are not neutral actors in this historic sequence, however; without proactive commitment otherwise, they do not merely pass on societal racism, but they also encourage and promote oppression and domination within their own institutional operations. Figure 32-6 summarizes this discussion by providing an overview of some of the ways in which racism may be altered in the operation of each element of higher educational organizations. The identification, diagnosis, and assessment of these patterns are necessary steps in planning changes to reduce institutional racism. Each element also carries a key to the change process, to the effort to combat and reduce racism. To the extent we can alter the mission, culture, power, structure or resources of higher educational organizations we can alter the institutional racism that permeates these organizations. In turn, as we alter institutional racism in colleges and universities, we also alter aspects of their organizational missions, cultures, power, structures and resources.

IV. Changing Institutional Racism In Higher Education[5]

In order to create change in the well-institutionalized character of racism in higher education a comprehensive planning process is required. Anything less will lack an integrative vision and design, will lead to piecemeal and sporadic efforts, and will fail to produce lasting results. False starts and minimalist or poorly planned efforts can make a situation worse by failing to anticipate resistance, failing to confront opposition forcefully, escalating stigmatizing reactions to intended beneficiaries of new policies, appearing to solve problems without real substance, etc.

Significant organizational change involves alterations in all components of the collegiate or university organization, including mission, culture, power, structure and resources. Even then, questions of feasibility remain; the kinds and extent of change required to significantly reduce racism may be impossible in the context of current organization forms and procedures. Indeed, some scholars and activists argue that universities, and racism itself, are so embedded in the political and economic structures of our society that no meaningful change is possible short of major societal transformation. Despite this potential, we think that even the limited organizational changes discussed here can have significant positive impact in and of themselves; they also can be key elements in a more sustained and far-reaching effort to alter institutional racism.

When "incidents" of racism surfaced on college and university campuses the primary responses of many local administrators were focused on eliminating conflict to achieve "image management." That is, a major initial concern was to protect the image of the university, sometimes by denying the importance of events, and to indicate a high level of concern when denial could not be maintained. In a recent issue of *Black Issues In Higher Education*, Warren (1988) confirms this impression, arguing that "Too often, attention is directed at crisis situations born out of daily incidents which have been ignored by all except the victims (p. 56)."

When it was clear that some action had to be taken, the usual first efforts were limited and short-range. Typical initiatives that were rapidly deployed included multiple meetings to talk about issues, special campaigns to recruit students and faculty of color, the commissioning of human relations or "sensitivity" training programs, the appointment of a special assistant for minority affairs, and the

MISSION
   Attend to societal/demographic transformations that require reducing racism.
   Attend to racism as a threat to institutional excellence, effectiveness, and goal attainment
   Attend to linkages between racism and other forms of oppression/exploitation
   Generate plural definitions of excellence—in research, teaching and service.
   Provide justification for anti-racism programs

CULTURE
   Recognize and celebrate multicultural norms and practices, and distinct cultural backgrounds and styles
   Advance scholarly epistemologies and curricula that embrace the world views and knowledge of different
      cultures
   Respond to conflict in ways which do not seek to dominate, repress or deny differences but rather to learn
      about problems and cherish differences (and potential commonalities)

POWER
   Provide people of color with access to decisional arenas
   Redistribute power to achieve broader sharing among various stake holders, including increased power
      for people of color.
   Utilize formal and informal power to combat racism
   Demonstrate senior administrative, faculty and staff commitment to change

STRUCTURE
   Alter patterns of interaction to promote collaboration across existing group and organizational boundaries
   Develop task designs and study/work groups that encourage formal and informal multi-racial
      collaboration
   Develop new priorities in teaching/curriculum and research that improve responsiveness to cultural and
      economic diversity
   Develop new courses, teaching methods, research methods, and topics that seek to understand and
      combat racism
   Develop policies and practices to identify and combat discrimination and harassment generally—and
      racial harassment specifically
   Provide ongoing support for people of color to achieve excellence, as well as to gain access to higher
      education

RESOURCES
   Seek and allocate financial resources to local efforts that promote organizational innovation and change
   Apply financial resources to reducing racism in research and teaching and university life as a priority
   Improve recruitment and enrollment/employment to address both diversity and excellence
   Provide spaces that are comfortable and supportive for the gathering, collaborating, and celebrating of
      under-represented groups

Figure 32-6 Keys to Potential Reduction of Racism in Higher Education

development of study skills' programs for students of color (Ransby, 1987). To the extent that the issues were raised by protesting student groups, first efforts also were likely to include meetings with aggrieved students or the formation of task forces to "study" or "solve" local problems.

Sometimes the gross symptoms of racism, including embarassing public conflict, can be temporarily alleviated through such piecemeal efforts, programmatic add-ons, and crash initiatives. However, these crisis-focused responses will not reduce institutional racism because they do not address the underlying organizational and institutional factors that are involved. These activities can be valuable components of more comprehensive and longer-range change programs, but by themselves they only raise false hopes for institutional change.

Comprehensive organizational change to reduce racism requires the top leadership of colleges and universities to make explicit decisions that commit the organization to major change. But these changes cannot be decided upon by the senior leadership themselves; the traditional white and male dominance of this leadership cadre must itself be challenged as part of the change process. Thus, major planning efforts and decisions must include: faculty, staff and students as well as administrators; students and faculty of color as well as whites; and women as well as men. Conflict will inevitably occur as a result of such widespread participation, but plural involvement also provides ideas that are more responsive to the needs of different groups of people throughout the organization. It may begin to develop, moreover, a more legitimate and effective multicultural educational environment by its very example. If "lower-level" organizational members have to be relied upon to implement any plan organizational leaders develop, they are more likely to do so to the extent that they and their representatives have been involved in the planning process and have developed programs relevant to their needs, mindsets and resources.

Efforts to reduce racism in organizations often are motivated primarily by the guilt of white administrators and faculty members, and the desire to ameliorate public protests or bad press. While such factors may contribute to initial efforts to reduce racism they are insufficient bases for pursuing long-term and lasting change. Other motivations must be developed for this endeavor. These other motivations can be grounded in several factors, including:

> The costs of institutional racism to the organization, both to whites and people of color.
> New potentials open to the organization and all of its members by reducing institutional racism.
> New internal organizational rewards for members or units which undertake positive efforts to reduce racism (and/or sanctions for resistance or continued racism).

If people and organizations are operating in racist ways they must be receiving some "benefit" from such activities. It must in some way be in their interest (real or perceived), at least in the short term, to continue such activities in the face of laws and moral codes to the contrary. Whether that self-interest is financial, positional (status), emotional, or cultural, may not matter as much as its existence, per se. Only change in the self-interest basis for behavior, the things that cause people and organizations to seek their own gain, will permanently cause (and support) change. This principle of organizational change is articulated clearly by the Stanford University self-study of campus

racism (Stanford University Committee on Minority Issues, 1989):

> Good intentions are not enough . . . At the departmental level, some managers find the University's pluralistic goals important and apply them to their particular office, but when others make half-hearted efforts or no efforts at all to recruit, develop, and retain minority staff, they face no repercussions . . . Until we impose real sanctions for willful failure to implement stated goals for diversity and inclusion in the workplace, the University will not be able to say that it acknowledges and opposes institutional racism—or that "bigotry is out." (pp. 9, 214).

As self-interests are redefined, based on a long term perspective on the future of social relations and institutional success, alternative motivations to reduce institutional racism in higher education may become more compelling. Such redefinition of self-interests also will require effective education and sustained incentives. For instance, if college or university leaders (or staff members or faculty members or students) do not experience rewards or gains for anti-racist behavior they are not likely to sustain that behavior for long. Similarly, if college or university leaders see very clearly the costs of racism for themselves and their institution, they will not (unless simultaneously seeing major gains) continue to engage in or support the operations that generate that cost. At the more micro-level of influencing the behavior of faculty members, Monaghan argues for the self-interest principle in the following terms:

> Colleges and universities should offer incentives and rewards to faculty members who show a commitment to cultural pluralism, and should hold administrators more accountable for advancing institutional goals to improve opportunities for minority scholars. (1989, p. A18)

Certainly there are potential costs to a meaningful change effort, and planning and implementation designs must be cognizant of the pain or threat that will occur to some peoples' values and interests, and their resultant resistance. It is our experience that while members of institutions of higher education often are ignorant of the long-term costs of current racist policies and procedures, and of the potential long-term gains of change, they are very sophisticated (often to the point of paralysis) regarding the short-term costs (and political resistance) involved in an anti-racism effort.

The attempt to plan and carry out a long-term change program can focus on some of the key challenges to institutional racism summarized in Figure 32-6. These organizational change options are grouped according to the 5 core elements of higher educational organizations outlined in Figure 32-4 and discussed in detail earlier. Since these 5 core elements, as well as the many individual program suggestions, interact with the are co-dependent upon one another, an integrated strategic plan is absolutely necessary.

Implementing these or other organizational change options also requires making a number of tactical choices, choices that determine the shape and conduct of a local change effort. A detailed discussion of such tactics is beyond the scope of this paper, but the reader is referred to our forthcoming companion piece for elaboration. Briefly, the following issues must be dealt with:

The balance between (or combination of) top-down and bottom-up change approaches.

The number and types of groups or constituencies to be involved in planning and implementing the change effort.

The role of people of color, especially students, in designing responses to their experience of racism.

The role and visibility (and accountability) of senior administrative officers and senior faculty.

The degree and type of involvement of external organizations and individuals in planning, implementing and evaluating the organizational change effort.

The balance between (or combination of) persuasion and coercion as change approaches.

The stance taken toward those passively resisting or actively opposing anti-racism efforts.

The maintenance of a thrust on countering counter organizational/institutional racism in the face of probable efforts to focus on individualistic analyses and solutions.

The linkage of anti-racism efforts to other change programs, such as anti-sexism and general designs to improve student learning and faculty working environs.

These problems and possibilities in the effort to reduce racism in institutions of higher education impress upon us the delicate, complex and immense natures of this task. At the same time, the cries of protesting students, the often muted voices of faculty and staff of color, and the analytic perspective offered earlier impress upon us the necessity of undertaking this task. Decisions made within the university both reflect and influence decisions made by students, faculty and administrators, policy makers and just plain citizens in their daily work and activity outside the university as well. The future of social justice and peace in our entire society and the world, not merely in our systems of higher education, rest on the efforts we can make to acknowledge, understand, and reduce the racism within our universities and colleges.

Notes

1. This working paper is a revised and expanded version of a chapter prepared for ETHICS IN HIGHER EDUCATION, edited by W. May (Macmillan, 1990). We plan to complement it later with another working paper, "Racism in higher education II: Designing and implementing organizational change."

2. Of course, it is uniquely visible, accessible and objectionable to us, as faculty of the University of Michigan.

3. This list of proposals from the United Coalition Against Racism is similar to a series of demands/proposals also made in the Winter of 1987 by the Black Action Movement III and the Hispanic Student Association.

4. From materials prepared and distributed by the Black Action Movement.

5. A separate paper (in preparation) will draw on the foregoing analysis to create an expanded discussion of some of the possibilities and strategies for changing institutional racism in higher education.

References

Alderfer, C., Aderfer, D., Tucker, L. and Tucker, R. Diagnosing race relations in management. *The Journal of Applied Behavioral Science.* 1980, 16(2): 135–166.

Allen, W. *Gender and Campus Race Differences in Black Student Academic Performance, Racial Attitudes and College Satisfaction.* Atlanta, Southern Educational Foundation, 1986.

Allen, W. Improving Black student access and achievement in higher education. *The Review of Higher Education.* 1988, 11(4), 403–416.

Astin, A. *Minorities in Higher Education.* San Francisco, Jossey-Bass, 1982.

Alvarez, R., & Lutterman, K (Eds). *Discrimination in Organizations.* San Francisco, Jossey-Bass, 1979.

Baldridge, V. and Deal, T. Overview of change processes in educational organizations. In Baldridge and Deal (Eds.), *Managing Change in Educational Organizations.* Berkeley, McCutchan, 1975.

Bayh, B. Let's tear off their hoods. *Newsweek,* 1989, April 17.

Bell, D. The price and pain of racial perspective. *Stanford Law School Journal.* 1986, May 9, 5.

Benjamin, E. Faculty responsibility for enhancing minority participation in higher education. *Academe.* 1989, 75(5), 64.

Birnbaum, R. Administrative commitment and minority enrollments: College president's goals for quality and access. *The Review of Higher Education.* 1988, 11(4), 435–458.

Blackwell, J. Mentoring: An action strategy for increasing minority faculty. *Academe.* 1989, 75(5), 8–14.

Blakey, M. The professional caucus: Place of refuge, source of change. *Academe.* 1989, 75(5), 15–18.

Blauner, R. *Racial Oppression In America.* New York, Harper & Row, 1972.

Brooks, R. Life after tenure: Can minority law professors avoid the Clyde Ferguson syndrome? *University of San Francisco Law Review.* 1986, 20, 419–427.

Brown, D. *Managing Conflict at Organizational Interfaces.* Cambridge, Addison-Wesley, 1983.

Campbell, A. and Schuman, H. *Racial Attitudes in Fifteen American Cities.* Ann Arbor, Institute for Social Research, 1968.

Carmichael, S., & Hamilton, C. *Black Power: The Politics of Racism in America.* New York, Vintage Books, 1976.

Checkoway, B. Unanswered questions about public service in the public university. *The University Record.* 1989, February 6, 10–12.

Clark, B. *The Distinctive College: Antioch, Reed and Swarthmore.* New York, Aldine, 1970.

Clark, K., and Plotkin, L. *The Negro Student at Integrated Colleges.* N.Y., National Scholarship Service and Fund for Negro Students, 1963.

Crenshaw, K. Foreword: Toward a race-conscious pedagogy in legal education. *National Black Law Journal.* 1989, 11(1), 1–14.

Dill, D. The management of academic culture: notes on the management of meaning and social integration. *Higher Education.* 1982, 11, 303–320.

Elmore, C. and Blackburn, R. Black and white faculty in white research universities. *Journal of Higher Education.* 1983, 54, 1–15.

Epps, E. Academic culture and the minority professor. *Academe,* 1989, 75(5), 23–26.

Exum, W. Climbing the crystal stair: Values, affirmative action, and minority faculty. *Social Problems.* 1983, 30(4), 383–399.

Feagin, J., & Feagin, C. *Discrimination American Style: Institutional Racism and Sexism.* Englewood Cliffs, Prentice Hall, 1986.

Fields, C. The Hispanic pipeline: narrow, leaking and needing repair. *Change.* 1988, 20(3), 20–27.

Finn, C. The Campus: "An island of repression in a sea of freedom." *Commentary.* 1989, September, 17–23.

Fiske, E. The undergraduate Hispanic experience: A case of juggling two cultures. *Change.* 1988, 20(3), 28–33.

Fleming, J., Gill, G. and Swinton, D. *The Case for Affirmative Action for Blacks in Higher Education.* Washington, D.C., Howard University Press, 1978.

Friere, P. *Pedagogy of the Oppressed.* New York, Seabury Press, 1970.

Gardner, A., Mason, C. & Matyas, M. Equity, excellence and just plain good teaching. *The American Biology Teacher.* 1989, 51(2), 72–77.

Gross, N. Universities as organizations: a research approach. *American Sociological Review,* 1968, 33, 518–543.

Hurst, F. *Report on University of Massachusetts Investigation,* Amherst, UMass, 1987.

Jackson, B., and Holvino, E. Multicultural organizational development. Ann Arbor, Program in Conflict Management Alternatives (Working Paper #11), 1988.

Jacobs, J. *The Death and Life of Great American Cities.* New York, Vintage, 1963.

Jones, J. *Prejudice And Racism.* Reading, Mass. Addison-Wesley, 1970.

Justus, S., Freitag, S. & Parker, L. *The University of California in The Twenty-First Century.* 1987.

Katz, J. Facing the challenge of diversity and multiculturalism. Ann Arbor, Program in Conflict Management Alternatives (Working Paper #13), 1988.

Katz, J. *White Awareness.* Norman, Oklahoma, University of Oklahoma Press, 1978.

Katz, D. and Kahn, R. *The Social Psychology of Organizations.* New York, Wiley, 1978.

Keller, E. *Reflections On Gender And Science.* New Haven, Yale University Press, 1985.

Kennedy, R. Racial critiques of legal academia. *Harvard Law Review.* 1989, 102(8), 1745–1819.

Kochman, T. *Black and White: Styles in Conflict.* Chicago, University of Chicago Press, 1981.

Knowles, R. and Prewitt, K. (eds.) *Institutional Racism in America.* Englewood Cliffs, Prentice Hall, 1969.

Martin, J., and Siehl, C. Organizational culture and counterculture: An uneasy symbiosis. *Organizational Dynamics.* 1983, Autumn, 52–64.

Maclay, K. Berkeley faculty considers mandatory minority course. *Black Issues In Higher Education.* 1988, 5(20), 15.

Masland, A. Organizational culture in the study of higher education. *The Review of Higher Education.* 1985, 8, 157–168.

McBay, S. *The Racial Climate on the Mit Campus.* Cambridge, MIT, 1986.

Michigan Alumnus. 1987, 94(1).

Monaghan, P. Action, not just policy change, seen needed to improve minority scholars' opportunities. *The Chronicle of Higher Education,* 1989, 35(26), A17–18.

Moore, W. and Wagstaff, L. *Black Faculty in White Colleges.* San Francisco, Jossey-Bass, 1974.

Omi, M. and Winant, H. *Racial Formation in the United States.* London, Routledge and Keegan Paul, 1986.

Payne, H. Hidden messages in the pursuit of equality. *Academe.* 1989, 75(5), 19–22.

Peterson, M., Blackburn, R., Gamson, Z., Arce, C., Davenport, R., & Mingle, J. *Black Students on White Campuses: The Impacts of Increased Black Enrollments.* Ann Arbor, Institute for Social Research, 1978.

Ransby, B. University goes for pushbutton solution. *Agenda,* 1987, October, 7–18.

Richardson, R., & de los Santos, A. The guest editors' introduction: From access to achievement: Fulfilling the promise. *The Review of Higher Education.* 1988, 11(4), 323–328.

Richardson, R., Simmons, H., & de los Santos, A. Graduating minority students: Lessons from ten success stories. *Change.* 1987, 19(3), 20–26.

Ridgeway, J. *The Closed Corporation.* New York, Ballantine, 1968.

Rosenberg, L. A battle far from won. *Yale.* 1988. November, 44–47.

Schuman, H., Steeh, C., and Bobo, L. *Racial Attitudes in America: Trends and Interpretations.* Cambridge, Harvard University Press, 1985.

Schwartz, B. and Disch, R. (eds.) *White Racism.* New York, Dell, 1970.

Smelser, N. and Content, R. *The Changing Academic Market.* Berkeley, University of California Press, 1980.

Stanford University Committee on Minority Issues. *Building a Multiracial, Multicultural University Community.* Stanford University, 1989.

Steele, S. The recoloring of campus life. *Harpers Magazine.* 1989, February, 48–55.

Sudarkasa, N. Black enrollment in higher education: The unfulfilled promise of equality. In Dewart (Ed), *The State of Black America.* 1988. New York, National Urban League, 1988.

Takaki, R. An educated and culturally literate person must study America's multi-cultural reality. *The Chronicle of Higher Education.* 1989, 35(26), B1–2.

Terry, R. The negative impact on white values. In Bowser & Hunt (Ed), *The Impact of Racism on White Americans.* Beverly Hills, Sahe Press, 1981.

Thomas, G. *Black Students in Higher Education: Conditions and Experiences in the 1970s.* Westport, Greenwood Press, 1981.

Tichy, N. *Managing Strategic Change.* New York, Wiley, 1983.

United States Commission on Civil Rights, *Affirmative Action in the 1980s: Dismantling the Process of Discrimination.* 1981 (Clearing House Publication #65).

Vetter, B., Babco, E., and Jensen-Fischer, S. *Professional Women and Minorities.* (3rd edition) Washington, D.C., Scientific Manpower Commission, 1982.

Wall Street Journal. The privileged class. 1989, September 19.

Warren, S. One step forward, two steps back. *Black Issues in Higher Education.* 1988, 5(6), 56.

Wilson, R. and Carter, D. *Minorities in Higher Education.* Washington, D.C., American Council on Education, 1988.

Wilson, R. Recruitment and retention of minority faculty and staff. *AAHE Bulletin.* 1987, February, 2–5.

Zorn, J. Ethics, values best imparted by example. *The University Record.* 1986, July 7, 8.

CHAPTER 33

HARNESSING A DIVERSITY OF VIEWS TO UNDERSTAND MULTICULTURALISM

PATRICIA L. NEMETZ AND SANDRA L. CHRISTENSEN

Formal diversity-training programs have been growing rapidly, but anecdotal literature suggests that many such programs garner negative reactions from participants. Charges of "political correctness" and "white-male bashing" may typify such responses. This article theorizes that fundamental beliefs and multiple sources of influence must be taken into account to predict a participant's reaction. Burrell and Morgan's (1979) work on paradigmatic differences is used to identify polar opposite beliefs about multiculturalism. Ideal states of multiculturalism are then defined and predicted from these fundamental beliefs. These belief systems are compared to sources of influence to predict reaction to a formal diversity-training program. We conclude with some cautionary dialogue about realistic expectations of diversity and the polarizing effects of Balkanizing rhetoric.

Corporate public relations officers and media sources have provided a barrage of information to promote efforts to "value diversity" (Copeland, 1988; Cox, 1991; Cox & Blake, 1991). Often, such information has been accompanied with evidence illustrating the changing demographics of this multicultural society, suggesting diversity is based on racial, ethnic, gender, or physical differences. Yet well-intentioned exhortations to diversify the workplace seem somewhat inadequate, given the confusion of issues surrounding "multiculturalism." Well-intentioned statements may simply serve to attenuate underlying conflicts without adequately addressing the racial tensions and cultural alienation inflicting the nation and its institutions. In media outlets, such as radio talk shows and campus speech events, much of the rhetoric about multiculturalism has been neither honest nor dignified, thus creating the possibility of long-term strained relations. Organizations that want to become more diverse frequently hire consultants to "take care of the problem" (Rossett & Bickham, 1994: 41). However, a review of diversity-training articles turns up such phrases as "white-male bashing or a pointless waste of time" (Lunt, 1994: 53), "punishment for the insensitive" (Rossett & Bickham, 1994: 41), "PC's final frontier" (Lynch, 1994: 32), "sensitivity overload" (Kaufman, 1994: 16), and "confusion, disorder, and hostility" (Thomas, 1994: 61).

We believe much of the controversy arises from two basic issues surrounding multiculturalism. The first issue stems from a failure to understand the most fundamental differences about how individuals view ideal or desirable states of multiculturalism in today's society and how these ideals have evolved or changed during the last 30 years. Whereas integration and equal treatment were once broadly prescribed remedies for the relief of racism, sexism, and other forms of discrimination, today's societal prescriptions have become much more complex and confusing. White separatist movements have been widely criticized as racist, whereas minority separatist movements have been regarded as remedies for racism. Some authors view the "mommy track" as highly supportive of women, whereas others view it as sexist. Similar differences apply to numerous other examples, yet formal programs often fail to take into account the origins of these different views.

A second issue stems from the fact that organizationally sanctioned diversity programs are only one source of influence for individuals. Many individuals also are influenced by sources of their own choosing, which may or may not reflect the view endorsed by the organization. In fact, many of the influences can be quite polarizing and mitigate the effect of formal diversity-training programs. Unless these influences are explored and recognized, we believe that diversity programs will cease to exist, regardless of their honorable intention or efficacy.

The purpose of this article is to provide a theory predicting how individuals react to various sources of influence shaping different views of diversity. We describe multiple dimensions of multiculturalism and predict an individual's ideal state of multiculturalism in society based on Burrell and Morgan's (1979) paradigmatic differences of the view of the nature of society. We continue development of the theory (a) by acknowledging that influencers and target individuals may not necessarily share the same ideal

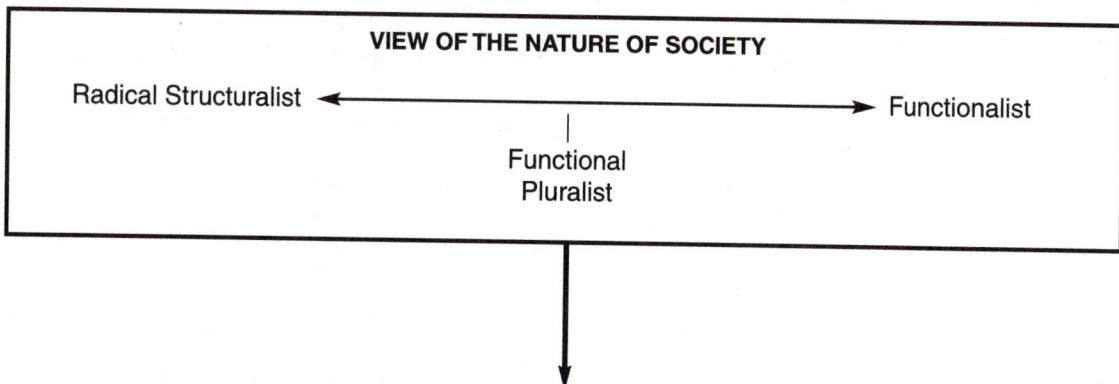

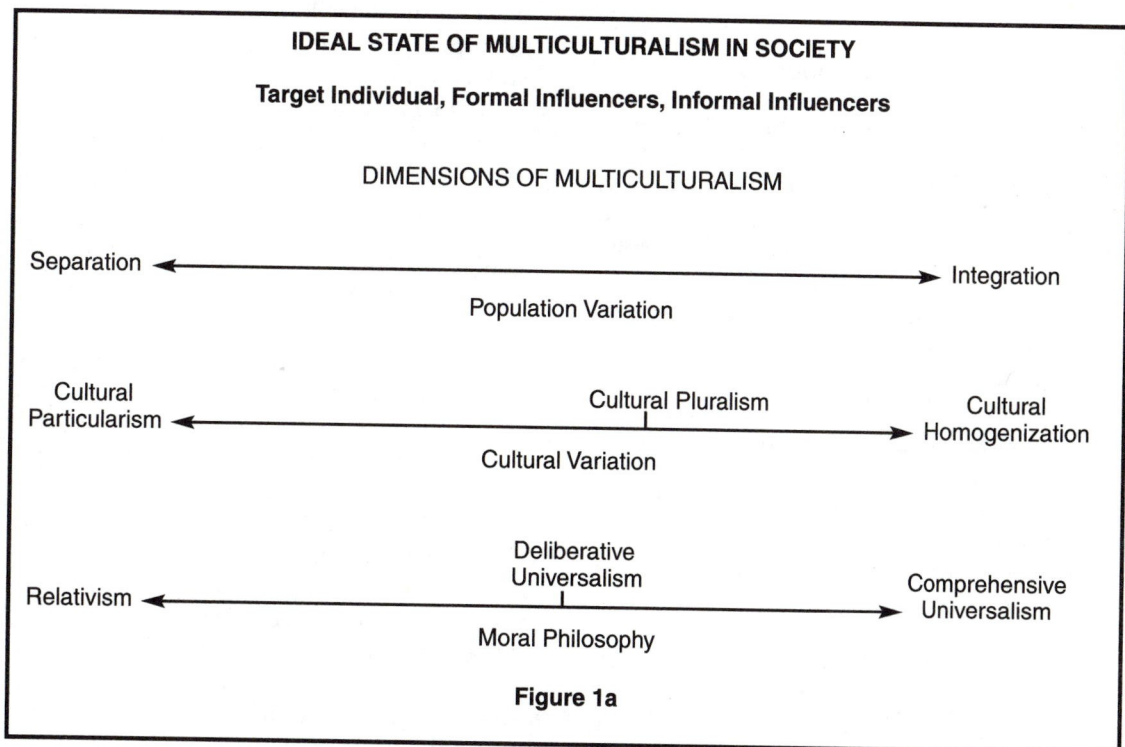

Figure 1a

Figure 33-1 View of the Nature of Society and Multiculturalism

of multiculturalism and (b) by predicting how individuals react to these differences. We then discuss the theoretical, research, and practical implications of the theory before concluding.

View of the Nature of Society and Multiculturalism

The first part of the theory is primarily concerned with defining an individual's predisposition toward a particular ideal state of multiculturalism based on a particular view of the nature of society. The view of the nature of society is based on the work of Burrell and Morgan (1979). In Figure 33-1, this relationship is illustrated and the various dimensions of multiculturalism are identified. According to the theory, individuals have certain ideals and views that may be expressed or latent. Further, the theory is reflective of late 20th-century thinking in modern democratic societies and would not be appropriate in other circumstances. We begin by defining and explaining key variables in the theory, and then we state hypothesized linkages among the variables. The process is then repeated as we examine multiple sources of influence. The unit of analysis is at the individual level.

View of the Nature of Society

Individuals interpret the world through various lenses or perspectives that form a framework of assumptions about the world. Kuhn (1962) labeled these frameworks *paradigms* and suggested they are changed only rarely through major knowledge revolutions. Burrell and Morgan's (1979) extensive work on various sociological paradigms identified "an individual's view of the nature of society" as an important way of distinguishing differences in how individuals interpret their world. Burrell and Morgan defined the concept as "two broad sociological perspectives in the form of a polarized dimension" (1979: 19). One polarity is labeled *the sociology of regulation* and the other *the sociology of radical change*. The term *sociology of regulation* refers to explanations of society that emphasize its underlying unity and cohesiveness. *Sociology of radical change* refers to explanations of the deep-seated structural conflict and modes of domination characterizing

modern society (Burrell & Morgan, 1979). Organization theorists who seek to explain social relations and events objectively through the sociology of regulation have been labeled *functionalists*, whereas those who have taken the *sociology of radical change* perspective have been labeled *radical structuralists* (Burrell & Morgan, 1979). These polar opposites view society from inherently different perspectives. Radical structuralists are interested in dramatic change, whereas functionalists are supportive of the status quo.

Radical Structuralism

Radical structuralism is rooted in the writings of Marx, who viewed capitalism as a new mode of societal organization, spawned by the dissolution of feudalism and beset by repression, oppression, and human bondage. According to radical structuralism, capitalism and its latter-day transmutations are characterized by gross economic inequalities and by vast discrepancies in power, which means that social life inevitably rests upon domination and conflict. The underlying purposes of activists who assume a radical structuralist view are to provide a critique of contemporary society and to propose social change through revolutionary and sometimes violent means (Burrell & Morgan, 1979). Radical structuralists assert that humans cannot assume a common value system built around consensus, but that a plurality of interests exist. Plurality is seen not as a purposeful exercise in democracy, but rather as a collection of central points of conflict (Worseley, 1985). Further, they view conflict resolution as an opiate and a tool of domination whose purpose is to prevent revolution and the shift of power to the oppressed. The growth of conflict between interest groups is a central and necessary feature of the movement for revolutionary change. Much of this ideology was adapted to specific problems in the United States during the 1960s and 1970s, notably the causes of minority groups and feminists, where oppression, domination, and economic inequality are recurring themes (Hughes, 1993). The viewpoint has become deeply embedded in contemporary liberal arts curricula, spawning the *dead white male* label to describe authors of traditional classics (Bloom, 1994; Hughes, 1993; Shulman, 1994). It is a substantial change in university tradition, and its effects on graduates entering the workforce may become increasingly noticeable.

Functionalism

Functionalism, by way of contrast, is a perspective whose proponents are highly supportive of the status quo, concerned with understanding society in a way that generates knowledge that can be put to practical use. They emphasize the importance of maintaining order in society and inducing social change through problem solving (Burrell & Morgan, 1979). They are essentially satisfied with society as is, though they recognize the need for ongoing activity in building consensus and social order, often within the boundaries of existing authoritative and control structures. Although their primary orientation is not activist in the same way as radical structuralists, their viewpoint may create backlash movements when serious threats to the status quo are created. Burrell and Morgan (1979) noted that most scholars, particularly those in organizational studies, assume this orientation.

Functional Pluralism

Within the functionalist perspective is a view that recognizes *functional pluralism*. Its followers emphasize conflict and power as factors affecting society, but they are primarily concerned with seeking a balance among these factors (Burrell & Morgan, 1979). To them, pluralism and controlled conflict are necessary elements in building democratic institutions through consensus. Conflict resolution is viewed as a useful exercise in creative problem solving. Change is sought primarily through results-oriented debate and consensus. Their pluralist orientation reflects reform, not revolution of oppressed against oppressor. In this respect, their approach to pluralism differs greatly from that of the radical structuralist.

Ideal State of Multiculturalism in Society

A state or condition of multiculturalism can be defined as an environment "designed for a combination of several distinct cultures" (*Webster's Collegiate Dictionary*, 1993: 764). But this definition lacks the clarity necessary to fully describe the concept's complexities in contemporary society.

A review of several streams of literature turns up three major dimensions of the multiculturalism construct. In ethnic studies concerning immigrants, two fundamental dimensions—*assimilation* and *acculturation*—have long been recognized as distinct processes underlying multicultural adaptations (Pratt, 1974). However, because multiculturalism often has been associated with groups whose ancestors have been in the country for many generations—blacks, feminists, gays, Native Americans, and so on (Fukuyama, 1993)—we prefer other terms. More inclusive terms for today's applications are *population variation* and *cultural variation*. In addition to these two dimensions, a moral dimension is evident in a variety of multiculturalism literature. A delineation of the distinctions among these dimensions is important to understanding an individual's ideal or desired state of multiculturalism in his or her society. Figure 33-1a illustrates the three dimensions with their polar labels. The continuum illustrating the state of multiculturalism ranges from an ultimate level of intergroup diversity on the left, to a complete absence of multicultural diversity on the right. Because functional pluralism is a subset of functionalism, functional pluralism and its relationships are shown slightly off-center and to the right.

Population Variation

Population variation can be defined as the extent of subgroup members' interactions and relationships with other subgroups (Pratt, 1974). Degrees of population variation exist on a continuum with complete *separation* at one extreme and complete *integration* at the other extreme. A fully integrated population is one in which relationships are randomly distributed without regard to race, ethnicity, gender, religion, or sexual orientation. Population separation, in contrast, might occur along any of these lines. Furthermore, separation might occur by choice or by imposition of an existing socioeconomic structure. For example, it has long been recognized that first-generation immigrants band together to protect themselves and to share their familiar ways of life (Worseley, 1985). Often, however, subgroups have been forced to live under ghetto conditions as the result of a social structure that affords little opportunity for access to society's goods (Sowell, 1975, 1981). However, separation also might be driven by political movements that seek to isolate majority or minority subgroups from the influence of other subgroups, such as that occurring in Yugoslavia today.

Cultural Variation

Cultural variation refers to the variety and concentration of values, behavior, and attitudes experienced and accepted by various groups within a society. At one end of the continuum is cultural particularism, and at the other end is cultural homogenization. A more centrist position is described by cultural pluralism.

Cultural particularism. *Cultural particularism* is a concept that emphasizes "within-group" similarities and "between-group" differences within a diverse society. It is most positively associated with values like solidarity, a local identity, and a "sense of community" *within a group* (Barber, 1992). According to Quincy Wright,

> A perfect community is objectively one which manifests cultural uniformity, spiritual union, institutional unity, and material unification in the highest possible degree and subjectively one with which the members resemble one another closely in evaluations, purposes, understandings, appreciations, prejudices, appearances, and other characteristics which any of them consider important. They are all in continuous contact with group sentiment, contributing to group policy and group decisions. (1964: 204)

Although providing a sense of pride and attachments to its adherents, cultural particularism in its more negative form can be parochial, isolationist, and prejudicial, "disparaging any common element [of] history, society, and culture" (Ravitch, 1991: 77). Solidarity is often secured through war (in various degrees) against outsiders, fanaticism, obedience to a hierarchy, and obliteration of individual self in the name of the group. Cultural separation is often viewed as a necessary precondition for cultural preservation.

Cultural pluralism. According to the concept, *cultural pluralism*, many cultures can coexist in the same society. It involves a process through which minority and majority culture members adopt some norms of the other group. Pluralism also means that members of a minority culture are encouraged to enact behaviors from an alternative culture as well as from the majority culture. They therefore are able to retain a sense of identity with their minority-culture group (Cox, 1991).

Cultural homogenization. *Cultural homogenization*, in contrast, is the creation of a modern, integrated society through the application of a common language, common currency, and common cosmopolitan behavior. Homogenization is the process of blending diverse elements into a smooth mixture (*Webster's Collegiate Dictionary*, 1993: 555). Homogenized societies *minimize* between-group differences through structural institutions at the societal level. In such societies, religion, culture, and nationality are marginal elements in a person's working identity (Barber, 1992). Although Sowell (1981) characterized this state as resulting from the give and take of majority and minority subgroups, others emphasize the importance of industrialization and commercialization as the driving force behind homogenization (Barber, 1992: Bloom, 1987). The question of the source of the "dominant" homogenized culture of America remains unresolved. Some critics characterize cultural homogenization as the imposition of a dominant, Eurocentric, technologically driven culture on less-than-vigilant subgroups (Worseley, 1985), whereas other critics point to the free and equal participation of all subgroups in a mass culture that appeals to the basest instincts of human existence (Bloom, 1987; Lasch, 1979). Although an offshoot of cultural homogenization might be an emphasis on the individual over the group, its major pathology is the alienation of some individuals from society at large through the marginalization of cultural and religious identity (Lasch, 1979, 1993).

Approach to Moral Philosophy

The third dimension evident in the multiculturalism literature defines differences in the approach to moral philosophy. The continuum on this dimension extends from relativism to comprehensive universalism, with deliberative universalism as a variant to comprehensive universalism. According to relativism, no common moral guidelines can be applied to all humankind, whereas according to universalism, common guidelines either exist or can be found.

Relativism. The argument from *relativism* has as its premise the well-known variation in moral codes from one society to another and from one period to another; it is also based on differences in moral beliefs between different groups and classes within a complex community (Mackie, 1987). Moral relativists assert that, ideally, tolerance of these differences is essential to openness among people. Finding common ground is not essential to the moral relativist. Moral relativism can create severe practical difficulties in a multicultural society, however, because such a wide variety of conflicts among gender, racial, ethnic, and religious groups can arise during the course of normal interaction (Wolin, 1993). Ideas of Western liberal democracy are subject to attack, even though a liberal democracy is the system most likely to make allowances for giving voice to such conflicts (Hughes, 1993). Furthermore, because moral relativism recognizes no objective moral truth, it gives great liberty to those who define all outcomes according to economic and power relationships (Shweder & Bourne, 1984). This attitude often leads to zero-sum thinking, in which the world is bifurcated into oppressors and victims, that is, a place where there is no chance for victims to better their positions unless at the expense of the oppressors. This argument, in turn, can lead to the so-called oppressors believing that they are victims of powerfully protected vocal subgroups, as in white male claims of victimization by affirmative action programs (Cox, 1991). Such dilemmas have no resolution under relativism because no guiding principle can be applied (Shweder & Bourne, 1984).

Comprehensive universalism. Proponents of universalism believe that an objective moral truth exists at a *fundamental* level and can be applied to all humankind (Taylor, 1987). Furthermore, they may take an evolutionist view and believe that some societies are more enlightened than others (Fukuyama, 1992; Shweder & Bourne, 1984). Often, these proponents support Enlightenment principles associated with the development of Western liberal democracy and argue that history is progressing linearly toward this goal (Fukuyama, 1992; Wilson, 1993). Enlightenment principles include such ideals as freedom, equality, human rights, meritocracy, and the rule of law. An alternative set of principles often is found in universalist religions, such as Christianity and Islam. A current example of such absolutist principles have been found in Pope John Paul II's encyclical, *Veritatis Splendor (The Splendor of Truth)* (Ostling, 1993). He emphasized stricter and more specific moral guidelines and suggested that they apply not only to Roman Catholics but also all humankind. Fundamentalist Protestant religions also endorse a strict and thorough set of moral guidelines based on their interpretation of the Bible. Gutman (1993) labeled such thorough sets of guidelines *comprehensive universalism*. These two examples illustrate quite clearly the problem associated with comprehensive universalist guidelines, that is, a disagreement over whose rules are *the* objective truth.

Deliberative universalism. Gutman (1993) suggested that a more viable approach in a multicultural democratic society is *deliberative universalism*. Deliberative universalists rely partly on a core of universal principles and partly upon publicly accountable deliberation to address fundamental conflicts concerning social justice. Deliberation is required in those instances of moral conflict where no substantive standard can legitimately claim a monopoly on reasonableness or justification. Deliberation encourages the search for common ground and the understanding of each other's point of view (Gutman, 1993). No guarantee exists that resolution can be found quickly, but some movement toward consensus is encouraged.

Beliefs about these three dimensions—population variation, cultural variation, and moral philosophy—can be combined to define an individual's ideal or desired state of multiculturalism. Many variations exist, not only in how the variables are combined but also in how many are accessed in one's ideals. Some people may prefer integration and hold no strong opinions on other dimensional aspects, whereas others may strongly prefer cultural particularism, separation, and judgment based on moral relativism. The ideal is unique to the individual and may remain unexpressed. Furthermore, an individual may hold to more than one ideal for different contexts, for example, favoring cultural homogenization at the workplace and cultural particularism at church.

The Relationship Between Nature of Society and Ideal State of Multiculturalism

Figure 33-1 identifies a linkage between *view of the nature of society and ideal state of multiculturalism*. We hypothesize relationships at the polar extremes and in the center based on the assumption that individuals' perceptions and ideals are influenced by their fundamental belief systems. We predict individuals who have extremely strong radical structuralist beliefs will support an ideal of multiculturalism that is consistent with separation, cultural particularism, and relativism, whereas individuals who have extremely strong functionalist beliefs will support an ideal that is consistent with cultural homogenization and comprehensive universalism. We predict that functional pluralists will support an ideal that is consistent with integration, cultural pluralism, and deliberative universalism.

Radical Structuralist View

Radical structuralists use Marxist theory to explain all relationships in terms of *material* (economic) structures. Marx took no account of individual character, moral conviction, or altruistic behavior, which have been viewed as social constructions of existing elites who seek the stabilization of their power base. Using this reasoning, morality and cultural practices are thus determined by who holds power. In Marx's writings, the primary determinant of behavior is membership in an economic class—the *bourgeoisie* is inherently oppressive; the *proletariat* is inherently alienated (Roberts, 1993). However, his theory is not particularly cultural. Adapting his theory to cultural groups leads to the inevitable classification of individuals according to group membership without taking into account individual circumstances or character. Males, whites, European-Americans, and/or heterosexuals, by virtue of their traditionally higher economic status, are seen as dominating existing structures and institutions in the United States; hence, they are oppressive (Hughes, 1993). Whereas Marx and radical structuralists have a utopian, post-revolutionary vision consistent with egalitarianism and social justice through economic equality, *revolutionary* activity

today requires the demonization of elitists and oppressors. Radical structuralists are likely to see the greatest threat as coming from the subtle influence of a dominant, all-powerful elite. Therefore, within present-day capitalist America, radical structuralists are most likely to espouse some degree of isolation from these elitist attitudes, consciousness raising to *illuminate* the truth of domination, the establishment of their own power base, and a *revolutionary* movement that includes separatism, an emphasis on between-group differences and moral relativism. Thus, we suggest that individuals who have extremely strong radical structuralist beliefs are likely to support an ideal of multiculturalism that is consistent with separatism, cultural particularism, and moral relativism.

Functionalist View

Functionalists, who prefer unity and social cohesion, are likely to see the greatest threat to society as coming from conflict and a failure to bind society together with common values; therefore, they are more likely to espouse cultural homogenization and comprehensive universalism. To them, the status quo and existing authority structures are the mechanisms for expressing society's common values; the inexorable movement toward homogenization (Barber, 1992) and the authoritative nature of comprehensive universalism are not problematic for them. Rather, those characteristics are seen as solutions to problems.

The functionalist position on population variation (integration-separation) is more complex. A functionalist's source of the common values that bind society together—whether secular or religious—must be examined to predict the relationship for this dimension. Functionalists who do not support certain types of comprehensive universalism or who support moral universalism based on secular Enlightenment principles would undoubtedly endorse integration. It is far more difficult to argue that all those at the functional extreme would support integration, particularly if their moral universalism is based on certain types of religious fundamentalism. For example, Kolchin (1993) indicated that a major tenet among religions of the American South came with the recognition that Christianity applied universally, even to slaves, but it was perfectly acceptable to separate black churches from white churches. Furthermore, some fundamentalist religions are absolute in their position on the role of women and acceptance of sexual behavior, often endorsing limited interaction between the genders and shunning those who deviate from their sexual and religious mores. Because of these fundamental differences over whose universalism is the truth, we cannot predict a correlation between functionalism and integration or between functionalism and separatism. We can, however, predict that individuals who have extremely strong functionalist beliefs are likely to support an ideal of multiculturalism that is consistent with cultural homogenization and comprehensive universalism.

Functional Pluralist View

Functional pluralists also are supportive of a society bound together by common values. However, rather than relying on existing control and authority structures, they seek the use of debate and conflict resolution to build consensus. In a diverse society, this behavior suggests they are essentially open to many differences as long as the ultimate endpoint is a commonality of values. The underlying belief is consistent with the idea that many individuals of different cultures can provide input into building integrated relationships through deliberation. Thus, individuals who have extremely strong functional pluralist beliefs are likely to support an ideal of multiculturalism that is consistent with integration, cultural pluralism, and deliberative universalism.

Multiple Sources of Influence

Formal influencers, informal influencers, and target individuals all have a view of the nature of society and a view of the ideal state of multiculturalism in society (hereafter referred to as *views* and *ideals*). Further, the examination of multiple sources of influence assumes that an individual targeted for a formal diversity program exists in an environment rich with opportunity for interaction with a variety of other people. Influence could originate with informal sources as well as with formal sources. We are concerned primarily with the target's reaction to a formal diversity program through which the formal influencer is motivated to create some change in a group of target individuals. A target

individual is an employee, student, or organizational participant who is required or encouraged to attend a formal diversity program.

Formal Influence

Formal influence is defined as organization-sponsored intervention intended to affect a target's attitudes, behaviors, and/or emotions toward multicultural diversity. Organizations engage in two major types of formal influence to promote diversity—training and setting policy.

Training. Diversity training exists in many different forms. Table 33-1 defines and describes several types and methodologies. Methodologies differ greatly among the different types; some are psychologically intensive and participative (psychotherapeutic approaches), and others are more superficial and less participative (lectures and listening). Some types of training have content that is consistent with a certain view of the nature of society, but most are adaptable to the trainer's view. Psychotherapeutic approaches generally involve functional pluralist views because they seek common ground through participative group therapy. However, other types are highly adaptive. Examples of techniques associated with different views are included in Table 33-1. For example, cultural awareness training can be used to uncover common stereotypes for the purpose of discrediting them and for building consensus about how to treat other people. This approach represents a functional pluralist view. Alternatively, cultural awareness training can be used to make *oppressive* employees aware of how *oppressed employees feel* (Caudron, 1993). This approach represents a radical structuralist approach. The view of the nature of society expressed in the training program and/or by the trainer is important because it may or may not coincide with the view of those who will be influenced.

Organization policy. Cox (1991) noted that organization policy is an important determinant of success when implementing diversity programs. Top management support is manifested through the provision of resources and inclusion of diversity in corporate strategy. In addition to voluntary implementation of such organization policies, affirmative action programs provide legal validation for promoting diversity efforts (Cox & Blake, 1991). However, formal organization policy may be somewhat

Table 33-1			
Types of Formal Diversity Training			
Types of Training	**Description**	**Sample Functionalist or Functional Pluralist Tactics**	**Sample Radical Structuralist Tactics**
Ethnic, Black, or Feminist Studies	Scholarly academic class using in-depth analysis to review status of minority group in dominant society	Studying the contributions of women and minority members to American society (National Public Radio, 1993)	Criticizing Western civilization using deconstructionist techniques, then promoting ethnocentric studies to dramatically overhaul beliefs about existing institutions (Jaroff, 1994)
Psychotherapeutic Approaches	Group therapy involving groups experiencing conflict. The approach is based on the belief that the roots of ethnic hostility lie in the infantile need to externalize unwelcome self-images; ethnic rival becomes target of projected guilt and self-loathing (Cullen, 1993)	Dwelling on the history of animosity and loss brought on by ethnic hatred. Acknowledging through group therapy with neighbors that wrongs occurred. Acting contrite if appropriate (Cullen, 1993)	—
Sensitivity Training	Sensitizing individuals to feelings provoked by discrimination (Smith, 1990; *Spokesman-Review*, 1993)	Separating individuals by eye color. Discriminating against one eye color arbitrarily to illustrate the underlying belief that all individuals are hurt by discrimination	Separating men from women. *Empowering* women to sexually harass men through role play to illustrate the underlying belief that women are victimized by men (Caudron, 1993)
Dissonance Creation	Purposely creating cognitive dissonance with the hope that the target will resolve dissonance by changing attitude (Leippe and Eisenstadt, 1994)	Requiring an individual who shows initial prejudice to write an essay showing the absurdities of stereotyping	Requiring an individual who shows initial prejudice to debate in favor of the idea that whites are oppressive
Cultural Awareness	Exploration of cultural or gender differences (Gordon, 1992)	Discussing stereotypes and unintentional slights. Building consensus on how to avoid them	Separating oppressed individuals from oppressive individuals. Encouraging oppressed individuals to express feelings to oppressive individuals (Caudron, 1993)
Legal Awareness	Explaining discrimination laws	Describing various activities that violate the law and stating the consequences of violation (Thomas, 1994)	Discussing unfairness and bias in laws and the injustice present in a white-male-dominated justice system (Schafran, 1993)

problematic when policymakers take a unidimensional view of multiculturalism. For example, Gordon (1992) asserted that most organizations use the term *diversity program* as a synonym for equal employment opportunity or affirmative action. Such organizations rely primarily on the integration-separation dimension of multiculturalism to define their programs and disregard the cultural variation and moral philosophy dimensions. Organizations that are truly multicultural are not only interested in hiring workers with various backgrounds but also in accepting some of the norms from the various backgrounds (Cox, 1991).

Informal Influence

Informal influence is that which is not sanctioned by formal authority, organizational policy, or certified expertise (Mintzberg, 1983). It is often conceptualized as a mass of competing power groups, each seeking to influence policy in terms of its own interests (Strauss, 1964). Informal influence can come from a variety of sources, such as reference groups (Bock, Beeghley, & Mixon, 1983; Hall, Varca, & Fisher, 1986; Hooper, 1982; Merton, 1958; Merton & Rossi, 1950; Montgomery, 1980), support groups and career networks (Ibarra, 1993), political activists, media rhetoric (Triandis, 1971) and organization culture (Martin & Siehl, 1983; Mintzberg, 1983; Smircich, 1983; Van Maanen & Barley, 1984). Informal influence often involves the search for a common understanding of acceptable behavior, communication with similar people, and an acknowledgment of roughly the same problems (Van Maanen & Barley, 1984). Although the sources of informal influence can be a consequence of the social circumstances to which an individual was born or directed, they often are chosen on the basis of self-categorization (Turner, 1982; Turner & Oakes, 1989). Also, some types of informal influence may be more influential than others; for example, media has been shown to have only a moderate impact (Becker, McCombs, & McLeod, 1975).

According to a number of theories and empirical studies, informal influence is particularly important in shaping the views of individuals, primarily through social-identity processes. Asch (1952, 1956), Moscovici (1976), and Turner and Oakes (1989) argued that the nor-

mative expectation of similar others is more important in shaping views than is information. They argued, along with dissonance theorists (Festinger, 1957; Simon, Greenberg, & Brehm, 1995), that disagreement with people with whom one expects to agree creates uncomfortable uncertainty that acts to align one's views with the other or to trivialize the issue. Furthermore, the influence of similar others is important for polarizing and extremitizing one's initially similar views. This concept is described as *group polarization*, which is the tendency of group discussion or some related manipulation to extremitize the average of group members' responses on some dimension from pre-to postdiscussion in the direction of the prevailing tendency (Moscovici & Zavalloni, 1969; Turner & Oakes, 1989). It arises because people seek to conform to what defines their social group as a whole in contrast to other groups (Turner & Oakes, 1989). This socializing process also is evident in work organizations, where organization leaders frequently achieve their positions by conforming to the *status quo*. Often, individuals in a position of organizational leadership believe their work group to be a primary reference group and are under severe pressure to conform to social norms. Kanter (1977) argued that the pervasiveness of conformity pressures and the development of exclusive management circles stem from the degree of uncertainty surrounding managerial positions. "The greater the uncertainty, the greater the pressures for those who have to trust each other to form a homogeneous group" (Kanter, 1977: 49).

A number of phenomena and empirical studies confirm the theoretical importance of informal influence when it is applied to issues of multiculturalism. Conventional wisdom suggests that an individual's view of other races and ethnic groups is strongly determined by the age of five under the influence of reference groups (Adorno, Frenkel-Brunswik, Levinson, & Sanford, 1950; Frenkel-Brunswik & Havel, 1953; Maddi, 1968; Triandis, 1971). In general, attraction to demographically similar others is strongly supported in empirical studies (Feldman, 1968; Hornstein, 1978; Hornstein, Fisch, & Holmes, 1968; Hornstein, Masor, Sole, & Heilman, 1971; Krebs, 1970; Piliavin, Rodin, & Piliavin, 1969; Stotland, 1969; Tafjel, Billig, Bundy, & Plament, 1971), and similarity exerts strong influence on views (McCroskey, Richmond, & Daly, 1975; McGuire, 1985). Insko, Nacoste, and Moe (1983) found that attraction and persuasive impact increase with ideological and demographic similarity, and ideological similarity has been increasing in importance in the United States. Myers and Bishop (1970) empirically verified a group-polarization effect on racial attitudes by showing that the intensity of initial attitudes increased after discussion with similar others. Stigmatizing language is an everyday manifestation of group-polarization effect, with *politically correct* and *patriotically correct* statements used to establish solidarity among like-minded participants, as in Pat Robertson's characterization of "a feminist agenda, a socialist anti-family political movement that encourages women to leave their husbands, kill their children, practice witchcraft, destroy capitalism, and become lesbian" (Wicker, 1991: A12). These informal-influence processes, in general, are thought to be the primary source of influence for individuals, with more formal informational influence playing a secondary role only in limited circumstances (Rajecki, 1990).

Individual's Commitment to His or Her Own Views and Ideals

The commitment to one's own views and ideals is a measure of the stability of one's initial views in the presence of new information and/or a measure of the lengths to which an individual will go to achieve a desirable state in society. Both political literature in the 1960s and literature on attitudinal change have dwelled extensively on this concept. Bell and Kristol (1965) labeled those who have an extreme commitment to their ideals *ideologues*. Ideologues, according to Bell and Kristol (1965), *preconceive reality* and attempt to engineer a *new utopia* (Bell, 1965). An *ideologue* differs from an *idealist* (one who is guided by one's ideals), in that he or she assumes one can place ideals before practical considerations. Both the idealist and idealogue, nevertheless, have a strong motivation to achieve a more desirable state of society. Lack of commitment, by way of contrast, may be characterized by apathy and/or alienation. An intermittent

stage has been defined as *latency* by Mann (1986). The idea of latency is especially important to radical structuralists, who believe revolution will occur if only individuals can be aroused from their latent state (Mann, 1986).

In the literature on attitude change, commitment to one's views is an important component in the integration (Siero & Doosje, 1993) of social judgment theory (SJT; Sherif & Hovland, 1961; Sherif, Sherif, & Nebergall, 1965) and the elaboration likelihood model (ELM; Petty & Cacioppo, 1986). According to SJT, every person has three latitudes of attitudinal commitment: a latitude of acceptance (opinions with which the person agrees), a latitude of noncommitment (opinions with which the person neither agrees nor disagrees), and a latitude of rejection (opinions with which the person disagrees). People are persuaded to change attitude most strongly by messages that are at moderate distance from the recipient's initial attitude (Freedman, 1964; Wittaker, 1965) and that are in the individual's latitude of noncommitment (Siero & Doosje, 1993). It is in the latitude of noncommitment that individuals are most likely to elaborately process new information that might change their views (Siero & Doojse, 1993); regarding other latitudes, individuals will remain committed to their initial views and distort new information (O'Keefe, 1990). Some evidence indicates that attitudes people consider personally important are resistant to change (Fine, 1957; Gorn, 1975) and stable over time (Krosnik, 1988; Schuman & Presser, 1981).

Reactions to Formal Diversity Programs

In defining reaction to a formal diversity program, we select two separate dependent variables to comprehensively define the terms—*behavior and attitude change* and *response to the diversity program itself.*

Behavior and Attitude Change

It has often been noted in the training literature that training evaluation is inadequate because it fails to measure the appropriate dependent variables (Bunker & Cohen, 1977;

Latham & Saari, 1979). Training evaluation should assess if the program accomplished what it intended to accomplish; it also should assess how the target individuals responded to the training itself (Latham & Saan, 1979). With this in mind, we begin with the assumption that diversity training is intended to provoke some change in *behavior* or *attitude*. Thus, a measure of such change becomes an important dependent variable.

Response to the Formal Diversity Program Itself

Response to the formal diversity program itself also is important because survival of diversity programs depends on this outcome. The interest in *response* also is clearly expressed in the practitioner literature, particularly when unusually intense organizational conflict has been generated by a program. The intended response to a formal diversity-training program is difficult to define because the goals of the program often are undetermined (Rossett & Bickham, 1994). Without well-defined organizational goals, the intention of the program may become intermixed with the personal intention of the trainer. If the trainer operates from a radical structuralist perspective, the goals may be to increase conflict among interest groups and to raise the consciousness of participants about oppression (as is typical in many university diversity programs). If the trainer operates from a functional pluralist perspective, the goal may be to increase harmony and productivity. Because of these differences, the definition of *response* must rest upon some assumptions about what is the desirable outcome. We define *response* according to anecdotal reports noted in the diversity literature, acknowledging that the literature exhibits a functionalist bias. *Negative response* to a formal diversity program includes emotions, attitudes, and behaviors consistent with confusion, disorder, hostility (Thomas, 1994), punishment (Rossett & Bickham, 1994), resentment, vulnerability, and anger (Caudron, 1993). *Positive response* includes emotions, attitudes, and behaviors consistent with bias reduction (Dovidio, 1993), harmony, inclusion, legal compliance (Rossett & Bickham, 1994), creativity, productivity (Cox, 1991), and approval (Thomas, 1994).

Dynamics That Influence Reactions to Formal Diversity-Training Programs

We predict reaction to formal diversity programs based on SJT (Sherif & Hovland, 1961; Sherif et al., 1965; Siero & Doosje, 1993) and the ELM (Petty & Cacioppo, 1986). According to SJT, the likelihood of change following a persuasive message is dependent on the discrepancy between the position advocated in the message and the target individual's initial view, with moderate discrepancy evoking the most change. However, the degree of discrepancy between a person's views and the message conveyed in a training program is not sufficient to explain reactions to the training program. A person's degree of commitment to an ideal or a view also affects how that person reacts. People who are weakly committed to an ideal or a view are more likely to be in a state that is receptive to new information and reasoning than are those who are strongly committed (Siero & Doosje, 1993; Triandis, 1971). In the case of diversity training, target individuals who agree in principle with the views and ideals of the formal diversity program would likely have a positive response to it. People who initially disagree but have a weak commitment to their own ideals may respond positively if they learn something that causes them to elaborately process the information (Petty & Cacioppo, 1986; Siero & Doosje, 1993). These individuals are the most likely candidates for behavioral and attitudinal change, but where target individuals have an initially strong disagreement with the views of the program, the probability and intensity of a negative response increases as the commitment to their own ideals increases. For example, an individual who regularly agrees with and contributes to conservative radio talk shows probably shows a high commitment to a functionalist point of view. Exposure to a radical structuralist viewpoint in a diversity-training program would likely create a very strong negative response and little or no change.

Another predictor for reaction to a formal diversity program is the predominant view expressed by informal influencers. If an individual has little exposure to informal sources of information on diversity, the issue is likely to have little personal importance (Boninger, Krosnick, & Berent, 1995), and the formal diversity program will be the most influential (Siero & Doosje, 1993). However, because informal sources of influence generally are chosen by the individual rather than recommended by the organization, they tend to be more influential than formal sources (Berent, Krosnick, & Boninger, 1993; Triandis, 1971). Further, informal influencers can offer social support for arguments that refute a formal influencer (Mitchell, 1982). Therefore, we predict that consistently self-selected informal influence takes precedence over formal influence. Where the two are not congruent, the probability of a negative response to a formal diversity-training program increases. For example, if friends and support groups operate from a radical structuralist viewpoint, they are not likely to favor greater productivity and harmony with the *dominant majority*. Programs that promote such goals will receive a negative reaction among target individuals with radical structuralist leanings.

Organizational Influence

Though organizations frequently announce formal organization policies to define their position on an issue, the formal announcement may be perceived as nothing more than a facade. The *real* views of the organization may be expressed more subtly through an organizational culture that negates formal pronouncements (Van Maanen & Barley, 1984). For diversity programs, this may be evidenced by much sloganeering with little or no resources dedicated to diversity (Cox & Blake, 1991). Further difficulties occur when organizations define diversity as forced affirmative action programs (Gordon, 1992), or when there are subtle messages to conform to the norms of exclusive management circles (Kanter, 1977). As a consequence of the mismatch between formal and informal organization practices and values, target individuals may become cynical about formal diversity programs. Little behavior and attitude change is likely to occur when the organization's diversity goals are not perceived as serious (Minizberg, 1983). Attendance at formal diversity-training programs also may be perceived as occasions for appearance's sake only. In such circumstances, nega-

tive responses to the formal diversity training are likely. Only when the informal organizational culture corresponds to the formal pronouncements of the organization will target individuals give due consideration to the seriousness of the issue. To summarize, behavioral change, attitudinal change, and positive responses to training are more likely to occur when the organization's informal influence is congruent with formal organization influence compared to when it is not.

Training Methodology

The importance of training methodology has long been recognized in the training literature, and participative methods have been particularly important for changing attitudes and eliciting positive responses (Carroll, Paine, & Ivancevich, 1972). Participation of individuals who have many different views may be even more important. Vinokur and Burnstein (1978) found that some group depolarization is likely to occur when members of a group with heterogeneous opinions participate in discussing an issue. The causal mechanism for this depolarization is believed to be a transition from normative social influences as primary determinant of attitude to informational influence as primary determinant. Normative influence is based on the desire to conform to the expectations of similar others, whereas informational influence is based on the acceptance of information of others as evidence about reality. When similar others are not available for comparison, informational influence has more impact. This is particularly true when multiple arguments and, thus, multiple choices are provided (Rajecki, 1990). From this argument, it follows that formal diversity-training programs that fully engage target individuals and promote open acknowledgment of multiple viewpoints are more likely to elicit a change in views and a positive response compared to those that do not.

Theoretical, Research, and Practical Implications

Theoretical Implications

Our theory is important because it provides a foundation for the concept of multiculturalism and an analysis of how different paradigmatic views create complexities in developing effective formal diversity programs. In public policy and liberal arts literatures, both prominent black scholars (Boynton, 1995) and white scholars (Hughes, 1993; Wilson, 1993) have begun to critically examine the meaning and limitations of multiculturalism, often in the form of essays. This article overcomes the *fuzzy thinking* that may be a part of critical essays because it provides a structured framework for the development of a common body of knowledge on the topic of multiculturalism. Because some of the knowledge generated in other disciplines may not yet have filtered into management literatures, we believe the theory represents state-of-the-art thinking about multiculturalism and cultural diversity.

Well-defined concepts and relationships are necessary for continued critical evaluation and the development of a meaningful dialogue about the consequences of paradigmatic differences when applied to multiculturalism. The challenge or paradox of diversity lies in the fact that diversity today is defined only along cultural lines, rather than according to differences of opinion. For example, it is paradoxical that proponents of *politically correct* speech codes often are active proponents of cultural diversity, yet speech codes restrict a diversity of opinion (as expressed through paradigmatic differences). Our theory offers a vehicle for respecting diversity of opinion while also recognizing the value of cultural diversity.

The theory also provides a balanced approach for assessing the reasons why diversity programs garner support or failure. Because of the highly charged emotions surrounding the issue of cultural diversity, researchers, formal influencers, and participants often interpret results on the basis of their own paradigmatic biases. Negative responses to diversity-training programs may be interpreted as racism or sexism, when, in fact, participants may be confused about programs that emphasize racial or gender differences when they had been taught in the past to be *color blind* or *gender neutral*. Although we do not refute that a negative response may be due to prejudice, in our theory we take into account a broader variety of reasons for the response and some basis for assessing the paradigmatic

biases of the trainer or researcher. We also examine the influence target in the full context of multiple sources of influence. Diversity programs often compete with informal influences, both inside and outside of the organization, which present formidable challenges; these influences must be included in assessing the likelihood of success in a diversity program.

We also suggest that Pfeffer's (1993) call to limit future organizational research to a single paradigmatic viewpoint may be premature. Pfeffer (1993) identified lack of consensus about theoretical structures as a serious limitation in advancing knowledge. Although we leave that particular argument to others, we believe that an individual's paradigmatic viewpoint can be a *very powerful* predictor of his or her behavior and attitudes. Failure to acknowledge these different viewpoints would limit a whole range of explanations that deserve merit. Certainly, the most plausible explanation for this decade's irrational international ethnic conflicts lies in the ability of demagogues to influence others to live by their paradigmatic viewpoints. These viewpoints must be thoroughly understood if a rational defense is to be mounted against destructive behaviors.

Several points of contention may arise from the theory. For example, conservative critics often portray Americans as far too entrenched in moral relativism and having little or no regard for universal moral reasoning (Bloom, 1987). Although we respectfully acknowledge this contention, we believe a majority of Americans are not radical structuralists; rather, we suspect that the difference between deliberative and comprehensive universalism has not been adequately addressed in these critiques. The critiques do, however, represent alternative theories that can be tested against this one. Other theorists may argue that radical structuralists have social integration in mind as the ultimate goal of social organization and do not favor separatism. We believe there is merit in this argument, but our theory is limited to American society as it exists today. In capitalist America, radical structuralists must continuously create conflict to relieve perceived oppression. The pursuit of such conflict often requires unrelenting commitment to such an extent that the radical structuralist can lose sight of the ultimate goal. This loss of sight can result in an unintended lifelong smuggle as conflict expands for such a person without ultimate end (revolution) or intermediate resolution (Tinder, 1989). Our theory assumes a certain stability of American society that precludes revolution any time soon; in such a sustained condition, conflict becomes the goal in and of itself.

Last, the theory raises the question of whether individuals' different paradigmatic viewpoints can or should be reconciled to improve the viability of diversity programs. Burrell and Morgan (1979) indicated that these viewpoints simply cannot be reconciled. Proponents of each viewpoint harbor suspicion about the hidden agenda of others. Suspicion is not conducive to reconciliation. Further, predictions that paradigmatic or ideological differences would resolve over time (Bell & Kristol, 1965) have not come to pass. Dionne (1991) noted that Bell's (1965:59) publication of *The End of Ideology* was "followed almost immediately by an intensely ideological period, especially in America." We must conclude, therefore, that theoretical efforts at this time should center on defining different viewpoints and predicting their relationships to behavior and attitudes. Further, this knowledge should be discussed openly, so that individuals can make an educated choice as to their beliefs.

Research Implications

Despite the rapid growth in diversity-training programs (Rossett & Bickham, 1994), little research has been conducted to assess their impact. Anecdotal evidence offers a pot pourri of advice, suggesting that empirical examination must begin before problems are worsened rather than improved (Kaufman, 1994; Lunt, 1994; Lynch, 1994; Rossett & Bickham, 1994; Thomas, 1994). We agree with this assessment but acknowledge that researchers must be especially careful in controlling for response bias when conducting research on this topic. For example, although most direct surveys show that Americans favor integration in general, they quickly alter their responses when questions about integration are applied to their own neighborhoods (Dovidio, 1993).

A substantial amount of instrument development and measurement must be conducted to assess the constructs defined in the theory. A number of unobtrusive techniques may be used to assess certain variables. For example,

scenarios with alternative explanations could be used to assess people's agreement with different paradigmatic viewpoints. Laboratory studies are useful for measuring the effect that rhetoric has on attitudes and behaviors. Experimental methods can be used to measure the effect of cultural diversity classes on university students. Most important, field studies can be conducted with the cooperation of organizations undergoing diversity training. In fact, researchers in this area appear to have a number of avenues to pursue and fewer impediments when compared to other subject areas.

A second approach that may yield interesting results is comparing the effects that various training programs have on different outcome variables. For example, if behavior is the outcome of most concern, legal awareness with a functional viewpoint may be the program most likely to yield positive results for the organization. By informing employees of the law and the consequences for breaking the law, the trainer may provide sufficient incentive for employees to engage in appropriate behaviors. Such training would not necessarily be enough, however, to change employees' attitudes about diversity. Psychotherapeutic approaches and dissonance creation may be more useful for changing people's attitudes.

In conclusion, research in this field appears to be reasonably feasible. The theory offers some guidelines for beginning a series of research projects that may enable greater understanding of multiculturalism. Furthermore, the methodologies necessary for adequate evaluation of training programs have received considerable attention in the training literature (Bunker & Cohen, 1977; Campbell, Dunnette, Lawler, & Wieck, 1970; Latham & Saari, 1979), so the research techniques are immediately available for a researcher's use.

Practical Implications

The theory has several important implications for practitioners, but we also should caution practitioners to have realistic expectations about the potential impact of formal diversity programs. First, the theory indicates that formal diversity programs are most likely to induce behavioral and attitudinal change under the following specific conditions: (a) when target individuals have not yet committed to strong paradigmatic views of their own, (b) when conflicting informal influence is absent, and (c) when the organizational culture supports a well-defined ideal of multiculturalism. Many target individuals may, in fact, have a wide latitude of noncommitment or be in a state of latency about multiculturalism, so formal diversity training may have far-reaching potential. Furthermore, formal diversity-training programs may provide useful information that causes target individuals to develop a view of multiculturalism that is congruent with the intent of the program. However, practitioners must be aware that they may be "awakening a sleeping elephant" when they broach the topic of multiculturalism. Informal influencers have as much potential to arouse individuals in the state of latency as do formal influencers. When individuals seek the support of informal influencers to refute the message of formal diversity programs, they may, in fact, become even more "dug in" in a paradigmatic viewpoint at variance with the formal program (Perloff, 1993: 205). Furthermore, this may arouse antidiversity-program activism by eliciting a negative response to the formal diversity program itself. For these reasons, we believe the most appropriate approach to formal diversity training is to use the foundation of knowledge developed in the theory as a basis for discussion of various viewpoints. It may, in fact, be useful to develop a certification process for trainers based on this foundation of knowledge.

Second, it may be unrealistic to assume that many individuals in organizations do not have a functionalist or functional pluralist bias. Trainers who have radical structuralist leanings may speculate on how to change this situation. Radical structuralist training programs have, in fact, been reported in the literature (see Table 33-1). However, we believe it is extremely difficult to change individuals to a radical structuralist viewpoint in a work organization setting. Radical structuralists question the very nature and purpose of work organizations, particularly in capitalist economies, where they are perceived as a major cause of oppression and domination. According to Mann (1986), the true radical structuralist must operate outside the boundaries of work organizations, encouraging escalating episodes of protest until revolution is ultimately achieved. Radical structuralists cannot rely on the gentle art of persuasion in a

training setting to fulfill radical ends. Trainers who take radical structuralism out of its appropriate context and who fail to convey the richness of its literature mistakenly assume that all individuals have a common understanding of concepts like oppression and domination. These concepts should remain in an educational setting where a thorough examination and critique of the viewpoint can be made.

Third, the theory encourages a methodology of open dialogue for formal diversity-training programs. Open discussion creates the possibility for individuals to choose what they believe in an educated manner. Presenting only a single viewpoint may appear to be a "salesmanship" job rather than serious discourse. Open discussion of various viewpoints also reduces the threat of normative sanction within the training session. If the threat is reduced, individuals are less likely to seek social support for their own point of view in a different setting. Long-term change is then more likely to occur.

Last, the theory suggests that practitioners must realistically evaluate their own willingness to undertake the difficult task of "valuing diversity," when the potential for intense criticism exists. In modern times, multiculturalism has been central to most memorable political events. Horrific wars, great acts of moral courage, and difficult civil rights movements have characterized the intensity of the struggle for greater inclusiveness of all peoples. The intensity of these events attests to the difficulty of changing attitudes about and behaviors regarding multiculturalism. Recent attacks on affirmative action provide fresh evidence that diversity programs remain a controversial topic. Practitioners must not be naive in assuming that everyone will accept diversity as a worthy goal.

Reflections and Conclusion

Lack of a well-defined foundation of knowledge about multiculturalism has created a situation whereby much of the information about multiculturalism comes in the form of rhetoric. However, rhetoric that polarizes, rather than informs, has characterized much of the debate accessed by average citizens. We note from history that the impulse toward tribalism, or Balkanization, destroys the civilization in which the impulse toward polarization has free rein. For this reason alone, debaters of multiculturalism must shift course to a more reasoned and civilized dialogue. Our theory provides a basis for such dialogue.

Our theory is not excessively optimistic about diversity; we attempt to firmly ground our expectations in reality. Philosophers have long recognized a tension between the individual and the community or between the smaller organizing unit and the larger society. Researchers must recognize that no utopian solution exists to resolve this tension. The unfortunate consequence of struggling for a utopian ideal is that the ideal turns into a tyranny once in practice (Tinder, 1989). History is also littered with lost civilizations that failed to set high standards for appreciating the uniqueness of others while also recognizing a common humanity. Part of the human condition is struggling for this balance. Our theory attempts to identify the differences that define the struggle.

Researchers and organizational participants must recognize that attachment to "one's own" is not easily abandoned, but as organizational citizens, people must also recognize that attachment to "one's own" is not all that matters. A sense of dissatisfaction and yearning may characterize typical sentiments about the alienating effects of organizational life, not just subgroup members' sentiments. Though people might hope for greater personal attachments and cultural meaning in their work life, the organization is limited in the intensity of diversity it can absorb before Balkanization occurs.

Organizations also have obligations to their citizens. Forced affirmative action plans may be insufficient to resolve the tensions associated with diversity. However, more important, organizations must recognize the performance limitations imposed by "organization-man" social conformity. Repression of unorthodox ideas may be far more damaging to individual initiative and organizational success than is political dissension. Broad-based and informal efforts to eliminate mediocrity by pursuing heterogeneous ideas may go further in relieving tensions than more formalized programs. To the extent that formalized programs are pursued, organizational leaders must be responsible for articulating a vision of diversity, for diligently examining the content of diversity programs, and for empirically evaluating the results of diversity training. Programs that exacerbate tensions surrounding diversity should be abandoned in favor of those that promote tolerance and curiosity.

Patricia L. Nemetz received her Ph.D. from the University of Washington. She is an associate professor of management at Eastern Washington University. Her research interests include the technology-human interface and both domestic and international multiculturalism, with an emphasis on Eastern Europe.

Sandra L. Christensen received her Ph.D. from the University of Washington. She is an assistant professor of management at Eastern Washington University. Her current research interests include ethics and public policy and environmental history.

References

Adorno, T. W., Frenkel-Brunswik, E., Levinson, D. J., & Sanford, R. N. 1950. *The authoritarian personality.* New York: Harper.

Asch, S. E. 1952. *Social psychology.* Engelwood Cliffs, NJ: Prentice Hall.

Asch, S. E. 1956. Studies of independence and conformity: A minority of one against a unanimous majority. *Psychological monographs: General and applied.* 70: 1–70 (Whole No. 416).

Barber, B. J. 1992. Jihad vs McWorld. *Atlantic Monthly,* 269(3): 53–63.

Becker, L. B., McCombs, M. E., & McLeod, J. M. 1975. The development of political cognitions. In S. H. Chattee (Ed.), *Political communication: Issues and strategies for research:* 21–63. Beverly Hills, CA: Sage.

Bell, D. 1965. *The end of ideology.* New York: Free Press.

Bell, D., & Kristol, I. 1965. What is in the public interest? *Public Interest,* 1(1): 3–5.

Berent, M. K., Krosnick, J. A., & Boninger, D. S. 1993. *Attitude importance and memory for attitude-relevant information.* Unpublished manuscript.

Bloom, A. 1987. *The closing of the American mind.* New York: Simon & Schuster.

Bloom, H. 1994. *The Western canon.* New York: Harcourt Brace Jovanovich.

Bock, E., Beeghley, W., & Mixon, A. J. 1983. Religion, socioeconomic status, and sexual morality: An application of reference group theory. *Sociological Quarterly,* 24: 545–559.

Boninger, D. S., Krosnick, J. A., & Berent, M. K. 1995. Origins of attitude importance: Self-interest, social identification, and value relevance. *Journal of Personality and Social Psychology,* 68: 61–80.

Boynton, R. S. 1995. The new intellectual. *Atlantic Monthly*, 275(3): 53–71.

Burrell, G., & Morgan, G. 1979. *Sociological paradigms and organizational analysis.* London: Heinemann.

Bunker, K. A., & Cohen, S. L. 1977. The rigors of training evaluation: A discussion and field demonstration. *Personnel Psychology*, 30: 525–541.

Campbell, J. P., Dunnette, M. D., Lawler, E. E., III, & Weick, K. E., Jr. 1970. *Managerial behavior, performance, and effectiveness.* New York: McGraw-Hill.

Carroll, S. J., Paine, F. T., & Ivancevich, J. J. 1972. The relative effectiveness of training methods—Expert opinion and research. *Personnel Psychology*, 25: 495–509.

Caudron, S. 1993. Training can damage diversity efforts. *Personnel Journal*, 72(4): 51–63.

Copeland, L. 1988. Valuing workplace diversity. *Personnel Administrator*, November: 65–88.

Cox, T. 1991. The multicultural organization. *Executive*, 5(2): 34–47.

Cox, T., & Blake, S. 1991. Managing cultural diversity: Implications for organizational competitiveness. *Executive*, 5(3): 45–56.

Cullen, R. 1993. Cleansing ethnic hatred. *Atlantic Monthly*, 272(2): 30–36.

Dionne, E. J. 1991. *Why Americans hate politics.* New York: Simon & Schuster.

Dovidio, J. 1993. The subtlety of racism. *Training & Development*, 47(4): 51–57.

Feldman, R. E. 1968. Response to compatriot and foreigner who seek assistance. *Journal of Personality and Social Psychology*, 10: 202–214.

Festinger, L. A. 1957. *A theory of cognitive dissonance.* Stanford, CA: Stanford University Press.

Fine, B. J. 1957. Conclusion-drawing, communicator credibility, and anxiety as factors in opinion change. *Journal of Abnormal and Social Psychology*, 54: 369–374.

Freedman, J. 1964. Involvement, discrepancy, and change. *Journal of Abnormal and Social Psychology*, 69: 290–295.

Frenkel-Brunswik, E., & Havel, J. 1953. Prejudice in the interviews of children: I. Attitudes toward minority groups. *Journal of Genetic Psychology*, 82: 91–136.

Fukuyama, F. 1992. *The end of history and the last man.* New York: Avon Books.

Fukuyama, F. 1993. Immigrants and family values. *Commentary*, 95(5): 26–33.

Gordon, J. 1992. Rethinking diversity. *Training*, 29(1): 23–31.

Gorn, G. J. 1975. The effects of personal involvement, communication discrepancy, and source prestige on reactions to communication on separatism. *Canadian Journal of Behavioral Science*, 7: 369–386.

Gutman, A. 1993. The challenge of multiculturalism. *Philosophy & Public Affairs*, 22(3): 171–206.

Hall, R. G., Varca, P. E., & Fisher, T. D. 1986. The effect of reference groups, opinion polls, and attitude polarization on attitude formation and change. *Political Psychology*, 7: 309–321.

Hooper, M. 1982. Explorations in the structure of psychological identifications with social groups and roles. *Multivariate Behavioral Research.* 17: 515–523.

Hornstein, H. A. 1978. Promotive tension and prosocial behavior: A Lewinian analysis. In L. Wispe (Ed.), *Altruism, sympathy, and helping*: 177–207. New York: Academic Press.

Hornstein, H. A., Fisch, E., & Holmes, M. 1968. Influence of a model's feeling about his behavior and his relevance as a comparison other on observer's helping behavior. *Journal of Personality and Social Psychology*, 10: 222–226.

Hornstein, H. A., Masor, H. N., Sole, K., & Heilman, M. 1971. Effects of sentiment and completion of a helping act on observer helping. *Journal of Personality and Social Psychology*, 17: 107–112.

Hughes, R. 1993. *Culture of complaint.* New York: Oxford University Press.

Ibarra, H. 1993. Personal networks of women and minorities in management: A conceptual framework. *Academy of Management Review*, 18: 56–87.

Insko, C. A., Nacoste, R. W., & Moe, J. L. 1983. Belief congruence and racial discrimination: Review of the evidence and critical evaluation. *European Journal of Social Psychology*, 13: 153–174.

Jaroff, L. 1994. Teaching reverse racism. *Time*, 142(17): 74–76.

Kaufman, L. 1994. Painfully aware. *Government Executive*, 26(2): 16–22.

Kanter, R. M. 1977. *Men and women of the corporation.* New York: Basic Books.

Kolchin, P. 1993. *American slavery 1619–1877.* New York: Hill & Wang.

Krebs, D. 1970. Altruism—An examination of the concept and a review of the literature. *Psychological Bulletin*, 73: 258–302.

Krosnick, J. A. 1988. Attitude importance and attitude change. *Journal of Experimental Social Psychology*, 24: 240–255.

Kuhn, T. 1962. *The structure of scientific revolutions.* Chicago: University of Chicago Press.

Latham, G., & Saari, L. M. 1979. Application of social-learning theory to training supervisors through behavioral modeling. *Journal of Applied Psychology*, 64: 239–246.

Lasch, C. 1979. *The culture of narcissism.* New York: Warner Books.

Lasch, C. 1993. Traditional values: Left, right, and wrong. *Harper's Magazine*, 287(1720): 13–16.

Leippe, M. R., & Eisenstadt, D. 1994. Generalization of dissonance reduction: Decreasing prejudice through induced compliance. *Journal of Personality and Social Psychology*, 67: 395–413.

Lunt, P. 1994. Should you do diversity training? *ABA Banking Journal*, 98(8): 50–55.

Lynch, P. R. 1994. Workforce diversity: PC's final frontier? *National Review*, 48(3): 32–35.

Mackie, J. L. 1987. The subjectivity of values. In G. Sher (Ed.), *Moral philosophy:* 177–200. San Diego: Harcourt Brace Jovanovich.

Maddi, S. A. 1968. *Personality theories.* Homewood, IL: Dorsey Press.

Mann, M. 1986. *Consciousness and action among the Western working class.* London: McMillan.

Martin, J., & Siehl, C. 1983. Organizational culture and counterculture: An uneasy symbiosis. *Organizational Dynamics*, 90(2): 52–64.

McCroskey, J. C., Richmond, V. P., & Daly, J. A. 1975. The development of a measure of perceived homophily in interpersonal communication. *Human Communication Research*, 1: 325–332.

McGuire, W. J. 1985. Attitudes and attitude change. In G. Lindzey & E. Aronson (Eds.), *Handbook of social psychology,* vol. 2: 233–346. New York: Random House.

Merton, R. K. 1957. Continuities in the theory of reference groups and social structure. In R. K. Merton (Ed.), *Social theory and social structure*: 335–440. New York: Free Press.

Merton, R. K., & Rossi, A. S. 1950. Contributions to the theory of reference group behavior. In R. K. Merton (Ed.), *Social theory and social structure*: 279–335. New York: Free Press.

Mintzberg, H. 1983. *Power in and around organizations.* Englewood Cliffs, NJ: Prentice Hall.

Mitchell, T. R. 1982. *People in organizations.* San Francisco: McGraw-Hill.

Montgomery, R. L. 1980. Reference groups as anchors in judgements of other groups: A biasing factor in "ratings tasks"? *Psychological Reports*, 47: 967–975.

Moscovici, S. 1976. *Social influence and social change.* London: Academic Press.

Moscovici, S., & Zavalloni, M. 1969. The group as a polarizer of attitudes. *Journal of Personality and Social Psychology*, 12: 125–135.

Myers, D. G., & Bishop, G. D. 1970. Discussion effects on racial attitudes. *Science*, 169: 778–779.

National Public Radio. 1993. Morning edition. October 23.

O'Keefe, D. J. 1990. *Persuasion: Theory and research.* London: Sage.

Ostling, R. N. 1993. A refinement of evil. *Time*, 142(14): 75.

Perloff, R. M. 1993. *The dynamics of persuasion.* Hillsdale, NJ: Erlbaum.

Petty, R., & Cacioppo, J. 1986. *Attitudes and persuasion: Central and peripheral routes to attitude change.* New York: Springer-Verlag.

Pfeffer, J. 1993. Barriers to the advance of organizational science: Paradigm development as a dependent variable. *Academy of Management Review*, 18: 599–620.

Piliavin, I., Rodin, J., & Piliavin, J. 1969. Good Samaritans: An underground phenomenon? *Journal of Personality and Social Psychology*, 13: 289–299.

Pratt, H. J. 1974. *Ethno-religious politics.* Cambridge, MA: Schenkman.

Rajecki, D. W. 1990. *Attitudes* (2nd ed.). Sunderland, MA: Sinquer Associates.

Ravitch, D. 1991. Pluralism vs. particularism in American education. *Responsive Community*, 1(2): 32–45.

Roberts, J. M. 1993. *History of the world.* New York: Oxford University Press.

Rossett, A., & Bickham, T. 1994. Diversity training: Hope, faith, and cynicism. *Training,* January: 41–46.

Schafran, H. L. 1993. Is the law male? Let me count the ways. *Chicago-Kent Law Review*, 69: 397–416.

Schuman, H., & Presser, S. 1981. *Questions and answers: Experiments on question form, wording, and context in attitude surveys.* New York: Academic Press.

Sherif, M., & Hovland, C. 1961. *Social judgment, assimilation and contrast effects in communication and attitude change.* New Haven, CT: Yale University Press.

Sherif, M., Sherif, C., & Nebergall, R. 1965. *Attitude and attitude change: The social judgement-involvement approach.* Philadelphia: Saunders.

Shulman, K. 1994. Bloom and doom. *Newsweek*, 124(15): 75.

Shweder, R. A., & Bourne, E. J. 1984. Does the concept of the person vary cross-culturally? In R. A. Shweder & R. A. Levine (Eds.), *Culture theory: Essays on mind, self, and emotion:* 158–199. London: Cambridge University.

Siero, F. W., & Doosje, B. J. 1993. Attitude change following persuasive communication: Integrating social judgment theory and the elaboration likelihood model. *European Journal of Social Psychology*, 23: 541–554.

Simon, L., Greenberg, J. & Brehm, J. 1995. Trivialization: The forgotten mode of dissonance reduction. *Journal of Personality and Social Psychology*, 68: 247–260.

Smirchich, L. 1983. Concepts of culture and organizational analysis. *Administrative Science Quarterly*, 28: 339–358.

Smith, A. 1990. Social influence and antiprejudice training programs. In J. Edwards, R. Scott Tindale, L. Heath, & E. J. Posavac (Eds.), *Social influence processes and prevention:* 183–196. New York: Plenum Press.

Sowell, T. 1975. *Race and economics.* New York: McKay.

Sowell, T. 1981. *Ethnic America: A history.* New York: Basic Books.

Spokesman-Review. 1993. German teachers receive training to fight bigotry. October 17: A8.

Stotland, E. 1969. Exploratory studies in empathy. In L. Berkowitz (Ed.), *Advances in experimental social psychology,* vol. 4: 271–314. New York: Academic Press.

Strauss, G. 1964. Workflow frictions, interfunctional rivalry, and professionalism: A case study of purchasing agents. *Human Organization*: 137–149.

Tafjel, H., Billig, M. G., Bundy, R. P., & Plament, C. 1971. Categorization and intergroup behavior. *European Journal of Social Psychology*, 1: 149–178.

Taylor, P. 1987. Ethical relativism. In G. Sher (Ed.), *Moral philosophy*: 146–160. San Diego, CA: Harcourt Brace Jovanovich.

Thomas, V. C. 1994. The downside of diversity. *Training & Development*, 48(1): 60–62.

Tinder, G. 1989. Can we be good without God? *Atlantic Monthly*, 264(6): 68–98.

Triandis, H. C. 1971. *Attitude and attitude change*. New York: Wiley.

Turner, J. C. 1982. Towards a cognitive redefinition of the social group. In H. Tafjel (Ed.), *Social identity and intergroup relations*: 15–40. Cambridge, England: Cambridge University Press.

Turner, J. C., & Oakes, P. J. 1989. Self categorization theory and social influence. In P. B. Paulus (Ed.), *Psychology of group influence* (2nd ed.): 233–275. Hillsdale, NJ: Erlbaum.

Van Maanen, J., & Barley, S. 1984. Occupational communities: Culture and control in organizations. In B. M. Staw & L. L. Cummings (Eds.), *Research in organization behavior*, vol. 1: 209–264. Greenwich, CT: JAI Press.

Vinokur, A., & Burnstein, E. 1978. Depolarization of attitudes in groups. *Journal of Personality and Social Psychology*, 36: 872–885.

Whittaker, J. 1965. Attitude change and communication—Attitude discrepancy. *Journal of Social Psychology*, 85: 141–147.

Wicker, T. 1991. The Democrats as the devil's disciples. *New York Times*, August 30: A12.

Wilson, J. Q. 1993. *The moral sense*. New York: Free Press.

Wolin, S. S. 1993. Democracy, difference, and re-cognition. *Political theory*, 21(3): 464–484.

Worseley, P. 1985. *Introducing sociology*. New York: Penguin Books.

Wright, Q. 1964. *A study of war*. Chicago: University of Chicago Press.

CHAPTER 34

RE-WRITING GENDER INTO ORGANIZATIONAL THEORIZING: DIRECTIONS FROM FEMINIST PERSPECTIVES

MARTA B. CALÁS AND LINDA SMIRCICH

By the time you get to this chapter you may feel there is little more to be said toward rethinking organization. The previous chapters have already pointed to at least two areas of concern in academic circles: world conditions are changing and our theories lag behind; and more generally, theorizing itself is now seen as a problematic activity. Similar to other authors in this book we address both concerns, but from a different point of departure and perhaps with a different 'destination' in mind.

With our title 'Re-writing Gender into Organizational Theorizing' we mean to suggest that gender has been written into organizational theorizing in incomplete and inadequate ways and that organizational analysis has understood gender very narrowly. We would like to alter that understanding.

A few years ago this may have been our only objective. That is, our earlier concerns were with how gender had been mis- or under-represented in organization theory, and we were concerned with correcting the record. Today, under the inspiration of feminist poststructuralist theory, we mean to suggest more with our title. We want to explore how the idea of 'gender' can be a strategy through which we can question what *has been represented* as organization theory. And further, we want to begin to discuss how that questioning may lead to a different way of writing 'organization'.

The ideas for this chapter are drawn from feminist theory, and the history of feminist theorizing has influenced how we have organized it. But despite the phrase 'feminist theory' there is no single feminist *theory*. Rather, feminist theory covers the scholarly terrain, from the biological sciences to the social sciences to literature and philosophy. Diverse theoretical perspectives are joined together under the name 'feminist' because of their shared concern with gender relations and gender arrangements, and because of their concern for social change.

Since the early 1970s there has been an explosion of production of feminist scholarship in various disciplines. However, with a few exceptions (such as Alvesson and Billing, nd; Balsamo, 1985; Calás and Smircich, 1989; Donelson et al., 1985; Grant, 1988; Hearn and Parkin,,1987; Hearn et al., 1989; Jacobson and Jacques, 1989; Marshall, 1984, 1989; Martin, 1990; Mills, 1988), this discussion has been going on *outside* the borders of organization theory. One point to emphasize at the start of our chapter is that feminist theorists would recognize that we are saying little that is new. The only thing new is its location—in a conversation about reshaping organizational theorizing. Another

"Re-writing Gender into Organizational Theorizing: Directions from Feminist Perspectives," by Marta B. Calás and Linda Smircich, in *Rethinking Organization: New Directions in Organization Theory and Analysis*, edited by Michael Reed and Michael Hughes, SAGE Publications, Inc., London, 1992.

caveat, we are writing from the standpoint of women academics in a school of management in the United States, and so our location orients us in particular ways. Others, located differently, may understand these ideas differently.

Our purpose is to summarize some of the important aspects of feminist literature and use them to help us rethink our field. Our purpose is not to argue that feminist theory is 'good' and that organization theory is 'bad', or that feminist theory should replace organization theory. Instead we wish to call attention to areas of intersection. It is our opinion, however, that while feminist theory won't replace organization theory, an encounter of organizational theory with feminist theorizing may render organization theory as we know it unrecognizable.

In the rest of the chapter we look very briefly from the vantage point of the history of feminist theorizing at the ways organization theory has considered gender. Then we begin to investigate how we may write gender differently. Our discussion is organized around three important activities in the history of feminist 'knowing' that we label: 're-vising' 're-flecting' and 're-writing'. After explaining these we discuss their implications for organizational theorizing. We do not intend to propose some possibly utopian views about feminine organizing and managing. Rather, we want to pose what we see as more immediate questions: How is organization theorizing (male) gendered and with what consequences? And how may organizational theorizing be rewritten through 'gender'?

What is Feminist Theorizing?

There is variety in feminist scholarship, yet it is all addressed to the subject of gender (for example, A. Ferguson, 1989). 'The single most important advance in feminist theory is that the existence of gender relations has been problematized. Gender can no longer be treated as a simple, natural fact' (Flax, 1987: 627).

At least two distinct issues are at the root of feminist theorizing: a particular form of gender relations—patriarchy—(male dominance), is fully assumed; and changes from this form of domination are sought. These are minimum conditions in the development of feminist theoretical positions; but they are ascribable to a wide range of social and political viewpoints,

and to an even wider range of issues from the personal to the institutional to society at large.

Early feminist theorizing distinguished between 'sex' (biologically based) and 'gender' (a social construction) (Oakeley, 1972). On a TV talk show recently this was explained simply as 'sex is between your legs and gender is between your ears'. While apparently helpful at first for opening a theoretical space to explore gender as a socially constructed category, feminist theorists realized this distinction could not be maintained for very long. Doing so obscures how humans live—in *both* a physical, material body and a socially, historically constituted ideational space. To oppose biological sex against socially constructed gender accepts the idea of a separate non-culturally mediated body. It maintains the idea that biology (the body) is separate from culture (the mind).

Later feminist theorizing does not accept this distinction. Instead its focus is on gender *relations*. It is through gender relations that 'men' and 'women,' two categories of persons, are created and their bodies connected to culture. From this perspective, both men and women are 'prisoners of gender,' although in different ways (Flax, 1987; Scott, 1986).

How Has Gender Been Written into Organizational Theorizing?

For the moment, the analytical distinction between sex and gender is helpful for understanding the situation in organizational theorizing. This is because organizational theorizing has been explicitly and primarily concerned with sex and not gender.

The organizational literature that supposedly considers gender has been labeled the 'women-in-management' literature. It is relatively recent, coinciding with the second wave of the women's liberation movement and associated civil rights legislation in the 1960s and 1970s which brought more women into previously male-dominated professions. The 'women in management' label reveals that gender is important to organizational theorizing only because the biological entities—women—suddenly arrived into management, changing the nature of the situation. Prior to the entrance of women there is (apparently) no 'gender' in *man*agement.

But, as we will argue later, gender *has* been present all along, even if ignored or repressed (Hearn et al., 1989). However, most organizational theorizing treats issues of gender as collapsed into the category of sex: a biologically determined variable easily measured. And further, sex is reduced to the category 'women'. This approach to sex/gender helps maintain organizational theorizing's traditional premises.

For example, Calás and Jacques (1988) found that the women in management literature represented issues and theories identical to traditional micro organizational behavior research. And Jacobson and Jacques (1989) noticed that it appeared as if only women were gendered. The implicit formula underlying the literature is gender = sex = women = problem. And 'solving the problem' has been mostly equivalent to 'masculinizing' the defective as a normalizing practice. Producing this literature required no 're-thinking'. Instead a concept—'women'—was grafted onto the pre-existing structures of questioning. The same pattern was seen in the USA in our professional organization, the Academy of Management, when a new Women in Management division was established; and it too was added onto the pre-existing structure.

What is missing is recognition of the wider operation of gender relations—how women are denied a normal presence in organization theory and how the male presence becomes the standard on the basis of that denial. Thus in spite of the pervasiveness of gender relations as a social issue in the USA, and of sex and gender in the workplace as dominant structural principles, organization theory has succeeded in 'taming' sex and ignoring 'gender' in its discourses of knowledge. But has it?

Writing Gender Differently: Three Activities in Feminist Theorizing with Relevance for Organizational Theorizing

In organizational analysis gender has been mostly another variable in an otherwise (presumably) neutral constellation of empiricist works. But there are other ways to consider gender, and feminist theories and theorizing offer powerful insights for understanding its dynamics. In our view the major 'new direc-

tion' that feminist theorizing offers to organizational analysis is that it raises the problem of the 'genderedness' of knowledge. It means asking the question: *How is organization theorizing (male) gendered, and with what consequences?*

We have organized our discussion around three epistemological activities from the history of feminist 'knowing': the *'activity of re-vising'*, the *'activity of re-flecting'*, and the *'activity of re-writing'*. These three activities seem to be, from our standpoint, necessary steps for formulating more appropriate conceptualizations for today's world, but only recently have they been conceived as distinct and necessary. Taken together, they comprise more fully formed theoretical positions than they would separately, even if—as we will discuss—paradoxically so. In conjunction they can provide a very strong basis for re-examining any traditional disciplinary body of knowledge. Thus, inspired by these activities, we raise some questions and issues that may help us reconceptualize organizational theorizing.

Revising the Record: How Patriarchy Shows Up in Knowledge

Feminist scholars have been re-examining and re-vising the production of knowledge in their disciplines. Early work called attention to exclusionary institutional arrangements. But then attention shifted from equity issues to examination of the consequences of women's absence as knowledge producers. They questioned the extent to which the historical under-representation of women as scholars skewed the choice of research problems and biased the design of research and the interpretation of results.

At the same time, universities in the USA established Women's Studies programs and departments in response to the women's movement. These provided the context for much of the feminist scholarship done since the 1970s. Faculty members teaching Women's Studies courses usually hold positions in a disciplinary department and split their time between units. This structure has contributed to the multidisciplinary character of much feminist scholarship.

Below we sketch very briefly the epistemological questioning feminist scholars addressed to their disciplines. For purposes of illustration we consider feminist writing in history, psychology, anthropology, and literature. Our review shows that feminist theorizing has problematized 'knowing' as an already (male) gendered sphere of action. It traces changing concerns, paraphrasing Sandra Harding, 'from the woman question in knowledge' to 'the knowledge question in feminism' (Harding, 1986). Furthermore, the review provides us with a list of questions, summarized in Table 34-1, showing new directions for organization theorists deriving from the activity of re-vising.

Examples of Re-vising Activities

History What is now referred to as the 'new history' in the USA had its roots in the black civil rights movement and the women's liberation movement. Historical research inspired by these social and political currents offered redefinitions of the American past and pointed out that what has been written as history over the last several hundred years is the history of white men (Degler, 1981; Bernstein, 1988).

For instance, historians researching women's experiences of the settlement of the American frontier by examining documents previously ignored by historians (diaries and letters written by women) found the women's side of the story was quite different. Rather than an heroic adventure, to women, western movement represented tremendous loss and suffering (Faragher and Stansell, 1975). Other accounts of women and slavery (Davis, 1972), women and the industrial revolution (Dublin, 1979), women and the US reform movements of the nineteenth and early twentieth centuries (Freedman, 1981), demonstrated that women were also active agents and not merely victims carried along by the forces of history/men.

Women's history, then, aims to re-write history as herstory, a narrative of women's experiences, and in so doing it fits a new subject—women—into received historical categories (Scott, 1987). These writings offer a more complex picture of history, in effect serving to complete and correct the historical record.

At the same time the very idea of what history is—with its focus on military, political and legal activity—came to be questioned. New

---

Table 34-1

Re-vising organizational theorizing: Directions from feminist revisions of knowledge

Completing/Correcting the Record

Implies recovering 'lost' women, accounting for women's absence and exclusion, both as subject of inquiry and author of knowledge.

Implies adding in women's contributions and women's experiences.

Assessing Gender Bias in Current Knowledge

Implies retracing the conceptual history of our field to assess the consequences of the under-representation of women.

Implies re-reading our important texts with different eyes. Is there misogyny/sexism in the great books?

Implies systematically retracing the pattern of questioning in multiple streams of research, such as motivation, leadership, career development, organizational life cycle, culture, effectiveness, population ecology, job design, and so on, to assess whose viewpoints are solicited in the research and whose viewpoints are absent?

Implies assessing the extent to which the concepts through which we produce knowledge are male gendered.

Implies reconsidering the underlying values that guide the interpretation of data.

Making the 'New' Organizational Theorizing

Implies that the narratives of organizational theorizing will be more diverse.

Implies that other topics, of more concern to women, will be written into organizational theorizing.

Implies re-thinking the grounds for judging what is true, good, beautiful in organizational theorizing.

topics of investigation such as child bearing, child rearing, prostitution and birth control became legitimate historical subjects (Degler, 1981; Gordon, 1977).

Psychology Feminist re-vising of knowledge in psychology has also been wide ranging, looking at who the research subjects were (and were not), what research questions were investigated (and which were not), and how results were interpreted, in order to assess the extent of male bias. Some investigated the one-sidedness of data-gathering (Meyer, 1988); for example, a series of experiments on interpersonal attraction from the late 1960s to mid-1970s all measured conditions under which men felt attracted towards women, but not vice versa. Even when the research was done by women (for example, Walster) it was concerned with assessing the male's reactions; females were only stimuli.

A well known example of the one-sidedness of data-gathering is Gilligan's revision of Kohlberg's research on moral development. Typical of much research practice, Kohlberg called his a theory of moral development, not a theory of moral development of white, privileged males— although they formed his sample (Minnich, 1986). When Gilligan did her study of moral development based on a sample of males and females, she derived two *different* systems of thinking rather than a single general model. Gilligan characterized these different patterns as moralities of rights and moralities of care. Gilligan's arguments about women's 'different voice' have generated a lot of debate. She is accused of sustaining a stereotypical view of women and of being guilty of the same universalizing tendencies that characterized Kohlberg's work. Nevertheless, her work was significant because it called attention to the gendered nature of standards that were supposedly neutral.

The imagery of women's 'different voice' was picked up by other researchers who examined 'women's ways of knowing' (for example, Belenky et al., 1986). Similar to the work of historians of women, these writings documented 'women's experience' and asserted it as valid knowledge in its own right. This research showed how certain values, more common to male socialization, had come to be accepted as the standard for human beings. It demonstrated that the presupposition involved in scientific

research—that there are generalizable standards for all humankind—was problematic.

Feminist re-analysis of psychological research shows also how gender, politics, and social conditions interweave with the workings of science. Consider, for example, Witkin's (1940s–70s) research on perception, which elaborated the psychological construct 'field dependence-independence'. Witkin concluded that 'as a general rule' women are more field dependent than men. But is this a neutral description of empirical reality?

Haaken (1988) noted that the name of a construct suggests embedded social assumptions. 'Dependence' has negative connotations in a society that values autonomy and independence. To Witkin, field independence represented the higher form of development; he compared field dependence to childlike behavior and an 'arrest' in development toward emotional maturity.

But, as Haaken argued, it is entirely possible to have interpreted field dependence in a positive way. That is, the 'inability to separate a stimulus from its embedded context' could mean greater sensitivity to contextual elements in matters of judgment and decision-making. Haaken's analysis detailed how Witkin's findings were consistent with and reproduced prevailing stereotypes of women during the post-war shift in ideas about essential differences between the sexes.

Other researchers questioned the meanings of psychological research on sex differences altogether (Weisstein, 1971; Sadker and Frazier in DuBois et al., 1987; Hochschild, 1973), suggesting that supposed sex differences had their origins in researchers' prejudices about women and in the social institutions in which sexism is sustained.

Anthropology The period 1972–1976 was characterized by many critiques of male bias in anthropology and by a heightened interest in women's roles (Lamphere, 1987). A well known example is Sally (Linton) Slocum's 'Woman the gatherer: Male bias in anthropology' (1975). Slocum's analysis maintains that the image of 'man the hunter' as the critical factor in human evolution ignored the cooperative activities of women. Traditional anthropological theory maintained that males' hunting activities were the important site for the development of the crucial social skills of cooperation and communication and tool making. In this societal portrait, women wait at home for men to return with dinner; left behind with the children, they contribute little to human evolution. Slocum formulated a theory of evolution that included women's activities in gathering, child bearing, and child rearing. She argued that women's gathering and child raising activities also required complex communication, sharing, cooperation, and tool and container making. Her analysis presented a counter-argument that women's gathering activities rather than men's big-game hunting were the key factor in human evolution. Her work demonstrated that it matters who is doing the interpreting.

In another critique of a male perspective on culture, Annette Weiner (1976) revised Malinowski's picture of the Trobrianders. Weiner believed that Malinowski did not give enough importance to women's roles in the exchanges so central to Trobriand life (Shapiro, 1981). She focused on the symbolic dimensions of exchange and argued that Trobriand men and women understood their exchange activities in terms of their beliefs about the complementary roles of women and men in reproduction. Weiner makes the case that Trobriand society values femaleness in a way that Malinowski (and with him male anthropology and male Western society) did not, and so did not see (Shapiro, 1981).

Many writers documented that in various societies the work women did, no matter what it was, was valued less than the work men did. There was variation in culture, but sexual asymmetry (women's subordination) seemed universal. Some anthropologists attempted to explain it (Rosaldo and Lamphere, 1974; Lamphere, 1987). Others challenged this thesis, claiming that the Eskimo and Hopi had egalitarian societies, characterized by separate, but equal, division of labor. Debates continue over how to characterize societies, as do debates over whether sexual asymmetry is universal. Today, however, the trend in anthropology is writing that deals with the particular and the local rather than the general and the universal.

Literature Feminist criticism of literature reassessed the texts that make up the literary canon, the generally accepted 'great books', and reassessed literary theories. Early feminist criticism exposed misogyny in literary practice, including stereotypical images of women in literature as saints or monsters and the exclusion of women from literary history (Showalter, 1985). When the literary canon was re-examined in light of the women's movement its male bias became apparent.

Where were the women authors on the lists of great books used for courses in English and Western civilization? What values guided the choices of masterpieces; which works were the ones that dealt with 'universal' themes? Immediately, similar to what was happening in history, scholars worked to recover the 'lost' or ignored writings of women. This excavation work led to the discovery that women writers had a literature of their own and that its artistic importance and historical and thematic coherence had been invisible under patriarchal values (Showalter, 1985: 6).

In a short time there was an outpouring of scholarship documenting women's literary history as well as developing the notion of a female aesthetic. The idea of a female aesthetic, incorporating the concept of a women's culture and a women's way of writing, paralleled the 'different voice' perspective in psychology. And similarly, it was the subject of controversy. To what extent can one speak of 'women's style', when lesbians and women of color had very different lives and expressive concerns? In the 1970s and 1980s literary studies saw increasing differentiation among types of readers and writers (women, lesbian, gay, people of color, for example). The change of attention, evident in anthropology, from the universal and general to the particular and local was taking place in literary studies as well. The emphasis on differences encouraged even more far reaching questioning about the conceptual grounds of literary criticism and the social practices of reading and writing that have been based entirely on male literary experiences (Showalter, 1985).

Re-vising: Implications for Organizational Theorizing

Based on the activities of re-vising, how would we re-write gender into organizational theorizing? What kinds of questioning would it lead us to ask in organizational theorizing? Table 34-1 summarizes possible new directions for organizational theorizing coming from feminist questioning of related disciplines. Following through with this agenda will enable organizational scholars to study the extent to which organizational theorizing is male gendered. As you read through them, consider to what extent these questions and concerns have made their way into organizational theorizing. And what would be the consequences of answering them?

Re-writing gender from the perspective of feminist re-vising takes at least two moves: recognizing that gender no longer equals women—therefore *the implicitly male gendered organizational theorizing practices get noticed*— and recognizing that the implicitly male gendered organizational theorizing has kept women's voices silent—therefore *women's voices begin to be written into organizational theorizing*.

In our judgment these moves are just beginning in organizational theorizing. The women's voice/women's experience perspective is beginning to be heard regarding organizational practices (for example, Marshall, 1984; Grant, 1988). Others are noticing the male genderedness of organizational theorizing (for example, Hearn and Burrell, 1989), or questioning the values that are represented in the choice of research questions and the modes of analysis (Calás and Smircich, 1989). However, it is our observation that few researchers discuss this issue. Dachler (1988: 283–4) is an exception in voicing these concerns in relation to leadership research.

> [When] mostly male researchers choose certain issues as important to describe in a primarily male leadership and management population, a choice is made regarding what is 'worthy' or 'interesting' or 'profitable' or 'status enhancing' to be described in the leadership and management world . . . Clearly the kind of leadership traits we choose to investigate, and the methods we use to measure them, tell a story about how we as intelligent and knowledgeable researchers see the subjects we are investigating.

A few years ago we would have stopped our chapter about here. We would have been calling for writing that demonstrates how male bias operates in our field, for work that corrects the record by adding the perspectives from women's voices, and for work that introduces and develops new topics of more concern to women. In fact, this is similar to what one of us did (Smircich, 1985) several years ago. But such a stopping place today would mean not taking part in the changing discourse of feminism. Although feminist theorizing in various disciplines offers blueprints for rethinking the organizational, the later profusion of feminist theorizing has generated additional, more wide ranging, questions that imply even more from us than revising knowledge.

Re-flections on 'Doing the Disciplines': Looking back at Re-vising

At first, feminist inquiry started out to add women in. In this sense, organizational analysis with its 'women-in-management' research paralleled feminist theory. But then feminist inquiry took different turns that organizational analysis has barely begun to consider. The 'women's voice/women's experience' or '(her)story' approaches went further than including women into traditional formulations, to more assertive stances about women's differences as a valid form of representing human experience. The writing moved from noticing the absence of women's accounts to seeing women as agents, to documenting their separate forms of action/writing, to questioning the traditions of the disciplines in which this acting and writing is taking place. It is clear that feminist scholarship represents both a sophisticated area of inquiry and a growth industry in academic publishing. But has it been successful?

From a conventional perspective many would raise an eyebrow to this question. Aren't 'Women's Studies' programs, and their acceptance and legitimation in academic circles, a clear measure of success? What more do women want?

However, in feminist circles there are second thoughts about the meanings of this 'success'. These concerns emerge from the *strong political awareness* underlying feminist epistemological positions, and from their mistrust of any definition of success which does not consider the complex consequences stemming from any one 'gain'.

Recent writings are repeatedly calling attention to feminist 'theoretical unrest'. As feminist scholars engaged in revisionist approaches to their disciplines, rather than a coherent 'feminist perspective', their efforts created fragmented feminist theorizing. They reproduced the plurality of disciplines and the plurality of approaches (such as liberal, socialist, Marxist, Freudian, Object Relations, and so on) rather than any unified feminist perspective. This theoretical variety has become problematic, especially when it is followed by the question 'which account is the best account?' (Jaggar and Rothenberg, 1984; Glazer, 1987; A. Ferguson, 1989). But the way the questioning has been posed in 'feminisms' is different from typical epistemological concerns about 'attaining good knowledge'. 'Which account is the best account?' has to be answered with regard to the consequences of the many accounts of feminism(s).

Knowledge on Knowing

The proliferation of feminist epistemological approaches accompanied by reflexivity over the multiplicity of theoretical accounts has returned feminism(s) to philosophy of science. The question, however, has changed from 'What is feminist epistemology?' or 'What is the distinctive character of feminist knowledge?' to 'What is the meaning of epistemological and multiplicity in feminism?'

This 'return to philosophy' raises questions beyond issues of the legitimacy of women's privileged claims to knowledge and the 'crisis' associated with these claims (for example, K. Gergen, 1988). That is, while there is clear awareness of the current problematics posed by knowledge claims based on diverse epistemological tenets and diverse women's experiences—including diverse women's experiences *in theorizing as an activity*—feminist scholars are addressing these issues, at the same time, with regard to their political implications.

Their reflections focus on the following. First, despite existing claims about 'women's ways of knowing', most 'feminist epistemologies' are revised versions of traditional nonfeminist epistemological approaches. In that sense the revisions may result only in critiques and distortions, by reversal, of the original theoretical claims while not creating any more adequate theoretical ground. And beyond the issue of epistemological adequacy, 'the very fact that we borrow from these theories', says

Sandra Harding (1987: 248), 'often has the unfortunate consequence of diverting our energies into endless disputes with the nonfeminist defenders of these theories: we end up speaking not to other women but to patriarchs'.

Second, even when some traditional epistemological positions provide tenable approaches for feminism, others have consequences which reinforce patriarchal arrangements. For example, feminist empiricism ends up at odds with the traditional model of positivist science when the tenets of neutrality and value-free knowledge are contested by feminist criticism, and when the feminist approach is labeled 'bad science'. Re-vising the record has been particularly difficult in those disciplines that hold on—nonreflexively—to the values of positivist science and empiricism. Feminist re-visions appear to have more impact in literature, history and anthropology than in psychology and sociology (Stacey and Thorne, 1985; Acker, 1987; Smith, 1979). Some feminist scholars still believe that there is no possible immediate resolution to this impasse in a world where scientific claims are *the* model of knowledge (for example, Harding, 1986, 1987). Others, however, consider the feminist critique of empiricism and of traditional epistemology in general, as part of a current critique of knowledge in which feminism should be involved (for example, Hawkesworth, 1989).

Third, the two previous issues become more politically relevant with the question 'Which women do theory?' As acknowledged by many (for example, Harding, 1987; Shotter and Logan, 1988; Spelman, 1988; Collins, 1989) the realization of the diversity of women's experiences, compounded by race and class, for example—and the difficulties in legitimizing these 'Others'' knowledge—makes the political nature of 'knowing' and knowledge claims even more salient. This problem extends beyond the particulars of any feminist theory—whether relevant or not to 'all women'—to the more general problem of the ways in which the practices of 'doing knowledge' are structured. This situation, thus, gives way to another strand in the 'activity of reflecting'.

The Structure of the Women's Place in the Academy

While the content of feminist knowledge has captured a lot of attention in academic circles and publications, what are the consequences of creating this knowledge within the structures of the academy? Thus, as part of feminist epistemology there is also the emerging reflexivity of sociology of knowledge (Morawski, 1988). There are several areas of immediate interest. For example, in moving from 'women' to 'gender' what happens to the political agenda which stood behind the creation of Women's Studies in the first place? And does widening the scope of questioning—from the problems of women to the problems of gender—in effect depoliticize feminist inquiry?

The task of going beyond women's studies has often taken the path of 'mainstreaming' women's issues into the traditional curriculum of the disciplines. Ideally, bringing feminism into the traditional curriculum means, at the same time, exposing the invisible paradigms that rule what is taught and how it is taught, and their relation to the ideologies of the dominant groups in society (see, for example, Andersen, 1987; Reinharz, 1985; Schuster and Van Dyne, 1985). While integrating feminist theory into the disciplines has been attainable in various cases, it seems that the critical force of this integration has more often than not failed (see, for example, Aiken et al., 1987; Glazer, 1987).

Similarly, the social structure of science has been resistant to the critical impetus brought about by feminist theorizing (for example, Hubbard, 1988; Andersen, 1987; Keller, 1983, 1985; Harding and Hintikka, 1983). The social construction of science has been explicitly addressed in feminist writings with questions such as 'Which women are excluded from science?' 'How is science taught?' 'What are the scientific research questions that, as feminists, we need to ask?' 'How is difference studied in scientific institutions?' and 'How is the exclusion of women from science related to the way science is thought and done?' (Andersen, 1987). But it seems that little has changed in the practice of science as a result of feminist perspectives.

Images of scientific work as integration of hand, brain and heart (Rose, 1987), or spinning and quilt-making (Rose, 1986), or craft-structured inquiry (Harding, 1987), or non-hierarchical science (Bleier, 1984), have had little impact in traditional scientific approaches. As many now recognize, this situation cannot be understood without recourse to the accorded prestige of the scientific enterprise in the university and society, and to the related emphasis on 'being scientific' which seems required of many disciplines outside the natural sciences (see, for example, Stacey and Thorne, 1985).

Still, other reflections pertain to the specific conditions of academic women as outsiders and marginal even when in tenured positions (see, for example, Aisenberg and Harrington, 1988). This is, indeed, a remark on the pervasiveness of patriarchal arrangements in the university despite many years of feminist theorizing. Patriarchy at 'the site of knowledge' becomes even more present when the possibility of *Men in Feminism* is considered (Jardine and Smith, 1987). It shows the distinct possibility of another privileged space for male academics when they speak 'from the woman's position' (see, for example, Heath, 1987).

Thus, is it even possible to come out of this paradox? Isn't 'doing knowledge' part and parcel of the reproduction of patriarchal conditions of power/knowledge? Explorations of these questions have brought feminism and postmodernism face to face, and into 'the activity of re-writing'. But before we get into that activity we consider some implications of 'the activity of reflecting' for organizational theorizing.

Re-flecting: Implications for Organizational Theorizing

From the theoretical debates in feminist theorizing some might infer that epistemology in feminism(s) is facing the same unrest which now plagues organizational theorizing. Are we to choose between paradigmatic pluralism or shall we engage in paradigm wars? Such an inference, however, loses sight of the political awareness which defines feminist theories every step of the way. Have we, organizational theorists, been willing to ask how has paradigmatic pluralism changed the ways we do academic life? How many of us are trying to re-evaluate forms of teaching, modes of engagement with the subject matter, research, consulting, relationships with students and colleagues, out of accepting paradigm plurality? We know that some are. But it seems that the only consistent result of at least ten years' worth of paradigmatic pluralism in organization theorizing is additional opportunities for creating 2 x 2 models—or similarly discrete models based on binary logic—to explain, one more time, the meaning(s) of paradigmatic pluralism (for example, Rao and Pasmore, 1989). Otherwise, effort has been spent in controlling pluralism by legislating theoretical or semantic agreements (for example, Webster and Starbuck, 1988; Bacharach 1989; Whetten, 1989), or by subsuming multiplicity into 'higher order constructs' (for example, Poole and Van de Ven, 1989; Osigweh, 1989). These are never-ending (phal)logocentric tasks under the guiding 'gaze' of patriarchy.

Feminism's reflections, on the other hand, notice epistemological multiplicity and question, first, the depoliticization and neutralization that pluralism and relativism, as much as any totalizing approach, may bring to feminist epistemologies. At the same time, feminism's reflections focus on the institutional norms, on the modes of existence brought about by the knowledge-making enterprise.

To embrace feminist re-visions means also to embrace a reflexivity that constantly assesses the relationship between 'knowledge' and 'the ways of doing knowledge'. The assessment evaluates approaches to knowledge as they reproduce or change existing gender relations and patriarchal models. That is, to move back and forth between 'saying' and 'doing' is a necessary activity for feminist epistemology.

Thus, adopting a feminist stance in organizational theorizing means more than just adding 'a feminist paradigm' to the existing multiplicity. It would mean more than engaging in a revisionary activity regarding exclusions and limitations embedded in content matters. Rather, it would mean embracing the political consequences of having recognized exclusions and limitations under feminist tenets. What would come to the fore would be the gendered principles sustaining the traditional knowledge-making enterprise, including the gendered principles embedded in current paradigmatic pluralism in organization theorizing. This current paradigmatic pluralism is only capable of 'talking about' pluralism, while the knowledge-making enterprise remains untouched.

In summary, the consequences of feminist reflexivity over epistemological issues in organizational theorizing would also imply political engagement over the limits of 'knowledge-making'. It would imply questioning the gendered nature of traditional epistemologies and institutional arrangements, and of the interests they have been serving under the guise of 'knowledge'.

Re-writing Gender Relations

And so we arrive at the space for which the rest of the chapter was the occasion, as if we were waiting to send what was sent already. From the beginning we were re-writing gender relations in organization theorizing. We were doing so *as if it were* others' writings; we were doing so *as* 'talking about re-vising'— showing oppositions and reversing them *as if* they were another's; we were doing so *as if* we were 'talking about re-flecting'—creating an undecidable present/future in a 'we must reflect'. And so we arrive at the 'trap' of the text. Where do feminism(s) stand (lie?) in postmodernity?

The relationship between feminist epistemology and postmodernism/post-structuralism is an ambiguous one. For example, one can think of the three 'feminist activities' in this paper as feminism's historical impulse towards deconstruction (reversal, undecidability, dissolution). As observed in some writings (for example, Scott, 1988) it is difficult to conceive of the postmodern space without considering that it shares a self-conscious critical and historical relationship with late-twentieth-century feminism. What kind of relationship is it? Before we review some feminist commentaries about this issue, let us acknowledge that the mere attempt to articulate postmodernism is a way to stay out of it. But isn't this also the case with feminism(s) today? Is it possible, then, to define other than a casual intersection between these elusive entities?

As in the previous sections of this chapter, we are focusing on the arguments 'making the rounds' in US academic settings. We are aware of non-American 'post-structuralist feminist' works and their influence in most of the American writings, but we have chosen not to mention them. We are explicitly creating in this writing the elements of our own location, of our own academic setting, and of the conditions under which we perform. And this text, neither inside nor outside of these conditions, should be taken likewise as a performance.

With these caveats in mind, we review some of the intersections and digressions ongoing between feminism(s) and postmodernism.

Postmodernism(s): Have critiqued totalizing theories of 'knowledge', 'justice', or 'beauty'. Consider these ideas rooted in the modernist pursuit of transcendent reason, able to separate itself from the body, and from historical time and place.

Feminism(s): Have enacted and supported the postmodernist critiques. They are consistent with feminist concerns regarding the masculine logic embedded in the notions of 'objectivity' and 'reason'. The critiques also provide a basis for avoiding the construction of 'feminist' theoretical accounts which generalize to all women the experiences of Western, white, middle-class women. Explicit discussions of the relationships between feminism(s) and postmodernism include views of feminist theory as possible correction for the androcentrism and political naiveté of postmodernism. Conversely, postmodernism would correct essentialist tendencies in feminism by replacing the unitary notions of 'woman' and 'feminine gender identity' with plural and complex conceptions of social identity, treating gender as one relevant strand among others (Fraser and Nicholson, 1988).

Some are skeptical. They see these critiques as a masculine reaction to the principles of the Enlightenment where, after all, only men participated. They question whether it may be too early for feminism to embrace positions against epistemology which would weaken feminist theories (for example, DiStefano, 1990). Others question the alternatives provided by postmodernist positions such as Lyotard's (1984), because on negating privilege to any meta-narrative while accepting the need to adjudicate knowledge claims one may end up privileging some domain of knowledge over others through a hidden criterion. Such would be an unfortunate occurrence if feminist theories had been discounted as just another meta-narrative (see, for example, Benhabib, 1984).

Postmodernism(s): Question the norms of neutrality and objectivity of the academy and its ruling values of universalism and the authority of science. Regarding methods of inquiry, there is a suspicion of generalizations which transcend time, culture, and region.

Feminism(s): Feminist scholarship emerged and gained legitimacy precisely by countering the ruling values of the academy, and by demonstrating how gender had influenced those values. Arguing that all scholarship reflected the perspectives of its creator, feminism promoted a view of the academy where narrowness of knowledge could only be avoided by the inclusion of a multitude of points of views, even if contradictory to one another (for example, Nicholson, 1990).

On the other hand, there are serious concerns regarding the consequences of postmodern relativism for feminism. Harding's (1987) feminist empiricism and standpoint theories are presented as ways to leave intact traditional understandings of the cumulative nature of scientific research and as a way to adjudicate knowledge claims while supporting feminist principles. A particular concern refers to the fate of 'theory' under postmodernism. If the relatively unified notion of 'woman' as theoretical construct has to be abandoned, 'feminist theorizing' may end up being nothing more than a nominalist ontology tied to an individualistic politics. Thus, feminism(s) worry about maintaining theoretical power without totalization (for example, Hartsock, 1987).

Postmodernism(s): Promote celebration of difference. Promotion of human experience(s) and the notion of 'self' as multiple, disjointed, and transient rather than unified, centered, and immutable.

Feminism(s): Recent feminist critiques of 'women's experience', which try to identify the 'ultimate factor' in women's oppression, point at the contradiction of a unitary perspective in feminism. The ideal of inclusiveness claimed by feminism is negated as that *one* 'ultimate factor' would not represent the experience(s) of all women. As expressed by Flax (1987: 633–4), postmodernism helps us see that 'reality can have *a* structure only from the falsely universalizing perspective of the dominant group', which may include privileged women. Thus, on promoting the partiality, ambiguity, and ambivalence of a postmodern 'feminism' she prefers to focus on 'gender relations', which include men and women involved in one of many forms of social domination. A postmodern view of these relations would also deconstruct their assumed stability and order.

Other views are not so comfortable with postmodernist critiques of 'experience' and 'self'. Bordo (1990) focuses on the *body* as both materiality and metaphor to insist that human bodies are limited in their mobility and flexibility and, therefore, situated somewhere and bounded. Theory, representing these limitations, is equivalent to the finite capabilities of human understanding. Bordo considers gender and the bodies of women as a theoretical stopping point which feminism(s) should not lose. Still, on this point it is difficult to find strong disagreements between feminism and postmodernism. As illustrated by Bordo's concerns, the disagreements are mostly expressed within the discourse of post-structuralism rather than outside of it. For example, Alcoff (1988: 435) while openly opposing postmodernism proposes the concept of 'positionality' which calls for a fluid identity of women, where 'being a "woman" is to take up a position within a moving historical context and to be able to choose what we make of this position and how we alter this context'.

Postmodernism(s): View political engagement as temporary alliances, discursive formations, negation of categorization, openness and indetermination.

Feminism(s): Perhaps this is the most difficult postmodern issue for feminism. Some support is found among those who consider postmodernism a viewpoint for current times, justified only by the conditions of the time. Particularly notable is Haraway's (1985) metaphor of Cyborgs as entities which, like the mixed values of the present, violate previous dominant categories. She sees the possibility of a postmodern politics for feminism which rests on a conscious negation of identification with fixed criteria. As such, feminist 'otherness' and 'difference' are paradoxical identities in their multiplicity and contradictions. Regarding the politics of discourse, Scott (1988) supports the power of deconstruction as a form of political engagement for feminism. In deconstructing 'equality-versus-difference' she demonstrates that in a world made up by discursive strategies perhaps the best political tool is a discoursive strategy.

However, many are ambivalent about the actual possibilities in these forms of political engagement. For example, Hawkesworth (1989) commends the ways in which post-structuralism has helped our understanding of power/knowledge constellations but she considers that 'rape, domestic violence, sexual harassment . . . are not fictions or figurations that admit of the free play of signification' 1989: 555). Her approach is to maintain a strategic position in the space between world and text while furthering the feminist agenda against patriarchy.

Repeatedly, then, these evaluations maintain the tension between feminism and postmodernism in ambivalent and partial acceptance of the tenets of postmodernism(s) (for example, Haraway 1985; Flax, 1987; Weedon, 1987; Diamond and Quinby, 1988; Kauffman, 1989; Harding, 1990; Nicholson, 1990), while maintaining a critical distance from them. It is clear that for feminism(s) the quarrel with postmodernism(s) is not around a naive hope for the promises of the Enlightenment or around faith in logocentric understandings. Rather, it is a quarrel around *the consequences* of completely abandoning the modern principles when *the powerful* may still be performing and oppressing under these principles. At the same time, the quarrel includes suspicion that the only possible postmodern space may be patriarchal.

Because of postmodern feminism(s)' strong awareness of conditions of domination it is possible for them to maintain a flexible relationship between the traditional 'women's experience' revisionist approaches more—inspired by a modern sensibility—and the newer 'post-structuralist-feminist' re-writings (for example, Flax, 1990; Kathy Ferguson, forthcoming). 'Post-structuralist feminism' exposes the apparently unimpeachable structures of truth and knowledge in society, and helps to debunk mythical social constructions which silence and oppress many of society's members. 'Women's experiences' construct new possible views. Together they stand in constant tension, since the 'post' position prevents 'women's experiences' from establishing themselves as 'the last word'. They need each other for creating the space which brings society, *constantly*, toward a more just state. But this is a never-ending task given the partiality, ambiguity, and complexity of any understanding in the postmodern. Thus, isn't this doubleness already a postmodern sensibility? And, more importantly, can any of us choose to live or not in the postmodern hyperspace now? Isn't any 'feminism' now necessarily postmodern?

Re-writing Organizational Knowledge

It is impossible to illustrate the contribution of 'postmodern feminism(s)' for organizational theorizing through a commentary. Re-writing *cannot be* a theoretical account (the modern 'talking about') of 'what *might be* re-writing'—even though it may be so if the 'theoretical' commentary is an indefinite deferral of saying 'what might be'. More typically, 're-writing' would be an activity where we can show the politics of a text by calling attention to the strategies of 'truth-making', while leaving the 'original' text under 'erasure'—that is, recognizing that the genre (in this case 'organization theory') must be defined under these strategies, but its 'truth' can still be doubted. At the same time, texts are the primary sites of our political engagement in the academy—they determine our 'location' through the institutional conditions of 'publish or perish' and the consequences of where and how we 'get published'. Our texts are the sites for re-writing.

The postmodern feminist political 'depoliticization' (deconstruction, re-writing) of the text is particularly compelling if one assumes that textual constructions in Western (modern) academic disciplines proceed under a rhetoric of gender relations, subordinating 'the feminine' under 'the masculine'. While this rhetoric is explicit in literature about gender in organizations (such as 'women-in-management'), it is even more interesting to notice its (metaphysical) presence in non-explicitly gendered organizational accounts. Thus, we engage now in some re-writing of 'organization theory' under premises (guise) of 'postmodern feminism'. In our example, gender is not part of the content but, as we will illustrate, it is none the less a very gendered text.

The example comes from a recent article by Karl Weick (Weick, 1989), and this choice, we believe, makes our points stronger. First, the article's topic is theory construction in organizational studies, thus it addresses 'the origin' of our concerns in this chapter. Second, the author is a widely known and admired organization theorist. Third, his ideas and approaches are different from 'the mainstream' in the field, favoring theoretical innovation and eclectic views. Fourth, we enjoy, quote, and support Weick's approaches, and we respect his scholarship. Fifth, we are personally aware of Weick's concern with possible 'sexism' in his work, and of his recent interest in feminist theorizing. For all these reasons, we hope that our re-writings of his words are not seen as an opportunity to engage in an adversarial academic 'game' but as a way to show the inescapable patriarchal (modern) condition of *published* organization theorizing.

Weick: 'Much as theorists may resist the notion, most theory construction depends on conjectures, preserved in well-crafted sentences, that are tested in substitute environments by people who have a stake in the outcome of the test and may be tempted to bias that outcome.'

Calás and Smircich's 're-writings': Establishes an opposition between theorists and people as a problem. [Theorist = Mind represented in well-crafted sentences, Mind as the origin of knowledge and language as transparent representation of Mind] [People = Body/the flesh, subject to temptation]

Theorists [Mind] may resist, but they/it still suffer from the bias of the People/[Body's] temptation. The opposition of thinker/doer (theorist/people) follows the mind/body Cartesian split and promotes a problematic—devalues—the concrete body versus the ideal mind. Adam/Eve, male/female, culture/nature, superior/subordinate can easily substitute the opposition theorist/people.

Weick: 'This is the drama that lies behind trial and error thinking, and it lies close to the surface in much theory construction. However, it is a manageable drama.'

Weick: 'The choice is not whether to do mental testing. Instead, the choice is how well this less than ideal procedure can be used to improve the quality of theoretical thinking.'

Weick: 'To do better theory, theorists have to "think better". That empty platitude takes on more substance when better thinking is interpreted to mean a more informed and deliberate use of a simulated evolutionary system' (1989: 529; end of text).

Calás and Smircich's 're-writings': The rhetorical strategy poses as dramatic the previously staged theorist/people opposition. But the danger that lies behind trial and error (the serpent?) can be resolved in the patriarchal dream of transcendence (it is manageable). Thus the drama is heroic not tragic; there can be a return to the site of the 'original sin' which can be overcome in the Promised Land. So the text proceeds:

Calás and Smircich's 're-writings': To arrive in the Promised Land (of knowledge) there is no alternative but to do mental testing ('shed the body'). Purifying oneself (of temptation), one can sacrifice pleasure of the flesh to achieve quality of thought.

Calás and Smircich's 're-writings': And the problem is solved. In the Hegelian process of Reason, mind and nature overcome their duality, or immature stage, into progressively higher levels of consciousness. The immature stage, however, remains as a memory in the wilderness of animal consciousness which has been superseded. [It allowed the first paragraph to be written.] This recognition of 'having superseded' constitutes, by allowing a comparison, the continuous presence of immature stages in relationship to more advanced ones. Thus, if one reads the Hegelian logic in Weick's paragraphs, the first three paragraphs enacted the stage for 'superseding' in this last one. And as it happened, in his writing Hegel related femininity to lesser stages in the advance of Reason (see, for example, Lloyd, 1984). So it is, after all, Hegel's promised Absolute Knowledge—in a logic 'transcending femininity' and ignoring its own genderedness—which fulfills the Promised Land of the text. 'Simulated evolutionary system' (a higher stage of consciousness) overcomes the mind/body, culture/nature, masculine/feminine splits since now 'the thinker' can simulate evolution [a technological feat?] and 'think better'. Paradoxically, this paragraph, then, closes the signification of this article [giving 'substance to emptiness] as a way to fulfill the promised progress] by keeping 'open' the possibility of 'better' organization theory.

It is important for us to reiterate that we are not criticizing Weick's intentions in this article, nor are we stating that his language is purposely anti-feminine. We are writing, instead, over his text—as a generic organization theory text—to show how 'the organization theory discourse' is sustained, and made possible, by traces of previous discourses of 'knowledge' and 'reason'. We should acknowledge that a feminist post-structuralist reading of these discourses does not differ significantly from other forms of deconstruction. Re-marking the male genderedness of philosophical discourse in general has often been a concern of deconstruction (for example, Derrida, 1978, 1986; Irigaray, 1985). Our readings here are a way to foreground the limit that 'woman' (the signifier) defines for theoretical discourse (the discourse of 'knowledge' and 'reason') which we all have inherited in what we call disciplines.

Thus we are also writing to argue the *inescapable* condition in which we all are, as we cannot avoid this discourse if we want to speak 'organization theory'. At the same time, our writing (re-writings) in this space, calling attention to organization theory's discursive formations through 'feminist theories', is a form of theorizing but is it organization theory? And since we cannot answer one way or the other to that question, we will have to leave it for you, the reader, to make the decision.

Concluding Comments

To summarize this chapter, in re-writing/deconstructing taken-for-granted discourses in organizational theory, our approach first used 're-vising from women's experiences' to notice the absence of women's values and concerns in organizational discourses. Then 'feminist reflections' helped us consider the political consequences of what we were doing. Who will benefit, who will perish under the structures of domination which control our discourses? Finally, it moved toward 'postmodern feminism' to help us notice how the signs 'woman' and 'feminine' function as general limits in our discourses and institutions, and how they can be deployed to create textual undecidability. In general, feminist re-writing allows us to understand how *normal* organization theorizing can be regarded as normal in so far as we don't question the gender orientation that sustains that 'normality'.

As we close our chapter we want to avow the ambivalence with which we have produced it. We supposed we should have been happy. We were invited to attend a conference, be amongst people whose work we respect, and to write a chapter for this volume. But we're skeptical. After all, although this book is staged for the purposes of re-thinking organizational analysis and pointing to new directions for research, its form is also one for promoting the School of Management at the University of Lancaster, for enhancing the careers of all who participate, and for making a product for Sage. And so it helps to sustain the circumstances it

is supposedly re-thinking. Such are the conditions under which we all work and write and speak, and the most we can do at this moment is to call attention to them.

And as we write these lines with the obligatory disclaimer 'You are welcomed to re-write the text we have just "re-written" because ours is not "the last word"', we realize that we have written as women can write in a writing that is already gendered. Thus, it seems we have come to occupy 'the women's position' which was written for us before we came into this text. We were asked to fill the space on women and organizations for the conference and the book and so we did.

And now you can return to the beginning of this text and read it all as 're-writing organization theory'.

Note

An earlier version of this chapter was presented at the conference on 'Re-Thinking Organization' held at the University of Lancaster on 6–8 September 1989.

References

Acker, J. (1987) 'Hierarchies and jobs: Notes for a theory of gendered organizations. Paper presented at the American Sociological Association Annual Meeting, Chicago, IL, August.

Aiken, S. H., Anderson, K., Dinnerstein, M., Lensink, J. and MacCorquodale, P. (1987) 'Trying transformations: Curriculum integration and the problems of resistance'. *Signs*. 12 (2): 255–75.

Aisenberg, N. and Harrington, M. (1988) *Women of Academe*. Amherst, MA: The University of Massachusetts Press.

Alcoff, L. (1988) 'Cultural feminism versus post-structuralism: The identity crisis in feminist theory', *Signs*, 13 (3): 405–36.

Alvesson, M. and Billing, Y. D. (nd) 'Gender and organization: Towards a differentiated understanding'. Unpublished manuscript, University of Stockholm.

Andersen, M. L. (1987) 'Changing the curriculum in higher education', *Signs*, 12 (2): 222–54.

Bacharach, S. B. (1989) 'Organizational theories: Some criteria for evaluation'. *Academy of Management Review*, 14 (4): 496–515.

Balsamo, A. (1985) 'Beyond female as a variable: Constructing a feminist perspective on organizational analysis'. Paper presented at the conference 'Critical Perspectives in Organizational Analysis'. Baruch College, September.

Belenky, M. F., Clinchy, B. M., Goldberger, N. R. and Tarule, J. M. (1986) *Women's Ways of Knowing*. New York: Basic Books.

Benhabib, S. (1984) 'Epistemologies of postmodernism: A rejoinder to Jean-François Lyotard', *New German Critique*, 33: 103–26.

Bernstein, R. (1988) 'History convention reflects change from traditional to gender studies', *New York Times*, 9 January.

Bleier, R. (1984) *Science and Gender*. Oxford: Pergamon.

Bordo, S. (1990) 'Feminism, postmodernism, and gender-skepticism', in L. J. Nicholson (ed.). *Feminism/Postmodernism*. New York: Routledge, pp. 133–56.

Burrell, G. (1984) 'Sex and organizational analysis', *Organization Studies*, 5 (2): 97–118.

Calás, M. B. and Jacques, R. (1988) 'Diversity or conformity?: Research by women on women in organizations'. Paper presented at the Seventh International Conference on Women and Organizations, Long Beach, CA.

Calás, M. B. and Smircich, L. (1989) 'Using the F word: Feminist perspectives and the social consequences of organizational research', Academy. of Management *Best Papers Proceedings*, Washington, DC, pp. 355–9.

Collins. P. H. (1989) 'The social construction of black feminist thought'. *Signs*, 14 (4): 745–73.

Dachler, H. P. (1988) 'Constraints on the emergence of new vistas in leadership and management research: An epistemological overview', in J. G. Hunt, B. R. Baliga, H. P. Dachler and C. A. Schriesheim (eds), *Emerging Leadership Vistas*. Lexington, MA: Lexington Books, pp. 261–85.

Davis, A. (1972) 'Reflections on the black woman's role in the community of slaves'. *Massachusetts Review*, 13: 81–100.

Degler, C. (1981) 'What the women's movement has done to American history', in E. Langland and W. Gove (eds), *A Feminist Perspective in the Academy: The Difference it Makes*. Chicago: The University of Chicago Press, pp. 67–85.

Derrida, J. (1978) *Spurs*. Chicago: University of Chicago Press.

Derrida, J. (1986) *Glas*. Lincoln: University of Nebraska Press.

Diamond, A. and Edwards, L. R. (1988) *The Autonomy of Experience*. Amherst, MA: The University of Massachusetts Press.

Diamond, I. and Quinby, I. (1988) *Feminism and Foucault*. Boston: Northeastern University Press.

DiStefano, C. (1990) 'Dilemmas of difference: Feminism, modernity, and postmodernism', in L. J. Nicholson (ed.) *Feminism/Postmodernism*. New York: Routledge, pp. 63–82.

Donelson, E., Van Sell, M. and Goehle, D. (1985) 'Gender biases in management research: Implications for theory and practice'. Paper presented at the Fourth Annual International Conference on Women and Organizations, San Diego, CA.

Dublin, T. (1979) *Women at Work. The Transformation of Work and Community in Lowell, Massachusetts, 1826–1860*. New York: Columbia University Press.

DuBois, E. C., Kelly, G. P., Kennedy, E. L., Korsmeyer, C. W. and Robinson, L. S. (1987) *Feminist Scholarship: Kindling in the Groves of Academe*. Urbana, IL: University of Illinois Press.

Faragher, J. and Stansell, C. (1975) 'Women and their families on the overland trail 1842–1867', *Feminist Studies*, 2: 160.

Farnham, C. (ed.) (1987) *The Impact of Feminist Research in the Academy*. Bloomington: Indiana University Press.

Ferguson, A. (1989) *Blood at the Root: Motherhood, Sexuality and Male Dominance*. London: Pandora.

Ferguson, K. E. (1984) *The Feminist Case Against Bureaucracy*. Philadelphia: Temple University Press.

Ferguson, K. E. (forthcoming) *Reversal and its Discontents: The Man Question*. Manuscript in preparation.

Flax, J. (1987) 'Postmodernism and gender relations in feminist theory', *Signs*, 12 (4): 621–43.

Flax, J. (1990) *Thinking Fragments: Psychoanalysis, Feminism and Postmodernism in the Contemporary West*. Berkeley: University of California Press.

Fraser, N. and Nicolson, L. J. (1988) 'Social criticism without philosophy: An encounter between feminism and postmodernism' in L. J. Nicholson (ed.), *Feminism/Postmodernism*. New York: Routledge, pp. 19–38.

Frazier, N. and Sadker, M. (1973) *Sexism in School and Society*. New York: Harper & Row.

Freedman, E. B. (1981) *Their Sisters' Keepers: Women's Prison Reform in America, 1830–1920*. Ann Arbor, MI: University of Michigan Press.

Freedman, S. M. and Phillips, J. M., (1988) 'The changing nature of research on women at work', *Journal of Management*, 14 (2): 231–51.

Gergen, K. J. (1988) 'Feminist critique of science and the challenge of social epistemology', in M. M. Gergen (ed.), *Feminist Thought and the Structure of Knowledge*. New York: New York University Press, pp. 27–48.

Gilligan, C. (1977) 'In a different voice: Women's conceptions of self and morality', *Harvard Educational Review*, 47: 481–517.

Glazer, N. Y. (1987) 'Questioning eclectic practice in curriculum change', *Signs*, 12 (2): 293–304.

Gordon, L. (1977) *Woman's Body, Woman's Rights: A Social History of Birth Control in America*. New York: Gron Publishers.

Grant, J. (1988) 'Women as managers: What they can offer to organizations', *Organizational Dynamics*, Summer: 56–63.

Haaken, J. (1988) 'Field dependence research: a historical analysis of a psychological construct', *Signs*, 13 (2): 311–30.

Haraway, D. (1985) 'A manifesto for Cyborgs: Science, technology, and socialist feminism in the 1980s', *Socialist Review*, 15 (80): 65–107.

Harding, S. (1986) *The Science Question in Feminism*. Ithaca, NY: Cornell University Press.

Harding, S. (1987) 'Conclusion: Epistemological questions', in S. Harding (ed.), *Feminism and Methodology*, Bloomington, IN: Indiana University Press, pp. 181–90.

Harding, S. (1990) 'Feminism, science, and the anti-Enlightenment critiques', in L. J. Nicholson (ed.), *Feminism/Postmodernism*. New York: Routledge, pp. 83–106.

Harding, S. and Hintikka, M. B. (eds) (1983) *Discovering Reality: Feminist Perspectives on Epistemology, Metaphysics, Methodology, and Philosophy of Science*. Dordrecht, Holland: Reidel.

Hartsock, N. (1987) 'Foucault on power: A theory for women?', in M. Leijenaar (ed.), *The Gender of Power: A Symposium*. Leiden: Vakgroep Vrouwenstudies/Vena.

Hawkesworth, M. E. (1989) 'Knowers, knowing, known: Feminist theory and claims of truth', *Signs*, 14 (3): 533–57.

Hearn, J. and Burrell, G. (1989) 'The sexuality of organization', in J. Hearn, D. L. Sheppard, P. Tancred-Sheriff and G. Burrell (eds), *The Sexuality of Organization*. London: Sage, pp. 1–28.

Hearn, J. and Parkin, W. (1987) *'Sex' at 'Work': The Power and Paradox of Organization Sexuality*. New York: St. Martin's Press.

Hearn, J., Sheppard, D. L., Tancred-Sheriff, P. and Burrell, G. (1989) *The Sexuality of Organization*. London: Sage.

Heath, S. (1987) 'Men and feminist theory', in A. Jardine and P. Smith (eds), *Men in Feminism*. London: Methuen, pp. 41–6.

Hochschild, A. (1973) 'A review of sex role research', in J. Huber (ed.). *Changing Women in a Changing Society*. Chicago: University of Chicago Press, pp. 249–67.

Hubbard, R. (1988) 'Some thoughts about the masculinity of the natural sciences', in M. M. Gergen (ed.), *Feminist Thought and the Structure of Knowledge*. New York: New York University Press, pp. 1–15.

Irigaray, L. (1985) *This Sex which Is Not One*. Ithaca: Cornell University Press.

Jacobson, S. W. and Jacques, R. (1989) 'Feminism(s) and organization studies: Possible contributions to theory from women's experiences'. Unpublished manuscript, University of Massachusetts, School of Management.

Jaggar, A. M. and Rothenberg, P. S. (1984) *Feminist Frameworks: Alternative Theoretical Accounts of the Relations Between Women and Men*. New York: McGraw-Hill.

Jardine, A. and Smith, P. (1987) (eds) *Men in Feminism*. London: Methuen.

Kauffman, L. (ed.) (1989) *Feminism and Institutions: Dialogues on Feminist Theory*. Oxford: Basil Blackwell.

Keller, E. F. (1983) 'Gender and science', in S. Harding and M. B. Hintikka (eds), *Discovering Reality: Feminist Perspectives on Epistemology, Metaphysics and Philosophy of Science*. Dordrecht, Holland: Reidel, pp. 187–205.

Keller, E. F. (1985) *Reflections on Gender and Science*. New Haven, CT: Yale University Press.

Kelly-Gadol, J. (1977) 'Did women have a Renaissance?', in R. Bridenthal and C. Koonz (eds), *Becoming Visible: Women in European History*. Boston: Houghton-Mifflin, pp. 137–64.

Lamphere, L. (1987) 'Feminism and anthropology: The struggle to reshape our thinking about gender', in C. Farnham (ed.), *The Impact of Feminist Research in the Academy*. Bloomington: Indiana University Press, pp. 11–33.

Lloyd, G. (1984) *The Man of Reason: 'Male' and 'Female' in Western Philosophy*. Minneapolis: University of Minnesota Press.

Lugones, M. C. and Spelman, E. V. (1983) 'Have we got a theory for you! Feminist theory, cultural imperialism and the demand for "The Woman's Voice"', *Women's Studies International Forum*, 9 (6): 573–81.

Lyotard, J. F. (1984) *The Postmodern Condition*. Minneapolis: University of Minnesota Press.

Marshall, Judi (1984) *Women Managers—Travellers in a Male World*. Chichester, UK: Wiley.

Marshall, Judi (1989) 'Re-visioning career concepts: a feminist invitation', in M. B. Arthur, D. T. Hall and B. S. Lawrence (eds.), *Handbook of Career Theory*. Cambridge, UK: Cambridge University Press, pp. 275–91.

Martin, J. (1990) 'Deconstructing organizational taboos: The suppression of gender conflict in organizations'. *Organization Science*, 1: 1–21.

Meyer, J. (1988) 'Feminist thought and social psychology', in M. M. Gergen (ed.), *Feminist Thought and the Structure of Knowledge*. New York: New York University Press, pp. 105–23.

Mills, A. J. (1988) 'Organization, gender and culture', *Organization Studies*, 9 (3): 351–69.

Minnich, E. K. (1986) 'Conceptual errors across the curriculum: Towards a transformation of the tradition'. A publication from the Research Clearing House and Curriculum Integration Project, Center for Research on Women. Memphis State University.

Morawski, J. G. (1988) 'Impasse in feminist thought?', in M. M. Gergen (ed.), *Feminist Thought and the Structure of Knowledge*. New York: New York University Press, pp. 182–94.

Nicholson, L. J. (ed.) (1990) *Feminism/Postmodernism*. New York: Routledge.

Oakeley, A. (1972) *Sex, Gender and Society*. London: Temple Smith.

Osigweh, C. A. B. (1989) 'Concept fallibility in organization science', *Academy of Management Review*, 14 (4): 579–94.

Poole, M. S. and Van de Ven, A. H. (1989) 'Using paradox to build management and organization theories', *Academy of Management Review*, 14 (4): 562–78.

Rao, M. V. H. and Pasmore, W. A. (1989) 'Knowledge and interest in organization studies: A conflict of interpretations', *Organization Studies*, 10 (2): 225–39.

Reinharz, S. (1985) 'Feminist distrust: Problems of context in sociological work', in D. N. Berg and K. K. Smith (eds), *Exploring Clinical Methods for Social Research*. Newbury Park, CA: Sage.

Rosaldo, M. and Lamphere, L. (eds) (1974) *Women, Culture and Society*. Stanford, CA: Stanford University Press.

Rose, H. (1986) 'Women's work: Women's knowledge', in J. Mitchell and A. Oakley (eds), *What is Feminism: A Re-examination*. New York: Pantheon, pp. 161–83.

Rose, H. (1987) 'Hand, brain, and heart: A feminist epistemology for the Natural Sciences', in S. Harding and J. F. O'Barr (eds), *Sex and Scientific Inquiry*. Chicago: The University of Chicago Press.

Schuster, M. and Van Dyne, S. (eds) (1985) *Women's Place in the Academy: Transforming the Liberal Arts Curriculum*. Totowa, NJ: Rowman and Allanheld.

Scott, J. W. (1986) 'Gender: A useful category of historical analysis', *American Historical Review*, 91 (December): 1053–75.

Scott, J. W. (1987) 'Women's history and the rewriting of history', in C. Farnham (ed.), *The Impact of Feminist Research in the Academy*. Bloomington: Indiana University Press, pp. 34–50.

Scott, J. W. (1988) 'Deconstructing equality-versus-difference: Or, the uses of poststructuralist theory for feminism', *Feminist Studies*, 14 (1): 33–50.

Shapiro, J. (1981) 'Anthropology and the study of gender', in E. Langland and W. Gove (eds), *A Feminist Perspective in the Academy: The Difference it Makes*. Chicago: Chicago University Press, pp. 110–29.

Shotter, J. and Logan, J. (1988) 'The pervasiveness of patriarchy: On finding a different voice', in M. M. Gergen (ed.), *Feminist Thought and the Structure of Knowledge*. New York: New York University Press, pp. 69–86.

Showalter, E. (1985) *The New Feminist Criticism*. New York: Pantheon.

Slocum, S. L. (1975) 'Woman the gatherer: Male bias in anthropology', in Rayna R. Reiter (ed.), *Toward an Anthropology of Women*. New York: Monthly Review Press.

Smircich, L. (1985) 'Toward a woman centered organization theory'. Paper presented at the Academy of Management national meeting, San Diego, CA.

Smith, D. E. (1979) 'A sociology for women', in J. A. Sherman and E. T. Beck (eds). *The Prism of Sex*. Madison: The University of Wisconsin Press, pp. 135–87.

Spelman, E. V. (1988) *Inessential Woman*. Boston, MA: Beacon Press.

Stacey, J. and Thorne, B. (1985) The missing feminist revolution in sociology', *Social Problems*, 32: 301–16.

Webster, J. and Starbuck, W. H. (1988) 'Theory building in industrial and organizational psychology', in C. L. Cooper and I. T. Robertson (eds), *International Review of Industrial and Organizational Psychology*, 3.

Weedon, C. (1987) *Feminist Practice and Poststructuralist Theory*. Oxford: Basil Blackwell.

Weick, K. E. (1989) 'Theory construction as disciplined imagination', *Academy of Management Review*, 14 (4): 516–31.

Weiner, A. (1976) *Women of Value, Men of Renown*. Austin: University of Texas Press.

Weisstein, N. (1971) 'Psychology constructs the female', in M. H. Garsk (ed.), *Roles Women Play: Readings Toward Women's Liberation*. Belmont, CA: Brooks/Cole, pp. 68–83.

Westkott, M. (1979) 'Feminist criticism of the social sciences', *Harvard Educational Review*, 49 (4): 422–30.

Whetten, D. A. (1989) 'What constitutes a theoretical contribution?' *Academy of Management Review*, 14 (4): 490–5.

CHAPTER 35

ACADEMIC STRUCTURE, CULTURE, AND THE CASE OF FEMINIST SCHOLARSHIP

PATRICIA J. GUMPORT

Patricia J. Gumport is assistant professor of education and, by courtesy, of sociology at Stanford University and the deputy director of the Stanford Institute for Higher Education Research. Earlier versions and portions of this article were presented at the annual conference of the Association for the Study of Higher Education, St. Louis, 3–6 November 1988 and at the annual conference of the American Educational Research Association, San Francisco 27–31 March 1989. Acknowledgments: Burton Clark, James Hearn, Gary Rhoades, Robert Silverman, and William Tierney provided thoughtful comments.

E pluribus unum—out of many, one. Higher education scholars have used this phrase both descriptively and prescriptively. Both as metaphor and motto, the phrase suggests that, despite a plurality of interests and specialties in academic life, there is cohesion within the organization of academic work and that this cohesion corresponds to lines of formal structure based on one's disciplinary and institutional affiliation. In this article, I call into question the utility of this idealized image as a conceptual frame for understanding complex variations in academic culture. Drawing on recent empirical data about the formation of intentional intellectual communities, I analyze feminist scholarship as a contemporary current in academic life.

Two significant findings are: (1) Faculty seek and find intellectual communities beyond lines of formal structure (e.g., department, institution); and (2) The departmental organization of academic work does not necessarily function as an integrating framework for resolving conflicting interests and advancing common ones. This analysis concludes with an invitation to rethink the premises about culture and structure that are implicit in prevailing conceptual frameworks for studying change in higher education organizations.

Frameworks for Understanding Academic Change

The current configuration of departments and disciplines across campuses evolved in an evolutionary process of intellectual and social differentiation, according to functionalist accounts of academic change in American higher education (e.g., Blau 1973; Clark 1983; Rudolph 1981; Trow 1984). From this perspective, disputes over curricula and new academic programs have been handled by additive solutions—that is, expanding to cover a plurality of interests rather than replacing what counts as worthwhile academic pursuits. Regardless of whether this explanation is the definitive historical explanation, it is apparent that differentiation has its limits. Fewer resources and more capital-intensive academic endeavors render infinite expansion an untenable solution for solving conflicting academic visions.

With varying degrees of urgency over the past decade, some scholars have challenged higher education to "pull itself together" against the current proliferation of new fields and the "blurring of genres" (Geertz 1983; Clark 1983, 1987). Other scholars have warned that "faculty are even more sharply divided than in previous years, . . . and the end of this . . . fragmentation is not in sight" (Bowen and Schuster 1986, 152). One assessment of this state of academic affairs is to assure us of *e pluribus unum*, that is an enduring, harmonious system where faculty are held together by a devotion to knowledge, dual commitments to one's discipline and institution, a unified system albeit constituted by a pluralistic landscape of interests, as Clark (1987, 145) has proposed. An alternative assessment is to view the contemporary scene as a site of oppositional discourses, imbued with fundamental conflicts of vision and resistance to new ideas, such that the revision of the current departmental organization may be imminent (Lincoln 1986).

Such divergent assessments of how things are and how they may be in the future compel us to reconsider some assumptions about academia. In the broadest sense, when we speak of the organization of academic work or of the academic profession, we usually presuppose some degree of integration, whether it be cohesion among people around a knowledge base by discipline or by department, or whether it be cohesion around a professional ideal of purpose or service.

Yet, both within and across disciplines as well as within and across departments on any given campus, such cohesion appears to be waning or, if present, is buried under an array of dramatically different visions of the nature and content of academic knowledge. Debates over the value of Euro-centric scholarship and Western culture undergraduate requirements in the curricula, to name two recent examples, illustrate not only different but conflicting interests. Although the metaphor of organizational culture has been implicitly used in higher education for over two decades (e.g., Clark 1970, 1972), the increased popularity and refinement of cultural perspectives among higher education researchers and managers

attest to the pervasive interest in understanding the glue that holds academia together. The theoretical and empirical work on organizational culture in higher education is, at least in part, a response to this functionalist concern.

Whether positing structural dimensions of organizations as a foil or merely as an analytical complement, deliberate cultural analysis in higher education settings has provided an alternative set of concepts and methods for studying cultural artifacts (e.g., myths, symbols, and rituals) in higher education organizations. The purpose of such research is to uncover beliefs and values among organizational participants, with the promise of more accurately portraying organizational life (Clark 1983; Dill 1982; Gumport 1988; Harman 1988; Masland 1985; Tierney 1988).

Most of such higher education research has been constructed and disseminated within a functionalist paradigm that implicitly seeks to uncover layers of academic order and mechanisms of integration. For example, Andrew T. Masland proposes that culture be seen as "a force that provides stability and a sense of continuity" (1985, 165). Along similar lines, William G. Tierney suggests that the study of cultural dynamics can help us "to decrease conflict" and "to understand and, hopefully, to reduce adversarial relationships" (1988, 18, 5).

Grounded in an *e pluribus unum* premise of organic solidarity (Durkheim 1933), such frameworks for understanding academic organization may be appealing for their currency as a motto, if not as a metaphor, for the hoped-for, ensuing coordination. However, as a conceptual frame for analyzing academic culture, the approach limits inquiry by assuming equilibrium rather than investigating it as an open empirical question. Conflict among organizational participants is seen as either a transient condition that erupts in an otherwise smoothly running system or as a more substantial difference of interest that nonetheless can and should be remedied or resolved. The solution may be structural (by creating a new organizational unit) or cultural (by accepting a divergence of beliefs). Conflict in academic culture is conceptually rendered part of a trend toward differentiation and pluralism.

An alternative starting point for the analysis of academic culture is to ask a different question than what glue is holding everything together, for it may be that things will fall apart or fall out along different lines. Rather than beginning with integration as an *a priori* analytical strait-jacket, we can examine what faculty do—"not what others think they do or should be doing," as George Kuh and Elizabeth Whitt have proposed (1988, 109). What becomes centrally problematic is to examine the nature of individuals' interests and commitments. In other words, the researcher should try not only to find out whether faculty really have dual commitments to their disciplines and institutions, but also to describe faculty perceptions of how their commitments are constructed in different academic settings. This approach leaves open the possibility for ambiguity, with an enduring interest in the sociology of knowledge and of science to determine the interplay between social structures and the development of ideas.

Accordingly, my analysis is framed by two questions: First, how do faculty seek and find intellectual community? And second, how do patterns of association differ in different campus organizational settings? I have found that the emergence of feminist scholarship and its associated academic networks call into question the accuracy of the *e pluribus unum* framework. The analysis is based on interview data from twenty-seven full-time faculty located on two campuses and case study data analyzing how different organizations frame the possibilities for forming intentional communities. These data are drawn from a larger two-year study in which I conducted seventy-five semi-structured, in-depth interviews with administrators and a stratified, random sample of women faculty across ten campuses and three disciplines (Gumport 1987). By supplementing the interviews with case study research and by conceptually anchoring faculty at the center of the analysis, I examined how faculty are constrained by, yet contribute to, their academic settings.

A major substantive line of inquiry in the interviews was examining whether and how these faculty became involved with feminist scholarship and its teaching arm, women's studies. Some of the faculty were located in conventional departments (sociology, history, and philosophy); others were in autonomous women's studies programs. Since they were all women who were in academia at a time of heightened gender consciousness, the contemporary emergence of academic feminism pro-vided a set of intellectual, social, and political interests that they could ignore or embrace. Voluntary association was the major mechanism whereby faculty became participants in this newly emerging, not-yet-legitimate academic specialty. Feminist scholarship is interdisciplinary, potentially of interest to faculty in a wide range of disciplines, and controversial. Some scholars interpret it as having an explicitly political and oppositional agenda. These factors make it a suitable empirical opportunity to examine contemporary lines of academic culture on different campuses.

Analysis

Through an iterative, grounded theory analysis of the interview data (Glaser and Strauss 1967), I discerned patterns that reflected a complex process of finding intellectual affinity and forming intentional networks that cross-cut structural lines of departments. Faculty described individual and group processes as characterized by ambiguity of purpose and conflict of vision as well as by an absence of forethought, conscious planning, or likelihood of academic rewards. In fact, more often than not, the reference group and source of authority were identified as outside the department and sometimes outside academia entirely. Visible communities of feminist scholars emerged across departments as well as across campuses.

Faculty career histories and intellectual biographies enable us to examine what compelled them to associate and what subsequent senses of intellectual and organizational community emerged. First, I address the individual level of how faculty conceive of their intellectual community. Second, I analyze the campus levels for the distinctive informal networks that emerged.

Although individual variations may be interesting in and of themselves, different patterns among individuals provide greater insight for the analysis of social action. The faculty in this sample may be grouped into the following four patterns: (1) scholars whose interests matched their conventional departments and who had no interest or participation in feminist thinking; (2) feminist scholars working primarily in their department and discipline of training but who had some dual or mixed loyalties; (3) feminist scholars in departments yet whose primary loyalty was to women's studies as an autonomous unit separate from the conventional department; and (4) feminist scholar-activists located in women's studies programs who saw themselves as change agents to develop women's studies as an autonomous unit, and whose primary affinity was to the broader national feminist movement.

In this sample, those in the first group were fewer in number, especially among those who entered graduate school in the 1960s. The other three groups reflected some involvement with feminist scholarship and conveyed varying experiences of fragmentation and conflict in academia, both internally and interpersonally. They expressed a sense of conflicting membership within their departments and even internally within an emerging women's studies subculture. I examine each group in turn.

Faculty Identifying with Departments

The scholars who were oriented to their department and discipline agendas did not see their work as intersecting with feminist scholarship in a meaningful way. They did not become involved with feminist research or teach women's studies, deeming them either irrelevant or inappropriate due to the perceived political nature of feminist scholarship.

Four quotations illustrate this sense of detachment. A philosopher commented, "I was conscious of there being a feminist movement; but since there weren't any differences for me as a woman at the time, I more or less ignored all of it."

"I could see it as an area of interest but not something that can stand alone," said a sociologist. "It could get into trouble if it becomes a matter of taking sides rather than material that can be analyzed and looked at critically. It's fine to see women as victims, but that should be separate from the academic milieu. I feel uncomfortable with that."

"I just don't understand it," admitted a second sociologist, and added, "I don't think I agree with it. It worries me a little. . .because I can see people saying we need a Catholic or Jewish sociology; we need a sociology of white supremacy or anti-white supremacy. It gets off into directions I feel real uncomfortable with. . . . I'm not very comfortable with a larger

political role. I don't have any problem with people trying to shift the agenda of the discipline as an intellectual activity, but I have problems with combining the roles—using their academic credentials to legitimate a particular political position. . . . I prefer to keep them separate."

"The label is a disservice," a historian charged. "I've had enough ideologies and dogmas. I have not found [feminist scholars] a natural audience. . . . I'm mistrustful. . . . They want something more doctrinaire, much more ideological."

These four scholars conceived of themselves and their sense of community as clearly anchored in their departments and disciplines. Their networks and associations were not problematic, since they followed the formal structure; but they were only a few voices in my sample.

Faculty with Mixed Loyalties

The second group tried to balance the dual loyalties of their department/discipline and their emerging interests in feminist scholarship.

For some, the balancing act worked. These were usually historians who found a niche in the emerging subfield of women's history. For example, one historian explained she "fell into" feminist scholarship "by accident." Initially she was worried about possible consequences and

> . . . toyed briefly with not telling anyone here that I was working on it, because I was afraid of how it might be perceived, especially as I was coming up for tenure at the time. But I decided not to. There was the practical reason that people would wonder what I was working on. . . . Then it also just didn't seem right. Then I presented some of it in the form of a paper to colleagues in my department. It went very well. I was amazed. Some of the issues that I dealt with are at the intersection of sex and power. They are interested in that. . . . They were very supportive and made good suggestions, and I was much relieved.

Recalling her relations with departmental colleagues prior to her feminist research, she realized in retrospect that there was no need to worry: "I had established such a moderate or really a conservative facade in my department that ... I felt it would not be detrimental." This scholar thus conceived of herself and her community as centered in history, yet able to accommodate a feminist research project.

Others found no convergence between interests in historical and feminist scholarship. They either felt pulled in two different directions or tried to enact a new kind of scholarly identity.

Another historian described herself as "balancing on women's history and French history. Each of them takes me in a direction away from the other. I do pursue women's history outside of France and French history outside of women's history. But in different periods of my life, I'm concentrating either on one or the other."

Her primary professional involvement was the American Historical Association, although she characterized that group as "not exciting." In contrast, she was "attached to" the Berkshire Conference of women's historians and feminist scholars with related interests: "It's special and it's a happening. To go to a place where you know you're going to be indulging your professional interests with other women ... perks you up in a sense because it takes away a burden you don't even know is there when you're working in a male-dominated place like this." In spite of her identification with those who attend the Berkshire Conference, her sense of her work and community was still problematic. She felt pulled apart, unable to find a home entirely in either location.

In trying to reconcile this kind of tension, some scholars in history, sociology, and philosophy generated a research agenda and tried to establish a new intellectual and organizational identity created from the intersection of disciplinary and feminist interests. Historians were most likely to succeed in making this a viable option, although others made concerted efforts.

One historian, who described herself as a pioneer, characterized her efforts:

> I was putting together the politics and the scholarship and feeling like it had to be done.... I still do it that way. You can see all my articles start out with the contemporary political issue and end up with it, too. And I do the history in between.... Now I define myself as someone in women's history and a feminist. I have a network of women's historians around the country. It's

an intellectual community: we read each others' work and comment on it ... and go to conferences. We also socialize at those gatherings and other times. It's also active as a political network.

She had a clear sense of belonging in a feminist scholarly community. Rather than feeling pulled in two separate directions or working in two separate worlds, she had constructed a new primary identity as a "feminist historian." Simultaneously she retained a strong disciplinary orientation, which reflected a comfortable congruence with her being located in the history department at a leading research university: "I'm very wedded to history," she described herself. "I read in other fields, but I really believe in history and in having strong disciplinary training, that without it people can float too much. So my primary identity is as a feminist historian."

It is noteworthy that both this historian and the one who described herself as "balancing" between feminism and history were in the same department at the same institution. Yet their experiences differed, one ending up with dual loyalties while the second ended up constructing a new sense of self and community.

Two philosophers also spoke of finding a new scholarly path which united their divergent scholarly interests. However, they characterized this orientation as more problematic, both in the process and in the outcome, than for the historians. Both philosophers described the difficulty of, first, establishing an intellectual and organizational niche and, second, finding an audience for their research.

The first philosopher observed, "In college I was definitely not a feminist," but over the past two decades, she became a self-described "feminist and a philosopher." She described the process: "The challenge for me as my own person and independent thinker was to get the blend that is desirable. I felt that it was too difficult ... to meet the narrow constraints of the discipline, so I shifted into a women's studies program for a while. That context was invaluable for me [in being] able to develop my thinking freely." Then she took a position in a philosophy department. Her sense of her work was that "it is not straight philosophy." Her most recent paper probably will not be accepted for the American Philosophical Association annual conference because "it's too bizarre in its multidisciplinary approach." In sum, this scholar did not see herself fitting comfortably into her discipline.

A second philosopher also sought to "have something to say to both feminist and philosophical audiences," a task she conceived of as doing something new for her field.

> I take the current [feminist] agenda and ask myself is there something useful a philosopher can do here. . . . When I'm speaking to a feminist audience . . . , I have to make my work relevant in ways that I don't have to when I'm speaking to a philosophical audience. . . . After the initial encounter between the disciplinary work and feminist concerns, then the work develops its own momentum and generates its own sort of questions, so that it no longer seems appropriate to talk about my work as bridging some gap between my subfield in philosophy and separate [feminist] concerns.

This philosopher still saw negative consequences for not "doing straight philosophy," so she spent time developing a feminist scholarly network and trying to publish in both feminist and philosophy journals.

In sum, the pattern characteristic of this group was mixed loyalties that they tried, with different degrees of success, to balance or blend through different strategies. Historians tended to find more resolution in carving out an intellectual and organizational niche for themselves and their community.

Faculty Identifying Primarily with Women's Studies

A third pattern in this sample was scholars who, although located in conventional departments, found their intellectual and social center outside the department. For the most part, they were extensively involved with a campus women's studies program and read, attended, and published primarily in women's studies forums. They consistently reported feeling "more and more distance" from their departments. (Not surprisingly, these scholars were employed at a comprehensive state university, not a research university, which is a point I will address later in the analysis.)

As an example of this pattern, a historian described how she has struggled with this dimension of academic life since graduate school in the late 1960s. She stayed in history, even though her identity and interests gradually moved into women's studies. As a graduate student, she recalled, the discipline was more a heavy hand than an intellectual home. "Where there was a question of my values being in direct conflict with the trajectory of the disciplinary career, I got slapped down and I was very well aware of that. I could see that happening. I cried. I wept. I said it was unfair. And I changed."

Years later, her intellectual affinities turned toward women's studies, even though she had a full-time position in a history department. She did not find it feasible to be in both worlds, so she, in effect, "dropped out of the history department." She remembered: "I wouldn't serve on any committees and I wouldn't socialize with anyone. I had nothing to do with the department. . . . All of my orientation was with the women's studies program. Because that was a confrontational program at the time, the separation was absolute. I could be here, or I could be there. But I couldn't be in both places."

In retrospect, she characterized herself as having been "professionally dumb" to make primary commitment to women's studies without thinking about the consequences. Still, her identification with women's studies was so strong that "if someone had said don't risk it, it would have to have been the leader of our feminist movement. If the chair of the [history] department had said to me, 'Look, I'm with you and I love what you're doing for the women's studies but I'm not going to be able to get you through the department,' I would have said 'screw you,'" She gained tenure in her department, probably because of her outstanding teaching record; her courses, which were cross-listed with women's studies, were popular and consistently well-enrolled.

Naturally faculty located in women's studies programs most frequently expressed the feeling of having an intellectual and organizational home in women's studies. Since they were not located in conventional departments, they would have a greater opportunity to find congruence between their interests, expertise, and organizational niche. However, such positions lacked the security of appointments in more traditional departments. Only some women's studies faculty had "retreat rights" to another department in the event of program dissolution. However, the perceived marginality of women's studies coupled with a lack of common intellectual interests made those future scenarios unsatisfactory. One women's studies program director, who was simultaneously a full professor in a sociology department, explained her own situation: "The loss of collegiality with my 'home' department is something I hadn't anticipated would happen. I no longer go to their meetings—on campus or nationally in the association. I can't do both." The center of her academic life was clearly in women's studies, locally, regionally, and nationally—an orientation shared by some other women's studies scholars who had departmental appointments.

Faculty Identifying with Feminism

Some faculty with positions in women's studies differed from their department colleagues in having a distinctive nonacademic orientation, where the faculty member conceived of her work and her community as lying outside the academy. In those cases, the primary loyalty and reference group became more the political movement than the academy.

For example, one faculty member reported having had a series of terminal appointments over the last seven years, part-time on and off, later full-time in a women's studies program. "Basically I've been a gypsy scholar and to me it [politics and academics] is not an internal conflict. If it's a choice between my political convictions and a job, the job can go to hell. . . . I will never make those kinds of compromises. It's not an internal conflict, but it's a conflict with the system." She identifies herself as a feminist scholar and black scholar who believes in women's studies programs as "an essential institutional power base . . . not . . . in it being a safe harbor, but in it being a real space for women . . . scholars and women students." She describes having a primary political agenda.

She is located in a women's studies program on a campus where the program functions much like a department; a handful of other full-time faculty in women's studies ostensibly share her feminist scholarly interests. However, this setting has not become a complete home. As a woman of color, she felt that she was hired to boost enrollments; and the other women's studies faculty felt threatened when she wanted to change things, "threatened enough to complain to the administration." She felt betrayed:

> Most of the tension has come in women's studies because they didn't realize what it'd mean to have a woman of color who is not a clone of traditional feminist theory. . . . They put on file with the administration a criticism saying that I was not collegial because I did not validate the work of the women who went before me, that I moved too fast. And they refused to talk with me about it. . . . So that's saying to me we don't want you here, and if we want you here we want you under our control.

Although this particular case may seem extreme, it is a useful reminder that the basic organizing units of academic life do not necessarily convey cohesion of purpose and loyalty. Both on the individual level and the interpersonal level, fragmentation and conflict may be pervasive. Even in a case where women's studies functions like a department, there may be less cohesion than we presume. In fact, faculty involved with women's studies and feminist scholarship admit to internal lack of consensus on program content, visions for change, and even who qualifies as members in their enterprise (Gumport 1990). As one director of a women's studies program observed: "People differ in what they mean by feminist and feminist scholarship, and some programs have been torn apart over it."

Campus Networks

These four patterns of faculty orientations also coincide with different higher education organizational settings. Individuals oriented toward conventional departments without interest or involvement in feminist work as well as individuals who felt pulled in two directions from conflicting departmental and feminist scholarly associations were located at a leading research university. Those whose primary affinities were in autonomous women's studies programs or who were highly politicized and oriented outside academia entirely were located at a comprehensive state university.

At the common-sense level and in a functionalist framework, this pattern is no surprise. One obvious hypothesis is that either the individual women self-selected organizational settings that matched their interests or the research-oriented and teaching-oriented institutions each selected faculty with orientations that fit their particular campus culture. However, rather than assuming conscious choice on either part, and examining desegregated individual behaviors, it is more illuminating to examine the kinds of informal networks that developed in each campus setting.

The reward system within research universities for departmental and disciplinary research and the emphasis in comprehensive state universities on teaching suggest that the different organizational settings provide different possibilities for cross-departmental networks among feminist scholars. The case study data from the two campuses point to a distinctive pattern: the comprehensive university had a thriving cross-departmental feminist, scholarly network; the leading research university had a floundering one.

At the comprehensive university, the faculty in general were described as "progressive" and "having a radical bent." The core of the feminist scholarly community revolved around the women's studies program, which was established in the early 1970s and, at the time of this research, boasted fifty undergraduate majors, eighteen courses a semester, and a dozen faculty (including part-timers) with women's studies appointments. The faculty network also included over a dozen more active feminists located in departments.

The faculty network originated in and has been sustained by students' grass-roots efforts to establish a women's studies program. In the early years, there was a student alliance, where students either ran the courses or taught them informally. Since the courses were well-enrolled and highly politicized, the administration took notice. As an administrator remembered: "It scared the administration. The mere size of the thing, the numbers of people involved, the energy generated around it! I think all that was significant enough to carry us ultimately into the women's studies program itself." Years later, the alliance became an ad hoc committee which has been the intellectual, social, and political center for feminist faculty and students ever since. Many departmental faculty became connected formally by cross-listing courses or serving on committees,

or informally by socializing. Their efforts are constrained by time; "we're all teaching heavy loads." Their focus shifted to formulating a master's program in women's studies and whether to make women's studies a general education requirement, thereby changing small, personal classes into large required ones.

As faculty described the campus milieu, they often referred to "the administration." "The administration," they said, "does not penalize us for being involved in women's studies." What seemed to count most was generating and sustaining high enrollment programs. Since departmental involvement and women's studies involvement were not differentially valued, participating in a feminist network on campus had a pay-off.

In contrast to the thriving feminist scholarly network at the comprehensive university, the research university has had a small though growing faculty group, whose members tended to keep an intellectual and organizational anchor in their departments. The women's studies program at the research university was small and had no permanent autonomous faculty lines; except for an occasional visitor, the program relied on cross-listed departmental courses. Established relatively late vis-a-vis the national scene, the program did not grant degrees; students petitioned individually to an interdisciplinary majors committee for a bachelor's degree in women's studies.

At the time of this research, the dozen or so most visible feminist faculty in the departments wanted the teaching program to flourish but recognized the constraints in faculty recruitment and hiring practices in the departments. A historian explained: "The reality of the university is so discipline-based that you do a disservice to create something outside the disciplines. . . . Strategically, people need to be based in the disciplines. . . . And it's not just strategically but intellectually as well." However, the women's studies program director acknowledges that the institution was willing to support women's studies, provided that it demonstrated "strong scholarship" and an "assurance of respectability." The willingness came from the competitive drive for excellence—the fact that "entrepreneurs get their way here. . . . it's survival of the fittest. . . . You survive if you get a high level of visibility, if you are judged by your peers as at the top."

Participating in an emerging informal feminist scholarly network on this campus would have little pay-off for faculty, given the strong disciplinary orientations and time constraints from pressure to publish. In addition, according to one observer in the humanities:

> It's a little risky that no matter how committed you are, you have to draw the line somewhere because there is so much to be done. There are considerations of practicality, of what you need to do and can do if you want to stay here. . . . Most people are much more cautious about getting involved in anything besides writing their books. . . . It's getting labeled—not as a feminist or a women's studies person per se. It's getting labeled as a person who will do non-scholarly, collaborative, student-oriented things. . . . It's the kiss of death.

In spite of the risk, participating in a feminist network on a small scale provides intellectual, social, or political support for faculty who are trying to balance or blend feminist with disciplinary interests. Although informal feminist networks connect people who would otherwise be dispersed and isolated in conventional departments, they may also do a disservice. A philosopher explained: "In general there isn't a location for feminist work in the field. . . . The status of feminist work is still fairly fragile. . . . It's mostly women doing it. And so, of course, [since] women are all engaged in this funny kind of work just really people's initial prejudice that women can't do real philosophy . . . [but] are doing this other thing which isn't real philosophy." In any case, despite the scrutiny and stigma, a scholar with this orientation may still seek a feminist scholarly network as an intellectual and organizational home. Another philosopher explained her own decision to do so and remarked on the same inclination of her colleagues:

> If you are working on feminist stuff, you are likely to feel embattled. . . . The women in philosophy who see themselves as feminist scholars will generally be the only person doing feminist work in a department and may sometimes be the only woman period. [They] may feel cut off or deprived of collegial relationships among departmental colleagues and may develop closer relationships with colleagues in women's studies [located] in other departments. . . . Those are the only places where you get both philosophical colleagueship and feminist colleagueship. You get both of them at the same time, in the same place, in the same sentence. And for most women philosophers that is extremely rare.

Thus, both the advantages and disadvantages of associating with a feminist scholarly network are heightened in the constraints of the research university than in the comprehensive university.

The contrast between two campuses raises questions about the organizational factors that might account for these differences. The inability of the research university to generate—let alone sustain—a thriving feminist scholarly network reflects a distinctive structure and culture which stand in dramatic contrast to that of the comprehensive university.

At the research university, faculty were oriented primarily to their disciplinary colleagues; and departments did the essential work of research and graduate education. In a sense, this peer culture became coercive, guiding faculty behavior and time management as a means of social coordination. In effect, it kept people on their assigned academic tasks, not only junior faculty who faced the "publish or perish" criteria for tenure but senior faculty who earned merit increases in promotion. Since departmental senior faculty held the power, other faculty were not inclined to spend too much time and energy on voluntary associations. Those who chose to do so essentially ran against the grain at their own risk by leaping across the discrete departmental building blocks on which the university organization rests. When it comes to peer review, they ran an even greater risk of not fitting in (Gumport 1990). A feminist scholar who had been denied tenure at a leading research university explained it this way: "It's harder to work when it's not fitting into your discipline in a particular way. You can't expect to get clear judgments and rewards, although you'll get different opinions about it. . . . The problem is the people who could judge it are out there and not in here in my department and my discipline."

In contrast, the locus of power at the comprehensive university lay with administrators, not with a departmental/disciplinary peer culture. Administrators' power was linked to their discretion over academic programs and teaching loads. Enrollment-driven data carried clout. Consequently, there was a greater organizational distance between the faculty and the central administration. Faculty and administrators ended up antagonists, no matter what voluntary associations faculty formed. Since course enrollments were the currency for leverage, it was less important whether a feminist faculty member was participating in women's studies centrally, marginally, or in a conventional department. The issue simply lacked the salience it assumed in the disciplinary peer culture of the research university.

In light of these fundamental differences in organizational settings it becomes clear that overarching academic beliefs like academic freedom and devotion to knowledge are mediated by local settings. Moreover, each setting coordinates academic work with a different emphasis so that faculty are encouraged to attend to different concerns. Thus, each setting is more likely to raise different possibilities for the formation of a cross-departmental feminist scholarly network. Although these patterns appear to warrant an *e pluribus unum* conclusion, such a conclusion would be overly simplistic and premature. As the first part of this analysis shows, participants interpret and reenact beliefs according to their subjective perceptions and have the potential to reconstitute the settings in which they work.

Conclusion

In an analysis of recent empirical data, I reexamine the functionalist premise of *e pluribus unum*—out of many, one. Rather than beginning with the assumption of the past, present, or future cohesion among organizational participants, as other higher education scholars have, I bring the analysis down to the level of individuals to examine how they enter, negotiate, and play out structural and cultural dimensions of their particular organizational settings. The interview data reveal that faculty conceive of their commitments and their sense of community in ways that do not always correspond with idealized conceptions of academic organization in which departmental and institutional affinities reign supreme.

Setting aside the sub-group in this small sample whose orientations did correspond to their departments, the three other groups of women scholars exemplify a kind of intellectual and social incongruence with their organizational locations. There are plenty of academics whose work does not fit neatly into their so-called home departments and disciplines. In fact, many of the quotations cited in the preceding analysis could have been spoken by faculty in such fields as area studies, urban studies, environmental studies, science policy studies, and ethnic studies—to name a few. These are contemporary fields whose scholarly content and practice do not match the current departmental organization. These are fields where, in an effort to reconstitute academic knowledge, people seek and find intentional communities that are cross-departmental and sometimes even nonacademic.

In a fundamental sense, the emergence of faculty with orientations that diverge significantly from their departments/disciplines of training remains a puzzle. Are they self-chosen outliers, deviants, or examples of inadequate disciplinary socialization? Do they reflect the particular dynamics of those with distinctive special interests? Or are their experiences characteristic of academics who are engaged in the formation of new specialties or interdisciplinary fields?

While I am not proposing generalizability from this small sample of women faculty, I am suggesting that the data may illuminate some persistent dynamics of conflict and ambiguity in academic life that are overlooked when one begins in the aggregate by attributing cohesion of purpose to departments and institutions. Whether it be for academics who engage in not-yet-legitimate academic pursuits or even for those who apparently have conventional disciplinary and departmental affiliations, the process of forming a scholarly identity, the nature of interpersonal communication, and positioning oneself within the academic reward system may be central features of academic organizational life that have been understudied and undertheorized.

The nature of academic organization needs to be reconceptualized because departmental units do not necessarily or inevitably determine behavior, interests, and, more profoundly, the pace and direction of knowledge change.

That is, the formation of intentional communities may be integral to the process of negotiating the tension between constraints of the academic reward structure and personal ambitions, between the designation of what is cutting edge versus trivial, and between determining what is legitimately innovative versus what is off the map. The consequences for innovation in higher education are significant, as there is a perennial need to consider which administrative frameworks foster scholarly creativity. As Dean MacHenry has noted: "In scholarship, as in farming, the most fertile soil may be under the fences, rather than at the center of long-established fields" (1977, ix). Similarly, Angela Simeone has proposed that "there are some who would argue that these networks constitute the most vital development within the recent history of American higher education" (1987, 99).

Functionalist conceptions do not make problematic how, where, and why faculty seek and find intellectual community, since a premise of overlapping memberships assures that affinities will converge along two primary lines of disciplinary and campus affiliations. Such an orientation assumes that beliefs lead to commitments (Clark 1987, 106–7) and commitments lead to community. Beliefs and increasingly specialized orientations more or less correspond to, or at least complement, one's departmental affiliation; otherwise, a new unit will be differentiated. A further functionalist presupposition is one of coordination, where the organization of academic work and knowledge acts as a "framework for both resolving conflicting interests and advancing common ones" (Clark 1987, 109). In spite of "narrow groups that in turn generate their own separate subcultures," cultural overlap emerges from a common commitment to shared, overarching principles and beliefs (Clark 1987, 109, 140–42).

While my analysis challenges Clark's rationalistic premises, one functionalist proposition finds support in this analysis: beliefs get played out differently in organizational settings (Clark 1987, chap. 5). At research universities, disciplinarity and cutting edge scholarship are valued; whereas in the comprehensive college sector, both faculty and administration, the "they" to whom faculty often refer, turn their attention to teaching and undergraduate enrollments. Using this analytical distinction, I examine how these different organizational settings may inhibit or foster informal, cross-departmental faculty networks.

As the analysis revealed, location was linked with distinctive patterns of association among faculty. Feminist scholarly activity at the comprehensive university most closely approximates a subculture, although this particular subculture seems more likely to subvert the status quo enterprise than enhance it. The research university could not generate and sustain a viable cross-departmental network; instead faculty behavior tended to either correspond to, or complement, lines of differentiation in the formal structure. Both patterns illustrate that structural and cultural features of organizational life may be a coercive force. Yet faculty are active agents who may try to reshape their immediate academic settings; further, faculty's innovative interests may be tied to the wider external culture. Thus, when supposedly shared beliefs are viewed in their respective organizational embodiments, far more variation, fragmentation, conflict, and ambiguity exist than the *e pluribus unum* framework presumes.

For those who study higher education, a theoretical and methodological directive is clear. The kinds of questions we need to ask about academic life need to reflect complexity, not only of structures but of processes; not of distinct levels but of the mechanisms that cross-cut and potentially undermine the levels; not of daily life inside an organization but of how daily life is necessarily situated in wider socio-cultural circumstances. The questions locate both the realities of organizational life and the potentials for change in people's subjective experiences, not solely in *a priori* notions of formal structure, dominant norms, and beliefs as determinative.

Indeed, an even further diversity of perspectives is necessary to understand something as complex as the nature of academic change. As illustrative of one emerging approach, a critical cultural perspective signifies a marked departure from functionalist premises in order to take seriously the interplay between prevailing social structures and individuals' perceptions of agency (Tierney 1991). The intention is to yield a more accurate portrayal, not only of the variation in academic life in its myriad settings, but also of the ways in which research from a functionalist perspective advance a myth of unity in pluralism. The aim is to examine how interests may conflict and come to be differently valued, "not to celebrate organization as a value, but to question the ends it serves" (Smircich 1983, 355). Nor is the intention to remain silent on the unresolved and unacknowledged controversies underlying established departmental categories, but rather "to think about them and to recognize they [themselves are] the product of theoretical choices" (Graff 1987, 8).

Although some proponents of this line of inquiry approach their data with an etic standpoint from the top down, other proponents of a critical cultural analysis advocate inductive inquiry that begins at the local level from the inside out. From either perspective, a cultural analysis makes problematic conventional functionalist analyses of such essential academic processes as curricular change, faculty hiring and promotion, and academic program planning. It forces us to rethink concepts such as hierarchy—an all-important context of academic life. For instance, rather than seeing hierarchy as an ordered arrangement that promotes coordination and excellence, hierarchy may also be examined as a means of social control which is contested between the Weberian bureaucratic interests of central administrators and the faculty's professional interests for self-regulation and autonomy.

From this line of inquiry, empirical study on the problem of social integration generates a wider range of questions worth pursuing, ultimately for revising theoretical explanations of the nature of academic organization. For example, how and under what conditions do academic organizations reflect enduring systemic disequilibria, either in the contemporary era or historically? Are there new types of social and intellectual integration that have emerged beyond the administratively decentralized, rational organizational order; if so, how has the formation of intentional communities played a role in academic change? Are current faculty commitments pointing to a disintegration of the modern academic role, or possibly to a postmodern legitimacy for explicit expression of political and economic commitments, or perhaps to an institutionally mediated academic role in which certain commitments and behaviors—such as political protest or economic

entrepreneurship—are deemed acceptable lines of partisanship in certain kinds of campus settings but not in others?

As researchers of higher education define directions for further organizational studies, they will determine whether the various structural and cultural analyses of higher education may be used in a complementary manner or may be judged incompatible on the basis of divergent directives for what to study, how to study it, and to what end. It remains to be seen whether this uncertainty should be interpreted as a sign of knowledge growth and differentiation in a maturing field of study or as a sign of impending fragmentation and cultural ambiguity in a field of study that is itself inescapably embedded in multiple nested contexts.

References

Blau, Peter. *The Organization of Academic Work.* New York: John Wiley & Sons, 1973.

Bowe, Howard, and Jack Schuster. *American Professors: A National Resource Imperiled.* New York: Oxford University Press, 1986.

Clark, Burton R. *The Distinctive College.* Chicago: Aldine, 1970.

———. "The Organizational Saga in Higher Education." *Administrative Science Quarterly* 17 (June 1972): 178–84.

———. *The Higher Education System: Academic Organization in Cross National Perspective.* Berkeley: University of California Press, 1983.

———, ed. *The Academic Life: Small Worlds, Different Worlds.* Princeton: The Carnegie Foundation for the Advancement of Teaching, 1987.

Dill, David D. "The Management of Academic Culture: Notes on the Management of Meaning and Social Integration." *Higher Education* 11 (May 1982): 303–20.

Durkheim, Emile. *The Division of Labor in Society.* 1933; reprint ed., New York: The Free Press, 1984.

Geertz, Clifford. "The Way We Think Now: Toward an Ethnography of Modern Thought." In his *Local Knowledge: Further Essays in Interpretive Anthropology,* 147–66. New York: Basic Books, 1983.

Glaser, Barney, and Anselm Strauss. *The Discovery of Grounded Theory: Strategies for Qualitative Research.* New York: Aldine, 1967.

Graff, Gerald. *Professing Literature: An Institutional History.* Chicago: The University of Chicago Press, 1987.

Gumport, Patricia J. "The Social Construction of Knowledge: Individual and Institutional Commitments to Feminist Scholarship." Ph.D. diss., Stanford University, 1987.

_____. "Curricula as Signposts of Cultural Change." *Review of Higher Education* 12 (Autumn 1988): 49–61

_____. "Feminist Scholarship as a Vocation." *Higher Education* 20 (October 1990): 231–43.

Harman, Kay. "The Symbolic Dimension of Academic Organization: Academic Culture at the University of Melbourne." Ph.D. diss., La Trobe University, 1988.

Kuh, George, and Elizabeth Whitt. *The Invisible Tapestry: Culture in American Colleges and Universities.* ASHE-ERIC Higher Education Reports, Washington, D.C.: Association for the Study of Higher Education, 1988.

Lincoln, Yvonna S. "Toward a Future-Oriented Comment on the State of the Profession." *Review of Higher Education* 10 (Winter 1986): 135–42.

MacHenry, Dean. "Preface." In *Academic Departments,* edited by Dean MacHenry and Associates, ix–xvi. San Francisco: Jossey-Bass, 1977.

Masland, Andrew T. "Organization Culture in the Study of Higher Education." *Review of Higher Education* 8 (Winter 1985): 157–68.

Rudolph, Frederick. *Curriculum: A History of the American Undergraduate Curriculum Since 1936.* San Francisco: Jossey-Bass, 1981.

Simeone, Angela. *Academic Women: Working Toward Equality.* South Hadley, Mass.: Bergin and Garvey, 1987.

Smircich, Linda. "Concepts of Culture and Organizational Analysis." *Administrative Science Quarterly* 28 (1983): 339–58.

Tierney, William G. "Organizational Culture in Higher Education: Defining the Essentials." *Journal of Higher Education* 59 (January/February 1988) 2–21.

_____, ed. *Culture and Ideology in Higher Education: Advancing a Critical Agenda.* New York: Praeger, 1991.

Trow, Martin. "The Analysis of Status." In *Perspectives on Higher Education,* edited by Burton Clark, Chap. 5. Berkeley: University of California Press, 1984.

PART VIII

CRITICAL APPROACHES TO ORGANIZATIONAL GOVERNANCE

CHAPTER 36

ORGANIZATION THEORY IN THE POSTMODERN ERA

KENNETH J. GERGEN

Why do we find it so congenial to speak of organizations as structures but not as clouds, systems but not songs, weak or strong but not tender or passionate? Is it because organizations physically resemble one but not the other, that we somehow discern through the clamorous hurly burly something that is structural, but not cloudlike, systemic rather than rhapsodic, strong but not tender? What kind of 'structure' could we have in mind that the continuous movements of eyeballs, arms, legs, words, papers, and so on should bear a physical resemblance? And are those who think they observe structure simply blind to systemic 'process', and those who spy 'strength' insensitive to obvious signals of 'tenderness'? No, there is little sense to be made of the assumption that organization theories are read off the world as it is, inductively derived from our experiential immersion in a world of continuous flux.

A far more promising alternative for understanding the intelligibility of organizations is to be found in the discursive context. For our theories of organizations are, first and foremost, forms of language. They are guided by existing rules of grammar, and constructed out of the pool of nouns and verbs, the metaphors, the narrative plots, and the like found within the linguistic context. In this sense, theories of the organization do not exist apart from or independent of the surrounding intelligibilities of the culture. As theorists we must 'make sense', and if we are to make sense within our own culture, we have no recourse but to obey the culture's rules of intelligibility. We thus borrow and steal from the cultural ways of talking about organizational life, for if we do not rely on our cultural surrounds we cannot serve as their insightful informants. This does not mean that we are simply redundant, speaking back to the culture what it already knows. Yes, the cultural intelligibilities must necessarily guide or inform our ways of speaking. However, as a profession we then act upon these intelligibilities—expanding and elaborating on the dominant metaphors, synthesizing, purifying, explicating, elaborating, and following their implicature into the realm of the as yet unspoken. So when we do our work well, the culture does indeed learn anew from our sayings.

This image of inter-discourses—in this case the cultural and the professional—provides a prelude to the major concerns I wish to address in this chapter. For I believe that organization theory of the present century has drawn its chief sustenance from two cultural leitmotifs, or hegemonic bodies of discourse. In the first case our theories have been enriched and informed by romanticist discourse of the nineteenth century, and in the second, by the modernist understanding of the person dominant within the twentieth century. However, in my view the gains to be acquired through continued intercourse with these traditions are diminishing. Already, romanticist discourse is largely displaced by modernist understandings. And at present the intellectual and cultural *Zeit-*

geist is substantially undermining the rhetorical force of modernism. As many believe, we are entering a period of postmodernism. And as we do so, new formulations are invited, formulations that are essential to the intellectual, political and practical significance of organization theory.

In what follows I shall first take a brief scan of the influence of romanticism and modernism on traditional and current accounts of the organization. I shall then outline what I believe to be critical ingredients of the postmodern turn within the intellectual sphere. Finally, I shall offer a preliminary scaffold for a postmodern theory of power and efficacy in the organization.

Romantic Dimensions of Organizational Life

Any intelligible theory of organizational life must be coherent with prevailing conceptions of the human being. The theorist cannot make sense about persons in relationship without relying on a forestructure of understandings concerning the nature of human functioning more generally. Yet, cultural conceptions of human functioning are hardly cumulative; they are subject to vast upheavals and decay across time. In this context, let us consider the romanticist discourse largely reaching its ascendancy within the nineteenth century. For, not only is there a coherence in this discourse across many sectors of Western culture—an array of interrelated and commonly held assumptions—but in many respects this emerging view of human functioning is both distinct in quality and profound in implication. Here I am not only speaking of the verbally articulate—of poets, novelists and philosophers, from Goethe, Hölderlin, in the early phases, through Byron, Keats, Shelley, and Wordsworth somewhere toward the center, to Nietzsche, Rimbaud and Edgar Allen Poe toward the latter phase. I am also including as purveyors of the romantic idiom artists (from Casper David Friedrich to the Pre-Raphaelites and symbolists), composers (from Beethoven and Brahms to Chopin and Rachmaninov), and architects (including both Victorian and Art Nouveau).

In my view the chief contribution of the romanticists to the prevailing concept of the person was their rhetorical creation of *the deep interior*. That is, what was truly significant about the individual, that which rendered persons uniquely identifiable as persons, is the existence of a repository of capacities or characteristics lying deeply within human consciousness. These capacities and characteristics are not given immediately to conscious rationality—simply there for the passing glance of any errant philistine. To understand them, to express them, and to appreciate them—either in oneself or others—requires special sophistication, an introspective sensitivity, a willingness to be wrenched from the contented perch of the ordinary. Among the chief constituents of the deep interior was the human soul, a concept resuscitated from medieval texts, and which served to give the individual inherent worth—a value above and beyond that assigned to marketplace commodities. To the deep interior was also allocated a powerful and mysterious energic force. For many this force was wondrous—nothing short of pure love—and its expression (both in committed love and friendship) furnished life its fundamental meaning. And, because of the power of this force, one might also experience grief (at the loss of the loved one) and a sense of longing or remorse so profound that suicide was its most appropriate mode of expression. For others, particularly the late romanticists, this force was also endowed with evil potential—possibly leading to madness. In addition to these constituents of the deep interior, romanticists located entities such as inspiration, creativity, and genius along with the power of will and the capacity for moral sensibility. The resources at a depth were rich indeed.

For many romanticists, the deep interior was also rooted in nature. No, it was not crassly biological nature—material, brute-like, there for medical inspection. Rather, in the great chain of being, which linked God at the uppermost, with the kingdom of animals and plants toward the lower spectrum, the deep interior was of God, but at the same time, endowed with natural forces. It was natural in that it was God-given, and not a product of human artifice. And it was natural in that it was at home within and vulnerable to the surrounding forces of worldly nature. Genius, inspiration, creativity, will power and moral sensibility were not, then, products of simple training and instruction. They were inherent gifts within the natural order.

Today the romanticist perspective is sustained largely by the arts, literature, religion, and the mass media. They urge people to find 'meaning in life', to 'give all to love', to achieve moral worth, to know oneself, and to express one's deepest impulses. And romanticism also furnishes a significant rhetorical legacy for theories of the organization. Let me cite only a few perspectives that owe their power or appeal largely to the romanticist language of the deep interior:

Work emanating from the Tavistock Institute (including Bion, Jacques, Menzies and Bridger) along with other psychoanalytically based theories of the organization (for example, Zaleznick) in which unconscious dynamics furnish the explanatory fulcrum.

Theoretical work inspired by Jung's theory of archetypical bases of action (for example, Denhardt, Mitroff).

Theory and research presuming fundamental human needs, including human resource management and human potential perspectives (for example, Mayo, Maslow, McGregor).

Positions emphasizing the personal resources essential for successful leadership (for example, Fiedler, Hollander).

That aspect of Japanese management theory, as made intelligible in the West, emphasizing organizational commitment, and bonds between organizations and their members which transcend market exigencies.

Inquiries into executive appreciation that emphasize the workers' needs for positive regard and the significance of empathy and dialogue to organizational success (for example, Cooperider and Srivastva).

It is essential to note at this point that by viewing these accounts as forms of language, not in themselves derived from what is the case, achieving their impact through rhetorical artifice, my aim is not at all derogatory. In my view the value of organization theory does not lie in its accuracy, how well it matches or reflects the

way things are. (In what way can words be matched against visual images, sounds, and the like?) Theory cannot be evaluated by its capacity to predict, for words in themselves are simply sounds or markings, lifeless and inert; words in themselves do not predict. Rather, theory gains its importance from the activities which it enables, which essentially means, by the way in which it figures in ongoing patterns of relationship. Thus, by drawing sustenance from the romanticist vocabulary, organization theorists hammer out intelligibilities that resonate with a significant part of the cultural vernacular. In this sense, they find an eagerly appreciative audience. Further, when such intelligibilities are inserted into organizational life, old practices seem wrong-headed, and new forms of organizational life are invited. It is not that the new practices are superior in some sense of 'truer' or more 'fundamental'. Rather, the new practices often enable people to live out their cultural meaning systems in ways that seem congenial or 'more fully expressive'.

From Romantic to Modernist Conceptions of the Organization

To be sure, romanticist vocabulary of understanding is still very much alive in Western culture; many would say that without it life ceases to have meaning. However, it is also a vocabulary in remission. In the intellectual world most particularly, romanticist voices largely speak from the margins. The chief replacement for the romanticist world-view is the modernist. There are as many reasons for the flourishing of modernism in the present century as there are pitfalls to overall characterization of the era. The interested scholar may wish to consult relevant works by Bradbury and McFarlane (1976), Berman (1982), Frisby (1985), and Habermas (1981). However, in very brief form,, I would characterize modernism as:

1. *A revival of Enlightenment beliefs in the powers of reason and observation*, linked importantly to Darwinistic views of species survival. Through observation we record the character of the world, and through reason we can develop and test theories about the world. As our

theories become progressively more accurate and predictive, so do our potentials for survival increase.

2. *A search for fundamentals or essentials.* Sustained by powers of reason and observation, we may lay bare the secrets of the universe, whether it be atomic particles, chemical elements, economic behavior, architectural form, or musical tonality.

3. *A faith in progress and universal design.* Because of the obvious gains in knowledge or understanding of fundamentals, we can be assured of a steadily improving future. As we succeed in mastering fundamental knowledge of energy, biological systems, psychological mechanisms, social structures and the like, we can move toward utopian societies. Knowledge of essentials is also universal knowledge, and thus we may have faith in rationally derived, large-scale designs for society.

4. *Absorption in the machine metaphor.* There are many reasons: the enormous social consequences of the industrial revolution, the efficiency of lifestyles increasingly engendered by the machine, and the Enlightenment presumption prevailing in science (and thus rational) of the world as 'one great machine'. In any case, the existing confluence of images and ideas gave rise to a prevailing metaphor of understanding: the machine. That is, whatever the essentials—from atoms to architecture—the model theoretical picture stresses the systematic (typically causal) relationships between or among basic elements. Thus, like any good machine, if one understands its internal functioning, and has control over the inputs, one can depend on a reliable product.

These various presumptions remain vital throughout contemporary culture, and they have left an indelible mark on theories of organization from early in the century to the present. Not only have modernist beliefs granted the scholar an honorable niche (grounded expertise in a given domain of inquiry), but they have promised the scholarly community

that with the assiduous application of research technology, fundamental progress can be attained in our understanding of organizational life. Such views, along with the associated metaphor of the machine, are variously represented in:

Scientific management theory along with time and motion methodology.

General systems theory in its various modifications and extensions, including contemporary contingency theory (for example, Lawrence and Lorsch).

Exchange theories (for example, Homans), along with related investigations of equity and bargaining and expectancy value analyses of individual behavior.

Cybernetic theory, in which organizations approximate sophisticated mechanical automata.

Trait methodology, which presumes the stability of individual patterns of behavior and the possibility of selecting individuals to fit different positions (for example Fiedler).

Cognitive theories of individual behavior (see Iligen and Klein's 1989 review).

Theories of industrial society based on rational laws of economic organization and development.

The Postmodern Transformation

To be sure, romantic and modernist discourses are hardly moribund. They have many champions and charges, and a great deal of research and organizational planning is carried out within their purview. And so it should be. However, for many these voices have lost their sense of lived validity. For many, they seem more akin to formalisms or to ideological mystifications. There is a yearning for alternatives. In my view, this sense of unease can largely be traced to what many see as the postmodern turn in intellectual and cultural life more generally. As in the preceding, I must be mercilessly brief in accounting for major contours and rationales. But for present purposes, let me summarize the postmodern turn in the following way.

For modernists there were essentials to be discovered through reason and observation, and to be reflected in language. The relationship of language to the essential was thus one of master to slave. The essentials of the universe (atoms, neurons, economies, and so on) served as masters, fixed and foremost, and the language was to be their servant—flexibly bending to the contours of the essential. The creditable language was thus one which depicts or maps the essentials as they truly are. I shan't review here all the many counter-currents that came to challenge this view. Among the initially prominent were certainly Wittgenstein's (1963) writings on language games, Quine's (1960) critique of the word-object link, Kuhn's (1970) account of paradigm incommensurability, Garfinkel's (1967) ethnomethodology, critical school challenges (Habermas, 1975) to interest-free knowledge, Nelson Goodman's (1978) views on world construction, and various discussions (for example, Pepper, 1972; Burke, 1968; White, 1978) of the metaphoric and rhetorical basis of knowledge. And of more recent vintage, one should have to mention feminist critiques (Harding, 1986; Keller, 1985) of the androcentric biases underlying seemingly neutral science, Foucault's (1978) analysis of the relationship of knowledge to power and control, inquiries in the sociology of knowledge (Latour, 1987; Knorr-Cetina, 1981; Barnes, 1974), social constructionist accounts (Gergen and Davis, 1985; Harré, 1986) of taken-for-granted knowledge, communicationist accounts of the negotiation of meaning.(Pearce and Cronen, 1980), inquiries into the discursive basis of ordinary understanding (Billig, 1987; Potter and Wetherall, 1987), and to be sure, the many semiotic (Barthes, 1964) and deconstructionist (Derrida,1974,DeMan, 1979) analyses of literary and philosophic works.

All of these movements across the disciplines conspire to reverse the modernist view of language as picturing the essentials of reality. Collectively they achieve a counter-intelligibility drawing heavily from three related arguments.

The Replacement of the Real by the Representational

For the modernist, language was simply a tool for the logical representation of the essential or the real. However, as the impossibility of a picture theory of language became increasingly clear, one might justifiably ask about other sources of representation (such as description and explanation). As demonstrated in these various lines of inquiry, one can make a compelling case that knowledge, as a body of discourse, is governed, influenced or constrained by ideological or valuational interests, by social processes, and by the rules or conventions of language formation itself. However, as attention is increasingly addressed to the forces governing representation—other than reality itself—reality becomes subject to erasure. That is, if what we call 'the real' is governed by the ideology of the caller, attempts to inform society of what is 'actually the case' must be regarded with suspicion. A genuine interest in discovering the nature of things in themselves seems both naive and misleading.

In this context, all the modernist attempts to determine through empirical investigation—through sensitive measuring devices, experimental variations and sophisticated statistical procedures—the actual nature of organizations become suspect. The entire empirical apparatus is a handmaiden to the traditional assumption that language is a pawn to nature; it presumes that with sufficiently rigorous research, we can eventually 'straighten the language out', rectify it with reality. Yet, as postmodern consciousness sets in, the empirical process is redefined. Rather than correcting the language of understanding, primary research is typically justificatory. It proceeds on the basis of assumptions, or discourses, already shared within the scientific sub-community, and generates evidence that is interpreted within this restricted discursive domain. Because it commences with theoretical views already intact, whatever data are produced by the research will inevitably be named or defined within this theoretical spectrum. In this sense the theoretical perspective is self-fulfilling; all that exists does so by virtue of theoretical definition. Research results do not stand as separate and independent vindicators of position; they are essentially reification devices for positions already embraced.

Representation as a Communal Artifact

Within the postmodern view, language loses its role as functionary in the realm of reality. However, for many contributors to this colloquy language is not thereby set free. Rather, it acquires a new master, and this master is the community. Language gains its meaning and significance through its placement within social interchange. Words fail to make sense (they remain nonsense) until there is at least one other person to give assent to their meaningfulness. Sense-making is thus a collective manifestation, or in John Shotter's (1980) terms, a *joint* action—requiring the coordinated participation of two or more persons. This view is favored by Wittgenstein's views of language games and meaning; it is implied by Kuhn's (1970) work on the history of paradigm shifts; it is articulated most clearly within certain sectors of the sociology of knowledge (Latour, 1987), discourse analysis (Billig, 1987) and social constructionism (Gergen, 1985). Further, the social basis of appropriate, just, or 'correct' description is congenial with feminist and critical school analyses of ideological bias, as well as postmodern literary theory (see especially Fish, 1980).

It is important to note in this regard that for many contributors to the postmodern turn, these developments have meant an abandonment of psychological explanation. This falling away from mental explanation is, first of all, an obvious conclusion to the replacement of reality by representation. That is, psychological events (motives, traits, rational decision processes) have traditionally been viewed as among the essential realities that scientists should seek to elucidate. However, as one becomes aware that representations of these realities cannot be dictated by their essence, then their essential nature becomes dubitable. Is not the very concept of 'essence' a move within the game of language? Or more directly, if we cannot move beyond the realm of representation, is the concept of mental events essential to our understanding?

However, by placing language in the hands of the community, the second major move in postmodernism, the mind is subjected to double jeopardy. For the traditional account of language held that it was a product of the individual mind, a conduit by which internal thought made its way into the public sphere. Yet, if mind is not something we can know about (in the sense of representation), then why must we posit a reasoning mind behind the sounds and markings that make up language?

As Derrida has phrased it, we fall heir to a *logocentric* bias, in which we presume an internal, reasoning agent. There are no grounds on which to justify such a view, and as Richard Rorty (1979) argues it is a view that leads to enormous philosophic confusion. Thus, to place language into relational space, an achievement of coordinated action, we need make no mention of knowing minds or reasoning powers. Language is not thus a means by which I overcome my Cartesian isolation. I do not express myself in relationships through language; relationships express themselves through me.

Ironic Self-Reflection

As Lawson (1985) has proposed, self-reflexivity, or critical suspicion of one's own suppositions, is a prevailing theme within many sectors of postmodernism. The chief reason for this self-critical attitude should be clear from the preceding. For, as it becomes painfully clear, all those propositions removing representation from the grip of reality are themselves representations. They treat as a putative reality both language and a world independent of this language. As a result, they fall heir to their own critical assessment. Or, in terms of the traditional argument against skepticism: how can an argument negating the concept of truth itself be true? Postmodernists have reacted to this irony in a variety of ways. Derrida engages in elliptical, intentionally ambiguous, and often self-negating practices, essentially deconstructing his own writings. French feminists such as Julia Kristeva (1980) see the Western metaphysics of language as itself androcentric, and attempt to escape through developing alternative forms of expression (nonsense within the traditional conventions, but as they believe, sensible within a primordial semiotic). Action researchers in a variety of disciplines attempt to escape the responsibilities of representing their subjects (as objects) by allowing the subjects to speak for themselves, to control their own voice as represented in the professional literature. Others propose that the scholar should play the fool or the dandy, or more provocatively, go piss in public (Sloterdijk, 1987).

If there is one theme that unites most of those confronting the postmodern irony, it is a certain sense of ludic humility. The view of knowledge-making as a transcendent pursuit, removed from the trivial enthrallments of daily life, pristinely rational, and transparently virtuous, becomes so much puffery. We should view these bodies of language we call knowledge in a lighter vein—as ways of putting things, some pretty and others petty—but in no sense calling for ultimate commitments, condemnations, or profound consequences. We should rather be more playful with our sayings. We who utter them are giving voice neither to reality as it is nor to internal possessions (insights, reasons, intentions). Rather we are engaging in public pastimes, rituals, or lifeforms and for such enterprises there are no vindicating foundations.

Let us briefly reconsider traditional organizational inquiry in this light, for one must be cautious regarding the distribution of levity in this case. For the greater part of the twentieth century the major approach to organizational study has been modernist, mixing both romanticist and modernist metaphors of human functioning, but in general attempting to lay bare the essentials. Or, in Lyotard's (1984) terms, organizational theorists have participated in the grand modernist narrative of progress. It is a story we repeat to ourselves in order to justify what we do, one that says that with a combination of rigorous rationality and methodology we can move ever closer to knowledge of the object (and thus toward rational decisions regarding its welfare). It is the seriousness of this grand narrative that postmodernists would challenge, for not only is it mystifying, but it generates zero-sum conflicts and suppresses a multitude of alternative voices. Rather than founders of 'the last word' (where in the beginning was the word of God), we should perhaps view ourselves as balloon craftsmen—setting aloft vehicles for public amusement.

And yet, this metaphor for the theorist is incomplete. For there is a more serious side to the enterprise that follows from the earlier treatment of language and social interdependence. As we find, languages of understanding are interlaced with what else we do; they are insinuated into our daily activities in such a way that without the languages the patterns of activity would be transformed or collapse. (Remove all talk of God, and what is left of religious ceremonies; abandon all talk of profit and loss and what happens to economic enterprise; abandon the language of emotions and

the love affair ceases to be a love affair.) It is in this sense that theories of organization are most fully subject to critique and to credit. They are subject to critique if and when we feel the theories lend themselves to repugnant patterns of social life. (Here consider Barry Schwartz's volume *The Battle for Human Nature* (1986), in which behavior theory and economic rationality theory are condemned for the sanctimonious selfishness they help to foster.) They are subject to credit, as well, for such theories may contribute to activities of positive consequence for organizations and society more generally. We shall return to this latter point shortly.

Toward Postmodern Theories of the Organization

Organization theory has hardly been immune to these various developments within the intellectual world. Indeed, the organizational community has made an active and important contribution to many of the issues at stake. Argyris' (1980) critique of inner contradictions of rigorous research, ideological critiques of organizational realities (see, for example, Salaman and Thompson, 1981), and critiques of the empiricist philosophy of science in the organizational context (Bhagat, 1983), were all important conceptual steps toward the postmodern. More focused work on paradoxical group processes (Smith and Berg, 1987), cooperative group inquiry (Reason, 1988), the social construction of leadership (Dachler, forthcoming; Srivastva and Barrett, 1988), and on action research (see, for example, Pasmore and Friedlander, 1982), moves importantly in the postmodern direction. Morgan's (1986) treatment of existing organizational theories as literary metaphors adopts a postmodern stance. As cybernetic systems theory has moved through its second-order phase, questioning the epistemological foundations of empiricism, and generating a keen appreciation of self-reflexive processes (see Steier, 1991) it has made a strong contribution to postmodernism in organizational theory. The corpus of work on organizations as cultural systems creating and generating symbolic realities (see summaries by Morgan, 1986; and by Schein, 1990), is both congenial with and makes a significant contribution to postmodern views of representation and reality. Reed's (1985) 'social practice framework' does much to orchestrate and develop many of their themes along postmodern lines. Further, theories of emerging heterogeneity, disorganization and information dependency in contemporary society (Lash and Urry, 1987; Piore and Sabel, 1984) all suggest that postmodern shifts in organization theory and practices may be essential to the continuing viability of organizations.

Yet, moving toward fully developed theory within the postmodern context is not an easy task. It is difficult, for one, to generate theories where there is no existing forestructure of intelligibility to be extended and elaborated. And the postmodern turn does remove the luster from traditional argots of understanding; that is, romanticist and modernist. So, if we do not base theories on conceptions of rationality, motivation, emotion and the like, where do we turn? Of equal importance, how can we take the process of theory construction seriously? If we cannot offer truth, objective accounts removed from our own valuational biases, then on what grounds can any new formulations be justified? If there are no foundations for theoretical formulations, and these are only linguistic constructions, then why play the fool—whose serious words turn to mere posturing in the hands of the deconstructionist critic?

As I have tried to indicate throughout this chapter, and most succinctly in my cautions about theoretical playfulness, the theorist is not rendered voiceless by postmodern argumentation. To be sure, there is little reason to suppose that theories are pictures, and that the concept of truth is more than hand waving. Yet, we are moved to silence only if persuaded by the modernist presumption that objective truth is the only game in town. If the function of theories is *not* derived from their truth value, but from their pragmatic implications, then the theoretical voice is restored to significance. And the potential of theoretical work is far greater than that assigned to it under modernist conditions. For under modernism, the proper theory should be fortified with years of research, and its application undertaken by yet another culture (the practitioners). In the postmodern context, the primary ingredient of theory is not its data base but its intelligibility, and the very communication of this intelligibility already establishes grounds for its utility. Theory and practice are inseparable.

The postmodern theorist confronts, then, the following condition: There is no language of understanding placed beyond the boundaries of potential. That is, the postmodern need not fear the resuscitation of romanticist language, nor abhor all that is modernist. All such formulations enable or abet certain patterns of action, or solve certain kinds of problems. Nor should these forms of discourse be viewed as our only sources of theoretical intelligibility. Not only does Western culture have a long and richly laminated history of conceptualization, but we are continuously in the process of absorbing other cultural intelligibilities into our own. Like the postmodern architect, we should feel free to draw from the entire repository of potentials within human history.

At the same time, we must pause before partaking, to ask more critically into the potentials of such work. We must inquire not only into the kinds of cultural patterns served or discredited by given theoretical positions, but also into the potential for theories to offer new alternatives and options to the culture (both organizational and otherwise). Elsewhere I have spoken of a *generative* criterion for evaluating theory; that is, evaluating a theory in terms of its challenge to the taken-for-granted and its simultaneous capacity to open new departures for action (Gergen, 1982). It is in this latter respect that I find myself currently drawn to bodies of postmodern writings themselves. For in my view, these writings furnish a new and exciting forestructure for theorizing about the organization. We may fruitfully extend, elaborate, and transform this argot of understanding in ways that open new options for action within the organization. It is to this latter possibility that the remainder of the present chapter is devoted.

Power, Signification and Organizational Efficacy

The concept of power has been of enormous significance to the traditional understanding of organizational life (see Clegg's 1989 review). At the same time, conceptions of power have typically been wedded to the existing conventions of understanding within the culture. Thus, from the romanticist perspective, power is often equated with personal capabilities: drive, determination, intelligence, inspiration, insight, charisma, and the like. With modernism, power is often associated with machine functioning. Thus, depending on the structure of the organizational machine, those occupying certain positions will possess more power than others. Power, on this account, is less a matter of personal depth than one's function within the structure. With Foucault's writings (1978, 1979) playing a pivotal role, however, we find these traditional views no longer viable within the postmodern sphere. And, while Foucault's work is richly suggestive, it does not fully articulate an alternative view of power. In this regard, I have viewed with keen interest the work of Robert Cooper and Gibson Burrell (1988) on postmodern organization analysis. They too have been drawn by the possibilities of elaborating postmodern discourse into a theory of organizational life. I would like to use two of the central concerns in their 1988 paper as the beginning point of the present offering. These concerns are, first, the indeterminacy of meaning and, second, the resulting tension between forces for organization and disorganization. I wish, however, to extend these concerns to lay out the conceptual scaffolding for a theory of organizational power and efficacy. For purposes of clarity, the arguments will be developed around five emblematic themes.

Indeterminate Rationalities

Let us begin with a simple focus on the organizational manager. For the most part managerial functions are essentially discursive; they are carried out by means of language. Further, it is incumbent on the manager to make sense within the confines of the organization. Thus, the typical manager will draw from the repository of wise, perspicacious or 'true' sayings within the particular subculture of the firm to generate intelligibility. Or to put it another way, he or she manages the available language conventions to achieve a sense of rationality as defined within the organization.

The postmodern drama begins, however, with the realization that the 'rational sayings' available to the individual are of indeterminate meaning. Derrida's (1974) concept of *différance* is

most applicable here for, as Derrida proposes, the meaning of any word or phrase is derived from a process of *deferral* to other words or phrases that *differ* from itself (with the single concept, *différance*, representing the simultaneous and conflated processes). Thus, for example, a bit of corporate rationality embodied in the words 'Let's be logical about this; the bottom line would be the closing of the Portsmouth division' does not carry with it a transparent meaning. Rather, its meaning depends on what we make of words like 'logical' 'bottom line' 'closing' and the like. These meanings require that we defer to still other words. What does the speaker mean by the term 'logical' for example? To answer we must defer to other words, like 'rational' 'systematic', or 'coherent'.

But the plot now thickens, for at the outset it is clear that there are multiple meanings for such terms as 'logical', 'bottom line' and the like. Or, as it is said, they are *polysymous*; they have been used in many contexts, and thus bear 'the trace' (in Derrida's terms) of many other terms. For example, 'logical' can also mean 'right thinking', 'conventional', or 'superior'. Which of these does the speaker really intend? Yet, again, convolutions of complexity; for, as we find, each term employed for clarifying the initial statement is itself opaque until the process of *différance* is again set in motion. 'Right thinking' can also mean 'morally correct', 'conventional' can also mean 'banal', and so on. And in turn, these terms bear the traces of numerous others in an ever-expanding network of significations. What seemed on the surface to be a simple, straightforward piece of wise advice, on closer inspection can mean virtually anything.

Cooper and Burrell (1988) are particularly concerned with the ironic self-negation underlying this spread of signification. Drawing importantly from Derrida's works, they see the possibility (if not the theoretical necessity) for every saying to imply its contradiction. To affirm something is to set in motion a chain of signification that simultaneously confirms its negation. (In simplest terms, for example, the exhortation 'Let's be logical about this . . .' is to make reference to the possibility of irrationality, which possibility is affirmed by the nature of the exhortation itself . . . which is not logically grounded.)

Social Supplementarity

Because of the fundamental undecidability of language meaning, it is often said by deconstruction theorists that signifiers are 'free floating'. Their meaning is never fixed, always in motion, ever demurring. Yet, while this is so in principle, in practice signifiers do not float freely. The advice 'Let's be logical . . .' does not, in practice, simply mean anything including its negation. Its definition is circumscribed or contained, and this containment is to be located within the social milieu. The speaker signifies, but a supplement is required to determine its meaning: it is the listener who supplies the supplement. More concretely, this is to say that managers themselves are never rational; their sayings are never wise or realistic. Their rationality, wisdom or objectivity is dependent on their colleagues, for it is their colleagues who supply the interpretations of the sayings. Rationality is preeminently a product of social collaboration.

It is important to emphasize at this point that such products are both transient and local. Both speakers and listeners are, in the first instance, free to resignify at any time. Managers may reframe their sayings over time; colleagues may reinterpret. Rationalities are never written in stone. Further, as a given saying proliferates across different social settings, its meanings may undergo further change. Each attempt to decode the original is yet another encoding. And these encodings are open-ended, undecidable until constrained by listeners. A manager's words, then, are like authorless texts; once the words are set in motion, the manager ceases to control their meaning. They are possessions of the community.

Power as Social Coordination

As this analysis makes clear, traditional conceptions of power as inhering either in individuals or in organizational flow charts must be abandoned. It is not individual actors who, either by dint of personal style or office location, possess power. Actors do not control the fate of their expressions; we are empowered only through the actions of others. Let us reconsider the problem of power, then, from a postmodern perspective. In particular, let us begin by defining power roughly as the *capac-*

ity to achieve specified ends. If we do so, then we find at least two components essential for the existence of power. First, it is necessary to *articulate criteria for the achievement of power*. (For many people, for example, the power of a corporation is defined in terms of its capital assets.) The achievement of this initial component is inherently social, requiring coordinated agreements among participants. In effect, there is a mutual agreement regarding the containment of the signifiers. As a second component of power, a range of *activities must be coordinated* around the achievement of these locally defined ends. Such activities will include both discourse and other forms of action. This is to say that participants must generate constraints over the free play of signifiers, and confine their activities to those which fit the language so constrained. (We may agree, for example, that 'bottom line' is a financial tally—gains minus losses—and that activities called 'investment' and 'market evaluation' are important to achieving a satisfactory bottom line.) In effect, then, power is inherently a matter of social interdependence, and it is achieved through the social coordination of actions around specified definitions.

Power as Self-Destructive

As social units achieve power, so do they simultaneously architect its undoing. This is chiefly so because the achievement of coordination within a group erects a barrier between it and adjoining communities of signification. Not only are its own signifiers prevented from escaping, or playing into the surrounding languages, but the languages of the surrounding milieu fail to enter the coordinated unit. In this sense the unit fails to achieve the kinds of supplementarity in meaning that would enable its self-contained definitions to be honored from without, and it fails to supplement the meanings of others in ways that would invite reciprocation and further coordination. To illustrate: within organizations divisions of marketing, personnel, planning, production and the like each attempt to achieve power of functioning. In doing so, each develops local definitions of the real and the good and coordinates its actions around these definitions. However, as power of functioning is achieved within each group, signification is solidified—as it must be for reliable coordination of actions among persons. And, as local criteria of the real and the good are solidified, so do members of these divisions become insulated against the realities of the adjoining divisions. Their languages seem progressively alien, unreal, possibly erroneous or foolish. And their own reality becomes rarefied and opaque within the adjoining worlds. In effect, as each unit becomes increasingly powerful within itself, so is the organization as a whole disenabled—with the ultimate end being the destruction of all.

Much the same situation holds in terms of the relationship of an organization to its broader social surrounds. With attention given to a common language—where all definitions of means and ends are shared—participants may coordinate themselves to achieve an efficient and effective organization. Conflict, misunderstandings, ambiguities, and the like are all minimized, and power is maximized. Yet, if their internal view of 'efficient production' is seen as a 'local sweatshop' from without, their 'effective disposal system' is defined from without as 'industrial pollution', their 'reasonable policy of equal employment' is regarded as 'racist', their 'effective computerization' is perceived as 'hopelessly out of date' and their 'innovative line of merchandise' is described as 'derivative', then the organization slowly perishes. Its local realities fail to penetrate the public arena, and the public array of signifiers fail to enter the internal system.

Heteroglossia and the Recovery of Efficacy

What we find is that as organizations strive to achieve power of operation, so must they coordinate themselves within. Such an achievement requires the arresting of meaning, the containment of signifiers. At the same time, this achievement carries with it an ultimate cost, which is the very negation of the power originally sought. Required, then, are means for sustaining organizational efficacy, for creating a dynamic tension between empowerment and disempowerment. Cooper and Burrell (1988) are again drawn to this possibility in their emphasis (following Lyotard) on the balance of consensus and dissensus. For them, full consensus within an organization robs it of its vitality, for that which makes consensus possible, namely dissensus, is negated. Organizational vitality thus depends on restoring the process of *differance*. My own argument rests less on principled issues of linguistic antinomy than on more practical considerations of language and social coordination. However, the resulting conclusion is much the same: to restore efficacy the signifiers must be set free. The result will threaten the power base of the organization as constituted; at the same time it will set in motion a process by which power will be reconstituted—but now within a broader social network.

To explicate, it is useful to draw again from the domain of literary theory. Specifically, the Russian literary theorist Mikahil Bakhtin (1981) has introduced the term *heteroglossia*, referring at least in one of its uses to the fact that the languages of any culture thrive on polyglot. Thus, as we speak English we are borrowing as well from the French, German, Norse, Spanish, Italian, and so on. And we are, as well, falling back on linguistic forms from previous cultural periods, and from a mixture of subcultures. Essentially, there are no thoroughbred languages, and the very capacities of the language for flexibility and multiple usage depend on this fact. In this case let us reconstitute Bakhtin's concept of heteroglossia as a dimension. That is, we can view organizations (or their sub-units) as varying in the degree to which they incorporate the discursive forms of surrounding cultures (or other organizational units). Following the argument that the constitution of power is ultimately self-destructive, it follows that organizations acting to increase internal heteroglossia, up to a point, are those most capable of surviving in postmodern society. That is, an active emphasis must be placed on (1) sharing organizational realities across sub-units within a firm, (2) exporting organizational realities into the outside culture, and (3) enabling external realities to enter freely into organizational life.

On a practical level such a conclusion leads in a variety of different directions. Attention is invited to ways in which members of various organizational sub-units can shift from one locale to another within the firm, incorporating diverse viewpoints, values, and modes of action. Such shifting should be undertaken in such a way that consensus within any unit is constantly contested. The emphasis is removed from developing, and implementing strong and rational leadership, the voice of which attempts to dominate decision-making throughout the firm. Centrality is displaced by heterogeneity and an *ad hoc*ing through the complexities of an ever shifting sea of meaning and action. Rationality becomes situated, expendable or defeasible as context and contingency are altered. Means must also be sought for pressing the localized realities of the organization into the public sphere. As they are shared within the surrounding cultures, they will be transformed. They will meet with resistance, alternative interpretations, metaphoric replacements, gouging and distortion. However, in the process the organizational realities are married to the realities of the surrounding culture. Although not in its own terms, the organization becomes intelligible to the social surrounds.

Finally, means must be sought for opening the organizational doors to alien realities. For example, minority voices, voices of dissensus within the organization, must be invited to speak out; and, although unsettling the fluid operation of the organization, their messages must be made intelligible, absorbed and integrated. Organizational members should also be encouraged in alternative pursuits—to master alternative argots, from various fields of study, politics, sports, the arts, foreign cultures, specialty clubs, and the like. Instead of detracting from the time devoted to organizational ends, and engendering 'peculiar' points of view, such extraneous pursuits will enrich the realm of signification within. Minority hiring should not be viewed as an obligation so much as an opportunity for expanding the discursive (and practical) capacities of the organization. And organizations might wisely invite criticism—from various political, intellectual and moral corners—not with an intent to improve their defensive skills, but to understand and incorporate alternative realities. Again, constant challenges to the smooth coordination of internal realities are essential to organizational vitality. Or, more bluntly, if everything is running smoothly the organization is in trouble.

The result of this constant challenge to naturally occurring tendencies toward consensus will be, from the present standpoint, the prevention of hegemonic tendencies of various sub-units (including high-level management) within the firm and the more complete integration of the organization into the surrounding environment. In the first instance, this will mean a more fully developed integration of the internal segments of the organization. In the second, it will mean that the organization and the surrounding culture will come to form a more thoroughly symbiotic relationship. The tendency to view the organization as an autonomous, self-contained system will recede, and instead, the organization's outcomes will become inseparable from those of the broader community. The misleading distinction between *inside* and *outside* the organization will blur. Ultimately we may be able to see the end of the Hobbesian view of cultural life, along with the demise of the free market as a zero-sum game. For as organizations join with their surrounding cultures for purposes of mutual empowerment, and the circle of interdependence is ever widened, we may become aware of the world as a total system.

References

Argyris, C. (1980) *Inner Contradictions of Rigorous Research.* NY: Academic Press.

Bakhtin, M. (1981) *The Dialogic Imagination: Four Essays by M. M. Bakhtin* (trans. M. Holquist). Austin, TX: University of Texas Press.

Barnes, B. (1974) *Scientific Knowledge and Sociological Theory.* London: Routledge & Kegan Paul.

Barthes, R. (1964) *Elements of Semiology.* London: Jonathan Cape.

Berman, M. (1982) *All that is Solid Melts into Air.* NY: Simon & Schuster.

Bhagat, R. (1983) 'Intellectual performance and utilization in a two-paradigm administrative and organizational science: A philosophy of science-based assessment', in R. H. Kilmann and K. Thomas and associates (eds), *Producing Useful Knowledge for Organizations.* NY: Praeger.

Billig, M. (1987) *Arguing and Thinking.* London: Cambridge University Press.

Bion, W. R. (1959) *Experience in Groups.* NY: Basic Books.

Bradbury, M. and McFarlane, J. (1976) *Modernism, 1890–1930.* Harmondsworth: Penguin.

Burke, K. (1968) *Language as Symbolic Action.* Berkeley: University of California Press.

Clegg, S. (1989) *Frameworks of Power.* London: Sage.

Cooper, R. and Burrell, G. (1988) 'Modernism, post modernism, and organizational analysis: An introduction', *Organizational Studies*, 91–112.

Cooperider, D. L. and Srivastva, S. (1987) 'Appreciative inquiry into organization life', *Research in Organizational Change and* Development, 1: 129–69.

Dachler, H. P. (forthcoming) 'Constraints on the emergence of new vistas in leadership and management research: An epistemological overview', Saint Gall Graduate School of Economics, Law, Business and Public Administration. Switzerland.

DeMan, P. (1979) 'Shelley disfigured', in H. Bloom, P. DeMan, J. Derrida, G. Hartman and J. H. Miller (eds), *Deconstruction and Criticism*. NY: Continuum.

Denhardt, R. B. (1981) *In the Shadow of Organization*. Lawrence, KA: Regents Press.

Derrida, J. (1974) *Of Grammatology*. Baltimore: Johns Hopkins University Press.

Fiedler, F., Chemers, M. and Mahan, L. (1976) *Improving Leadership Effectiveness: The Leader Match Concept*. NY: John Wiley & Sons.

Fish, S. (1980) *Is there a Text in this Class? The Authority of Interpretive Communities*. Cambridge, MA: Harvard University Press.

Foucault, M. (1978) *The History of Sexuality*. NY: Random House.

Foucault, M. (1979) *Discipline and Punish*. NY: Vintage.

Frisby, D. (1985) *Fragments of Modernity*. Oxford: Polity.

Garfinkel, H. (1967) *Studies in Ethnomethodology*. Englewood Cliffs, NJ: Prentice-Hall.

Gergen, K. J. (1982) *Toward the Transformation in Social Knowledge*. NY: Springer-Verlag.

Gergen, K. J. (1985) 'Social pragmatics and the origin of psychological discourse', in K. J. Gergen and K. E. Davis (eds), *The Social Construction of the Person*. NY: Springer-Verlag.

Gergen, K. J. and Davis, K. E. (eds) (1985) *The Social Construction of the Person*. NY: Springer-Verlag.

Goodman, N. (1978) *Ways of Worldmaking*. NY: Hackett.

Habermas, J. (1975) *Legitimation Crisis*. Boston, MA: Beacon Press.

Habermas, J. (1981) 'Modernity versus postmodernity', *New German Critique*, 22: 3–14.

Harding, S. (1986) *The Science Question in Feminism*. Ithaca, NY: Cornell University Press.

Harré R. (1986) 'The social constructionist viewpoint', in R. Harré (ed.),*The Social Construction of Emotion*. Oxford: Basil Blackwell.

Hollander, E. (1958) 'Competence, status and idiosyncrasy credit', *Psychological Review* 65: 117–27.

Homans, G. C. (1974) *Social Behavior in its Elementary Forms*. NY: Harcourt Brace Jovanovich.

Iligen, D. and Klein, H. (1989) 'Organizational behavior', in M. Rosenzweig and L. Porter (eds), *Annual Review of Psychology*, 40: 327–52.

Jacques, E. (1955) 'Social systems as a defense against persecutory and depressive anxiety', in M. Klein (ed.), *New Directions in Psycho-analysis*. London: Tavistock.

Keller, E. F. (1985) *Reflections on Gender and Science*. New Haven: Yale University Press.

Knorr-Cetina, K. D. (1981) *The Manufacture of Knowledge*. Oxford: Pergamon.

Kristeva, J. (1977) *Polylogue*. Paris: Seuil.

Kristeva, J. (1980) *Desire in Language: A Semiotic Approach to Literature and Art*. NY: Columbia University Press.

Kuhn, T. S. (1970) *The Structure of Scientific Revolutions* (second revised edition). Chicago, IL: University of Chicago Press.

Lash, S. and Urry, J. (1987) *The End of Organized Capitalism*. Cambridge: Polity Press.

Latour, B. (1987) *Science in Action*. Cambridge, MA: Harvard University Press.

Lawrence, P. and Lorsch, J. (1967) *Organization and Environment*. Cambridge, MA: Harvard Graduate School of Business Administration.

Lawson, H. (1985) *Reflexivity, the Post Modern Predicament*. London: Hutchinson.

Lyotard, J. F. (1984) *The Post Modern Condition: A Report on Knowledge*. Minneapolis: University of Minnesota Press.

McGregor, D. (1960) *The Human Side of Enterprise*. NY: McGraw-Hill.

Maslow, A. H. (1961) 'Peak experiences as acute identity experiences', *American Journal of Psychoanalysis*, 21: 254–60.

Mayo, E. (1933) *The Human Problems of an Industrial Civilization*. NY: Macmillan.

Menzies, I. (1960) 'A case study in the functioning of social systems as a defense against anxiety', *Human Relations*, 13: 95–121.

Mitroff, I. (1984) *Stakeholders of the Mind*. San Francisco: Jossey-Bass.

Morgan, G. (1986) *Images of Organization*. London: Sage.

Pasmore, W. and Friedlander, F. (1982) 'An action research program for increasing employee involvement in problem solving', *Administrative Science Quarterly*, 27: 343–62.

Pearce, W. B. and Cronen, V. E. (1980) *Communication, Action and Meaning*. NY: Praeger.

Pepper, S. (1972) *World Hypotheses*. Berkeley: University of California Press.

Piore, M. J. and Sabel, C. F. (1984) *The Second Industrial Divide: Possibilities for Prosperity*. NY: Basic Books.

Potter, J. and Wetherall, M. (1987) *Discourse and Social Psychology*. Beverly Hills: Sage.

Quine, W. V. 0. (1960) *Word and Object*. Cambridge, MA: MIT Press.

Reason, P. (1988) *Human Inquiry in Action*. London: Sage.

Reed, M. (1985) *Re-directions in Organizational Analysis*. London: Tavistock Publications.

Rorty, R. (1979) *Philosophy and the Mirror of Nature*. Princeton: Princeton University Press.

Salaman, G. and Thompson, K. (1981) *Control and Ideology in Organizations*. Cambridge, MA: MIT Press.

Schein, E. H. (1990) 'Organizational culture', *American Psychologist*, 45: 109–19.

Schwartz, B. (1986) *The Battle for Human Nature*. NY: Norton.

Shotter, J. (1980) 'Action, joint action and intentionality', in M. Brenner (ed.), *The Structure of Action*. Oxford: Basil Blackwell.

Sloterdijk, P. (1987) *Critique of Cynical Reason*. Minneapolis: University of Minnesota Press.

Smith, K. and Berg, D. (1987) 'A paradoxical conception of group dynamics', *Human Relations*, 40: 633–58.

Srivastva, S. and Barrett, F. J. (1988) 'The transforming nature of metaphors in group development: A study in group theory', *Human Relations*, 41: 31–64.

Steier, F. (ed.) (1991) *Research and Reflexivity*. London: Sage.

White, H. (1978) *Tropics of Discourse*. Baltimore: Johns Hopkins University Press.

Wittgenstein, L. (1963) *Philosophical Investigations*. G. Anscombe. NY: Macmillan.

Zaleznick, A. (1970) 'Power and politics in organizational life', *Harvard Business Review*, 48: 47–60.

CHAPTER 37

CRITICAL LEADERSHIP AND DECISION MAKING IN A POSTMODERN WORLD

WILLIAM G. TIERNEY

Due in large part to the fiscal belt-tightening that occurred throughout the 1980s, administrators have increasingly turned to strategic planning as a decision-making style. The intended goal of strategic planning is to give a cohesive direction and purpose to an institution beset by all too common problems such as declining enrollments, an increasingly competitive marketplace, and a physical plant in dire need of capital improvements.

"Strategic planning," notes one of its central architects, George Keller, "could not have been devised at a better time for American higher education" (1983, p. 118). Keller maintains that, due to the myriad of problems that beset academe, administrators need to have a "battle plan" just as the military have strategies to defeat their enemies. In effect, strategic planning bolsters the rational idea that individuals are not only able to be, but must be, in charge of their own organizational destinies if colleges and universities are to survive.

In this chapter, I offer a case study of an institution that has recently engaged in strategic planning. Huntsville College (a pseudonym) is a small, private liberal arts institution where a president began a strategic plan in a manner that has become commonplace in the world of academe. A new president was hired and one of his first decisions was that the institution needed to have a better sense of where it was going and what it wanted to do. "We didn't know who we were," reflected the president four years after the process had been put in motion. "I thought strategic planning would help us focus more."

My purpose in this chapter is to take issue with assumptions such as the president's and in doing so highlight the underlying tenets of strategic planning and, by inference, leadership. By way of a case study of Huntsville College, I offer a portrait of the different constituencies at Huntsville, their reactions to the manner in which strategic planning was carried out, and their definitions of leadership. The idiosyncrasies we find at Huntsville should not be of concern to us; however, the institution brings into focus larger issues about higher education's purposes and decision-making processes. I suggest that the manner in which administrators manage the institution and the form used for institutional decision making centrally affect how the institution acts and is defined; that is, an analysis of decision making not only tells us what decisions were made by whom, but it also helps explain the culture and ideology of the institution.

Huntsville is also a good case study because the president and the designers of the strategic planning process have tried to create collective decision making based on a collegial model, but as we will see, most individuals are dissatisfied with the outcomes and process. As with so many

"Critical Leadership and Decision Making in a Postmodern World," by William G. Tierney, from *Building Communities of Difference: Higher Education in the Twenty-First Century*, Bergin & Garvey, Westport, CT, 1993.

other institutions, the problems that beset Huntsville do not lend themselves to simple-minded solutions: the replacing of a president or an infusion of funds will not settle all conflicts. In large part, the president and his team have struggled to deal with the college's manifold problems, and they have tried to do so in an equitable manner. Accordingly, I suggest that Huntsville's challenges provide three questions for discussion:

1. How might we define critical leadership in a postmodern world?

2. What should be the goal of strategic planning?

3. What are preliminary organizational points that are based on agape and critical postmodernism?

The chapter is divided into three parts. First, I will offer a brief overview of previous discussions of academic planning and decision making. I will then provide a brief historical sketch of the institution before developing the case study of Huntsville College. In so doing, I discuss the challenges the constituents faced with the strategic planning process. In the third section, I will consider each of the questions raised above.

My point here is not to paint the failure of an institution in its attempts at strategic planning, but rather to highlight the differing perceptions individuals have about the nature of their lives and their institution. My goal is to attempt to reorient academe's definition of leadership and decision making so that it is more in keeping with the discussion raised in the previous chapters. I argue that we ought to move away from developing goals that are externally driven and move toward a concern for internal processes. I suggest that in academe we need to focus our energies more on the internal dynamics with which we coexist with one another and less on perceived external demands from the environment.

Strategic Leadership and Decision Making

In the managerial revolution that took place in the 1960s, academic institutions changed from essentially simple organizational forms composed of a handful of administrators and the faculty, to complex organizations in which a variety of individuals took responsibility for numerous managerial tasks. The assumption that a president and academic vice president could simultaneously shoulder responsibilities of a dean of students, development officer, fiscal officer, or a multitude of other organizational roles quickly became an idea of the past. Instead, we observed the proliferation of administrative roles and responsibilities.

To some, the rise of administration and bureaucracy created a cadre of individuals who could also set the direction for the institution. Such a decision-making style, commonly known as *linear strategy*, was in vogue in the 1960s and early 1970s as the idea of administration in academe became increasingly professionalized. "As the word 'linear' suggests," notes Ellen Chaffee, "in this mode, strategy is methodical, direct, sequential, and plan-based" (1989, p. 25). The notion either that an institution existed in the shadow of a college president or that an organization was a collegium where the faculty set the direction fell by the wayside.

Administrative teams composed of president and "cabinet" became the decision makers for colleges and universities. They set goals, generated plans to achieve them, and decided which route was preferable in order to reach their market. Although the president was no longer a charismatic "great man" considered with the likes of Charles Eliot of Harvard or Robert Hutchins of Chicago, a president still maintained sweeping authority over the academic enterprise. Eventually, decision makers felt the need for another decision-making style in large part due to the unpredictability of academe's environment in the 1970s and the multiplicity of goals that colleges and universities had to pursue simultaneously.

The "boom" of the higher education bubble had burst; fewer traditionally-aged students attended academe and less money was available from federal and state governments. Students demanded services, such as day care for their children or health care, that had not been previously needed, and these demands created additional fiscal strains for the institution. Thus, students of organizational theory rejected the idea that a small group, of individuals could set the agenda for an organization irrespective of an external environment, as if the structure were a walled institution that merely needed to define its goals and the rest would follow. Commonly, known as *open systems*, these new ideas presaged a vast array of literature about the environment and the need for administrators to take into account the needs of the marketplace.

Linear strategy gave way to *adaptive strategy*, in which individuals in organizations no longer worked in isolation; rather, administrators struggled to adapt to the demands of the external environment. "Students" became "markets." The importance of information that would help decision makers read the market accurately took on increased significance. The assumption was that perfect information was available, and the task of the decision maker was to arrive at the correct analysis of market trends. Visionary leadership became less important, and management and interpretation took on precedence.

Into the organizational fray came organizational planners, theorists, and consultants who coined the phrase "strategic management." Following hot on the heels of adaptive strategy, this more recent concept works from a slightly different set of assumptions. Although strategic planners assume that one must take into account the vagaries and demands of the environment, unlike adaptive strategists, they neither assume that a decision maker can necessarily accumulate all of the requisite information needed for a decision, nor do they believe that one solution necessarily exists. Either explicitly stated in their work, as does Ellen Chaffee (1984, 1985), or implicitly stated in their discussion, as does George Keller (1983), strategic planners have adopted a view of the world based on *cultural functionalism*: organizations have cultures, and different structures, people, ceremonies, and the like have functions to be maintained if the organization is to function effectively. The task of the leader is to ensure that these functions are effective and efficient for system maintenance. The managers of the system strive for dynamic equilibrium.

Such a theory holds that all organization is created by the interactions of the participants, the institution's history, and an awareness of the present context. Administration, management, leadership, and governance are the four key ingredients of strategic planning that ensure institutional health and renewal.

Administration pertains to the effective coordination of activities, and management sees that the right decisions are made. Leadership is charismatic and inspires the "troops," and governance refers to efficient decision making. Unlike adaptive strategists, strategic planners not only need to read their environment, but they need to interpret that environment to a multitude of different constituencies. Organizational leaders manage the institution through communication and design. As with linear and adaptive planning, strategic planning derives from the business world. As Keller notes:

> Colleges and universities across the land are realizing that they must manage themselves as most other organizations in society do; they are different and special but not outside the organizational world. Money, markets, competitors, and external forces matter as well as traditions, academic freedom, devotion to ideas and internal preferences. Design is better than drift. . . . Thought is preferable to squabbling (1983, p. 118).

The purpose, then, of strategic management is to "plan the defeat of one's enemies through the effective use of resources" (Keller, 1983, p. 74). A college's enemy might be defined as a competitor who seeks to gain a toehold in one of the institution's markets, or the enemy might be thought of less personally as the market forces that have created the possibility of a fiscal nightmare. In one light it is difficult to disagree with Keller's dramatic language. Who would argue that it is better to squabble than to think? Few individuals want their institution to drift mindlessly.

Robert Birnbaum states the obvious: "Of course, institutions must be aware of their environments, must manage resources prudently, and cannot be indifferent to changing markets without placing themselves in jeopardy" (1988, p. 222). Like Birnbaum, I am hard pressed to see how people desire their institutions not to be aware of environmental threats or engage in resource management. The problem with strategic planning, however, is that Keller has framed the problem as either-or, when actually a variety of options exist. Either an institution plans, or it drifts. Either individuals think logically or they squabble. Such a line of thinking is similar to discussions about effectiveness and efficiency. Who desires ineffectiveness or inefficiency?

The assumption in this text is that we must first have an epistemological understanding of our positions and then develop agendas for action. Strategic planners, however, often go immediately to action plans. They neither consider what a philosophy of education ought to be nor do they develop a philosophy of decision making. The problem is that, as with the manner in which Keller has written about strategic planning, we overlook the assumptions that guide his suggestions. As Nancy Hartsock states, "Theory is always implicit in our activity and . . . includes our understanding of reality. We can either accept the categories given us or we can develop a critical understanding of the world" (1979, p. 57). When we overlook these theoretical assumptions, we implicitly buy into epistemological ideas about the nature of education and community.

From a critical postmodern perspective, however, we see that an investigation of the basic premises of education and decision making enables us to develop alternative epistemological possibilities that move us away from either-or thinking on an action level. Critical postmodernists are neither for inefficiency nor against effectiveness. The fundamental concern with market-oriented decision-making strategies is that they all are epistemologically consistent in terms of how they view the organizational world. That is, although linear, adaptive, and strategic management differ in how individuals ostensibly define the actions of leaders and managers, they are remarkably similar in their epistemological assumptions and outlook.

"The definition of community implicit in the market model," points out Patricia Hill Collins, "sees community as arbitrary and fragile, structured fundamentally by competition and domination" (1991, p. 223). The organization is a market that has goods to sell to consumers. As Keller (1983) noted, academic organizations are like business organizations; economic goals drive the enterprise. And if postsecondary institutions are businesses, then we should rightfully utilize business models to run the organization.

Critical postmodernists offer a dramatically different paradigm to critique and to think about organizational life, one which stresses connection, caring, and difference. Rather than modernist appeals to equilibrium, critical postmodernism seeks to keep institutions in flux so that norms are constantly reconfigured in light of new awareness. Issues of justice and equity rather than economic profit are of central concern. The organization is a community and not a market; we engage in dialogue with one another, and we view organizational activity as intellectual rather than transactual.

Leadership is geared less to management and governance and more toward an intellectual involvement pertaining to justice and equity. As Kenneth Gergen aptly notes, "From the postmodern standpoint, leaders lose their credibility as 'superior knowers' and guiding rationales prove empty" (1991, p. 250). The idea that an individual or group of planners can determine the actions of the community is rejected, for those individuals see the world in a particular, privileged manner. Instead, decisions are shared across groups, and discussion develops within the entire community.

If strategic planning is too bureaucratic or managerial, the idea that decision making is to be shared across groups sounds anarchic. Keller and others may rightfully argue that discussion is fine but decisions often need to be made expeditiously; the idea that decision making is to be consensual provokes visions of academic logjams where nothing gets done. I turn to the case study of Huntsville for one example of how strategic planning itself can result in a logjam. I then return to a discussion of how critical postmodernism might resolve such a dilemma

Strategic Planning At Huntsville

Background

Huntsville is a small, private liberal arts college founded more than a hundred years ago in a rural area in the Northeast. Most of the 1,100 students are full-time and reside on campus; many of them are first generation college-goers. There are about seventy-five full-time faculty. As with many other institutions, Huntsville's faculty in many areas is an aging one whose members have begun to retire in increasing numbers.

Eighty percent of those students who apply to Huntsville are accepted, and their average SAT scores are in the 1000 range. The college has garnered some repute for its natural science departments, and students and faculty alike point to the relatively high percentage of the student body who go on to attain graduate degrees as evidence that the college has good programs. The college is coed but neither racially nor ethnically diverse. The student body is drawn primarily from throughout the region. A vast percentage of students qualify for, and receive, financial aid. There are no fraternities or sororities, but there is an extensive array of student activities that everyone is encouraged to join.

When a new president arrived four years ago, the college heaved a collective sigh of relief. In particular, many of the faculty had been demoralized by the previous president's term; they had sought a president who was collegial and believed in the importance of communication and dialogue. "We had a president," commented one individual in a group discussion, "who felt he was the only one to make decisions." "The faculty voice was considerably lessened," added a second. "We were sure to look for someone different, someone who would listen," continued a third. But a fourth person stated, "I've been involved in choosing three presidents here and I must say as I get older I get considerably more pessimistic about democracy. The process isn't right."

If the previous president was at one end of the spectrum in terms of collegiality and dialogue, it is safe to say that the current president occupies the opposite end of that spectrum. Views of the president's style vary. The students are highly complimentary. "The president's a good guy," commented a student. "He's easy to talk to and he knows most of the students' names," said a second. "He goes to the football games, everything. He always cheers the loudest," commented another student.

The faculty also pointed out how the president was very open and easy to talk with, but their comments were not always as positive. "He is easy to talk to, I'll grant that," conceded one faculty member. Another professor said, "I want someone who can make a decision. I'm confused about the vision of Huntsville now, where I wasn't before." A third individual agreed, "The president seems to have so much faith in us that he thinks we can be all things to all people." "His mistakes," added another, "are well-intentioned mistakes. He communi-

cates, sure. But we don't know where we're going. I wish he'd just get on with it." "I disagree," stated another individual who heard the previous comment. "The president has gotten us thinking about what we want to be. He's on the mark." "There seems to be this intense desire to please," concluded another. "You get the feeling that if you engage in dialogue that we like one another, but that's not leadership."

The faculty view of presidential leadership brings into focus the wider topic of decision making in general, and faculty governance in particular. Because the faculty is relatively small, there is no faculty senate with elected representatives. Instead, the faculty meet as a whole body, and the academic dean chairs the meeting. The result is that there is no structural role in the organization that signifies who is a leader among the faculty. "We've had leaders sometimes," reflected a longtime faculty member, "but that was many years ago." "The department chairs might fill the role, but they don't," added another. "What this does is create a vacuum," explained a relative newcomer to the institution. "Everyone speaks up, but no one provides direction."

At the same time, faculty felt they were deeply involved in the governance of the college through the committee structure. "We are all on too many committees," said one individual. Another person explained:

> We tend to be here all day. We teach a lot, and then everyone is also called on to serve on different committees. And the committees have subcommittees. The way things get done around here is through people talking with one another on committees. You also find out what is going on in other parts of the college.

Everyone mentioned the dedication of the faculty and the ability to see faculty on a relatively easy basis. The students, in particular, had enthusiastic opinions about the faculty: "They really work hard. I can even go see my advisor on a Friday afternoon, without an appointment," said one student. "The faculty at Huntsville—not everyone, but a lot—want to get to know you," commented another. "I like faculty who don't just read from a lecture, but get involved in and out of the class, and there are a lot here who do that," added another. Still another student continued, "The wall between students and teachers needs to be torn down. People come here because they think they'll be able to find faculty to talk to and you usually do."

The Huntsville faculty do not seem demoralized, but they mention how busy they are. "It's not the teaching, but the committee work that kills you," offered one individual. The confusion about who directs change, and by inference, the role of the faculty and administration, is akin to what was heard at Sherman College. "For an idea to work here," commented one Huntsville individual in a faculty group, "it's got to come from the faculty." A few moments later an individual said, "The president needs to set the parameters, make decisions, and stop forming task forces." When I pointed out the seeming contradiction between the two statements—one saying that the faculty should manage change and the other suggesting it was the president's role—the faculty seemed content to accept both ideas. When I queried other faculty about the contradiction, they too, were comfortable with both ideas. One said, "Our problem has always been this, working out the two sides." Another added, "It's a schizophrenia of desire. We want to run things, but we also know the president should more forcefully set the agenda."

Some faculty also mentioned that the academic dean also had a role, but in general, the comments about the dean's role were relatively few. "We have a first-time president and a first-time dean. They're feeling their way along," said one individual. "The dean can stimulate communication and conversation, but not much else," added a second person. A third person summarized, "The dean's an administrator, not a faculty member. It is a little strange that she runs the faculty meeting, but that's the way it's been."

In some respects, Huntsville recalls college life in the 1950s. Full-time, white, traditional college-aged students live in residence halls and interact with their faculty during class and office hours. Ceremonies and activities such as homecoming abound and are quite important in the life of the community.

Huntsville, however, also faces particular challenges typical of the 1990s. Buildings need to be renovated or built. The library must be upgraded. An aging faculty will gradually retire and need to be replaced. The demand for

student financial aid outweighs what can be given. Although faculty governance seems a bit inefficient, there does not seem to be a high degree of animosity or dissatisfaction. In part, this is due to the work of the president, who led a new administrative team into office four years ago and wanted to "provide a clearer image of who we are." We turn to a discussion of the manner in which Huntsville's image was to become clearer.

Strategic Planning at Huntsville

"When I arrived," the president recalled, "I thought we were too fuzzy about what we were about. We had implicit values—'community' appears in our mission statement three times—but we needed greater clarity." The president believed that not only was there a need for a more shared sense of what Huntsville was, but there was also a need for what Huntsville might become. He continued:

> In Huntsville's culture, there has always been a view toward outcomes, student outcomes, but we needed to state that more explicitly, more up front. I also want us to move up a notch in quality. I want strength across the curriculum and not just in a few areas. We need a better understanding of the freshman-year experience. And to my surprise, we did not have a facilities plan; we had no idea of a unified picture of the physical plant.
>
> We also do not market ourselves well to the outside. People do not know us. We brought in a consultant who thought our mission statement was "too vanilla." So all these things went along with my reason for starting a strategic plan.

The president's use of both the present and past tense in his statement reflects how the strategic planning process is still not finished. The implementation of strategic planning was threefold. The president named a senior administrator to lead the process. Initially, faculty and staff seemed to buy into the notion. "You know faculty," an individual sighed. "We're task oriented and we like to talk. The president had a task, and it required talk—lots of it. We went along." A "mission" committee composed of faculty, administrators, and students discussed the goals of the college. One individual remembered, "It gave us a common sense of what it meant." Another participant recalled, "People read into it what they wanted, but it was a good start. It said that talking about the mission and goals was important." "The committee was very inclusive, very participatory. It was a broadbrush kind of thing, diagnostic," recalled another individual.

The other two committees addressed internal and external assessment. As described by numerous faculty, the internal assessment committee resembled the kind of committee that colleges create for accreditation reports. Departments were asked to assess their strengths and weaknesses and what kind of resources they needed to improve. One example of a weakness is a liberal arts department in which they rely on part-time faculty to teach, due to either departures or retirements that have not been replaced. The external assessment committee studied the external environment and outlined the opportunities or threats that existed for Huntsville both in the present and future. One opportunity highlighted by the committee was the prediction that by the mid-1990s the declining demographic curve will turn up and the college-age cohort will, in turn, increase. What must be viewed as both a threat and an opportunity was that college-age students desired technologically current educational instruction and support. The problem was the cost needed to develop such classes, and yet the opportunity for creating a new market niche also existed.

Obviously, internal and external assessments may be in conflict or agreement. A liberal arts department may well need an additional faculty member to achieve excellence, but if an external assessment forecasts less need for liberal arts courses and more need for technical coursework, then difficult choices exist. Presumably, a college's mission ought to provide some direction about how to choose among the many difficult options that exist. A liberal arts college where the philosophy department has long been well respected and prominent is probably not well advised to downscale the department in favor of vocational education courses. Again, the point of strategic planning is not simply to adapt to the demands of the environment, but to assess the manifold arenas in which a college operates in order to develop a cohesive and holistic approach to needs changes and innovations.

At Huntsville by the end of the first phase of the strategic planning process, individuals felt good about their respective committees, but they did not yet see how each of the parts provided a sense of direction about where Huntsville should go. "The mission committee and the other ones were okay," said one individual. "It got us going." A second person agreed, "I thought the mission committee did its task relatively well." "I don't like departmental assessments, they seem to always be asking that—what are your strengths and weaknesses," commented another, "but it was an honest attempt."

To most of the faculty, however, the next major step in the process was viewed as a disaster. Logically, the task before the college was to take the various recommendations and analyses of the different committees and incorporate them into a unified document about which areas the college would emphasize and how specific actions might occur. By inference, of course, the college had to decide which departments and programs would not be emphasized.

"We met over the summer and we decided to form five task forces that would outline what was needed to be done," remembered the academic dean. "What a mistake that was," said a faculty member. "First they—primarily administrators—get together over the summer and refine things, and then set up these task forces." Another administrator said, "The tasks were not well defined. We had to prioritize what needed to be done, and one group assumed no resource constraints, and other groups worked within fiscal constraints." "The process," summarized one individual, "was timely and destructive." The president said forthrightly, "I did not exercise enough leadership. It was a mistake." A longtime faculty member explained how the mistake eventually exploded:

> It became the biggest disaster I've seen here. It was a very fractious three months. Because people perceived their tasks differently, the reports were different. So we found departments fighting one another. Some said, "Our department needs to be increased because the others have had enough," and then the other departments got angry. There was no follow-up, and the subsequent actions, like adding a member in Geology, or avoiding a discussion about what to do with the foreign languages,

made me feel that the whole process was an enormous waste of time that produced more ill will than any sense of where we're going.

"I disagree," countered one professor. "The history department got full support for conducting a national search in the manner in which they desired because of the plan. It had never been done before." "But the same did not happen in other departments—look at the foreign languages," countered another individual. "That's what makes the whole process look whimsical."

"Part of the problem is endemic to Huntsville," explained one professor. "The fellow who was in charge of the whole process was an administrator, and we don't trust him." Another faculty member added, "My sense is the president, vice presidents, and the advisory group have a clear idea of what they want. We don't." A senior administrator agreed in part, "Perhaps the problem is not with what we decided, but how we decided them. The process broke down because there was no natural group leadership of the faculty. We need to work on that and get the planning process back on track."

A faculty member concurred by reflecting on another example of misunderstanding in part due to the structure of communication at Huntsville: "It's akin to the freshman year fiasco where the dean thought she had this neat idea, got money from a foundation, chose the wrong people to get involved and then there was this firestorm of protest from the faculty when we heard about it."

The dean essentially agreed with the analysis by saying, "It was a good idea, but I see now that if you want faculty change they have to believe it. What killed it, or at least stalled it for the time being, was that it was seen as a violation of turf and the way the group was composed." A third individual commented, "We didn't think anything was wrong with the freshman-year experience, and then we found out that something was going to be done. We just put a stop to it. It seemed she wanted the project because her previous institution had one."

In part, each of these issues—the problem of strategic planning, and the initiation of a new project—stems from three misunderstandings that pertain to (1) the overall goals of the

college, (2) the kind of information that is gathered to make a decision, and (3) the manner in which that data is disseminated. Ironically, the strategic planning process was supposed to create greater understanding of the college's purpose, yet it seems to have done the opposite. "I don't even know what 'student-oriented outcomes' is, but that's what they say we're about. Where did it come from?" asked one individual. "We've gotten mixed messages," elaborated another person. "We hear that student outcomes and assessment are important, and then it seems that the president wants us to be more [Ivy League]." A new professor said, "I heard that research would be more important from some people, and this was a teaching institution from other people."

"People hide information," commented one professor. "Administrators have different kinds of facts and figures to justify why one department should be enhanced, another should be strengthened, and others should just be maintained." "'Student outcomes' is supposed to be information-based," commented another, "but so far I haven't seen any of that information." "The process has just broken down," ended one individual. "All this time spent on committees doing this and that, and for what?"

One final point pertains to the purpose of a strategic plan in the minds of the organization's participants. The president pointed out why he wanted such a planning process, but after four years of effort, what were the participants' reflections? "We needed a better marketing tool," said one. "Strategic planning is externally motivated," commented a second. "It's external in the sense that you get the idea that everyone else is doing it and you should too. That accrediting groups want you to do this. It's in the air." "It will help us with our student recruiting," said an advocate. "We have a better idea of which groups have come to Huntsville, and how we need to tap into other groups." Thus, most individuals thought strategic planning was driven either by a new president's desire to better understand the institution for himself or by external demands.

Ironically, other than the individual in charge of the process, it seemed that no one was able to assess strategic planning except in generalized terms. One might think that an institution that committed itself to "Student-oriented outcomes" would be able to assess its own actions in specific ways. Yet, the participants either commented in the negative fashion heard above, or in a positive light such as, "If there hadn't been strategic planning, I would have had to make sense of where to go, what to do anyway." "I'm glad we've done it," said another. "It's one of those things you ought to go through every so often. It could have been done better, but the attempt was admirable." "I don't think it's affected me, my office, in any way," concluded a mid-level administrator, "but it's good to talk about institutional image."

Discussion

I stated at the outset of this chapter that the process in which Huntsville was engaged tells us about (1) the nature of academic leadership and strategic planning, (2) the goals of strategic planning, and (3) the manner in which decision making takes place. Before I turn to those three points, it is incumbent upon me to comment on the overall view I have about Huntsville. Although I am suggesting that strategic planning did not work particularly well at Huntsville, the participants do not demonstrate a high degree of conflict or disagreement with one another. It would not be accurate to say that Huntsville is an institution that reflects different constituencies at odds with one another. The negative views that the faculty hold about strategic planning have not frozen attitudes toward the administration to the point that no communication occurs whatsoever. Indeed, morale among administration, faculty, and, in particular, students seems quite high. Yet during my visit, most people did not suggest that strategic planning had helped the process of communication and goal attainment; if anything, strategic planning has hindered the process.

The administration expresses a high degree of goodwill and a desire to include different constituencies in decision making. Although the administration still maintains a strong belief in its ideas and strategic planning, the president and academic dean seem particularly forthright about the mistakes that have been made, and what they should have done both with strategic planning and the idea for changing the freshman-year experience.

Similarly, although I suggest that Huntsville has focused too highly on the external environment, threats do exist that all institutions need to take into account. Markets that once existed may no longer be available to an institution, for example, or opportunities might exist that should be taken. However, Huntsville's constituents seem to have engaged in strategic planning not for themselves but for others. My central concern here is particularly with such an institution's focus. How might an educational institution remain competitive and communicate an aura of quality to external constituencies and at the same time engage in processes that highlight intergroup communication and solidarity?

Critical Leadership and Strategic Planning

At first glance, it may seem paradoxical that the faculty wanted the president to make decisions while, at the same time, they also believed that any substantive decisions had to come from the faculty. From a critical perspective, however, academic leadership in strategic planning enables different constituencies to set the framework for decision making and to develop those decisions. At Huntsville, such actions are difficult, if not impossible. The structure of the organization has developed so that administrators control—however benevolently—information and communicative processes.

There are instrumental actions that might be taken; a faculty member might be put in charge of strategic planning, for example, and somehow the professoriate needs an academic structure through which they have a voice. Whether that voice comes from the chair of a faculty senate or from a presidential cabinet that includes a chair of the faculty is irrelevant; what matters is that faculty have a voice and structure that is distinct from the administration's. From a postmodern perspective, decentralization enables distinctly different voices to arise, and from a critical perspective, decentralization enables oppositional voices to speak.

Huntsville's administration acknowledges the importance of communication, yet what appears to be lacking is a unified perspective about how communication and, hence, decisions best occur. Any small organization has a high degree of informal dialogue and contact, and such is the case at Huntsville. Huntsville's constituents also believe they have an over-abundance of formalized opportunities for communication through their committee structure. Strategic planning (and now preparation for an accreditation visit) creates another layer of committee meetings. From the data developed here, I am not convinced that such an elaborate committee structure is in the best interests of either the individuals involved in the process or for decision making in general. To be sure, committees serve various functions as symbolic entities, as overseeing bodies, and as disseminators of information. However, committees also serve to reinforce bureaucratic structures and often have two destructive consequences. First, decisions that might be made in a relatively short time frame often take countless weeks of discussion. Second, individuals who must attend committee meetings do not become engaged in intellectual tasks but bureaucratic ones. The strategic planning process at Huntsville is a good example.

Huntsville's faculty and administrators spent countless hours discussing a mission statement and found when they finished that they had arrived back from where they had started. No one can point to how Huntsville's 1990s mission statement has changed Huntsville, and the statement remains "too vanilla," in one person's words. The hours spent in meetings eventually devolved the activities to a few individuals who wrote the documents and the others who critiqued the pages, to change words from "enhance" to "strengthen," for example.

The point is not to deride the process, but rather to suggest that academic leadership ought to present a more forceful intellectual presence so that the community engages with one another not in bureaucratic forms where internecine fights eventually erupt over terms, but rather the community participates in a process in which they are able to speak from their own personal experiences about the life of the community. Henry Giroux has commented on the kind of leadership I am suggesting. He states that a transformative intellectual "exercises forms of intellectual and pedagogical practice that attempt to insert teaching and learning directly into the political sphere by arguing that schooling represents both a struggle for meaning and a struggle over power relations" (1988a, p. 174). Such a definition suggests a leader distinctly different from a strategic manager concerned with marketing and effectiveness. Rather than moving the organization toward equilibrium, the individual strives to understand differences and encourages reflexive discourse aimed at orienting the organization toward agape.

A leader of the kind I am suggesting assumes two contradictory stances. On the one hand, the individual sets an intellectual, rather than a bureaucratic, tone for the institution. On the other hand, the leader creates the conditions by which diverse dialogues about the nature of the institution take place. Thus, the leader is both a listener who voices and a participant who offers a particular view. Such a view of leadership is distinctly different from the old-fashioned view of a leader as a "great man" who sets the direction of the institution, or of leadership as a synonym for management. Instead, the leader views his/her task as an intellectual process that necessitates ongoing multivocal dialogue.

Strategic Goals

Rightfully or not, many in Huntsville's community believed that the goals of strategic planning were to develop marketing tools for external constituencies. The ultimate goal—student-oriented outcomes—was one that will enable Huntsville to communicate how well they are doing to the outside world. The strength of such an approach is easily understandable. Educational foundations appreciate knowing that a college has increased student learning from one point to another. Parents and students like to know that the college of their choice is increasing in quality along several different dimensions.

My concern in this regard, however, is what we lose by concentrating so heavily on developing goals that are understandable to external constituencies. As I noted in the previous chapter, Americans in the late twentieth century seem to have an almost obsessive desire to quantify different issues and topics. A college or university ought to be able to satisfy the demands of different external constituencies about how quality is judged. Yet such a task should not be the work of the university community, but rather should be assigned to an individual involved with university relations.

From a critical postmodern perspective, the fabric of an educational community is the members' fealty to a discourse concerned with the life of the intellect, "Agape enjoins one to identify with the neighbor's point of view," notes Gene Outka, "to try imaginatively to see what it is for him to live the life he does. . . . The other's right to assume a point of view different from one's own is also affirmed" (1972, p. 311). For such discussions to occur, we create committees that concentrate on the development of fellowship among one another, rather than on how to satisfy the perceived demands of external groups. Education is a process that ought to involve dialogue about one's place in society and within our own communities. To develop such a community, we necessarily raise questions about what kind of community we want to be. And these questions are not worked out by way of formalized goals, but rather they are enacted on a daily basis among one another.

Decision Making in a Postmodern World

Educational organizations are not business organizations, and we ought not to be forced into trying to become such. By that I mean that a for-profit business organization ultimately assesses itself through an analysis of a profit margin. Colleges and universities should not be made to think that students are markets that need to be tapped or products that need to be improved; such assumptions lose sight of what education is and insult virtually all of the constituencies involved in the educational process.

Strategic management and other functionalist theories of organization are, as Robert Merton noted more than a quarter of a century ago, "oriented toward the needs of management" (1968, p. 625). The problems chosen as well as the focus of their solutions have developed from a managerial frame of decision making. Many alternate frames exist, and the one utilized here is based on critical postmodernism. Such an approach focuses on the structural relations of power in the organization and on how reality is constructed. Rather than assume that the purpose of organizational life is to act rationally and achieve stasis, we investigate how to develop dialogue among often competing interests. Although I will expand on these ideas in Chapter 7, I set the stage, so to speak, with five

approaches to decision making: (1) structure, (2) hierarchy, (3) committees, (4) pedagogy and structure, and (5) comparative awareness.

Structure. The interests of faculty and administration are not always alike. Administrators may have greater needs for dealing with external constituencies, and faculty may have more desire to improve the relations within the classroom. Administrators may think of how they can reduce the costs of sizable blocs of resources—such as faculty salaries—and faculty may resist paying a senior administrator an income that the board of trustees feels is justified.

I raise these specific examples not because they are issues at Huntsville, but simply to point out that when we speak of a "community of difference," we are assuming that different individuals and groups have unique interests, and, of consequence, an organization needs to incorporate those interests through a structure that enables voices to develop. An example at Huntsville would be the creation of a faculty senate that is run by the faculty and develops an agenda distinct from that of the administration.

Reduce Hierarchy. To a certain extent, postmodern organizations thrive on contradictions, and at first glance, this suggestion seems to contradict the first point. I am suggesting that administrative and faculty roles be less clearly defined so that all individuals seize decision-making responsibility rather than let it reside primarily in one arena. Even though decision making becomes blurred in a postmodern world, different groups do not have to have unique structural entities. In essence, postmodern organizations have a twofold task: (1) of creating arenas where individuals who have distinct interests may congregate, debate, recommend, and decide, and (2) of developing a sense of community where decisions are based on the debate of the whole.

Such a portrait suggests that faculty become involved in areas such as student life and, conversely, that student affairs administrators have something to say about curricular matters. This point pertains particularly to senior administrators. Often we find that "administrators administer"; I am suggesting not only that decision making be shared, but also that roles become intertwined. To be sure, we often think that faculty have a role in governance, but we also need to reinsert administrators and staff into the teaching and learning process. Such a suggestion implies that at a teaching institution everyone will be involved in teaching.

Temporary Committees. If the life of the community is geared toward the intellect, then we need to focus our time more centrally on intellectual tasks. Just like at countless institutions, at Huntsville individuals complained of the overwhelming amount of committee work that often produced few, if any, tangible results. Again, a contradiction exists with this suggestion in comparison with my point about structure, for the idea here is to reduce the committee structure and develop a more fluid decision-making style.

Committees might develop specific charges and meet as quickly as possible in order to dispense with an issue. Standing college committees often have leisurely agendas and meet once a month throughout the academic year, and the committee's apparent purpose is of little more than symbolic import. Yet such symbols all too often depress people about the meaninglessness of their input. Instead, why not create committees that "go out of business" within a very short time frame rather than debate issues seemingly ad nauseam?

Obviously, certain decisions cannot be made in a month's time, but as anyone knows who serves on college committees such as the ones discussed at Huntsville, the vast majority of decisions are not so involved that they necessitate a year's worth of consideration. We do ourselves a disservice both instrumentally and ideologically by discussing the vast array of academic items at a snail's pace. Instrumentally, decisions get bogged down; more importantly, individuals remove themselves from committees—either in body or in mind—when they feel that the tasks before them are trivial.

Pedagogy and Structure. If some committees are trivial, others deserve more prominence. If some tasks can be solved in a brief moment, others require concerted, sustained inquiry. The debate that rages in academe about curriculum and interdisciplinary foci demands more structured attention from college communities than it is presently given. Again, committees that meet over minute items once a month are not necessarily able to engage in the sort of dialogue that I am suggesting here.

Huntsville spoke in broad brushstrokes about its mission and about how to increase departmental allotments. Such discussions are the norm. I am suggesting, however, that individuals involve one another in the most intense dialogues over the nature of learning. Outside speakers might be brought in, and readings might be included. The point is the process. Rather than a task that has a goal of deciding which department to increase and which to decrease, we need to rediscover how to speak intellectually to one another. I appreciate that faculty and administrators are too busy; in large part, my suggestion about reducing trivial committee work feeds into this suggestion.

Community does not simply happen; we need to enable mutual dialogues of respect and difference to take place. To meet one another in an intellectual dialogue demands that we have the time and desire. At present most faculties have neither the time nor the desire. To create the stimulus for change demands leadership of the kind that the Huntsville faculty implicitly suggested. The president of an institution needs to redirect his/her energies from that of an external agent to that of one who is a transformative intellectual willing and able to foment dialogue across constituencies.

Comparative Awareness. I offer yet another contradiction. However strong an organization's culture and ideology may be, there are times when such cultural strength breeds insularity. We must constantly remind ourselves that previous ideas of community often based themselves on notions that absented women, people of color, and others from the community. A postmodern version of organizational culture demands a comparative awareness of other institutional cultures—their structures, interactions, and ideologies.

As I noted in the previous chapter, to the extent that the community's individuals can have others visit the campus or that they can visit campuses themselves, they will be able not simply to learn about another culture but to reflect on their own. I am suggesting something different from faculty attending a conference to present a paper. Although helpful, such conferences speak more to a faculty's disciplinary culture than to institutional culture. Instead, an institution will be improved if individuals are able to spend a day or two at another campus and then report on what they found in an open forum; institutions might even develop a faculty exchange program through which faculty spend a semester teaching at another institution. Such a suggestion does not have to involve vast sums of resources, and the potential for self-learning in the community is great.

Finally, let me reemphasize that I am not suggesting that we cease to consider whether the organization is acting in a manner that is both efficient and effective. Countless nonprofit organizations have streamlined their activities by learning from profit-making businesses. Postsecondary institutions also have been aided by consultants who have helped them tap into markets that the college otherwise would not have considered. However, such actions ought to be viewed for what they are—incremental adjustments to improve the ultimate task of the institution. And the ultimate task is the manner in which we engage one another as educational citizens.

CHAPTER 38

ORGANIZATIONAL CHANGE AS PARADIGM SHIFT

HASAN SIMSEK AND KAREN SEASHORE LOUIS

Introduction

Since the mid-1960s, systems theory has dominated the study of organizational change [43]. By viewing organizations as adaptive organisms that strive toward equilibrium under changing environmental conditions, systems theory shifted the focus of organizational research from exclusive attention to internal conditions to a concern with the relationships between the organization and its environment [10, 20, 24, 41]. Metaphors originating from the systems perspective have resulted in many new directions in organizational change research [32].[1] Common to most systems theorists is the assumption that, in the absence of dramatic changes in the environment, organizations will best be served by slow, adaptive change. Other theorists [50] have argued that educational organizations are unusual systems, in that they are "loosely coupled," a characteristic that makes large-scale change less likely to occur rapidly or to affect the whole organization in dramatic ways. The only strong alternative to the systems theory/incremental change perspective over the past two decades has been a political perspective [1]. This is perhaps best exemplified by Cohen and March's [8] image of universities as "organized anarchies," in which change is unpredictable because of the random but politicized nature of the involvement of different actors with different agendas and interests. Again, however, this perspective points toward the limited possibility of rapid, strategic change.

Along with these approaches to organizations, a new stream of cultural organizational research that incorporates a systems perspective, concern with metaphors, and anthropological theory appeared [11, 16, 34, 36, 40, 45, 46]. Cultural perspectives on organizations emphasize the maintenance of strong organizational cultures as a strategy linked to higher performance [36] and thus point to the conclusion that strategic management in successful organizations usually involves anticipatory adaptation rather than radical change.

An alternative perspective is grounded in Kuhn's [23] analysis of scientific progress, which also emphasizes the role of shared beliefs, values, and norms of behavior but points to the importance of radical shifts as a mechanism for maintaining vitality and progress in a system. It is this latter perspective that motivates the central question being investigated in this article: To what degree can major organizational changes in universities be said to be characterized by a change in a collectively understood paradigm that is reflected in metaphors, stories, or myths that reflect underlying values

"Organizational Change as Paradigm Shift: Analysis of the Change Process in a Large, Public University," by Hasan Simsek and Karen Seashore Louis, *Journal of Higher Education*, Vol. 65, No. 6 (November/December 1994). Copyright © 1994 by the Ohio State University Press.

and shared understandings of how these metaphors and myths are enacted? To explore this question, we have investigated a strategic change process in a large, public university.

Organizational Change as Paradigm Shift

The terms "paradigm" and "paradigm shift" are part of the popular language of change at the present time. However, the concept of paradigm is usually misapplied and is typically used to refer to any set of beliefs that precipitates action. To investigate the applicability of a paradigm model to universities requires a more precise conceptual foundation. Our article is based on several assumptions, which will be further developed below: (1) Organizations are defined by their paradigms, that is, the prevalent view of reality shared by members of the organization. Under a particular dominant paradigm, structure, strategy, culture, leadership and individual role accomplishments are defined by this prevailing world view; and (2) radical change in organizations may be construed as a discontinuous shift in this socially constructed reality.

Kuhn [23] argued that the evolution of scientific theories is always punctuated by revolutionary leaps in which the entire shape of scientific activities and world views are altered. Change in scientific activities follows a predictable path where a long period during which the dominant scientific theories are barely questioned is punctuated by noncumulative, radical breaks. Since the late 1970s, a handful of researchers have been interested in translating this perspective into a theory of organizational change [3, 17, 31, 37, 38, 44].[2] These studies emphasized that organizations can be understood as enacted realities that define what to do and what not to do in organizations as a symbolic resource. More specifically, an organizational paradigm can be defined as a world view, a frame of reference, or "a set of assumptions, usually implicit, about what sorts of things make up the world, how they act, how they hang together, and how they may be known" [3, p. 373]. This world view is composed of three interrelated components: (1) a way of looking at the world which creates an image of the subject matter about the world's phenom-

ena and constructs a system of beliefs; (2) a way of doing things that provides the methods and instruments needed to apply fundamental beliefs to internal and external realities; and (3) an interaction among human agents to support both the belief system and the normative behavior, including social networks that support the adoption and practice of a particular paradigm [31, 38].

However, these initial attempts at theory development fell short of a concrete, conceptually strong and methodologically sound model of organizations as paradigms and organizational change as paradigm shifts, and empirical investigations in this promising area have not materialized. In the following section we will further develop a model that can be empirically tested.

A Model of Organizations as Paradigms

Figure 38-1 is a representation of a model of organizations as paradigms in which three domains are in continuous interaction. In the figure, *background assumptions*—a way of looking at the world—are central to the model and comprise the abstract and often tacit dimension of organizational paradigms defined as myths. They are the forms of selectively collected and integrated pieces of knowledge that shape the underlying belief system in the organization. They are called myths because long-lasting beliefs generally turn into a mythical phenomenon which later becomes quite resistant to change.[3] Metaphors, on the other hand, are convenient short-hand descriptions of a particular belief system or myth—an expressive (language-related) form that facilitates communication in understanding the tacit assumptions of a belief system. Metaphors filter and define reality in a simple fashion such as "Richard is a lion," "the brain is a computer" [47, p. 98], or "organizations are machines," "organizations are organisms" [32]. Metaphors are powerful in describing the most important features of a complex array of variables in a simple form, but only provide part of a whole picture. Exemplars and models are directly drawn from the dominant myth(s) and guide the action in organizations. They are the most visible part of any paradigm, for they are the collection of typical organizational strategies and actions [15, 18]. They are examples of what an organization typically does in accomplishing the required organizational tasks.

The relationship between organizational assumptions and action is moderated by the organization's environment. The lower domain shown at the bottom of figure 38-1 identifies the *specific/unique organizational realities* to which the paradigm principles are applied. The actions of any organization are guided by a set of background assumptions grounded in the details of particular settings, actors, and history of successes and failures. In providing explanations for how major changes occur in organizations, we also need to consider that "no organization is an island." Rather, each belongs to a population that performs similar functions and shares, at least in part, a common perspective and set of beliefs—values [14]. The upper domain thus represents a *constructed body of knowledge* (scientific or nonscientific)

that is shared by a number of organizations in a particular industry or sector. It is a tacit symbolic source of the dominant understanding of the world, current technologies, market relations, use of resources and many other characteristics in an industry.

Following Kuhn, knowledge structures may change in a revolutionary manner due to changes in the environment, such as when a technological breakthrough occurs that has the potential of altering the entire industry/sector. In education, however, the knowledge structure is more likely to respond to changes in the external environment than to technological invention; demographic shifts have had more impact than, for example, changing information technologies such as computer hardware and software [7, 13].[4] Because changes in educational knowledge are often ambiguous, this domain usually contains more than one

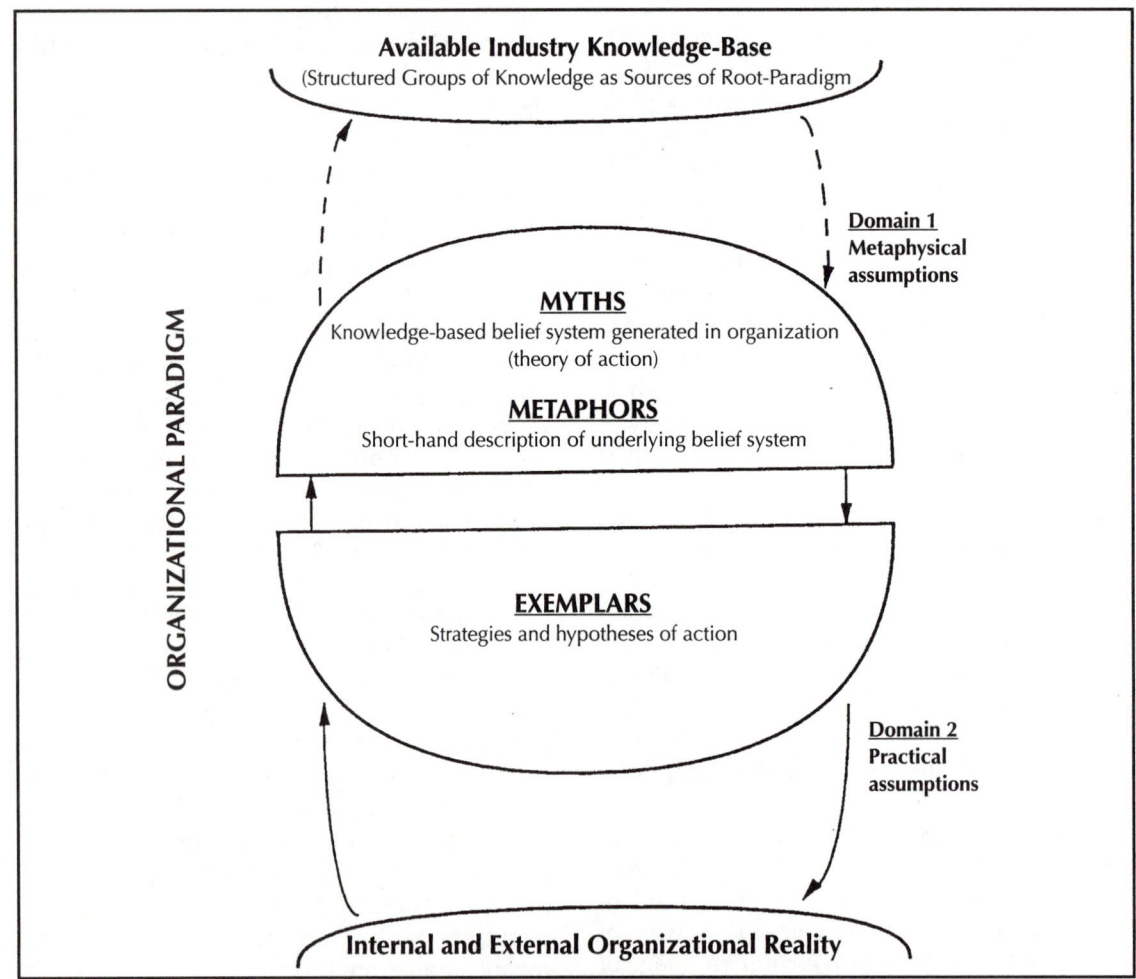

Figure 38-1 Organization as Paradigm: An Interpretive Process

paradigm that represent the "facts" behind each technological/environmental revolution. While a particular knowledge paradigm may dominate an entire industry,[5] the more ambiguous the knowledge, the more likely it is that there will be a dominant paradigm coexisting with several strong, but less popular "world views."

Between the upper and lower domains of figure 38-1, the organization enacts its particular reality largely through social interaction and formal and informal sharing of experience. At a particular time and place, a dominant world view directs the organizational activities.[6] This frame of reference, or paradigm, is defined by an underlying belief system/background assumptions that are tacit and abstract and by exemplars and models that are concrete and observable.

A Model of Organizational Change as Paradigm Shift

Figure 38-2 is a representation of a dynamic organizational change model that takes into consideration the fundamental characteristics of the Kuhnian change perspective and the distinctive realities of organizational life. The model comprises five separate and consecutive phases: normalcy, confrontation of anomalies, crisis, selection (revolution), and a new normalcy period.

1. *Normalcy*: This period is characterized by adaptive organizational activities and a slow pace of change. It is assumed that a particular paradigm has established dominance in guiding the organizational activities and imposing a set of tacit organizational knowledge as reference to those activities [3]. Background assumptions and the model and exemplars provided by the ruling paradigm are not questioned seriously when inconsistencies occur between expected and actual outcomes.

2. *Confronting Anomalies*: Anomalies can result either from facing unresolved puzzles or from sudden changes occurring within and outside the organization. In order to view problems as anomalies, they must provide uncertain stimuli within the organization for an extended period. Thus the discovery of anomalies is a matter of perception. Managerial elites (like Kuhn's scientific elites) generally perceive the world view associated with their paradigm as taken-for-granted and avoid any questioning of their ideology [44].

3. *Crisis*: If organizations experience anomalies (reduced market share, low morale among employees, or continued poor performance in the primary mission) over a long period of time, they

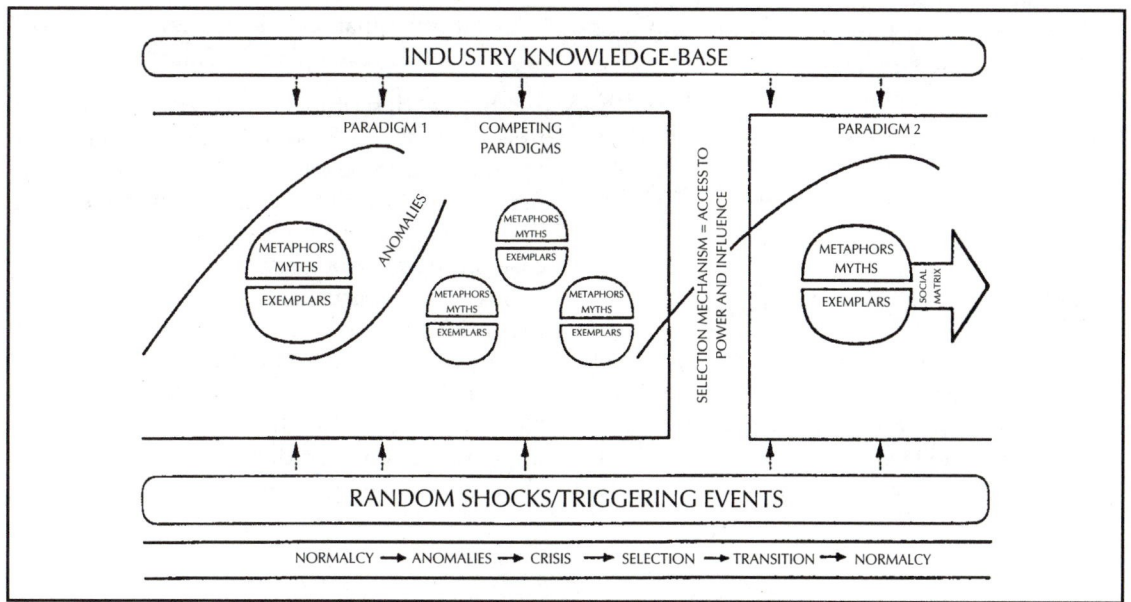

Figure 38-2 Organizational Change as Paradigm Shift

may trigger the beginning of a crisis period in which the organization's paradigm is questioned. Members begin to look for new ways of thinking which either spring from within their own sector, or are transferred from paradigms available in other organizational industries or sectors. A new leader is often seen as a catalyst to solve the crisis.

4. *Selection*: During the crisis period, the competition between available, but largely untested, paradigms is intense [47]. Logically, they have an equal chance to be the next dominant paradigm in the organization until another organizational reality is factored in: "the imposition of [a paradigm] reality by more powerful groups" [3, p. 375]. Thus, in figure 38-1, the selective mechanism for preferring one paradigm over others is access to power and influence. Note that this component of a paradigm shift is absent from Kuhn's perspective but is consistent with studies of decision-making and change in higher education [8, 1].

5. *Renewed Normalcy*: As a new paradigm becomes dominant, a wave of enthusiasm appears in the organization. This coincides with the establishment of new power relations and the appearance of new actors on stage. Instability characterizes the initial policy formation period of the new paradigm, in which new organizational structures, procedures and systems are initiated [19, p. 157]. Under new sets of metaphors, myths, models, and exemplars another paradigm life-cycle begins, and the social matrix of the paradigm continues to extend within the organization.

Statement of the Problem

The explanatory power of the model was tested using the strategic reorientation process in the University of Minnesota that began in the late seventies. The following questions guided the data collection and analysis process:

1. *Exploring the old paradigm:* What was the dominant paradigm in the organization prior to the paradigm replacement period?
   - What metaphors served as the shorthand description of the old paradigm?
   - What myth(s)/set of beliefs guided the organizational activities?
   - What exemplars and models defined the paradigm-in-action?

2. *Exploring anomalies:* Were there anomalies that led to the emergence of the paradigm-in-use in the organization and, if so, what were their nature and characteristics?

3. *Sector knowledge:*
   - Were any root-paradigms or available models of action available in the higher education sector during the anomalies period?
   - Did particular external events and trends trigger the paradigm replacement process?
   - Were there competing paradigms or world views in the organization prior to the selection of the paradigm-in-use?

4. *Nature and characteristics of the selection process.*

5. *Characteristics of the new dominant paradigm:* What are the current metaphors, myth(s), exemplars, and models?

Before describing our methods, we will first provide background information about the planning process at the University of Minnesota, in which the case study was conducted. The University of Minnesota was selected as a case study site not only because of its convenience but because existing research suggested that efforts to create change at this institution were present over a relatively long period of time. This made it an excellent site in which to "test" the degree to which efforts to reorient a large university could result in a paradigm shift, rather than incremental change.

Strategic Planning in the University of Minnesota

The planning process at the University of Minnesota dates back to the mid 1970s. Clugston [9] divided the strategic planning process in the university into four phases: Between 1974 and 1979, the structure and framework for planning began with the appointment of a planning council by the president. After this preparatory discussion, the first cycle of planning occurred between 1979 and 1982. The second cycle, which occurred between 1982 and 1984, was an attempt by the university to link the in-process program prioritization with budget reallocation decisions as a response to a severe cut in state funding caused by a budget shortfall. The third cycle (1984–85) focused on letting each unit find ways to develop strategies in order to implement identified priorities. The fourth cycle (1985) required each unit to reexamine its mission in light of the second and third cycles of the planning process [9, p. 96].

This formal planning process was interrupted by [interim] President Kenneth Keller (previously the vice-president for academic affairs). His *Commitment to Focus* proposal, announced in the early months of 1985, was largely based on the previous committee recommendations—although it was a personal interpretation—and it gained the support of the majority of the faculty as well as the governing board [12].

The plan laid out the following assumptions [21]:

1. Efforts of higher education institutions in the state should be coordinated, and/or duplicative efforts should be minimized;

2. Faculty should be released from certain involvements, such as a heavy teaching load;

3. The university is out of balance in terms of the ratio of undergraduates to graduates;

4. Quality should not be sacrificed in order to preserve breadth of programs;

5. Various university campuses should be coordinated through a number of rearrangements.

Keller's plan initially received wide support from inside and outside the university. By the time it was announced, the search was on for a new president, and Keller was appointed by the governing board in 1986, owing in large measure to his plan. Described by many as an intelligent and visionary leader, he managed to convince the legislature on a key proposal that decoupled state funding from undergraduate enrollment.

However, he resigned in March 1988 as a result of a public controversy regarding the financial management of the university [12]. The new president, Nils Hasselmo, was recruited in 1989 from an administrative position at the University of Arizona. During his previous tenure at the University of Minnesota, he had served on many committees related to the initial phases of the strategic planning process. In his inauguration address, he demonstrated his strong support for the fundamental spirit of *Commitment to Focus*. However, the plan was renamed "Access to Excellence" in order to overcome some public charges that the original plan was elitist, and the educational improvement emphasis was shifted from graduate to undergraduate education.

Research Design and Methodology

To answer the questions posed earlier, we used a qualitative case study design [52]. Because a paradigm is a socially constructed reality, subjective perceptions of the organizational members are the logical source of metaphors, myths, exemplars, and models [38], and such data are difficult to collect through survey instruments or unobtrusive measures. We focused on faculty as informants, because they are viewed as carrying a special status of responsibility for conserving the university and typically have a longer time perspective than administrators, who, at least at the University of Minnesota, often occupy their positions for five or fewer years.

An open-ended interview schedule was developed. Each question dealt with a particular dimension of the change model depicted in figure 38-2, although it was designed to use language that could be understood by faculty in a variety of disciplines. The interview was pilot-tested on four members of the university community, including one professor who also occupied an administrative position, and was refined to eliminate confusion about meaning and language [52, p. 75].

A "multiple embedded case design," which involved sampling several departments within the university, was used in order to increase the validity of the study [52, pp. 44–47]. After consulting with knowledgeable members of the faculty, five departments from four large colleges in the university were selected: Strategic Management (School of Management), Political Science and English (College of Liberal Arts), Mathematics (Institute of Technology), and Food Science (College of Agriculture). The departments were chosen to reflect a wide variety of disciplinary backgrounds, because they are largely isolated from each other both physically and intellectually and because they have contributed at very different rates to faculty governance. It was assumed that if common metaphors, myths, and exemplars could be found among such a diverse set of faculty members, we would have some confidence that we were observing a shared organizational paradigm.

In each department we obtained a list of faculty members who had been in the institution for at least ten years and randomly selected five primary and three substitute respondents from these lists. Potential respondents were contacted by a letter followed by telephone call. Uninterested or unavailable faculty were replaced from the substitute list. A total of twenty-four faculty members was interviewed (one appointment could not be scheduled within the time frame). A typical interview ran about forty-five minutes and was tape-recorded and later transcribed by a professional typist. About 190 single-spaced pages of interview transcripts were produced.

In analyzing the data, systematic qualitative methods were followed [28, 35]. First, the researchers produced a coding scheme based on the issues and questions. Each interview transcript was sorted without changing the original word structure or phrasing as used by respondents, so that each piece of information was grouped under a related category. Then each posted item under a particular category was given a "tag" describing the whole sentence. Following this procedure, tags under each category were compared across five inter-

view transcripts for each department and then grouped. For example, program eliminations, closings, mergers, and consolidations made up a group of exemplars [actions] of the paradigm-in-use.

Results

Identifying the Old Paradigm

Metaphors:[7] A total of thirty-two metaphors was produced by twenty-two respondents, of which more than one-third were mentioned by more than one faculty member: octopus, elephant, amoeba, and a wildly growing garden/vegetable. Other metaphors can be combined with these. Cow and buffalo, like elephant, target the size of the institution. By the same token, metaphors such as "a tangled up ball of twine," "an enormous Chinese menu of offerings," "unruly group of school children," "a feudal-medieval landscape containing many fiefdoms with their own princes and princesses," "a wagon train going different directions for different purposes" and "a beehive going different directions, doing their own separate jobs" can be combined with the metaphor of "a wildly growing garden or vegetable," because all of them explain an organized anarchy in terms of lack of control, lack of coordination and collaboration, and uncontrolled growth in organizational activities.

By combining the metaphors in terms of their contextual similarities, we found the following images: amoeba (3), octopus (5), elephant and related metaphors (5), a wildly growing garden/vegetable and related metaphors (8).

Reading these metaphors in terms of their most visible characteristics, we can make some interpretations about the nature of the old paradigm. For example, an amoeba is a one cell living organism which is essentially shapeless and multiplies by fission. The metaphor refers to the fact that the organization was not characterized by a strong/solid identity, perhaps "being all things for all people" as a land-grant university, and that it was in a constant process of multiplication, which is closely related to "a wildly growing garden or vegetable" metaphor. On the other hand, the elephant, cow, and buffalo are all visible with their size and massive body. The metaphors identify an organization characterized by its mass and impressive size that has traditionally been one of the largest public universities in the nation. The octopus, however, is easily identified with its multi-armed body. In explaining their choice of this metaphor, many faculty members pointed out that "the university was like an octopus with its eight arms embracing different constituencies simultaneously." Moreover, the metaphors of "wildly growing garden or vegetable" and other related ones, as listed above, characterize an uncontrolled and continuous growth and expansion in the program areas and activities in the organization. As will be pointed out below, each metaphor was strikingly linked to a group of central exemplars and anomalies that led to a crisis situation in the institution.

Besides the metaphors provided for the old paradigm, respondents used adjectives in an attempt to define the meaning of the metaphors that they identified. The list of adjectives included: big, large, sloppy, ponderous, very slow, departmentalized, multi-limbed, stumbling, dividing, decentralized, unplanned, unruly, opportunist. Again, these adjectives are closely connected to types of exemplary actions in the organization—which later became the anomalies.

Myths/exemplars: Myth(s), or the "stories" that identify the belief system in an organization, are usually derived from the exemplars and models. Because a belief system, background, or metaphysical assumptions are tacit and abstract, organizational members usually explain them by using some central examples [18]. Five activities were identified by respondents as concrete applications or exemplars of the belief system of the old paradigm: (1) growing, expanding, diversifying program areas or increasing variety/offering many programs (78 percent); (2) giving priority or emphasizing the teaching mission of the university (50 percent); (3) growing size resulting from an open access policy and low admission standards (41 percent); (4) highly decentralized decision making, with virtually complete freedom granted to units to develop desired programs (36 percent); and (5) emphasizing the service mission of the university (30 percent).

What type of organizational myth do these exemplars describe? The teaching and service emphasis and large size resulted from open access policy; low admission requirements and quantity emphasis can be linked to a dominant myth that the primary responsibility of the institution is to educate sons and daughters of the citizens of the state, which in turn is linked to the perceived populist/agrarian socialist history of public policy in Minnesota. Faculty interviews have clearly pointed out the validity of this statement: 71 percent (17 out of 24 respondents) in one way or another suggested populism as the belief system in the university. This myth can be stated as follows: "The mission of the university is to educate all who live in the state of Minnesota. Access to university is an entitlement of citizenship."

Although closely linked to a populist myth, faculty identified another distinctive myth: the continual growth, expansion, and diversity in program areas and activities, which was fostered by unit autonomy and decentralization in the decision-making structure. While some linked size with populism, an institution whose primary responsibility is mass education need not always be a decentralized one; a centralized and much more highly coordinated higher education system, as is found in a number of other states, might well satisfy the same ends. Thus, the second internally driven myth is associated with exemplars that point to "an entrepreneurial spirit" and an institutional value placed on independent, expansionist behavior.

Identifying the anomalies: Seven problems were identified as anomalies resulting from the old paradigm. The growth and expansion exemplar discussed above was identified as putting a burden on increasingly limited finances of the institution (79 percent), thinly spreading resources (54 percent), which also caused a decline in the overall quality of the programs (46 percent). The fourth anomaly (size of the student population) is linked to the size-related exemplar, but was also noted as creating a high student-faculty ratio and an increase in undergraduates at the expense of graduate students (46 percent). Thus, the faculty's teaching load was expanded, ultimately weakening research and graduate level studies.

A fifth anomaly, "duplication of efforts in the state higher education system (38 percent)," was highlighted by the *Commitment to Focus* proposal. In this document, Interim President Keller argued that teaching and undergraduate functions traditionally allocated to the university could be shifted, in part, to expanded state university and community college systems, asserting also that the open-access mission of the university was designed at a time when there were no other higher education opportunities in the state. The sixth anomaly, "lack of leadership" (21 percent), helps to account for why units became so decentralized and activities were uncoordinated. Some respondents pointed out that the reason why Keller initially had so much support from inside and outside the university was that he provided a sense of leadership and vision for the institution.

Sector knowledge: Twenty-two out of twenty-four respondents (92 percent) agreed that there were other higher education institutions trying to do similar things in or before the mid 1980s. More than fifteen institutions were named as being involved in similar reorientations, but the most frequently named higher education institutions were those that completed or achieved a successful reorientation in the late 1970s and early 1980s. These included the University of California system and the Michigan system in general (46 percent) and Berkeley and the University of Michigan in particular (25 percent). The content of their change efforts was stated as a renewed emphasis on research, reorganization for more efficiency, reduction of size, restriction of admissions, clearer separation of research and teaching functions within the state higher education system, and upgrading of quality. Also, according to the faculty, these change efforts originated as a response to centralized planning, "the accountability movement," financial retrenchment, efforts to advance in the national ratings, and a trend toward more research and graduate level emphasis.

Triggering events: Faculty also pointed to particular external events and trends that helped to trigger an examination of anomalies, five of which were identified by multiple respondents. The first was the recession in the state economy in the early 1980s (46 percent) which resulted in a reduction in the allocation of state funds for the university. Next was Reagan's higher education policy at the federal level, which was described as antipopulist (42 percent). The third triggering event, as cited by the respondents (33 percent), was the election of an activist governor, who demanded that the University limit its activities. The fourth (29

percent) was a combination of national concerns that emerged in the early 1980s, such as increasing global competition, concern about quality of education at all levels, and, in particular, the national perception that there was a drop in academic performance in higher education institutions. The final event, recalled by 24 percent, was a demographic forecast that demand for higher education and student enrollments would decline.

Competition between old and new paradigms: In his analysis of scientific progress, Kuhn argued that there would always be a clash between the new and the old paradigms in the paradigm replacement period [23]. According to the respondents in this study, the strongest opposition against the *Commitment to Focus* proposal was from the believers of the old land-grant philosophy (what we have called "populism") according to 75 percent of the respondents. Specifically identified were rural constituents from "Greater Minnesota," legislators representing these areas, and some faculty who identified with this group. A second source of opposition came from those units and departments that were threatened by the proposal (63 percent). Those were various autonomous service units and small, expensive, or low priority programs. The third source of opposition (29 percent) was founded in the old belief system that rewarded teaching, service, and undergraduate education, as mentioned in the exemplars section. This group consisted largely of older or senior faculty.

Nature of the selection process: According to faculty members, the Board of Regents' adoption of the *Commitment to Focus* proposal as its formal institutional policy was actually a result of the personal, political, and leadership skills of a new, energetic, young, visionary president (83 percent). His skills played an important role in gaining support from faculty, regents, the governor, legislators, and the business community. The proposal was strongly backed by these power sources according to the respondents (58 percent). We also note that these groups were much more likely to reflect the interests of the growing urban sectors of the state as opposed to "Greater Minnesota." Also, the president carefully cultivated the support of a diverse group of faculty who normally had little in common—those who were oriented toward research and graduate-level teaching and those who were concerned about the declining quality in undergraduate education (54 percent).

What Is the Dominant Paradigm Today?

Metaphors: A total of twenty-four metaphors was produced by twenty-one faculty members. The list exhibits greater variety and less consensus than in the descriptions of the old paradigm, with the exception of the "lion" metaphor, which was repeated three times. However, the adjectives used suggest that the current organization *is* different from the previous one in terms of being more directed, focused, and purposeful in its strategic orientation, smaller and trimmed down in its size and structure, and more coordinated in its internal decision making. The adjectives and verbs used as explanations for the metaphors included: more powerful, aggressive, trimmed down, directed, focused, stabilized, faster, smaller, self-sufficient, better hunter, bit ruthless, clever, pruned, coordinated, seeks, searches, scaled down. We infer that a new paradigm is still in the process of development and has not yet created a strong image. In addition, the departure of the president who designed the *Commitment to Focus* may have had a destabilizing effect. Although the new president has expressed strong commitment to the original plan, changes in language and modest changes in emphasis detract from the process of image formation.

Exemplars and models: Seven groups of exemplars and models were identified by the interviewed faculty. The first, the reallocation plan laid out in the *Commitment to Focus* proposal (67 percent), was intended to distribute resources differentially (from low priority programs/units to high priority programs/units) as opposed to the previous practice of across-the-board distribution. The second and third group of exemplars were related to reductions in scope: cuts in student enrollment and/or reducing the size of the university (67 percent) or other activities intended to lessen program and campus diversity by closing or merging departments, units, or programs (63 percent). Fourth and fifth among those mentioned was a focus on quality, especially at the levels of teaching and undergraduate education in the

university (42 percent), an increased emphasis on research, and more priority given to graduate education (38 percent). The sixth exemplar was a trend toward more central coordination through planned activities and an emphasis on collaborative work among the units (33 percent), while the final group describes a university that has aggressively directed itself toward external funding through endowed chairs, fund raising activities, and grants for research (25 percent).

The emerging action image of the university seems to be aimed at addressing anomalies that emerged from the old paradigm. For example, whereas the old paradigm praised the quantity that resulted in inflated size, the emerging one attempts to reduce it. In order to overcome financial anomalies, the new paradigm generates a partial solution by distributing the resources differentially and trying to find ways to get external funding. In order to solve the problem of diversity, complexity, and "diseconomized scale" the paradigm that is appearing attempts to create criteria or a rationale for expanding, maintaining, or eliminating programs. To do all these, the central administration has gained a more central integration function in the internal affairs. Lastly, as a response to eroding or declining quality, the new paradigm emphasizes quality.

Assessment of the current myth: The comparisons discussed above show that the dominant myths before and after *Commitment to Focus* are not the same, yet they are not opposite. The emerging myth is neither the old populist myth, nor is it elitist. A comparison between the first four examples resulting from the *Commitment to Focus* initiative and the first four anomalies created by the old belief system suggests that the new paradigm is in the process of providing solutions to the accumulated anomalies. The new myth might be called "managed populism" in terms of the nature of the exemplars and models it has generated.

Discussion and Summary

Observers of universities are more often struck by the stability of these institutions than by their adaptability; . . . many shifts and alterations in the way a university does things occur every year. Yet these often do not add up to institutional change; rather they merely patch up the existing system [25, p. 91].

The above remarks summarize an embedded assumption that has dominated research on higher education organizations for many years. Popular evolutionary and adaptation theories of organizational change have set the background for this line of inquiry in studying universities as organizations. However, this study demonstrates that a radical change in the ways in which faculty in a large, public university view the nature and purpose of their institution can occur within a relatively short period of time (approximately a decade). The paradigm or world view that once dominated the institution was transformed from "entrepreneurial populism" to "managed populism" through a series of stages consistent with the process of paradigm shift as outlined above. We will summarize the five-step paradigm shift model as presented in figure 38-2 to describe the discontinuous change at the University of Minnesota and reflect on the applicability of the paradigm shift model to the data presented.

The Paradigm Perspective Applied to the University of Minnesota

The initial period of normalcy: "Entrepreneurial populism" captures the two dimensions of the myth that dominated the university until the mid-1980s: the idea of "the servant university" dated back to an earlier period in which the university was the only public higher education institution in the state. Between the late 1950s and the early 1970s, the university faced an increased demand for higher education as a result of changing demographics, the push toward technological superiority and the subsequent increase of federal monies to universities, the civil rights movement, and increased enrollment and demands from minorities and women. But, these were also years in which resources were abundant: the state had one of the fastest-growing economies in the nation, invested heavily in education, and there were a variety of incentives that supported the drift toward opportunism. The university's growth supported decentralization and a deemphasis on coordination, as the lower layers of the institution became stronger and demonstrably successful in marketing their services. Up to a

point, the old entrepreneurial populism myth generated a sense of impressive success for the university, which became one of the largest in the nation in terms of student enrollments, among the most research intensive as measured by external funding, and much commended for the opportunities offered to various constituencies in the state.

The period of anomalies: The late 1970s marked a turning point for the university: resources began to decline, enormous size (once a privilege) was perceived as a burden, overemphasis on teaching and service weakened the research mission, and quality started eroding [12]. As a response to the anomalies, the university adopted a strategic planning process to solve the problems. However, the incremental changes and loose linkages of the past forty years created tensions that the initial phases of strategic planning seemed unable to fix.

The period of crisis and selection: The strategic change process took a dramatic turn in 1985 by the announcement of the *Commitment to Focus* proposal, which, despite high levels of leadership turnover, became the framework in guiding the change efforts. A wide public debate took place internally and externally, which laid out a need for a discontinuous change in the university and which concentrated on the obsolescence of the old belief system and its anomalistic outcomes as discussed above.

As expected, opposition came from the internal and external supporters of the old paradigm. However, strong interpersonal and leadership skills from the architect of the new paradigm amassed political support of a coalition by key urban power holders which permitted the new paradigm to persist in the face of the lessened political influence of the largely rural adherents of the older paradigm. These results are important in supporting our conceptual model, because they confirm that (1) paradigm shifts coincide with a new leader on the scene, (2) any selected paradigm needs to be supported by an eclectic group of key power holders in and around the organization, and (3) the exercise of political coalition building skills may be essential for a paradigm shift in organizational settings where the knowledge base is ambiguous.

The period of renewed normalcy: Under attack, the new paradigm was adjusted but not significantly altered by a new president. The paradigmatic shift that has been described as a transformation from "an entrepreneurial populist" image to "a managed populist" one occurred in the mid-1980s.

How Well Does the Paradigm Shift Model "Fit"?

We conclude, based on the above summary, that the paradigm shift model based largely on Kuhn's [23] theory fits our data well. As noted, however, a certain amount of fuzziness is evident in the metaphors provided by the faculty concerning the new paradigm. Perhaps this should not be surprising, since Imershein argues that "the full possibilities for a paradigm's use are rarely seen at its initial inception; such awareness comes only with the growth and extension of the paradigm, so a certain degree of diversity is understandable" [18, p. 41]. This can be provided for in figure 38-2 by inserting an intermediary stage between selection (revolution) and renewed normalcy. The emerging paradigm at the University of Minnesota appears to be in this stage, in which parts of the old and new paradigm are meshed, with the new one gradually eliminating the old. We would argue, based on the data, that in social organizations, "revolutionary changes" do not occur rapidly and may, more likely than in scientific paradigms, incorporate elements of the old paradigm (while redefining their meaning) rather than fully rejecting them. Since our data were collected, for example, the University of Minnesota has developed several key task forces to examine different elements of the "land-grant mission," which we interpret as part of a process of constructing a new interpretation of populism. We also suggest that a paradigm revolution can only be interpreted as such after the fact: unlike a political revolution (where discontinuity is visible from the start), the beginning and end of a paradigm shift are harder to identify.

While Kuhn emphasizes the importance of shared disciplinary perspectives, we did not anticipate that the "invisible college" of ideas about higher education reform would be well developed. Yet, sector knowledge was surprisingly well distributed among faculty, many of whom were able to cite specific strategies used to reorient and redesign other institutions which they believed to be part of the University of Minnesota's reference group. The importance of sector knowledge clearly challenges the notion that faculty are "loosely connected" to ideas regarding institutional environment and direction, although it is very likely that their understanding of sector knowledge was moderated by selective communication from top university administrators, who were in closer contact with developments in other universities, either directly or through consultation with the faculty governance system. The relevance of sector knowledge to faculty members' understanding of the paradigm shift draws attention to the observation that, in a relatively participatory, decentralized change process, communication networks can spread relatively esoteric and specialized information through a broad segment of a very large (over three thousand member) faculty. This suggests that, at least in higher education, internal paradigm shifts may need to be justified in terms of a larger community of organizations.

Also notable is the importance of coalition building on the part of university leaders, an aspect of paradigm change that is not discussed by Kuhn. While the ideas articulated by the "visionary leader" were described as a rehashing of existing statements, what was new was his ability to develop a coalition of external and internal constituents who supported an alternative to the existing paradigm. Most of the members of this coalition had nothing in common beyond their belief that the university should be streamlined and quality should be improved. They ranged from radical professors to right-wing business leaders; from well-established political figures to obscure government administrators. This case underscores the need to elaborate the macropolitics of higher education organizations, a topic that has been neglected in favor of micropolitical perspectives, such as those articulated by Baldridge et al. [1] and Cohen and March [8].

Additional Implications for Organizational Research in Higher Education

We are aware that a single case study cannot prove or disprove the enduring value of a theoretical framework for the study of higher education organizations. However, the change perspective outlined at the beginning of this article suggests that the revolution-based paradigm approach can be used effectively in explaining strategic behavior within higher education organizations. We draw three tentative conclusions from our study:

The need for longer time frames in studying change in higher education: The dominant theories of change in universities have emphasized their inherent incremental nature. In the past two decades, the "open systems" theory of change, which bases its assumption of the desirability of slow adaptation on a biological survival analogy, has been augmented by more recent theories that have dominated research on decision making and change in educational settings. Universities are viewed as "organized anarchies" [8], which have a structure that is best characterized as "loosely coupled" [50]. Both of these characteristics lead to decentralization of decision making, limited impacts of leaders, and localized adaptation within subunits. Research on strategic turnarounds in smaller institutions [7, 13] might have been viewed as challenging this dominant theoretical assumption but did not result in significant reorientation within educational research.

Our summary suggests that those perspectives are descriptive of the historical phase in which universities enjoyed prosperous growth that was facilitated by an "anarchic orientation" to strategy and a highly decentralized structure. According to Miller and Friesen [29, 30], when organizations find a strategic path that initially brings them success, they usually tend to stay in the same course. Thus, for example, the rise of the "multiversity" in the postwar period created a large, loosely linked enterprise that was, by internal as well as external standards, remarkably successful at both mass education and the production of high-quality research. However, as the paradigm change perspective outlined at the beginning of this article suggests, following a successful course over a long period of time creates excesses that turn initially successful orientations into anomalies that cannot be addressed by "more of the same" or by maintaining the same assumptions about the essential nature of the institution. This argument is supported by the results of the study. According to faculty members, the incremental change and loose linkage of the past forty years created tensions that the initial phases of strategic planning

seemed unable to fix. The mid-1980s saw the beginning of a paradigmatic shift away from loose linkage and organizational anarchy and toward more trimmed down/coordinated structural arrangements. The implementation of this paradigm shift is clearly incomplete. However, most faculty members interviewed seemed convinced that a permanent and radical change had occurred.

The need for interpretive perspectives in studying change in higher education: This case study has used a framework adapted from Kuhn, but it is part of a broader tradition of interpretive studies of organizations noted earlier in this article. According to Morgan [33], the interpretive perspective suggests the following: (a) we must understand organizations as *socially constructed* phenomena; (b) organizational members (including administrators) should be sensitive to the importance of understanding organizations as contextually based systems of meaning; (c) organizational practice is a continuous process of enactment; and (d) organizational contexts are enacted domains. This broader interpretive perspective is clearly compatible with the paradigm-shift model presented here, and it stands in opposition to the more common alternative which focuses on the role of leaders in generating and guiding "transformations" that are based on rationally planned changes in structure and procedures. Our data suggest that changes in structure and procedures (while they might be excellent indicators that a change has taken place) are difficult to carry out and do not produce much change in behavior (exemplars and models) until there has been a genuine shift in the underlying assumptions and values (myths and metaphors).

The implications of the interpretive framework are significant for administrative as well as organizational theory. They imply, for example, that real organizational change requires leadership strategies that emphasize interpretation of organizational values and meaning rather than emphasize organizational restructuring and administrative control. Leaders, for example, must become effective story tellers rather than commanders-in-chief, and must learn to become "post-heroic" in the sense that they must give up the hope that they can personally control the destiny of the organization. Managing meaning is a considerably more slippery endeavor than traditional models of leadership would suggest.

The need to rethink the role of strategic planning: Despite what the strategic management and planning models assume, change is a highly decentralized yet community-based activity. Change that is orchestrated from the top (as is typically suggested in the strategic planning literature) and which reflects the "vision" or subjective realities of an elite group cannot define an institution-wide change process unless it takes into account the alternative competing paradigms that have typically emerged in different parts of the organization. Our data suggest that changing a paradigm in a research university is far more complicated than creating a visionary statement of the future and that visions that articulate the direction of a paradigm shift may emerge as a consequence of strategic planning rather than as a stimulus to it. This perspective is consistent with Bryson's [4] argument that strategic planning in public organizations rarely begins with a strategic vision.

Strategic planning may work on the surface, particularly in smaller colleges, such as those studied by Chaffee [7] and Hahn [13], where collective discussions about assumptions and values are easier to manage. It is not, by itself, capable of stimulating changes in principles of action, background assumptions, and myths and metaphors that constitute the organizational paradigm. Without incorporating the significance of these factors in a large-scale transformative process, strategic planning will not be able to address the chaotic and unpredictable phases of change that are characteristic of more complex, decentralized organizations such as research-intensive universities.

In conjunction with the above point, our analysis suggests that change is both evolutionary and revolutionary. The first decade of planning at the University of Minnesota was not a failure; change happened—but not radical, university-wide change [25]. We hypothesize that traditional strategic planning and change techniques may be extremely helpful as tools for designing changes within large institutions during a "normalcy period," but may be less helpful when there is a need to change socially constructed meanings across the entire organization. However, the analysis in this article reveals that even apparently easy targets of

change in organizations (admitting fewer undergraduates and raising admissions standards) are deeply connected through the paradigm to more difficult, unstated targets of the change process (the need to challenge deeply held beliefs about the meaning of populism). Furthermore, strategic planning and management models hold a largely unrealistic premise concerning the change capabilities of the existing management in organizations. Our data suggest that strategic planning at the University of Minnesota was largely ineffective until new actors with new beliefs and values emerged and publicly challenged the existing paradigm.

Many of the managerial and strategic planning models are one-shot proposals to solve problems in organizations, which may be repeated every few years, but are not assumed to be continuous. The change model implied by this study assumes an unbroken change effort lasting many years, because the process of testing new meanings cannot be separated into episodic planning efforts. According to the data presented in this study, typical strategic planning efforts in the evolutionary (normalcy) phase result in the paradigms.

Notes

1. The life-cycle metaphor, for example, has described organization on the basis of birth, maturity, and death. Organizational ecology has used the Darwinist analogy of the "survival of the fittest," and has examined the mimetic character of successful organizations [14]. Contingency theories, on the other hand, have generated a metaphor of situation-specific adjustment between organizational variables and environmental situations [24].

2. Kuhn's models have always been controversial, beginning with the strong attacks by Popper and other "positivist" philosophers of science. A key criticism of Kuhn's notion of paradigms has been recently expressed by Bartley [2], who argues that they are overly relativistic: Scholars love the concept because it offers them an opportunity to legitimize any investigative behavior under the rubric of "it's part of my paradigm." In addition, it overstates the importance of repressive group values as contrasted to the entrepreneurial spirit of individuals and thus corresponds to socialist and communist political ideology, as contrasted with the market economy ideal. Some have questioned the applicability of Kuhn's paradigm model to organizational

analysis, and Kuhn himself has expressed discomfort with "abusive" use of his concept by others. Nevertheless, the application of Kuhn's ideas to organizations is consistent with a growing interest in interpretive or constructivist approaches in social science generally [39]. Burrell and Morgan's [6] influential discussion of research traditions in social science identifies the interpretive perspective as one of four key frameworks for analysis. Thus, while we are sensitive to the fact that the terms "paradigm" and "paradigm shift" have been popularized in ways that misconstrue the original intent of the theory, our effort here has been sensitive to the underlying philosophical premises of an interpretive approach to understanding radical change.

3. Therefore, myth in the model denotes Kuhn's metaphysical assumptions.

4. The process of radical change or revolution may take generations to complete, during which time change is limited and slow, as perceived by both insiders and outsiders. Thus, for example, many observers of U.S. universities would agree that the last radical shift occurred during the post-WWII period, which saw major changes in the scope of research funding and a concomitant increase in the differentiation of functions among different institutions of higher education. For most members of the university who did not live through this shift, there is little or no recognition that this change occurred—a reflection of the depth of the current paradigm.

5. Using Kuhn's terms, this would result in the conversion of others into a particular paradigm.

6. This assertion is not inconsistent with the notion of "muddling through," or the organizational "garbage can." We assume that one of the reasons why the accumulation of individual quasi-rational decisions may appear appropriate or even strategic in hindsight is that individual decisions are guided by similar paradigms and interpretations of specific local needs/information.

7. To elicit metaphors and myths, two types of questions were designed: direct and indirect. The direct question (Which metaphor, image or analogy would best describe this institution before 1985? After 1985?) was relatively unsuccessful in terms of collecting striking images. However, the indirect question (Which animal or living organism would best describe this institution before 1985? After 1985?) elicited rich material. The indirect method was suggested by Gareth Morgan, at an informal seminar at the University of Minnesota.

References

1. Baldridge, J. V., D. V. Curtis, G. Ecker, and G. L. Riley. *Policy Making and Effective Leadership:* *A National Study of Academic Management.* San Francisco: Jossey-Bass, 1978.

2. Bartley, W. W. *Unfathomed Knowledge, Unmeasured Wealth: On Universities and the Wealth of Nations.* La Salle, Ill.: Open Court, 1989.

3. Brown, R. H. "Bureaucracy as Praxis: Toward a Political Phenomenology of Formal Organizations." *Administrative Science Quarterly,* 23 (1978) 365–82.

4. Bryson, J. *Strategic Planning for Public and Nonprofit Organizations: A Guide to Strengthening and Sustaining Organizational Achievement.* San Francisco: Jossey-Bass, 1988.

5. Burke, W., and H. A. Hornstein. *The Social Technology of Organization Development.* Washington, D.C.: N.T.L. Institute, 1972.

6. Burrell, G., and G. Morgan. *Sociological Paradigms and Organizational Analysis.* London: Heinemann, 1979.

7. Chaffee, E. "Successful Strategic Management in Small Private Colleges." *Journal of Higher Education,* 55 (March/April 1984) 212–41.

8. Cohen, M., and J. March. *Leadership and Ambiguity: The American College President.* New York: McGraw-Hill, 1974.

9. Clugston, R. "Strategic Adaptation in Organized Anarchy: Priority Setting and Resource Allocation in the Liberal Arts College of a Public Research University." Ph.D. Dissertation, University of Minnesota, 1987.

10. Emery, F. E. (ed.). *Systems Thinking.* Harmondsworth, England: Penguin, 1969.

11. Feldman, S. P. "Stories as Culture Creativity: On the Relation between Symbolism and Politics in Organizational Change." *Human Relations,* 43 (1990), 809–28.

12. Foster, E. "Planning at the University of Minnesota." *Planning for Higher Education,* 18 (1989–90), 25–38.

13. Hahn, D. "A Study of the Process of Curriculum Change and Instructional Development Designed to Increase Enrollment at Selected Private Colleges." Ph.D. Dissertation, University of Minnesota, 1992.

14. Hannan, M. and J. H. Freeman. "The Population Ecology of Organizations." *American Journal of Sociology,* 32 (1977), 929–64.

15. Hedberg, B. "How Organizations Learn and Unlearn." *In Handbook of Organizational Design,* vol. 1, edited by Paul C. Nystrom and William H. Starbuck. New York: Oxford University Press, 1981.

16. Hofstede, G., et al. "Measuring Organizational Cultures: A Qualitative and Quantitative Study across Twenty Cases." *Administrative Science Quarterly,* 35 (1990), 286–316.

17. Imershein, A. W. "Organizational Change as Paradigm Shifts. *Sociological Quarterly,* 18 (1977), 33–43.

18. _____. "The Epistemological Bases of Social Order. Toward Ethnoparadigm Analysis." In *Sociological Methodology,* edited by David R. Heise. San Francisco: Jossey-Bass, 1977.

19. Jonsson, S. A., and R. A. Lundin. "Myths and Wishful Thinking As Management Tools." In *Prescriptive Models of Organizations,* vol. 5, edited by Paul C. Nystrom and William H. Starbuck. Amsterdam: North-Holland Publishing Company, 1977.

20. Katz, D., and R. L. Kahn. *The Social Psychology of Organizations.* 2nd ed. New York: John-Wiley, 1978.

21. Keller, K. H. "A Commitment to Focus: Report of Interim President Kenneth H. Keller to the Board of Regents." University of Minnesota, 1985.

22. Kostouros, J. "Higher Education, Lower Expectations." *Minnesota* (July/August 1991), 29–34.

23. Kuhn, T. S. *The Structure of Scientific Revolutions.* 2nd. ed. Chicago: University of Chicago Press, 1970.

24. Lawrence, P. R., and J. W. Lorsch. *Organization and Environment.* Cambridge, Mass.: Harvard Graduate School of Business Administration, 1967.

25. Louis, K. S. "Surviving Institutional Change: Reflections on Curriculum Reform in Universities." In *Improving Undergraduate Education,* edited by Carol Pazendak. New Directions for Higher Education, Number 66. San Francisco: Jossey-Bass. 1989.

26. March, J., and H. Simon. *Organizations.* New York: John-Wiley, 1958.

27. Meyers, J. W., and B. Rowan. "Institutionalized Organizations: Formal Structure as Myth and Ceremony." *American Journal of Sociology,* 83 (1977), 340–63.

28. Miles, M., and M. Huberman. *Qualitative Data Analysis.* Beverly Hills, Calif.: Sage, 1984.

29. Miller, D., and P. H. Friesen. "Momentum and Revolution in Organizational Adaptation." *Academy of Management Journal,* 23 (1980), 591–614.

30. _____. *Organizations. A Quantum View.* Englewood Cliffs, N.J.: Prentice-Hall, 1984.

31. Mohrman, A. M., Jr., and E. Lawler III. "The Diffusion of QWL as a Paradigm Shift." In *The Planning of Change,* 4th ed., edited by W. G. Bennis. K. D. Benne, and R. Chin. New York: Holt, Rinehart and Winston, 1985.

32. Morgan, G. *Images of Organization.* Newbury Park, Calif.: Sage Publications, 1986.

33. _____. "Paradigm Diversity in Organizational Research." In *The Theory and Philosophy of Organizations,* edited by J. Hassard and D. Pym. New York: Routledge, 1990.

34. Pascale, R., and A. Athos. *The Art of Japanese Management.* New York: Warner Books, 1981.

35. Patton, M. *Qualitative Evaluation Methods.* Beverly Hills: Sage, 1980.

36. Peters, T. J., and R. H. Waterman. *In Search of Excellence.* New York: Harper & Row, 1982.

37. Pfeffer, J. "Management as Symbolic Action: The Creation and Maintenance of Organizational Paradigms." In *Research in Organizational Behavior,* vol. 3, edited by L. L. Cummings and B. M. Staw. Greenwich, Conn.: JAI Press, 1982.

38. _____. *Organizations and Organization Theory.* Boston: Pitman, 1982.

39. Phillips, D. C. *Philosophy, Science, and Social Inquiry.* Oxford: Pergamon, 1987.

40. Pondy, L. R., P. Frost, G. Morgan, and T. Dandridge (eds.). *Organizational Symbolism.* Greenwich, Conn.: JAI Press, 1983.

41. Quinn, J. B. *Strategies for Change: Logical Incrementalism.* Homewood, Ill.: Irwin, 1981.

42. Scalzo, T. "Reallocation: The Next Chapter." *Minnesota* (May–June 1991), 27–29.

43. Scott, R. *Organizations: Rational, Natural, and Open Systems.* New York: Prentice-Hall, 1982.

44. Sheldon, A. "Organizational Paradigms: A Theory of Organizational Change." *Organizational Dynamics* (Winter, 1980), 61–80.

45. Smircich, L. "Concepts of Culture and Organizational Analysis." *Administrative Science Quarterly,* 28 (1983), 339–58.

46. Sproull, L. S. "Beliefs in Organizations." In *Handbook of Organizational Design.* vol. 2, edited by P. Nystrom and W. H. Starbuck. London: Oxford University Press, 1981.

47. Sterman, J. D. "The Growth of Knowledge: Testing a Theory of Scientific Revolutions with a Formal Model." *Technological Forecasting and Social Change,* 28 (1985), 93–122.

48. University of Minnesota. "Enrollment Data," Minneapolis, Minn.: Office of Management, Planning, and Information Services, 1990.

49. University of Minnesota. "A Mission and Policy Statement for the University of Minnesota." Minneapolis, Minn.: University Board of Regents, 1974.

50. Weick, K. "Educational Organizations as Loosely Coupled Systems." *Administrative Science Quarterly,* 25 (1976), 1–19.

51. Westerlund, G., and S. E. Sjostrand. *Organizational Myths.* New York: Harper & Row, 1979.

52. Yin, R. *Case Study Research.* Beverly Hills, Calif.: Sage, 1984.

An earlier version of this article was presented at the annual meeting of the University Council for Educational Administration, Baltimore, Md., October 1991. We would like to thank two anonymous reviewers, Robert Silverman, Melissa Anderson, and Richard Heydinger for their helpful comments. Correspondence should be addressed to Karen Seashore Louis, 104 Burton Hall, University of Minnesota, Minneapolis, MN 55455.

Hasan Simsek is assistant professor of educational administration, Middle East Technical University, Ankara, Turkey. and Karen Seashore Louis is professor of educational-policy and administration and associate dean for academic affairs, College of Education. University of Minnesota.

CHAPTER 39

POSTMODERNISM AND HIGHER EDUCATION

HARLAND G. BLOLAND

Postmodern perspectives, terms, and assumptions have penetrated the core of American culture over the past thirty years. Postmodernism's primary significance is its power to account for and reflect vast changes in our society, cultures, polity, and economy as we move from a production to a consumption society, shift from national to local and international politics, commingle high and low culture, and generate new social movements. Postmodernism has captured our interest because it involves a stunning critique of modernism, the foundation upon which our thinking and our institutions have rested. Today, modernist values and institutions are increasingly viewed as inadequate, pernicious, and costly. Postmodernists attack the validity and legitimacy of the most basic assumptions of modernism. Because higher education is quintessentially a modern institution, attacks on modernism are attacks on the higher education system as it is now constituted. The modern/postmodern debate began in the United States in the 1960s in the humanities, gained momentum in the 1970s in the arts and social theory, and by the early 1980s became, as Andreas Huyssen noted, "one of the most contested terrains in the intellectual life of Western society" [59, p. 357]. Today, having swept through the humanities and social sciences, the modern/postmodern debate has ebbed, and in literary studies at least, scholars refer to the current period as "post-theory" [101, p. A9].

In anthropology and other social sciences, postmodernism has had transformational effects, but currently many scholars who have been influenced by it distance themselves from the term, asserting that it identifies others, but not them [70, p. 563]. In literary studies, scholars continue to employ postmodern conceptualization extensively, while they assume that those who use the words also know the theory. No such assumption can be made in higher education studies concerning familiarity with modern/postmodern theory. Despite its significance in the past three decades the modern/postmodern debate has had relatively little direct impact on the study of higher education. The term "postmodern" appears with increasing frequency in the titles of presentations on postsecondary education in American Educational Research Association presentations, but few of the discussions address directly the background of the modern/postmodern divide that provides the vocabulary for the issues addressed.[1]

The paucity of literature in higher education on postmodernism is surprising, because the postmodern debate has been in the foreground for many education scholars who write about the public schools, particularly in the fields of curriculum studies, school administration, and educational theory [3, 37, 68]. Still, we rarely find postmodernism studies in the ASHE Reader series, in the ASHE/ERIC monographs, the *Journal of Higher Education*, the *Review of Higher Education*, or *Change* magazine. Postmodernism does find a place in *The Chronicle of Higher Education* articles, but they are not authored by higher education professors. The meagerness of higher educationists' general engagement with the postmodern is unfortunate, for despite the fact that the high tide of debate seems to be waning, the postmodern/modern discussion continues to have an unsettling but significant impact on the way in which we now think about society, politics, economics, and education. Thus, the terms and concepts of this debate are still with us, and the postmodern critique affects every field of inquiry that deals with human society.

Perhaps nowhere are the issues of the postmodern/modern debate more sharply drawn, more clearly illuminated, and more difficult to acknowledge than in higher education in the United States. For higher education is so deeply immersed in modernist sensibilities and so dependent upon modernist foundations that erosion of our faith in the modernist project calls into question higher education's legitimacy, its purpose, its activities, its very raison d'être. In attacking modernism, postmodernism presents a hostile interpretation of much of what higher education believes it is doing and what it stands for.

This study examines postmodernism and higher education by presenting four seminal postmodernist authors' ideas that provide a framework for discussions for much of the literature on postmodernism:

Jacques Derrida, Michel Foucault, Jean-François Lyotard, and Jean Baudrillard. Derrida and Foucault are viewed as representative of poststructuralist thought from which postmodernism as a perspective is derived, and Lyotard and Baudrillard are reflective of the view of postmodernism as a historical period. The postmodern concepts of these authors are discussed in terms of their implications for merit, community, and autonomy, three crucial characteristics of modernist higher education as it is situated in American society. Twelve reactions to the postmodern are introduced, each of which purports to interpret the consequences and illuminate the uses of postmodern thought. A summary of postmodernism's legacy for higher education concludes the discussion.

Postmodernism as a Perspective

The terms "modern" and "postmodern" occupy no fixed positions; their meanings are imprecise and highly contested. Despite this ambiguity, however, these concepts are critical reference points for discussions that try to make sense of what appear to be disparate cultural, economic, political, and social changes taking place in architecture, art, philosophy, literary criticism, the social sciences, in every day life, in popular culture, in industry, business, technology, and education.

Modernism

Modernism requires faith that there are universals that can be discovered through reason, that science and the scientific method are superior means for arriving at truth and reality, and that language describes and can be used as a credible and reliable means of access to that reality. With its privileging of reason, modernism has long been considered the basis for the emancipation of men and women from the bonds of ignorance associated with stagnant tradition, narrow religions, and meager educations. Championing democracy, modernism promises freedom, equality, justice, the good life, and prosperity. Equating merit with high culture, modernism provides expectations of more rigorous standards for and greater enjoyment of the arts and architecture. Through science and scientific method, modernism promises health, the eradication of hunger, crime, and poverty. Modernist science claims to be progressing toward true knowledge of the universe and to be delivering ever higher standards of living with effectiveness and efficiency. Modernism promises stability, peace, and a graspable sense of the rational unfolding of history. Modernism equates change with progress, which is defined as increasing control over nature and society.

Perhaps the most important means for understanding and carrying out the modernist project is education. Higher education is deeply embedded in the ideals, institutions, and vocabulary of modernism. Higher education trusts that merit should be rewarded through good jobs, promotions, higher status, and prestige. Higher education defends the notion that knowledge and expertise are important for problem solving in the society. Higher education assumes that science, scientific methods, and the science sensibility are better means for discovering and creating truth than tradition. Higher education treats high culture as separate from and better than popular culture. Higher education values differentiation, recognizing that there are different discourse communities in the academy and that there is a difference between the inside and outside of institutions of higher education. While valuing diversity, colleges and universities treasure community and institutional autonomy.

Higher education assumes that middle-class values are good for society and for individuals, that parents and students want middle-class status, and that the road to upward mobility and the way to prevent downward mobility or skidding is through education. Higher education assumes that progress is possible and good, and that the way to move in that direction is through education. Higher education assumes that community is good, that some fundamental set of values, some basic accepted rules of conduct, and some sense of limits are good.

However, over time, modernism has displayed another, quite negative face. Although modernism has been a spectacularly successful and powerful orientation, it has also organized and constructed its own serious failures. For Max Weber (a doubting, skeptical modernist), reason in the form of instrumental rationality has generated the overorganized modern economic order which in turn has imprisoned people in an "iron cage" of work incentives. As Weber writes, "This order is now bound to the technical and economic conditions of machine production which today determine the lives of all the individuals who are born into this mechanism . . . with irresistible force" [97, p. 181]. The highly rationalized world Weber described as our modern fate is characterized as having lost the sense of enchantment that tradition provides for societies [41, p. 155]. The Frankfort school of critical social theory, with such luminaries as Theodore Adorno, Max Horkheimer [1], and Herbert Marcuse [71] offered pessimistic interpretations of modernism, seeing in it the rise of faceless, characterless mass societies. Even Jürgen Habermas, the current generation's premier Frankfort school intellectual who believes in Enlightenment values and goals and whose project is to save modernism, sees rationality as having strayed from its proper direction, resulting in highly dysfunctional institutions in the world society [51, 52].

Many of the Frankfort school's ideas have been incorporated into the postmodern diatribe against modernism. Instrumental rationality in its current postmodern reading is seen as having forged the consumer society, in which commodification, the definition of persons and activities solely in terms of their market value, has become dominant. Science is now associated as much with death through annihilation, environmental problems, and uncontrollable technology as it is with progress and benign innovation.

Richard Bernstein reminds us that the terms, "reason" and "rationality" now "evoke images of domination, oppression, repression, patriarchy, sterility, violence, totality, totalitarianism, and even terror" [12, p. 32]. Thus, fascism, nazism, and communism, as well as democracy, are associated with modernism. As Stephen White writes, "The costs of Western modernization or rationalization are being progressively reestimated upward" [99, p. 5]. In this negative image of modernism, postmodernists deeply implicate higher education.

Postmodernism and Poststructuralism: Derrida and Foucault

Postmodernism may be seen as a perspective [67, p. 14], a means for understanding the conditions we now live in. It may also be viewed as a new epoch, or a new historical era. In either case, the major concepts and ideas of postmodernism provide a devastating attack on modernism. This assault renders as questionable the major assumptions and assertions of our modern culture. That is, it makes problematic what is taken for granted in a wide range of topics. The postmodern problematic zeroes in on hierarchies of any kind—and hierarchies are inherent in modern life—with the view that "there are no natural hierarchies, only those we construct" [57, p. 13].

Postmodernism interrogates the modern system, which is built on continuing, persistent efforts, to totalize or unify, pointing out that totalization hides contradictions, ambiguities, and oppositions and is a means for generating power and control. Institutions of modernity come under critical postmodern scrutiny, and among the primary institutions open to questioning are the college and university. To see postmodernism as a way of understanding the limits of modernism is to view our world in the midst of profound change and to concentrate on the disillusionment we are experiencing with some of our deepest assumptions and cherished hopes relating to our most important institutions. We seek rational solutions in a world that increasingly distrusts reason as a legitimate approach to problem solving. We try to move forward in our lives and through our institutions in a milieu of declining faith in the possibility of progress. We act on dimly apprehended foundational assumptions, for example, faith in science and the scientific method, even as we grow increasingly suspicious of all grand narratives.

Postmodernism as a perspective (often printed "postmodern" rather than "post-modern," defined as an era) borrows extensively from the definitions and concepts of poststructuralism. Thus it focuses upon the indeterminacy of language, the primacy of discourse, the decentering and fragmentation of the concept of self, the significance of the "other," a recognition of the tight, unbreakable power/knowledge nexus, the attenuation of a belief in metanarratives, and the decline of dependence upon rationalism. Poststructuralist thought developed in France in the 1970s as a reaction to the French structuralist attempts to build a rigorous, objective, scientific analysis of social life through the discovery of the underlying, deep structural linguistic and social rules that organize language and social systems [13, pp. 18, 20]. Poststructuralist concepts have been appropriated, broadened, and extended by the international movement of postmodernism, which has applied the poststructural ideas to a much larger number of topics in its wide-ranging attacks on modernism.

What do these poststructural/postmodern concepts mean and what is their significance for society and for higher education? Much of this orientation is related to poststructuralist views of language and of how language is used. Two poststructuralists who have transformed our ideas about language are Jacques Derrida and Michel Foucault.

Derrida

Derrida attacks basic modernist assumptions about languages and reality. The usual assumption is that there are thoughts and realities prior to language and that language is the vehicle for communicating ideas and of describing reality. He asserts, instead, that language comes before knowledge and that the meaning of words is constantly changing. Language becomes indeterminate and difficult to control. For Derrida, the meanings of words are permanently in flux. Word meanings continually escape their boundaries as these meanings are negotiated and renegotiated in social settings. The Derridian strategy is to search out and illuminate the internal contradictions in language and in doing so show how final meaning is forever withheld or postponed in the concepts we use. The means for carrying out this project is deconstruction [29].

Deconstruction involves a close reading of a text,[2] examining and bringing to the surface concealed hierarchies and hidden oppositions, inconsistencies, and contradictions in the language [29]. The method of deconstruction includes "demystifying a text, tearing it apart to reveal its internal, arbitrary hierarchies and its presuppositions" [86, p. 120].

The central arguments of a text are ignored as deconstruction looks to the margins and to that which has been omitted, erased, or withheld. The Derrida position is that "the binary oppositions governing Western philosophy and culture (subject/object, appearance/reality, speech/writing, and so on) work to construct a far-from-innocent hierarchy of values which attempts not only to guarantee truth, but also serves to exclude and devalue allegedly inferior terms or positions. This binary metaphysics thus works to positively position reality over appearance, speech over writing, men over women, or reason over nature, thus positioning negatively the supposedly inferior term" [13, p. 21].

The purpose of deconstruction is not simply to unmask or illuminate hierarchies and demonstrate their arbitrariness, to delegitimate them, but to do so without replacing them with other hierarchies and so create tensions without resolving them. Thus, as Rosenau points out, "deconstruction attempts to undo, reverse, displace, and resituate the hierarchies in polar opposites . . . But the goal is to do more than overturn oppositions, for this would permit new hierarchies to be reappropriated" [86, p. 120].

Deconstruction and higher education. Derrida's powerful attack upon hierarchies of the modernist world can be used with great effect in challenging higher education's hierarchies and illuminating its exclusions. Higher education is composed of hierarchies. The disciplines are arranged within institutions of higher education in a loose hierarchy of discourses[3] that give preference to the physical sciences over the social sciences and humanities and to the arts and sciences over education and other marginal professions.

Research is above teaching, doctoral studies over masters, and bachelors over associate degree studies. Private education is over public education, professors over students, administrators over professors, tenured over non-tenured professors. The list is long. To deconstruct these discourses is to indicate first that they are social constructions and did not emerge from some inherent, universalistic rationale or logic. It is to point out the hidden contradictions, inconsistencies, and ambiguities within academia, to show just how much hierarchy is based on what look like arbitrary exclusions, and to illuminate how much they serve to put other ideas and people on the margin or exclude them entirely. Concepts that lend credence to faith in reason, science, progress, and the Enlightenment are privileged in the modernist world, and especially in the university and college. Once their legitimacy is called into question, all sorts of hierarchies become suspect in the university—science over the humanities, high culture over popular culture, literary canons over wider definitions of literature, classical over popular music. This erosion of faith in the legitimacy of the assumptions embedded in the hierarchical academic order provides a series of cracks in the dominant culture of the university, encouraging historically marginal groups, such as persons of color, gay and lesbian groups, and women, to claim space in these institutions, even as this erosion delegitimates the dominant modernist culture for its assumptions of superiority.

The delegitimation goes well beyond simply allowing space for those individuals traditionally thought to be marginal in the universities. Delegitimation encompasses harsh questioning of universities and colleges about their reward structures, the purposes and practices in which they are engaged, and the claims of those now in positions of power and responsibility to their right of office. If the hierarchies of academia are falsely assembled, are arbitrary, and illegitimate, the question becomes why are these particular professors and administrators, rather than others, now sitting in their superior positions benefiting from the modernist academic hierarchies?

Colleges and universities are particularly susceptible to the postmodern critique that denigrates hierarchy because institutions of higher education see themselves as institutions with the responsibility to create and distribute knowledge, civic values, and meaning to new generations. They act as sorting mechanisms and as institutions that maintain the middle-class status of students (class being another modernist hierarchical concept), while also creating the means for upward mobility of students. Institutions of higher education are the generators of large numbers of professionals and of the professional sensibility. Expertise, the primary attribute of professionals, is suspect, for it places clients and lay people in an inferior position. These concepts, when directed toward higher education, provide a powerful delegitimating lever that interrogates the purposes, structure, and activities of higher education as it now operates in its modernist context.

Deconstruction provides reasons and arguments supporting the accusations that excluded groups make against institutions of higher education. Some authors are particularly good at providing the ideas and language that speak to marginality. No one is clearer in pointing out the exclusionary character of modern language and institutions than Derrida. As Richard Bernstein says of Derrida, "Few contemporary writers equal him in his sensitivity and alertness to the multifarious ways in which the 'history of the West'—even in its institutionalization of communicative practices—has always tended to silence differences, to exclude outsiders and exiles, those who live on the margins. . . . This is one of the many good reasons why Derrida 'speaks' to those who have felt the pain and suffering of being excluded by the prevailing hierarchies embedded in the text called 'the history of the West'—whether they be women, Blacks, or others bludgeoned by exclusionary tactics" [12, pp. 51, 52].

However, this depriviledging is dangerous and can easily backfire for marginal groups. If there are no legitimate bases for rewarding the privileged in our society, there are also no foundational standards for rewarding marginal groups. There are no grounded assumptions or moral grounds from which marginal groups can claim privilege. From this postmodern perspective there is no compelling reason for controlling groups to give ground to others.

Merit and community. Higher education is a modern institution that has the concept "merit" deeply embedded in its value structure. Derrida's hostility toward hierarchies is an attack on merit, for merit creates standards that separate and hierarchicalize those who meet them from those who do not. Deconstruction can be used to demonstrate that merit or standards are not only capricious and without foundation, but are arbitrarily exclusive in their consequences. They instantly create marginality. Because higher education places high value on scholarly merit—attempting to find a way to keep it, but make it fair—it is constantly structurally creating and justifying exclusions. Derrida would not eliminate merit, although in his thought there are no foundational reasons for claiming that one standard for merit is better than another; rather, he would keep a continuous tension between what is viewed as merit and what is not, thus making the merit boundaries more open and presumably less exclusionary.

Deconstruction celebrates differences, but refers not to the difference of heterogeneity, which is intrinsic to modernism, but to the difference of disruption, tension, and the withholding of closure. The modernist idea of community also celebrates difference, but emphasizes that which unites people, smooths over disruption, and places limits on the depth and intensity of differences. The creation of community generally is a process of setting boundaries, and this means that communities always have those excluded and those created as marginals. An extreme anticommunity perspective is developed by Iris Marion Young, who believes that a politics of difference should be organized which would have as its chief characteristics "inexhaustible heterogeneity" and "openness to unassimilated otherness," a system that would completely eliminate community with its exclusions of others [102, p. 301].

Higher education promotes the idea of community and is interested in community on several levels. Disciplines are conceived of as communities of scholars, and institutions are viewed as communities of scholars, students, and administrators. The promotion of community is a constant in higher education, and one of its assumptions is that it fosters a concept of citizenship that is an idea of community. Higher education teaches and promotes identification with the larger differentiated community.

Foucault

Both Derrida and Foucault give discourse theory a central place in their writings. Foucault deals initially with what he terms an archaeological approach to discourse. Foucault asks, "What rules permit certain statements to be made; what rules order these statements; what rules permit us to identify some statements as true and some false; what rules allow the construction of a map, model, or classificatory system [78, p. 69].

Archaeology. Archaeology seeks out the rules that designate what will be true or false in a discourse and create the possibility of organizing a discipline, a field of knowledge such as physics or psychology. When academic disciplines, especially the human sciences, are looked at in this archaeological way, they have histories that do not resemble mainstream, modernist notions of how history explains things. Instead of smooth continuities and totalizing explanations, one gets discontinuities and disruptions. As Gibson Burrell points out, Foucault's "aim is to attack great systems, grand theories and vital truths, and to give free play to difference, to local and specific knowledge, and to rupture, contingency, and discontinuity. In Foucault, there is no unity of history, no unity of the subject, no sense of progress, no acceptance of the History of Ideas" [15, pp. 223, 229].

Genealogy. Foucault later expanded his archaeological approach to concentrate on the power/knowledge relationships that exist in institutions. For Foucault, knowledge and power are inextricably bound together. That is, there is no knowledge without a power question arising, and no power without knowledge. This power/knowledge connection has a confounding effect on our understanding of knowledge in the academy. If Foucault is correct about the power/knowledge relationship, there can never be anything approaching neutral, objective knowledge. That is, whatever knowledge comes from research in the disciplines is always implicated in power considerations. This is very different from the modernist assumption in higher education that each discipline can be a separate and independent intellectual enterprise that exists above and outside of politics. Rather, Foucault and the postmodernists view disciplines as completely involved with politics, economics, culture, and other external influences. In Foucault's terms, this means there is little interest in the substance of a discipline or in whether it has legitimate rules for determining meritorious from mediocre work. The interest is only in what power relations are permitted and assumed. The power/knowledge relationship is embedded in discourses, and discourses are the locations where groups and individuals battle for hegemony and over the production of meaning. Disciplines become sites for power contests for control of subject matter through language. As Val Rust writes, "Discourse analysis and cultural studies are really fundamentally studies of power. They should reveal who wields power, in whose interest it is wielded, and with what effects" [89, p. 619].

Power and politics in Foucault's thought. Foucault views power not in terms of a commodity that someone or some group uses or has over others, but as a system or network. Power is pervasive, but it is not in the hands of anyone or any institution, such as the state. Thus one does not ask, Who has power? but, What are the consequences of applying power? Foucault is interested in power in terms of its results, or power at the point where it is wielded. This places his interest at the local level. The Foucaultian analysis provides a species of politics at the margin, ineluctably plural, and on the microlevel. "Foucault calls for a plurality of autonomous struggles throughout the microlevels of society, in the prisons, asylums, hospitals, and schools" [13, p. 56].

Negatively, the Foucaultian perspective is disinterested in what politically could build a larger, better society. His micropolitical perspective favors small communities at the margins of institutions, such as those formed through identity politics. Modernist notions of politics are usually couched in terms of what cross-cutting political activism would add to the larger community. Thus, modernist politics uses such categories as class, or class struggle, or the state and political party action, or the unions and union activities, categories that are justified on the basis of their commitment to an improved macrocommunity and to universals.

As Todd Gitlin argues, in a discussion that employs traditional right/left political orientations, "A troubling irony: the right, traditionally the custodian of the privileges of the few, now speaks in the general language of merit, reason, individual rights, and virtue that transcends politics, whereas much of the left is so preoccupied with debunking generalizations and affirming the differences among groups—real as they often are—that it has ceded the very language of universality that is its birthright" [45, pp. 16, 18, 19].

This politics at the microlevel, or the politics of everyday life, is significant for universities and colleges in terms of the idea of community. Institutions of higher education recognize and encourage differences among disciplines in methods, orientations, languages, and scholarly commitments by individual professors. Colleges and universities recognize that disciplinary discourses may be incommensurate. But even incommensurate academic discourses are assumed to identify with a broad, common set of values that include respect and reward for academic rigor, intellectual creativity, academic freedom, peer review, and general respect for the rules of scholarship. Incommensurate social and cultural discourses are much more difficult to encompass within academia, for institutions have trouble reconciling academic values as they are interpreted within the institutions of higher education with the incommensurate cultural values that are apparent between marginal groups and mainstream academia. The usual method for trying to create community in this situation is for colleges and universities to broaden their interpretations of merit and justice in such a way as to include other cultural values and thus preserve community through the traditional common values. But this modernist strategy in colleges and universities is failing.

For marginal groups, such modernist concepts as freedom, equality, and justice provide the vocabulary for legitimating incommensurate cultural discourses, but their meanings are so contested that they do not provide the same sense of having common values that academia assumes it has, and hence they do not provide the foundations for commitment to a larger community. The larger community values of academia and the language in which they are communicated are viewed in the Foucaultian argument as elements of a hegemonic discourse that places minorities and others at the margins of the institution and directly benefits those who created and sustain the discourse of scholarship and community. The knowledge/power nexus cuts in a different direction that also affects higher education. As Sarup points out, for Foucault "knowledge ceases to be liberation and becomes a mode of surveillance, regulation, discipline" [90, p. 73]. This view of knowledge as surveillance and discipline is in contradistinction to the modernist view that knowledge is emancipating and liberating. And it flies totally in the face of what colleges and universities are traditionally about in a modernist world, for they are the master institutions that preach freedom, liberation, and emancipation through knowledge.

Postmodernism as a Historical Period

The concepts embedded in the notion of postmodernism as a perspective feed into and provide a basis for looking at postmodernism as a new historical era. Viewing postmodernism as a new historical phase is a means for approaching a number of important questions that higher education is involved in and must deal with. To see our postmodern condition through the lens of a new era is to focus on the rapid and unfamiliar changes that are taking place in the world. Looking at postmodernism as a new era dovetails with the intense interest we have in societal change generated by the rapid approach of a new century. Postmodernism as a new era concentrates our attention on the impact of the information age, consumer society, commodification, performativity, multinational corporations, and similacra. Perhaps most disconcerting, this new age is characterized by increasingly shattered cultural orders and growing levels of disorganization in such significant institutions as the state, society, and the economy.

Lyotard

Although Lyotard sees postmodernism as a condition or mood, not an epoch [67, p. xiii], he can be viewed as a transitional figure because his analysis takes on characteristics of a historical period. Lyotard picks up the assault upon modernism, particularly in terms of a denigration of rationalism, but concentrates on what he calls "metanarratives"' those large universals that undergird our orientations toward the modern world, the grand stories that provide the foundation for modern life. Metanarratives are the foundational stories that legitimate discourses and are criticized by postmodernists as locking society in a prison of restrictive, totalizing systems of thought. In Stephen K. White's description, metanarratives, "focusing on God, nature, progress, and emancipation, are the anchors of modern life" [99, p. 5]. For Lyotard the postmodern is defined "as incredulity toward metanarratives" [67, p. xxiv]. The erosion of belief in metanarratives fits with the Derridian and Foucaultian notions that language is not a path to truth or a means for describing reality, but simply a series of discourses socially created in varying contexts, none of which have superior truth claims. The disbelief in metanarratives again foregrounds a questioning of hierarchies, including those of higher education.

The questioning of metanarratives is important for higher education, because metanarratives are the foundation of modern university and college life, especially as they undergird the scientific-technological aspects of higher education, but also higher education's assumptions about progress, knowledge, and socialization. Unlike Derrida and Foucault, who avoid the term postmodern in describing their works, Lyotard writes specifically about postmodernism, and his most influential book is called *The Postmodern Condition: A Report on Knowledge* [67].

Lyotard is interested in the changing circumstances of contemporary science and technology in what he sees as a postmodern society. This concern allows him to look at a number of questions about society, many of which are related to university and college organization and circumstances. He specifically discusses the changing university and the future status of the professor. Lyotard predicts a dim future for higher education as it is now constituted. His notion that performativity is the only viable criterion in a postmodern world means that higher education's sole reason for existence is its ability to contribute directly to the performativity of the economic system. For Lyotard, the task of universities and colleges is to "create skills, and no longer ideals. . . . The transmission of knowledge is no longer designed to train an elite capable of guiding the nation towards its emancipation, but to supply the players capable of acceptably fulfilling their roles at the pragmatic posts required by its institutions" [67, p. 48].

Teaching by professors is still necessary, but it is reduced to instructing students in the use of the terminals [67, p. 50]. If you do not have legitimate grand narratives, you do not need professors to teach them, but you can rely upon machines to teach students what they need to know in a performatively driven society. Lyotard is quite explicit about the death of the professorship. In the cases of both the production and transmission of knowledge, he asserts that "the process of delegitimation and the predominance of the performance criteria are sounding the knell of the Professor" [67, p. 53].

Like Foucault, Lyotard is concerned with questions of power and language. Lyotard has an interest in legitimacy and how it is created. He sees discourses as language games in which players' speech is viewed as "moves" directed at legitimating their language game and proving its superiority over other language games. As Keane describes Lyotard's perspective, "players within language games are always embedded in relations of power—power here understood as the capacity of actors wilfully to block or to effect changes in speech activities of others within the already existing framework of a language game which itself always prestructures the speech activities of individuals and groups" [62, p. 86].

The discourse of science and higher education. Modernism is associated with science and the scientific mode of thinking and doing, and science is tightly connected to higher education. For one hundred fifty years, higher education has promoted the concept that science and its forms, science research, scientific methods, and the progress that results from science, are the principal guarantors of the legitimacy of higher education. The belief in science and its assumptions and methods has provided the basis for creating and justifying the prestige hierarchies among and within colleges and universities and the reward structures among academics. Much of higher education's argument for autonomy is premised on scientific values relating to creativity, objectivity, and neutrality. The social sciences strive for legitimacy through claiming that what they do is scientifically grounded. Even where science and the scientific method are not dominant, as in the humanities, there are constant debates concerning whether the humanist disciplines ought to be more scientific, and if they decide that they are not, they are still consumed by notions of discovery, of objectivity, and of cumulative knowledge, notions that are derived from perceptions of how science proceeds in its work. Higher education as it is currently organized, constituted, and structured is committed to a search for truth, is dependent for its legitimacy on a belief in the scientific method and science as a way of obtaining this goal. Such a search has the assumption that as the search becomes more sophisticated and knowledge information accumulates, progress will result. Problems will be solved. Life will become better. Science has operated as an independent sphere with its own rules, much of its own structure, and though not unaffected by the market, government, and the institutions in which it has been housed, it has, nevertheless, been viewed as clearly differentiated from them. It has had a superior position in the academy, has lived by its own standards of excellence and good work, and has been able to impose its perspectives on large areas within the academy.

In the postmodern world this position is jeopardized. Lyotard, who writes extensively on science and technology in *The Postmodern Condition*, denigrates this view of science on two grounds. First, science is just one more metanarrative and has no more legitimacy than any other metanarratives. Second, science in the postmodern world becomes judged by efficiency and effectiveness and turns into technology. Postmodernism thus makes science and the scientific method problematic, less a basis for legitimacy or for determining good work. Science is viewed, not as a value-free, disassociated form of knowledge, above and outside of social and political values, but as a discourse like any other discourse, a political terrain where power struggles take place for the control of meaning. If science is a discourse equal to any other discourse, then there is no meritocratic basis for privileging science over creationism, astrology, or any number of noxious theories about race and gender. It means there is no rational argument for keeping any discourse from finding a place in the curricula of colleges and universities. What is left is a series of power positions and contested viewpoints vying for a place in academe with no real set of standards by which to judge their relative merits and no rules to follow that allow anyone to say yes or no to questions of inclusion and exclusion in the curriculum. This is the extreme consequence of relativism that is involved in extreme readings of the postmodern critique.

Performativity. In the postmodern world described by Lyotard, performativity is viewed as the most powerful criterion for judging worth, taking the place of agreed upon, rational, modernist criteria for merit. Crook, Pakulski, and Waters describe performativity as "the capacity to deliver outputs at the lowest cost, replaces truth as the yardstick of knowledge" [24, p. 31]. That is, efficiency and effectiveness become the exclusive criteria for judging knowledge and its worth in the college and university. Knowledge becomes "technically useful knowledge." The criterion of technically useful knowledge is its efficiency and its translatability into information (computer) knowledge. Therefore, the questions, "'Is it true?', 'Is it just?', 'Is it morally important?' become reduced to 'Is it efficient?', 'Is it marketable?', 'Is it sellable?', 'Is it translatable into information quantities?'" [62, p. 108].

Baudrillard

Baudrillard also identifies himself as a postmodern thinker. His significance lies in what he has to say about the consumerism, fashion, and the media/information society. His ideas about simulation, implosion of boundaries, hyperreality, and simulacra destabilize our sense of the boundaries within institutions of higher education and between them and the external world [6].

His political stance is similar to that of Derrida, Foucault, and Lyotard. That is, he is inter-

ested in micropolitics, politics at the margin, with emphasis upon differences. In Baudrillard's case, it is a micropolitics that emphasizes lifestyle and communication changes that would free individuals from a repressive modernist society. For Baudrillard, the postmodern society is a world in which the images or simulations, which are an intrinsic aspect of computerization, media, and information processing generally, replace modern production as the basis for organizing our lives [13, p. 118].

Perhaps the most significant of his concepts is that of implosion. This involves a process that leads to boundary collapses in a wide variety of circumstances. Implosion simply means that the boundary between a simulation and reality is erased, that is, implodes, and the basis for determining the real is gone. A telling example of postmodern implosion is the collapse of the boundary between the political and the image, in which the image of the politician in our society replaces the reality of the political. One of his most startling concepts is "hyperreality," a post modernist state in which models become the basis for determining the real, thereby replacing the real. According to Linda Hutcheon, Baudrillard "has argued that mass media has neutralized reality for us and it has done so in stages: first reflecting, then masking reality, and then masking the absence of reality, and finally, bearing no relation to reality at all. This is a simulacrum, the final destruction of meaning" [57, p. 223].

Higher education implosions in the postmodern era. If we accept Baudrillard's concept of implosion, we see in education that the collapsing of boundaries may be drastically changing the organization, purposes, and activities of higher education. As the metanarratives of progress, rationality, and science are undermined and deprivileged, the boundaries and hierarchies they sustain are weakened and move toward collapse. Thus, academic disciplines based on these metanarratives find their borders dissolving and the bases for their hierarchical structures attenuated. Also threatened are those boundaries that define the difference between the inside and outside of organizations, institutions, groups, and individuals. In the postmodern era, there is danger of the collapse of the distinction between knowledge inside the academy and outside of it, with the result that certain kinds of knowledge that used to be the monopoly of the academy are now shared with institutions outside of the academy. As Geyer writes, "Students no longer get their knowledge about the world from the universities, which are losing their 'paternal authority'. . . . TV entertainment, news and documentary spectacles, radio talk shows, and for that matter, the religious revival and the instruction that comes with it have developed a power commensurate with university education. They are our competition, replacing rapidly the remnants of civic and transcivic education that have survived the past decade" [42, p. 511].

With the collapse of boundaries between the inside and outside of the academy, there is pressure for the inclusion of new subjects waiting to be taught, brought in by groups who believe they should be a part of the curriculum without the impediment of the usual modernist criteria as a restraint. This means that the boundaries between modern differentiating curricula based on rationality, the discipline's standards, and the model that science offers are breaking down. These boundaries have always been contested and in flux. But now, curricular boundaries are contested by religious, racial, ethnic, gender, and new cultural perspectives that seek to establish their own potentially incommensurable criteria for inclusion in higher education curricula. The idea of the canon is a concept from literary studies concerning what the boundaries of a discipline should be. As the canons are contested, the boundaries of various disciplinary discourses become more vulnerable to disintegration. However, this collapsing, like other aspects of the postmodern changes, is occurring slowly and sporadically. For example, in the teaching of literature, where some of the most divisive and rancorous arguments over the canon have been occurring, the 1990 MLA biennial survey of English departments indicates that some changes have taken place, such as the introduction of feminist perspectives and heightened interest in the relationship of race, class, and gender to literature generation and interpretation. The authors go on to say, "These innovations, however, have not displaced traditional classroom goals or approaches to literary study" [39, p. 42].

Implosion of cultures and other boundary collapses. An implosion often noted in postmodern discussion is the collapse of the distinction between high culture and popular culture.

What is its significance for higher education? The postmodernist collapse of boundaries entails a mixing together of high and low culture. Intellectuals, including academic intellectuals, enter the world of popular culture and interpret it. As intellectuals become associated with popular culture and identified with it, they begin to lose their hierarchical station as experts [95, p. 4].

Another example of the collapse of the boundary between the college or university and its city environment is that campuses are now viewed as the scenes of crimes that are simply a part of the same density and pattern of crime that any urban center generates. The campus is rapidly losing its identity as an enclave. None of the racial, poverty, health, and environmental problems of the city or the surroundings of the campus can be avoided by institutions of higher education. The boundaries between city and campus continue to weaken.

Postmodernism, Economic Life, and Higher Education

Some of the most striking postmodern changes are associated with economic life viewed in terms of performativity, and these changes profoundly affect the place of higher education in the society. The changes affect what kind of education may be offered by higher education, the methods of delivery, the autonomy of the colleges and universities, and the competitive position of institutions of higher education. The postmodern society is a postindustrial society. The changes taking place are striking. The workforce is moving out of industrial production to service jobs. A primary change for United States citizens is from the centrality of work to the centrality of consumption. We now emphasize the production of information over the manufacturing of goods. Corporations are less constrained by national and state boundaries and are entering a world of multinational manufacturing and trade, relying on telecommunications networks and using foreign local work forces for producing goods and services. Large, industrial conglomerates are giving way to small, highly specialized businesses confined to single sites and run by a relatively small cadre of highly entrepreneurial owners.

Service jobs. When postmodernism is viewed as a new historical era, it illuminates the potentiality for higher education to play a much different and potentially attenuated role in the postmodern society of the future. The changes put considerable strain on the conventional purposes and activities of institutions of higher education. However, institutions of higher education respond by introducing conventional changes in curriculum, under the increasingly questionable assumption that the changes will allow institutions of higher education to continue to educate middle-class managers and professionals in hierarchically arranged, large scale, now global bureaucracies. Thus the optimistic assumption is that educating for service jobs means preparing people for professional careers, and that the information society requires large numbers of professionals at many levels to operate it. In fact, service jobs may turn out to be low-paying, noncareer-producing positions that require vocational and technical education. Although the impact of the information society is very much in a muddle at this point, there may be only a small number of opportunities for autonomous, highly skilled information professionals, what Jencks has called a "cognitariat" [60].

Multinational corporations. There is an assumption that multinational, globally oriented corporations will need many persons fluent in foreign languages, able to understand diverse cultures, willing to move easily to foreign sites which will act as way stations in the corporate ladder. Many higher education institutions are initiating programs of global studies with this scenario in mind. However, it has become more apparent with time, that multinational corporations find local work forces to have great advantages over imported American experts. Local workers are knowing about the local culture and language, will often work for lower wages and salaries, and have less desire to globe trot in order to move up the corporate ladder.

The aggressive activities of multinational corporations, the great fluidity of capital, and the increasing cross-national mobility of labor mean that multinational corporations with their Eurocentric cultures must incorporate great chunks of the cultural assumptions and, indeed, of the cultural orientations of the Third world. The global system itself may be drastically changing the culture of business. In doing so, Eurocentric culture becomes diffused and

the Eurocentric cultures of multinational corporations may be watered down.

Dirlik has a fascinating interpretation of the complex interplay of incentives, actions, and consequences that arise from what are usually perceived to be the contradictory perspectives on the multiculturalism of the academy and business. "Focusing on liberal arts institutions, some conservative intellectuals overlook how much headway multiculturalism has made with business school administrators and the managers of transnational corporations. . . . While in an earlier day it might have been Marxist and feminist radicals, with the aid of a few ethnics, who spearheaded multiculturalism, by now the initiative has passed into the hands of 'enlightened' administrators and trustees who are quite aware of the 'manpower needs' of the new economic situation. . . . Among the foremost and earliest of United States advocates of transnationalism and multiculturalism is the *Harvard Business Review*" [32, 354–55].

Consumer culture. Perhaps most foreign of all, and potentially most disruptive to the higher education curricula, is the notion that the United States is now a consumer culture. The conventional interpretation of this in higher education is that a consumer culture education prepares persons to supply consumer goods and services to a population that is awash in conspicuous displays of television and other electronic devices, a population that seeks an ever greater supply and variety of consumer goods. But the postmodern interpretation is that consumer activity is now "the cognitive and moral focus of life, the integrative bond of the society, and the focus of systemic management" [93, p. 63]. In Baudrillard's perception of postmodern society, commodities through advertising in the media, become "codes, shared systems of meaning . . . without material foundation" [24, p. 132].

Such an orientation, if it is an accurate description, would call for higher education to prepare students, not simply to be producers and sellers of consumer goods, but to be intellectually and philosophically skillful and knowing consumers. But higher education has such formidable competition for attention from the mass media that it is almost unthinkable that it would be viewed as the legitimate institution which teaches consumerism. Learning what a consumer society should or wants to consume comes not from the teachings of professors in a university or college, but from television, the information highway, or another mass media alternative.

Much of what students want to consume that higher education has supplied in the past is either in the process of erosion, for example, high culture, or can be supplied by other sources (science education, education for the professions). To say that students are extremely consumption-oriented at this time is to say that they have choices, can do comparative shopping, and can find much of what they want outside the walls of the traditional colleges or university. Institutions of higher education, over much of our history, have defined to a large extent the nature and shape of an education and have confidently and accurately assumed that the legitimacy that education conferred was not only a societal but a private good. Students as consumers are rapidly reaching a point where they are asking for a different education, and they are willing to look for this education in a variety of locations. As Robert Zemsky writes, "Students today want technical knowledge, useful knowledge, labor related knowledge in convenient, digestible packages" [103, p. 17].

At present, institutions of higher education are still able to offer legitimacy and credentials that promise to give graduates a jump start on middle-class careers. But the changes in the economy and culture make this promise highly problematic for the future. A consumer culture calls into question the assumption that the academy has a monopoly of knowledge. This delegitimates belief in professors as experts, particularly as ultimate authorities on the subjects they teach.

The Loss of State Authority in the Postmodern Era

The changes taking place that increase the power and reach of multinational organizations and the reality of a truly global world mean a potential reduction of the strength and legitimacy of the state, historically the chief financial supplier for higher education. It also means the continuation and expansion of research, but for competitive, consumer, and international interests.

In this postmodern era, institutions rely increasingly on their own efforts to acquire funding in the face of weakened state and federal agencies to grant needed resources. There is more dependence on multinational organizations for funding. A consequence is that research is judged on its ability to aid in the competitive position of the multinational organizations. A totally utilitarian view of research is a logical consequence. Science as a totally commodified enterprise becomes simply technology.

The loss of authority of governments is paradoxical. Centralization, which includes increased regulatory demands by government upon institutions and more means of control, is occurring simultaneously with loss of control by government. Persons within institutions of higher education feel increasingly burdened by the addition of more rules and stringent regulations from the state. This seems to demonstrate that the state is becoming stronger as the institutions of higher education become weaker and lose more of their autonomy. Paradoxically, the increase in regulations can be seen as a loss of authority by the state. The state, through government, has great difficulty in maintaining a taxing capacity that will allow it to do its business. Governments find it harder to make necessary but unpopular decisions. Governments are hampered by the explosion of interest groups with incompatible interests, whose collective weight easily vetoes government decisions. The state finds it more difficult to permit institutions of higher education the autonomy they need to fulfill their purposes.

Changes related to postmodernism must be viewed in a long time frame, such as the time it has taken tradition to give way to modernism. We can expect to see changes occur in fits and starts, discontinuously, with some aspects of the world in accelerated change, and some changing slowly, while in some areas of life there is no change at all. Thus, as we see that both the traditional and the modern are very much alive in today's society, we also become increasingly aware of postmodernism in our world.

What is the impact of the ideas of our four representative authors on the whole field of higher education? How can higher education retain three modern metanarratives, the ideas of merit, community, and autonomy, all three of which are extremely questionable in the post-structuralist, postmodern modes of thought? These essentialist characteristics, community, merit, and autonomy, are sorely tested by the deconstructive and postmodern descriptions of boundary collapse, the celebration of differences, the close connection of power to knowledge, the strength of micropolitics that take the form of identity politics, the rising disbelief in metanarratives, and the destruction of reality that is a part of the similacrum.

Solutions

The postmodern world is a place of contradictions. It is rife with uncertainty, ambiguity, and contradiction. In reaction to the devastating critique of modernism, a number of voices, positive and negative, have been raised that tell us how we might react to the postmodern assault and/or the postmodern world. Some see in postmodernism a return to a kind of right-wing barbarism that seeks to undo all of the progress associated with the Enlightenment. Others see postmodernism as a basis for the organization of a new, freer, more open society, capable of allowing the individual to create his/her own life in ways that have not been conceived of previously, picking and choosing parts of lifestyles that appear everywhere.

Presented next are some voices from among the many who have taken seriously and commented on the consequences of the postmodern sensibility. It is not meant to be exhaustive but to give some perspectives on postmodernism and what its meaning might be for our society.

The Social Conservative Position

This response to a postmodern society is to pull back to an ideal time, a period when the country's values were homogeneous, where hierarchy reigned, distinctions between high and low culture were ironclad and backed by money, government, tradition, and a belief in experts. The politics of nostalgia can be used to promote elements of both a premodern tradition and a modern sensibility. The argument is that we should return to a time that seems in retrospect enchanted, more stable, more predictable, and safer. One modernist source of such

enchantment is the romance of technology when viewed optimistically. Attempts to capture the enchantment of a traditional world often emanate from religious fundamentalism and political conservatism.

There is also in this social conservatism, a good deal of talk about how a particular institution previously had been characterized by community, but is now rife with fractiousness and depersonalization. But, as most marginalized persons and groups are aware, such a community was hegemonically white, male, Western European, and exclusive. Such communities marginalized minorities and women in ways that are unacceptable in a postmodern world.

Hardcore Postmodernism

At the other extreme is what Rosenau calls "skeptical postmodernism" [86, p. 15]. Its adherents use postmodernism to attack and delegitimate modernism, but essentially offer no real way to organize a society or a university. They see a collection of autonomous discourse groups operating in a university, responding entirely to their own vocabularies and sets of values, which are assumed not to be commensurable with other discourses, groups of discourses without any hierarchical principles and eschewing the values of merit and the larger college or university community. It is not clear how this apparently anarchic organization would work, because it seems clear that some discourses are going to be more equal than others, and some are going to have more power, more resources, richer vocabularies, and definitions of merit that work better than others. The result will again be hierarchy, but without the values of merit, neutrality, or objectivity. It will be based strictly on power.

Although power seems to be at the center of much of the discussion about postmodernism, in its most extreme form, postmodernism so assaults as foundational any standards for justifying the assertion of power that actual political intervention to change things has only weak reasons to motivate action by anyone. This is one of the reasons why post-post modernists, new historicists, and students of cultural studies find themselves in such an ambiguous relationship to postmodernism. They want to act, to change the modernist world, and in order to do so they need strong reasons to do so, foundational reasons.

The Project of Unfulfilled Modernism

Habermas, the defender of modernism, agrees with much of the critique by postmodernists, but sees postmodernism as a retrogressive conservative force pushing modernism toward a premodern unenlightened stage. In contrast, he seeks to develop a renewed modernism, a rationality based on communication; open, free, and engaged in by all, as a means for preserving and improving democracy, freedom, equality, and progress. Habermas has strongly asserted that "we can never escape the demand to warrant our validity claims, to defend them by the best possible arguments and reasons which are available to us. This is the 'truth' in the Enlightenment tradition that needs to be preserved and defended" [12, p. 26].

Yet Habermas has been strongly criticized for depending too much upon the possibility of building institutions that could and would sustain what sounds like perfect communication. So much dependence upon the communication process seems extremely precarious in a postmodern moment, when we are discovering the extent to which meanings shift and slide and disappear across cultures and time contexts.

Feminist Perspectives on Postmodernism

Feminists have conflicting views on postmodernism. For those who have viewed themselves as marginal and excluded because of gender, postmodern criticism is helpful. Postmodernism is used to attack many of the major philosophical perspectives of modernism, such as essentialism, foundationalism, and the assumption of universals, which have been used to create hierarchies that place women in positions inferior to men and then legitimate that subordination. Best and Kellner assert that modernist discourses since the time of Plato and Aristotle have generated "antithetical sets of characteristics that position men as superior and women as inferior. This scheme includes dichotomies between rational/emotional, assertive/passive, strong/weak, or public/private" [13, p. 207]. Feminists are sympathetic to attacks on modernist academic assumptions about neutrality and objectivity, for these assumptions are associated with the maintenance of the binary oppositions that subordinate women. Feminists find that the postmodern notions of difference, plurality—including plural selves, transience, marginality, otherness, and disjointedness—are compatible with many feminist perspectives [16, p. 108; 39, pp. 34–35]. However, feminists are concerned that the elimination of essentialist assumptions, that is, metanarratives, weakens the possibility of doing theory and of having a strong philosophical basis for political change and change in gender relations [16, pp. 107–8].

Feminists are bothered by postmodernism's potential for a relativist reading of feminist agendas and goals that severely attenuates the basis for political and social action to change the male-dominated status quo in and out of universities. As Best and Kellner point out, "Modern categories such as human rights, equality, and democratic freedoms and power are used by feminists to criticize and fight against gender domination, and categories of the Enlightenment have been effectively mobilized by women in political struggles and consciousness-raising groups; indeed, the very discourse of emancipation is a modern discourse" [13, p. 208]. Also, empiricist and standpoint theories that maintain as legitimate the modernist scientific and academic standards are negated by postmodernist perspectives.

Marxist Responses to Postmodernism

Many Marxists are critical of postmodern thought [17], but others see postmodernism as a new, higher stage of capitalism [61]. Frederick Jameson, in particular, has written extensively about postmodernism, which he sees as a historical period in which culture has penetrated all forms of social life, including economics. The postmodern era is characterized for Jameson by a global capitalism far more extensive than ever before, with considerable cultural fragmentation and differences in how a person experiences time and space [61]. His perspective takes into consideration the impact of media and information and their relationship to an almost total commodification of social and political life.

Jameson's critics see him as one who tries to introduce postmodernist concepts into a traditional foundational Marxist emphasis upon class and economic determinism. Because the concept of a Marxist metanarrative would seem to be incompatible with the anti-metanarrative orientation of postmodernism, he is accused of inconsistency in his position [13, pp. 187–88]. As Cohen writes, "The fundamental charge is that Jameson cannot have it both ways" [21, p. 339]. Nevertheless, he has greatly reinvigorated the Marxist position.

The Post-Marxist Reaction

As Post-Marxists, Ernesto Laclau and Chantel Mouffe embrace postmodernism but are interested in political action as well [65]. They attempt to find a path to change the order of things in the university and in society. This means that they accept the idea of discourse theory and assert that it implies "the commitment to show the world for what it is: an entirely social construction of human beings which is not grounded on any metaphysical 'necessity' external to it—neither God, nor 'essential forms' nor the 'necessary laws of history'" [65, p. 198].

These theorists differ from Marxists in their views on class struggle. As post-Marxists they are no longer convinced that the analysis of classes is relevant in the struggle against capitalism. They emphasize, instead, the need for a variety of forms of resistance.

Cultural Studies

Cultural studies is one of several movements—this one highly interdisciplinary—that attempt to reflect the diversity, the plurality, the diffuseness, and the blurring of boundaries of academic disciplines and between disciplines and the external world. Its orientation is to what has been called the "new politics of difference—racial, sexual, cultural, transnational" [69, p. 393]. It overlaps with postcolonial studies and uses concepts and vocabulary from postmodernism and poststructuralism. It seems to be in a fluid state by choice, and has not gelled into a discipline with its own methodology. It draws from anthropology and tends to be humanistic in its orientation. There is a strong predilection to think in terms of political action in relation to marginal groups [49].

New Historicism

In the aftermath of the powerful impact of poststructuralism and postmodernism upon

English departments in the nineteen-seventies, literary studies in the United States began to focus on the historical, political, and cultural contexts in which literary texts are written and read [72, p. 392]. The major figure leading this movement was Stephan Greenblatt, who coined the term "new historicism" to describe this form of literary criticism [9, p. 32]. Retaining many of the concepts from postmodernism, such as Foucault's ideas about power, disbelief in the metanarratives related to objectivity or neutrality, new historicist scholars are particularly concerned about the boundaries that result from the continual struggle for control over meaning in literary studies. New historicists penetrate the borders that separate literary studies from history, anthropology, art, economics, science, cultural studies, and other disciplines. "The boundaries to be reckoned with in literary studies range from national, linguistic, historical, generational, and geographical to racial, ethnic, social, sexual, political, ethical, and religious" [47, p. 4].

New historicists are accused by some feminists of speaking in a "neutral, authoritative, putatively interest-free voice" (10, p. 93). Conservative critics deplore the new historicist's politicization of literary studies and are hostile to the boundary collapse that seems to eliminate "the distinction between good art, bad art, and non-art" [9, p. 32].

Postcolonialism

The postcolonial perspective has developed from the efforts of third world intellectuals. They want to dismantle Eurocentrism, which has in the past dominated not only the territories of the third world, but also their histories, their perceptions of self, and their political lives. Their aim is to "abolish all distinctions between center and periphery as well as other 'binarisms' that are allegedly a legacy of colonial(ist) ways of thinking and to reveal societies in their complex heterogeneity and contingency" [32, p. 329].

Postcolonialism is related to postmodernism in that metanarratives are repudiated, which means that the premises and concepts of European enlightenment, and therefore of modernism, are deeply criticized. Postcolonialists have a strong affinity for local politics, local histories, and fragmentation of the national into the local. A strong criticism of the postcolonial approach is that "within the institutional site of the First World academy, fragmentation of earlier metanarratives appears benign (except to hidebound conservatives) for its promise of more democratic, multicultural, and cosmopolitan epistemologies. In the world outside the academy, however, it shows in murderous ethnic conflict, continued inequalities among societies, classes, and genders, and absence of oppositional possibilities that, always lacking in coherence, are rendered even more impotent than earlier by the fetishization of difference, fragmentation, and so on" [32, p. 347].

Postmodernism and Chaos Theory

An optimistic perspective on postmodernism links it with chaos theory. Both postmodern and chaos theory give center stage to ideas about disorder, indeterminacy, undecidability, and fragmentation in their emphasis upon complexity. But in its two most frequently argued versions, that is, order hidden in chaos and order rising out of chaotic systems [54, p. 12], chaos theory gives a structure and hope for controlling complexity that is not found in several of the reactions to postmodernism discussed above—for example, hardcore postmodernism, social conservatism, and new historicism.

In an optimistic reading of postmodernism, the affinity with chaos theory is striking. What could be more optimistic for the postmodern emphasis upon the marginal and the local than the concept of nonlinearity, in which small causes result in large consequences (the butterfly effect—that is, the butterfly flapping its wings in China through a long, complex chain of causes and effects results in a hurricane in Guatemala). It would seem to give hope to a number of politically conscious groups whose focus is the micropolitical stage, but who seek large changes in the society, such as postcolonialists, those interested in cultural studies, and post-Marxists. At the same time, however, the idea of the butterfly effect from chaos theory should lead to pessimism for those with specific political agendas, because it emphasizes that those who initiate local actions will have no power to predict or control the consequences that follow on the macrolevel.

But the most important convergence, or relationship, between chaos theory and post-modernism lies in the area where one branch of chaos theory emphasizes the possibility of the creation of order from disorder. This concept when transferred to postmodernist conceptions of society, or of narratives and texts, provides strong reason for using deconstruction to attack seemingly settled metanarratives, to generate discontinuities, and to point to the void that lies beneath language. Chaos theory seems to promise that out of the nothingness that results from deconstructing the language, will arise a new, albeit tenuous, and constantly shifting order that will provide space for new voices and new perspectives to be heard and granted legitimacy.

Border Crossing and Border Pedagogy

Henry A. Giroux combines postmodernisin, feminism, postcolonialism, and culture studies to promote a social, cultural, political, educational agenda that invites teachers, students, and cultural workers to critique, then challenge and oppose the institutions, the knowledge claims of disciplines, and the social relationships that now dominate our society. This process he calls "border crossing." The means for helping and effecting this crossing is "border pedagogy," and the purpose of border crossing is to create "border-lands" or "alternative public spaces" [44, p. 22], where the partial, shifting nature of negotiated and constructed realities allows students, among others, "to rewrite their own histories, identities, and learning possibilities" [44, p. 30]. These constructed border-lands are realms where democratic political and ethical revolutionary battles are to be waged, and the values of this crusade are to be firmly grounded in what appear to be modernist readings of such values as freedom, equality, liberty, and justice [44, p. 32].

Postmodern language is invoked when the author discusses how educators might understand marginality, the life world of the Other, and the positive qualities of difference and radical pluralism. While border pedagogy speaks of revolutionary change in society, it takes a long and benign road to that end by focusing first on the transformation of individuals; only later, when radical changes in individuals have occurred, will quick changes in society and its institutions happen.

The Liberal, Pragmatist Approach

Liberal thinking continues to dominate higher education today, and liberalism is quintessentially modernist in its orientation and in its effects. It is clear that this approach does not dismantle the ideas of merit, democracy, progress, science, and rationality, but expands and modifies them so that new ideas and orientations will be accommodated. The strategy in current higher education thinking, in an era of greatly increasing multicultural consciousness, is to redouble efforts to bring marginal persons and ideologies into an expanded modernist college and university. Mainstream educators assume that given educational opportunities and access, ethnic, minority, and religious groups and individuals will be socialized into liberal modernist culture. Administrators and faculty hope that this strategy will change the structure and life of the college and university, but not the metanarratives.

This solution is attractive in that it preserves merit, autonomy, and community, but it does require considerable modification to have credibility with the marginal and excluded groups to whom it is directed. Richard Rorty's distinction between public and private life provides a possible justification for the use of a liberal, pragmatic approach that is postmodern in orientation, strong, but flexible, yet retains room for merit, community, and autonomy. In the Rorty perspective, such modernist Enlightenment concepts should be fostered, not on the basis of any objective or foundational superiority, but because they are historically, traditionally, and habitually shared by enough people in academe to make it worthwhile to preserve them, albeit not in as rigid a basis as before. Rorty takes his justification from Jefferson's view of politics and religion: "Jefferson maintained that religion is essentially 'irrelevant to social order but relevant to, and possibly essential to individual perfection.' The gist of this insight, formulated as the 'Jefferson compromise,' is that any ideas used to shape public policy, which are bound to some larger commitments—whether religious, philosophical, or ideological—must be capable of defense in terms of views and traditions widely shared by a given polity. If such ideas cannot be defended on these grounds, then they must be rebuffed and the individual must sacrifice her conscience on the 'altar of public expediency.'

Politics is about common-sensical argument that appeals to the values and traditions shared by a given 'public' and commitment which falls outside this grouping, or cannot be translated to appeal to citizens must be relegated to the private realm.... This direction reflects his deep misgivings about philosophy as well as his sense that people could agree about a wide range of problems and share common practices while maintaining vastly different cultural and ethnic backgrounds as well as religious and philosophical convictions" [100, p. 553].

However, the feminist scholar Nancy Frazer is strongly critical of Rorty's separation of the public and private spheres. Feminists argue that the private is the public. From this perspective, practical politics have always emanated from what modernists have thought of as nonpolitical, that is, "the domestic and the personal" [100, p. 555]. Thus, if the private and the public are separated, the result is the retention of the modernist status quo with its built-in superior/inferior oppositions.

Nevertheless, Rorty does address this problem through his version of pragmatism and irony. As Wicks points out, the ironist "acts to negotiate the boundaries of the private and the public" [100, p. 554]. Ironists are especially sensitive to and capable of showing us where we do not understand our biases. "We may expand the logical space of reasons to include, and socially embrace, alternative understanding of practices that do not oppress. It is this capacity for empathetic understanding, vocabulary switching, and metaphor construction which makes the role of the ironist . . . so vital to oppressed groups" [100, p. 557].

This perspective does two things for the maintenance of the college and university and their values of merit, community, and autonomy. It expands the space for having multiple definitions for the three terms, while perhaps indicating limits to what those definitions might contain. At the same time, as with Jefferson's desire to keep religion out of politics, we can justify severely limiting the inclusion as truth in the curriculum, assumptions inherent in fundamentalist religions, for example, or contained in extreme ideological positions.

But for those who have been heavily influenced by the postmodern critique, the foundational premises of liberalism do not have the legitimacy they used to have. This is why Rorty is significant. He believes in the postmodern critique but asks of us that we embrace a liberal stance, knowing full well that it does not provide the foundations that modern notions of liberalism assume but only that its practical consequences are better than other ideologies. But others, particularly Richard Bernstein, add an especially significant caveat: the necessity for dialogue. In fact, Rorty, Bernstein, Derrida, Habermas, all place a heavy burden on listening and dialogue.

The Legacy of Postmodern Thought for Higher Education

An important consequence of postmodern thought is that almost no responsible scholar today is unaffected by the arguments that displace essentialism, or metanarratives. Postmodernism makes us aware of the destabilization and uncertainty that we confront not only in society, but in higher education. We are in a crisis in which the standard categories of modernism fail to account for—that is, to explain and make predictable—the conditions we face in the world today. The specter of relativism hangs over all our institutions. Higher education is not an exception. It cannot act as though it spoke truths; it can argue only that what it does is useful, but not that it is true.

The modernist orientation is to resolve problems; the postmodern perspective not only points to the contradictions in discourses, but makes a virtue of preserving that essential tension. It may be that opposing perspectives need to be kept alive and in tension with the dominant model. This would mean that institutions of higher education must be able to sustain and cope permanently with considerable unresolved conflict and contradiction.

If there is a transformation in higher education, what should it be? Is there a need for a set of values that transcend group values, for a vocabulary that will speak to all groups within the academy? Or should there be a wide open conglomeration of presumably incommensurate values, ethics, standards? Some poststructuralist thought seems to indicate that we already have this incommensurability among discourses. The destruction of the belief in eter-

nal verities and the attenuation of the drive to search for truth mean that higher education's task may be to pay much more attention to values, what they mean, where they come from, what their function is, and how to forge new values that fit the higher education world and its mission.

Because the borders of colleges and universities are becoming more permeable in the postmodern world and the great sustainers of the independence of higher education, the state and governments, are becoming weaker, institutions need to find ways of maintaining autonomy in the face of multinational corporate resources and power, the debilitating effects of the increased proliferation of active interest groups, and the encroachment of extreme local power.

In the world of simulacra and the power that comes from creating images, the universities' task may be to seek and sustain a kind of authenticity of information and knowledge. In this it needs to create a consistent and useful concept of merit; it cannot rely as heavily upon the strictures of science or the rules of a broken canon. But it needs to sustain the value of merit and find with all the contradictions, the plural voices, the lack of a sense of progress, and the continual tension an interest in and pursuit of means for measuring, judging, and rewarding merit. As the boundary between higher education and the market collapses, some means for organizing and sustaining autonomous sanctuaries, oases, or enclaves in universities should be found that do not simply respond to the drive for performativity and the standards of the market. Institutions of higher education need ways to construct and sustain community, and community at several levels: community on the campus and community in the larger society, a commitment to citizenship.

The emphasis upon the other, the marginal, the outsider, in postmodern thought needs to be kept in the foreground in higher education. Colleges and universities need to find ways of encompassing the other, of taking in marginal people and ideas. However, it should not be done in the usual liberal strategy of simply adding courses on multinationalism, women's studies, and cultural studies. These need to be included in academia more on the basis of their own standards. But the argument here is that this inclusion does not mean that the search for and creation of standards of merit is compromised. An important means for ensuring this is to follow the advice that a number of postmodern writers have offered, namely, to listen very hard and openly. As Cornel West has written, "I hope that we can overcome the virtual de facto segregation in the life of the mind in this country, for we have yet actually to create contexts in which black intellectuals, brown intellectuals, red intellectuals, white intellectuals, feminist intellectuals, genuinely struggle with each other" [98, p. 696].

At the same time, we need to pay attention to Richard Bernstein's caution, "There can be no dialogue, no communication unless beliefs, values, commitments, and even emotions and passions are shared in common. . . . Dialogical communication presupposes moral virtues—a certain 'good will' at least in the willingness to really listen, to seek to understand what is genuinely other, different, alien, and the courage to risk one's more cherished prejudgments. But too frequently this commonality is not really shared, it is violently opposed" [12, p. 51].

Just how difficult the process of authentic listening to "others" and creating and sustaining meaningful dialogue is, may be illustrated by U.S. business as it becomes globalized. We must face the fact that moral boundaries may blur as we face a world in which the center, the Eurocentric center, is in transition, perhaps moving to the periphery, while the marginal is becoming central. Thus, a business overseas may encounter the moral dilemma of responding to the situation in Saudi Arabia, in which "it is illegal to hire female managers for most jobs" [33, p. 11]. The lines of morality become very fuzzy indeed. A kind of in-between moral relativism may result. Thus, "If Thai tolerates the bribery of public officials, then Thai tolerance is no worse than Japanese or German intolerance. . . . If Switzerland fails to find insider trading morally repugnant, then Swiss liberality is no worse than American restrictiveness" [33, p. 11].

Although no other institution in our society is as capable of listening and of dialogue as the colleges and universities, institutions of higher education find themselves confronting similar problems as they seek to relate to other cultures, internationalize the curriculum, and enter also into the globalized world. It is not just a matter of responding with open arms to different dress and celebrations of new holidays, or of taking in new languages and literatures; it is dealing fairly but firmly with customs and values that have been morally repugnant to higher education.

Conclusion

The term postmodern is disappearing from the vocabularies of excluded groups, social scientists, humanist intellectuals, scholars of all kinds. But postmodern terms and concepts remain very much alive and in constant use. Postmodernism is disappearing because of its relativistic connotations and because, by accepting the corpus of the postmodern perspective, a group with a political agenda places its own position in jeopardy. For those drawn to the postmodern critique, who have political, cultural, social, and/or economic agendas, including feminists and ethnic and cultural groups, postmodern concepts are an extremely effective weapon to discredit and delegitimate modernism, the status quo, and colleges and universities as they are now constituted. However, if the metanarratives of modernism and higher education have no philosophical foundation, the metanarratives of marginal and excluded groups do not have essentialist foundations either. This is what engenders the profound ambivalence toward postmodernism of those who are most critical of the current modernist world. By avoiding the term "postmodernism" and by declining to identify oneself as a postmodernist, critics may and do continue to use the terminology of postmodernism, while retaining their own necessary metanarratives to justify their political, cultural agendas.

If we accept the implications of postmodernism and see it as a critique that applies both to modernists and to those critical of modernism, we can reach a point where the postmodern stricture to listen and listen very hard and long to the "other" has strong credibility. If neither side has any foundational credentials, there is space for real and continuing dialogue. The result of such listening and the pursuit of dialogue under such conditions could mean the retention in universities and colleges of the values of merit, community, and autonomy, and their justification in Rorty's terms, on the basis of agreement that these are, in some form, even as the particulars are contested, an integral part of our higher education heritage. For the excluded "others" this kind of dialogue could well provide the basis for changing the meaning and terms of merit, community, and autonomy in ways that are satisfactorily inclusive and representative of the plurality of "others'" cultures and politics. Currently, we are precariously poised between a modern/postmodern incommensurable hostility and the conditions for tough authentic dialogue. In higher education our course is clear. We need to increase and sustain the dialogue, even as we acknowledge that the tension will not, and perhaps should not, be resolved.

Notes

1. One set of notable exceptions published in the *Journal of Higher Education* involved an article by Gary Rhoades which used both Derrida and Foucault [81]. This stimulated a lively and provocative exchange (two critiques and a rebuttal) in a subsequent issue [19, 66, 82].
2. In addition to referring to the words of a speech or piece of writing, texts should be understood as events and relationships. Almost anything can be a text. This means that events and relationships as well as words can be deconstructed to indicate contradictions, tensions, oppositions, hierarchies, hidden meanings, withheld meanings, and multiple interpretations [82, pp. 34–41].
3. "Discourses are about what can be said and thought, but also about who can speak, when and with what authority ... Meanings ... arise not from language but from institutional practices, from power relations. Words and concepts change their meaning and their effects as they are deployed within different discourses" (5, p. 2).

References

1. Adorno, T., and M. Horkheimer. *The Dialectic of Enlightenment*. London: Verso, 1979.
2. Alexander, J., and S. Seidman (eds.). *Culture and Society: Contemporary Debates*. Cambridge: Cambridge University Press, 1990.
3. Aronowitz, S., and H. A. Giroux. *Postmodern Education*. Minneapolis: University of Minnesota Press, 1991.
4. Ashley, D. "Habermas and the Completion of 'The Project of Modernity'." In *Theories of Modernity and Postmodernity*, edited by B. S. Turner, pp. 88–107. Newbury Park, Calif.: Sage, 1990.
5. Ball, S. J. (ed.). *Foucault and Education*. London: Routledge, 1990.
6. Baudrillard, J. *Simulations*. New York: Semiotext(e), 1983.
7. _____. *America*. Trans. C. Turner. London: Verso, 1989.
8. Bauman, Z. "Is There a Postmodern Sociology?" *Theory, Culture, and Society*, 5 (1988), 217–37.
9. Begley, A. "The Tempest around Stephen Greenblatt." *New York Times Magazine*, 28 March 1993, p. 32.
10. Bender, J. "Eighteenth-Century Studies." In *Redrawing the Boundaries*, edited by S. Greenblatt and G. Gunn, pp. 79–99. New York: The Modern Language Association, 1992.
11. Bernstein, R. J. (ed.). *Habermas and Modernity*. Cambridge, Mass.: MIT Press, 1985.
12. _____. *The New Constellation*. Cambridge, Mass.: MIT Press, 1992.
13. Best. S., and D. Kellner. *Postmodern Theory*. New York: The Guilford Press, 1991.
14. Bloland, H. G. "Higher Education and High Anxiety: Objectivism, Relativism, and Irony." *Journal of Higher Education*, 60 (September/October 1989), 519–43.
15. Burrell, G. "Modernism, Post Modernism, and Organizational Analysis 2: The Contribution of Michel Foucault." *Organization Studies*, 9 (1988), 221–35.
16. Calas, M. B., and L. Smircich. "Re-Writing Gender into Organizational Theorizing: Directions from Feminist Perspectives." In *Women in Higher Education: A Feminist Perspective*, edited by J. Glazer, E. M. Bensimon, and B. Townsend, pp. 97–117. Needham Heights, Mass.: Ginn Press, 1993
17. Callinicos, A. *Against Postmodernism: A Marxist Critique*. Cambridge: Polity Press, 1989.
18. Cherryholmes, C. H. *Power and Criticism: Poststructural Investigations in Education*. New York: Teachers College, Columbia University, 1988.
19. Cinnamond, J. "Replicating Rhoades: Deconstructing a Deconstructionist." *Journal of Higher Education*, 62 (November/December 1991), 694–706.
20. Clegg, S. R. *Modern Organizations: Organization Studies in the Postmodern World*. Newbury Park, Calif.: Sage, 1990.
21. Cohen, W. "Marxist Criticism." In *Redrawing the Boundaries*, edited by S. Greenblatt and G. Gunn, pp. 320–48. New York: Modern Language Association, 1992.
22. Connolly, W. E. *Political Theory and Modernity*. New York: Basil Blackwell. 1989.
23. Cooper, R., and G. Burrell. "Modernism, Postmodernism, and Organizational Analysis: An Introduction." *Organization Studies*, 9 (1988), 91–112.
24. Crook, S., J. Pakulski, and M. Waters. *Postmodernization*. Newbury Park, Calif.: Sage. 1992.
25. Curti, L. "What is Real and What is Not: Female Fabulations in Cultural Analysis." In *Cultural Studies*, edited by L. Grossberg, C.

Nelson, and P. A. Treichler, pp. 134–53. New York: Routledge, 1992.

26. Davidson, A. "Archaeology, Genealogy, Ethics." In *Foucault: A Critical Reader*, edited by D. C. Hoy, pp. 221–33. Cambridge, Mass.: Basil Blackwell, 1986.

27. Denzin, N. K., and Y. S. Lincoln (eds,). *Handbook of Qualitative Research*. Thousand Oaks, Calif.: Sage, 1994.

28. _____. "Preface." In *Handbook of Qualitative Research*, edited by N. K. Denzin and Y. S. Lincoln, pp. ix–xii. Thousand Oaks, Calif.: Sage, 1994.

29. Derrida, J. *Of Grammatology*. Baltimore: Johns Hopkins University Press, 1976.

30. _____. *Positions*. Chicago: University of Chicago Press, 1981.

31. _____. *Writing and Difference*. Trans. A. Bass. Chicago: University of Chicago Press, 1978,

32. Dirlik, A. "The Postcolonial Aura: Third World Criticism in the Age of Global Capitalism." *Critical Inquiry*, 20 (1994), 329–56.

33. Donaldson, T. "Global Business Must Mind Its Morals." *New York Times* 13 February 1994, p. 11.

34. Doyle, K. "The Reality of a Disappearance: Frederick Jameson and the Cultural Logic of Postmodernism." *Critical Sociology*, 19 (1992), 113–27.

35. Dreyfus, H. L., and P. Rabinow. *Michel Foucault: Beyond Structuralism and Hermeneutics*. 2nd ed. Chicago: University of Chicago Press, 1983.

36. Esch, D. "Deconstruction." In *Redrawing the Boundaries*, edited by S. Greenblatt and G. Gunn, pp. 374–91. New York: Modern Language Association, 1992.

37. Foster, W. *Paradigms and Promises: New Approaches to Educational Administration*. Buffalo, N.Y.: Prometheus, 1986.

38. Foucault, M. *Discipline and Punish*. New York: Vintage Books, 1979.

39. Franklin, P., B. J. Huber, and D. Lawrence. "Continuity and Change in the Study of Literature." *Change*, 24 (1992), 42–48.

40. Frazer, N., and L. J. Nicholson. "Social Criticism without Philosophy: An Encounter between Feminism and Postmodernism." In *Feminism/Postmodernism*. edited by L. J. Nicholson, pp. 19–38. New York: Routledge, 1990.

41. Gerth, H. H., and C. W. Mills (eds. and translators). *From Max Weber: Essays in Sociology*. New York: Oxford University Press, 1958.

42. Geyer, M. "Multiculturalism and the Politics of General Education." *Critical Inquiry*. 19 (1993), 499–533.

43. Giddens, A. *The Consequences of Modernism*. Stanford, Calif.: Stanford University Press, 1990.

44. Giroux, H. A. *Border Crossings*. New York: Routledge 1992,

45. Gitlin, T. "The Left, Lost in the Politics of Identity" *Harpers*, 287 (1993), 16–20.

46. Glazer, J. S., E. M. Bensimon, and S. K. Townsend (eds.). *Women in Higher Education*. Needham Heights. Mass.: Ginn Press, 1993.

47. Greenblatt, S., and G. Gunn. "Introduction." In *Redrawing the Boundaries*. edited by S. Greenblatt and G. Gunn, pp. 1–11. New York: The Modern Language Association. 1992.

48. _____. *Redrawing the Boundaries*. New York: The Modern Language Association, 1992.

49. Grossberg, L., C. Nelson, and P. A. Treichler (eds.). *Cultural Studies*. New York; Routledge, 1992.

50. Habermas, J. "Modernity versus Postmodernity." *New German Critique*, 22 (1981), 3–11.

51. _____. *The Theory of Communicative Action*. Vol. 1: *Reason and Rationalization of Society*. Trans. T. McCarthy. Boston: Beacon Press, 1981.

52. _____. *The Theory of Communicative Action*. Vol. 2: *Lifeworld and System*. Trans. T. McCarthy. Boston: Beacon Press, 1987.

53. Hassan, I. *The Postmodern Turn: Essays in Postmodern Theory and Culture*. Columbus: Ohio State University Press, 1987.

54. Hayles, N. K. "Introduction: Complex Dynamics in Literature and Science." In *Chaos and Disorder*, edited by N. K. Hayles, pp. 1–33. Chicago: University of Chicago Press, 1991.

55. _____ (ed.). *Chaos and Disorder: Complex Dynamics in Literature and Science*. Chicago: University of Chicago Press, 1991.

56. Hazzard, J., and M. Parker (eds.). *Postmodernism and Organizations*. Newbury Park, Calif.: Sage, 1993.

57. Hutcheon, L. *A Poetics of Postmodernism*. London: Routledge, 1988.

58. Hoy, D. C. (ed.). *Foucault: A Critical Reader*. Cambridge, Mass.: Basil Blackwell, 1986.

59. Huyssen, A. "Mapping the Postmodern." In *Culture and Society: Cultural Debates*, edited by J. C. Alexander and S. Seidman, pp. 355–75. Cambridge: Cambridge University Press, 1990.

60. Jencks, C. *What is Post-Modernism?* 2nd ed. London: Academy, 1987.

61. Jameson, F. "Postmodernism, or the Cultural Logic of Late Capitalism." *New Left Review*, 146 (1984), 53–93.

62. Keane, J. "The Modern Democratic Revolution: Reflections on Lyotard's 'The Postmodern Condition'." In *Judging Lyotard*, edited by A. Benjamin, pp. 81–98. London: Routledge, 1992.

63. Kerrigan, W. "Seventeenth-Century Studies." In *Redrawing the Boundaries*, edited by S. Greenblatt and G. Gunn, pp. 64–78. New York: Modern Language Association. 1992.

64. Kiziltan, M. U., W. J. Bain, and A. M. Canizares. "Postmodern Conditions: Rethinking Public Education." *Educational Theory*, 40 (1990), 351–69.

65. Laclau, E., and C. Mouffe. "Post-Marxism without Apology." *New Left Review*, 66 (1987). 79–106.

66. Lokke, V., and D. Jaeckle. "Plastic Buffalo Humps: Theory as Sludge in the *Journal of Higher Education*." *Journal of Higher Education*, 62 (November/December 1991), 683–94.

67. Lyotard, J. F. *The Postmodern Condition*. Minneapolis: University of Minnesota Press, 1984.

68. McLaren, P. "Review Article—Postmodernity and the Death of Politics: A Brazilian Reprieve." *Educational Theory*, 36 (1986), 389–401.

69. Mani, L. "Cultural Theory, Colonial Texts: Reading Eyewitness Accounts of Widow Burning." In *Cultural Studies*, edited by L. Grossberg, C. Nelson, and P. A. Treichler, pp. 392–405. New York: Routledge, 1992.

70. Marcus, G. E. "What Comes (just) after 'Post'?: The Case of Ethnography." In *Handbook of Qualitative Research*, edited by N. K. Denzin and Y. S. Lincoln, pp. 563–74. Thousand Oaks, Calif.: Sage, 1994.

71. Marcuse, H. *One Dimensional Man*. Boston: Beacon Press, 1964.

72. Montrose, L. "New Historicisms." In *Redrawing the Boundaries*, edited by S. Greenblatt and G. Gunn, 392–418. New York: The Modern Language Association, 1992.

73. Nelson, C., P. A. Treichler, and L. Grossberg. "Cultural Studies: An Introduction." In *Cultural Studies*, edited by L. Grossberg, C. Nelson, and P. A. Treichler, pp. 1–16. New York: Routledge, 1992.

74. Nicholson, C. "Postmodernism, Feminism, and Education: The Need for Solidarity." *Educational Theory*, 39 (1989), 197–205.

75. Nicholson, L. J. (ed.). *Feminism/Postmodernism*. New York: Routledge, 1990.

76. Nuyen, A. T. "Lyotard on the Death of the Professor." *Educational Theory*. 42 (1992), 25–37.

77. Parker, M. "Post-Modern Organizations or Postmodern Organization Theory?" *Organization Theory*, 13 (1992), 1–17.

78. Philp, M. "Michel Foucault." In *The Return of Grand Theory in the Human Sciences*, edited by Q. Skinner, pp. 65–81. Cambridge: Cambridge University Press, 1985.

79. Rasmussen, D. M. *Reading Habermas*. Cambridge, Mass.: Basil Blackwell, 1990.

80. Reed, M. I. "Organizations and Modernity: Continuity and Discontinuity in Organization Theory.' In *Postmodernism and Organizations*, edited by J. Hazzard and M. Parker, pp. 163–82. Newbury Park, Calif.: Sage. 1993.

81. Rhoades, G. "Calling on the Past: The Quest for the Collegiate Ideal." *Journal of Higher Education*, 61 (September/October 1990). 512–34.

82. _____. "Vive la 'Differance': Poststructural Analysis of Education." *Journal of Higher Education*, 62 (November/December 1991), 706–21.

83. Rorty, R. *Contingency, Irony, and Solidarity*. New York: Cambridge University Press, 1989.

84. _____. "Habermas and Lyotard on Postmodernity." In *Habermas and Modernity*, edited by R. J. Bernstein, pp. 161–75. Cambridge, Mass.: MIT Press, 1985.

85. _____. *Objectivism. Relativism, and Truth*. New York: Cambridge University Press, 1991.

86. Rosenau, P. M. *Post-Modernism and the Social Sciences*. Princeton, N.J.: Princeton University Press, 1992.

87. Ross, A. (ed.). *Universal Abandon? The Politics of Postmodernism*. Minneapolis: University of Minnesota Press, 1988.

88. Rowe, J. C. "Postmodern Studies." In *Redrawing the Boundaries*, edited by S. Greenblatt and G. Gunn, pp. 179–208. New York: Modern Language Association, 1992.

89. Rust, V. "Postmodernism and Its Comparative Education Implications." *Comparative Education Review*, 35 (1991), 610–26.

90. Sarap, M. *An Introductory Guide to Post-Structuralism and Postmodernism*. Athens: The University of Georgia Press, 1989.

91. Skinner, Q. (ed.). *The Return of Grand Theory to the Human Sciences*. Cambridge: Cambridge University Press, 1985.

92. Smart, B. *Michel Foucault*. London: Tavistock Publications, 1985.

93. _____. *Postmodernity*. New York: Routledge, 1993.

94. Tichi, C. "American Literary Studies to the Civil War." In *Redrawing the Boundaries*, edited by S. Greenblatt and G. Gunn, pp. 209–31. New York: Modern Language Association, 1992.

95. Turner, B. S. "Periodization and Politics in the Postmodern." In *Theories of Modernity and Postmodernism*, edited by B. S. Turner, pp. 1–13. Newbury Park, Calif.: Sage, 1990.

96. _____. (ed.). *Theories of Modernity and Postmodernity*. Newbury Park, Calif.: Sage, 1990.

97. Weber, M. *The Protestant Ethic and the Spirit of Capitalism*. Trans. T. Parsons. New York: Charles Scribner Sons, 1958.

98. West, C. "The Postmodern Crisis of the Black Intellectuals." In *Cultural Studies*, edited by L. Grossberg, C. Nelson, and P. A. Treichler, pp. 689–96. New York: Routledge, 1992.

99. White, S. *Political Theory and Postmodernism*. Cambridge: Cambridge University Press, 1991.

100. Wicks, A. C. "Divide and Conquer? Rorty's Distinction between the Public and the Private." *Soundings*, 76 (1993), 551–69.

101. Winkler, K. "Scholars Mark the Beginning of the Age of 'Post-Theory'." *Chronicle of Higher Education*, 13 October 1993, pp. 9, 16, 17.

102. Young, I. M. "The Ideal of Community and the Politics of Difference." In *Feminism/Postmodernism*, edited by L. Nicholson, pp. 300–323. New York: Routledge, 1990.

103. Zemsky, R. "Consumer Markets and Higher Education." *Liberal Education*, 79 (1993), 14–17.

CHAPTER 40

THE POWER OF SYMBOLIC CONSTRUCTS IN READING CHANGE IN HIGHER EDUCATION[1]

HASAN SIMSEK

Abstract. Based on interviews with 24 faculty members at a large, public university, this article reports the use of metaphors as a new conceptual strategy to analyze change in higher education organizations. Results of the study indicate that strategic choices guiding the behavior of the organization under study and the metaphorical images held by the faculty members about their organization show a high degree of congruence. Implications for change and maintenance of enacted realities in higher education organizations are discussed.

Introduction

As the base of the organization theory expands (Burrel and Morgan 1983), new terms, concepts, analytical and methodological tools are increasingly used in ways that are consistent with these emerging new themes. In particular, with the emergence of the symbolic or cultural perspective on organizations (Bolman and Deal 1991; Smircich 1983), anthropological concepts such as myths, sagas, symbols, ceremonies, beliefs and values as well as some linguistic concepts such as metaphors have received a great deal of attention. Using these concepts, organizations are analyzed as enacted cultural realities that bind and hold an entire community and its membership.

"A metaphor is a figure of speech in which a term or a phrase with a literal meaning is applied to a different context in order to suggest a resemblance" (Sackmann 1989, p. 465). Besides its transformative power as a language form, metaphor also denotes a way of knowing: For example, scientists view the world metaphorically in developing their framework for analysis (Morgan 1980, p. 611). Furthermore, Lakoff and Johnson argued that less concrete and inherently more vague concepts are restructured in terms of more concrete concepts that have clear meanings, understanding and familiarity in our daily life. Thus, through metaphor, the unknown is explained by known experiences (Lakoff and Johnson 1982, p. 112; reported in Sackmann 1989, p. 465).

According to Morgan, "the creative potential of metaphor depends upon there being a degree of difference between the subjects involved in the metaphorical process" (Morgan 1980, p. 611), one being more concrete than the other when used to explain the target phenomenon. In most cases, while the commonalties are emphasized, differences are suppressed in a selective comparison (Morgan 1980, p. 611). On the other hand, metaphors transmit entire systems or domains of meaning by under-emphasizing individual and isolated concepts or phenomena. They create a mental picture which substitutes for thousands of words in describing an entire situation. This makes

"Metaphorical Images of an Organization: The Power of Symbolic Constructs in Reading Change in Higher Education Organizations," by Hasan Simsek in *Higher Education*, Vol. 33, No. 3, April 1997.

metaphors very powerful communication tools with their picture-like nature since they transmit a complete story visually using only one image (Sackmann 1989, pp. 467–68).

Metaphors transfer schema from one area to another, they filter and define reality in a simple fashion such as "Richard is a lion," "the brain is a computer," "capitalist economies are markets" (Sterman 1985, p. 98), or "organizations are machines," "organizations are organisms," "organizations are flux and transformation," etc. (Morgan 1986). Metaphors are very powerful in describing the most important features of a complex array of variables in a simple form, but they only provide part of a whole picture (Morgan 1980; Sterman 1985).

It is useful in the following ways to employ metaphors to explain tacit background assumptions in organizations:

1. to clarify the enacted reality in organization which emphasizes commonalities between the nature of organization and of the used metaphor,

2. to draw an approximate visual picture of the organization in terms of the dominant strategic orientation guided by the underlying enacted reality,

3. to provide somewhat detailed information about the organization by containing certain linguistic components, specifically adjectives and adverbs used in a metaphorical description (Simsek 1992).

Thus, metaphor is an expressive (language-related) form that facilitates communication in understanding the tacit assumptions widely shared in an organization. These tacit assumptions in turn define the mode and direction of behavior in organizations.

A growing literature has examined the use of metaphors in a variety of social settings ranging from the process of theory construction in science, to the behavior of firms, to procedures by which children in grade school classroom learn (Morgan 1986; Sackmann 1989; Sterman 1985). The value of metaphors come from their rich linguistic character and their relationship with explication of reality: "All languages have deeply embedded metaphorical structures that are reflective of and influential in the meaning of reality . . . become[ing] vehicles of vernacular

for expressing one's understanding of one's environment within a specific cultural, historic context" (Bredeson 1985, p. 30). The important reflection of a cultural and historic context through metaphorical linguistic forms has been widely recognized in studies explaining construction and perception of reality in organizational settings (Lakoff and Johnson 1982; Sackmann 1989; Bredeson 1985; Simsek and Louis 1991; Louis and Simsek 1994).

Several authors emphasize the importance of metaphors in knowledge creation and defining ways of knowing the world through a process of interpretation (Smircich 1983; Morgan 1986). By using metaphors, Morgan (1986), for example reinterpreted mainstream organization theories by identifying their metaphorical imagery. Similarly, Sackmann (1989) demonstrated how metaphors were used by executives in a private firm's restructuring process to redefine their changing reality. Her results showed that the metaphors of "gardening" (cutting, pruning, gathering, nurturing) were effectively used to change the firm's overall identity.

Bredeson (1985), on the other hand, analyzed the bases of three metaphorical images held by a number of school principals about their jobs: maintenance, survival and vision. The maintenance metaphor was represented by an image of caretaker or overseer who keeps the school doors open and the process going. The metaphor of survival was depicted by an image of a constant flow of day-to-day and immediate activities. The metaphor of vision, on the other hand, reflected their broad understanding of the future on certain educational issues concerning their schools, surrounding community and the state at large.

This discussion proves two powerful uses of metaphors in organizational analysis: First, there is enough evidence of the uses of metaphorical analysis in reading the present nature of organization. It is like taking the picture of an often implicit and tacit world view that overwhelmingly defines the behavior of an organization. Thus, in this mode of inquiry, metaphors are tools to read the situation. Second, some scholars use metaphors not as a reading tool but as a catalyst for change as reported in Sackmann's study (1989). Sackmann argued that metaphors may be used to inject a particular vision in the organization. Since metaphors have picture-like qualities, they may potentially constitute a powerful medium for communication of an often abstract and tacit future orientation. A simple metaphor may substitute a thousand-word document in prescribing particular actions to be taken or a particular path to be followed. In this study, metaphorical analysis was used in the first sense, that is, in reading the organization.

On the other hand, organization theory in higher education is based on five powerful models: the bureaucratic or structural frame, the collegial or human resource frame, the political frame, the organized anarchy frame and the symbolic frame. The bureaucratic or structural frame involves a hierarchical, rule-based administrative scheme in which change is explained as structural reconfiguration of organizational apparatus as the environment demands (Emery 1969; Katz and Kahn 1978; Lawrence and Lorsch 1967). The collegial or human resource frame considers higher education institutions as a collegium "where differences in status are deemphasized, people interact as equals in a system that stresses consensus, shared power and participation in governance, and common commitments and aspirations" (Bensimon, Neumann and Birnbaum 1989, p. 54). In this frame, change is through community-wide consensus and participative decision-making. The political frame sees the higher education institutions as essentially political entities where there exists more than one interest group or coalition. Change, under the political frame, is a dynamic politicking process among various groups struggling for more control and influence (Baldridge et al. 1978). The organized anarchy frame (Cohen and March 1974), on the other hand, explains higher education organizations as essentially unpredictable entities where change is random because of "politicized nature of the involvement of different actors with different agendas and interests" (Simsek and Louis 1994, p. 671).

Of the symbolic frame, one of the least utilized perspectives to higher education organizations as part of a general trend in the organization theory is that "the symbolic side of modern organizations has been vastly understated in research" (Clark 1983, p. 73). However, starting with Clark's seminal work on organizational sagas (Clark 1972), scholars have devoted attention to the symbolic side of academic organizations in terms of beliefs, ideologies, stories, legends and sagas. In a recent study, for example, Simsek and Louis argued that changes in organizational structure and procedures in higher education institutions may not produce much change in behavior unless there is a genuine shift in the underlying organizational paradigm, namely assumptions and values (Simsek and Louis 1994, p. 690).

Departing from a symbolic orientation, and, by using a case study design, the purpose of this article is to present how metaphors as symbolic constructs can be used in the analysis of change in higher education organizations.

Statement of the Problem

The following questions guided the data collection and analysis process:

1. *Before the Commitment to Focus Plan*

   1a. What metaphor, image or analogy were used by the faculty members to describe the University before the Commitment to Focus Plan?

   1b. What institutional strategies or policies were perceived by the faculty to describe the University before the Commitment to Focus Plan?

   1c. Is there any relationship or contextual congruence between the metaphors, images or analogies and institutional policies or strategies from the perspectives of faculty members concerning the period before the Commitment to Focus Plan?

2. *After the Commitment to Focus Plan*

   2a. What metaphor, image or analogy were used by the faculty members to describe the University after the Commitment to Focus Plan?

   2b. What institutional strategies or policies were perceived by the faculty to describe the University after the Commitment to Focus Plan?

   2c. Is there any relationship or contextual congruence between the metaphors, images or analogies and institutional policies or strategies from the perspectives of faculty members concerning the period after the Commitment to Focus Plan?

Before describing the method of study, it would be relevant to provide background information about the planning and change at the University of Minnesota.

The Case: Strategic Planning in the University of Minnesota

According to Foster (1989–90), the University of Minnesota has a number of unique roles that distinguish it from other higher education institutions in the United States:

- It is the land-grant university for a state that is a center for both agriculture and technology, so that education in 'agriculture and the mechanic arts' is an important responsibility; it is the state's only source for higher education in agriculture and related fields and, until 1983, its only source of engineering education. The university maintains the strong commitment to public service and statewide outreach that such a combination implies.

- The university's Twin Cities campus serves as the urban university for the Minneapolis–St. Paul metropolitan area, with a population of 2.5 million; its evening extension classes serve 37,000 students per year.

- It is the state's only research university (Foster 1989–90, p. 26)

A number of internal and external calamities forced the university to undertake a strategic planning process. Externally, the reasons laid within the state's financial difficulties in the late 1970s and the early 1980s. Internally, on the other hand, many observed an erosion of quality over the previous forty years as a number of departments' national reputation declined. Especially, the university's undergraduate education was criticized in several areas: an impersonal campus climate, large classes, long lines, bureaucratic rules, and very few faculty who showed interest in their students (Foster 1989–90 p. 26).

Although a strong planning orientation was started in the early 1980s, the planning process at the University of Minnesota dates back to the mid 1970s. Clugston (1987, p. 91), for example, divided the strategic planning process of the University into four phases. During the period between 1974–79, the structure and framework for planning was started with the appointment of a planning council by the president. Following this preparation phase, the first cycle of planning occurred between the spring of 1979 and the spring of 1982. Following a centrally developed planning statement, all units, including colleges, were required to submit their goals and objectives under the direction of guidelines defined by the central planning document for the 1980s.

The second cycle covered the period between 1982–84. A severe budget shortfall in the state economy in the early 1980s (1981–83) resulted in a four percent cut in the state's allocation for the university. This unexpected development forced the university to immediately link the already-in-process program prioritization with the budget decisions in terms of internal resource allocation (Clugston 1987, p. 95).

The third cycle, covering the period between 1984–85, let each unit find ways or develop strategies in order to implement set targets in program prioritization. The fourth cycle, on the other hand, was designed to give feedback to the first cycle through which each unit would re-examine its mission in light of the second and third cycles of the planning process (Clugston 1987, p. 96). During this planning process at least seven university committees were dealing with different issues confronting the university [—such as undergraduate and graduate education, research, outreach and technology transfer, and improving the management of the university—]. The result of this committee work was a vast array of diagnoses, prescriptions and recommendations (Foster 1989–90, p. 26).

By the time the university was busy with the planning and committee work. an incidental event occurred which sparked a series of momentous events in the planning and change process of the university:

> In late 1984, while the university was attempting to digest the many committee recommendations and to set a direction for concerted action, an activist governor visited to tell the interim president that the university was trying to do too much and should focus its activities if it hoped for

support in the governor's budget recommendations to the legislature (Foster 1989–90, pp. 26–27).

The response to this challenge came from Kenneth Keller, vice president for academic affairs, then interim president and subsequently president. His "Commitment to Focus" proposal announced in 1985 was largely based on the previous committee recommendations, although it was a personal interpretation of those recommendations. The proposal gained the support of the majority of the faculty as well as the governing board (Foster 1989–90, p. 27).

In the report, the foundation of the Commitment to Focus plan was described as the governing board's mission statement and the institution-wide planning activities. The Commitment to Focus plan was put forth as an effort to make the university one of the five top public universities in the nation with emphasis on being an international research university, a land-grant institution, a metropolitan university carrying out the functions of research, teaching and service, and, fundamentally serving a clientele composed of professional, graduate and undergraduate students (Keller 1985).

The Commitment to Focus Plan: A Vision for Change

The plan was basically laid out on the following dimensions:

1. Efforts of higher education institutions in the state should be coordinated, or duplication of efforts should be minimized.

2. Faculty should be released from certain involvements such as heavy load of teaching.

3. The university is out of balance in terms of ratio of undergraduates to graduates.

4. Quality should not be sacrificed in order to preserve the breadth of programs.

5. Various campuses in the system should be coordinated through a number of rearrangements (Keller 1985).

To release faculty from certain involvements and to reduce the undergraduate/graduate ratio, the plan recommended that undergraduate enrollments should be reduced (which would lead to reduced undergraduate class sizes) and the number of graduates should be increased. The cuts in the undergraduate numbers could easily be absorbed by other higher education institutions in the state. By doing so, the principle of equal educational opportunity would not be harmed.

In order to reduce the breadth of programs which had resulted in increasing financial burden and declining quality, the plan proposed eliminating and reducing a number of programs and units.

Of the declining quality, it was proposed that the admission requirements should be increased to recruit high-ability undergraduates, and the quality of undergraduate programs should be improved through increased admission standards and reduced class sizes.

On the issue of coordinating campuses, the plan proposed that the mission of each campus should be focused and sharpened. The University's attention should be focused on the Twin Cities campus, and entrance standards should be increased and unified across all undergraduate colleges on this campus (Keller 1985).

The plan received wide support from inside and outside the university. By the time the plan was announced, the university was in search of its new president. Then, Kenneth Keller was appointed as president by the governing board in 1986, no doubt owing to his Commitment to Focus Plan. This was a "green light" signaling the approval to implement the strategies developed in the plan. Described by many as an intelligent and visionary leader, he managed to convince the legislature on the funding issues. The state's support for the University was going to remain the same even as enrollment declined. This was an unusual and impressive success for the university in general and for the new president in particular. On the other hand, a considerable amount of private funding was provided through a series of successful fund raising campaigns.

However, the president resigned in March 1988 as a result of a public controversy due to alleged financial mismanagement of the University (Foster 1989–90, p. 35). The new president, inaugurated in October 1989, had served on numerous university committees since the initial phases of the strategic planning process. In his inauguration address, he laid out his plan for the University demonstrating his strong commitment to the fundamental spirit of the Commitment to Focus plan. However, the name of the plan was changed to "Access to Excellence" in order to overcome charges of elitism levied against the original plan. Additionally, he emphasized his priority as upgrading the quality of undergraduate education.

Data Collection and Analysis

The Interview Schedule

The interviews were held in the summer of 1992, seven years after the Commitment to Focus proposal was announced. In order to elicit the metaphors that describe the University after and before the Commitment to Focus initiative and their relation to most cited strategic choices with which the University was identified, four types of open-ended interview questions were designed:

Before Commitment to Focus:

- What metaphor, image or analogy would best describe the University as a higher education institution before the Commitment to Focus Plan?[2]

- What particular policies, strategies or organizational actions could best describe the University before the Commitment to Focus Plan?

After Commitment to Focus:

- What metaphor, image or analogy would best describe the University as a higher education institution after the Commitment to Focus Plan?

- What particular policies, strategies or organizational actions could best describe the University after the Commitment to Focus Plan?

Pilot Test, Sampling and Interview

The interview schedule was initially pilot-tested on six randomly selected faculty members representing six departments from different colleges. Then, a "multiple embedded case design" (Yin 1984 pp. 44–47) was used to form the sample which involved five departments from the four largest colleges. These departments and colleges were chosen after the researcher's consultations with knowledgeable members of the faculty. Of particular concern was that the selected departments should not be involved in similar professional circles which might yield a routine interaction as a result of overlapping responsibilities or similar professional and intellectual backgrounds. The sample involved the following departments: Strategic Management (School of Management), Political Science and English (College of Liberal Arts), Mathematics (Institute of Technology), and Food Science (College of Agriculture). In each department, a list of faculty members was obtained. Since the researcher was interested in exploring the degree of shared understanding in terms of symbolic images and subjective perceptions held by the faculty members about their institution, professional experience and length of tenure in the institution was used as a sampling criterion rather than the academic ranks of the faculty. For this, the researcher decided that the faculty member should have been in the institution for at least ten years to ensure that the perception of faculty would reflect the differences (if any) between the two phases of the change process in the institution.

From each department, a list of five primary and three substitute faculty members were selected through a random sampling procedure. As a result, the sample involved faculty members from various academic ranks who were actively teaching. Potential respondents were contacted first by letter and then by telephone. Disinterested or unavailable respondents were substituted by others through similar stages. A total of 24 faculty members from five departments were interviewed. All interviews were tape-recorded and later transcribed verbatim by a professional typist.

Although the researcher is aware of the fact that the universities involve various levels, this study only deals with the perceptions of the faculty members. As was explained elsewhere, "we focused on faculty as informants, because they are viewed as carrying a special status of responsibility for conserving the university and typically have a longer time perspective that administrators, who, at least at the University of Minnesota, often occupy their positions for five or fewer years" (Simsek and Louis 1994, p. 678).

Qualitative Data Analysis and Reporting

To analyze the data, a qualitative method was followed. Particularly, in identifying the strategic choices that the university was most engaged in before and after the Commitment to Focus initiation, the interview transcripts were content analyzed to find out themes and patterns (Patton 1987, p. 149). By using a word processing program, each interview transcript was sorted under four question categories by cutting and pasting without changing the original word structure or phrasing used by respondents, so each piece of information could be accurately grouped under a related category. The procedure was carefully constructed in an effort to avoid any distortion of the information at the primary level of analysis. Then, each pasted item in each category was given a name or a tag describing each intact sentence. Finally, the tags under each category were compared across five interview transcripts for each department, and then they were grouped in their contextual similarity. This analysis procedure is called "open coding" by Strauss and Corbin (1990, pp. 61–74).

Qualitative analysis and reporting may range from pure narrative to statistical forms and graphic presentations (Wolcott 1994, pp. 17–32). The nature of data at hand and the nature of the problem posed may dictate different analysis and reporting strategies, but, in many cases, the same data can be treated in both ways based on the priorities identified by the researcher. In this study, extensive interview data were reduced to thematic categories based on the general categories stated in the research problems. The purpose in doing so was to compare two phases of organizational change at the University of Minnesota from the perspectives of the faculty members, to relate these findings to the planning efforts of the university administration, and to explore the likelihood of any congruence between the metaphorical images and organizational strategies generated by the faculty members. So, an analysis and reporting strategy which was more categorical based on simple frequencies,

and less narrative (see Exhibit 2 and Exhibit 4) seemed appropriate for this purpose.

The following points should be made for better understanding of the findings which will be presented later:

1. As mentioned earlier, Nils Hasselmo, the new president replacing Kenneth Keller, who designed the Commitment to Focus Plan, did not alter the fundamental spirit of the Commitment to Focus Plan other than changing the name of the plan to Access to Excellence to overcome negative charges against the original plan and to emphasize the quality of the undergraduate education. For these reasons, interviewees were asked to generate metaphors/images/analogies as well as institutional strategies and policies only about the periods before and after the Commitment to Focus Plan. Since Access to Excellence can not be called a radically different plan per se, the findings that will be presented later only concern two distinct institutional phases, namely pre-1985 (before the Commitment to Focus initiation), and post-1985 (after the Commitment to Focus initiation).

2. Since the interviews were held in the summer of 1992, the post 1985 period covers a seven year time span during which most of the proposed strategies in the Commitment to Focus Plan were already put into action (e.g. program closures to solve the problems of duplication and of quality deterioration, reduction in the undergraduate student population in favor of an increase in the graduate student number). Because of this, and of the way the research questions were designed, the following findings reflect the faculty's perception of the changes at the University of Minnesota in reference to the Commitment to Focus Plan.

3. Although the sampling design was carefully constructed to ensure diversity and representation of the general faculty population, one generic weakness of qualitative research holds true in this study as well: ". . . a lone qualitative researcher, working with inevitable limitations of time and resources . . ." (Wolcott 1994, p. 183) studying large organizations such as

the University of Minnesota. In this respect, findings of this study should be considered more of an exploratory effort to bring forth a new analytical tool in higher education organization research such as metaphors rather than to make generalizable descriptive inferences to the larger population.

Findings

Q1. *Results reading the period before the Commitment to Focus Plan*

1a. *Metaphorical images*

A total of 32 metaphors were produced by 22 respondents (Exhibit 1). More than one-third of them were match: Octopus=5, elephant=3, amoeba=3, and a wildly growing garden or vegetable=2. Some of the images can still be grouped under these four broad categories in terms of their contextual similarity.[3] For example, "cow" and "buffalo" metaphors can be added to the "elephant" metaphor, since all three metaphors emphasize the massive size of the institution. By their contextual similarities, other metaphors such as the following can be grouped together, and linked to the metaphor of "a wildly growing garden or vegetable:" "a tangled up ball of twine," "an enormous size, Chinese menu catalog of offerings," "unruly group of school children," "a feudal-medieval landscape containing many fiefdoms with their own princes and princesses," "a wagon train going different directions for different purposes" and "a beehive going different directions, doing their own separate jobs." From an organizational perspective, these metaphorical images can be interpreted in two ways. On the one hand, they may confirm an organized anarchy in terms of lack of control, lack of coordination and collaboration, and uncontrolled growth in organizational activities. On the other hand, they may simply confirm the fact that the University of Minnesota is one of the largest and most complex universities in the U.S. Both of these interpretations seem to confirm the organization change literature that there is a positive association between the size of the organization, and differentiation and structural complexity, as well as more decentralization (Hage and Aiken 1967; Pugh et. al. 1969; Blau and Schoenherr 1971; Scott 1992).

Thus, by combining the metaphorical images in terms of their contextual similarities, we reach the following picture:

Amoeba=3, Octopus=5, Elephant and related metaphors=5, A wildly growing garden and related metaphors=8

1b. *Institutional strategies*

Faculty members identified four clusters of dominant strategic behaviors that identified the University before the Commitment to Focus Plan (Exhibit 2):

1. Growth and expansion in program areas, and in program diversity, variety of offerings, opening and creating many small departments and programs.

2. Teaching and service emphasis as rewarded and praised faculty behavior.

3. Large student population and emphasis on quantity, open access and guaranteed admission, and low admission standards.

4. Independent unit activities, freedom to develop programs; autonomy and decentralized/collegial decision making granted to colleges, units and departments.

1c. *The match between metaphors and institutional strategies*

The following interpretation can be drawn from these four central metaphors in relation to the four clusters of institutional strategies:

1. The amoeba metaphor represented an image of the University as a land grant institution that lacked a solid/strong identity. Many referred to the University as an institution "being all things for all people." Additionally. it was in a constant process of growth similar to the amoeba's multiplication by fission.

2. The elephant and related metaphors (cow and buffalo) provided an image that is significant by its size and massive body. They refer to the institution that has traditionally been one of the largest public universities in the nation.

3. The octopus, however, is easily identified with eight arms on a single body. As several faculty members remarked "the university was like an octopus with its

eight arms embracing different constituencies simultaneously." The organization was explained as a single body attempting to satisfy the demands of many constituencies at the same time.

4. The metaphors of "wildly growing garden or vegetable," and other related images listed above, characterize an uncontrolled and continuous growth and expansion in the program areas and activities in the University. As a result, the metaphorical images used by the faculty in describing the most noticeable features of their organization are strikingly linked to the most salient institutional strategies, with each metaphor representing a group of central institutional strategies.

Q2 *Results reading the period after the Commitment to Focus Plan*

2a. *Metaphorical images*

A total of 24 metaphors were produced by 21 faculty members (Exhibit 3). In this case, there is considerable diversity and less consensus over the metaphors chosen compared to the metaphors used for describing the period before Commitment to Focus, except the "lion" metaphor which was repeated three times. However, respondents see the current organization as being different than the prior one in terms of being more directed, focused, powerful and purposeful in its strategic orientation, smaller and trimmed down in size and structure, and more coordinated in its internal decision making.

A careful examination of metaphors reveals that almost half of the metaphors generated by the faculty in describing the university after the Commitment to Focus plan show a metaphoric continuity. Although a minority, some faculty were not convinced that a real change was evident in the university. Rather, the situation was worsened as revealed by such metaphors as "a great, big, multi-limbed, stumbling animal," "an enormous Chinese menu catalog of offerings," "a sick octopus," "a jungle," "a wounded buffalo," "an amoeba." On the other hand, a number of faculty added a qualitative improvement (often in a positive manner) in the university's overall image. "A grazing bull" implies a still large body but it is more powerful and aggressive to go after

things, "a hippopotamus" but little faster, smaller, more trimmed down and directed, "a rhinoceros" but a self sufficient organism, still "an octopus" but smaller in size, still a wagon train but more coordinated, "a large bear" which is still a large body but smaller than an elephant, scaled down, however, still an indiscriminate eater (Exhibit 3).

On the other hand, a third group of metaphors reveal a rather sharp change in the overall image of the university that might be ascribed to the Commitment to Focus plan. The "lion" metaphor which was repeated three times by three faculty members who had quite different disciplinary or departmental orientations indicate a rather focused and powerful image for the university. Perhaps the content of the image was best described by a faculty member from political science: "a better hunter, a bit ruthless, and the head triumph over the heart" which explains a focused and selective attention for vision and organizational goals, a rational and logical emphasis on organizational structure, process and commitments.

Other images such as "fox," "fish," "a pruned tree," "an ant colony," a hunting dog," and, "a neatly set up garden" describe a context which is close to the qualitative richness of the "lion" metaphor. Various qualities of these metaphors ascribed to the used images by the faculty members provide rich insights into the nature of this new strategic orientation at the university such as clever and faster, more focused movement, but still darting around, focused on a task, seeks, searches and finds (Exhibit 3).

Compared to the images that described the university before the Commitment to Focus plan, the sort of fuzziness and diversity in the content of provided metaphors can be explained in three ways: (1) if an organization is identified with incremental and slow change, metaphorical images may provide a rather strong picture of the organization. Change, on the other hand, distorts this continuity and clarity of the images like taking of picture of a moving target. Thus, fuzziness and diversity in the metaphorical images may prove that change is in order in the organization. (2) Metaphorical fuzziness may, however, also be due to people being able to judge the past more clearly than the present.

2b   *Institutional strategies*

Results show that 7 groups of emerging strategies were identified by the interviewed faculty. The first policy or action, the reallocation plan which was originally defined in the Commitment to Focus proposal, was designed to distribute resources differentially. Following the identification of the priority areas among the programs, the plan proposed that the available resources should be shifted from low-priority to high-priority programs. It seems that this strategy directly addresses an immediate need to remedy the declining resources of the University by offering an internal solution to the problem.

The second group of strategies concerns access issues or reduction in size of the University. As the interviewed faculty perceived, enrollment and class size are reduced by raising admission and preparation standards.

The third group of strategies focused on certain activities designed to reduce already-expanded units, programs and campus diversity in the university. To do this, certain departments, units or programs have either been closed, merged or their budgets cut.

According to the results concerning the fourth policy, there appears to an emphasis on quality, especially at the levels of teaching and undergraduate education.

Along with the quality concern, there seems to be a tendency towards more emphasis on research and publication expected from the faculty, and more priority has been given to graduate level education.

The sixth strategy indicates, as reported by the faculty, that there is a trend towards more centralization in the internal affairs of the university through planned activities and an emphasis on collaborative work among the units.

The seventh group of policies show that the university has more aggressively sought outside funding by creating endowed chairs, increasing fund raising activities and applying for more research grants.

Regarding these results, first, if a comparison is made between the period before and after the Commitment to Focus, the new or proposed policies seem to be constructed to reverse the trend. For example, while the previous policy was praising the quantity that ended up in an inflated size, the new one attempts to reduce it. In order to overcome the financially problematic situation, the new set of policies were created to generate a partial solution by distributing the resources differentially as well as finding ways of generating external funding. In order to solve the problem of massive program diversity, complexity and expansion or a "diseconomized scale," the new policies and strategies are developed to streamline the institutional and program complexity. To do all these, central administration gained more control in the internal affairs. Lastly, as a response to eroding or declining quality, upgrading quality especially in the undergraduate education was given the highest priority after the Commitment to Focus.

These findings lend some support to Miller and Friesen's discussion that revolution in the strategy and structural variables in organizations first attempts to reverse the excesses of the period preceding any discontinuous change initiative (Miller and Friesen 1980).

There appears another important point concerning the order of the proposed policies (Exhibit 4). It seems that the order of strategic choices with respect to their percentage ratios from high to low define the level of concreteness, as perceived by the respondents. The highly-rated ones are those in which the university administration is actively promoting the resolution of the problems inherited by the previous policies.

2c.   *The match between metaphors and emerging institutional strategies*

Although the congruence between the provided images and the emerging institutional strategies is not as strong as in the case of the period prior to Commitment to Focus, the images are, however, rich in context in terms of describing the university's overall strategic direction.

1. As discussed earlier in relation to the metaphors describing the period after the Commitment to Focus, whereas the same images were used by the faculty, we observed some qualitative differences in each image. Although the emerging images did not sharply contrast with the previous images, a qualitative improvement was evident as in the following examples: from "a grazing cow" to "a grazing bull" from "an elephant" to "a hippopotamus" (faster, smaller, trimmed down and more directed), from "a coral reef" to "a stabilized coral reef," from a free-flowing "wagon train"

to "a coordinated wagon train," from "a kitten" (sits there and loves to be petted) to "a hunting dog" (seeks, searches and finds), from "a wildly growing vegetable" to "a pruned tree," from "a garden without strict gardeners" to "a neatly set up garden."

These metaphors indicate a strategic continuity or an incremental change in the strategic orientation of the university. Change was not seen as radical or discontinuous, rather as focused on trimming the extremities of the previous institutional strategies. This analysis was supported through the analysis of the strategic choices that the new strategies were designed to treat the ills of the prior period. Metaphorical images clearly showed this connection as the faculty members used the same metaphors, but in the second case, with more positive attributes.

2. On the other hand, some metaphorical images sharply contrasted with the dominant metaphors characterizing the university's past and the present. The metaphorical images of bull, lion, fox, fish and hunting dog all resemble a different character for the university, the one that has slimmer, swifter, lean and focused qualities of emerging strategic inclination. For example, the reallocation plan, the program, campus closures and consolidations are well described by the image of a "lion" that is a little bit ruthless and puts the head over the heart. This is contrasting with the university's image of "attempting to satisfy everybody's willy-nilly" with a rationalistic approach of efficiency and effectiveness.

Images that are related to the size of the university were clearly evident in the scaled down versions of the previously used metaphors: from elephant to hippopotamus, from octopus to smaller octopus, from elephant to a large bear, from a jungle to a pruned tree, etc.

The imagery of the emerging strategic orientations related to planned, coordinated and collaborative activities; and, more central direction in the university was hidden in the previously cited metaphors of bull, lion, fox, fish and hunting dog. Such organisms do have more control, coordination and swifter qualities in their movements compared to rather sloppy and slow organisms such as elephant, octopus and cow. The university is no more a "free enterprise, a tangled up ball of twine, an unruly group of school children, a feudal-medieval landscape," but moving towards a more centralized, coordinated and unified configuration.

Discussion and Conclusions

Land grant universities endure on a populist image originated from an agrarian socialism. This populist land-grant philosophy was explained by a University of Minnesota faculty as follows:

> It was highly populous, a belief that the university had to be all things to all people, a general world view that we just serve everybody's demands willy nilly (Simsek and Heydinger 1993, p. 20).

After the Second World War, this populist image transformed into an "entrepreneurial populism" under the influence of the growth years (late 1950s and early 1970s) (Simsek 1992; Simsek and Heydinger, 1993; Simsek and Louis 1994). During these years, institutions engaged in a number of strategies that resulted in an uncontrolled expansion in program areas, diversity in institutional missions, growth in size and decentralization in decision making. The metaphorical analysis in this article shows that dominant images (metaphors) among faculty are matched with sets of institutional strategies provided by the same professionals, and verified by individuals involved in articulating those strategies.

In the case of the University of Minnesota, the era of "entrepreneurial populism" was terminated by the 1985 Commitment to Focus plan. As the reported results show, the institution was trying to reverse the extremities of the entrepreneurial populist strategies as well as providing a vision for the future.

This article draws the following four implications from the study:

(1) *Since metaphors provide simple ways of knowing and seeing the world, organization members' sense of reality and their role accomplishments will be consistent with these implicit images. These images provide the necessary framework that limit or delimit the members' accomplishment of organizational roles.* According to interpretive organization theorists, "the world is, essentially, an ambiguous realm of experience that is made concrete by the people who interpret it, and who act on the basis of these interpretations. People's interpretations construct reality and,

through subsequent actions based on those interpretations, actually shape future realities. Realities are not given; they are *made!*" (Morgan 1989, p. 93: emphasis original). From the images provided by the University of Minnesota faculty, a large number of images show an improvement in the image of the University compared to the previous period. A man-made, constructed reality which defines the University as more coordinated, focused, scaled down, and directed prescribes individual actions and a criterion for role accomplishments by the faculty members consistent with these images. Moreover, a faculty member's image of the University as "a sick octopus," or "a great, big, multi-limbed, stumbling animal," or "an enormous, Chinese menu catalog of offerings" will prescribe a different set of individual actions on the part of these community members. Similarly, if a faculty member sees the University as "a fox who is clever and devious," then he or she will be cynical about the University's, especially about the administration's, agenda of change that will frame this particular faculty member's daily job routine.

(2) *These images are shared across a population of organization members.* As we discussed elsewhere (Simsek 1992; Simsek and Heydinger 1993; Simsek and Louis 1994), an enacted or socially constructed reality in organizational settings can be reframed as an organizational paradigm. An organizational paradigm is a cognitive map that guides and directs organizational activities. As was originally put forward by Kuhn (1970), every paradigm creates its own language pattern, its unique concepts and principles. This language form is disseminated among the members of a community, the process which is called the social matrix. The full use of any paradigm comes into existence when the social matrix is close to the maximum level of membership. At this phase, the image of paradigm reality is shared among the majority of the community members. In the University of Minnesota case, we were able to find out almost the same, sometimes similar, semantic approaches in the faculty's description of the university. Faculty members with quite dissimilar professional and departmental interests articulated similar metaphors in describing the university.

On the other hand, *if the shared reality is orderly, dominating images are strong, clear and agreed. If the constructed reality is chaotic and disorderly, images are correspondingly fuzzy and weak.* As you may recall, the metaphors describing the University of Minnesota prior to the Commitment to Focus plan were stronger and consensus was higher compared to the period after the Commitment to Focus. The diversity and relative lack of consensus on the metaphors related to the period after the Commitment to Focus may indicate that change is underway, and that it is directly reflected by the provided metaphors. This eventually creates a fuzzy imagery or picture of the organization under study.

(3) *Changes in strategic choices create changes in members' image of their organization. Conversely, effective management of images may create a situation where certain desired strategic choices can easily be implemented.* This was evident in the case of the University of Minnesota in such a way that the Commitment to Focus plan altered "the entrepreneurial populist image" in this public university. Any change in strategic choices that are a direct extension of an implicit world view may distort the image of the community members about their organization. Conversely, the process may work the other way. Any alteration in the images may create a situation where certain strategies can be disseminated in the organization. This second case was not the purpose of this study. However, as earlier reported from Sackmann's study (1989), creating a particular vision and articulating new strategic choices may be achieved through alterations of dominant images in an organization.

(4) The results regarding the metaphorical images used by faculty members in describing the period prior to the Commitment to Focus plan (before 1985) are supportive of the three theory bases to higher education organizations as applied to the case under study. *The study provides evidence that theories such as "loose-coupled systems" (Weick 1976), "organized anarchies" (Cohen and March 1974), and "multiversities" explain the most important characteristics of the university organization before the 1980s.* The metaphorical images of "octopus," "amoeba," and "a wildly growing garden or vegetable" are able to define the most salient characteristics of the University of Minnesota before 1985 defined by others as a loosely-coupled system, an organized anarchy, or a multiversity. How-

ever, the results of this study show that all these descriptions of the academy of the 1970s were some essential components of one socially enacted image, what Simsek and Louis (1994) called the paradigm of "entrepreneurial populism." The imagery representing the University of Minnesota presented in this article describes the general characteristics of a large university organization of the early 1970s in which these theories were offered: a loosely-linked structural configuration, independent and decentralized decision making, multiple, sometimes conflicting, mission and vision in a single institution. What is important here is the fact that each of these three theories simply focused on only one dimension of the higher education institutions. At least in the University of Minnesota case, metaphorical images presented in this article provide a perspective that fundamental aspects of these three theories are interconnected. This may lend some proof to the temporal dimension of theories in describing social phenomena of the time in which a particular theory is developed.

On the other hand, the University of Minnesota has traditionally been one of the largest public universities in the U.S. Our findings of metaphorical imagery associated with loose-coupling and organized anarchy are equally important in confirming the findings in organization theory—when translated into the context of higher education organization—that growth in size, leads to differentiation and complexity in structure of organization and decentralization in decision making (Hage and Aiken 1967; Pugh et al., 1969; Blau and Schoenherr 1971; Scott 1992).

Notes

1. An earlier version of this article was presented at the annual meeting of the University Council For Educational Administration (UCEA), Philadelphia. PA, USA (October, 1994). The author would like thank three anonymous reviewers and editor Grant Harman for their helpful comments.
2. In cases where this direct question did not work in eliciting striking images, the researcher alternatively used the following question, which, in most cases, worked well: "Which animal or living organism would best describe this institution before 1985? After 1985?" This method was suggested by Gareth Morgan at an informal seminar at the University of Minnesota.
3. If you consult Exhibit 1 and Exhibit 3, you will see an extensive list of metaphorical images generated by the faculty about their institution. The discussions under 1a and 2a were limited only to cover the metaphors that are contextually similar or the ones that have, one way or another, relevance to the institutional strategies. The images which seem to be random in the responses list were left untreated.

References

Baldridge, J. V., Curtis, D. V., Ecker, G. and Riley, L. (1978). *Policy Making and Effective Leadership: A National Study of Academic Management*. San Francisco: Jossey-Bass.

Bensimon, E. M., Neumann, A. and Birnbaum, R. (1989). *Making Sense of Administrative Leadership: The "L" Word in Higher Education*. ASHE-ERIC Higher Education Report 1, Washington D.C.: The George Washington University, School of Education and Human Development.

Blau, P. M. and Schoenherr, R. (1971). *The Structure of Organizations*. New York, NY. Basic Books.

Bolman, L. G. and Deal, T. E. (1991). *Reframing Organizations: Artistry, Choice, and Leadership*. San Francisco, CA: Jossey-Bass.

Bredeson, P. V. (1985). 'An analysis of the metaphorical perspectives of school principals', *Educational Administration Quarterly*, 21(1), 29–50.

Burrell, G. and Morgan, G. (1983). *Sociological Paradigms and Organizational Analysis*. London: Heinemann Educational Books.

Clark, B. R. (1972). 'The organizational saga in higher education', *Administrative Science Quarterly*, 17, 178–183.

Clark, B. R. (1983). *The Higher Education System: Academic Organization in Cross-National Perspective*. Berkeley, CA: University of California Press.

Clugston, R. (1987). *Strategic Adaptation in Organized Anarchy: Priority Setting and Resource Allocation in the Liberal Arts College of a Public Research University*. Ph.D. Dissertation, University of Minnesota.

Cohen, M. D. and March, J.G. (1974). *Leadership and Ambiguity: The American College President*. New York, NY:McGraw-Hill.

Emery, F. E. (1969). *Systems Thinking*. Harmondsworth, England: Penguin.

Foster, E. (1989–90). 'Planning at the University of Minnesota'. *Planning for Higher Education*, 18(2), 25–38.

Hage, J. and Aiken, M. (1967), 'Program change and organizational properties: a comparative analysis', *American Journal of Sociology*, 72, 503–519.

Katz, D. and Kahn, R. L. (1978). *The Social Psychology of Organizations*, 2nd ed. New York, NY. Wiley.

Keller, K. H. (1985). *A Commitment to Focus: Report of Interim President Kenneth H. Keller to the Board of Regents*. University of Minnesota.

Lakoff, G. and Johnson, M. (1982). *Metaphors We Live By*. Chicago, IL: University of Chicago Press.

Lawrence, P. R. and Lorsch, J. W. (1967). *Organization and Environment*. Cambridge, MA: Harvard Graduate School of Business Administration.

Louis, K. S. and Simsek, H. (1991). 'Paradigm shifts and organizational learning: some theoretical lessons for restructuring schools'. *Paper presented at the annual meeting of the University Council for Educational Administration*. Baltimore, MD.

Miller, D. and Friesen, P. H. (1980). 'Momentum and revolution in organizational adaptation', *Academy of Management Journal*, 23, 591–614.

Morgan, G. (1980). 'Paradigms, metaphors and puzzle solving in organization theory', *Administrative Science Quarterly*, 25, 605–622.

Morgan, Gareth (1986). *Images of Organization*. Newbury Park, CA: Sage.

Patton. M. Q. (1987). *How to Use Qualitative Research in Evaluation*. Newbury Park, CA: Sage.

Pugh, D., Hickson, H., Hinings, C. R. and Turner, C. (1969). 'The context of organizational structures', *Administrative Science Quarterly*, 14, 91–114.

Sackmann, S. (1989). 'The role of metaphors in organization transformation', *Human Relations*, 42, 463–485.

Scott, W. R. (1992). *Organizations: Rational, Natural and Open Systems*, 3rd ed. Englewood Cliffs, NJ: Prentice-Hall.

Simsek, H. (1992). *Organizational Change as Paradigm Shift: Analysis of Organizational Change Processes in a Large, Public University by Using a Paradigm-Based Change Model*. Ph.D. Dissertation, Minneapolis, MN: University of Minnesota.

Simsek, H. and Heydinger, R. B. (1993). 'An Analysis of the Paradigmatic Evolution of U.S. Higher Education and Implications for the Year 2000', in Smart, J.C. (ed), *Higher Education: Handbook of Theory and Research*, New York, NY: Agathon Press, Vol. 9, 1–49.

Simsek, H. and Louis, K. S. (1994). 'Organizational change as paradigm shift: analysis of the change process in a large, public university', *Journal of Higher Education*, 65(6), 670–695.

Smircich, L. (1983). 'Concepts of culture and organizational analysis', *Administrative Science Quarterly*, 28, 339–358.

Sterman, J. D. (1985). 'The growth of knowledge: testing a theory of scientific revolutions with a formal model', *Technological Forecasting and Social Change*, 28, 93–122.

Strauss, A. and Corbin, J. (1990). *Basics of Qualitative Research: Grounded Theory Procedures and Techniques*. Newbury Park, CA: Sage.

Weick, K. E. (1976). 'Educational organizations as loosely coupled systems', *Administrative Science Quarterly*, 21, 1–19.

Wolcott, H. F. (1994). *Transforming Qualitative Data: Description, Analysis and Interpretation*. Thousand Oaks, CA: Sage.

Yin, R. (1984). *Case Study Research*. Beverly Hills, CA: Sage.

[Exhibit 1]

Metaphors Describing The University Before Commitment To Focus Plan

Strategic Management

I. A grazing cow = sturdy, big, dependable, very slow
   A tangled up ball of twine
   A highly departmentalized hierarchy

2. A great, big multi-limbed, stumbling animal
   (A cross b/w centipede & elephant)
   An octopus

3. A big, non-thinking bureaucracy
   An elephant
   An octopus
   "Communiversity"

4. A dog = takes resources, but returns something to environment
   A good quality, faculty run, democratic inst.

5. An enormous size, Chinese menu catalog of offerings

Political Science

1. Amoeba=constantly dividing,
   "U of Lake Wabegon" = decentralized, unwilling to make hard decisions
   Unruly group of school children, all going & doing separate things

2. An octopus = with all eight arms embracing different constituencies and concerns

3. A ship = sailing in the smoother waters

4. A healthy octopus

English

1. Amoeba
   A free enterprise

2. An octopus

3. A coral reef

4. A feudal-medieval landscape

5. A wildly growing vegetable

Food Science

1. A free enterprise
   A wagon train = going different directions for different purposes

2. A healthy buffalo

3. A beehive = going different directions, doing their own separate jobs

4. A kitten = sits there & loves to be petted

Department Of Mathematics

1. Amoeba = if something comes along that you haven't planned for, just go out and grab it
   = if you push it one place, it pops out in another place

2. An elephant = large, sloppy, slow, ponderous, eats large amounts

3. A garden without strict gardeners

Octopus=5, Elephant=3, Amoeba=3,
A wildly growing garden/vegetable=2

Sturdy, big, very slow, departmentalized, multi-limbed, stumbling, dividing, decentralized, opportunist, unplanned, sloppy, large, ponderous, unruly.

[Exhibit 2]

Dominant Policies, Strategies Or Organizational Actions By The University Before Commitment To Focus Plan

1. Growth/expansion in program areas,
Variety/many offerings,
Growth in program diversity,
Opening/creating many small departments/programs
Diverse/too many programs

StrMan	PolSci	English	FoodSci	Math	Tot. #
4/4	3/5	4/5	4/5	3/4	18/23(78%)

2. Teaching emphasized, praised, rewarded

StrMan	PolSci	English	FoodSci	Math	Tot.#
3/4	3/5	3/5	1/5	1/3	11/22(50%)

3. Large student population
Emphasis on quantity
Open access
Too many admissions
Large/guaranteed admission
Low admission standards

StrMan	PolSci	English	FoodSci	Math	Tot.#
2/4	1/5	3/5	1/5	2/3	9/22 (41%)

4. Independent activities,
Freedom to develop programs
Autonomous, collegial decision making
Unit autonomy
Decentralized decision making

StrMan	PolSci	English	FoodSci	Math	Tot.#
0/4	3/5	2/5	3/5	0/3	8/22 (36%)

5. Service emphasized, praised, rewarded

StrMan	PolSci	English	FoodSci	Math	Tot.#
4/4	0/5	0/5	0/5	0/3	4/20 (20%)

[Exhibit 3]

Metaphors Describing The University After Commitment To Focus Plan

Strategic Management

1. A grazing bull = more powerful & aggressive to go after things & to do things

2. A great, big, multi-limbed, stumbling animal. A cross b/w a centipede & an elephant

3. A hippopotamus = little bit faster, smaller, more trimmed down, more directed

4. A lion = grabs resources from the environment, but contributes little

5. An enormous, Chinese menu catalog of offerings

Political Science

1. A rhinoceros = a self sufficient organism

2. A lion = better hunter, a bit ruthless, the head triumph over the heart

3. A fox = clever, devious, operate w/o being seen, moves faster

4. A centipede
A sick octopus
A jungle

English

1. A fish = more focused movement, but still darting around

2. A smaller octopus

3. A stabilized coral reef

4. 19th Century German Uni. model = research, publication, graduate studies oriented

5. A pruned tree

Food Science

1. A coordinated wagon train = wagons rounding up into a circle
A lion = aggressive, not easy to prey on

2. An ant colony = busy, working hard, focused on a task

3. A wounded buffalo

4. A hunting dog = seeks, searches and finds

Department Of Mathematics

1. Amoeba = no change in the image

2. A large bear = smaller than elephant, scaled down, but still an indiscriminate eater

3. A neatly set up garden

Lion = 3

More (powerful, aggressive, trimmed down, directed, focused, stabilized), faster, smaller, self sufficient, better hunter, bit ruthless, clever, pruned, coordinated, seeks, searches, scaled down.

[Exhibit 4]

Dominant Policies, Strategies Or Organizational Actions By The University After Commitment To Focus Plan

1. Reallocation Plan

StrMan	PolSci	English	FoodSci	Math	Tot.#
4/5	4/5	4/5	1/5	3/4	16/24(67%)

2. Reduced/limited enrollment
Higher preparation/admission standards
Limited course offerings
Smaller classes

StrMan	PolSci	English	FoodSci	Math	Tot.#
2/5	3/5	4/5	3/5	4/4	16/24(67%)

3. Program/campus closings
Program consolidation
Program/unit mergers/cuts

StrMan	PolSci	English	FoodSci	Math	Tot.#
3/5	3/5	4/5	2/5	3/4	15/24(63%)

4. Emphasis on quality
Quality teaching
Quality undergraduate education

StrMan	PolSci	English	FoodSci	Math	Tot.#
2/5	2/5	1/5	2/5	3/4	10/24(42%)

5. More emphasis on research, publication, graduate level

StrMan	PolSci	English	FoodSci	Math	Tot. #
4/5	1/5	0/5	0/5	3/4	8/24(33%)

6. Planned/coordinated/collaborative activities
More central direction
Planned activities for setting priorities, defining areas of strengths

StrMan	PolSci	English	FoodSci	Math	Tot. #
1/5	1/5	2/5	3/5	1/4	8/24(33%)

7. Endowed chairs
Fund raising activities
Orientation towards external funding

StrMan	PolSci	English	FoodSci	Math	Tot.#
2/5	2/5	1/5	1/5	0/3	6/24(25%)

ADDITIONAL READINGS
(with the assistance of Eboni M. Zamani)

References

Aguirre, A. Jr., & Messineo, M. (1997). Racially motivated incidents in higher education: What do they say about the campus climate for minority students? *Equity & Excellence in Education*, 30(2), 26–30.

Altbach, P. G., Berdahl, R. O., & Gumport, P. J. (1994). *Higher education in American society*. Amherst, New York: Prometheus Books.

Altbach, P. G., & Kelly, D. H. (1985). *Higher education in international perspective: A survey and bibliography*. Bronx, NY: Mansell Publishing Limited.

Amada, G. (1994). *Coping with the disruptive college student: A practical model*. Asheville, NC: College Administration Publications.

American Academy of Arts and Sciences. (1971). *The Assembly on university goals and governance*. Cambridge, Massachusetts. The Academy of Arts and Sciences.

American Council on Education. (1994). *Dialogues for diversity: Community and ethnicity on campus*. Phoenix, AZ: Oryx Press.

Association of Governing Boards of Universities and Colleges (1996). *Ten public policy issues for higher education in 1996*. Washington, DC: AGB Publications.

Astin, A. W. (1993). *Higher education and the concept of community*. Urbana: University of Illinois.

Bailey, S. K. (1975). Education and the state. In J. F. Hughes, (Ed.) *Education and the state*. Washington, DC: American Council on Education.

Baird, L. L. (1990). Campus Climate: Using surveys for policy-making and understanding. *New Directions for Institutional Research*, 17(4), 35–45.

Baldridge, J. V. (1971). *Academic governance*. Berkeley: McCutchan.

Baldridge, J. V., Curtis, D., Ecker V. G., & Riley, G. L. (1980). *Policy making and effective leadership*. San Francisco: Jossey-Bass.

Benjamin, R. & Carroll, S. J. (1996). Impediments and imperatives in restructuring higher education. *Educational Administration Quarterly* 32, 705–719.

Birnbaum, R. (1988). *How colleges work: The cybernetics of academic organizations and leadership*. San Francisco: Jossey-Bass.

Boulding, K. E. (198 9). *Three faces of power*. Newbury Park, CA: Sage Publications.

Bowen, H. R. (1982). *The state of the nation and the agenda for higher education*. San Francisco: Jossey-Bass.

Boyle, P., & Bowden, J. A. (1997). Educational quality assurance in universities: An enhanced model. *Assessment & Evaluation in Higher Education*, 22(2), 111–21.

Brown, M. C. (1999). *The quest to define collegiate desegregation: Black colleges, Title VI compliance, and post-Adams litigation*. Westport, CT: Bergin & Garvey.

Brown, M. C. (1999). Public black colleges and desegregation in the United States: A continuing dilemma. *Higher Education Policy*, 12, 15–25.

Callan, P. M. (1994). *The gauntlet for multicampus systems*. Trusteeship 2(3), 16–20.

The Carnegie Commission on Higher Education. (1973). *Governance of higher education*. New York: McGraw-Hill.

The Carnegie Foundation for the Advancement of Teaching. (1982). *The control of the campus: A report on the governance of higher education*. Washington, DC: Author.

Chait, R. P. & Associates (1996). *Improving the performance of governing boards*. Washington, DC: American Council on Education.

Chambers, G. S. (1991). Creative governance in the 1990s. *AGB Reports* 33 (5), 611.

Chandler, T. L. (1993). Incorporating diversity into the professoriate. *New Directions for Teaching & Learning*, 54, 91–101.

Cheng, T. C. E. (1993). Operations research and higher education administration. *Journal of Educational Administration*, 31, 77–90.

Chin, J. (1997). Mobilizing for social change: An Asian American's perspective. *Race, Gender & Class*, 4(3), 112–21.

Chronister, J. L., & Truesdell, T. C. M. (1991). Exploring faculty issues and institutional planning for the twenty-first century. *Review of Higher Education*, 14(4), 467–84.

Clark, B. R. (1997). Small worlds, different worlds: The uniqueness and troubles of American academic professions. *Daedalus*, 126, 21–42.

The Commission on the Academic Presidency (1996). *Stronger leadership for tougher times*. Washington, DC: AGB.

Cook, R. W. & Zallocco, R. L. (1983). Predicting university preference and attendance: Applied marketing in higher education administration. *Research in Higher Education*, 19(2), 197–211.

Corak, K. (1992). Do big decisions committees work? *Planning for Higher Education*, 21, 20–24.

Corson, J. J. (1975). *The governance of colleges and universities*. New York: McGraw-Hill.

Cowley, W. H. (1980). *Presidents, professors, and trustees: The evolution of American academic government*. San Francisco: Jossey-Bass.

Courts, P. L., & McInerney, K. H. (1993). *Assessment in higher education: Politics, pedagogy, and portfolios*. Westport, CT: Praeger Publishers.

Cress, C. M., & Sax, L. J. (1998). Campus climate issues to consider for the next Decade. *New Directions for Institutional Research*, 25(2), 65–80.

Currie, J., & Newson, J. (1998). *Universities and globalization: Critical perspectives*. Thousand Oaks, CA: SAGE Publications.

Daxner, M. (1995). Intimations to academic governance. *Higher Education Policy*, 8(3), 11–14.

Deegan, W. L. & J. F. Gollattsheck (198 5). *Ensuring effective governance*. New Directions for Community Colleges, Report #49. San Francisco: Jossey-Bass.

Eaton, G. M., & Miyares, J. (1995). Integrating program review in planning and budgeting: A systemwide perspective. *New Directions for Institutional Research*, 86, 69–79.

Edelson, P. J. (1995). Historical and cultural perspectives on centralization/ decentralization in continuing education. *Continuing Higher Education Review*, 59(3), 143–56.

El-Khawas, E. (1994). *Campus trends 1994*. Washington, DC: American Council on Education.

Engel, M. (1984). Ideology and the politics of higher education. *Journal of Higher Education*, 55, 19–34.

Epstein, L. D. (1974). *Governing the university*. San Francisco: Jossey-Bass.

Eulau, H., & Quinley, H. (1970). *State officials and higher education: A survey of the opinions and expectations of policy makers in nine states*. New York: McGraw-Hill.

Finn, C. E., & Manno, B. V. (1996). What's wrong with the American university? *The Wilson Quarterly*, 20, 44–53.

Fleming, J. S. (1986). The Eisenhower college silver dollar legislation: A case of politics and higher education. *Journal of Higher Education*, 57(6), 569–605.

Floyd, C. E. (1995). Governing boards and trustees. *The Review of Higher Education*, 19(1), 93–110.

Floyd, C. E. (1994). Faculty participation and shared leadership. *The Review of Higher Education*, 17(2), 197–209.

Franklin, K. K. (1998). Looking in the looking glass: How administrators define institutional effectiveness. *Metropolitan Universities: An International Forum*, 9 (3), 7–18.

Frost, S. H., Hearn, J. C., & Marine, G. M. (1997). State policy and the public research university. *Journal of Higher Education*, 68(4), 363–397.

Glenny, L. A. (1971). The anonymous leaders of higher education. *Journal of Higher Education*, 43, 9–22.

Glenny, L. (1959). *The autonomy of public colleges*. New York: McGraw-Hill.

Gold, S. D. (1995). *The fiscal crisis of the states*. Washington, DC: Georgetown University Press.

Gove, S. K., & Floyd, C. E. (1975). Research on higher education administration and policy: an uneven report. *Public Administration Review*, 35, 111–118.

Gove, S. K., & Solomon, B. W. (1968). The politics of higher education. *Journal of Higher Education*, 39, 181–195.

Gumport, P. J. (1997). Public universities as academic workplaces. *Daedalus*, 126(4), 113–136.

Hannah, S. B. (1996). The Higher Education Act of 1992: Skills, constraints, and the politics of higher education. *Journal of Higher Education*, 67(5), 498–527.

Haynes, L. J. (1985). Skills of the effective academic administrator: Structuring the curriculum. *Review of Higher Education*, 8(4), 275–94.

Henry, W. J., & Nixon, H. L. (1994). Changing a campus climate for minorities and women. *Equity & Excellence in Education*, 27(3), 48–54.

Hodgkinson, H. L., & Meeth, L. R. (1971). *Power and authority: The transformation of campus governance*. San Francisco: Jossey-Bass.

Houle, C. O. (1996). *The design of education*. Second Edition. San Francisco, CA: Jossey-Bass.

Hufner, K. (1987). The role of performance indicators in higher education: The Case of Germany. *International Journal of Institutional Management in Higher Education*, 11 (2), 140–48.

Husen, T. (1994). *The role of the university: A global perspective*. Paris: United Nations Educational, Scientific, and Cultural Organization.

Ingram, R. T. (1993). *Governing public colleges & universities*. Washington, DC: AGB.

Johnson, R., & Associates (1990). *Assessing assessment: An in-depth status report on the higher education assessment movement in 1990*. Washington, DC: American Council on Education.

Johnstone, D. B., Dye, N. S., & Johnson, R. (1998). Collaborative leadership for institutional change. *Liberal Education*, 84(2), 12–19.

Jones, G. A., & Skolnik, M. L. (1997). Governing boards in Canadian universities. *Review of Higher Education, 20*(3), 277–95.

Kauffman, J. F. (1980). *At the pleasure of the board: The service of the college & university president.* Washington, DC: American Council on Education.

Kerr, C. (1994). *Troubled times for American higher education: The 1990s and beyond.* Albany: SUNY Press.

Konrad, A. M., & Pfeffer, J. (1991). Understanding the hiring of women and minorities in educational institutions. *Sociology of Education, 64*(3), 141–57.

Krotseng, M. V. (1990). Profiles of quality and intrusion: The complex courtship of state governments and higher education. *The Review of Higher Education, 13*(4), 557–566.

Lazerson, M. (1997). Who owns higher education? The changing face of governance. *Change, 29*(2), 10–15.

Leslie, D. W. (1996). Strategic governance: The wrong questions? *The Review of Higher Education, 20,* 101–112.

Leslie, L. L. (1995). What drives higher education management in the 1990s and beyond? The new era in financial support. *Journal for Higher Education Management, 10*(2), 5–16.

LeVasseur, P. M. (1996). 1970–1995: An IMHE perspective on higher education in Transition. *Higher Education Management, 8*(3), 7–14.

Lewis, L. S. (1993)). *The cold war and academic governance: The Lattimore case at Johns Hopkins.* Ithaca, NY: State University of New York Press.

Luke, C. (1997). Quality assurance and women in higher education. *Higher Education, 33*(4), 433–51.

Lynch, J. (1993). The politics of higher education: An analysis using the parallel political marketplace conceptualization. *Journal of Marketing for Higher Education, 4,* 91–106.

MacTaggert, T. J. (1998). *Seeking excellence through independence: Liberating colleges and universities from excessive regulation.* San Francisco, CA: Jossey-Bass.

MacTaggart, T. J. & Associates (1996). *Restructuring higher education: what works and what doesn't in reorganizing governing systems.* San Francisco: Jossey-Bass.

Marcus, L. R. (1997). Restructuring state higher education governance patterns. *Review of Higher Education, 20*(4), 399–418.

Marcus, L. (1994). A new way for states to fund higher education. *Planning for Higher Education, 23*(2), 11–15.

Marginson, S. (1997). How free is academic freedom? *Higher Education Research & Development, 16*(3), 359–69.

McDaniel, O. C. (1996). The paradigms of governance in higher education systems. *Higher Education Policy, 9*(2), 137–58.

McGuinness, A. C., Jr. (1994). The changing structure of state higher education leadership. *State post-secondary education structures handbook.* A. C. McGuinness, R. M. Epper, & S. Arredondo, Eds. Denver: Education Commission of the States.

McGuinness, A. C., Jr. (1994). The states and higher education. In P. G. Altbach, R. O. Berdahl, & P. J. Gumport (Eds.), *Higher education in American society.* Amherst, New York: Prometheus Books.

Millett, J. D. (1984). *Conflict in higher education: State government coordination versus institutional independence.* San Francisco: Jossey-Bass.

Millett, J. D. (1980). *Management, governance, and leadership.* New York: American Management Association.

Millett, J. D. (1978). *New structures of campus power.* San Francisco: Jossey-Bass.

Mingle, J. R. (1995). *The case for coordinated systems of higher education.* Denver: State Higher Education Executive Officers.

Moos, M., & Rourke, F. E. (1959). *The campus and the state.* Baltimore: Johns Hopkins.

Mortimer, K. P. & McConnell, T. R. (1979). *Sharing authority effectively.* San Francisco: Jossey-Bass.

Nettles, M. T. (1995). The emerging national policy agenda on higher education assessment: A wake-up call. *Review of Higher Education, 18*(3), 293–313.

Obiakor, F. E., & Barker, N. C. (1993). The politics of higher education: Perspectives for African Americans in the 21st century. *Western Journal of Black Studies, 17*(4), 219–26.

O'Brien, G. D. (1998). *All the essential half-truths about higher education.* Chicago, IL: University of Chicago Press.

Peterson, M. W. & Associates (1993). *Total quality management in higher education: From assessment to improvement: An annotated bibliography, Second Edition.* Ann Arbor, MI: University of Michigan, Center for the Study of Higher Education.

Peterson, M. W., & Metts, L. A. (1987). *Key resources on higher education governance, management, and leadership.* San Francisco: Jossey-Bass.

Rhoades, G. (1984). Conditioned demand and professional response. *Higher Education, 13*(2), 139–69.

Ringle, P. M., & Savickas, M. L. (1983). Administrative leadership: Planning and time perspective. *Journal of Higher Education, 54*(6), 649–61.

Rosovsky, H. (1990). *The university: An owner's manual.* New York: W. W. Norton.

Ruppert, S. S. (1994). *Charting higher education accountability.* Denver: Education Commission of the States.

Sabloff, P. L. W. (1997). Another reason why state legislatures will continue to restrict public university autonomy. *Review of Higher Education, 20*(2), 141–62.

Saeed, K. (1996). The dynamics of collegial systems in the developing countries. *Higher Education Policy, 9,* 75–86.

Savenije, B. (1992). University budgeting: Creating incentives for change? *Research in Higher Education*, 33 (5), 641–56.

Schick, E. G., Novak, R. J., Norton, J A., & Elam, H. G. (1993). *Shared visions of public education governance: Structures and leadership styles that work*. Washington, DC: AGB.

Schofield, A. (1995). *The management of higher education: An annotated bibliography*. London (England): Commonwealth Higher Education Management Service.

Schmidtlein, F. A., & Milton, T. H. (1988). College and university planning: Perspectives from a nationwide study. *Planning for Higher Education*, 17(3), 1–19.

Schuster, J H., Miller, L. H., & Associates (1989). *Governing tomorrow's campus*. New York: Macmillan.

Schuster, J. H., Smith, D. G., Corak, K. A., & Yamada, M. M. (1994). *Strategic governance: How to make big decisions better*. Phoenix: Oryx Press.

Sheheen, F. R. (1988). The role of state boards of higher education in influencing access and retention of minorities in higher education. *Peabody Journal of Education*, 66, 20–38.

Shoemaker, C. C. J. (1998). *Leadership in continuing and distance education in higher education*. Needham, MA: Allyn & Bacon.

Stevens, M. L. & Williams, J. L. (1988). *Organizational effectiveness in higher education: The management of organized anarchy*. College & University, 63(2), 168–79.

St. John, E. P. (1995). Hard decisions, retrenchment and the faculty role. *The NEA Higher Education Journal*, 21, 25–42.

Tierney, W. G. (1998). *The responsive university*. Baltimore: Johns Hopkins.

Tierney, W. G. (1983). Governance by conversation: an essay on the structure, function, and communicative codes of a faculty senate. *Human Organization*, 42(2), 172–177.

Trow, M. (1998). Governance in the University of California: The transformation of politics into administration. *Higher Education Policy*, 11 (2–3), 201–15.

Trow, M. (1990). The academic senate as a school for university leadership. *Liberal Education*, 76, 231–27.

Twale, D. J., & Shannon, D. M. (1996). Gender differences among faculty in campus governance: nature of involvement, satisfaction, and power. *Initiatives,* 57(4), 11–19.

Volkwein, J., Fredericks, M., & Shaukat, M. (1997). State regulation and administrative flexibility at public universities. *Research in Higher Education*, 38, 17–42.

Welzenbach, L. F. (1982). *College & university business administration*, Fourth Edition. Washington, D.C.: National Association of College and University Business Officers.

Wolfe, A. (1996). The feudal culture of the postmodern university. *The Wilson Quarterly*, 20, 54–66.

Wilson, C. H. (1997). Catholic colleges and civil law: Benefits and burdens of government involvement in higher education. *Current Issues in Catholic Higher Education*, 18, 3–66.

Wilson. C. E.. & Benveniste, H. S. (1994). A framework for surveying communication effectiveness in institutions of higher education. *Journal of the Association for Communication Administration*, 2, 115–23.

About the Editor

M. Christopher Brown II is a professor in the higher education program at the University of Illinois at Urbana-Champaign. His research investigates the systemic and structural challenges to effective and efficient functioning of postsecondary institutions. Dr. Brown is the author of *The Quest to Define Collegiate Desegregation: Black Colleges, Title VI Compliance, and Post-Adams Litigation,* and the editor of *Black Colleges at the Millennium: Perspectives on Policy and Practice* (with Kassie Freeman). He has also written numerous other articles and book chapters on organization and governance in higher education.